1 MONTH OF
FREE
READING

at

www.ForgottenBooks.com

By purchasing this book you are eligible for one month membership to ForgottenBooks.com, giving you unlimited access to our entire collection of over 1,000,000 titles via our web site and mobile apps.

To claim your free month visit:

www.forgottenbooks.com/free1247954

ISBN 978-0-428-60215-4
PIBN 11247954

MINUTES

OF THE

TRUSTEES

OF THE

Internal Improvement
Trust Fund

State of Florida

VOLUME XXXVIII

From July 1, 1970 to June 30, 1972

Published Under Authority of Trustees of Internal
Improvement Trust Fund

TALLAHASSEE, FLORIDA

1973

MINUTES

OF THE

TRUSTEES

OF THE

Internal Improvement
Trust Fund

State of Florida

VOLUME XXXVIII

From July 1, 1970 to June 30, 1972

Published Under Authority of Trustees of Internal
Improvement Trust Fund

TALLAHASSEE, FLORIDA

1973

Tallahassee, Florida

July 7, 1970

The State of Florida Board of Trustees of the Internal Improvement Trust Fund met on this date in Senate Hearing Room 31 with the following members present:

The minutes of the meeting of June 23, 1970, were approved as submitted.

BREVARD COUNTY - Confirmation of Contract Sales.

In accordance with recommendation of the Department of Legal Affairs that at least five of the seven members of the Board of Trustees vote on sales due to present statutory requirements, motion was made by Mr. Faircloth, seconded by Mr. Williams and adopted without objection, that the Trustees confirm sales and issuance of deeds in the following instances:

A. On November 23, 1965, the Trustees confirmed the sale of a parcel of submerged land in the Indian River in Section 22, Township 22 South, Range 35 East, City of Titusville, Brevard County, to Roy F. Roberts, Edna Mae Roberts and Roy F. Roberts, Jr. Under the policy effective at that time the applicants entered into purchase contract No. 24167(1733-05) that had been paid in full and said grantees were entitled to receive a deed.

B. On November 23, 1965, the Trustees confirmed the sale of a parcel of submerged land in the Indian River in Section 15, Township 22 South, Range 35 East, Brevard County, to Louis D. Harris. Under the policy effective at that time the applicant entered into purchase contract No. 24122(1710-05) that had been paid in full and the said grantee was entitled to receive a deed.

MONROE COUNTY - File Nos. 2178-2179-2180-44-253.42
Land Exchange and Confirmation of Sale.

On May 12, 1970, the Trustees considered the application of The Wacouta Corporation of Miami, Florida, represented by James T. Glass, for conveyance of 10.11 acres of sovereignty land in Newfound Harbor abutting Sections 26 and 35, Township 66 South, Range 29 East, Big Pine Key, Monroe County. In exchange the applicant would convey to the Trustees 4 parcels containing 4.63 acres of upland, would quitclaim to the Trustees approximately 8 acres lying bayward of the mean high water line and within erroneous meander lines.

Other reasons cited by the applicant to show that the project was in the public interest were that construction of navigation channels would increase the flow of water to tidal ponds which would become stagnant when uplands were filled to usable level, applicant would dedicate by plat an additional 4.9 acres as a private conservation tract, and the project would provide many waterfront homesites in Big Pine Key.

The biological report of April 15, 1969, was adverse and the applicant had modified his plans to provide for the conservation areas and reduce the area and design of the navigation channel. The perimeter channel would be dredged in part on applicant's uplands.

The application was advertised in the Key West Citizen and several objections were received, mainly related to zoning and not taking into consideration the conservation areas to be conveyed to the state. Action was deferred on June 30, the advertised sale date.

An appraisal by the staff appraiser of the 10.11 and 4.63 acres indicated a difference in value of $2,400 which applicant agreed to pay in addition to defraying the cost of the appraisal.

Based on an opinion that the areas to be conveyed to the state would offset the damage caused by dredging and filling, that the appraisal was equitable and sale would be in the public interest, the staff recommended approval.

On motion by Mr. Williams, seconded by Mr. Christian and adopted without objection, the Trustees overruled the objections and confirmed the land exchange and sale at the appraised value subject to applicant paying the cost of appraisal.

LEE COUNTY - File No. 2337-36-253.12(6), Quitclaim Deed

Deferred last week when only four members were present was the application of L. K. Thorne, Jr., represented by Stephen L. Helgemo for a quitclaim deed under provisions of Section 253.12(6) Florida Statutes, to a parcel of filled sovereignty land in Yacht Basin of Charlotte Harbor embracing 0.125 acre abutting Section 23, Township 43 South, Range 20 East, Gasparilla Island in Lee County.

The land was filled prior to June 11, 1957, all required exhibits were furnished, and the parcel was appraised at $500.

Action was deferred by the Trustees last week when only four members were present. On this date motion was made by Mr. Williams, seconded by Mr. Faircloth and Mr. Christian and adopted without objection, that the Board authorize issuance of the quitclaim deed for the $500 appraised value and payment of appraisal cost by the applicant.

BROWARD COUNTY - File No. 2353-06-253.03, Spoil Easement.

The Florida Inland Navigation District applied for a spoil easement in the Atlantic Ocean embracing 1.84 acres abutting Section 5, Township 48 South, Range 31 East, Deerfield Beach, Broward County.

Easements had been obtained from abutting upland owners. Bureau of Beaches and Shores reviewed the project and had no objections. Upland owners within 1,000 feet of the spoil area were notified and filed no objections.

On motion by Mr. Faircloth, seconded by Mr. Williams and adopted without objection, the Trustees authorized issuance of the easement requested by Florida Inland Navigation District.

CLAY COUNTY - File No. 2354-10-253.03
            Right of Way Easement.

The Seaboard Coast Line Railroad Company requested right of
way easement across 1.25 acres of Black Creek bottom lands
abutting Sections 12 and 40, Township 5 South, Range 25 East,
Clay County, for construction of a new railroad bridge. The
existing bridge would be removed.

Construction plans were reviewed, no dredging or filling was
proposed within the easement area, and the Department of
Natural Resources had no objection to the project.

On motion by Mr. Adams, seconded by Mr. Faircloth and adopted
without objection, the Trustees authorized issuance of the
easement for $100 processing fee.

MARTIN COUNTY - File No. 2350-43-253.03
              Spoil Easement.

Deferred last week when only four members of the Board were
present was the application from Central and Southern Florida
Flood Control District for a spoil easement to the United
States Corps of Engineers for five permanent spoil areas
embracing 40 acres in the St. Lucie River in Martin County
adjacent to Sections 2, 3, 4 and 12, Township 38 South, Range
41 East, Martin County, to be used in connection with maintenance dredging of the Okeechobee Waterway.

The Department of Natural Resources reviewed the application
and had no objection to the project.

On motion by Mr. Christian, seconded by Mr. Williams and
adopted without objection, the Trustees authorized issuance
of the easement as requested.

HOLMES AND WASHINGTON COUNTIES - Right of Way Easement,
                                 File No. 2351-30 and
                                 67-253.03.

The Department of Transportation requested right of way easement across 3.74 acres of bottom lands of the Choctawhatchee
River abutting Section 15, Township 4 North, Range 16 West,
in Holmes and Washington Counties, for construction of a
bridge on State Road 8 (I-10), Section 61001-2401. Action
was deferred last week when only four members of the Board
were present.

Construction plans were reviewed, no dredging or filling
was indicated, and the Florida Game and Fresh Water Fish
Commission had no objection.

On motion by Mr. Williams, seconded by Mr. Dickinson and
adopted without objection, the Trustees authorized issuance
of the easement.

FRANKLIN COUNTY - Power Line Easement.

Florida Power Corporation requested an easement six feet wide across a parcel of land in Section 29, Township 8 South, Range 6 West, for electrical service to a new Highway Patrol Station.

The Department of Highway Safety and Motor Vehicles had approved the application and staff recommended approval.

On motion by Mr. Dickinson, adopted without objection, the Trustees authorized issuance of the easement for power line to the Highway Patrol Station in Franklin County.

MARION COUNTY - Power Line Easement.

Florida Power Corporation requested an additional easement thirty feet wide over state lands at Lowell in Township 14 South, Range 21 East, Marion County, adjacent to the existing transmission line crossing said land. Applicant offered $1,300 for the easement.

The Department of Health and Rehabilitative Services and other state agencies using the land had reviewed and approved the request.

Mr. Adams asked why a charge was not made in the preceding application in these minutes. The Director advised that if there was a direct benefit, a state facility was to be served, the policy was to make no charge for the easement crossing state land.

On motion by Mr. Dickinson, adopted without objection, the Trustees authorized issuance of the easement for consideration of $1,300.

LEON AND ALACHUA COUNTIES - Reconfirmation of three applications approved last week by four members of the Board of Trustees.

1. LEON COUNTY - Application for a lease covering the A and M University Hospital to the City of Tallahassee and Leon County for an additional two years for hospital purposes, as recommended by the General Counsel of the Board of Education.

2. LEON COUNTY - Application for an easement to the City of Tallahassee over lands of Florida State University in Sections 3 and 4, Township 1 South, Range 1 West, for construction and maintenance of electric transmission lines as approved by the Board of Regents.

3. ALACHUA COUNTY - Road right of way easement applied for by the Board of County Commissioners of Alachua County over certain land of the University of Florida for paving Southwest 23rd Terrace as approved by the Board of Regents.

On motion by Mr. Williams, seconded by Mr. Christian and Mr. Adams, and adopted without objection, the Trustees reconfirmed approval of the above three applications.

COLLIER COUNTY - Oil and Gas Lease.

On April 28, 1970, the Trustees with the concurrence of the

Board of Education authorized advertisement for sealed bids for a five-year primary term oil and gas drilling lease covering the full interest held by the Trustees in Section 16, Township 49 South, Range 31 East, containing 640 acres, more or less, in Collier County. The lease required an annual rental of $1 per acre, one-eighth royalty, at least one test well every 2½ years, and a $50,000 surety bond. The successful bidder was required to pay all advertising costs and the Board reserved the right to reject any or all bids.

Invitation to bid was published in the Tallahassee Democrat and the Naples Daily News pursuant to law, with bids to be opened on June 30. However, since only four members of the Board of Trustees were present on that date, the sealed bids were held unopened until this date.

Mr. James T. Williams of the Trustees' staff read the following bids: (1) Sun Oil Company offered a bonus bid of $2,246.40 and $640 for the first year's rental or a total amount of $2,886.40; and (2) Phillips Petroleum Company offered a bonus bid of $16,396.80 and $640 for the first year's rental or a total amount of $17,036.80.

On motion by Mr. Christian, seconded by Mr. Williams and by the Attorney General, the Trustees received the bids and awarded the lease to the high bidder, Phillips Petroleum Company. Also by the same motion the Board of Education confirmed the action.

CHARLOTTE COUNTY - Oil and Gas Lease.

On December 23, 1969, the Trustees with the approval of the Game and Fresh Water Fish Commission authorized advertisement for sealed bids for a five-year primary term oil and gas drilling lease covering the full interest held by the State of Florida in the C. M. Webb Wildlife Management Area containing 59,221.17 acres, more or less, in Charlotte County. The lease required an annual rental of $1 per acre, one-eighth royalty, at least one test well every 2½ years, and a $50,000 surety bond. The successful bidder was required to pay all advertising costs and the Board reserved the right to reject any or all bids.

Invitation to bid was published in the Tallahassee Democrat and The Herald News of Punta Gorda, Florida, pursuant to law, with bids to be opened on June 30. However, since only four members of the Board of Trustees were present on that date, the sealed bids were held unopened until this date.

Mr. James T. Williams of the Trustees' staff read the following bids: (1) Sun Oil Company offered a bonus bid of $137,985.33 and $59,221.17 for the first year's rental or a total amount of $197,206.50; (2) Frank A. Ashby, Jr., offered a bonus bid of $92,385.03 and $59,221.17 for the first year's rental or a total amount of $151,606.20; and (3) E. M. Smith offered a bonus bid of $657,947.20 and $59,221.17 for the first year's rental or a total amount of $717,168.37.

On motion by Mr. Christian, seconded by Mr. Williams and adopted without objection, the Trustees received the bids and awarded the lease to the high bidder, E. M. Smith of New Orleans, Louisiana.

SANTA ROSA AND ESCAMBIA COUNTIES - Oil and Gas Lease.

On April 28, 1970, the Trustees authorized advertisement for sealed bids for a five-year primary term oil and gas drilling lease covering the sovereignty land owned by the Trustees in the Escambia River and its tributaries in Townships 5 and 6 North, Ranges 29 and 30 West, containing 205 acres, more or less, in Santa Rosa and Escambia Counties. The lease required an annual rental of $1 per acre, one-eighth royalty, at least one test well every 2½ years, and $50,000 surety bond. The lease would contain an additional provision that wells will not be drilled on the submerged leased area without prior written consent of the Trustees, and in the event production is obtained on adjoining lands directional wells shall be drilled under the lease area. The successful bidder was required to pay all costs of advertising and the Board reserved the right to reject any or all bids.

Invitation to bid was published in the Tallahassee Democrat and the Pensacola News-Journal and Milton Times, pursuant to law, with bids to be opened on June 30. However, since only four members of the Board of Trustees were present on that date, the sealed bids were held unopened until this date.

Mr. James T. Williams of the Trustees' staff read the one bid received, as follows: Marshall R. Young Oil Company offered a bonus bid of $177,295 and $205 for the first year's rental or a total amount of $177,500. Treasurer Williams made a motion that the bid be approved but discussion followed and the motion was not adopted.

Mr. Christian said it might be wise to reject the one bid and readvertise, and Governor Kirk agreed. The Director suggested that if only one company had leased the uplands on both sides of the river, that would account for only one bid being received, as any directional drilling under the river would be from the leased uplands.

Mr. Tom Smith, an attorney representing the bidder, said that was the case, and he doubted that readvertising would bring any additional bids. He and Mr. Kelly Young, vice president of the Marshall R. Young Oil Company, explained further with respect to a unit agreement and efficient operations in this type of drilling. Mr. Young said that the delay of readvertising might obstruct operations on the lands contiguous to the river bottoms. But in view of the promising aspects of oil drilling in northwest Florida, some members were in favor of readvertising.

On motion by Mr. Christian, seconded by Mr. Adams, and approved by all other members except Mr. Dickinson, who voted "No", the Trustees rejected the one bid received from Marshall R. Young Oil Company and directed the staff to readvertise for bids at a later date.

HENDRY COUNTY - Oil and Gas Lease.

On April 28, 1970, the Trustees authorized advertisement for sealed bids for a five-year primary term oil and gas lease covering the reserved one-half interest of the Trustees in privately owned Section 27, N½ and SE¼ of Section 33, and W½ of Section 35, all in Township 47 South, Range 32 East, containing 1,440 surface acres in Hendry County.

The lease required an annual rental of $1 per net mineral acre, one-eighth royalty, at least one test well every 2½ years, and a surety bond of $50,000. The successful bidder was required to pay all advertising costs and the Board of Trustees reserved the right to reject any or all bids.

Invitation to bid was published in the Tallahassee Democrat and The Hendry County News pursuant to law, with bids to be opened on this date.

Mr. James T. Williams of the Trustees' staff read the one bid received, as follows: Sun Oil Company offered a bonus bid of $6,912 and $702 for the first year's rental, or a total amount of $7,632 for lease covering the one-half interest reserved by the Trustees. The Director said that company had a lease of the privately-held one-half interest.

On motion by Mr. Christian, seconded by Mr. Adams and adopted without objection, the Trustees accepted the bid and awarded oil and gas drilling lease covering the reserved one-half interest of the Trustees to the bidder, Sun Oil Company.

In answer to Mr. Adams' question, Director Randolph Hodges of the Department of Natural Resources said that before any actual drilling is done under a lease, a drilling permit would have to be approved and issued by that department.

PASCO COUNTY - Offshore Campsite Lease.
William B. Bennett, represented by Sam Y. Allgood, Jr., applied for an offshore campsite lease in Township 25 South, Ranges 15-16 East, 1.2 miles northwesterly of Cow Key in the Gulf of Mexico in Pasco County. An existing structure was severely damaged by Hurricane Gladys in October 1968, and under the policy adopted on April 7, 1970, by the Trustees, the application was for lease of an area not to exceed one acre with annual rental of $100 for a one-year lease and option to renew for four additional years.

On motion by Mr. Christian, seconded by Mr. Dickinson and adopted without objection, the Trustees authorized issuance of the campsite lease.

HILLSBOROUGH COUNTY - SAJSP Permit 66-383.
Staff recommended that the Board of Trustees officially object to reissuance of SAJSP Permit 66-383 as modified. The District Engineer, Jacksonville District, United States Corps of Engineers, had requested that an overall state position be indicated.

At the time the original federal permit issued on February 13, 1967, the Trustees had no clear-cut authority to act on these matters within the boundaries of the Tampa Port Authority, where the land involved was located. The Marine Bank and Trust Company obtained a permit from that Authority on June 22, 1967 (to expire June 21, 1972) to dredge and fill submerged lands in Tampa Bay abutting Section 19, Township 29 South, Range 18 East, Hillsborough County. As the permit issued prior to effective date of Chapter 67-1503, a biological study was not executed.

The deed to submerged lands subject to be filled is in escrow, release being contingent upon the lands being filled to an appropriate elevation complying with the local zoning requirements. If the company fails to secure necessary permits it appears that the agreement between the Tampa Port Authority, which acquired the land by Legislative Act, and the Marine Bank and Trust Company will be invalid.

The Florida Game and Fresh Water Fish Commission filed an objection to issuance of the subject permit with the District Engineer on September 5, 1969, on the basis that the area was highly productive for estuarine resources. The Trustees' staff recommended that the Board officially object to reissuance of SAJSP Permit 66-383 as modified.

7-7-70

Mr. Leo Foster of Tallahassee was present to introduce Mr. Lewis H. Hill, an attorney representing the Marine Bank and Trust Company, applicant for the permit from the Corps of Engineers. Mr. Hill reviewed the history of the matter including establishment of the bulkhead line in 1960 and approval by the Trustees, application made in 1967 to fill a portion of the land but showing the plan for development of the entire parcel, approval of the project by the Tampa Port Authority, Hillsborough County Commission, City of Tampa, Chamber of Commerce, Central and Southern Florida Flood Control District and the Trustees. Mr. Hill said that upon application by the company to the Corps of Engineers for permit to finish the fill project, objections were filed by the Interior Department and subsequently by the Game and Fresh Water Fish Commission. In view of prior approvals and completed fills that made of this parcel a pocket that was not valuable biologically, according to an independent biologist's survey, Mr. Hill urged approval for completion of development of the area which he said was mud flats exposed at low tide.

The Director advised that the only reason the Board was involved was that the Corps of Engineers, having received conflicting reports, desired the Trustees to indicate the state's position. He reiterated the staff recommendation against issuance of the Corps permit based on the reports of the Game and Fresh Water Fish Commission but pointed out that the land was owned by Tampa Port Authority. Mr. Adams felt it would be inconsistent to go against the staff recommendation in view of the Board's self-imposed mandate of the public purpose in matters of this kind. Mr. Christian said it was difficult to decide the public purpose aspect, but it was a pocket between other fills and could be made more valuable and useful by the proposed development. Mr. Dickinson said it was a just issue before them, that the work started in 1967 and it might not be in the public interest to protect the small pocket, that to fill any water area would affect biological resources, and he would like a delay until the Board could take a look at the site.

On motion by Mr. Dickinson, seconded by Mr. Williams and adopted without objection, the Trustees postponed further consideration for two weeks.

DADE COUNTY - Dredge Permit, Section 253.123 Florida Statutes. Willis H. duPont applied for permit for maintenance dredging in an existing channel in Biscayne Bay in Township 55 South, Range 41 East, Dade County, which the biological report stated would have little adverse effect on marine biological resources.

On motion by Mr. Christian, seconded by Mr. Adams and adopted without objection, the Trustees authorized issuance of the permit for $50 processing fee subject to recommendations of the staff that all spoiling be done above the line of mean high water, the spoil area be adequately diked to prevent silt and other suspended material from re-entering the bay, and the dredging be done in such a way as to minimize turbidity.

DADE COUNTY - Utility Permit for Aerial Cable Crossing, Section 253.03(7)
On motion by Mr. Williams, seconded by Mr. Adams and adopted without objection, the Trustees authorized issuance of a permit for $100 processing fee, to Florida Power and Light Company for installing an aerial line over the Intracoastal Waterway in Section 14, Township 52 South, Range 42 East, Dade County.

LAKE COUNTY - Utility Permit for Aerial Cable Crossing,
                    Section 253.03(7)
On motion by Mr. Williams, seconded by Mr. Adams and adopted
without objection, the Trustees authorized issuance of a permit for
$100 processing fee, to the Florida Telephone Corporation of
Leesburg, Florida, for installing an aerial wire crossing Haimes
Creek in Section 2, Township 19 South, Range 25 East, Lake County.

PALM BEACH COUNTY - Dredge Permit, Utility Installation,
                    Section 253.123(2)(b)
On motion by Mr. Williams, seconded by Mr. Adams and adopted
without objection, the Trustees authorized issuance of a dredge
permit for $100 processing fee, to Teleprompter, Inc., for
installing a TV cable in Lake Worth in Sections 2 and 3, Township
45 South, Range 43 East, Palm Beach County. The biological survey
report was not adverse.

PALM BEACH COUNTY - State Commercial Dock Permit, Section 253.03.
On motion by Mr. Williams, seconded by Mr. Adams and adopted
without objection, the Trustees authorized issuance of a state
commercial dock permit for $100 processing fee, to Paradise Harbor
Condominium, represented by William G. Wallace, Inc., for constructing a dock in Lake Worth adjacent to upland in Section 16, Township
42 South, Range 43 East, Palm Beach County, to be used exclusively
by members of the condominium association.

LEASE INCOME REPORT - The Trustees accepted for the record the
report of remittances to Florida Department of Natural Resources
from holders of dead shell leases, as follows:

Lease No.	Name of Company	Amount
1718	Radcliff Materials, Inc.	$ 7,007.06
1788	Benton and Company, Inc.	23,918.47
2233	Bay Dredging & Construction Co.	5,774.25
2235	Fort Myers Shell & Dredging Co.	1,078.35

TRUSTEES FUNDS - The Department of General Services requested
commitment of Trustees funds in an amount not to exceed $29,000
for site preparation of the proposed state motor pool. The release
of funds would be based on bids for the work contained in the
estimate prepared by General Services. The commitment would be
consistent with the Board's policy regarding use of funds and
subject to approval by the Secretary of Administration.

The Director said that the motor pool would be in the area that
had been recommended by the capitol center planners.

On motion by Mr. Williams, seconded by Mr. Christian and adopted
without objection, the Board agreed to commit an amount not to
exceed $29,000 subject to approval by the Secretary of Administra-
tion, as recommended by the staff.

LITIGATION - Coastal Petroleum Co. vs. Secretary of the Army of
                the United States, Trustees of the Internal Improvement
                Trust Fund of the State of Florida, et al.
The Director presented the Board's counsel in the above case,
Mr. Neal P. Rutledge, who discussed the litigation and the
memorandum opinion dated June 30, 1970, of Judge C. Clyde Atkins,

United States District Judge. Mr. Rutledge advised the Board that
the judge had found that the lease was valid and the Corps of
Engineers had no authority to deny the permit for the company to
proceed to mine limerock from Lake Okeechobee. But the court found
that the mining operations would have a potentially disastrous effect
on the ecology and fresh water supply of the central and south
Florida area, and in what Mr. Rutledge called an unprecedented type
of decision the court would deny the injunctive relief sought by
Coastal and not order the Corps of Engineers or Trustees to permit
it; but as an alternative the court would impose a liability for
whatever loss of profit Coastal will be able to show at a subsequent
hearing set for October of this year.

As it was not a final or appealable ruling, Mr. Rutledge recommended
procedure of a special appeal which would be discretionary with the
Court of Appeals and Judge Atkins. Another case now pending, Zabel
v. Tabb, involving some of the same legal questions, was mentioned
as also greatly affecting the power and right of the sovereignty of
the state to protect lands for the people of Florida. The Board
could still appeal the final opinion in the litigation.

Motion was made by Mr. Dickinson, seconded by Mr. Adams and Mr.
Williams, and adopted without objection, that Mr. Rutledge be
instructed to proceed with the special appeal.

SUBJECTS UNDER CHAPTER 18296

REFUND - On motion by Mr. Christian, seconded by Mr. Williams and
adopted without objection, the Trustees authorized refund of $30 to
Peters, Maxey, Shupack, Short and Morgan, Attorneys at Law, whose
applications for release of state road right of way reservations
had been withdrawn.

HOLMES COUNTY - Murphy Act Land Conveyance.
On motion by Mr. Adams, seconded by Mr. Williams and adopted
without objection, the Trustees authorized conveyance under provisions of Chapter 21684, Acts of 1943 (Section 197.350 Florida
Statutes 1969), to the Department of Transportation for $100, without
advertisement and public sale, of Lots 16, 18, 19 and 20, Block 40
of Ponce DeLeon Park Subdivision, being in Section 34, Township
4 North, Range 17 West, Holmes County. The lots had been certified
to the state under tax sale certificate No. 1561 of September 4,
1933.

On motion duly adopted, the meeting was adjourned.

GOVERNOR - CHAIRMAN

ATTEST:

EXECUTIVE DIRECTOR

7-7-70

Tallahassee, Florida
July 14, 1970

The State of Florida Board of Trustees of the Internal Improvement
Trust Fund met on this date in Senate Hearing Room 31 with the
following members present:

Claude R. Kirk, Jr.	Governor
Tom Adams	Secretary of State
Earl Faircloth	Attorney General
Fred O. Dickinson, Jr.	Comptroller
Broward Williams	Treasurer
Floyd T. Christian	Commissioner of Education
Doyle Conner	Commissioner of Agriculture

James W. Apthorp   Executive Director

The minutes of the meeting of June 30, 1970, were approved as
submitted.

CITRUS COUNTY - Bulkhead Line, Section 253.122 Florida Statutes.
The Board of County Commissioners of Citrus County by resolution on
April 7, 1970, established a bulkhead line 4,040 feet long in
Sleepy Lagoon and around Parker Island in Section 28, Township 18
South, Range 17 East, Citrus County.

The biological survey report stated that the line around Sleepy
Lagoon followed existing shorelines or concrete seawalls, and the
line around Parker Island was well located and about as conserva-
tive as surveyed lines would permit.

On motion by Mr. Williams, seconded by Mr. Adams and adopted
without objection, the Trustees approved the bulkhead line as
located by Citrus County Commissioners.

CITRUS COUNTY - Bulkhead Line, Section 253.122 Florida Statutes.
The staff recommended that the rules be waived for consideration
of a bulkhead line that had not been placed on an advance agenda.
Without objection, the Trustees accepted the recommendation.

The Board of County Commissioners of Citrus County by resolution
adopted on May 19, 1970, established a bulkhead line 999.34 feet
long in the Gulf of Mexico near Fort Island in Sections 13 and 14,
Township 18 South, Range 16 East, Citrus County. The area landward
of the line was to be developed into a public beach and recreation
facility to be constructed with the help of a federal grant on a
matching fund basis.

The biological survey report was adverse to the proposed dredging
and filling, but the Trustees' staff recommended the project as
being in the public interest.

On motion by Mr. Williams, seconded by Mr. Adams and adopted
without objection, the Trustees approved the bulkhead line as
located by Citrus County Commission for a public recreation area.

SARASOTA COUNTY - Bulkhead Line Relocation, Section 253.122 F. S.
Logan Smith Company, Inc., submitted an application to Sarasota
County Water and Navigation Control Authority which by resolution
adopted on November 18, 1969, approved Major Work Permit No. 69-4-M
relocating a bulkhead line on the east shore of Roberts Bay in Section
6, Township 37 South, Range 18 East, Sarasota County. The Authority
approved application to fill the land purchased and dredge a perimeter navigation channel. On February 17, 1970, the Trustees
deferred consideration because of questions raised about unauthorized
activities by the applicant.

The original application was based upon use of 0.7 mean sea level
as the mean high water line in this area; however, the line has been
redefined by the county. Based upon 1.46 ft. m.s.l. elevation, an
encroachment has occurred and the following tentative settlement was
worked out by the staff and the company:

1. The Authority would rehear the matter and relocate the bulkhead
   line to preserve the mangrove islands.

2. Offer to purchase 1.277 acres of land lying between the 1.46 ft.
   m.s.l. elevation and the proposed bulkhead line. A valuation
   of $2,593 per acre was determined by appraisal.

3. Pay for 2,450 cubic yards of material to be dredged from
   navigation channel.

4. A reconveyance of 0.388 acre of submerged land acquired from
   the Trustees, lying adjacent to the area in the application.

The staff recommended approval of the bulkhead line relocation and
settlement because (1) a definitive boundary would be established
between public and private lands, (2) submerged lands heretofore
conveyed would be returned to the Trustees, (3) the utilization of
0.7 ft. m.s.l. elevation would be abandoned in that area, and (4) it
would allow an orderly development of the upland into homesites.

The Director called attention to the purchase application from Logan
Smith Company, Inc., for 1.277 acres of sovereignty land mentioned
in the above settlement, for which the biological report was
adverse. The applicant had modified his plans in accordance with
suggestions in the report; and staff felt the offer was fair and
the sale would be in the public interest because of the settlement
proposal.

Mr. Adams said the Trustees' policy required a penalty payment for
an encroachment. The Director advised that the settlement amounted
to not less than three times the value and an extenuating circumstance was the reliance on mean sea level elevation of 0.7 feet in
accordance with surveying practice in the area for a number of years.
Also, the city had approved the work done under proper permit. Mr.
Conner said the staff had worked out a very difficult situation.

Motion was made by Mr. Adams, seconded by Mr. Christian and
Mr. Conner, that the staff recommendation be approved.

Mr. William E. Robertson represented Hold the Bulkhead-Save Our Bays
Association in strenuous objection to the application. Using three
sketches, he discussed filling by the applicant and removal
required by the county on two occasions, objected to the proposed
settlement which he said would still go through mangrove areas,
and requested that the conservation report and map be followed in
the solution of the problem.

The Trustees referred to the sketches and asked questions in an effort to understand the objections to the staff recommendation. It was noted that the difference in the amount of land that would be in the purchase application was very small. The Director had had no opportunity to study the sketches brought by Mr. Robertson and it was suggested that the objector meet with the staff.

Motion was made by Mr. Faircloth, seconded by Mr. Adams and adopted without objection, that the Trustees defer action until next week.

MONROE COUNTY - Lease Old State Armory.
The Monroe County Historical Restoration and Preservation Commission by resolution adopted on June 8, 1970, requested transfer of the old state armory building at Key West to the commission for restoration and preservation. The building at the corner of White and Southhard Streets, built in 1902, had served as a meeting place for civic and Boy Scout groups after being declared surplus many years ago but was condemned by the city due to neglect and lack of maintenance.

The building had been determined by several historians to be valuable both historically and architecturally and the commission had budgeted $9,500 of its $10,000 appropriation for necessary repairs. After restoration, the building could be used by the community as a meeting place by various public and civic associations under jurisdiction of the commission.

On motion by Mr. Dickinson, seconded by Mr. Williams and Mr. Christian, and adopted without objection, the Trustees approved leasing the building to the Monroe County Historical Restoration and Preservation Commission.

BREVARD COUNTY - Contract Sale No. 24258(1642-05)
On July 13, 1965, the Trustees confirmed sale of a parcel of submerged land in the Indian River in Section 10, Township 22 South, Range 35 East, Brevard County, to M. T. Broyhill Enterprises and Broyhill Investment Corporation and under policy effective then, the applicant entered into a contract to purchase.

Contract No. 24258(1642-05) issued and was paid in full. The assignee, Berkshire Life Insurance Company, a Massachusetts corporation, was now entitled to receive a deed.

In accordance with the recommendation of the Department of Legal Affairs that at least five of the seven members of the Board of Trustees vote on sales due to present statutory requirements, motion was made by Mr. Dickinson, seconded by Mr. Adams and adopted without objection, that the Trustees confirm the sale and authorize issuance of the deed.

GLADES COUNTY - Land Sales.

1. File No. 2301-22-253.36. Mr. J. R. Click, represented by Fred E. Click, applied for a parcel of reclaimed lake bottom land in Lake Okeechobee lying between the 17 ft. contour line and the right of way line of Levee L-50 in unsurveyed Section 24, Township 40 South, Range 32 East, Glades County, containing 4.39 acres valued by the staff appraiser at $1,367 per acre, $6,000 for the parcel.

2. File No. 2302-22-253.36. Mr. S. D. Dewell, represented by Fred E. Click, applied to purchase 1.77 acres of reclaimed lake bottom land in Lake Okeechobee lying between the 17 ft. contour line and the right of way line of Levee L-50 in unsurveyed Section 24, Township 40 South, Range 32 East, valued by the staff appraiser at $805 per acre, $1,425 for the parcel.

On June 16 the applicants were present, the applications were fully discussed, and action was deferred for the reason that only four members were present. The staff recommendation, renewed on this date, was that the sales be denied as not being in the public interest. The applicants were again present but there was no demonstration that the sales were in the public interest.

Mr. Adams said he understood the staff recommendation in the light of the Trustees' policy, but the applications had been pending for a long time, certain assurances had been given to applicants who had donated land for a road, and the circumstances warrant approval. Mr. Christian and Mr. Dickinson agreed, the latter pointing out that not a single objection had been received, the application was made long before the policy adoption, and no detriment to the public interest had been shown.

Motion was made by Mr. Dickinson that the two sales of reclaimed lake bottom land be confirmed at the price of $475 per acre as agreed to by the Trustees' staff in April, 1968. Instruments of conveyance shall contain protective covenant to the Central and South Florida Flood Control District holding them harmless from damages due to flooding by future regulations of water level in Lake Okeechobee.

Mr. Faircloth seconded the motion, explaining that the applicants had been promised something by governmental officials (Flood Control District) when they gave up right of way for the flood control project, and in the absence of any representation that it was contrary to the public interest he approved the sales.

The motion to confirm the sales was adopted without objection.

MONROE COUNTY - File No. 2123-44-253.12, Land Sale.
On March 24 the Trustees considered application of William S. Clark, represented by James T. Glass, for a parcel of sovereignty land in Largo Sound abutting Section 14, Township 61 South, Range 39 East, Key Largo, Monroe County, containing 0.08 acre appraised at $100 for the parcel, desired for constructing a small jetty into Largo Sound to protect a boat basin constructed on applicant's upland. The biological survey report was not adverse.

As the parcel abutted Key Largo Waterway, some protection was needed from wave action of passing boats. No objection was received as a result of notice of sale published in the Key West Citizen. In the opinion of the staff, sale would be in the public interest as construction of the small jetty would prevent erosion of the uplands and damage to boats in the basin, caused by wave action of passing boats in the waterway.

On motion by Mr. Christian, seconded by Mr. Adams and Mr. Dickinson and adopted without objection, the Trustees confirmed sale at the appraised value subject to the applicant paying the appraisal cost.

LAKE COUNTY - Land Acceptance and Lease.
Staff recommended acceptance of a Lake Griffin park site from the City of Leesburg and authority to lease the site back to the city

for park purposes only. Details of the park plans were included in the agenda of the Department of Natural Resources on this date.

On motion by Mr. Adams, seconded by Mr. Dickinson and adopted without objection, the Trustees approved the recommendation subject to the lease containing a reverter to the Trustees in the event the city failed to use the parcel for public park purposes.

GLADES COUNTY - File No. 2359-22-253.03, Easement.
The Central and Southern Florida Flood Control District requested a canal right of way easement embracing 2.0 acres in Turkey Creek abutting Section 26, Township 42 South, Range 30 East, Glades County, the right of way to extend northerly approximately 1,560 feet from the intersection of Turkey Creek with the Caloosahatchee River. The easement was to be used to accommodate dredge permit issued to H. E. Walker on June 9, 1970.

There was an adverse biological survey report from the Game and Fresh Water Fish Commission. Staff recommended approval.

Motion was made by Mr. Christian, seconded by Mr. Dickinson and adopted, that the canal right of way easement be granted. Mr. Adams voted "No" based on previous action by Mr. Walker in entering suit when the Flood Control District project required his riparian rights.

PALM BEACH COUNTY - File No. 2357-50-253.03, Spoil Easement.
The Port of Palm Beach, represented by James E. Weber, applied for permanent spoil easement to the U. S. Corps of Engineers embracing 55 acres in the Atlantic Ocean in theoretical Sections 34 and 35, Township 42 South, Range 43 East, Palm Beach County, to accommodate spoil from channel maintenance dredging at Lake Worth Inlet. The Trustees had granted temporary easement on the same area on January 27, 1970. The Department of Natural Resources had no objections.

On motion by Mr. Adams, seconded by Mr. Christian and adopted without objection, the Trustees authorized issuance of the easement.

MARION COUNTY - Land Exchange.
The Department of Health and Rehabilitative Services requested an exchange of a 15.56 acre parcel of land under control of the Division of Adult Corrections at Lowell, for a 16.06 acre parcel owned by Southern Materials Corporation. The exchange would be mutually beneficial to the state and the corporation as the land acquired by the state would act as a noise and dust buffer zone between the limerock processing plant and a residential development for state institution personnel.

An appraisal of both parcels was furnished, reporting a value of $450 per acre on the 16.06 acres to be received in exchange and $300 per acre on the state land. The State Geologist indicated relatively little difference in mineral value.

In view of the recommendations by Dr. Bax and Mr. Wainwright and the staff, motion was made by Mr. Williams, seconded by Mr. Dickinson and adopted without objection, that the exchange be approved subject to Marion County being offered the state tract for recreational purposes pursuant to Section 253.111 Florida Statutes, and title evidence being furnished guaranteeing clear title to the parcel to be received by the state.

HIGHLANDS COUNTY - Grazing Lease.
Cleveland Boney requested a three-year grazing lease on Lot 1,
Section 21, Township 35 South, Range 30 East, Highlands County,
33.14 acres on the north side of Lake Istokpoga formerly under
Lease No. 2271 to Julian O'Neal who did not wish to renew. The
staff appraiser recommended continued grazing use as the land lacked
access, and recommended increase of annual rental from $2 to $5 per
acre.

On motion by Mr. Williams, seconded by Mr. Dickinson and adopted
without objection, the Trustees authorized issuance of three-year
grazing lease to Cleveland Boney for $5 per acre annual rental, with
30-day cancellation privilege by the Board of Trustees.

BREVARD COUNTY - Dredge Permit and Fill Permit,
                File No. 23775(790-05)-253.124.
Edward Shablowski, represented by Eric W. Pappas, requested consider-
ation of dredge and fill permit issued by the City of Melbourne on
August 29, 1969, to dredge 17,035 cubic yards of material from the
Indian River to be deposited on 1.76 acres of submerged land
purchased from the Trustees on November 6, 1963.

A request was submitted that the application be considered under the
hardship provisions of the July 1 policy. The biological report was
adverse and staff had not presented the application because of
failure of the City of Melbourne to relocate any of its bulkhead
lines pursuant to recommendations of the Interagency Advisory
Committee and policy adopted by the Trustees on December 31, 1968.

Staff recommended denial of the dredge permit and deferral of action
on the fill permit until the city relocates bulkhead lines in accordance with Interagency Advisory Committee recommendations.

On motion by Mr. Adams, seconded by Mr. Dickinson and adopted
without objection, the Trustees accepted the staff recommendation
as the action of the Board.

BROWARD COUNTY - Dredge and Fill Permit, File No. 253.123-598 and
                253.123-130.
A. C. N. Y. Agency Company, Inc., represented by J. Lewis Hall, Jr.,
applied for a permit to dredge connections for two 70 ft. wide
interior canals with South Fork New River in the City of Fort Lauderdale in Section 9, Township 50 South, Range 42 East, Broward County,
and to fill lands landward of the bulkhead line approved by the
Trustees on June 23, 1970.

The land to be filled landward of the bulkhead line lay within an
area platted as "Harbor Island", Plat Book 59, Page 29, public
records of Broward County, and according to resolution No. C-70-22
adopted by the city, the bulkhead line followed the existing mean
high water line as closely as practicable conforming to the platted
boundary of lands abutting the river.

The Director advised that the city permit had been received and the
staff recommended approval. The biological report indicated that
the area was marginal with little marine productivity.

On motion by Mr. Adams, seconded by Mr. Christian and adopted
without objection, the Trustees authorized issuance of dredge
permit under Section 253.123 and approved the fill permit under
provisions of Section 253.124 Florida Statutes.

BROWARD COUNTY - Dredge Permit, Section 253.123, File 587.
The Director advised that Governor Kirk had requested deferment of
an application by Port Everglades Authority for a dredge permit.

Without objection, the Board deferred action pending discussion by
the county and the port authority.

MONROE COUNTY - Dredge Permit to Improve Navigation,
                Section 253.03 Florida Statutes.
Carlton E. Regan, represented by James T. Glass, applied for a
permit for dredging a 400 ft. long, 30 ft. wide and 5 ft. deep
navigation channel in Florida Bay adjacent to applicant's property
in Section 7, Township 63 South, Range 38 East, Monroe County. The
application was filed prior to the effective date of the policy
requiring $50 processing fee.

The material removed would be placed on upland. The biological
report was adverse and the applicant amended his plan to comply
with the recommendations in the report. Supplemental biological
report stated that the revised project was more oriented to conservation.

On motion by Mr. Conner and Mr. Williams, seconded by Mr. Christian
and adopted without objection, the Trustees approved issuance of
dredge permit for the revised application.

MARTIN COUNTY - Dredge Permit to Improve Navigation,
                Section 253.123 Florida Statutes.
Sailfish Marina, represented by Cal Montgomery, applied for a
dredging permit for a marina approximately 165 feet wide, 400 feet
long and 6 feet deep in Manatee Pocket in Section 26, Township 38
South, Range 41 East, Martin County.

Applicant submitted $300 for the overdredge material. The applica-
tion was filed prior to the effective date of the policy requiring
a $50 processing fee.

The biological report was adverse; however, the applicant amended
the plans in accordance with the recommendations in the report
and supplemental biological report was not adverse.

On motion by Mr. Williams, seconded by Mr. Dickinson and adopted
without objection, the Trustees authorized issuance of the dredge
permit to improve navigation.

DADE COUNTY - Utility Permit, Section 253.03 (7) Florida Statutes.
On motion by Mr. Dickinson, seconded by Mr. Williams and adopted
without objection, the Trustees approved the application from
Southern Bell Telephone and Telegraph Company for a permit to lay
a telephone cable loosely on the bottom of Intracoastal Waterway
in Section 6, Township 54 South, Range 42 East, Dade County, for
which the required processing fee of $100 had been tendered.

Mr. Adams again raised questions with respect to the fees for
permits and easements, noting that charge was made where the permit
allows exclusive private use of the public domain or limits use
by the public.

The Director said no charge was made for submarine cables, and
in other cases there was a permit fee unless some public purpose
was being served by the application.

7-14-70

PALM BEACH COUNTY - Commercial Dock Permit, Section 253.03 F. S.
Lost Tree Village Club Suites, represented by Tom McCarthy and
Associates, applied for a state commercial dock permit for construc-
tion of a marginal dock in Little Lake Worth adjacent to upland in
Section 4, Township 42 South, Range 43 East, Palm Beach County, to be
used exclusively by members of the condominium association.

Motion was made by Mr. Christian, seconded by Mr. Williams, that the
application be approved.

Mr. Adams questioned the philosophy used for such permits when in
other cases a license is issued with a charge for use of the water
column. He said the condominium dock increased the value of the
property by using the public domain and it limited the public use.
In his opinion private docks or commercial docks were obstructing
the public use of the water column the same as marinas or aquaculture
leases.

The Director said the difference was that this applicant's principal
business was not the use of the public land for profit and a man with
a private dock was not, but the staff could work out a proposal that
would make a square foot charge applicable not just to marinas. Under
present policy, there is a $10 charge for a private dock permit,
$100 fee for a commercial dock permit, and two cents per square foot
annual license for a marina.

In view of the tenor of the discussion, Mr. Christian withdrew his
motion.

Mr. Dickinson renewed the motion for approval as he thought the
application on the agenda should not be held up for a possible policy
change, that each application should stand on its own merits and he
thought it was in the public interest to have a dock for the use of
the people of Lost Tree Village Club Suites. He did not object to
the staff trying to develop a policy for applications where the
private use impairs the public domain, but made no commitment as to
how he would vote on such a proposal.

Mr. Christian said a private dock at a man's home was in a different
category from a dock at an apartment house or condominium. Mr.
Williams also indicated that private docks were in a different category
from marinas and condominiums.

After further discussion, Mr. Dickinson's motion to approve the application was seconded by Mr. Williams and adopted on the following
vote: Ayes by Governor Kirk, Messrs. Faircloth, Williams, Dickinson
and Conner; Noes by Messrs. Adams and Christian.

The Director said he would bring in an alternative to the present
policy for consideration by the Trustees.

————

POLICY - Utility Crossings.
The staff requested authority to issue permits for utility installation crossings over waterways and dredging permits for submarine
utility crossings in waterways without bringing such matters before
the Board. Such action would not be inconsistent with authority
previously granted relating to issuing permits for private dock
permits.

The staff did not contemplate waiving any biological hydrographic
reports that might be required. In the event an applicant desired
to have any requirements waived, such request would be presented
to the Trustees.

7-14-70

On motion by Mr. Williams, seconded by Mr. Faircloth and Mr. Christian, the Trustees approved the staff request.

———

LAKE COUNTY - Dredge Permit, Section 253.123 Florida Statutes. On motion by Mr. Adams, seconded by Mr. Christian and adopted, the rules were waived to allow consideration of an addendum to the agenda.

The Game and Fresh Water Fish Commission requested permission to test the effectiveness of muck removal equipment in Trout Lake in Section 2, Township 19 South, Range 26 East, Lake County. If the method proved satisfactory, water quality in eutrophic lakes could be improved.

The material removed would be placed on upland. Notice of intent to perform the work was published in the local newspaper and no objections were filed. Staff requested waiver of the biological study, as Trout Lake was eutrophic and had doubtful biological value.

On motion by Mr. Williams, seconded by Mr. Christian and adopted without objection, the Trustees approved the application.

———

VOLUSIA COUNTY - Sky Tower at Daytona Beach. Mr. Stephen Boyles, State Attorney for the 7th Judicial Circuit, said he was present on behalf of the State of Florida, that in October of 1969 the City of Daytona Beach had issued a building permit for the erection of a sky tower on Daytona Beach which had been placed approximately 80 feet seaward of the existing seawall. A competitor filed suit and after examining the suit Mr. Boyles decided the State of Florida should intervene. The court allowed it and the State Attorney filed cross complaint including that the sky tower was being built east of the mean high water mark on sovereignty land and that it was being built on the soft sand area of the beach to which the public had a prescriptive right.

Mr. Boyles requested the Trustees to seek to intervene as a party plaintiff in the law suit, which appeared necessary to him for litigation of the question of where the mean high water mark is located.

Mr. Faircloth commended the State Attorney for maintaining this action and made a motion, seconded by Mr. Christian, that the Trustees seek to intervene in the suit. The motion was adopted without objection.

———

TRUSTEES' OFFICE. Secretary of State Adams, speaking for himself and some others, said the Board had supported the request for additional staff as it had been obvious that the effort as Trustees required investigation of matters of increasing importance, thorough review by the staff and briefing for the information of the Trustees. He said it was necessary to reevaluate the responsibilities, that it was no criticism of the dedicated effort of the staff, but more needed to be done and additional representatives should be in the field.

Mr. Adams suggested that the members give serious consideration to the suggestions contained in a memorandum from the Governor which expressed concern that the Trustees might not be meeting their responsibilities in the area of protection of sovereignty land from illegal dredge and fill violations and other violations because of the problem of inadequate staffing of field investigators in the Trustees' office.

Mr. Apthorp said he would make a study for the Board to consider in two weeks, that he thought the objective the Board gave him was to convert the function from a passive title holder of the public's land to a manager of the public's land and in some respects that had been done. In order to become more effective in management, he appreciated the opportunity to review the situation and report to the Trustees within two weeks.

On motion duly adopted, the meeting was adjourned.

GOVERNOR - CHAIRMAN

ATTEST:

EXECUTIVE DIRECTOR

* * *

Tallahassee, Florida
July 21, 1970

The State of Florida Board of Trustees of the Internal Improvement Trust Fund met on this date in Senate Hearing Room 31 with the following members present:

Claude R. Kirk, Jr.	Governor
Tom Adams	Secretary of State
Earl Faircloth	Attorney General
Floyd T. Christian	Commissioner of Education
Doyle Conner	Commissioner of Agriculture
James W. Apthorp	Executive Director

The minutes of the meeting of July 7, 1970, were approved as submitted.

SARASOTA COUNTY - Bulkhead Line Relocation,
Section 253.122 Florida Statutes.
Logan Smith Company, Inc., had applied to Sarasota County Water and Navigation Control Authority which by resolution adopted on November 18, 1969, approved Major Work Permit No. 69-4-M relocating a bulkhead line on the east shore of Roberts Bay in Section 6, Township 37 South, Range 18 East, Sarasota County. The Authority approved application to fill the land purchased and dredge a perimeter navigation channel. On February 17, 1970, the Trustees deferred consideration for investigation of reported unauthorized work by the applicant.

On July 14 the staff recommended approval of the bulkhead line relocation and a settlement, the details of which were set out in minutes of that date. Objections were presented by Mr. William E. Robertson on behalf of the Save Our Bays Association and the Board deferred action for a week. After the meeting the staff met with Mr. Robertson and provided him various documents that supported the proposed settlement. The staff had not been advised whether or not the objections were withdrawn but had added a further recommendation that dredging and filling would be subject to requirements that turbidity be controlled and that mangrove islands lying outside the proposed channel be protected from damage.

In connection with the bulkhead line relocation and settlement, the staff recommended approval to advertise for objections the Logan Smith Company's application to purchase a 1.277 acre parcel of sovereignty land in Roberts Bay abutting Section 6, Township 37 South, Range 18 East, Sarasota County, appraised at the value of $3,311.26 for the parcel. Applicant offered that price and reconveyance of 0.388 acres previously purchased, lying adjacent to the area in the application.

The biological survey report was adverse, stating that the proposed fill area would consume valuable mangrove islands. The applicant had modified his plans according to suggestions in the report for alternate channel and fill areas.

Mr. John Fite Robertson renewed the objections expressed last week by his son on behalf of the Save Our Bays Association. He said that to make any concession or change in the bulkhead line might lead to other such requests and they strenuously protested. Mr. Christian said it was unfortunate that an agreement could not be reached. But the staff renewed its position that it was in the public interest to approve the settlement because (1) a definitive boundary would be established between public and private lands, (2) submerged lands heretofore conveyed would be returned to the Trustees, (3) the utilization of 0.7 ft. m.s.l. elevation would be abandoned in that area, and (4) it would allow an orderly development of the uplands into homesites.

Motion was made by Mr. Christian, seconded by Mr. Conner and adopted without objection, that the Trustees approve the staff recommendation for approval of the bulkhead line relocation and advertisement of the 1.277 acre parcel for objections only.

PINELLAS COUNTY - File No. 2316-52-253.12, Application
for Land Sale Confirmation.
George L. Mallory, et al, represented by H. H. Baskin, Trustee, applied to purchase a parcel of sovereignty land in St. Joseph Sound abutting the vacated portion of Albert Street in the City of Dunedin containing 0.22 acre in Section 34, Township 18 South, Range 15 East, Pinellas County, appraised at $530 for the parcel.

The biological survey report dated June 6, 1969, was adverse to the proposed work; however, applicant had amended the plan so that there would be only limited adverse effects. The Trustees approved the bulkhead line location on March 24, 1970. The Director said the purchase application came pursuant to that approval and had been filed with the staff for several months, prior to the adoption of the public interest criteria policy for sales. The staff recommended approval because it was an integral part of the March approval of bulkhead line relocation. The bottom lands on both sides had been conveyed and were controlled by the applicant.

Mr. Christian made a motion that the sale be approved.

Mr. Adams called attention to the fact that while the parcels on each side of the application area had been sold, no authority had been granted to dredge and fill them. He said the Board of Trustees now had a public purpose criteria for sales and he did not consider the reason cited by the applicant that additional housing was needed in the area a valid public purpose. Mr. Christian, noting the position of the small parcel on the map, thought it would be better to allow the continuous shoreline development to the approved bulkhead line; and while he did agree with the public interest policy he pointed out that the application was filed prior to its adoption.

Mr. Faircloth said he would vote against the sale on the basis that an insufficient public purpose was presented.

Speaking for the applicant, Mr. Howard Rives pointed out that it was an old application, that it would be in the public interest as it would be the only condominium complex in the City of Dunedin within walking distance of the public park, marina and other public facilities, that it was approved by the Pinellas Authority, that it was an old street in 1883 but was not a street in its present state and had been vacated.

Mr. Christian questioned whether there could be any other use for the area, and Governor Kirk agreed.

The motion for approval by Mr. Christian was seconded by Mr. Conner and adopted on vote of three to two, Messrs. Adams and Faircloth voting "No." Since there were not five votes for the sale, Mr. Christian said it would have to be reconsidered or denied. The Director said it amounts to a denial.

ST. JOHNS COUNTY - Application to Advertise Two Adjacent Parcels for Sale; File Nos. 2360 and 2361-55-253.12. Staff requested waiver of the usual two weeks advance agenda notice and authority to advertise the following two sale applications for objections only.

File No. 2360-55-253.12. J. Carver Harris of St. Augustine, Florida, offered the $100 minimum set by the staff appraiser for a 0.04 acre parcel of sovereignty land in the St. Johns River lying between established bulkhead line and Lot 5 of Palamo Subdivision in Section 39, Township 6 South, Range 27 East, St. Johns County.

File No. 2361-55-253.12. Dr. Emilio D. Echevarria offered the $100 minimum set by the staff appraiser for a 0.06 acre parcel of sovereignty land in the St. Johns River lying between the established bulkhead line and Lot 4 of Palamo Subdivision in Section 39, Township 6 South, Range 27 East, St. Johns County.

The biological report dated October 24, 1969, prepared for the bulkhead line application, was adverse. Both applicants desired to construct seawalls and backfill to prevent damage to upland property and dwellings. The sale would allow restoration of an old wooden seawall and backfilling under the houses. The Trustees approved the bulkhead line location on May 12, 1970.

On motion by Mr. Christian, seconded by Mr. Adams and adopted without objection, the Trustees authorized advertisement of the two parcels for objections only.

PASCO COUNTY - Offshore Campsite Lease.
Staff recommended issuance of a campsite lease for private purposes
to W. D. Little, represented by Sam Y. Allgood, Jr., New Port Richey,
Florida, for one year with option to renew for four additional years,
at $100 annual rental. The application complied with the policy
established on April 7, 1970. The area would not exceed one acre.
Applicant had a structure offshore in Pasco County which was
severely damaged by Hurricane Gladys in October of 1968, and
desired to replace the destroyed structure.

On motion by Mr. Christian, seconded by Mr. Adams and adopted
without objection, the Trustees authorized issuance of a campsite
lease as recommended by the staff.

BROWARD COUNTY - Quitclaim Deeds, File No. 2330-06-253.12(6)
                    and File No. 2331-06-253.12(6)
(1) Richard L. and Bruce W. Burkard of Fort Lauderdale, Florida,
represented by Harold Zinn and Associates, applied for quitclaim
deed to a parcel of filled sovereignty land embracing 0.007 acre
in Lake Mayan abutting Section 13, Township 50 South, Range 42
East, Fort Lauderdale, Broward County. The parcel was appraised at
$216.60, or $28,750 per acre.

(2) Walter Michner, et al, of Miami, Florida, represented by Harold
Zinn and Associates, applied for quitclaim deed to a parcel of
filled sovereignty land embracing 0.026 acre in Lake Mayan abutting
Section 13, Township 50 South, Range 42 East, Fort Lauderdale,
Broward County. The parcel was appraised at $733.40, or $28,750
per acre.

On motion by Mr. Adams, seconded by Mr. Faircloth and adopted
without objection, the Trustees authorized issuance of quitclaim
deeds to the two applicants in compliance with Section 253.12(6)
Florida Statutes, at the appraised value of each parcel, provided
each applicant pays $100 processing fee and the appraisal costs.

BROWARD COUNTY - Road Easement.
On motion by Mr. Christian, seconded by Mr. Conner and adopted
without objection, the Trustees approved the request of the Department of Transportation for an easement for widening and improving
State Road No. S-817 in Sections 16 and 21 of Township 51 South,
Range 41 East, and temporary use of additional land for sloping
and grading purposes.

The Department of Health and Rehabilitative Services agreed to
issuance of the easement for use of the land that had been used
as part of the South Florida State Hospital grounds.

HILLSBOROUGH COUNTY - Easements.
On motion by Mr. Christian, seconded by Mr. Adams and adopted
without objection, the Trustees granted the request of the City
of Tampa, approved by the Department of Health and Rehabilitative
Services, for two easements 10 feet by 30 feet for the purpose of
installation and service of water meters to serve the new mental
health facility at Fletcher Avenue and 30th Street in Tampa,
Hillsborough County.

DIXIE COUNTY - Dredge to Improve Navigation. Section 253.123 F. S.
John Irwin of Steinhatchee, Florida, applied for dredge permit to
connect a 50 ft. wide by 5 ft. deep boat slip to the Steinhatchee

River in Section 25, Township 9 South, Range 9 East, Dixie County, for which the $50 processing fee had been remitted.

Mr. Adams noted that the biological report said that dredging would eliminate portions of productive marsh but the project was small with limited adverse effects as long as all spoil material was placed on upland and not on the marsh. The Director said that requirement would be written into the permit.

On motion by Mr. Adams, seconded by Mr. Christian and adopted without objection, the Trustees authorized issuance of the dredge permit to improve navigation.

FRANKLIN COUNTY - Dredge to Improve Navigation, Section 253.123 F. S. Dr. A. C. Tuck, represented by Mr. Jerrol Raymond, applied for a permit for a navigation channel 200 ft. long, 42 ft. wide and 4 ft. deep in Alligator Harbor adjacent to Section 6, Township 7 South, Range 1 West, Franklin County. The Director said there was an objection, but upon on-site inspection and survey by a field man on the Trustees' staff it was determined that the work done by the applicant was not below the line of mean high water and staff recommended approval of the application.

The members had understood that this application would be deferred, however, Mr. Raymond was present with a letter from the applicant agreeing that deposit of spoil material would be in accordance with recommendations of the Department of Natural Resources. The main objection had been that spoil would be deposited on marsh areas.

Since postponement had been recommended at the meeting of the Trustees' staff members, on motion by Mr. Adams, seconded by Mr. Christian and adopted without objection, the application was deferred for further consideration.

MARTIN COUNTY - Dredge to Improve Navigation, Section 253.123 F. S. Scott Construction Co., in care of the Department of Transportation, applied for a permit to dredge two 150 ft. wide channels in the St. Lucie River at Palm City Bridge in Section 17, Township 38 South, Range 41 East, Martin County, so that the old bridge structure could be removed. The material would be deposited at the site and later returned to the dredge area. The biological report was not adverse.

Staff recommended approval subject to the dredging being done with extreme care, no material stockpiled on adjacent grass flats, and the dredge material being returned to the dredge area after completion of the project.

On motion by Mr. Adams, seconded by Mr. Christian and adopted without objection, the Trustees approved issuance of the permit with requirements recommended by the staff.

MARTIN COUNTY - Dredge to Improve Navigation, Section 253.123 F. S. Bill V. Neff, represented by Evans Crary, Jr., applied for a permit to dredge a navigation channel 80 ft. long, 50 ft. wide and 5 ft. deep in South Fork St. Lucie River adjacent to Section 5, Township 38 South, Range 41 East, Martin County. The application was filed prior to adoption of the $50 processing fee requirement.

The material removed would be placed on applicant's upland, and the biological survey report was not adverse.

7-21-70

On motion by Mr. Adams, seconded by Mr. Faircloth and adopted without objection, the Trustees authorized issuance of the dredge permit to improve navigation without the $50 processing fee.

PALM BEACH COUNTY - Fill Permit, Section 253.124 Florida Statutes. File No. 24981(1991-50)
The motion for rehearing in that cause styled DiVosta Rentals, Inc., v. Claude R. Kirk, et al, Case No. 69-1219 Second Judicial Circuit, Leon County, had been denied.

The staff requested authority to issue fill permit to DiVosta Rentals, Inc., which the Trustees had denied on October 21, 1969.

Motion was made by Mr. Christian, seconded by Mr. Conner and adopted without objection, that the permit be issued on order of the court.

PINELLAS COUNTY - Dredge to Improve Navigation, Section 253.123 F.S.
T. D. Allissandratos of Tarpon Springs, Florida, was granted a dredge-only permit by Pinellas County Water and Navigation Control Authority, subject to Trustees' approval, to dredge a navigation channel 30 ft. wide, 5 ft. deep and 240 ft. long in Whitcomb Bay adjacent to Section 14, Township 27 South, Range 15 East, Pinellas County. The material removed would be hauled away and the biological survey report was not adverse.

The Authority recommended that the Trustees waive the $50 processing fee, as the permit was filed prior to adoption of the policy.

On motion by Mr. Adams, seconded by Mr. Christian and adopted without objection, the Trustees authorized issuance of the dredge permit without the $50 processing fee requirement.

HILLSBOROUGH COUNTY - SAJSP Permits 66-383.
On July 7 the Trustees postponed action for two weeks on consideration of the request of the District Engineer, Jacksonville District, United States Corps of Engineers, that an overall state position be indicated by the Trustees in connection with reissuance of SAJSP Permit 66-383 as modified, to the Marine Bank and Trust Company which had a permit from the Tampa Port Authority to dredge and fill submerged land in Tampa Bay abutting Section 19, Township 29 South, Range 18 East, Hillsborough County.

The Director stated that the Attorney General had requested deferment.

It was so ordered.

ST. JOHNS COUNTY - Dock Permit, Section 253.03 F. S.
Loran A. Brown, represented by Emmett W. Pacetti, requested approval of modification of a dock to be constructed under state commercial dock permit No. CD-1705 in Matanzas Bay adjacent to applicant's upland in David Shores Subdivision in Township 7 South, Range 30 East, St. Augustine, Florida.

Staff recommended approval of the revised location that was proposed due to an objection filed by an adjacent owner.

On motion by Mr. Conner, seconded by Mr. Christian and adopted without objection, the Trustees authorized revision of the state commercial dock permit.

RESOLUTION - Revision.
Revision of the resolution adopted by the Trustees on June 2 was
suggested by the Cabinet in the Department of Natural Resources meeting on June 9 and discussed by the Trustees on June 16. The Director,
after much discussion with representatives of the Trustees, proposed
a redraft that requires sales of state-owned land be made only in
the public interest with applicant to demonstrate compliance with
that policy, and provides that no lease of public land would be for
more than fifteen years and not contrary to the public interest.

Mr. Faircloth favored a reduced term of five years and avoiding any
structures under a lease which might affect use of the state land in
the future. He said the Department of Natural Resources should be
consulted in matters of this kind, as both leases and sales would
divest the Board of use of the sovereignty land. Mr. Adams suggested
a lease term of ten years would comply with the law, and mentioned
that in agricultural leases drainage facilities or structures were
erected but in any event the structures on leased land would become
property of the state after the lease term expired.

On motion by Mr. Christian, seconded by Mr. Conner and Mr. Adams,
adopted without objection, the Trustees waived the rules for action
on the policy resolution, and approved revision of the resolution
as recommended by the Director but with a lease term of ten years
only, as follows:

RESOLUTION

WHEREAS, Florida's publicly-owned land is a vitally important
resource which should be preserved for the use of all her
citizens; and

WHEREAS, past sales of this publicly-owned land have
significantly depleted this vital resource; and

WHEREAS, stringent measures must now be adopted to preserve
what remains of this resource for future generations; and

WHEREAS, the State of Florida Board of Trustees of the
Internal Improvement Trust Fund had fiduciary duty to act on
behalf of all the citizens of Florida; NOW

THEREFORE, BE IT RESOLVED, that the State of Florida Board
of Trustees of the Internal Improvement Trust Fund does hereby
declare that no further sales of state-owned land will take
place unless the applicant for the sale can affirmatively demonstrate
that same would be in the public interest; and be it

FURTHER RESOLVED, that no lease of public land shall be
executed for a term in excess of ten years and that no such
lease shall be contrary to the public interest; and be it

FURTHER RESOLVED, that the Trustees' staff is hereby directed
to include in its recommendations on each sale a statement as
to whether same would be in the public interest and on each lease
a statement as to whether same would be contrary to the public
interest.

DONE in the Capitol, Tallahassee, Florida, this 21st day
of July, A. D. 1970.

WEST FLORIDA COUNTIES - Hurricane Becky.
Riparian properties along the Gulf of Mexico coast, bays and bayous
of West Florida counties might experience damage as a direct result
of Hurricane Becky advancing toward Pensacola. The Director
requested certain emergency authority be granted, if recommended
by an inspection team consisting of Board of Trustees and Department
of Natural Resources personnel.

On motion by Mr. Christian, seconded by Mr. Adams and adopted without
objection, the Trustees granted permission to the staff to administratively authorize installation of protection devices in and
restoration of these critical areas after, but only after, an on-site
inspection and investigation reveals that the damage was a direct
result of the hurricane.

Secretary of State Tom Adams, joined by Mr. Christian and other
members, requested the Director for a complete public presentation
and briefing of the Trustees on activities in Collier County relating
to Wiggins Pass-Vanderbilt Beach, Parkshores-Point Royal developments involving the Trustees and the Department of Natural Resources
and about which there was great misunderstanding and considerable
correspondence.

The Director said he would make a full report at the next meeting.

SANTA ROSA AND ESCAMBIA COUNTIES - On July 7, 1970, the Trustees
received one bid from Marshall R. Young Oil Company in response to
an advertised lease of land in the Escambia River. In view of
promising aspects for oil drilling in that area the members thought
a higher bid might be expected and rejected the bid.

Mr. Apthorp said the staff had no instruction as to when the oil
and gas drilling lease should be readvertised.

On motion by Mr. Christian, seconded by Mr. Adams and adopted
without objection, the rules were waived and the Trustees ordered
readvertisement for new bids on the oil and gas drilling lease
covering the sovereignty land owned by the Trustees in the Escambia
River and its tributaries in Townships 5 and 6 North, Ranges 29 and
30 West, containing 205 acres, more or less, in Santa Rosa and
Escambia Counties.

SUBJECTS UNDER CHAPTER 18296

On motion by Mr. Faircloth, seconded by Mr. Christian and adopted
without objection, the Trustees approved Report No. 970 listing two
regular bids for sale of Murphy Act land in Pasco and Seminole
Counties under provisions of Chapter 18296, Acts of 1937, Section
197.350 Florida Statutes, as follows: (1) sale of a parcel of land
in Pasco County to William F. Rawlinson et ux, for $300, and (2) sale
of a lot in Seminole County to M. G. Hodges for $200; and the
Trustees authorized execution of deeds pertaining thereto.

REFUND - On motion by Mr. Adams, seconded by Mr. Christian and
adopted without objection, the Trustees authorized refund of $15
to each of the following two applicants for the reason that the
Department of Transportation declined to recommend release of the
state road right of way reservations contained in the Murphy Act
deeds as listed below:

28

Panama Title Company - Bay County Deed No. 351
Roy W. Caldwell - Lake County Deed No. 02-Chapter 21684

On motion duly adopted, the meeting was ad'   .   /

ATTEST: _James W Apthorp_
EXECUTIVE DIRECTOR

GOVERNO   CHAIRMAN

Tallahassee, Florida
July 28, 1970

The State of Florida Board of Trustees of the Internal Improvement
Trust Fund met on this date in Senate Hearing Room 31 in the Capitol,
with the following members present:

Claude R. Kirk, Jr.	Governor
Earl Faircloth	Attorney General
Fred O. Dickinson, Jr.	Comptroller
Broward Williams	Treasurer (Present part time)
Floyd T. Christian	Commissioner of Education
Doyle Conner	Commissioner of Agriculture
James W. Apthorp	Executive Director

The minutes of July 14 were approved as submitted.

DADE COUNTY - File No. 2329-13-253.12, Land Sale.
On June 2, 1970, the Trustees considered application from H. P.
Forrest, Trustee, represented by William J. Roberts, to purchase a
parcel of sovereignty land in Biscayne Bay containing 4.4026 acres
abutting Section 22, Township 53 South, Range 42 East, in Miami Beach,
Florida, for construction of Island View Post-Graduate Hospital. The
applicant offered $95,000 - the $92,500 appraisal reviewed and adjusted
by the staff appraiser. The proposed sale was advertised for objections
only in the Miami News, proof of publication filed, and several
objections were received from individuals on Sunset Island No. 4 and
from owners of a condominium on Lincoln Court.

The biological survey report showed that sale and development would
have adverse effects on the small amount of remaining marine life
in the area.

Staff was of the opinion that the sale was in the public interest
based on a study submitted by the applicant that showed a need for
additional hospital beds and a post-graduate hospital in the area.
Therefore, recommendation was that the objections be overruled and
the sale confirmed at the adjusted appraised value.

7-21-70

Motion was made by Mr. Williams, seconded by Mr. Christian, that the sale be confirmed.

Mr. Faircloth voted against sale, stating that while hospitals are generally in the public interest this one is a private hospital and possibly could be built elsewhere. He suggested more time to study items on the agenda that require consideration of the public interest. The Director explained that sales and bulkhead lines are shown on an advance agenda two weeks before consideration by the Trustees, and, when authorized, advertisement of proposed sale ran for four weeks before consideration of confirmation of sale. In reply to Mr. Faircloth's question about pollution, the Director reported that the staff referred any application involving possible pollution to the Air and Water Pollution Control staff for report and recommendation. A longer period of advance agenda notification was discussed.

Mr. Roberts, applicant's attorney, explained that this was for a private non-profit hospital which accepted indigent patients and had a teaching and complete research program, which did serve a public purpose.

On the motion by Mr. Williams, seconded by Mr. Christian and approved by Governor Kirk, Mr. Dickinson and Mr. Conner, the Board confirmed the sale with Mr. Faircloth voting "No."

MONROE COUNTY - File No. 2309-44-253.12, Land Sale Denied.
On June 16 the Trustees considered application from D. R. Gaines, represented by James T. Glass, to purchase a parcel of sovereignty land in Florida Bay abutting Section 6, Township 66 South, Range 33 East, at Key Vaca, Monroe County, containing 1.93 acres in the original application but reduced to 0.87 acre to lessen adverse biological effects and eliminate a mangrove island as recommended by the biological report and the staff.

Navigation channels would be placed almost entirely within the purchase area which would be used for a low income housing development. Mr. William J. Roberts, present on behalf of the applicant, said this was a federal Housing and Urban Development project needed in the area. The applicant offered the appraised value of $750 for the parcel ($858 per acre).

Mr. Christian made a motion, seconded by Mr. Williams, that the sale be approved. Mr. Faircloth and Governor Kirk voted "No" and the sale was denied, lacking five votes for disposition of the land. Mr. Faircloth said he favored low income housing but did not see that it had to be constructed on the water.

BREVARD COUNTY - File No. 2315-05-253.12, Application to Advertise.
Orval M. Bradford, Jr., and Floyd H. Criswell, represented by Leonard Spielvogel, applied for a 0.341 acre parcel of sovereignty land in the Indian River abutting fractional Section 2, Township 25 South, Range 36 East, at Merritt Island in Brevard County.

The biological report secured at the time the bulkhead line was established was not adverse. The Trustees approved the bulkhead line on June 24, 1969, and again on January 27, 1970. Based on existing information, the sale appeared to be in the public interest as it would allow straightening of the shoreline between existing seawalls, eliminating a mosquito breeding stagnant pocket and providing an orderly upland development, clearly delineating the boundary between public and private lands.

On motion by Mr. Christian, seconded by Mr. Williams and adopted without objection, the Board authorized advertisement for objections only.

MONROE COUNTY - File No. 2349-44-253.12(6) Quitclaim Deed. W. F. VanSweringen, represented by James T. Glass, requested issuance of a quitclaim deed to a parcel of filled sovereignty land containing 0.14 acre in Tarpon Basin abutting Section 22, Township 61 South, Range 39 East, Key Largo, Monroe County, Florida, appraised at $100, or $715 per acre, prior to filling.

On motion by Mr. Williams, seconded by Mr. Faircloth and adopted without objection, the Board authorized issuance of quitclaim deed in compliance with provisions of Section 253.12(6) Florida Statutes at the appraised value, applicant to pay $100 processing fee and cost of the appraisal.

PALM BEACH COUNTY - File No. 2346-50-253.12(6), Quitclaim Deed. Leon A. Robbins, represented by Grover C. Herring, requested issuance of a quitclaim deed to a parcel of filled sovereignty land covering 1.929 acres in Lake Worth abutting Section 15, Township 45 South, Range 43 East, Town of Manalapan, Palm Beach County, appraised at a value of $100 prior to filling.

On motion by Mr. Williams, seconded by Mr. Faircloth and adopted without objection, the Board authorized issuance of quitclaim deed in compliance with Section 253.12(6) Florida Statutes, at the appraised value, applicant also to pay the $100 processing fee, cost of the appraisal and $722.42 for fill material.

SPOIL ISLANDS; OKALOOSA ISLAND AUTHORITY REQUEST. The agenda listed consideration of spoil island policy and the request of Okaloosa Island Authority for dedication of a spoil island in Okaloosa County; however, the Director advised that the Secretary of State had asked for deferment for two weeks because of his absence.

The Board agreed to the deferment, but heard Representative J. G. (Jerry) Melvin who had come to make a presentation on behalf of Okaloosa Island Authority.

Mr. Melvin said the Authority already had three miles of islands developed under protective regulations and areas for public purposes. The spoil island in question was being used by people now, with no one responsible for cleaning up the debris, and the Authority desired to have it under their jurisdiction in the public interest. Mr. Melvin did not object to the deferment for two weeks.

TRUSTEES FUNDS - Staff requested authority to spend up to $800 for aerial photography of Cudjoe Key in Monroe County. The majority of land on the key was owned by Rimersburg Coal Company and El Radabob Liquidation Trust, which firms desired to enter into boundary line agreement with the Board to clear land titles and had agreed to defray half of the total $1,600 cost to obtain the photography needed to work out suitable boundary lines.

On motion by Mr. Christian, adopted without objection, the Trustees authorized expenditure of Trustees funds up to $800 for the aerial photography requested by the staff.

ESCAMBIA COUNTY - Spoil Easement.
The United States Department of the Navy requested permission to
place on uplands within Fort Pickens State Park in Escambia County
spoil material that would result from maintenance dredging of the
ship channel to be completed by November 1971.

The Division of Recreation and Parks, Department of Natural
Resources, reviewed and approved the project; and on this date the
Board approved the item on the agenda of the Department of Natural
Resources in connection with dredging by the Corps of Engineers of
the passage from the Gulf of Mexico into Pensacola Bay.

On motion by Mr. Faircloth, seconded by Mr. Christian and adopted
without objection, the Trustees authorized spoil easement for the
purpose.

DADE COUNTY - Corrective Deed.
L. Jules Arkin requested issuance of a deed superseding and
correcting Trustees Deed No. 21159 dated March 13, 1956, issued to
Edith L. Trees who became deceased 13 days prior to the date of the
deed. The grantee in the corrective deed would be the present
record owner of the property.

On motion by Mr. Williams, seconded by Mr. Christian and adopted
without objection, the Trustees authorized issuance of corrective
deed to Doris Kaskel, et al, for $25 processing fee.

BROWARD COUNTY - Dredge Permit to Improve Navigation,
                Section 253.123 F. S., File 587.
Port Everglades Authority had applied for a dredge permit for a
channel 15 ft. deep, 100 ft. wide, and 600 ft. long in and parallel
to the old F. E. C. canal, and to dredge an area in the Intracoastal
Waterway 425 ft. wide, 600 ft. long and minus-36 ft. deep in Section
24, Township 50 South, Range 42 East, Broward County, with the spoil
to be placed on upland. The Port Authority by resolution requested
waiver of the requirement of 10¢ per cubic yard payment.

The biological report was not adverse, noting that it was a heavily
industrialized port area, but objection was filed by the Board of
County Commissioners on the basis that the proposed dredging
would adversely affect the county park. On July 14 the Trustees
deferred action because of the county objection. Motion to approve
was made by Mr. Faircloth, seconded, and discussed. Port Attorney
Linwood Cabot, Chairman Jack Clark and Dr. L. F. Wicker of
Hydrospace Research Corporation, discussed the application,
negotiations for leasing 4½ acres owned by the Port Everglades
Authority and zoned for many years for industrial use, the intended
use of the land on the Intracoastal Waterway for oceanographic
research. Mr. Cabot said the Trustees should not be placed in the
position of a planning and zoning board, that the Authority members
were an elected body and should be allowed to use port-owned land
as planned, and he urged approval of the dredge permit.

Carl F. Thompson, Director of Parks, representing Broward County
Commission, objected that the county had plans to use the area in
connection with the county beach, if it could get the land (owned
by the Port Authority). The county was not against Hydrospace
but suggested some other location might be used that would not be
so near the county beach. Governor Kirk asked about access to
the county beach and possibility of a tunnel which Mr. Thompson
said was a plan for the future.

Harry J. Vardemeier, Jr., of Broward County Area Planning Board,
and Al Barill, Area Planning Director, also strongly objected to
the Port Authority plans, charging that it would damage the tourist
oriented activities and the environment, and would use an area needed
for expansion of the county beach.

Treasurer Broward Williams left the meeting during this discussion.

Mr. Christian made a motion that the application be denied, which
was seconded by Mr. Faircloth. There was further discussion and no
vote on the motion. The motion was withdrawn.

Mr. Apthorp pointed out that the question before the Board was an
application from the Port Authority to remove material from the
waterway in front of the site and from the Intracoastal Waterway
which would be used to raise the site for building the Hydrospace
facility, that the biological report was not adverse, that the
county obviously wanted the land that was owned by the Port Authority.

After the additional discussion and explanation by Dr. Wicker of the
research plans, Mr. Faircloth said he might be in favor of the application but since there was an allegation that it would impair the
county beach, he would like to know the reaction of the Department
of Natural Resources Divisions of Beaches and Shores and Recreation
and Parks. Mr. Christian suggested deferment until reports were
available from those agencies.

The Director said the staff would secure reports, and would meet
with the various parties before again placing the application on the
agenda for consideration by the Trustees.

MONROE COUNTY - Dredge Permit to Improve Navigation,
            Section 253.03 Florida Statutes.
Ernest Leder applied for permission to dredge a channel 50 ft. wide,
minus-5 ft. mean low water depth, 900 ft. long, in the Atlantic
Ocean in Section 19, Township 65 South, Range 34 East, at Grassy
Key, Monroe County. The application was filed prior to the effec-
tive date of the $50 fee policy.

The project was approved on August 8, 1967 without a biological
study; therefore, when applicant requested an extension of time
a biological study was required. It cited limited adverse effects,
suggested revisions, and applicant modified channel as recommended.

On motion by Mr. Christian, seconded by Mr. Faircloth and adopted
without objection, the Trustees authorized issuance of the dredge
permit.

DADE COUNTY - Permit for Channel Markers, Section 253.03 F. S.
On motion by Mr. Faircloth, seconded by Mr. Christian and adopted
without objection, the Trustees waived the $100 processing fee and
authorized issuance of state permit to the Dade County Public Works
Department, Water Control Division, for installation of five channel
markers in Biscayne Bay offshore from upland in Section 40, Township
54 South, Range 41 East, Dade County.

POLICY FOR DOCK PERMITS - At the request of the Secretary of State
who was not present on this date, the Trustees deferred consideration
of alternatives to the present policy regarding dock permits.

HILLSBOROUGH COUNTY - SAJSP Permits 66-383.
Consideration of the Marine Bank and Trust Company permit was
again deferred. Attorney General Faircloth said the applicant had
obtained another biological survey report and the Board would like
a staff recommendation on it.

BROWARD COUNTY - Parker-Dorado Litigation.
The staff had been working with the Attorney General with respect
to litigation now pending against Parker-Dorado interests in Broward
County, had turned up additional evidence indicating that the seawall
appeared to be constructed seaward of the mean high water mark, and
requested that the Cabinet authorize the Attorney General to proceed
on behalf of the Trustees in the suit.

On motion by Mr. Christian, seconded by Mr. Faircloth, it was so
ordered.

TRUSTEES OFFICE - The Trustees postponed consideration of the
report of the Executive Director on expanding the personnel and
operations of the office pending completion of the budget requirements.

On motion duly adopted, the meeting was adjourned.

GOVERNOR - CHAIRMAN

ATTEST:
EXECUTIVE DIRECTOR

* * *

Tallahassee, Florida
August 4, 1970

The State of Florida Board of Trustees of the Internal Improvement
Trust Fund met on this date in Senate Hearing Room 31, with the
following members present:

Tom Adams   Secretary of State, Acting Chairman
Earl Faircloth   Attorney General
Fred O. Dickinson, Jr.   Comptroller
Floyd T. Christian   Commissioner of Education
Doyle Conner   Commissioner of Agriculture

James W. Apthorp   Executive Director

The minutes of the meeting of July 21, 1970, were approved as
submitted.

8-4-70

BREVARD COUNTY - File No. 23775(790-05), Dredge and Fill Permits.
An application from Edward Shablowski that was denied by the Board
of Trustees on July 14, 1970, was placed on the agenda for further
consideration at the request of Mr. Dickinson for the reason that
through an oversight the staff had failed to notify the applicant
that the matter was to be considered.

However, Mr. Dickinson stated that counsel for the applicant had
asked for a delay, and the Director added that they would like a
delay of three weeks.

Without objection, the application was deferred until August 25.

CITRUS COUNTY - Dredge and Fill Permits, Sections 253.123 and
253.124 Florida Statutes.
The Board of County Commissioners of Citrus County applied for
permission to remove muck and silt from the beach area on Fort
Island in Section 16, Township 18 South, Range 16 East, Citrus County
in the Gulf of Mexico. Beach material would be hauled in to replace
the removed muck and silt, for the purpose of creating a public
beach. On July 14, 1970, the Trustees approved the establishment
of a bulkhead line for the project and although the biological survey
report was adverse, staff recommended approval of the application
as the work would create a public beach in an area where there was
none.

Answering Mr. Adams' question regarding the public nature of the
project, the Director stated that the county was to construct the
beach, and it would be a public beach.

On motion by Mr. Christian, seconded by Mr. Dickinson and adopted
without objection, the Trustees approved the application.

DUVAL COUNTY - Dredge Permit, Maintenance Dredging for Navigation,
Section 253.123, File 608.
Jacksonville Electric Authority applied for a permit authorizing
maintenance dredging to improve navigation in the St. Johns River
in Township 2 South, Range 27 East, in Jacksonville in an area 800
feet long, 150 feet wide and minus-36 feet in depth. Applicant
tendered $50 application fee.

The biological survey report dated July 24, 1970, was not adverse.
Staff recommended approval subject to the dredging and spoiling
being carefully done to minimize siltation and water turbidity.

On motion by Mr. Dickinson, seconded by Mr. Christian and adopted
without objection, the Trustees approved the application subject to
the provisions recommended by the staff.

HIGHLANDS COUNTY - Rescind Permit; Refund.
On February 4, 1969, the Trustees approved issuance of a dredge
permit (File 253.03-91) for removal of 700 cubic yards of material
from Lake June-in-Winter in Highlands County; however, the applicants requested refund of the $70 as they no longer intend to remove
the material from the lake.

On motion by Mr. Dickinson, seconded by Mr. Christian and adopted
without objection, the Trustees authorized refund of $70 to Mr. and
Mrs. Steven Hudeck and rescinded the permit.

LEE COUNTY - Permit No. 253.123-137.
Permit No. 253.123-137 was issued on March 18, 1969, to Sunset Realty
Company, represented by Earl Drayton Farr, Jr., to dredge a by-pass
navigation channel in Sections 11, 12, 13 and 14, Township 43 South,
Range 20 East, on Gasparilla Island in Lee County. A field
inspection indicated applicant's dredge operator had performed
additional work, had deepened and widened the existing channel
northward to the bridge at 16th Street which had been previously
approved under a Corps of Engineers permit, now expired. Apparently
the dredge operator was given copies of the Corps permit as well
as the state permit. The dredge operator thought both permits
covered the same work area and proceeded to make the additional cut.

At the staff's request, the applicant furnished cross-section of
the dredge area and volume of material removed and offered to pay
for the 32,267 cubic yards of material at the standard rate of 10¢
per cubic yard. Staff recommended issuance of permit for the
overdredge at penalty rate of 30¢ per cubic yard or $9,680.

Mr. Farr had indicated that he would like to be heard on the rate
to be charged for the material. Mr. Adams pointed out that the
rules also provided that a charge might be made up to the maximum
rate of three times the rate per cubic yard prevailing in the
locality at time of discovery which could be considerably more.
Mr. Apthorp said the staff had advised Mr. Farr of that policy,
that the reason for the penalty was consideration of the biological
damage, and the applicant thought the dredging in the channel
covered by the Corps of Engineers permit was also included in the
state permit.

Motion was made by Mr. Christian and adopted without objection,
that the Board accept the staff recommendation for issuance of the
permit upon receipt of $9,680.

MONROE COUNTY - Dredge Permit to Improve Navigation,
                File No. 253.03-167.
R. E. Scharf applied for a dredge permit for a navigation channel
1,300 feet long, 50 feet wide and 5 feet mean low water depth in
Hawk Channel in Section 27, Township 67 South, Range 26 East,
Monroe County. The application was filed prior to the $50 fee
policy was adopted.

The April 14, 1970, biological survey report was adverse and
recommended certain revisions. The project was amended as requested
and a supplemental biological report dated July 21 recognized a
definite improvement in the plans. Staff recommended approval.

Mr. Adams asked the elevation of the land on which the material
was to be deposited, noting that there were many channel dredging
applications where it appeared that fill material was needed.
Explanation of the background of the application was made, including the fact that Mr. Scharf originally applied to purchase
fifteen acres which was denied because of adverse biological conditions, that he had revised his plans as suggested by the staff
so that he would not need to purchase submerged land, that he
would secure fill material from a system of interior canals, that
the perimeter channel would provide access and the adjacent property
owner would tie unto the channel, also. The staff felt that this
was a legitimate navigation project.

The motion that had been made by Mr. Conner and seconded by Mr.
Dickinson was withdrawn and at the request of Mr. Adams the

application was deferred for two weeks for further investigation.

ST. LUCIE COUNTY - Dredge Permit to Improve Upland, Section 253.123.
Florida Power and Light Company, represented by A. M. Davis, vice
president, requested permission to remove 800,000 cubic yards of
material from Big Mud Creek adjacent to Sections 8 and 17, Township
36 South, Range 41 East, St. Lucie County, in addition to the
700,000 cubic yards approved under a dredge permit on June 16, 1970.
Much of the material being removed lacked the quality necessary for
the foundation of the plant being constructed, the biological survey
report was not adverse, and applicant tendered check for $80,000 for
the additional material.

Staff recommended approval subject to spoil area being diked to
prevent silt from returning to the waters and subject to dredging
being done so that turbidity of the water will not exceed 50 Jackson
Units above base.

On motion by Mr. Dickinson, seconded by Mr. Christian and adopted
without objection, the Trustees approved issuance of permit for the
additional material subject to the conditions recommended by the
staff.

PINELLAS COUNTY - State Construction Permit, Erosion Control,
                  Section 253.03 Florida Statutes.
The Pinellas County Public Works and Engineering Department requested
a permit without charge for the installation of sheet piling and
rock rubble for erosion control and emergency repairs at the
Madonna Boulevard Bridge in Tierra Verde in Section 17, Township
32 South, Range 16 East, Pinellas County.

The Department of Natural Resources indicated that no adverse
effects were expected.

On motion by Mr. Dickinson, seconded by Mr. Faircloth and Mr.
Christian, and adopted without objection, the Trustees approved the
application and waived the processing fee for the public project.

MANATEE COUNTY - File Nos. 253.123-561 and 253.124-126,
                 Dredge and Fill Permits.
N. J. Cowart, Trustee, and C. H. Wooten applied for a permit for
dredging 314,000 cubic yards of fill material from existing and
proposed navigation channels and deposit of fill material on submerged lands purchased from the Board by the Estate of Bessie Richards
in Deed Nos. 24887 and 24888(455-41). The City of Palmetto had
granted a permit on July 20, 1970, in accordance with Section 253.124
Florida Statutes.

The biological survey report of July 1, 1970, stated that the proposed
dredging and filling would have significant adverse effects on
productive nursery and feeding grounds.

The original plan submitted to the staff called for massive excavation within the boundaries of the submerged lands in private
ownership. In accordance with staff recommendations the applicant
revised the project to lessen the damage to the environment. All
dredging, except for areas lying within the privately owned lands,
was to be done in existing channels. By increasing channel size
to 125 feet wide by minus-10 feet deep, future maintenance will be
unnecessary and potential damage to ecology reduced.

In consideration for fill material from the channels, the applicants proposed to reconvey two mangrove islands containing approximately 1.6 and 1.2 acres respectively, lying within private ownership. The major portion of the project Terra Ceia Bay will be pulled back from the bulkhead line that will commit an additional 4.36 acres to public use in the form of navigation channels.

The Director reviewed the history of the application, the action of the Trustees approving the sale in 1968 to clear title to the land, and Mr. Christian recalled that the applicant had said they were purchasing twice land on which they had paid taxes for many years. Mrs. Richards had conveyed right of way to the county which in turn agreed to assist her in securing submerged land from the Trustees. The staff recommended approval of the permits because of the situation that existed regarding the land sale.

Mr. Adams recalled the contingent circumstances given consideration at the time of the sale but said great caution should be taken, an actual on-the-site survey might be needed and a determination of whether the portions of mangrove islands to be reconveyed were equal in value to the fill material. Mr. Christian suggested an appraisal.

The Director said the staff would be glad to develop any specific information desired by the members and could have an appraisal made.

Without objection, action was deferred for two weeks.

STATE PARK AND RECREATION AREA LEASE AGREEMENTS. On motion by Mr. Christian, seconded by Mr. Dickinson and adopted without objection, the Trustees approved the request of the Division of Recreation and Parks of the Department of Natural Resources that the Board enter into the following listed lease agreements authorized by the departments as noted:

1. Eden State Park in Walton County, Division of Recreation and Parks
2. Patten Property (Gamble Mansion) in Manatee County, Division of Recreation and Parks
3. Lake Kissimmee State Park (Zipprer Ranch) in Polk County, Division of Recreation and Parks
4. Caloosahatchee River State Park in Lee County, Division of Recreation and Parks
5. Ichetucknee Springs, Columbia and Suwannee Counties, Division of Recreation and Parks
6. Sebastian Inlet, Brevard County, Division of Recreation and Parks
7. Flagler Beach in Flagler County, City of Flagler Beach
All of the above authorized by the Department of Natural Resources on February 17, 1970.

8. Melbourne Beach in Brevard County, Town of Melbourne Beach
9. Wekiwa Springs in Seminole County, Division of Recreation and Parks
10. Apollo State Park in Volusia County, Division of Recreation and Parks
The above three authorized by the Department of Natural Resources on October 21, 1969.

11. Gold Head Branch State Park in Clay County, Division of Recreation and Parks - authorized by Department of Natural Resources on December 16, 1969.

DUVAL COUNTY - Easement. On motion by Mr. Dickinson, adopted without objection, the Trustees granted an easement to the Jacksonville Electric Authority needed to provide electrical service to the site of the new Regional Community Mental Retardation Center in Section 35, Township 2 South, Range 28 East, and Section 2, Township 3 South, Range 28 East, in Duval County, as approved by the Division of Retardation of the Department of Health and Rehabilitative Services.

PINELLAS COUNTY - File No. 2316-52-253.12, Sale Application. Without objection, the Trustees deferred for an indefinite time an application for purchase of a parcel of sovereignty land in St. Joseph Sound abutting the vacated portion of Albert Street in the City of Dunedin from H. H. Baskin, Trustee, on behalf of George L. Mallory, et al. The matter was considered on July 21 and there were not five votes for the sale. At the request of a member of the Board the staff had placed the application on the agenda on this date but the applicant requested postponement.

COLLIER COUNTY - The Director made a status report, requested by the Secretary of State, on several areas of reported illegal dredging in Collier County. Three platted units in the Florida Vanderbilt development were in question, and when the Trustees' field representative had requested cessation of work it was stopped. Upon investigation it was found that there were questions about the location of the mean high water line which the staff was trying to resolve by surveys and aerial photography. The mangrove areas destroyed without a permit would be evaluated and if on state land, a penalty or compensation would be sought.

Mr. Adams was concerned at evidence he had seen on a trip to Collier County of operations without bulkhead lines or dredge and fill permits and said it was just a matter of how much trespass. He said one party to the south continued to fill after being stopped, that there were many problems including disclaimers that had been issued, letters misinterpreted, but that the Board should take some action pending the resolving of basic questions of ownership. He noted that development began in the fifties when no permits were required and was concerned lest some responsible developer be inappropriately criticized but equally concerned that the public domain be protected.

Mr. Apthorp said that five property owners were planning for long-range development of the area on up to Wiggins Pass that would be acceptable to the county and to the Trustees, and with an expanded staff that would be requested next week there would be field men and survey parties to assist the Board.

Mr. Elliot Messer, attorney for Florida Vanderbilt, explained that his client had relied on the advice of counsel, engineers, title information, information from the Trustees' office several years ago, and thought they were working on their own land. The firm would cooperate with the Trustees in any way proper and pay whatever was reasonable and fair to work it out. No further work would be done until the Trustees said it was all right, and then there would be a comprehensive development plan that the staff approved.

Mr. Baker, vice president of Florida Vanderbilt, also defended the company's operations that were within the law according to all the legal advice they had relied on. He said they had deeded some parcels which presented a problem.

The Director discussed what had been done in the Park Shores area nearer to the City of Naples, where an arrest had been made but the prosecutor decided not to proceed against the owner or the dredge operator until two major questions were resolved: first, whether permits were required to operate in that area, and second, whether the meander line should be relied on or the shoreline. The staff needed to seek a judicial solution to the question of ownership. Mr. Adams said that would be a civil proceeding.

Mr. Faircloth said he would make a motion that the Director be authorized to take whatever action was necessary to have these determinations made by the proper court. A resolution had been prepared by Mr. Adams and on motion by Mr. Faircloth, adopted without objection, the Board waived the rules and adopted the following:

R E S O L U T I O N

WHEREAS, the Trustees of the Internal Improvement Trust Fund are vested and charged with the administration, management, conservation, protection and disposition of all lands owned by the State of Florida; and

WHEREAS, in Collier County, Florida, serious questions have been raised as to the trespass of sovereignty lands and those privately owned submerged lands which the Trustees are empowered by statute to regulate through the issuance of permits and the establishing of bulkhead lines; and

WHEREAS, these alleged violations demonstrate the immediate need for a cessation of all dredging, filling, and seawalling activity in the concerned areas until a thorough study and investigation can be made;

NOW, THEREFORE, BE IT RESOLVED by the Trustees of the Internal Improvement Trust Fund that the staff of the Trustees is instructed to seek injunctive relief or other appropriate legal action to prevent any further dredging, filling, or construction of seawalls or further encroachments on state lands in Collier County, Florida; and

BE IT FURTHER RESOLVED, that independent legal counsel be employed by the Trustees for the purpose of making a thorough study and legal determination of the state's title to the lands in question and recommend legal action, both criminal and civil, for any violations which may have occurred, and

BE IT FURTHER RESOLVED, that the areas in question in Collier County be surveyed under the direction of the staff of the Trustees.

The resolution was executed at the meeting by those members present.

The Trustees were given copies of a memorandum from the Governor concurring in the resolution and asking that action be taken to speed up the Coast and Geodetic Survey work in these tidal areas. The staff had an appointment with the Department of the Interior, the federal agency responsible for government surveys. The surveys relied on in Collier County were originally done by the United States and new surveys should be executed by the federal agency.

Mr. Adams spoke of many reported violations, some on a large scale, that must be followed up, many illegal operations in lakes reported over a period of years which the staff just was not equipped to handle; but now, the Board must face up to the task of protecting the public domain.

Mr. George Vega, attorney for Park Shores, said his clients would cooperate with the state and welcomed a lawsuit to properly determine questions of land title and public policy.

Mr. Richard D. DeBoest, attorney for General Acceptance Corporation, said they inherited the problems of the old Gulf American Company, had worked with the staff and fifteen months ago had suggested a settlement, and were continuing to negotiate with the state to try to finalize a settlement. Mr. G. Turner, vice president of GAC, said they would honor their commitments and were anxious to solve the problems.

In view of the late hour, the members noted that no action would be taken on Cape Coral today and they would prefer a written report that would show the fill material yardage figures.

The Trustees heard the following parties speaking on conservation and the need to protect the valuable marine resources and prosecute all violators.

Mr. Bradford Patton from Lee County approved adoption of the resolution and expressed that county's pride in its many vital coastal areas remaining unspoiled.

Mr. Thomas M. Provisano, for himself and Collier County Conservancy, pointed out that tourism depended on the many outdoor aspects of Florida and called for protection of the lands with no compromises or after-the-fact permits.

Mr. Bill Prennen, Director of Big Cypress Nature Center in Naples, called attention to the decreasing amount of land and shoreline owned by the state and the need to preserve it for the future.

Mr. George Matthews, reviewing something of the history of Florida sovereignty and swamp lands and in particular the changes made in the area of Collier and Lee Counties, emphasized that the land was held in trust and the state should back up the cases to prosecute violators.

Mr. Loring Lovell presented a written statement from Conservation 70s, as the time was late.

Mr. Adams reminded those present that when Florida was growing in the past development was needed and encouraged; but now the times were changing, this Board had done much to correct serious problems, and with an increased staff and new laws they would continue to make progress. He thanked those interested parties and concerned citizens who appeared on this date and on many other occasions before the Board.

SUBJECTS UNDER CHAPTER 18296

On motion by Mr. Dickinson, seconded by Mr. Christian and adopted without objection, the Trustees approved Bidding Report No. 970 listing one regular bid for sale of Murphy Act land in Alachua County to Roger W. Williams for $500, under provisions of Chapter 18296, Acts of 1937, Section 197.350 Florida Statutes, and authorized execution of deed pertaining thereto.

On motion duly adopted the meeting was adjourned.

8-4-70

SECRETARY OF STATE - ACTING CHAIRMAN

ATTEST:

EXECUTIVE DIRECTOR

*   *   *

Tallahassee, Florida
August 11, 1970

The State of Florida Board of Trustees of the Internal Improvement
Trust Fund met in Senate Hearing Room 31 in the Capitol, with the
following members present:

Claude R. Kirk, Jr.	Governor
Tom Adams	Secretary of State
Earl Faircloth	Attorney General
Fred O. Dickinson, Jr.	Comptroller
Broward Williams	Treasurer (Present part time)
Floyd T. Christian	Commissioner of Education
Doyle Conner	Commissioner of Agriculture

| James W. Apthorp | Executive Director |

On motion adopted without objection, the Board approved the minutes
of the meeting of July 28, 1970.

Attorney General Faircloth moved the adoption of a resolution asking
that on all applications for sales of land and all dredge and fill
permits the staff advise the Board of the reaction from the Air
and Water Pollution Control Board as to the possible polluting effect
from whatever the applicants propose to do with the land when sold
or dredged or filled. Mr. Faircloth said he would like to have
that additional information as it affects the potentiality for
polluting the environment. Mr. Adams seconded the motion.

The Director explained that under the present procedure the staff
requested the reports required in the statutes and then presented
applications to the Board, that the staff and the Air and Water
Pollution Control Department had agreed on the procedure as they
were not equipped to comment on every application. Under the
federal statutes applicants must secure required certificates.

Mr. Nathaniel P. Reed read portions of the law and commented on the
procedures called for which the Air and Water Pollution Control
Department was totally unprepared to implement for lack of staffing
and funds. He said it was a burdensome process and he did not
foresee any problems under the existing setup except in very large
projects, such as Caladesi Island; and while the resolution was
well thought of, it placed him in a predicament in that there was
not enough staff or money to take the mass that came to Mr. Apthorp's
office - of which only a percentage came to the Board which was
cutting down on those applications, also. Mr. Reed said it was
more involved than giving a reaction, that other things were called

8-11-70

for such as publicizing applications in a newspaper, allowing a 10-day waiting period, holding public hearings; and he would ask the Legislature for funds to implement the law. He added that it was a strong law and if strictly observed he thought any dredging operation in the State of Florida would be in violation.

Mr. Faircloth said he wanted to take full advantage of the new law, that the Board should be very careful and the additional recommendation should help the Board when the staff recommended a sale or dredge and fill permit, but he recognized the problems of implementing the new law.

Mr. Reed said the Air and Water Pollution Control Department would try to live within the spirit of the Attorney General's resolution, would go to the Legislature for sufficient funds, and they would continue to work with the Trustees' staff.

CHARLOTTE COUNTY - Bulkhead Line, Section 253.122 Florida Statute. On June 18, 1968, the Board of County Commissioners of Charlotte County established a bulkhead line in Lemon Bay adjacent to Section 8, Township 41 South, Range 30 East, near Englewood in Charlotte County, located coincidental with the boundary line of submerged land conveyed by the Trustees in Deed No. 22081(177-08) dated March 25, 1959, containing 4.19 acres of bay bottom.

The biological report submitted on May 2, 1968, recommended that the bulkhead line be established at the mean high water line. The staff recommended that the line be denied.

On motion by Mr. Christian, seconded by Mr. Adams and adopted without objection, the Trustees denied approval of the bulkhead line.

OKALOOSA COUNTY - Bulkhead Line, Section 253.122 Florida Statutes. The Board of County Commissioners of Okaloosa County by resolution adopted on July 2, 1970, established a bulkhead line along the mean high water line of Santa Rosa Island in Santa Rosa Sound and Choctawhatchee Bay in Township 2 South, Ranges 23 and 24 West, Okaloosa County. The biological survey report was not adverse, and the staff recommended approval of the line.

On motion by Mr. Adams, seconded by Mr. Christian and adopted without objection, the Trustees approved the bulkhead line established by Okaloosa County on July 2, 1970.

SPOIL ISLANDS - Policy. Pursuant to the request of the Secretary of State that the staff and the Division of Recreation and Parks study the possibility of using spoil islands on the east and west coasts of Florida as a system of marine parks, Mr. Apthorp had advised the Board by memorandum dated July 23 and on this date presented recommendations to the Board for consideration. The Division did not consider it feasible to think in terms of state park development of the spoil islands except in limited instances, setting forth the reasoning in letter of June 19 from Director Ney C. Landrum, copy of which was attached to the staff memorandum and recommendations. Mr. Adams said that letter should be accepted as supplemental material to the policy.

Mr. Adams suggested that the Trustees proceed to inventory all spoil islands, and that the state take appropriate action to evict all squatters. From time to time, the Director advised, a sheriff had been called on to assist in removing squatters.

The recommended policy for future use, concurred in by the Division of Recreation and Parks, recognized the aesthetic and recreational value of spoil islands as they are, with no development. Any use of spoil islands by local government or private persons, as provided for in the policy, would be contingent on showing that a higher public purpose would be served.

On motion by Mr. Christian, seconded by Mr. Faircloth and adopted without objection, the following recommendations of the staff were accepted as the Board's policy with respect to spoil islands:

1. Spoil islands should be left in their natural state unless a greater public purpose would be served by development. If non-state development is to take place, it should be undertaken under lease by the Trustees, rather than sale and consistent with guidelines set forth in Section 253.111 Florida Statutes.

2. Proposals for public development of any spoil island should be authorized only after consultation with appropriate state agencies to see if any better public purpose might be served.

Mr. Christian included in his motion, which was adopted, that the Trustees proceed to inventory all spoil islands.

OKALOOSA COUNTY - Okaloosa Island Authority.
On July 28, 1970, the Trustees deferred action on a resolution from the Okaloosa Island Authority dated May 14, 1970, requesting dedication of a spoil island and other spoil areas to the Authority for management in accordance with the policies and regulations under which it had developed other areas under its jurisdiction. Mr. Adams mentioned a lease under a definite plan of development, instead of dedication.

Honorable J. G. Melvin, Representative from District 7, said the island was in need of cleaning, that it had no facilities but was being used by campers, and the Authority would like to develop it as the other islands, with the title vested in Okaloosa County.

The members felt that the title should remain in the state, and the Director said he would work up a lease proposal with the applicant and bring it back to the Trustees for consideration.

POLK COUNTY - Crooked Lake.
The staff requested authority to select hearing officer and conduct public hearing for the purpose of gathering evidence that would provide a means of establishing a boundary line for Crooked Lake in Polk County. Under provisions of Chapter 70-97, Acts of 1970, one method to establish boundary line is to hold public hearing at such time evidence is submitted upon which a boundary line can be adopted by the Board. The Director said there was much controversy with reference to the boundary of this lake.

On motion by Mr. Conner, seconded by Mr. Faircloth and Mr. Adams, the Trustees approved the request.

MANATEE COUNTY - File No. 2153-41-253.12, Land Sale.
Mr. O. R. Icard, represented by Mr. Dewey Dye, Jr., in order to

clear title to a 2.18 acre parcel of sovereignty land adjacent to Bolees Creek abutting Section 26, Township 35 South, Range 17 East, Manatee County, made application to purchase the parcel at the appraised value of $1,193 per acre or $2,600 for the parcel. The parcel is landward of the bulkhead line approved by the Board on February 6, 1970. The application was on the advance agenda on May 19, was authorized to be advertised on June 2 before adoption of the resolution requiring all sales to be in the public interest.

The Trustees' office received 11 protests of which 6 were withdrawn, and 21 letters in favor of the application. A letter from the County Engineer stated that the sale would aid in the drainage flow of Bolees Creek. Most of the protests were based on an existing eagle's next which was determined to be some distance from the sale area. The biological report was adverse, stating that "The proposed 'inland lagoon' purchase area appears to be a draglined canal extending off Bowlees Creek . . . The inland lagoon has definite value to marine life." (The canal and spoil area can be seen in a 1947 aerial.)

The Director discussed the study by the staff narrowing down the available alternatives to the only proper approach - that the applicant offer to purchase the artificially dug canal area. The staff felt that if the Trustees and the public had any interest there should be compensation for clearing the title.

Attorney General Faircloth said he appreciated the reasons given, but since there was a title question and the state might own the parcel, and the biological report was adverse, he would make a motion that the sale be denied. Mr. Adams seconded the motion.

Explanation of the background and application was made by Mr. Dye and Mr. Thomas F. Icard, including that the canal was dug in 1941 on applicant's property, that efforts to secure a disclaimer for clearing title began two years ago with the Trustees' office, that affidavits and other proof were in the file and they knew of no evidence that the canal was not dug on the Icard upland property.

Mr. Dickinson commented that they needed a court decree quieting title or an instrument from the Board. Mr. Adams said if applicant owned it there was no reason to buy it a second time, and if the applicant did not own it he found it hard to consider that sale was in the public interest. Mr. Dye pointed out that this was not the usual sale of land bordering on the waterfront.

On the motion by Mr. Faircloth, seconded by Mr. Adams, and adopted without objection, the Trustees denied the sale.

PUTNAM COUNTY - File No. 2185-54-253.03, Proposed Settlement. On May 13, 1969, after a considerable period of time and staff investigation, the Trustees denied sale of 3.86 acres of Lake Swan bottom land that had been filled without authorization. As a consequence of the controversial matter, policies were developed that provided the staff with guidelines for final disposition of encroachments, trespasses and other unauthorized activities affecting lakes. The staff recommended the following proposals to resolve the Lake Swan application of Carl C. Carnes:

1. That Mr. Carnes execute an appropriate instrument that would provide a public easement to the lake
2. That Mr. Carnes dredge a minimal boat access channel into the open waters of the lake
3. That dredged material be spoiled in such a manner as to

provide a 1-acre vehicular parking area
4. That Mr. Carnes execute an instrument which would remove any interest in title to Lots 1 through 7, Johnston's unrecorded Subdivision No. 4, that he may have
5. That Mr. Carnes be allowed to purchase the filled 2.43 acre parcel at the rate of $1,200 per acre. The original appraisal evaluated the 3.86 acre application parcel at a nominal value of $400. Approximately 3/5 of the 2.43 acre parcel would be encumbered with a restrictive covenant prohibiting construction of any building.

6. The staff would process such permits as may be necessary to complete the transaction if approved by the Trustees.

The staff had secured an agreement from an intervening upland owner that would provide for an easement from the county road to Mr. Carnes' property. The Game and Fresh Water Fish Commission had been consulted about a boat launching site, but public access easements are necessary before any construction funds for such a purpose can be secured. The staff felt that the above settlement would provide public access to Lake Swan, allow the construction of a boat launching ramp and parking area, allow those owners of Lots 1 through 7, Johnston's unrecorded Subdivision No. 4, to clear title to their lands, and close the file on this long-pending matter.

Mr. Adams, noting that many interested parties were present, spoke of after-the-fact dredge permit for the little channel, the spoil deposited on state property, and his feeling that the state should keep the land. He suggested that Mr. Carnes be allowed to continue dredging the canal to make access to the lake, deposit the material on the state's upland northerly of the canal, that the land not be sold, that Mr. Carnes execute an instrument that would give the state access to its property, and that the state assert title to everything waterward of the meander line.

Representative Ralph C. Tyre, District 17, said he had known the area for many years, that it was a question of who owned what and the state might not own the land in question as it was once upland pasture land, that someone might be unjustly ridiculed, and a new law effective on August 1 provided guidelines for setting boundaries for meandered fresh water lakes. Mr. Adams assured him that the state was not trying to encroach on private ownership.

Mr. David Anderson, spokesman for Lake Swan property owners, expressed opposition to every point of the proposed settlement, and to Mr. Adams' suggestion that the canal dredging be completed. Mr. Adams pointed out that turbidity in the lake could be avoided by a barrier until the operation was finished.

Mr. Christian also opposed the settlement, as the property owners had not been consulted. He said that eventually the problem must be resolved, that Mr. Carnes and the others have to be considered and possibly some agreement could be reached on another solution.

Mr. Christian made a substitute motion, seconded by Mr. Faircloth, that the staff recommendation be denied and the staff meet with the property owners and make a recommendation at a later date.

Mr. Carnes called attention to how long the matter had been pending, that the fill material was put on high ground and pushed back to where it was not on state property - but Mr. Adams pointed out that it was waterward of the meander line. Mr. Carnes said he had purchased in good faith and the title read "from this point following the water's edge to another point" and all the fill would be inside that description.

Representing Conservation 70s, Mr. Loring Lovell and Mr. Lyman Rogers urged the Board to make an example of this case of illegal trespass, that the Legislature had provided the intent in such cases and the Cabinet should interpret and carry it out to preserve Florida waters, that the matter of public access should be treated as a separate issue and attention focused on protection of the marsh areas as being the primary public interest, that the guilty party should remove all of the fill on state lands to restore the lake to the original level.

Mr. Christian thought those suggestions were too drastic, that there was no law requiring removal of the fill (some of which was dredged by a predecessor in title) under penalty, that replacing the material in the lake would damage the lake waters. He said the Board had stopped the filling operation, established that the state owned the land, and now was trying to work out a problem in a manner that would be fair to the tax payers without excessive punishment to the party at fault, considering all the facts.

Mr. N. E. Bingham, one of the protesting property owners, said they were all concerned that they had not been consulted about the staff proposal. On being asked by the Governor if he had any other suggestion, Mr. Anderson responded as spokesman that the Secretary of State's recommendation was more acceptable - to deny everything with the exception of the possible completion of the canal under circumstances acceptable to the staff that would not disrupt the ecology of the lake.

At this point Mr. Carnes proposed as a solution that the lake, being meandered, should have public access and he offered to give an easement across his property, smooth off an acre of land for a parking lot, cut an access channel if necessary to permit boat launching, and pay the state for any land it doesn't care to use in order to clear up the whole matter, with all the details worked out by the staff.

Mr. Faircloth said the staff would consider all the various proposals made here today.

Secretary of State Tom Adams restated the proposal he had made, as follows: that the state assert its ownership waterward of the meander line that has been established, that at this time no land be sold to anyone, that Mr. Carnes be allowed to complete the canal dredging provided a barrier can be provided to protect the lake from siltation, that the spoil material be deposited on the state upland, and that Mr. Carnes execute an appropriate instrument to the state giving access to the state property.

Mr. Conner said he would like to consider that as a recommendation that the staff could study along with the other suggestions made on this date. Mr. Anderson said the interested parties would like to have a decision made today.

Mr. Adams' recommendation, taken as a motion, was seconded by Mr. Faircloth.

Mrs. Wayne R. Conway objected to any more dredging in Lake Swan, as all affected owners had taken that position at a local public meeting held before this date. She objected to Mr. Carnes' offer to give public access, pointing out that this was a small lake and that he should make that offer with respect to the lake that he lived on,

47

and that the dredging had already muddied the beaches and hurt the
other property owners. Mr. Adams and Mr. Christian tried to explain
why the motion appeared to be a good solution, and Governor Kirk
assured her that the Board would consider the residents in determining the proper solution.

The motion made by Mr. Adams, seconded by Mr. Faircloth, was adopted
without objection.

CITRUS COUNTY - Release.
Mr. Colin English requested release of flooding rights held by the
Trustees covering privately-owned Lot 60 of River Heights Subdivision,
Plat Book 1, Page 57, of Citrus County public records. Flooding
rights were acquired by Florida Power Corporation in 1948 and assigned
to the Trustees in 1965 at the time Florida Power donated the
Withlacoochee and Backwaters property (Lake Rousseau) to the state
for public recreational purposes.

The flooding rights were held by the Trustees for the use and
benefit of the Canal Authority of the State of Florida in connection
with the barge canal project. The Canal Authority had no objection
to the release, as Lot 60 is exceptionally high land and will not
be required for either construction or a maintenance spoil area.

Subject to approval of the Division of Recreation and Parks, the
staff recommended release of flooding rights affecting Lot 60 to the
present record owner, Exchange National Bank of Tampa as Trustee,
for handling charge of $15.00.

On motion by Mr. Faircloth, seconded by Mr. Adams and adopted
without objection, the Board adopted the staff recommendation
subject to approval of the Division of Recreation and Parks.

ESCAMBIA COUNTY - Surplus Towersite.
Staff recommended reconveyance without cost to Frontis W. Sherrill,
John H. Sherrill, Jr., Alan P. Sherrill, Margaret S. Bach and Mary
S. Baranco, heirs of J. H. and Mary A. Sherrill, of a 10-acre
parcel formerly used as the Walnut Hill Towersite but now not needed
by the Division of Forestry because of a change in the forest fire
protection system. All fixed improvements had been removed or sold.

The parcel was donated to the Board of Forestry on December 14,
1937, by J. H. and Mary A. Sherrill. Although the deed did not
contain a reverter clause, the Department of Agriculture and Consumer
Services recommended return of the land at no cost to the donors'
heirs who own all the adjacent land. Staff counsel advised that
there did not appear to be any legal impediments in that procedure.

Motion for approval was made by Mr. Adams, but Mr. Faircloth asked
for deferment so that he might review the legal situation. It was
so ordered. Mr. Conner commented that in his opinion it would be
in the interest of the state, that when other parties contributed
sites they should be returned when no longer needed.

SANTA ROSA COUNTY - Power Line Easement.
The Escambia River Electric Cooperative, Inc., requested an easement
over and across 0.58 acre in Section 12, Township 3 North, Range
27 West, and Section 7, Township 3 North, Range 26 West, Santa Rosa
County, for a power line to serve two residences, traversing the
Red Rock Picnic area and providing for future development of a
park in the Blackwater River State Forest.

The Division of Forestry, Department of Agriculture and Consumer Services, recommended approval.

On motion by Mr. Christian, seconded by Mr. Adams and adopted without objection, the Trustees authorized issuance of the easement.

HIGHLANDS COUNTY - File No. 253.123-544, Dredge Permit.
Kenneth M. Knox made application, prior to the adoption of the $50 fee policy, for a dredge permit for a proposed navigation canal 200 ft. long, 20 ft. wide and 3 ft. deep for access to Lake Huntley at Lake Placid, Florida, in Section 5, Township 37 South, Range 30 East, Highlands County.

The biological report was not adverse, and the canal would be on the applicant's upland property.

On motion by Mr. Christian, seconded by Mr. Adams and Mr. Faircloth, adopted without objection, the Trustees approved issuance of the permit without charging the $50 fee.

MARTIN COUNTY - File No. 253.123-383, Dredge Permit.
Richard B. Dunning, represented by W. R. Scott, tendered the $50 application fee for a dredge permit for maintenance dredging in North Fork St. Lucie River in Section 32, Township 37 South, Range 41 East, Martin County. The biological report was not adverse for the project 20 ft. long, 40 ft. wide and 6 ft. deep.

On motion by Mr. Faircloth, seconded by Mr. Christian and adopted without objection, the Trustees approved issuance of the permit for maintenance dredging.

POLICY FOR DOCK PERMITS.
On July 14 the Board had discussed the various permits for docking facilities and asked the Director to review the current policy and suggest revisions, particularly with respect to large apartments or condominiums.

The present policy provided for three classes of authorization:
(1) annual licenses for marinas, charter boat docks and other commercial mooring that severed sovereignty land and the water column from free, unobstructed and unlimited public use, with license issued after approval by the Board and receipt of the first annual payment of no less than 2¢ per year for each square foot of sovereignty land severed from public use; (2) commercial dock permits for other commercial operations such as docks for tenants of hotels, motels, apartments and condominiums, wharfs, piers and other structures of a commercial nature as well as docks for the use of clubs and organizations, with a flat $100 one-time payment for the permit; and (3) private dock permits issued by the staff for a flat $10 one-time fee.

The Director had prepared three alternatives for consideration, the first being to combine (1) and (2) and apply the marina license concept to all commercial docks, so that all docks except those to be used exclusively by the owner, his family and occasional guests, would be subject to the annual licensing procedure outlined in number one above.

The staff proposed that all existing structures would be "grandfathered." Any modifications to existing structures would be subject to a permit. These permits would apply to piers, defined as a structure extending from the solid land out into the water, affording convenient passage for persons and cargo to and from vessels moored along the sides of such structures and to wharfs, defined as a structure on the margin of navigable waters along which vessels can be brought to be loaded or unloaded, and docks, being defined as a slip or waterway extending between two piers or projecting wharfs for reception of vessels.

Motion was made by Mr. Adams, seconded by Mr. Faircloth and adopted without objection, that the policy with respect to dock permits be changed to provide for only two classes of permits and licenses, the first to combine (1) and (2) above, applying the marina license concept to all commercial docks which would be subject to an annual licensing procedure with license to be issued after the Board's approval and receipt of first annual payment which shall be no less than 2¢ per year for each square foot of sovereignty land severed from public use; and the second class of permit to be for private docks used exclusively by the owner, his family, and occasionally by guests, with the permit to be issued by the staff upon submission of a drawing of the proposed structure, the consent of adjoining property owners, and payment of a $10 fee.

Mr. Adams suggested further consideration regarding the "grandfather clause." He pointed out that under the new policy monies would be engendered that might be used to finance rejuvenation of ecological resources.

PALM BEACH COUNTY - Marina License.
Old Port Cove Condominiums of Palm Beach, Florida, represented by Joe Jacobs, applied for a marina license to construct and operate a marina in Lake Worth in conjunction with the condominium units in the Village of North Palm Beach in Section 9, Township 42 South, Range 43 East, Palm Beach County.

The marina will occupy two sites presently encumbered with maintenance spoil easements granted by the Trustees to the Florida Inland Navigation District. The District in turn conveyed its interest in the spoil easements to the United States. A petition for release of MSA 625-B and MSA 626-B was submitted to the District which by resolution on November 14, 1969, recommended release of the easements.

By letter of August 4, 1970, the Chief, Engineering Division of Jacksonville District Engineer, offered no objection to an exchange of spoil areas provided the plan is approved by appropriate state and federal agencies.

The minimum yearly license fee for the two areas embracing a total of 573,055 square feet, would be $11,461.10. Staff recommended approval under certain conditions.

On motion by Mr. Faircloth, seconded by Mr. Christian and adopted without objection, the Trustees approved a marina license conditioned upon the applicant securing approval of appropriate state and federal agencies of any alternate maintenance spoil area that may be necessary, the effective date of the license to coincide with the date of release of the spoil areas by the United States Corps of Engineers.

BROWARD COUNTY - Artificial Reef Permit No. 2329,
Section 253.03 Florida Statutes.
On motion by Mr. Faircloth, seconded by Mr. Christian and adopted

without objection, the Trustees granted two-year extension of the permit approved on April 30, 1968, to Broward Artificial Reef, Inc., for installation of a series of artificial reefs in the Atlantic Ocean 1,800 yards offshore from and parallel to Fort Lauderdale beaches. All of the reefs originally proposed had not been installed.

WAKULLA COUNTY - Dredge Permit for Navigation, and Dock Permit. On motion by Mr. Conner, seconded by Mr. Faircloth and Mr. Adams and adopted without objection, the Trustees approved the request from Olin Corporation of St. Marks, Florida, for the following:

1. Dredge permit under Section 253.123 F. S. to improve navigation in the Wakulla River at St. Marks, Florida, by dredging a channel 300 ft. long, 50 ft. wide and 4 ft. deep. Application filed prior to the adoption of $50 application fee policy. Biological report was not adverse.

2. Commercial dock permit to construct an employees' recreational dock in the Wakulla River adjacent to the applicant's upland property in Section 33, Township 3 South, Range 1 East, Wakulla County. $100 processing fee was submitted by applicant.

LEASE INCOME REPORT - The Trustees accepted for the record the following report of remittances to Florida Department of Natural Resources from holders of dead shell leases:

Lease No. 1718   Radcliff Materials, Inc. $4,457.90
Lease No. 2233   Bay Dredging & Construction Co.   4,451.29

TRUSTEES OFFICE - The Director requested authorization from the Board to request the establishment of thirty new positions, to increase the staff particularly in the Field Operations Division in view of the Board's request and the Governor's memorandum. Mr. Apthorp said the staff had been at its present number for six months and review of the work showed that during the period about one hundred matters needing survey and field inspection had accumulated.

Motion was made by Mr. Christian, seconded by Mr. Faircloth, that the request for additional staffing be approved.

Mr. Adams was in favor of adding four complete survey teams rather than the two proposed under field operations.

Mr. Conner asked for postponement so that he could study the request in view of the large number of new positions at a cost of about $300,000 without legislative authority. He suggested that help might be obtained from other agencies. The Governor was in favor of increasing the staff. Mr. Adams pointed out that the Board had asked the Director to do this, that it was not enough when it concerned every lake and the entire shore line of Florida and the Legislature had told the agency to operate from money it generated to manage all the areas under its jurisdiction. Mr. Christian explained that his motion was for the positions requested by the Director and if additional ones were needed they could be requested later.

The motion authorizing the establishment of the thirty new positions made by Mr. Christian, seconded by Mr. Faircloth, was adopted on the following vote: Ayes, Messrs. Christian, Faircloth, Adams and Governor Kirk; Nays, Messrs. Conner and Dickinson. Mr. Williams was not present.

51

TRUSTEES OFFICE - On motion by Mr. Adams, seconded by Mr. Faircloth and adopted without objection, the Trustees authorized the Director to retain the firm of Holland and Knight in Tampa, and specifically Mr. Henry M. Kittleson of that firm, as outside special counsel to review the situation in Collier County and work on the many land title questions.

Also, the Director advised that Mr. Neal P. Rutledge, who had been representing the Board in the Coastal Petroleum litigation, would be teaching law out of the state in the fall; therefore, other counsel was recommended.

On motion by Mr. Faircloth, seconded by Mr. Adams and adopted without objection, the Trustees authorized the Director to retain the firm of Robert J. Beckham and Tom W. McAliley, Jr.

On motion duly adopted, the meeting was adjourned.

GOVERNOR   CHAIRMAN

ATTEST:
EXECUTIVE DIRECTOR

Tallahassee, Florida
August 18, 1970

The State of Florida Board of Trustees of the Internal Improvement Trust Fund met in Senate Hearing Room 31 in the Capitol, with the following members present:

Claude R. Kirk, Jr.	Governor
Tom Adams	Secretary of State
Broward Williams	Treasurer
Floyd T. Christian	Commissioner of Education
Doyle Conner	Commissioner of Agriculture
James W. Apthorp	Executive Director

On motion adopted without objection, the Board approved the minutes of the meeting of August 4, 1970.

MONROE COUNTY - Bulkhead Line, Section 253.122 Florida Statutes. The Board of County Commissioners of Monroe County by Resolution No. 29-1970 adopted on April 28, 1970, established a bulkhead line along the right of way line of State Road No. 5 (U. S. No. 1) between Stock Island and Boca Chica in Sections 25 and 26, Township 67 South, Range 25 East, and in Section 30, Township 67 South, Range 26 East, Monroe County. Staff recommended approval, as four - laning of the highway was needed.

The biological survey report by the Department of Natural Resources stated that filling of the area within the proposed bulkhead line would have adverse effects on marine life in that and surrounding areas.

Motion was made by Mr. Williams, seconded by Mr. Adams and adopted without objection, that the Board approve the bulkhead line established by Monroe County in connection with improvement of the highway.

PALM BEACH COUNTY - File Nos. 2310 and 2311-50-253.12.
The Trustees deferred consideration of the following applications to purchase parcels of sovereignty land in Lake Worth, in the Town of Lantana, that were advertised for sale on this date:

    File No. 2310-30-253.12 - Application of Paul Maddock
                              for 0.123 acre
    File No. 2311-50-253.12 - Application of William E. Benjamin II
                              for 0.412 acre

for the reason that additional time was needed for the staff appraiser to review the appraisals.

GLADES COUNTY - Lease No. 1694.
Request was made for assignment of Grazing Lease No. 1694 expiring in January 1972 covering 22.1 acres in Glades County, from W. E. Perry to Ellie H. Yaun. Executed copy of assignment was filed and staff legal counsel approved the request. However, information had been received after preparation of the agenda that about eleven acres was being used for growing sugarcane. The Director requested deferment for further information, pointing out that with additional field men leased lands could be inspected more often.

Mr. Christian suggested cancellation of the lease as the Board could probably get more than one dollar per acre if the land could be used for other than grazing purposes.

Mr. Adams said that a more adequate field force could find out such things, that in the past the staff in many instances had only the information in the applications and no field men to make regular inspections. Mr. Apthorp added that the Trustees' appraiser, employed last fall, had been reviewing leases and sale prices.

The request for lease assignment was deferred.

PALM BEACH COUNTY - File No. 2339-50-253.12, Application for
                    Advertisement of Proposed Land Sale.
Mayfran, Inc., represented by Brockway, Owen and Anderson Engineers, applied to purchase a parcel of sovereignty land in Lake Worth abutting Section 11, Township 44 South, Range 43 East, in the Town of Palm Beach, Palm Beach County, containing 0.698 acre, at the appraised value.

The parcel was landward of the established bulkhead line, the Area Planning Board of Palm Beach County had no objection to sale, and the Town of Palm Beach endorsed sale and filling of the area.

The application claimed that the sale for private residential purposes would be in the public interest as the parcel lying between two existing seawalls was a debris-collecting pocket and a haven for water rats. The staff recommended advertisement.

8-18-70

The biological report was adverse, showing that mangroves on the subject parcel had been destroyed which lessened the productivity of the area. Mr. Adams commented on this report, and recommended no action until checking the possibility of trespass on state land.

Without objection, the Board deferred action pending further investigation by the staff.

DADE COUNTY - Dredge and Fill Permits, Sections 253.124 and 253.123
          Florida Statutes, File No. 203.
Saul J. Morgan and Norman Cohen, represented by Richard P. Kenney, requested amendment of the dredge permit authorized by the Board on February 18, 1969, for removal of 522.500 cubic yards from the southern part of Dumfoundling Bay in Section 10, Township 52 South, Range 42 East, Dade County, to be dredged to a depth of 15 feet mean low water. Applicant paid $52,250 for the fill material.

The applicant now asked for permission to remove an additional 677,500 cubic yards from the same location to a depth of 30 feet m.l.w. and tendered $67,750 in payment. Applicant had a valid Corps of Engineers permit and submitted an affidavit from the dredging company showing that as of August 10, 1970, 346,478 cubic yards had been removed from the authorized dredge area. At the completion of the project, applicant will submit another affidavit as to the final quantity of material removed and if the authorized yardage is exceeded payment for the overdredge material will be made at the standard rate of 10¢ per cubic yard.

The dredged material will be placed on land heretofore conveyed. The biological report prepared for the initial permit was adverse. The Director said the applicant had intended to take some material from the upland but found it was not suitable for use, and that the depth indicated no damage as areas nearby had been dredged to fifty or sixty foot depths. Metropolitan-Dade filed letter of no objection.

On motion by Mr. Christian, seconded by Mr. Adams and adopted without objection, the Trustees approved amendment of the dredge permit as requested.

LEE COUNTY - Dredge Permit to Improve Navigation, File 253.123-605.
Caloosa Bayview Corporation, represented by Duane Hall and Associates, requested a permit for dredging an access channel in the Caloosahatchee River at Negro Head in Section 16, Township 45 South, Range 24 East, Lee County, 700 feet long, 50 feet wide and 5 feet deep mean low water.

The biological survey report cited limited adverse effects and some objections to the project had been filed. Objectors were notified of consideration of the application on this date.

Staff recommended approval subject to the spoil area being adequately diked to prevent silt and run-off from entering the river.

On motion by Mr. Christian, seconded by Mr. Adams and adopted without objection, the Trustees authorized issuance of the permit subject to the provisions recommended by the staff.

MADISON COUNTY - Dredge Permit for Bridge Construction,
            File No. 253.123-606.
Soule Construction Company of Pensacola, Florida, made application

for a dredge permit for two areas to be blasted 40 feet long, 22 feet wide and 9 feet deep in the Suwannee River in Section 35, Township 1 South, Range 11 East, Madison County, for a bridge to be constructed for the Department of Transportation.

The biological survey report was not adverse and the Division of Interior Resources of the Department of Natural Resources had no objection to the proposed work.

On motion by Mr. Christian, seconded by Mr. Williams and adopted without objection, the Trustees authorized issuance of the dredge permit.

MANATEE COUNTY - Dredge Permit to Improve Navigation,
                File No. 253.123-618.
The City of Palmetto applied for a dredge permit for improving navigation in the Manatee River in Section 23, Township 34 South, Range 17 East, Manatee County. The project area will be 700 feet long, 50 feet wide and 5 feet deep, with the spoil material to be placed on city-owned uplands. The biological survey report cited limited adverse effects.

A resolution from the City Council of Palmetto requested waiver of the $50 processing fee.

On motion by Mr. Williams, seconded by Mr. Christian and adopted witnout objection, the Trustees authorized issuance of the permit at no charge.

 MONROE COUNTY - Dredge Permit to Improve Navigation,
                File No. 253.03-167.
On August 4, 1970, the Trustees deferred action on the request from R. E. Scharf, represented by Joe M. Trice, for a permit to dredge a navigation channel 1,300 ft. long, 50 ft. wide top cut, 5 ft. deep m.l.w., in Hawk Channel adjacent to Section 27, Township 67 South, Range 26 East, Monroe County.

The quantity to be removed will be calculated by the engineer. The applicant offered to purchase all the material and deposited $1,300 on account. Mr. Adams said that apparently the application did involve more than navigation, that some fill material was needed since the applicant agreed to pay for the material.

On motion by Mr. Christian, seconded by Mr. Adams and adopted without objection, the Trustees approved issuance of the dredge permit subject to receipt of payment for the dredged material.

PASCO COUNTY - Fill Permit Time Extension, Section 253.124 F. S.,
               File No. 2006-51.
On March 12, 1968, the Trustees approved a fill permit to J. D. Brown to fill 77.77 acres of submerged land previously conveyed under Deed No. 24677. Applicant completed about two-thirds of the project, completely diked the area, and requested a nine-month extension of the fill permit. The expiration date will coincide with the permit from the U. S. Corps of Engineers.

On motion by Mr. Conner, seconded by Mr. Christian and adopted without objection, the Trustees extended the expiration date of the fill permit to December 31, 1971.

PINELLAS COUNTY - Dredge Permit, Section 253.123, File 134;
            Fill Permit, Section 253.124.
Subject to the Trustees' approval, Pinellas County Water and Navigation Control Authority issued Permit No. DF-268 to Rebma Florida,
Incorporated, to dredge, fill and seawall in Boca Ciega Bay in
Section 25, Township 31 South, Range 15 East, Pinellas County. All
dragline work would be on submerged land in private ownership,
seawalls constructed and 30,000 cubic yards of material removed
from the channels used as backfill.

The biological survey report was partially adverse.

On motion by Mr. Christian, seconded by Mr. Williams and adopted
without objection, the Trustees authorized issuance of the dredge
permit and approved the fill permit subject to inclusion in the
permit of recommendations contained in the biological report.

PINELLAS COUNTY - Dredge Permit, File No. 253.123-629;
            Fill Permit, File No. 253.124-135.
Subject to Trustees' approval, Pinellas County Water and Navigation
Control Authority issued Permit No. DF-263 to Harvern Enterprises,
Incorporated, for dredging 30,000 cubic yards of material in Boca
Ciega Bay in Section 31, Township 31 South, Range 16 East, to fill
approximately 3.0 acres of privately-owned land. The project
dimensions were 2,100 ft. long, 80 ft. wide and 10 ft. deep, and
all dragline work would be on submerged land in private ownership.

The biological survey report was not adverse. The project had
been modified to comply with recommendations contained in the
report.

On motion by Mr. Williams, seconded by Mr. Christian and adopted
without objection, the Trustees authorized issuance of the dredge
permit and approved the fill permit to Harvern Enterprises, Inc.

PINELLAS COUNTY - Dredge Permit, File No. 253.123-633.
Subject to Trustees' approval, Pinellas County Water and Navigation
Control Authority issued Dredge Only Permit No. DO-189 to Belleview
Biltmore Hotel for maintenance dredging in Clearwater Harbor in
Sections 20 and 29, Township 29 South, Range 15 East, Pinellas
County. $50 application fee was tendered for the project 2,300 ft.
long, 100 ft. wide and minus-8 ft. deep m.l.w., which would be an
extension of work authorized by the Board on December 2, 1969.

The biological survey report was not adverse, but objections were
filed by Suncoast Active Volunteers for Ecology (SAVE).

Staff recommended approval subject to certain conditions, receipt
of certified estimate of yardage, and payment for the material.
The application involved removal of 4,060 cubic yards of material.
Mr. Adams questioned whether all the dredging previously done had
been properly permitted and mentioned purchase of property by
United States Steel, former ownership of an island by Ed Wright,
and court action removing a bulkhead line. If the application
was part of the large project, Mr. Adams said the applicant should
make the overall development plans available for review. The
Director explained that the permit was for access into a boat
basin at the hotel, the applicant had a Corps permit, the material
was to be placed in a previously designated and diked disposal
area. The proposed U. S. Steel project involving Sand Key was to
be altered radically in order to get the necessary approvals, and

56

was across the Intracoastal Waterway from this site in Clearwater. Mr. Adams and Mr. Christian requested deferment, having received communications indicating the need for additional information.

Without objection, action was deferred.

SANTA ROSA COUNTY - Dredge Permit to Improve Navigation, File No. 253.123-542.
Barba Investment Company applied, prior to the adoption of the $50 application fee policy, for a dredge permit for a navigation channel in Santa Rosa Sound 150 ft. long, 50 ft. wide and 5 ft. deep m.l.w. in Section 32, Township 2 South, Range 28 West, Santa Rosa County.

The project would be a continuation of work authorized by the Board on February 25, 1969, under Permit No. 253.123-191. With respect to the initial application the biological report was adverse. Applicant modified his plan in part to conform to recommendations in the report.

On motion by Mr. Christian, adopted without objection, the Board approved issuance of the dredge permit.

COLLIER COUNTY - Secretary of State Tom Adams said that although parties present on August 4 had professed a desire to cooperate completely with the Trustees pending the resolving of land title and dredge violation questions in Collier County, he had information that Collier County had issued certain permits for work that indicated a lack of cooperation and some action should be taken.

The Director reported that Mr. Henry Kittleson, special attorney employed last week, was reviewing a great deal of information and would meet with the staff this week.

Governor Kirk said they should be certain there was cooperation and other members of the Board were kept informed.

SUBJECTS UNDER CHAPTER 18296

REFUNDS - On motion by Mr. Conner, seconded by Mr. Christian and adopted without objection, the Trustees authorized refunds of $15 to each of the following applicants for the reason that the Department of Transportation did not recommend release of the state road right of way reservations contained in the Murphy Act deeds listed below:

Applicants	Murphy Act Deeds
W. J. Vaughn	Brevard County Deed No. 109
C. John Coniglio	Citrus County Deed No. 236
Mid-South Properties, Inc.	Franklin County Deed No. 323
Roy Christopher	Lake County Deed No. 2706
Berrien Becks, Jr.	Volusia County Deed No. 3389

The Cabinet decided not to meet on September 8, as those who might need to appear would find it inconvenient on election day.

On motion duly adopted, the meeting was adjourned.

8-18-70

57

Tallahassee, Florida
August 25, 1970

The State of Florida Board of Trustees of the Internal Improvement
Trust Fund met in Senate Hearing Room 31 in the Capitol, with the
following members present:

On motion duly adopted, the Board approved the minutes of the
meeting of August 11, 1970.

DADE COUNTY - Bulkhead Line.
Because of late objections received by the staff, the Director
requested deferment of consideration of a bulkhead line set by the
City of Miami at Dinner Key in Biscayne Bay in Section 22, Township
54 South, Range 41 East, Dade County. The areas inside the proposed bulkhead line would be used as spoil disposal areas for
dredging of the Dinner Key Marina.

Secretary of State Tom Adams said he had questions, also, particu-
larly with respect to construction of additional spoil areas. The
Director said the staff would confer with Mr. M. L. Reese, City
Manager of Miami, who was here on this date.

Without objection, the Trustees deferred action on the bulkhead line.

PALM BEACH COUNTY - File No. 2310-50-253.12, Land Sale.
On June 9 the Trustees authorized advertisement for objections
only pursuant to application from Paul Maddock for purchase of a
parcel of sovereignty land in Lake Worth abutting Government Lot
6 in Section 3, Township 45 South, Range 43 East, containing 0.123
acre, more or less, in the Town of Lantana, Palm Beach County.
Applicant offered the appraised value of $450 for the parcel to be
used to construct a seawall and backfill, which would prevent
erosion of uplands and would straighten the shoreline.

The narrow strip of submerged land was sandy and unvegetated and
the biological report indicated no significant adverse effects on

marine resources from the small fill project. The Area Planning
Board of Palm Beach County and the Town of Lantana had no objection
to the sale. The parcel did not extend to the established bulkhead
line, and at maximum extended only twenty-five feet from the
present shoreline. The staff recommended sale in the public
interest. The parcel was advertised and no objection was received
to the sale.

On motion by Mr. Adams, seconded by Mr. Dickinson and adopted without
objection, the Trustees confirmed sale of the advertised parcel at
the appraised value, the applicant to pay the appraisal costs.

PALM BEACH COUNTY - File No. 2311-50-253.12, Land Sale.
On June 9 the Trustees authorized advertisement for objections only
pursuant to application from William E. Benjamin II of Palm Beach,
Florida, for purchase of a parcel of sovereignty land in Lake Worth
abutting Government Lot 6 in Section 3, Township 45 South, Range 43
East, 0.412 acre in the Town of Lantana, Palm Beach County. Applicant offered the appraised value of $1,450 for the parcel to be
used to construct a seawall and backfill, which would prevent
erosion of uplands and straighten the shoreline.

The biological survey report stated that the narrow strip of
submerged land was sandy, unvegetated, and filling should not have
significant adverse effects on marine biological resources. The
Area Planning Board of Palm Beach County and the Town of Lantana had
no objection to the sale. Staff was of the opinion that the sale
would be in the public interest. The parcel did not extend out to
the established bulkhead line and at maximum extended only 25 feet
from the present shoreline. The parcel was advertised and no
objection received to the sale.

On motion by Mr. Adams, seconded by Mr. Dickinson and adopted
without objection, the Trustees confirmed sale of the advertised
parcel at the appraised value, the applicant to pay the appraisal
costs.

DADE COUNTY - File No. 2364-13-253.03, Dedication.
The City of Miami by Resolution No. 41563 adopted May 13, 1970,
requested dedication of a parcel of sovereignty land embracing
0.092 acre in Biscayne Bay abutting Section 39, Township 54 South,
Range 41 East, City of Miami, Dade County. The city proposed to
construct a seawall and fill the parcel which was landward of the
established bulkhead line as confirmed by the Interagency Advisory
Committee and at the terminus of Southeast 15th Road abutting a
parcel recently conveyed by the Trustees.

A biological survey report was not adverse. The staff was of the
opinion that dedication was in the public interest, as it would
prevent a pocket and create a smooth shoreline.

On motion by Mr. Dickinson, seconded by Mr. Williams and adopted
without objection, the Trustees authorized the parcel to be
advertised for objections only.

MONROE COUNTY - File No. 2352-44-253.12(6), Quitclaim Deed.
Noah H. Swayne of Islamorada, Florida, applied for quitclaim deed
to two parcels of filled sovereignty land embracing 0.12 acre in
the Straits of Florida abutting Section 24, Township 63 South,
Range 37 East, and Section 19, Township 63 South, Range 28 East,
Plantation Key, Monroe County. The land was appraised at $2,082

per acre or $250 for the two parcels.

Staff recommended issuance of quitclaim deed in compliance with
Section 253.12(6) Florida Statutes, at the appraised value, the
applicant to pay the $100 processing fee and appraisal costs.

On motion by Mr. Williams, seconded by Mr. Dickinson and adopted
without objection, the Trustees accepted the staff recommendation.

BREVARD COUNTY - File No. 2320-05-253.03, Easement.
Canaveral Port Authority represented by Edward M. Jackson, requested
perpetual easement embracing 16.18 acres in the Atlantic Ocean for
installation of a trestle to accommodate a sand transfer plant in
Section 12, Township 24 South, Range 37 East, Brevard County, to
pump sand from the north side of the channel entrance into Canaveral
Harbor, to a spoil area heretofore granted by the Board on April
14, 1970.

On motion by Mr. Dickinson, seconded by Mr. Williams and adopted
without objection, the Trustees granted the perpetual easement
requested.

BREVARD COUNTY - File No. 23775(790-05), Dredge and Fill Permit
                 Applications.
Edward Shablowski, represented by the law firm of Storms, Pappas
and Krasny, had applied for a dredge permit and approval of a fill
permit that the Trustees denied on July 14, re-agendaed on August 4
because of failure to notify the applicant, and deferred at the
request of the applicant until this date. The City of Melbourne
on August 29, 1969, issued dredge and fill permit to dredge 17,035
cubic yards of material from the Indian River to be deposited on
1.76 acres of submerged land purchased from the Trustees on November 6, 1963.

In compliance with policies adopted on July 1, 1969, the application had been held pending action by the City of Melbourne to review
and relocate bulkhead lines pursuant to the recommendations of the
Interagency Advisory Committee and policy adopted by the Trustees
on December 31, 1968. On July 14 the matter was on the agenda for
consideration under the hardship provisions of the July 1 policy.

The biological survey report of March 24, 1969, stated that the
"project would have definite adverse effects on marine life."

Staff recommended that the dredge permit be denied and the fill
permit deferred until the City of Melbourne relocated bulkhead
lines in accordance with Interagency Advisory Committee
recommendations. Mr. Apthorp advised the members that the City of
Melbourne had been contacted and replied that they did not intent
to relocate bulkhead lines at this time. In any event, the staff
did not recommend approval of the dredge permit to take material
from the large dredging area indicated on the application. He said
there were areas where no submerged land had been sold and the city
had not taken action in those areas, that the city would not be
required to relocate the line at the Shablowski property.

Mr. Elting L. Storms reviewed some background facts to show that
this was a hardship on his client, that other sales had been made
and the submerged land filled in the area, that the city had held
hearings at which no one spoke in favor of relocating the lines
and the city made no decision to change the lines which would be
an engineering expense, that the biological report was not so

adverse as to be contrary to the public interest. He called attention
to the July 1 policy statement that where the Trustees had approved
bulkhead lines prior to and inconsistent to the Interagency reports
and submerged land had been sold to such lines, action should not
be taken at this time to require relocation of the bulkhead lines.
His client was caught in the crossfire, he said, between the city
and the Trustees trying to compel change of the lines. He urged
approval of the public applications, as not to allow Mr. Shablowski
to use that land would be a taking without compensation, he said.

Mr. Dickinson made a motion, seconded by Mr. Williams, that the
application be approved.

Mr. Adams recalled that the Board had held up applications in other
areas until the county or city officials were willing to comply with
the Interagency report based on recommendations of the ecologists
and biologists for preservation of coastal areas. He said there was
no disagreement on the facts of this case, that any change in bulkhead lines had to emanate from the local level and this was the only
lever the Board could utilize effectively, that by not acting the
city was penalizing this application, and the Board had taken a
strong position on this policy.

Mr. Dickinson made a motion that the Board waive its policy as an
aggrieved citizen was entitled to relief. But he thought the city
should take action to move the bulkhead lines.

Mr. Adams made a substitute motion that the application be denied
as recommended by the staff (dredge permit denied and fill permit
deferred), and Governor Kirk agreed, noting that the applicant
would get relief as soon as the city acted and it might be possible
for the matter to be reagendaed next week in that case. Messrs.
Christian and Dickinson voted against the substitute motion.

Mr. Conner raised questions regarding the authority of the local
governing board as against the recommendations of the Interagency
Advisory Committee on changing bulkhead lines. He agreed to vote
for the substitute motion, to let the city have another opportunity
to change its mind about relocating the bulkhead lines. Mr.Williams
suggested that a staff member attend a city hearing to explain the
Board's position. Mr. Apthorp pointed out that relocation did not
have to be actually completed but that the city should make some
progress toward the recommendations of the Interagency report that
the Board of Trustees had adopted as criteria.

The action of the Board was to sustain the staff recommendation to
deny the dredge permit and defer action on fill permit. The
Governor expressed it as technical deferment, and he hoped the city
would show good faith by reviewing the bulkhead lines.

BROWARD COUNTY - File No. 253.123-587,
                    Dredge Permit to Improve Navigation.
Port Everglades Authority applied for a dredge permit for a channel
15 ft. deep, 100 ft. wide and 600 ft. long parallel to and adjoining
the old F. E. C. canal, and to dredge from Intracoastal Waterway to
minus-36 ft. deep by 425 ft. wide and 600 ft. long. The material
removed would be placed on uplands owned by the Authority.

The biological report was not adverse, noting that it was a heavily
industrialized port area.

On July 28 after a lengthy hearing the Board deferred action for additional reports. The Bureau of Beaches and Shores subsequently advised that the dredge material would not be suitable for beach nourishment purposes. The Executive Director of the Department of Natural Resources advised that the proposed work would not have any material adverse effect upon the Broward County park; however, it was indicated that the spoil site would be suitable for incorporation into the county park system. In view of the additional reports, the Trustees' staff renewed its recommendation for approval of the dredge permit.

Mr. Linwood Cabot, attorney for the Authority, considered this a routine request for a dredge permit to improve navigation, and land use and zoning matters should not be before the Cabinet. He said that the Authority-owned parcel proposed to be leased to Hydrospace Research Corporation was across the waterway from a shipyard, was no picnic or swimming area and not on the Atlantic Ocean, that a few years ago the authority tried to trade that very parcel to the county, that in 1966 the county favored use of the parcel by E.S.S.A. for oceanographic research but now opposed use by Hydrospace for oceanographic and pollution research under a contract with the United States. As for the tidal creek, the deepening and widening would aid in recreational use of Whiskey Creek and the county land.

Maps were examined and many questions asked by the Board. It was noted that the county property was east of the creek and on the ocean side, that a road separated it from the proposed spoil area, that county long-range plans indicated a desire to encompass land of the Port Authority. Mr. Adams asked if there was any difference in the activities of Hydrospace and Nova, the latter already in operation with county approval. The Governor said that after granting the dredge permit the land use problem could still be solved on a local basis.

Mr. Bob Whelan, Chairman of Broward County Commission, opposed issuance of the permit, would like to see Hydrospace in some other location in the county, and thought the best use of the subject parcel would be public recreation and Whiskey Creek was called the key to the recreation area. He said the county tried to purchase the parcel proposed to be leased, desired to acquire additional land now under litigation, that industry should be located on the west side of the waterway. He felt that approval of the dredge permit would activate the lease to Hydrospace for ten years with an option to renew, thereby interfering with the county long-range plans.

Motion was made by Mr. Dickinson, seconded by Mr. Adams, that the Board approve issuance of the dredge permit to Port Everglades Authority. Governor Kirk voted in favor of the motion. Messrs. Christian, Williams and Conner voted in opposition. On this three to three vote, the motion failed and the permit was denied.

DADE COUNTY - Dredge Permit, File No. 253.123-626.
John Donnell Yachts, represented by John S. Bristol, applied for a dredge permit for a boat basin 160 ft. wide on upland in Section 7, Township 52 South, Range 42 East, Dade County, and connection to Little River (Canal C-7). The $50 application fee was tendered and biological report was not adverse.

On motion by Mr. Christian, seconded by Mr. Adams and adopted without objection, the Trustees authorized issuance of the dredge permit.

OSCEOLA COUNTY - Lake Tohopekaliga.
The Central and Southern Florida Flood Control District by Resolution
No. 930 dated July 24, 1970, requested cooperation of the Board of
Trustees in issuance of dredging permits to upland owners for navigation and irrigation channels in Lake Tohopekaliga where the District
and the Game and Fresh Water Fish Commission are involved in an
experiment to drawdown the lake in an effort to oxidize nutrients
in the lake.

The staff would continue an investigation of fences placed on
sovereignty bottoms in this lake. Mr. Apthorp said the drawdown
period might be a good time for removal of the fences, and Governor
Kirk suggested that the Division of Corrections could be of assistance.

On motion by Mr. Christian, seconded by Mr. Adams and adopted without
objection, the Board approved the request of Central and Southern
Florida Flood Control District.

DADE COUNTY - Canal Right of Way.
On motion by Mr. Adams, seconded by Mr. Dickinson and adopted without
objection, the Trustees authorized issuance of an easement for canal
purposes to the Central and Southern Florida Flood Control District
over the South 50 ft. of the S½ of the SE¼ of Section 28, Township
53 South, Range 40 East, Dade County. The easement would supersede
canal easement No. 21755 over the South 100 ft. of Section 28 that
had been determined excess to needs of the District and Dade County.

HENDRY COUNTY - Oil Lease Assignments.
On motion by Mr. Adams, seconded by Mr. Dickinson and adopted
without objection, the Trustees approved assignments dated June 16,
1970, of oil and gas drilling lease Nos. 2441-S and 2443 from Craig
Castle to Exchange Oil and Gas Corporation, a Delaware corporation.
Assignments and instruments of acceptance were filed and approved by
legal counsel.

ST. LUCIE COUNTY - Dock Permit, Section 253.03 F. S., File CD-1692.
Estate Capital Development Corporation, represented by Arthur F.
Wood, applied for an extension of six months to complete the
construction of a dock under State Commercial Dock Permit No.
CD-1692 adjacent to applicant's upland at Faber Cove in the Indian
River in Section 1, Township 35 South, Range 40 East, St. Lucie
County.

On motion by Mr. Christian, seconded by Mr. Dickinson and adopted
without objection, the Trustees granted the time extension.

PALM BEACH COUNTY - Marina License.
The Sailfish Club of Florida, represented by Gee and Jenson, applied
for a marina license to expand an existing facility in Lake Worth
adjacent to upland in Palm Beach in Section 3, Township 43 South,
Range 43 East, Palm Beach County. The minimum yearly license fee
for the area to be used would be $1,896.30.

All dredged material would be placed behind a seawall reconstructed
along the shoreline. The biological survey report was not adverse.

On motion by Mr. Dickinson, seconded by Mr. Christian and Mr.
Williams, the Board authorized issuance of the marina license.

Mr. Adams asked what progress the staff was making in the investigation, that he wanted to support, of the U. S. Steel application for dredging in Pinellas County. He had information that areas under permit had been overdredged and hoped a master plan could be worked out.

Also, Mr. Adams asked about the pending settlement of the Cape Coral overdredge case.

The Director discussed these matters briefly and was instructed to bring in a staff recommendation on the Cape Coral settlement.

On motion duly adopted, the meeting was adjourned.

GOVERNOR   CHAIRMAN

ATTEST:

EXECUTIVE DIRECTOR

Tallahassee, Florida
September 1, 1970

The State of Florida Board of Trustees of the Internal Improvement Trust Fund met in Senate Hearing Room 31 in the Capitol, with the following members present:

Tom Adams	Secretary of State, Acting Chairman
Earl Faircloth	Attorney General
Broward Williams	Treasurer
Floyd T. Christian	Commissioner of Education
Doyle Conner	Commissioner of Agriculture
James W. Apthorp	Executive Director

Without objection, the minutes of August 18 were approved as submitted.

COLLIER COUNTY - Bulkhead Line, Section 253.122 Florida Statutes. The Board of County Commissioners of Collier County adopted a resolution on March 31, 1970, establishing a bulkhead line 2,604.84 feet long near the intersection of the Marco River and Goodland Bay in Section 18, Township 52 South, Range 27 East, in Collier County.

The biological survey report stated that "Filling to the limits of the proposed bulkhead line would have definite adverse effects on the marine biological resources in the subject area."

9-1-70

The staff recommended denial of the line and suggested revision to
coincide with the limits of proposed construction. The Department
of Transportation had been notified that the bulkhead line would be
considered on this date.

On motion by Mr. Williams, seconded by Mr. Christian, the Trustees
denied approval of the bulkhead line based on the adverse biological
report and the staff recommendation.

DADE COUNTY - Bulkhead Line; Dredge and Fill Permits.
The City of Miami by resolution adopted July 1, 1970, established a
bulkhead line at Dinner Key in Biscayne Bay in Section 22, Township
54 South, Range 41 East, Dade County, enclosing areas to be used for
disposal of spoil from the proposed dredging of the Dinner Key Marina
facility. The project is to expand the yacht mooring facilities and
improve navigation at the Dinner Key Yacht Basin. All the submerged
land involved had been conveyed to the city.

The project had been endorsed by the Coconut Grove Sailing Club,
Marine Council of Greater Miami, Coconut Grove Chamber of Commerce,
Fleet of the Country Club of Coral Gables, and Coconut Grove Exchange
Club.

The biological survey report from the Department of Natural Resources
was not adverse as to dredging or filling within that portion designated as Area No. 3; however, areas designated as 4A and 4B are
vegetated with seagrass and dredging or filling those areas would
have adverse effects on marine biological resources.

Staff recommended approval of the bulkhead line encompassing the
area designated as Area No. 3 and the dredge and fill permit, but
recommended denial of bulkhead line and dredge and fill permit for
4A and 4B areas.

Mr. Adams asked about the three-foot elevation to which the spoil was
proposed to be deposited. The Director explained that it was necessary in order to dispose of all the spoil in the designated spoil
area.

Without objection, the Trustees accepted the staff recommendation
for approval of the bulkhead line for Area No. 3 and the dredge and
fill permit for this area, and denied approval of the bulkhead line
and permits for the areas designated as 4A and 4B based on the
adverse biological report.

Mr. M. L. Reese, City Manager of Miami, and Mr. Paul Andre' ,
president of Coconut Grove Chamber of Commerce, were present and
urged approval of the complete plan. Operating under instructions
from the city, Mr. Reese said he could not agree to exclusion of a
portion of the plan without further explanation that the area was
needed for mooring boats for the boating public. He said the city
could secure another biological report that would not indicate too
much damage to marine resources. Mr. Adams noted that about three-
fourths of what the city asked for had been approved, but the Board
could reopen the matter.

Mr. Conner made a motion, seconded by Mr. Christian and adopted,
that the Board reconsider the city's application, rescinding the
previous vote. Mr. Reese was asked to furnish the additional
information for reevaluation by the Board and Mr. Williams asked that
the matter be reagendaed at a later date.

Mr. Andre' asked that the proposed dredging be allowed to proceed under the first approval as a contract had been let and some preliminary work could be done on the part recommended for approval by the staff. Mr. Adams said that with the Area No. 3 portion cleared, which had been the first motion, the city could proceed to supply additional information for reevaluation of the remainder of the application. The city representatives agreed that this was the proper procedure.

On motion by Mr. Faircloth, adopted without objection, the Board approved the bulkhead line encompassing the area designated as Area No. 3 and the dredge and fill permit for that area, withholding approval with respect to the area designated as 4A and 4B until a later date.

_____

ST. JOHNS COUNTY - File No. 2360-55-253.12, Land Sale and Permit. The Trustees on July 21, 1970, authorized advertisement of a parcel of sovereignty land in the St. Johns River lying between the established bulkhead line and Lot 5, Palamo Subdivision in Section 39, Township 6 South, Range 27 East, St. Johns County, applied for by J. Carver Harris who desired to construct a seawall and backfill to prevent damage to upland property and a dwelling. The 0.04 acre parcel was advertised in The Record, St. Augustine, Florida, and no objection to the sale was received.

The biological report prepared for consideration of the bulkhead line was adverse. On May 12, 1970, the Trustees approved the bulkhead line, and staff recommended sale in the public interest because of the potential damage to the property if applicant is not allowed to restore an old wooden seawall and backfill under the dwelling.

The applicant also requested approval of construction permit issued by the St. Johns County Commission on July 16, 1970, for rebuilding and backfilling a seawall to be located at the established bulkhead line. The biological report for this area had been adverse but staff recommended approval of the permit for construction in view of the necessity of rebuilding the existing shoreline and protecting the owner's dwelling. The improvements were constructed between fifteen and twenty years ago and it appears that such improvements were legally permissable under the provisions of Chapter 8537, Laws of 1921 (the Butler Act).

On motion by Mr. Williams, seconded by Mr. Faircloth and adopted without objection, the Trustees confirmed sale at the $100 minimum price recommended by the staff appraiser, and approved construction permit under provisions of Section 253.124 Florida Statutes.

_____

ST. JOHNS COUNTY - File No. 2361-55-253.12, Land Sale and Permit. The Trustees on July 21, 1970, authorized advertisement of a parcel of sovereignty land in the St. Johns River lying between the established bulkhead line and Lot 4, Palamo Subdivision, containing 0.06 acre, more or less, in Section 39, Township 6 South, Range 27 East, St. Johns County, applied for by Emilio D. Echevarria who desired to construct a seawall and backfill to protect his upland property and a dwelling. The proposed sale was advertised in The Record, St. Augustine, Florida, and no objection to the sale was received.

The biological report prepared for consideration of the bulkhead line was adverse. On May 12, 1970, the Board approved the bulkhead line and staff recommended sale in the public interest because of the potential damage to property if the applicant is not allowed to restore an old wooden seawall and backfill under the dwelling.

The applicant also requested approval of construction permit issued by the St. Johns County Commission on July 16, 1970, for rebuilding and backfilling a seawall at the established bulkhead line. The biological report for this area had been adverse, but the staff recommended approval of the permit for construction in view of the necessity of rebuilding the existing shoreline and protecting the owner's dwelling. The improvements were constructed between fifteen and twenty years ago and it appears such improvements were legally permissible under the provisions of Chapter 8537, Laws of 1921 (the Butler Act).

On motion by Mr. Williams, seconded by Mr. Faircloth and adopted without objection, the Trustees confirmed sale at the $100 minimum price approved by the staff appraiser, and approved construction permit under provisions of Section 253.124 Florida Statutes.

GLADES COUNTY - File No. 2365-22-253.36, Application to Advertise. Mr. Henry F. Seels had requested deferment of consideration of his application to purchase a parcel of reclaimed lake bottom land abutting State Lot 2 in Section 12, Township 40 South, Range 32 East, containing 3.8 acres in Lake Okeechobee, Glades County. He could not be present on this date because of illness in his family.

On motion by Mr. Conner, seconded by Mr. Christian and adopted without objection, the Trustees postponed consideration of the application.

DADE COUNTY - File No. 2225-13-253.12, Application to Advertise. Paul L. E. Helliwell, Trustee, represented by Thomas B. DeWolf, applied to purchase 4.96 acres of sovereignty land in Biscayne Bay abutting Section 6, Township 55 South, Range 42 East, Key Biscayne, Dade County, for a residential subdivision.

The biological report for this area at Mashta Point was adverse, stating that "While the submerged land proposed for purchase is not as well vegetated as those lands farther offshore, its sale and subsequent development would eliminate the marine habitat now occurring in the subject area."

The parcel was landward of the bulkhead line approved by the Trustees on January 28, 1969. The applicant submitted letter from Dade County endorsing the sale in the public interest. Staff was of the opinion that the applicant did not submit sufficient reasons why the sale would be in the public interest, and recommended denial and deactivation of the file.

On motion by Mr. Faircloth, adopted without objection, the Board accepted the staff recommendation for denial of the application.

DUVAL COUNTY - Lease, Institution Land.
The Division of Forestry, Department of Agriculture and Consumer Services, requested a lease of the former Highway Patrol Station site on U. S. Highway 90 west of Jacksonville in Section 21, Township 2 South, Range 25 East, Duval County. The facility had been leased to the Department of Law Enforcement since 1968 when it was declared surplus to the Department of Public Safety, will be vacated and the lease terminated on September 15, and the Division

of Forestry desired to use the location for a Division Office.

On motion by Mr. Williams, seconded by Mr. Conner and adopted
without objection, the Trustees authorized issuance of a lease to
the Division of Forestry, Department of Agriculture and Consumer
Services.

ESCAMBIA AND SANTA ROSA COUNTIES - Oil and Gas Drilling Lease.
On July 21 the Trustees ordered readvertisement for new bids on a
five-year oil and gas drilling lease covering a portion of the
Escambia River containing 205 acres, more or less. Earlier advertisement for bids resulted in one bid from Marshall R. Young Oil
Company, which the Board on July 7 rejected. New bid invitation
was published pursuant to law in the Tallahassee Democrat, Pensacola
Journal and the Milton Press-Gazette, bids to be opened on this
date. Successful bidder was required to pay all advertising costs
and the Board reserved the right to reject any or all bids.

The lease required $1 per year per acre annual rental, one-eighth
royalty, $50,000 surety bond and at least one test well every 2½
years of the lease term. An additional provision was that wells
will not be drilled on the submerged leased areas without prior
written consent of the Trustees, and in event of production on
adjoining lands directional wells shall be drilled under the lease
area.

Mr. Apthorp reported one bid from Marshall R. Young Oil Company of
$187,500, being one dollar per acre rent for the first year on the
205 acres plus a bonus bid. Mr. Christian noted that the Board
received $10,000 more than the first bid rejected in July.

Motion was made by Mr. Christian, seconded by Mr. Williams, that
the bid be accepted.

Mr. Martin Northrup, assistant director of Florida Audubon Society,
opposed the lease and requested a moratorium on all oil leasing
until better environmental safeguards are adopted. He thought
leasing the river bed might be a bad precedent. Mr. Adams said
any wells would be drilled on upland, the bid was from the only
eligible bidder, the surrounding uplands were in private ownership
under lease with exploration already in progress. The Board had
tried to follow every safeguard, no offshore wells were being
drilled and conservation areas were being withheld from oil exploration, and the Board should receive credit for these efforts.

Without objection, the Board adopted the motion by Mr. Christian
to accept the bid of Marshall R. Young Oil Company and issue oil
and gas drilling lease.

MANATEE COUNTY - File Nos. 253.123-561 and 253.124-126.
The application of N. J. Cowart, Trustee, and C. H. Wooten for
dredge and fill permits was deferred at the request of the applicants.

MONROE COUNTY - Campsite Lease for Private Use.
On motion by Mr. Faircloth, seconded by Mr. Christian and adopted
without objection, the Trustees approved application of John M.
Koenig for a private campsite lease near Man Key in the Gulf of
Mexico of a 1-acre site at annual rental of $100 for one-year lease
with option to renew for four additional years, in accordance with
the policy adopted April 7, 1970, which stated, in part, "Require

all structures in existence to be under lease for so long as the structure remains in existence."

MONROE COUNTY - Dredge and Fill Permit, Section 253.03.
The Director requested deferment of the application from M. D. Siderius for a permit to dredge a navigation channel, for the reason that the staff had not been able to get in touch with the applicant with respect to questions raised by members of the Board.

Mr. Adams brought up again questions regarding dredging of many navigation channels and whether the Board should make a charge for the material removed from state submerged land, which might be used to make dry land out of wet land.

Without objection, the Board deferred consideration of the application.

MONROE COUNTY - File No. 253.03-212, Fill Permit.
The Department of Transportation applied for a fill permit covering approximately 1.5 acres in Boca Chica Channel in Section 25, Township 67 South, Range 25 East, and Section 30, Township 67 South, Range 26 East, Monroe County, in connection with bridge and approaches on State Road 5.

The biological report was adverse; however, the Department of Natural Resources stated that there was no reasonable alternative to filling alongside the existing roadway to accommodate the four-laning of U. S. 1, and therefore removed objection to the filling. The staff recommended approval.

Mr. Adams inquired about the kind of structure and whether it would restrict the flow of water in Boca Chica Channel. He said it was tragic that while the Trustees were concerned with trying to conserve the environment there are other agencies whose projects destroyed the environment - noting that Department of Transportation structures often created problems. He asked for opportunity to look at the plans for the subject structure and deferment until there was a decision on where the fill material would come from for widening the bridge and approaches at Boca Chica Channel. Mr. Apthorp advised that no more restriction of the water flow was anticipated than from the original bridge.

Mr. Faircloth agreed with Mr. Adams on this matter. Mr. Christian asked if the Department was involved in a contract, agreed with the remarks in general, but pointed out that in Monroe County dredging was often necessary because of the geographical conditions.

The Trustees adopted a resolution on May 19, 1970, placing responsibility for examination of plans of structures to be placed on sovereignty lands that might affect the environment in the Board of Trustees, and the staff had been reviewing plans of public projects such as causeways, roads, bridges and other works and would continue to do so. The Director said there had been more cooperation from the agencies.

On motion by Mr. Faircloth, adopted without objection, action was deferred for further examination of the plans and determination of the dredge area for this project.

MONROE COUNTY - Dredge and Fill Permit, Section 253.03 F. S.
On motion by Mr. Williams, adopted without objection, the Board

deferred consideration of the application from Wacouta Corporation
to dredge to improve navigation and to place the material on
submerged land in private ownership in accordance with a plan
proposed on July 7 when an exchange and boundary line agreement
was authorized.

PALM BEACH COUNTY - Marina License, Section 253.03 F. S.
On motion by Mr. Christian, seconded by Mr. Conner and adopted
without objection, the Board approved issuance of a marina license
to Bills Sailfish Club, for expansion of an existing facility in
Lake Worth adjacent to Section 26, Township 42 South, Range 43 East,
Palm Beach County, for which no dredging was required. The applicant tendered $100 processing fee and $255 for the first year's
license fee for the 12,750 square feet of sovereignty land encom-
passed by the marina.

POLICY - Permits for Navigation Aids and Mooring Facilities.
Staff requested authority to issue permits for navigational aids
such as day marks, day beacons, lighted beacons, buoys, and other
similar devices in navigable waters to facilitate safe navigation
by the general public. Also, staff asked for authority to issue
permits for permanent mooring devices such as dolphins, piles, anchor
buoys, and other similar devices if they are to be available to the
general public without cost.

The permits would be issued only after securing approval of the
Department of Natural Resources, and all installations would be
subject to final review and approval by the Corps of Engineers or
the U. S. Coast Guard.

Motion was made by Mr. Christian and adopted without objection,
that the staff be authorized at its discretion to issue such permits
described above without processing fee if the facilities are
unconditionally available to the general public.

MARIFARMS, INC. - Aquaculture Lease.
The Director presented a matter pertaining to the lawsuit filed by
Organized Fishermen of Florida. On motion by Mr. Faircloth,
seconded by Mr. Williams and adopted without objection, the Board
waived the rules for consideration of a matter not on the agenda.

Also on motion by Mr. Faircloth, seconded by Mr. Williams and
adopted without objection, the Board accepted the bond of Marifarms,
Incorporated, required by the aquaculture lease awarded by the
Board on February 3, 1970. Bond was posted in the amount of
$180,000 by the company, and $25,000 cash bond was placed in a
savings account with the pass book to be held by the Board.

CAPE CORAL REPORT. The Board last week asked for a report on
progress being made on a settlement of the long-pending Cape Coral
overdredge matter. Mr. Apthorp recommended that the Board require
from G. A. C. Properties, Inc., a penalty settlement of $765,383.78
including payment for 5,069,918 cubic yards of fill material
removed from the Caloosahatchee River without permits during a
period from 1959 to 1965 by the Gulf American Company, payment
for 172 acres of sovereignty land filled that should be valued at
approximately $1,000 per acre (from $750 to $1,200 per acre), and
engineering costs. He said that 11¢ per cubic yard was more than
twice the usual price for fill material from 1959 to 1965 when
the violations occurred, that the recommendation took into account

the policies of the Board at the time the work was done and took into account the earlier negotiations of the staff of the Trustees and the present owner of the project, that the value of the land was figured on the basis of its value today.

Motion was made by Mr. Faircloth, seconded by Mr. Christian, that the report be received and agendaed at some time in the future. It was noted that the recommended penalty settlement figure had not been discussed with the company - and that the Trustees had only received the report on this Lee County dredging.

Mr. J. G. Turner, vice president of the company, said their engineers would need some time to evaluate the report and the Director had said they would have an opportunity to study the engineering figures.

On motion by Mr. Williams, the Trustees directed that the matter be placed on the agenda in a month.

Mr. Adams said this was a clear case of trespass, there was no bulkhead line, dredging and filling had been done with permits, the company had made a profit of roughly two million dollars from selling the land which he thought should be the penalty payment required by the Board.

SUBJECTS UNDER CHAPTER 18296

On motion by Mr. Williams, seconded by Mr. Conner and adopted without objection, the Trustees approved Report No. 972 and one regular bid for sale under provisions of Chapter 18296, Acts of 1937, Section 197.350 Florida Statutes, of a lot in Volusia County to Daytona Beach No. 1, Inc., for $101.00. The lot had been certified to the State of Florida with a 1932 assessed value of $10 under tax sale certificates 5987 of 1930 and 21825 of 1933. The Board authorized execution of the deed pertaining to this Murphy Act sale.

On motion duly adopted, the meeting was adjourned.

_____
SECRETARY OF STATE - ACTING CHAIRMAN

ATTEST:

_____
EXECUTIVE DIRECTOR

*   *   *   *   *

9-1-70

Tallahassee, Florida
September 15, 1970

The State of Florida Board of Trustees of the Internal Improvement
Trust Fund met in Senate Hearing Room 31 in the Capitol, with
the following members present:

Claude R. Kirk, Jr.	Governor
Tom Adams	Secretary of State, Present part time
Earl Faircloth	Attorney General
Fred O. Dickinson, Jr.	Comptroller
Broward Williams	Treasurer
Floyd T. Christian	Commissioner of Education
Doyle Conner	Commissioner of Agriculture

James W. Apthorp   Executive Director

Without objection, the minutes of the meeting on August 25, 1970,
were approved as submitted.

On motion by Mr. Dickinson, seconded by Mr. Christian and adopted
without objection, the Board authorized correction of the minutes
of July 14, 1970, page 4 of the duplicated minutes, as follows:
in the fifth paragraph relating to File Nos. 2301 and 2302-22-
253.36, strike the period and insert "at the price of $475 per
acre as agreed to by the Trustees' staff in April, 1968. Instruments
of conveyance shall contain protective covenant to the Central and
Southern Florida Flood Control District holding them harmless from
damages due to flooding by future regulations of water level in Lake
Okeechobee."

VOLUSIA COUNTY - Bulkhead Line.
The City Council of the City of Port Orange on October 25, 1968,
relocated a bulkhead line along the south side of Port Orange
Causeway in the Halifax River in Section 3, Township 16 South,
Range 33 East, Volusia County. The biological reports concluded
that the proposed construction behind the bulkhead line would have
adverse effects on marine biological resources, could interfere
with a nearby bird rookery, and some debris might collect in part
of the area due to poor circulation. The staff recommended that
the bulkhead line relocation not be approved by the Board, and
that the staff be given authority to file a condemnation suit for
the property under the provisions of Chapter 70-358, Acts of 1970,
for the purpose of reacquiring the submerged land.

The submerged lands lying partially within the bulkhead line were
purchased from the Trustees in 1952 for $150 per acre, and 4.45
acres were conveyed by Trustees Deed No. 20181. An attempt to
negotiate a repurchase from the present owner, C. K. Walley,
failed due to a difference in opinion as to value. Trustees' staff
appraiser placed a value of $8,200 per acre or $36,500 for the
4.45 acres which in Mr. Walley's opinion should be $100,000.

Numerous objections had been received by the Trustees' office
relating to the relocated bulkhead line. The Audubon Society
was interested in the nearby bird rookery.

Senator Frederick B. Karl, representing C. K. Walley, said his client
was concerned with ecology but the biological reports in this case were
vague and uncertain, he had paid taxes for years, was in the dredge and
fill business as a commercial enterprise, and if the Board was unwilling
for him to develop his land and it was determined to be in the public int
to keep it in its natural state, then the owner should be paid for the la
sold to his predecessor in title in 1952.

Mr. Adams noted that there might be a number of other similar situations
and suggested delay to allow opportunity to study all that was involved.
The Director said this would be the first time action under the new law
was recommended, and while Mr. Walley would like to see the matter resolv
postponement should not cause any damage.

Governor Kirk directed postponement for a week, which was approved.

BREVARD COUNTY - File No. 2315-05-253.12, Land Sale.
On July 28, 1970, the Trustees considered application from Leonard
Spielvogel, on behalf of Orval M. Bradford, Jr., and Floyd H. Criswell,
for purchase of 0.341 acre parcel of sovereignty land in the Indian
River abutting fractional section 2, Township 25 South, Range 36 East,
Merritt Island, Brevard County, appraised at $400 for the parcel
($1,172 per acre) as adjusted by staff appraiser. Notice of sale was
published in the Cocoa Tribune, proof of publication filed, and no
objection to the sale received.

The biological report was not adverse. Staff recommended approval of
the sale, requested by the applicant in order to close the gap between
adjacent seawalls.

Mr. Adams, noting that the public interest emanated from the fact that
a stagnant pocket existed at the site, made a motion that the sale be
confirmed at the adjusted appraised price, applicant to pay for the
appraisal. Motion was seconded by Mr. Williams and adopted without
objection.

SARASOTA COUNTY - File No. 2207-58-253.12, Land Sale.
On July 21, 1970, the Trustees considered application from Logan Smith
Company, Inc., for the Purchase of a parcel of sovereignty land in Roberts
Bay abutting Section 6, Township 37 South, Range 18 East, containing
1.277 acres, more or less, in Sarasota County, appraised at $2,593 per
acre or $3,311.26 for the parcel. Applicant offered the appraised price
and reconveyance of 0.388 acre previously purchased. Notice of sale
was published in the Sarasota Herald, proof of publication filed, and
several objections were received. On the advertised sale date, September
8, there was no meeting and all objectors were notified that the applicat
would be considered on this date.

The biological survey report was adverse, stating that the area to be
filled for residential development would consume valuable mangrove island
The applicant had modified his plans according to suggestions in the repo
for alternate channel and fill areas.

Staff was of the opinion that the offer of $3,311.26 for the parcel and
reconveyance of 0.388 acre previously conveyed was fair and the sale in
the public interest because (1) a definite boundary would be established
between public and private lands, (2) the utilization of 0.7 ft. m.s.l.
elevation will be abandoned in the area, and (3) it will allow for orderl
development of uplands into homesites.

The Director said that several additional objections were received but no information that was not previously considered, that one good result of this application was that Sarasota County on the Trustees' recommendation had changed the tidal data that had been used to locate the line of mean high water. Staff recommended the objections be overruled and the sale confirmed.

On motion by Mr. Conner, seconded by Mr. Dickinson and adopted without objection, the Trustees overruled the objections and confirmed sale as recommended.

PALM BEACH COUNTY - File No. 2339-50-253.12, Application to Advertise. On August 18 the Trustees deferred action for further staff investigation of the application from Owen H. Libby, Jr., on behalf of Mayfran, Inc., for the purchase of 0.698 acre parcel of sovereignty land in Lake Worth abutting Section 11, Township 44 South, Range 43 East, Town of Palm Beach, Palm Beach County, to be used for a private residence.

The biological survey report was adverse, remarking that mangroves on the parcel had been destroyed which lessened the productivity of the area. A report from the applicant was requested, and the land-clearing contractor advised that the foreshore area of the lot resembled a city dump due to debris that had collected in the mangroves over the years. No dredging or filling has occurred. The parcel is landward of the established bulkhead line. The Area Planning Board had no objections, the Town of Palm Beach endorsed the sale and filling of the area, and adjacent neighbors were in favor of the application.

Applicant said that sale would be in the public interest as the parcel was between two existing seawalls and was a pocket where debris collected.

The Director said that the land-clearing contractor had removed some mangroves that bordered the shoreline very closely and had served to collect debris, but no dirt had been moved. Answering Mr. Adams' question, he did not think there was any basis for a penalty for destroying the mangroves.

On motion by Mr. Adams, adopted without objection, the Board authorized advertisement of the parcel for objections only.

FILL MATERIAL - Review.
On motion by Mr. Faircloth, seconded by Mr. Williams and adopted, the Trustees authorized a review of the value of fill material secured from state-owned lands, for the purpose of making recommendations as to guidelines. The following committee members recommended by the Director were approved and travel and per diem authorized:

1. Chairman, Richard B. Hellstrom, P.E. (Engineer with Biendorf & Assoc., Consulting Engineers, Vero Beach)
2. P. J. White, P.E. (Assistant State Highway Engineer of Construction, Department of Transportation, Tallahassee)
3. James T. Glass, Registered Land Surveyor (Post, Bailey & Glass, Islamorada)
4. A. J. Capeletti (Contractor, rock, fill and earth moving, Miami)
5. J. I. Wilson, M.A.I. (Fee appraiser, Miami)

6. N. R. Boutin, M.A.I. (Trustees of the Internal Improvement Trust Fund)

ORANGE COUNTY - Lease.
The Department of Highway Safety and Motor Vehicles request a long-term lease of 5 acres of unused state land adjacent to the State Office Building at Winter Park described as Lots 1 through 8, Block "A", Hills Addition to Winter Park, Plat Book C, Page 50, for construction of a building for the Driver License Office and Motor Vehicle Division District Office to serve Orange County. The Department of General Services had reviewed and approved the request.

On motion by Mr. Williams, seconded by Mr. Faircloth and adopted without objection, the Trustees approved issuance of 99-year lease to the Department of Highway Safety and Motor Vehicles.

DADE COUNTY - Duplicate Deed.
On motion by Mr. Dickinson, seconded by Mr. Faircloth and adopted without objection, the Trustees approved issuance of a duplicate deed for $25 processing charge pursuant to request from Joseph A. Barley. Trustees Deed No. 30-D-18 dated August 1, 1934, was lost or misplaced prior to being recorded in the public records.

MONROE COUNTY - Release Restriction Covenants, Deed No. 19550.
The City of Key West by Resolution No. 70-73 adopted on August 17, 1970, requested release of restrictive covenants contained in Deed No. 19550 dated December 27, 1949, that conveyed certain sovereignty land to the city for public purposes. In order to obtain street right of way through land in private ownership, the city had worked out an agreement to exchange an area of 48,530 sq. ft. for an equal area. Before such exchange can be effectuated, the restrictive covenants that prohibit sale, conveyance or lease to private parties, must be released.

On motion by Mr. Williams, seconded by Mr. Dickinson and adopted without objection, the Board agreed to release the restriction as to the area requested by the city.

CITRUS COUNTY - Dredge Permit to Improve Navigation,
            File No. 253.123-612.
Katherine S. Bowld, represented by Allen F. Kisinger of Crystal River, Florida, applied for permission to dredge a navigation channel 140 ft. long, 20 ft. wide and 3 ft. deep in the Crystal River in Section 21, Township 18 South, Range 17 East, Citrus County, in an area where the biological report was not adverse. Applicant tendered $50 application fee.

On motion by Mr. Williams, seconded by Mr. Dickinson and adopted without objection, the Trustees authorized issuance of the dredge permit.

CITRUS COUNTY - Dredge Permit to Improve Navigation,
            File No. 253.123-589.
Tommy Jordon of Tampa, Florida, applied for permissin to dredge a navigation channel 1,800 ft. long, 30 ft. wide and 5 ft. deep, in the Withlacoochee River in Section 23, Township 17 South, Range 19

East, Citrus County, in an area where the biological report was not adverse. Applicant tendered $50 application fee. A plug would remain at the entrance of the river until dredging of the lagoon is complete and all spoil would be placed above the mean high water line.

On motion by Mr. Williams, seconded by Mr. Dickinson and adopted without objection, the Trustees authorized issuance of the dredge permit subject to compliance with the recommendations regarding the dredging as stated above.

LEE COUNTY - Fill Permit for Lands Artificially Eroded,
          File No. 253.124(7)-140, Chapter 70-333, Acts of 1970.
Mary Simmons Estate, represented by Duane Hall of Fort Myers, Florida, applied for permission to fill land lost due to artificially induced erosion from wave action from passing boats in Matlacha Pass in Section 24, Township 44 South, Range 22 East, covering approximately 0.069 acre in Lee County.

Under provisions of Chapter 70-333, Acts of 1970, a construction permit may be issued by the local governing body to restore lands that have been subject to artificially induced erosion or avulsion, such construction to be within 25 feet of the existing shoreline.

Staff recommended approval of the permit issued by Lee County on August 5.

On motion by Mr. Faircloth, seconded by Messers. Williams and Christian, the Trustees approved the application under provisions of the new law.

LEE COUNTY - Permit for Maintenance Dredging,
          Section 253.123, File No. 577.
Florida Power and Light Company applied for a permit for maintenance dredging in Charlotte Harbor adjacent to Section 26, Township 43 South, Range 20 East, Lee County, in an area where the biological report was not adverse.

The applicant tendered $50 processing fee. Applicant agreed to give the Department of Natural Resources, Bureau of Beaches and Shores, a $35,000 grant for a beach erosion control project on the southern tip of Gasparilla Island, and will make available 50% of the material (13,000 cubic yards) from the dredge area.

Staff recommended approval of the permit and recommended no charge for the 26,000 cubic yards of material to be removed, one-half of which would be made available for the erosion control project.

On motion by Mr. Williams, seconded by Mr. Faircloth and adopted without objection, the Trustees accepted the staff recommendation for approval at no charge, since the applicant had committed $35,000 to fund the beach erosion control project.

MONROE COUNTY - Dredge and Fill Permit, Section 253.03, F.S.
Wacouta Corporation, represented by James T. Glass, applied for a permit to dredge a channel 50 ft. wide and 5 ft. deep in Section 35, Township 66 South, Range 29 East, for navigation in Newfound Harbor, Big Pine Key, in Monroe County, and to place the material on submerged land privately owned. The Board had agreed in principle to the proposed plan on July 7 when the exchange and boundary line agreement was authorized. The revised biological report was

partially adverse, and the application was deferred on September 1.

Governor Kirk by memorandum had requested a deferment on consideration until a later meeting.

Mrs. Irene Hooper, president of Seacamp Association, Inc., a non-profit educational association, said the dredging would adversely affect the program at Cupon Bight where study and research were participated in by high school and college students because this was a relatively undistrubed area.

On the Governor's request, the application was deferred for one week.

MONROE COUNTY - Dredge Permit to Improve Navigation,
        Section 253.03, File 172.
Bahia Shores, Inc., represented by James T. Glass, applied for permission to dredge two navigation channels in Big Spanish Channel in Section 16, Township 66 South, Range 30 East, Monroe County, one a perimeter channel 350 ft. long, 30 ft. wide and 1.0 ft. deep and the other an access channel 300 ft. long, 50 ft. wide and 5 ft. deep. The application was filed prior to the adoption of the $50 processing fee policy.

The biological report on the original application was adverse. The plan was revised as suggested in the report from the Department of Natural Resources, and the subsequent biological report was not adverse.

On motion by Mr. Faircloth, seconded by Messers. Christian and Williams, the Board of Trustees approved issuance of the permit.

PALM BEACH COUNTY - Dredge Permit to Improve Navigation,
        File No. 253.123-636.
Old Port Cove Venture, represented by Perry E. Willits, applied for permission to dredge a boat slip connection only, 67 ft. wide and 4 ft. deep in Section 9, Township 42 South, Range 43 East, Lake Worth in Palm Beach County, in an area where the biological report was not adverse. Applicant submitted $50 application fee.

On motion by Mr. Christian, seconded by Messers. Williams and Faircloth, the Trustees approved issuance of the dredge permit.

PINELLAS COUNTY - Permit for Maintenance Dredging, Section 253.123.
Subject to Trustees' approval, the Pinellas County Water and Navigation Control Authority issued Dredge-Only Permit No. 184 for maintenance dredging in 16 channels throughout the City of St. Petersburg. Dredging would be done with a dragline and spoil would be placed along the sides of the channels.

The biological report was not adverse and staff recommended approval subject to the dredging being coordinated with the Department of Natural Resources.

On motion by Mr. Faircloth, seconded by Messers. Williams and Christian, the Trustees approved issuance of permit to the city as recommended by the staff.

PINELLAS COUNTY - Dredge Permit to Improve Navigation,
Section 253.123, Dredge-Only No. 188.
Subject to Trustees' approval, Pinellas County Water and Navigation
Control Authority issued a permit to install a seawall and dredge
a perimeter channel 30 ft. wide by 15 ft. deep in Section 4, Township 31 South, Range 15 East, Pinellas County, to Bernard Greenbaum
and Associates. The biological report was not adverse.

The material removed from applicant's land would be used to backfill
behind the seawall. Applicant tendered $50 processing fee. Staff
recommended no charge for the backfill material that would be
excavated from applicant's submerged land and recommended approval
of the application subject to the draglining being limited to an area
not more than 30 ft. from the seawall.

On motion made by Mr. Williams, seconded by Messrs. Christian and
Conner, and adopted without objection, the Trustees approved issuance
of the dredge permit as recommended by the staff.

_____

OKALOOSA COUNTY - Dredge Permit to Improve Navigation,
File No. 253.123-634.
C. B. S. Development Corporation, represented by Jim Dennis of
Gulf Breeze, Florida, applied for permission to dredge a navigation
channel 500 ft. long, 30 ft. wide and 5 ft. deep in Old Pass Lagoon
in Township 2 South, Range 22 West, at Block "F", Holiday Isle in
Okaloosa County. Applicant tendered $50 application fee.

The biological report from the Department of Natural Resources was
not adverse. Staff recommended approval subject to the spoil area
being adequately diked to prevent silt from returning to the bay.

On motion made by Messrs. Conner and Christian, seconded by Mr. Williams,
and adopted without objection, the Trustees approved issuance of the
dredge permit with the provision recommended by the staff.

_____

DADE COUNTY - Marina License, Section 253.03 Florida Statutes.
On motion by Mr. Williams, seconded by Mr. Christian and adopted
without objection, the Trustees authorized issuance of a marina license
to Sunbeam Television Corporation for $100 minimum annual fee, for a
marina including a marginal dock in Biscayne Bay adjacent to uplands
in Section 9, Township 53 South, Range 42 East, Dade County.

_____

LEVY COUNTY - State Construction Permit.
On motion by Mr. Williams, seconded by Mr. Faircloth and adopted without
objection, the Trustees authorized issuance of state construction
permit to International Oceanographic Corporation for $100 processing
fee, for the construction of racks for supporting strings for commercial
oyster culture within an aquaculture lease area authorized by the
Trustees on June 30, 1970, in the Gulf of Mexico near Cedar Keys in
Levy County.

_____

ST. LUCIE COUNTY - Permit and Management Agreement.
Marine Science Center, Inc., represented by Richard B. Hellstrom,
applied for a permit to manage approximately 320 acres of sovereignty
land in the Indian River in unsurveyed Sections 8 and 9, Township 34
South, Range 40 East, St. Lucie County, for scientific research and
associated purposes within a designated area consistent with the
conditions set forth in Section 3 (B) of the General Aquatic Preserve
Resolution adopted by the Trustees on November 24, 1969. That would
allow activities designed to enhance the quality or utility of not
only the Indian River Aquatic Preserve (A-9) but the other preserves,
from the knowledge gained through permitted activities.

The applicant desired permission to construct docks, piers, wharfs and
similar structures, and structures to house laboratory equipment used in

connection with ecological research and water control, measuring and monitoring devices. The permit would be subject to revocation in the event of any activity that would significantly reduce the biological value of the management area or interfere with reasonable navigational requirements.

Secretary of State Tom Adams described some of the accomplishments and research activities of Dr. E. A. Link, president of the applicant company, and recommended approval of the application.

On motion by Mr. Adams, seconded by Mr. Williams and adopted unanimously, the Trustees granted the request for permit and management agreement conditioned upon the applicant promulgating to appropriate governmental agencies any information, data and conclusions obtained through operation of the project. and furnishing quarterly reports of activities.

SUBJECTS UNDER CHAPTER 18296

On motion by Mr. Conner, seconded by Mr. Dickinson and adopted without objection, the Trustees approved Report No. 973 and authorized execution of deeds pertaining to two regular bids for sale of Murphy Act land under provisions of Chapter 18296, Acts of 1937, Section 197.350 Florida Statutes, as follows:

> 1 parcel of land in Section 39, Township 8 South, Range 30 East, St. Johns County, to the Deltona Corporation for the high bid of $600;

> Lot 9, Block 70, Vermont Heights, St. Johns County, to Amelia E. Terry for the high bid of $100.

ALACHUA COUNTY - Sale under Section 197.355 Florida Statutes. Irene Jacobs Hicks applied for conveyance of a parcel of land certified to the State of Florida under tax sale certificate No. 789 of November 4, 1895, described as Lot 30, Stoughton's Addition to Micanopy as per plat thereof recorded in Plat Book A Page 31 of the Public Records of Alachua County, Florida, of which she was the former owner on June 9, 1939, the date title vested in the state under Section 192.38, now 197.350 Florida Statutes.

On motion by Mr. Williams, seconded by Mr. Faircloth and adopted without objection, the Trustees approved the application under the so-called "Hardship Act" and authorized issuance of deed for $200.

REFUNDS - Murphy Act.
On motion by Mr. Conner, seconded by Mr. Williams and adopted without objection, the Trustees authorized refund to two applicants for release of state road right of way reservations contained in Murphy Act deeds but which the Department of Transportation did not recommend be released, as follows: (1) $45 refund to Ruth Morat, Dade Deeds 3126-EDDJ, 3821-EDDJ and 4740; (2) $15 refund to Tampa Abstract Division Chelsea Title and Guaranty Company, Hillsborough County Deed No. 4707.

On motion duly adopted, the meeting was adjourned.

GOVERNOR   CHAIRMAN

ATTEST: _James W Apthorp_
EXECUTIVE DIRECTOR

* * *   * * *

Tallahassee, Florida
September 22, 1970

The State of Florida Board of Trustees of the Internal Improvement
Trust Fund met in Senate Hearing Room 31 in the Capitol, with the
following members present:

Claude R. Kirk, Jr.	Governor, Present Part Time
Tom Adams	Secretary of State
Fred O. Dickinson, Jr.	Comptroller
Broward Williams	Treasurer
Floyd T. Christian	Commissioner of Education

James W. Apthorp   Executive Director

On motion duly adopted, the minutes of September 1, 1970 were
approved as submitted.

At Mr. Adams' suggestion because a number of persons were present
interested in dredge and fill matters appearing at the end of the
agenda, the Trustees began with the application numbered "30" and
considered the items in the reverse order.

ESCAMBIA COUNTY - Temporary Construction Permit,
                  Section 253.03 Florida Statutes.
The City of Pensacola applied for a partial after-the-fact temporary
construction permit to erect an earthern cofferdam in Escambia Bay
to facilitate installation of a concrete headwall for a storm
sewer outfall. The cofferdam, to be removed after the headwall
has been installed, was erected without permit but the work ceased
when the city was advised that a permit was required. The biological
report was not adverse, and staff recommended approval for a 90-day
period.

Motion was made by Mr. Williams, seconded by Mr. Adams and adopted
without objection, that the Trustees approve temporary permit to
the City of Pensacola for a period of 90 days.

VOLUSIA COUNTY - City of Daytona Beach had requested approval of
a lease arrangement between the City and other parties to develop
and operate a marina on lands deeded to the city for public
purposes only.

Parties who had requested a hearing by the Board had found it
impossible to be here on this date. Without objection, the
Trustees deferred consideration for two weeks.

DADE COUNTY - Marina License, Section 253.03 Florida Statutes.
The City of Miami applied for a state marina license, without fee,
for installation of a public marina facility in Biscayne Bay at
Dinner Key in Section 22, Township 54 South, Range 41 East, Dade

9-22-70

County. All required exhibits were submitted and staff recommended approval and waiver of the fee. Mr. Williams made a motion for approval.

Mr. Nathaniel P. Reed said the Department of Air and Water Pollution Control raised the issue of water quality standards, that for a period of thirty or forty years hundreds of boats had dumped raw sewage in the bay, that now the city wanted to enlarge the marina site by pumping up material and there were many problems to be solved. He thought this was the time to insist on installation of pipes to remove waste, but had not had an opportunity to discuss the application with Mr. Apthorp.

Mr. Williams withdrew his first motion and made a motion, adopted without objection, that the application by the City of Miami be postponed until a recommendation from the Air and Water Pollution Control Department was available.

SARASOTA COUNTY - Amendment to Dredge Permit No. 253.123-395. Mara Beach, Incorporated, represented by Richard W. Cooney, applied for amendment of an existing permit to allow dredging a 100 ft. wide, 296 ft. long and 7 ft. deep boat basin that applicant's boat needed for safe maneuvering. A total of 881.7 cubic yards of over-dredge material would be removed, for which payment of $38.17 was tendered, and $50 processing fee was paid. The biological report was adverse. Sarasota County approved the amended permit on September 1, 1970.

On motion by Mr. Adams, seconded by Mr. Williams and adopted without objection, the Trustees approved issuance of the permit amendment.

OKALOOSA COUNTY - Dredge Permit to Improve Navigation,
             File No. 253.123-594.
Gary E. Lee applied for permission to dredge a navigation channel in Choctawhatchee Bay in Section 4, Township 2 South, Range 23 West, Okaloosa County, 1,467 ft. long, 30 ft. wide and 5 ft. deep. Application fee of $50 was paid. The material removed would be placed behind an existing seawall to replace that lost by erosion due to hurricanes. The biological survey report was not adverse, and the Bureau of Beaches and Shores approved the application.

On motion by Mr. Williams, seconded by Mr. Adams and adopted without objection, the Trustees approved issuance of the dredge permit.

MONROE COUNTY - Dredge and Fill Permit, Section 253.03 F. S. ,
To Improve Navigation and Submerged Land Heretofore Conveyed. Wacouta Corporation, represented by James T. Glass, applied for a permit for dredging a Y-shaped channel 50 ft. wide and 5 ft. deep in Section 35, Township 66 South, Range 29 East, for navigation in Newfound Harbor at Big Pine Key, Monroe County. Material removed would be placed on submerged land in private ownership as part of the applicant's plan agreed to in principle on July 7 when the Trustees authorized an exchange and boundary line agreement with the Wacouta Corporation. The plan had been modified to reduce damage to biological resources, but the revised biological report was partially adverse.

On September 1 the Trustees deferred action on the dredge and fill application. On September 15 at the Governor's request action

was again deferred, but the Board heard objections presented by
Mrs. Irene Hooper of Seacamp Association Inc.

Numerous objections had been received. Representative William G.
Roberts of Monroe County requested deferment for further study.
Mrs. Hooper had requested the Advisory Committee on Aquatic Preserves
to establish a preserve in Cupon Bight to protect the unique ecology,
and urged denial of the application on the basis that it was harmful
to the ecology and not compatible with the environment. She said
Seacamp objected to the entire project but the staff had advised
that the objections should be presented at the time the dredge and
fill permits were considered.

Mr. Adams expressed concern at the information that a staff member
was carried to the site by a developer associated with an overfill
at Summerland Key, which had connotations requiring an investigation as it was highly inappropriate for staff members to travel
with land developers whose approach was different from the objec-
tives of the Board. He said that representations had been made with
respect to a conservation area in this project that were not now
being honored, that this particular area had not been subject to
intense development, and when this matter was again considered after
the deferment suggested by other members he would vote to deny the
permit and set this area aside as an aquatic preserve.

Mrs. Hooper said that particular developer's name had never been
mentioned with the applicant firm. Mr. Christian expressed concern
at the vagueness of the references and cautioned against implications involving the party in the previous litigation; but he wanted
an investigation to exonerate the staff members.

Mr. Bill Roberts, attorney for the project engineer, said to his
knowledge Mr. Phil Toppino had no involvement with the corporation,
the upland was platted for single family homesites for which access
channel to deep water was desired, the channel design was modified
as recommended by the staff, there would be a tertiary treatment
plant with outfall in the Atlantic Ocean, the land exchange
approved in July was for the purpose of letting the state acquire
valuable submerged bottoms and to clarify title questions arising
from erroneous government surveys. He said what was asked for
would do minimum damage, that the applicant and purchasers of the
homesites did not desire to destroy the fishing and other
recreation benefits.

Mr. Apthorp said the term "conservation area" on the drawing was
probably misleading, that the file indicated community use, that
he knew the staff had inspected the application site but not the
details of the transportation, that when the Secretary of State
and the Attorney General were involved in the lawsuit on Summerland
Key the Director had been an employee in the office of the Secretary
of State. Mr. Apthorp felt that when the Board agreed to the land
exchange it carried some commitment as to dredging, but he did not
know whether the exchange deeds had been issued.

Mr. Christian wanted to defend the education project at Seacamp
but not to get involved in other implications. He thought action
should be deferred for securing a recommendation from the Air and
Water Pollution Control Department. The Governor said the
associations should be looked into. He knew the area well, and
there were evident conditions to indicate stagnation and other
unfavorable results from the proposed dredging. If the application came back to the Board in its present form, the Governor and
the Treasurer said they would vote against it.

On motion by Mr. Christian, seconded by Mr. Williams and adopted
without objection, the Trustees deferred consideration for clearing
up the several questions raised on this date.

On motion by Mr. Williams, seconded by Mr. Christian and adopted
without objection, the Board directed that the exchange deeds be
held if they had not already been issued.

MONROE COUNTY - Dredge and Fill Permit, Section 253.03 F. S.,
To Improve Navigation and Submerged Land Heretofore Conveyed, File 169.
The Branigar Organization, Inc., represented by James T. Glass,
applied for a permit for dredging a 1,312 ft. long, 50 ft. wide and
5 ft. deep navigation channel adjacent to Sections 20 and 21, Township 64 South, Range 36 East, in Florida Bay, Monroe County. The
15,000 cubic yards of material would be placed on upland and on
submerged land previously conveyed in Trustees Deed No. 20770. The
applicant tendered $1,500 for the material. The application was
filed prior to adoption of the $50 processing fee requirement. The
biological report was adverse. However, the dredge and fill area
had been reduced to minimize adverse effects.

On motion by Mr. Adams, seconded by Mr. Dickinson and adopted
without objection, the Trustees approved issuance of the permits.

MONROE COUNTY - Dredge Permit to Improve Navigation, File 253.03-205.
William E. Olson applied for permission to dredge a navigation
channel 400 ft. long, 45 ft. wide and 5 ft. deep in Pine Channel
at Big Pine Key in Section 27, Township 66 South, Range 29 East,
Monroe County. The biological report was partially adverse but the
applicant had revised the plan in accordance with recommendations
of the biological report.

At Mr. Adams' request, the Trustees deferred action for two weeks.

LEE COUNTY - Dredge Permit to Improve Navigation, File 253.123-638.
John T. Sheets applied for permit to dredge a navigation channel
2,800 ft. long, 50 ft. wide top cut, 5 ft. deep (M.L.W.) in Manatee
Bay, Matlacha Pass, in Section 23, Township 45 South, Range 25 East,
Lee County. The biological report indicated limited adverse effects
and staff recommended construction of dikes to contain the silt.
The site was south of Aquatic Preserve G-12.

At Mr. Adams' request the Trustees deferred action for two weeks.
Mr. Adams wanted to know if, in fact, the deposit of the dredged
material would constitute sufficient improvements of the upland that
the Board should make a charge for the fill material.

DUVAL COUNTY - Dredge Permit 253.123-622, Fill Permit 253.124-132,
                SAJSP Permit (70-400)
Dunn's Terminal Corporation, represented by Lake G. Ray, Jr., Harbor
Engineering Company, applied for approval of dredge and fill permit
issued by the City of Jacksonville on May 12, 1970. It was proposed
to dredge 327,000 cu.yds. of material from the St. Johns River,
from areas that are "sandy and unvegetated, remaining generally
below the zone of effective sunlight penetration" according to the
biological survey report. In accordance with the report and staff
recommendations, the applicants had agreed to modifications of the
project and agreed to convey to the state 5.3 acres of marsh land
bordering on Wynn Creek. Further modification of the seawall

configuration should diminish adverse hydrographic effects as
indicated by a report from the Coastal Engineering Laboratory.
Applicant tendered $22,800 for 228,000 cubic yards of material to
be removed from sovereignty land.

Numerous objections were filed and objectors present were represented by Hans Vige, Jr., Hans Vige, Sr., Mrs. Rosemary Furman and
Miss Alberta James who based protests on their past opposition to
sale of the land to be filled, the many different maps representing
modifications of the engineering plans but causing confusion and
doubt that the current plan was that one approved by Jacksonville
City Council, adverse biological and hydrological reports, drainage
in the area of Dunns and Wynns Creeks, and opposition to industry
moving into the area. A petition was filed with over two thousand
signatures, opposing the application.

Representing the applicant, Gardner T. Gillett advised the Board
that the parcel was zoned for industry, the bulkhead line established, all requirements had been met, drainage would be properly
taken care of to protect the area as well as his client's other
property, and in the process of meeting requirements and adverse
reports there had been modifications and changes in the engineering
maps. He offered to try to talk further with objectors to resolve
protests, if possible, in the event the Trustees desired to defer
action.

Members asked questions, expressed concern for the business man as
well as the residents in an area being changed by industrial zoning,
and in view of the technical questions raised by the objectors and
differences in maps and other exhibits that could not be resolved
at a board meeting, motion was made by Mr. Williams, seconded by
Mr. Dickinson and adopted without objection, that action be
deferred for additional information and a clearer presentation of
the application with pertinent maps.

Governor Kirk thanked the concerned citizens for their work and
presence, assured them that the facts would be brought out in a
more orderly form for a decision to be made by the Board at a
later meeting at which they might be represented if they desired
to be heard again. Governor Kirk left the meeting at this time.

DADE COUNTY - Fill Permit, Section 253.124 Florida Statutes.
Albert J. Bacskay, represented by James P. Shiskin, requested
approval of a fill permit granted by Dade County for filling 0.086
acre parcel damaged by erosion in Section 14, Township 52 South,
Range 42 East, Intracoastal Waterway in Dade County. All fill
material would be hauled to the site, and the biological report
indicated only limited adverse effects on marine life in the area
from the filling.

On motion by Mr. Dickinson, seconded by Mr. Williams and adopted
without objection, the Trustees approved the fill permit.

DADE COUNTY - Dredge Permit to Improve Navigation, File 253.123-653.
On motion made by Messrs. Williams and Dickinson, seconded by Mr.
Christian and adopted without objection, the Trustees authorized
issuance of dredge permit without fee to Dade County Public Works
Department for a boat slip connection in Section 5, Township 54
South, Range 42 East, Biscayne Bay, Dade County. The biological
survey report was not adverse.

BAY COUNTY - Dredge Permit to Improve Navigation, File 253.123-639.
Miss S. E. Wright applied for permission to dredge a navigation
channel 250 ft. long, 50 ft. wide and 5 ft. deep in Grand Lagoon
in Section 9, Township 4 South, Range 15 West, Bay County. The
biological report cites limited adverse effects.

At Mr. Adams' request, the Trustees deferred action for two weeks.

SHELL LEASE INCOME REPORT - The Board of Trustees accepted for the
record the following report of remittances to Florida Department
of Natural Resources from holders of dead shell leases:

Lease No. 1718	Radcliff Materials, Inc.	$ 2,078.68
Lease No. 1788	Benton & Company, Inc.	16,223.02
Lease No. 2233	Bay Dredging and Construction	5,451.22

CHARLOTTE AND COLLIER COUNTIES - At the request of Governor Kirk,
the Board deferred consideration of requests from Sun Oil Company,
Humble Oil and Refining Company, and Amerada Hess Corporation, for
advertisement of oil and gas leases on land of the Trustees and
the Board of Education.

TRUSTEES FUNDS - On motion by Mr. Williams, seconded by Mr. Dickinson,
and adopted without objection, the Trustees authorized contribution
of funds for the following purposes:

(1) $250,000 for continuation of the cooperative agreement with
    the Unites States Geological Survey dated February 27, 1969,
    for accelerated topographic mapping program. The federal
    government will match said amount. The 1970 Legislature
    included payment of that amount in the budget of the
    Trustees of the Internal Improvement Trust Fund. '

(2) Trustees funds to match contributions of various counties
    and conservation districts, approximately $13,000, the
    total amount of which is matched with federal funds for the
    purpose of continuing water resources investigations during
    the 1970-71 year under an agreement with the United States
    Department of the Interior, Geological Survey. Funds are
    provided in the current operating budget of the Trustees of
    the Internal Improvement Trust Fund.

BREVARD COUNTY - Refund, Contract 24760(423-05)253.12.
Stanley Wolfman, on behalf of Hampton Homes Inc. of Cocoa, requested
refund of the amount paid on Contract No. 24760(423-05) for purchase
of 34.67 acres of sovereignty land in Newfound Harbor abutting
Section 25, Township 24 South, Range 36 East, Brevard County. The
applicant had paid to date $40,527.68, principal and interest,
and in event of refund, agreed to withdraw the suit styled Hampton
Homes Corp. Inc. of Cocoa, Pettitioner, vs the Board of Trustees
of the Internal Improvement Fund of the State of Florida, Respondent,
Case No. 0-82, in which the Office of Legal Affairs represented the
Board of Trustees.

On motion by Mr. Williams, seconded by Mr. Dickinson and adopted
without objection, the Trustees authorized refund and cancellation
of the contract conditioned upon Hampton Homes agreeing to
dismissal of the suit in accordance with stipulation being prepared
by Department of Legal Affairs.

9-22-70

TRUSTEES FUNDS - Grant-in-Aid: Fresh Water Lakes Study.
The Environmental Engineering Department, University of Florida,
received a federal grant of $26,666 from the Office of Water
Resources Research, Department of the Interior, for a two-year
study for the purpose of locating the high water lines of fresh
water lakes. Dr. W. H. Morgan, Associate Professor of Environmental
Engineering, and Dr. John H. Davis, Jr., Professor of Botany,
requested funds from the Trustees to augment the federal grant.

The proposed study will have definite use in the Lake Cypress
(Osceola County) matter, and staff recommended grant of $11,000
for a two-year study period. That amount might be transferred
from the funds earmarked for tidal mean high water line survey
and mapping.

On motion by Mr. Williams, seconded by Mr. Dickinson and adopted
without objection, the Trustees granted $11,000 to augment the
federal grant for the two-year study period.

PALM BEACH COUNTY - Power Line Easement.
Florida Power and Light Company requested an easement across lands
of the University of Florida Experimental Station, Morikomi Farm,
in Section 27, Township 46 South, Range 42 East, in Palm Beach
County, for an electrical power line to serve the station. The
Board of Regents approved the request.

On motion by Mr. Williams, seconded by Mr. Dickinson and adopted,
the Trustees authorized issuance of the easement for power line.

DUVAL COUNTY - Road Right of Way.
The Jacksonville Expressway Authority by Special Resolution
No. 205 requested an easement across two small parcels in Sections
8 and 9, Township 3 South, Range 28 East, for use in constructing
interchanges on Jose-Vedra Boulevard.

The parcels were a part of the new University of North Florida
and the interchange will be beneficial to the University. Officials
of the University and the Board of Regents approved the request.

On motion by Mr. Williams, seconded by Mr. Dickinson and adopted
without objection, the Trustees authorized issuance of the easement.

DADE COUNTY - Temporary Borrow Area Easement.
The Department of Transportation applied for a borrow area of
approximately 23 acres in Dumfoundling Bay in theoretical Sections
2 and 3, Township 52 South, Range 42 East, Dade County, for removal
of material to be used on uplands in connection with construction
of State Road 852 (192nd Street).

The biological report dated April 20, 1970, was adverse. Applicant
advised that an alternate area with suitable material could not
be located within the vicinity of the proposed construction. The
adjacent bottoms of Dumfoundling Bay have been subjected to
extensive dredging.

Mr. Christian made a motion for approval, which Mr. Adams and Mr.
Williams voted against. Mr. Dickinson said he would second the
motion made by Mr. Christian.

William J. Roberts, representing the engineering firm employed by
the Department of Transportation, explained that this area was

being relinquished by the developers of Biscayne Village project,
that use of this dredge material would save the Department of Transportation over $400,000 for having material trucked in. He
reminded the Board that parties previously allowed to dredge in
Dumfoundling Bay had made a commitment of $100,000 to create
artificial reefs to help rebuild fisheries in the area.

Mr. Adams referred to dredging in Indian River for highway construction - that has caused much pollution. Although the Board had
approved dredging in Dumfoundling Bay when the bulkhead lines for
South Dade County were being considered, he was concerned about
digging another hole in the Bay.

Mr. Dickinson made a motion that the application be approved,
which was seconded by Mr. Christian. However, as Messrs. Williams
and Adams voted "No" and only four were present, the motion failed
on a tie vote.

Mr. Christian then made a motion that the application be reagendaed,
and it was so ordered.

SARASOTA COUNTY - Quitclaim Deed, File 2356-58-12(6)
C. Archer Smith, represented by J. Douglas Arnest, applied for a
quitclaim deed to a parcel of filled sovereignty land containing
0.45 acre in Little Sarasota Bay abutting Sections 19 and 20,
Township 37 South, Range 18 East, Sarasota County, appraised at
$475 for the parcel by the staff appraiser.

On motion by Mr. Dickinson, seconded by Mr. Williams and adopted
without objection, the Board authorized issuance of the quitclaim
deed in compliance with Section 253.12(6), Florida Statutes, at
the appraised value plus $100 processing fee and the appraisal costs.

OSCEOLA COUNTY - Lake Cypress
Arthur Steed, an attorney representing Bronson's Inc., applied for
a quitclaim deed or disclaimer to the bottoms of Lake Cypress in
Osceola County, a large non-meandered fresh water lake within
the Kissimmee River chain of lakes that is presumed to be navigable.
Title to the lake bottoms is sovereignty in character and not
susceptible of being conveyed. The applicant requested that the
Trustees, in the event they refuse to issue the desired instrument,
consent to a quiet title suit to be filed and heard in Osceola
County.

On motion by Mr. Williams, seconded by Mr. Dickinson and adopted
without objection, the Trustees denied the request for a quitclaim
or disclaimer to the lake bottoms, and agreed to the suit being
filed in Osceola County. The Director recommended that Mr. Henry
Kittleson handle the case for the Trustees.

PALM BEACH COUNTY - Corrective Deed and Disclaimer
The Parini Land and Development Company, successors in title to
Calig Land Company, through their representative, Robert I.
Shapiro, requested issuance of corrective instruments to supplement
Trustees Deed No. 22884(924-50) and Disclaimer No. 22885(924-50)
which contained errors in certain dimensions and require correc-
tion before title insurance can be obtained.

9/22/70

On motion by Mr. Dickinson, seconded by Mr. Williams and adopted without objection, the Trustees authorized issuance of corrective instruments for the usual charge of $25 each.

MARTIN COUNTY - Corrective Deed.
On motion by Mr. Dickinson, seconded by Mr. Williams and adopted without objection, the Trustees authorized issuance of corrective deed for $25 that was requested by Evans Crary, Jr., representing Laurel Court, Inc., the Grantee in Trustees Deed No. 24961(1820-43) dated June 30, 1969, for the reason that the original deed had referred to Block "C" instead of Block "B" of Riverside Park Subdivision.

DADE COUNTY - File No. 2225-13-253.12, Application to Advertise
On September 1 the Board, on the recommendation of the staff, denied the application from Paul L. E. Helliwell, Trustee, represented by Thomas B. DeWolf, for advertisement of a proposed purchase of 4.96 acres of sovereignty land in Biscayne Bay abutting Section 6, Township 55 South, Range 42 East, Key Biscayne , Dade County. Sufficient reasons had not been submitted to the staff as to the public interest justifying the sale.

The biological report for the Mashta Point area was adverse, but the original plans were modified to eliminate dredging in the shallow area. The parcel was landward of the bulkhead line approved by the Board on January 28, 1969.

Through error a request from the applicant for deferment had not reached the Board on September 1, and the application was again placed on the agenda; however, the staff had not received from the applicant any additional reasons as to why the sale would be in the public interest. Dade County had endorsed the sale by letter.

Mr. Apthorp explained that under the standards set by the Board, the fact that the applicant desires to purchase the area for permanent homesites and neighbors favor the application, would not constitute a showing of public interest. Therefore, the staff recommended denial.

Mr. DeWolf pointed out the written approval by Dade County after numerous alterations of the engineering plan, approval of the bulkhead line at Mashta Point after numerous studies and revisions, the engineering report on development of single family residences, and the present hazardous and undesirable conditions on the point of land. He said Mashta Island Association favored the application. and that the applicants would do required maintenance dredging at Hurricane Harbor and modify dredging areas.

Mr. Christian pointed out that the Board expected the staff to review such information as Mr. DeWolf had presented to the members on this date, and Mr. Adams said they should know just where the fill would come from.

On motion by Mr. Christian, seconded by Mr. Dickinson and adopted without objection, the application was deferred for receipt from the applicant of sufficient information on the public purpose to be served by the sale and further details of the complete project.

<u>VOLUSIA COUNTY</u> - Bulkhead Line Denied; Condemnation.
On September 15, at request of the Governor the Board deferred
action on a bulkhead line relocated by the City Council of Port
Orange on October 25, 1968, along the south side of Port Orange
Causeway in the Halifax River in Section 3, Township 16 South, Range
33 East, Volusia County. (See minutes of September 15, 1970.)

The staff recommended that approval of the bulkhead line be denied,
in view of the fact that the biological report stated that the
dredge and fill project proposed for the area within the bulkhead
line would not be in the best interest of marine conservation and
development activity could be expected to lessen the value to birds
of a nearby rookery. The staff also recommended that authority be
granted for the staff to file a condemnation suit for the 4.45 acres
that had been previously conveyed by the Trustees.

On motion by Mr. Dickinson, seconded by Mr. Christian and adopted
without objection, the Trustees denied approval of the bulkhead
line and authorized condemnation suit for the property under the
provisions of Chapter 70-358, Acts of 1970, for the purpose of
reacquiring the submerged lands.

On motion duly adopted, the meeting was adjourned.

GOVERNOR - CHAIRMAN

ATTEST:
EXECUTIVE DIRECTOR

*   *   *   *

Tallahassee, Florida
October 6, 1970

The State of Florida Board of Trustees of the Internal Improvement
Trust Fund met in Senate Hearing Room 31 in the Capitol, with the
following members present:

Claude R. Kirk, Jr.	Governor
Tom Adams	Secretary of State
Fred O. Dickinson, Jr.	Comptroller
Broward Williams	Treasurer
Floyd T. Christian	Commissioner of Education
Doyle Conner	Commissioner of Agriculture

James W. Apthorp	Executive Director

On motion duly adopted, the Trustees approved the minutes of
September 15 and 22, 1970, as submitted.

10-6-70

FRANKLIN COUNTY - Bulkhead Line, Section 253.122 Florida Statutes.
The Board of County Commissioners of Franklin County by resolution
adopted on June 15, 1970, established a bulkhead line 948.19 feet
long in Alligator Harbor at the Alligator Point Marina in unsurveyed fractional Sections 2 and 3, Township 7 South, Range 2 West,
Franklin County. The biological survey report was not adverse,
and the staff recommended approval.

Motion was made by Mr. Williams, seconded by Mr. Dickinson,
that the bulkhead line be approved.

This was an area where some unauthorized dredging and filling had
been done which was under investigation by the staff. Mr. Adams
said there was some question as to just when the fill was placed
there, that the bulkhead line would surround. He suggested that
action be withheld.

Without objection, the Trustees deferred action for further study
and consideration.

GADSDEN COUNTY - Release of Option.
On May 9, 1969, the Board of Trustees was granted an option by
Frank L. Pittman to purchase four parcels of land for Bear Creek
State Park in Gadsden County, three of which had been acquired by
the Division of Recreation and Parks, Department of Natural
Resources.

On September 22 the Department approved release of the option to
purchase the fourth parcel of approximately 34 acres. Mr. Pittman
requested execution of a release of option which runs to September
20, 1971.

On motion by Mr. Williams, seconded by Mr. Adams and adopted
without objection, the Trustees authorized execution of an
instrument of release of option as to the fourth parcel.

BAY COUNTY - Land Transfer.
Pursuant to action on March 31, 1970, the Department of Natural
Resources requested conveyance of Government Lot 4, Section 15,
Township 4 South, Range 15 West, Bay County, to the Gulf Coast
Junior College for oceanographic and related purposes connected
with the school curriculum. The small, unused parcel in the
St. Andrews State Park acquired from the United States in 1948 and
restricted for park and recreational purposes had not been used as
part of the park due to its separation from the park by the waters
of Grand Lagoon.

The restrictions imposed on the parcel by the United States had
been changed to recreational and educational uses. The United
States Department of the Interior had authorized transfer of title
to the Junior College.

On motion by Mr. Williams, seconded by Mr. Adams and adopted without
objection, the Trustees approved transfer of title without cost to
the Gulf Coast Junior College for oceanographic and related
purposes only by appropriate instrument.

ST. JOHNS COUNTY - Road Easement.
By resolution adopted on August 25, 1970, the St. Johns County
Commission requested an easement for public road purposes across

a portion of the Frank B. Butler State Park containing 0.05 acre in the northeast corner of the park. The Department of Natural Resources approved issuance of the easement that would allow access to land owned by Frank Butler, who donated the portion of the park on which the parcel was located.

On motion by Mr. Christian, seconded by Mr. Williams and adopted without objection, the Trustees authorized issuance of the easement for public road purposes.

ALACHUA COUNTY - Easement.
On motion by Mr. Christian, seconded by Mr. Williams and adopted without objection, the Trustees authorized issuance of an easement approved by the Board of Regents on September 18, to the City of Gainesville for extending sanitary sewer lines over lands of the University of Florida in Section 18, Township 10 South, Range 20 East, in Alachua County.

BREVARD COUNTY - Dedication, File No. 2328-05-253.03.
By resolution adopted June 23, 1970, the City of Cocoa requested dedication of 4.45 acres of sovereignty land in the Indian River abutting Sections 33 and 34, Township 24 South, Range 36 East, Brevard County, landward of the bulkhead line approved by the Board of Trustees on January 27, 1970, for use as a wayside park adjacent to State Road No. 520 to be constructed by the Department of Transportation.

The City of Cocoa had reconveyed to the Trustees land previously dedicated in the area, as required by the Trustees in meeting of January 27, 1970. The biological report dated August 15, 1969, made at the time the bulkhead line was being relocated, was adverse to filling and there had been some controversy as to where the park should be located. The proposed 10-acre fill had been reduced to 4.45 acres, and while the biological report was adverse as to all the site, the parcel would provide a public park.

On motion by Mr. Christian, seconded by Mr. Adams and adopted without objection, the Trustees waived the two-weeks' advance agenda period and authorized advertisement of the parcel for objections only.

SARASOTA COUNTY - Disclaimer, File No. 2366-58-253.129.
On motion by Mr. Christian, seconded by Mr. Adams and adopted without objection, the Trustees authorized issuance of disclaimer in compliance with provisions of Section 253.129 Florida Statutes, for $100 processing fee, applied for by William Neil Benton on behalf of Michael J. Furen, for a parcel of filled sovereignty land embracing 0.42 acre in Roberts Bay abutting Section 1, Township 37 South, Range 17 East, Sarasota County.

SARASOTA COUNTY - Quitclaim Deed, File No. 2356-58-253.12(6)
On motion by Mr. Christian, seconded by Mr. Williams and adopted without objection, the Trustees confirmed action by four members on September 22 approving issuance of a quitclaim deed in compliance with provisions of Section 253.12(6) Florida Statutes, to filled sovereignty land embracing 0.45 acre in Little Sarasota Bay abutting Sections 19 and 20, Township 37 South, Range 18 East, Sarasota County, at the appraised value of $475 for the parcel, plus $100

processing fee and the appraisal costs. The applicant for the quitclaim deed was C. Archer Smith, represented by J. Douglas Arnest.

DADE COUNTY - The Department of Transportation requested further deferment of its request for a temporary borrow area easement of approximately 23 acres in Dumfounding Bay in Dade County for fill material to be used on uplands in connection with construction of State Road 852 (192nd Street).

Mr. Adams said he was prepared to vote against this application again, was pleased that it was deferred, and hoped a solution could be reached that would not only save some money but would preserve more estuarine areas. The Director said no reason for the request for deferment was given.

PALM BEACH COUNTY - Marina License, Section 253.03 Florida Statutes. On motion by Mr. Dickinson, seconded by Mr. Adams and adopted without objection, the Trustees approved issuance of a marina license to Ronald G. Sinn who had submitted payment of $128.69 for the first year's fee for a marina facility in Lake Worth adjacent to upland in Section 28, Township 42 South, Range 43 East, Palm Beach County, for the mooring of applicant's charter fishing boat.

LEVY COUNTY - Aquaculture Lease.
Staff requested authority to advertise for bids and objections on an aquaculture lease application from Ocean Farms, Inc., by Gerald Golub, president, embracing approximately 40 acres near Cedar Key in Levy County for cultivating oysters. The biological survey report was not adverse.

Mr. Adams noted that this was the company that had caused some difficulty in the Indian River by creating some obstruction, and he thought the Board should determine just what was proposed to be done before authorizing advertisement.

The Director had received word that the County Commission might oppose this application.

Without objection, action was deferred pending receipt of further information.

POLICY - Offshore Campsite Lease Rentals.
The staff, thinking that fees should be more representative of current conditions and competitive with private campsite rental fees, requested authority to increase rentals for offshore (stiltsville) campsite leases when such leases are renewed. The following rates were suggested: $300 year minimum for one-fourth acre or less, $500 per year for one-half acre, and $900 per year for one acre.

The present rate was $100 for a one-acre site, which the staff had compared with rates for other similar small structures. The Director recommended that one-fourth acre become the standard size rather than one acre, and that the application for a site in Monroe County on this date be considered on the basis of the increased rate.

On motion by Mr. Christian, seconded by Mr. Adams and adopted

without objection, the Trustees increased the rentals for offshore
campsite leases when such leases are renewed to the rates suggested
by the staff.

MONROE COUNTY - Campsite Lease for Private Use of Offshore Site.
W. B. Hannum, Jr., applied for a campsite lease for an existing
structure near Man Key in the Gulf of Mexico in Monroe County. The
lease area would not exceed one-fourth acre, the current annual
rental was $100 for one-year lease with option to renew for four
additional years. The staff placed the application on the agenda
and recommended lease in accordance with the policy adopted on April
7, 1970, which stated, in part: "Require all structures in existence
to be under lease for so long as the structure remains in existence."

On motion by Mr. Christian, seconded by Mr. Adams and adopted without
objection, the Trustees approved issuance of the campsite lease
under the new rental rate of $300 per year for the one-fourth acre
site.

COLLIER COUNTY - At the request of Governor Kirk, the Director
suggested deferment of consideration of oil and gas drilling lease
applications from Sun Oil Company and Humble Oil and Refining Company. The Governor said that supporting maps were on hand this
week, but Mr. Christian said he would like further study made.

Without objection, the Trustees again deferred consideration of the
applications for advertising of oil and gas drilling leases in
Collier County.

CHARLOTTE COUNTY - Oil and Gas Drilling Lease Advertisement.
Amerada Hess Corporation requested advertisement for sealed bids
for an oil and gas drilling lease of the reserved one-half interest
of the Board of Education in the Petroleum in privately-owned
Section 16, Township 41 South, Range 27 East, Charlotte County.

The State Geologist concurred in the staff recommendation that the
Trustees advertise for sealed bids for a five-year oil and gas
lease covering the reserved one-half interest of the Board, lease
to require annual rental of one dollar per net mineral acre, one-
eighth royalty, $50,000 surety bond and at least one test well every
two and one-half years to a depth of six thousand feet or to the
top of the Lower Cretaceous, whichever is deeper.

On motion by Mr. Christian, seconded by Mr. Dickinson and adopted
without objection, the Trustees accepted the staff recommendation
for advertisement for sealed bids.

CITRUS COUNTY - Dredge Permit for Maintenance Dredging,
                File No. 253.123-589A.
J. Thomas Jordon requested permit for maintenance dredging to
improve navigation in Old Channel of Withlacoochee River in Section
24, Township 17 South, Range 19 East, Citrus County, 500 ft. long,
30 ft. wide and 5 ft. deep, for which $50 application fee was
submitted and the biological report was not adverse.

On motion by Mr. Adams, seconded by Mr. Dickinson and adopted
without objection, the Trustees approved the staff recommendation
for issuance of the permit subject to requirement that a plug shall
remain at the river entrance until completion of dredging in the
old channel, and all spoil material will be placed above mean high
water line.

DUVAL COUNTY - Dredge Permit for Maintenance Dredging,
             File No. 253.123- 635.
Jacksonville Electric Authority applied for maintenance dredging
permit to improve navigation in the St. Johns River in Section 24,
Township 1 South, Range 27 East, Duval County, for which $50 appli-
cation fee was submitted and the biological report was not adverse.

On motion by Mr. Adams, seconded by Messrs. Dickinson and Christian
and adopted without objection, the Trustees accepted the staff
recommendation for approval subject to requirement that spoiling
be done on upland and dikes maintained at all times to contain the
spoil material.

ESCAMBIA COUNTY - Dredge Permit for Beach Nourishment,
                 Section 253.123(2)(c)
On motion by Mr. Adams, seconded by Messrs. Dickinson and Conner
and adopted without objection, the Trustees approved the application
of William Soule to dredge 30,000 cubic yards of material from
Pensacola Bay adjacent to Sections 50 and 51, Township 2 South,
Range 30 West, Escambia County, to be deposited on beach areas
lost by erosion resulting from Hurricane Camille. The biological
report was not adverse, and the Bureau of Beaches and Shores had
no objection to the project.

OKALOOSA COUNTY - Section 253.03 Florida Statutes.
Horace H. Higdon applied for a permit to reclaim a portion of his
upland lost by avulsion caused by Hurricane Camille. Field investigation by staff members of the Trustees and the Department of
Natural Resources in September and October 1969 confirmed the loss
and authorized the construction subject to applicant filing formal
application. All required exhibits including $50 for the material
to be removed from Five Mile Bayou were submitted.

On motion by Mr. Conner, seconded by Mr. Adams and adopted without
objection, the Trustees approved the application for permit.

HILLSBOROUGH COUNTY - Maintenance Dredging Permits.
On motion by Mr. Adams, seconded by Mr. Dickinson and adopted
without objection, the Trustees approved two applications from
Tampa Electric Company for $50 each, provided the spoil was placed
in existing spoil areas authorized under SAJSP Permit (57-463), the
projects described as follows:

    (1) File No. 253.123-646 for dredging 250 ft. long,
         150 ft. wide and minus-32 ft. deep in Port Sutton
         Channel in Section 33, Township 30 South, Range 19
         East, Hillsborough County.

    (2) File No. 253.123-649 for dredging 570 ft. long, 25 ft.
         wide and minus-32 ft. deep in Sparkman Channel in
         Section 19, Township 29 South, Range 19 East,
         Hillsborough County.

The biological report was not adverse.

BAY COUNTY - Dredge Permit to Improve Navigation, Section 253.123.
The Board of County Commissioners of Bay County requested permit
to dredge a channel in Grand Lagoon in Township 4 South, Range 15
West, from which the material would be deposited on the beach as

approved by the Bureau of Beaches and Shores and Recreation and Parks. The biological report was not adverse to the dredging and supplemental report approved the new spoil area.

On motion by Mr. Christian, seconded by Mr. Adams and adopted without objection, the Trustees authorized issuance of the permit.

INDIAN RIVER COUNTY - Dredge Permit to Improve Navigation,
                        File No. 253.123-654.
The City of Vero Beach requested permission to dredge a temporary channel 1,250 ft. long, 50 ft. wide and 4.5 ft. deep (MLW) in the Indian River in Sections 17 and 18, Township 33 South, Range 30 East, Indian River County, to improve navigation for installing a power line. $50 application fee was submitted, the biological report was not adverse, and the spoil would be replaced by applicant after completion of the project.

On motion by Mr. Adams, seconded by Mr. Dickinson and adopted without objection, the Trustees approved the application for dredge permit.

LEE COUNTY - Seawall and Backfill, Section 253.03 F. S., SAJSP Permit
             (70-388)
The application of Elmer E. Handy for a permit to construct a seawall and backfill along the foreshore of the Caloosahatchee River (FCD Canal C-43) to prevent erosion and loss of upland, was deferred at Mr. Adams' question regarding the source of the backfill material.

LEE COUNTY - Dredge Permit to Improve Navigation, File 253.123-640.
Old Bridge Park Corporation applied for a dredge permit to improve navigation in the Caloosahatchee River in Section 1, Township 44 South, Range 24 East, Lee County. The biological report indicated limited adverse effects might be expected from this channel 2,200 ft. long, 50 ft. wide top cut, and 5 ft. deep (MLW). $50 application fee was submitted.

On motion by Mr. Christian, seconded by Mr. Williams and adopted without objection, the Trustees approved the staff recommedation for issuance of the permit subject to requirement that the spoil be placed on upland in accordance with biologists' recommendations, behind adequate dikes, and waste water wiers be directed back into the channel and not through adjoining marsh and mangrove.

LEE COUNTY - Dredge Permit to Improve Navigation,
             Section 253.123 Florida Statutes.
On September 22 the Board deferred action on the application from John T. Sheets for a permit to dredge a navigation channel 2,800 ft. long, 50 ft. wide top cut, 5 ft. deep (MLW) in Manatee Bay, Matlacha Pass, adjacent to Section 23, Township 45 South, Range 22 East, in Lee County. The applicant tendered $50 application fee and subsequent to that date he agreed to pay the standard fee for the 10,000 cubic yards of material to be removed. The biological report indicated limited adverse effects on marine life from the project.

Mr. Apthorp said an objection was received on October 5 from the Organized Fishermen of Florida. He said this was a legitimate navigation need but the applicant had agreed to pay for the material and staff recommended approval subject to receipt of $1,000 payment.

Mr. Adams pointed out that it was difficult for the staff in the light of present criteria to determine just when fill material should be charged for and when it should not, but recently when applicants had requested permits for navigation channels they had offered payment for material for use on low-lying lands. Mr. Adams suggested a policy change, which his staff members had been considering and would discuss with the Trustees' office staff.

On motion by Mr. Adams, seconded by Mr. Dickinson and adopted without objection, the Trustees approved Mr. Sheet's application for a dredge permit to improve navigation subject to receipt of payment for the spoil material.

MANATEE COUNTY - Dredge and Fill Permits,
             File Nos. 253.123-561 and 253.124-126.
N. J. Cowart, Trustee, and C. H. Wooten applied for permit to dredge a total of 314,000 cubic yards of fill material from existing and proposed navigation channels and to deposit fill upon submerged lands purchased from the Board by the Estate of Bessie Richards, Deed Nos. 24887 and 24888(355-41). It was determined that 264,100 cubic yards of the total amount would be dredged from state-owned land. The Trustees deferred action on August 4 (see minutes of that date) and directed that the land be appraised to determine if the exchange of fill material for land proposed to be reconveyed to the Trustees would be comparable in value. The staff appraiser valued the 7.16 acres of land at $4,500. A computation of fill material indicated that 264,100 cubic yards would be valued at $26,410. On the basis of an equal exchange from a monetary standpoint, the applicant should remit $21,910 for the fill.

Staff recommended approval of permit upon payment of $21,910 for material and conveyance of 7.16 acres of land valued at $4,500.

William C. Grimes, attorney representing the applicants, said the original application requested permission to dredge and fill entirely within lands owned by the applicants, that applicant had agreed to modify the plan, to convey a portion of their land to the state, and to get the necessary material by dredging existing channels. Applicants were willing to abide by the staff recommendation, he said, except for the money involved. They would agree to pay what they considered a fair amount as a solution, $4,930, and the deepening of existing channels would be a public benefit. Mr. Adams discussed the prices mentioned and the reconveyance of land to the state, stating that he thought the Board had no basis for going beyond the figure fixed by the staff. The staff appraiser had found the islands of less value than it appeared at first, and the Director said the difference of $21,910 was the only basis the staff could recommend.

Mr. Adams made a motion, seconded by Mr. Christian, that the staff recommendation be accepted. Instead of accepting the staff recommendation, Mr. Grimes requested approval of the applicants' original application to dredge and fill entirely within the limits of the property owned by the applicants. The Director said that original application had never been before the Board, but the staff could bring it to the Trustees for consideration.

The Trustees adopted the motion made by Mr. Adams that the staff recommendation for approval of permit upon payment of $21,910 for material and conveyance of 7.16 acres of land valued at $4,500 be accepted as the action of the Board. In the event the applicants do not accept that proposal, they might bring an alternate proposal to the Trustees for consideration.

OKEECHOBEE COUNTY - Dredge Permit to Improve Navigation,
                    File No. 253.123-637.
Taylor Creek Isles, Inc., applied for permission to dredge four
channel connections 80 ft. wide and 6 ft. deep in Taylor Creek in
Sections 26 and 35, Township 37 South, Range 35 East, Okeechobee
County. $50 application fee was submitted.

Central and Southern Florida Flood Control District had no objection,
and Florida Game and Fresh Water Fish Commission biological report
was not adverse.

On motion by Mr. Christian, seconded by Mr. Adams and adopted without,
objection, the Trustees accepted the staff recommendation for approval
of the dredge permit subject to requirement that a plug shall be left
in the canal at Taylor Creek until upland dredging is completed and
all material removed shall be placed above the mean high water line.

MONROE COUNTY - Dredge Permit to Improve Navigation,
                Section 253.03 Florida Statutes, File No. 32.
Charles Kinsell applied for a permit for the construction of a
perimeter channel 50 ft. wide, 5 ft. deep and 12,500 ft. long, and
five access channels 150 ft. long and 5 ft. deep in Section 36,
Township 60 South, Range 39 East, Lake Surprise and Sexton Cove,
Monroe County. The application was filed prior to adoption of the
policy requiring $50 processing fee.

The biological report was partially adverse. The original application filed in 1968 was totally adverse but applicant revised plans
to lessen the adverse effects. The material removed would be placed
above the mean high water line.

On motion by Mr. Adams, seconded by Mr. Christian and adopted without
objection, the Trustees approved issuance of the dredge permit to
improve navigation.

PALM BEACH COUNTY - Dredge Permit to Improve Navigation,
                    File No. 253.123-599.
Investment Corporation of Florida, represented by Gee and Jenson,
applied for permission to dredge a navigation channel 30 ft. long,
100 ft. wide, 5 ft. deep, in Lake Wyman in Section 17, Township 47
South, Range 43 East, Palm Beach County. Applicant submitted $50
application fee and $50 minimum payment for the material to be
removed. The biological report indicated limited adverse effects.

On motion by Mr. Adams, duly adopted, the Trustees authorized issuance of the dredge permit.

PUTNAM COUNTY - Dredge Permits.
(A) Dredge Permit to Improve Navigation, File 253.123-540.
     Ernest K. Combs applied for a dredge permit for a navigation
channel 700 ft. long, 50 ft. wide and 5 ft. deep in the St. Johns
River in Section 33, Township 11 South, Range 26 East, Putnam County.
Applicant submitted $50 application fee. The biological report from
the Department of Natural Resources was not adverse.

Staff recommended approval subject to requirement that no spoiling
be done below the elevation of 1.1 ft. mean sea level.

(B) Dredge Permit and Post Dredging Settlement, Section 253.123 F.S.

Ernest K. Combs applied for permission to complete construction of a navigation channel and to make a connection to an upland boat basin (constructed on applicant's upland) in the St. Johns River adjacent to his upland in Crosby Grant in Township 12 South, Range 26 East, Putnam County. The channel will be 50 ft. wide paralleling the shoreline, 350 ft. long and 5 ft. deep, and approximately 100 ft. of channel had been completed before applicant was asked to stop work and make application for the required state permit. The biological report from the Department of Natural Resources was not adverse.

Applicant tendered check for $1,028.30 as payment for 3,427.66 cubic yards of material, representing payment for all material at the penalty rate of 30¢ per cubic yard. The Director pointed out that this would exceed the penalty rate for that part done without permit.

Motion was made by Mr. Williams, seconded by Mr. Christian and adopted without objection, that the dredge permits be approved as recommended by the staff.

VOLUSIA COUNTY - Dredge Permit to Improve Navigation,
                      Section 253.123 Florida Statutes.
B. F. Goodrich made application prior to adoption of the policy requiring $50 processing fee, for permission to dredge a perimeter channel 136 ft. long, 40 ft. wide top cut and 5 ft. deep (MLW), and an access channel 50 ft. long, 30 ft. wide top cut, and 5 ft. deep (MLW) adjacent to Section 5, Township 19 South, Range 35 East, in the Indian River in Volusia County.

The biological report was not adverse. Applicant tendered $86.80 in payment for 868 cubic yards of material to be removed, as the project was located within an aquatic preserve. Answering Mr. Adams' question regarding dredging in an aquatic preserve, the Director referred to the policy adopted by the Trustees on November 18, 1969, permitting reasonable navigation channels but requiring payment for all material excavated at 10¢ per cubic yard to compensate for damage to the marine biological environment in an aquatic preserve.

Without objection, the Trustees approved issuance of the dredge permit for navigation channels.

LEE COUNTY - Cape Coral Survey and G. A. C. Settlement.
The Director discussed the matter of encroachment and overdredging in the Caloosahatchee River done between 1959 and 1965, negotiations begun before he became director, conferences between representatives of the Trustees and General Acceptance Corporation, and a settlement recommended by the staff in accordance with the report to the Board on September 1, 1970. To conclude the matter the Director recommended (1) that settlement in the amount of $731,503.78 be used as a credit by the Board to acquire lands owned by G.A.C. in the Fakahatchee Strand, the valuation of such land to be determined by an appraisal by a M.A.I. appraiser; (2) that timetable for such acquisition be coordinated with the Department of Natural Resources, Division of Recreation and Parks and their acquisition program of the Strand, that Department administering the acquisition; (3) that $33,800 cash be tendered to the Board by G.A.C. in payment for the surveys contracted and executed for and on behalf of the Trustees in connection with this settlement, such monies to be deposited with the Board within ninety days; (4) that the subject surveys and methods of survey in no way be considered as establishing a

precedent for locating boundary lines or determining quantities of fill removed from state lands in any future matters requiring surveys or earthwork computations between the Board and G.A.C.; (5) that an appropriate instrument clearing title to the area affected by encroachment be issued by the Board to G.A.C. or others as may be required to perfect title to the subject lands, this action in the settlement conveying title to be considered as a land exchange between the Board and G.A.C.

Important in the consideration was the fact that the title of about 280 parties who had purchased lots from G.A.C. was clouded by the illegal dredging and filling of Gulf American, predecessor in title of G. A. C. Properties, Inc.

The Director explained the penalty approach used by the staff. The profit approach considered with the assistance of the Trustees' appraiser had resulted in about the same settlement figure, and the Director renewed his recommendation of a total settlement of $765,303.78.

Mr. Joel Kuperberg, representing Conservation 70s, read a letter from Lee County Conservation Association which stated that they considered the proposal inadequate compensation for the trespass on sovereignty state lands and steps should be taken to penalize the illegal operation. As executive director of Collier County Conservancy, Mr. Kuperberg expressed concern at the difference in surveying methods and urged the Board to preserve the entire marsh area that supports the Ten Thousand Islands.

Secretary of State Adams said the Board had the responsibility to resolve the situation as it relates to the public interest and also to the property owners. He thought the settlement was not sufficient and would recommend $1,621,000 as the required settlement amount. He was also concerned at the different approaches taken by the two surveyors in determining the high water mark, since by one technique it appeared that the state would be surrendering many acres of estuarine fringes. Thirdly, Mr. Adams said the Board should evaluate the Fakahatchee Watershed as a whole to try to determine what can be done to preserve the estuarine system.

The Director discussed some of the points raised, said that many of the lots were only partially affected by the overfill, and he reviewed the appraiser's approach in making an estimate of what the developer's profits might have been. With reference to the surveys, the staff had employed two reputable surveying firms and had two pieces of engineering work done by professional engineers. Both methods used were valid, he said, as a method of locating the line of mean high water which was difficult to do with legal sufficiency in areas such as these. Someone professionally competent had to make that determination, and the staff would go to court if necessary to defend the public's land, and would hope to sustain in court the Board's right to assess penalties.

In view of Mr. Adams' concern, Mr. Christian made a motion, seconded by Mr. Williams, that the Trustees defer action pending a study of the survey methods.

Mr. G. J. Turner, vice president of G.A.C. Properties, Inc., spoke of his previous appearance before the Board then, the offer that had been presented to the Board then, the difference in surveying techniques, and stated for the record that they did not feel there was any trespass on the state's land. The firm had filed for after-the-fact permits before penalties were set up, and felt that the matter should be settled as quickly as possible and not deferred as it could go on for many years.

Mr. Richard D. DeBoest, attorney for the firm, said he had worked on this matter with staffs of the Trustees for three and a half years, that the work started in 1958 shortly after passage of the Bulkhead Act followed the usual practice of developers, the value of estuarine fringes was not commonly known, nobody knew where the mean high tide line was until substantially all this development work had been completed, and the Florida Supreme Court had stated that when the mean high tide line could not be determined by ordinary engineering methods they could use the meander line - which in this case was actually much further out in the river. The firm made applications in many areas in the original Cape Coral section that were approved but due to a failure of communications were not followed through, and now many years later they find one member of the Board asking for a settlement more than twice what their actual profit was. He said the company had also offered some 20,000 acres of the Fakahatchee land to the state, and had appeared before the Board in good faith ever since 1967 in an effort to resolve the matter, being delayed first by moratoriums, then engineering and survey reports - and in the meantime ecology became more and more a matter of public interest and people consider the land more and more valuable. He protested that the application filed in 1967 has been delayed for years and the company had made every effort to explain the situation and get it settled.

Mr. Adams agreed that a settlement should be reached, but it should be equitable and in the light of conflicting surveys the Board had to be assured. Governor Kirk noted that this was the first time the staff had brought a complete recommendation to the Board, and members might want to examine parts of it.

The Director said the staff could make a written report to the Board on the points discussed and others with respect to engineering techniques and the values that had been considered.

On the motion made by Mr. Christian, seconded by Mr. Williams and adopted without objection, the Trustees deferred action.

SUBJECTS UNDER CHAPTER 18296

REFUNDS - Murphy Act. On motion by Mr. Christian, seconded by Mr. Dickinson and adopted without objection, the Trustees authorized refund of $15 each to three applicants for release of state road right of way reservations contained in Murphy Act deeds for the reason that the Department of Transportation did not recommend release of the reservations, as follows:

(1) $15 refund to Real Estate Title Company - Hillsborough County Murphy Act Deed No. 08-Chapter 21684
(2) $15 refund to Bornstein, Petree and Gluckman - Orange County Murphy Act Deed No. 382
(3) $15 refund to Gordon C. Huie - Polk County Deed No. 570.

On motion duly adopted, the meeting was adjourned.

GOVERNOR - CHAIRMAN

10-9-70

100

ATTEST: _James W Apthorp_
EXECUTIVE DIRECTOR

Tallahassee, Florida
October 13, 1970

The State of Florida Board of Trustees of the Internal Improvement
Trust Fund met in the Capitol with the following members present:

Claude R. Kirk, Jr.	Governor
Tom Adams	Secretary of State
Earl Faircloth	Attorney General
Fred O. Dickinson, Jr.	Comptroller
Broward Williams	Treasurer
Floyd T. Christian	Commissioner of Education
Doyle Conner	Commissioner of Agriculture

James W. Apthorp	Executive Director

FLAGLER COUNTY - Dredge Permit to Improve Navigation,
Section 253.123 Florida Statutes.
ITT Levitt Development Corporation applied for permission to connect
three canals 200 ft. wide top cut, 12 ft. deep mean low water, to
the Intracoastal Waterway at the following locations: Canal 1 in
Section 29, Township 10 South, Range 31 East; Canal 2 in Section 32,
Township 10 South, Range 31 East; and Canal 3 in Section 38,
Township 11 South, Range 31 East, Flagler County. Applicant
tendered $50 processing fee for the permit.

The biological survey report was not adverse.

On motion by Mr. Adams, seconded by Mr. Williams and adopted without
objection, the Trustees authorized issuance of the dredge permit.

LAKE COUNTY - Dock Permit, Section 253.03 Florida Statutes.
W. R. Henderson applied for after-the-fact dock permit for a private
dock with covered deck in Lake Louisa adjacent to his upland property
in Government Lot 4, Section 7, Township 23 South, Range 26 East, Lake
County. The dock had been constructed with all required local permits,
but without state permit for this particular structure. The covered
deck had the appearance of living quarters, but the applicant advised
the staff that it would be used for games, outboard motor and fishing
gear storage, and not for living purposes.

Through negotiation the staff instructed Mr. Henderson to submit
$100 as payment for permit, which he did. The staff recommended
approval.

On motion by Mr. Williams, seconded by Mr. Adams and adopted
unanimously, the Trustees authorized issuance of after-the-fact
dock permit as recommended by the staff.

10-13-70

LEE COUNTY - Construction of Seawall and Backfill,
             Section 253.03 F. S., SAJSP Permit (70-388)
Elmer E. Handy applied for permit for a seawall and backfill along
the foreshore of the Caloosahatchee River (FCD Canal C-43) in
Section 19, Township 43 South, Range 27 East, Lee County, with the
material to be trucked in. The construction will be above normal
high water line of the river; however, it would be affected by the
impoundment of water and Central and Southern Florida Flood
Control District issued letter of no protest to the project. The
construction will prevent erosion and loss of upland, and will
reduce turbidity in the area.

On motion by Mr. Adams, seconded by Mr. Williams and adopted
without objection, the Trustees authorized issuance of the permit.

MARION COUNTY - Dredge Permit to Improve Navigation,
               Section 253.123 Florida Statutes.
Charles A. Savage applied for permission to dredge a navigable
channel 4,500 ft. long, 30 ft. wide top cut, 5 ft. deep mean low
water, and a boat basin 200 ft. long, 100 ft. wide and 5 ft. deep
in Halfmoon Lake in Sections 31 and 32, Township 15 South, Range
25 East, Marion County.

The application was revised in accordance with the recommendations
in the biological report. The project was now considered to be
acceptable. All material removed would be placed on uplands.

Mr. Adams noted that a portion of the dredging would be done on
privately-owned land and asked if applicant would be required to
pay for the material dredging from state land. The Director
explained that the channel bordered national forest land principally, that the National Forest Service in granting permit to the
applicant required a number of protective measures and required
him to make an embankment along the channel and plant grass. In
view of that, the staff felt that permit should be granted without
payment for material.

On motion by Mr. Williams, seconded by Mr. Dickinson and adopted
without objection, the Trustees approved issuance of the dredge
permit.

MONROE COUNTY - Dredge Permit to Improve Navigation,
               File No. 253.03-205.
William E. Olson applied for permission to dredge a navigation
channel 400 ft. long, 45 ft. wide and 5 ft. deep in Pine Channel
at Big Pine Key in Section 27, Township 66 South, Range 29 East,
in Monroe County. $50 application fee was tendered and $106.30
as payment for 1,063 cubic yards of material to be removed. The
latter payment was offered after the application was deferred on
September 22 at Mr. Adams' request. The biological report was
partially adverse, but applicant had revised his work plan in
accordance with the recommendations.

On motion by Mr. Adams, seconded by Mr. Dickinson and adopted,
without objection, the Trustees approved issuance of the dredge
permit.

NASSAU COUNTY - Dredge Permit to Improve Navigation,
               File No. 253.123-474.
On April 28, 1970, the Trustees approved a permit to Interpace
Corporation to connect a 100-ft. wide navigation channel to

Kingsley Creek in Nassau County, which was subsequently revised in accordance with recommendations of the United States Fish and Wildlife and other concerned agencies.

Applicant requested permission to amend the project in accordance with recommendations by dredging a channel 2,200 ft. long, 6 ft. deep, 100 ft. wide, in Amelia River and on applicant's upland in Sections 63 and 64, Township 3 North, Range 28 East, Nassau County, the spoil from which will be placed on upland property. The biological report was partially adverse. Applicant had stated that all spoiling would be done above mean high water and staff recommended approval. Mr. Williams made a motion for approval.

Mr. Adams noticed on the map that depths in the Amelia River were indicated in some places as 6 ft., 12 ft., 16 ft., commenting that it would not be necessary to dredge to get a 6 ft. deep channel in those areas. The Director suggested that a stipulation could be written into the permit to allow dredging where necessary to get a minimum 6 ft. depth for navigation.

On that basis motion was made by Mr. Adams, seconded by Mr. Dickinson and adopted without objection, that the application be approved.

PASCO COUNTY - Fill Permit, Section 253.124(7), to Reclaim Lands
                Lost by Artificially-induced Erosion,
                Chapter 70-333, Acts of 1970.
On motion by Mr. Faircloth, seconded by Mr. Williams and adopted unanimously, the Trustees approved the request of the City of New Port Richey for a permit to reclaim land lost by artificially-induced erosion caused by boat traffic and existing seawalls in Section 32, Township 25 South, Range 16 East, Pithlachascotee River in Pasco County. The fill area would be seawalled, the material trucked in, and proposed construction would be within 25 feet of the existing mean high water line.

PINELLAS COUNTY - Dredge and Fill Permit Deferred.
At the request of the Director, the Trustees deferred consideration of an application from Madeira Garden Apartments for a maintenance dredging permit, because of information received by the staff after preparation of the agenda. Mr. Adams pointed out that this was one of a number of violations previously discussed and efforts were being made to resolve the problem with the owners.

ST. LUCIE COUNTY - Dredge Permit, Section 253.123 Florida Statutes,
                File No. 253.123-623.
On motion by Mr. Williams, seconded by Messrs. Faircloth and Adams, and adopted without objection, the Trustees approved the application from Florida Power and Light Company to revise its permit approved by the Board on June 16, 1970, to increase the dredge depth from 40.0 to 55.0 feet. There would be no change in the size of the dredge area or the quantity of material, but it had been found that material from a lesser depth was not suitable for filling.

ESCAMBIA, WALTON, GADSDEN AND JEFFERSON COUNTIES - Lease.
Surplus welcome stations in the above counties, no longer needed due to changes in tourist traffic flow, were made available by the Department of Commerce and all state departments had been notified. The staff was advised that the Department of Agriculture and Consumer Services had need of all four stations, and 10-year lease with option to renew was recommended.

On this date the Director reported that the Department of Agriculture and Consumer Services had requested a deferment, which was granted.

SANTA ROSA COUNTY - Oil and Gas Lease to be Advertised.
Sun Oil Company requested advertisement for sealed bids for an oil and gas drilling lease of the reserved one-half petroleum interest held by the State of Florida in the privately-owned land described as the South 22-1/2 chains of Government Lot 2, Section 12, Township 5 North, Range 30 West, Santa Rosa County, containing 44.995 acres, more or less. The reserved interest of the state was by virtue of Murphy Act Deed No. 272 dated January 5, 1945.

The staff recommended an increase from the usual one-eighth to one-sixth minimum royalty due to the close proximity of this tract to the discovery well in Jay, Florida. The State Geologist concurred in the staff recommendation to advertise the land for sealed bids for a five-year oil and gas drilling lease pursuant to law, lease to require an annual rental of $1 per net mineral acre, one-sixth royalty, $50,000 surety bond, and at least one test well every 2 1/2 years of the lease term to a depth of 6,000 feet or to the top of the Smackover Formation, whichever is deeper.

On motion by Mr. Christian, seconded by Mr. Conner and adopted without objection, the Board authorized advertisement for bids as recommended by the staff.

SHELL LEASE INCOME REPORT - The Trustees accepted for the record the following report of remittances to Florida Department of Natural Resources from holders of dead shell leases:

Lease No.	Company	Amount
1718	Radcliff Materials Inc.	$ 151.03
1788	Benton and Company, Inc.	12,352.58
2233	Bay Dredging & Construction Co.	5,801.39

PALM BEACH COUNTY - Marina License, Section 253.03 Florida Statutes.
Norman A. Cortese, Vice President of Arvida Corporation, applied for a marina license for a docking facility in Lake Boca Raton adjacent to upland in Section 29, Township 47 South, Range 43 East Palm Beach County, to be used by owners at the Lake House South Condominium. Staff recommended approval at the minimum annual fee of $231.83.

On motion by Mr. Williams, seconded by Mr. Adams and adopted without objection, the Trustees authorized issuance of marine license to the applicant.

On motion duly adopted, the meeting was adjourned.

GOVERNOR - CHAIRMAN

ATTEST:
EXECUTIVE DIRECTOR

* * * *

Tallahassee, Florida
October 20, 1970

The State of Florida Board of Trustees of the Internal Improvement
Trust Fund met in the Capitol with the following members present:

Claude R. Kirk, Jr.	Governor
Tom Adams	Secretary of State
Earl Faircloth	Attorney General
Fred O. Dickinson, Jr.	Comptroller
Broward Williams	Treasurer
Floyd T. Christian	Commissioner of Education
Doyle Conner	Commissioner of Agriculture
James W. Apthorp	Executive Director

The minutes of the meeting on October 6, 1970, were approved as
submitted.

ESCAMBIA COUNTY - Bulkhead Line Location, Section 253.122 F. S.
              Right of Way Easement, File 2367-17-253.03
              Fill Permit, Section 253.124 Florida Statutes
On motion by Mr. Faircloth, seconded by Mr. Adams and adopted
without objection, the Trustees approved three applications relating
to state highway construction in Escambia County, as follows:

(1) Bulkhead Line Location. The Board of County Commissioners
by resolution adopted August 2, 1970, established a bulkhead line
460.72 feet long in Perdido Bay at Millview in Section 14, Township
2 South, Range 31 West, Escambia County, to accommodate construction
of State Road 298. The biological report was not adverse, and all
fill material would be trucked to the site.
(2) Right of Way Easement. The Department of Transportation was
granted an easement embracing 0.32 acre in Perdido Bay that would
be filled in Section 14, Township 2 South, Range 31 West, and an
easement embracing 0.16 acre in Robinson Bayou in Sections 13 and
14, Township 2 South, Range 31 West, for which construction plans
did not indicate any dredging or filling in Robinson Bayou. The
biological report dated July 7, 1970, was not adverse to filling
the parcel in Perdido Bay with trucked-in fill material.
(3) Fill Permit. The Department of Transportation was granted
a permit to fill approximately 0.32 acre of submerged land adjacent
to Section 14, Township 2 South, Range 31 West, in Perdido Bay,
Escambia County, with material trucked in from an upland borrow area.
The permit will issue to the successful contractor. Biological
report was not adverse.

DADE COUNTY - Disclaimer, File 2368-13-253.129.
Mercy Hospital, Inc., a Florida corporation not for profit, represented
by Wyatt Johnson, applied for a disclaimer pursuant to Section 253.129
Florida Statutes, to a parcel of land filled prior to May 29, 1951,
in Biscayne Bay abutting a portion of Tract 4 Vizaya - James Deering
Estate, Plat Book 34, Page 46 of the Public Records of Dade County.
The parcel also abuts Section 40, Township 54 South, Range 41 East,
Jonathon Lewis Donation and contains 7.755 acres, more or less.

On motion by Mr. Williams, seconded by Mr. Adams and adopted without
objection, the Trustees authorized issuance of the disclaimer for
the usual $100 processing fee. The Board executed the instrument
that had been properly prepared and approved by the office of the
Attorney General.

MONROE COUNTY - Fill Permit, File No. 253.03-212,
             and Temporary Borrow Easement.

On motion by Mr. Adams, seconded by Mr. Faircloth, and adopted without
objection, the Board approved the following two applications from the
Department of Transportation related to road work at Boca Chica in
Monroe County:

(1)   The Department of Transportation was granted approval of fill permit for approximately 1.5 acres in Boca Chica Channel in Boca Chica Channel in Section 25, Township 67 South, Range 25 East, and Section 30, Township 67 South, Range 26 East, Monroe County, in connection with State Road 5, bridge and approaches over Boca Chica Channel. The biologi report was adverse; however, the Department of Natural Resources stated that there was no reasonable alternative to filling alongside the existin roadway to accommodate the four-lanning of U. S. 1. The dredge and fill permit would issue to the contractor.

Applicant also was granted permit to dredge 1,004,000 cubic yards of fill material from a 23.25 acre borrow area in the Gulf of Mexico adjacent to Racoon Key in Township 67 South, Range 25 East, Monroe County. The biological report was not adverse, and the Bureau of Beaches and Shores indicated that there should be no adverse hydrographic effects from this project.

The fill within the borrow area must be removed upon completion of the project, and no spoil will remain above the natural bottom elevation either in the borrow area or on adjacent submerged lands. Dredging and filling must be done in such a way that turbidities in the project area do not exceed 50 Jackson Units above base for the area.

(2)   The Department of Transportation was granted a temporary easement for a borrow area of 23.25 acres in the Gulf'of Mexico adjacent to Raccoon Key in Township 67 South, Range 25 East, Monroe County, for removing material to be used in construction of State Road 5. The biological report was not adverse and location of the borrow area was recommended by the Department of Natural Resources.

BREVARD COUNTY - Dredge Permit Amendment,
                File No. 253.123-470
On motion by Mr. Christian, seconded by Mr. Williams and adopted without objection, the Trustees approved request of the City of Satellite Beach for amendment of dredge permit approved on May 26, 1970, to allow the channels to be dredged to minus-6 feet. The original permit depth was minus-4 feet, but the Coast Guard would not approve the city's bridge permit unless channels were deeper. The revised biological report was not adverse.

COLLIER COUNTY - Dredge Permit, to Improve Navigation
                Section 253.123 Florida Statutes
Key Island, Inc., represented by Tri-County Engineering, Inc., applied for a permit to perform maintenance dredging in Gordon Pass Lagoon in Section 21, Township 50 South, Range 25 East, in Collier County. The material removed would be placed above the mean high water line.

Applicant tendered $90 as payment for overdredge material and $50 processing fee. Channel dimensions were minus-8 ft. deep, 85 ft. wide and 400 ft. long.

The biological report was not adverse and the City of Naples had approved the maintenance dredging project.

Mr. Adams, noting that normal navigation channels were only 5 feet in depth, was informed by the Director that the craft of some applicants required greater depth, such as sail boats. Mr. Adams asked why all the material dredged out should not be paid for and Mr. Apthorp said that the staff was working on a proposed policy change. The staff had been recommending payment under the current policy in instances where it was obvious that the application was made to obtain fill material rather than solely for navigation.

Motion was made by Mr. Williams, seconded by Mr. Christian and adopted without objection, that the dredging permit be approved.

MONROE COUNTY - Dredge and Fill Permit, Section 253.03 F. S.
Rene R. Veliz and Miguel Aquilera, represented by James T. Glass,
had revised their original application to fill approximately 3.5
acres of privately-owned submerged land because of an adverse
biological report. The revised application was for a dredge permit
to excavate a boat basin within a 4.55-acre parcel of submerged land
heretofore conveyed by the Trustees in Section 18, Township 63 South,
Range 38 East, and to dredge a navigation access channel 5 ft. deep,
50 ft. wide and 550 ft. long.

The supplemental biological report suggested further revision of the
project; however, the applicant declined to make further modifications.

Staff recommended approval of permit to dredge boat basin and navigation channel and to fill approximately 2 acres of privately-owned
submerged land in consideration for reconveyance of approximately 2
acres of submerged land by the applicant. Mr. Apthorp said this
applicant had been very cooperative.

On motion by Mr. Adams, seconded by Mr. Faircloth and adopted without
objection, the Trustees approved issuance of the dredge and fill permit
on the basis recommended by the staff.

MONROE COUNTY - File No. 2182-44-253.12, Application for Filled Land.
The application of Donald L. Wollard, represented by William J. Roberts,
to purchase 0.25 acre parcel of filled sovereignty land in Little Basin,
Florida Bay, abutting fractional Section 12, Township 63 South, Range
37 East, Upper Matecumbe Key, was considered by the Board on June 10, 196
and was removed from the agenda for the purpose of obtaining an appraisal
and determining a penalty for the unauthorized filling.

An appraisal indicated that the 0.25 acre parcel in its filled and
seawalled state was valued at $1,065, or $4,260 per acre. The original
value suggested by the staff was $833.33 per acre for unimproved land,
or $519.33 for the parcel including $311 for fill material hauled in by
the applicant.

As a penalty for the unauthorized filling, the staff determined a
revised value of $346.50 for the fill material purchased from upland
sources by the applicant and hauled to the site. The total settlement
comes to $1,461.50 which included $50 to defray cost of the appraisal.
Due to financial difficulties the applicant had asked to be allowed to
pay $100 per month until the required amount was paid in full; but
upon insistence of the staff for full payment, the $1,461.50 was finally
remitted.

In the opinion of the staff the recently adopted policy requiring a
showing that sale of submerged land is in the public interest is not
applicable, as this application was formally considered and held in
abeyance for determining an appraisal and penalty payment for a settlement. Staff recommended that the sale be confirmed.

Mr. Adams, referring to the policy adopted on July 1, 1969, to sell
state-owned sovereignty land that has been filled without authority
at three times the value of the land in its filled condition without
regard to the price spent on improvements, said the reason this
application was held up was for the policy to be developed and it
did not appear to him that the staff recommendation for settlement
was based on that policy. The Director said the staff had computed the
settlement amount on the basis of a penalty charge for the fill material,
since the application had been considered prior to the July 1 policy.
He added that from time to time there would be some cases on either side
of the policy, on which settlement might have to be determined.

At Mr. Adams' request, the Board deferred action.

VOLUSIA COUNTY - City of Daytona Beach Application for Release of
                 Restriction in Deed No. 20798
The City of Daytona Beach requested release of restrictive covenants
contained in Trustees Deed No. 20798 (that granted lands to the city
for one dollar) in order to allow the city to lease the Daytona Beach

Municipal Yacht Basin to be operated by private interests. The
city did not have sufficient funds to repair the existing facilities
nor make capital improvements such as proper sanitary facilities
and expanded electrical distribution system. Installation of a
sanitary disposal system would cost approximately $25,000, and
there remained a debt of $143,687 with an annual debt service of
$17,960 from the bonded indebtedness of $327,443 on the Yacht Basin
incurred after approval by voters in a 1947 referendum of the City
of Daytona Beach.

The staff recommended release of the public purposes restriction
only insofar as it applied to leasing and only for a 5-acre parcel,
conditioned upon Trustees' approval of the lease agreement between
the city and the successful bidder to operate the Yacht Basin.

The city also requested a marina license without charge for 14
acres of water area upon which mooring facilities are constructed.
The city desired to lease the area and use the marina rental toward
paying off its bonded indebtedness. The staff recommended denial
of that request and suggested that issuance of a marina license be
considered as a separate matter, and that the successful bidder for
lease agreement with the city be required to apply for a state marina
license.

Attorney J. Kermit Coble said the city's application was unusual,
that the city some years ago spent a large sum installing docks
on what they thought was their land and, having difficulty financing
improvement, the city proposed leasing to a private marina operator
and using the rent for retiring the city debt. The marina facilities
were public; the private yacht club was not included in the application.
Mr. Coble explained that the city, lacking up-graded facilities, had
not been able to charge a rate sufficiently high to make the yacht
basin a profitable operation. Mr. Adams questioned whether the city
should not be able to manage the yacht basin successfully itself.
Mr. Dickinson said if private enterprise could do it better, he saw
no harm in complying with the city's request but agreed to a delay
suggested by Mr. Adams.

City Attorney John C. Chew said the city, having financial problems,
was trying to help itself, was exploring several avenues, and he
urged issuance of a marina license to the city without charge. The
Director thought that a decision should first be made as to who would
operate the marina. Members assured Mr. Chew that the Trustees desired
to help the city, and Mr. Williams pointed out that during the period
of a brief deferment the questions now being raised might be answered.

Mr. Adams asked for two weeks' delay. Since there would be no meeting
on election day, Governor Kirk said the matter might be brought back
next week if it was in order for further consideration. Without
objection, action was deferred.

DADE COUNTY - Lease Assignment.
On motion by Mr. Christian, seconded by Mr. Adams and adopted without
objection, the Board approved assignment of Campsite Lease No. 2146
from William V. Southard to Cornelia D. Dinkler.

LEE COUNTY - Dredge Permit to Improve Navigation
            File No. 253.123-607
Ross Mayer, represented by James DeLozier, Jr., applied for a permit
to dredge a navigation channel 850 ft. long, 50 ft. wide top cut,
5 ft. deep mean low water, adjacent to Sections 1 and 2, Township
46 South, Range 21 East, Pine Island Sound, Lee County. The material
removed would be placed above the mean high water line, and applicant
tendered $350 for 3,500 cubic yards of material to be taken in an
aquatic preserve, and $50 for processing fee.

The application was completely revised to comply with recommendations
in the original biological report, and supplemental report was not
adverse. Staff recommended approval.

On motion by Mr. Adams, seconded by Mr. Christian and adopted, the Trustees authorized issuance of the dredge permit.

MARTIN COUNTY - Corrective Deed Reconfirmed.
Due to the fact that only four members were present on September 22 when the Board approved issuance of a corrective deed, and the staff was advised by the office of the Attorney General that five are required, motion was made by Mr. Conner, seconded by Mr. Dickinson and adopted without objection, that the Trustees approve issuance of corrective deed to supplement Trustees Deed No. 24961 (1820-43) issued by the Trustees on June 30, 1969, requested by Evans Crary, Jr. for the reason that the description in the original deed referred to Block C of Riverside Park Subdivision whereas it should cite Block B.

SARASOTA COUNTY - Emergency Dredge Permit, Section 253.123 F. S.
On motion by Mr. Conner, seconded by Mr. Dickinson and adopted without objection, the Trustees granted the request from Quinlan Marine Attractions (Floridaland) for an emergency dredge permit to reconstruct porpoise pens adjacent to Section 14, Township 38 South, Range 18 East, Dryman Bay in Sarasota County. Approximately 1,100 cubic yards of material will be removed from an area minus-8 feet deep mean low water, 30 ft. wide top cut, and 130 ft. long.

Until the new pens are ready the porpoises are being contained in too small an area, and one porpoise had already died. Because of the emergency, the Board without objection waived the biological report as provided in Section 253.123(3)(a), as amended by Chapter 70-118, Acts of 1970.

SUBJECTS UNDER CHAPTER 18296

On motion by Mr. Williams, seconded by Mr. Dickinson and adopted without objection, the Trustees approved Report 974 listing two regular bids for sale of Murphy Act land under provisions of Chapter 18296, Acts of 1937, Section 197.350 Florida Statutes, described as follows:

(1) A parcel of land in Section 8, Township 4 South, Range 14 West, Bay County, certified to the state under tax sale certificate 7178 of 1933, sold to Mrs. Ola Brown Lunsford for high bid of $250;

(2) A parcel of land in Section 17, Township 1 South, Range 15 East, Hamilton County, certified to the state under tax sale certificates 83 of 1897 and 99 of 1938, sold to L. R. Taylor for high bid of $40.

Deeds pertaining thereto were approved for execution.

On motion duly adopted, the meeting was adjourned.

CHAIRMAN

ATTEST:
EXECUTIVE DIRECTOR

Tallahassee, Florida
October 27, 1970

The State of Florida Board of Trustees of the Internal Improvement
Trust Fund met in the Capitol with the following members present:

Tom Adams	Secretary of State, Acting Chairman
Earl Faircloth	Attorney General
Broward Williams	Treasurer
Floyd T. Christian	Commissioner of Education
Doyle Conner	Commissioner of Agriculture

James W. Apthorp	Executive Director

The minutes of the meeting of October 13, 1970, were approved as
submitted.

VOLUSIA COUNTY - Bulkhead Line, Dedication, Dredge and Fill Permit,
and Marina License
By Resolution No. 70-78 adopted on October 15, 1970, the Board of
County Commissioners of Volusia County established a bulkhead line
for the City of Daytona Beach 3,621 feet long in the Halifax River
embracing approximately 6.35 acres of sovereignty land and portions
of upland owned by Volusia County. At the hearing on October 1 there
were objections to the project; at the October 15 hearing no objections were filed. The bulkhead line was to accommodate construction
of a Small Craft Harbor, Federal Project No. 09-0024, and a marina
for general public use. The county required approximately 6.35
acres of additional sovereignty land for the project toward which
the county had obtained $75,000 federal grant commitment to expire
on December 31, 1970 (Unless action had been taken).

It was proposed to dredge 68,880 cubic yards of material from the
small craft harbor and the navigation entrance channel to be dredged
to minus-5 feet mean low water and 80 ft. wide, more or less, top
width. All of the material would be deposited behind the bulkhead
line on lands subject to dedication and on county-owned uplands.

The initial biological report was adverse, however, the project was
modified pursuant to the biologist's recommendations.

At the request of the county, the staff recommended waiver of the
two weeks' advance agenda notice. In view of the public nature of
the project and the fact that it was modified to conform to recommendations in the biological survey report, the staff recommended (1)
approval of the bulkhead line; (2) issuance of dedication for public
park, marina and associated public use, and to waive advertising (not
required by law) for dedicating a 6.35 acre parcel, more or less, of
sovereignty land in the Halifax River abutting a parcel of county-
owned land lying in Township 15 South, Range 33 East, City of
Daytona Beach, Volusia County; (3) approval of dredge and fill permit
issued by the City of Daytona Beach on August 24, 1970, to the county;
and (4) although the county did not apply for a marina license, the
staff was of the opinion that the license would complete the project
package, and the staff recommended issuance of marina license to the
county without fees as the project would be for the general public
and was being constructed with public funds.

Motion was made by Mr. Faircloth, seconded by Mr. Williams, that
the application be approved.

The Director reported a few objections were received before the county
asked for waiver of advance agenda notice because of the urgency of
their schedule, and that twenty-three objections were filed, mainly
from apartment owners in a condominium across the street from the county
property.

Stanley D. Kupiszewski, Jr., representing objecting property owners,
objected to this use of public funds as the city had an existing
similar facility immediately adjacent to the proposed site and was
having difficulty meeting it bond obligations. He pointed out that
at the public hearing on October 1 the Board of County Commissioners
voted to abandon the project and subsequently on October 15 without

further notice the county reconsidered and adopted the proposal. Mr. Kupiszewski, retained on October 22 to represent certain objectors, criticized the procedures followed by the Board of County Commissioners and urged the Board of Trustees to reject the project as one not needed by the city.

Mr. Faircloth noted that the first hearing on October 1 was properly advertised and everybody was heard, and that the county had reconsidered on the 15th.

Representing the Daytona Beach Outboard Club and pursuing the matter for the county, J. Kermit Coble discussed the project of a small boat harbor with ramps, parking for boat trailers, and a beautified park area, serving a different purpose than the existing yacht basin. He explained the points raised by the objector, the redesigning of plans to comply with the biological report, water flow improvement expected from the dredging, and to illustrate support for the project he filed a petition with more than 1,000 signatures. Mr. Coble said the project was not involved with that application from the city on the agenda last week.

The Director reviewed the proposal and recommended approval of the project, based on all the circumstances.

The motion by Mr. Faircloth, seconded by Mr. Williams, to approve the bulkhead line, dedication, dredge and fill permit, and marina license, was adopted with one dissenting vote by Mr. Adams.

GLADES COUNTY - Application to Advertise,
                 File No. 2365-22-253.36
Henry F. Seels and wife applied to purchase 3.8 acres of reclaimed Lake Okeechobee bottom land abutting State Lot 2 in Section 13, Township 40 South, Range 32 East, between the 17-ft. contour line and the levee right of way line. The only access to the parcel was across applicant's upland property, but applicant submitted no justification of the sale in the public interest.

The Director said this riparian owner made a proper application in May, however on June 2 the Board adopted a policy that no sale would be made unless it was in the public interest - and in view of the policy the staff recommended against the sale.

Motion was made by Mr. Christian, seconded by Mr. Williams, and pronounced adopted by Mr. Adams, that the application be denied as recommended by the staff.

It was called to the attention of the Board that the applicant would like to be heard. Mr. Seels said he bought a small home site twenty-five years ago, gave concessions to the state three times for rights of way for State Road 78, State Road 721, and for building the dike which took his riparian rights, but he was told he would have the right to purchase the reclaimed parcel between his property and the levee. Mr. Christian examined the map and asked questions, and then asked to be allowed to withdraw his motion. Mr. Williams withdrew his second.

Mr. Adams pointed out that the motion had been adopted, before they knew there was anyone to be heard. Motion was made by Mr. Christian, seconded by Mr. Williams and adopted without objection, that the matter be reconsidered.

Mrs. Anna Ruth Seels said she went to the property as a ten-year old girl, now as a retired nurse it was her homesite but access to the rim canal was needed, and she asked for the Board's consideration of their riparian rights.

Mr. Christian said the staff should give some consideration to the rights of way given by these owners which he thought was the public purpose in this application. The Director reported that the staff had about a dozen similar applications, not all ready for presentation to the Board, but under present policy it was difficult for the staff to recommend the sales in the public interest without some further standards from the Trustees. Mr. Adams said there must be some value judgment rendered as to mitigating circumstances that might create a different interpretation of what is the public interest, and the consensus of the members was that the staff should bring back to the Board a reconsidered evaluation. Mr. Christian said the applicants should be notified, and the Board should consider each application on its merits. Mr. Williams said other similar applications should be disposed of in the same way. Mr. Apthorp said that he thought the public interest would be what the Board considered was in the public interest, that it was other agencies that had made commitments to the owners regarding purchase of the reclaimed lake bottom - but that would be only in the event the state wanted to sell.

On the basis of the discussion, action was deferred.

DADE COUNTY - Dedication No. 23991
Two members of the Board had requested deferment of consideration of the request from the City of North Miami for approval of a lease agreement pertaining to Spoil Island No. 1 in Biscayne Bay previously dedicated to the city for public park and recreation.

Without objection, action was deferred.

GLADES COUNTY - File 2369-22-253.03, Dedication
The Central and Southern Florida Flood Control District requested dedication of a parcel of land embracing 5.74 acres in unsurveyed Sections 21 and 28, Township 42 South, Range 32 East, Lake Hicpochee, Glades County, to be developed as a recreation site adjacent to Canal C-4

On motion by Mr. Williams, adopted without objection, the Trustees dediacated the parcel to the Flood Control District as a recreation area.

GLADES COUNTY - File 2224-22-253.03, Spoil Area.
The Central and Southern Florida Flood Control District requested relocation of a spoil area in unsurveyed Sections 21 and 28, Township 42 South, Range 32 East, Lake Hicpochee, Glades County, in order to provide for a recreation area adjacent to Caloosahatchee Canal (C-43). The original spoil area location had been granted on June 24, 1969.

On motion by Mr. Faircloth, seconded by Mr. Christian and adopted without objection, the Trustees granted the request for relocation of the spoil area.

DADE COUNTY - Lease Renewal
On motion by Mr. Christian, seconded by Messrs. Faircloth and Williams, and adopted without objection, the Trustees approved the application from Cornelia D. Dinkler, assignee of Campsite Lease No. 2146, for one-year renewal with option to renew for four additional years at $300 annual rental. The request conformed to the policy of April 7, 1970, that required lease as long as the structure remained on the site, and the policy of October 6, 1970, that established an annual rental of $300 for a quarter-acre site.

DADE COUNTY - Lease Assignment and Renewal
On motion by Mr. Christian, seconded by Mr. Williams and adopted without objection, the Trustees approved the following:

(1) Assignment of Campsite Lease No. 2167 from Karl Mongelluzzo to Coconut Grove Marine Properties, Inc., for which executed copies of assignment and acceptance of terms of the lease were filed with the staff:

(2) Renewal of Campsite Lease No. 2167 for one year with option to renew for four additional years at an annual rental of $300, conforming to the Trustees' policy of April 7, 1970 that required lease as long as the structure remained on the site, and the policy of October 6, 1970, that established an annual rental of $300 for a quarter-acre site.

ESCAMBIA COUNTY - Oil and Gas Drilling Lease to be advertised
Louisiana Land and Exploration Company requested advertisement for
sealed bids for an oil and gas drilling lease of the reserved one-
half petroleum interest held by the Trustees in privately-owned land
described as Government Lot 3, Section 36, Township 6 North, Range
30 West, containing 2.8 surface acres in Escambia County.

The State Geologist concurred in the staff recommendation to advertise
for sealed bids for a five-year oil and gas drilling lease pursuant
to law, annual rental of $1 per net mineral acre, 1/6 royalty, $50,000
surety bond, and at least one test well every 2 1/2 years of the lease
term to a depth of 6,000 feet or to the top of the Smackover formation,
whichever is deeper.

On motion by Mr. Williams, seconded by Mr. Christian and adopted
without objection, the Trustees approved the staff recommendation to
advertise for sealed bids on the reserved interest.

ESCAMBIA COUNTY - Lease
On October 13 action was deferred on leasing four surplus Welcome
Stations no longer needed due to changes in tourist traffic flow.

At the request of the Department of Agriculture and Consumer Services,
The Board of Trustees on motion by Mr. Williams, seconded by Mr. Conner
and adopted without objection, authorized ten-year lease to that Departme
with option to renew, with respect only to the one Welcome Station locate
in Escambia County on U. S. Highway 90 in Section 11, Township 1 South,
Range 32 West, Escambia County. The Welcome Station will be used by
the Division of Dairy Industry.

OKALOOSA COUNTY - Road Right of Way.
The Board of County Commissioners of Okaloosa County by resolution adopte
on January 27, 1970, requested an easement 80 ft. wide for the improvemen
and paving of an existing public road known as the Beaver Creek Road,
that passed through four parcels of land owned by the Trustees and in use
by the Division of Forestry of the Department of Agriculture and Consumer
Services as the Blackwater River State Forest. That Department approved
the request as the road improvement would benefit the state forest.

On motion by Mr. Faircloth, seconded by Mr. Williams and adopted without
objection, the Board granted the easement to the Board of County Commissioners of Okaloosa County.

DUVAL COUNTY - Road Right of Way.
At the request of the Board of Regents, the Trustees removed from the
agenda a request from the Jacksonville Expressway Authority for an easement in Sections 8 and 9, Township 3 South, Range 28 East, Duval County
on land of the new University of North Florida.

PALM BEACH COUNTY - Power Line Easement
On motion by Mr. Faircloth, seconded by Mr. Williams and adopted with-
out objection, the Trustees reconfirmed action by four members on
September 22 approving an easement to Florida Power and Light Company
across lands of the University of Florida Experimental Station,
Morikomi Farm, in Section 27, Township 46 South, Range 42 East, in
Palm Beach County, for an electrical power line to serve the station
as approved by the Board of Regents.

PUTNAM COUNTY - Power Line Easement.
The Clay Electric Co-Operative, Inc., Keystone Heights, Florida, requeste
easement for a 110 K.V. transmission line across a portion of the Univers
of Florida Conservation Reserve at Welaka. The easement would be in
Government Lot 7, Section 22, Township 12 South, Range 26 East, Putnam
County, 100 ft. wide and 427 ft. long, containing 0.977 acre.

The Board of Regents recommended the easement that would be a definite benefit as a protective fire line in a critical area at no expense to the state.

On motion by Mr. Christian, seconded by Mr. Conner and Mr. Williams and adopted without objection, the Trustees authorized issuance of the power line easement.

BAY COUNTY - Marina License, Section 253.03 Florida Statutes.
On motion by Mr. Christian, seconded by Mr. Williams and adopted without objection, the Trustees approved application from Miracle Strip Yacht Basin for a marina license in St. Andrews Bay adjacent to uplands in Section 34, Township 3 South, Range 15 West, Bay County, for which applicant had submitted payment of $570 for the first year's fee.

VOLUSIA COUNTY - Marina License, Section 253.03 Florida Statutes.
On motion by Mr. Christian, seconded by Mr. Williams and adopted without objection, the Trustees approved the application from Edward F. Brennan, Engineering Director of the City of South Daytona, for a marina license to construct and maintain a public fishing dock in the Halifax River in Section 33, Township 15 South, Range 33 East, Volusia County. The Board waived all fees for this public facility for the City of South Daytona.

ST. LUCIE COUNTY - Construction Permit.
On motion by Mr. Faircloth, seconded by Mr. Christian and adopted without objection, the Trustees authorized issuance of a construction permit for $100 processing fee to the General Development Corporation, Miami, Florida, for the construction of a foot bridge for pedestrian traffic across the North Fork of St. Lucie River abutting Section 22, Township 36 South, Range 40 East, St. Lucie County, to be four feet wide and adjoining the existing bridge for vehicular traffic. The Coast Guard had approved the bridge application.

BREVARD COUNTY - Fill Permit Deferred.
At the request of the Director, the Trustees deferred consideration of application of Kenneth L. Sagrans for approval of a fill permit for 0.37 acre in the Indian River in Brevard County.

NASSAU COUNTY - Dredge Permit for Utility Installation
              Section 253.123(2)(b)
ITT Rayonier, Inc., Fernandina, Florida, applied for a dredge permit for the installation of two effluent outfall lines in the Atlantic Ocean adjacent to Section 16, Township 3 North, Range 29 East, Nassau County, to comply with an order from the Air and Water Pollution Control Department that had certified the two lines. The biological report was not adverse. ' The temporary structure in connection with the project will be removed when work is completed and the lines will be covered and beach area leveled to its original contour.

On motion by Mr. Williams, seconded by Mr. Christian and adopted without objection, the Trustees authorized issuance of the dredge permit for $100 processing fee.

RESOLUTION - Material Removed from Navigation Channels.
The Director requested consideration of a resolution regarding charge for material dredged from navigation channels in navigable waters of the State of Florida. He said it would be a less difficult policy to administer with no question about whether the applicant should pay for the material removed, and the staff would like to work with the Department of Natural Resources to locate suitable areas in the water where conditions might be improved by placement of material, for instance, to raise deep-bottomed areas so that seagrasses might grow.

On motion by Mr. Williams, adopted without objection, the Board of Trustees adopted the following resolution:

RESOLUTION

WHEREAS, by authority of Sections 253.03 and 253.123 of the Florida Statutes the Trustees of the Internal Improvement Trust Fund are charged with the responsibility of regulating the dredging and maintenance of navigation channels in navigable waters of the state,

WHEREAS, there is presently no charge for fill removed as the result of dredging and maintaining minimum-sized navigation channels in navigable waters of the state when the fill is placed on land above the line of mean high water, and

WHEREAS, in many instances the applicant benefits greatly from depositing the fill on his land above the line of mean high water because it raises the elevation of his land so as to make it suitable for construction, and

WHEREAS, this fill is a ligitimate source of revenue for the Trustees of the Internal Improvement Trust Fund which is not being utilized;

NOW, THEREFORE, BE IT RESOLVED that all applicants for dredging or maintaining navigation channels in navigable waters of the state as authorized by Sections 253.03 and 253.123 of the Florida Statutes be charged the customary rate for fill where the fill is placed on private property above the line of mean high water.

BE IT FURTHER RESOLVED that there will be no charge for material removed from such channels if the applicant deposits spoil in a specified area as determined by the Department of Natural Resources.

* * *

BAY COUNTY - Dredge Permit to Improve Navigation,
       Section 253.123 Florida Statutes, File 639.
Miss S. E. Wright applied for permission to dredge a channel 50 ft. wide top cut, 5 ft. deep mean low water, 250 ft. long, in Grand Lagoon adjacent to Sec. 9, Twp. 4 South, Rge. 15 West, Bay County. A total of 465 cubic yards of material would be removed and placed on upland property of Chas. S. Weeks Company. The applicant tendered minimum payment of $50 and $50 processing fee. On September 22 the Trustees had deferred action at Mr. Adams' request. The biological report indicated limited adverse effects.

On motion by Mr. Faircloth, seconded by Mr. Williams and adopted without objection, the Trustees authorized issuance of the dredge permit as recommended by the staff.

––––––––––

DIXIE COUNTY - Dredge Permit, Maintenance Dredging,
       Section 253.123 Florida Statutes, File 673.
The Board of County Commissioners of Dixie County requested approval of the dredge permit issued by the county for maintenance dredging in a channel 2,000 ft. long, 50 ft. wide top cut, 5 ft. deep mean low water, adjacent to Section 14, Township 12 South, Range 10 East, in Horseshoe Bay, Dixie County. Approximately 6,000 cubic yards of material would be removed and placed on county-owned uplands. The biological report was not adverse. The applicant had agreed to spoil away from the marsh.

On motion by Mr. Conner, seconded by Mr. Williams and adopted without objection, the Trustees waived the $50 processing fee and approved the dredge permit without charge to the county.

––––––––––

LEVY COUNTY - Aquaculture Lease Denied.
Ocean Farms, Inc., by Gerald Golub, president, applied for an aquaculture lease of approximately 40 acres near Cedar Keys in Levy County for cultivating oysters. The biological reports were not adverse. On October 6 the Board deferred action. The Board of County Commissioners of Levy County by resolution on October 20, 1970, objected to the proposed lease as outlined in the provisions of Section 253.68 Florida Statutes.

Since the county objected, the Director thought it would be pointless to proceed to advertise the lease. The applicant had requested a delay.

Motion was made by Mr. Faircloth, seconded by Mr. Christian, that the application be denied based on the county resolution. Mr. Williams suggested that the applicant might consider other areas in the state for the proposed oyster culture. The Director said this company used a method in cultivating oysters ("tire beads") which some boaters objected to as a navigation hazard.

Representing Organized Fishermen of Florida, A. W. Hemphill said the method used by the company in the Indian River was a great problem, which was why his group complained to the Department of Natural Resources about it. He requested denial of the lease.

Without objection, the motion by Mr. Faircloth, seconded by Mr. Christian, to deny the lease application was adopted.

MANATEE COUNTY - State Dredge Permit No. 253.123-456. Jack Van Norman, staff field inspector, reported that Suncoast Realty Company had violated the terms of state dredge permit No. 253.123-456 granted on May 19, 1970, for improvement of navigation and upland property. Staff requested authority to temporarily suspend the permit until a thorough survey can be made and the extent of unauthorized work determined.

On motion by Mr. Christian, adopted without objection, the Board suspended state dredge permit No. 253.123-456 as requested.

TRUSTEES OFFICE - Budget and Funds. The Director had advised the Board that with the increased operations of the Trustees office, the trust fund was sufficient for current support but eventually, since state lands are not now being sold as before, there might have to be other sources of funds. He suggested that the operations be funded from general revenue, leaving the revenues generated in the trust fund to be used for reacquisition of submerged lands. The proposed change could be presented to the Legislature for approval of funding from general revenue.

The Trustees recognized that the budget might have to be adjusted when the need arose but indicated that the department should continue to be self-supporting for the present. Mr. Adams suggested that the Trustees seek to develop a funding program with the Legislature. Mr. Conner said when the master land plan was developed there would probably still be a considerable amount of unsold land, and when additional need was evident it could be budgeted then. He suggested collection of old debts, implementing revenue measures, and review of leases. The Director advised that the Board had collected practically no royalty from oil leases. Mr. Williams said the Legislature might be advised that since the Board was not now selling state land as before, something should be worked out to properly fund the Department when it becomes necessary.

The consensus was that the staff should continue to prepare and submit the budget based on the trust fund.

SUBJECTS UNDER THE MURPHY ACT

On motion by Mr. Williams, seconded and adopted without objection, the Trustees approved Report 975 listing two regular bids for sales of Murphy Act lands under Section 197.350 Florida Statutes, as follows: (1) Citrus County, Lot 9, Block 11, Town of Hartshorn, certified to the State of Florida under tax sale certificates 49 of 1909, 22 of 1912, and 470 of 1934, sold to Shirley McCoy for high bid of $350; (2) Nassau County, Lots 1, 2, 3, 6, 9 to 16 inclusive, and 24, Block 201 Town of Hilliard, certified to the State of Florida under tax sale certificates 2662, 2663, 2664 and 2665 of 1933 (and others) sold to D. W. Franklin for high bid of $325.

Deeds pertaining thereto were approved for execution.

PUTNAM COUNTY - Quitclaim Deed.
In order to remove a cloud on the title of land owned by Thos. J.
Butler, Inc., a Florida corporation, Thomas B. Dowda applied for a
quitclaim deed to 6.2 acres, more or less, in Section 48, Township 9
South, Range 27 East, conveyed to E. B. O'Hara in Putnam County
Murphy Act Deed No. 520 dated August 22, 1941, for $35 plus costs.
On January 18, 1945, E. B. O'Hara and wife erroneously quitclaimed
this land to the Governor of the State of Florida, instead of to the
rightful owner at the time.

On motion by Mr. Williams, seconded by Mr. Conner and adopted without
objection, the Trustees authorized issuance of quitclaim deed for
$25 handling charges.

On motion duly adopted, the meeting was adjourned.

_____
SECRETARY OF STATE - ACTING CHAIRMAN

ATTEST: _____
EXECUTIVE DIRECTOR

*   *   *

Tallahassee, Florida
November 10, 1970

The State of Florida Board of Trustees of the Internal Improvement
Trust Fund met in the Capitol with the following members present:

Claude R. Kirk, Jr.	Governor
Tom Adams	Secretary of State
Floyd T. Christian	Commissioner of Education
Doyle Conner	Commissioner of Agriculture
James W. Apthorp	Executive Director

The minutes of the meetings held on October 20 and 27, 1970, were
approved as submitted.

Because there were only four members of the Board present, several
applications on the agenda were deferred, including the following:

1. Brevard County. Request for authority to issue deeds for land
   sold by the Trustees on November 16, 1965, and under policy
   effective at that time the applicant entered into contracts to
   purchase No. 24177 and 24178 that were paid in full and grantee
   now entitled to receive deeds.

2. Palm Beach County. Application from Mayfran, Inc., File No. 2339-
   50-253.12, to purchase 0.698 acre parcel of land that had been
   advertised and an objection received.

3. Dade County. Metropolitan Dade County by Resolution R-831-70
   requested a drainage easement. File No. 2371-13-253.03.

4. St. Lucie County. Board of County Commissioners of St. Lucie
   County requested approval of a land exchange between the
   county and the adjoinint owner, William E. Glover, Trustee.

5. Murphy Act Land Sale Report No. 976. Request for approval of
   14 regular bids for sale of lots in St. Johns County to
   X. L. Pellicer, Jr., under provisions of Section 197.350
   Florida Statutes.

11-10-70

MONROE COUNTY - City of Key West, Deed No. 20949.
On March 10, 1970, the Trustees released a parcel of land from certain
restrictive covenants contained in Deed No. 20949 to the City of
Key West, grantee, on the condition that the license should be approved
before it would be binding upon the city and the licensee, and subject
to review of plans and specifications of the facility.

The Board of Trustees General Counsel approved the license as to form
and legality, and the staff approved the proposed plans and specifications. The Director recommended a time limit until January 1, 1972,
for construction to get under way.

On motion by Mr. Christian, seconded by Mr. Conner and adopted without objection, the Board approved the license as recommended by the
Director.

DADE COUNTY - Lease Assignment.
Because five members of the Board of Trustees were not present on this
date, action was deferred on request for approval of an assignment of
that part of Oil and Gas Drilling Lease No. 1939-1939-S held by RK
Petroleum Corp. to Exchange Oil and Gas Corporation.

DADE COUNTY - Marina License, Section 253.03 Florida Statutes.
Keystone Harbor Condominium, represented by Keys and Keys, attorneys
at Law, made application for a marina license for the construction
and maintenance of a mooring facility of 7,875 square feet in New Arch
Creek adjacent to applicant's upland in Section 28, Township 52 South,
Range 42 East, Dade County. The annual fee of $157.50 was tendered
and staff recommended approval.

On motion by Mr. Christian, seconded by Mr. Adams and adopted without
objection, the Trustees authorized issuance of the marina license.

MARTIN COUNTY - Marina License, Section 253.03 Florida Statutes.
John A. Herbert of Jupiter, Florida, applied for a marina license
to construct and maintain a mooring facility of 19,020 square feet
in Section 19, Township 40 South, Range 43 East, Martin County.

On motion by Mr. Christian, seconded by Mr. Adams and adopted without
objection, the Board authorized issuance of the marina license for
annual fee of $380.40.

TAYLOR COUNTY - Marina License, Section 253.03 Florida Statutes.
L. E. Files of Steinhatchee, Florida, applied for a marina license for
an area of 5,000 square feet in the Steinhatchee River adjacent to
Section 25, Township 9 South, Range 9 East, Taylor County. An existing
facility would be expanded to include an overhead marine hoist to launch
and beach fishing boats. Applicant tendered the minimum annual fee of
$100.

On motion by Mr. Christian, seconded by Mr. Adams and adopted without
objection, the Board authorized issuance of the marina license.

BROWARD COUNTY - County Park Lease.
Because five members were not present on this date, the Board of
Trustees deferred consideration of a development plan of Broward County
that was acceptable to the Division of Recreation and Parks and issuance
of a 95-year lease of a 50-acre spoil island in Section 5, Township
48 South, Range 43 East, for public park and recreation uses subject
to Chapter 70-449.

CAPITOL CENTER - Surplus Buildings.
The staff requested authority to advertise for sealed bids for dispositio
of ten buildings located on recently acquired property in the Capitol Cen
described as follows:

    1-story frame residences at (1) 311 W. St. Augustine Street,
    (2) 214 Bloxham Street, (3) 216/218 Bloxham Street,
    (4) 220 Bloxham Street, (5) 222 Bloxham Street,
    (6) 815 Bronough Street, (7) 817 Bronough Street,
    (8) 814 Blount Street; (9) 2-story frame garage apartment at
    311 1/2 West St. Augustine Street; and (10) 1-story brick residence
    at 306 West Gaines Street.

The Bureau of Property Management, Department of General Services, has
determined that the ten buildings were of no use to the State of Florida.

When Mr. Christian questioned the advisability of allowing houses in bad
condition to be moved and erected elsewhere to be eyesores, Mr. Conner
noted that some might provide better shelter than a possible purchaser no
had. The Director said some of the buildings were in very bad shape but
might be usable. After removal of buildings, the purchasers would be
allowed a certain time to clean up the lots.

Governor Kirk suggested that the staff advise the city and county of the
situation. The members accepted that suggestion and on the motion by
Mr. Adams, duly adopted, the staff was authorized to advertise for sealed
bids for disposition of the ten buildings in the Capitol Center.

REFUND - Murphy Act.
On motion by Mr. Christian, adopted without objection, the Board authoriz
refund of $15 to Dalton S. Payne, applicant for release of a state road
right of way reservation contained in Lake County Murphy Act Deed NO. 192
for the reason that the Department of Transportation did not recommend
release of the reservation.

COLLIER COUNTY - Dredge and Fill Permit,
                File Nos. 253.123-677 and 253.124-148.
Marco Island Development Corp., represented by Edgar M. Moore, Attorney
at Law, requested approval of a dredge and fill permit issued by the
Board of County Commissioners of Collier County on October 27, 1970.
The proposed work would be done in the Collier-Read Tract in Sections
19, 20, 21, 28, 29, 30 and 33, Township 51 South, Range 26 East, and
approximately 524,000 cubic yards of material would be dredged from
state-owned lands.

In consideration for the material obtained which would be valued at
$52,400, the applicant proposed to convey to the Trustees 25.86 acres
of mangrove valued at $1,900 per acre, and 9.25 acres of water area
valued at $1,500 for a total of $63,009, based upon a recent appraisal
of similar lands in a nearby township.

The Trustees on November 25, 1969, agreed in principle to the overall
Collier-Read plan of development and received 500 acres as a result of
the agreements. The project had been modified as a result of cooperation
between representatives of the Nature Conservancy and the applicant where
it was determined that the additional area to be deleted from the project
would have beneficial effects from an environmental standpoint. The
biological report prepared for establishment of the bulkhead line stated:
"This bulkhead line represents a compromise between maximum development
and no disturbance of the subject area .... to protect certain productive
areas from dredging and filling."

In view of the fact that the project increased areas to be left intact,
the staff recommended approval of the dredge and fill permit. The Direct
said this was the final step necessary to complete the project, noting th
there had been a change of ownership since the project was begun two year
ago.

Mr. Adams said that time and values continued to change, but at the time the overall plan was approved it was a tremendous step in the right direction. He called attention to benefits ecologically and aesthetically from use of riprap bulkheading rather than prepoured concrete seawalls, asked the Director to contact the developer and suggest consideration of this type of construction.

On motion by Mr. Adams, seconded by Mr. Christian and adopted without objection, the Trustees approved the dredge and fill permit contingent upon Board decision as to the nature of the bulkheading to be used for this project.

COLLIER COUNTY - File No. 253.123-679, Dredge Permit.
The Marco Island Development Corp. also submitted application to dredge 2,111,999 cubic yards of fill material from 64.35 acres in Collier Bay. The Board of County Commissioners of Collier County approved the permit on October 6 and 27, 1970. The dredging area was modified and supplemental biological report indicated that the modified plan was less adverse than the original design.

After lengthy negotiations the applicant had agreed to reconvey 3 parcels of mangrove islands and submerged land heretofore conveyed by the Trustees, in lieu of payment for fill material. The parcels were identified as 7/E-2 containing 118.52 acres, 4/F-1 containing 11.4 acres, and 5/F-1 containing 1.8 acres, totalling 131.72 acres. An appraisal prepared by the staff appraiser determined the value of the 118-acre parcel to be $190,000 at the rate of $1,603 per acre. At the $1,603 per acre, valuation, the 131.72 acres to be reconveyed to the Trustees is worth $211,147 and the fill material to be dredged is worth $211,199.

Staff was of the opinion that the exchange of undeveloped mangrove and submerged land for fill material was fair and would increase the land inventory following the pattern of the Collier-Read plan.

The Air and Water Pollution Control Department was not in favor of the project. Mr. Nathanial P. Reed was present and expressed willingness to speak on the water quality standard on this date or another date, if Mr. Adams' suggestion for deferment was adopted.

Mr. Adams said there still appeared to be some inconsistencies between the original government survey and the resurvey, and in addition the Air and Water Pollution Control Department had some questions. He did not oppose the application but requested a delay so that some of the questions that existed might be examined further

On motion by Mr. Adams, seconded by Mr. Christian and adopted without objection, the Board deferred action until November 24.

MONROE COUNTY - Dredge Permit, to Improve Navigation,
                Section 253.03 Florida Statutes, File No. 209
B. M. Manno of Marathon, Florida, applied for permission to remove 2,000 cubic yards of material from an area in Hawk Channel that had silted in, adjacent to Section 35, Township 65 South, Range 33 East, Monroe County. The material removed will be placed on upland property. Applicant tendered $200 payment for material and $50 processing fee. A breakwater installed by applicant's predecessor will be removed during the dredging operation.

The biological report was not adverse and the Bureau of Beaches and Shores did not require a hydrographic study.

On motion by Mr. Christian, seconded by Mr. Adams and adopted without objection, the Board approved issuance of the dredge permit.

NASSAU COUNTY - Amendment to Permit No. 253.123-474.
On motion by Mr. Christian, seconded by Mr. Adams and adopted without objection, the Board granted the request of Interpace Corporation, represented by Reynolds, Smith and Hills, for amendment to dredge permit issued October 13, 1970, providing for channel depth of minus-12 feet mean low water. Through error the original permit was issued for channel depth of minus-6 feet, and information showed the tidal range in the area was 6 feet.

PALM BEACH COUNTY - Dredge Permit, to Improve Navigation,
                    Section 253.123, File No. 674
Jess Kemberling, represented by M. R. Baggett, applied for a permit
to dredge an existing channel in Lake Worth 100 ft. wide top cut,
8 ft. deep mean low water, and to dredge a 245 ft. wide, 270 ft. long,
8 ft. deep mean low water, turning basin in Lake Worth adjacent to
Section 11, Township 43 South, Range 32 East, Palm Beach County.
Applicant tendered $3,860 for the material and $50 processing fee.
The material will be placed on upland above the mean high water line.

The Town of Palm Beach had approved the project. The biological
report was not adverse. Dredging and spoiling would be done in such
a way that turbidities in the area would not exceed 50 Jackson units
above background.

On motion by Mr. Christian, seconded by Mr. Adams and adopted without
objection, the Trustees approved issuance of the dredge permit.

COLLIER COUNTY - Seawall and Dredge Permit
Miles Scofield of Naples, Florida, requested approval of a permit
issued by the Board of County Commissioners of Collier County for
the construction of a seawall on filled land landward of the established
bulkhead line in Section 17, Township 48 South, Range 25 East, in the
Cocohatchee River. The seawall will be constructed 5 feet landward
of the bulkhead line. The Department of Natural Resources reported that
the project should not have significant adverse effects on marine
biological resources.

The Trustees and the Corps of Engineers in 1965 approved a dredge and
fill permit to fill this land, the permit expired in 1967, and subsequently applicant removed 4,550 cubic yards of material before
being stopped by staff personnel. The material previously placed inside
the bulkhead line had sloughed off into the river due to the lack of
retaining walls. Applicant tendered check for $1,365 as payment at
the rate of 30¢ per cubic yard for the material removed without permit.
The material lying riverward of the proposed seawall should be removed and
replaced landward thereof.

On motion by Mr. Adams, seconded by Mr. Christian and adopted without
objection, the Trustees accepted the staff recommendation for approval
of the dredge permit.

LEE COUNTY - Dredge Permit, Section 253.123 Florida Statutes.
Without objection, at the request of Mr. Adams the Trustees deferred
consideration of the application of First Development Corporation for
a partial after-the-fact navigation channel and removal of additional
material from Whiskey Creek in Section 10, Township 45 South, Range 24
East, Lee County.

PALM BEACH COUNTY - Because there were only four members of the Board
of Trustees present, action was deferred on an exchange of land with
the City of Boca Raton involving Florida Atlantic University property,
that had been approved on this date by the Board of Education.

DADE COUNTY - Corrective Deed, File No. 2189-13-253.12.
Because only four members were present, the Trustees deferred action on
a corrective deed requested by Joseph W. Bradham, Jr., on behalf of
S. P. J. Inc.

MANATEE COUNTY - On motion by Mr. Adams, seconded by Mr. Christian
and adopted without objection, the rules were waived for consideration
of a matter not on the agenda but of an emergency nature, according
to brief explanation by the Executive Director and Mr. Frank Schaub,
State Attorney of the Twelfth Judicial Circuit.

Motion was made by Secretary of State Tom Adams, seconded by Commissioner
of Education Floyd T. Christian, and carried without objection, that the
following resolution be adopted by the Board of Trustees:

121

RESOLUTION

WHEREAS, the Board of Trustees of the Internal Improvement Trust Fund of the State of Florida authorized the dredging and removal of certain submerged lands for purposes of both providing an access channel and for filling certain lands for port purposes for the Manatee County Port Authority and did thereby designate certain specific fill areas for the disposition of any surplus land so dredged as reflected by Exhibit A attached hereto and,

WHEREAS, the said Board of Trustees of the Internal Improvement Trust Fund on June 4, 1968, approved the fill permit issued by the Board of County Commissioners of Manatee County, Florida, to the Manatee County Port Authority under provisions of Section 253.124, Florida Statutes, to fill the 36.91 acres of land in Tampa Bay in Section 1, Township 33 South, Range 17 East, in Manatee County, Florida, designated for port purposes and,

WHEREAS, thereafter certain of the lands dredged for the construction of said channel were placed upon acreage immediately south of said port site, without approval or authority of this Board, said lands being the property of the Hendry Corporation, comprising approximately 40 acres, and,

WHEREAS, it appears that a sale of such unauthorized fill is contemplated very shortly to the Florida Power and Light Company,

BE IT RESOLVED that the Hendry Corporation as the abutting upland owner do remove any fill created in violation of this Section upon the above-mentioned lands, and upon failure to do so this Board will remove it at its own expense, such fill in the course thereof shall become a lien upon the property of said Hendry Corporation as abutting upland owner, and the Executive Director of the Board is hereby directed to give notice of this Resolution to the Hendry Corporation and to Florida Power and Light Company pursuant to Chapter 253 of the Laws of the State of Florida.

On motion duly adopted, the meeting was adjourned.

GOVERNOR - CHAIRMAN

ATTEST: _____
EXECUTIVE DIRECTOR

*   *   *

Tallahassee, Florida
November 17, 1970

The State of Florida Board of Trustees of the Internal Improvement Trust Fund met in the auditorium of the Department of Transportation building in Tallahassee with the following members present:

Claude R. Kirk, Jr.	Governor
Tom Adams	Secretary of State
Earl Faircloth	Attorney General
Fred O. Dickinson, Jr.	Comptroller
Doyle Conner	Commissioner of Agriculture

James W. Apthorp	Executive Director

11-17-70

With reference to the minutes of last week which would be presented
for approval on November 24, Mr. Adams said it was his intention that
action be held up on a dredge and fill permit for Marco Island
Development Corp. until the matter of using rip-rap bulkheading could
be evaluated. The Director said he would review the transcript with
Mr. Adams' staff.

BREVARD COUNTY - Confirmation of Contract Sales.
On November 16, 1965, the Trustees confirmed sale of two parcels of
submerged land in the Banana River in Sections 9 and 10, Township
25 South, Range 37 East, Brevard County, to River Isles Development
Company. Under policy in effect at that time, the applicant entered
into contracts 24177 and 24178 have been paid in full, and grantee was
entitled to receive deeds. The Department of Legal Affairs having
advised that such matters should be presented for action by five members
of the Board, the Director recommended approval on this date.

Governor Kirk asked if the land was not in an aquatic preserve, suggesting that the property might be bought back. Mr. Adams asked if
he wanted to hold up issuance of the deeds, but the Governor replied
there was no way to hold up the deeds for land purchased by installment
sale but repurchase might be investigated.

On motion made by Mr. Adams, seconded by Mr. Faircloth and adopted
without objection, the Trustees authorized issuance of the deeds and
directed the staff to look into the possibility of buying back the
land in the aquatic preserve.

DADE COUNTY - Corrective Deed, File No. 2189-13-253.12.
On motion by Mr. Faircloth, seconded by Mr. Adams and adopted without
objection, the Trustees authorized issuance of a corrective deed to
S. P. J., Inc., for $25 for the purpose of revising a minor error in
the legal description of the land conveyed in Deed No. 24983(21890-13)
dated July 29, 1969.

MONROE COUNTY - File No. 2182-44-253.12, Application for
                Filled Land.
The Director asked for deferment requested by a member of the Board,
on consideration of Donald L. Wolland's application to purchase a
0.25 acre filled parcel of sovereignty land in Little Basin, Florida
Bay, in Monroe County.

Without objection, consideration of the application was deferred.

BREVARD COUNTY - Confirmation of Contract Sale.
On April 12, 1966, the Trustees confirmed the sale of 26.36 acres
of submerged land in Newfound Harbor in Section 31, Township 24 South
Range 37 East, Brevard County, to Eightkap, Inc., a Florida corporation.
Under policy in effect at that time, the applicant entered into contract
to purchase, Contract No. 24270 has been paid in full, and grantee was
entitled to receive a deed. The Department of Legal Affairs having
advised that such matters should be presented for action by five members
of the Board, the Director recommended approval on this date.

Motion was made by Mr. Dickinson, seconded by Mr. Adams and adopted
without objection, that the deed be issued. Governor Kirk added that
the staff should find out if the land was in an aquatic preserve.

PALM BEACH COUNTY - Land Exchange.
On motion by Mr. Adams, seconded by Mr. Faircloth and adopted without
objection, the Board approved an exchange of land with the City of
Boca Raton involving a portion of the Florida Atlantic University
property. The exchange was approved by the Board of Education on
November 10, but was deferred by the Trustees for the reason that five
members were not present on that date.

11-17-70

ST. LUCIE COUNTY - Land Exchange.
Deferred last week when five members of the Trustees were not present
was the request from the Board of County Commissioners of St. Lucie
County for favorable consideration of a land exchange between the
county and the adjoining owner, William E. Glover, Trustee.

On January 15, 1946, by Deed No. 19115 the Trustees conveyed the
S 1/2 of Lot 8, Section 19, Township 35 South, Range 41 East, containing
19.71 acres, for bathing beach purposes. The lot conveyed to the
county had approximately 275 feet of Atlantic Ocean frontage out of
a total of approximately 1,320 feet of lot width. The adjoining owner
proposed to exchange a portion of his land fronting the ocean in
Section 20, Township 35 South, Range 41 East, St. Lucie County, which
would provide the county an additional 600 feet, more or less, of
ocean frontage and would provide the private owner a usable lot depth.
Staff recommended approval.

On motion by Mr. Adams, seconded by Mr. Dickinson and adopted without
objection, the Trustees approved the exchange and authorized preparation of suitable instruments to effectuate the exchange that would
contain the usual restrictive covenants as to recreational and
public purposes.

BROWARD COUNTY - County Park Lease.
On August 23, 1966, the Board of Commissioners of Florida Inland
Navigation District dedicated to the Trustees for 99 years a 50-acre
spoil island in Section 5, Township 48 South, Range 43 East, Broward
County, for public park and recreation use subject to certain existing
spoil disposal uses. Due to the limited size and location of the
island, the Division of Recreation and Parks of the Department of
Natural Resources determined that development and operation for park
purposes could best be accomplished as a county park. On November
10, 1970, the Department of Natural Resources approved lease to
Broward County that had submitted a development plan and schedule
acceptable to the Division of Recreation and Parks.

The 1970 Legislature by Chapter 70-449, Laws of Florida, authorized
5 acres of this spoil island to be used for oceanographic studies
by the Florida Atlantic University Foundation, Inc. The County
and the Division of Recreation and Parks agreed to work out details
for the additional use of a 5-acre portion of the island, with the
Foundation.

Last week because five members were not present, the Board of Trustees
took no action.

Motion was made by Mr. Conner, seconded by Mr. Dickinson and Mr. Adams,
and adopted without objection, the Trustees authorized issuance of
a 95-year lease to Broward County of the 50-acre spoil island for
public park and recreation uses subject to Chapter 70-449, Laws of Florid
and completion of the county park plan within 10 years.

DADE COUNTY - Campsite Lease Renewal, Assignments.
(1) Lease No. 2138. Safety Valves, Inc. holder of campsite lease
in Biscayne Bay, Dade County, requested approval of assignment to
Herbert W. Hoover, Jr. Said assignee requested renewal of Lease 2138
for one year with option to renew for an additional four years at
$300 annual rental.

(2) Lease No. 2142. William A. Daniel, D. R. Burden and R. D. Slaton,
holders of Campsite Lease No. 2142 in Biscayne Bay, requested one-year
renewal with option to renew for four additional years at $300 annual
rental.

(3) Lease No. 2139. Martin Woolin requested renewal of Campsite
Lease No. 2139 in Biscayne Bay for one year with option to renew
for four additional years at $300 annual rental.

The three requests conformed to policy of April 7, 1970, that allows lease as long as the structure remains on the site, and the policy of October 6, 1970, that established an annual rental of $300 for a quarter-acre site.

On motion made by Mr. Adams, seconded by Mr. Dickinson and adopted without objection, the Board approved the assignment and renewal of Lease No. 2138, and renewal of Lease Nos. 2142 and 2139 as requested.

DADE COUNTY - Oil and Gas Lease Assignment.
Deferred last week because five members were not present, and presented on this date with staff recommendation for approval, was the request for assignment of that part of Oil and Gas Lease No. 1939-1939-S held by RK Petroleum Corp. to Exchange Oil and Gas Corporation. Assignment and acceptance executed by both parties had been reviewed and approved by staff legal counsel. This lease was issued by the Board of Education and the Trustees on September 24, 1963, covering 24,830 net mineral acres at Forty Mile Bend.

Motion was made by Mr. Conner, seconded by Mr. Dickinson, that the assignment be approved. But Mr. Adams said he had been told that there was some question as to performance under this lease of an area contiguous to the Big Cypress. The Director would make a report to the Board on performance under the lease covenants. Mr. Conner had no objection to deferment.

Without objection, the Board directed the matter to be brought back next week.

COLLIER COUNTY - Oil Lease Assignment.
On motion by Mr. Adams, adopted without objection, the Board approved assignment of an undivided one-half interest in Oil and Gas Drilling Lease No. 2447-S from Phillips Petroleum Company to Mobil Oil Corporation. Executed copy of assignment had been reviewed and approved by staff legal counsel.

SHELL LEASE INCOME REPORT - The Trustees accepted for the record the following report of remittances to Florida Department of Natural Resources from holders of dead shell leases:

Lease No.	Company	Amount
1718	Radcliff Material, Inc.	$ 103.57
1788	Benton and Company, Inc.	18,163.98
2233	Bay Dredging and Construction Co.	4,589.26

MONROE COUNTY - Sand Lease Assignment.
On motion by Mr. Faircloth, seconded by Mr. Dickinson and adopted without objection, the Board approved assignment of Sand Lease No. 2381, issued by the Board of Trustees on June 1, 1969, from Allied Electrical Co., Inc., to Keys Sand and Salvage Co. of Monroe County. Lease assignment and acceptance of the terms of the lease were approved by staff legal counsel.

DADE COUNTY - City of North Miami, Dedication No. 23991.
On April 7 and June 16, 1970, the City of North Miami came before the Trustees requesting approval of a proposed revocable license for operation of a concession on Spoil Island No. 1 in Biscayne Bay, one of the spoil islands dedicated in 1965 to the city for public purposes. There was no action on April 7, and on June 16 the request was deferred for the purpose of development of a policy for spoil islands throughout the state. On August 11 the Board adopted the following policy: (1) Spoil islands should be left in their

natural state unless a greater public purpose could be served by development. Any non-state development should be undertaken under lease by the Trustees, rather than sale and consistent with guidelines set forth in Section 253.111 Florida Statutes; and (2) Proposals for public development of any spoil island should be authorized only after consultation with appropriate state agencies to see if any better public purpose might be served.

The City of North Miami submitted a proposed license agreement with a private concessionaire, but no plan of development was furnished. In view of the fact that the policy adopted required that spoil islands be left in their natural state and that the city to date had not developed the island dedicated on May 11, 1965; and, furthermore, in view of the fact that the city had not carried out the conditions of the dedication which states: "In the event the said City of North Miami shall (1) use said lands for other than public park and recreational purposes, or (2) for a period of three consecutive years shall fail and neglect to maintain and use the same for said purposes, the dedication hereby made shall at the option of said Trustees be subject to termination upon sixty days' notice in writing by the Trustees to said city"; the staff recommended denial of lease agreement and notification that the dedication would be rescinded in accordance with conditions in Trustees Dedication No. 23991. On October 27 the Board deferred consideration of the above staff recommendation that was placed on the agenda again at the request of a member of the Board.

Mayor Sheppard Broad of the Town of Bay Harbor Islands objected to the lease agreement at previous hearings. He said he supported the staff recommendation to deny the lease and rescind the dedication. He would not object to the City of North Miami retaining the dedication if the spoil islands were left in their unspoiled state as recommended for such islands by the June 19 letter from the Division of Recreation and Parks, as green relief was needed in the area with many concrete seawalls.

Mr. Adams pointed out that it had been the Board's policy to extend the right to public bodies to use such areas as were within their jurisdiction, and if the City of North Miami could assure the Board that the dedicated areas would be used for proper public purposes in public control, it might be desirable. Mr. Adams made a motion that the request for approval of the lease agreement be denied. The motion was seconded by Mr. Faircloth and adopted without objection.

The second thing to be considered was the dedication. Mr. Elton T. Gissendanner pointed out that the dedication specifically required some development of the island by the city, which was why the license agreement was proposed. He added that the city would be happy for the islands to remain in their natural state, would have them patrolled by police, and would resist having the dedication rescinded. He suggested some amendment of the terms of the dedication. With reference to Mr. Adams' statement that the islands had not been kept clean and needed better supervision, Mr. Gissendanner said he was not aware that such report had been made, that it was not a factual report, that supervision of the islands was a continuing job.

The Director recommended change in the terms of the dedication in line with the Board's new policy for spoil islands, since the original dedication contemplated recreational development, boating, beach and other facilities or construction. That would be contrary to the intent of the new policy to leave spoil islands in their natural state for the most part, unless under state control.

Motion was made by Mr. Adams, seconded by Mr. Faircloth and adopted without objection, that the dedication be continued but amended in accordance with the recently adopted policy for spoil islands throughout the state.

DADE COUNTY - Drainage Easement, File No. 2371-13-253.12.
On motion by Mr. Adams, seconded by Mr. Faircloth and adopted without
objection, the Trustees granted request of Metropolitan Dade County
by Resolution No. R-831-70 dated July 14, 1970, for an easement for
secondary drainage in the Oleta River (Big Snake Creek) in Section 33,
Township 51 South, Range 42 East, and Section 4, Township 52 South,
Range 42 East, Dade County. The Central and Southern Florida Flood Contr
District had concurred in the request.

PALM BEACH COUNTY - Maintenance Spoil Easement,
                    File No. 2374-50-253.03
Florida Inland Navigation District requested alternate spoil area to
replace MSA 625B and MSA 626B in Lake Worth adjacent to Section 9, Township 42 South, Range 43 East, Palm Beach County. On August 11, 1970, the
Board authorized a marina license to Old Port Cove Condominiums that
would allow a marina on the two spoil areas, conditioned upon applicant
securing the approval by public agencies of alternate spoil areas. The
Department of Natural Resources had no objection to the alternate site
if no feasible upland sites were available, and Florida Inland Navigation
District recommended substitution of the proposed site.

On motion by Mr. Adams, seconded by Mr. Faircloth and adopted without
objection, the Board authorized issuance of the easement requested by
FIND.

PALM BEACH COUNTY - Commercial Dock Permit, Time Extension
On motion by Mr. Adams, seconded by Mr. Faircloth and adopted without
objection, the Board approved a time extension for State Permit No.
CD-1719 issued to Arvida Corporation for a marginal wharf along the
Intracoastal Waterway, to be used by the Coast Guard Auxiliary.

OKALOOSA COUNTY - Marina License, Section 253.03, Florida Statutes.
Motel Miramar Apartments, represented by Rhett E. Cadenhead, applied
for a state marina license for installation of mooring facilities
occupying 4,480 square feet in Santa Rosa Sound in Section 23, Township
2 South, Range 24 West, Okaloosa County.

On motion by Mr. Faircloth, seconded by Mr. Adams and adopted without
objection, the Board authorized issuance of a marina license for the
minimum payment of $100.

VOLUSIA COUNTY - City of Daytona Beach Yacht Basin.
On October 20 the Trustees heard a full presentation of the request
from the City of Daytona Beach for release of restrictive covenants
contained in Trustees Deed No. 20798 to allow the city to lease
its yacht basin to be operated by private interests. The city also
requested a marina license without charge for 14 acres of water area
upon which was constructed the mooring facilities, and expected to
lease the water column and bottoms at the usual rate of 2¢ per square
foot, using the money derived therefrom toward paying off the bonded
indebtedness on the yacht basin.

Staff renewed its two-fold recommendation (1) that the request for a
marina license be denied, that such license be a separate matter to be
considered by the Board, that the lease agreement between the city and
successful bidder require that bidder file an application for a marina
license to be granted by the Trustees under such terms and conditions
as they may deem appropriate; and (2) that request for release of
restrictive covenant contained in Deed NO. 20798 be granted only insofar as it applies to leasing and only to a 5-acre portion, the release
to be conditioned upon Trustees' approval of lease agreement between
the city and successful bidder.

City Attorney John C. Chew stated that Daytona Beach, finding itself
unable to finance certain repairs and capital improvements in the
form of proper sanitary facilities and expanded electrical distribution system, had asked for proposals for private developers for which
release of deed restrictions was needed. But in the event the Board
did not agree to release restrictions for this lease, the city needed
a marina license for the operation of its marina and requested waiver
of the 2¢ charge per square foot. Mr. Chew said the city would like
the option to do what is financially best for the city.

Mr. Apthorp said the staff's most serious disagreement with the
city was the matter of payment of the marina license fee, that if the
city was given a license and allowed to transfer it to a private
operator, that operator should pay the fee to the Trustees for operating
on sovereignty lands as other marina licensees had to do. The Director
recommended that any marina license given to the city should be non-
transferable.

Mr. Edgar Dunn, attorney for a prospective lessee of the city yacht
basin area, indicated agreement with the Director's recommendations,
specifically that the city should have a marina license, and did
not ask for a waiver of public revenue (the 2¢ per square foot fee).

Mr. J. Kermit Coble, representing another prospective lessee, said
his client did not ask for preferential treatment but proposed that
the 2¢ fee be paid to the city to go toward paying off its bonded
indebtedness. Governor Kirk felt that would be taking revenue that
should go to the entire state, not just the city. Mr. Coble referred
to the fact that the city at great expense some twenty years ago
built the docks, that the project was for public use, that the sewage
facilities were needed, that the city had consulted the staff
and tried to work up proposals but without waiver of the 2¢ Mr. Coble
did not think any private operator would be able to enter into a
lease.

There was further discussion and the consensus of the Board was
against waiver of the fee in event the city desired to assign the
operation of the marina to private parties. Mr. Adams expressed
opposition to release of public purpose covenants on sovereignty
lands.

Motion was made by Mr. Adams, seconded by Mr. Dickinson and adopted
without objection, that a non-assignable marina license be issued
to the City of Daytona Beach without the 2¢ per square foot fee
and, as suggested by the Governor, that all provisions required by
the Air and Water Pollution Control Department be complied with by
the yacht basin.

On the matter of release of the restrictive covenant in Deed No.
20798, motion was made by Mr. Faircloth, seconded by Mr. Dickinson,
and approved on a vote of four to one, with Mr. Adams voting "No",
release subject, however, to the city furnishing the project plans
for examination by the Board.

Since there were not five affirmative votes for release of the public
purpose covenant, the effect was a denial. At the request of a
Board member, that might be brought again to the members for
reconsideration.

PALM BEACH COUNTY - Dredge Permit to Improve Navigation,
                     Section 253.123 File 579
Arvida Corporation applied for permission for maintenance dredging
in an existing boat slip 75 ft. wide, 75 ft. long and 4 ft. deep
m.l.w., in Boca Raton Inlet in Section 28, Township 47 South, Range
43 East, Palm Beach County. Approximately 300 cubic yards of
material will be removed and placed behind an existing seawall in
an area that has had erosion. Applicant tendered $50 minimum payment
for dredge material and $50 processing fee.

The City of Boca Raton approved the project. The biological report
was not adverse and staff recommended approval.

On motion by Mr. Faircloth, seconded by Mr. Dickinson and adopted
without objection, the Trustees approved the application.

PINELLAS COUNTY - Dredge and Fill Permit denied.
On motion by Mr. Adams, seconded by Mr. Faircloth and adopted without
objection, the Trustees concurred in denial of a dredge
and fill permit denied by Pinellas County Water and Navigation
Control Authority on October 20, 1970, DFNo. 269 to the City of
St. Petersburg to dredge 270,000 cubic yards of material from
Tampa Bay and to fill 7.7 acres, more or less, in Tampa Bay for
extension of runway at Albert Whitted Airport.

DUVAL COUNTY - Dredge Permit 253.123-622; Fill Permit 253.124-132;
                SAJSP Permit (70-400)
On September 22, 1970, the Trustees heard a full presentation
from the applicants and the objectors with regard to a dredge and
fill permit application from Dunn's Terminal Corporation that had
been approved by the City of Jacksonville on May 12, 1970, for
removing 327,000 cubic yards of material from the St. Johns River
from areas sandy and unvegetated, according to the biological
report. Applicant tendered $22,800 for material to be removed from
sovereignty land, agreed to convey 5.3 acres of marsh land bordering
on Wynn Creek to remain intact and unmolested in accordance with
recommendations in the biological report, and further modification
of the seawall configuration should diminish adverse hydrographic
effects as indicated by a report from the Coastal Engineering
Laboratory. The Department of Natural Resources had advised that
a hydrological report was not needed.

The Director had tried on three occasions to meet with the objectors
and the applicant to attempt to resolve problems, but the objectors
would not participate and still objected. The City of Jacksonville,
requested by objectors to reconsider its action, refused to reconsider.
Mr. Apthorp reviewed the matter and exhibited a map showing the
application area. The staff still recommended approval.

Mr. William L. Durden, attorney representing the sellers of the
land, added further explanation of the project, history of the
area, and approval of the application by the area planning and zoning
board, Council and County Commission. He said it was in an industrial
area, across the river from Blount Island.

Strong objections were expressed by Messrs. Hans Vige, Jr., and
Hans Vige, Sr., Miss Alberta James, and Mrs. Rosemary Furman. Many
other objectors were present and additional petition and letters were
offered to be filed. Reasons given for objecting to the dredging and
filling included ecological and hydrographical considerations, drainage,
protection of residences from the undesirable automobile body shredding
plant proposed for the site to be filled, advice from various parties
that further technical information was needed, and lack of understanding
of maps and other things relating to the application. Mr. Vige, Sr.,
called attention to the vote at the last election on the constitutional
amendment to protect submerged land in the public interest.

Motion was made by Mr. Faircloth, seconded by Mr. Adams, that the
staff recommendation for approval be adopted. With respect to the
various reports submitted, the Board said they depended on the advice
of the Department of Natural Resources and while they understood the
concern of the residents, they felt that there had been a lack of
understanding rather than any attempt to mislead anyone. The staff
had attempted to schedule a meeting for the objectors to have some
of their questions answered. Mr. Adams said that in recent litigation
the court had said the law vests zoning in the local authority and
zoning was not a problem to de discussed here. Both Mr. Adams and
Mr. Dickinson assured the objectors that no one was trying to withhold
anything, that it was complicated, the staff was trying to get all
the answers and the applicant had been cooperative.

The Director said this was not the first time there had been divergent biological reports, that Dunns Creek and Wynnes Creek and drainage should not be adversely affected, that the permit would contain a clause requiring careful control of the dredging and filling to prevent siltation, the matter of water quality would be handled by certification from the Department of Air and Water Pollution Control, and the staff recommended approval of the application.

The motion to approve was adopted without objection.

PASCO COUNTY - Dredge and Fill Permit,
Section 253.123 and 253.124 Florida Statutes.
Lindrick Corporation, represented by Walter A. Cassin, Jr., applied for permission to remove two spoil banks containing 172,882 cubic yards of material, and to perform maintenance dredging in two existing channels adjacent to Sections 12 and 13, Township 26 South, Range 15 East, in the Gulf of Mexico in Pasco County. Material from the spoil banks would be deposited on submerged land previously conveyed in an area where dikes were constructed to contain the spoil. Material from the two navigation channels would be spoiled alongside the channels on existing spoil banks. Each spoil bank would be a maximum of 300 ft. long and 100 ft. wide with a minimum of 150 ft. between the spoil banks to provide for tidal circulation The total dredge area was 7.75 acres with approximately 55 acres subject to filling, and applicant tendered $17,288.20 for the material.

The biological report was not adverse. The project was approved by Pasco County. The staff recommended approval of a permit containing the usual conditions regulating dredging and spoiling.

On motion by Mr. Faircloth, seconded by Mr. Adams and adopted without objection, the Board authorized issuance of the requested permit.

DADE COUNTY - Artificial Reef Permit.
Snyder and Des Rocher, Inc., applied for a permit for an artificial reef in the Atlantic Ocean at 25° 02' 00" North Lat., 80° 04' 06" W. Long., Dade County. Applicant tendered $50 processing fee. The material used should attract marine life and later, sport and commercial fishermen. The Department of Natural Resources suggested that metal parts be anchored and that care should be taken to prevent inadvertent introduction of pollutants into the water from the junk materials.

Motion was made by Mr. Faircloth, seconded by Mr. Adams and adopted without objection, that the Board approve the application for an artificial reef permit.

OKALOOSA COUNTY - Fill Permit, Section 253.124 Florida Statutes,
Chapter 70-333, File 150.
Okaloosa Island Authority, represented by Representative Jerry Melvin, requested approval of a fill permit issued by Okaloosa County Board of County Commissioners to reclaim land lost through artificially induced erosion in Santa Rosa Sound, commencing at the southeast corner of Lot 25, Block 13, and terminating at the east side of Sixth Beach Freeway in Okaloosa County. No filling will be done beyond the established bulkhead line.

The biological report prepared on January 30, 1970, in connection with establishment of the bulkhead line, was not adverse.

On motion by Mr. Adams, seconded by Mr. Faircloth and adopted without objection, the Board approved the fill permit.

130

DADE COUNTY - Fill Permit, Section 253.124 Florida Statutes,
              Deed File No. 2268-13-253.12
Delphi Investment Company, represented by James R. Shiskin, requested
approval of a fill permit issued by the City of Miami to fill 2.665
acres of submerged land in Biscayne Bay adjacent to Section 12,
Township 54 South, Range 41 East, Dade County. The parcel of
submerged land was conveyed by the Trustees on April 7, 1970. The
material to fill the parcel will be trucked in from upland sources.

The biological survey report was adverse. The Bureau of Beaches
and Shores advised that no hydrographic study was required.

On motion by Mr. Conner, seconded by Mr. Faircloth and adopted without
objection, the Board approved the fill permit.

LEE COUNTY - Settlement and Dredge Permit, Section 253.123 F. S.
First Development Corporation, represented by Duane Hall and Associates,
made application for a settlement and permission to construct a
navigation channel 1,200 feet long, 5 feet deep and varying from
50 to 200 feet wide in Whiskey Creek in Section 10, Township 45 South,
Range 24 East, Lee County. Approximately 325 cubic yards of material
had been removed from Whiskey Creek before the project was stopped.
Applicant desired to remove an additional 2,000 cubic yards of material
from Whiskey Creek which, according to the Lee County Engineer, is
the main outlet of a major drainage basin of the Iona Drainage District
and needed improvement to handle the increased water runoff caused by
subdivision development in the area. All required exhibits including
$50 processing fee had been submitted. Consideration of the application
was deferred last week at the request of the Secretary of State.

The Department of Natural Resources recommended that no filling of
submerged land be permitted and that fill presently placed on red
mangroves be removed and the red mangroves be replanted.

To resolve the matter applicant offered (1) to pay damages for fill
previously removed at a penalty rate of $1 per cubic yard, (2) to pay
for additional material at standard yardage rates of 10¢ per cubic
yard, (3) to reduce depths of platted lots, (4) to cooperated with
marine biologists and others to insure proper development of its
holdings, and (5) to plant red mangroves on the offshore mangrove
island in Whiskey Creek.

Staff recommended approval of permit upon receipt of payment of
$325 for the material already removed, payment of $200 for material
to be removed, and a bond for $500 to insure replanting of red
mangroves.

On motion by Mr. Adams, seconded by Mr. Faircloth and adopted without
objection, the Board accepted the staff recommendation as the action
on this application.

SUBJECTS UNDER CHAPTER 18296

On motion by Mr. Adams, seconded by Mr. Faircloth and adopted without
objection, the Trustees approved Report No. 976 and the 14 regular
bids listed thereon for sale of lots in St. Johns County under provisions
of the Murphy Act, Section 197.350 Florida Statutes, to X. L. Pellicer, J
for the highest bids totalling $2,960. Deed pertaining thereto was approv
for execution.

On motion duly adopted, the meeting was adjourned.

GOVERNOR - CHAIRMAN

ATTEST:
EXECUTIVE DIRECTOR

* * * * * *

11-17-70

Tallahassee, Florida
November 24, 1970

The State of Florida Board of Trustees of the Internal Improvement
Trust Fund met in the Capitol in Tallahassee with the following
members present:

On motion by Mr. Adams, seconded by Mr. Christian and adopted without
objection, the Board approved the minutes of November 10 subject to
amendment of page four to show approval of dredge and fill permit
(File Nos. 253.123-677 and 253.124-148) contingent upon Board decision
as to the nature of the bulkheading to be used for this project.

Discussing the construction of bulkheads, Mr. Adams suggested that
thought should be given to the use of riprap material which might be
of greater benefit ecologically than poured concrete, and he would
like an opportunity to evaluate a report on the subject. The dredge
and fill application could then be agendaed for action of the Board.

FRANKLIN COUNTY - Bulkhead Line, Marina License.
The Board of County Commissioners of Franklin County by resolution
established a bulkhead line 948.19 feet long in Alligator Harbor at
the Alligator Point Marina in unsurveyed fractional Sections 2 and
3, Township 7 South, Range 2 West, Franklin County. The biological
survey report was not adverse. On October 6 the Board deferred
action for additional information.

The area subject to the location of the bulkhead line was filled
around 1959 by the applicant's predecessor in title, now deceased.
Applicant, Alligator Point Marina, Inc., Peter Fenn, president,
submitted invoices showing the number of hours that trucks operated
removing material from the marina site which included areas owned
by the applicant. It was estimated that 7,219 cubic yards of
material was dredged from sovereignty land for which the applicant
will pay $2,165.70, at the penalty rate of 30¢ per cubic yard. The
project would have limited temporary adverse effects on the marine
biological environment. The Bureau of Beaches and Shores advised
that a hydrographic survey was unnecessary.

The marina area to be licensed consisted of 0.68 acres of filled,
seawalled and improved sovereignty land and 1.73 acres of unimproved
sovereignty land upon which floating piers are installed. For the
total area of 104,979.60 square feet the annual license would be
$2,099.59. The effective date would be December 1, 1969.

The applicant planned to engage in maintenance dredging in the future,
and the staff recommended deposit of all spoil material on the gulf
front beach without cost to the state in areas designated by the
Bureau of Beaches and Shores for beach nourishment purposes. The
Director recommended no conveyance but that a marina license be issued.

Motion was made by Mr. Adams, seconded by Mr. Conner and Mr. Dickinson,
and adopted without objection, that the Board approve the bulkhead line
located by Franklin County and issuance of a marina license effective
December 1, 1969, in accordance with the staff recommendations.

MONROE COUNTY - File No. 2182-44-253.12, Application for filled land.
On October 20 at Mr. Adams' request, the Board deferred action on
the application of Donald L. Wollard to purchase 0.25 acre parcel
of filled land in Monroe County.

Mr. Adams, noting that the financial condition of the applicant had
been considered, felt that the penalty should be charged and reading
of the transcript and minutes showed that the application had been
held in abeyance for the expressed reason of developing policy. The
Director said the staff would prepare the next agenda for the Wollard
application in accordance therewith.

INDIAN RIVER COUNTY - Bulkhead Line Relocation, Section 253.122 F. S.
The Board of County Commissioners of Indian River County by Resolution
No. 70-38 adopted September 9, 1970, relocated a bulkhead line 446.98
feet long in the Indian River in Section 8, Township 31 South, Range
39 East, following an existing seawall encompassing sovereignty land
filled a number of years ago. The biological report was not adverse.

The property of Wallington G. Bosworth, deceased, for which the bulkhead line was established, was bequeathed to Florida State University
and Miami University. The executor of the estate needed clear title
for disposal of the property, establishment of the bulkhead line being
the first step.

On motion by Mr. Christian, seconded by Mr. Faircloth and adopted
without objection, the Board approved the bulkhead line as relocated
by Indian River County on September 9, 1970.

RESOLUTION - Canoe Trails.
On motion by Mr. Dickinson, seconded by Mr. Faircloth, and adopted
unanimously, the Trustees adopted the following resolution that
designated portions of the Withlacoochee River from the Georgia-Florida
state line to its confluence with the Suwannee River as a canoe trail,
setting in motion a program of state-wide canoe trails as part of the
state recreation program. The designation of waterways as state canoe
trails required Trustees' concurrence with the Executive Board of the
Department of Natural Resources.

R E S O L U T I O N

WHEREAS, the State of Florida, by virtue of its sovereignty, is
the owner of the beds of all navigable waters; and

WHEREAS, title to these sovereignty and certain other lands
has been vested by the Florida Legislature in the State of Florida
Board of Trustees of the Internal Improvement Trust Fund, to be held,
protected and managed in the public interest for the people of Florida;
and

WHEREAS, the said Board of Trustees as part of its overall
management program for Florida's state-owned lands, does desire to
insure the perpetual protection, preservation and public enjoyment of
exceptional value and quality by designating these certain areas as
canoe trails; and

WHEREAS the Executive Board of the Department of Natural Resources
in meeting on October 13, 1970, approved a statewide system of canoe
trails as a part of the state recreation program; and

WHEREAS, the implementation of designation of waterways as
state canoe trails requires the concurrence of the State of Florida
Board of Trustees of the Internal Improvement Trust Fund;

NOW, THEREFORE, BE IT RESOLVED by the State of Florida Board of
Trustees of the Internal Improvement Trust Fund:

THAT it does hereby concur with the Executive Board of the
Department of Natural Resources approving a statewide system of
canoe trails as a part of the state recreation program; and

THAT it does specifically designate the Withlacoochee River from
the Georgia-Florida state line to the Suwannee River State Park
as a canoe trail; and

THAT it does hereby recognize that portions of the Withlacoochee
River lying within the State of Georgia as being included in the
canoe trail system; and

BE IT FURTHER RESOLVED by the State of Florida Board of
Trustees of the Internal Improvement Trust Fund that it recognizes
this project represents a cooperative effort between the State of
Georgia and the State of Florida.

VOLUSIA COUNTY - Dedication, File No. 2376-64-253.03
The Board of County Commissioners of Volusia County by Resolution
No. 70-13 adopted February 19, 1970, requests the dedication of
6.35 acres of sovereignty land in the Halifax River abutting county-
owned land in Township 15 South, Range 33 East, Volusia County, the
land to be used for public park, marina, and associated public use.

On October 27, 1970, five members were present and the vote was four
to one for approval of bulkhead line, dredge and fill permit, marina
license and dedication. Staff felt that five affirmative votes
were needed for the dedication.

Mr. Adams recalled that the county had urged immediate action
because of the time schedule with respect to a federal grant. He
called attention to a similar operation, the Daytona Beach Yacht
Basin (see minutes of October 20 and November 17), which he had
investigated and found out that the reason the city marina was short
of funds was that other city expenses were being charged to the
marina funds. The Director said the sites were adjacent, but the
dedication recommended by the staff was for the county facility.

On motion by Mr. Faircloth, seconded by Mr. Dickinson and adopted
without objection, the Trustees approved the dedication to the
county of land to be used for public park, marina, and associated
public use.

DESOTO COUNTY - Interest in Estate
Under the will of Dolores Ruthenberg, one-third of her residuary
estate was bequeathed to the Council for the Blind and one-third
to the State Board of Health. On behalf of the Department of Health
and Rehabilitative Services, the Trustees acquired an interest in
Lots 1 to 24 inclusive, Block 11, Subdiv. 4, Section 19, Township
38 South, Range 27 East, DeSoto County. Because the property and
two-thirds interest would be of no value to the agency beneficiaries
in their statutory responsibilities, the executor advised that the
only buyer would be Bailey M. Theus, the other residuary beneficiary,
who offered $100 for the interest of the state. The offer was
higher than the value placed on the land by a M.A.I. appraiser.

On motion by Mr. Conner, seconded by Mr. Adams and adopted without
objection, the Board authorized sale of the interest of the Trustees
to Mr. Theus by appropriate instrument and transfer of the $100 to
the Department of Health and Rehabilitative Services for distribution
to the Division of Health and the Bureau of Blind Services.

DADE COUNTY - Temporary Borrow Easement
On the agenda on September 22 and October 6, and deferred, was the
application from the Department of Transportation for a borrow area
of approximately 23 acres in Dumfoundling Bay, Dade County, in
theoretical Sections 2 and 3, Township 52 South, Range 42 East, for
material to be used on uplands in connection with construction of
State Road 852 (192nd Street).

The biological report dated April 20, 1970, was adverse to dredging
but applicant stated that an alternate area with suitable material
could not be located within the vicinity of the proposed construction.

The adjacent bottoms have been and are still subjected to extensive dredging. The dredge permit will be issued to the contractor after contract was awarded. Dredging would be done in such a manner that turbidities in the dredge area would not exceed 50 Jackson units above base. The spoil area would be diked to prevent silt from re-entering the bay. In addition, the Director reported that the Department of Transportation had given assurance that the dredging would be limited to areas of greater depth than five feet to preserve marine biological growth.

Motion was made by Mr. Christian and by Mr. Adams, seconded and adopted without objection, that the application for temporary borrow easement be approved on the basis of dredging being done in areas five feet or deeper.

BAY COUNTY - Spoil Area Easement

The Board of County Commissioners of Bay County requested a spoil area for immediate and future maintenance channel dredging in Grand Lagoon and the ship channel in the Vicinity of St. Andrews State Park. The Division of Recreation and Parks recommended that dredge material suitable for beach nourishment be placed on the gulf shore line of the park to replenish eroded beaches. The Department of Natural Resources approved the project on this date.

On motion by Mr. Faircloth, seconded by Mr. Adams and adopted without objection, the Trustees approved issuance of a perpetual easement to Bay County permitting placement of suitable spoil material on the designated area subject to issuance of a coastal construction permit by the Department of Natural Resources.

MANATEE COUNTY - File No. 2318-41-253.12, Land Sale.

On May 12, 1970, the Trustees authorized advertisement for objections only of two parcels of filled sovereignty land containing a total of 2.798 acres, more or less, in the Manatee River in Section 26, Township 34 South, Range 17 East, applied for by the City of Bradenton so that it could convey land to upland owners to conform with agreements entered into by the city in developing waterfront lands. The parcels were a part of the 54.25 acre tract dedicated to the city by the Trustees on February 27, 1968. The city will quitclaim rights encumbering the parcels acquired under the dedication.

On June 30 the appraisal had not been received and the Board deferred action. An appraisal valued the 1.113 acre parcel at $36,362 and the 1.685 acre parcel at $36,699. The valuation reflected the improved condition of the land on which the cost of filling and cost of fill material were not deducted. The fill material was obtained from the river without cost consistent with the Trustees' policy in effect at the time of the dedication, but rescinded on May 14, 1968.

Staff recommended sale at the appraised valuation of a total of $73,061, less estimated cost of filling of $11,284.88, or the amount of $61,776.12 for the two parcels. The value included the usual 10¢ per cubic yard charge for fill material.

The Director explained that the conveyance was an arrangement worked out at the time the state dedication was made to the City of Bradenton, that the riparian owners were to receive the two small parcels of land as their riverfront property was eliminated by the dedication to the city. The city will convey the parcels to those riparian owners as compensation for cutting off their riparian rights.

On motion by Mr. Christian, seconded by Mr. Adams and adopted without objection, the Board confirmed the land sale as recommended by the staff.

11-24-70

PINELLAS COUNTY - File No. 2316-52-253.12, Land Sale
At the request of a member of the Board, the application of George
L. Mallory, et al, for purchase of a parcel of sovereignty land
in St. Joseph Sound abutting the vacated portion of Albert Street
in the City of Dunedin in Section 34, Township 28 South, Range 18
East, Pinellas County, containing 0.22 acre, more or less, appraised
at $530.00, was again presented to the Trustees for consideration.
Applicant had amended his plan so that only limited adverse effects
might occur to the marine biological resources. High-rise rental
units or a condominium was planned and applicant submitted evidence
that the small parcel applied for was a pocket in which debris
collected.

The application was advertised and sale recommended by Pinellas
County Water and Navigation Control Authority. On July 21 the
Trustees approved the sale on the vote of three to two - which
amounted to a denial without five affirmative votes. On August 4
a member had requested reconsideration, which was deferred at the
applicant's request.

Staff recommended the sale and approval of a fill permit under
Section 253.124 Florida Statutes granted by Pinellas County on
February 17, 1970, for two parcels of submerged land previously
conveyed and for the 30-ft strip considered on this date.

The Director said the applicant owned property on either side of the
strip and had agreed to reconvey three acres of submerged land that
he would not fill lying riverward of his property. There did not
appear to be any public use of the 30 ft. strip of land, and it did
appear to be in the public interest to reacquire the three acres
of bay land. Answering Mr. Adams' question about a marina license,
the Director said when it was land owned by the applicant the staff
did not charge a license fee.

On motion by Mr. Faircloth, seconded by Mr. Christian and adopted
without objection, the Trustees confirmed the sale of the advertised
parcel, approved fill permit for two parcels of submerged land
previously conveyed, and approved fill permit for the parcel
confirmed on this date.

PALM BEACH COUNTY - File No. 2372-50-253.12, Application to
                    Advertise
William E. Benjamin II, represented by Raymond W. Royce, made application to purchase 4 parcels of sovereignty land in Lake Worth abutting
a parcel of filled sovereignty land in Section 10, Township 45 South,
Range 43 East, containing 4.928 acres in the Town of Manalapan,
Palm Beach County, landward of the established bulkhead line. Applicant proposed to use the parcels for single family residential
construction to complete development begun approximately 13 years ago,
to increase the tax base, to straighten an irregular shoreline. The
small parcels are not usable by the public and Resolution No. 11-70
adopted by the Town Commission of the Town of Manalapan approved the
application.

The biological report dated April 24, 1970, was adverse. The Director
said the applicant was caught by a policy change, that he did not
think the reasons given represented the public interest in accordance
with the Board's criteria, and that improvement by straightening the
shoreline would serve the property owner but was not for public use.
The staff recommendation should be adverse.

Treasurer Broward Williams said the work was started in the fifties,
the applicant had agreed to limit the work to the four small parcels
to straighten the shoreline to make it look better. He did not think
the work would damage fisheries, and making the property usable was
in the public interest.

Secretary of State Tom Adams commented that there had been cases where
prior arrangements or commitments or work begun under the Old Butler
Act were considered by the Board, that these small parcels were useless
in their present state. In talking to the applicant he found out that

rip rap would be used for much of the work which would aid the
ecology; also, the applicant would transplant a large portion of
the mangroves where feasible - all subject to staff approval.

For the above three reasons, Mr. Adams made a motion that the
Board agree to advertise the parcels for objections only. Messrs.
Faircloth and Dickinson seconded the motion. Governor Kirk said
he was not going to object, but as a resident of Palm Beach County
the concept of riprap did not please him as it might cause vermin
and flies and collection of debris. When the applicant came to the
Board for a fill permit that matter would be considered, Mr. Apthorp
advised.

Another motion approving the application for advertisement was made
by Mr. Faircloth, seconded by Mr. Williams and adopted without
objection. The Governor said he would vote against rip rap when
the fill permit was under consideration.

TRUSTEES RULES - Repeal 18-031 and 18-1.032
On motion by Mr. Christian, seconded by Mr. Williams and adopted
without objection, the Trustees repealed Administrative Rules
18-031 and 18-1.032 which set forth certain restrictions in
leasing of reserved fractional interest in oil and gas held by the
Trustees in privately-owned land. The two rules were no longer
necessary because of the enactment by the 1969 Legislature of
Chapter 69-369, Laws of Florida (Section 253.451 Florida Statutes),
which broadened the term "land the title to which is vested in the
state" to encompass lands previously held by the state or any
agency thereof, in which mineral rights were retained. The statutes
now prescribe the manner in which oil and gas leases or reserved
interest shall be leased.

CHARLOTTE COUNTY - Lease Assignment
On motion by Mr. Dickinson and Mr. Christian, seconded by Mr.
Williams and adopted without objection, the Trustees approved the
assignment of Oil and Gas Drilling Lease No. 2448 dated July 7,
1970, covering the Webb Wildlife Management Area, from E. M. Smith
to Shell Oil Company. Instrument of assignment and acceptance
executed by both parties had been reviewed and approved by staff
legal counsel.

DADE COUNTY - Lease Assignment.
Staff recommended approval of assignment of that part of Oil and
Gas Drilling Lease No. 1939-1939-S held by RK Petroleum Corp. to
Exchange Oil and Gas Corporation. The lease, issued by the Board
of Education and the Trustees on September 24, 1963, covered
24,830 net mineral acres at Forty Mile Bend. Assignment and
acceptance executed by both parties were approved by staff legal
counsel.

Action was deferred on November 17 due to question being raised
regarding the lessee's compliance with provisions of the lease.
All terms and conditions have been complied with by the lessee.

On motion by Mr. Christian, seconded by Mr. Williams and adopted
without objection, the Board of Trustees approved the lease
assignment.

COLLIER COUNTY - Advertise Oil and Gas Lease
Sun Oil Company requested the Board to advertise for sealed bids
for an oil and gas drilling lease of the reserved one-half interest
of the Board of Education in the petroleum in privately-owned
Sections 16, Township 46 South, Ranges 29 and 30 East, containing
1,280 surface acres in Collier County.

On September 22 and October 6 the Board deferred action due to a
question with respect to the location. The two sections appear to
be immediately to the north of the north line of the Big Cypress
watershed.

The State Geologist concurred in the staff recommendation to
advertise for sealed bids for a five-year oil and gas lease covering
the reserved one-half interest of the Board, lease to require
an annual rental of $1 per net mineral acre, 1/8 royalty, $50,000
surety bond and at least one test well every 2 1/2 years to a depth
of 6,000 feet or to the top of the Lower Cretaceous, whichever is
deeper.

On motion made by Mr. Dickinson and Mr. Christian, seconded by
Mr. Williams, and adopted without objection, the Board authorized
advertisement for sealed bids for lease of the reserved interest.

HENDRY COUNTY - Application to Advertise Oil and Gas Lease
At the request of the Governor, consideration of an application
from Sun Oil Company was deferred. Applicant desired advertisement
for sealed bids for an oil and gas drilling lease of reserved one-
half interest held by the Board of Education in privately-owned
Section 16, Township 47 South, Range 33 East, Hendry County, which
was located approximately three miles south of the northerly
limits of the Big Cypress drainage area.

CHARLOTTE COUNTY - Oil and Gas Lease
On October 6 the Trustees authorized advertisement for bids for a
five-year oil and gas drilling lease of the reserved one-half
interest of the Board of Education in Section 16, Township 41 South,
Range 27 East, Charlotte County, containing 640 surface acres
(320 net mineral acres). Invitation to bid was published pursuant
to law in the Tallahassee Democrat and the Herald-News, Punta Gorda,
Florida, and bids were opened at 10:00 A.M. on this date.

Amerada Hess Corporation, the only bidder, offered $1,280 which
included offer of rental for the first year at the rate of $1 per
net mineral acre, for a state drilling lease for oil, gas and
other petroleum products, covering the reserved one-half interest
in the advertised land.

On motion by Mr. Faircloth, seconded by Mr. Williams and adopted
without objection, the Trustees accepted the bid of Amerada Hess
Corporation for an oil and gas drilling lease under the usual
terms and conditions stated in the lease.

SANTA ROSA COUNTY - Oil and Gas Lease
On October 13 the Trustees authorized advertisement for bids for a
five-year oil and gas drilling lease covering the reserved one-
half interest of the State of Florida under Chapter 18296, the Murphy
Act, in a parcel of privately-owned land described as the South
22 1/2 chains of Government Lot 2, Section 12, Township 5 North, Range
30 West, containing 44.995 surface acres (22.497) net mineral acres).
Invitation to bid was advertised in the Tallahassee Democrat and the
Press-Gazette of Milton, Florida, pursuant to law, and bids were
opened at 10 a.m. on this date. The land was in the Jay area.

Bids submitted were $24,929.71 from Sun Oil Company of Dallas,
Texas, $45,156.86 from G. Thomas Smith of Tampa, Florida, and
$112,894.97 from M. B. Rudman of Dallas, Texas, which included the
first year's rental of $22.50.

On motion by Mr. Christian, seconded by Mr. Williams and adopted
without objection, the Trustees accepted the high bid from
M. B. Rudman for lease of the advertised reserved one-half interest in
the Santa Rosa County land previously sold under provisions of the
Murphy Act.

MONROE COUNTY - Fish Camp Lease
"Alabama" Jack Statham and wife applied for lease of a 0.93 acre
parcel of sovereignty land along the southwesterly side of Card
Sound Road in the SW 1/4 of Fractional Section 18, Township 59 South,
Range 40 East, Monroe County, under certain terms as described on
the agenda. The lessee proposed to rent boats, motors, fishing
tackle, and operate a concession stand open to the general public.
The staff recommended approval of a lease with the effective date
of January 1, 1971.

On motion by Mr. Williams, seconded by Mr. Christian and adopted
without objection, the Board approved the terms and conditions of
a lease recommended by the staff.

BROWARD COUNTY - Dredge Permit to Improve Navigation,
                Section 253.123 Florida Statutes, File 587
A cabinet member requested consideration of an application denied
on August 25 on a three-to-three tie vote from Port Everglades
Authority for a dredge permit for a channel parallel to and
adjoining the Old F. E. C. Canal, and to dredge from Intracoastal
Waterway and place the material on upland property of the Authority.
On August 25 the staff recommended approval, in view of the fact
that the biological report was not adverse to dredging and the
dredging was not adverse to the Broward County Park.

The Director said deferment was requested by a member of the Board,
but there were persons present who desired to be heard. The
Authority desired to improve the canal and prepare a site to serve
the needs of Hydrospace Research Corporation for oceanographic
and pollution research. Mr. Apthorp reported to the Board that the
chairman of the Board of County Commissioners of Broward County
by telegram received this morning stated objection, and had received
the notice mailed last Wednesday only yesterday. It appeared that
notice to the applicant's representative was also delayed in the
mail, but both parties had known of the matter being scheduled on
the agenda in time to be present to be heard by the Trustees.

Mr. Linwood Cabot spoke briefly for the applicant, commenting that
this was his third appearance on the matter.

Motion was made by Mr. Faircloth, seconded by Mr. Dickinson and
adopted without objection, that the dredge permit be approved.

COLLIER COUNTY - Dredge Permit, File 253.123-679
The Marco Island Development Corporation applied for a permit to
allow dredging 2,111,999 cubic yards of fill material from 64.35
acres in Collier Bay. The Board of County Commissioners had issued
a permit, the dredging area was modified to reduce adverse effects,
and after project modifications the Department of Air and Water
Pollution Control no longer objected. The developer would be
expected to comply with that Department's provisions to contain the
silt and control the turbidity, Mr. Nathaniel P. Reed said.

The applicant had agreed to reconvey three parcels of mangrove
islands and submerged lands heretofore conveyed in lieu of payment
for fill material. Staff thought that the exchange of undeveloped
mangrove and submerged land was fair and increased the land inventory
in the pattern of the Collier-Read plan. Staff recommended approval
of the dredge permit.

Mr. Adams raised a number of questions regarding surveys, deed
descriptions that were vague in the original conveyance, and he
suggested delay for clearing up such questions before the land trade
was considered. The Director was agreeable to deferment, said that
staff surveys indicated no questions in the sites involved in the
proposed trade, but agreed that in all the holdings of the company
there might be uncertainties regarding surveys and title to be
cleared up. Mr. Christian suggested deferment for checking the
appraisal. Governor Kirk said he was ready to vote based on the
staff work.

Motion was made by Mr. Faircloth, seconded by Mr. Williams, that
the staff recommendation be accepted. Mr. Christian voted against
the motion, and made a substitute motion, seconded by Mr. Adams, to
defer for two weeks for review of the deed description.

Mr. Jack Peeples, representing the applicant, assured the Board of
the title sufficiency of the parcels involved in the proposed land
exchange, did not oppose another deferment, but asked that a time
be scheduled for action. He also discussed the Collier-Read tract
application previously deferred at Mr. Adams' request, which at the
time the bulkhead line was established had been referred to as an
example of good planning by all concerned and a development that his
client was very proud of because development was planned in a way
to preserve and improve conservation and ecological resources.

Mr. Peeples commented on the lack of conservation objections to
the Collier Bay application, the great amount of work by the staff
that helped the developer to maintain the natural state as much as
possible, the report on use of riprap prepared on short notice at
Mr. Adams' request for information although his client had no
particular background in that type construction; and he asked for
information regarding the question of imposing a riprap requirement
on this application or as a general matter of policy. Mr. Adams
said he would not propose retroactive action that was unfair but in
the public interest the Board should study techniques that would
improve conservation and ecology wherever possible. Mr. Adams
desired deferment to be sure that any action taken would be based
on fact.

Without objection, the substitute motion for deferment for two
weeks was adopted.

COLLIER COUNTY - Seawall Replacement, Section 253.03 F. S.
On motion by Mr. Faircloth, seconded by Mr. Adams and adopted without
objection, the Board approved the application of Key Island, Inc.,
represented by Paul T. O'Hargan, to replace an existing wooden
seawall with a concrete seawall in Cutlass Anchorage adjacent to
Gordon Pass Channel in Section 21, Township 50 South, Range 25
East, Collier County. The project had been approved by the county
and the Department of Natural Resources had no objection.

LAKE COUNTY - Settlement and Dredge Permit
Mrs. Esther Lackey of Flagler Beach, Florida, applied to construct
a navigation channel 800 ft. long, 90 ft. wide, 10 ft. deep, in
Section 37, Township 16 South, Range 28 East, in Lake County. She
had connected two land canals with the St. Johns River and removed
15,767 cubic yards of material, and now desired to remove an
additional 38, 194 cubic yards to be placed on the upland. Applicant
tendered check for $8,549.50 as payment at 30¢ per cubic yard for
material already removed and 10¢ per cubic yard for the additional
material she needed.

Florida Game and Fresh Water Fish Commission was unable to evaluate
the biological resources in the area because part of the work had
been done. The staff made an investigation and recommended a
settlement and issuance of the dredge permit.

Motion was made by Mr. Faircloth, seconded by Mr. Christian and
adopted, with the Governor and Secretary of State voting "No"
that the staff recommendation be accepted.

Mr. Adams opposed settlement, commenting that under the law a
person doing such work without a permit could be prosecuted or
required to replace the material, and the price charged could be
three times the local price for such material. He said the Board
should get tough in such cases.

PINELLAS COUNTY - Dredge and Fill Permit,
              Sections 253.123, File 683; 253.124, File 151
Madeira Garden Apartments, Inc., submitted an application approved
by Pinellas County Water and Navigation Control Authority for
maintenance dredging to minus-8 feet m.l.w., 50 ft. wide top cut,
in two existing channels, and to dredge one channel that same depth
and width and 700 ft. long in Boca Ciega Bay adjacent to Sections
3 and 4, Township 31 South, Range 15 East, Pinellas County. Spoil
placed on upland and privately-owned submerged land will fill 0.69
acre of submerged land. Applicant tendered $75.90 for 759 cubic
yards of material to be removed from sovereignty land in an aquatic
preserve.

The application was deferred on October 13 for checking a reported
violation. The work reported as a violation, however, was actually
performed on upland. The area was originally filled under BDF
Permit No. 70 issued by Pinellas County prior to July 25, 1961. The
biological report was partially adverse. Staff recommended approval
with certain requirements. The 8 ft. depth of the channel, rather
than the minimum 5 ft., was noted by Mr. Adams and discussed.

On motion by Mr. Christian, seconded by Mr. Williams and adopted
without objection, the Board approved the permits subject to the
requirement that dikes be constructed to contain all spoil, and waste
water weirs be installed to minimize silting.

HILLSBOROUGH COUNTY - SAJSP Permit 66-383
On July 7 the Board postponed action on the request of District
Engineer, Jacksonville, District, that the Board indicate an overall
state position on reissuance of SAJSP Permit 66-383 as modified.
At the time the original federal permit issued on February 13, 1967,
the Trustees had no clear-cut authority to act on these matters
within the boundaries of the Tampa Port Authority.

The Marine Bank and Trust Company obtained a permit from Tampa Port
Authority on June 22, 1967, to expire June 21, 1972, to dredge and
fill submerged land in Tampa Bay abutting Section 19, Township 29
South, Range 18 East, Hillsborough County. The permit issued prior
to the effective date of Chapter 67-1503 did not require a biological
study.

The Game and Fresh Water and Fish Commission has objected to the permit
on the basis that the area is highly productive for estuarine
resources. The Trustees deferred action on response to the District
Engineer in meetings on July 21 and July 28, 1970. Deed to submerged
land subject to be filled granted to the company was in escrow with
release of the deed contingent upon the land being filled to an
appropriate elevation complying with local zoning requirements. If
the company failed to secure the necessary fill permits, it appeared
that the agreement between Tampa Port Authority and the Marine Bank
and Trust Company would be invalid.

The staff recommended that the Board officially object to reissuance
of SAJSP Permit 66-383 as modified. Mr. Adams said that because
of the previous jurisdiction of the Tampa Port Authority, the
bulkhead lines had not been re-examined. He and the Governor said
they should be reviewed and relocated. The Director advised that
the 1970 act clearly applied to dredge and fill permits, but might
not apply to bulkhead lines. A legal interpretation was needed.

11-24-70

A memorandum dated November 24 from Mr. Nathaniel P. Reed, Chairman of the Department of Air and Water Pollution Control, recommended development of a comprehensive plan for Tampa Bay and its shoreline and stated that after approving the Marine Bank and Trust project the Department would issue no further dredge and fill permits except where there is a clear public emergency. Mr. Reed suggested that the Trustees hold the line on issuing any further dredge and fill permits except for public emergencies or in accord with an overall bay plan. He offered a resolution for consideration by the Trustees.

Mr. Joseph Phillip Phyler, attorney, made a presentation on behalf of the applicant, reviewing the background of the property in the Hillsborough County Port Authority, now Tampa Port Authority, the setting of bulkhead lines, hearings, dredge and fill permit for the subject parcel, the objections in 1969 by the Department of Interior and state agencies based on biological reports. The applicant had obtained independent biological reports, desired to fill in line with Sheldon bulkhead limits, and would improve a muck pocket now in a deteriorating condition.

Mr. Christian said he knew the property collected debris and saw no reason not to allow filling in line with previously filled land.

On motion by Mr. Williams, seconded by Mr. Christian, for approval, Mr. Adams pointed out that to "no protest" the Corps permit was not the staff recommendation; and the Governor conditioned his approval on Mr. Reed's memorandum to the Trustees. Mr. Conner felt that he needed an opportunity to study the memorandum and would like the permit application and consideration of the memorandum and resolution handled separately.

Mr. Dickinson was in favor of the permit and the memorandum; but he said he did not know all the implications of the language in the memorandum and reserved the right to look at any application in the future on its merits because circumstances ecologically and otherwise might necessitate adjustments.

Mr. Phyler commented that the resolution appeared to redeem the Trustees' jurisdiction with respect to bulkhead lines in Tampa Bay but might raise a legal question. He said the memorandum and resolution imposed a moratorium on dredge and fill permits pending overall planning for Tampa Bay.

With the reservations expressed above by Mr. Conner and Mr. Dickinson, the motion by Mr. Williams, seconded by Mr. Christian, that the Trustees approve issuance of the Corps of Engineers permit provided the development implementation of the plan shall be in strict keeping with the recommendation contained in Mr. Reed's memorandum of November 24, 1970, to the Board, approve said memorandum, and adopt the resolution as suggested by Mr. Reed was carried unanimously.

RESOLUTION

WHEREAS, the Board of Trustees of the Internal Improvement Trust Fund has reviewed the application of Marine Bank and Trust Company to the United States Army Corps of Engineers, SAJSP Permit (66-383), and

WHEREAS, the Corps of Engineers has requested that the State of Florida take official position with respect to the reissuance of said permit as modified, and

WHEREAS, after closely reviewing the various aspects of the proposed project,

NOW, THEREFORE, BE IT RESOLVED, that the said Board on behalf of the State of Florida does not object to reissuance of said permit conditioned upon the declaration of a moratorium on the issuance of any further dredge and fill permits for Old Tampa Bay until such time as a master plan of development has been implemented for the Bay.

BE IT FURTHER RESOLVED, that the development and

implementation of said master plan should be in strict keeping
with the recommendations contained in Mr. Nathaniel P. Reed's
memorandum of November 24th, 1970, to the Board.

BE IT FURTHER RESOLVED that there will be no further
dredge and fill permits approved by the Trustees for Old
Tampa Bay until such time as bulkhead lines have been
relocated and the master plan of development has been
implemented.

TRUSTEES LEGISLATIVE BUDGET - On motion by Mr. Faircloth, seconded
by Mr. Christian, the Board approved the 1971-72 Legislative Budget
as submitted.

SARASOTA COUNTY - Bulkhead Line, Dredge and Fill Permit,
           File No. 253.123-682
The Sarasota County Water and Navigation Control Authority on
November 2, 1970, established a bulkhead line 9,958.22 feet long
along the Myakka River in Sections 34 and 35, Township 39 South,
Range 20 East, Sarasota County. The original biological report
dated March 11, 1970, was adverse and recommended certain changes
to preserve portions of the marsh and mangrove area. Objections
based on potential damage to the ecology were overruled at the
local hearing, and the Authority established the bulkhead line and
issued dredge and fill permits. Objections were filed with the
Trustees.

The applicant agreed to reconvey approximately 8.1 acres of marsh
to the state conditioned upon their success in obtaining all dredge
and fill permits required to commence development. Deed for the
land will be held in escrow for six years from date of issuance of
all necessary dredge and fill permits. If the grantor fails to
direct delivery of the deed, the escrow agent will automatically
deliver the deed after expiration of the six-year period.

Applicant submitted $611.11 payment for 6,111 cubic yards of fill
material to be removed from a 1,100 ft. by 50 ft. by 5 ft. perimeter
navigation channel alongside the Myakka River, and paid the $50
processing fee. Staff recommended approval.

Mr. Adams suggested that the terms as to how the work should
proceed that were outlined in a November 9th memorandum from Mr.
John DuBose to Mr. Dallas Gray in the Trustees' office should be
incorporated in the approval, as requirements. He made a motion
to that effect, that was seconded by Mr. Christian and adopted
without objection.

TRUSTEES FUNDS - Litigation Expenses
The State of Florida is a party defendant in litigation styled
the United States vs. Maine. Pursuant to discussion with Attorney
General Faircloth and Attorney General Elect Shevin, the Director
recommended that the Trustees bear the expense of the litigation
which involves about 40 to 50 thousand square miles of offshore
territory in the Atlantic Ocean which may come to the state as a
result of the lawsuit. The Trustees would be the immediate
beneficiary if successful in the suit, as title to the land
would come to the Trustees.

On motion by Mr. Adams, seconded by Mr. Christian and adopted without objection, the Board of Trustees authorized an amendment to the
budget of $24,509 to support the cost of the litigation from
December 1, 1970 through June 30, 1971, as recommended by the
Director.

11-24-70

SUBJECTS UNDER CHAPTER 18296

On motion by Mr. Conner, seconded by Mr. Adams and adopted without objection, the Trustees approved Murphy Act Bidding Report No. 977 and issuance of deed for sale of a parcel of land in Jefferson County under provisions of Section 197.350 Florida Statutes to Willie Taylor, Sr., for the high bid of $150. The land was certified to the State of Florida under tax sale certificates 6 of 1929, 15 of 1930, 32 of 1933, described as two acres in E 1/2 of SW 1/4 of Section 16, Township 1 North, Range 3 East, Jefferson County.

On motion duly adopted, the meeting was adjourned.

GOVERNOR — CHAIRMAN

ATTEST:

EXECUTIVE DIRECTOR

*   * *

Tallahassee, Florida
December 1, 1970

The State of Florida Board of Trustees of the Internal Improvement Trust Fund met in the Capitol in Tallahassee, Florida, with the following members present:

Claude R. Kirk, Jr.	Governor
Tom Adams	Secretary of State
Earl Faircloth	Attorney General
Fred O. Dickinson, Jr.	Comptroller

James W. Apthorp	Executive Director

The minutes of the meeting of November 17 were approved as submitted.

BREVARD COUNTY - File No. 2328-05-253.03, Dedication.
On October 6, 1970, the Board authorized advertisement of a proposed dedication of 4.45 acres of sovereignty land in the Indian River abutting Sections 33 and 34, Township 24 South, Range 36 East, to the City of Cocoa to be used for a wayside park adjacent to State Road 520. The park was to be constructed by the Department of Transportation. The city had reconveyed to the Board land previously dedicated, as required by the Trustees' action on January 27, 1970.

The biological report dated August 15, 1969, made at the time the bulkhead line was being relocated, was adverse to filling the area. The Director explained that the biological report was made on the entire site of about 10 acres, but about one-half of the area, the most productive portion, was eliminated from the plan. The staff recommended issuance of dedication instrument for public purposes.

On motion by Mr. Adams, seconded by Mr. Faircloth and adopted without objection, the Board authorized issuance of the dedication for public purposes to the City of Cocoa.

LEVY COUNTY - Shoreline Survey.

Robert Wigglesworth of M. K. Flowers and Associates, Gainesville, Florida, submitted a proposal to conduct an aerial photographic survey of Township 15 South, Range 13½ East, on an experimental basis in an attempt to establish a bulkhead line in an area relatively inaccessible by conventional transportation. It was proposed to take infrared, color, and black and white photography and by scientific techniques to locate the mean high water line. The project would be unique as the area was subject to a recent dependent resurvey to which aerial photography can be related to visible, locatable monuments. The position of the United States Government meander line can be compared to photo-interpreted mean high water lines. Infrared photography owned by the Trustees, now in cold storage, would be used for the project.

As part of the cooperative project, the Board of County Commissioners of Levy County on November 3, 1970, agreed to expend funds in the amount of $1,000 to match a similar amount to be provided by the Trustees.

On motion by Mr. Adams, seconded by Mr. Faircloth and adopted without objection, the Board authorized expenditure of Trustees' funds (matching funds) not to exceed $1,000 for the project, payable to M. K. Flowers and Associates.

PALM BEACH COUNTY - File Nos. 2074-50-253.12 and 2075-50-253.12. Applications from two riparian owners, Eugene N. Uvanile and Dependable Enterprises, Inc., for purchase of parcels of sovereignty land in Lake Worth in the Town of Riviera Beach, Florida, were placed on the agenda for consideration on this date. The biological reports were not adverse but the applicants had not submitted any reasons why the sales would be in the public interest, and the staff recommended denial and refund of the monies deposited toward the purchase price.

Mr. Apthorp said the applicants had been notified of the listing on the agenda on this date and had requested deferment. Mr. Adams suggested that in two weeks' time the applicant might prepare information for the public purpose requirement.

Without objection, the Board deferred consideration for two weeks.

LEE COUNTY - Boundary Line Agreement and Land Exchange.

Mr. Apthorp said that with only four members present the land exchange could not be made. Mr. Leif Johnson was present representing the applicant. The Julius Wetstone suit concluded about two years ago resulted in the Court ruling that since the state failed to locate the mean high water line, the Court had no choice but to use the meander line as the boundary line between private and state property. However, in some places the meander line cut across upland and in other places was out in the water. Therefore, the Supreme Court decision did not help the Trustees or Mr. Wetstone, who discussed a proposed exchange with the staff as indicated on a map exhibited by the Director.

Mr. Faircloth approved the proposed agreement and exchange. Mr. Adams brought up the matter of the bulkhead line which he thought should be adjusted to limit the submerged area that some future owner might desire to apply for and fill. Mr. Johnson advised the Board that he did not think there would be any objection locally to adjustment of the bulkhead line.

The consensus was that those present approved the boundary line agreement and land exchange contingent upon adjustment of the bulkhead line to separate public and private ownership; but since only four were present the matter will be reagendaed.

12-1-70

BAY COUNTY - Easement for Road Right of Way
On motion by Mr. Faircloth, seconded by Mr. Adams and adopted without objection, the Board approved an easement to the Department of Transportation covering 0.92 acre of land in Section 3, Township 1 South, Range 12 West, Bay County, for public highway purposes as approved by the Division of Forestry, Department of Agriculture.

DADE COUNTY - Easement for Road Right of Way
On motion by Mr. Adams, seconded by Mr. Dickinson and adopted without objection, the Board granted request of the Board of County Commissioners of Dade County for an easement for public road purposes across the South 55 feet of Tracts 65 and 66 in Section 31, Township 51 South, Range 41 East, Dade County. The Department of Health and Rehabilitative Services approved this use of land in Dade County Sunland Training Center.

ST. JOHNS COUNTY - Spoil Easement
At the request of the Department of Air and Water Pollution Control, the Board deferred a request for perpetual spoil easement made by St. Augustine Port, Waterway and Beach Commission on behalf of the United States in connection with maintenance dredging of the harbor.

VOLUSIA COUNTY - Temporary Easement Extension
On motion by Mr. Adams, seconded and duly adopted, the Board authorized extension of the time limit to June 1, 1971, as requested by Ponce DeLeon Port Authority, sponsoring agency for the federal stabilization project of Ponce DeLeon Inlet. Temporary Easement No. 2326 expiring January 1, 1971, was for pipelines to be used in construction of the North Jetty, and was granted by the Board in 1968 with no objection from the Florida Board of Conservation.

SARASOTA COUNTY - Easement and Fill Permit, File 2378-58-253.03
The Department of Transportation requested an easement across 6.4 acres of Sarasota and Roberts Bay bottom lands abutting Section 36, Township 36 South, Range 17 East, and Section 31, Township 36 South, Range 18 East, Sarasota County, for construction of bridge and causeway for State Road 789, Section 17080-2505. Construction plans were reviewed by the staff, no dredging was proposed within the easement, approximately 1.1 acres along the north side of an existing causeway at the easterly end of the easement was to be filled with material from upland sources placed landward of the established bulkhead line. The biological report was not adverse. The Bureau of Beaches and Shores found no indication of any substantial adverse effects. A fill permit was issued by the City of Sarasota by resolution adopted May 20, 1968, after consideration of the biological report.

On motion by Mr. Adams, seconded by Mr. Dickinson and adopted without objection, the Trustees granted the request of the Department of Transportation for right of way easement and fill permit.

SUWANNEE COUNTY - Right of Way Easement, File 2377-61-253.03
On motion by Mr. Adams, seconded by Mr. Dickinson, and adopted without objection, the Board granted the request of the Department of Transportation for an easement across 0.73 acre of Suwannee River bottom lands abutting Section 17, Township 1 South, Range 14 East, Suwannee County, for the construction of a bridge on State Road 51, Section 37040-2510. The construction plans were reviewed, no dredging or filling was proposed within the easement area, and there were no objections from the Department of Natural Resources and the Game and Fresh Water Fish Commission.

DADE COUNTY - Campsite Lease Assignment
On motion by Mr. Adams, adopted without objection, the Board approved assignment of Campsite Lease 2185 in Biscayne Bay from Frank D. Tolin to Jay I. Kislak. Executed assignment and acceptance of the lease terms and conditions had been filed in the Trustees' office. The present lease would expire on April 26, 1971. The Director said there was an existing stilt-house on the site.

POLICY - Campsite Lease Assignments
The staff requested authority to assess a $25 fee for processing a
campsite lease assignment that requires the same staff effort as
the issuance of duplicate or corrective instruments. At present
no charge was made for such assignments.

On motion by Mr. Adams, adopted without objection, the Board
authorized a charge of $25 to be made for each campsite lease
assignment in the future.

MONROE COUNTY - Dredge and Fill Permit, Section 253.03 F. S.
The application of Wacouta Corporation for an amended navigation
channel dredging permit had been placed on the agenda again at the
request of a member of the Board of Trustees. On this date the
Director advised that there was a request for further deferment,
which was agreeable to the members present. The staff previously
had been directed to hold up any instruments incident to action
taken with respect to the application of this applicant. The
deeds had not been issued.

FRANKLIN COUNTY - Dredge Permit to Improve Navigation,
                  Section 253.123 Florida Statutes
Dr. A. C. Tuck, represented by Mr. Jerrol Raymond, attorney, applied
for a permit to dredge a navigation channel in Alligator Harbor
adjacent to Section 6, Township 7 South, Range 1 West, Franklin
County. The Trustees had deferred consideration at the regular
meeting on July 21, 1970. Mr. Raymond requested that action be
taken on this date.

The applicant had submitted $50 processing fee and $77 in full payment
for 770 cubic yards of material to be removed, as the project was in
the Alligator Harbor Aquatic Preserve. The material would be placed
on applicant's upland and the staff recommended approval subject to
a provision that no spoil material will be deposited on the marsh land.

Objections were filed. The biological report was adverse, stating
that some dredging had already been done in the intertidal marsh.
However, the mean high water line of the project location was
established by the staff Field Operation Division and it was
determined that the intertidal marsh land referred to in the report
was above the mean high water line. No dredging had been done
below the mean high water line. Applicant had agreed to spoil in
accordance with the recommendations of the Department of Natural
Resources.

On motion by Mr. Adams, seconded by Mr. Faircloth and adopted without
objection, the Board deferred action.

PINELLAS COUNTY - Settlement, Permit No. 253.123-423
An inspection made by the Field Operations Division revealed that the
work had exceeded the authorized widths and depths of the channel under
Trustees Permit No. 253.123-423 issued to the Belleview Biltmore Hotel,
that authorized a channel 70 feet wide and minus-7 feet deep. The chann
constructed was 100 feet wide and an average depth of minus-8 feet. The
overdredging was 8,900 cubic yards of material. The Director said that
the permit issued by the Trustees did not carry the dimensions but
the scale shown on the application would have been approximately
70 feet wide. However, in applying to the Corps of Engineers the
dimension was stated as 100 feet wide and that width was in the Corps
of Engineers permit. Mr. Adams commented that the Trustees' office
had "no protested" that Corps permit. The dredge operator made the cut
according to the Corps permit, which was the only information supplied
to him, and the work was completed before the error was discovered.
Pinellas County Water and Navigation Control Authority had approved the
70 ft. width.

The applicant tendered $2,700 as payment for the overdredge material
at the penalty rate, and the staff recommended approval of the
settlement. Replying to Mr. Faircloth's questions, the Director said
that the applicant would not get an after-the-fact permit, and that acti
by five members was not required for disposition of material as that
was not defined as real property. Mr. Adams said it appeared to be an
equitable settlement.

12-1-70

On motion by Mr. Adams, seconded by Mr. Faircloth and adopted without objection, the Board accepted the settlement.

Mr. Adams pointed out that U. S. Steel had not furnished a master plan for development of the area of which the settlement today was a part, that the spoil was placed on an island owned by the firm but formerly owned by Ed Wright, that as a result of litigation the bulkhead line was invalidated and there was no bulkhead line around the island. It appeared that the developer should make his plans known so that the Trustees could work with him. The Director said that was true, Sand Key was also involved, and he would make inquiry regarding plans for development of the area.

On motion by Mr. Dickinson, seconded by Mr. Faircloth and adopted, the Board approved Mr. Adams' suggestion that an effort be made to work with the developer toward an overall master plan for the area.

LEE COUNTY - Cape Coral Survey and G. A. C. Settlement
The Trustees deferred consideration of the Cape Coral survey and G. A. C. Settlement for a week. By memorandum to the Board on this date, the Director outlined engineering questions and renewed his earlier recommendation, but suggested some alternatives.

Mr. Adams commended the staff for their work, but indicated that the settlement should be about one and a half million dollars in land and should be based on 1970 values. He discussed different engineering approaches to the establishment of mean high water lines, both consistent with certain procedural instructions and both sustainable in court; but he proposed that the Board as a policy require the approach that would be more beneficial to the state in preserving sovereignty areas, which would greatly aid the staff in the future in defining the boundaries of ownership.

Mr. Apthorp was requested to prepare such a policy to be considered by the Board.

The Florida Vanderbilt and Park Shores developments in Collier County would be considered next week, about which a thorough report had been made by Mr. Henry Kittleson, Trustees' special legal counsel. Consideration should also be given to developing a master plan for the area from Florida Vanderbilt northward to the Lee County line, about fifteen miles involving about five large ownerships.

COLLIER COUNTY - Dredge and Fill Permit,
              File 253.123 - 677 and 253.124-148
On November 10 the Board approved a dredge and fill permit to Marco Island Development Corp., subject to decision as to the nature of the bulkheading to be used for the project, as Mr. Adams had asked that riprap be considered for the construction.

On this date the application was on the agenda at the request of Mr. Adams. He made a motion to approve the application with the understanding that prepoured vertical concrete seawalls might be used and said he would not pursue riprap at this time. Mr. Dickinson seconded the motion, which was approved by the Board without objection.

The work would be done in the Collier-Read Tract in Section 19, 20,21, 28, 29, 30 and 33, Township 51 South, Range 26 East, in Collier County, under conditions explained in the minutes of November 10, 1970.

OKEECHOBEE COUNTY - Easement
On motion by Mr. Adams, seconded by Mr. Faircloth and adopted without objection, the Trustees waived the rules and approved a request presented by Mr. Bernie Goode, on behalf of the United States Corps of Engineers, for modification of a right of way easement previously grante for the outlet of Canal C-59 into Lake Okeechobee in Section 6, Township 38 South, Range 36 East, in Okeechobee County. Approval was made subjec to the return of the easement previously granted.

On motion duly adopted, the meeting was adjourned.

GOVERNOR - CHAIRMAN

ATTEST:

EXECUTIVE DIRECTOR

* * * * *

Tallahassee, Florida
December 8, 1970

The State of Florida Board of Trustees of the Internal Improvement
Trust Fund met on this date in the Capitol with the following
members present:

Claude R. Kirk, Jr.	Governor
Tom Adams	Secretary of State
Fred O. Dickinson, Jr.	Comptroller
Broward Williams	Treasurer
Doyle Conner	Commissioner of Agriculture
James W. Apthorp	Executive Director

The minutes of the meeting of November 24, 1970, were approved
as submitted.

LEE COUNTY - Cape Coral Survey and G. A. C. Settlement
At the request of Governor Kirk, the Board deferred for a week
consideration of the Cape Coral and G. A. C. matter.

On December 1 with a quorum of four members present, the Trustees
approved the following applications that it was determined require
five votes. On this date the approval was reconfirmed on motion by
Mr. Adams, seconded by Mr. Dickinson, and adopted without objection.

1. BAY COUNTY - Road right of way easement to the Department
    of Transportation covering 0.92 acre in Section 3, Township
    1 South, Range 12 West, Bay County.

2. BREVARD COUNTY - Dedication, File No. 2328-05-253.03, to the
    City of Cocoa covering 4.45 acres of sovereignty land in the
    Indian River abutting Sections 33 and 34, Township 24 South,
    Range 36 East, to be used for a wayside park adjacent to
    State Road 520.

3. DADE COUNTY - Road right of way easement requested by the
    Board of County Commissioners of Dade County covering the
    South 55 Ft. of Tracts 65 and 66 in Section 31, Township 51
    South, Range 41 East.

4. OKEECHOBEE COUNTY - Right of Way easement to the United States
    Corps of Engineers, Jacksonville District, to change the outlet
    of Canal C-59 in Section 6, Township 38 South, Range 36 East,
    lying within Lake Okeechobee.

5. SARASOTA COUNTY - File No. 2378-58-253.03. Right of Way
    Easement and Fill Permit to the Department of Transportation
    covering 6.4 acres abutting Section 36-36-17 and Section 31-36-18

across bottoms of Sarasota and Roberts Bay for construction of
a bridge and causeway for State Road 789.

6. SUWANNEE COUNTY - File No. 2377-61-253.03. Right of Way
   easement to Department of Transportation across 0.73 acre of
   Suwannee River bottoms abutting Section 17, Township 1 South,
   Range 14 East, for a bridge on State Road 51 in Suwannee County.

7. LEE COUNTY - Little Pine Island boundary line agreement and
   land exchange with Goodman Banks, Trustee, represented by Leif
   Johnson. In this case motion for reconfirming last week's
   approval was made by Mr. Adams, seconded by Mr. Williams, and
   adopted without objection.

Further description of the above applications was made in the minutes
of December 1, 1970.

ESCAMBIA COUNTY - Oil and Gas Drilling Lease
On October 27, 1970, the Board authorized advertisement for sealed
bids for an oil and gas drilling lease of the reserved one-half
interest of the Trustees in Government Lot 3, Section 36, Township
6 North, Range 30 West, Escambia County, containing 2.8 surface acres
(1.4 net mineral acres). Invitation to bid was published pursuant
to law in the Tallahassee Democrat and Pensacola Journal for bids on
the underlying petroleum and petroleum products. The lease required
royalty payments of one-sixth in kind or in value for oil and gas
produced from said land, annual rental of $1 per net mineral acre,
rental to increase by five percent of such original annual rental
after the first two years, a test well to be drilled every two and
one-half years of the lease to a depth of 6,000 feet or to the top
of the Smackover Formation (whichever is deeper), a five-year primary
lease term, and a surety bond of $50,000 required prior to drilling.
Sealed bids were to be opened on December 8 at 10:00 a.m.

The only bid received was from the Louisiana Land and Exploration
Company, a Maryland corporation, in the amount of $2,550 cash
consideration including the first year's rental plus a bonus bid.

On motion by Mr. Williams, seconded by Mr. Adams and adopted without
objection, the Board accepted the bid and authorized issuance of oil
and gas drilling lease to the bidder.

ESCAMBIA AND SANTA ROSA COUNTIES - Spoil Area Easement Applications.
At the request of Mr. Adams, approval was withheld on the requests
from the United States Corps of Engineers, Mobile District, for two
spoil area easements, one embracing 22 acres in Pensacola Bay
adjacent to Section 59, Township 2 South, Range 30 West, Escambia
County, and the second embracing 1,390 acres in Blackwater Bay and
East Bay in Township 1 North and 1 South, Range 28 West, Santa Rosa
County. The Department of Natural Resources had no objections to
the proposed spoil areas.

Mr. Adams was concerned regarding turbidity control as required for
dredge and fill projects by private parties. Mr. Apthorp advised
that the Corps of Engineers usually took the position that navigation
was paramount and state permits were not required for public works.
Mr. Adams thought controls to protect the environment should also be
required on public projects and the appropriate federal environmental
agency should be contacted.

Governor Kirk said that action would be withheld on the two applications (File Nos. 2379-17 and 2380-57-253.03) until the Trustees
receive some assurance of turbidity control.

PASCO COUNTY - Fill Permit, Section 253.124(7)
On motion by Mr. Dickinson, seconded by Mr. Adams and adopted without objection, the Board approved the application of Henry J. Kunda
for a permit approved by Pasco County to seawall and backfill an
area averaging 7 feet wide by 57 feet long in the Anclote River
in Section 21, Township 26 South, Range 16 East, where river flood
stages caused by heavy rains each year result in erosion.

MONROE COUNTY - Amendment to Dredge Permit
On September 15, 1970, the Trustees approved State Dredge Pemit No.
253.03-172 to Bahia Shores, Inc., to dredge a perimeter channel
1.0 foot deep, and an access channel, in Big Spanish Channel at No
Name Key. The one foot depth was an error on the engineering
drawing and the applicant asked that the permit be amended to allow
the correct depth of 5.0 feet.

On motion by Mr. Dickinson, seconded by Mr. Adams and adopted without
objection, the Board authorized issuance of amended dredge permit.

PUTNAM COUNTY - Dredge Permit to Improve Navigation,
                Section 253.123, File No.667
Beckham and Robertson Development Corporation applied for permission
to dredge a 200 ft. long, 60 ft. wide, 5 ft. deep m.l.w., navigation
channel in the St. John's River adjacent to Section 40, Township 9
South, Range 27 East, Putnam County. Applicant tendered check for
$185 for 1,850 cubic yards of material to be removed and deposited
on upland, and $50 processing fee.

The project had been approved by the county. The biological survey
report was not adverse.

On motion by Mr. Dickinson, seconded by Mr. Adams and adopted
without objection, the Board approved the permit subject to the
requirement that a plug remain in the canal until the upland
dredging has been completed as recommended by the staff.

DADE COUNTY - File No. 2362-13-253.12, Application to Advertise
Mr. Apthorp said the staff recommended denial but a request had been
received for deferment of an application from James T. Barnes and
Company, represented by Norman D. Tripp, to purchase 1.303 acres
of sovereignty land in Biscayne Bay abutting Section 33, Township
52 South, Range 42 East, Dade County, for use as a recreation area
in connection with a condominium to be constructed on applicant's
upland property in North Miami, Florida. The application appeared to
interfere with statutory riparian rights of other upland owners.

Mr. Williams made a motion that the application be denied.

Mr. William J. Roberts, attorney representing the applicant, requested
the Board to defer action to allow him to work out a suitable alternate
plan with the other riparian owners that might be involved.

Mr. Williams offered an amended motion for deferment for one week,
which was adopted without objection.

12-8-70

LEE COUNTY - Boundary Line Agreement
Jack Windsor, Trustee, represented by Howard S. Rhoads, applied for
approval of a boundary line agreement covering land in Township 46
South, Range 24 East, that adjoins the Estero Bay Aquatic Preserve.
A suit to quiet title was filed against the Trustees by the Windsor
interests to determine the limits of their ownership as it appeared
impracticable to locate the mean high water line. It was determined
by actual field survey that location of the mean high water is
feasible, but due to the sinuosities of such a line rational
development of the tract would be impracticable. The Windsor tract
embraces approximately 5,147 acres.

The Trustees' staff, together with representatives of the Department
of Natural Resources and the Windsor interests, delineated a line
which separates valuable marine biological resources from the
tract, thereby protecting the integrity of the Estero Bay Aquatic
Preserve and allowing reasonable development of the remaining land.
This line would provide a clear-cut, readily locatable boundary
line and would lead to a settlement of the litigation.

As part of the settlement and agreement, the Board would agree in
principle to navigation channels with their location, number and
dimensions, subject to approval of the Department of Natural Resources;
and any material removed from such channels outside or bayward of
the proposed boundary line would be subject to the going rate at the
time permit is issued. The Director thought that any planning or
development of a master plan should be considered after the end of
the litigation.

Due to a dispute between the Windsor interests and the Estate of
Ed C. Wright over location of a section line common to Sections 26
and 27, Township 46 South, Range 24 East, Lee County, action on
boundary line agreement between Windsor and the Trustees affecting
the enumerated sections would be held in abeyance until differences
have been resolved.

On motion by Mr. Adams, seconded by Mr. Williams and adopted without objection, the Board approved the boundary line agreement in
accordance with staff recommendations.

———————

COLLIER COUNTY - Settlement. Park Shore, represented by Mr. George
Vega, Jr., attorney, offered to pay the appraised price for the land
in the disputed area in Section 16, Township 49 South, Range 25 East,
Collier County, at the rate of $720 per acre or $3,800 for the 5.28
acres, plus the cost of the appraisal. The staff recommended
acceptance of the offer for settlement. The Trustees previously had
given a disclaimer to the site in question and it might be difficult
to successfully assert title.

Mr. Adams commented on the extensive investigative work by the staff
of the Trustees and the Department of Natural Resources, by Mr.
Henry Kittleson, special counsel of the Board, and the cooperation
from the owners of the Park Shore development north of Naples on the
west coast in Collier County. The proposed settlement appeared to
Mr. Adams to be most equitable and in the state's interest.

On motion by Mr. Adams, seconded by Mr. Williams and adopted without
objection, the Board approved the settlement in accordance with the
recommendation of the Staff.

———————

COLLIER COUNTY - Settlement. Florida Vanderbilt Corporation,
represented by Mr. Elliot Messer, attorney, offered to settle the
dispute involving land in Baker Carroll Units I and II and in Wiggins
Pass Landings Unit I in Sections 20 and 29 in Township 48 South,
Range 25 East, Collier County, in the following manner:

1. As a result of its investigation, staff determined that Florida
   Vanderbilt's proposed development of the platted subdivisions
   known as Baker Carroll Unit II and Wiggins Pass Landings Unit I
   will intrude into areas lying below the line of mean high water

and consequently claimed by the state by right of its sovereignty. There was no controversy relative to Baker Carroll Unit I. Florida Vanderbilt maintained that the areas in controversy consisting of 4.15 acres in Baker Carroll Unit 2 and 3.64 acres in Wiggins Pass Landings Unit I are not owned by the state but are property of the company.

2. In order to resolve the dispute without the delay and expense of litigation, Florida Vanderbilt agreed to convey to the state a reasonably compact and contiguous parcel of land consisting of 23.37 acres, the location to be selected by the state from any of the company's lands situated outside of its platted subdivisions and located in the vicinity of Turkey Lake. As a part of this agreement the state will disclaim to Florida Vanderbilt those areas lying below the mean high water line within the recorded boundaries of Baker Carroll Unit II and Wiggins Pass Landings Unit I. The settlement will result in the state's acquisition of an undeveloped area comprising three times the acreage in issue located within the platted subdivisions. It is understood by the parties that the settlement will not constitute a waiver or release of any rights which either party claims with respect to properties located beyond the two recorded plats.

3. Florida Vanderbilt, other owners and Collier County are in the process of developing studies for the utilization of their lands extending north of Wiggins Pass Landings Unit I to the Lee County line. Florida Vanderbilt has assured the state that it will not develop any of these lands (including Turkey Lake and the tributary thereto) except pursuant to a comprehensive plan of development approved by the state or in the absence of state approval of such plan, only after a court of competent jurisdiction confirms the company's title to the areas which would be developed. Since the comprehensive plan of development as presently contemplated will be based on an ecological study to be conducted by the Rosenstiel School of Marine and Atmospheric Science, University of Miami, and will involve participation by federal, state and county agencies, it is believed that further disputes regarding ownership may be unnecessary and can be avoided.

Mr. Richard B. Lansdale, attorney representing the A. L. Daugherty Company, said the company as mortgage holder on land involved in the settlement had no objection now but would like deferment for two weeks to allow further study of the proposal. Governor Kirk and the Director expressed the opinion that deferment was not necessary for that reason.

On motion by Mr. Adams, seconded by Mr. Williams and adopted without objection, the settlement was approved in accordance with the recommendation by the staff, with the understanding that bulkhead lines would be established and the proper application made for dredge and fill permits.

––––––––

CITRUS COUNTY - Dredge Permit, Material for Beach Area,
                File 253.123-624
The Board of County Commissioners of Citrus County requested a permit to remove 18,200 cubic yards from a borrow area 465 ft. long, 270 ft. wide, 7 ft. deep m.l.w., in the Gulf of Mexico adjacent to Section 16, Township 18 South, Range 16 East, Citrus County, to place on the beach at Fort Island. On August 4 the Trustees had approved a permit to remove muck and silt from the beach area and backfill with trucked-in material, but that was not feasible.

The biological report was adverse. The Bureau of Beaches and Shores of the Department of Natural Resources approved the project with a stipulation that the sand bag "current trainers" be modified or removed at the direction of that division, after proper notice, if adjacent shoreline property was adversely affected.

On motion by Mr. Adams, seconded by Mr. Dickinson and adopted without objection, the Board granted the permit to Citrus County.

QUATERLY REPORT. The Director submitted to the Board a report of operations of the State of Florida Board of Trustees of the Internal Improvement Trust Fund for the three-month period from July 1, 1970, through September 30, 1970. The report was accepted.

On motion duly adopted, the meeting was adjourned.

GOVERNOR - CHAIRMAN

ATTEST: _____
EXECUTIVE DIRECTOR

*   *   *

Tallahassee, Florid
December 15, 1970

The State of Florida Board of Trustees of the Internal Improvement Trust Fund met on this date in the Capitol with the following members present:

Claude R. Kirk, Jr.	Governor
Tom Adams	Secretary of State
Earl Faircloth	Attorney General
Fred O. Dickinson, Jr.	Comptroller
Broward Williams	Treasurer
Floyd T. Christian	Commissioner of Education
Doyle Conner	Commissioner of Agriculture
James W. Apthorp	Executive Director

The minutes of the meeting of December 1, 1970, were approved as submitted.

DADE COUNTY - File No. 2362-13-253.12, Application to Advertise. The application from James T. Barnes and Company to purchase 1.303 acres of sovereignty land in Biscayne Bay abutting Section 33, Township 52 South, Range 42 East, Dade County, was deferred last week and the staff renewed a recommendation that the application be denied and the file deactivated because the proposed purchase area extended in front of two other lots and there was no indication that the sale was in the public interest. The applicant had been advised of the unfavorable recommendation.

Motion was made by Mr. Christian, seconded by Mr. Adams and adopted, that the staff recommendation for denial be accepted.

12-15-70

PALM BEACH COUNTY - File No. 2339-50-253.12, Land Sale.
On August 18 the Board deferred action for further staff investiga-
tion of the application of Mayfran, Inc., to purchase a parcel of
sovereignty land in Lake Worth abutting Section 11, Township 44
South, Range 43 East, 0.698 acre in the Town of Palm Beach, Palm
Beach County, appraised at $20,000 for the parcel.

The parcel was landward of the established bulkhead line, the
Area Planning Board of Palm Beach County and the Town of Palm
Beach approved the application that appeared to be in the public interest because the parcel was a pocket between two existing seawalls.

The adverse biological report stated that mangroves on the parcel
had been destroyed, lessening the productivity of the area. The
applicant reported that the land-clearing contractor stated that
the foreshore of the lot resembled a city dump due to debris that
had collected in the mangrove area over the years. No dredging
and filling had been done. A landscape firm appraised the value of
the 16 clumps of destroyed mangroves at $1,200 or $75 per tree.

On motion by Mr. Christian, seconded by Mr. Faircloth and adopted
without objection, the Board accepted the staff recommendation for
sale of the advertised parcel at the appraised value of $20,000
and payment of $1,200 for unauthorized removal of mangroves.

VOLUSIA COUNTY - Bulkhead line, Section 253.122 Florida Statutes
The City Commission of New Smyrna Beach by Ordinance No. 800
adopted June 23, 1970, established a bulkhead line 5,061.30 feet
long around Yacht Club Island in the Indian River in unsurveyed
portion of Section 20, Township 17 South, Range 34 East, Volusia
County. The biological report was adverse to any diking or filling
below the mean high tide line, and a hydrographic report recommended
the installation of an energy-absorption seawall.

The applicant in connection with this request for establishment
of a bulkhead line desired to purchase three parcels of sovereignty
land containing a total of 1.37 acres, and to dredge a navigation
channel 75 ft. wide, 2,100 ft. long, minus-6 ft. deep, to remove
approximately 17,500 cubic yards of material. The staff recommended
denial of the purchase application because no public interest was
indicated as required by Trustees' policy; but the dredging permit
was recommended for approval contingent upon the applicant placing
all material upon upland and paying $1,750 for dredged material.

Staff recommended that the bulkhead line along the intracoastal
waterway fronting applicant's upland ownership be approved, that
the remainder of the line be denied without prejudice with the
understanding that the line will be relocated to coincide with
property boundary lines, and that the sale be denied.

Mr. Hal S. McClamma, attorney, and Mr. John C. Gross, president
of Yacht Club Island Corporation, requested approval. The former,
authorized to speak also for the City of New Smyrna, said the
application had wide local support, most of the small island was
privately-owned, suitable for development of garden apartments in
the City, had been approved by the Corps of Engineers and Florida
Inland Navigation District, and Mr. Gross had an agreement with
the contractor doing maintenance dredging in the inland waterway
east of and adjacent to the island to allow deposit of spoil
material. He said the staff had been very helpful but there was
a difference of opinion which he explained further with the aid of
a map.

Mr. Adams said that under the policy of the Board and the new
amendment to the Florida Constitution, the staff recommendation
was proper as public lands cannot be sold unless it is in the
public interest. But he suggested a possible trade of land owned
by the applicant that was outside the bulkhead line.

On motion by Mr. Christian, seconded by Mr. Adams and adopted
without objection, the Trustees deferred action for a week
although Mr. Gross urged action to enable him to take advantage
of the agreement with respect to deposit of maintenance spoil
material.

155

DADE COUNTY - Release of Sandspur Island Spoil Area
On behalf of Inter-American Authority, Mr. George R. Headley,
Director of Site Development, requested the Board to submit to the
United States District Engineer and Florida Inland Navigation District a request for release of Sandspur Island in Biscayne Bay
from a maintenance spoil area easement. Interama requested that
the spoil island be granted to the Authority to be maintained as
a permanent wind and wave break to protect a proposed marina.

On March 11, 1969, the Trustees instructed the Director to take
appropriate action to preserve the island in its natural state.

On motion by Mr. Dickinson, seconded by Mr. Christian and adopted
without objection, the Board authorized request be made for release
of the island from the easement to the United States and that the
island be dedicated as a preserve area when clear title becomes
vested in the Board of Trustees.

SHELL LEASE INCOME REPORT. The Trustees accepted for the record the
following report of remittances to the Florida Department of Natural
Resources from holders of dead shell leases:

Lease No.	Company	Amount
1718	Radcliff Material, Inc.	$ 199.58
1788	Benton and Company	18,954.80
2098	East Bay Enterprises	2,500.00
2233	Bay Dredging & Construction Co.	4,293.67

MONROE COUNTY - Fish Camp Lease; Road Right of Way
On November 24 the Board had approved a lease of 0.93 acre of
sovereignty land along the southwesterly side of Card Sound Road
in the SW 1/4 of Fractional Section 18, Township 59 South, Range 40
East, Monroe County, to "Alabama" Jack Statham. Partly because of
a staff error, a county request for road right of way easement had
been overlooked. The lease had not been issued and the staff
recommended that the lease be allowed subject to the road right of
way easement with the understanding that when the county was ready
to four-lane the road the lessee would be asked to move his operation - which would be a binding condition of the lease.

Representing the Board of County Commissioners of Monroe County,
Mr. Gerald Saunders said the county did not object to the fish camp
serving the public but the road would have to be widened and the
facility should not be leased but be on a month to month basis until
the area was needed by the county.

Mr. Howard Post, Monroe County Engineer, spoke of the serious
traffic conditions along Card Sound Road, had asked the staff to
investigate ingress and egress from unauthorized shacks and fish
camps, and requested that the lease be subject to future road
requirements with the proceeds going to Monroe County instead of
the state and no future leases allowed because of the traffic
hazards. The Director said it was state land, the lease had been
in existence many years ago, and the negotiated rental amount
of $300 per month (subject to certain increases) should come to the
Trustees.

Mr. Williams made a motion, seconded by Mr. Adams, that the lease
be approved on the terms and conditions recommended by the staff
subject to the county road right of way. The motion was adopted.
Mr. Christian made a further motion that no other leases be
granted in the area pending future planning; but when Governor Kirk
asked if that would apply also to Dade County, Mr. Christian withdrew his motion and asked the Director to bring a recommendation to
the Board for Consideration.

BROWARD COUNTY - Corrective Deed
On motion by Mr. Adams, seconded by Mr. Christian and adopted without objection, the Board authorized issuance of a corrective deed
to correct an error in Trustees Deed No. 20851 dated July 29, 1959,
to Arvida Corporation, wherein it was recited that Arvida was a
Florida Corporation instead of a Delaware corporation.

BROWARD COUNTY - Power Line Easement
On motion by Mr. Adams, seconded by Mr. Williams and adopted without objection, the Board approved the request from Florida Power
and Light Company for a five foot wide easement for widening University Drive on land of the South Florida State Hospital. The request had been approved by the Department of Health and Rehabilitative Services.

HILLSBOROUGH COUNTY - Road Right of Way
On motion by Mr. Faircloth, seconded by Mr. Christian, and Mr.
Williams, the Board approved the request from the Department of
Transportation for an easement for public highway purposes over
8.12 acres of land in Section 35 and 36, Township 27 South, Range 20
East, within the Hillsborough River State Park. On December 1 the
Department of Natural Resources approved issuance of the easement.

FRANKLIN COUNTY - Dredge to Improve Navigation, Section 253.123 F.S.
On July 21 and December 1, 1970, the Board had considered an
application from Dr. A. C. Tuck for a permit to dredge a navigation
channel in Alligator Harbor adjacent to Section 6, Township 7 South,
Range 1 West, in Franklin County, for which the applicant had
submitted $50 processing fee and $77 in full payment for 770 cubic
yards of material to be excavated within Alligator Harbor Aquatic
Preserve and placed on upland property. The staff recommended
approval subject to the provision that no spoiling will be done
on the marsh land.

The possibility of a connection with an existing channel on another
owner's land was not an acceptable solution to the applicant. The
Director said the basin site would be inland on land above the mean
high water, but part of the access channel would involve state land.

Mr. Leo Foster, attorney, said Dr. Tuck asked for access from his
upland property to navigable water, such as the Board gave to other
property owners. He cited history of the area and court decisions
that validated land titles in the Forbes Purchase, said there was
no question regarding his client's title, but suggested that if the
Board did question the title he might begin dredging and the Board
could bring an injunction and the court would then decide the title
question. He referred to the staff review and recommendation, said
his client would follow the recommendation as to disposal of the
spoil, did not plan a marina or commercial use, but was entitled
to access to navigable water.

Mr. Adams referred to an opinion by the then Attorney General in
1958 which concluded that submerged land under the Ochlockonee River
and Bay were not included in the Forbes Purchase and thus passed to
state ownership. Mr. Adams was not averse to allowing access but
felt that the title question should be decided by the court.

Mr. Dickinson made a motion to approve the staff recommendation
which did not receive a second.

Objections based on protection of marsh land and ecology of a
valuable biological area were expressed by Mr. Loring Lovell,
Mr. Jack Rudloe, Dr. Robert Livingston, Dr. Andre Pool, and Mr.
Jack Hanway. It was said that the navigation channel was a small
project but it would continue and increase damage of the estuarine
area, and the accuracy of a survey and the mean high water line
location were questioned.

Mr. Christian made a motion that the permit be denied and the
Board ask the court to determine the legal ownership. Then he
withdrew his motion and seconded a motion by the Comptroller
that the Board request its legal counsel to immediately initiate
proceedings for a declaratory decree to determine the validity
of the fee simple title and all of the rights and privileges
attendant thereto of the property in question, and that Dr. Tuck's
application for a permit be held in abeyance for final determination pending the outcome of the litigation. The motion was seconded
by Mr. Christian and adopted without objection.

BROWARD COUNTY - Dredge Permit to Improve Navigation, Section
253.123
Port Everglades Authority requested approval of a dredge permit
from the City of Hollywood to deepen the South Extension of the
Turning Basin in Lake Mable in Section 24, Township 50 South,
Range 42 East, Broward County, for a dredge area 1,648 ft. long,
1,300 ft. wide, minus-34 and minus-37 ft. deep located entirely
within applicant's ownership, from which approximately 130,000
cubic yards of material will be removed and placed on applicant's
upland.

The biological report was not adverse but recommended that the
outside toe of the proposed dike be a sufficient distance landward of the existing mean high water line in order to preserve the
shallow water marine habitat below the mean high water line and to
prevent excessive siltation.

On motion by Mr. Christian, seconded by Mr. Adams and adopted
without objection, the Board authorized issuance of the permit
subject to compliance with the recommendations of the Department
of Natural Resources.

DADE COUNTY - Dredge Permit, Intake and Discharge Canal,
Section 253.123 Florida Statutes.
Florida Power and Light Company, represented by Mr. A. M. Davis,
vice-president, requested approval of a permit granted by Dade
County to dredge a 6,500 ft. long perimeter channel varying from
250 ft. wide top cut, to 180 ft. wide top cut, and in depth from
minus-20 ft. m.l.w. to minus-10 ft. m.l.w., and an access channel
700 ft. long, 280 ft. wide top cut, minus-20 ft. deep m.l.w.,
in Biscayne Bay adjacent to Sections 27 and 28, Township 57 South,
Range 40 East; also, a discharge channel 450 ft. wide top cut,
minus-20 ft. deep m.l.w., 500 ft. long, in Card Sound adjacent to
Section 27, Township 58 South, Range 40 East, Dade County. A total
of 256,000 cubic yards of material is to be removed below the mean
high water line, but only 174,686 cubic yards from state-owned
sovereignty land. Applicant tendered $50 processing fee and
$17,468.60 for the dredge material. Objections had been received.

The biological report dated February 20, 1970, was adverse. The
Bureau of Beaches and Shores recommended a model study and monitoring program of the canalization. An October 1970 report from
the University of Miami indicated that tidal interference caused by
discharge would be minimal but suggested a continuing study while
the plant is in operation, to counteract any unforseen problems.

The staff recommended approval of the dredge permit subject to
the applicant agreeing to the recommendations of the Bureau of
Beaches and Shores. The Air and Water Pollution Control Board had
not yet granted a permit and would have a hearing in February.
Certification from that department and compliance with federal
requirements would be necessary, after the state permit is issued.
The Director advised that a stockholders' lawsuit would not have
any bearing on issuance of the dredging permit.

Motion was made by Mr. Faircloth, seconded by Mr. Christian and
adopted,that the staff recommendation be adopted.

Mr. J. F. Redford, president, Mangrove Chapter of Izaak Walton
League in Dade County, urged delay until many questions have
been answered regarding possible thermal pollution of the water
that might destroy marine life.

Mr. Nathaniel P. Reed said that three and one-half years had
been spent on the problem of cooling the waters from the Turkey
Point Power Plant, one of the most involved and precedent-making
projects in the country, and that approval of this permit would
not affect the decision of the Department of Air and Water Pollution Control and the federal requirements.

Mr. Davis urged approval of the permit so that engineering could
get under way as time was extremely critical and without this
electric plant there would be a shortage of electricity in South
Florida. The channel system that would handle the cooling system
had been approved by Dade County after lengthy hearings, but its
construction could begin only after state and federal approval.

Another motion for approval was made by Mr. Williams, seconded
by Mr. Dickinson. Governor Kirk said approval of the permit was
an orderly process. A number of questions were raised and discussed by members of the Board with Mr. Davis and Mr. Reed.
Mr. Reed made no recommendation but if any problem arose the Board
would be fully advised and nothing would be done without proper
permits. Mr. Williams moved approval, seconded by Mr. Christian.

Without objection, the Trustees approved the dredge permit under
Section 253.123 Florida Statutes subject to the conditions recommended by the staff.

DUVAL COUNTY - Dredge Permit, Maintenance Dredging,
              Section 253.123 Florida Statutes
Jacksonville Shipyards, Inc., applied for a permit for maintenance
dredging in the St. Johns River at three locations, (1) South
Yard in Section 44, Township 2 South, Range 26 East, (2) North
Yard in Sections 13 and 38, Township 2 South, Range 26 East, and
(3) St. Johns Yard in Section 45, Township 2 South, Range 27 East,
and Section 13, Township 2 South, Range 26 East, Duval County.
The material would be placed in a spoil area in the St. Johns River
previously granted by the Trustees. The applicant tendered $50
processing fee.

The biological report dated September 21, 1970, was partially
adverse. A supplemental report dated December 4, 1970, indicated
that there was no feasible alternate areas and recommended that
spoiling be allowed as requested.

On motion by Mr. Williams, seconded by Mr. Christian and adopted
without objection, the Board approved the dredge permit.

MONROE COUNTY - Dredge Permit to Improve Navigation,
                Section 253,03 Florida Statutes, File No. 222
On motion by Mr. Faircloth, seconded by Mr. Christian and adopted
without objection, the Board approved the application of Theodore
C. Behrens for a permit to dredge a 110 ft. long, 30 ft. wide top
cut, and 4 ft. deep m.l.w. channel in Pine Channel, Section 34, Township 66 South, Range 29 East, Monroe County, for which $50 processing
fee had been tendered.

The applicant had conformed to the biologist's recommendation by
reducing the channel width. The channel would be dredged on
submerged land in private ownership, conveyed by Trustees Deed
No. 22808.

JACKSON COUNTY - Transfer of Institution Land
The Jackson County Port Authority requested transfer of 152 acres
of land in the NE 1/4 of Section 1, Township 3 North, Range 7
West, Jackson County, now under jurisdiction of the Apalachee
Correctional Institution as part of its agricultural and timber
production land, to the Authority to increase its land ownership
to 200 acres to qualify for federal financing.

The Department of Health and Rehabilitative Services agreed to
the request provided the Correctional Institution would have
continued use of the tract, title would revert to the Trustees if
the land was not used for industrial purposes within five years,
and in the event of sale of the property by the Port Authority
all proceeds, less cost of improvements, would accrue to the
appropriate state agency. The Director suggested a change of the
latter provision concerning sale to provide that any land disposal
would be handled as an exchange so that the institution did not
have a net loss of land.

Mr. Adams desired to cooperate with Jackson County in the effort
to develop the Port Authority, but in view of the Board's resolution
and the constitutional amendment relative to disposition of land
only in the public interest he cautioned against using the Port
Authority as a conduit for disposing of land unless in the public
interest. Representative Wayne Mixon was not of the opinion that
the constitutional amendment precluded any possible private use
of land, but that the conveyance must be in the public interest.
Based on that terminology he thought it could be worked out.

On motion by Mr. Williams, seconded by Mr. Faircloth and adopted
without objection, the Board approved the land exchange on the
basis recommended by the Director.

––––––––––––

LEE COUNTY - Cape Coral Survey and G. A. C. Settlement
The Board gave further consideration to a settlement with General
Acceptance Corporation Properties, formerly Gulf American Land
Company, in connection with development of Cape Coral that the
state claimed had been dredged and filled beyond the permit limits.
The staff had furnished several memoranda concerning the engineering costs and value of the land in question, that were discussed
in previous meetings. The Director had recommended a total
settlement of $765,303.78 and on December 1 offered several
alternatives.

The Director provided an additional alternative using a settlement
figure based on the 1962 value profit approach, that year representing the average date of sale of lots involved in the development,
as a basis for compromise. That proposed settlement was $950,000
plus $33,800 for engineering costs of determining the amount of
land involved, or a total of $983,800. Mr. Apthorp said the Board
also should consider use of the settlement amount as a credit to
acquire land in the Fakahatchee Strand from the company, and that
value of the land to be received by the state should be based on
the same year, 1962.

Mr. J. G. Turner, general counsel and vice president of the firm,
said he was authorized to accept the original proposal ($765,303.78)
but the settlement was not to set a precedent as the company felt
it owned the land which was in question because of the difference
in engineering techniques. He could not accept the $983,800 proposal
until his company had an opportunity to study it.

Motion was made by Mr. Williams, seconded by Mr. Christian and
adopted without objection, that the Trustees accept the $983,800
settlement recommendation including $33,800 for engineering costs,
the $950,000 to be credited toward acquisition of G. A. C. land
in the Fakahatchee Strand based on the 1962 value of land in the
Fakahatchee Strand.

––––––––––––

Mr. Apthorp had prepared a draft of a telegram to be sent to the
Secretary of the Army regarding dredging by the Corps of Engineers
in Florida.

––––––––––––

MEAN HIGH WATER - Policy for Surveying
The rules were waived and on motion by Mr. Williams, seconded by
Mr. Adams, and adopted without objection, the Board adopted the
following policy statements relative to future surveys of state-
owned submerged land, setting criteria for determining the mean
high water line - the legal boundary between state-owned land and
privately owned upland property. The Director explained the
method briefly as finding some known point on the land and proceeding
toward the water until the first indication of the line of mean
high water is found.

LOCATION OF MEAN HIGH WATER LINE OF
TIDAL NAVIGABLE BODIES OF WATER

1. The intent of a mean high water line survey is to locate the
    riparian boundary segregating sovereignty lands vested in
    the Trustees from private uplands.

2. Any survey purporting to locate the mean high water line of
    tidal navigable bodies of water shall commence at an interior
    section corner, quarter corner or other acceptable monument,
    and shall run the line of survey toward the body of water
    to be surveyed.

3. When a line is run toward the body of water and such line first
    intercepts a continuous line of mean high water, this first
    intercept shall be considered as the proper line to be
    surveyed locating the riparian boundary.

4. The point of first intercept can be identified by a change
    in vegetation from upland varieties to varieties that can
    survive frequent periodic inundation such as daily tidal
    action.

5. The density of the vegetative cover shall not be construed as
    a barrier to tidal action as many species of trees require an
    ample supply of water to survive.

DADE COUNTY-File No. 2262-13-253.03
By telegram Mr. Logan Manders had requested an opportunity to
speak with reference to litigation on certain land in Dade County.
The Director explained that the Trustees on January 27, 1970,
approved a settlement which upon payment of $45,000 would convey
any interest the state might have in approximately three acres of
land in the Oleta River (Big Snake Creek) in Fractional Section 9,
Township 52 South, Range 42 East, Dade County. However, the
payment was not forthcoming for which the staff was authorized
to disclaim any interest that the state has.

The members felt that the matter should be properly placed on an
agenda, but agreed to hear Mr. Manders who spoke of a bill now
pending in the United States Congress, a resolution that he
desired the Trustees to adopt setting forth no objection to the
bill that he said would have the effect of declaring the Oleta
River non-navigable, and an extension of the contract. He asked
that the Trustees' counsel be directed to join in an injunction
preventing any further activity on the land in question until
proper title could be established.

The Director said the only action he could recommend was an
extension of the contract entered into with Mr. Manders, but
only assuming that at some point the matter would be terminated and
the Board would receive the money for the land in question.
Mr. Christian suggested that the money be placed in escrow. Mr.
Manders indicated that would be agreeable but that there was a
pending mortgage foreclosure that included the land in question.
The Director did not think the Board should take any position in
the mortgage foreclosure except to protect the state's interest.
It was pointed out that the Board had agreed to disclaim interest
it might have for $45,000.

12-15-70

The Board was not willing to take any action and directed that the matter be placed on an agenda for proper consideration.

On motion duly adopted, the meeting was adjourned.

GOVERNOR   CHAIRMAN

ATTEST:

EXECUTIVE DIRECTOR

*   *   *

Tallahassee, Florida
December 22, 1970

The State of Florida Board of Trustees of the Internal Improvement Trust Fund met on this date in the Capitol with the following members present:

Claude R. Kirk, Jr.   Governor
Tom Adams   Secretary of State
Fred O. Dickinson, Jr.   Comptroller
Broward Williams   Treasurer
Floyd T. Christian   Commissioner of Education
Doyle Conner   Commissioner of Agriculture

James W. Apthorp   Executive Director

The minutes of the meeting of December 8, 1970, were approved as submitted.

OKALOOSA COUNTY - Bulkhead Line, Section 253.122 Florida Statutes.
The Board of County Commissioners of Okaloosa County adopted a resolution on November 10, 1970, fixing a bulkhead line 976 feet long in Rocky Bayou at State Road 20 in Sections 10 and 15, Township 1 South, Range 22 West, Okaloosa County, to accommodate road construction on State Road 20. All material was to be trucked in and the biological survey report was not adverse.

On motion by Mr. Adams, seconded by Mr. Williams and Mr. Dickinson, and adopted without objection, the Trustees approved the bulkhead line as established by Okaloosa County.

Right of Way Easement and Fill Permit, File 2384-46-253.03
The Department of Transportation requested an easement for right of way across bottoms of Rocky Bayou embracing 7.05 acres abutting Sections 10 and 15, Township 1 South, Range 22 West, Okaloosa County, required for construction of a new bridge on State Road 20. Also, the Department requested approval of a fill permit that was approved by Okaloosa County for filling 0.16 acre landward of the bulkhead line described above. The fill material would be obtained from upland sources. The Department of Natural Resources reviewed the plans and indicated that the filling should not cause adverse effects. No dredging was proposed.

The staff reviewed the construction plans and recommended issuance of the easement and approval of the fill permit to be issued to the contractor.

On motion by Mr. Adams, seconded by Mr. Dickinson and adopted without objection, the recommendation was accepted as the action of the Board.

PALM BEACH COUNTY - File No. 2075-50-253.12, Application of Dependable Enterprises, Inc., and File No. 2074-50-253.12, Application of Eugene N. Uvanile, et ux.

Applications for advertisement of proposed purchases for Dependable Enterprises, Inc., and Eugene N. Uvanile and wife, represented by David H. Bludworth, were on the agenda with staff recommendation for denial for the reason that there was no indication of a public interest. The biological report was not adverse, stating that the land was within a heavily developed area of Lake Worth shoreline.

Mr. Bludworth circulated pictures and sketches to show that it would be in the public interest to have the indentures in the shoreline sold and filled, to restore land that had washed away, remove material to improve navigation, in line with properties north and south of his clients' upland in the City of Riviera Beach.

Mr. Apthorp said it did not appear that sale for private purposes came within the definition of the public interest, and if the applicants needed fill material or navigation channels, perhaps other applications could be processed rather than sales.

The action of the Board was to deny the applications to purchase, authorize the files deactivated and monies deposited toward the purchase price to be refunded. The applicants' representative indicated that other applications would be submitted later.

The following applications were deferred:

1. St. Lucie County - Boundary Line Agreement and Land Exchange requested by Mr. Frank Fee representing Lucie Properties, Inc.

2. Volusia County - Bulkhead Line Location and Exchange Proposal for John C. Gross, represented by Hal McClamma.

MANATEE COUNTY - Town of Longboat Key

By resolution adopted on December 2, 1970, the Town of Longboat Key requested consent of the Trustees for conveyance of "Town Islands" to the National Audubon Society. The small islands were conveyed to the town by the Trustees on November 26, 1958, for $1, to be used for public purposes only. Subsequently, the Trustees denied permits for dredging and filling the area with the result that the town located its municipal complex on an upland site.

An offer was made by the National Audubon Society and others to purchase the islands at their present appraised value for the establishment of a bird sanctuary. The proceeds from the sale would go to the town. An objection to the town's request was received from Argus, a local civic association. Trustees' staff recommended denial and authorization for taking appropriate steps to have the islands, together with an access easement previously granted, reconveyed to the Board and an appropriate no-fee dedication of the islands prepared in favor of the National Audubon Society for a bird sanctuary.

Motion was made by Mr. Christian, seconded by Mr. Adams, that the staff recommendation be adopted.

Mr. John R. Wood, attorney for Longboat Key, disagreed with the recommendation, discussed a plan worked out by Mayor Sam Gibbon and Mr. Myron Gibbons of Tampa, attorney for the Audubon Society, their hope that the Board would join in the town's dedication to the Audubon Society, in exchange for which the town would reconvey to the Trustees the easement strip of bottom land. He pointed out that in some cases other land dedicated for public purposes only had been used in other ways and that the town needed the $50,000, to be paid partly by a large donation. The Audubon Society wanted the proposal accomplished and the town took the position that if it couldn't sell the islands it should keep them.

Mr. Adams recalled the circumstances of the dedication to the town, subsequent hearings and denial of the fill permit, and explained the Board's position. Mr. Christian pointed out that the town had not used the islands for public purposes and should reconvey them. Mr. Apthorp said the town's title was encumbered with the public purpose covenant, that if the town desired to protect the islands they should be allowed to revert to the Trustees with the understanding that an agreement would be made with the Audubon Society, with the State of Florida retaining title.

The motion by Mr. Christian, seconded by Mr. Adams, was adopted without objection, that the staff recommendation be accepted as the action of the Board.

BREVARD COUNTY - Confirmation of Contract Sale
On April 12, 1966, the Trustees confirmed sale of submerged land in Newfound Harbor in Section 31, Township 24 South, Range 37 East, Brevard County, to Florida-Ozier Enterprises, Inc., which entered into a contract to purchase under policy effective then. Contract No. 24269(1749-05) issued, was subsequently assigned to the Oakland Consolidated Corporation, all contract payments had been paid and assignee was entitled to a deed. Staff recommended approval. Mr. Apthorp said there was no question about the deed description, the confirmation was really a ministerial function of the Board, and the price had been paid.

Some question had been raised at the Board's staff meeting and it was understood that the matter would be deferred. Mr. Jay Hall asked to be advised what the problem was so that he could inform his client. Mr. Adams stated that he would be advised.

Without objection, the Board deferred action.

DUVAL COUNTY - Road Right of Way Easement.
On motion by Mr. Dickinson and Mr. Williams, seconded by Mr. Christian and adopted without objection, the Board granted the request from Jacksonville Expressway Authority for an easement across 4.42 acres, in Section 8, Township 3 South, Range 28 East, Duval County, at the southwest corner of the University of North Florida property to accommodate an interchange in the Jose-Vedra Expressway. The Board of Regents had approved the request.

COLUMBIA AND SUWANNEE COUNTIES - Road Right of Way Easements.
On motion by Mr. Dickinson, seconded by Mr. Christian and adopted
without objection, the Board approved the request of the Department
of Natural Resources for two easements 80 ft. wide for a road
through Ichetucknee Springs State Park, to replace an existing
county road through the park area in order to provide better
utilization of the property. Both Columbia and Suwannee Counties
by resolutions had abandoned that portion of the existing county
road that would be replaced by the new right of way in Section 12
Township 6 South, Range 15 East, in Suwannee County, and Section 7,
Township 6 South, Range 16 East, in Columbia County.

DADE COUNTY - Land Exchange
Florida Power and Light Company in developing its Turkey Point
Power Plant requested fee ownership of a 71.66 acre parcel in
Section 32, Township 57 South, Range 32 East, Dade County, to comply
with a requirement of the Atomic Energy Commission for site control.
The company offered to exchange a 72.12 acre parcel in Section 29,
Township 57 South, Range 40 East, Dade County, that has 444 ft.
frontage on Palm Drive, for the 71.66 acre parcel owned by the Board
that was presently without access and surrounded on three sides by
applicant's property and on one side by Sea Dade Industries. An
appraisal of both parcels (FP & L $68,500 and TIITF $55,000) was
reviewed by staff appraiser and the values appeared equitable.

The Trustees parcel was subject to Easement No. 22249A issued to
Central and Southern Florida Flood Control District for canal rights
of way, but due to realignment of Levee L-31-E none of the parcel
would be needed in the future except a small amount adjacent to
the south section line. The District agreed to relinquish its
easement rights if the exchange was made subject to the company
furnishing whatever future right of way was needed in this section
without charge, to which the company agreed.

The staff recommended the exchange. The Director advised that
specific provisions in the statutes relate to exchange, and do not
require advertisement.

On motion by Mr. Christian, seconded by Mr. Adams and Mr. Dickinson,
and adopted without objection, the land exchange was approved.

DUVAL COUNTY - Land Exchange.
On motion by Mr. Adams, seconded by Mr. Dickinson and adopted, the
Board concurred in action of the Department of Natural Resources in
the approval of exchange of a 2.05 acre parcel of state land on the
north side of Hecksher Drive at the western approach to the toll
bridge across Fort George Inlet that had been occupied under lease
for over 30 years by Mr. Allen K. Overall as a fish camp. Mr. Overall
offered in exchange a 28.8 acre marsh tract contiguous to state land
that was a part of Huguenot Historic Memorial. Both parcels were
surveyed and appraised. The 28.8 acres tract was appraised as 22% more
valuable than the 2.05 acre state land less improvements erected
by Mr. Overall.

COLLIER COUNTY - Grazing Lease Renewal, Thomas H. Baker.

On motion by Mr. Dickinson, seconded by Mr. Williams and adopted,
the Board approved renewal of Grazing Lease No. 2308-S for three
years at annual rental of 75¢ per acre with the other terms and
conditions remaining the same. The lease covering Section 16,
Township 49 South, Range 31 East, 640 acres, contained a provision

12-22-70

for cancellation by the Trustees after 90-day written notice.
The land had formerly been leased at 44¢ per acre annually.

SANTA ROSA COUNTY - Advertise Oil and Gas Lease.
On motion by Mr. Dickinson, seconded by Mr. Williams and adopted
without objection, the Board authorized advertisement for sealed
bids, requested by Humble Oil and Refining Company, for a five-year
oil and gas drilling lease pursuant to law, of the reserved one-
half petroleum interest held by the State of Florida in privately-
owned land described as the SW¼ of NW¼ of NE¼, the NW¼, SW¼, the SW¼
of SE¼ of NW¼, and two parcels containing 10 acres in the NE¼ of
SW¼, all in Section 20, Township 5 North, Range 29 West, containing
a total of 70 surface acres, more or less. The lease would require
an annual rental of $1 per net mineral acre, 1/6 royalty, $50,000
surety bond and at least one test well every 2½ years of the lease
term to a depth of 6,000 feet or to the top of the Smackover
Formation, whichever is deeper.

The State Geologist concurred in the staff recommended for
approval.

LEE COUNTY - Spoil Area Easement and Channel Right of Way,
          File No. 2385-36-253.03.
Central and Southern Florida Flood Control District, sponsoring
agent on behalf of Jacksonville District Engineer, requested six
spoil areas 600 ft. by 600 ft. and a channel right of way easement
in the Caloosahatchee River from Beautiful Island westerly to the
east city limits of Fort Myers, for a project to enlarge the
existing minus-8 ft. by 90 ft. channel of the Okeechobee Waterway
to a minus-10 ft. by 100 ft. approximately five miles long.

The Federal Water Pollution Control Administration reported that
short-term adverse effects from dredging can be expected, but
long-range effects would not be significant as far as water quality
is concerned provided recommendations as to diking are followed.
The biological report stated that the proposed sites appeared to
conform with recommendations made during a joint agency field
review.

On motion by Mr. Dickinson, seconded by Mr. Williams and adopted
without objection, the Board granted the request for easement and
right of way.

COLLIER COUNTY - Dredge Permit, File No. 253.123-679.
On November 10 and 24 the Board at Mr. Adams' request deferred an
application from Marco Island Development Corporation to dredge
2,111,999 cubic yards of material from 64.35 acres in Collier Bay
for which the county had issued a permit. The dredging plan had
been modified and the applicant agreed to reconvey three parcels
of mangrove islands and submerged land in lieu of payment for fill
material. The staff appraiser determined the value of the land
and the staff advised that the exchange of undeveloped mangrove
and submerged land for fill material was fair and would increase
the land inventory in the pattern of the Collier-Read plan.

Mr. Dickinson made a motion for approval, seconded by Messrs.
Williams and Conner.

Mr. Adams proposed an amended motion for approval of the dredge
permit provided no spoiling below the mean high water line would
take place until the Trustees determined what submerged land Marco
Island had a valid claim to below the mean high water line and
whether the bulkhead line extended beyond any submerged areas
claimed by Marco Island. Mr. Christian seconded the amended
motion, which was adopted without objection.

Mr. Adams mentioned several areas that the staff should check
including three connections in the sovereignty waters that
apparently were unauthorized, two recent resurveys of Marco Island

properties, and the elevation being used to determine the mean high
water line. The Director said the staff would review the data and
check the accuracy of elevations used.

DUVAL COUNTY - Settlement.
The Field Operations Division, along with personnel from the
Department of the Interior, U. S. Fish and Wildlife Service, State
of Florida Department of Natural Resources, and the Game and Fresh
Water Fish Commission, inspected work done on Pearson Island by
Associated Investment and Development Corporation consisting of
excavating a perimeter canal across uplands and the marsh surrounding Pearson Island. 39,119 cubic yards of material was removed
from the canal, some placed on upland and some on the marsh.

Staff recommended that (1) all material be removed from the marsh,
(2) all material removed from the canal be purchased at 10¢ per
cubic yard, (3) the canal be dedicated for public use, (4) those
parcels of upland lying landward of the G. L. O. meander line be
conveyed by quitclaim deed to the state in exchange for a quitclaim
deed to the state lands lying landward of the canal, (5) a minimum
of three culverts be installed in the existing county road leading
to Pearson Island to provide for water flow through the marsh on
either side of the road, with the size of the openings in the dike
and the removal of material subject to recommendations of the
Department of Natural Resources.

The staff recommendations were approved on motion by Mr. Dickinson,
seconded by Mr. Williams, adopted unanimously.

MARTIN COUNTY - Settlement.
The Field Operations Division discovered an unauthorized operation
by Mr. R. Stratton Justice, Justice Marine Sales, Inc., consisting
of deepening and filling in a man-made canal which would not be a
violation of Section 253.123 Florida Statutes. However, 70 cubic
yards of material had been removed from sovereignty land in Hobe
Sound-Intracoastal Waterway adjacent to Government Lot 1 in Section
19, Township 40 South, Range 43 East, Martin County. Mr. Justice
tendered $100 penalty payment and the staff recommended acceptance.

On motion by Mr. Williams, seconded by Messrs. Conner and Christian,
adopted without objection, the Board accepted $100 as settlement.

COLLIER COUNTY - Extension of Dredge Permit, File 253.123-678 and
253.124-149, Deed 17748 issued September 14, 1926.
On January 30, 1968, the Trustees approved the reactivation and
reissuance of an expired fill permit granted on October 22, 1964.
The Board of County Commissioners of Collier County considered a
biological report dated December 21, 1967, and issued a new dredge
and fill permit on December 19, 1967. A biological report prepared
on December 21, 1967, recommended modifications that the Marco
Island Development Corporation complied with and requested the
Trustees to extend the time on the existing permit. Corps of
Engineers permit SAJSP 64-413 would expire on December 31, 1971.

Staff recommended extension of permit to coincide with expiration
date of the Corps permit, filling to be limited to Sections 8, 9,
10 and 16 in Township 52 South, Range 26 East, and dredging in
Marco River from the mouth of John Stevens Creek to the projected
west line of Section 4. As payment for 3,825,000 cubic yards of
fill remaining to be removed, the applicant offered to convey sufficient land to equal $382,500 in value.

The project contemplated dredging approximately 307 acres of
sovereignty land and filling 475 acres owned by the applicant.
Two areas had been identified, containing approximately 71.07
acres of mangrove islands and 136.43 acres of submerged land valued
at a total of $332,500.

Motion was made by Mr. Christian that extension be approved as

12-22-70

recommended by the staff. At Mr. Adams' request, Mr. Christian amended the motion to include provisions that were included in File No. 253.123-679 on this date (no spoiling below mean high water line until the Trustees determined what submerged land Marco Island had a valid claim to below the mean high water line, and whether the bulkhead line extended beyond any submerged areas claimed by Marco Island). Mr. Adams seconded the motion that was adopted unanimously.

BAY COUNTY - Dredge Permit, File No. 253.123-693.
Grand Lagoon Company by Thomas P. Malloy, Vice President, applied for a dredge permit for two channels. The entire project had been revised to conform to the biologist's recommendations. A portion of the channels would be on applicant's upland property, and applicant desired agreement in principle for a boat basin, the precise location of which would be selected to conform to recommendations of the Department of Natural Resources.

Motion was made by Mr. Williams, seconded by Mr. Dickinson, that the application be approved. Mr. Adams requested deferral for resolving certain questions relating to the recommendations of the Department of Natural Resources and others. Without objection, the matter was deferred.

LEE COUNTY - Dredge Permit Amendment, File No. 253.123-640.
Old Bridge Park Corporation, by H. L. Stamm, applied for amendment to an existing permit to dredge an additional 145,000 cubic yards of material from a perimeter navigation channel in the Caloosahatchee River adjacent to Section 1, Township 44 South, Range 24 East, Lee County. In consideration for fill material the applicant proposed to convey approximately 11 acres of marsh land valued at $14,500. The biological report dated November 6, 1970, endorsed the staff's attempt to preserve a marsh area in private ownership, and the staff recommended approval of the application conditioned upon receipt of a warranty deed conveying title to the marsh free and clear from all title defects, liens and other encumbrances.

On motion by Mr. Williams, seconded by Mr. Christian and adopted without objection, the Board adopted the staff recommendation.

MONROE COUNTY - Dredge and Fill Permit, Section 253.03, File 197.
M. D. Siderius applied for a permit to dredge to improve navigation and submerged land conveyed in Trustees Deed No. 22744. He desired to dredge a 50 ft. wide top cut, 5 ft. deep m.l.w., and 450 ft. long channel adjacent to Section 32, Township 63 South, Range 37 East, Florida Bay, 250 ft. of it on sovereignty land and 200 ft. on submerged land in private ownership. Material would be placed on submerged land previously conveyed. $50 processing fee was tendered, a total of 2,600 cubic yards would be removed, and $70 was tendered for 700 cubic yards to be removed from state-owned land. The application had been deferred on September 1 because of a question raised regarding charge for dredge material.

The biological report was adverse. Applicant agreed to quitclaim to the state approximately 0.29 acre of submerged land to compensate for adverse effects on marine life.

On motion by Mr. Christian, seconded by Mr. Williams and adopted, the Board approved the application as recommended by the staff, subject to receipt of reconveyance of submerged land to the state as offered by the applicant, and normal stipulations as to dredging and filling.

OSCEOLA COUNTY - Dredge Permit, Section 253.123, File No. 501.
Thomas L. Reblk applied for permission to dredge 4,500 cubic yards of material from East Lake Tohopekaliga adjacent to Section 28, Township 25 South, Range 30 East, Osceola County, from an area 928 ft. long, 30 ft. wide top cut, 4 ft. deep m.l.w. The material would be placed on applicant's upland above the 61.0 ft. contour line. Applicant tendered $450 as payment and had modified the

application to lessen the adverse effects on marine life. The Central and Southern Florida Flood Control District offered no objection. On June 9 the Board had deferred action on this application. The Director said the lake was down as a result of drought conditions, was one of the bodies of water to be "drawn down" and the material would be removed during that period.

On motion by Mr. Williams, seconded by Mr. Christian and adopted without objection, the Board approved the dredge permit.

ST. LUCIE COUNTY - State Dredge Permit Amendment, Permit No. 253.123-487.
Marine Science Center, Inc., by Richard B. Hellstrom, requested approval of a dredge permit from the county to amend state dredge permit be allowing an approach wing to be dredged on the existing access channel. The dredge area would cover approximately one acre. There would be no additional charge for material as the 26,000 cubic yards of material authorized under the existing permit covered the amended area. The $50 processing fee was tendered.

The Department of Natural Resources on December 9 offered no objection to the proposal.

On motion by Mr. Williams, seconded by Mr. Christian and adopted without objection, the Board approved the dredge permit amendment.

MONROE COUNTY - Dredge Permit to Improve Navigation, Section 253.03 Florida Statutes, File No. 168.
Joseph R. Harrison, represented by William J. Roberts, attorney, applied for a permit to dredge a perimeter navigation channel in Barnes Sound adjacent to Sections 9 and 16, Township 60 South, Range 40 East, 9,500 ft. long more or less, 5 ft. deep m.l.w., and 50 ft. wide top cut; a 6,000 ft. long, 8 ft. deep m.l.w., 50 ft. wide top cut perimeter channel; and a 2,000 ft. long, 8 ft. deep, and 50 ft. wide access channel adjacent to Sections 10 and 15, Township 60 South, Range 40 East, Monroe County. Approximately 25,000 cubic yards will be removed from the Barnes Sound channel at no charge, as the submerged land was acquired through Murphy Act deeds.

That part of the application pertaining to a boat basin was withdrawn from the agenda at this time. Applicant tendered check for $2,300 as payment for 23,000 cubic yards to be removed from the channels in the Atlantic. $50 processing fee was tendered. Plans and other information relating to a marina license will be presented to the Board when the marina plans have been completed.

The Division of Recreation and Parks had no objection to the project that conformed to a comprehensive plan being prepared for a network of navigation channels within the John Pennekamp Coral Reef State Park. The biological report was partially adverse and recommended location of the perimeter channel on the Atlantic side above the red mangroves. The proposed 8 ft. deep dredging was for a valid navigation need.

Subject to modification of the application to eliminate the boat basin portion, the Trustees approved the dredge permit as recommended by the staff on the motion made by Mr. Conner, seconded by Mr. Dickinson, and adopted without objection.

POLK COUNTY - Marina License, Section 253.03 Florida Statutes.
Lakeside Hills Estates, Inc., in care of T. J. Oxford, Jr., applied for a state marina license for a floating fishing pier in Lake Gibson in Section 25, Township 27 South, Range 23 East, Polk County, for use by occupants of a mobile home park. All required exhibits including $346.50 payment for occupying the 17,325 sq. ft. in the lake were submitted. No dredging was required. All sanitary facilities will be connected to the sewer system of the City of Lakeland.

169

On motion by Mr. Christian, seconded by Mr. Williams and adopted
without objection, the Board approved issuance of the marina license.

GULF COUNTY - File No. 2383-23-253.12, Application for Advertisement
The St. Joe Paper Company applied to purchase a parcel of filled
sovereignty land in St. Joseph's Bay abutting Government Lots 4, 7
and 8, in Section 35, Township 7 South, Range 11 West, Gulf County,
containing 9.32 acres, more or less, to be used in conjunction with
a proposed project to construct industrial and municipal waste
treatment facilities. The bulkhead line will be scheduled for
consideration by the Trustees prior to the date for considering
confirmation of the sale. The area has been subjected to filling
without authorization and the staff recommended that in event of
sale the price should be three times the appraised value in accordance with the Trustees' policy. The Attorney General's office
indicated that action on the matter would not adversely affect
or interfere with current litigation.

On motion by Mr. Christian, seconded by Mr. Williams and adopted
without objection, the Trustees authorized advertisement of the
parcel for objections only.

TRUSTEES FUNDS - The Department of General Services requested
allocation of $61,407 to cover costs of relocating personnel from
the Holland Building, as follows: $4,200 moving expense; $15,359
for rent in Larson Building; $8,990 for expenses (supplies, etc.);
and $32,858 for renovation of the Larson Building space.

Use of Trustees funds for the purpose requested would be an exception to the policy set by the Trustees on June 30, 1970, and the
Director said he could only recommend the amount for renovations
but it should be clearly understood that it would constitute an
exception to the Board's policy. Legislative appropriations from
the Operating Trust Fund already exceed the total of cash on hand
and short term investments. It was assumed that the operating
receipts would be enough to cover that deficiency.

The recommendation was that the Board allocate $32,858 from the
Operating Trust Fund (2-750-0100) for the cost of renovation and that
the Senate be requested to allocate funds for the payment of moving
expenses, rent and other costs. However, Mr. Adams requested
deferment. He and other members questioned such use of Trustees
funds while recognizing that General Services Department had to
vacate the Holland Building at the request of the Legislature and
had to prepare office space in the Larson Building. Mr. Blakemore
explained that he had requested the Department of Administration
for funds from any legal source.

Mr. Dickinson said that funds would have to be generated for
alterations in the Holland Building for the Legislature, in the
Larson Building for General Services, and for a Cabinet Room.
Mr. Adams thought the new administration would address itself to the
problem. The members indicated that Mr. Blakemore could proceed
to do what was necessary and within a short time a legal source of
funds would be decided upon by those concerned.

Mr. Apthorp presented a statement of the cash balance and the
condition of the Trustees' funds, calling attention to overcommitment
of operating funds and efforts made during the year to offer better
protection of such funds which he thought should properly be used

for acquisition of land and operation of the Department.

DADE COUNTY - File No. 2262-13-253.03.
Mr. Logan Manders was present again with regard to a matter not on
the agenda, discussed last week, and the Director renewed his
recommendation that the Board take no action until receipt of the
$45,000 in payment for the state's interest in the land in question.
By agreement, the Board would then issue a disclaimer or quitclaim.
However, Mr. Manders proposed resolutions for the Board to consider
on this date, said the amount of $50,000 had been placed in escrow
with the Lawyers Title Insurance Company at Miami, and asked for
certain action by the Board to clarify the court proceedings.

Mr. Dickinson noted that no new ground was presented. The Governor
said the facts of the matter were clear. Mr. Apthorp, reviewing
the action, said the Trustees intervened in the lawsuit to protect
any interest the state might have, the court accepted the Trustees
as a party and recognized that the state might have an interest,
and about a year ago Mr. Manders asked to purchase whatever interest the Trustees had in the land which was appraised and a
price agreed upon. Upon receipt of that amount, any interest of
the state will be conveyed to Mr. Manders.

The Board felt that no further action was called for.Mr. Christian
made a motion, seconded by Mr. Dickinson and unanimously adopted,
that the Board adhere to the Director's recommendation.

Executive Director Apthorp, having been appointed as an assistant
to Governor-Elect Reubin Askew effective January 5, 1971, expressed
to the Trustees his appreciation for their support during his
past year and a half. Since the first meeting of the Board under
the new administration would be on January 12, he suggested that
Mr. Fred Vidzes be designated as the interim director until a
permanent director has been selected.

On motion by Mr. Christian, seconded by Mr. Adams and adopted
without objection, the Board accepted that suggestion and named
Mr. Vidzes as interim executive director of the Board of Trustees
of the Internal Improvement Trust Fund.

On motion duly adopted,the meeting was adj   d.

RNOR

ATTEST: _____
        EXECUTIVE DIRECTOR

12-22-70

171

Tallahassee, Florida
January 12, 1971

The State of Florida Board of Trustees of the Internal Improvement
Trust Fund met on this date in the auditorium of the Haydon Burns
Building in Tallahassee with the following members present:

Reubin O'D. Askew	Governor
Richard (Dick) Stone	Secretary of State
Robert L. Shevin	Attorney General
Fred O. Dickinson, Jr.	Comptroller
Thomas D. O'Malley	Treasurer
Floyd T. Christian	Commissioner of Education

Fred Vidzes	Interim Director

The Board approved the minutes of December 15 as corrected on page
nine by the addition of "based on the 1962 value of land in the
Fakahatchee Strand." The minutes of December 22, 1970, were approved.

The Board adopted the following resolution, traditional at the
beginning of a new administration:

RESOLUTION

WHEREAS, it has been the custom of the State of Florida
Board of Trustees of the Internal Improvement Trust Fund
to organize by designating the incoming Governor as Chairman
of the Board of Trustees; NOW, THEREFORE,

BE IT RESOLVED that the Board of Trustees of the Internal
Improvement Trust Fund designate the Honorable Reubin O'D.
Askew, Governor of Florida, as Chairman, and, pursuant to
custom, in his absence the next member of the Trustees,
according to the order in which their names appear designated
in the Act creating the Internal Improvement Trust Fund,
shall preside as Chairman.

A resolution proposed by Secretary of State Richard (Dick) Stone
regarding efforts to improve the Miami River was withdrawn from
the agenda for the reason that the matter was considered by the
Department of Natural Resources and a similar resolution was adopted
by that Board.

On motion by Mr. Christian, seconded by Mr. Dickinson, and carried
unanimously, the following resolution was adopted:

RESOLUTION

WHEREAS, James W. Apthorp was appointed Executive Director
for the Board of Trustees of the Internal Improvement Trust
Fund effective August 1, 1969, after having served the State
of Florida as Deputy Secretary of State, and

WHEREAS, James W. Apthorp, as one of his first accomplishments
as Executive Director, did organize and implement an improved
internal restructuring of the Board of Trustees' staff with
the result that the Board is more effectively managing,
conserving, and protecting the public's land as directed by
the Laws of Florida, and the public is being provided with
a more efficient promulgation of information regarding the
Board of Trustees' responsibilities in the area of land
management, and

WHEREAS, James W. Apthorp has been actively involved in some
of the most significant matters ever to come to the Board's
attention, such as the State's (and Nation's) first aquaculture lease, establishment of the State's first system of
aquatic preserves, and establishment of new policies governing
the protection of the State's lands, and

1-12-71

WHEREAS, James W. Apthorp in his capacity as Executive Director did effectively represent the Board of Trustees on many committees, namely, the Coastal Coordinating Council, the Advisory Committee on Aquatic Preserves, the Outdoor Recreation Advisory Committee, the Advisory Council to Bureau of Historic Sites and Properties, and the Ecology Advisory Council to the Florida State Department of Transporation, and

WHEREAS, James W. Apthorp by his example and leadership during his tenure as Executive Director did instill in his staff a high degree of loyalty, respect, and a desire to better serve the people of Florida, and

WHEREAS, James W. Apthorp by his impartial, professional approach to all matters coming before the Board of Trustees did provide the necessary guidance and assistance required for the Board to fulfill its obligations mandated by the people of Florida, and

WHEREAS, James W. Apthorp has submitted his resignation as Executive Director for the Board of Trustees of the Internal Improvement Trust Fund;

NOW, THEREFORE, BE IT RESOLVED that the Board of Trustees of the Internal Improvement Trust Fund, in recognition of his outstanding contributions to the Board of Trustees and to the State of Florida, does extend to him its official appreciation for the high standards he has set, as well as its sincere tribute for his dedication in the discharge of the responsibilities placed on his as Executive Director, and

BE IT FURTHER RESOLVED that the Board of Trustees does hereby extend to him its best wishes for his continued success as he further serves the State of Florida as Senior Executive Assistant to the Governor.

BREVARD COUNTY - Confirmation of Contract Sale.
Staff recommended approval for issuance of a deed for land sold by the Trustees on April 12, 1966, in Newfound Harbor in Section 31,Township 24 South, Range 37 East, Brevard County, to Florida-Ozier Enterprises, Inc. Under policy then in effect, the applicant entered into a contract to purchase. Contract No. 24269(1749-05) was issued and subsequently assigned to the Oakland Consolidated Corporation, a Michigan corporation. All contract payments were paid and the assignee was entitled to a deed. On December 22, 1970, the Board deferred action on this request.

Motion was made by Mr. Christian, seconded by Mr. Dickinson and adopted without objection, that the deed be issued to the assignee.

DADE COUNTY - Dedication, File 2364-13-253.03.
The Board deferred action on a request from the City of Miami for dedication of a parcel of sovereignty land containing 0.092 acre in Biscayne Bay abutting Section 39, Township 54 South, Range 41 East, in the City of Miami, pending receipt of a supplemental biological report.

PALM BEACH COUNTY - Quitclaim Deed, Section 253.12(6) F. S.
                    File 2383-50-253.12(6)
At the request of the Attorney General, the Board deferred for two weeks consideration of an application from William E. Benjamin II of Manalapan, Florida, represented by Raymond Royce, for a quitclaim deed to 8.262 acres of filled sovereignty land in Lake Worth abutting Section 10, Township 45 South, Range 3 East, in Palm Beach County, that was filled under a valid Corps of Engineers permit in 1957.

PALM BEACH COUNTY - Application for Confirmation of Sale,
File 2372-50-253.12

At the request of Attorney General Shevin, the Board deferred for
two weeks the consideration of confirmation of sale of four parcels
of sovereignty land in Lake Worth abutting filled sovereignty land
in Section 10, Township 45 South, Range 43 East, Palm Beach County.

On November 24, 1970, the Board authorized advertisement for
objections only, and objections were received along with several
letters from owners within the abutting subdivision approving sale.
Staff had recommended modification of the area that might be
considered for sale. The biological report was adverse.

The proposed sale had been advertised in the Palm Beach Post
four consecutive weeks and on December 29, the sale date shown in
the notice, there was no meeting of the Board. Therefore, the
application from William E. Benjamin II had been listed on the
agenda on this date.

VOLUSIA COUNTY - Bulkhead Line, Section 253.122 Florida Statutes

The Board of County Commissioners of Volusia County by Resolution
No. 70-81 adopted on November 5, 1970, established a bulkhead line
21,750 feet long along the east bank of the Halifax River approximating the mean high water line and existing seawalls in Townships
13 and 14 South, Range 32 East, Volusia County.

The biological survey report by the Department of Natural Resources
was not adverse. Staff recommended approval of the line.

Motion was made by Mr. Christian, seconded by Mr. Dickinson and
Mr. O'Malley, and adopted without objection, that the Board approve
the bulkhead line as established by Volusia County.

DADE COUNTY - City of Islandia, Dedication No. 23048

The staff requested authority to give the City of Islandia proper
notice, as required in Dedication No. 23048, that the dedication
of 109 acres of sovereignty land between Totten and Old Rhodes Key
will be revoked. The dedication granted by the Trustees on December
5, 1961, contained a non-use and reverter provision requiring the
city to use the land for public municipal purposes, file a report
concerning the uses and plan for using the land, and providing for
revocation for non-use at the option of the Trustees upon giving
the city 90 days' notice in writing. The city had been notified
that the matter was on the agenda on this date.

Request had been made by the Jacksonville District Engineer,
acting as land acquisition agent for Biscayne National Monument,
that the Trustees rescind the dedication so that the land subject
to the dedication might be acquired for the Monument.

On motion by Mr. O'Malley, seconded by Mr. Christian and adopted
without objection, the Board authorized the staff to notify the
City of Islandia that the reverter provision would be exercised
for non-use, as provided in the dedication instrument.

MORATORIUM - Fill Material, Dredge and Fill Permits

Attorney General Shevin made a motion to impose a moratorium on
the sale of any state-owned fill material and issuance of any
dredge and fill permits until such time as the committee appointed
by the Trustees on September 15, 1970, shall have submitted its
recommendations and the Trustees shall have adopted a revised
schedule of charges and procedure for assuring that, when and
if such material are lawfully sold or exchanged, the proceeds
to be returned to the Trustees, and ultimately to all citizens and
taxpayers, shall be as near the prevailing commercial market rate
as it is possible to ascertain.

Motion was made by the Attorney General, seconded by Mr. Christian
and adopted without objection, that the rules be waived and the
Board consider the moratorium.

Mr. Stone seconded the motion for a moratorium.

In the discussion that followed Mr. Shevin explained that he
wanted to make certain that the committee will bring recommendations
to the Board as soon as possible and that hopefully the Board will
adopt a policy raising the price from the present 10¢ per cubic
yard and requiring appraisals on each project over $1,000 in
value of fill material.

Governor Askew said there might be consideration as to whether the
Trustees should sell any material except for legitimate navigational
needs, that applicants might truck in material instead of dredging.
Mr. Christian pointed out that part of the revenue goes to the
state school fund. Mr. Stone commented that there would be many
things to consider when the committee recommendations were reviewed.

Mr. Vidzes advised the Board that the committee had met, that
recommendations were being drafted by the chairman of that committee, but that there might be certain emergency situations that
required consideration. The Governor said that the Board might
agree to grant permits in emergency situations provided the applicants understand that payment would have to be made at the new
rates to be established.

There being no further discussion, the motion by Mr. Shevin,
seconded by Mr. Stone, was adopted without objection.

BREVARD COUNTY - City of Titusville Dredge Permit 253.123-694
                 and Fill Permit 253.124-155
Because of adoption of the moratorium, the Board deferred
consideration of an application from Dr. Kenneth L. Sagrans for
approval of a dredge and fill permit issued by the City of Titusville on February 16, 1970, to fill a 0.37 acre parcel of submerged
land in the Indian River previously conveyed by the Trustees, and
to dredge 4,000 cubic yards of material from a borrow area in the
Indian River below the one fathom contour in accordance with
recommendations in the biological report. The biological report
had been adverse, although it recognized that a reduction of 66%
in the fill area had been made as a result of staff effort.

OSCEOLA COUNTY - State Utility Permit No. 253.03(7)-232
The City of Kissimmee had been granted a state utility permit on
November 20, 1970, in accordance with a policy adopted by the
Board on July 14, 1970. Mr. Arthur Steed on behalf of a number
of local citizens had asked for an opportunity to appear before
the Board to request that the permit be rescinded. He was not
present, however, as the matter appeared to have been resolved.
Mr. Vidzes reported that the City of Kissimmee had agreed to
relocate their power transmission lines, removing them from the
proposed area of Lake Tohopekaliga. As the line will not cross
state-owned land, refund of the $100 application· fee was requested.

On motion by Mr. Stone, seconded by Mr. Christian and adopted
without objection, the Board authorized the permit rescinded and
the $100 refunded.

DUVAL COUNTY - Dredge Permit, Section 253.123 F. S.

Harrell's Marina, represented by Lake G. Ray, Jr., applied for
permission to perform maintenance dredging in an existing basin in
Section 23, Township 2 South, Range 29 East, Duval County, in the
Intracoastal Waterway, to redredge to six and eight feet deep an
area approximately 650 ft. long and 200 ft. wide. Applicant had
tendered $50 processing fee and $1,050 for the 10,500 cubic yards
of material to be removed and placed within a diked area on the

upland.

The City of Jacksonville Beach had approved the project. The
spoil area was revised in accordance with the biological report of
September 21, and the supplementary report of November 13 was not
adverse.

Because of the request of the Attorney General on this date, the
Board deferred consideration of this application.

PALM BEACH COUNTY - Fill Permit, Section 253.124, File 156,
                   Deed No. 24284-1807-50
Arvida Corporation applied for approval of a fill permit from the
City of Boca Raton to fill approximately 0.094 acre, more or less,
of submerged land acquired under Deed No. 24284 in Lake Boca Raton
in Section 29, Township 47 South, Range 43 East, Palm Beach County.
No dredging was contemplated and the biological report was not
adverse.

Mr. Shevin agreed to remove his objection provided the permit
carried a stipulation that in addition to the material in the
subject permit application being trucked in, the Board could be
assured that there would not be a subsequent application for a
permit to dredge. The applicant's representative, Mr. Elliott
Messer, said there was no intention to dredge or require any
fill material from state-owned lands, that the project contemplated
obtaining material from the owner's property or by purchase from
another source.

Motion was made by Mr. Dickinson, seconded by Mr. O'Malley and
adopted without objection, that the Board approve the fill permit
subject to inclusion of a written stipulation as requested by the
Attorney General and accepted by the applicant's representative.

MONROE COUNTY - The Board deferred for one week the consideration
of a request from the U. S. Army Corps of Engineers and the U. S.
Department of Interior that the Trustees join in an effort
to alleviate the problem of unauthorized stilt houses in the
Marquesas Keys area, which lies within the Key West National
Wildlife Refuge in Monroe County, Florida.

There were about 17 stilt houses in the area, some under state
permit. Mr. Christian made a motion to post removal notices on
the unauthorized cabins. Mr. Dickinson made a substitute motion to
defer action to give the Attorney General an opportunity to
review the matter and advise the Board with reference to any
implications involved as to structures under state permits.

Without objection, the substitution motion for deferment was
adopted.

BAY COUNTY - Dredge Permit, File 253.123-693
On December 22 the Board deferred action on an application from
Grand Lagoon Company for a permit to dredge two channels and a
boat basin and perform maintenance dredging in an existing channel
in Sections 10 and 15, Township 4 South, Range 15 West, in Grand
Lagoon, Bay County.

The Attorney General requested deferment for two weeks, and noted
that the dredging of 48,600 cubic yards of material might come
within the moratorium. Mr. Dickinson commented that some of the
members had been thoroughly briefed on the application, but that
the new members had not had an opportunity to study the request.

A representative for the applicant was present but agreed to
withhold the presentation until the appropriate time. The Governor
advised him that he would not be in favor of the boat basin taking
up state water bottoms, but that it might be located on the applicant's upland.

The Attorney General's request for deferment was accepted by the
Board on motion made by Mr. Stone, adopted without objection.

REFUNDS - Murphy Act Deeds
On motion by Messrs. Dickinson and Stone, seconded by Mr. Christian
and adopted without objection, the Board authorized issuance of
refunds to three applicants for quitclaim deeds releasing state
road right of way reservations contained in Murphy Act deeds which
the Department of Transportation did not recommend be released,
as follows:

        $15 refund to Kurt Wellisch - Dade County Deed 1810
        $30 to Herman I. Bretan   - Dade County Deed 1191 & 1427
        $15 to Regional Building, Inc. - Leon County Deed 176

GADSDEN COUNTY - Land Transfer for School Purposes.
The Board of Public Instruction of Gadsden County requested transfer of 28.12 acres of land in Sections 33 and 34, Township 4 North,
Range 6 West, Gadsden County, to the Board of Public Instruction,
for public school purposes.

The parcel was under the control of Apalachee Correctional Institution and used for timber production. The Division of Corrections
approved the transfer provided that use of the land be restricted
to public school purposes only and title would revert to the Board
of Trustees in the event school construction was not commenced
within five years from date of the conveyance. The School Board
agreed to such restrictions and to the harvesting of all marketable
timber by the state prior to school construction.

Motion was made by Mr. Stone, seconded by Mr. Christian and adopted
without objection, that the Trustees approve conveyance of the
28.12 acre parcel to the applicant subject to the use and time
restrictions recommended.

OKEECHOBEE COUNTY - Temporary Road Easement.
The Department of Transportation requested a temporary road
easement to terminate on January 1, 1974, across the South 25 Ft.
of Lots 2, 4, 25 and 26 of Block 60, Okeechobee Gardens Subdivision,
Plat Book 2, at Page 30, Okeechobee County, for the purpose of a
temporary detour in connection with construction of a new bridge
on State Road 70.

Motion for approval was made by Mr. Stone, seconded by Mr. Christian.

During the discussion Mr. Stone called attention to the possibility
of the detour creating damage to the body of water, as projects of
the Department of Transportation in past years had been one of the
major offenders. Mr. Vidzes said that department was aware of the
problems in the area of water pollution and turbidity, and the staff
relied on that department to check on the contractors and the work.
The Governor said he would confer with the Secretary of Transportation on this very valid consideration.

The motion for approval was adopted without objection.

POLK COUNTY - Right of Way Easement
The Department of Transportation requested an easement for road
purposes covering 0.43 acre of land in S 1/2 of N 1/2 of Section 7,
Township 26 South, Range 27 East, Polk County. The required parcel
was part of the Citrus Experiment Station at Lake Alfred and the
Board of Regents and Department of Transportation had reached a

satisfactory settlement with respect to compensation for a number
of citrus trees being grown for experimental purposes. An agreement had been drawn and approved by both agencies whereby the Board
of Regents would receive $900 for the citrus trees.

On motion by Mr. Christian, seconded by Mr. Dickinson and adopted
without objection, the Board approved the agreement and right of
way easement.

ST. LUCIE COUNTY - Ocean Beach Park Lease.
Staff recommended acceptance of a deed from the Board of County
Commissioners of St. Lucie County conveying to the Board of
Trustees title to 3.25 acres of beach property and issuance of a 99-year
lease to the county for developing, preserving and maintaining the
land for outdoor recreational, park, conservation and related uses.

The Outdoor Recreation Advisory Committee on December 18 approved
granting $50,000 from the 15% Fund of the Land Acquisition Trust
Fund to St. Lucie County for development of this property, provided
the title was vested in the State of Florida.

The Department of Natural Resources on this date approved the deed,
and 99-year lease to St. Lucie County.

On motion by Mr. Christian, seconded by Mr. Dickinson and adopted
without objection, the Board authorized acceptance of the deed
from the county and issuance of 99-year lease to the county as
recommended.

SANTA ROSA COUNTY - Oil Lease Assignment
On motion by Messrs. O'Malley and Stone, seconded by Mr. Christian,
and adopted without objection, the Board of Trustees approved
assignment of Oil and Gas Drilling Lease No. 2475 dated November 24,
1970, from M. B. Rudman to Rudman Resources, Inc., a Texas corporation.

COLLIER COUNTY - Oil and Gas Lease Bids
On November 24 the Board authorized advertisement for sealed bids
for a five-year oil and gas drilling lease covering the reserved
one-half interest of the Board of Education in Section 16, Township
46 South, Range 29 East, and Section 16, Township 46 South, Range 30
East, containing 1,280 surface acres, more or less, in Collier
County. Invitation to bid was advertised pursuant to law, in the
Tallahassee Democrat and the Naples Daily News, and bids were to
be opened at 10:00 A.M. (EST) on this date.

The two bids received were for an identical amount of consideration,
$1,920. Sun Oil Company submitted $1,920 total consideration,
consisting of $640 for first year's rental plus a bonus of $1,280.
Robert Mosbacher submitted $1,920 total consideration, consisting
of $320 for first year's rental plus $1,600 bonus amount.

The Director suggested deferment to review the identical bids to
determine if both bids were equal, due to the fact that there was
a variation in the bonus amount and first year's rental making
up the consideration.

Without objection, action was deferred.

ESCAMBIA COUNTY - Messrs. Dave Nelson and Lee Goodwick were present
to make request for an emergency dredge permit in Chico Bayou in
Pensacola. They explained that dredging was required to allow a
gas barge to enter the terminal of the Water and Gas Petroleum Company.
However, the staff had not had an opportunity to review the application a
a number of questions were raised by the members. Mr. Vidzes said
the problem was that no emergency provision allowed issuance of
a permit for such dredging, that the law required the applicant to
secure a permit from the local governing body (city or county),
before issuing such a permit a biological report is required unless

waived by a majority vote of the Board of Trustees, and sometimes from six to eight weeks were required for processing such an application.

Governor Askew said the Board had not been furnished all the information required to determine the full consequences of any action it might take at this time. He recommended that the staff meet with the applicants and make a recommendation at the next meeting.

It was so ordered.

On motion adopted without objection, the meeting was adjourned.

GOVERNOR   -   CHAIRMAN

ATTEST: _Fred Vidzes_
INTERIM EXECUTIVE DIRECTOR

.   *   *   *

Tallahassee, Florida
January 19, 1971

The State of Florida Board of Trustees of the Internal Improvement Trust Fund met on this date in the auditorium of the Haydon Burns Building in Tallahassee with the following members present:

Reubin O'D. Askew	Governor
Richard (Dick) Stone	Secretary of State
Robert L. Shevin	Attorney General
Fred O. Dickinson, Jr.	Comptroller
Thomas D. O'Malley	Treasurer
Floyd T. Christian	Commissioner of Education
Doyle Conner	Commissioner of Agriculture

Fred Vidzes	Interim Executive Director

GULF COUNTY - Bulkhead Line, Section 253.122 Florida Statutes
The Board of County Commissioners of Gulf County by resolution adopted on September 30, 1970, and the City Commission of the City of Port St. Joe by Resolution No. 422 adopted October 6, 1970, established a bulkhead line 3,836 feet long along the easterly bank of St. Joseph Bay in Section 35, Township 7 South, Range 11 West, in Gulf County.

The biological report was not adverse and the staff recommended approval of the line. Mr. Vidzes explained that the line was fixed in relation to a proposed sale so that Port St. Joe Paper Company could proceed to install a seawall.

Mr. Stone said that upland development was not contemplated but rather anti-pollution measures, and he made a motion, seconded by Mr. Dickinson, that the bulkhead line be approved.

Mr. Shevin pointed out that usually bulkhead lines were established prior to advertising proposed sales, and Governor Askew referred to pending litigation and requested two weeks' deferment to determine what effect the bulkhead line establishment might have on the lawsuit. He asked the staff to confer with the Attorney General and the Department of Air and Water Pollution Control on the matter.

Without objection, the Board deferred action for two weeks.

VOLUSIA COUNTY - Bulkhead Line, Section 253.122 Florida Statutes
The Staff recommended reconfirmation of a bulkhead line established by the Board of County Commissioners of Volusia County by Resolution No. 70-88 adopted November 19, 1970, for the City of Daytona Beach in the Halifax River abutting upland in Section 39, Township 15 South, Range 33 East, in Volusia County.

On October 27 the Trustees approved the county's Resolution No. 70-78 establishing a bulkhead within the small craft harbor. Questions raised at the meeting concerning legality of the establishment of the line were resolved, as the line was properly advertised and the public hearing properly held.

On motion by Mr. Christian, seconded and adopted unanimously, the Board reconfirmed approval of the bulkhead line.

INDIAN RIVER COUNTY - File No. 2386-31-253.12 Application for Sale
In order to clear land title, Robert F. Lloyd representing the Estate of W. G. Bosworth, deceased, applied to purchase a parcel of filled sovereignty land in the Indian River abutting Section 8, Township 31 South, Range 39 East, 0.5 acre in Indian River County, for $100. The parcel was landward of the bulkhead line approved by the Trustees on November 24, 1970, and the staff recommended advertisement for objections only.

Monies from the estate were to be distributed to certain heirs and to two state universities. Governor Askew said the state should receive the full value if the land is sold. Mr. Dickinson agreed and asked that the Attorney General be fully informed in this matter.

Motion was made by Mr. Dickinson, seconded by Mr. Christian and adopted without objection, that the land be advertised for objections only with the understanding that the land will not be sold for less than the full value. The staff would secure an appraisal.

ST. LUCIE COUNTY - Boundary Line Agreement, Land Exchange
Lucie Properties, Inc., represented by Frank Fee, applied for a boundary line agreement and land exchange affecting land in and abutting Government Lots 1 and 2, Section 22, and Government Lot 2 in Section 23, in Township 34 South, Range 40 East, St. Lucie County. The lots had been granted to the state pursuant to the Swamp Land Grant, were conveyed by the Trustees to William L. Moor by Deed No. 14726 dated September 22, 1892, and the original government surveys of the area did not accurately reflect the true configuration of existing land. Meander lines cross over sovereignty land and swamp land which caused title to be clouded.

So that marketable title might be procured, the applicant desired to exchange four parcels containing 46.4 acres including open water areas, for three parcels containing 52.4 acres. The exchange would block up the applicant's holdings and eliminate any interest in contiguous swamp and sovereignty lands. The staff appraiser had reviewed the proposal and an appraisal submitted by the applicant, and had determined that an equitable exchange would be the payment of $10,925 plus transfer of the four parcels containing 46.4 acres to the Trustees. The applicant's appraiser developed two valuations, (1) assigning a value of $41,475 for the applicant's interest and (2) assigning two values for the Trustees' interest, one $52,400 and the other $38,000. This appraiser concluded by stating: "... it appears to this appraiser that it would be equitable to exchange the properties with no monetary considerations from either party."

1-19-71

The boundary line would be the metes and bounds traverse of the outside toe of the existing mosquito control dike that encompasses the entire tract.

The Trustees deferred action on December 22. On January 12 this application was placed on the advance agenda for consideration on this date. The Director had received a request from a member of the Board for deferment, but had not been able to advise the applicant's representative who was present.

Mr. Fee discussed the problems caused by the old survey not agreeing with the true ground conditions. He said the land exchange would be in the interest of the state and the citizens, that all parties should have their property lines established, and the approach to the valuations was fair in his opinion.

Mr. Stone had asked the Attorney General for an opinion on whether such a procedure, an exchange of land, should be advertised. Mr. Shevin advised the Board that he saw no difference in a consideration of money or of land when a sale was made, and he thought the Board should adopt a policy that any exchange of land be treated as a sale requiring a biological report and advertising for objections. The Governor shared in the concern that an exchange that was in effect a sale be advertised, but in some instances it was settling a boundary dispute and he suggested the policy be prepared in writing in order to take everything into consideration.

The Board postponed action on the policy change pending preparation of a written policy for the consideration of the members. The Comptroller pointed out that there was a different statutory procedure for exchanges than for sales and the Attorney General might want to call to the attention of the Legislature any new policy regulations that might require statutory changes.

The Governor thanked Mr. Fee for explaining the application, also deferred by the above action.

PALM BEACH COUNTY - Marina License, Section 253.03 Florida Statutes
On motion by Mr. Stone, seconded by Mr. Dickinson and adopted without objection, the Board approved the application of Bay Park Towers, Inc., represented by James D. Carlton Registered Engineers and Sand Surveyors, for a marina license for construction of a fishing and mooring facility over 4,041 square feet in Lake Worth adjacent to applicant's upland in Section 34, Township 43 South, Range 43 East, Palm Beach County, for the minimum annual fee of $100.

DADE COUNTY - Marina License, Section 253.03 Florida Statutes
On motion by Mr. Dickinson, seconded by Mr. Conner and adopted without objection, the Board approved the application of Whitehouse Inn and Boatel, represented by Clayton and Dufficy, for a state marina license for installation of mooring facilities occupying 5,383 square feet in Biscayne Bay adjacent to upland in Section 28, Township 52 South, Range 42 East, Dade County, for the annual fee of $107.66.

COMMERCIAL DOCK PERMITS - Time Extension
On motion by Mr. Dickinson, seconded by Mr. Christian and adopted without objection, the Board granted time extension of 180 days for each of the following state commercial dock permits for the reason that construction was delayed due to delay in obtaining permits from the United States Army Corps of Engineers:

Martin County - Permit No. CD-1688 issued April 14, 1970, to Henry Crane, 904 South Dixie Highway, Stuart, Florida.

Sarasota County - Permit No. CD-1751 issued June 18, 1970, to Fisherman's Cove, Inc., 1549 State Street, Sarasota, Florida.

PALM BEACH COUNTY - Marina License, Section 253.03 Florida Statutes
City Manager Carl L. Kopp, for the City of Lake Worth, applied for

a state marina license for the replacement and extension of a
public fishing pier existing in the Atlantic Ocean abutting
upland in Section 26, Township 44 South, Range 43 East, Palm Beach
County. The new structure will occupy about 21,600 square feet
of submerged land. The Department of Air and Water Pollution Control
had no objections to the project.

On motion by Mr. Dickinson, seconded by Mr. Stone and adopted without objection, the Board approved issuance of state marina license
for the public facility without fee.

VOLUSIA COUNTY - Bulkhead Line Location, Yacht Club Island,
       and Exchange Proposal
At the request of a member of the Board of Trustees, action was
deferred on the application of John C. Gross of New Smyrna Beach,
represented by Hal McClamma, for a bulkhead line, purchase and dredge
proposal.

BAY COUNTY - Dredge Permit, File No. 253.123-697
Tyndall Air Force Base, Panama City, Florida, requested approval of
a dredge permit issued by Bay County for maintenance dredging of
six sites in St. Andrews Bay and Sound, Sites 1-5 in Section 18,
Township 6 South, Range 12 West, for a Life Support School, and
Site 6 in an existing marina in Section 33, Township 4 South,
Range 14 West, Bay County. A total of 15,100 cubic yards of
material would be removed and placed on upland. The Bureau of
Beaches and Shores did not object, but the biological report was
adverse as to dredging in Sites 2,3,4 and 5.

The staff thought the application might fall within hardship provisions of the dredging moratorium. Mr. Shevin felt that it was
an exception because the federal government did not pay for the
material and the moratorium was for the purpose of fixing appropriate
prices for fill material. He had some questions about the location
and would probably vote against such an application if it was
not from the federal government. The Governor said it was for a
public purpose.

On motion by Mr. Dickinson, seconded by Mr. Christian and adopted
without objection, the Board approved the dredge permit.

MANATEE COUNTY - Dredge Permit Amendment, File 253.123-456
The Staff recommended reinstatement and amendment of an existing permit to Suncoast Realty by relocating the navigation channel closer
to the shoreline, eliminating the need for a temporary spoil site.
Payment of $120 was tendered for an additional 1,200 cubic yards
of material to be excavated.

On October 27, 1970, the permittee's dredging permit was temporarily
suspended on the basis that a violation had been reported. Subsequent
field investigation showed that the navigation channel had been
completed in accordance with conditions contained in the permit.
However due to limited capabilities of the earth-moving equipment,
spoil was temporarily placed on an unauthorized site. If the application had been properly filed to indicate a temporary spoil site,
no violation would have occurred.

The Governor noted that the firm would pay one dollar per yard for
the material placed on the unauthorized spoil area and would pay
for additional fill at the price to be determined. He asked for
a letter accepting those two provisions. Mr. William J. Roberts,
agent for the applicant firm, said the penalty provision was
accepted and requested permission to complete the remaining 100
ft. of the 2,000 ft. long channel on a hardship basis.

Motion was made by Mr. Stone, seconded by Mr. O'Malley and adopted,
that reinstatement and amendment of the permit be approved subject
to receipt of check for the penalty payment and a letter further
agreeing to the new charge for the additional fill material.

BREVARD COUNTY - Mosquito Control Project C-12A

On motion by Mr. Dickinson, seconded by Mr. Conner and adopted
without objection, the Board approved the application from Brevard
Mosquito Control District to impound 110 acres of state-owned
island marsh in the Banana River in Section 16 and 21, Township
25 South, Range 37 East, Brevard County. A perimeter dike would
be constructed for water improvement purposes. The Department of
Natural Resources and the Game and Fresh Water Fish Commission
concurred in the project.

RECLAIMED LAKE BOTTOM LANDS
The Interim Executive Director recommended adoption of the policy
for administration and management of reclaimed lake bottom lands
that was adopted on January 20, 1970, providing that the Board
of Trustees may sell or otherwise dispose of reclaimed lake bottoms
if determined not to be contrary to the public interest, each
application to be considered on its own merits and no application
to be entertained until a specific contour or other acceptable
boundary line representing the new, permanently lowered ordinary
high water level shall have been determined and approved by the
Trustees. By memorandum dated January 11, 1971, Mr. Vidzes had
explained his recommendation to use this policy for reclaimed lake
bottoms rather than the policy "... that no further sales of
state-owned land will take place unless the applicant for the
sale can affirmatively demonstrate that same would be in the
public interest..." The House Joint Resolution No. 792 stated
in part: "The title to lands under navigable waters ... is held
by the state, by virtue of its sovereignty, in trust for all
the people. Sale of such lands may be authorized by law, but
only when in the public interest."

Since reclaimed lake bottom lands were no longer under navigable
waters, and in October 1970 the Board had considered some applications for reclaimed Lake Okeechobee land and it was difficult to
define the public interest regarding those applications, the Board
had directed the staff to review its recommendations based upon
existing mitigating circumstances and to dispose of other pending
applications in the area accordingly. Such reclaimed lake bottoms
existed as a result of lowered levels of certain other lakes in
Florida. Also Mr. Vidzes said the staff would continue to check
with Central and Southern Florida Flood Control District, Southwest Water Management District, local county commissions, as
well as the Department of Natural Resources before recommending
a sale of reclaimed lake bottom lands.

Mr. Stone said his interpretation of the legislative intent was
that "in the public interest" should apply to all lands. Mr. O'Malley
thought the public interest could be demonstrated for such cases
without restriction to the criteria of health, safety and welfare.
The Governor pointed out that it was not easy to determine what
was clearly in the public interest, that there was a question as
to whether reclaimed lands should be in the same category as
sovereignty lands, and he saw no harm in using the policy of
"not contrary to the public interest" which was strong in itself.

Mr. Christian moved the adoption of the Director's recommendation.
Mr. Conner seconded the motion, commenting that such sales did not
do violence to the Board's policy. Mr. Dickinson agreed, stating
that the public interest was still the paramount test and each sale
would have to come to the Board for consideration and protection of
the public interest.

Mr. Stone requested two weeks' deferment to try to prepare reasonable
guidelines of what is in the public interest in this circumstance
rather than to adopt the former policy of not contrary to the
public interest. Without objection, the deferment was ordered.

MONROE COUNTY - Stilt Houses in Marquesas Keys
On motion by Mr. Christian, seconded by Mr. Dickinson and adopted
without objection, the Board of Trustees agreed to join with the
United States Army Corps of Engineers and Department of the
Interior, Bureau of Sport Fisheries and Wildlife, in posting

removal notices on unauthorized stilt houses in the Marquesas Keys area lying within the Key West National Wildlife Refuge in Monroe County as established on August 8, 1908, by Executive Order 923 signed by President Theodore Roosevelt. The Bureau was concerned that the proliferation of stilt cabins might ultimately have an adverse effect on the Refuge.

COLLIER COUNTY - Oil and Gas Lease Bids
On motion by Mr. Conner, seconded by Messrs Christian and O'Malley, the Trustees rejected the two bids received last week in response to an invitation to bid for a five-year oil and gas lease covering the reserved one-half interest of the Board of Education in Section 16, Township 46 South, Range 29 East, and Section 16, Township 46 South, Range 30 East, Collier County. Sun Oil Company and Robert Mosbacher each submitted a consideration of $1,920, with a variation in the bonus amount and first year's rental making up the total consideration amount. Staff legal counsel recommended rejection and readvertisement.

The Board authorized the staff to readvertise for new bids.

LEE COUNTY - Spoil Areas
The City of Fort Myers by Resolution No. 70-36 adopted on December 21, 1970, requested concurrence in granting of easements by the city to the U. S. Corps of Engineers for spoil areas and channel right of way in the Caloosahatchee River (Okeechobee Waterway) in Lee County. The land was granted to the City by act of the Legislature June 2, 1915. The Board of Trustees on December 22, 1970, approved spoil areas and channel right of way in connection with the project.

On motion by Mr. Christian, seconded by Mr. O'Malley and adopted without objection, the Board of Trustees concurred in the action of the City of Fort Myers.

QUARTERLY REPORT - For the Record
On motion by Mr. Conner, seconded by Mr. Dickinson and adopted without objection, the Board accepted the report of operations of the State of Florida Board of Trustees of the Internal Improvement Trust Fund for the three-month period from October 1, 1970, through December 30, 1970.

SHELL LEASE INCOME REPORT - The Board accepted for the record the following report of remittances to the Florida Department of Natural Resources from holders of dead shell leases:

Lease No.	Company	Amount
1718	Radcliff Material, Inc.	$ 304.20
1788	Benton and Company, Inc.	19,901.01
2233	Bay Dredging & Construction Co.	4,280.57

Governor Askew recommended that Mr. Fred Vidzes be given the salary of the Director during the time he is serving as acting director, retroactive from the time he assumed that responsibility.

On motion by Mr. Stone, adopted without objection, it was so ordered.

On motion duly adopted, the meeting was adjourned.

GOVERNOR   -   CHAIRMAN

ATTEST: Fred Vidzes
INTERIM EXECUTIVE DIRECTOR

1-19-71

Tallahassee, Florida
January 26, 1971

The State of Florida Board of Trustees of the Internal Improvement
Trust Fund met on this date in the auditorium of the Haydon Burns
Building in Tallahassee with the following members present:

Reubin O'D. Askew	Governor
Richard (Dick) Stone	Secretary of State
Robert L. Shevin	Attorney General
Fred O. Dickinson, Jr.	Comptroller
Thomas D. O'Malley	Treasurer
Floyd T. Christian	Commissioner of Education

Fred Vidzes	Interim Executive Director

The Trustees approved the minutes of January 12, 1971, and approved
correction of the minutes of December 8, 1970, consisting of
deletion of "with the understanding that bulkhead lines would be
established and the proper applications made for dredge and fill
permits" from the Collier County-Park Shore settlement minutes
and inserting that quoted portion in the Collier County-Florida
Vanderbilt Corporation minutes.

BAY COUNTY - Dredge Permit, File No. 253.123-693
The Grand Lagoon Company, Panama City, Florida, applied for
a permit to dredge two navigation channels, perform maintenance
dredging in an existing channel, and dredge a boat basin 200
ft. wide, 1,250 ft. long, 5 ft. deep, in Sections 10 and 15,
Township 4 South, Range 15 West, in Grand Lagoon, Bay County.
The applicant tendered $50 processing fee and payment for 48,600
cubic yards of material to be removed and placed on upland property.

A marina license would be applied for at a later date for approximately 4.38 acres for an annual fee of about $4,207.

The project had been modified to diminish adverse effects on
marine life. The biological report for the revised application
indicated scattered growths of turtle grass and some Cuban
shoalweed in the basin and channel areas, and while the new location of the boat basin contained less vegetation it still would
not be in the best interests of marine conservation. The Trustees'
staff recommended approval of the dredge permit.

Governor Askew suggested that the boat basin be located on upland property of the applicant. Mr. Shevin objected to that part
of the application as the biological report was adverse as to
the boat basin.

Senator Dempsey J. Barron said that digging into the bank to
create the basin could create an erosion problem, impair the
aesthetic plan, and cause additional expense and delay of a project on which the applicant had tried to comply with every request
of the government.

He said the area was explicity excluded from the aquatic preserve
and the project was completely endorsed by all local governing
bodies and other local groups. He filed a number of resolutions
in favor of the application with the Trustees.

Treasurer O'Malley had obtained information from many in Bay
County and found unanimous endorsement of the application. He
made a motion that the dredge permit be approved with the
additional requirement that the applicant post the necessary security
bond to guarantee payment for the fill material at the rate to be

established. Mr. Dickinson seconded the motion.

At the Governor's suggestion, a vote was taken only on adoption of the surety bond requirement. Without objection, on motion by Mr. O'Malley, seconded by Mr. Dickinson, the Board adopted that requirement.

Attorney General Shevin recommended amendment of the dredge permit by inserting the provision that the boat basin must be on the owner's upland pursuant to the recommendation of the Department of Natural Resources. Mr. Christian seconded that amendment.

Mr. Stone suggested deferment for obtaining further information and recommendations with respect to the possibility of erosion and a stagnant pocket being caused by digging the basin into the upland. He read a letter from Mr. John Robert Middlemas stating that the project was well-planned in close cooperation with the staff recommendations, and the proposed marina area was not as valuable as typical shallow submerged flats because of previous extensive dredging.

The Governor was concerned but also recognized that each case should be decided on its merits, and wanted to be sure that erosion and stagnant pocket problems would not be created. He felt it would be helpful in the future to have a rule requiring use of the upland for marinas.

Previous motion for approval of the dredge permit was withdrawn and the Treasurer's motion for two weeks' deferment was adopted.

———————

The Following action was taken by the Cabinet as the Department of General Services, and then as the Board of Trustees of the Internal Improvement Trust Fund:

TRUSTEES' FUNDS. Without objection the rules were waived, and the Comptroller made a motion, seconded by the Secretary of State and adopted without objection, that for the purpose of necessary repairs to the Capitol building, an amount not to exceed $100,000 be borrowed from Internal Improvement Trust Funds as an exception to the policy adopted by the Trustees on June 30, 1970, that limited the use of such funds. Mr. Dickinson said repayment could be made at the proper time and the Trustees' fund was the most prudent and accessible source from which to borrow. Mr. Shevin commented that repayment would have to be a direct appropriation by the Legislature, which Mr. Stone said should not be difficult as it was for maintenance of the capitol building used by the Legislature.

———————

Mr. Christian had to leave the meeting to attend the Florida Teacher of the Year Luncheon.

———————

BREVARD COUNTY - City of Titusville, Dredge Permit 253.123-694
                 and Fill Permit 253.124-155
Dr. Kenneth L. Sagrans applied for approval of a dredge and fill permit issued by the City of Titusville on February 16, 1970, to fill a 0.37 acre parcel of submerged land in the Indian River conveyed by the Trustees by Deed No. 19253. Consideration was scheduled for this date at the time of deferral prior to the January 12 meeting.

The applicant proposed to dredge 4,000 cubic yards of fill material from a borrow area in the Indian River below the one fathom contour in accordance with recommendations of the biologist, whose report was adverse although it recognized that a reduction of 66% in the fill area had been made as a result of staff effort. Applicant submitted $50 dredge application fee and $400 for the fill material, and the staff recommended approval. The dredge area was 1,600 ft. offshore at depths below the sunlight penetration, and would have limited adverse effect on marine biological resources.

It was explained that the applicant had difficulty arranging his
schedule and although there was a moratorium on dredge and fill
applications, he would be heard. The Director said the area to
be filled was on the Indian River waterfront in Titusville sold
a number of years ago, landward of the established bulkhead line.

Dr. and Mr. Sagrans spoke at length of the plan, delays and post-
ponements, changes in policies and regulations, modifications of
their application, expense and frustrations leading up to this
appearance at the cabinet meeting three years after purchase of the
property. In view of these things, Dr. Sagrans thought his application should be considered as an emergency and some action taken.

The Governor expressed understanding of the situation but pointed
out that four of the Trustees only recently became members of the
Board. The Director explained that approval was recommended
provided the applicant furnished a security bond in the amount of
the difference in price of material, since the committee was now
working to determine fill material values for adoption by the Board.
Mr. Shevin recommended $1 per cubic yard as the surety bond basis.

Motion was made by Mr. Dickinson, seconded by Mr. O'Malley, and
adopted on a vote of three to two, with the Governor voting in
favor and Messrs. Shevin and Stone voting "Nay", that the application be approved subject to Dr. Sagrans providing a sufficient
security bond to cover the increased cost of fill material, the
cost of material to be determined by the Board after receipt of the
report from the technical fill material committee.

HENDRY COUNTY - Oil and Gas Lease Assignment
The staff recommended approval of assignment of an undivided
11.258725% interest in Oil and Gas Lease No. 2443 dated June 16,
1970, covering the reserved one-half interest of the Board of Trustees
in the E 1/2 of Section 11, W 1/2 and NE 1/4 of Section 23, Township
46 South, Range 32 East, from Exchange Oil and Gas Corporation to
the South Coast Corporation, both Delaware corporations. Instrument
of assignment was approved by the staff legal counsel as to form
and legality.

On motion by Mr. O'Malley, seconded by Mr. Stone, and adopted without objection, the Board approved the assignment.

HENDRY COUNTY - Oil and Gas Lease Assignment
Staff recommended approval of assignment of an undivided 11.258725%
interest in Oil and Gas Lease No. 2441-S dated June 16, 1970,
covering the reserved one-half interest of the Board of Education
in Section 16, Township 46 South, Range 33 East, from Exchange Oil
and Gas Corporation to the South Coast Corporation, both Delaware
corporations. Instrument of assignment was approved by staff
legal counsel as to form and legality.

On motion by Mr. O'Malley, seconded by Mr. Stone and adopted without objection, the Board approved the assignment.

BAY COUNTY - Bulkhead Line, Section 253.122 Florida Statutes
The Board of County Commissioners of Bay County by resolution
adopted June 16, 1970, established a bulkhead line 16,870 feet long
in Grand Lagoon and St. Andrews Bay in Sections 10, 11, 14 and 15,
Township 4 South, Range 15 West, Bay County. The biological report
was adverse.

The staff recommended denial. The staff further recommended that
the applicant work with the staff of the Trustees and Department of/
Natural Resources to revise the proposed bulkhead line in such a
manner as to preserve the integrity of the marsh area.

On motion by Mr. Stone, seconded by Mr. Dickinson and adopted without objection, the staff recommendations were accepted as the action of the Board. The applicant had agreed to abide by the staff recommendations.

BAY COUNTY - Bulkhead Line, Section 253.122 Florida Statutes.
The Board of County Commissioners of Bay County by Resolution No. 508-A established a bulkhead line 3,264 feet along the southerly bank of Grand Lagoon in Section 16, Township 4 South, Range 15 West, Bay County, following the line of mean high water. The biological survey report was not adverse.

On motion by Mr. O'Malley, seconded by Mr. Dickinson and adopted without objection, the Board approved the bulkhead line as established by the county.

VOLUSIA COUNTY - Spoil Area, Section 253.03 F. S.
The Florida Inland Navigation District requested the Board of Trustees to reconfirm a spoil area easement granted to the United States Corps of Engineers on December 28, 1938. The original easement contained a reverter clause and the Corps of Engineers through an error had conveyed the area to the City of New Smyrna Beach. The city had quitclaimed its interest in the spoil area.

On motion by Mr. Stone, seconded by Mr. O'Malley and adopted without objection, the Board reconfirmed the spoil area easement as requested.

DADE COUNTY - Campsite Lease Renewals.
The staff recommended approval of the following two requests for renewal of offshore campsite leases in Biscayne Bay, Dade County, that both conformed to the policy of April 7, 1970, that allowed a lease as long as the structure remained on the site, and the policy of October 6, 1970, that established an annual rental of $300 for a quarter-acre site:

  1. Campsite Lease No. 2159 held by Frank L. FitzPatrick
  2. Campsite Lease No. 2158 held by Robert R. Bellamy and
     Read S. Ruggles, Jr.

The Attorney General suggested that renewals be on a year-to-year basis. Mr. Vidzes replied that that policy was followed, although the agenda did not so state.

On motion by Mr. O'Malley on the first lease, and by Mr. Dickinson on the second lease, seconded by Mr. Stone in both cases, and adopted without objection, the Trustees approved the requested campsite lease renewals.

SANTA ROSA COUNTY - Marina License, Section 253.03 Florida Statutes.
The Department of the Navy applied for a marina license for the construction of a fishing and mooring facility over 3,600 square feet in the Blackwater River abutting Section 35, Township 2 North, Range 28 West, Santa Rosa County.

At the request of the Attorney General, action was deferred.

Governor Askew requested a biological report from the Game and Fresh Water Commission, as the area was in a fresh water river.

DUVAL COUNTY - Corrective Deed.
On motion by Mr. O'Malley, seconded by Mr. Dickinson and adopted without objection, the Trustees authorized issuance of a corrective deed for $25 to correct an error in the legal description of the parcel of filled sovereignty land in the St. Johns River in Duval County conveyed in Trustees Deed No. 24765 to Denyse Stancell and Gerald Sohn (File No. 2098-16-253.12).

1-26-71

MONROE COUNTY - Bulkhead Line, Dredge and Fill Permit.

Florida Keys Aqueduct Authority was the applicant for a bulkhead line approved and established by the Board of County Commissioners of Monroe County in Resolution No. 60-1970. The line was 1,960 feet long at Stock Island in Section 35, Township 67 South, Range 25 East, and Section 2, Township 68 South, Range 25 East, Monroe County. The Authority planned expansion of an existing desalination plant. The County Commission had also granted permits to dredge and fill submerged land conveyed under Trustees Deed No. 24409. The biological report was adverse.

Motion was made by Mr. Stone, seconded by Mr. Dickinson, that the application for bulkhead line, dredge and fill permits be approved. Mr. Stone said he was in favor of the project and would like to discuss it when there was sufficient time. Governor Askew suggested deferral, as his staff had some questions regarding the application.

Without objection, action was deferred.

DADE COUNTY - Dredge Permit Amendment, File 253.123-218.
Donarl of Florida, Inc., represented by William J. Roberts, applied for amendment of State Dredge Permit No. 253.123-218 to allow dredging a channel that was inadvertently omitted from the initial application and is required to provide access to a proposed marina.

At the request of the Attorney General, consideration was deferred because it conflicted with the moratorium.

MARCO ISLAND DEVELOPMENT CORPORATION.
The staff had placed on the agenda the consideration of boundary line agreement and clarification of title questions relating to the Marco River dredge and fill permit.

Mr. Stone made a motion for approval, commenting that it was an extension of a permit with 90% of the job already completed. Mr. Dickinson also made a motion for approval.

Mr. Vidzes had reviewed some of the facts in a recent memorandum to the Board. The Marco Island Development Corporation's state permit would expire on January 31. If the state permit expired, the Corps permit would automatically expire although the valid Corps of Engineers permit ran to December 31, 1971. Mr. Vidzes briefly discussed certain questions that were raised by the previous members and staff recommendations to reconcile the matter of land title and boundaries.

Comptroller Dickinson said the staff should be commended for driving a hard bargain and securing compliance from the applicants with every state requirement. He thought renewal of the permit was in order. Mr. Shevin had no objection to renewal of the permit for one year but recommended deferment of any additional items regarding land title, noting that legal counsel had been employed to render an opinion on the title so that it could be determined which was state sovereignty land and which land was properly owned by the corporation.

Mr. Shevin proposed a substitute motion to extend the permit, but to take no further action at this time with regard to exchange of land.

Governor Askew expressed concern that he and other members were newcomers with respect to this matter, that the biological report was approximately three years old, that this was not a continuing body and he was trying to assert independent judgment. He suggested extension of the permit with a provision for review, whereupon Mr. Vidzes said that 90-day extension of the existing permit might allow sufficient time for review in the light of present policies by the present Board of Trustees.

In answer to Mr. Shevin's question regarding diligence to complete the project, Mr. Jack Peeples, representing Marco Island Development Corporation, pointed out that two years of the state permit time had expired before the Corps permit was obtained and construction begun, and if the state permit was renewed and a current biological report indicated that it should be revoked, the permit was revokable.

Mr. Stone made a substitute motion suggested by the Governor that was adopted without objection, that the Board grant a 90-day extension of the permit and require an updated biological report so that at the end of the temporary extension the members would be in a better position to determine whether they would approve completion of the work. The Governor recognized some moral commitment to the previous Board but said the applicant should appreciate the members' greater commitment to the public interest.

RESOLUTION REGARDING EXCHANGES OF STATE SOVEREIGNTY LANDS.
Attorney General Shevin offered a resolution for adoption as policy of the Board that had been recommended at a previous meeting by him and Secretary of State Stone, who felt that the legislative intent in requiring publication of notice of sales, notices to riparian owners, biological reports, was that land disposed of by exchanges should be subject to these requirements, also. In the event an exchange appeared to involve no ecological values the Board might make an exception to the policy. In answer to Mr. Vidzes' question regarding application of the policy to sovereignty land only, Mr. Stone and the Governor said it would apply to any sale (or exchange) and to all lands.

The Governor suggested deferment, as three members were not present. Mr. Dickinson agreed that exchanges should require advertising but also noted that the absent members might like to discuss the policy.

Since the resolution would be circulated for execution by all of the Board, Mr. Shevin made a motion, seconded by Mr. Dickinson, and adopted without objection, that the following resolution be adopted as policy henceforth:

RESOLUTION OF THE TRUSTEES OF THE INTERNAL
IMPROVEMENT TRUST FUND REGARDING EXCHANGES
OF STATE SOVEREIGNTY LANDS

WHEREAS, The Trustees of the Internal Improvement Trust Fund are charged with the conservation and protection of all lands to which they have title under Chapter 253, Florida Statutes; and
WHEREAS, exchanges of sovereignty lands with private owners involve the conveyance or relinquishment by the State of title to public properties; and full information concerning these properties which would be of interest to the public should be in possession of the Trustees before any such disposition of said lands;
NOW THEREFORE BE IT RESOLVED that the policy of the Board of Trustees of the Internal Improvement Trust Fund shall henceforth be that the conveyance or relinquishment of any title, right, claim, or interest in sovereignty lands of the State of Florida in connection with an exchange of lands with or without some cash consideration, with a private owner, shall not be undertaken prior to compliance with the publication and notice requirements of Section 253.12 Florida Statutes, in the same manner as is presently done prior to cash sales of sovereignty lands;
NOW THERFORE BE IT FURTHER RESOLVED that prior to any such conveyance or relinquishment of any title, right, claim or interest, pursuant to an exchange of sovereignty lands under Section 253.42, Florida Statutes, the biological reports required by Section 253.12, Florida Statutes, shall be obtained and the conservation findings required by the said section shall be made in the same manner as is presently done prior to cash sales of sovereignty lands.

IN WITNESS WHEREOF, we set our hands and seals this
26th day of January, 1971.

REUBIN O'D. ASKEW
Governor

RICHARD (DICK) STONE
Secretary of State

ROBERT L. SHEVIN
Attorney General

FRED O. DICKINSON, JR.
Comptroller

THOMAS D. O'MALLEY
Treasurer

FLOYD T. CHRISTIAN
Commissioner of Education

DOYLE CONNER
Commissioner of Agriculture

AQUATIC PRESERVES - Presentation of the Interagency Advisory
Committee report on aquatic preserves was postponed, as Mr.
Randolph Hodges, Chairman of the Committee, and several of the
Trustees were not present.

A delegation was present from St. Lucie County, including
Mr. E. E. Green, Chairman of the County Commissioners, Mr. Weldon
B. Lewis, County Administrator, and Mr. George D. Price, Commissioner. The request of the County Commissioners, supported also
by the City Commission of Ft. Pierce, the Chamber of Commerce,
various property owners' associations and the various drainage
districts within the community, was presented by Mr. Lewis.
They requested that the aquatic preserve be limited to the original
reach proposed that was limited on the north by White City
Road, rather than extending further north. Secondly, they
requested that the resolution creating the aquatic preserve
include provisions for hydraulic improvements for entrance
channels for water control purposes and provisions for maintenance
of the river bottom to prevent shoal build-up, to assure free
passage of storm water drainage. Since the delegation was present
for the scheduled aquatic preserves matter deferred by the
Board. Mr. Lewis asked whether they should be present again
next week or whether today's presentation would suffice.

The Governor thanked Mr. Lewis for the information he presented
and expressed appreciation for his understanding the necessity
of postponing action.

PALM BEACH COUNTY - Quitclaim Deed, Section 253.12(6) F. S.,
File No. 2383-50-253.12(6)

The Board deferred for two weeks consideration of the request
from William E. Benjamin II, represented by Raymond Royce, for
a quitclaim deed to filled sovereignty land in Lake Worth in
Palm Beach County.

PALM BEACH COUNTY - Land Sale, File No. 2372-50-253.12
The Board also deferred consideration of confirmation of sale
of four parcels of sovereignty land in Lake Worth abutting filled
sovereignty land in Section 10, Township 45 South, Range 43 East,
Palm Beach County, applied for by William E. Benjamin II,
represented by Raymond Royce.

SUBJECTS UNDER CHAPTER 18296

On motion by Mr. Dickinson, seconded by Mr. Stone and adopted
without objection, the Board approved Report No. 978 and
execution of deeds pertaining to the following:

1. Sale of a parcel of land in Columbia County under provisions of Section 197.350 Florida Statutes, to Bertha P. Monroe Williams for the high bid of $50. The 0.3 acre parcel in Section 33, Township 6 South, Range 16 East, was certified to the State of Florida under tax sale certificate No. 2549 of September 4, 1933

2. County of Dade Deed No. 974-Corrective to Catherine A. Drislane, et al, to be issued in lieu of a deed dated February 24, 1941, for the purpose of correcting the name of the grantee in the Murphy Act deed.

On motion duly adopted, the meeting was adjourned.

_____
GOVERNOR   -   CHAIRMAN

ATTEST: _____
INTERIM EXECUTIVE DIRECTOR

Tallahassee, Florida
February 2, 1971

The State of Florida Board of Trustees of the Internal Improvement Trust Fund met on this date in the auditorium of the Haydon Burns Building with the following members present:

Reubin O'D. Askew	Governor
Richard (Dick) Stone	Secretary of State
Fred O. Dickinson, Jr.	Comptroller
Thomas D. O'Malley	Treasurer
Floyd T. Christian	Commissioner of Education
Doyle Conner	Commissioner of Agriculture

Fred Vidzes	Interim Executive Director

The minutes of the meeting of January 19, 1971, were approved as submitted.

TRUSTEES' FUNDS - The Board discussed the action taken last week to lend an amount not to exceed $100,000 of Internal Improvement Trust funds to be used for necessary repairs to the capitol building.

Governor Askew emphasized that the Board was not waiving the policy adopted on June 30, 1970, " that funds accruing to the Internal Improvement Trust Fund may be used only for internal improvement of state-owned lands, or the purchase of needed lands, or the improvement, repair or rehabilitation within one year of purchase of any depreciable asset, except for that portion accruing to this fund which is required for operating expenses of the Board of Trustees in the administration of state lands and other related subjects, and such fund shall not be disbursed as loans or grants to any other state department, governmental unit, political subdivision or municipality." The Governor said the loan was an exception to presently existing policy and the cabinet would make every effort to have the Legislature appropriate money to repay the Internal Improvement Fund.

2-2-71

Mr. Dickinson agreed that the rule was not being waived but that an exception was being made for this one purpose, that if repairs are not now made much more expense would be incurred than the amount of interest that might be lost in liquidating some of the Trustees' present investments, and the Trustees were able to make this expenditure. He said he would inform members of the Legislature what was done and why the exception was made. Mr. Christian added that the neglect of repairs to the capitol building had been going on for a long time.

Mr. Kenneth Ireland, Secretary of the Department of Administration, indicated that the Trustees' action was in keeping with action by the Legislature last year in making an appropriation for repairs and renovations from this fund.

On motion by Mr. Dickinson, seconded by Mr. Stone and adopted without objection, the Trustees reaffirmed last week's action as an exception to the present policy limiting the use of Trustees' funds, and authorized the Department of General Services to proceed.

GULF COUNTY - Bulkhead Line, Section 253.122 Florida Statutes
On motion by Mr. Christian, seconded by Mr. Stone and adopted without objection, the Board considered a matter deferred for further study on January 19 and approved the bulkhead line established by the Board of County Commissioners of Gulf County by resolution adopted on September 30, 1970, and by the City Commission of Port St. Joe by Resolution No. 422 adopted October 6, 1970, located along the easterly bank of St. Joseph Bay, 3,836 feet long in Section 35, Township 7 South, Range 11 West, in Gulf County. The biological report was not adverse.

DUVAL COUNTY - Bulkhead Line, Section 253.122 Florida Statutes

On motion by Mr. Conner, seconded by Mr. Christian and adopted without objection, the Board approved the bulkhead line established by the City Council of the City of Jacksonville by Ordinance No. 70-1105-565 adopted December 22, 1970, located at the United States Coast Guard Base, Mayport, 663.30 feet long on the St. Johns River abutting unsurveyed Section 30, Township 1 South, Range 29 East, Duval County. The biological report was partially adverse. The area was needed to support rescue service facilities.

DUVAL COUNTY - Dedication, File No. 2387-16-253.03
On motion by Mr. Conner, seconded by Mr. Christian and adopted without objection, the Board of Trustees authorized issuance of a dedication to the United States Coast Guard covering a 0.25 acre parcel of sovereignty land in the St. Johns River abutting unsurveyed Section 30, Township 1 South, Range 29 East, City of Jacksonville, Duval County, landward of the bulkhead line approved by the Trustees on this date.

The parcel was needed for expansion of the Coast Guard facilities at Mayport. Governor Askew noted that the biological report was adverse as to part of the proposed fill area, but the application was for a public necessity.

ST. LUCIE COUNTY - Advertise Land Exchange
On January 19 the Board deferred action on the application from the Lucie Properties, Inc., represented by Frank Fee, for a boundary line agreement and land exchange affecting land in and abutting Government Lots 1 and 2, Section 22, and Government Lot 2 in Section 23, Township 34 South, Range 40 East, St. Lucie County.

On January 26 a resolution offered by the Attorney General was adopted by the Board, that required compliance with the publication and notice requirements of Section 253.12 Florida Statutes, in the same manner as is presently done prior to cash sales of sovereignty land, prior to any conveyance such as would be effected in the land exchange proposed by Lucie Properties. The staff requested authority to advertise the land exchange. In order to

block up the applicant's holdings and eliminate any interest in
contiguous swamp and sovereignty lands, the applicant desired
to exchange four parcels containing 46.4 acres including open
water areas, for three parcels containing 52.4 acres. The
boundary line would be the metes and bounds traverse of the outside toe of the existing mosquito control dike that encompasses
the entire tract. The lands had been appraised and a basis for
exchange recommended by the staff.

On motion by Mr. O'Malley, seconded by Mr. Christian and adopted
without objection, the Board authorized advertisement of the
land exchange.

MONROE COUNTY - Application to Purchase, File 2122-44-253.12
J. A. Sansone of Miami, Florida, had submitted an application
dated May 10, 1968, with application fee of $75, for purchase
of a parcel of sovereignty land embracing 1.4 acres in Bogie
Channel, Big Pine Key, Monroe County. The applicant requested
that the application be withdrawn.

The staff recommended that the file be deactivated and application
fee refunded, as the fee was paid prior to adoption of the policy
making such fee non-refundable.

On motion by Mr. Stone, seconded by Mr. Christian and adopted without objection, the Board accepted the staff recommendation.

DADE COUNTY - Corrective Deed
On motion by Mr. Stone, seconded by Mr. O'Malley and adopted without objection, the Board authorized issuance of a deed to correct
an error in Deed No. 21159-A-Corrective dated August 6, 1970.
Although the deed was executed by all members of the Board, the
testimonial clause erroneously recited that the legally designated
agent of the Board signed the deed.

DADE COUNTY - Campsite Lease Renewal

Joseph A. Caldwell and Thomas A. Wills, holder of Campsite Lease
No. 2157 in Biscayne Bay, Dade County, requested renewal for one
year with option to renew on a year-to-year basis for four additional
years at an annual rental of $300. The request conformed to the
Trustees' policies of April 7 and October 6, 1970.

On motion by Mr. Stone, seconded by Mr. Christian and adopted
without objection, the Trustees approved one-year renewal of the
campsite lease.

SANTA ROSA COUNTY - Advertise Oil and Gas Lease
On motion by Mr. Stone, seconded by Mr. Christian and adopted
without objection, the Board authorized advertisement for sealed
bids for a five-year oil and gas drilling lease of the reserved
one-half interest of the State of Florida in the petroleum and
petroleum products in all of Lot 2, Section 12, Township 5 North,
Range 30 West, less the South 22 1/2 chains, containing 56.235
surface acres, more or less (28.117 net mineral acres), under the
following terms and conditions: annual rental of $1 per net mineral
acre, $50,000 surety bond, one-sixth royalty, and at least one test
well every two and one-half years of the lease. The State Geologist
concurred in the staff recommendation to advertise for lease bids.

HENDRY COUNTY - Assign Oil and Gas Lease
On motion by Mr. Christian, seconded by Mr. O'Malley and adopted
without objection, the Board approved an assignment from Mobil Oil
Corporation, holder of Oil and Gas Drilling Lease No. 2442-S dated
June 16, 1970, of an undivided one-half interest of this lease to
Phillips Petroleum Company. The staff legal counsel approved the
assignment as to form and legality.

2-2-71

MANATEE COUNTY - Dredge Permit for Utility Installation
Section 253.123(2)(b), File 700
The Town of Longboat Key requested a dredge permit authorizing
the placement of a sixteen-inch water main in Longboat Pass in
Section 15, Township 25 South, Range 16 East, Manatee County,
and asked for waiver of the $100 processing fee. The biological
report was not adverse.

Mr. Vidzes said that ordinarily the permits for utilities were
issued by the staff under authority given by the Trustees, but
in this case the town requested waiver of the usual fee.

On motion by Mr. O'Malley, seconded by Mr. Conner and adopted
without objection, the Board approved the request of the Town of
Longboat Key for a permit without charge.

PASCO COUNTY - Artificial Reef Permit No. 2002
The New Port Richey Jaycees applied for a permit to complete
construction of an artificial reef in the Gulf of Mexico, South
9° 05' East a distance of 48.00 feet from Anclote Light. Applicant tendered $50 processing fee. The Department of Natural Re-
sources recommended that the permit be granted.

On motion by Mr. Stone, seconded by Mr. Christian and adopted
without objection, the Board approved the application.

DADE COUNTY - Artificial Reef Permit
Miami Sportfishing Club applied for a permit for three artificial
reefs adjacent to Hawk Channel, (1) Reef A at 25° 25' 21" North
Latitude and 80° 06' 45" West Longitude, (2) Reef B at 25° 31'
41" North Latitude and 80° 05' 16" West Longitude, and (3) Reef C
at 25° 33' 42" North Latitude and 80° 05' 02" West Longitude.
$50 fee was tendered.

The Department of Natural Resources made certain recommendations
as buoyancy might be a problem in placement of reef materials at
the water depths indicated.

Motion was made by Mr. Stone, seconded by Mr. Christian and adopted
without objection, that the reef permit be approved subject to the
applicant drilling air holes to reduce the buoyancy of the tires
to the satisfaction of the Department of Natural Resources.

DADE COUNTY - Dedication, File No. 2364-13-253.03
The City of Miami by Resolution No. 21564 adopted May 13, 1970,
requested dedication of a parcel of sovereignty land embracing
0.092 acre abutting Section 39, Township 54 South, Range 41 East,
in Biscayne Bay, Dade County, in the City of Miami, for construction of a seawall and filling the parcel that is landward of the
established bulkhead line as confirmed by Interagency Advisory Committee. The parcel was at the terminus of Southeast 15th Road
abutting a parcel recently conveyed by the Trustees and the city
expected the owners of the adjacent land to bulkhead and fill the
parcel, making a smooth shoreline in this area of Biscayne Bay. The
staff had not received an application for a fill permit from the
abutting owner.

On August 25 the Board authorized advertisement of the parcel and
notice of the proposed dedication was published in the Miami Herald
on four consecutive weeks showing December 29 as the date for the
Board's consideration. No objections were received. On January 12,
1970, the first meeting after the cancelled meeting of December 29,
the Board deferred consideration of the application pending receipt
of a current biological report.

Secretary of State Stone suggested deferment pending checking by the
staff of additional projects and developments in that general area.
The Governor agreed that problems might be created if other projects
were not taken into consideration.

Without objection, the matter was deferred at the request of the
Secretary of State.

DADE COUNTY - Emergency Dredge and Fill Permit,
            Sections 253.123 and 253.124(8), Chapter 70-333
The City of Miami Beach requested approval of an emergency permit
to dredge 3,000 cubic yards of material from Biscayne Bay to fill
approximately 0.35 acre, more or less, Dade County. The area was
purchased from the state in 1919 under Deed 16801, was filled, and
has eroded in such a way that Flagler Memorial Monument was being
undermined.

Under provisions of Section 253.124(8), land lost through avulsion
or artificially induced erosion can be reclaimed without establishing
a bulkhead line, and the city was in the process of fixing a bulkhead
line. The biological report was not adverse to dredging but stated
that filling will eliminate a vegetated and productive small area
of bay bottom.

On motion by Mr. Stone, seconded by Mr. Conner and adopted without
objection, the Board approved the emergency dredge and fill permit.

MONROE COUNTY - Dredge Permit, File 253.03-158
Chester F. Tingler, represented by Robert S. Appleton, was present
in connection with review of a permit previously issued to dredge
109,700 cubic yards of material from submerged land owned by the
applicant and 560 cubic yards from state-owned land in Hawk Channel
adjacent to Boot Key in Monroe County.

Mr. Stone requested deferment for two weeks and the Governor suggested the possibility of a new beginning on this permit. The
Board agreed to receive any information the parties present might
offer but made it clear that it was not the intention of the Trustees
to take final action on this date.

Mr. Appleton said the application filed in 1968 and argued through
1969 was issued in 1970 after the Board's requirements apparently
were satisfied, the Corps of Engineers permit was issued and Mr.
Tingler started with the fill operation on land he had purchased
from the state fourteen years ago. He was removing fill material
from land he purchased from the state and depositing it on his own
property and did not think there was any problem. The Governor
mentioned the state's position that it had jurisdiction over the
water column, and Mr. Stone asked the applicant to furnish his
office information. Mr. Appleton advised that after complete investigation the Board had issued the permit.

Governor Askew pointed out that four members of the Board were new,
they wanted to be sure what was in the best public interest, and he
felt that there were some property rights to be considered as this
was in a different category from taking of fill from sovereign lands.

At the request of the Secretary of State, the Trustees deferred
further consideration.

MONROE COUNTY - Dredge Permit No. 253.03-154
On December 29, 1969, a dredge permit was issued to Fred Henning
to excavate 205,000 cubic yards, to be paid for at the rate of 15¢
per cubic yard due on the 10th of each month for material removed
for the preceding month. The applicant had failed to remit payments
within the time provided, required continuous reminders of payments
due, and the staff had placed a recommendation on the agenda that
the permit be suspended until the applicant could provide assurance
that the payments would be made on time.

Mr. Vidzes requested withdrawal of that recommendation, as the
applicant's representative by letter with check enclosed to be
placed in escrow, had made provision to insure payments on time.

No action was required at this time and Mr. Vidzes recommended that the applicant be allowed to continue to operate.

It was so ordered.

DUVAL COUNTY - Temporary Spoil Easement
The Jacksonville Port Authority requested an alternate spoil area adjacent to the St. Johns River in Township 1 South, Range 27 East, embracing 150 acres, more or less. The spoil area granted for Area CSA-10A on January 14, 1969, on which the biological report was adverse, would br reconveyed to the Trustees. A biological report dated January 13, 1971, indicated that less damage would be caused if the requested alternate area is used.

The Trustees deferred action for two weeks at the request of Mr. Stone, who had asked some conservation organizations in the Jacksonville area if they could suggest an alternate site on which to deposit the spoil material.

RECLAIMED LAKE BOTTOM LAND - Governor Askew requested deferment of consideration of a policy with regard to sale of reclaimed lake bottom land, which was very technical, until a time when the Attorney General was present at the meeting. He added that the Corps of Engineers had suggested careful study because land around a lake, Lake Okeechobee in particular, served an important purpose of filtering adverse particles from water draining into the lake. That was one of the problems in Lake Apopka.

Without objection, the Trustees deferred consideration of a policy.

AQUATIC PRESERVES - The report of the Interagency Advisory Committee was presented by Mr. Vidzes, a member of that committee, on behalf of Senator Randolph Hodges, the chairman. He reviewed the creation of the committee and selection of five additional areas considered appropriate for aquatic preserves, with particular attention to the preserve in St. Lucie and Martin Counties described as North Fork St. Lucie River in Townships 36 and 37 South, Range 40 East. Public hearings had been held on all five proposed preserves, and because of testimony introduced at the hearing on North Fort St. Lucie River that had as its north boundary the White City Road, the committee decided to move the north boundary about 2 1/2 miles northerly to Selvitz Road. However, that northerly extension had not been advertised and objections were received from the Board of County Commissioners of St. Lucie County, the North St. Lucie Drainage District, the City of Fort Pierce, and others concerned with the drainage works both proposed and existing in that area. Also, the committee had postponed making a recommendation on the Ochlockonee Bay Preserve area in Wakulla and Franklin Counties because of many local objections.

Governor Askew suggested a hearing on the northerly extension of North Fork St. Lucie River Preserve, noting that the committee was asked to stay in existence for another 90 days to clear up the Ochlockonee Bay recommendation.

Mr. Vidzes said the technical advisory committee considered recommending the extension of the boundaries to Selvitz Road but, however, providing in the resolution that due consideration be given for the unique drainage situation. The Governor said the Board could take action on that portion that was originally recommended, up to White City Road. The spokesmen present to oppose the further extension were noted, but it was suggested that they make their presentation at the local public hearing on the northerly extension.

Mr. Weldon Lewis, St. Lucie County Administrator, County Commissioners George Price and Ed Green, and Agriculture Agent Hugh Welch were present. Mr. Stone expressed concern that proper provisions be made to insure that improper effluent won't affect the aquatic preserve area, which might require the inclusion of the area northerly to Selvitz Road.

Mr. Vidzes advised the Board that the General Development Corporation, major land owner on both sides of the river and islands, concurred in the concept of creating aquatic preserves but also was concerned with the drainage problems and indicated willingness to work with the state in developing a plan by utilizing some of their own land. The five areas proposed as aquatic preserves were as follows:

1. North Fork St. Lucie River, St. Lucie and Martin Counties
2. Cockroach Bay, a part of Tampa Bay, in Township 32 South, Range 18 East, in Hillsborough County
3. Waccasassa Bay near Cedar Key in Levy County, in Townships 15-17 South, Ranges 14-15 East
4. (a) Cupon Bight at Big Pine Key, Township 66 South, Range 29 East, Monroe County. (b) Lignumvitae Key, Shell and Indian Keys, Township 63-64 South, Ranges 36-37 East, Monroe County
5. Ochlockonee Bay in Franklin and Wakulla Counties

On motion by Mr. Stone, seconded by Mr. O'Malley, and adopted without objection, the Trustees approved area number one as originally proposed up to White City Road, deferring the northerly extension.

On motion by Mr. Stone, seconded by Mr. O'Malley and adopted, the Trustees approved area number two, Cockroach Bay Aquatic Preserve. The Director called attention to the fact that through several legislative acts the lands in Tampa Bay were vested in the Tampa Bay Port Authority. The managing director of the Authority had indicated concurrence and would forward a resolution committing Cockroach Bay to the aquatic preserve. The Trustees owned no land there but would take careful look at all dredge and fill applications in that area designated as a preserve. In answer to the Governor's question, Mr. Vidzes said the committee might not have known the extent of Tampa Port Authority ownership in that area. Objections were filed to the establishment of the preserve by upland owners.

The third area, Waccasassa Bay Aquatic Preserve, was approved on motion by Mr. O'Malley, seconded by Mr. Dickinson, and adopted without objection. Areas 4(a) and 4(b) were approved as an aquatic preserve on motion made by Mr. O'Malley, seconded by Mr. Dickinson, and adopted without objection.

Mr. Vidzes recommended deferment of the fifth area, Ochlockonee Bay, and that a select committee be appointed to study it further. The Governor said that the motion by Mr. O'Malley, seconded by Messrs. Stone and Dickinson, for 90-day deferment extended the life of the committee that would consider the Ochlockonee Bay area further and hold a hearing on one portion of the North Fork St. Lucie River area.

TRUSTEES' FUNDS - Appraiser's Assistant, Special Legal Counsel, Cooperative Agreement on Shoreline Mapping.
On motion by Mr. Stone, seconded by Mr. O'Malley and adopted without objection, the Board authorized use of Internal Improvement Trust Funds for the following:

1. Employment of an assistant for the staff appraiser for the month of February to gather preliminary appraisal data such as property titles, legal descriptions and comparative sales, which greatly increases the production of the appraiser and helps insure timely appraisal reports. February will be the fourth month this assistance has been used on a temporary basis during this fiscal year.

   Governor Askew suggested employment of a full-time assistant.

2. Retain Mr. J. Kenneth Ballinger as special legal counsel for another 90-day period beginning January 8, 1971, for which funds are available in the current operating budget. Mr. Ballinger had done legal work on Trustees' matters for many years and was working on several incomplete cases. Recently authorized in-house counsel positions had not been filled due to lack of suitable space, but it was anticipated that the authorized positions would be filled to handle all Trustees' matters by the end of the 90-day period.

3. Continue the cooperative agreement dated April 18, 1969, for the shoreline mapping program. The agreement provides for a $125,000 yearly contribution by the Trustees to the United States Coast and Geodetic Survey to be matched by federal funds. The 1970-71 budget request scheduled this item for payment from the Department of Natural Resources (General Revenue), but since the Legislature appropriated the continuation of the program from the Trustees, the staff requested authority to make the $125,000 transfer to United Coast and Geodetic Survey.

FILL MATERIAL COMMITTEE - On motion by Mr. O'Malley, seconded by Mr. Stone, and adopted without objection, the Board appointed Mr. Loring Lovell, Executive Director of Conservation 70s, to the Technical Advisory Committee on Fill that was appointed on September 15, 1970, and payment of travel and per diem was authorized.

SUBJECTS UNDER CHAPTER 18296

MURPHY ACT REPORT NO. 979. The staff requested approval of Report No. 979 and execution of deed for sale of a parcel of Murphy Act land in Bay County under provisions of Section 197.350 Florida Statutes, to James R. Meyers for the high bid of $320. The parcel, certified to the State of Florida under tax sale certificates 276 for 1930 taxes, and 277 of August 1, 1932, was described as Lot 16, Block 45, Calloway Plat, Section 18, Township 4 South, Range 13 West, Bay County.

On motion by Mr. Conner, seconded by Mr. Christian and adopted without objection, the Board approved the Murphy Act sale and authorized execution of deed pertaining thereto.

On motion duly adopted, the meeting was adjourned.

_____
GOVERNOR   -   CHAIRMAN

ATTEST: _Fred Vidzes_
INTERIM EXECUTIVE DIRECTOR
*   *   *   *   *

Tallahassee, Florida
February 16, 1971

The State of Florida Board of Trustees of the Internal Improvement Trust Fund met on this date in the Auditorium of the Haydon Burns Building, with the following members present:

Reubin O'D. Askew — Governor
Richard (Dick) Stone — Secretary of State
Robert L. Shevin — Attorney General
Fred O. Dickinson, Jr. — Comptroller
Thomas D. O'Malley — Treasurer (Present part time)
Floyd T. Christian — Commissioner of Education

Fred Vidzes — Interim Executive Director

DUVAL COUNTY - Temporary Spoil Easement. The Jacksonville Port Authority request for an alternate spoil area adjacent to the St. Johns River in Township 1 South, Range 27 East, embracing 150 acres, more or less, was deferred on February 2 at the request of the Secretary of State for contacting conservation groups for suggestions for a spoil area that might be less damaging to biological resources.

2-16-71

Mr. Vidzes said the staff recommendation in favor of the alternate spoil area still stands, that the biological report indicated it would be less damaging than the spoil area already authorized for use by the Corps of Engineers, and the Corps through the Jacksonville Port Authority had agreed to reconvey the Hannah Mills marsh area to the state.

Mr. O'Malley moved denial, stating that he would like to have additional information on the alternate site. Mr. Christian made a motion to approve the staff recommendation that died for lack of a second.

Mr. O'Malley pointed out adverse effects on the Back River area mentioned in the biological report and asked if there weren't other alternatives. It was brought out in the discussion that the area had been carefully reviewed by the staff and Mr. Woodburn, that a place for deposit of the spoil from the maintenance project had to be found, and that an area already designated could be used but the alternate site would cause less biological damage.

Mr. Stone had been advised by Mrs. Paul L. Bird (Southeastern Environmental Council representative) that the alternate site is better and she recommended that he vote for it; but Mr. W. Curtis Lovelace recommended seven other alternate sites that Mr. Stone thought should be evaluated. He requested deferral for one week. The Direc tor indicated that Mr. Woodburn was so thoroughly familiar with the area that one week might be sufficient for review of the seven suggested alternate sites. Mr. Christian withdrew his motion.

Without objection, action was deferred for another week.

———————

BAY COUNTY - Dredge Permit, File No. 253.123-693.
The application from the Grand Lagoon Company for a dredge permit for two navigation channels, maintenance dredging, and a boat basin in Sections 10 and 15, Township 4 South, Range 15 West, in Grand Lagoon in Bay County, was deferred on January 26 and considered further on this date. What concerned the Trustees with respect to the boat basin had been reconciled, the Governor said, and the position taken by the applicant was corroborated by the staff.

On motion by Mr. Stone, seconded by Messrs. Christian and Dickinson, and adopted without objection, the Trustees approved the dredge permit to Grand Lagoon Company.

———————

On motion by Mr. Stone, adopted without objection, the Board approved minutes of the meeting of January 26, 1971.

———————

DUVAL COUNTY - Bulkhead Line, Section 253.122 Florida Statutes.
The City Council of Jacksonville by Ordinance No. 69-541 adopted on September 4, 1969, established a bulkhead line 5,450 feet long along the easterly shore of Mill Cove adjacent to upland in Section 32, Township 1 South, Range 28 East, in Duval County.

The biological report was adverse.

On motion by Mr. Christian, seconded by Mr. Stone and adopted without objection, the Board accepted the staff recommendation that the bulkhead line be denied and the applicant be requested to work with the staff to locate the bulkhead line at the mean high water line.

———————

MONROE COUNTY - Bulkhead Line, Dredge and Fill Permit,
          Sections 253.122, 123, 124 Florida Statutes.
The Trustees again deferred consideration of an application from Florida Key Aqueduct Authority.

———————

2-16-71

VOLUSIA COUNTY - Bulkhead Line, Land Exchange, Fill Permit.
The City Commission of New Smyrna Beach by Ordinance No. 800 adopted
on June 23, 1970, established a bulkhead line around Yacht Club
Island in the Indian River in unsurveyed portion of Section 20,
Township 17 South, Range 34 East, Volusia County.

Mr. John C. Gross, represented by Mr. Hal McClamma, appeared before
the Trustees on December 15, 1971, requesting approval of the
bulkhead line, an application to purchase sovereignty land, and a
dredge permit. Action was postponed for working out a proposal for
exchange of submerged land owned by the applicant lying within
Intracoastal Waterway right of way for a strip of filled sovereignty
land abutting the applicant's upland.

On December 22 action was deferred since it had been alleged that
the applicant had filled submerged land without authorization and
destroyed mangrove trees adjacent to the island. There had been
approximately 200 ft. of cord grass skimmed off the submerged land
at the south 200 feet of the property. In this area the applicant
will replant destroyed mangroves under supervision of representatives of the Department of Natural Resources representing a penalty
for unauthoriz ed encroachment on state-owned sovereignty land. On
the easterly side of the island, a portion of the dike had been
pushed on the Intracoastal Waterway right of way. This segment of
the dike was on upland and at the staff's request that material was
pushed back onto Mr. Gross' property. Action was again deferred
on January 19.

Mr. Vidzes inspected the island and determined that all of the red
mangroves that had been destroyed were within the applicant's
property line. Part of the land in the proposed exchange is covered
with a dense mangrove grpwth and will be preserved if the exchange
occurs. A proposal was prepared under which the applicant will
convey a 0.55 acre parcel of submerged land for a 0.51 acre parcel
of sovereignty land, and in addition he will pay $1,815 for the
parcel, a value concurred in by the staff appraiser. To prevent
further destruction of remaining mangroves owned by the applicant,
an additional land exchange was proposed covering an area of
approximately 0.08 acre.

Mr. Shevin said he approved the application, but in his opinion the
statement on the agenda that these mangroves were in private ownership and could be harvested was inaccurate. He expressed the view
that the Board has the same authority under Section 253.03 to protect
against the cutting of mangroves as against the destruction of
aquatic plant life by dredging. In response to the Governor's
question, Mr. Shevin said his opinion would be that the law requires
five affirmative votes for a land exchange as for a sale.

The applicant had obtained a permit from the City of New Smyrna
Beach to fill sovereignty land conveyed by the Trustees, and would
procure fill material from a dredger under contract to the Corps of
Engineers engaged in maintenance dredging of the waterway. The
alternate site, Yacht Club Island, was reviewed by the various
environmental agencies and all reports concurred in preferring the
site for spoiling purposes.

The staff requested the applicant to tender bond for $20,000 which
had been posted in the Bank of New Smyrna, to secure payment for
20,000 cubic yards of material. The staff had learned that in
maintenance dredging of congressionally authorized public navigation channels, dredging contractors may secure alternate spoil
areas in private ownership. An agreement is entered into between
the contractor and private owner to deposit state-owned material
from the channel onto private lands. A small rebate is given
to the Corps of Engineers where this situation exists. The
staff requested authority, which was given, to advise the
District Engineers of Mobile and Jacksonville Districts that

2-16-71

payment for material will be expected from recipients when
state-owned spoil material from maintenance dredging is given
to private owners.

On motion by Mr. Shevin, seconded by Mr. Christian and adopted
without objection, the Board approved staff recommendations for
approval of a portion of the bulkhead line, the fill permit, and
advertisement of the land exchange.

DIXIE COUNTY - Wilderness Area
Under the provisions of Chapter 70-355, Acts of 1970, "State
Wilderness System Act", the Board of Trustees is authorized to
establish a wilderness area. As the first of such areas,the staff
recommended that the Pepperfish Keys, containing 127.39 acres of
swamp lands and 1240.23 acres of sovereignty land encompassing the
islands, a total of 1367.62 acres in Dixie County, be included in
the wilderness system under the new state law.

On motion by Mr. Christian, seconded by Mr. Shevin and adopted
without objection, the Board authorized advertisement of a public
hearing on the proposed Pepperfish Keys Wilderness Area.

BREVARD COUNTY - Land to the State
The Board of County Commissioners of Brevard County offered to the
State without cost a tract of 102.47 acres in Section 36, Township
23 South, Range 35 East, for use by the Division of Corrections for
a new correctional institution. A title insurance binder was furnished by the county, evidencing clear title to the property that
was one mile west of U. S. 1 and three miles north of Cocoa. The
Department of Health and Rehabilitative Services recommended
acceptance of the property with the restriction that title would
revert to the county in the event construction of correctional
institution buildings is not commenced within two years or the
property should cease to be utilized for a correctional institution.

Governor Askew said it should be made clear that acceptance of the
land did not obligate the state to build an institution there,
that the land might be used for a community correctional institution.

On motion by Mr. Christian, seconded by Mr. Stone and adopted
without objection, the Board accepted the land from the county.

GULF COUNTY - File No. 2383-23-253.12, Land Sale
St. Joe Paper Company applied for a parcel of filled sovereignty
land in St. Joseph Bay abutting Government Lots 4,7, and 8 in
Section 35, Township 7 South, Range 11 West, containing 10.0 acres
in Gulf County, to be used as an industrial waste treatment site.
The area was affected by dredging, siltation, pollution, and deposit
of foreign materials. The biological report was not adverse to the
bulkhead line that the Trustees approved on February 2, 1971. No
objections were received to sale of the filled parcel advertised for
consideration on February 9 and held over until this date.

The sale was represented as being in the public interest, so that
a bulkhead line could be constructed to contain materials along the
shoreline to prevent them from becoming dislodged during high
water and deposited on beaches in the area.

Sale had been recommended at three times the appraised value, and
motion was made by Mr. Stone, seconded by Mr. Christian, for
approval.

The Director explained that representatives of the company were
present, that certain circumstances had been brought to the
staff's attention, that there were some options to consider because of litigation pending, and he would change his recommendation

to acceptance of a $50,000 settlement offer.

The Governor and the Attorney General discussed the details of the settlement, the fact that three times the value did not apply to this case, and the offer if accepted would be approving the sale at the appraised value of $22,000 for the parcel, plus $8,000 to cover the actual cost of the litigation as incurred by the State, and $20,000 as a penalty. Then the litigation would terminate. Mr. Shevin recommended that such a settlement be entered into by the Board. Mr. Dickinson commended the Attorney General and the staff for working out the settlement in this manner, and Mr. Stone added that as a result the bark that continued to go into the bay would be disposed of by the proposed treatment.

The previous motion was withdrawn and on motion by Mr. Shevin, seconded by Mr. Stone and adopted without objection, the Trustees accepted the modified recommendation of the staff and approved the $50,000 settlement offered by St. Joe Paper Company that included sale of the parcel of land.

PALM BEACH COUNTY - File No. 2383-50-253.12(6), Quitclaim Deed, and No. 2372-50-253.12, Land Sale
The applicant, William E. Benjamin II, had requested further deferment of his application for a quitclaim deed to 8.262 acres of filled sovereignty land in Lake Worth and sale of four parcels containing 3.928 acres abutting the filled land. There was no objection to deferment and Mr. Dickinson suggested a period of three or four weeks.

Attorney General Shevin expressed the opinion that the Board was not obligated to give a quitclaim deed to the eight acres of very valuable waterfront land, because of the statute applied only to land on which the filling was completed prior to June 11, 1957. Also, he did not think it should be sold at $394 per acre. Mr. Dickinson indicated that the staff should address itself to these points.

MONROE COUNTY - File No. 2182-44-253.12, Land Sale
Mr. Vidzes reported that the applicant had consented to pay three times the appraised value for a parcel of filled sovereignty land containing 0.25 acre in Florida Bay abutting Section 32, Township 63 South, Range 37 East, Upper Matecumbe Bay in Monroe County; therefore, he changed his recommendation to approval of sale of the parcel to Donald L. Wollard for $3,195.

Application for the parcel to be used in connection with operation of a marina had been on the agenda June 10, 1969, October 20, 1970; and on November 24, 1970, consideration was deferred at the request of Mr. Adams who thought the penalty rate of three times the appraised value should be considered. The appraisal was $4,160 per acre, $1,065 for the parcel, and the applicant had offered the appraised value for the parcel plus $346.50 penalty plus $50 for the appraisal, or a total of $1,461.50. Since the Director had recommended denial at that price, Mr. Wollard finally agreed to the three times the value price.

Governor Askew commented that this was the first time that penalty had been implemented. Mr. Shevin wondered how long the marina had been in operation, whether it was on state land and a fee should be charged. It was explained that it was on the applicant's land.

Motion was made by Mr. Christian, and adopted without objection, that the filled parcel be sold at the price offered by Mr. Wollard of $3,195. Mr. Stone seconded the motion.

DADE COUNTY - Campsite Lease Renewal
On motion by Mr. Dickinson, seconded by Mr. Stone and adopted without objection, the Trustees authorized renewal of Campsite Lease No. 2163 in Biscayne Bay, Dade County, to Newell A. Horne, E. E. Bergquist, Malcolm E. Gracy, Arthur DesRocher and R. A. Mullins, for one year with option to renew on a year-to-year basis for four additional years at an annual rental of $300.

PINELLAS COUNTY- Easement
On motion by Mr. Stone, seconded by Mr. Christian and adopted without objection, the Trustees approved the application from Florida Power Corporation for a ten-foot wide easement over and across the site of the new state office building on Mirror Lake Drive in St. Petersburg for electrical service to the new state office building, as approved by the Department of General Services.

ESCAMBIA COUNTY - Emergency Dredge Permit, Section 253.123 F. S.
Warren Petroleum Company requested an emergency dredge permit to allow removal of silt and sand from applicant's barge slip 165 ft. long, 15 ft. wide, and 7 ft. deep, in Section 59, Township 2 South, in Escambia County, to enable barges to be moored against the dock and reduce danger of fuel spills. The material was eroded from applicant's land and will be replaced. The biological report is not adverse.

The dredge permit was approved on motion by Mr. Stone, seconded by Mr. Christian and adopted without objection.

HILLSBOROUGH COUNTY - Dredge Permit, File 253.123-701, Department of Transportation Project 10060-3519.
Bay Dredging and Construction Company requested approval of a dredge permit issued by Tampa Port Authority to dredge an area 80 ft. wide, 330 ft. long and 4 ft. deep in Section 18, Township 32 South, Range 19 East, in Little Manatee River, Hillsborough County. The dredging is required to enable applicant to maneuver a flotation barge in place to assist in bridge construction. The material removed would be placed adjacent to the channel and replaced in the dredge area when the project is complete.

The biological report is not adverse, $50 application fee was paid and the staff recommended approval.

On motion by Mr. Stone, seconded by Mr. Dickinson and adopted without objection, the Trustees approved the dredge permit.

MONROE COUNTY - Modify Dredge Permit, Refund, File No. 253.03-160
Rimersburg Coal Company, represented by John G. McKay, Jr., was issued a permit on April 21, 1970, to dredge a perimeter channel and three access channels 50 ft. wide, 500 ft. long, and 5 ft. deep, in Kemp Channel in Monroe County. The firm paid $7,500 for 75,000 cubic yards of material.

The United States Fish and Wildlife Service filed an objection to the project with the Corps of Engineers and after several conferences, applicant agreed to move the perimeter channel landward so as to leave a strip of red mangroves on the seaward side. Only 6,653 cubic yards of material will be removed from state-owned land.

On motion by Mr. Dickinson, seconded by Mr. Christian and adopted without objection, the Trustees authorized issuance of amended permit and refund of $6,834.70.

MANATEE COUNTY - State Construction Permit, Public Boat Ramp
On motion by Mr. Dickinson, seconded by Mr. Stone and adopted without objection, the Trustees approved issuance of a permit under Section 253.03 Florida Statutes, to the Manatee County Highway Department for construction of a public boat ramp in the Manatee River at Bradenton in Section 20, Township 34 South, Range 17 East, Manatee County.

2-16-71

PINELLAS COUNTY - State Dock Permits, Section 253.03 F. S.
On motion by Mr. Stone, seconded by Mr. Dickinson and adopted
without objection, the Board authorized issuance of state commercial dock permits for the following applications approved by
Pinellas County Water and Navigation Control Authority prior to
the August 11, 1970, policy changes relative to Marina licenses:

1. H. L. Bayless, Treasure Island
   Pinellas Authority Permits 5494 and 5495

2. F. H. Downward, Treasure Island
   Pinellas Authority Permit 5464

3. Regency West Apartments No. 2, St. Petersburg
   Pinellas Authority Permit 5482

4. Ronald Barnard, Madeira Beach
   Pinellas Authority Permit 5477

OSCEOLA COUNTY - Lake Tohopekaliga Draw-Down Project
On August 25, 1970, the Trustees agreed to cooperate with Central
and Southern Florida Flood Control District in issuance of dredging
permits for navigation and irrigation channels in Lake Tohopekaliga
for a draw-down project conducted under the auspices of the Game
and Fresh Water Fish Commission.

As the lake is lowered it will become difficult to control cattle
in the area; therefore, fence extension will be necessary. The
Osceola County Cattlemen's Association, Osceola County Farm Bureau,
Senator Irlo Bronson and a delegation of interested parties
requested that fences with suitable markings be allowed in exposed
portions of the lake. The staff asked for authority to issue the
necessary permits at staff level until termination of the project
on advice of the Flood Control District.

Governor Askew cautioned the public not to expect the sale of any
exposed lake bottoms, as it would be a temporary condition. Also,
it should be understood that the fences would be removed.

On motion by Mr. Stone, adopted without objection, the Trustees
approved the request to allow extension of fences subject to the
conditions stated by the Governor, the staff to issue the necessary
permits to be terminated upon advice of the Central and Southern
Florida Flood Control District. The Game and Fresh Water Fish Commission will coordinate the project.

The Director asked for withdrawal from the agenda of his recommendation on Interagency Advisory Committee membership.

It was so ordered.

LITIGATION. The Director requested the legal assistance of the
Department of Legal Affairs (Attorney General) to institute proceedings for a declaratory decree with respect to the Albert C. Tuck
application considered by the Board on December 15, 1970, and in
that cause styled Gables by the Sea, Inc., appellees vs Claude R.
Kirk, Jr., et al, appellants, Appeal No. 0-167, First District
Court of Appeal.

Attorney General Shevin said he had no objection and would provide
assistance. He might ask for a new policy to be adopted by the
Board, as he did not agree that the title question was the basic
legal premise.

TRUSTEES FUNDS - Office Building in Capitol Center
In order to provide urgently needed office space for the authorized,
increased staff of the Trustees, the staff requested authority to
enter into a contract with T. T. Jones Construction Company whose
adjusted total bid of $37,255 was low for converting into offices
a four-unit brick apartment building at 206 West Madison Street in
Tallahassee. The Department of Legal Affairs, Staff General Counsel
and Department of General Services were consulted, and the architect
was Forrest A. Coxen, A. I. A. Payment would be made from budgeted

2-16-71

funds.

On motion by Mr. Stone, seconded by Mr. Christian and adopted without objection, the Board authorized the staff to enter into the contract.

SUBJECTS UNDER CHAPTER 18296

MARION COUNTY - Murphy Act Land

Israel Cummings, heir of the former owner on June 9, 1939, date title vested in the State of Florida under Section 192.38 Florida Statutes (now 197.350 F. S.), offered $660 for a parcel of land that was certified to the State of Florida under tax sale certificate No. 826 of June 3, 1918, described as follows:

> South 215 ft. of North 718 ft. of East 594 ft. of NE 1/4 except North 40 ft. of East 148 ft. and except North 80 ft. of East 100 ft. of South 140 ft. in Section 14, Township 15 South, Range 21 East, 2.61 acres, more or less, in Marion County.

On motion by Mr. Dickinson, seconded by Mr. Christian and adopted without objection, the Board approved the staff recommendation for approval of the application and issuance of deed under provisions of Chapter 28317, Acts of 1953 (Section 197.355 F. S.), the so-called "Hardship Act."

REFUNDS - Murphy Act
On motion by Mr. Dickinson, seconded by Mr. Stone and adopted without objection, the Board authorized issuance of refunds of $15 each to the following two applicants for release of the state road right of way reservations contained in the Murphy Act deeds listed below, for the reason that the Department of Transportation did not recommend release of the reservations:

1. Real Estate Title Company - Hillsborough County Murphy Act Deed No. 3923

2. Donald J. Della Valle - Lee County Murphy Act Deed No. 257

SANTA ROSA COUNTY - Oil and Gas Lease
On December 22, 1970, the Trustees authorized the staff to advertise for sealed bids for a five-year oil and gas drilling lease covering the reserved one-half interest of the State of Florida (Chapter 18296, the Murphy Act) in 70 surface acres of privately-owned land in Section 20, Township 5 North, Range 29 West, Santa Rosa County, comprising 35 net mineral acres.

Invitation to bid was advertised pursuant to law, in the Tallahassee Democrat and the Press-Gazette of Milton, Florida, with bids to be opened at 10:00 a.m. on February 9. As there was no meeting on that date, the bids were held for opening on this date.

Two bids were received, one from Sun Oil Company for $40,880 and the other from Humble Oil and Refining Company for $70,735.

On motion of Mr. Stone, seconded by Mr. Dickinson and adopted without objection, the Board accepted the high bid from Humble Oil and Refining Company and authorized issuance of the oil and gas drilling lease to this bidder.

On motion duly adopted, the meeting was adjourned.

GOVERNOR - CHAIRMAN

ATTEST: _Fred Vidzes_
INTERIM EXECUTIVE DIRECTOR

2-16-71

Tallahassee, Florida
February 23, 1971

The State of Florida Board of Trustees of the Internal Improvement
Trust Fund met in the auditorium of the Haydon Burns Building, with
the following members present:

Richard (Dick) Stone   Secretary of State, Acting Chairman
Robert L. Shevin   Attorney General
Thomas D. O'Malley   Treasurer
Doyle Conner   Commissioner of Agriculture

Fred Vidzes   Interim Executive Director

On motion by Mr. O'Malley, duly adopted, the Trustees approved the
minutes of February 16 as submitted.

SARASOTA COUNTY - Bulkhead Line, Section 253.122 Florida Statutes
The Staff requested approval of a bulkhead line adopted on February
15, 1967, by the Sarasota County Water and Navigation Control
Authority, located along the southern bank of Forked Creek in
Sections 14 and 15, Township 40 South, Range 19 East, Sarasota
County. The line was approved by the county prior to enactment of
Chapter 67-393, Laws of Florida; therfore, no biological survey
report was submitted.

At the time the original application was presented the staff took
the position that the Trustees had no jurisdiction in the matter.
Mr. Vidzes explained that approval of the line would be an after-
the-fact action, a ministerial action by the Board of Trustees,
that it would allow the county and the Board to take a more active
interest in the creek waters that had become navigable due to dredging
work that completely channelized what had originally been natural
meanderings of the creek.

Mr. Stone and Mr. O'Malley criticized the fact that an old map was
furnished. Mr. Vidzes said that map would be filed in the county
records showing the before and after condition, the latter indicated
by a red line that was the seawall line of the channel created to
allow navigability.

Mr. Stone requested deferment for one week, which was agreed without objection.

MONROE COUNTY - File No. 2169-44-253.12
Key West Seaside Park, Inc. requested withdrawal of its application
dated January 29, 1969, filed with $75 application fee for purchase
of a parcel of sovereignty land in Similar Sound, Big Coppitt Key,
in Monroe County,

Staff recommended deactivation of the file and refund of the fee
that was paid prior to adoption of the policy making such fees
non-refundable.

On motion by Mr. O'Malley, seconded by Mr. Conner and adopted
without objection, the Board authorized the file closed and the
$75 fee refunded to the applicant.

MONROE COUNTY - Artificial Reef Permit No. 2101
On motion by Mr. O'Malley, seconded by Mr. Conner and adopted
without objection, the Board approved the extension recommended
by the Department of Natural Resources for Artificial Reef Permit
No. 2101 to allow completion of the installation of three artificial
reefs in Calda Channel and Smith Shoal by the City of Key West.

CHARLOTTE COUNTY - City of Punta Gorda
On may 7, 1969, the City of Punta Gorda submitted an application
to acquire an 11.7 acre parcel of sovereignty land in the Peace
River abutting Section 6, Township 41 South, Range 23 East, in
Charlotte County, for the purpose of developing a municipally-
owned mobile home park.

The biological report submitted on June 11, 1969, was adverse.

The staff did not recommend approval and had advised a delegation
from the city of that position.

On motion by Mr. O'Malley, seconded by Mr. Conner and adopted
without objection, the Board denied the dedication application
and authorized the staff to deactivate the file.

DADE COUNTY - Rescind Temporary Easement
On November 24, 1970, the Trustees approved issuance of a temporary
borrow easement to the Department of Transportation embracing about
23 acres in Dumfoundling Bay, Dade County. The Board overruled an
adverse biological report because the applicant had not located an
alternate site containing suitable material in the vicinity of the
proposed construction.

It had been brought to the staff's attention that fill material
was being hauled to the construction site from an upland source.
In view of the fact that suitable material had apparently been
located at another site, the staff recommended that the action of
the Board on November 24, 1970, be rescinded.

On motion by Mr. O'Malley, seconded by Mr. Conner and adopted
without objection, the Board approved the staff recommendation.
Mr. Stone commended the Department of Transportation for finding
a way to avoid dredging and filling.

PUTNAM COUNTY - Swan Lake Settlement
The Board deferred consideration of this matter for one week.

DADE COUNTY - Renew Campsite Lease
On motion by Mr. O'Malley, seconded by Mr. Conner and approved
without objection, the Board authorized renewal of Campsite Lease
No. 2156 in Biscayne Bay, Dade County, held by Gilbert L. O'Neal
for one year with option to renew on a year-to-year basis for four
additional years at $300 annual rental.

HILLSBOROUGH COUNTY - Fill Permit, Section 253.124, File 161
The Tampa Port Authority requested approval of a permit to fill a
71-acre tract 300 ft. wide, 10,300 ft. long, at Port Sutton in
Section 3, Township 30 South, Range 19 East, Hillsborough County.
1,092,000 cubic yards of material will be removed from an area at
Port Sutton and Pendola Point. As the dredge and fill areas are
within the boundaries of Tampa Port Authority, there was no charge
for the material.

The project was approved by the Board of County Commissioners of
Hillsborough County. The biological report dated January 26, 1971,
was adverse.

Action was deferred for one week at the request of Mr. Stone.

ESCAMBIA AND SANTA ROSA COUNTIES - Advertise Oil Lease.
The staff requested authority to advertise for competitive sealed
bids for a five-year oil and gas drilling lease covering a portion
of the Escambia River, 330.5 acres, more or less, in Township 5
North, Range 30 West. The lease would contain a special provision
prohibiting drilling in the river, provisions for one-sixth royalty,
annual rental of $1 per acre, $50,000 surety bond, at least one test
well to 6,000 feet or to the sediments of the Jurassic Age, whichever
is deeper, and that drilling be on contiguous pooled drilling units.
The State Geologist had reviewed and approved the terms and conditions.

2-23-71

Mr. O'Malley and Mr. Stone asked a number of questions, and Mr. Conner said the Board would not wish to be inconsistent but if there was any danger it should be established. There was no motion for approval and Mr. Stone said his vote would be "no" but action might be deferred for a week for a more detailed report to be submitted.

Without objection, the application was deferred for one week.

SHELL LEASE INCOME - For the record
On motion by Mr. Conner, adopted without objection, the Board accepted for the record the report of income received by the Department of Natural Resources from holders of dead shell leases:

Lease No.	Company	Amount
1718	Radcliff Materials, Inc.	$ 79.98
2233	Bay Dredging & Construction Co.	3,971.67
2235	Fort Myers Shell & Dredging Co.	679.95
2235	Fort Myers Shell & Dredging Co.	2,966.57

TRUSTEES RULES - On motion by Mr. O'Malley, seconded by Mr. Conner and adopted without objection, the Board authorized amendment of Rule 18-2.04(4) to bring the rules into conformity with the provisions of Section 253.122 Florida Statutes.

DUVAL COUNTY - Temporary Spoil Easement Revocation
The Board had previously deferred consideration of the request of the Jacksonville Port Authority for an alternate spoil area (CDA-34) adjacent to the St. Johns River in Township 1 South, Range 27 East, embracing 150 acres, more or less, in Duval County, that was proposed to be used instead of a spoil area (CSA-10A) in the Hannah Mills creek marshes. The Secretary of State had been advised through efforts of active conservationists in Duval County that there were other alternate areas available.

The staff had been advised by Mr. Paul Dettor of the Jacksonville Port Authority and by the Jacksonville District office of the Corps of Engineers that the dredging project had progressed to a point that the alternate spoil area could not be used, and that all spoil was being placed on existing upland spoil areas.

As incorrect information had been received as to the alternate sites, Mr. O'Malley said it indicated the need for checking more closely in the future on Jacksonville Port Authority projects.

On motion by Mr. O'Malley, seconded by Mr. Conner and adopted without objection, the Board authorized the file deactivated and requested the Corps of Engineers to reconvey the Hannah Mills marsh spoil area to the Trustees as recommended by the staff.

OSCEOLA COUNTY - Lake Boundaries
Under provisions of Chapter 70-97, Acts of 1970, one method of establishing lake boundaries includes holding public hearings at which time evidence is submitted that can be utilized by the Board of Trustees.

On motion by Mr. Shevin, seconded by Mr. O'Malley and adopted without objection, the staff was authorized to request the Central and Southern Florida Flood Control District to hold public hearings on behalf of the Board of Trustees for the purpose of gathering evidence that would provide a means of establishing boundary lines for Lake Kissimmee, Lake Tohopekaliga, East Lake Tohopekaliga, Alligator Lake and Lake Lizzie, lying within Osceola County.

As only four members of the Board of Trustees were present on this date, consideration was deferred with reference to a report on the status of litigation, Coastal Petroleum Company vs Secretary of the Army of the United States, USDC Southern District No. 68-951-CIV-CA and 69-699-CIV-CA Consolidated.

2-23-71

Mr. Shevin asked for information on a report to be presented to the Board by the Technical Advisory Committee on Fill. A moratorium on dredging and filling was imposed on January 12 pending a determination of appropriate prices for fill material, and several applications had been approved subject to payment for the material at the price to be decided by the Board.

The Committee had met again, and the Director said a report was being prepared that would make some significant recommendations, and the Board should be able to consider the detailed report in two weeks.

SUBJECTS UNDER CHAPTER 18296

MARTIN COUNTY - Murphy Act Land Sale.
Mr. Conner made a motion, seconded by Mr. O'Malley and adopted that the Board approve sale of a parcel in Martin County under provisions of Section 197.350 Florida Statutes.

The Director advised that five affirmative votes were required for a land sale, whereupon the Trustees reconsidered their action and deferred consideration of the sale for one week.

On motion duly adopted, the meeting was adjourned.

_____
SECRETARY OF STATE - ACTING CHAIRMAN

ATTEST: _Fred Vidzes_____
INTERIM EXECUTIVE DIRECTOR

Tallahassee, Florida
March 3, 1971

The State of Florida Board of Trustees of the Internal Improvement Trust Fund met on this date in the Capitol, with the following members present:

Reubin O'D. Askew	Governor
Richard (Dick) Stone	Secretary of State
Robert L. Shevin	Attorney General
Fred O. Dickinson, Jr.	Comptroller
Floyd T. Christian	Commissioner of Education
Doyle Conner	Commissioner of Agriculture

Fred Vidzes	Interim Executive Director

The minutes of the meeting of February 16 were approved as submitted.

COLLIER COUNTY - Bids for Oil and Gas Lease.
On January 19, after receiving two bids which were identical, the Board authorized readvertisement for bids for a five-year oil and gas drilling lease covering the reserved one-half

3-3-71

interest of the Board of Education in privately-owned Section 16, Township 46 South, Range 29 East, and Section 16 in Township 46 South, Range 30 East, containing 1,280 surface acres (640 net mineral acres) in Collier County.

Invitation to bid was advertised pursuant to law, in the Tallahassee Democrat and the Naples Daily News, with bids to be opened at 10:00 a.m. on March 2. There being no meeting on that date, the bids were held and opened on March 3.

Two bids were received, one from Sun Oil Company for $2,310.40 and the second from Shell Oil Company for $2,598.40.

At the Director's suggestion, action was deferred for one week.

OKALOOSA AND SANTA ROSA COUNTIES - Oil Lease Assignment.
On motion by Mr. Christian, seconded by Mr. Stone and adopted without objection, the Board approved assignment from Beard Oil Company to Maui Oil Corporation of an undivided 20% of Beard's 25% interest in its oil and gas lease issued by the Florida Board of Forestry dated March 24, 1969.

Instrument of assignment was approved by the staff legal counsel and by the Division of Forestry. The lease covers 3,665 net acres in the Blackwater River State Forest.

GLADES COUNTY - Grazing Lease Renewal.
On motion by Mr. Conner, seconded by Mr. Christian and adopted without objection, the Board approved renewal of Grazing Lease No. 2107 to Tommy Bronson for three years at $5.50 per acre annual rental, with lease to provide for cancellation by the Board after 90-day written notice and to require lessee to pay any and all lawfully assessed taxes.

The former lease rental was 50¢ per acre for the 320.86 acre tract of reclaimed Lake Hicpochee bottom land in Section 25, Township 42 South, Range 31 East, and Sections 19, 20 and 30, Township 42 South, Range 32 East, adjacent to Mr. Bronson's upland ownership. The land was appraised by the staff appraiser who recommended $5.50 per acre as fair annual rental.

Approval for continued grazing on the reclaimed lake bottom was received from the Game and Fresh Water Fish Commission and Central and Southern Florida Flood Control District.

MANATEE COUNTY - File 2390-41-253.03, Dedication.
The National Audubon Society, represented by Myron G. Gibbons of Tampa, Florida, requested dedication of Whale Island and the sovereignty land within 400 feet of the island in Sarasota Bay adjacent to Section 31, Township 35 South, Range 17 East, Manatee County, to be used as a Wildlife Sanctuary.

The Department of Natural Resources reported that dedication of the island and nearby sovereignty land would give the highly productive biological area an extra measure of protection.

On motion by Mr. Dickinson, seconded by Mr. Christian and adopted without objection, the Board authorized the land advertised for objections only.

OKALOOSA COUNTY - State Commercial Dock Permit, Section 253.03 F. S.
The City of Fort Walton Beach applied for a post construction permit for two docks in Choctawhatchee Bay adjacent to uplands in Section 19, Township 2 South, Range 23 West, Okaloosa County. The facility at the municipal beach park was constructed prior to the August 11,

1970, dock policy change. $100 processing fee was submitted.

On motion by Mr. Dickinson, seconded by Mr. Christian and adopted without objection, the Board approved issuance of the dock permit.

PINELLAS COUNTY - Marina License, Section 253.03 F.S.
Mr. Wesley Mill, Jr., applied for a marina license for construction of a mooring facility for an apartment complex in Clearwater Harbor abutting Section 5, Township 29 South, Range 15 Ease, Pinellas County. He tendered the minimum annual license fee of $100. No dredging would be required.

The application was approved by the City of Clearwater and Pinellas County Water and Navigation Control Authority. The Department of Air and Water Pollution Control had no objection to the project.

On motion by Mr. Christian, seconded by Messrs. Stone and Dickinson, adopted without objection, the Board approved the permit with the effective date of January 1, 1971.

PINELLAS COUNTY - Marina License, Section 253.03 F.S.
Mr. Charles C. Hickox, president, Stowaway Marinas, Inc., applied for a marina license for construction of a fueling dock over 3,200 square feed in Boca Ciega Bay abutting Section 25, Township 31 South, Range 15 East, Pinellas County. No dredging was required. The minimum annual license fee of $100. was tendered.

The Department of Air and Water Pollution Control had no objection to the project.

On motion by Mr. Dickinson, seconded by Mr. Conner and adopted without objection, the Board approved issuance of marina license to the applicant.

TRUSTEES FUNDS - Legal Counsel.

The Board on August 11, 1970, retained the firm of Holland and Knight, and specifically Mr. Henry Kittleson of that firm, as outside special counsel for a period of six months. That period of time had expired and the staff requested extension of the existing arrangement for another six months, as Mr. Kittleson was working on Collier County land title questions and would be involved in pending Lake Cypress litigation.

Motion was made by Mr. Conner, seconded by Mr. Stone, for approval. Then Mr. Conner said he would withdraw his motion for the reason Mr. Shevin expressed objection, not on the basis of Mr. Kittleson's ability but for the reason that the law firm on occasion represents clients whose interests differ from the Board's. The possibility of there being a conflict of interests involved here was discussed, and also the fact that no reflection on the integrity of the attorney was intended. The Governor mentioned the extremely technical title matters that were involved in the special work being done by Mr. Kittleson, but deferring to the judgment of the Board's attorney, the Attorney General, a postponement was suggested.

At the request of Mr. Shevin, the Board deferred action for one week.

OSCEOLA AND POLK COUNTIES - Lake Hatchineha Boundary Agreement,
Conveyance, and Channel Permit.
The request from Florida Ridge Cattle Company for the Trustees to
enter into a boundary line agreement establishing the 52.5 ft.
mean sea level elevation by traverse as the public-private
boundary line as to a particular area of Lake Hatchineha was
deferred by the Trustees for two weeks at the request of the
Secretary of State.

BAY COUNTY - At the request of the Attorney General, action
was deferred for two weeks on a request from Marifarms, Inc.,
for a lease amendment to Mariculture Lease NO. 2408 covering
West Bay submerged land.

PUTNAM COUNTY - Utility Dredge Permit, Section 253.123(2) (b) F.S.
Hudson Pulp and Paper Corporation of Palatka, Florida,
requested approval of a dredge permit to install a forty-eight
inch force main in Rice Creek in Section 27, Township 9 South,
Range 26 East, Putnam County, as part of a larger multi-million
dollar project to provide secondary treatment for approximately
thirty-five million gallons of Hudson waste water per day.
Applicant tendered $100 processing fee. The biological report
was not adverse, indicating that the treatment might improve
water quality in the creek and in the St. Johns River.

On motion by Mr. Stone, seconded by Mr. Christian and adopted
without objection, the Board approved the application.

SARASOTA COUNTY - Bulkhead Line, Section 253.122 Florida Statutes.
The Sarasota County Water and Navigation Control Authority by
resolution adopted on February 15, 1967, established a bulkhead
line 3,795 feet long, along the southern bank of Forked Creek
in Sections 14 and 15, Township 40 South, Range 19 East, in
Sarasota County. The bulkhead line was approved by the county
prior to the enactment of Chapter 67-393, Laws of Florida;
therefore, no biological report was submitted. At the time
the original application for approval of the bulkhead line was
submitted the staff took the position that the Trustees did not
have jurisdiction in the creek.

The bulkhead line is landward of the original mean high water
line, and that area between the bulkhead line and the original
mean high water line had been dredged to create a channel.
Forked Creek was a non-meandered navigable body of water that
connected with Lemon Bay, and in the past the staff had declined
to assert jurisdiction in non-meandered navigable bodies of water.
The present staff recommended that whether or not a body of water
is meandered should have no bearing on the Trustees' asserting
jurisdiction, but that the true test for asserting jurisdiction
is whether or not a body of water is susceptible of navigation.
Therefore, the staff recommended approval of the bulkhead line
because it would preclude encroachment on a non-meandered
navigable body of water.

Mr. Stone said the explanation was completely satisfactory
and he made a motion, seconded by Mr. Christian, that the
bulkhead line be approved. Without objection, the motion was
adopted.

Mr. Shevin called attention to the many times that staff is called upon to make a decision on whether the Trustees have jurisdiction, sometimes litigation resulting later on such as a case the Department of Legal Affairs is now pursuing. He recommended that the Board make decisions on jurisdictional questions.

On motion by Mr. Shevin, seconded by Mr. Christian and adopted without objection, the Trustees as a matter of policy directed the staff to bring all questions of whether or not the Board has jurisdiction to the Board prior to sending out any type of letter or information.

MONROE COUNTY - The Florida Keys Aqueduct Authority application for bulkhead line, dredge and fill permit was removed from the agenda.

PUTNAM COUNTY - Swan Lake Settlement.
On January 29, 1970, the Executive Director executed an agreement with Mrs. Eleanor L. Johnston that would provide an access easement through her property in consideration for an instrument clearing title to filled marginal lands of Swan Lake. The easement would provide access to a parcel of filled lake bottom land owned by the Trustees.

On February 23 the Board deferred action as only four members were present to consider the staff recommendation for confirmation of the agreement and issuance of an ex parte disclaimer.

On motion by Mr. Christian, seconded by Mr. Conner and adopted without objection, the Board approved the staff recommendation.

HILLSBOROUGH COUNTY - Fill Permit, Section 253.124, File 161.
At the request of the Secretary of State, the Board deferred for one week consideration of the application from Tampa Port Authority.

ST. LUCIE COUNTY - Dredge Permit Amendment,
                    File No. 253.123-623 Florida Statutes.
Florida Power and Light Company requested amendment of its existing permit to allow removal of an additional 1,600,000 cubic yards of material from Big Mud Creek, for which payment of up to $1 per cubic yard will be made when the moratorium is lifted and the new fee established. The present authorized dredge depth of minus-55 feet will not be exceeded, but a larger area will be dredged.

Also, the applicant requested that the permit be amended to allow cutting a 200 ft. wide channel into the upland to obtain additional fill material from lands in private ownership in Sections 17 and 18, Township 36 South, Range 41 East, St. Lucie County.

The biological report showed that submerged lands in Big Mud Creek were not vegetated, the bottom consisted of either mud or a mixture of mud and sand, dredging should not have significant adverse effects on the marine life of the area that had been subject to removal of approximately three million cubic yards of material to date.

Governor Askew raised the question of possibility of creating an anaerobic condition, referring to such a condition in the Escambia River. It was explained that an impoundment area and a supply of water was needed for cooling purposes in the event of an emergency such as a hurricane that might require the Hutchison Island plant to have to shut down operations.

On motion by Mr. Stone, seconded by Mr. Christian and adopted without objection, the Board approved both requested amendments.

ESCAMBIA AND SANTA ROSA COUNTIES - Advertise for Oil Lease Bids. On motion by Mr. Christian, seconded by Mr. Dickinson and adopted without objection, the Trustees authorized advertisement for competitive sealed bids for a five-year oil and gas drilling lease covering a portion of the Escambia River containing 330.5 acres, more or less, in Township 5 North, Range 30 West, Escambia and Santa Rosa Counties. The lease will prohibit drilling in the river and will contain provisions for one-sixth royalty, annual rental of $1 per acre, $50,000 surety bond, and require at least one test well drilled on contiguous pooled drilling units to 6,000 feet or the sediments of the Jurassic Age, whichever is deeper.

State Geologist Robert O. Vernon had approved the terms and conditions and advised the Board that no well would be drilled in or under the river, and he would furnish the members complete information.

Action was deferred on a report on litigation between Coastal Petroleum Company and Secretary of the Army of the United States, USDC Southern District No. 68-951-CIV-CA and 69-699-CIV-CA Consolidated.

AEROJET GENERAL SETTLEMENT OFFER - On September 8, 1969, Aerojet-General Corporation moved to exercise its option to purchase some 25,000 acres of south Dade County land under a 1961 lease-option contract with the Board of Trustees and the Board of Education. Subsequently, on October 21, 1969, the defendant boards, on the Trustees' agenda, voted to "void" the lease-option contract.

By order of September 21, 1970, the United States District Court for the Northern District of Florida granted Aerojet's motion for summary final judgment, finding the lease-option contract to have been valid and Aerojet to have been entitled to specific performance by the defendant boards. The case was on appeal.

In settlement of this matter and to extinguish the state's appeal, Aerojet made a bona fide offer to pay—over and above the original contract purchase price--$100,000 cash on closing and to give back a deed to 1674 acres of land, more or less, to form a conservation buffer zone along the west and south sides of the subject property bordering on the Everglades National Park.

Counsel to the Board of Education and the Board of Trustees recommended acceptance of the settlement offer.

Attorney General Shevin had requested deferment but suggested that the Board might hear Mr. George Wright, representing Aerojet, who was present on this date. Mr. Wright discussed the settlement proposal resulting from conferences held at the inviation of counsel to the Trustees and the Board of Education with the hope of amicably resolving the pending litigation. He said the offer was made in good faith, his client considered it reasonable, and if the Board did not, his client would proceed with the lawsuit.

Mr. Christian recommended acceptance of the settlement. Governor Askew said that although entering into the contract might not have been a good deal for the state, it had been held legally binding and he felt Aerojet's offer was in good faith.

Mr. Philip S. Bennett, chief counsel to the Board of Trustees, reviewed the background on the case that came to him from the previous Attorney General, the summary final judgment and his decision as to a basis of appeal, his discussions with Mr. Wright and Mr. Stephen Marc Slepin, then counsel to the Board of Education, on the proposed settlement, land appraisal and selection of land to be a buffer zone adjacent to Everglades National Park, Mr. Slepin and Mr. Bennett had recommended acceptance.

Mr. Stone was in favor, and the Governor indicated that position but noted that Mr. Shevin had requested deferral. Mr. Conner raised the question of compliance with stipulations in the original contract as to performance which Mr. Bennett explained. Other questions were raised regarding performance and the basis that might be used for appeal.

Mr. Wright said he would contact his client regarding the requested two-weeks' deferment. He added that the industry did come in and unfortunately came to a halt in 1965 due to the failure of the federal government to proceed with the solid-fuel rocket program, that it was terminated through no fault of Aerojet. He agreed to communicate to his client the Board's expressions and the request that the offer remain open at least until March 17.

Without objection, action was deferred for two weeks.

SUBJECTS UNDER CHAPTER 18296

MARTIN COUNTY - Murphy Act Land Sale.
The staff requested approval of sale and execution of deed for a parcel of Murphy Act land in Martin County sold under provisions of Section 197.350 Florida Statutes, the Beulah V. Johns for the high bid of $100 as reported on Bidding Report No. 980. The parcel was certified to the State of Florida under tax sale certificates 215 of July 5, 1926, and 1909 of August 7, 1933, described as the East 35 feet of Lot 155, Unrecorded Plat of Sinclair Subdivision, Tract 40, Palm City Farms, Section 2, Township 39 South, Range 40 East, Martin County.

On February 23 action was deferred for the reason that only four members were present.

On motion by Mr. Christian, seconded by Mr. Stone and adopted without objection, the Board approved the sale and execution of deed pertaining thereto.

On motion duly adopted, the meeting was adjourned.

_____
GOVERNOR   -   CHAIRMAN

ATTEST: _Fred Vidzee_____
INTERIM EXECUTIVE DIRECTOR

3-3-71

Tallahassee, Florida
March 9, 1971

The State of Florida Board of Trustees of the Internal Improvement
Trust Fund met on this date in the Haydon Burns Building in
Tallahassee, Florida, with the following members present:

Reubin O'D. Askew	Governor
Richard (Dick) Stone	Secretary of State
Robert L. Shevin	Attorney General
Fred O. Dickinson, Jr.	Comptroller
Thomas D. O'Malley	Treasurer
Floyd T. Christian	Commissioner of Education
Doyle Conner	Commissioner of Agriculture

Fred Vidzes   Interim Executive Director

The minutes of the meeting of February 23 were approved.

BROWARD COUNTY - Erosion Control Line.
The Town of Hillsboro Beach by Resolution No. 141 adopted on
December 15, 1970, approved and submitted to the Board a proposal
for the establishment of a line defining the limits between ownership of the Atlantic Ocean from the north limits of the town
southerly 5,000 feet, following the mean high water line as nearly
as practicable. The "erosion control line", when approved and
recorded, may be used as the boundary between public and private
ownership. Appropriate instruments may be exchanged to clearly
define limits of interest.

Motion was made by Mr. O'Malley, seconded by Mr. Dickinson and
adopted without objection, that the Trustees approve the line
established by the Town of Hillsboro Beach.

INDIAN RIVER COUNTY - File No. 2386-31-253.12, Sale Deferral.
The Trustees deferred consideration of the purchase application
from the Estate of W. G. Bosworth, Deceased, represented by Robert
F. Lloyd, for a parcel of filled sovereignty land in the Indian
River abutting Section 8, Township 31 South, Range 39 East, Indian
River County. The staff requested the deferment until the applicant
submits information requested and the appraisal is received.

SANTA ROSA COUNTY - Oil and Gas Lease.
On motion by Mr. Christian, seconded by Mr. O'Malley and adopted
without objection, the Board authorized the staff to advertise
for competitive sealed bids for a five-year oil and gas drilling
lease covering that portion of the 100-ft. wide right of way of
State Road 89 in Section 40, Township 5 North, Range 29 West,
containing 13.662 acres, more or less, in Santa Rosa County. The
Department of Transportation approved advertising for bids on this
portion of the right of way which extends northward from the
center of the Town of Jay.

Pursuant to Section 253.61 (a), Florida Statutes, the governing
authority of the Town of Jay will be requested to consent by
resolution to issuance of the lease that will contain a special
provision prohibiting drilling on the road right of way. Other
terms will be one-sixth royalty, annual rental of one dollar per

acre, $50,000 surety bond, and the requirement that at least one test well be drilled every 2½ years to a depth of 6,000 feet or to the sediments of the Jurassic Age, whichever is deeper, on contiguous pooled drilling units.

The State Geologist reviewed and approved the terms and special conditions.

OKALOOSA, SANTA ROSA AND ESCAMBIA COUNTIES - Seismic Permit. Geophysical Service, Inc., requested permission to conduct seismic exploration operation covering the ownership of the Trustees in the Perdido, Escambia and Yellow Rivers. Using air guns mounted on small boats and pontoons, the applicant will explore by reflection method and will not use explosive charges. The entire operation will take place between January and June 30, 1971.

The Department of Natural Resources issued Permit 98 dated January 19, 1971, for this exploration.

On motion by Mr. Christian, seconded by Mr. O'Malley and adopted without objection, the Board approved the request of Geophysical Service, Inc.

GLADES COUNTY - Grazing Lease Renewal.
Mr. Billy Rogers applied for renewal of Grazing Lease No. 2127 covering 142.23 acres of reclaimed Lake Okeechobee bottom land in Section 3, Township 40 South, Range 33 East, Glades County, traversed by State Road 78 and adjacent to applicant's upland.

The two tracts were appraised by the staff appraiser who recommended $4.30 per acre as the current fair annual rental. The former lease rental was $2.46 per acre.

Motion was made by Mr. Conner, seconded by Mr. Christian, that the lease be renewed as recommended by the staff, at $4.30 per acre annual rental, subject to cancellation by the Board after 90-day written notice, and lessee to pay any and all lawfully assessed taxes.

There was discussion on a question raised by the Governor as to a provision for maximum grazing density. Mr. Conner commented that it would be to the detriment of the owner of the livestock to impair the land by overgrazing, but that consideration might be given to preventing any erosion condition that might develop. The staff would prepare a report covering suggestions made for protecting the land from impairment.

There was no objection to issuance of the renewal on the terms recommended by the staff, and the motion was adopted.

DADE COUNTY - Campsite Lease.
On motion by Mr. Stone, seconded by Mr. Christian and adopted without objection, the Board authorized renewal of Campsite Lease No. 2173 held by Miami Springs Power Boat· Club, Inc., represented by Mr. Arthur Margerison, for one year with option to renew for four additional years on a year-to-year basis at an annual rental of $300.

Renewal conformed to the April 7, 1970, policy allowing a lease

as long as the structure remains on the site, and the policy of
October 6, 1970, that established an annual rental of $300 for a
quarter-acre site.

ESCAMBIA AND SANTA ROSA COUNTIES - Utility Dredge Permit,
                                             Section 253.123(2)(b) F.S.
Humble Oil and Refining Company requested approval of a dredge
permit to install two 4-inch flow lines in the Escambia River in
Sections 31 and 33, Township 6 North, Range 29 West, in Escambia
and Santa Rosa Counties. The staff suggested deferment to allow
a company representative to be present to explain measures to
contain any leakage.

The Board deferred action as requested.

GULF COUNTY - Dredge Permit Amendment, File 253.123-527,
                       and Fill Permit File 253.214-163.
On the request of the Secretary of State, action was deferred on the
request from Port St. Joe Authority to amend its permit to allow
removal of an additional 68,000 cubic yards of accumulated bark and
other material along the shoreline in St. Joseph Bay in Section 35,
Township 7 South, Range 11 West, Gulf County.

PINELLAS COUNTY - State Marina License, Section 253.03 F. S.
On motion by Mr. Stone, seconded by Mr. O'Malley and adopted without
objection, the Board approved the application from Field Hotel
Corporation for a marina license for construction of a mooring
facility on 28,213.62 square feet of sovereignty land in Clearwater
Harbor adjacent to uplands in Section 17, Township 29 South, Range
15 East, Pinellas County. Applicant had tendered $564.27 for the
first year's fee.

No dredging was required and the Department of Air and Water
Pollution Control had no objection to the project.

PINELLAS COUNTY - State Marina License, Section 253.03 F. S.
On motion by Mr. O'Malley, seconded by Mr. Stone and adopted
without objection, the Board approved the application from H. F.
Hallock, Inc., for a marina license for construction of a fishing
and sunning facility in Boca Ciega Bay adjacent to upland in Section
14, Township 31 South, Range 15 East, Pinellas County. The
applicant tendered the minimum annual fee of $100 for the 265 square
feet.

No dredging was required and the Department of Air and Water
Pollution Control had no objection to the project.

NASSAU COUNTY - Power Line Easement.
On motion by Mr. Conner, seconded by Mr. O'Malley and adopted
without objection, the Board authorized issuance of a 30-ft. wide
easement to Florida Public Utilities Company for an electric power
line and existing poles, lines and fixtures over and across
portions of Sections 10, 11 and 12, Township 3 North, Range 28
East, and Sections 7 and 8, Township 3 North, Range 29 East, in
Fort Clinch State Park at Fernandina Beach.

The Department of Natural Resources approved and authorized
issuance of the easement.

TRUSTEES' FUNDS - Appraisals.
On motion by Mr. Stone, seconded by Messrs. Christian and O'Malley, adopted without objection, the Board authorized the staff to retain an assistant for the staff appraiser for an additional four-month period beginning March 1, 1971, at the rate of $800 per month.

It appeared from the increasing workload that assistance for the staff appraiser will continue to be needed to properly administer the appraisal needs of the agency. Therefore, the staff also requested authorization to request establishment of the position of Assistant to Appraiser.

The Board granted approval on the condition that creation of the position will be justified to the Department of Administration, and the matter will be brought back to the attention of the Cabinet for decision based on the recommendations of the staff and of the Department of Administration.

PALM BEACH COUNTY - Modify Marina License.
In order to equal the minimum life expectancy of its marina structure and to allow time to redeem municipal bonds issued for the project, the City of Lake Worth requested modification of the standard marina license requirements contained in State Marina License No. ML-19 approved on January 19, 1971, to allow a time period of twenty years with option to renew for an additional twenty years.

On motion by Mr. O'Malley, seconded by Mr. Christian and adopted without objection, the Board authorized modification of the marina license as requested.

COLLIER COUNTY - Bids for Oil and Gas Lease.
On January 19, after receiving two identical bids for an oil and gas lease of the reserved one-half interest of the Board of Education in privately-owned Section 16, Township 46 South, Range 29 East, and Section 16, Township 46 South, Range 30 East, 640 net mineral acres in Collier County, the Trustees authorized readvertisement for bids for a five-year oil and gas lease. Invitation to bid was advertised pursuant to law, in the Tallahassee Democrat and the Naples Daily News, with bids to be opened at 10:00 a.m. on March 2, 1971.

As there was no meeting on March 2, the bids were held and opened at the meeting on March 3, 1971, and action was deferred until this date. Two bids were received, $2,310.40 from Sun Oil Company and $2,598.40 from Shell Oil Company.

On motion by Mr. Christian, seconded and adopted without objection, the Board accepted the high bid of $2,598.40 from Shell Oil Company and authorized issuance of lease to that firm.

TRUSTEES' FUNDS - Outside Legal Counsel.
On March 3 the Board deferred action on the request to extend for another six months the existing arrangement with the law firm of Holland and Knight, and specifically Mr. Henry Kittleson, as outside special counsel. Subsequently, Mr. Shevin conferred with Mr. Kittleson by telephone and expressed himself as satisfied with the propriety of the situation and that the firm was very sensitive and would avoid anything in any way involving a conflict of interest.

Motion was made by Mr. Shevin, seconded by Mr. Christian, and adopted unanimously, that Mr. Kittleson be retained as outside special counsel for an additional six months.

HILLSBOROUGH COUNTY - Consideration of the fill permit requested by Tampa Port Authority (Section 253.124, File 161) was postponed at the recommendation of the staff until the bulkhead lines have been re-established by the Authority.

FRANKLIN COUNTY - Dredge Permit, Section 253.123 F.S., File 718.
                  Dredge to Improve Navigation.
The Department of Natural Resources made application for a permit authorizing maintenance dredging in a navigation channel 500 ft. long, 50 ft. wide and 5 ft. deep in Section 1, Township 6 South, Range 2 West, in Ochlockonee Bay, Franklin County. Spoil from the channel would be deposited adjacent to the channel in the bay. The biological report was not adverse to either the dredging or spoiling of the 2,000 cubic yards of material.

On motion by Mr. Stone, seconded by Mr. O'Malley and Mr. Christian, and adopted without objection, the Trustees approved issuance of the dredge permit.

PALM BEACH COUNTY - Lake Osborne.
In compliance with Chapter 19133, Laws of Florida, Acts of 1939, the then Trustees executed Deed No. 18516 conveying Lake Osborne to Palm Beach County for park and forest purposes under the custody and control of the Board of County Commissioners of Palm Beach County. On December 8, 1970, the Board of County Commissioners renewed a sand dredging contract for dredging in the lake. Numerous objections to the dredging activity were filed with the Trustees' office, and the staff discussed the matter with the Attorney General's staff, requesting advice. It had been recommended that action be taken to preclude further dredging in Lake Osborne. Therefore, the staff requested authority to transmit a letter requesting the Board of County Commissioners of Palm Beach County to have the dredging stopped and submit a full report on the subject.

Mr. Malcolm Anderson, representing the Federated Conservation Council and also adjacent property owners on Lake Osborne, urged immediate cessation of the dredging which he charged was damaging to the ecology and wildlife in adjacent marsh areas and was not complying with the conditions in the conveyance for forest and park purposes.

Attorney General Shevin summarized his memorandum dated February 23, responding to the Director's request on February 8 for advice, pointed out that he had recommended that the staff take action to halt the dredging immediately and if not halted, to take the necessary steps to enforce the possibility of reverter including, if necessary, a suit to recover possession of the land including damages. He added that his memorandum of this date to the Board pointed out that action should already have been taken, and with reference to the agenda item, a telegram instead of a letter should be sent to the County Commission to stop the dredging immediately.

Mr. O'Malley expressed concern that the staff had not taken the immediate action recommended by the Attorney General's memorandum, and the Director explained that the staff required board authority on matters of jurisdiction.

The Governor thought there was some difference of opinion as to whether or not the state retains sovereignty making it a question of jurisdiction, but the situation might have been brought to the Trustees' attention sooner, and if there had not been compliance with the deed provisions Lake Osborne might be subject to reversion. Mr. Shevin did not consider it an issue of jurisdiction and said the dredging on sovereign lands was of an emergency nature and should be stopped immediately by telegram followed by a letter.

Motion was made by Mr. O'Malley that the Attorney General's recommendations be followed. Mr. Stone seconded the motion.

Mr. Michael Small from the County Attorney's office, representing the Palm Beach County Commissioners, said they desired to do only what was best for the greatest majority of the tax payers, that the area had been used for recreation even before the dredging started in 1960 which had created a lake from a swampy marsh, that the county had constructed a roadway all along the park, that the sand dredging lease had been renewed at least three times. He understood the Trustees' authority with respect to exercise of the reverter clause, but his presentation of recreational use of the area appeared to show compliance with the terms of the deed. Mr. Small was not prepared to make a complete report on the question of dredging, having received notice of this meeting on the Friday preceeding this date; but asked for a deferment for three weeks in order to have certain tests made to determine the effects of the dredging. He said that litigation brought by the objectors was pending in Palm Beach County and an accurate reading of the biological effects could not be made if the dredging conditions were changed now.

Dr. Dwight Goforth, a biologist with the Game and Fresh Water Fish Commission, said that now Lake Osborne was navigable because of the dredging, but continued dredging would damage the submerged marsh areas, increase turbidity and other adverse effects. He was involved in the suit to seek a permanent injunction to stop the dredging, having appeared before the County Commission and failed in an attempt to have the dredging stopped. The county had renewed the sand dredging lease.

The members asked many questions and after considerable discussion, and feeling that dredging activity violated the covenants in the deed and there was no permit for the dredging to begin with, it was the consensus that the county should be notified to cease and desist until such time as the permit is properly brought before the Board to determine whether further dredging would be permitted in the navigable body of water, and also to determine whether there has been satisfaction on the question of reverter. Mr. Stone made that as a motion, and it was seconded by Mr. Shevin. With Messrs. Shevin, Conner, Dickinson and Stone voting "Aye", and no objections, the motion was adopted.

The Director was instructed to notify the county by telegram, and with a follow-up letter which the Attorney General would assist the staff to prepare.

———————

FRANKLIN COUNTY - Attorney General Shevin reported briefly on the application for a dredge permit to improve navigation for Dr. A.C. Tuck that was considered by the Trustees on December 15, 1970, which he had been asked to assist with in the meeting on February 16, 1971.

The staff surveyors, asked by the Attorney General's office to make a new survey, had been denied access and then the applicant's attorney asked for a formal letter requesting permission before the surveyors will be allowed to make a survey. Mr. Shevin pointed out that whatever delay had been occasioned was because of the applicant's action.

Mr. Shevin made a motion, seconded by Mr. Stone and adopted without objection, that the staff be directed to send the requested letter so that the survey can proceed.

On motion duly adopted, the meeting was adjourned.

GOVERNOR — CHAIRMAN

ATTEST: _Fred Vidzes_
INTERIM EXECUTIVE DIRECTOR

***   ***

Tallahassee, Florida
March 16, 1971

The State of Florida Board of Trustees of the Internal Improvement Trust Fund met on this date in the auditorium of the Department of Transportation, with the following members present:

Reubin O'D. Askew	Governor
Richard (Dick) Stone	Secretary of State
Robert L. Shevin	Attorney General
Fred O. Dickinson, Jr.	Comptroller
Thomas D. O'Malley	Treasurer, present part time
Floyd T. Christian	Commissioner of Education
Doyle Conner	Commissioner of Agriculture
Fred Vidzes	Interim Executive Director

The minutes of the meeting of March 3 were approved as submitted.

PALM BEACH COUNTY - Lake Osborne Dredging.
On March 9 the Board directed the staff to notify the Board of County Commissioners of Palm Beach County to stop dredging in Lake Osborne until the matter of a permit is properly brought before the Board and the Board determines whether there has been compliance with the deed provisions.

3-16-71

Mr. Herbert Benn, Assistant Attorney General, filed a petition to intervene in the suit styled Federated Conservation Council vs. Board of County Commissioners, Palm Beach County, et al, seeking temporary injunction against dredging in the lake and a permanent injunction against further activities affecting the lake on the basis that title to the lake bottom was in question and that the dredging failed to obtain appropriate permits from the State of Florida. The court heard the state's argument for temporary injunction on March 12 and allowed the hearing to be continued on March 16 for introduction of additional testimony.

In view of the necessity to take immediate action in the litigation, motion was made by Mr. Stone, seconded by Mr. Shevin and adopted without objection, that the Trustees confirm the action taken by Mr. Vidzes requesting Mr. Benn to plead the state's cause in this matter. This action was considered out of order at the beginning of the meeting, so that the state's representative could be promptly notified. Mr. Shevin briefly explained what his office had done with respect to this situation.

DADE COUNTY - Aerojet-General Settlement Offer.
On March 3 the Board considered an offer from Aerojet-General Corp. to pay--over and above the original contract purchase price--$100,000 cash on closing and to give back a deed to 1674 acres of land, more or less, to form a buffer zone along the west and south sides of the 25,000 acres of south Dade County land covered by a 1961 lease-option contract with the Trustees and the Board of Education, for a settlement and to extinguish the state's appeal in the litigation brought when the boards voted to "void" the lease-option contract. Many questions were raised and the Trustees deferred action until this date.

While the case might be difficult Attorney General Shevin recommended that the cabinet continue litigation, as he thought there were criteria on which to prosecute the appeal and possibly win it. He thought the over-riding consideration should be that the firm failed to establish the industrial facility, and the issue had not been totally presented to the court. He would vote against the offered settlement as he thought the value of the land outweighed the risk, the state or county might get a buffer zone by condemnation, and the case should be vigorously pursued.

Motion was made by Mr. O'Malley, seconded by Mr. Stone and Mr. Dickinson, that the settlement offer be rejected formally and the Attorney General be requested to join in pursuit of the appeal with the general counsel of the Board of Education and the Trustees.

Mr. Conner expressed the opinion that at the time of the original contract the state had given the firm an incentive with land for $50 and acre and the state would have gone through with its part, but had the firm lived up to the bargain?

In view of what might be lost Mr. Christian expressed doubts, as the general counsel of the Board of Education and the Trustees had recommended settlement; but he accepted the Attorney General's recommendation in order to try to get the land back.

Mr. Conner and Governor Askew noted that the apparent failure to establish the facility might have been through no fault of the firm.

Mr. Alston Fisher's presence on behalf of Aerojet-General Corp. was recognized, but he made no statement for the record.

The biological report stated that restoration of the filled area to
its previous condition by removing the fill was a questionable
solution, and recommended removal of a small part of the fill at the
south end to provide connection of a marsh area to open water. The
applicant had agreed to remove the fill as suggested in that report
and agreed to pay three times the appraised value. He represented
that the sale would be in the public interest because the alternative
would not be in the public interest.

The staff recommended advertisement for objections only. Mr. Vidzes
said the party had been completely unaware of state requirements as
to filling and it was a very small parcel.

Mr. Conner made a motion, seconded by Mr. Stone, for approval.

Mr. Shevin made a substitute motion that the price be $2,500 instead
of $1,500, pointing out that the policy for sale of land filled
without authority required payment of three times the appraised
value as a minimum. Mr. Christian seconded this motion. Mr. Vidzes
explained that this would be an awkward situation, the applicant
might not purchase the parcel that would then just lie there, and the
Board could consider the price further after the advertising period.
Mr. Stone agreed, and Mr. Christian withdrew his second to the
substitute motion.

Mr. Vidzes advised that with respect to the biologist's recommendation for a connection of the marsh area to open water, the staff
would not issue a deed until the work was done.

On the first motion, adopted with Mr. Shevin voting "No", the Board
authorized advertisement of the parcel for objections only, the matter
of price to receive further consideration at the time for confirmation
of the sale. On the same motion the bulkhead line was approved.

TRUSTEES APPOINT DIRECTOR.
The Governor requested consideration of Mr. Joel Kuperberg to be
executive director for the Board of Trustees, to become effective
April 5. At least four affirmative votes are required for confirmation of an appointment by the Governor.

Motion was made by Mr. Christian, seconded by Mr. O'Malley, that
the appointment be confirmed. The motion was adopted on a vote of
six to one, Mr. Stone voting "No". Mr. Shevin spoke of his conference
with Mr. Kuperberg and his satisfaction that he could fill the
position well.

Because of afternoon appointments, Mr. O'Malley found it necessary to
leave the board meeting that had extended well into the afternoon
after a lunch recess during the presentation of the lengthy agenda
of the Board of Natural Resources.

PALM BEACH COUNTY - Bulkhead line, Section 253.122, Florida Statutes.
The City of Lake Worth by Ordinance No. 70-21 adopted on July 20,
1970, relocated an existing bulkhead line 590.77 feet long in Lake
Worth adjacent to State Road 802 (Lake Avenue) in Sections 26 and
27, Township 44 South, Range 43 East, Palm Beach County, to
accommodate construction of a four-lane bridge and road relocation
immediately adjacent to an existing causeway. This bulkhead line
appeared on the advance agenda on October 6, 1970.

The biological report indicated that the area to be affected by the new fill approach is not a shallow grassy bottom, but care should be taken to contain the trucked-in fill material at the fill site.

On motion by Mr. Christian, seconded by Mr. Stone and adopted without objection, the Board approved the bulkhead line established by the City of Lake Worth.

PALM BEACH COUNTY - File No. 2394-50-253.03, Easement, Fill Permit. The Department of Transportation requested an easement across a parcel of sovereignty land in Lake Worth embracing 4.01 acres abutting Sections 26 and 27, Township 44 South, Range 43 East, City of Lake Worth, Palm Beach County, for causeway and bridge right of way on State Road 802.

The Department also requested approval of a fill permit authorized by the City of Lake Worth Resolution No. 69-70 adopted December 7, 1970, for 2.77 acres for causeway construction. Trucked-in fill material will be used to fill the parcel that is landward of the bulkhead line above. The Area Planning Board of Palm Beach County had no objection.

The biological report dated August 31, 1970, was not adverse to the bridge construction over Lake Worth, but cited limited adverse effects to be expected from the filling.

The staff recommended that the easement be issued and the fill permit approved, the latter to be issued in the name of the contractor with a stipulation that all material be obtained from upland sources and the work be subject to normal stipulations as to filling.

On motion by Mr. Christian, seconded by Mr. Stone and adopted without objection, the Board approved the staff recommendations.

HILLSBOROUGH COUNTY - Lease Assignment.
On motion by Mr. Stone, seconded by Mr. Christian and adopted without objection, the Board consented to assignment of a Lease Agreement dated August 15, 1961, between the State Board of Education and the Trustees of the Diocese of Central Florida, to the Diocese of Southwest Florida, Inc.

The property was part of the campus of the University of South Florida. The instrument of assignment was reviewed and approved as to form and legality by the general counsel for the Board of Education.

PALM BEACH COUNTY - Road Right of Way.
On motion by Mr. Christian, seconded by Mr. Stone and adopted without objection, the Board approved a request from the Department of Transportation, also approved by the Department of Health and Rehabilitative Services, for an easement for road right of way in connection with State Road 9 (I-95) embracing 0.055 acre in the SE¼ of Section 33, Township 44 South, Range 43 East, Palm Beach County, being part of A.G. Holley State Hospital property in Lantana.

The Department of Transportation had agreed to relocate a fence at that departments expense.

DADE COUNTY - Campsite Lease.
On motion by Mr. Stone, seconded by Mr. Conner and Mr. Christian, adopted without objection, the Board approved the application from Isaac Dalton Cathey and John C. Tucker for renewal of Campsite Lease No. 2172 in Biscayne Bay for one year with option to renew on a year-to-year basis for four additional years, at an annual rental of $300. The request conforms to the policy of April 7, 1970, allowing lease as long as the structure remains on the site, and the October 6 policy establishing an annual rental of $300 for a quarter-acre site.

DADE COUNTY - Fill Permit, Section 253.124(8), File No. 164.
Public Works Department of Metropolitan Dade County requested a permit to fill two eroded areas along Rickenbacker Causeway, as follows: (1) Station 22+00 to Station 55+50 not exceeding 25 ft. wide and consisting of 1.89 acres in Section 54, Township 13 South, Range 41 East, and (2) from Station 110+50 to 131+00 not exceeding 25 ft. wide and consisting of 1.2 acres in Section 54, Township 13 South, Range 41 East, Dade County. The material would be trucked from an upland area.

Motion was made by Mr. Stone, seconded by Mr. Christian, and adopted that the permit be approved provided the county explore the feasibility of placing riprap to retain the fill material as suggested by Governor Askew.

PINELLAS COUNTY - State Dock Permit, Section 253.03 F.S.
On motion by Mr. Christian, seconded by Mr. Stone and adopted without objection, the Board approved the application of Jenard M. Gross for a state commercial dock permit for a dock application that was approved by Pinellas County Water and Navigation Control Authority under Permit No. 5527 prior to August 11, 1970, the date of policy change relative to state marina licenses.

POLK COUNTY - Marina License, Section 253.03 F.S.
At the request of Attorney General Shevin, action was postponed one week on the application of Stephen W. Keen for a marina license for construction of a mooring facility in Crooked Lake.

MARTIN COUNTY - Settlement.
The Field Operations Division reports an unauthorized operation by Julian B. Slevin consisting of connecting an upland boat basin to the St. Lucie River. Nineteen cubic yards of material had been removed from sovereignty bottoms in the St. Lucie River adjacent to the applicant's upland property in Section 35, Township 36 South, Range 41 East, Martin County.

The staff recommended acceptance of the applicant's check for $100 as penalty payment for the material removed, and $50 application fee.

On motion by Mr. Conner, seconded by Mr. Christian and adopted, the settlement was approved without objection.

PINELLAS COUNTY - Bulkhead Line Revision and Dredge and Fill
                  Permit Denial.
On February 16, 1971, Pinellas County Water and Navigation Control Authority denied the request of H. Sage Thompson for a bulkhead line revision and modification of Dredge-Only Permit No. 187 in

St. Joseph's Sound. The biological report from the Department of
Natural Resources dated July 9, 1970, was adverse.

On motion by Mr. Christian, seconded by Mr. Stone and adopted
without objection, the Board concurred with Pinellas County's
action denying the application, as recommended by the staff.

GULF COUNTY - Artificial Reef Permit.
The City of Port St. Joe requested permission to construct ten
artificial reefs at specified locations in the Gulf of Mexico, Gulf
County, each reef to consist of twenty cars in groups of five and
165 ft. long, 24 ft. wide, 5 ft. high and 400 yards apart, as
recommended by the Department of Natural Resources.

On motion by Mr. Dickinson, seconded by Mr. Stone and adopted
without objection, the Board approved issuance of the permit for
$50 processing fee.

SANTA ROSA COUNTY - Oil and Gas Drilling Lease.
On February 2 the Trustees authorized the staff to advertise for
sealed bids for a five-year oil and gas drilling lease of the
one-half reserved interest of the State of Florida in all of Lot 2,
Section 12, Township 5 North, Range 30 West, less the South 22½
chains, containing 56.235 surface acres (28.117 net mineral acres).
Invitation to bid was advertised in the Tallahassee Democrat and
the Milton Press-Gazette pursuant to law, proof of publication
filed in the Trustees' office, and the three bids received were
opened at 10:00 a.m. on this date.

The following bids were received; Humble Oil & Refining Company,
$58,528.12; Sun Oil Company, $38,042.98; and Pennzoil United, Inc.,
$2,839.87. The Director recommended acceptance of the high bid.

On motion by Mr. Stone, seconded by Mr. Dickinson and adopted
without objection, the Board accepted the high bid and authorized
issuance of the oil and gas drilling lease to Humble Oil & Refining
Company.

LEE COUNTY - Advertise Oil and Gas Lease.
Staff requested authority to advertise for sealed bids for a five
year oil and gas drilling lease covering a tract owned by the Trustees
approximately 12 miles southeast of Fort Myers described as Government
Lots 3 and 4, Section 2, Township 46 South, Range 26 East, containing
80.28 acres, more or less, in Lee County.

The State Geologist reviewed and concurred in the following terms
and conditions: 1/8 royalty, annual rental $1 per acre, $50,000
surety bond, and one test well every 2½ years to a depth of 6,000
feet or to the top of the Lower Cretaceous, whichever is deeper.

On motion by Mr. Dickinson, seconded by Mr. Conner and Mr. Christian,
adopted without objection, the Board authorized the advertisement
for bids.

MONROE COUNTY - Minutes Amended.
On motion by Mr. Dickinson, seconded by Mr. Christian and adopted
without objection, the Board authorized amendment to the minutes
of February 16, 1971, pertaining to the Rimersburg Coal Company

dredge permit in order to add the dimensions of the three access
channels 50 ft. wide, 500 ft. long, and 5 ft. deep.

The agenda had shown 10 ft. deep, but the depth was modified to 5 ft.

SHELL LEASE INCOME - For the Record.
On motion duly adopted, the Board received for the record the
report of income received by the Department of Natural Resources
from the following holders of dead shell leases:

Lease No.	Company	Amount
1718	Radcliff Materials, Inc.	$40,000.00
1718	Radcliff Materials, Inc.	6.30
2233	Bay Dredging & Construction Co.	4,607.29
2235	Ft. Myers Shell & Dredging Co.	630.90

BAY COUNTY - Mariculture Lease Amendment.
At the request of Secretary of State Stone, the Board deferred for
one week consideration of the request from Marifarms, Incorporated,
for amendment of Mariculture Lease No. 2408 covering West Bay
submerged land in Bay County.

SANTA ROSA COUNTY - Marina License, Section 253.03 F.S.
The staff recommended approval without fee for a public facility
requested by the Department of the Navy, Commanding Officer,
Southern Division, Naval Facilities Command, consisting of a
fishing and mooring facility over 3,600 square feet in the Blackwater River abutting Section 35, Township 2 North, Range 28 West,
Santa Rosa County, that was deferred by the Trustees on January 26.

No dredging would be required. The Department of Air and Water
Pollution Control had no objection, and the biological report from
the Florida Game and Fresh Water Fish Commission was not adverse.

On motion by Mr. Dickinson, seconded by Mr. Stone and Mr. Christian,
and duly adopted, the Board approved the marina license without
charging a fee for the public facility.

MONROE COUNTY - Stilt Houses in Marquesas Keys.
On January 19 the Board agreed to join with the District Engineer
and the Bureau of Sport Fisheries and Wildlife in posting notices
on stilt houses constructed without authorization in the area
lying within the boundaries of Key West National Wildlife Refuge
in Monroe County established on August 8, 1908, by Executive Order
signed by President Theodore Rossevelt. The posting was completed
and the notices to owners requested that plans be furnished by
March 11 for complying with the Board's directive to remove the
structure from the premises.

By telegram Congressman Dante B. Fascell requested the Board to
grant a 90-day extension for the purpose of holding public hearings,
to afford the affected individuals due process. Mr. William Ashe,
representative of the United States Fish and Wildlife Service in
Atlanta, indicated no objection to holding such hearings.

The staff recommended extension of the notice period for 90 days
commencing March 11, and that the staff participate in the public
hearings.

On motion by Mr. Stone, seconded by Mr. Christian and adopted without objection, the Board accepted the staff recommendations.

Governor Askew expressed appreciation on behalf of himself and the cabinet to Mr. Fred Vidzes for serving as Interim Executive Director for the Board of Trustees during a very difficult time, pending the appointment of a permanent director.

On motion duly adopted, the meeting was adjourned.

GOVERNOR — CHAIRMAN

ATTEST: *Fred Vidzes*
INTERIM EXECUTIVE DIRECTOR

Tallahassee, Florida
March 23, 1971

The State of Florida Board of Trustees of the Internal Improvement Trust Fund met on this date in the Haydon Burns Building in Tallahassee, Florida, with the following members present:

Reubin O'D. Askew	Governor
Richard (Dick) Stone	Secretary of State
Robert L. Shevin	Attorney General
Fred O. Dickinson, Jr.	Comptroller
Thomas D. O'Malley	Treasurer
Floyd T. Christian	Commissioner of Education
Doyle Conner	Commissioner of Agriculture

Fred Vidzes	Interim Executive Director

The minutes of March 9 were approved as submitted.

With reference to the minutes of March 16 that would be submitted for approval next week, Mr. Christian had requested clarification and Governor Askew said the minutes should reflect that the request of the Board to ask the Attorney General to intervene in the Aerojet-General Corporation suit was that he do it in the nature of associate counsel and not with the idea of trying to displace the principal counsel.

PALM BEACH COUNTY - Lake Osborne.
On March 9 and 16 the Board had considered the dredging in Lake Osborne, notified the county to stop immediately and subsequently through Mr. Herbert Benn, Assistant Attorney General, filed a petition to intervene in a suit styled Federated Conservation Council vs. Board of County Commissioners, Palm Beach County, et al, and requested Mr. Benn to plead the state's cause in this matter.

3-23-71

Attorney General Shevin advised the Board regarding a hearing and
that the Circuit Judge did enter a temporary injunction preventing
the county from continuing to dredge in Lake Osborne; but the county
had filed a motion for a rehearing on the temporary restraining
order and also filed a motion to advance the final hearing. Mr. Shevin
felt confident that the Board could get a permanent injunction to
prevent the county from dredging, but he pointed out that they were
also seeking a reversion of the land because of the serious questions
as to whether the county had used it for park and recreational
purposes. The two positions that had been advanced were with respect
to the reversion and that the county had failed to obtain proper
dredging permits from the Trustees.

Governor Askew thanked the Attorney General for the explanation.

MARTIN COUNTY - File No. 2130-43-253.12, Application Withdrawn.
Fadina Price and Bettie B. Hoppe of Jensen Beach, Florida,
represented by W.R. Scott of Stuart, Florida, had submitted an
application dated June 6, 1968, with application fee of $75 for
purchase of a parcel of sovereignty land in the Indian River in
Martin County. Subsequently the applicant requested withdrawal
of the application.

The staff recommended deactivation of the file and refund of the
$75 application fee that was paid prior to adoption of the December
23, 1969, policy making such a fee non-refundable.

On motion by Mr. Christian, seconded by Mr. Stone and adopted
without objection, the staff recommendation was approved as the
action of the Board.

VOLUSIA COUNTY - File No. 2393-64-253.129, Disclaimer.
On motion by Mr. Christian, seconded by Mr. Conner and adopted
without objection, the Board authorized issuance of a disclaimer for
$100 processing fee, to Eileen H. Butts, represented by Jay D. Bond, Jr.
attorney, for a parcel of filled sovereignty land embracing 1.4 acres
in the Halifax River abutting Section 14, Township 14 South, Range
32 East, Volusia County, for which all required exhibits had been
furnished including three affidavits indicating that the parcel was
filled by a predecessor in title prior to May 29, 1951.

PINELLAS COUNTY - State Construction Permit, Swimming Safety Line.
The Holiday Inn of Clearwater on February 23, 1971, was denied a
permit to place a swimmers' safety line adjacent to an existing
channel near Clearwater Pass by the Pinellas County Water and
Navigation Control Authority. The Authority had denied the request
previously, on November 10, 1970.

On motion by Mr. Stone, seconded by Mr. Christian and adopted
without objection, the Board concurred with the Pinellas County
Authority's action denying the application.

PINELLAS COUNTY - Marina License, Section 253.03 F.S.
Sea Island Apartments Condominium No. 3 applied for a marina
license for an existing mooring facility covering 615 square feet
in Clearwater Harbor abutting Section 5, Township 29 South, Range
15 East, Pinellas County. $100 minimum annual fee was tendered,
no dredging was required and the Department of Air and Water
Pollution Control had no objection to the project.

Motion was made by both Mr. Christian and Mr. Stone, seconded by
Mr. O'Malley, and adopted without objection, that the Board approve
issuance of a marina license with effective date of January 1, 1971.

PINELLAS COUNTY - Marina License, Section 253.03 F. S.
W. R. Marsh of Madeira Beach, Florida, applied for a marina license
for an existing mooring facility containing 265 square feet in Boca
Ciega Bay abutting upland in Section 15, Township 31 South, Range
15 East, Pinellas County. $100 minimum annual fee was tendered,
no dredging was required, and the Department of Air and Water
Pollution Control had no objection to the project.

Motion was made by Mr. Stone, seconded by Mr. Christian and Mr.
O'Malley, and adopted without objection, that the Board approve
issuance of a marina license with effective date of January 1, 1971.

PALM BEACH COUNTY - Corps of Engineers Notices.
Thomas J. Birmingham, Kelly Defee, Dan Burcham, Jim Trapp, and Carl
Wegener, represented by William G. Wallace, Inc., requested a permit
from the United States Corps of Engineers to seawall and fill in an
area in a land-cut section of Intracoastal Waterway in Section 5,
Township 42 South, Range 43 East, Palm Beach County.

It appeared that the provisions of Section 253.124 did not apply to
the project located within a land-cut, and the staff requested authority
to issue a letter of no objection to the Corps of Engineers' notice.
Mr. Vidzes explained that this question of jurisdiction was presented
to the Board, and the staff opinion was that no permit was required
for the reason that these lands were upland into which a canal had
been dug.

Governor Askew commented that it was an artificial waterway in which
the applicant desired to construct a backup seawall.

Mr. Stone made a motion for approval. Mr. Shevin made a motion that
the staff recommendation be denied but there was no second to his
motion. Mr. Christian then seconded the motion made by Mr. Stone.

Mr. Shevin based his position on his view that the application would
come within Florida Statutes 253.124 under the key phrase "bordering
on" or in navigable waters of the state, and a dredge permit must
be obtained.

Governor Askew suggested deferment until the Board has a legal opinion
from the Attorney General, whereupon Mr. Stone withdrew his motion
and requested a two weeks' deferrment and an Attorney General's
opinion on whether or not the application comes within the statutory
requirement. It was so ordered.

RECORDS DISPOSAL, TRUSTEES' OFFICE.
On motion by Mr. Conner, seconded by Mr. Christian and adopted
without objection, the Board authorized the Interim Executive Director
to execute a request for records disposal to the Division of Archives,
History and Records Management, Department of State, for a large
volume of letters, form letters, and petitions containing over 9,000
signatures received in 1968 from the "Save Our Waterways Committee"
on a moratorium on land sales. All statistical data had been
tabulated and recorded and the records had no further value.

PATENTS, TRADEMARKS AND COPYRIGHTS - Chapter 70-440 F. S.
Under Chapter 70-440 legal title to any patent, trademark or copyrights
held or acquired by the State was transferred to the Board of Trustees
with authority to enforce the rights of the State in these matters,
protect against improper and unlawful use and infringement, enforce
collections of any sums due. The law also provided for the Board of
Trustees to sell any of the patents, trademarks or copyrights and
to execute any and all instruments on behalf of the State necessary to
consummate any such sale; and the law provided authority to license,
lease, assign to any person, firm or corporation for the manufacture
or use on a royalty basis or other consideration.

Chancellor Robert B. Mautz of the State University System requested
transfer to the Board of Regents of any rights and interest held by
the Board of Trustees in a Device for Automatic Speech Sound Recognition
and Control developed by Dr. Anthony Holbrook, a faculty member of
Florida State University. It had been indicated that the device
probably would not be capable of being patented to any worthwhile degree;
however, a non-profit corporation, Saber, Inc., was interested in
attempting further development and marketing. Should the efforts
succeed the University would benefit from the revenue and utilize it
in its research program.

Motion was made by Mr. Stone, seconded by Mr. Christian, and adopted
without objection, that the Board of Trustees transfer to the Board
of Regents any rights and interest held by the Trustees under Chapter
70-440 in the device.

INDIAN RIVER COUNTY - File No. 2386-31,253.12, Sale Deferred.
Consideration of sale of a parcel of filled sovereignty land in the
Indian River abutting Section 8, Township 31 South, Range 39 East,
Indian River County, was removed from the agenda at the request of
the applicant, the Estate of W. G. Bosworth, Deceased, represented
by Fobert F. Lloyd, who desired to have an appraisal made by an
appraiser of his choice.

BAY COUNTY - Mariculture Lease No. 2408 Amendment.
The staff requested authority to execute an amendment to Mariculture
Lease No. 2408 covering West Bay submerged land in Bay County. The
amendment, approved by Staff Counsel, was an acknowledgment of
prepaid rent with a clarification as to when rental payments will be
due in the future.

On motion by Mr. Conner, seconded by Mr. Christian and adopted
without objection, the Board authorized execution of the amendment
to Lease No. 2408.

Mr. Shevin said he voted affirmatively, but allegations in a suit
filed by a fishing association against Marifarms, Inc., should be
brought to the attention of the Trustees and investigated to see if
they constitute a violation of the lease agreement, and whether
or not the Trustees would want to cancel the lease if, in fact, a
violation has occurred.

POLK COUNTY - Marina License, Section 253.03 F. S.
On the request of the Director, the application of Stephen W. Keen,
Keen Fruit Company, for a marina license for a mooring facility
in Crooked Lake, Polk County, was withdrawn from the agenda.

During the deferment the staff would investigate a reported illegal dredging and filling.

SARASOTA COUNTY - Seawall Permit.
F. Warren Rice requested authority to install a seawall above mean high water line of Little Sarasota Bay in Section 9, Township 38 South, Range 18 East, Sarasota County.

The staff requested authority to issue a letter of no objection for the installation, since the seawall would be above the mean high water line.

On motion by Mr. Christian, seconded by Mr. Stone and adopted without objection, the Board approved the request.

DUVAL COUNTY - Dredge Permit.
A request from Commodores Point Terminal Corporation had been placed as an addendum on the agenda, but on this date the Director asked for removal of the addendum.

It was so ordered.

SUBJECTS UNDER CHAPTER 18296

ST JOHNS COUNTY - Corrective Murphy Act Deed, Report No. 981.
On motion by Mr. Stone, seconded by Mr. Conner and adopted without objection, the Board authorized issuance of County of St. Johns Deed No. 999-Corrective to the Deltona Corporation in lieu of a deed dated Septermber 25, 1970, to the same grantee, for the purpose of correcting an error in the description of the land.

REFUND - Murphy Act.
On motion by Mr. Christian, seconded by Mr. Stone and adopted without objection, the Board authorized issuance of $15 refund to Sidney Efronson, an applicant for release of the State Road right of way reservation contained in Dade County Murphy Act Deed No. 2807, for the reason that the Department of Transporation did not recommend release of the reservation.

On motion duly adopted, the meeting was adjourned.

_____
GOVERNOR   -   CHAIRMAN

ATTEST: _____
INTERIM EXECUTIVE DIRECTOR

3-23-71

Tallahassee, Florida
March 30, 1971

The State of Florida Board of Trustees of the Internal Improvement
Trust Fund met on this date in the Haydon Burns Building in
Tallahassee, Florida, with the following members present:

Reubin O'D. Askew	Governor
Richard (Dick) Stone	Secretary of State
Robert L. Shevin	Attorney General
Fred O. Dickinson, Jr.	Comptroller
Thomas D. O'Malley	Treasurer
Floyd T. Christian	Commissioner of Education
Doyle Conner	Commissioner of Agriculture

Fred Vidzes	Interim Executive Director

The minutes of the meeting of March 16 were approved as submitted.

TECHNICAL ADVISORY COMMITTEE ON FILL - Report.
On September 15, 1970, the Board authorized a review of the value
of fill material secured from state-owned lands. The Technical
Advisory Committee on Fill had submitted a report to all members
signed by Mr. Richard B. Hellstrom, chairman of the committee.

On motion by Mr. Dickinson, seconded by Mr. Stone and adopted without
objection, the Board received the report that would be considered on
April 13.

BAY COUNTY - State Marina License, Section 253.03 F.S.
On February 3, 1970, the Trustees approved issuance of a State
Commercial Dock Permit (CD-1635) to Major Clyde Weber for a
commercial marina facility in Pitts Bayou in St. Andrews Bay in
Section 24, Township 4 South, Range 14 West, Bay County. All
required exhibits were furnished and no objections had been
received at the time of issuance of the permit.

The City of Parker issued license No. 209 to the applicant on
February 13, 1970. The city has no current zoning regulations
or other building limitations in Pitts Bayou.

Numerous objections (25) were received from local residents
subsequent to issuance of the state permit. An on-site investigation by Field Operations indicated that the primary objection
by local residents is directed toward further commercial expansion
in Pitts Bayou. Objectors were notified that an application for
a marina license would be considered today.

Due to delay in issuance of the Corps of Engineers permit, the
applicant was unable to begin construction within the required
time limit of 120 days as provided by the state permit granted at
that time. Major Weber reapplied for state approval under a
marina license for 115-foot, 10-slip facility. The previously
authorized structure was 170 feet long and provided 22 slips.
The area of the proposed marina is 5190 square feet, and annual
license fee will be $103.80.

The Department of Air and Water Pollution Control, the Department of Natural Resources and the Game and Fresh Water Fish Commission had no objections. The Corps of Engineers had established no official pier line in Pitts Bayou; however, a tentative line had been set and was being used as a guide line for issuing permits. Any structure falling landward of the proposed pier line should not interfere with navigation, that would be considered a reasonable distance to extend a pier into the Bayou, and the proposed marina was landward of the proposed pier line.

The staff recommended that the applicant be granted a marina license and that the $100 fee paid for permit CD-1635 be applied toward the first year's license fee.

Motion was made by Mr. Dickinson, seconded by Mr. Stone, that the application be approved.

Mr. Emerson Sweat, representing objectors, filed petitions against issuing the marina license and spoke against allowing further commercialization in Pitts Bayou in a residential area that he said had reached the saturation point and the marina environment would create erosion problems, pollution, and adversely affect marine life and public recreational use in the relatively small bayou.

The members pointed out the city had zoning authority but had not adopted any zoning regulations, that the application had received no objections from state agencies from the ecological or pollution standpoint, and although the members understood the residents' objections they could not superimpose zoning authority over the City of Parker.

The above motion was not adopted and a motion was made by Comptroller Dickinson, seconded by Secretary of State Stone, and adopted without objection, that action be deferred for two weeks to allow the objectors to contact their elected city officials and to secure some affirmative action by the city toward zoning the Pitts Bayou area. Governor Askew did not say that the Board would deny this application, but he thought the interested parties would be in a better position if the city had made a commitment.

BAY COUNTY - Dredge Permit, Section 253.123 Florida Statutes, File No. 729.
The Town of Mexico Beach applied for a maintenance dredge permit authorizing removal of 2,500 cubic yards from an existing canal 200 ft. long, 50 ft. wide, 5 ft. deep, adjacent to Section 22, Township 16 South, Range 12 West, in the Gulf of Mexico, Bay County. The applicant requested a permit valid for three years because of constant siltation of the channel. All material removed would be used for adjacent down-drift public beach nourishment.

The biological report was not adverse. The Bureau of Beaches and Shores concurred in the project.

On motion by Mr. Dickinson, seconded by Mr. Christian and Mr. O'Malley, adopted without objection, the Board approved the permit for $50 processing fee, subject to the requirement that the town notify the the staff prior to each dredging operation.

DUVAL COUNTY - Emergency Dredge Permit, Section 253.123, F. S.
        File 658
Harrell Marine, Inc., applied for an emergency maintenance dredge
permit authorizing removal of 10,500 cubic yards of silt material
from an existing boat basin in Section 32, Township 2 South, Range
29 East, Intracoastal Waterway, in Duval County. The application
was on the agenda on January 12 and deferred because of the moratorium.
The area is approximately 650 ft. long, 200 ft. wide, and will be
redredged to 6 ft. and 8 ft. deep. The dredged material will be
placed within a diked area on the upland. The engineer stated that
the material has no value for commercial use. Applicant posted a
bond and a check representing one dollar per cubic yard for the
material.

The biological report dated September 21, 1970, was adverse to
depositing the spoil in low marsh areas. After revision of the
spoil area, the biological report of November 13, 1970, was not
adverse.

The Secretary of State requested deferment for one week, but after
hearing the details of the application as presented by Mr. Eli H. Fink,
representing the applicant, Mr. Stone withdrew his deferment request.
He noted that the later biological report was not adverse.

Mr. Fink said the permit was urgently needed, that the marina existing
at that location for about fifteen years had to dredge silt from the
channel and slips about every four years to allow boats to get in and
out, that at low tide now the boats in the slips rest on mud. The
applicant firm had tried to meet every requirement of the various
state agencies since the request was submitted last fall and about a
month ago Mr. Fink's law firm was called on for assistance in securing
the permit. He stressed the necessity of opening the channel and
basin for the applicant to continue to operate the marina.

Motion was made by Mr. Dickinson, seconded by Mr. Conner and adopted
without objection, that the emergency dredge permit be approved.

PASCO COUNTY - Core Boring Permit.
Florida Power Corporation requested authority to make eleven core
borings in its proposed water discharge channel in the Gulf of Mexico
adjacent to Section 27, Township 26 South, Range 15 East, Pasco County.

The work would be done with a floating drill rig, would take approximatel
thirty days, and would be performed in accordance with staff recommendations to determine the type of material that is in the proposed
dredge area as a preliminary to the dredge permit application. The
staff recommended approval.

Mr. Shevin desired to know about the total project, expressing
concern about considering a permit on a piece-meal basis without
seeing the complete plan. The Director explained that the staff
had been told of the complete comprehensive project, had brought
in other state agencies, and a conference was requested with the
cabinet aides. The core borings were needed to locate where the
canal should be placed for the oil-fired steam-electric generating
station on the applicant's property on the Anclote River.

At Mr. Shevin's request, the Trustees deferred consideration for two
weeks and asked for a report on the position of the Department of
Air and Water Pollution Control on the proposed project.

3-30-71

239

PINELLAS COUNTY - Dredge and Fill Permit Denial.
On March 2, 1971, Pinellas County Water and Navigation Control
Authority denied the application of Stanley J. Reynolds for a permit
to dredge and fill in St. Joseph's Sound at Crystal Beach in Section
3, Township 28 South, Range 15 East, Pinellas County.

The biological report was adverse and the staff recommended
concurrence in the denial.

On motion by Mr. Conner, seconded by Mr. Christian and adopted
without objection, the Board concurred in the county's action denying
the dredge and fill permit.

PINELLAS COUNTY - State Dock Permit, Section 253.03 F. S.
The staff recommended issuance of a state commercial dock permit for
an application from Paul Piedmont that was approved by Pinellas
County Water and Navigation Control Authority under Permit No. 5426
prior to August 11, 1970, the effective date of the Trustees' policy
changes relative to marina licenses. The applicant had tendered $100
processing fee.

On motion by Mr. Stone, seconded by Mr. Dickinson and adopted
without objection, the Board approved issuance of the permit.

DUVAL COUNTY - Dredge and Fill Permit, Files 253.123-737,
253.124-169.
The United States Coast Guard requested approval of a permit for
removal of 12,000 cubic yards of material from an area 330 ft. long,
130 ft. wide, 10 ft. deep, to fill 0.25 acre, more or less, in the
St. Johns River adjacent to unsurveyed Section 30, Township 1 South,
Range 29 East, Duval County.

The proposed fill area was dedicated to the applicant on February
2, 1971, was landward of the bulkhead line approved on that date,
and the project was deemed a public necessity. The biological
report of March 9, 1970, was adverse to filling but not to dredging.

On motion by Mr. Stone, seconded by Mr. Dickinson and adopted
without objection, the Board approved the dredge and fill permit
requested by the Coast Guard.

OSCEOLA AND POLK COUNTIES - Lake Hatchineha boundary line agreement,
conveyance and navigation access channel.
Florida Ridge Cattle Company requested the Board to enter into a
boundary line agreement establishing the 53.0 ft. mean sea level
elevation by traverse as the boundary line between public and private
lands relating only to this area of Lake Hatchineha abutting Sections
33,34 and 35, Township 28 South, Range 29 East, and Section 2,
Township 29 South, Range 29 East, Polk County. The agreement would
not be construed to mean that either party admits to ownership of the
other party of any portion of the lands subject to the boundary line
agreement. A major development was planned for the upland and the
applicant desired to have the boundaries resolved before any further
planning. Representatives of the applicant and developer indicated
that no construction would occur lakeward of the crest of the
existing natural escarpment, which would be included as a covenant
in the articles of agreement.

3-30-71

In consideration for entering into the agreement the applicant would convey to the Trustees approximately 145 acres of land adjacent to and including Catfish Creek lying within Sections 13 and 14, Township 29 South, Range 28 East, Polk County. It is proposed that the creek and its marginal lands be included in a Wilderness Area pursuant to Chapter 70-355, "State Wilderness System Act." A verbal report by the Game and Fresh Water Fish Commission approved Catfish Creek as a desirable addition to the Wilderness System.

Also, the applicant will relinquish any right, title and interest he may have in Big Gum Lake, a non-meandered lake that was conveyed into private ownership by the United States through direct patent. Before any instruments would be accepted from the applicant, he would be required to furnish a title certificate showing that the lands are free from all liens and encumbrances, together with prepayment of any taxes due on the lands subject to conveyance.

As part of the package the applicant request approval of three navigation channels connecting uplands with the lake. The biological report recommend that channels be limited to a 30 Ft. top width. Maximum depth of each channel will vary from 6.5 ft. at 53.0 m.s.l. diminishing 0.00 ft. at 46.0 ft. m.s.l. An estimated total quantity of 7000 cu. yds. will be excavated from the channels. Satisfactory assurances were submitted that an amount up to $7,000, representing $1 per cubic yard charge for material, will be made available payable to the Trustees.

The 55.0 ft. mean sea level elevation would be the upper limit of the flood plain referred to·in the articles of agreement. The agreement would contain a hold-harmless covenant that would save the Flood Control District and the Trustees from any liability due to flooding of lands up to and including the 55.0 ft. elevation, by virtue of any future regulation of lake levels under the Central and Southern Florida Flood Control project.

The staff recommended approval of the boundary line agreement as explained above.

Motion was made by Mr. Dickinson, seconded by Mr. Stone, that the recommendation be approved.

Mr. Shevin referred to the lengthy opinion from Mr. Henry Kittleson and questioned the 53 ft. mean sea level elevation. Mr. Vidzes said that would provide a needed meets and bounds description, that the Central and Southern Florida Flood Control District would try to maintain the top level of 53 ft. stage elevation in that lake, that would be a 53 ft. traverse and the point where the boundary between public and private ownership would occur. The hold-harmless clause would protect the state and the District against any liability due to flooding. Mr. Vidzes pointed out on a map the holdings of the Florida Ridge Cattle Company, the proposed boundary lines and the wilderness area that would be conveyed to the state, and a part of Big Gum Lake to be conveyed to the state as additional consideration. He thought the Catfish Creek wilderness area might be protected from any. adverse activity occurring in the privately owned parcel. The applicant had agreed to convey lands on either side of Catfish Creek necessary to preserve the area in its natural state. It was explained that Big Gum Lake was conveyed in its entirety by the United States, the State never had any interest or clear-cut jurisdiction, but obtaining a portion of it might give the Board an opportunity of asserting jurisdiction.

3-30-71

Mr. Bruce Wilson, engineer with the applicant firm, showed photographs of the Catfish Creek area that would be dedicated as a wilderness area. Mr. Stone suggested that the state should acquire the privately-owned parcel.

Mr. Don Williams, owner of a fishing camp on the river near the project, objected because the state would not have the access parcels into Lake Pierce on one end and Lake Hatchineha on the other. The Governor said the applicant did not own the outlets into the lakes. Mr. Williams further objected that there should be a biological study on the effect of the 53 ft. contour on these lakes.

Mr. O'Malley questioned the advisability of the procedures used for establishing the proposed boundary lines, pointing out the specific criteria in the statutes; and he asked for more detailed information on the effect of the agreement on the area between the water marsh and the dike and tree line along the berm, and just what jurisdiction the state would retain in the future development around the lake. Mr. Vidzes explained that this was for only part of the lake, the Trustees had already conveyed to the 52½ ft. contour on the east side a number of years ago, the 53 ft. contour was very close to the original ordinary high water mark, the staff had studied the factual material and went into this matter very thoroughly, the 53 ft. elevation would not be binding elsewhere, and the staff had tried to furnish complete information to the cabinet aides. The Department of Air and Water Pollution Control had considered the project and would check on the internal canal structure designs. The covenant would restrict any development from the top of the berm toward the lake. A flowage easement above the 53 ft. to the 55 ft. contour indicated that this area will be susceptible to flooding. The control elevation had been determined by the Corps of Engineers and the Central and Southern Florida Flood Control District, predetermined by a hydrological study conducted in conjunction with the overall drainage project of the District.

The applicant requested approval of three navigation channels and the staff had requested biological report from the Game and Fresh Water Fish Commission, copy of which was furnished to each member. It did not appear to offer sufficient information for the members, however.

Mr. O'Malley requested deferment because of his concern as to the specific steps outlined in the statutes to determine boundary lines, his concern as to the effect of dredging and spoil areas, and the need for a more specific biological report. Governor Askew suggested an opinion from the Attorney General if there was any question about following the statutes.

Mr. Milton Bevis, attorney with the firm of Helliwell, Melrose and DeWolf, representing the owner, spoke of their four-month's work and adjustments at each state agency's request, their plan not to develop the lake front, an independent opinion by Mr. Henry Kittleson, and a memorandum Mr. Bevis' firm presented to the staff three months ago.

Mr. O'Malley felt that he did not have sufficient information to exercise good judgment. Motion was made by Mr. O'Malley, seconded by Mr. Conner and adopted (Mr. Dickinson having withdrawn his earlier motion), that the matter be deferred for six weeks to secure a biological report on the effect of the canalization of the property and to obtain an opinion from the Attorney General on the legal authority of the Board to enter into this type of agreement without exercising the criteria in the statutes.

Attorney General Shevin made a brief report to the Board on his action
pursuant to the direction of the Trustees, to file two motions in the
Aerojet General Corporation case requesting scheduling at a later date
and permission to file supplementary material.

SUBJECTS UNDER CHAPTER 18296

OKALOOSA COUNTY - Murphy Act Sale.
On motion by Mr. Dickinson, seconded by Mr. Stone and adopted with-
out objection, the Trustees approved sale and execution of a deed
under provisions of Section 197.350 Florida Statutes to Robert E.
Helms for the high bid of $100 for a parcel of land in Okaloosa
County described as Lot 12, Box 12, Garden City, certified to the
State of Florida under tax sale certificate No. 143 of August 6, 1923.
The sale was reported on Murphy Act Bidding Report No. 982.

On motion duly adopted, the meeting was adjourned.

_____
GOVERNOR   -   CHAIRMAN

ATTEST: _____
INTERIM EXECUTIVE DIRECTOR

Tallahassee, Florida
April 6, 1971

The State of Florida Board of Trustees of the Internal Improvement
Trust Fund met on this date in the Haydon Burns Building in Tallahassee,
Florida, with the following members present:

Reubin O'D. Askew	Governor
Richard (Dick) Stone	Secretary of State
Robert L. Shevin	Attorney General
Thomad D. O'Malley	Treasurer
Floyd T. Christian	Commissioner of Education
Doyle Conner	Commissioner of Agriculture

Joel Kuperberg	Executive Director

The minutes of the meeting of March 23 were approved as submitted.

ESCAMBIA AND SANTA ROSA COUNTIES - Utility Dredge Permit,
                          Section 253.123(2)(b) F. S.
Humble Oil and Refining Company requested a dredge permit for the
installation of two 4-inch flow lines in the Escambia River in
Sections 31 and 33, Township 6 North, Range 29 West, and tendered
$100 processing fee.

The biological report was not adverse but recommended that the spoil
be placed on the upland. The permit would be issued in accordance

with the report recommendations. The staff had authority to issue utility permits of this kind, but brought the request to the Board for informational purposes. The Game and Fresh Water Fish Commission offered no objection.

The grade of pipe used exceeds all minimum requirements and as a protective device in the event of a break or a leak, an Otis Safety Shutdown Valve will be installed on the line crossing the river that will automatically shut off the oil flow.

On March 9 the staff recommended approval but suggested deferment to allow a company representative to be present to explain measures to contain any leakage. Members had suggested shut-off valves on each side of the river.

Mr. Stone made a motion that the dredge permit be approved contingent upon the company having Otis Safety Shutdown Valves installed on each side of the river. The Board desired to provide optimum precautionary measures to protect the river from spillage. Discussion followed, during which Mr. John Everett and Mr. Jerry Higgs, representing the company, testified to the integrity of the pipe to be used, that there was practically no chance of its breaking, that because of the unsuitableness of the area manual shutdown equipment could not be used and automatic equipment would be subject to vandalism and in fact, probably would incur more damage that the precautionary measures originally proposed by the company and recommended by the staff and Dr. Robert Vernon, State Geologist with the Department of Natural Resources.

Motion was made by Mr. O'Malley, seconded by Mr. Christian, adopted without objection, that the Board accept the original staff recommendation for approval of the dredge permit for installation of the pipelines with shutdown valves as planned on each side of the river.

ST. LUCIE COUNTY - Boundary Line Agreement, Land Exchange. The application of Lucie Properties, Inc., was deferred at the request of the Governor's Office.

PALM BEACH COUNTY - Corps of Engineer Notices.
1. Sam G. Crupi requested a permit from the Corps of Engineers to place a seawall along the mean high water line in a land-cut section of the Intracoastal Waterway in Section 5, Township 42 South, Range 43 East, Palm Beach County.

2. Thomas J. Birmingham and others requested a permit from the Corps of Engineers to seawall and fill an area in a land-cut section of the Intracoastal Waterway in Section 5, Township 42 South, Range 43 East, Palm Beach County.

The Board had requested an opinion from the Attorney General as to whether the applications came under the provision of Section 253.124 Florida Statutes. The Trustees' office received copy of the opinion just prior to the meeting that placed jurisdiction in the Board of Trustees.

Mr. O'Malley said that the seawall had already been constructed, according to a report he had received. He had information that the Palm Beach Area Planning Board had under consideration a violation order in the case.

At the suggestion of Governor Askew, the Board deferred action for one week on Mr. Stone's motion.

BREVARD COUNTY - Temporary Borrow Easement No. 2258,
                Dredge and Fill Permit.
On May 23, 1967, the Trustees approved issuance of temporary easement No. 2258 embracing 9.23 acres to the Department of Transportation for a borrow area in the Indian River abutting Section 34, Township 24 South, Range 36 East, Brevard County. The Department of Transportation requested that the date of expiration of the easement, May 1, 1971, be extended to May 1, 1974. The 83,000 cubic yards of material from the borrow area will be used for the construction of a wayside park adjacent to State Road 520.

The Department of Natural Resources reviewed the project plan and recommended no dredging of the westerly 40 feet of the borrow area. The applicant modified its plan accordingly. The Department of Air and Water Pollution Control had certified the project.

The Trustees on December 8, 1970, approved dedication of 4.45 acres of sovereignty land in the Indian River to the City of Cocoa for a wayside park. The dedication was landward of the established bulkhead line. The City of Cocoa issued a dredge and fill permit to the Department of Transportation on February 9, 1971, to dredge 83,000 cubic yards of material and fill 4.45 acres.

On motion by Mr. Christian, seconded by Mr. Conner and adopted without objection, the Board approved the staff recommendation for approval of the dredge and fill permit containing the normal stipulation with respect to dredging and filling to be issued by the contractor, and approved the requested extension of the easement.

DADE COUNTY - File No. 2396-13-253.03, Easement.
The staff requested withdrawal from the agenda of a request from the Department of Transportation for a right of way easement over 2.96 acres in Biscayne Bay abutting Sections 9 and 10, Township 53 South, Range 42 East, Dade County.

It was so ordered.

VOLUSIA COUNTY - Easement for Power Line.
Florida Power and Light Company requested an additional electric transmission line right-of-way 60 feet wide adjacent to an existing 110 foot wide right-of-way through Section 16, Township 18 South, Range 31 East, Volusia County. The company offered $800 per acre compensation for easement over the 6.37 acres. An appraisal report furnished by the applicant was reviewed by the Trustees'. Staff Appraiser, who agreed that the compensation offered was equitable.

The Section 16 was under lease to the Volusia County Board of Public Instruction for use by Future Farmers of America. That Board had no objection to the easement provided the FFA chapter would be allowed to harvest any timber in the right-of-way. The applicant agreed to that provision.

On motion by Mr. Conner, seconded by Mr. Stone and adopted without objection, the Board authorized issuance of the easement to Florida Power and Light Company subject to the provision requested by the Volusia County Board of Public Instruction.

COLLIER COUNTY - Mobil Oil Corporation.
Mobil Oil Corporation held oil and gas drilling lease No. 2350-S
issued October 15, 1968, covering the one-half petroleum interest
of the Board of Education in Section 16, Township 47 South, Range 28
East, Collier County. The lease required commencement and completion
of drilling of at least one test well within the first 2½ years of the
lease, or not later than April 15, 1971. Mobil did drill the No. 1
Barron Collier Well in the SE¼ of Section 9, adjacent to the north
of said Section 16. That well was completed as a producer of oil on
May 25, 1969, for 118 barrels of oil and 78 barrels of water per day.
Due to the excessive amount of water the well was reworked and
re-completed on September 12, 1969, for 157 barrels of oil and 1
barrel of water per day. Production of oil has now declined to 68
barrels per day.

The time involved in evaluating the performance of the marginal
production from No. 1 Barron Collier Well resulted in a delay in
commencing to drill an offset well on the area covered by the state
lease. Therefore, Mobil requested that State Lease No. 2350-S be
amended to provide for operations for the drilling of a Sunniland
test well to be commenced on or before June 15, 1971, and drilled
to completion as required by the terms of the lease.

The Department of Natural Resources had approved and issued permit
No. 477 for drilling a test well on this leased area.

On motion by Mr. Christian, seconded by Mr. O'Malley and adopted
without objection, the amendment was approved.

On motion duly adopted, the meeting was adjourned.

GOVERNOR   -   CHAIRMAN

ATTEST:

EXECUTIVE DIRECTOR

* * *   * * *

Tallahassee, Florida
April 13, 1971

The State of Florida Board of Trustees of the Internal Improvement
Trust Fund met on this date in the Haydon Burns Building in
Tallahassee, Florida, with the following members present:

Reubin O'D. Askew   Governor
Richard (Dick) Stone   Secretary of State
Robert L. Shevin   Attorney General
Fred O. Dickinson, Jr.   Comptroller
Thomas D. O'Malley   Treasurer
Floyd T. Christian   Commissioner of Education
Doyle Conner   Commissioner of Agriculture

Joel Kuperberg   -.-   Executive Director

4-13-71

The minutes of the meeting of March 30 were approved as submitted.

Policy recommendation listed on the agenda with reference to environmental impact was withdrawn from consideration on this date.

OSCEOLA COUNTY - City of Kissimmee Dredge and Fill Permit.
At the request of the City of Kissimmee, consideration of dredge and fill plans was withdrawn from the agenda.

DADE COUNTY - Canal Right-of-Way.
Central and Southern Florida Flood Control District requested an easement for canal and drainage right-of-way in the South 165 feet of Section 16, Township 52 South, Range 39 East, Dade County, a section that was leased to Dade County for public purposes.

The Metro Dade County Public Works Department approved the canal and drainage right-of-way location and staff recommended approval.

On motion by Mr. Dickinson, seconded by Messrs. Conner and Shevin, adopted without objection, the Board authorized issuance of the easement.

DADE COUNTY - Offshore Campsite Lease Renewals.
Two applications were presented for renewal of offshore campsite leases for one year with option to renew on a year-to-year basis for four additional years at an annual rental of $300, from the following lessees:

1. Alan Wylie, holder of Campsite lease No. 2178 in Biscayne Bay, Dade County

2. Jay I. Kislak, holder of Campsite Lease No. 2185 in Biscayne Bay, Dade County

The applications conformed to the April 7, 1970, policy allowing a lease as long as the structure remains on the site, and the October 6, 1970, policy that established an annual rental of $300 for a quarter-acre site.

On motions by Mr. Stone and Mr. Dickinson, seconded by Mr. Christian, and adopted without objection, the Board approved renewal of the two campsite leases as requested.

PASCO COUNTY - Core Boring Permit.
On March 30 the Board had deferred action on a request from Florida Power Corporation for permission to make eleven core borings in its proposed water discharge channel in the Gulf of Mexico adjacent to Section 27, Township 26 South, Range 15 East, Pasco County. Representatives of the firm were present on this date.

Motion was made by Mr. Christian, seconded by Mr. Dickinson, that the application be approved.

Mr. Shevin had requested deferment until more was known of the complete plan. Executive Director Kuperberg explained that the borings were needed to determine the nature of the material in the proposed channel area, that the overall project was a power plant near the mouth of the Anclote River, and the Department of Air and

Water Pollution Control had offered no objection to the core borings.

Without objection, the Board approved the request.

MARTIN COUNTY - Utility Installation, Section 253.03(7)
                SAJSP (56-241).
Staff requested authority to issue a letter of no objection to the
United States Corps of Engineers for the Florida Power and Light
Company to revise and modify a permit issued on July 13, 1956, by
the Corps to the company for the installation of an aerial power
line over the St. Lucie Canal in Section 12, Township 39 South, Range
40 East, Martin County. That would allow the replacement of the
west crossing pole landward of the canal and raising of the line by
ten feet on the existing facility.

On motion by Mr. Christian, seconded by Mr. Conner and adopted
without objection, the Board approved the request.

BAY COUNTY - State Marina License, Section 253.03 F. S.
On March 30, 1971, the Board of Trustees considered the application
from Major Clyde Weber for a state commercial marina license for
a facility in Pitts Bayou in St. Andrews Bay in Section 24, Township
4 South, Range 14 West, Bay County, in the City of Parker. The
Trustees had approved issuance of State Commercial Dock Permit No.
CD-1635 in February 1970, but the applicant's construction time
limit expired due to delay in issuance of the Corps of Engineers
permit. He reapplied for state approval under a marina license
covering an area of 5,190 square feet for which the annual license
fee would be $103.80.

The concerned state agencies had no objection, but numerous local
residents did object to further commercial operations in Pitts
Bayou. Action was deferred on March 30 to allow objectors to
contact their elected city officials and to secure some affirmative
action by the city toward zoning the Pitts Bayou area. In 1970
the City of Parker had issued License No. 209 to the applicant
but the city had no current zoning regulations or other building
limitations in Pitts Bayou.

The city had advised by letter that they had had the first reading
of a construction permit ordinance and a proposed zoning ordinance
would be voted upon on Septermber 20, 1971. Governor Askew suggested
a week's delay to ascertain the scope of the city ordinance that
might be passed. Treasurer O'Malley had been in the area, talked
with Mayor Earl Gilbert of Parker and offered the assistance of his
office in furnishing model zoning ordinances. He said they indicated
no objections as the city had issued a permit previously. The
objectors at the March 30 meeting had not represented the city but
waterfront property owners.

At the request of Secretary of State Stone, the Trustees deferred
action one week pending further information regarding the proposed
city ordinances.

ESCAMBIA AND SANTA ROSA COUNTIES - Oil and Gas Drilling Lease.
On March 3 the Board of Trustees authorized advertisement for sealed
bids for a five-year oil and gas drilling lease covering a portion
of the Escambia River in Township 5 North, Range 30 West, containing
330.5 acres, more or less, Escambia and Santa Rosa Counties. Lease

will contain a special provision prohibiting drilling in the river, one-sixth royalty, annual rental of $1 per acre, $50,000 surety bond, and requirement that at least one test well be drilled on contiguous drilling units to 6,000 feet or sediments of the Jurassic Age, whichever is deeper.

Invitation to bid was advertised pursuant to law in the Tallahassee Democrat, Milton Press-Gazette and Pensacola Journal, with bids to be opened at 10:00 a.m. on April 13.

A member of the staff, Mr. James T. Williams, stated that one bid was received, from the Louisiana Land and Exploration Company, in the amount of $34,702.50 (first year's rental of $330.50 plus a cash bonus). He explained that the lease required drilling on contiguous parcels, not necessarily slant drilling as the Governor mentioned, and prohibited drilling in the river.

Mr. Stone advised the members that this bid was comparable to bids received in Louisiana and Texas.

On motion by Mr. Christian, seconded by Mr. Stone and adopted without objection, the Board accepted the bid from The Louisiana Land and Exploration Company and authorized issuance of the oil and gas drilling lease.

OKALOOSA COUNTY - Advertise Oil and Gas Drilling Lease.
Amoco Production Company requested the Trustees to offer for lease the 25% interest held by the Board in the oil and gas in a portion of the Blackwater River State Forest, covering approximately 26,400 surface acres of which Amoco had leased the Federal Government's 75% interest. The Division of Forestry had no objections.

The State Geologist concurred with the staff recommendation to advertise for sealed bids on three separate leases with annual rental of $1 per net mineral acre, five-year primary lease term, $50,000 surety bond, and at least one test well to be drilled to 6,000 feet or to a depth sufficient to test the Norphlet Sands, whichever is deeper, with royalty and acreage for each lease as follows: (1) 5,542.05 surface acres in Township 5 North, Range 24 West and Township 5 North, Range 25 West, one-sixth royalty; (2) 7,681.26 surface acres in Township 4 North, Range 24 West and Township 5 North, Range 24 West, one-eighth royalty; and (3) 13,168.09 surface acres in Township 4 North Range 24 West, and Township 4 North, Range 25 West, one-sixth royalty.

Mr. Kuperberg said the lease phraseology protected the water bottoms. The Game and Fresh Water Fish Commission had reviewed the application, did not object, but asked for advance notice.

On motion by Mr. Dickinson, seconded by Mr. Christian and adopted without objection, the Board authorized advertisement of the oil and gas drilling lease.

DADE COUNTY - Revocation of Dedication No. 23048.
On January 12, 1971, the Board authorized the staff to notify the City of Islandia that the reverter provision in Dedication No. 23048 would be exercised for non-use of the 109 acres of sovereignty land between Totten Key and Old Rhodes Key that the Trustees on December 5, 1961, pursuant to request by the city, had dedicated for public and recreational purposes under supervision and management of the city.

The City of Islandia was notified by certified mail on January 13 that final action would be taken by the Trustees on this date, and in accordance with that action the dedication was officially revoked as of this date on motion by Mr. Christian, seconded by Mr. Dickinson, adopted without objection.

Mr. Joseph C. Jacobs, attorney representing the City of Islandia, Mr. Ralph Fossey, City Councilmen, and certain citizens and taxpayers in the area, reviewed certain facts regarding the history of Islandia, actions of the Trustees and Federal Government, and legal actions now pending. He admitted that the dedication area had not been used, explaining how the possibility of the creation of Biscayne National Park had chilled the development of the entire area, and urged the Board to take no action until the Court had made a decision on pending matters. Also, he questioned whether the Board had authority under constitutional law to give away 94,000 acres. Members questioned Mr. Jacobs, who in closing asked for a week's deferment.

The consensus of opinion was that no benefit would be gained by delay, the Board had already acted by notifying the city that the reverter provisions were being exercised, and Mr. O'Malley felt that no affirmative action was required on this date.

Upon Mr. Shevin's recommendation that the Board act on the matter, motion was made by Mr. Christian, seconded by Mr. Dickinson and adopted without objection, that the Trustees reaffirm their prior action of exercising the reverter and the dedication was officially revoked as of this date.

COLLIER COUNTY - Permit Extension.
A. File No. 253.123-51. Marco Island Development Corporation requested extension of its permit so that its expiration would coincide with the Corps of Engineers permit (SAJSP 67-762) on December 31, 1972, to allow dredging of approximately 3,930,000 cubic yards of material from Roberts Bay, Collier County.

The original permit expiring on April 15 allowed the dredging of 9.1 million cubic yards of material from Smokehouse Creek and Roberts Bay to be placed on lands claimed to be vested in the corporation. Payment was received for only 73,250 cubic yards at the rate of 5¢ per cubic yard in accordance with the policy in effect at that time. It was also contended that the corporation owned the majority of the submerged lands subject to the proposed dredging.

Some questions had arisen relative to title to certain areas subject to dredging and filling. For the purpose of ascertaining the extent of the Trustees' interest in the lands in question, the staff required additional time before any final action is taken on the request for time extension. The applicant had been so advised. The staff recommended that the permit be temporarily extended to May 18, 1971.

B. File No. 253.123-678, 253.124-149. On January 26, 1971, the Trustees granted 90-day extension of the numbered permits for the purpose of determining if the permits would be allowed to run concurrently with the present Corps of Engineers permit (SAJSP 64-413) expiring on December 31, 1971. The Trustees would consider this on April 27; however, in view of the fact that the questions raised on January 26 apply to (A), both items should be considered concurrently.

The staff recommended that the permit expiring on May 2, 1971, also be extended to May 18, 1971.

On motion by Mr. Dickinson, seconded by Mr. Christian and adopted without objection, the Board approved the staff recommendation for temporary extension of both permits to May 18, 1971.

The applicant had requested consideration, at the end of that period, of further time continuation. The Governor said that was not before the Board at this time.

The Director advised the members that he was from Collier County, had knowledge of this work by Marco Island Development Corporation, and expected to continue study and staff investigation in the future with the assistance of Mr. Henry Kittleson, special attorney

PINELLAS COUNTY - City of Madeira Beach.
The staff had been directed to agenda a request from the City of Madeira Beach regarding the establishment of the boundary line between public and private lands along the Gulf of Mexico beach. The city by Resolution No. 71-11 requested the Trustees to adopt the present mean high water line as a demarcation line between private property and sovereignty lands along the gulf beach within the City of Madeira Beach. The city contended that utilization of the 1954 mean high water line as a boundary line, in accordance with recommendations of the Bureau of Beaches and Shores, Department of Natural Resources, would be unfair and unjust, and held the view that accretions caused by construction of groins funded through assessments levied upon upland property owners should be vested in those riparian upland owners.

It was indicated to the staff that evidence was being secured to show the manner in which the beach front was lost prior to the construction of groins. Until such evidence was submitted and evaluated, the staff could make no recommendations. The 1971 mean high water tide line extended several hundred feet beyond the 1954 line. The Director said the question was in what manner the beach was lost and in what manner had it been restored. If rapid erosion was determined, then private waterfront property owners had a right to restore what they had lost; but if it was gradual and imperceptible erosion since 1954, any accretion as a result of the beach restoration program accrued to the public, to the state.

Governor Askew suggested that with no recommendation before the Board, the problem had been presented as information and discussion appeared premature at this time. The Director explained that the Bureau of Beaches and Shores had determined the line to be the 1954 mean high tide mark and had agreed to a variance from that line in an effort to resolve construction problems of a Holiday Inn Franchise holder (purchaser from a water front property holder); however the variance was insufficient to permit the planned construction and a seawall already constructed was based on the present mean high tide line and not the 1954 line.

Mr. Dickinson said it was an emergency, and Mr. Christian expressed the opinion that it was a real problem and the Board would have to decide which mean high tide line was right as construction had been started. Director Randolph Hodges, Department of Natural Resources, called on Mr. William T. Carlton, Bureau of Beaches and Shores, who advised the Board of his extensive survey that revealed no evidence that the beach ever extended any farther, or much farther, than the 1954 mean high tide line that coincided with surveys in 1954, 1950 and very nearly with a 1931 survey. He recommended that no structure be allowed on the accreted beach, and said that all evidence indicated that the accretion was artificial. Mr. Shevin pointed out that the law was

4-13-71

clear that artificial accretion would benefit the state - not the upland owner. The Trustees are empowered in such cases to make an appraisal of the factual situation affecting riparian rights. Mr. John Neilson, Mayor of the City of Madeira Beach, present on this date with the City Attorney, City Manager and others, explained the city's position, indicated that there had been avulsion and accretion over a period of about thirteen years, and emphasized that the future economic growth and development of the city depended upon the decision on the situation now before the Trustees. Members asked Mr. Neilson many questions, and Mr. Christian suggested there was merit in the City's position, and any evidence to support its claim should be given further study. The Governor said the Board has to make decisions, constantly balancing equities as to conservation and the economic impact, but first the facts should be determined and the law applied to those facts.

Mr. Theodore C. Taub, attorney representing the property owners, recounted the facts that he considered important, attempts to resolve the problem, the situation with respect to their title insurance that required them to proceed with the construction, and suggested that a portion of the accretion might be attributed to natural causes as opposed to the view of the Bureau of Beaches and Shores that all of the accretion resulted from the installation of the groins. In view of his clients' attempts to accommodate the state agencies' requests and time spent to resolve a very serious problem, Mr. Taub asked if there might be a reasonable middle ground that would make it economically feasible for property owners to utilize their property. The Board requested the work stopped.

Governor Askew said the Board could not negotiate away public land and suggested further exchange of information between the city, the owners, and the staff of the Department of Natural Resources and Trustees to verify where the mean high water line is, a factual determination. Mr. O'Malley agreed, noting that the decision would set an entire pattern for the whole strip shown on an aerial photograph. Mr. Stone brought up the possibility of ordering construction stopped until a determination was made, and Mr. Shevin felt that after a policy decision was reached there would probably be legal action on this matter.

Without objection action was deferred for one week, the period of time suggested by Mr. Randolph Hodges.

TECHNICAL ADVISORY COMMITTEE ON FILL - Report.
Mr. Richard B. Hellstrom, Chairman of the Technical Advisory Committee on Fill, Mr. N.R. Boutin, M. A. I., and Mr. Loring Lovell, members, were present to answer questions or give additional information on the committee's report on its review of the value of fill material secured from state-owned lands that was received by the Trustees at the March 30 meeting and scheduled for consideration on this date.

Mr. Hellstrom outlined the three recommendations of the committee as follows:

1. If fill material is secured from state-owned lands and is placed upon privately-owned lands for the use and benefit of the private owner, then the applicant should pay the state for the material, regardless of the purpose of the removal, whether it be for navigational access or any other purpose. Conversely, if fill material is removed from State-owned

lands, but is <u>not</u> placed on privately-owned lands, then the applicant should not be charged for the material.

2. Fill material removed from State-owned lands, regardless of the purpose of the removal, and placed upon privately-owned lands for the use and benefit of the private owner, should be paid for by the applicant on the following basis:

For quantities less than 10,000 cubic yards: 50 cents per cubic yard for each cubic yard of material removed.

3. For quantities greater than 10,000 cubic yards: $5,000 plus 50 cents per cubic yard for each cubic yard of fill material removed in excess of 10,000 cubic yards; or at the option of either the applicant or the Board, an appraisal may be made to lend guidance and assistance to the Board and its staff in determining the rate to be applied for the cost above $5,000, but in no event shall the rate be less than 20 cents per cubic yard for each cubic yard removed above that covered by the $5,000 minimum.

4. Appraisals for the guidance of the Board in determining the value of fill material shall be performed in accordance with requirements established by the Board or its agents, shall be performed by a qualified appraiser, and shall be paid for by the applicant.

Mr. Hellstrom indicated that the Board might use the appraisal as a guide line, that a separate appraisal in each instance might not be advisable, and careful research had determined the state's highest royalty for such material was 22 cents per cubic yard.

Governor Askew suggested a rule requiring the applicant to be bound by the appraisal figure except not less than 20 cents. The Attorney General thought payment should always be required, at a straight 50 cents per cubic yard. The Director had not been present when the committee started its work and, expressing concern for productive marine bottom lands, he recommended that the Board receive the report and allow the staff an opportunity to comment on it.

On motion by Mr. O'Malley, adopted without objection, the report was received and further action deferred pending receipt of staff comments. The Governor noted that the fact that values might be set for fill material did not mean that the Board necessarily would permit dredging of material. He expressed appreciation for the work of the Technical Advisory Committee on Fill.

<u>DADE COUNTY</u> - File No. 2396-13-253.03,
Easement and Construction Permit.
The Department of Transportation requested (1) an easement over 2.96 acres in Biscayne Bay abutting Sections 9 and 10, Township 53 South, Range 42 East, Dade County, and (2) a construction permit to allow erection of a bridge and seawalls for State Road 828 (Northeast 79th Street), for which no dredging or filling would be required as the water depth is sufficient to support flotation equipment and a special clause in the contract prohibits dredging.

The Department of Natural Resources had no objection to the work. The Department of Air and Water Pollution Control reviewed the plan and advised the staff that no certification would be required.

On motion by Mr. O'Malley and Mr. Conner, seconded by Mr. Dickinson, and adopted without objection, the Board granted the request for right-of-way easement and construction permit.

PALM BEACH COUNTY - Corps of Engineers Notices.
The Trustees had considered previously requests from (A) Sam G. Crupi for a permit from the Corps of Engineers to place a seawall along the mean high water line in a land-cut section of the Intracoastal Waterway in Section 5, Township 42 South, Range 43 East, Palm Beach County, and (B) Thomas J. Birmingham, et al, for a permit from the Corps of Engineers to seawall and fill an area in a land-cut section of the Intracoastal Waterway in the same section. Action was deferred pending receipt of an opinion from the Attorney General on an issue of jurisdiction under Chapter 253, Florida Statutes, in that section of the waterway that was formerly upland but which bordered on the navigable waters of the state.

Attorney General's Opinion No. 071-59 held that the Board had full authority to promulgate rules covering the filling of such "land-cut" areas bordering on navigable waters. Therefore, the staff had advised the applicants, the Corps of Engineers, and the local governing authority, that permits would be required for such construction.

Mr. Kuperberg advised the Board that staff field work was in progress to check on the reported unauthorized seawall construction.

SUBJECTS UNDER CHAPTER 18296

HAMILTON COUNTY - Easement, Murphy Act Land.
On motion by Mr. Christian, seconded by Messrs. Dickinson and Conner, adopted without objection, the Board granted the request from the Department of Transportation for an easement for highway purposes across a parcel of land certified to the State of Florida under tax sale certificates No. 124 of 1912 and No. 1419 of 1933, being a portion of Lot 10, Block 16, Reneau's Survey, in Section 7, Township 2 South, Range 16 East, containing .07 acre, more or less, in the Town of White Springs in Hamilton County.

On motion duly adopted, the meeting was adjourned.

GOVERNOR _ CHAIRMAN

ATTEST:

EXECUTIVE DIRECTOR

4-13-71

The State of Florida Board of Trustees of the Internal Improvement
Trust Fund met on this date in the Haydon Burns Building in Tallahassee,
Florida, with the following members present:

Reubin O'D. Askew	Governor
Richard (Dick) Stone	Secretary of State
Robert L. Shevin	Attorney General
Thomas D. O'Malley	Treasurer
Floyd T. Christian	Commissioner of Education
Doyle Conner	Commissioner of Agriculture

Joel Kuperberg	Executive Director

The minutes of the meeting of April 6 were approved as submitted.

ST. LUCIE COUNTY - Boundary Agreement, Land Exchange.
At the request of the staff the Board deferred for two weeks, for
further review, the application from Lucie Properties, Inc., for a
boundary line agreement and confirmation of a land exchange affecting
land in and abutting Government Lots 1 and 2 in Section 22, and
Government Lot 2 in Section 23 in Township 34 South, Range 40 East,
St. Lucie County. The lots granted to the State of Florida pursuant
to the "Swamp Land Grant" were conveyed by the Trustees to William
L. Moor by virtue of Deed No. 14726 dated September 22, 1892. The
original government surveys of the area do not accurately reflect
the true configuration of existing land. Meander lines cross over
sovereignty land and swamp land, causing title to be clouded.

CHARLOTTE COUNTY - Dredge Permit, Section 253.123 Florida
Statutes, File No. 733.
At the request of the staff the Board deferred for two weeks the
request from the City of Punta Gorda for a maintenance dredge permit
to widen and deepen an existing channel in Charlotte Harbor adjacent
to Section 15, Township 41 South, Range 22 East, Charlotte County,
for which a supplemental biological report would be obtained.

MONROE COUNTY - Regulatory Buoy Markers.
The Division of Recreation and Parks of the Department of Natural
Resources requested permission to install 10 regulatory floating
buoy markers at John Pennekamp Coral Reef State Park in Township 62
South, Range 39 East, and Township 59 South, Range 42 East, Monroe
County, needed to more clearly define the boundaries of the park and
mark dangerous or special interest areas.

The staff requested authority to issue a letter of no objection for
the installation of the buoy markers. Approval would be required
also from the United States Coast Guard, Corps of Engineers and the
Department of Natural Resources.

On motion by Mr. Stone, seconded by Mr. Christian and adopted without
objection, the Board approved the staff recommendation.

DADE COUNTY - Lease No. 2429.
Seminole Rock Products, Inc., was awarded Lease No. 2429 by the
Trustees on April 14, 1970, for mining limerock from a 1,000-acre
tract in Sections 22 and 23, Township 53 South, Range 39 East, Dade
County, following advertisement for sealed bids. The lease had a
term of ten years with option to renew for two succeeding ten-year
periods, royalty of 7¢ per short ton on material mined and sold, and
annual advance rental of $25,000 for each of the first two years and
$40,000 per year thereafter, to be applied as advance royalty. The
lease further required the mining project to conform to a master
recreation plan that required the mining operation to leave the
premises suitable and ready for installation of facilities and ready
for enjoyment by the public as a recreation area.

The recreation plan was approved by the Trustees and the Department
of Recreation and Parks subject to approval of Dade County. Lessee
submitted the plan to Dade County that approved the zoning variance
necessary to conduct mining in the area, approved certain modifications, and the county further requested that the site be transferred
to the county for development following completion of the mining.

The Division of Recreation and Parks recommended acceptance of the
modified plan and transfer of the property to Dade County for park
development at the appropriate time.

The staff recommended approval of the modified plan and requested
authority to lease the area to Dade County for public recreational
purposes following completion of the mining operations.

On motion by Mr. O'Malley, adopted without objection, the staff
recommendation was approved as the action of the Board.

GLADES COUNTY - Agriculture Lease Renewal.
U. S. Sugar Corporation, holder of Agriculture Lease No. 2205
covering 6.5 acres of reclaimed lake bottom land in Section 19,
Township 42 South, Range 34 East, requested extension of the lease
for an additional five years following expiration of the present
lease on July 27, 1971. The firm had control of the surrounding
land either by ownership or lease.

The staff appraiser had inspected the parcel and recommended that
the fair rental value for agriculture purposes be increased from
$25 to $33 per acre. The staff recommended extension of the present
lease for five years at annual rental of $33 per acre, with option
for an additional five years at a rental to be determined by an
appraisal. The lease provides that the lessee is responsible for
any and all taxes lawfully assessed against the property.

Governor Askew thought the Board should consider whether such
valuable muck lands should be leased for agriculture because of
the danger of oxidation and depletion of the soil. Mr. Conner
said that proper management was the answer, and while food crops
were needed the Board might develop some management policies not
now included in the leases. Mr. Christian mentioned the benefit
of the money to the state school fund.

The Governor suggested that the Board consider some policy in the
area, some guidelines for leasing without depletion of the soil.
He recommended indefinite postponement pending staff recommendations.
Mr. Kuperberg, noting that the Everglades was the largest body
of organic soil in the world, said a way must be found to produce
food and the staff would undertake to research the questions
discussed.

4-20-71

BREVARD COUNTY - Contract No. 24387(1854-05)
On September 30, 1966, the Trustees issued Purchase Contract No.
24387(1854-05) to Pecony, Inc., a New York Corporation, for 8.68
acres of submerged land in the Banana River in Section 34, Township
24 South, Range 37 East, Brevard County. All contract payments
having been made, the contract purchaser was entitled to receive a
deed. The staff requested ratification by at least five affirmative
votes of the present Board of Trustees in accordance with the former
Attorney General's recommendation to the staff in such matters.

The Governor commented on the filling done in a portion of this land
under a fill permit, as reported by the staff.

On motion by Mr. O'Malley, seconded by Mr. Christian and adopted
without objection, the Trustees authorized issuance of deed to the
contract purchaser.

MARTIN COUNTY - Reported Violation.
The Board of County Commissioners of Martin County requested a permit
authorizing completion of a seawall and backfill of land that had
been lost due to erosion along Jensen Beach Causeway, work that had
been commenced without the benefit of a permit. The project was shut
down and under investigation by the Field Operations Division of the
Trustees Office, and a biological report requested. However, the
county advised that the project should be completed to protect its
beach and 275 lineal feet of new seawall.

The staff suggested deferment for two weeks pending receipt and
evaluation of a biological report, but the Governor pointed out that
with the work in its present condition that period of time might not
be advisable and the Board should move as expeditiously as possible
for the protection of the beach in that area at the edge of the state
road right-of-way. The Director said there was danger of storm damage,
referred to restoration of a coastal structure if not more than
twenty-five feet into the water, and noted that at some places this
project was more than that distance out into the water.

The Board approved deferral with the understanding that the staff
will reagenda the application as soon as possible.

BAY COUNTY - State Marina License, Section 253.03 Florida Statutes.
On April 13 the Board deferred for one week the consideration of the
application from Major Clyde Weber for a commercial mariana facility
in Pitts Bayou in St. Andrews Bay in the City of Parker which had
been protested by a number of local residents.

The City of Parker on April 12 submitted copies of a proposed zoning
ordinance to control commercial development within the city.
Therefore, the staff recommended that the application for a marina
license be denied without prejudice.

Mr. O'Malley made a motion that the application be denied without
prejudice.

Mr. Kuperberg said the applicant had retained legal counsel, who
requested deferral pending an opportunity to review the matter and
appear before the Trustees. Governor Askew was agreeable, noting
that the objectors had been allowed a deferment period.

On motion by Mr. O'Malley, seconded by Mr. Christian and adopted without objection, the Trustees deferred the pending motion for one week in deference to the applicant, to allow his attorney to make a presentation to the Board.

PINELLAS COUNTY - City of Madeira Beach Boundary Line Between Public and Private Lands Along the Gulf Beach.
On April 13 the Trustees deferred action on the request from the City of Madeira Beach regarding establishment of the boundary line between public and private lands along the Gulf of Mexico beach where construction of a seawall encroached on state property according to the research and advice of the Bureau of Beaches and Shores, Department of Natural Resources.

Conferences had been held and would be continued between the representatives of the city, the property owners and staffs of the Trustees and Department of Natural Resources, seeking to resolve the technical questions.

The Director reported that the Trustees, through its general counsel and the office of the state attorney for the Sixth Judicial Circuit, filed a complaint against Madeira Beach Nominee, Inc., asking for injunctive relief and a temporary restraining order against any activity gulfward of the 1954 high water line, and further asking that the court order the defendant to remove all material and equipment which it has placed upon sovereignty lands. Mr. Kuperberg said that only the seawall was involved, as there was no problem regarding the building structures that were entirely within the 1954 mean high water line. It was indicated at the previous meeting that the title company would not permit the contractor to stop work, and it appeared that a temporary injunction was appropriate under the circumstances.

Without objection, the Trustees deferred this matter that was still under review by the staff.

SHELL LEASE INCOME - For the Record; Change of Procedure.
The Trustees received the report of income received by the Department of Natural Resources from the following holders of dead shell leases:

Lease No.	Company	Amount
2233	Bay Dredging and Construction Co.	$ 3,555.95
1788	Benton and Company, Inc.	17,144.25

The staff recommended that in the future such reports be eliminated from the agenda and minutes of the Trustees, as the revenue accrued to the Department of Natural Resources and the reports should be handled by that department.

It was so ordered.

MONROE COUNTY
Attorney General Robert L. Shevin gave to each member a memorandum setting forth in detail a matter of some urgency involving a threat of injury to state-owned lands in the Glades and the Keys and asking for it to be placed on the agenda next week so that the Trustees might take some action.

Governor Askew suggested that the matter be referred to the staff and placed on the agenda as soon as it could be brought back with a recommendation, within a week if possible.

It was so ordered.

_____

POLK COUNTY - Avon Park Correctional Institution.
The Department of Health and Rehabilitative Services recommended
acquisition of the 455.32 acre surplus portion of the Avon Park
Air Force Bombing Range from General Services Administration for
$425,000, the value set by G. S. A. Staff recommended approval of
the purchase and requested authority for the Executive Director to
execute on behalf of the Board a formal offer to purchase and other
documents necessary to finalize the purchase.

The Division of Corrections had leased the property from the U.S.
Air Force since 1957 for $1 per year utilizing and maintaining the
World War 2 barracks as a correctional institution. The Air Force
declared the property surplus in 1968 following unsuccessful efforts
by the Florida Congressional delegation to secure the land and
improvements without cost. General Services Administration offered
the 581.6 acres of land to the state for the U. S. appraised value
of $650,000. A 126.28 acre portion of the tract was transferred to
the U. S. Department of Health, Education and Welfare and deeded to
the State of Florida without cost subject to use for educational
purposes for thirty years and other restrictions.

The remaining 455.32 acres on which is located certain improvements
necessary to the operation of the institution was made available for
a limited time by G. S. A. for a negotiated purchase price of $425,000
from the state. Title to the remainder of the tract is needed in order
to construct needed sewage treatment plant and provide other necessary
improvements. Clear and unencumbered title will be received by purchase.
The Department advised that the purchase price had been appropriated
by the Legislature.

On motion by Mr. Stone, seconded by Mr. O'Malley and adopted without
objection, the Trustees approved the purchase and authorized the
execution of necessary documents by the Executive Director on behalf
of the Trustees.

_____

TRUSTEES FUNDS
The Board's approval was requested for an overlap of the position of
Executive Director as far as salary is concerned for Mr. Fred Vidzes
for an interim training period not to exceed three months for which
there were sufficient funds in the budget and the Auditor General's
office had verbally given approval, as long as proper approval is
obtained. Mr. Vidzes was the acting director in the interim period
between the resignation of the former Executive Director of the
Department and Mr. Kuperberg's appointment.

Governor Askew said he did a good job, but he thought the overlap
period should be limited to thirty days as normally applied to
other overlap positions within state government.

On motion by Mr. Christian, seconded and adopted without objection,
the Trustees approved the overlap for a thirty-day period.

_____

SUBJECTS UNDER CHAPTER 18296
NASSAU AND SUMTER COUNTIES - Murphy Act Land Sales.
On motion by Mr. Stone, seconded by Mr. Conner and adopted without
objection, the Trustees approved Bidding Report No. 983 and the
sales listed thereon under the provisions of Section 197.350 Florida
Statutes, and authorized execution of deeds pertaining thereto.

The land was described as follows:

Lot 3 Block 153 Town of Hilliard, Nassau County, certified to the State of Florida under tax sale certificate No. 2474 of 1933, sold to the high bidder, Leon Nelson, for $60.00.

Lots 56, 57 and 58, Coleman Heights Subdivision in Section 30, Township 19 South, Range 23 East, Sumter County, certified to the State of Florida under tax sale certificates 1452 of 1928 and 3734 of 1933 (Lot 56), 1576 of 1927, 1453 of 1928 and 3735 of 1933 (Lots 57 and 58), sold to the high bidder, Tommie Coleman, for $90.00.

REFUNDS - Murphy Act Land.
On motion by Mr. Christian, seconded by Mr. O'Malley and adopted without objection, the Trustees authorized issuance of refunds as follows:

$16.00 to George W. Eyles who withdrew his application for release of oil and mineral reservations in Indian River County Murphy Act Deed No. 871.

$15 to Berrien Becks for the reason that the Department of Transportation did not recommend release of the state road right-of-way reservation contained in Volusia County Murphy Act Deed No. 1579.

On motion duly adopted, the meeting was adjourned.

GOVERNOR - CHAIRMAN

ATTEST:

EXECUTIVE DIRECTOR

Tallahassee, Florida
April 27, 1971

The State of Florida Board of Trustees of the Internal Improvement Trust Fund met on this date in the Haydon Burns Building in Tallahassee, Florida, with the following members present:

Reubin O'D. Askew	Governor
Richard (Dick) Stone	Secretary of State
Robert L. Shevin	Attorney General
Fred O. Dickinson, Jr.	Comptroller
Thomas D. O'Malley	Treasurer
Floyd T. Christian	Commissioner of Education
Doyle Conner	Commissioner of Agriculture

Joel Kuperberg	Executive Director

4-20-71

The Trustees approved the minutes of the meeting of April 13 as submitted.

-1-

GLADES COUNTY - Grazing Lease Violation.
W. E. Perry, Winter Haven, Florida, is the holder of Grazing Lease No. 1694 dated January 15, 1962, for a ten year term covering 22.1 acres of reclaimed lake bottom land in Section 18, Township 42 South, Range 33 East, lying approximately 1½ miles east of Moore Haven in Glades County.

On May 27, 1971, consent of the Trustees to assign this lease to Ellie H. Yaun was received, following by a request to expand terms of the grazing lease to include planting of sugar cane. The staff appraiser's inspection of the 22.1 acres to determine fair rental value for agriculture purposes revealed that a portion of the tract was planted in sugar cane. Mr. John Yaun, son of the proposed assignee of the existing lease, advised that this area was 3-year old cane planted for the former owner of adjoining uplands, W. E. Perry. The Yauns acquired the uplands on May 29, 1970.

Mr. Perry, advised of the apparent violation of the terms of the grazing lease, responded through his attorney, stating that cane had been planted for him for the past two or three years on approximately 4 acres of the state land by reason of insufficient advice as to the terms of his lease.

Additional staff research and survey of the 22.1 acre tract revealed that as of November 10, 1970, 13.1 acres was planted in old cane and the balance in new cane. It has also been learned that an annual average of 6.28 acres had been planted in cane for the years 1965 through 1969.

In view of these facts and the established violation of the terms of the grazing lease, Mr. Perry was advised that the staff was willing to recommend a settlement as follows: The full present day rental of $27 per acre be assessed on the entire 22.1 acres for each year that the lease terms had been violated by cane planting (1965-1970) plus 10% penalty. This would amount to $3,580.20 plus 10% or a total of $3,938.22. The staff approach to this settlement was that the terms of the lease were changed to a higher and better use without authority, and additional rental is justified due to higher productivity of the land.

Another avenue of approach would be to assess Mr. Perry rental for the land actually planted in cane for the years 1965 through 1970. Using acreage figures obtained from the County Extension Director, an average of 7.75 acres was planted each year for the last six years. This would amount to 46.5 acres times $27 per acre rental, amounting to $1,255.50 plus a penalty of three times the value or $3,766.50 and cost of survey, $275, totaling $4,041.50.

The staff recommended (1) settlement of violation of lease terms, (2) approval of assignment of lease from W. E. Perry to Ellie H. Yaun, and (3) approval of change of lease to agriculture lease at $27 per acre with appropriate terms and provisions.

ACTION OF THE TRUSTEES:

Commissioner of Agriculture Doyle Conner had investigated this matter and recommended that the individuals pay as a penalty twice the agricultural rent for the acres used, making Mr. Perry's prorated share $1,463.40, and Mr. Yaun's $1,047.60 plus the survey cost of $275, or $1,322.60. Mr. Conner's information from the County Agent's office indicated the total acreage used by Mr. Perry in 1965-68 was 27.1 acres, and a total of 19.4 acres used by Mr. Yaun in 1969-70.

Mr. Conner made a motion that the above recommendation be adopted, seconded by Mr. O'Malley, supported by Mr. Stone, and adopted by the Trustees without objection. The old lease would be cancelled and a new agricultural lease issued to Mr. Yaun at $27 per acre annual rental.

Governor Askew spoke of his concern in the future, that consideration be given to determining what profit was made from any improper use of leased land. Mr. Conner said that would depend on such factors as the market, and pointed out that this land was not muck land but salt-and-pepper soil.

---

2. <u>LEE COUNTY</u> - Consideration of Oil and Gas Lease Bids.
On March 16 the Trustees authorized advertisement for sealed bids for a five-year oil and gas drilling lease covering all of the underlying petroleum and petroleum products in Government Lots 3 and 4, Section 2, Township 46 South, Range 26 East, Lee County, containing 80.28 acres, more or less. The lease will require one-eighth royalty, annual rent of $1 per acre, $50,000 surety bond, and one test well to a depth of 6,000 feet or to the top of the Lower Cretaceous, whichever is deeper.

Invitation to bid was advertised in the Tallahassee Democrat and the Fort Myers News pursuant to law, with bids to be opened at 10:00 a.m. on April 27. The staff recommended consideration of the bids.

ACTION OF THE TRUSTEES:

Motion was made by Mr. Christian, seconded and adopted without objection, that the one bid received, from Dalco Oil Company in the amount of $506, be accepted and the oil and gas drilling lease awarded to that bidder.

---

3. <u>SANTA ROSA COUNTY</u> - Consideration of Oil and Gas Lease Bids.
On March 9 the Trustees authorized advertisement for sealed bids for a five-year oil and gas drilling lease covering all of State Road 89 right-of-way lying in Section 40, Township 5 North, Range 29 West, containing 13.62 acres, more or less.

The lease will contain a provision prohibiting drilling on the road right-of-way, one-sixth royalty, annual rent of $1 per acre, $50,000 surety bond, and requirement that at least one test well be drilled on contiguous drilling units to 6,000 feet or to the sediments of the Jurassic Age, whichever is deeper.

Invitation to bid was advertised pursuant to law in the Tallahassee Democrat and the Press-Gazette of Milton. Prior to the issuance of this lease, a resolution from the Town of Jay will be necessary, consenting to the issuance of the lease as required by Section 253.61(a) Florida Statutes. The staff recommended consideration of the bids.

ACTION OF THE TRUSTEES:

Bids covering the cash consideration and rental for the first year were received from the following:

4-27-71

Chevron Oil Company $42,917.00
Pennzoil United, Inc.   2,737.62
Amerada Hess Miss-Fla Corporation   35,520.96

On motion by Mr. Christian, seconded by Mr. Conner and adopted
without objection, the Trustees accepted the highest bid and awarded
the oil and gas lease to Chevron Oil Company conditioned upon receipt
of a resolution from the Town of Jay consenting to the issuance of the
lease as required by Section 253.61(a), Florida Statutes.

4. LEE COUNTY - Contract No. 24374. This was on the advance
    agenda but was not placed on the agenda for consideration
    on this date.

5. COLLIER COUNTY - Electric Transmission Line Easement.
The Lee County Electric Co-Operative, Inc., requested a 12-foot wide
easement over and across a portion of the Immokalee State Farmers
Market in Section 34, Township 46 South, Range 29 East, and Section
3, Township 47 South, Range 29 East, for transmission and distribution
of electricity to the market.

The Department of Agriculture and Consumer Services reviewed and
approved the request, and the staff recommended issuance of the
easement.

ACTION OF THE TRUSTEES:

Motion was made by Mr. Stone, seconded by Mr. Christian and adopted
without objection, that the Trustees grant the easement requested.

6. MARION COUNTY - Drainage Easement.
The City of Ocala by Resolution No. 71-33 dated April 6, 1971, requests
an easement across the West 20 feet of the South 570 feet of the NW¼
of NW¼ of Section 22, Township 15 South, Range 22 East, for storm
drainage purposes. This land in Marion County is a part of the
Florida School for Girls property at Ocala.

The Department of Health and Rehabilitative Services approved the
request. The staff recommended issuance of a drainage easement.

ACTION OF THE TRUSTEES:

On motion made by Mr. Conner, seconded by Mr. Christian and Mr. Stone,
adopted without objection, the Trustees granted the request of the
City of Ocala for a drainage easement.

7. BAY COUNTY - State Marina License, Section 253.03 F. S.
On February 3, 1970, the Trustees approved issuance of State Commercial Dock Permit No. CD-1635 to Major Clyde Weber for a commercial
marina facility in Pitts Bayou in St. Andrews Bay in Section 24,
Township 4 South, Range 14 West, Bay County, in the City of Parker.
Due to delay in issuance of the Corps of Engineers permit, the
applicant was unable to begin construction within the required time
limit of 120 days provided by the state permit granted at that time.
Major Weber has now reapplied for state approval under a marina
license for a 115-foot, 10-slip facility. The previously
authorized structure was 170 feet long and provided 22 slips.

The City of Parker on April 12 submitted copies of a proposed zoning ordinance to be voted upon September 20 and a construction permit ordinance to become effective May 20, 1971.

On April 13 action was deferred for one week for further information regarding the city action.

In view of the fact that the City of Parker is proposing an ordinance to control commercial development within the city, staff recommended that the application for a marina license be denied without prejudice.

ACTION OF THE TRUSTEES:

The Trustees heard Mr. William J. Roberts, applicant's attorney, who reviewed the efforts made by Major Weber to get the required permits for his proposed dock facility on the Pitts Bayou shoreline in a commercial area. The opposite shoreline was residential making the problem one of zoning, a local responsibility.

Mr. O'Malley expressed the opinion that the Trustees should not hold up the permit on zoning grounds and he made a motion, seconded by Mr. Stone, that the application be approved.

The Governor asked Mr. Roberts several questions. It was brought out that the reason for the delay in action on the zoning ordinance was that September was the time for the next regular city election. Since the Trustees had deferred action to allow the objectors to try to get local action on zoning, and no great concern on the part of the city was evident, clarification of the city's position appeared to be desirable.

Mr. O'Malley withdrew his motion for approval and made a motion for two weeks' deferral, that was adopted without objection.

Governor Askew asked the Director to notify the City of Parker of the deferment and that the Board desired a representative to be present to explain the position of the city so that the matter might be disposed of properly.

8. MARTIN COUNTY - Violation.
The Board of County Commissioners of Martin County requested a permit to complete a seawall and backfill lands that have been lost due to erosion along Jensen Beach Causeway. The work was commenced without benefit of a permit. However, the county states that it needs to complete the project to protect its beach and 275 lineal feet of new seawall.

The Department of Natural Resources biological report indicated that as long as draglining is limited to the shoaled and stagnant bottoms at the western relief bridge and filling is limited to the eroded areas along the causeway, there should be no adverse effects on marine biological resources from this emergency work.

The Game and Fresh Water Fish Commission reported no objection to this project provided filling is confined to only those areas along the causeway. No additional areas should be filled under any circumstances. Heavy equipment should be confined to those areas that have become stagnant and shoaled at the western relief bridge.

The Department of Air and Water Pollution Control indicated no objections to the completion of the seawall by the Martin County

Commission. It is felt that to complete the project rather than
to leave it in a partially completed state will tend to improve
the water quality.

The staff had received a permit drawing from Martin County, reviewed
the application, and recommended issuance of the necessary permit.

ACTION OF THE TRUSTEES:

Motion was made by Mr. Dickinson, seconded by Mr. Christian and
adopted without objection, that the Board approve the permit
authorizing Martin County to complete the seawall and backfill the
land lost due to erosion.

---

9. AQUATIC PRESERVES - Ochlockonee Bay in Wakulla and Franklin
                       Counties, and North Fork St. Lucie River
                       in St. Lucie and Martin Counties.
A 90-day deferment was granted on February 2, 1971, in order that
the Interagency Advisory Committee on Aquatic Preserves might consider
the Ochlockonee Bay area further and hold a hearing on that portion
of the North Fork St. Lucie River between White City Road and Selvitz
Road.

It had been determined that the expiration date of May 3, 1971, would
not afford sufficient time for these matters to be properly considered.
Therefore, it was recommended that an additional 90-day extension be
granted.

ACTION OF THE TRUSTEES:

Governor Askew expressed the opinion that the extension was justified
but he hoped the study and hearing could be completed within the
next ninety days.

On motion by Mr. O'Malley, seconded by Mr. Dickinson and adopted
without objection, the Trustees allowed an additional 90-day
extension.

---

10. MONROE COUNTY - Development work reported to affect drainage
                    in the Everglades.
The Executive Director called attention to correspondence he had
received on the previous afternoon concerning the Monroe County
mainland area that was the subject of the memorandum of the Attorney
General. It was reported that the drag lines were at work in the
Loop Road area.

Governor Askew said that Mr. Henry Kittleson, special counsel for
the Trustees, had corroborated the position of the Attorney General
and in effect recommended that an injunction be sought.

Attorney General Shevin reviewed his memorandum concerning a vast
amount of private development going on that affects drainage and
the water supply of South Florida, and under the statutes he
thought the Trustees should take legal action.

On motion by Mr. Stone, seconded by Mr. Dickinson and adopted,
the Trustees waived the rules to allow discussion of an item not
on the agenda, and on the same motion requested the Attorney General
to take the necessary action for an injunction.

On motion duly adopted, the meeting was adjourned.

[signature]
GOVERNOR - CHAIRMAN

ATTEST: _[signature]_
EXECUTIVE DIRECTOR

Tallahassee, Florida
May 4, 1971

The State of Florida Board of Trustees of the Internal Improvement Trust Fund met on this date in the Haydon Burns Building in Tallahassee, Florida, with the following members present:

Reubin O'D. Askew	Governor
Richard (Dick) Stone	Secretary of State
Robert L. Shevin	Attorney General
Fred O. Dickinson, Jr.	Comptroller
Thomas D. O'Malley	Treasurer
Doyle Conner	Commissioner of Agriculture

Joel Kuperberg	Executive Director

The Trustees approved the minutes of the meeting of April 20 as submitted.

-1-

MONROE COUNTY - File No. 2255-44-253.12, Denial of Application

   STAFF DESCRIPTION: A parcel of sovereignty land in Florida Bay abutting Section 11, Township 66 S. Range 32 East, Key Vaca, Marathon, Monroe County, 1.1 acres.

A. CITY AND COUNTY: Marathon, Monroe County

B. APPLICANT: James B. Tharpe
             Post Office Box 427, Marathon, Florida 33050

C. ACREAGE: 1.1 acres
   RATE PER ACRE: Appraised value

D. APPRAISAL: None requested

E. PURPOSE: Expansion of Motel Property

F. BIOLOGICAL REPORT: Dated October 8, 1969; adverse.
   Remarks: "Sale and development of the 1.1 acre parcel would have adverse effects on marine biological resources."

G. STAFF REMARKS: Applicant stated that the parcel was a shallow swampy area that collected debris, that snakes and other pests inhabit the area, and

5-4-71

that the shallow water created noxious odors.

Staff was of the opinion that the reasons
stated were not sufficient to demonstrate
that the sale would be in the public interest.

H. RECOMMENDATION: That application be denied and file deactivated,
and that the application fee of $75 be refunded
as the application was filed prior to adoption
of the policy making application fees non-refundable.

Applicant was advised of the staff recommendation.

ACTION OF THE TRUSTEES:

The applicant had advised the staff by telegram on this date that
he desired no action on his application and would substitute a
navigation channel application instead of his dredge and fill
plan for the submerged parcel he had applied to purchase.

Motion was made by Mr. Stone, seconded by Mr. Dickinson and
adopted without objection, that the application be denied as
recommended, without prejudice to the filing of another type
of application.

ESCAMBIA COUNTY - Bulkhead Line
                 Right of Way Easement
                 Dredge and Fill Permit

The Department of Transportation requested approval of

A. Bulkhead line established by the Board of County Commissioners
of Escambia County by resolution adopted on March 11, 1971,
145 feet long in Bayou Chico at "W" Street in Section 39,
Township 2 South, Range 30 West. The Bulkhead line coincides
with the limits of a proposed box culvert.

B. Easement embracing 0.02 acres in Bayou Chico which will be
used for construction of a state road.

C. Dredge Permit to remove 5,676 cubic yards of material from
Bayou Chico and to fill 0.02 acre, more or less, lying landward of the above proposed bulkhead line. Also, a construction
permit to allow the placement of a 10 ft. x 6 ft. box culvert
within the dredge area.

The biological report indicated that the project as a whole should
have only limited adverse effects on marine life and wildlife if
certain precautions were taken during construction of the proposed
road bed and installation of the culvert.

The project was certified by the Department of Air and Water
Pollution Control. The Game and Fresh Water Fish Commission
issued a letter of no objection to the project.

RECOMMEND: (1) approval of the bulkhead line, (2) issuance of the
easement, and (3) approval of the dredge, fill and
construction permits subject to normal stipulations
for dredging and filling and to the recommendations
outlined in the biological report.

ACTION OF THE TRUSTEES:

Motion was made by Mr. Dickinson, seconded by Mr. O'Malley and
adopted without objection, that the staff recommendation be
approved.

3

ESCAMBIA COUNTY - Bulkhead Line
                  Right of Way Easement
                  Partial Post Construction Permits (Dredge/Fill)

The Department of Transportation, Applicant.

On April 14, 1971, the Trustees' Field Operations Division made an
on-site inspection of the project location and reported the following:

> Material had been hauled in and placed for a roadbed and a
> small amount of excavation had taken place in the area where
> box culverts are to be installed. The creek was 20 to 25 ft. wide
> at the site, and the proposed box culverts would occupy 20 feet.
> The stream was approximately 2 feet deep, installation of the
> culverts would not restrict the flow of water in the creek, and
> the box culverts would provide the same latitudinal cross
> section that a bridge would provide.

The Department of Transportation requested approval of:

A. Bulkhead Line established by the Board of County Commissioners
   of Escambia County by resolution adopted March 4, 1971, 342.08
   feet long in Bayou Grande at State Road No. 292A in Section
   5, Township 3 South, Range 31 West, Escambia County. The
   bulkhead line lies coincidental with the limits of the
   proposed box culverts.

B. Easement embracing 0.08 acre, more or less, in Bayou Grande,
   to be used for construction of State Road No. S-292-A.

C. Dredge Permit to complete removal of 1,809 cubic yards of
   material, fill permit to fill approximately 0.08 acre, and
   construction permit to place two 10 x 10 ft. box culverts in
   the dredge area.

The biological survey report indicated damage to marine biological
resources has already occurred due to previous work.

The Department of Air and Water Pollution Control has certified the
project, and the Game and Fresh Water Fish Commission has issued a
letter of no objection.

RECOMMEND: (1) approval of bulkhead line, (2) issuance of easement,
            and (3) approval of dredge, fill and construction permits,
            subject to normal stipulations as to dredging and filling
            and subject to the recommendations outlined in the bio-
            logical report.

ACTION OF THE TRUSTEES:

Motion was made by Mr. Stone, seconded by Mr. O'Malley and
adopted without objection, that the staff recommendation be
approved.

4

OKALOOSA COUNTY - Marina License, 253.03 F. S.

The Okaloosa Island Authority, c/o Mrs. Doris Jordan, Executive
Manager, 105 Santa Rosa Boulevard, Fort Walton Beach, Florida,
applied for a state marina license for a public fishing pier
in the Gulf of Mexico abutting upland in Township 2 South, Range
28 West, Okaloosa County. The proposed facility would occupy
approximately 18,500 square feet of submerged lands.

Due to the public nature of the facility, the Island Authority
requested waiver of all fees and modification of the standard time

requirement to allow a time period of twenty years with option to renew for an additional twenty years. The minimum life expectancy of this pre-stressed concrete pier was fifty years.

The Department of Air and Water Pollution Control had no objections to the proposed project. The Department of Natural Resources, Bureau of Survey and Management, had no objection; however, the Bureau of Beaches and Shores required that the applicant obtain a construction variance.

RECOMMEND approval, subject to receipt of above mentioned variance.

ACTION OF THE TRUSTEES:

Motion was made by Mr. Stone, seconded by Mr. Dickinson and adopted without objection, that the staff recommendation be approved.

MONROE COUNTY - Investigation of Dredge Operations

In response to the Governor's question, Mr. Kuperberg reported that the Trustees' staff had organized a federal and state agency joint task force that for the past two weeks had reviewed the problems of unauthorized dredge and fill operations in Monroe County.

Aerial photographs of the entire 103-mile run of the Keys, obtained with the help of the Department of Transportation, were checked against the permit files and about 105 operations were found that apparently were unauthorized. Staff of the state and federal agencies were making investigations on the site, and citations would be made in those cases where they were indicated.

On motion duly adopted, the meeting was adjourned.

GOVERNOR   CHAIRMAN

ATTEST:

EXECUTIVE DIRECTOR

Tallahassee, Florida
May 11, 1971

The State of Florida Board of Trustees of the Internal Improvement Trust Fund met on this date in the Haydon Burns Building in Tallahassee, Florida, with the following members present:

Reubin O'D. Askew	Governor
Richard (Dick) Stone	Secretary of State
Robert L. Shevin	Attorney General
Fred O. Dickinson, Jr.	Comptroller
Thomas D. O'Malley	Treasurer
Floyd T. Christian	Commissioner of Education
Doyle Conner	Commissioner of Agriculture
Joel Kuperberg	Executive Director

The minutes of the meeting of April 27 were approved as submitted.

r o i a   irustees oi the internai improvement irust
Fund for the three-month period from January 1 through March
31, 1971.

-2-

SARASOTA COUNTY - Bulkhead Line, Section 253.122, Florida Statutes

The Sarasota County Water and Navigation Control Authority by
resolution adopted November 7, 1968, established a bulkhead
line 252.54 feet long, along the southern bank of Grand Canal
in Section 1, Township 37 South, Range 17 East, Sarasota County.

The biological survey report was not adverse.

The bulkhead line lay at, or landward of, the original mean high
water line. This portion of Grand Canal was a navigable non-
meandered body of water.

The staff recommended approval of the bulkhead line.

ACTION OF THE TRUSTEES:

On motion by Mr. Christian, seconded by Mr. Stone and adopted
without objection, the Trustees approved the bulkhead line as
established by Sarasota County.

-3-

MARTIN COUNTY - Right of Way Easement, File 2399-43-253.03,
                and Construction Permit 253.03 F. S.

Central and Southern Florida Flood Control requested an
easement embracing 1.08 acres in Lake Okeechobee contiguous to
Levee 47 in Martin County. The right of way would be used for
the construction of a breakwater and stilling basin for the
protection of Structure 135 (Locks). The breakwater would
be constructed of rubble material obtained from upland sources,
with no dredging within the lake.

The Department of Natural Resources recommended approval of the
project. The Game and Fresh Water Fish Commission and the Department
of Air and Water Pollution Control had no objections to the project.

The staff recommended approval of the right of way easement and
issuance of a construction permit subject to approval of construction plans by the Department of Air and Water Pollution Control.

ACTION OF THE TRUSTEES:

Motion was made by Mr. Stone, seconded by Mr. Conner and
adopted without objection, that the easement and permit be
approved subject to the approval of the Department of Air and
Water Pollution Control.

-4-

OKEECHOBEE COUNTY - Right of Way Easement, File 2400-47-253.03
                    and Construction Permit, Section 253.03 F. S.

Central and Southern Florida Flood Control District requested an
easement embracing 1.92 acres in Lake Okeechobee contiguous to
Levee 47 in Okeechobee County. .The right of way would be used
for the construction of a breakwater and stilling basin for the
protection of Henry Creek Lock. The breakwater would be constructed of rubble material obtained from upland sources, with

5-11-71

no dredging within the lake.

The Department of Natural Resources recommended approval of the project. The Game and Fresh Water Fish Commission and the Department of Air and Water Pollution Control had no objections to the project.

The staff recommended approval of the right of way easement and issuance of a construction permit subject to approval of construction plans by the Department of Air and Water Pollution Control.

ACTION OF THE TRUSTEES:

Motion was made by Mr. Stone, seconded by Mr. Conner and adopted without objection, that the easement and permit be approved subject to the approval of the Department of Air and Water Pollution Control.

-5-

ESCAMBIA COUNTY - Marina License, Termination and Refund

On April 28, 1970, the Trustees authorized the issuance of Marina License No. 2 to

> Quadricentennial, Inc., c/o William Soule,
> Soule Construction Company, P. O. Box 1550,
> Pensacola, Florida.

The applicant requested that the marina license be terminated and the first year's fee of $1,548.40 be refunded. A report from the Field Operations Division indicated that no work was done on proposed project.

The staff recommended cancelling the license and refunding the annual fee.

ACTION OF THE TRUSTEES:

Motion was made by Mr. Conner, seconded by Mr. Stone, that the staff recommendation be approved.

Mr. O'Malley did not favor refund of the fee and made an amended motion to cancel the license without refunding the fee. There was no second to the amended motion.

On Mr. Conner's motion the staff recommendation was accepted.

-6-

PALM BEACH COUNTY - Marina License, Section 253.03 F. S.

> Mystan Marina, c/o Mock, Roos, and Searcy, Inc.,
> 2930 Okeechobee Road, West Palm Beach, Florida,

applied for a marina license to add 9,200 square feet to an existing facility in the Loxahatchee River in Section 31, Township 40 South, Range 43 East, Palm Beach County. The minimum annual fee of $184 was tendered.

No dredging was required. The Department of Air and Water Pollution Control, the Department of Natural Resources, and the Game and Fresh Water Fish Commission had no objections to the project.

The staff recommended approval.

ACTION OF THE TRUSTEES:

On motion by Mr. Dickinson, seconded by Mr. Christian and
adopted without objection, the Trustees approved issuance of
a marina license to the applicant.

-7-

MARTIN COUNTY - Marina License, Section 253.03 F. S.

Sailfish Marina, c/o Greenlees, Arbogast & Montgomery, Inc.
P. O. Box 92, Stuart, Florida,

applied for a marina license for a mooring facility containing
37,600 square feet in Manatee Pocket of the Indian River abutting
uplands in the Hanson Grant near Port Salerno, Martin County.
No dredging was required. The minimum annual fee of $725 was
tendered.

The Board of County Commissioners of Martin County, the Game and
Fresh Water Fish Commission, the Department of Air and Water
Pollution Control, and the Department of Natural Resources,
had no objections to the project.

The staff recommended approval.

ACTION OF THE TRUSTEES:

On motion by Mr. Dickinson, seconded by Mr. Stone and adopted
without objection, the Trustees approved issuance of the
marina license.

-8-

SANTA ROSA COUNTY - Marina License, Amendment to Time Limit

On March 16, 1971, the Trustees approved Marina License No. 26
to the

United States of America, Department of the Navy,
Charleston, South Carolina,

for a fishing and mooring facility in the Blackwater River in
Section 35, Township 2 North, Range 28 West, Santa Rosa County.

The Department of the Navy has requested an amendment to the
"one year with option to renew for a period of one year" provision,
to provide for a term of twenty years with right of renewal for
an additional twenty years.

The staff recommended approval.

ACTION OF THE TRUSTEES:

On motion by Mr. Stone, seconded by Mr. Dickinson and adopted
without objection, the Trustees approved amendment of the marina
license as requested.

-9 and 10-

DADE COUNTY - Two oil lease assignments were removed from the
advance agenda for further checking.

5-11-71

-11-

OKALOOSA AND SANTA ROSA COUNTIES - Oil Lease Assignment

On March 24, 1969, an oil and gas lease was issued by Florida Board of Forestry to Arthur E. Meinhart covering the 1/4 interest in petroleum held by the State in 14,648.04 acres in Blackwater River State Forest. Beard Oil Company as successor to this lease by assignment desired to assign a 50% undivided interest to Maui Oil Corporation.

Executed assignment was reviewed and approved by staff legal counsel as to form and legality.

Division of Forestry approved the assignment.

The staff recommended approval of assignment.

ACTION OF THE TRUSTEES:

On motion by Mr. Dickinson, seconded by Mr. Stone and adopted without objection, the Trustees approved the assignment.

Prior to presentation of these minutes for approval, an error in the agenda was discovered. The request should have been for assignment from Beard Oil Company and Maui Oil Corporation to Continental Oil Company. With this correction, the assignment was approved.

-12-

COLLIER COUNTY - Grazing Lease Renewal

> D. Wayne Pringle, Immokalee,
> and R. B. Hemleben, Ocala,

requested renewal of Grazing Lease No. 2184-S covering Section 16, Township 49 South, Range 32 East, containing 640 acres, more or less.

The land was located 3 miles north of Alligator Alley and 20 miles southeast of Immokalee. The section supported a reported 15 to 20 head of cattle for grazing, with approximately 500 acres being flooded or unusable for grazing from 4 to 7 months each year.

A current appraisal by the staff appraiser indicated an annual fair rental of 75¢ per acre. Former lease rental was 35¢ per acre.

The staff recommended renewal of grazing lease for an additional three years at increased rental, ninety-day cancellation clause and requirement that lessee pay any and all taxes which may be lawfully assessed.

ACTION OF THE TRUSTEES:

The Director pointed out that the recommendation should have included "three years" as the additional period of the renewal.

On motion by Mr. Christian, seconded by Mr. Stone and adopted without objection, the Trustees approved renewal of the grazing lease for an additional three years at increased rental, ninety-day cancellation clause and requirement that lessee pay any and all taxes which might be lawfully assessed.

-13-

COLLIER COUNTY - Grazing Lease Renewal

Mrs. Lois A. Crews, Immokalee, requests renewal of Grazing Lease No. 2320-S covering all of Section 16, Township 49 South, Range 33 East, containing 640 acres, more or less, Collier County.

The land is located three miles north of Alligator Alley, 24 miles southeast of Immokalee. Access was by fair weather road with half of the section remaining flooded or unusable for grazing all of the time. The tract would support a reported 20 head of cattle for grazing.

A current appraisal by staff appraiser indicated an annual fair rental of 75¢ per acre. Former lease rental was 30¢ per acre.

The staff recommended renewal of grazing lease for an additional three years at increased rental, ninety-day cancellation clause and requirement that lessee pay any and all taxes which may be lawfully assessed.

ACTION OF THE TRUSTEES:

On motion by Mr. Christian, seconded by Mr. Stone and adopted without objection, the Trustees approved renewal of the grazing lease for an additional three years at increased rental, ninety-day cancellation clause and requirement that lessee pay any and all taxes which might be lawfully assessed.

-14-

POLK COUNTY - A request for approval of a   land exchange was removed from the advance agenda.

-15-

PALM BEACH COUNTY - The Board of County Commissioners of Palm Beach County adopted a resolution on March 30, 1971, requesting that the Trustees order a moratorium on all dredging operations in the public waters of Palm Beach County, including certain fresh water lakes, until it can be ascertained that "dredging will not permanently degrade water quality nor cause irreversible damage to marine ecosytems."

Staff requested authority be given that an immediate inquiry be made based on the county's resolution to determine the imposing of a moratorium and the extent thereof.

ACTION OF THE TRUSTEES:

Mr. Dickinson made a motion to approve the staff recommendation.

Mr. Shevin did not understand why the staff had difficulty ascertaining whether there were any existing permits that might be affected. The Director explained that the resolution was most comprehensive, ordering a moratorium for an undetermined length of time on all dredging operations in the public waters of the county including presently permitted private and public operations. Letters objecting to the resolution had been forwarded to the Board from Mr. W. T. Carlton of the Bureau of Beaches and Shores, Department of Natural Resources, because of beach nourishment and maintenance projects, and from the Area Planning Board of Palm Beach County.

Mr. Kuperberg said the resolution was unworkable in his judgment as it requested suspension of all dredging for an indefinite time for judgments that would be extremely difficult to determine and would have to be funded. He suggested as an alternate measure that the Board might declare a moratorium on the issuance of dredge and fill permits in Palm Beach County.

Mr. Shevin asked that some action be taken within a week or two. Mr. Stone thought a one-county moratorium would be unrealistic, that the staff should confer with the County Commission and bring the Board a conservation-minded, realistic recommendation.

On the motion by Mr. Dickinson, seconded by Mr. Christian, the Trustees delayed action until the staff investigation was completed, within two weeks if possible.

5-11-71

MONROE COUNTY - Mr. James G. Pace requested an opportunity
to be heard regarding the Trustees' action on April 27 in
connection with the Loop Road property in Township 54 South,
Range 33 East, Monroe County (Gum Slough area).

Representing owners of about 10,000 acres of land purchased
in 1963 South of the Loop Road (an extension of Tamiami Trail),
north of Everglades National Park, Mr. Pace discussed his
clients' plan to use 1,800 acres for experimental farming
where farming had been done in the 1930's, containing and
regulating the water within the private land by diking. He
displayed maps and soil maps, discussing the soil, the use
of trace minerals as fertilizer, the natural drainage in
the area and the diking effect of the Tamiami Trail at the
present time, the Gum Slough that acts as east-west natural
drainage for part of the property. He did not see that
the private owners' use of their land would damage the ecology
or ruin the Park. He pointed out that many acres in the Park
had not been purchased from the private owners but had been
used for about fourteen years.

Mr. Pace spoke of the owners' effort to form a drainage district under the General Drainage Law of Florida. Now, taking
a small portion of their property, the private owners were
trying to find out if their experimental farming plans would
work. While they were not ecologists or conservationists, they
were aware of the trend and were trying to conform to the
objections.. They had done nothing illegal and objected to
criticism and litigation to prevent them from using their own
land for farming or raising cattle.

Attorney General Shevin had brought this matter to the attention
of the Trustees several weeks ago and recommended immediate
action to protect the state-owned land and coastal waters that
were threatened with damage as evidenced by the action of the
Circuit Court in ruling against the establishment of a drainage
district. Mr. Shevin said the Trustees should take action
to protect the state lands from a cut-off of water and a
resulting disruption of the natural food chain in the area, as
well as affecting the water supply of the public, relying on
the Circuit Court ruling on the drainage district and seeking
an injunction on the basis that the development would detrimentally
affect the state. The facts brought out by Mr. Pace should be
brought out in the court. Mr. Kittleson had also recommended
filing of a suit, which Mr. Shevin's office had almost ready
to file in an effort to protect state land from damage that
might result from the proposed diking.

Governor Askew said it was not the intent of the Trustees to deprive
owners of the lawful use of their land, but in that particular area
it appeared that the use of some land might have an adverse effect on
other land and the Board decided on the advice of the Attorney General
that it should be litigated to determine the extent of individual
rights as opposed to the larger areas that might be detrimentally
affected. It posed a serious problem, and the Board appreciated
the information Mr. Pace had offered.

-17-

PALM BEACH COUNTY - Dredge Permit, Section 253.123 F. S.

The application from Vista Builders, Inc. , for permission to
install a seawall and perform maintenance dredging was withdrawn at the request of the Palm Beach County Planning Board.
The matter would be reviewed with that agency.

-18-

OKALOOSA COUNTY - Fill Permit, Section 253.124(8)-171

    Dr. R. S. Ellis
    P. O. Box 685, Niceville, Florida 32578

requested approval of a permit issued by Okaloosa County on
January 12, 1971, to construct a seawall and backfill land subject
to avulsion. The land would be filled by trucking in material in
Choctawhatchee Bay lying adjacent to Section 21, Township 1 South,
Range 22 West. An area with dimensions of 140 ft. by an average
width of 15 ft. would be filled.

The purpose of the permit was to prevent further erosion and to
prevent loss of several large oak trees. The applicant stated that
since the application was submitted further erosion had occurred
to a point where the dwelling now lay within 15 ft. of the shoreline.

Request authority to issue permit subject to recommendation of
the Department of Natural Resources that the area to be filled be
reduced by one-fourth.

ACTION OF THE TRUSTEES:

On motion by Mr. Stone, seconded by Mr. Dickinson and adopted
without objection, the Trustees authorized issuance of the
fill permit subject to compliance with the recommendation of the
Department of Natural Resources that the area to be filled be
reduced by one-fourth.

Mr. Shevin, noting that the report of the Technical Advisory
Committee on Fill was received on April 13, asked the Director
if he was in a position to make a recommendation. Mr. Kuperberg
advised that the delay was caused by the work on the Marco Island
matter, and he expected to be able to report within a week or two.

-19-

BAY COUNTY - State Marina License, Section 253.03 F. S.

On February 3, 1970, the Trustees approved issuance of State
Commercial Dock Permit No. CD-1635 to Major Clyde Weber for
a commercial marina facility in Pitts Bayou in St. Andrews
Bay in Section 24, Township 4 South, Range 14 West, Bay County,
in the City of Parker. Due to delay in issuance of the Corps
of Engineers permit, the applicant was unable to begin construction within the required time limit of 120 days provided
by the State permit granted at that time. Major Weber reapplied
for state approval under a marina license for a 115-ft, 10-slip
facility. The previously authorized structure was 170 feet
long and provided 22 slips.

The City of Parker on April 12 submitted copies of a proposed
zoning ordinance to be voted upon September 20 and a construction
permit ordinance to become effective May 20, 1971.

On April 13 action was deferred for one week for further information regarding the city action. In view of the fact that the
City of Parker was proposing an ordinance to control commercial
development within the city, on April 27 the staff recommended
that the application for a marina license be denied without
prejudice.

On April 27 the Trustees deferred action for two weeks and the
Governor directed the Executive Director to notify the city of
the deferment and that the Board desired a representative to be
present to explain the position of the city so that the matter
might be disposed of properly. This had been done, and it had
been indicated to the staff that a representative from the City
of Parker would be in attendance to present the city's position.

ACTION OF THE TRUSTEES:

Mr. William J. Roberts and his client, Major Clyde Weber, were present. Mr. Roberts pointed out that the city objected to further commercial development in Pitts Bayou, but in fact it was already heavily commercial on the side of the Bayou where Mr. Weber's property was located, including tugboat and barge facilities. His client had purchased it for commercial use, and had previously received a permit for a dock from the state and a permit from the city. The Corps of Engineers had indicated that the dock would not interfere with navigation, no dredging was required, and the construction would be subject to building permit requirements of the city.

City Councilman Donald L. Benoit, representing the City of Parker, discussed the small city's situation and based objections on the previous letters from the city and four letters of objection. He said the young community had many problems, that this area was a recreation area, and the city council wanted the people to indicate whether or not they actually desired the zoning.

Mr. O'Malley said his motion two weeks ago was seconded and deferred to allow the city to explain its position. It had been pointed out that tugboats and barges used the bayou and he was concerned about getting involved in zoning matters that were local issues. He noted that the Board had approved other marina licenses on this date. Mr. Christian agreed with him.

Governor Askew spoke of the councilman's reference to sewage problems but pointed out that there were no objections to this application from the Department of Air and Water Pollution Control. The Trustees had delayed a decision in deference to the city, but it was not certain that the people of Parker in September would vote against commercial zoning for this area.

On the motion by Mr. O'Malley, seconded by Mr. Stone and adopted without objection, the Trustees approved the application of Major Weber for a state marina license.

On motion duly adopted, the meeting was adjourned.

GOVERNOR   -   CHAIRMAN

ATTEST:

EXECUTIVE DIRECTOR

Tallahassee, Florida
May 18, 1971

The State of Florida Board of Trustees of the Internal Improvement Trust Fund met on this date in the Haydon Burns Building, with the following members present:

Reubin O'D. Askew	Governor
Richard (Dick) Stone	Secretary of State
Fred O. Dickinson, Jr.	Comptroller
Thomas D. O'Malley	Treasurer
Floyd T. Christian	Commissioner of Education
Doyle Conner	Commissioner of Agriculture

Joel Kuperberg	Executive Director

The minutes of May 4 were approved as submitted.

-1-

VOLUSIA COUNTY - Land Exchange File No. 2395-64-253.42

John C. Gross as President of Yacht Club Island Corporation, New Smyrna Beach, Florida, represented by Mr. Hal McClamma, requested the Board of Trustees to exchange 0.51 acre parcel of sovereignty land for two parcels of submerged land embracing 0.55 acre and 0.08 acre. The two parcels of submerged land were within an area previously conveyed by the Board. In addition, applicant agreed to pay $1,815, the difference in the appraised value of the 0.51 acre parcel and the 0.55 acre parcel.

The parcel to be conveyed was landward of the bulkhead line approved by the Board on February 16, 1971. The exchange was advertised for objections and two objections were received.

The objections concern what the proposed development might do to land values, ecology, and aesthetic values.

On February 16, the Trustees granted the applicant a fill permit to fill his uplands.

All material to fill the area would be obtained from the maintenance dredging of the Intracoastal Waterway. A bond in the amount of $20,000 for 20,000 cubic yards of material was posted in the Bank of New Smyrna payable to the Trustees. Applicant also agreed to replant mangroves at the southerly end of the island under the supervision of the Department of Natural Resources.

A supplemental biological report dated May 5, 1971, from the Department of Natural Resources found that the exchange would result in the state acquiring a small productive area containing valuable marine habitat, for a parcel that was sandy and unvegetated.

Recommend that the Trustees enter into the exchange.

ACTION OF THE TRUSTEES:

Motion was made by Mr. O'Malley, seconded by Mr. Stone and adopted without objection, that the Trustees enter into the land exchange with Mr. John C. Gross as president of Yacht Club Island Corporation.

-2-

POLK AND OSCEOLA COUNTIES - Lake Hatchineha

Consideration of a conveyance of lands to be included in a proposed wilderness area and granting of a navigation channel dredge permit was withdrawn from the advance agenda pending receipt of a resolution from the Florida Game and Fresh Water Fish Commission. The Director said the staff hoped to have the matter on the agenda on May 25.

-3-

COLLIER COUNTY - Consideration of Permit Extension

    (A)   File No. 253.123-51

    (B)   File Nos. 253.123-678, 253.124-149

    Applicant: Marco Island Development Corporation.

In accordance with action taken by the Trustees on April 13, this matter was scheduled on May 18 for further consideration.

ACTION OF THE TRUSTEES:

The Director had reviewed the entire matter involving the
Marco Island permit extension request. The Big Marco River
permit was originally issued by the Army Corps of Engineers
in 1964, expired, was reissued and again expired in January,
was extended for ninety days during which time the extension
of Smokehouse Creek-Roberts Bay permit was considered, and
both permits had been extended until this date.

The staff presented a series of preliminary recommendations
and set two deadlines. On June 1, the staff would report to
the Trustees on the progress made with Marco Island Development
Corporation toward an agreement, and on June 15, would submit
that agreement to the Trustees or indicate that no agreement was
reached.

Mr. Kuperberg explained that during the negotiations, the staff
was trying to resolve the entire matter involving some 19,500
acres of land in M. I. D. C. ownership so that consideration
could be given to a revised plan for the ecological impact of
the development. He had searched for a solution at the federal
level also, because a settlement unacceptable to federal agencies
that issue permits would not solve the problem.

The Director recommended approval of the applicant's request for
extension of the two permits until June 15, pending the Trustees'
consideration of the staff recommendations.

On motion by Mr. O'Malley, seconded by Mr. Dickinson and adopted
without objection, the Trustees approved all the following
recommendations of the staff:

1. Marco River and Roberts Bay renewal applications:

That these permit areas be further examined, in cooperation with
the applicant, to determine if modifications can be made within
the framework of the existing development. (Modifications such
as use of riprap seawalls where feasible; further limitations on
dredge areas; establishment of experimental mangrove areas, etc.)

2. Areas which have been platted but not yet permitted; or are
    conditionally permitted; or await permits from other agencies:

That in addition to the same examination as specified in (1) above,
the staff and applicant jointly examine the possibility of a conveyance by applicant to the State or other appropriate authority
of an undisturbed area or areas which would include submerged
lands and uplands owned by the applicant and consist of a complete and viable ecosystem and would at least equal the total
area to be disturbed.

3. Areas not platted; or which await permits from other agencies:

That a series of ecological constraints be developed which will
give maximum protection to the marine ecosystems. Property law
principles shall yield in favor of these ecological constraints.

4. That a study period be provided to June 1, 1971, thus giving
the Trustees time to study the information submitted, providing
the applicant time to discuss the above recommendations with the
staff, and providing the applicant sufficient time to file information responsive to these preliminary recommendations.

5. On June 15, 1971, the staff will present to the Trustees its
proposed agreement (or nonagreement) with the applicant and make
its detailed recommendation. At that time the applicant may be
heard if necessary.

6. The applicant has requested that the two permits subject to
the renewal applications be extended to June 15, 1971, pending
Trustees' consideration of staff recommendation.

Governor Askew commended the Director on his work on the Marco
Island matter and his good faith in trying to seek a solution
to a very difficult problem.

279

-4-

CORRECTIVE DEED - Murphy Act

Request approval of Murphy Act Report No. 984 listing one
corrective deed:

> County of Manatee Deed No. 826-Corrective to H. H. Adams
> and Vera Adams to be issued in lieu of Manatee County
> Deed No. 826 dated December 9, 1944, to H. H. Adams or
> Vera Adams. Purpose of the correction was to change "or"
> to "and" in the name of the grantee.

ACTION OF THE TRUSTEES:

On motion by Mr. O'Malley, seconded by Mr. Stone and adopted
without objection, the Trustees approved issuance of the
corrective deed.

-5-

PATENTS, TRADEMARKS AND COPYRIGHTS

Under Chapter 70-440 legal title to any patent, trademark or
copyright held or acquired by the State was transferred to
the Board of Trustees with authority to enforce the rights of
the State in these matters, protect against improper and unlawful
use and infringement, enforce collections of any sums due. The
law also provided for the Board of Trustees to sell any of the
patents, trademarks or copyrights and to execute any and all
instruments on behalf of the State necessary to consummate any
such sale. The law provided authority to license, lease, assign
to any person, firm or corporation for the manufacture or use
on a royalty basis or other consideration.

Chancellor Robert B. Mautz of the State University System has
requested transfer to the Board of Regents of any rights and
interest held by the Board of Trustees in an invention called
"Spectrometer System" which was developed by Dr. David T. Williams,
a member of the faculty of the University of Florida. The transfer
would afford the Board of Regents the opportunity to pursue the
matter with Spectrometrics of Florida, Inc. to the best interest
of the University of Florida and the State University System of
Florida.

This invention arose out of activities assisted by a U. S.
Department of Health, Education and Welfare grant. That department
had first right of ownership in the invention and agreed to allow
the University to assume ownership for purposes of development
but would not lease this right to the State of Florida.

Recommend that Trustees assign to the Board of Regents for the use
and benefit of the University of Florida the full and exclusive
rights to the application and patent that may be issued.

ACTION OF THE TRUSTEES:

On motion by Mr. Christian, seconded by Mr. Stone and adopted
without objection, the Trustees approved the assignment as
recommended.

-6-

LITIGATION - Coastal Petroleum Company

Staff reported to the Board on the status of the litigation,
Coastal Petroleum Company vs. Secretary of the Army of the
United States, USDC Southern District No. 68-951-CIV-CA and
69-699-CIV-CA Consolidated.

The firm of Beckham and McAliley had been representing the
Trustees in this litigation.

5-18-71

The final judgment in this suit was received and the court declared that as to issue (1), Leases 224-A, 224-B, and 248 were declared to be valid and existing leases and that limestone was a mineral within the meaning of that term as used in Lease 248.

As to issue (2), the United States had the right to deny issuance of a permit to mine within the area subject to application for permit with the determination that there was no taking of Coastal's property by reason of denial of permit and no liability to Coastal assessed to the Flood Control District or the Trustees for the material used in construction of Levee 47 on Lake Okeechobee.

The order further stated that Coastal's obligations as lessee under the terms of the several leases were suspended and that the suspension shall not expire until a reasonable time after the time for appeal of issue (1) of the judgment has run, or the receipt of the mandate on appeal by the Clerk of the Court after appeal challenging issue (1) of this judgment.

On the basis of the reasons set forth in the memoranda furnished to the Board, the staff recommended that appeal be taken on this matter and further recommended that the firm of Beckham and McAliley continue to be retained to represent the Trustees.

ACTION OF THE TRUSTEES:

The Governor commented that the state had everything to gain and nothing to lose by pursuing an appeal.

On motion by Mr. Christian, seconded by Mr. Stone and adopted without objection, the Trustees authorized the appeal and retained the firm of Beckham and McAliley to represent the Boards.

On motion duly adopted, the meeting was adjourned.

_____
GOVERNOR   -   CHAIRMAN

ATTEST: _____
EXECUTIVE DIRECTOR

* * *   * * * *   * * *   * * * *   * * * *

Tallahassee, Florida
May 26, 1971

The State of Florida Board of Trustees of the Internal Improvement Trust Fund met on this date in the conference room of the Governor in the Capitol, with the following members present:

Reubin O'D. Askew	Governor
Richard (Dick) Stone	Secretary of State
Robert L. Shevin	Attorney General
Thomas D. O'Malley	Treasurer
Floyd T. Christian	Commissioner of Education
Joel Kuperberg	Executive Director

On motion by Mr. Stone, duly adopted, the Trustees approved the minutes of May 11 as corrected to show approval of an oil lease assignment from Beard Oil Company and Maui Oil Corporation to Continental Oil Company in the item numbered eleven.

-1-

MANATEE COUNTY - Dedication, File No. 2390-41-253.03

The National Audubon Society, represented by Myron G. Gibbons
of Tampa, Florida, requested dedication of Whale Island and
the sovereignty land within 400 feet of the island in Sarasota
Bay, embracing approximately 26 acres adjacent to Section 31,
Township 35 South, Range 17 East, Manatee County, to be used
as a wildlife sanctuary.

The Department of Natural Resources reported that dedication
of the island and nearby sovereignty land would give the highly
productive biological area an extra measure of protection.

The parcel was advertised for objections and no objections were
received.

Recommend that dedication be issued containing a reverter clause
in the event the area is abandoned as a wildlife sanctuary.

ACTION OF THE TRUSTEES:

On motion by Mr. O'Malley, seconded by Mr. Christian and
adopted without objection, the recommendation of the staff
was approved as the action of the Board.

-2-

COLLIER COUNTY - Artificial Reef Permit, Section 253.03 F. S.

    Marco Island Development Corporation
    Post Office Box 280, Miami, Florida 33129

requested a permit to install an artificial reef in the Gulf of
Mexico one and two-tenths (1.2) miles west of Marco Island. The
reef would be one (1) mile long and one-half (1/2) mile wide.
The corner locations would be:

    25° 56' 24" North Lat.   81° 46' 15" West Long.
    25° 56' 24" North Lat.   81° 45' 45" West Long.
    25° 55' 32" North Lat.   81° 45' 45" West Long.
    25° 55' 32" North Lat.   81° 46' 45" West Long.

The applicant would install approximately 15,000 tires per year
for a period of five years (anchored in place with concrete blocks).

The biological report was not adverse.

The Department of Natural Resources recommended approval subject
to the site being adequately marked by buoys on all four corners
to prevent damage or entanglement of fishermen's nets.

The Department of Air and Water Pollution Control and the Game
and Fresh Water Fish Commission had no objections.

$50 processing fee was tendered.

The staff recommended approval of the project.

ACTION OF THE TRUSTEES:

On motion by Mr. Stone, seconded by Mr. Christian and adopted
without objection, the Trustees approved the project and
authorized issuance of the artificial reef permit.

282

-3-

DUVAL COUNTY - Utilities Easement

The City of Jacksonville requested an easement for the construction of electric transmission lines, water mains and sewer
lines over, under and across a parcel 105 feet wide and 2,568.96
feet long. The easement is across a portion of the University
of North Florida campus. The Board of Regents approved issuance
of the easement at its April 5 meeting. The Game and Fresh Water
Fish Commission inspected the site and approved the proposed
easement route.

Recommend issuance of the easement as requested.

ACTION OF THE TRUSTEES:

On motion by Mr. Christian, seconded by Mr. Stone and adopted
without objection, the Trustees authorized issuance of the easement to the City of Jacksonville.

-4-

ESCAMBIA COUNTY - Emergency Dredge Permit,
                 Section 253.123 F. S.

    Warren Petroleum Company, c/o R. S. Taylor
    P. O. Box 1589, Tulsa, Oklahoma

On February 16, 1971, the Trustees approved State Dredge Permit
No. 253.123-707 to allow removal of silt and sand from applicant's
barge slip 165 ft. long, 15 ft. wide and 7 ft. deep in Section
59, Township 2 South, Range 30 West, Escambia County. The dredging
was required to enable barges to be moored against the dock to
reduce the danger of fuel spills. The material removed was to
be placed on the applicant's upland.

No fees for dredge material were required because the area subject to dredging was filled as a result of sloughing off adjacent
bank into the mooring site.

The Department of Natural Resources biological report dated
January 29, 1971, was not adverse. The Department of Air and
Water Pollution Control stated that there was reasonable
assurance that the project would be executed in a manner which
would not violate applicable water standards.

Corps of Engineers Notice 61-67 indicated a dredge depth of
minus-12 feet mean low water. A review of the file with the
applicant's engineer indicated that the agenda item of February 16,
1971, should have specified a dredge depth of minus-12 feet mean
low water. So that both the state permit and Corps permit would
correspond, it was necessary to correct the state permit to indicate a minus-12 mean low water rather than a minus-7 mean low
water from the existing subsurface.

Staff requested authority to issue a corrected permit to allow
dredging to minus-12 feet mean low water.

ACTION OF THE TRUSTEES:

Mr. Kuperberg explained that it was not a new dredge permit
but modification of an existing permit.

On motion by Mr. Stone, seconded by Mr. Christian and adopted
without objection, the Trustees approved issuance of the corrected
permit as requested.

5-26-71

-5-

HILLSBOROUGH AND MANATEE COUNTIES - State Construction Permit
                                   Instrumentation Platform
                                   Pilings.

    Florida Power and Light Company
    P. O. Box 3100, Miami, Florida 33101,

applied for a state construction permit for the placement of
three oceanographic instrumentation platforms in Townships 32
and 33 South, Range 17 East, in Lower Tampa Bay, Hillsborough
and Manatee Counties. A $100 processing fee was tendered.

The stations would be used to house electronic equipment to
measure water temperature, salinity, current speed and direction
for determining baseline data and the effects of heated effluent
discharged from the proposed Port Manatee electric generating
facility.

The Department of Air and Water Pollution Control , the Game
and Fresh Water Fish Commission, the Department of Natural
Resources, the Tampa Port Authority and the Board of County
Commissioners of Manatee County had no objections to the project.

The staff recommended approval of the project.

ACTION OF THE TRUSTEES:

On motion by Mr. Christian, seconded by Mr. Stone and adopted
without objection, the Board approved the application for state
permit.

-6-

PINELLAS COUNTY - State Marina License, Section 253.03 F. S.
                  Ref. PCWNCA File No. 5798

    Concord Arms Apartments, Inc.
    2566 Gary Circle, Dunedin, Florida,

applied for a marina license for a docking facility covering
218 square feet in St. Joseph Sound in Section 15, Township 28
South, Range 15 East, Pinellas County.

The Pinellas County Water and Navigation Control Authority
approved the application on March 9, 1971.

No dredging was required. The minimum annual fee of $100 was
tendered.

The Department of Natural Resources had no objection to the proposed facility, the Department of Air and Water Pollution Control
had no objection to the location, and the Game and Fresh Water Fish
Commission had no comments.

Staff recommended approval.

ACTION OF THE TRUSTEES:

On motion by Mr. Christian, seconded by Mr. Stone and adopted
without objection, the Trustees approved issuance of a state
marina license to the applicant.

-7-

MONROE COUNTY - Refund - Donald L. Wollard
                TIITF File No. 2182-44-253.12

The Board in meeting on February 16, 1971, confirmed the sale
of a parcel of filled sovereignty land embracing 0.25 acres in

5-26-71

Florida Bay, Monroe County, to Donald L. Wollard for 3 times
the appraised value or $3,195 and $50 to cover cost of appraisal,
total $3,245. Applicant submitted a cashier's check for $3,345.

Request authorization to refund the $100 excess that was submitted.

ACTION OF THE TRUSTEES:

The Director said the staff had learned that there was authority
for such refunds without bringing each one to the attention of
the Board.

Governor Askew suggested that the refund be withdrawn from the
agenda and handled by the staff administratively.

It was so ordered.

-8-

REFUNDS - Murphy Act

Request authority for issuance of refunds to applicants for
release of state road right of way reservations contained in
Murphy Act deeds that the Department of Transportation did not
recommend be released at this time, as follows:

$15 to Biscayne Title & Mortgage Co. - Dade County Deed No. 2221
$15 to Cassel and Benjamin - Dade County Deed No. 3474
$15 to Van Buren Vickery - Dade County Deed No. 3665
$15 to Charles R. Bennett - St. Johns County Deed No. 658

ACTION OF THE TRUSTEES:

On motion by Mr. O'Malley, seconded by Mr. Stone and adopted without objection, issuance of the four refunds was approved.

-9-

CORRECTIVE DEED - Murphy Act

Request approval of Murphy Act Report No. 984 listing one
corrective deed:

> County of Pasco Deed No. 950-Corrective to Pearl Lackey
> Thompson and Laura Lackey Matthews a/k/a/ Laura Lackey
> Mathews, to be issued in lieu of Pasco County Deed No.
> 950 dated November 17, 1944, to B. H. Hermanson.

The purpose of the correction was to change the name of the
grantee from B. H. Hermanson, who was deceased on the date of
the original Murphy Act deed, to Pearl Lackey Thompson and
Laura Lackey Matthews a/k/a/ Laura Lackey Mathews. Staff
counsel approved the corrective deed.

ACTION OF THE TRUSTEES:

Motion was made by Mr. Christian, seconded by Mr. Stone and
adopted without objection, that the corrective deed be approved.

-10-

POLK AND OSCEOLA COUNTIES - Navigation Channel Dredge Permit

> Florida Ridge Cattle Company,
> P. O. Box 1399, Winter Haven, Florida 33881,

originally applied for a boundary line agreement and a permit
for 3 navigation channels into Lake Hatchineha. The matter

285

was deferred so that a biological report could be secured to
determine whether the proposed boundary line agreement and
navigation channel dredging would cause any biological damage.
After consultation with representatives of the Game and Fresh
Water Fish Commission and local conservation interests, the
applicant agreed to withdraw its request for a boundary line
agreement.

In accordance with recommendations contained in a letter dated
May 4, 1971, from the Game and Fresh Water Fish Commission,
the applicant now proposes to convey to the Trustees all lands
lying lakeward of a line that delineates the tree line as shown
on an aerial photograph (Exhibit "A") landward of an existing
escarpment. This line is to be surveyed and plats are to be
furnished by the applicant within 120 days after the Board's
final affirmative action in accepting the conveyance and approval
of the dredge permits, with the understanding that:

   (1) the area to be conveyed will be designated a wilderness
       area, with the applicant being permitted to:

        a. remove Spanish moss to improve visibility, but
            no trees shall be cut or pruned;
        b. create paths for pedestrian traffic and water
            access;
        c. remove man-made debris and litter;
        d. spray for mosquito control using pesticides
        . approved by the Game and Fish Commission; and
        e. maintain proposed navigation channels subject
            to receipt of required permits.

Said wilderness area is to be characterized as a biological
and aesthetic type. Use of the area by the public shall
be to the extent compatible with this type and as set forth
in Section 258.21, Florida Statutes, with the exception
of hunting, picnicking and camping, which shall not be
allowed. No oil or mineral exploration or recovery shall
be allowed.

   (2) A portion of the area to be conveyed will be converted by
the developer into a public bathing beach not to exceed
500 front feet along the shoreline. The Game and Fresh
Water Fish Commission shall have authority to alter the
location of this beach up to 300 yards in any direction
along the shore. Use of the beach will be subject to the
following conditions:

        a. No trees will be removed or cut.
        b. No permanent or portable structures such as concession
            stands, restrooms or locker rooms, etc., will be
            placed on the beach or wilderness area without valid
            authorization.
        c. No land alteration will be permitted lakeward of the
            demarcation line without approval of the managing
            agency and the Board of Trustees.
        d. The area dedicated as a public beach shall be and will
            remain as state-owned property.
        e. After the location has been finalized, the applicant
            or his successor in title shall cause to be prepared a
            plat defining the location of the beach and of the
            wilderness area. Said plat shall be reviewed on behalf
            of the Trustees by the chief cadastral surveyor, signed
            by him and recorded in the public records.

   (3) As the recommending agency, the Game and Fresh Water
Fish Commission shall be designated as the duly
authorized agent of the Board of Trustees of the
Internal Improvement Trust Fund and shall be responsible
for the management of the wilderness area.

   (4) The 3 navigation channels originally requested will
be permitted with dimensions to comply with recommendations
of the Game and Fish Commission.

5-26-71

(5) The applicant will convey its right, title and interest
in Big Gum Lake to the State of Florida.

(6) The delivery of the instruments conveying the wilderness
area and Big Gum Lake will be contingent upon the applicant
acquiring all dredge permits, said instruments to be delivered
to the Trustees' staff 90 days after the applicant or his
successor is granted a Corps of Engineers permit.

(7) The applicant further agrees to execute a flowage easement
up to 55 ft. m.s.l., agreeing to hold harmless the Central
and Southern Florida Flood Control District and the State
of Florida by virtue of any future regulation of lake levels
under the Central and Southern Florida Flood Control project,
the instrument granting the easement to be delivered 90
days after receipt of the Corps of Engineers permit.

The Department of Air and Water Pollution Control has certified
the navigation channels in conformance with the federal water
quality act, Public Law 91-224.

The Game and Fresh Water Fish Commission has indicated by resolution adopted May 21, 1971, that it will accept the responsibility
of managing the wilderness area. The preservation of this margin
of cypress trees on the lake will be beneficial in maintaining
the water quality, fish habitat, sport fisheries and aesthetic
beauty of this area.

The applicant has submitted $7,000 in payment for an estimated
quantity of 7,000 cubic yards of material to be excavated from
the channels, which represents a $1 per cubic yard charge, with
the understanding that any balance will be refunded when a final
value has been determined by the Trustees for this material.

The applicant and successors in interest understand that the
permit to be granted regarding the construction of the three
proposed channels and boat basins includes only the construction
of those channels and boat basins and does not include the right
to improve any existing canals or to connect new canals with the
proposed channels and boat basins without further specific approval
of the Trustees of the Internal Improvement Trust Fund and other
involved governmental agencies.

The conditions and stipulations contained in this agenda item
will form the basis of Articles of Agreement to be executed by
the Trustees and the applicant and successor in interest, with
the details of the agreement to be worked out with the staff, the
applicant, and successor in interest.

The staff recommended that the Trustees accept the conveyance from
the applicant in accordance with the conditions hereinbefore
stated, subject to the Game and Fresh Water Fish Commission's
resolution of May 21, 1971, accepting the management responsibilities, with the further condition that all property and
drainage taxes be paid by the applicant up to the time that the
instruments of conveyance are delivered, the applicant to furnish
a title certificate showing that the lands are free from all
encumbrances.

The staff further recommended that the Trustees grant navigation
channel dredge permits.

ACTION OF THE TRUSTEES:

Mr. Kuperberg said that the matter actually was an agreement
to agree, details of the agreement to be worked out with the
staff, the applicant and the successor in interest.

With a comment that it was an excellent solution to a problem,
Mr. Christian made a motion, seconded by Mr. O'Malley, that
the staff recommendations be approved.

Mr. Shevin called attention to lengthy statutory procedures
to be followed in taking lands for a wilderness area, and asked
if there would be any conflict with a resolution passed by the
Trustees in January 1970 against dredging in state-owned lakes.

Mr. Kuperberg reassured the Board, stating that the resolution
referred to dredging and filling or encroachment upon lakes.
There would be no filling or encroachment in Lake Hatchineha
in this application that involved only three navigational
entries into the lake in a three and one-half mile length of
shoreline, and 145 acres being given to the State of Florida
to be dedicated as a wilderness area. As a biologist he would
like to see all the marsh preserved but as a realist the Director
knew the marsh was in private ownership and unless purchased by
the State there was no way, according to legal counsel, to prevent
the owner from developing that upland. The articles of agreement
would reflect the fact that there must be a local hearing, the
statutes would be followed, this appeared to be a significant step
forward, and further improvements might be made.

The Governor commended the staff for working out with the Game
and Fresh Water Fish Commission the plans for the agreement.

Mr. O'Malley said the agreement was a valuable precedent ecologically
and commended his staff for studying the application in great detail
and working closely with the Director and Trustees' staff on a
very workable and sound solution.

On Mr. Christian's motion, seconded by Mr. O'Malley and adopted
without objection, the Trustees approved the recommendations with
the understanding that the staff would proceed in accordance with
the statutes.

-11-

PALM BEACH COUNTY - Dredge Permit, Section 253.123 F. S.

> Vista Builders, Inc.
> c/o Winningham & Lively, Inc.
> 1040 Northeast 45 Street, Fort Lauderdale, Florida,

(1) requested authorization to install a seawall along the mean
high water line of the Intracoastal Waterway in Section 33, Township 47 South, Range 43 East, and

(2) requested a permit to perform maintenance dredging in a
3,860 ft. length of the Intracoastal Waterway in Section 33, Township 47 South, Range 43 East.

The channel would be dredged from the existing depth of minus-12
ft. to a depth of minus-16 ft. The width would remain at 150 ft.
The purpose for overdredging was to provide for the release of a
perpetual maintenance spoil area (MSA-654) to enable the parcel
to be used by the record fee owner. The Trustees did not appear to
have any fee interest in either the waterway right of way or MSA-654.
The release of the spoil area was cleared by Florida Inland Navigation District.

The applicant agreed to pay the newly-established rate if the
Trustees demonstrated an interest in any portion of the 40,000
cubic yards of dredge material which would be removed and placed on
upland. A title opinion was requested to determine ownership
of the area subject to dredging.

The biological report stated that there was no significant amount
of marine life in the area but recommended that mangroves growing
within the Intracoastal Waterway right of way be left for use by
wildlife.

5-26-71

The Department of Air and Water Pollution Control certified this project, and the Game and Fresh Water Fish Commission issued a letter of no objection to the project.

The item was withdrawn from the agenda of May 11 for the purpose of reviewing objections submitted by the Area Planning Board of Palm Beach County. The Area Planning Board withdrew its objections insofar as release of the easement is concerned. The matter of seawall realignment was to be considered at the next regular meeting.

The applicant agreed not to construct the seawall until the local review was completed. However, he desired to stockpile landward of the mean high water line the material removed from the waterway.

The staff requests authority to issue permit, for dredging only, subject to applicant depositing a bond to guarantee payment for materials removed if it is determined that the Trustees have a fee interest, and further subject to location of the stockpile on an upland site.

ACTION OF THE TRUSTEES:

The previously considered matter had been placed by mistake on the advance agenda for June 1 and subsequently was placed on the agenda of May 26 as an addendum.

Mr. Stone made a motion that the rules be waived and the matter considered. There was some discussion as to whether a matter prepared as an addendum, properly circulated and received in time, required a vote on waiver of the rules in order to be considered. Governor Askew said that would be checked out, procedurally. Mr. O'Malley then seconded the motion to waive the rules for discussion of the Vista Builders application.

Mr. Shevin asked for a two-weeks' deferment in order for his staff to ascertain whether the County Commissioners objected, in view of their resolution requesting a moratorium on all dredging. He suggested a delay until some action was taken on the resolution. Mr. Stone agreed.

Mr. Kuperberg advised the Board that a previous deferment was due to an objection from the Palm Beach County Area Planning Board that thought the land was in public ownership. The land was privately owned, under a spoil easement to the Army Corps of Engineers, and under a policy of the Corps the area would be released from the easement if the stretch of waterway was over-dredged. The land on both sides of the waterway was largely developed, the application appeared reasonable, and the staff recommended it.

Mr. Albert J. Marinello, for the applicant, urged approval by the Board in view of the fact that over a period of about a year the applicant had satisfied the criteria of the Department of Natural Resources, Game and Fresh Water Fish Commission, Air and Water Pollution Control Board, the Corps of Engineers, the Area Planning Board of Palm Beach County, and the City of Boca Raton. The Governor, pointing out that any member was granted a two-weeks' deferment on request, suggested that Mr. Marinello meet with the staff to reconcile any questions.

On Mr. Shevin's request, the application was deferred.

—————————

The Director reported briefly with respect to the moratorium requested by Palm Beach County. He called attention to the many active permits in Palm Beach County for dredging and filling, his telephone conversations with the Palm Beach County Conservation Council and the County Attorney, and the conclusion that the resolution drafted in haste would place legal and economic burdens on the State of Florida. He indicated that a revised resolution would be presented to the Palm Beach County Commission by the conservation group of which Mr. Bob Bair was a member.

Mr. Kuperberg assured the Trustees that he was anxious to resolve the problems of dredging where there was no reason to dredge.

Governor Askew expressed the Board's appreciation for the Director's efforts to work out those things and asked the staff to work with the Attorney General's office in the preparation of recommendations to be considered by the Trustees.

On motion duly adopted, the meeting was adjourned.

GOVERNOR - CHAIRMAN

ATTEST:

EXECUTIVE DIRECTOR

* * *   * * *

Tallahassee, Florida
June 1, 1971

The State of Florida Board of Trustees of the Internal Improvement Trust Fund met on this date in the Haydon Burns Building, with the following members present:

Reubin O'D. Askew	Governor
Richard (Dick) Stone	Secretary of State
Robert L. Shevin	Attorney General
Fred O. Dickinson, Jr.	Comptroller
Thomas D. O'Malley	Treasurer
Floyd T. Christian	Commissioner of Education
Doyle Conner	Commissioner of Agriculture
Joel Kuperberg	Executive Director

The minutes of May 18, 1971, were approved as submitted.

-1-

BAY COUNTY - Confirmation of Sale
      File No. 2392-03-253.12

    Staff Description: 1.273 acre parcel of filled sovereignty land in East Bay, abutting Section 18, T 5 S, R 12 W.

A. CITY AND COUNTY: Bay County

B. APPLICANT: Donald Ray Gore
                         Box 91 Wewahitchka Star Route
                         Panama City, Florida

C. ACREAGE: 1.273
    RATE PER ACRE: $392.77, $500 for the parcel, staff adjust-
                         ment
    TOTAL OFFER: $1500 - three time the upward adjusted
                         appraised value
D. APPRAISAL: $290 for the parcel
    DATE: December 16, 1970
    APPRAISER: David T. Nolen, M.A.I., adjusted
                         by staff appraiser

E. PURPOSE: Residential Development

F. BIOLOGICAL REPORT: Attached, dated February 16, 1971.
    Results not adverse. Remarks: Restoration of the filled area
    to its previous condition by removing the fill would be a
    questionable solution or recommendation. However, recommend
    removal of a small part of the fill at the south end to
    provide connection of a marsh area to open water.

G. STAFF REMARKS: The parcel was landward of the bulkhead line
    approved by the Trustees on March 16, 1971.

    Applicant agreed to remove the fill as suggested by the
    biological report and agreed to pay three times the appraised
    value for the parcel. Applicant stated that the sale would
    be in the public interest as the alternative would not be
    in the public interest.

    Staff requested Mr. Gore to remove a portion of a dike in
    compliance with recommendation of Department of Natural
    Resources. To date, the applicant had not responded to the
    Staff request. This matter was advertised for consideration
    on this date.

H. Recommend that action be deferred until applicant complies
    with request.

ACTION OF THE TRUSTEES:

The Director said that word was received yesterday from Mr. Gore
reporting the removal of the fill material that the staff had
requested him to remove, but on-site inspection had not yet
been made.

The Trustees deferred action at the request of the Director.

-2-

BROWARD COUNTY - Deactivate File
               File No. 2283-06-253.12
               Application to Purchase

    B. C. Deuschle, Sr., et ux
    2856 East Oakland Park Boulevard
    Ft. Lauderdale, Florida 33306,

submitted an application for purchase of a 0.129 acre parcel
in Middle River adjacent to Government Lot 2, Section 36, Township
49 South, Range 42 East, Broward County.

A suit was instituted to determine if the Trustees had any
interest in the submerged lands subject to the application. The
Court ruled in favor of the applicant, affirming title in him.

Staff requested authority to deactivate file.

ACTION OF THE TRUSTEES:

On motion by Mr. Christian, seconded by Mr. O'Malley and adopted
without objection, the Trustees authorized deactivation of the
file.

6-1-71

-3-

<u>HILLSBOROUGH COUNTY</u> - Right of Way Easement
TIITF File 2407-29-253.03

The Department of Transportation

requested an easement embracing 1.0 acre across the bottoms of
Little Manatee River abutting Section 25, Township 32 South,
Range 19 East, Hillsborough County, to be used for the construction
of a bridge on State Road 43 (U. S. 301).

Dredging or filling for the project was not required.

The Department of Air and Water Pollution Control, the Department
of Natural Resources, and the Game and Fresh Water Fish Commission had no objections to the project.

<u>Recommend that easement be issued</u>.

ACTION OF THE TRUSTEES:

On motion by Mr. O'Malley, seconded by Mr. Stone and adopted
without objection, the Board authorized issuance of the easement.

-4-

Consideration of a Resolution submitted by Pinellas County Water
and Navigation Control Authority.

The Pinellas County Water and Navigation Control Authority adopted
a resolution on May 18, 1971, requesting that the Trustees amend
their present policy applying to issuance of permits and marina
licenses for construction of non-commercial and commercial
mooring facilities.

The Trustees' current policy requires a marina license for all
commercial facilities regardless of whether or not revenue is
derived from occupancy of sovereignty lands and the water column.
A single $10 fee is charged for private mooring facilities.

The Authority desired a policy modification that would create
a commercial mooring facility permit that would apply where no
direct revenue was derived from use of the water column. This
policy would apply to hotels, motels, apartment houses and other
similar multiple occupancy uses.

By recently adopted resolutions, the City of Treasure Island and
Treasure Island Chamber of Commerce endorsed the Authority's
request.

<u>The staff recommended that this third category be reestablished</u>.

<u>The staff further requested the following rules be adopted to
implement the proposed policy change</u>:

> Any pier, wharf or other mooring facility constructed
> over state-owned submerged bottom lands or sovereignty
> lands used as an adjunct to commercial operations such as
> hotels, motels, apartments, dining facilities or commer-
> cial cargo handling facilities, would require a commercial
> dock permit. This requirement would apply to private,
> non-profit, social or fraternal organizations where
> dockage fees were not assessed.

> A non-refundable application fee of $100, in addition, a
> minimum annual charge of 2¢ per square foot but in no
> event less than $100 for the area subject to severence
> from public use, must be remitted when applying for a
> commercial dock permit.

> Refund of the charges for area severed from public use
> would be allowable when the applicant could show that

6-1-71

(1) the Corps of Engineers has denied issuance of a
federal permit, (2) local governing bodies denied
issuance of a building permit or other permits that
may be required by such authorities, (3) such facility
would be contrary to public interest.

The last rule would also be applicable to marina licenses.

ACTION OF THE TRUSTEES:

The Director stated that Pinellas County representatives had
attended a conference with the Trustees' staff members, and it
was found that there was an area that needed further discussion.
Deferment was recommended.

Without objection, the Trustees deferred action.

-5-

MONROE COUNTY - Public Recreation Lease

On April 1 the Outdoor Recreation Advisory Committee approved
a grant of $50,000 to the City of Key West for development
of recreational facilities on Smathers Beach. The Department
of Natural Resources gave its approval of the project on
April 13.

The City of Key West forwarded a deed transferring ownership
to the Trustees in return for a 99-year lease of the property
consisting of 1,500 feet of beach and the grant.

Recommend acceptance of the deed and issuance of 99-year lease
to the city restricting use of the property to public recreational
purposes under the supervision of the Department of Natural
Resources.

ACTION OF THE TRUSTEES:

The Director stated that the lease would contain a cancellation clause whereby the Trustees would regain control in
the event of non-compliance with terms of the lease.

On motion by Mr. Christian, seconded by Mr. Dickinson and
adopted without objection, the Trustees accepted the deed and
authorized issuance of the lease as recommended.

-6-

PINELLAS COUNTY - Marina License, 253.03, F. S.

  Samuel D. Pettito
  197 - 116 Avenue
  Treasure Island, Florida

applied for a marina license for an existing fishing pier covering
864 square   feet in Boca Ciega Bay abutting Section 23, Township
31 South, Range 15 East, Pinellas County.

The Pinellas County Water and Navigation Control Authority
approved the project on March 16, 1971. Construction of the
facility was completed about April 16, 1971. No dredging was
required.

The Department of Natural Resources and the Game and Fresh Water
Fish Commission had no objection to the facility. The Department
of Air and Water Pollution had no objection to the location of
the facility.

Staff recommended approval of the license with an effective date
of April 16, 1971.

ACTION OF THE TRUSTEES:

Because action had been deferred on consideration of policy
with respect to dock permits and marina licenses, the Director
requested that agenda items 6 and 7 be considered under the
marina license classification.

On motion by Mr. Dickinson, seconded by Mr. O'Malley and Mr.
Conner, adopted without objection, the Trustees authorized
issuance of a marina license with the effective date of
April 16, 1971, as recommended.

-7-

ST. LUCIE COUNTY - Marina License, Section 253.03 F. S.

    Hoyt C. Murphy
    P. O. Box 446
    Fort Pierce, Florida 33450

applied for a marina license for a fishing dock facility
covering 1,150 square feet in the Fort Pierce Inlet abutting Section
36, Township 34 South, Range 40 East, St. Lucie County. No dredging
would be required. The minimum annual fee of $100 was tendered.

The Department of Natural Resources, the Corps of Engineers and
the Game and Fresh Water Fish Commission had no objection to the
project. The Department of Air and Water Pollution Control had
no objection to the location of the project.

Staff recommended approval.

ACTION OF THE TRUSTEES:

The proposed fishing dock would be cantilevered.

On motion by Mr. Dickinson, seconded by Mr. Stone and adopted
without objection, the Board authorized issuance of a marina
license to Mr. Murphy.

-8-

PALM BEACH COUNTY - Dredge Permit, Section 253.123 F. S.

The application of Vista Builders, Inc., had been deferred
at the request of Attorney General Shevin. In response to
Mr. Shevin's question regarding the effect of the moratorium
requested by Palm Beach County and the resolution to be considered
by the Trustees on this date, Mr. Kuperberg said the staff felt
it could make a determination of whether or not this dredging
was in the public interest.

The application was deferred until next week as requested by
the Attorney General.

-9-

DADE COUNTY - Dredge Permit, Section 253.123 F. S.
               Dredging for Navigation

    MacMillan Bloedel, Ltd.
    1075 W. Georgia St.
    Vancouver 105, British Columbia, Canada,

applied for a permit to dredge for navigation in Section 31,
Township 53 South, Range 42 East, Biscayne Bay, Miami, in an
area 1,665 ft. by 200 to 915 ft. 140,000 cubic yards of
material would be removed and deposited on Burlingame Island

6-1-71

according to the recommendation of the Department of Natural Resources.

The Department of Air and Water Pollution Control and the Game and Fresh Water Fish Commission had no objections.

The submerged lands subject to dredging vested in the City of Miami by virtue of Chapter 8305, Acts of 1919. Therefore, no fee was being charged for materials dredged.

Staff requested authority to issue the permit.

ACTION OF THE TRUSTEES:

At the request of the Secretary of State, action was deferred for two weeks.

-10-

SARASOTA COUNTY - Utility Dredge Permit
                  Section 253.123(2)(b)
                  File No. 253.123(2)(b) - 773

    Key Towers Apartments, Stanley Goldman
    P. O. Box 1359, Sarasota, Florida,

applied for a permit to install an 8-inch outfall pipe to accommodate condensate discharge from air conditioning equipment, to replace an installed outfall in Section 35, Township 36 South, Range 17 East, in the Gulf of Mexico. The area dimensions would be 150 cubic yards, the depth minus-6 feet maximum to minus-3 feet minimum and the length 800 feet.

The outfall would be securely anchored. The installation would comply with recommendations of the Bureau of Beaches and Shores, Department of Natural Resources. The Department of Air and Water Pollution Control and the Game and Fresh Water Fish Commission had no objections.

Request authority to issue the utility installation permit.

ACTION OF THE TRUSTEES:

On motion by Mr. Dickinson and Mr. Christian, seconded by Mr. Conner and adopted without objection, the Board approved issuance of the utility installation permit.

-11-

PALM BEACH COUNTY - The Board of County Commissioners of Palm Beach County adopted a resolution on March 30, 1971, requesting that the Trustees order a moratorium on all dredging operations in the public waters of Palm Beach County, including certain fresh water lakes, until it could be ascertained that "dredging will not permanently degrade water quality nor cause irreversible damage to marine ecosystems."

The staff recommended adoption of a resolution responding to the request of the Board of County Commissioners.

Comptroller Dickinson said the Director deserved great commendation for working out this matter.

On motion by Mr. Dickinson, seconded by Mr. O'Malley and carried without objection, the Trustees adopted the following resolution:

<u>R E S O L U T I O N</u>

WHEREAS, the Board of County Commissioners of Palm Beach County, by Resolution adopted March 30, 1971, did request that the Board of Trustees of the Internal Improvement Trust Fund order a moratorium on all dredging operations in the public waters of Palm Beach County until such time as it can be determined that continued dredging will not permanently degrade water quality nor cause irreversible damage to marine ecosystems, and

WHEREAS, the Bureau of Beaches and Shores, Department of Natural Resources, and the Area Planning Board of Palm Beach County have filed objections to the ordering of such moratorium, and

WHEREAS, this request has been reviewed with representatives of concerned private and public bodies from Palm Beach County, together with a study of the record of the Board of County Commissioners' meeting dealing with the subject resolution, and

WHEREAS, it has been concluded that the imposition of a moratorium on all dredging may have widespread legal ramifications and, further, that such a moratorium would stop beach nourishment, inlet maintenance, and public navigation projects where dredging is required;

NOW, THEREFORE, BE IT RESOLVED by the Board of Trustees of the Internal Improvement Trust Fund, assembled in regular meeting on this the <u>1st</u> day of <u>June</u>, A. D. <u>1971</u>, that the said Board of Trustees hereby declares a moratorium on the issuance of all dredge permits in Palm Beach County save those instances in which it can be shown that the issuance of such permits would be in the public interest.

BE IT FURTHER RESOLVED that this moratorium shall continue in force until such time as the Board of County Commissioners of Palm Beach County shall determine that continued dredging will not permanently degrade water quality nor cause irreversible damage to marine ecosystems, or until such time as said Board of County Commissioners shall otherwise determine that the present requirements for certification by the Department of Air and Water Pollution Control and the biological surveys and ecological studies by the Department of Natural Resources provide sufficient protection of water quality and marine ecosystems; and that, upon having made such a determination, the Board of County Commissioners shall by resolution notify the Board of Trustees of the Internal Improvement Trust Fund of such determination and request the moratorium be lifted.

IN TESTIMONY WHEREOF, the members of the State of Florida Board of Trustees of the Internal Improvement Trust Fund have hereunto subscribed their names and have caused the official seal of said State of Florida Board of Trustees of the Internal Improvement Trust Fund to be hereunto affixed, in the City of Tallahassee, Florida, on this the <u>1st</u> day of <u>June</u>, A. D. <u>1971</u>.

REUBIN O'D. ASKEW
Governor

RICHARD STONE
Secretary of State

(SEAL)　　　　　　　　　　　ROBERT L. SHEVIN
State of Florida　　　　　　Attorney General
Board of Trustees of
the Internal Improvement　 FRED O. DICKINSON, JR.
Trust Fund　　　　　　　　　 Comptroller

6-1-71

THOMAS D. O'MALLEY
Treasurer

FLOYD T. CHRISTIAN
Commissioner of Education

DOYLE CONNER
Commissioner of Agriculture

The Attorney General asked about progress on the G. A. C.
matter.

The Director advised that the work had been discussed with
the Attorney General's aides. It involved an appraisal of
about 28,000 acres in the Fahkahatchee swamp, and did require a
considerable amount of work.

On motion duly adopted, the meeting was adjourned.

GOVERNOR   -   CHAIRMAN

ATTEST:

EXECUTIVE DIRECTOR

* * *   * * *

Tallahassee, Florida
June 8, 1971

The State of Florida Board of Trustees of the Internal Improvement Trust Fund met on this date in the Haydon Burns Building in
Tallahassee, with the following members present:

Reubin O'D. Askew	Governor
Richard (Dick) Stone	Secretary of State
Robert L. Shevin	Attorney General
Thomas D. O'Malley	Treasurer
Floyd T. Christian	Commissioner of Education

Joel Kuperberg	Executive Director

Without objection, the minutes of May 26 were approved.

-1-

CHARLOTTE COUNTY - Application to Purchase - Withdrawal
                   TIITF File No. 1985-08-253.12

Leslie J. Inglis and wife of Englewood, Florida, represented
by I. W. Whitesell, Jr., submitted an application on April 3,
1967, to purchase a parcel of sovereignty land embracing 0.93
acre in Lemon Bay abutting Section 17, Township 41 South, Range
20 East, Charlotte County.

6-8-71

Applicant requested that the application be withdrawn and the
application fee of $50 be refunded.

The staff recommends that the file be deactivated and the application fee of $50 refunded, since the fee was submitted prior to
adoption of the policy making application fees non-refundable.

ACTION OF THE TRUSTEES:

Motion was made by Mr. Stone, seconded by Mr. Christian and
adopted without objection, that the file be deactivated and
$50 refunded.

-2-

DADE COUNTY - Migrant Housing Land Transfer

The Board of County Commissioners of Dade County by resolution
adopted on May 18, 1971, requested transfer of title covering
the W 1/2 of NE 1/4 of NW 1/4 of Section 2, Township 58 South,
Range 38 East, containing 20 acres, more or less, to Dade County
for the location of a migrant housing facility.

The property was used by the Department of Transportation as a
former road prison camp, that had been closed for a number of
years. The property was recently used by the Department as
a maintenance facility. The Department reviewed this request
and agreed to relinquish further use of the property in order
that it could be transferred to Dade County for migrant housing
use. Dade County advised that because Federal funds would be
used to finance construction of the housing facility, fee
title was required.

It is recommended that title be conveyed to Dade County by deed
containing a reverter whereby title would automatically revert
to the Trustees in the event (1) the land was used for purposes
other than migrant housing, or (2) if not used for 3 consecutive
years.

ACTION OF THE TRUSTEES:

Mr. Ralph Carey, Director of the H. U. D. agency for Dade County,
was present.

On motion by Mr. Stone, seconded by Mr. Shevin and Mr. O'Malley,
and adopted without objection, the recommendation was approved
as the action of the Board.

-3-

POLK COUNTY - Land Exchange

The Department of Highway Safety and Motor Vehicles requested
consideration by the Trustees of a proposed land exchange.
The Department desired to obtain a 9.5 acre parcel owned by
the City of Lakeland. The City agreed to lease this 9.5
acre parcel to the Department for 50 years, receiving in
exchange title to state-owned lots 14, 15, and 16, Block 17,
Shore Acres Subdivision, located in East Lakeland.

The 9.5 acre parcel was determined by the Department to
be ideal for development of a field office complex, including
a driver examining facility, future relocation of the Highway
Patrol Station and a Motor Vehicles Division complex.

The three lots owned by the Department since 1946 in a residential area, were not of a size and configuration suitable for
the needed new facilities of the Department.

6-8-71

An appraisal by an M.A.I. appraiser estimated the value of the three unimproved lots as $13,000. A fifty-year lease-hold interest in the 9.5 acre tract was appraised at $91,500. The 9.5 acre tract was located at the intersection of Robson Street and Lakeland Hills Boulevard near Interstate 4.

Recommend exchange as requested.

ACTION OF THE TRUSTEES:

On motion by Mr. O'Malley, seconded by Mr. Stone and adopted without objection, the Trustees approved the land exchange.

-4-

VOLUSIA COUNTY - Temporary Easement Extension
Easement No. 2326-B

The Ponce de Leon Port Authority, sponsoring agency for the federal project to stabilize Ponce de Leon Inlet, requested a time extension to March 30, 1972, for temporary easement No. 2326-B.

The existing easement that expired June 1, 1971, provided for use of pipelines in constructing the North Jetty.

The consulting engineer indicated the project was 89% completed. The delay in completing the project resulted from an underestimate of rock required in constructing the jetty, a delay in acquiring rock from the mines, and the strike in the railroad industry.

The Florida Board of Conservation initially reviewed the project plans and offered no objections when the Trustees considered the request on April 2, 1968.

The staff recommends that the temporary easement be extended to March 30, 1972.

ACTION OF THE TRUSTEES:

On motion by Mr. Stone, seconded by Mr. Christian and adopted without objection, the Trustees approved extension of the temporary easement to March 30, 1972.

-5-

MURPHY ACT REPORT NO. 986 - Sale of Alachua County Land

Request approval of Bidding Report No. 986 and execution of deed for sale of a parcel of Murphy Act land in Alachua County under provisions of Section 197.350 Florida Statutes, to Grace M. Hall for the high bid of $300.

The land, certified to the state of Florida under tax sale certificates 1803 of 1930 and 7469 of 1933, was described as Lots 30 and 31 Block C, Lakeview Subdivision in Section 26, Township 10 South, Range 22 East, Alachua County. The lots were approximately 25' x 110' each.

ACTION OF THE TRUSTEES:

On motion by Mr. Stone, seconded by Mr. O'Malley and adopted without objection, the Trustees approved the report and authorized execution of the deed for the sale of Murphy Act land.

-6-

ALACHUA COUNTY - Easements for Road and Drainage

The Department of Transportation requested an easement for
drainage ditch purposes and an easement for road right of
way covering 0.62 acres in Section 20, Township 10 South,
Range 20 East, Alachua County. The easements are within
the recently purchased Payne's Prairie property south of
Gainesville.

The request was reviewed by the Division of Recreation and
Parks and approved by the Department of Natural Resources
at its meeting April 27.

The staff recommended issuance of the easements.

ACTION OF THE TRUSTEES:

Mr. Kuperberg advised that there was no objection to the work.

On motion by Mr. O'Malley, seconded by Mr. Stone and adopted
without objection, the Trustees approved the easement for road
and drainage purposes.

-7-

BROWARD COUNTY - File No. 1387-06-253.12.

On November 29, 1966, the Trustees considered an application from
W. D. Horvitz, president of Hollywood, Inc., to purchase a tract
of sovereignty land in New River Sound in Section 25, Township
50 South, Range 42 East, in the City of Hollywood, Florida,
containing 44.1 acres, more or less. The Trustees deferred
action for a period of ninety days in response to a request from
Honorable John U. Lloyd, County Attorney of Broward County,
for deferment to permit a new survey to be made of the area
in question.

The new survey was completed and reviewed by the Staff, and on
request from the Staff the Attorney General on April 7, 1967,
advised that the upland ownership of the applicant, Hollywood,
Inc., with respect to the easterly one-half of New River Sound
of the N 1/2 of Section 25, Township 50 South, Range 42 East,
(which upland ownership was shown as Government Lot 1), is no
longer in existence and therefore the applicant could no longer
be construed as an upland owner with the right to purchase
this portion of New River Sound. The letter from the Attorney
General further stated that no evidence was available to indicate
the exact cause of the disappearance of Government Lot 1, but
it could be presumed that such disappearance occurred by reason
of a gradual and natural process.

On the basis of this advice from the Attorney General, the
Staff recommended deferment of any action concerning the application of Hollywood, Inc., for a period of sixty days to permit
the applicant to institute legal proceedings to resolve all
legal questions involved in this matter, and in the absence of
the commencement of litigation within this period, that the
Trustees reject the application as to the entire area.

On April 25, 1967, motion was made by Mr. Williams, seconded by
Mr. Dickinson, and adopted unanimously, that the Trustees defer
any action for sixty days as recommended by the Staff, and if
the applicant had not commenced litigation within that time, that
the Trustees reject the application as to the entire area.

The applicant did file suit on May 5, 1967, in conformity with
the Trustees' action. An Order of Dismissal issued from the
Circuit Court of the 2nd Judicial Circuit, Leon County, on November
13, 1970.

An appraisal by an M.A.I. appraiser estimated he value of the three unimproved lots as $13,000. A fifty-yea lease-hold interest in the 9.5 acre tract was appraised a $91,500. The 9.5 acre tract was located at the intersectior of Robson Street and Lakeland Hills Boulevard near Interstate 4

Recommend exchange as requested.

ACTION OF THE TRUSTEES:

On motion by Mr. O'Malley, seconded by Mr. Stce and adopted without objection, the Trustees approved the lnd exchange.

-4-

VOLUSIA COUNTY - Temporary Easement Extension
Easement No. 2326-B

The Ponce de Leon Port Authority, sponsoring aenoy for the federal project to stabilize Ponce de Leon Init, requested a time extension to March 30, 1972, for tempoary easement No. 2326-B.

The existing easement that expired June 1, 19'., provided for use of pipelines in constructing the North Jety.

The consulting engineer indicated the projectvas 89% completed. The delay in completing the project resulted com an underestimate of rock required.in constructing the jetty, aielay in acquiring rock from the mines, and the strike in the rairoad industry.

The Florida Board of Conservation initially reiewed the project plans and offered no objections when the Trusies considered the request on April 2, 1968.

The staff recommends that the temporary easemnt be extended to March 30, 1972.

ACTION OF THE TRUSTEES:

On motion by Mr. Stone, seconded by Mr. Chrisian and adopted without objection, the Trustees approved extesion of the temporary easement to March 30, 1972.

-5-

MURPHY ACT REPORT NO. 986 - Sale of Alachua Cinty Land

Request approval of Bidding Report No. 986 an execution of deed for sale of a parcel of Murphy Act land n Alachua County under provisions of Section 197.350 Flcida Statutes, to Grace M. Hall for the high bid of $300.

The land, certified to the state of Florida uder tax sale certificates 1803 of 1930 and 7469 of 1933, as described as Lots 30 and 31 Block C, Lakeview Subdivisin in Section 26, Township 10 South, Range 22 East, AlachuaCounty. The lots were approximately 25' x 110' each.

ACTION OF THE TRUSTEES:

On motion by Mr. Stone, seconded by Mr. O'Maley and adopted without objection, the Trustees approved the eport and authorized execution of the deed for the saleof Murphy Act land.

6-8-71

ALACHUA COUNTY - Easements for Road and Drainage

The Department of Transportation requested an easement
drainage ditch purposes and a easement for road right
way covering 0.62 acres in Section 20, Township 10
Range 20 East, Alachua County. The easements are with
the recently purchased Payne's Prairie property south
Gainesville.

The request was reviewed by th Division of Recreation and
Parks and approved by the Department of Natural Resources
at its meeting April 27.

The staff recommended issuance of the easements.

ACTION OF THE TRUSTEES:

Mr. Kuperberg advised that there was no objection to the work.

On motion by Mr. O'Malley, seconded by Mr. Stone and adopted
without objection, the Trustee approved the easement for road
and drainage purposes.

———— ————

7-

BROWARD COUNTY - File No. 1387)6-253.12.

On November 29, 1966, the Trustees considered an application from
W. D. Horvitz, president of Holywood, Inc., to purchase a tract
of sovereignty land in New Rivr Sound in Section 25, Township
50 South, Range 42 East, in th City of Hollywood, Florida,
containing 44.1 acres, more orless. The Trustees deferred
action for a period of ninety ays in response to a request from
Honorable John U. Lloyd, Count Attorney of Broward County,
for deferment to permit a new survey to be made of the area
in question.

The new survey was completed al reviewed by the Staff, and on
request from the Staff the Attorney General on April 7, 1967,
advised that the upland ownersip of the applicant, Hollywood,
Inc., with respect to the eastrly one-half of New River Sound
of the N 1/2 of Section 25, Township 50 South, Range 42 East,
(which upland ownership was shwn as Government Lot 1), is no
longer in existence and therefre the applicant could no longer
be construed as an upland owne with the right to purchase
this portion of New River Sour. The letter from the Attorney
General further stated that ncavidence was available to indicate
the exact cause of the disapperance of Government Lot 1, but
it could be presumed that such disappearance occurred by reason
of a gradual and natural proces.

On the basis of this advice frn the Attorney General, the
Staff recommended deferment ofany action concerning the application of Hollywood, Inc., fora period of sixty days to permit
the applicant to institute lecl proceedings to resolve all
legal questions involved in trs matter, and in the absence of
the commencement of litigatior within this period, that the
Trustees reject the applicatic as to the entire area.

On April 25, 1967, motion was ade by Mr. Williams, seconded by
Mr. Dickinson, and adopted unaimously, that the Trustees defer
any action for sixty days as rcommended by the Staff, and if
the applicant had not commence litigation within that time, that
the Trustees reject the appliction as to the entire area.

The applicant did file suit or May 5, 1967, in conformity with
the Trustees' action. An Orde of Dismissal issued from the
Circuit Court of the 2nd Judical Circuit, Leon County, on November
13, 1970.

6-8-71

298

An appraisal by an M.A.I. appraiser estimate the value of the
three unimproved lots as $13,000. A fifty-yar lease-hold
interest in the 9.5 acre tract was appraisedat $91,500. The
9.5 acre tract was located at the intersectin of Robson Street
and Lakeland Hills Boulevard near Interstate 4.

Recommend exchange as requested.

ACTION OF THE TRUSTEES:

On motion by Mr. O'Malley, seconded by Mr. £one and adopted
without objection, the Trustees approved the land exchange.

-4-

VOLUSIA COUNTY - Temporary Easement Extensia
Easement No. 2326-B

The Ponce de Leon Port Authority, sponsorin agency for the
federal project to stabilize Ponce de Leon ılet, requested
a time extension to March 30, 1972, for temprary easement
No. 2326-B.

The existing easement that expired June 1, 971, provided for
use of pipelines in constructing the North etty.

The consulting engineer indicated the projet was 89% completed.
The delay in completing the project resulte from an underestimate
of rock required.in constructing the jetty,a delay in acquiring
rock from the mines, and the strike in the ailroad industry.

The Florida Board of Conservation initiallyreviewed the project
plans and offered no objections when the Tıstees considered
the request on April 2, 1968.

The staff recommends that the temporary easment be extended to
March 30, 1972.

ACTION OF THE TRUSTEES:

On motion by Mr. Stone, seconded by Mr. Chıstian and adopted
without objection, the Trustees approved eɪension of the
temporary easement to March 30, 1972.

-5-

MURPHY ACT REPORT NO. 986 - Sale of Alachu County Land

Request approval of Bidding Report No. 986and execution of
deed for sale of a parcel of Murphy Act laɪ in Alachua
County under provisions of Section 197.350Florida Statutes,
to Grace M. Hall for the high bid of $300.

The land, certified to the state of Florid under tax sale
certificates 1803 of 1930 and 746'9 of 193, was described
as Lots 30 and 31 Block C, Lakeview Subdivsion in Section
26, Township 10 South, Range 22 East, Alacua County.
The lots were approximately 25' x 110' eac.

ACTION OF THE TRUSTEES:

On motion by Mr. Stone, seconded by Mr. O'alley and adopted
without objection, the Trustees approved te report and
authorized execution of the deed for the ɪle of Murphy Act
land.

6-8-71

ALACHUA COUNTY - Easements for Roa and Drainage

The Department of Transportation requested an easement for
drainage ditch purposes and an easement for road right of
way covering 0.62 acres in Section 20, Township 10 South,
Range 20 East, Alachua County. Th easements are within
the recently purchased Payne's Pracie property south of
Gainesville.

The request was reviewed by the Division of Recreation and
Parks and approved by the Departmet of Natural Resources
at its meeting April 27.

The staff recommended issuance of he easements.

ACTION OF THE TRUSTEES:

Mr. Kuperberg advised that there ws no objection to the work.

On motion by Mr. O'Malley, seconde by Mr. Stone and adopted
without objection, the Trustees ap oved the easement for road
and drainage purposes.

-7-

BROWARD COUNTY - File No. 1387-06-53.12.

On November 29, 1966, the Trustees considered an application from
W. D. Horvitz, president of Hollywd, Inc., to purchase a tract
of sovereignty land in New River Sind in Section 25, Township
50 South, Range 42 East, in the Cit of Hollywood, Florida,
containing 44.1 acres, more or les. The Trustees deferred
action for a period of ninety days n response to a request from
Honorable John U. Lloyd, County Atorney of Broward County,
for deferment to permit a new surv· to be made of the area
in question.

The new survey was completed and riewed by the Staff, and on
request from the Staff the Attorne General on April 7, 1967,
advised that the upland ownership the applicant, Hollywood,
Inc., with respect to the easterly ne-half of New River Sound
of the N 1/2 of Section 25, Township 50 South, Range 42 East,
(which upland ownership was shown Government Lot 1), is no
longer in existence and therefore he applicant could no longer
be construed as an upland owner wit the right to purchase
this portion of New River Sound. .e letter from the Attorney
General further stated that no evi nce was available to indicate
the exact cause of the disappearan· of Government Lot 1, but
it could be presumed that such disappearance occurred by reason
of a gradual and natural process.

On the basis of this advice from t Attorney General, the
Staff recommended deferment of any ction concerning the application of Hollywood, Inc., for a pciod of sixty days to permit
the applicant to institute legal pcceedings to resolve all
legal questions involved in this meter, and in the absence of
the commencement of litigation witln this period, that the
Trustees reject the application as o the entire area.

On April 25, 1967, motion was made y Mr. Williams, seconded by
Mr. Dickinson, and adopted unanimouly, that the Trustees defer
any action for sixty days as recommnded by the Staff, and if
the applicant had not commenced litgation within that time, that
the Trustees reject the application as to the entire area.

The applicant did file suit on May , 1967, in conformity with
the Trustees' action. An Order of ismissal issued from the
Circuit Court of the 2nd Judicial Crcuit, Leon County, on November
13, 1970.

The Staff considered the status of the litigation and the motion
by the Trustees on April 25, 1967, indicating that the application
be rejected and further based upon the advice in a letter dated
April 7, 1967, from the then Attorney General.

The staff recommended that the application for purchase be denied
and the file be deactivated.

ACTION OF THE TRUSTEES:

Mr. Kuperberg said in the judgment of the staff the land involved
was sovereignty land that by accretion was raised to an elevation
above sea level and was state land.

On motion by Mr. O'Malley, seconded by Mr. Stone and adopted
without objection, the staff recommendation was approved as the
action of the Board.

-8-

COLLIER COUNTY - Oil and Gas Lease Assignment

Recommend consent to assignment of an undivided 1/2 interest
in Oil and Gas Drilling Lease No. 2522-S from Shell Oil
Company to Robert Mosbacher.

The lease was issued by the Trustees covering the reserved
1/2 interest of the Board of Education in the petroleum in
privately-owned Section 16, Township 46 South, Range 29 East,
and Section 16, Township 46 South, Range 30 East, Collier
County.

The instrument of assignment was reviewed and approved as to
form and legality by staff legal counsel. The lease provided for
assignment subject to approval and consent of the lessor.

ACTION OF THE TRUSTEES:

On motion by Mr. O'Malley, seconded by Mr. Stone and adopted
without objection, the Trustees consented to the assignment
as recommended.

-9-

OKALOOSA COUNTY - Consideration of Oil and Gas Lease Bids

On April 13 the Trustees authorized advertisement as requested
by Amoco Production Company for sealed bids for three (3) oil
and gas drilling leases covering a total of 26,400 surface
acres in the Blackwater River State Forest in which the State
held an undivided 1/4 mineral interest.

Each lease would prohibit drilling operations in the waters
of streams, rivers, and ·lakes within the leased area. The lessee
would be required to notify the Division of Forestry and the
Game and Fresh Water Fish Commission prior to entering the land
to conduct exploration operations.

The leases would require an annual rental of $1 per net mineral
acre, $50,000 surety bond and at least one test well every
2 1/2 years to a depth of 6,000 feet or to the Norphlet Sands,
whichever is deeper.

The royalty and acreage of each lease was as follows:

Tract 1 - ·5,542.05 surface acres at 1/6 royalty
Tract 2 - 7,681.26 surface acres at 1/8 royalty
Tract 3 - 13,168.09 surface acres at 1/6 royalty

Invitation to bid was advertised pursuant to law in the Tallahassee
Democrat and Okaloosa News-Journal with bids to be opened at 10:00
AM (DST) on June 8, 1971 for consideration by the Trustees.

ACTION OF THE TRUSTEES:

On Mr. Stone's motion, seconded by Mr. O'Malley, that the bids
be received and considered, Mr. James T. Williams reported the
following bids.

For Tract 1, Mellon Creek Exploration Co. submitted a bid of
$34,291.37, and Amoco Production Company offered $24,371.12.

On motion by Mr. Christian, seconded by Mr. Stone and Mr. O'Malley,
and adopted without objection, the Trustees awarded the lease of
Tract 1 to the high bidder, Mellon Creek Exploration Co.

Governor Askew noted that under all the leases, drilling would
be prohibited in streams, rivers, and lakes.

For Tract 2, one bid was received from Amoco Production Company
in the amount of $9,928.05. Mr. Williams recommended acceptance
of the bid.

On motion by Mr. Stone, seconded by Mr. Christian and adopted
without objection, the Board awarded lease of Tract 2 to Amoco
Production Company.

For Tract 3, one bid was received from Amoco Production Company
in the amount of $17,019.74. Mr. Williams recommended acceptance.

On motion by Mr. Stone, seconded by Mr. O'Malley, and Mr. Christian,
and adopted without objection, the Board awarded lease of Tract
3 to Amoco Production Company.

-10-

LEVY COUNTY - Shoreline Survey

On December 1, 1970, the Trustees authorized the expenditure of
$1,000 matching a similar amount from the County Commissioners
of Levy County, for a cooperative pilot mean high water shoreline survey in Levy County. This survey was to be executed by
M. K. Flowers and Associates, 532 S. E. 5th Avenue, Gainesville,
Florida.

To date the survey firm had not accomplished the survey nor
indicated when it will be accomplished. The Board of County
Commissioners and M. K. Flowers have been notified that the staff
will recommend that the Trustees' commitment be terminated.

The staff recommended that matching funds commitment be terminated.

ACTION OF THE TRUSTEES:

On motion by Mr. O'Malley, seconded by Mr. Stone and adopted
without objection, the Trustees terminated the matching funds
commitment since the survey was not undertaken.

-11-

PALM BEACH COUNTY - Dredge Permit, Section 253.123 F. S.

    Vista Builders, Inc.
    c/o Winningham & Lively, Inc.
    1040 Northeast 45 Street, Fort Lauderdale, Florida,

(1) requested authorization to install a seawall along the mean
high water line of the Intracoastal Waterway in Section 33, Township 47 South, Range 43 East, and

(2) requested a permit to perform maintenance dredging in a
3,860 ft. length of the Intracoastal Waterway in Section 33, Township 47 South, Range 43 East.

6-8-71

for the construction of two new bridges replacing the existing
bridge, to allow for four lanes of traffic.

No dredging or filling will be required. The Department of
Natural Resources, the Game and Fresh Water Fish Commission and the
Department of Air and Water Pollution Control offered no objections
to the project.

Staff recommends approval.

ACTION OF THE TRUSTEES:

On motion by Mr. Conner, seconded by Mr. Christian and adopted
without objection, the Board authorized issuance of the easement to the Department of Transportation.

-2-

LEE COUNTY

On October 6, 1966, the Trustees issued Contract No. 24374
(1817-36) to Shorehaven of Lee County, Inc., for the purchase
of 13.57 acres of submerged land in the Caloosahatchee River
in Section 28, Township 44 South, Range 24 East. This was on
advance agenda of April 27 and deferred for on-site inspection.

On-site inspection revealed that there had been no encroachment
on the public lands and no dredging and filling had been done
in the purchase area.

All contract payments have been paid and under the terms of the
contract, the purchaser is entitled to deed.

Recommend issuance of deed.

ACTION OF THE TRUSTEES:

On motion by Mr. Christian, seconded by Mr. Stone and adopted
without objection, the Board authorized issuance of the deed
to the purchaser.

-3-

MURPHY ACT REPORT NO. 987 - Sale of Lots in Alachua
and Gadsden Counties

Request approval of Bidding Report No. 987 listing 22 regular
bids for sale of lots in Alachua and Gadsden Counties under
provisions of Section 197.350 Florida Statutes. The land
had been certified to the State of Florida under tax sale
certificates.

Alachua County: R. H. Wyrosdich offered the high bid of $150
for 3 lots (two lots 25' x 120' and one a small triangle) in
Block 21, Archer, Section 17, T 11 S, R 18 E. The Tax
Assessor's value estimate for the land was $50.

Gadsden County: Adrian C. Fletcher offered the high bid of
$310 for 40 lots (25' x 107') in Washington Park Subdivision,
Section 18, T 2 N, R 6 W. Trustees' staff appraiser reported
$7.66 per lot as an equitable price. The bid was $7.75 per lot.

Request authority for execution of deeds.

ACTION OF THE TRUSTEES:

The Director explained briefly the reason for the rather low
lot values. The staff recommended approval of the sales.

On motion by Mr. Conner, seconded by Mr. Christian and adopted
without objection, the Trustees approved the Murphy Act report
and authorized execution of deeds pertaining thereto.

6-15-71

DADE COUNTY - The dredge permit application of MacMillan Bloedel, Ltd., was approved by the Trustees on June 8.

-5-

HOLMES, WASHINGTON, AND WALTON COUNTIES - Snag Removal to Improve Navigation in Choctawatchee River and Holmes Creek.

The Game and Fresh Water Fish Commission requested a permit authorizing removal of snags to improve navigation in the Choctawhatchee River and Holmes Creek. The work will be done during a six-month period beginning June 1, 1971.

Disposal of debris will be on property owned by International and St. Regis Paper Companies sufficiently distant from the shoreline to insure that it will not re-enter the river.

Staff recommends approval.

ACTION OF THE TRUSTEES:

On motion by Mr. Stone, seconded by Mr. Dickinson and adopted without objection, the Trustees approved issuance of the permit requested by the Game and Fresh Water Fish Commission.

-6-

LAKE AND ORANGE COUNTIES - Dredge Permit

The Game and Fresh Water Fish Commission requested a permit to engage in an experimental dredging project in Lake Carlton for the purpose of redistributing sediments.

A sand suction dredge will be used to obtain sand under deep muck deposits and redeposit it over areas presently covered with a thin layer of muck.

There will be no fill exposed above the lake's surface.

Staff requests authority to issue permit.

ACTION OF THE TRUSTEES:

Mr. Stone made a motion, seconded by Mr. Christian and adopted without objection, that the dredge permit be approved. Mr. Stone also urged the Director to study the possibility of an experimental program in the model project approach in the Miami River.

-7-

OKALOOSA COUNTY - Spoil Island Lease 2224

Rhett E. Cadenhead, W. F. Davis, and M. P. Cox requested renewal of their lease which expires July 6, 1971, for an additional five year period under provisions of the option stated in paragraph 2 of said lease.

The Board of Trustees adopted a policy on August 11, 1970, whereby all spoil islands would be left in their natural state to insure their preservation.

The staff has received numerous objections to the commercial development of this spoil island.

Staff legal counsel and the Attorney General's Office state there is no legal obligation to renew the lease for an additional term.

Staff recommends that the lease not be renewed and the file be deactivated upon expiration of the present lease.

The channel would be dredged from the existin
ft. to a depth of minus-16 ft. The width wou
The purpose for overdredging was to provide f
perpetual maintenance spoil area (MSA-654) tc
to be used by the record fee owner. The Trus
have any fee interest in either the waterway
The release of the spoil area was cleared by
tion District.

The applicant agreed to pay the newly-establ
Trustees demonstrated an interest in any poı
cubic yards of dredge material which would '
upland. A title opinion was requested to d
of the area subject to dredging.

The biological report stated that there wa
of marine life in the area but recommendec
within the Intracoastal Waterway right of
wildlife.

The Department of Air and Water Pollutioı
this project, and the Game and Fresh Wat
issued a letter of no objection to the ľ

The item was withdrawn from the agenda
of reviewing objections submitted by th
of Palm Beach County. The Area Planniɾ
objections insofar as release of the eı
matter of seawall realignment was to b
regular meeting.

The applicant agreed not to construct
local review was completed. However,
landward of the mean high water line
the waterway.

<u>The staff requests authority to issı
subject to applicant depositing a b
materials removed if it is determiɾ
fee interest, and further subject ↑
on an upland site.</u>

ACTION OF THE TRUSTEES:

Mr. Kuperberg explained that the
ultimately would be required by t
in a designated intracoastal watı
approval of that portion of the

On motion by Mr. O'Malley, secoɾ
without objection, the Trustees
for dredging only, subject to t
to guarantee payment as recommє
subject to location of the stoˌ

———

ᴣᴄ
.e
R
.d ʍ

<u>DADE COUNTY</u> - Dredge Permit,
                 Dredging for Nɑ

        MacMillan Bloedel, Ltd.
        1075 W. Georgia St.
        Vancouver 105, British

applied for a permit to drє
Township 53 South, Range 4
area 1,665 ft. by 200 to 9
material would be removed
according to the recommenˌ
Resources.

The Department of Air anˌ
and Fresh Water Fish Com

The submerged lands sub·

Bloedel,

:o
aek.

ermit
the
be done

national
·om the
/er.

ınd adopted
of the
Commission.

ed a permit
ı Lake Carlton

ınd under deep
ently covered

s surface.

·istian and adopted
approved   Mr. Stone
lity of an ex erı
in the Miami Ri

?. ox reques
1, or an add.
opion stated

on Agust 11, 1970,
: in heir natural st⌴

:ions o the commercial

Genera's Office state
/ the lase for an additional

be reneıd and the file be
present ease.

The channel would be dredged from the existing depth of minus-12 ft. to a depth of minus-16 ft. The width would remain at 150 ft. The purpose for overdredging was to provide for the release of a perpetual maintenance spoil area (MSA-654) to enable the parcel to be used by the record fee owner. The Trustees did not appear to have any fee interest in either the waterway right of way or MSA-654. The release of the spoil area was cleared by Florida Inland Navigation District.

The applicant agreed to pay the newly-established rate if the Trustees demonstrated an interest in any portion of the 40,000 cubic yards of dredge material which would be removed and placed on upland. A title opinion was requested to determine ownership of the area subject to dredging.

The biological report stated that there was no significant amount of marine life in the area but recommended that mangroves growing within the Intracoastal Waterway right of way be left for use by wildlife.

The Department of Air and Water Pollution Control certified this project, and the Game and Fresh Water Fish Commission issued a letter of no objection to the project.

The item was withdrawn from the agenda of May 11 for the purpose of reviewing objections submitted by the Area Planning Board of Palm Beach County. The Area Planning Board withdrew its objections insofar as release of the easement is concerned. The matter of seawall realignment was to be considered at the next regular meeting.

The applicant agreed not to construct the seawall until the local review was completed. However, he desired to stockpile landward of the mean high water line the material removed from the waterway.

The staff requests authority to issue permit, for dredging only, subject to applicant depositing a bond to guarantee payment for materials removed if it is determined that the Trustees have a fee interest, and further subject to location of the stockpile on an upland site.

ACTION OF THE TRUSTEES:

Mr. Kuperberg explained that the dredging was work that ultimately would be required by the Army Corps of Engineers in a designated intracoastal waterway. The staff recommended approval of that portion of the application.

On motion by Mr. O'Malley, seconded by Mr. Stone and adopted without objection, the Trustees authorized issuance of a permit for dredging only, subject to the applicant depositing a bond to guarantee payment as recommended by the staff, and further subject to location of the stockpile on upland.

-12-

DADE COUNTY - Dredge Permit, Section 253.123 F. S.
           Dredging for Navigation

     MacMillan Bloedel, Ltd.
     1075 W. Georgia St.
     Vancouver 105, British Columbia, Canada,

applied for a permit to dredge for navigation in Section 31, Township 53 South, Range 42 East, Biscayne Bay, Miami, in an area 1,665 ft. by 200 to 915 ft. 140,000 cubic yards of material would be removed and deposited on Burlingame Island according to the recommendation of the Department of Natural Resources.

The Department of Air and Water Pollution Control and the Game and Fresh Water Fish Commission had no objections.

The submerged lands subject to dredging vested in the City of

Miami by virtue of Chapter 8305, Acts of 1919. Therefore, no fee was being charged for materials dredged.

Staff requested authority to issue the permit.

ACTION OF THE TRUSTEES:

On June 1 the Board had deferred action for two weeks. The application was scheduled for June 15 but subsequently, at the request of the Secretary of State, it was circulated as an addendum to the agenda of this date. No objections were received. Mr. Stone had investigated and found that the Board could not require payment for the fill material.

On motion by Mr. Christian, seconded by Mr. Shevin and adopted without objection, the rules were waived for consideration of the application on this date.

On motion by Mr. Stone, seconded by Mr. Christian and adopted without objection, the Trustees authorized issuance of the dredge permit.

On motion duly adopted, the meeting was adjourned.

_____
GOVERNOR   -   CHAIRMAN

ATTEST: _____
EXECUTIVE DIRECTOR

Tallahassee, Florida
June 15, 1971

The State of Florida Board of Trustees of the Internal Improvement Trust Fund met on this date in the Haydon Burns Building in Tallahassee, with the following members present:

Reubin O'D. Askew	Governor
Richard (Dick) Stone	Secretary of State
Robert L. Shevin	Attorney General
Fred O. Dickinson, Jr.	Comptroller
Floyd T. Christian	Commissioner of Education
Doyle Conner	Commissioner of Agriculture

Joel Kuperberg	Executive Director

Without objection, the minutes of June 1 were approved as submitted.

-1-

LEVY COUNTY - Right of Way Easement
          TIITF No. 2403-38-253.03

The Department of Transportation requested an easement embracing 0.64 acres across the bottom of the Withlacoochee River abutting Sections 2 and 3, Township 17 South, Range 16 East, Levy County,

6-15-71

for the construction of two new bridges replacing the existing bridge, to allow for four lanes of traffic.

No dredging or filling will be required. The Department of Natural Resources, the Game and Fresh Water Fish Commission and the Department of Air and Water Pollution Control offered no objections to the project.

Staff recommends approval.

ACTION OF THE TRUSTEES:

On motion by Mr. Conner, seconded by Mr. Christian and adopted without objection, the Board authorized issuance of the easement to the Department of Transportation.

-2-

LEE COUNTY

On October 6, 1966, the Trustees issued Contract No. 24374 (1817-36) to Shorehaven of Lee County, Inc., for the purchase of 13.57 acres of submerged land in the Caloosahatchee River in Section 28, Township 44 South, Range 24 East. This was on advance agenda of April 27 and deferred for on-site inspection.

On-site inspection revealed that there had been no encroachment on the public lands and no dredging and filling had been done in the purchase area.

All contract payments have been paid and under the terms of the contract, the purchaser is entitled to deed.

Recommend issuance of deed.

ACTION OF THE TRUSTEES:

On motion by Mr. Christian, seconded by Mr. Stone and adopted without objection, the Board authorized issuance of the deed to the purchaser.

-3-

MURPHY ACT REPORT NO. 987 - Sale of Lots in Alachua
                              and Gadsden Counties

Request approval of Bidding Report No. 987 listing 22 regular bids for sale of lots in Alachua and Gadsden Counties under provisions of Section 197.350 Florida Statutes. The land had been certified to the State of Florida under tax sale certificates.

Alachua County: R. H. Wyrosdich offered the high bid of $150 for 3 lots (two lots 25' x 120' and one a small triangle) in Block 21, Archer, Section 17, T 11 S, R 18 E. The Tax Assessor's value estimate for the land was $50.

Gadsden County: Adrian C. Fletcher offered the high bid of $310 for 40 lots (25' x 107') in Washington Park Subdivision, Section 18, T 2 N, R 6 W. Trustees' staff appraiser reported $7.66 per lot as an equitable price. The bid was $7.75 per lot.

Request authority for execution of deeds.

ACTION OF THE TRUSTEES:

The Director explained briefly the reason for the rather low lot values. The staff recommended approval of the sales.

On motion by Mr. Conner, seconded by Mr. Christian and adopted without objection, the Trustees approved the Murphy Act report and authorized execution of deeds pertaining thereto.

6-15-71

-4-

DADE COUNTY - The dredge permit application of MacMillan Bloedel, Ltd., was approved by the Trustees on June 8.

-5-

HOLMES, WASHINGTON, AND WALTON COUNTIES - Snag Removal to Improve Navigation in Choctawatchee River and Holmes Creek.

The Game and Fresh Water Fish Commission requested a permit authorizing removal of snags to improve navigation in the Choctawhatchee River and Holmes Creek. The work will be done during a six-month period beginning June 1, 1971.

Disposal of debris will be on property owned by International and St. Regis Paper Companies sufficiently distant from the shoreline to insure that it will not re-enter the river.

Staff recommends approval.

ACTION OF THE TRUSTEES:

On motion by Mr. Stone, seconded by Mr. Dickinson and adopted without objection, the Trustees approved issuance of the permit requested by the Game and Fresh Water Fish Commission.

-6-

LAKE AND ORANGE COUNTIES - Dredge Permit

The Game and Fresh Water Fish Commission requested a permit to engage in an experimental dredging project in Lake Carlton for the purpose of redistributing sediments.

A sand suction dredge will be used to obtain sand under deep muck deposits and redeposit it over areas presently covered with a thin layer of muck.

There will be no fill exposed above the lake's surface.

Staff requests authority to issue permit.

ACTION OF THE TRUSTEES:

Mr. Stone made a motion, seconded by Mr. Christian and adopted without objection, that the dredge permit be approved. Mr. Stone also urged the Director to study the possibility of an experimental program in the model project approach in the Miami River.

-7-

OKALOOSA COUNTY - Spoil Island Lease 2224

Rhett E. Cadenhead, W. F. Davis, and M. P. Cox requested renewal of their lease which expires July 6, 1971, for an additional five year period under provisions of the option stated in paragraph 2 of said lease.

The Board of Trustees adopted a policy on August 11, 1970, whereby all spoil islands would be left in their natural state to insure their preservation.

The staff has received numerous objections to the commercial development of this spoil island.

Staff legal counsel and the Attorney General's Office state there is no legal obligation to renew the lease for an additional term.

Staff recommends that the lease not be renewed and the file be deactivated upon expiration of the present lease.

ACTION OF THE TRUSTEES:

The staff had received protests from about ninety-one individuals
and many objectors were present to be heard. However, Mr. Cadenhead
had advised that the matter came to his attention only yesterday
and had asked for postponement. Because of that, Mr. Christian
requested deferment.

Governor Askew pointed out that the Board, acting in good faith,.
recognized that the lessee had property rights and required legal
notice. Members were prepared to support the staff recommendation
but the matter would be reagendaed, and the Board would appreciate
it if those who could come back would reserve their comments
until a later date.

Mrs. Henry A. Boudolf, President of the League of Women Voters
of Okaloosa County, had filed many petitions of objection
and read a statement protesting lease of the spoil island
that she said was used extensively for recreation by residents and tourists. She agreed with the staff recommendation
and indicated that the group of objectors would return when
the Board considered the matter.

The Board deferred disposition for two weeks.

-8-

Request authority to transfer $18,000 to the Department of
Natural Resources, Division of Interior Resources, for the
continuation of the Shoreline Survey project. These funds will
be used by the Department of Natural Resources for the installation, maintenance, and monitoring of tide gauges and bench marks
along the coastline. Funds have been budgeted for the project
and are available within the approved operating budget.

ACTION OF THE TRUSTEES:

On motion by Mr. Stone, seconded by Mr. Christian and adopted
without objection, the Board authorized the transfer of
$18,000 as requested.

-9-

The Executive Director will present his comments regarding the
report of the Technical Advisory Committee on the proposed fee
schedule for fill material obtained from sovereignty lands.

ACTION OF THE TRUSTEES:

On April 13 the Board had deferred action on the report of
the Technical Advisory Committee 6n Fill, pending receipt of
staff comments.

Mr. Kuperberg said that three categories were established
based on supporting data provided by the Coastal Coordinating
Council, (1) unavailability of fill material, (2) demand for
fill material, and (3) damage to the environment. The intention
was to place a true value on the fill material that would involve
the loss of annual income in marine productivity, whereas the
Technical Advisory Committee report was on a strict appraisal
basis and did not involve any environmental considerations.

Mr. Kuperberg presented the following recommendations:

> STAFF RECOMMENDATIONS AS TO THE VALUE OF FILL
> MATERIAL SECURED FROM STATE-OWNED LANDS

After a lengthy review of the report of the Technical Advisory
Committee on Fill, the following recommendations are submitted
by staff in response to the Trustees' request for guidelines:

1. There should be no dredging permitted except for navigational
purposes, of sovereignty lands shallower than one fathom at mean
low water.

2. A premium price should be placed on fill material where project feasibility depends upon the use of sovereignty lands as a source of fill.

3. The cost, in place, of fill material taken from sovereignty lands should not be less than the in-place cost of fill from other sources based upon consideration of the total quantity of fill required for the project.

4. Cities, counties and special districts should pay the State for sovereignty fill material used for public projects which, by their nature, do not require waterfront locations.

5. Public navigation projects should receive special consideration with regard to the disposal of spoil.

6. The economic value of Florida's beaches is such that upon the recommendation of the Department of Natural Resources, the State should not charge for the material used to nourish beaches.

7. The following categories of minimum prices should be established.

> I. $1.50 per cubic yard -- Monroe County
> Explanation: See recommendation number two.
>
> II. $1 per cubic yard -- Bay, Brevard, Broward, Charlotte, Collier, Dade, Duval, Escambia, Hillsborough, Lee, Manatee, Palm Beach, Pasco, Pinellas and Sarasota.
>
> Explanation: The most populous coastal counties, which comprise 70.01 percent of Florida's total population, where there has been a demand for fill or where bulkhead lines are still located well offshore the line of mean high water despite the recommendations of the State interagency advisory committee on submerged land management.
>
> III. $.50 per cubic yard -- all other counties
> Explanation: Lightly populated coastal counties with little present demand for fill material or counties where aquatic preserves comprise a significant portion of the shoreline and submerged lands. Aquatic preserves preclude borrow areas for fill material.

Motion was made by Mr. Stone, seconded by Mr. Dickinson and adopted without objection, that the staff recommendations be approved as the policy of the Board with respect to the value of fill material secured from state-owned lands.

Governor Askew said the staff should be commended because in his opinion the recommendations were innovative, conservation-oriented, and certainly in the public interest. Mr. Shevin said they were excellent recommendations.

-10-

COLLIER COUNTY - Permit Extension
>   (A) File No. 253.123-51
>   (B) File Nos. 253.123-678, 253.124-149

Applicant: Marco Island Development Corporation

On April 13, 1971, the Trustees extended to May 18, 1971, the Roberts Bay and Big Marco River permits on a temporary basis to allow the new executive director the opportunity to review the request of the applicant for sufficient time to complete the subject dredge and fill projects.

On May 18, 1971, the staff submitted an agreement outline for the Trustees' consideration. The recommendations were approved, including an extension of the two permits to June 15, 1971, at which time the staff was to make a detailed recommendation.

Negotiations with the applicant have been slower than anticipated
partly because of an incapacitating accident to the applicant's
senior planner. As a result, the applicant's unacceptable proposal was not received in time to permit discussions prior to
agenda publication.

The staff recommends that the subject permits be extended to
June 29, 1971.

ACTION OF THE TRUSTEES:

The executive director had not been able to finalize the negotiations
and therefore recommended the short extension.

Motion was made by Mr. Dickinson, seconded by Mr. Christian and
adopted without objection, that the subject permits be extended
to June 29, 1971.

On motion duly adopted, the meeting was adjourned.

GOVERNOR - CHAIRMAN

ATTEST:

EXECUTIVE DIRECTOR

* * *

Tallahassee, Florida
June 22, 1971

The State of Florida Board of Trustees of the Internal Improvement
Trust Fund met on this date in the auditorium of the Department
of Transportation in Tallahassee, with the following members
present:

Reubin O'D. Askew   Governor
Richard (Dick) Stone   Secretary of State
Fred O. Dickinson, Jr.   Comptroller
Thomas D. O'Malley   Treasurer
Floyd T. Christian   Commissioner of Education
Doyle Conner   Commissioner of Agriculture

Joel Kuperberg   Executive Director

Without objection, the minutes of June 8 were approved.

At the suggestion of the Governor, the cabinet decided that
meetings in July and August would be held every other week.
Mr. Conner suggested that department heads be urged to notify
as many as possible that the meetings would be scheduled for
July 6, 20, August 3, 17 and 31, in order to minimize any
inconvenience to the public that had come to expect cabinet
meeting each Tuesday.

It is proposed that a continuing interagency advisory committee
for State wilderness systems be created in compliance with the
provisions of Chapter 70-355, State Wilderness System Act.
Section 12 of this Act states: "The Trustees shall create a
continuing interagency advisory committee to assist in the
selection of wilderness areas, to act at the request of the
Trustees and to initiate proposals of its own for new wilderness
areas, and in formulating rules and regulations for use of such
areas."

Membership of the committee shall be comprised of the directors
of the following bodies or their designees:

    Board of Trustees of the Internal Improvement Trust Fund
    Department of Natural Resources
    Department of Agriculture
    Department of Air and Water Pollution Control
    Game and Fresh Water Fish Commission
    Coastal Coordinating Council

Payment of travel and other necessary expenses in connection with
committee work will be authorized by the Trustees' staff from
Trustees' funds.

Staff recommends the creation of a continuing interagency advisory
committee for State wilderness systems and authorization to pay
necessary expenses.

ACTION OF THE TRUSTEES:

On motion by the Secretary of State, seconded by Mr. Dickinson
and Mr. O'Malley, and adopted without objection, the Trustees
accepted the staff recommendation for creation of a continuing
interagency advisory committee with the suggested membership
and authorized payment of necessary expenses.

Governor Askew suggested the designation of Mr. Kuperberg as
chairman of the committee, which was approved on motion by
Mr. Dickinson, seconded by Mr. Stone and Mr. Conner, and
adopted without objection.

-2-

MONROE COUNTY - Florida Keys Aqueduct Authority Application

At the Executive Director's request, the application by Florida
Keys Aqueduct Authority was withdrawn from the agenda. The
applicant had been notified of the withdrawal.

-3-

BAY COUNTY - Confirmation of Sale
          File No. 2392-03-253.12

    Staff Description: 1.273 acre parcel of filled
                            sovereignty land in East Bay,
                            abutting Section 18, T 5 S, R 12 W.

A. CITY AND COUNTY: Bay County

B. APPLICANT: Donald Ray Gore
                      Box 91 Wewahitchka Star Route
                      Panama City, Florida

C. ACREAGE: 1.273
    RATE PER ACRE: $392.77, $500 for the parcel, staff adjustment
    TOTAL OFFER: $1500 - three times the upward adjusted
                            appraised value.
D. APPRAISAL: $290 for the parcel, Nolen appraisal
    DATE: December 16, 1970
    APPRAISER: David T. Nolen, M.A.I., adjusted
                      by staff appraiser

E: PURPOSE: Residential Development

F. BIOLOGICAL REPORT: Attached, dated February 16, 1971.
    Results not adverse. Remarks: Restoration of the filled
    area to its previous condition by removing the fill would be a
    questionable solution or recommendation. However, recommend
    removal of a small part of the fill at the south end to
    provide connection of a marsh area to open water.

G. STAFF REMARKS: The parcel was landward of the bulkhead line
    approved by the Trustees on March 16, 1971.

    Applicant agreed to remove the fill as suggested by the
    biological report and agreed to pay three times the appraised
    value for the parcel. Applicant stated that the sale would
    be in the public interest as the alternative would not be
    in the public interest.

    Staff requested Mr. Gore to remove a portion of a dike in
    compliance with recommendation of Department of Natural
    Resources.

    A field investigation on June 10, 1971, by a Marine Patrol
    Officer disclosed that the dike has been removed in accordance
    with the instructions of this agency.

H. Recommend that the sale be made at three times the upward
    adjusted appraised value.

ACTION OF THE TRUSTEES:

On motion by Mr. O'Malley, seconded by Mr. Stone and adopted
without objection, the Board confirmed sale of the advertised
parcel to Mr. Gore at three times the upward adjusted appraised
value.

-4-

DUVAL COUNTY - Dredge Permit, Section 253.123

    Jacksonville Electric Authority
    222 East Bay Street, Jacksonville, Florida

on April 29, 1970, applied for a permit to dredge a cooling water
discharge channel 800 ft. long, 6 ft. deep, 200 ft. in width, in
the west fork of San Carlos Creek in Section 13, Township 1 South,
Range 28 East, Duval County.

Approximately 25,000 cubic yards of mud, silt and sand would
be removed and placed on adequately diked upland belonging
to the applicant.

The biological report indicated that the sand, silt and mud bottoms
were unvegetated, and dredging these areas would not have significant adverse effects on marine resources. However, the report
was adverse to removal of two marsh islands.

Staff requested channel alignment be revised to save a portion
of the larger marsh island. The revised biological report indicates
this revision will do less damage to productive marine habitat.
Staff believes this is the least damaging channel location that can
be designed to serve this marsh site.

The Game and Fresh Water Fish Commission and the Department of Air
and Water Pollution Control have no objections to the issuance
of the requested permit.

Recommend approval of revised application, and that all fees be
waived.

ACTION OF THE TRUSTEES:

On motion by Mr. Christian, seconded by Mr. Conner and adopted
without objection, the Trustees approved waiver of all fees
and issuance of permit for the revised application.

-5-

DADE COUNTY - Florida East Coast Railway Company Application

Consideration of the application for fill permit for Florida
East Coast Railway Company was deferred for two weeks at the
request of the Attorney General.

Mr. W. P. Simmons, Jr., and others were present representing
the applicant, not having known it would be deferred. Mr. Simmons
indicated that they would return in two weeks, and would like to
know if there were any objections to the application.

-6-

SANTA ROSA COUNTY - Fill Permit Amendment, File 253.124-116;
                   and State Construction Permit, Boat Ramp

    Department of Transportation

(1) requested amendment of the fill permit authorized by the
     Trustees on December 2, 1969, so that an additional 0.43
     acre parcel of submerged land in Section 5, T 3 S, R 29 W,
     might be filled for installation of a boat ramp; and

(2) requested a state construction permit for a public boat
     ramp adjacent to State Road 30 at Gulf Breeze in Section
     5, T 3 S, R 29 W.

The submerged land to be filled was conveyed in 1967 under Deed
No. 24630.

All work will be within existing right of way and an established
bulkhead line.

The biological report dated June 1, 1971, from the Department
of Natural Resources was not adverse. The Department of Air and
Water Pollution Control and the Game and Fresh Water Fish Commission filed letters of no objection to the project.

The staff recommends amendment of the fill permit and issuance
of the construction permit without fee.

ACTION OF THE TRUSTEES:

On motion by Mr. Dickinson, seconded by Mr. Christian and
adopted without objection, the Trustees approved amendment
of the fill permit and issuance of the construction permit
without charge.

-7-

BREVARD COUNTY - Marina License, Section 253.03, F. S.

    Board of County Commissioners of Brevard County
    Post Office Box 1496, Titusville, Florida 32780

applied for a marina license for a public docking pier in the
Indian River adjacent to North Grange Island in Section 34,
Township 29 South, Range 38 East, Brevard County.

The structure would occupy approximately 2,960 square feet of
sovereignty land.

No dredging would be required. The county requested that all
fees be waived as the project was for public recreation purposes.

The Department of Natural Resources, the Game and Fresh Water
Fish Commission, the Department of Air and Water Pollution Control,
and the Florida Inland Navigation District had no objection to the
project.

The staff recommends approval.

6-22-71

ACTION OF THE TRUSTEES:

On motion by Mr. Dickinson, seconded by Mr. Stone and adopted
without objection, the Trustees approved issuance of the
marina license to the Board of County Commissioners of Brevard
County without charge.

-8-

CHARLOTTE COUNTY - Dredge Permit, Section 253.123 Florida Statutes
                  File No. 733

    City of Punta Gorda
    c/o Tri County Engineering, Inc.
    121 East Charlotte Avenue
    Punta Gorda, Florida 33950

requests a maintenance dredge permit to widen and deepen an
existing channel in Charlotte Harbor adjacent to Section 15,
Township 41 South, Range 22 East, Charlotte County.

The new channel will be 1735 ft. long, 80 ft. wide and 8 ft. deep,
with 14,920 cubic yards of material to be removed. $14,920 has
been remitted in payment for fill material.

The revised spoil area will be approximately 1000' inland on land
owned by Punta Gorda Isles, in the Northeast corner of Sec. 14,
Township 14 South, Range 22 East.

The application has been revised and the supplemental biological
report of the Department of Natural Resources states that "The
revised project should not have significant adverse effects on
marine biological resources if dredging is carefully done to
minimize siltation."

The Department of Air and Water Pollution Control has indicated
that the project would be certified if no objections were filed.

The Game and Fresh Water Fish Commission concurs with the Department of Natural Resources report.

Request authority to issue permit.

ACTION OF THE TRUSTEES:

On motion by Mr. Stone, seconded by Mr. O'Malley and adopted
without objection, the Trustees authorized·issuance of the
dredge permit to the City of Punta Gorda.

-9-

TRUSTEES POLICY - Fill Material Rates

On June 15, 1971, the Trustees adopted recommendations submitted
by the staff for new charges for material removed from sovereignty
lands and other criteria related to dredging.

In view of the change in policy, it is necessary to amend existing
administrative rules and regulations relating to this matter.
Trustees approval of this matter would also have the effect of
terminating the moratorium on processing dredge and fill applications.

Request authority to proceed with execution of appropriate
emergency and regular rule-making provisions of Chapter 120,
Florida Statutes, to·implement the policy adopted on June.15.

ACTION OF THE TRUSTEES:

On motion by Mr. O'Malley, seconded by Mr. Stone and adopted without objection, the Trustees authorized filing of appropriate emergency and regular rules to implement the policy adopted on June 15, 1971.

For the record, attention is called to the fact that approval of the new charges for material removed from state sovereignty lands terminated the moratorium on processing dredge and fill applications.

The Executive Director distributed to the Trustees copies of a report dated June 11, 1971, "Repairing the Florida Everglades Basin" by Arthur R. Marshall of the Center for Urban Studies, University of Miami.

The Secretary of State expressed gratitude that the report by this technically qualified group not only pointed out damages and indicated areas of further danger to the water supply of the Everglades, but also offered constructive alternatives.

On motion duly adopted, the meeting was adjourned.

GOVERNOR   -   CHAIRMAN

ATTEST: EXECUTIVE DIRECTOR

Tallahassee, Florida
June 29, 1971

The State of Florida Board of Trustees of the Internal Improvement Trust Fund met on this date in the auditorium of the Department of Transportation, with the following members present:

Reubin O'D. Askew	Governor
Richard (Dick) Stone	Secretary of State
Robert L. Shevin	Attorney General
Fred O. Dickinson, Jr.	Comptroller
Thomas D. O'Malley	Treasurer
Floyd T. Christian	Commissioner of Education
Doyle Conner	Commissioner of Agriculture

Joel Kuperberg	Executive Director

The minutes of June 15 were approved as submitted.

6-29-71

PALM BEACH COUNTY - 1. Establish Bulkhead
                      2. Application to advertise for
                         purchase, TIITF File No. 2370-50-253.12
                      3. Dredge and fill permits, 253.123-794 and
                         253.124-182

Multicon Properties, Inc.
3081 East Commercial Boulevard, Ft. Lauderdale, Florida 33308,

requests approval of:

1. Bulkhead line established by City of Boca Raton by Ordinance
   No. 1485 adopted April 6, 1971, establishing a bulkhead line
   1889.92 feet long along the northwesterly shore of the Hillsboro
   Canal in Section 31, Township 47 South, Range 43 East, Palm
   Beach County;

2. Application to advertise for purchase of six parcels of sovereignty land embracing a total of 3.67 acres landward of the
   proposed bulkhead line. The applicant has submitted the
   following reasons why the sale would be in the public interest:

   a. The elimination of a vermin-infested swampy area;
   b. The elimination of debris collecting pockets;
   c. The beautification of a heavily traveled highway
      and waterway.

   The staff has received numerous letters of endorsement from
   local agencies and persons.

3. Dredge Permit to remove 5,285 cubic yards of fill material
   from four proposed channels and to fill 3.67 acres of submerged land lying landward of proposed bulkhead line.

The Department of Air and Water Pollution Control, the Area
Planning Board of Palm Beach County and the Game and Fresh
Water Fish Commission have no objections to the project.

The biological report indicates that approval of the proposed
bulkhead line and later development within it would not have
significant adverse effects on marine biological resources.

If the Trustees authorize sale of sovereignty lands, the bulkhead
line must be approved and dredge and fill permits will be required
to develop the lands purchased.

Staff requests authority to advertise the sovereignty land sale.

ACTION OF THE TRUSTEES:

The Executive Director explained that the staff was presenting
all phases of this application for consideration at one time.
Mr. Stone expressed approval, as the total project could be
studied rather than the first step.

Mr. Shevin said that no position had been taken other than to
advertise for objections. The staff had made it clear to the
applicant that convincing evidence must be submitted that the
sale was in the public interest. Mr. Shevin also asked for some
documentation as to the present bad condition of the area as
cited by the applicant.

Motion was made by Mr. Stone, seconded by Mr. Christian and
adopted without objection, that the land sale be advertised
for objections only.

-2-

BREVARD COUNTY - Application to advertise proposed purchase
of sovereignty land.
Trustees IITF File No. 2363-05-253.12(5)

Marquis Realty, Inc.
377 Main Avenue
Norwalk, Connecticut 06851

Represented by: Richard A. Lawrence, Sr.
P. O. Drawer 818
Melbourne, Florida 32901

requests authority to advertise for purchasing 1.85 acres of
filled sovereignty land in the Indian River abutting a portion
of Lot N, plat of Tillman, Section 24, Township 28 South, Range
37 East, Brevard County.

The proposed acquisition area is land filled during the construction
of U. S. 1 lying between the upland property owned by the applicant
and the present high water line of the Indian River.

The applicant states that this sale would be in the public interest
because placing the land on the tax roll would add to the public
revenue. In the staff's opinion, this is an insufficient reason.

Staff recommends that the application to advertise be denied and
the file be deactivated.

ACTION OF THE TRUSTEES:

On motion by Mr. Stone, seconded by Mr. O'Malley and Mr. Dickinson,
and adopted without objection, the Board accepted the staff recommendation for denial because the public interest had not been
demonstrated, and authorized deactivation of the file.

-3-

PINELLAS COUNTY - Beach Nourishment, Treasure Island

The Board of County Commissioners
of Pinellas County,

local sponsors for the Beach Erosion Control Project of Treasure
Island, require 66,000 cubic yards of sand to nourish the Treasure
Island public beach in Sections 23 and 26, Township 31 South,
Range 15 East, Pinellas County.

This is an addition to the existing project in which the Trustees
granted borrow area easements and pipeline easements on October 15,
1968. Federal funds will be available until June 30, 1971.

The Department of Natural Resources issued a coastal construction
permit (BBS-71-14) for this project on June 8, 1971.

The Game and Fresh Water Fish Commission and the Department of Air
and Water Pollution Control has no objections. The biological
report is not adverse.

Staff requests authority to issue a construction easement, pipeline easement, and borrow easement.

ACTION OF THE TRUSTEES:

On motion by Mr. Christian, seconded by Mr. Stone and Mr. Dickinson,
adopted without objection, the Trustees approved the application
of Pinellas County for a construction easement, pipeline easement
and borrow easement in connection with beach nourishment at
Treasure Island.

6-29-71

OKALOOSA COUNTY - Spoil Island Lease 2224

Rhett E. Cadenhead, W. F. Davis, and M. P. Cox requested renewal of their lease which expires July 6, 1971, for an additional five year period under provisions of the option stated in paragraph 2 of said lease.

The Board of Trustees adopted a policy on August 11, 1970, whereby all spoil islands would be left in their natural state to insure their preservation.

The staff has received numerous objections to the commercial development of this spoil island.

Staff legal counsel and the Attorney General's Office state there is no legal obligation to renew the lease for an additional term.

Staff recommends that the lease not be renewed and the file be deactivated upon expiration of the present lease.

ACTION OF THE TRUSTEES:

Mr. David Palmer, attorney representing the three lessees, filed a memorandum with the Board setting forth reasons why they thought the lease should be renewed, citing need for additional facilities at that location for the boating and fishing public.

Mrs. Henry Boudolf said she represented the Okaloosa County League of Women Voters, three other organizations, and other individuals that opposed leasing the spoil island for commercial development and called for protecting its natural resources and scenic beauty for recreational use by all citizens and tourists.

Governor Askew thanked those present for their interest. He pointed out that in the five years of the lease there had been no development and there was other land available for that purpose, and that the Trustees had a philosophy of maintaining all spoil islands in their natural condition.

On motion by Mr. O'Malley, seconded by Mr. Christian and adopted without objection, the Trustees accepted the staff recommendation against renewal of the lease.

-5-

BREVARD COUNTY - County Park Lease

Request authority to lease to Brevard County for 99 years for recreational purposes a 2.65 acre parcel of ocean-front beach known as Satellite Beach, in Section 1, Township 27 South, Range 37 East, between Highway A1A and the Atlantic Ocean with approximately 293 feet of ocean frontage.

Development will be by the county under the supervision of the Division of Recreation and Parks, Department of Natural Resources.

The Department of Natural Resources authorized purchase of this property and lease to Brevard County on January 12, 1971.

ACTION OF THE TRUSTEES:

On motion by Mr. Christian, seconded by Mr. Shevin and adopted without objection, the Trustees approved the lease to Brevard County.

The Executive Director assured Mr. Shevin that the lease would provide for reversion to the Trustees in the event the land was not used as authorized.

BREVARD COUNTY - County Park Lease

Request authority to lease a parcel containing 142.54 acres to
Brevard County for 99 years for public outdoor recreational purposes.
This parcel in Section 30, Township 24 South, Range 35 East, was
acquired by the county for $60,000 and deeded to the State on
February 4, 1971, in order to qualify for a grant of $50,000 from
the Department of Natural Resources' 15% fund. The grant will be
utilized in developing the area in the expansion of the adjoining
Lone Cabbage County Park. The development by the county will be under
the supervision of the Division of Recreation and Parks, Department
of Natural Resources.

The grant and lease were approved by the Department of Natural
Resources on October 13, 1970.

ACTION OF THE TRUSTEES:

On motion by Mr. Christian, seconded by Mr. Shevin and adopted
without objection, the Trustees approved the lease to Brevard County.

The Executive Director assured Mr. Shevin that the lease would
provide for reversion to the Trustees in the event the land was not
used as authorized.

WALTON, GADSDEN AND JEFFERSON COUNTIES

On October 13, 1970, the Trustees were advised that four Welcome
Stations had been declared surplus by the Department of Commerce.
After notification to all state departments of the availability of
these properties, the Trustees were advised that the Department of
Agriculture desired to utilize all four stations. The station near
Pensacola was leased to the department for use by its Division of
Dairy Industries. The department later determined that it could not
use the other three stations and released them.

The Department of Transportation has now requested that the three
remaining stations be made available for public wayside parks.

It is recommended that the three stations identified as the Monticello,
Paxton and Havana Welcome Stations be leased to the Department of
Transportation for ten years with option to renew.

ACTION OF THE TRUSTEES:

On motion by Mr. Christian, seconded by Mr. Conner and adopted
without objection, the Trustees approved leasing the three stations
as recommended by the staff.

SANTA ROSA COUNTY - Advertise Oil and Gas Lease.

    The Louisiana Land and Exploration Company

requests the Trustees to offer the 25% interest in the oil and gas
held by the State in a portion of the Blackwater River State
Forest for lease.   The land is located in large scattered parcels
in Township 3 North, Range 26 West and Township 4 North, Range 27
West, Santa Rosa County, containing approximately 6,949.51 surface
acres of which Louisiana Land and Exploration Company has under
lease the 75% reserved interest of the federal government.

The Division of Forestry and the Game and Fresh Water Fish
Commission offer no objections to leasing the land.

This request has been reviewed with the state geologist who

concurs in the following recommendation.

Recommend advertising for sealed bids for lease with an annual
rental of $1 per acre, 1/6 royalty, 5-year primary term, $50,000
surety bond and at least one test well required to be drilled to
6,000 feet or to a depth sufficient to test the Norphlet Sands,
whichever is deeper.

ACTION OF THE TRUSTEES:

On motion by Mr. Christian, seconded by Mr. Conner and adopted
without objection, the Trustees authorized advertisement for
sealed bids for the oil and gas drilling lease.

Mr. Kuperberg explained that routine procedures protected the State
of Florida in that there would be no drilling in water bodies,
and wherever drilling was proposed in a park or preserve area
request was first made to the managing agents.

-9-

DADE COUNTY - Oil Lease Assignment

Exchange Oil and Gas Corporation,

owner of certain undivided interest in Oil and Gas Drilling
Lease No. 1939-1939-S issued by the Board of Trustees of the
Internal Improvement Trust Fund and the Board of Education,
requests approval and consent to assign to Mobil Oil Corporation
an undivided 50% of Exchange's interest in this lease.

Executed copy of assignment has been approved as to form and
legality by staff legal counsel.

Recommend approval of assignment.

ACTION OF THE TRUSTEES:

On motion by Mr. Christian, seconded by Mr. Stone and adopted
without objection, the Trustees approved the oil lease assignment that also had been approved by the State Board of Education.

-10-

DADE COUNTY - Oil Lease Assignment

Mobil Oil Corporation,

owner of certain undivided interest in a 1,120 acre portion of
Oil Lease No. 1939-1939-S issued by the Board of Trustees of the
Internal Improvement Trust Fund and the Board of Education, requests
approval and consent to assign to Exchange Oil and Gas Corporation
an undivided 50% of Mobil's interest in this acreage.

Executed copy of assignment has been approved as to form and
legality by staff legal counsel.

Recommend approval of assignment.

ACTION OF THE TRUSTEES:

On motion by Mr. Christian, seconded by Mr. Stone and adopted
without objection, the Trustees approved the oil lease assignment that also had been approved by the State Board of Education.

-11-

HENDRY COUNTY - Oil Lease Correction

Request authority to issue an instrument correcting an error
in the legal description in Oil and Gas Drilling Lease No. 2443,
dated June 16, 1970, issued to Craig Castle and assigned to
Exchange Oil and Gas Corporation.

The text of the lease indicated 320 net mineral acres. The
acreage is actually 400 net mineral acres as correctly stated
in the lease exhibit which describes the property under lease.

ACTION OF THE TRUSTEES:

On motion by Mr. Stone, seconded by Mr. Conner and adopted without
objection, the Trustees authorized issuance of the corrective
instrument.

-12-

Request authorization to permit the Executive Director to execute
instruments for the purpose of correcting deeds, leases and other
instruments where errors were made, such as misspelling and incorrect legal descriptions.

This authority shall not be used to amend, change or alter the
terms or provisions of any legal document.

ACTION OF THE TRUSTEES:

Mr. Kuperberg said the authority requested would take care of
the correction of such clerical or typographical errors as cited
in the preceding agenda application.

Motion was made by Mr. Stone, seconded by Mr. O'Malley and
adopted unanimously, that the Executive Director be authorized
to execute such corrective instruments.

-13

WALTON COUNTY - Building Encroachment

It has been brought to the attention of the staff that the
state-owned two-story brick and frame building in DeFuniak Springs
on the north 65 feet of Lot 760, according to the map of
Lake DeFuniak by W. J. Van Kirk, encroaches on adjoining Lot
761 owned by Southeastern Telephone Company. The state building
is occupied by the Division of Family Services, Department of
Health and Rehabilitative Services.

The encroachment of the building wall on Lot 761 is .8 feet,
the eaves 1 foot, and a retaining wall encroaches .2 feet
according to a survey prepared by W. E. Overstreet, Registered
Land Surveyor.

An agreement has been drawn and approved by staff counsel as
to form and legality whereby Southeastern Telephone Company
agrees that so long as the encroaching building wall, eaves
and retaining wall remain standing, the State shall have the
right to encroach and remain on the Southeastern Telephone
Company land.

It is recommended that the Executive Director be authorized
to execute this agreement on behalf of the Trustees.

ACTION OF THE TRUSTEES:

On motion by Mr. Stone, seconded by Mr. Christian and adopted
without objection, the Executive Director was authorized to
execute the agreement on behalf of the Board.

6-29-71

-14-

DADE COUNTY - Marina License

    City of Miami
    Miami, Florida,

applies for a marina license for the installation of a public
marina facility covering 12,000 square feet of state-owned
land in Biscayne Bay at Dinner Key in Section 22, Township
54 South, Range 41 East, Dade County.

The city requests waiver of all fees. The item appeared on the
September 22, 1970, agenda and was deferred for comments from
Air and Water Pollution Control.

The Department of Air and Water Pollution Control has issued
Water Quality Certificate No. DF-13-48.

The Department of Natural Resources and the Game and Fresh
Water Fish Commission have no objections to the project.

Staff recommends approval of license and waiver of fees.

ACTION OF THE TRUSTEES:

Mr. Kuperberg explained that a small dock would be removed and a
larger dock constructed on the same site.

On motion by Mr. Stone, seconded by Mr. O'Malley and adopted
without objection, the Trustees approved issuance of the marina
license to the City of Miami without charge.

-15-

SANTA ROSA COUNTY - Marina License, Section 253.03, F. S.

    City of Gulf Breeze

applies for a marina license for the enlargement of an existing
public boat ramp and mooring facility, containing approximately
470 square feet in Santa Rosa Sound abutting Section 9, Township
3 South, Range 29 West, Santa Rosa County.

No dredging is required. The city requests waiver of fees.

The Department of Air and Water Pollution Control, the Game and
Fresh Water Fish Commission and the Department of Natural Resources
have no objections to the project.

Application for the proposed groin construction has been scheduled
to appear on the Department of Natural Resources agenda for June
29, 1971.

Staff recommends approval of license and waiver of fees.

ACTION OF THE TRUSTEES:

On motion by Mr. O'Malley, seconded by Mr. Stone and adopted
without objection, the Trustees approved the marina license
to the City of Gulf Breeze without charge.

-16-

TRUSTEES' FUNDS

Staff requests authority to retain an assistant for the staff
appraiser for an additional 90-day period beginning July 1, 1971,
at the rate of $800 a month. As authorized previously, the re-
quest has been initiated for establishment of the position of
Assistant to Appraiser, IIF; however, due to a delay in the
processing of the request, this additional 90-day period is
needed in which to finalize the matter of the permanent position.

ACTION OF THE TRUSTEES:

Motion was made by Mr. Dickinson, seconded by Mr. Stone and adopted without objection, that the staff request be approved.

-17-

CAPITOL CENTER - Surplus Buildings

Request authority to advertise for sealed bids for disposition of two surplus buildings located on recently acquired Trustees' property in Tallahassee.

1. 1-story small frame residence
   811 South Bronough Street

2. 1-story frame residence
   818 South Duval Street

The Bureau of Property Management, Department of General Services, has determined that the two buildings are of no use to the State.

ACTION OF THE TRUSTEES:

The Director said that a request to the staff for deferral had been removed as the problem had been resolved.

On motion by Mr. Stone, seconded by Mr. Christian and adopted without objection, the Trustees authorized advertisement for sealed bids for disposition of the surplus buildings.

-18-

COLLIER COUNTY - Marco Island Development Corporation

The Executive Director presented a report of staff negotiations with principals and representatives of Marco Island Development Corporation. The staff had worked for a long time to reach a settlement that would tie together the whole project and resolve not only the dredge permits but also the overall situation of lands sold for which fill permits were not issued. Mr. Kuperberg thought that residing in that area for seventeen years had helped him to arrive at a justifiable recommendation, and in the staff's judgment the counter offer of the corporation was unacceptable.

Mr. O'Malley suggested an additional extension and deferment until July 20 for further negotiation. Mr. Dickinson seconded the motion but pointed out that this was a very important matter and members had busy schedules in addition to the meetings that had been cancelled.

Governor Askew was reluctant for dredging to continue for three weeks in an area that gave the greatest concern, and made it clear that he would not want any dredging if deferred beyond that time. He thought there were indications that agreement might be reached on this very difficult problem, that the company had done nothing other than what they were legally able to do at the time, but there was substantial law on the Board's side in the event it chose to deny an extension short of an agreement. He asked the Attorney General to advise the members on his research of the law.

Mr. Shevin felt that the additional period of negotiation might resolve what appeared to be an impasse. Mr. O'Malley said there was merit on each side and hoped a settlement could be reached that would not be harmful but would protect the legal interest of the property owner within reason. Staff assistants were to be included during negotiations and a field inspection was suggested to view the area considered so important ecologically by Mr. Kuperberg and so important for development reasons by Marco Island Development Corporation. Mr. Stone said he was reluctant to have the work continue, and a decision should be reached by July 20 with no extensions after that.

Mr. Frank Mackle answered questions regarding the work to be done during the deferment period, said the company would be reasonable, and at the request of the members agreed that the level of the dredging work would not be increased and the new, larger dredge would not be used in this three weeks' time.

Mr. Kuperberg thought an overall settlement should be reached before any additional work was done, but since the settlement was taking longer than anticipated he agreed that Mr. Mackle's statement would be helpful.

On motion by Mr. O'Malley, seconded by Mr. Dickinson and adopted without objection, the Board approved deferment and extension until July 20 with the understanding that the dredging in progress will not be increased or speeded up during that period.

On motion duly adopted, the meeting was adjourned.

GOVERNOR   -   CHAIRMAN

ATTEST: _____
EXECUTIVE DIRECTOR

*

Tallahassee, Florida
July 6, 1971

The State of Florida Board of Trustees of the Internal Improvement Trust Fund met on this date in the auditorium of the Department of Transportation, with the following members present:

Reubin O'D. Askew	Governor
Richard (Dick) Stone	Secretary of State
Robert L. Shevin	Attorney General
Thomas D. O'Malley	Treasurer
Floyd T. Christian	Commissioner of Education
Doyle Conner	Commissioner of Agriculture

Joel Kuperberg	Executive Director

The minutes of June 22 were approved as submitted.

Request authority to correct the minutes of May 26, 1971, concerning Artificial Reef Permit to Marco Island Development Corporation, Collier County. The correct corner locations should be:

    25° 56' 24" N. Lat., 81° 46' 15" W. Long.
    25° 56' 24" N. Lat., 81° 45' 45" W. Long.
    25° 55' 32" N. Lat., 81° 45' 45" W. Long.
    25° 55' 32" N. Lat., 81° 46' 45" W. Long.

This is to correct the previous description furnished by the applicant.

ACTION OF THE TRUSTEES:

Motion was made by Mr. Stone, seconded by Mr. Christian and adopted without objection, that the minutes of May 26 be corrected as requested.

-2-

BAY COUNTY - Bulkhead Line - Section 253.122, F. S.

The Board of County Commissioners of Bay County by resolution
adopted March 16, 1970, established a bulkhead 2842.76 feet long
in Poston Bayou in Section 26, Township 3 South, Range 15 West,
Bay County. The bulkhead line follows existing seawalls and
approximates the mean high tide line.

The biological report is not adverse.

The Game and Fresh Water Fish Commission and the Department of
Air and Water Pollution Control have no objections to the proposed line.

Staff recommends approval.

ACTION OF THE TRUSTEES:

On motion by Mr. Christian, seconded by Mr. Stone, adopted without
objection, the Trustees approved the bulkhead line as established
by the Board of County Commissioners of Bay County on March 16, 1970.

-3-

HILLSBOROUGH COUNTY - Relocation of Bulkhead Lines
                      by Tampa Port Authority

In accordance with request of the Trustees on March 9, 1971, the
Tampa Port Authority has relocated bulkhead lines to the mean
high water line throughout Hillsborough County, with the following
areas excepted:

    In the terminal areas adjacent to channels maintained by
    the Federal Government, including the Inner Harbor, East
    Bay, Port Sutton terminal area, Alafia terminal area,
    Big Ben Terminal area, Port Tampa terminal area and McKay Bay.

It further excepted areas where valid dredge and fill permits are
in effect or under review and where submerged lands have previously been sold where there are legal contractual rights in
existence.

A biological report submitted by the Department of Natural
Resources states that "this revision is in the best interest of
marine conservation and no further biological studies are
required."

Staff recommends that with the exception of McKay Bay, the
relocated bulkhead lines be approved and that the moratorium
on issuance of dredge and fill permits in Hillsborough County
be terminated.

ACTION OF THE TRUSTEES:

Governor Askew suggested that the moratorium be withdrawn con-
ditionally for 45 days in order for the staff to be assured of
receiving additional needed information. Mr. Kuperberg said that
would be helpful.

On motion by Mr. Stone, seconded by Mr. Christian and adopted without objection, the Trustees approved a 45-day conditional lifting
of the moratorium in Hillsborough County with a review to be made
at the end of that period, and approved the relocated bulkhead
lines with the exception of McKay Bay under that condition.

7-6-71

BROWARD COUNTY - Beach Nourishment, Hallandale

City of Hallandale, local sponsor for the Beach Erosion Control
Project of City of Hallandale, requires 340,000 cubic yards of
sand to nourish 4,000 feet of the City's public beach in Sections
25 and 26, Township 51 South, Range 42 East, Broward County. The
Department of Natural Resources issued a coastal construction
permit (BBS-71-11) on June 8, 1971.

Staff requests authority to issue borrow easement.

ACTION OF THE TRUSTEES:

On motion by Mr. O'Malley, seconded by Mr. Conner and Mr. Christian
and adopted without objection, the Trustees authorized issuance
of the borrow easement for the Hallandale beach nourishment
project.

-5-

DADE COUNTY - Fill Permit
               TIITF File No. 253.124-180

     Florida East Coast Railway Company
     Post Office Drawer 1048, St. Augustine, Florida 32084,

applied for a permit to fill an area 850 feet by 750 feet with
380,000 cubic yards of material contiguous to old P & O docks
in the City of Miami in Section 37, Township 54 South, Range 42
East. All fill material would be hauled to the site. No dredging
was contemplated. In consideration for the permit, the applicant
was committed to remove the old railroad trestle across Miami
River.

The City of Miami issued a permit on December 21, 1970. The
Department of Air and Water Pollution Control had no objection.
The biological report from the Department of Natural Resources
was adverse, but is offset by the applicant's cooperation in the
effort to clean up the Miami River.

Staff recommends that the fill permit be issued.

ACTION OF THE TRUSTEES:

Mr. Kuperberg explained that there were some marine grasses in
this commercial port area but the staff felt that ultimately it
would be lost and therefore recommended approval of the permit.

Motion was made by Mr. Conner, seconded by Mr. Christian, that
the recommendation be accepted.

Answering Mr. Stone's question for the record, Mr. William P.
Simmons, Jr., attorney, and Mr. W. L. Thornton, president of
Florida East Coast Railway Company, assured the Trustees that the
old trestle would be removed by the company without delay.

Mr. Shevin, commenting on a recent decision by city officials to
condemn and rezone this land, recommended deferment 60 days to
ascertain the city's plans. Mr. Kuperberg had received information
on this only the night before and was unable to contact city
officials before this meeting, but the city had issued a fill
permit. The material would be transported and not dredged, and
the staff had considered the application on its merits with removal
of the old trestle as an added factor. Questioned as to the
intended use for the land, Mr. Simmons explained it had been
zoned for many years for port purposes including barge operations
and was still used for that, and while no specific plans could be
made until the land was filled, it would be developed for lawful
purposes under zoning regulations. The city had granted a fill
permit, there were no basic environmental objections, and Mr.
Simmons saw no reason for delay of their application filed five
months ago.

The Governor, noting that this was similar to a case in Bay County involving zoning, said it was hard to find a basis for denial and to delay might be tantamount to denial. He thought the basis for considering denial should be the adverse biological report.

Mr. O'Malley sympathized with the Attorney General's desire to save the city money in the event of condemnation, but he had studied the request, his main concern was the adverse biological report, and in view of the staff recommendation he was prepared to approve the fill permit.

Mr. Stone had been informed by city officials that the fill permit would not affect rezoning or condemnation. The city knew of the FEC application but had made no effort to amend the city fill permit. Mr. Stone suggested approval conditioned upon no filling being done within thirty days. The Izaac Walton League had advised that there was little of substantial value to be saved in this area.

Mr. Conner expressed the opinion that the applicant probably could fill the area at less expense than the city. Mr. Christian objected that the City of Miami should have informed the Board of its plans.

Mr. Simmons argued that the city had not asked the Board to take this action, which would place the company in an unfair position, but he did not object to a delay of sixty days suggested by the Governor.

The motion by Mr. Stone, seconded by Mr. O'Malley and adopted without objection, was to approve the fill permit conditioned upon no actual filling taking place within sixty days and conditioned upon the company's commitment to remove the old trestle.

-6-

OSCEOLA COUNTY - Fill Permit, 253.151(5)(b), Lake Tohopekaliga Southport Park Recreational Area.

The Central and Southern Florida Flood Control District has been developing the Southport Park recreation area on Lake Tohopekaliga in Osceola County. The lands subject to development are owned by the Trustees who, on behalf of the Outdoor Recreational Council, leased the land to Osceola County.

A fill permit has been granted by the Board of County Commissioners of Osceola County to fill approximately 1.1 acre portion of the exposed lake bottom above the controlled water level of the lake. All material will be hauled to the site.

The purpose of the fill is to combat erosion adjacent to the existing boat basin and navigation channel.

The Game and Fresh Water Fish Commission biological report indicates that damage to tne environment would occur; however, it recognizes that the project is in the public interest and does not object to issuance of a permit.

The Department of Natural Resources offers no comment on the project. The Department of Air and Water Pollution Control has no objection to the project.

Staff requests authority to issue permit.

ACTION OF THE TRUSTEES:

On motion by Mr. Christian, seconded by Mr. Stone and adopted without objection, the Trustees authorized issuance of the fill permit.

-7-

ESCAMBIA COUNTY - Navigation channel dredge permit
File No. 253.123-797

Richard E. Dunham
115 Sabine Drive, Pensacola Beach, Florida

applies for a navigation channel dredge permit in Santa Rosa
Sound adjacent to Villa Sabine on Santa Rosa Island in Township
2 South, Range 29 West, Escambia County.

The proposed channel will have the following dimensions:

-5.0 ft. m.l.w. x 50 ft. wide (top cut) x 900 ft. long.

An estimated 2900 cubic yards will be removed. Payment of $2900
for material has been remitted at the rate of $1 per cubic yard,
the established rate in Escambia County.

The Department of Natural Resources, Game and Fresh Water Fish
Commission and the Department of Air and Water Pollution Control
have no objections to the project.

The Board of County Commissioners of Escambia County has granted
a permit for this project.

Staff requests authority to issue dredge permit.

ACTION OF THE TRUSTEES:

On motion by Mr. Stone, seconded by Mr. Christian and Mr. Conner,
adopted without objection, the Trustees approved issuance of
the dredge permit.

-8-

HILLSBOROUGH COUNTY - Maintenance Dredge Permit

File No. 253.123-807
Eastern Associated Terminals
P. O. Box 18666, Tampa, Florida 33609, and

File No. 253.123-808
Seaboard Coast Line Railroad Terminals
P. O. Box 5025, Tampa, Florida 33605,

apply for a maintenance dredge permit authorizing dredging alongside existing terminal facilities in East Bay, Port Sutton and
Hookers Point. All dredging is to be accomplished by dragline
method and the excavated material deposited on approved spoil
areas.

The biological report recommends spoiling on the Hookers Point
spoil area or along Cut "C" between the Alafia River and Port
Sutton. The Department of Air and Water Pollution Control
recommends spoiling only on Hookers Point.

An emergency navigational maintenance permit was issued to the
applicants by the Tampa Port Authority on June 15, 1971.

Staff requests authority to issue dredge permit subject to all
spoil being placed on uplands at Hookers Point.

ACTION OF THE TRUSTEES:

It was pointed out that the moratorium on dredge and fill permits
was lifted for forty-five days only, in Hillsborough County.

Mr. Guy Verger of Tampa Port Authority had requested that the
permit require the spoil material to be placed on uplands, rather

than to specify that the uplands be at Hookers Point. Mr. Kuperberg said he saw no objection to that.

On motion by Mr. O'Malley, seconded by Mr. Christian and adopted without objection, the Trustees approved the maintenance dredge permit with the understanding that the moratorium was lifted only for forty-five days and that the spoil would be placed on uplands.

-9-

MARTIN COUNTY - Maintenance Dredging
           File No. 253.123-774

    David H. Lowe, III
    Rocky Point, Port Salerno, Florida 33492,

applies for a dredge permit to excavate 1275 cubic yards of material from an existing boat basin and mooring site on Manatee Pocket, Hanson Grant, Township 38 South, Range 41 East, Martin County. All spoil will be placed on uplands.

The $50 application fee and $1,275 for material representing payment at the rate of one dollar per cubic yard, have been tendered. The applicant will be entitled to a refund of $637.50 as charge for material in Martin County is only 50¢ per cubic yard.

The biological report is not adverse and the Department of Air and Water Pollution Control has no objections.

The Game and Fresh Water Fish Commission has no objection providing the dredge area is "diapered" and the spoil area is adequately diked.

The staff recommends issuance of the dredge permit.

ACTION OF THE TRUSTEES:

On motion by Mr. Conner, seconded by Mr. O'Malley and adopted without objection, the Trustees approved issuance of the dredge permit.

-10-

MARTIN COUNTY - Navigation access channel dredge permit
           File No. 253.123-602

    George E. Spicer
    Treasure Cove
    Post Office Box 253, Hobe Sound, Florida 33455,

applies for a dredge permit to connect two upland canals in Treasure Cove Subdivision with the intracoastal waterway through Hobe Sound.

The first channel connection dimensions will be -5 ft. deep, m.l.w. x 100 ft. long x 50 ft. wide (top cut), and the second will be -5 ft. deep m.l.w. x 80 ft. long x 100 ft. wide (top cut.) The total quantity of material to be excavated is 541 cubic yards, to be deposited on uplands. Payment of $270.50 has been tendered representing 50 cents per cubic yard for material, the established rate in Martin County.

The Department of Natural Resources biological report dated February 9, 1971, is favorable. The project was amended in accordance with recommendations of the Game and Fresh Water Fish Commission which indicated that channel connections should be reduced in size, the mangrove fringe preserved, and spoil deposited on uplands.

The Air and Water Pollution Control has no objection to this project.

Staff requests authority to issue dredge permit.

7-6-71

ACTION OF THE TRUSTEES:

On motion by Mr. O'Malley, seconded by Mr. Christian and Mr. Conner, adopted without objection, the Trustees authorized issuance of the dredge permit.

-11-

DADE COUNTY - Assignment Campsite Lease No. 2158A

Robert R. Bellamy & Read S. Ruggles, Jr.
810 Alfred I. DuPont Building, Miami, Florida,

holders of Campsite Lease No. 2158A which expires February 1, 1976, request assignment of the lease to Stiltsville, Inc., c/o Eugene M. Nesic, President, 250 Bird Road, Coral Gables, Florida.

Instrument of assignment and acceptance of terms and conditions, executed by both parties, have been approved by staff legal counsel.

Applicants have tendered $25 assignment fee in accordance with the Trustees' policy of December 1, 1970.

The staff recommends approval of assignment of Lease No. 2158A to Stiltsville, Inc.

ACTION OF THE TRUSTEES:

Mr. Kuperberg said there were no sanitary requirements in the stilthouse lease. The Governor noted that this was an assignment of an old lease, not an initial lease.

On motion by Mr. O'Malley, seconded by Mr. Christian and adopted without objection, the assignment was approved.

-12-

ESCAMBIA AND SANTA ROSA COUNTIES - Oil Lease Assignment

Marshall R. Young Oil Co., holder of Oil and Gas Drilling Lease No. 2464 dated September 1, 1970, covering a 205-acre portion of the Escambia River, requests approval of assignment

(1) of all of its interest in Parcel 1 of the leased area to the Louisiana Land and Exploration Company;

(2) an undivided one-half interest in Parcel 2 to each of the following: The Louisiana Land and Exploration Company and Humble Oil and Refining Company; and

(3) a 15-acre portion of the leased area identified as Parcel 3 to W. A. Moncrief, William K. Young, George M. Young, Frank G. Young and Marshall R. Young, Jr.

Assignment and acceptance executed by all parties has been reviewed and approved by staff counsel as to form and legality.

Recommend approval of assignment.

ACTION OF THE TRUSTEES:

The lease prohibited drilling in the river but would allow the state to obtain royalties from its fair share of the area.

On motion by Mr. Christian, seconded by Mr. O'Malley and adopted without objection, the Trustees approved the assignments.

329

-13-

<u>TRUSTEES' OFFICE</u>

<u>Staff requests authority</u> to retain Mr. J. Kenneth Ballinger
as special legal counsel for another 90-day period beginning
July 8, 1971. The need for his continued assistance is two-
fold: to continue working on the several cases in which he
has been involved; and to bridge the gap during the period
in which the new attorneys, being employed to fill the positions unfilled because of previous space limitations, are
assuming their new responsibilities.

ACTION OF THE TRUSTEES:

Mr. O'Malley questioned the wisdom of having as special legal
counsel for the Trustees a retired state employee who was a
registered lobbyist for a real estate organization. Mr. Kuperberg
explained that Mr. Ballinger was in the employ of the Board before
he became its Executive Director, had rendered real service on
special matters, and was held in very high regard for his integrity.

Governor Askew suggested a delay, without reflecting anything
adverse upon Mr. Ballinger, to allow the matter to be discussed
with Mr. Ballinger.

Without objection, action was deferred.

_____

-14-

<u>BAY COUNTY</u> - Consideration of a bulkhead line and advertisement
of a parcel of filled sovereignty land for sale to St. Andrews
Bay Yacht Club was withdrawn from the agenda.

_____

-15-

<u>PALM BEACH COUNTY</u> - Dredge Permit, 253.123-794

    Multicon Properties, Inc.
    3081 East Commercial Boulevard, Ft. Lauderdale, Florida,

requests that the Board consider issuing a <u>dredge permit only</u>
to cut four navigation entrance channels into the Hillsboro
Canal so that the applicant may proceed to obtain certification
from the Department of Air and Water Pollution Control which
would then allow submission of an application to the Corps of
Engineers for the federal permit. The applicant agrees not
to engage in any work authorized by the state permit until
the Trustees have taken appropriate action on the application
for approval of bulkhead line and the proposed sale.

The permit would allow removal of 5,285 cubic yards of material
from the four proposed channels to be stockpiled on the site
without any encroachment upon the sovereignty land being
advertised for sale.

The applicant has been advised that granting the dredge permit
would in no way commit the Trustees to sale of the 3.67 acres
now being advertised.

The Department of Air and Water Pollution Control and the Game
and Fresh Water Fish Commission have no objections to the
dredging. The Department of Natural Resources has indicated
that the proposed development would not have significant adverse
effects on the marine biological resources.

<u>Staff recommends that dredge permit only be granted, with the
understanding that it does not commit the Trustees to approve the
bulkhead line or sale of the submerged land applied for by
Multicon and with further understanding that this would merely
allow the applicant to obtain a water quality certificate and
file an application with the District Engineer.</u>

7-6-71

ACTION OF THE TRUSTEES:

By letter dated June 30, 1971, Multicon Properties, Inc., had acknowledged that the grant of this permit would not in any way obligate the Trustees to sell or otherwise dispose of the sovereignty land in question, and the corporation agreed not to engage in any work under the permit until the Trustees take action on the proposed sale and bulkhead line.

The Governor asked that the letter be made a part of the permit.

On motion by Mr. Stone, seconded by Mr. Christian and adopted without objection, the Trustees authorized issuance of the dredge permit on the conditions recommended by the staff and the commitment made by the corporation.

-16-

PALM BEACH COUNTY - Agriculture Lease Assignment

Recommend approval of assignment of Agriculture Lease No. 1766 from R. W. Bishop, Clewiston, Florida, to United States Sugar Corporation. The lease issued on June 1, 1962 for 20 years covers a 231.4 acre parcel of land in Section 27, Township 44 South, Range 35 East, Palm Beach County, located approximately six miles south of Lake Harbor.

Executed instrument of assignment and acceptance of all terms and conditions by U. S. Sugar Corporation has been reviewed and approved as to form and legality by staff legal counsel.

ACTION OF THE TRUSTEES:

Motion was made by Mr. Christian, seconded by Mr. Stone, that the assignment be approved.

Mr. O'Malley expressed unwillingness to accept assignment unless the applicant agreed to the inclusion of a provision currently placed in leases, but not in this older one, that the lessee shall not take land out of production to obtain federal subsidies. The Attorney General was asked to report at the next meeting whether the Trustees could require that additional provision, in the event the parties were not agreeable to its inclusion.

The motion as amended by Mr. Conner, adopted without objection, was that the assignment be approved subject to the parties agreeing to an additional provision prohibiting removal of the land from production to obtain a subsidy, the Attorney General to assist in drafting the provision.

-17-

ALACHUA COUNTY - Road Right of Way

On July 7, 1970, the Trustees authorized issuance of Easement 25139 for road purposes over and across a portion of the University of Florida campus, for the paving of SW 23rd Terrace.

Subsequently, the county has found it desirable to alter the route slightly and requests a new easement covering a portion of the existing right of way and the revised route.

The revised easement has been reviewed and approved by the University of Florida and Board of Regents. It rescinds and supersedes the previous easement.

Recommend issuance of the revised easement.

ACTION OF THE TRUSTEES:

On motion by Mr. Stone, seconded by Mr. Christian and adopted without objection, the Trustees authorized issuance of the revised easement.

Mr. Robert Thomas spoke with reference to an application in Hillsborough County that he said was similar to that numbered "8" on this date, but he had been unable to have it placed on the agenda because of the various reports from state environmental agencies causing delay in processing. He described it as a request for approval for disposition of spoil material dredged in widening a channel in the Port of Tampa.

Mr. Kuperberg explained that it was on the agenda early this year but was deferred for relocation of bulkhead lines by Tampa Port Authority and because the Department of Air and Water Pollution Control had not approved it. Mr. Thomas said he had a letter of approval from that department.

Governor Askew said the staff would explore the feasibility of placing the application on the agenda in the near future.

Attorney General Shevin discussed the Florida boundaries case, United States vs. Maine, in which the State of Florida was a party, and explained that the state was now litigating its own action in the case styled United States vs. Florida.

Mr. Shevin said the state boundaries were in dispute as to whether the three leagues boundary would be carried through Florida Bay, that almost a million acres in the Atlantic Ocean and the Gulf of Mexico were at stake for either the state or the federal government, and the basic problem was trying to establish that the Gulf Stream runs into the Atlantic. The outcome would be significant, he said, in connection with drilling and mining as well as various other aspects of ownership.

The Governor thanked Mr. Shevin for the report.

On motion duly adopted, the meeting was adjourned.

GOVERNOR   -   CHAIRMAN

ATTEST: _____
EXECUTIVE DIRECTOR

* * * *   * * * *

Tallahassee, Florida
July 20, 1971

The State of Florida Board of Trustees of the Internal Improvement Trust Fund met on this date in the auditorium of the Department of Transportation, with the following members present:

7-20-71

The minutes of June 29 were approved without objection.

-1-

MANATEE COUNTY - The request of Mr. A. M. Davis, Vice President
of Florida Power and Light Company, to be heard regarding
proposed dredging, was withdrawn from the agenda.

-2-

ESCAMBIA COUNTY - Road Right of Way

The Department of Transportation requests an easement over and
across 0.19 of an acre of land in the N 1/2 of Lot 2, Section 17,
Township 2 South, Range 30 West, in order to widen and improve
Leonard Avenue in Pensacola. The area requested is a portion
of a six-acre parcel under control of the Division of Health,
Department of Health and Rehabilitative Services, and used for
various Escambia County offices.

Both the Department of Health and Rehabilitative Services and
Escambia County have reviewed and approved the proposed easement.

Recommend issuance of the easement.

ACTION OF THE TRUSTEES:

On motion by Mr. Stone, seconded by Messrs. Dickinson and
Christian, and adopted without objection, the Trustees approved
issuance of the easement to the Department of Transportation.

-3-

DADE COUNTY - Lease Assignment

Recommend approval of assignment of Lease No. 1177 from Canaveral
Groves Development Company, Inc., to Sea Research, Inc., a Maine
corporation.

This lease dated April 15, 1958, is for a term of 30 years and
covers a 1.39 acre parcel located on the Miami River at 3300 N.W.
North River Drive in Miami. The assignment and acceptance of
assignment have been reviewed and approved by staff legal counsel
as to form and legality.

ACTION OF THE TRUSTEES:

On motion by Mr. Stone, seconded by Mr. Dickinson and adopted
without objection, the Trustees approved the lease assignment.

-4-

BROWARD COUNTY - Marina License, Section 253.03, Florida Statutes

   Jungle Queen, Inc. c/o McLaughlin Engineering Company
   400 Northeast 3rd Avenue, Fort Lauderdale, Florida 33301,

applies for a marina license for an area containing 2,100 sq. ft.
for enlargement of an existing facility in the South Fork of
New River abutting Section 17, Township 50 South, Range 42 East,
Broward County. No dredging is required. The minimum annual fee
of $100 has been tendered.

The Department of Natural Resources, the Game and Fresh Water
Fish Commission and the Department of Air and Water Pollution
Control have no objections to the proposed project.

Staff recommends approval.

ACTION OF THE TRUSTEES:

On motion by Mr. Christian, seconded by Mr. Dickinson and Mr.
O'Malley, and adopted without objection, the Trustees approved
issuance of the marina license.

-5-

DUVAL COUNTY - Dredge Permit, 253.123-738

   Wilfred R. Godard
   Post Office Box 26274, Jacksonville, Florida,

requests a dredge permit to connect an upland canal with the
land cut segment of the Intracoastal Waterway in Section 1,
Township 1 North, Range 28 East, Black Hammock Island, Duval County.

Applicant requests that there be no charge for the 5,000 cubic
yards of spoil material to be placed on uplands, since the
project lies within a land cut of the Intracoastal Waterway
and applicant has title to said lands. Staff field investigation
supports this claim.

The biological report for the modified project is not adverse.
The Game and Fresh Water Fish Commission and Air and Water
Pollution Control have no objections.

Staff recommends authority to issue a dredge permit and that
fee for spoil material be waived.

ACTION OF THE TRUSTEES:

On motion by Mr. Conner, seconded by Mr. Christian and adopted
without objection, the Trustees authorized issuance of the dredge
permit and waived the fee for the spoil material.

-6-

FRANKLIN COUNTY - Dredge Permit Modification 253.123-718

   Department of Natural Resources
   Larson Building, Tallahassee, Florida

requests modification of an existing project authorized by the
Trustees on March 10, 1971, that allowed maintenance dredging
of a channel 500 ft. by 50 ft. (top cut), excavating 2,000
cubic yards of material.

The modification would permit maintenance dredging of a channel
2770 ft. x 50 ft. (bottom cut), excavating approximately 22,000

7-20-71

cubic yards in Ochlockonee Bay, Section 1, Township 6 South, Range 2 West, Franklin County.

The biological report is not adverse. The Department of Air and Water Pollution Control certified the original project on March 25, 1971 (DF-19-205).

Staff requests authority to modify the dredge permit.

ACTION OF THE TRUSTEES:

On motion by Mr. O'Malley, seconded by Mr. Dickinson and adopted without objection, the Trustees authorized modification of the existing permit as requested by the Department of Natural Resources.

-7-

MONROE COUNTY - Construction Permit, Section 253.03 F. S.

    Key West Power Squadron
    Post Office Box 5, Key West, Florida,

requests after-the-fact construction permit for an existing shelter and piers in Mudd Key in Township 66 South, Range 26 East, Monroe County. Applicant requests that fees be waived because the facility provides dockage and shelter for the squadron and the general public for recreation and in times of emergency.

The Department of Natural Resources, Game and Fresh Water Fish Commission, and the Department of Air and Water Pollution Control have no objections.

Staff recommends authority to issue construction permit and that all fees be waived.

ACTION OF THE TRUSTEES:

On motion by Mr. Stone, seconded by Mr. Dickinson and adopted without objection, the Trustees authorized waiver of the fees and issuance of the construction permit.

-8-

Philip S. Bennett has resigned as General Counsel of the Board of Trustees of the Internal Improvement Trust Fund effective July 31, 1971. Mr. Bennett has requested to withdraw as attorney of record in all pending cases.

Staff recommends that Mr. Bennett be permitted to file a withdrawal on each case in which he is attorney of record.

ACTION OF THE TRUSTEES:

On motion by Mr. Dickinson, seconded by Messrs. Christian and Stone, and adopted without objection, the recommendation was accepted as the action of the Board.

Governor Askew extended the appreciation of the members to Mr. Bennett for the service he had rendered to the Trustees. Mr. Dickinson added that it was a job well done.

Mr. Kuperberg advised that background material on qualifications of the new staff counsel, Mr. Steve Turner, was being distributed to the members. Mr. O'Malley said he recognized the Director's responsibility to make his own choice in employing staff counsel, but as a member of the Board he would like to be informed in advance who was being considered to fill such a sensitive position. The Governor said the request would be accepted as from the Board for information to be furnished on a procedural basis in the future when consideration was being given to filling such a position as general counsel.

7-20-71

-9-

PATENTS, COPYRIGHTS AND TRADEMARKS

The Department of Citrus requested the Trustees to transfer all
of their right, title and interest in and to eight certain
patents and patent applications to the Department of Citrus.

Under Section 286.021, Florida Statutes, the Trustees are vested
with title to all patents, trademarks and copyrights held by the
State or any of its boards, commissions or agencies. Section
286.031, Florida Statutes, charges the Trustees with the use,
management and control of patents, copyrights, etc. Staff legal
counsel is of the opinion that the Trustees can permit the Department of Citrus to perform almost any act concerning the patents,
but the title must remain in the Trustees. The Attorney General
in 1969 by letter to the Department of Citrus and Opinion 069-81,
indicated a license arrangement would be the proper means of
granting use of patents to other boards, commissions or agencies
of the State. It is recommended that the Trustees grant authority
to the Department of Citrus by license or agreement to develop,
receive royalties and engage in other acts that may be necessary
with respect to the eight patents and patent applications.

ACTION OF THE TRUSTEES:

Secretary of State Stone understood the legislative intent was to
centralize all properties of the state in one department, and
the Trustees' records would show each transaction or disposition.

Mr. O'Malley pointed out that the staff recommendation was based
on the Attorney General's recommendation. He made a motion for
approval.

Mr. Monterey Campbell, attorney for the Citrus Commission, objected
to the recommendation, requesting transfer by assignment. He
discussed the position of the Citrus Commission, the historical
basis for his request and expressed the opinion that it could be
done at the Board's discretion as title was needed by the Commission in negotiating with companies on the patents. He said
that royalties had not entered into the picture in the past but
rather improvement of the citrus industry.

Mr. Conner felt that when trust funds can generate revenue it was
commendable and lightened the burden of general revenue. He
would like to see the benefits accrue to those attempting to be
self-supporting.

At the request of the Governor, action was delayed for two weeks.

-10-

PALM BEACH COUNTY - Fill Permit 253.124-187, and
                    Amendment to Dredge Permit 253.123-762

The application of Vista Builders, Inc., was deferred two weeks
at the request of the staff.

-11-

DUVAL COUNTY - Dredge Permit 253.123-787

    Harrell's Marine, Inc.
    2315 Beach Boulevard, Jacksonville, Florida 32250,

requests a dredge permit for maintenance excavation of existing
navigation channels. The 3,727 cubic yards of spoil material
will be deposited on previously-used spoil areas on upland
adjacent to Intracoastal Waterway in Section 32, Township 2 South,
Range 29 East, Duval County. All material will be retained
within adequate dikes.

Applicant requests that the $1.00 per cubic yard fee for fill
material be waived, and provided a signed affidavit from Lake
G. Ray, Jr. Professional Engineer, stating that the spoil
material consists entirely of silt and muck with no value what-
soever for use as fill.

Department of Air and Water Pollution Control has no objections.
The Game and Fresh Water Fish Commission has no objections providing
the spoil is adequately diked. The biological report is not adverse.

Staff recommends issuance of the dredge permit and that the fee not
be waived.

ACTION OF THE TRUSTEES:

Mr. Stone made a motion, seconded by Mr. Dickinson, that the
staff recommendation be accepted.

The staff had discussed the matter with the applicant, and as
the dredge was ready to proceed he had agreed to pay for the
material. Mr. Kuperberg said that while the material being removed from sovereignty land was certified as being without value
and the applicant would have to pay for depositing it on upland,
the staff had no core borings, only twelve on the staff to cover
the whole state on investigations, and an extension of a waiver
policy on other major projects might be difficult to administer.

Treasurer O'Malley felt that the state should not make a charge
for a waste item. Mr. Conner agreed, commenting that the Board
would get the reputation of being arbitrary.

Mr. Douglas Crane, representing Harrell's Marine, Inc., explained
that maintenance was a continuing process, dredging was required
about every four years and the silt was totally worthless and
disposition was an expense to the applicant.

Mr. O'Malley recognized the staff problem but thought it should
not be the state's responsibility to make the determination. He
was not satisfied with a signed affidavit but would want some
type of test borings. He offered an amendment to the motion,
accepted by Mr. Stone, that the permit be issued with a provision
that if the applicant provided evidence acceptable to the Director
that borings have been made showing the material to be of no
value as fill material, then the total fee might be waived.

Governor Askew suggested that the staff study a proposed policy
for a situation where there is reason to believe that all is
not silt.

Without objection, the Trustees adopted the amended motion, seconded
by Mr. Stone, to grant the permit and waive payment conditioned upon
the Director receiving adequate evidence that the material removed is
worthless, this waiver not to be considered a precedent.

-12-

COLLIER COUNTY - Marco Island Development Corporation
            (a) File No. 253.123.51
            (b) File Nos. 253.123-678. 253.124-149

Results of negotiations with Marco Island Development Corporation
will be reported.

ACTION OF THE TRUSTEES:

Mr. Kuperberg thanked the Mackles for their cooperation, the
Trustees for their patience, and the Governor for his active
participation in the negotiations between the Executive Director

and Marco Island Development Corporation (and its parent company The Deltona Corporation both referred to as MIDC). Copy of a letter from Mr. Frank Mackle and attached Memorandum of Understanding had been furnished to each member, outlining the results of the negotiations with respect to the terms and conditions under which development of MIDC's holdings in Townships 51 South, 52 South and 53 South, Collier County, would proceed. The further purpose of the memorandum was to form a basis for the drafting and implementation of a definitive agreement.

Mr. Kuperberg recommended the extension of the Roberts Bay permit (File 253.123-51) to December 1972, and the Marco River permit (File 253.123-678, 253.124-149) to December 1971, to correspond with the existing Corps of Engineers permits, the time of extension to be conditioned upon the execution of the final agreement within 45 days.

Motion was made by Mr. Christian, seconded by Mr. O'Malley, that the recommendation be accepted.

Governor Askew commended Mr. Kuperberg, the staff and the representatives of Deltona for the tremendous amount of time spent and the excellent results. He pointed out that the state would be given valuable land including Kice Island with two miles of beachfront and Liquor Still Key, dredge requirements were restricted leaving undisturbed mangrove areas around the border of Horr's Island; and together with the possibility of acquisition of lands by the federal government and securing lands from Collier Conservancy and the Nature Conservancy plus the possible state acquisition of Cape Romano, a tremendous conservation package would be put together. The Governor thanked the Mackles for the extent they were willing to go to work out a problem that had not been a violation of the law at the time, but the law had changed and the Mackles were making the change and a substantial contribution to the state.

Governor Askew made it clear that in granting the permits, the Trustees set a time limit of 45 days from today in which a final agreement should be executed consistent with the Memorandum of Understanding, or the permits would be subject to revocation.

Motion with the 45-day time limit amendment was made by Mr. Stone, seconded by Mr. O'Malley and adopted without objection.

Mr. Dickinson expressed the appreciation of the Trustees for the excellent solution for the Mackles and the State of Florida.

Mr. George Salley was heard at the request of Mr. Conner, with regard to the sugar industry of Florida. On behalf of Okeelanta Sugar Mill owned by the Food Products Division of Gulf and Western Industries, Mr. Salley proposed an exchange of land owned by Okeelanta for two sections of state-owned land practically the same distance from Lake Okeechobee, that would open up about 2,800 acres for sugarcane cultivation and therefore would benefit the state.

Mr. Conner said the staff might not be prepared to make a recommendation but might explore the possibility of a trade that would not be to the disadvantage of the state. The Governor added that there might be something as an incentive to the state, and a trade would have to be advertised.

Mr. O'Malley brought up the need for a waiver of the rules, whereupon motion was made by Mr. Conner and seconded by Mr. Christian that the rules be waived.

Mr. Conner then made a motion, seconded by Mr. Dickinson, that the staff be instructed to evaluate Mr. Salley's request and bring the Board a recommendation.

The Governor said the waiver of the rules passed with five votes, the matter had been discussed and the request was made to Mr. Kuperberg to come back with some policy.

Mr. Conner expressed the opinion that the information package offered by Mr. Salley was very important, and misunderstandings about subsidies should be clarified. A portion of the amount that had been assessed to the growers was a rebate for compliance with the sugarcane act, not a subsidy.

Mr. Salley asked the Trustees to tour the sugarcane area at the invitation of the Florida Sugarcane League to gain a better understanding of the industry and the good conditions provided for agricultural workers.

On motion duly adopted, the meeting was adjourned.

GOVERNOR   -   CHAIRMAN

ATTEST:

EXECUTIVE DIRECTOR

*   *   *   *   *   *   *

Tallahassee, Florida
August 3, 1971

The State of Florida Board of Trustees of the Internal Improvement Trust Fund met on this date in the auditorium of the Department of Transportation, with the following members present:

Reubin O'D. Askew	Governor
Robert L. Shevin	Attorney General
Fred O. Dickinson, Jr.	Comptroller
Thomas D. O'Malley	Treasurer
Joel Kuperberg	Executive Director

The minutes of the meeting held on July 6, 1971, were approved as submitted.

-1-

PALM BEACH COUNTY - Application to Advertise
          TIITF File No. 2414-50-253.36

     Clewiston Syrup Mill, Inc., c/o Howard S. Rhodes
     Post Office Box 1480, Collins Arcade, Ft. Myers, Florida

Staff requests authority to advertise for objections only the sale of a 100 ft. strip of reclaimed lake bottom in Sections 18 and 19, Township 43 South, Range 35 East, embracing 3.78 acres in Palm Beach County. The land would be used for a public recreational camping park.

The Board of County Commissioners of Palm Beach County and of Hendry County, the City Commission and the Board of Directors of the Chamber of Commerce of Clewiston, all state that the creation of the proposed recreational camping park would be in the public interest.

8-3-71

The Department of Natural Resources, the Game and Fresh Water Fish Commission and the Department of Air and Water Pollution Control have no objections.

Staff requests authority to advertise for sale this surplus canal right-of-way.

ACTION OF THE TRUSTEES:

On motion by Mr. Dickinson, seconded by Mr. Shevin and adopted without objection, the Trustees authorized advertisement of the surplus canal right-of-way for sale.

-2-

MONROE COUNTY - Application for Quitclaim Deed
                File No. 2391-44-253.12(6)

The application of the Branigar Organization, Inc., was withdrawn from the agenda because only four members of the Board were present.

-3-

MURPHY ACT REPORT - Sale of lots in Nassau, Marion and
                    Okaloosa Counties

Consideration of Report No. 988 listing 24 regular bids for sale of lots under provisions of Section 197.350, Florida Statutes, was withdrawn from the agenda because only four members of the Board were present.

-4-

ESCAMBIA COUNTY - Advertise Oil and Gas Lease

    Southeastern Exploration, Ltd.,
    Jackson, Mississippi,

requests the Board to advertise for sealed bids for a five-year oil and gas drilling lease covering the reserved one-half interest of the State in the petroleum and petroleum products in a 3.1 acre parcel in NW 1/4 of NW 1/4 of Section 11, Township 5 North, Range 33 West, Escambia County.

This request has been reviewed by the State Geologist, who concurs in the following recommendation.

Recommend advertising for sealed bids for lease with an annual rental of $1 per net mineral acre, 1/6 royalty, five-year primary term, $50,000 surety bond and at least one test well required to be drilled to 6,000 feet or to a depth sufficient to test the Norphlet Sands, whichever is deeper.

ACTION OF THE TRUSTEES:

On motion by Mr. O'Malley, seconded and adopted without objection, the Trustees authorized advertisement for sealed bids for an oil and gas lease as recommended by the staff.

8-3-71

-5-

SANTA ROSA COUNTY - Advertise Oil and Gas Lease

    The Louisiana Land and Exploration Company
    New Orleans, Louisiana,

requests the Board to advertise for sealed bids for a five-year
oil and gas drilling lease covering the reserved one-half interest
of the State in the petroleum and petroleum products in Lots 1 and
2 , Section 28, Township 6 North, Range 29 West, containing 80
surface acres in Santa Rosa County.

This request has been reviewed by the State Geologist who concurs
in the following recommendation.

Recommend advertising for sealed bids for lease with an annual
rental of $1 per net mineral acre, 1/6 royalty, five-year primary
term, $50,000 surety bond and at least one test well required to
be drilled to 6,000 feet or to a depth sufficient to test the
Norphlet Sands, whichever is deeper.

ACTION OF THE TRUSTEES:

On motion by Mr. O'Malley, seconded and adopted without objection,
the Trustees authorized advertisement for sealed bids for an oil
and gas lease as recommended by the staff.

-6-

SANTA ROSA COUNTY - Advertise Oil and Gas Lease

    Sun Oil Company,
    Dallas, Texas,

requests the Board to advertise for sealed bids for a five-year
oil and gas drilling lease covering the reserved one-half interest
of the State in the petroleum and petroleum products in the
N 1/2 of NW 1/4 of SE 1/4 of SE 1/4, Section 22, Township 5 North,
Range 29 West, containing 5 surface acres in Santa Rosa County.

This request has been reviewed by the State Geologist, who
concurs in the following recommendation.

Recommend advertising for sealed bids for lease with an annual
rental of $1 per net mineral acre, 1/6 royalty, five-year primary
term, $50,000 surety bond and at least one test well required to
be drilled to 6,000 feet or to a depth sufficient to test the
Norphlet Sands, whichever is deeper.

ACTION OF THE TRUSTEES:

On motion by Mr. O'Malley, seconded and adopted without objection,
the Trustees authorized advertisement for sealed bids for an oil
and gas lease as recommended by the staff.

-7-

CLAY COUNTY - Right of Way Easement, File 2404-10-253.03
               Dredge Permit 253.123-864
               Fill Permit 253.124-199

    Department of Transportation
    Tallahassee, Florida,

requests a right-of-way easement embracing 3.0 acres of sovereignty
land in Black Creek abutting Sections 28 and 38, Township 5 South,
Range 26 East and right-of-way easement embracing 2.41 acres of
sovereignty land in Governor's Creek abutting Section 37, Township
6 South, Range 26 East, Clay County, necessary for the construction
of two bridges for State Road No. 15.

The Department of Air and Water Pollution Control, the Game and Fresh Water Fish Commission and the Department of Natural Resources have no objections to the proposed easements.

Dredging and filling are not required for the Governor's Creek project. The Black Creek project will require the excavation of 1,700 cubic yards of muck to be placed on upland and replaced with 600 cubic yards of fill material obtained from uplands.

The Department of Air and Water Pollution Control certified the dredge and fill operations on July 21, 1971. The biological report for the project is not adverse. The Game and Fresh Water Fish Commisssion offers no objections.

The Board of County Commissioners of Clay County granted a dredge and fill permit on June 8, 1971.

Staff recommends issuance of the two right-of-way easements, approval of the county's action and requests authority to issue the neces- sary permits.

ACTION OF THE TRUSTEES:

On motion by Mr. Dickinson, seconded by Mr. Shevin and Mr. O'Malley, and adopted without objection, the Trustees approved issuance of the two right-of-way easements to the Department of Transportation, approved the action of the Board of County Commissioners of Clay County, and authorized issuance of the necessary permits.

-8-

DUVAL COUNTY - Right of Way Easement
            TIITF No. 2409-16-253.03

> Department of Transportation
> Tallahassee, Florida,

requests a right of way easement covering 3.2 acres of sovereignty land in the Ortega River in Section 42 (McIntosh Grant), Township 3 South, Range 26 East, Duval County.

The easement is necessary for construction of a bridge crossing at Timuquana Road. No dredging or filling will be required.

The Department of Natural Resources, the Game and Fresh Water Fish Commission and the Department of Air and Water Pollution Control have no objections.

Staff requests authority to issue the easement.

ACTION OF THE TRUSTEES:

On motion by Mr. Dickinson, seconded by Mr. Shevin and Mr. O'Malley, and adopted without objection, the Trustees approved issuance of the right-of-way easement to the Department of Transportation.

-9-

DADE COUNTY - Fill Permit 253.124-190

> Department of Transportation
> Tallahassee, Florida,

requests a permit to fill approximately 10 acres south of State Road 826 (79th Street Causeway) in Biscayne Bay, conveyed to Dade County by Trustees Deed No. 18251, dated July 31, 1934, for public purposes only.

8-3-71

A portion of the project has been previously filled under Fill
Permit No. 253.124-101 dated October 29, 1969. The fill will be
hauled to the site and the area elevated to a +4.0 feet. The
City of Miami approved the project by Resolution No. 42535
dated April 22, 1971.

The biological survey report stated that the proposed filling would
have limited adverse effects on marine biological resources.

The Game and Fresh Water Fish Commission had no objections, as the
project will be in the public interest and on unproductive bottoms.
The Department of Air and Water Pollution Control had no objection.

Staff recommends that a fill permit be approved subject to the
public purpose covenant contained in the referenced Trustees' Deed.

ACTION OF THE TRUSTEES:

On motion by Mr. O'Malley, seconded by Mr. Dickinson and Mr. Shevin,
and adopted without objection, the Trustees approved issuance of
the fill permit to the Department of Transportation subject to
the public purpose covenant in Deed No. 18251.

-10-

DUVAL COUNTY - Fill Permit, File No. 253.124(8)-184

Tilly Adams, c/o Eagle Marine,
1604 Kingswood Road, Jacksonville, Florida 32207,

requests approval of a fill permit issued by the City of Jacksonville by Resolution 71-107-52 to construct a seawall and
backfill on a private lot adjacent to St. Johns River.

The fill material is stockpiled on the upland and applicant
proposes to fill only an area lost by avulsion and artificially
induced erosion.

The Department of Natural Resources and the Game and Fresh Water
Fish Commission have no objections. Our Field Operations report
substantiates the claim that applicant is applying in accordance
with Chapter 253.124(8) pertaining to reclamation of land lost by
avulsion and/or artificially induced erosion.

Staff recommends approval of the fill permit issued by the City of
Jacksonville.

ACTION OF THE TRUSTEES:

The Director pointed out that under the special act, parties have
the right to restore land lost by avulsion or artificially induced
erosion.
On motion by Mr. Dickinson, seconded by Mr. O'Malley and adopted
without objection, the Trustees approved the fill permit issued
by the City of Jacksonville to Tilly Adams.

-11-

DUVAL COUNTY - Fill Permit 253.124(8)

Kathryn Fortson
3875 Ortega Boulevard, Jacksonville, Florida 32210,

requests approval of permit issued by the City of Jacksonville by
Resolution 70-1229-421 to restore a seawall and backfill on
Lot 2, Ortega Subdivision bordering on the St. Johns River, in
accordance with the provisions of Chapter 253.124(8) pertaining
to reclamation of land lost to avulsion and artificially induced
erosion.

The fill material will be trucked in.

The Department of Natural Resources and the Game and Fresh Water Fish Commission have no objections.

Staff recommends approval of the fill permit issued by the City of Jacksonville.

ACTION OF THE TRUSTEES:

On motion by Mr. Dickinson, seconded by Mr. O'Malley and adopted without objection, the Trustees approved the fill permit issued by the City of Jacksonville to Kathryn Fortson.

-12

GULF COUNTY - Dredge and Fill, Seawall, and Jetties Construction, TIITF No. 253.123-796

 Department of Natural Resources,
 Division of Recreation and Parks
 J. Edwin Larson Building
 Tallahassee, Florida 32304

requests a dredge permit to excavate approximately 4,500 cubic yards of spoil from an existing boat basin and channel in St. Joseph State Park in Section 24, Township 8 South, Range 12 West, in Gulf County. The spoil will be placed along the shoreline to establish a low energy beach behind proposed jetties of concrete bags.

The biological report is not adverse. The Department of Natural Resources issued a coastal construction permit (BBS 71-15) on June 8, 1971.

The Game and Fresh Water Fish Commission has no objection. The Department of Air and Water Pollution Control certified the project on July 7, 1971.

Staff requests authority to issue a dredge permit.

ACTION OF THE TRUSTEES:

On motion by Mr. Dickinson, seconded by Mr. O'Malley and adopted without objection, the Board authorized issuance of the dredge permit to the Department of Natural Resources.

-13-

OKALOOSA COUNTY - Fill Permit 253.124(8) - 188

 Robert Maxon, c/o Barrow & Holly
 Crestview, Florida,

requests a permit to fill areas in Section 6, Township 2 South, Range 23 West, below the present mean high water line behind a proposed seawall that generally follows the present mean high water line in Garniers Bayou.

The applicant requests permission to fill in accordance with Chapter 253.124(8) pertaining to reclamation of land lost by avulsion or artificially induced erosion. The biological report and our Field Operations Division report substantiate the claim that former upland property has eroded away.

The fill material will be trucked in.

Staff requests authority to issue a fill permit.

8-3-71

ACTION OF THE TRUSTEES:

On motion by Mr. O'Malley, seconded by Mr. Dickinson and adopted without objection, the Board authorized issuance of a fill permit for this land restoration project.

-14-

PALM BEACH COUNTY - Fill Permit, 253.124-187

    Vista Builders, Inc., c/o Albert J. Marinello
    2 North Federal Highway, Boca Raton, Florida 33432,

requests approval of a fill permit issued by the City of Boca Raton on June 29, 1971, to construct a seawall and backfill along Intracoastal right-of-way line. The proposed project is located in Sections 32 and 33, Township 46 South, Range 43 East, Palm Beach County. The marginal lands proposed to be filled with approximately 10,000 cubic yards of material are in private ownership. The Trustees granted a dredge permit No. 253.123-762 on June 8, 1971, to overdredge the Intracoastal Waterway to -16 feet adjacent to this area.

The biological report is not adverse; however, Department of Natural Resources recommends that a small area of white mangroves growing in this area should not be disturbed.

The Department of Air and Water Pollution Control has granted a water quality certificate for the project. The Game and Fresh Water Fish Commission and Palm Beach County Area Planning Board have no objection to the proposed project.

The field investigation revealed minor filling done upon the director of the City of Boca Raton for the purpose of establishing property corners of the lands subject to filling.

Staff recommends that fill permit granted by the city be approved.

ACTION OF THE TRUSTEES:

In answer to questions by Mr. Shevin and the Governor, Mr. Kuperberg said he was satisfied that the work was in accordance with requirements. There had been a minor technical violation in that some material was pushed into place in order to locate the property boundaries or the seawall line, and the staff had carefully reviewed the work several times. He added that the party who had lodged a complaint had not contacted the Trustees' office.

On motion by Mr. O'Malley, seconded by Mr. Dickinson and adopted without objection, the Board approved the fill permit issued by the City of Boca Raton.

-15-

COLLIER COUNTY - State Construction Permit
               Automatic Recording Tide Gauges

    Marco Island Development Corporation
    Post Office Box 68, Marco Island, Florida 33937,

applies for a state construction permit for placing three automatic recording tide gauges in the Gulf of Mexico, Big Marco River and Barfield Bay, in Township 52 South, Range 26 East, Collier County.

Staff recommends approval of permit subject to applicant submitting $100 processing fee.

ACTION OF THE TRUSTEES:

On motion by Mr. O'Malley, seconded by Mr. Dickinson and adopted without objection, the Trustees authorized issuance of a state construction permit upon receipt of the $100 processing fee.

-16-

VOLUSIA COUNTY - Dredge Permit 253.123-826
Marina License

> Florida Power and Light Company
> c/o Norris R. Kincaid
> Post Office Box 3100, Miami, Florida 33101,

applies for a permit to dredge approximately 3,500 cubic yards in
Section 16, Township 19 South, Range 30 East, from an existing
boat basin to enlarge docking space in St. Johns River adjacent
to Florida Power and Light plant near Lake Monroe, Volusia County.
The applicant has tendered check for $3,500 representing $1 per
cubic yard for material to be removed from sovereignty lands.
This material will be placed on applicant's upland.

Applicant also proposes to install six additional mooring dolphins
covering an area of 14,428 sq. ft. The marina license fee of
$288.56 has been tendered.

The biological report prepared by the Game and Fresh Water Fish
Commission under the direction of the Department of Natural
Resources is not adverse.

The Department of Air and Water Pollution Control certified the
project on April 21, 1971.

The staff requests authority to issue dredge permit and marina
license.

ACTION OF THE TRUSTEES:

On motion by Mr. Dickinson, seconded by Mr. O'Malley and adopted
without objection, the Board approved issuance of the dredge
permit and marina license.

Mr. Kuperberg explained that under Trustees' permit procedures
there was no other way to classify the application, which was
not for a commercial marina but a place to dock oil barges.

-17-

DADE COUNTY - Marina License - Section 253.03, F. S.

> R. E. J. Investments, Inc.
> c/o Auto Marine Engineers, Inc.,
> 3464 NW North River Drive, Miami, Florida 33142,

requests a marina license for existing mooring pilings covering
674 square feet in the Miami River adjacent to Section 1, Township 54 South, Range 41 East, Dade County. The minimum annual
fee of $100 has been tendered. No dredging is required.

The Department of Natural Resources, the Game and Fresh Water
Fish Commission, the Department of Air and Water Pollution Control,
and the Florida Inland Navigation District have no objections to
the facility.

Staff recommends approval.

ACTION OF THE TRUSTEES:

On motion made by Mr. O'Malley, seconded by Mr. Dickinson and
adopted without objection, the Trustees authorized issuance of
the marina license at the minimum fee of $100.

8-3-71

-18-

MARTIN COUNTY - Marina License, Section 253.03, Florida Statutes

>   Stuart Land Development, Inc.
>   c/o Thurlow and Thurlow
>   Post Office Box 775, Stuart, Florida 33494,

applies for a marina license covering 8,696 square feet in the
Indian River abutting Section 30, Township 37 South, Range 42
East, Martin County. No dredging is required. The minimum annual
fee is $173.92.

The Department of Natural Resources, the Game and Fresh Water Fish
Commission, and the Department of Air and Water Pollution have
offered no objections.

Staff recommends approval of the marina license.

ACTION OF THE TRUSTEES:

On motion made by Mr. Dickinson, seconded by Mr. O'Malley and
adopted without objection, the Trustees authorized issuance of
the marina license.

-19-

OKEECHOBEE COUNTY - Marina Licenses, Bait and Tackle Shops,
                    Section 253.03, F. S.

(1)   Ray's Fish Camp, c/o Ray Watson
      601 West North Street, Okeechobee, Florida

(2)   Earl's Fish Camp, c/o Earl W. Bertram
      1310 Avenue B, Okeechobee, Florida

Pursuant to investigations by Field Operations Division, applications have been filed by the above parties for after the fact
marina licenses for the existing bait and tackle sales barges
along the northwest shore of Lake Okeechobee.

The Corps of Engineers, the Game and Fresh Water Fish Commission,
and the Department of Natural Resources have no objections.

The Board of County Commissioners of Okeechobee County and the
Central and Southern Florida Flood Control District have objected
to the existing facilities. The Department of Air and Water Pollution Control has withheld comment.

Staff recommends denial and requests authorization to have the
facilities removed from the premises.

ACTION OF THE TRUSTEES:

Motion was made by Mr. Shevin and seconded by Mr. Dickinson that
the Board follow the staff recommendations and deny both requests.

Mr. O'Malley, noting that there was no objections from three
agencies and that denial would put two people out of business,
asked for deferral for study of the basis for objections as well
as the non-objections.

The previous motion and second were withdrawn. On a motion by
Mr. O'Malley, seconded by the Comptroller and adopted without
objection, the Trustees deferred action until August 31 pending
further study.

POLK COUNTY - Marina License, Section 253.03, Florida Statutes

    Fountainview Estates
    c/o Nelson Steiner, Lake Development Co.
    8800 Sheldon Road, Tampa, Florida 33615,

applies for a marina license for a fishing pier facility covering
1,700 square feet in Lake Gibson abutting Section 25, Township
27 South, Range 23 East, Polk County. No dredging is required and
the minimum annual fee of $100 has been tendered.

The Department of Natural Resources and the Department of Air
and Water Pollution Control have no objections to the proposed
project.

The Game and Fresh Water Fish Commission indicated that an alleged
unauthorized dredge and fill operation has taken place at the site.
An inspection by the Field Operations Division indicates less than
one-fifth of an acre has been cleared of aquatic vegetation and
no encroachments were witnessed at the proposed marina facility.

<u>Staff recommends issuance of marina license.</u>

ACTION OF THE TRUSTEES:

Motion was made by Mr. O'Malley, seconded by Mr. Dickinson and
adopted without objection, that the marina license be approved.

-21-

SARASOTA COUNTY - Marina License Section 253.03, Florida Statutes

    Frederick F. Lutz
    1810 Phillippi Shores Drive, Sarasota, Florida 33581,

applies for a marina license for a docking and unloading facility
covering 1,870 square feet in Phillippi Creek abutting Section 7,
Township 37 South, Range 18 East Sarasota County. The minimum
annual fee of $100 has been tendered.

The Sarasota County Water and Navigation Control Authority has
granted a minor work permit No. 71-16 for the project. No
dredging is required.

The Department of Natural Resources, Game and Fresh Water Fish
Commission and the Department of Air and Water Pollution Control
have offered no objections.

<u>Staff recommends approval.</u>

ACTION OF THE TRUSTEES:

Motion was made by Mr. O'Malley, seconded by Mr. Dickinson and
adopted without objection, that the marina license be approved.

-22-

MARTIN COUNTY - Fill Permit, Seawall
                 File No. 253.124(8)-189

    Hobe Sound North, Inc.
    Gee & Jenson, Consulting Engineers, West Palm Beach, Florida,

requests approval of a permit issued by Martin County to fill
an area landward of the west right of way line of the artificial
cut of the Intracoastal Waterway, Jupiter River section, Gomez
Grant in Township 39 South, Range 42 East, in accordance with the
provisions in Chapter 253.124(8) pertaining to reclaiming land lost
by avulsion or artificially induced erosion.

A field inspection report states that erosion has occurred due to
wakes from heavy boat traffic on the Intracoastal Waterway.

940 cubic yards of fill will be obtaine ｌ ｏ ｌ ．．．sources and
no dredging will occur.

Staff requests authority to issue a fill permit.

ACTION OF THE TRUSTEES:

On motion by Mr. Dickinson, seconded by Mr. O'Malley and adopted
without objection, the Board approved issuance of the fill permit.

-23-

PRIVATE DOCK PERMITS - Procedure

In the interest of better serving the public and to reduce the
handling time required to issue a private dock permit, after
August 10, 1971, private dock permits will be processed by
the Trustees' area offices as follows:

1. Applications will be accepted by the area office
    and assigned to a field inspector.
2. The field inspector will make an on-site inspection
    indicating on a sketch the dimensions and the location
    of the proposed dock with respect to the applicant's
    waterfront ownership.
3. The area office will mail application and exhibits
    along with applicant's check for $25 to the Trustees'
    Tallahassee office.
4. A dock permit will be issued and mailed to applicant with
    copy to the area office.
5. Area office will make final inspection and close file,
    if in order.

Recommend increasing the processing fee for private docks to
$25 and approval of the above procedure.

ACTION OF THE TRUSTEES:

The Director requested affirmation of a procedure whereby the
regional offices would assist in processing more rapidly the many
private dock permit applications. An increased fee of $25 was
proposed to cover two inspection trips to check the site and the
completed construction, often a concern or dispute between adjoining property owners.

The proposed fee increase was discussed. The Governor said it should
be fair to the state to offset the cost of the inspection trips.
Since that might depend on the distance to be traveled by field
operations staff, the Comptroller suggested a schedule of fees
taking such factors into account, to be brought back to the Board
for study.

On motion by Mr. Shevin, seconded by Mr. O'Malley and adopted without objection, the Board approved the private dock permit procedure
recommended by the staff. The Director was asked to review the
permit fees and recommend action to take care of the costs in any
instances where the regional office could not handle inspections
without extra expense.

-24-

MANATEE COUNTY - Dredge Permit Application, Florida Power and
                 Light Company

The staff was prepared to agenda and recommend on this application
but upon request of the applicant, the matter was deferred so that
the company might make further preparation for a presentation.

-25-

TRUSTEES' PERSONNEL

The Director of the Land Management Division, Fred Vidzes, has
submitted his resignation effective August 31, 1971, and it has
been accepted by the Executive Director with regret.

Governor Askew complimented Mr. Vidzes for his many years of
service to the Trustees, particularly for that period of time
when he served as acting director.

-26-

HILLSBOROUGH COUNTY - Dredge Permits

    Eastern Associated Terminals (253.123-807)
    Post Office Box 18666, Tampa, Florida 33608, and

    Seaboard Coast Line Railroad Terminals (253.123-808)
    Post Office Box 5025, Tampa, Florida 33605

request that dredge permits 253.123-807 and 808 authorized by the
Board on July 6, 1971, be amended by striking the words, "all
dredging is to be accomplished by dragline method."

The change of the spoil area, as requested by the staff, from
Hookers Point to an upland area east of the terminal and north
of Delaney Creek (relocated) necessitates the use of a hydraulic
dredge rather than a dragline.

The Department of Air and Water Pollution Control, the Department
of Natural Resources and the Game and Fresh Water Fish Commission
have no objections.

Staff recommends that the two dredge permits be amended to permit
hydraulic dredging.

ACTION OF THE TRUSTEES:

On motion by Mr. Dickinson, seconded by Mr. O'Malley and adopted
without objection, the Trustees approved amendment of the two
dredge permits to allow hydraulic dredging.

Governor Askew commented on the report, "Organic Soil Survey of
Agricultural Area South of Lake Okeechobee." The Director said
he hoped all members could read this very significant report
requested by the Governor. He expected to review it with Commissioner of Agriculture Conner and make specific recommendations
as a result of the report.

On motion duly adopted, the meeting was adjourned.

                                        GOVERNOR - CHAIRMAN

ATTEST:

           EXECUTIVE DIRECTOR

    *   *   *   *

8-3-71

Tallahassee, Florida
August 17, 1971

The State of Florida Board of Trustees of the Internal Improvement Trust Fund met on this date in the auditorium of the Department of Transportation, with the following members present:

Richard (Dick) Stone   Secretary of State, Acting Chairman
Robert L. Shevin   Attorney General
Fred O. Dickinson, Jr.   Comptroller
Thomas D. O'Malley   Treasurer
Floyd T. Christian   Commissioner of Education
Doyle Conner   Commissioner of Agriculture

Joel Kuperberg   Executive Director

The minutes of the meeting of July 20, 1971, were approved as
submitted.

-1-

QUARTERLY REPORT - For the record

A report of operations of the State of Florida Board of Trustees
of the Internal Improvement Trust Fund for the three-month period
from April through June 30, 1971, was received by the Board.
The quarterly report was received.

-2-

PRINTING TRUSTEES' MINUTES, VOLUME 37

Request authority to invite bids for printing and binding 150
copies of Volume 37 of the minutes of the Trustees, the repro-
duction to be by photo-lithographic process, 10 copies in full
sheepskin binding and balance paper cover stock uniform with
the preceding volume. Funds are available within the approved
operating budget.

ACTION OF THE TRUSTEES:

Mr. Kuperberg said it was a regular request for the usual printing
of the minutes that was done every two years.

Commenting that it was public records, Mr. Dickinson made a
motion, seconded by Mr. O'Malley and adopted without objection,
that the staff be authorized to invite bids for printing and
binding Volume 37 of the minutes.

-3-

HILLSBOROUGH COUNTY - Relocation of Bulkhead lines

On July 6 the Trustees withdrew the moratorium on issuance of
dredge and fill permits in Hillsborough County for a 45-day conditional
period pending receipt by the Trustees of further information.

Since the end of the conditional period would expire prior to the
next scheduled meeting of the Board on August 31, Mr. Kuperberg
reported that a resolution had been received from the Tampa Port
Authority restoring all bulkhead lines in the area to the line of
mean high water, save those instances where there is some contractual
agreement in force. It appeared that no action by the Trustees
was necessary, but if such action had not been taken by the Authority
the moratorium would have been reinstated.

4

ST. LUCIE COUNTY - Bulkhead Line, Section 253.122 F. S.

The Trustees deferred consideration of a bulkhead line 1,169.0 feet long in the Indian River abutting Section 11, Township 37 South, Range 41 East, located by the Board of County Commissioners of St. Lucie County by Resolution No. 71-7 adopted on January 19, 1971. The staff had recommended denial.

PALM BEACH COUNTY - 1. Bulkhead Line Establishment
                  2. Application to Purchase
                    File No. 2370-50-253.12
                  3. Dredge and Fill Permits,
                    253.123-794 and 253.124-182

     Multicon Properties, Inc., applicant

On June 29 the Board authorized advertisement for objections to a proposed sale of 3.67 acres of sovereignty land along the north bank of the Hillsboro Canal in Section 31, Township 47 South, Range 43 East, City of Boca Raton, Palm Beach County. The notice showed August 17 as the date for consideration of the proposed sale.

Recommend deferral, as requested by the applicant.

ACTION OF THE TRUSTEES:

Since the application of Multicon Properties, Inc., was advertised in the Boca Raton News for consideration by the Board on this date, it was placed on the agenda but with recommendation for deferral.

Treasurer O'Malley called attention to photographs that had been furnished to him concerning intrusion on the land that apparently was now under purchase application. In comparison with photographs taken in October of 1970, some mangrove swamps appeared to have been bulldozed and filled adjoining land on which the applicant now had construction in progress. Mr. O'Malley also had some correspondence describing vegetation that had existed at the site.

Mr. Kuperberg said the local Audubon Society had brought the matter to his attention but he had not seen the photographs. He had scheduled a conference with the applicant and notified him to stop all work if there was any question that he was operating on public lands.

MURPHY ACT REPORT - Sale of Lots in Nassau, Marion and Okaloosa Counties

Request approval of Report No. 988 and authority for execution of deeds pertaining to 24 regular bids for sale of lots in Nassau, Marion and Okaloosa Counties under provisions of Section 197.350, Florida Statutes.

The lands reverted to the State of Florida by virtue of various state-owned tax sale certificates that were four years old or older on June 9, 1939, the effective date of the Murphy Act.

1. Nassau County

    (a) New Zion Baptist Church offered the high bid of $60 for the East 20 feet of North 1/2 of Lot 2, Block 53, City of Fernandina Beach (20 ft. x 50 ft.). The church owns the adjacent land. The 1971 assessed value based on full just value by the Nassau County Tax Assessor was $20.

(b)   Leon A. Nelson offered the high bid of $1,300 for
Lots 12 through 24, Block 173, Town of Hilliard, in
Section 8, Township 3 North, Range 24 East. The staff
appraiser reported a total valuation of $1,275 for the
lots. Each lot is 25 feet x 125 feet.

2.   Marion County

(a)   Brown Ray offered the high bid of $2,880 for 16 lots in
Section 29, Township 12 South, Range 22 East, which is
more than three times the 1970 assessed value. The
applicant owns all the surrounding land, and there is no
access to the 16 lots except through the applicant's
property.

(b)   Boise Handy offered the high bid of $860 for a parcel
of land described as "Com. 420 ft. E of SW cor. of
N 1/2 of NE 1/4; thence E 420 ft. N 210 ft. W 420 ft.,
S 210 ft. to POB in Section 11, Township 13 South, Range
21 East, 2 acres." The staff appraiser reported a market
value of $860 for the land.

(c)   Thomas M. Kilgore offered the high bid of $405 for Lot 7
Block K, and Lots 16 through 21, Block G. West Ocala
Heights, in Section 15, Township 15 South, Range 21 East.
The current assessed value of the lots is $30 per lot.

3.   Okaloosa County

O. F. Norris offered the high bid of $50 for a parcel
of land in Section 4, Township 2 North, Range 25 West
described as Begin 140 ft. East of Northwest corner of Lot
2, Section 4, Township 2 North, Range 25 West; thence
South 75 feet; thence East 40 feet; thence North 75 feet;
thence West 40 feet to beginning. The Okaloosa County Tax
Assessor reported the 1971 value as $15.75.

ACTION OF THE TRUSTEES:

On motion by Mr. Dickinson, seconded by Mr. Christian and
adopted without objection, the Trustees approved all the Murphy
Act sales on Report No. 988 as listed above, and authorized
execution of deeds pertaining thereto.

-7-

SANTA ROSA COUNTY - Consideration of Oil and Gas Lease Bids

On June 29 the Trustees authorized advertisement for sealed bids
for a five-year oil and gas lease covering the one-quarter
undivided interest held by the State in scattered parcels
containing approximately 6,949.51 surface acres entirely within
the Blackwater River State Forest.

The lease will prohibit drilling operations in the waters of
streams, rivers and lakes within the leased area. The lessee
will be required to notify the Division of Forestry and the
Game and Fresh Water Fish Commission prior to entering the
land to conduct exploration operations.

The lease requires an annual rental of $1 per net mineral acre,
$50,000 surety bond, 1/6 royalty and at least one test well
every 2 1/2 years to a depth of 6,000 feet or to the Norphlet
Sands, whichever is deeper.

Invitation to bid was advertised pursuant to law in the Tallahassee Democrat and the Milton Press-Gazette with bids to
be opened at 10:00 a.m. (DST) on August 17, 1971, for consideration by the Trustees.

ACTION OF THE TRUSTEES:

On motion by Mr. Dickinson, seconded by Mr. Shevin and adopted, that the bids be opened, Mr. James T. Williams opened and read the one bid received from the Louisiana Land and Exploration Company in the total amount of $13,303.35. The bid was in order and acceptance was recommended. No objections had been received.

On motion by Mr. Christian, seconded and adopted without objection, the Trustees accepted the bid of the Louisiana Land and Exploration Company and authorized issuance of the lease to that firm.

-8-

ESCAMBIA COUNTY - Advertise for Oil and Gas Lease

> Southeastern Exploration, Ltd.,
> Jackson, Mississippi,

requests the Board to advertise for a five-year oil and gas drilling lease covering the reserved one-half interest of the State in the petroleum and petroleum products in 6.9-acre parcel in the NE 1/4 of NE 1/4 of Section 10, Township 5 North, Range 33 West, Escambia County.

This request has been reviewed by the State Geologist who concurs in the following recommendation.

Recommend advertising for sealed bids for lease with an annual rental of $1 per net mineral acre, 1/6 royalty, five-year primary term, $50,000 surety bond and at least one test well required to be drilled to 6,000 feet or to a depth sufficient to test the Norphlet Sands, whichever is deeper.

ACTION OF THE TRUSTEES:

On motion by Mr. Christian, seconded by Mr. Shevin and adopted without objection, the Trustees authorized the advertisement for oil and gas lease of the reserved interest.

-9-

DADE COUNTY - Campsite Lease 2157A

> Clifford F. Knauer, Paul J. Slayden, James A.
> Harden and Joseph A. Caldwell
> 601 Ferre Building, Biscayne Boulevard, Miami, Florida,

make application for a campsite lease in Biscayne Bay. The request conforms to the policy of April 7, 1970, that allows a lease as long as the structure remains on the site.

On February 2, 1971, the Trustees approved renewal of Campsite Lease No. 2157A embracing this property to Thomas Willis and James A. Caldwell.

On May 24, 1971, Mr. Willis requested permission to assign his interest in the lease to James A. Harden.

Since Lease No. 2157A to Thomas Willis and James A. Caldwell was improperly executed, staff recommends that the Board grant a new lease naming all four principals, with the annual rental of $300 per 1/4 acre.

ACTION OF THE TRUSTEES:

On motion by Mr. Conner, seconded by Mr. Christian and adopted without objection, the Trustees authorized issuance of the new lease to the four principals at the annual rental of $300 per one-fourth acre.

8-17-71

-10-

CHARLOTTE COUNTY - Dredge Permit and Fishing Pier
TIITF 253.123-845

Mary-Lu Mobile Home Park
Tri-County Engineering, Inc.
121 East Charlotte Avenue, Punta Gorda, Florida,

requests a permit to dredge an access boat channel 700 feet
by 50 feet by -5 feet mean low water and to construct a fishing
pier covering 2,000 square feet adjacent to the proposed channel,
in the Peace River in Section 30, Township 40 South, Range 23 East.
Approximately 1,630 cubic yards of material will be removed and
placed behind a seawall on uplands. A check for $1,630 has been
tendered for the dredged material. The minimum annual fee for
the pier would be $100.

The biological report is not adverse. The Game and Fresh Water
Fish Commission has no objection providing the spoil area is
entirely above the mean high water line and properly diked. The
Department of Air and Water Pollution Control has no objection.

Staff recommends issuance of a dredge permit and marina license.

ACTION OF THE TRUSTEES:

On motion by Mr. Dickinson, seconded by Mr. O'Malley and adopted
without objection, the Trustees approved the application for a
dredge permit and marina license.

-11-

DUVAL COUNTY - Marina License and Construction Permit,
Section 253.03 F. S.

Atlantic Dry Dock Corporation
8502 McKenna Road, Fort George Island, Florida 32226,

applied for a marina license for an area covering 9280 square
feet for installation of an access pier and mooring dolphins
in the St. Johns River abutting Section 26, Township 1 South,
Range 28 East, Duval County. Applicant also requests a
construction permit for installation of a 350 foot marine
railway adjacent to the proposed pier.

No dredging is required. The minimum annual fee of $185.60
and all processing fees have been tendered.

The Department of Air and Water Pollution Control, the Department of Natural Resources and the Game and Fresh Water Fish
Commission have no objections to the proposed project.

The staff recommends approval of the marina license and for
the pier and dolphins, and a construction permit for the
marina railway subject to applicant furnishing a performance
bond in an amount of three times the cost of installing the
marine railway in the event the Trustees require that the
railway be removed, it being understood that no appurtenant
structures shall be installed adjacent to the proposed railway that would impede unrestricted use of the water column over
the railway.

ACTION OF THE TRUSTEES:

On motion by Mr. Dickinson, seconded by Mr. O'Malley and adopted
without objection, the Trustees approved the application for a
marina license and construction permit subject to the bond and
other requirements recommended by the staff.

8-17-71

-12-

ESCAMBIA COUNTY - Dredge Permit No. 253.123-850

> Grand Lagoon Properties, Inc., Ben White, President
> Post Office Box 5725, Pensacola, Florida 32505

requests authority to dredge a navigation channel 575 feet by 50 feet by -5 feet (mean low water) in Big Lagoon, Section 22, Township 3 South, Range 31 West, Escambia County. The applicant proposes to excavate 1,700 cubic yards of material to be placed on upland. A check for $1,700 has been tendered.

The Game and Fresh Water Fish Commission requested a 50-foot channel to avoid a productive turtle grass flat. Applicant has agreed to the 50-foot channel. Biological report states there should be no significant effects on marine biological resources. The Department of Air and Water Pollution Control has no objections.

Staff recommends issuance of a dredge permit.

ACTION OF THE TRUSTEES:

On motion by Mr. Dickinson, seconded by Mr. O'Malley and adopted without objection, the Trustees approved the application for a dredge permit.

-13-

OKALOOSA COUNTY - Dredge Permit, 253.123-854

> Howard C. Marler, Jr.
> Post Office Box 262, Destin, Florida 32541,

requests a permit to perform maintenance dredging in an existing entrance channel and an area around applicant's docks. Approximately 150 cubic yards of material will be excavated and placed on applicant's upland in Township 2 South, Range 24 West, Okaloosa County. Applicant has tendered $75 check for fill material at the rate of 50¢ per cubic yard.

The project was certified by the Department of Air and Water Pollution Control on April 12, 1971. The biological report states that approval of this small project should not have significant effects on marine biological resources. The Game and Fresh Water Fish Commission has no objection.

Staff requests authority to issue a dredge permit.

ACTION OF THE TRUSTEES:

On motion by Mr. Dickinson, seconded by Mr. Christian and Mr. O'Malley, adopted without objection, the Trustees approved issuance of the dredge permit.

-14-

OSCEOLA COUNTY - Fill Permit

Request confirmation for the issuance of a permit to the City of St. Cloud, Florida, to fill a dredged hole 300 feet offshore from the public bathing beach in East Lake Tohopekaliga. The filling will be done under the direction of the Florida Game and Fresh Water Fish Commission regional biologist.

This hole, about 60 feet wide, 100 feet long and 22 feet deep, was created when the City of St. Cloud pumped up a public bathing beach on the south side of Lake Tohopekaliga. There have been several drownings in this area over the past several years. The most recent one was the tragic loss of five lives on August 1, 1971.

8-17-71

ACTION OF THE TRUSTEES:

Motion was made by Mr. Christian, seconded by Mr. O'Malley and
adopted without objection, that the Trustees confirm the issuance
of an emergency permit to allow filling of the dredged hole for
safety purposes.

-15-

ST. LUCIE COUNTY - Dredge Permit 253.123-825

> Florida Power and Light Company, c/o Norris R. Kincaid,
> Administrative Assistant
> Post Office Box 3100, Miami, Florida 33101,

requests a permit to excavate 5,000 cubic yards for a barge
unloading slip 225 feet by 40 feet by -9 feet in Big Mud Creek,
in Section 16, Township 36 South, Range 41 East, near the
Hutchinson Island Plant in St. Lucie County. All dredging will
be done landward of the mean high water line on uplands owned
by the applicant. Therefore, payment for this material is not
required.

The biological report is not adverse. The Game and Fresh Water
Fish Commission and the Department of Air and Water Pollution
Control have no objections.

Staff recommends issuance of a dredge permit.

ACTION OF THE TRUSTEES:

Motion was made by Mr. Conner, seconded by Mr. O'Malley and
adopted without objection, to approve issuance of the dredge
permit that would allow expansion of an existing barge
unloading area landward of the mean high water line. The dredged
material would be placed on upland property.

-16-

SARASOTA COUNTY - Fill Permit 253.124(8)-194

> Roy and Ruth Waite
> 18 Oxford Street, Northport, New York 11768,

request approval of a fill permit issued by Sarasota County
Water and Navigation Control Authority (Minor Work Permit
No. 71-38) in accordance with the provisions of Section 253.124(8)
pertaining to reclamation of land lost by avulsion and/or
artificially induced erosion and the rebuilding of an existing
seawall.

The Field Operations Division substantiates that the new seawall will be constructed in the same location as the existing
broken seawall, which is to be removed.

The fill area is less than 25 feet waterward of the mean high
water line in Section 25, Township 40 South, Range 19 East, Sarasota
County. Fill material will be trucked in.

Staff recommends approval of the permit issued by the Sarasota
County Water and Navigation Control Authority.

ACTION OF THE TRUSTEES:

On motion by Mr. Christian, seconded by Mr. O'Malley and adopted
without objection, the Trustees approved the fill permit issued
by the Sarasota County Water and Navigation Control Authority in
accordance with provisions of Section 253.124(8) Florida Statutes.

8-17-71

-17-

ESCAMBIA AND SANTA ROSA COUNTIES - Bulkhead Line,
                                   Right of Way Easement
                                   No. 2417-17-57-253.03
                                   Fill Permit No. 253.124-203

The Department of Transportation requested approval of

A. Bulkhead line approved by Board of County Commissioners
    of Escambia County by Resolution adopted February 4, 1971,
    and by the Board of County Commissioners of Santa Rosa
    County by Resolution adopted November 10, 1970. The total
    combined length of the lines is 1,721.34 feet.

B. An easement embracing two parcels of sovereignty land in
    Santa Rosa Sound, Section 10, Township 3 South, Range 29
    West totaling 1.42 acres to be used for highway and bridge
    construction on State Road No. S-399.

C. A fill permit issued by the Board of County Commissioners
    of Escambia County on April 29, 1971, embracing .52 acre
    in Section 10, Township 3 South, Range 29 West, and a
    fill permit issued by the Board of County Commissioners
    of Santa Rosa County issued on February 9, 1971, embracing
    0.7 acre in Section 10, Township 3 South, Range 29 West.
    Fill material will be trucked to the site.

The biological report is not adverse. The Game and Fresh Water
Fish Commission has no objections providing "care is taken to
confine all siltation to the immediate (fill) area." The Department of Air and Water Pollution Control has no objections.

Staff requests approval of the bulkhead line, the easement and
the fill permits.

ACTION OF THE TRUSTEES:

On motion by Mr. Conner, seconded by Mr. Christian and adopted
without objection, the Trustees approved the bulkhead lines as
established by Escambia and Santa Rosa Counties with the total
combined length of 1,721.34 feet, authorized issuance of the
requested right-of-way easement, and approved the fill permit issued
by the Board of County Commissioners of Escambia and Santa Rosa
Counties to the Department of Transportation.

————————

-18-

PINELLAS COUNTY - Marina License
                  Section 253.03 F. S.

    Madeira Garden Apartments, Inc.
    c/o Hilborn, Werner, Carter & Associates
    1630 South Myrtle Avenue, Clearwater, Florida 33576,

applies for a marina license covering 5,000 square feet in
Boca Ciega Bay abutting privately-owned submerged lands and
uplands in Section 3 and 4, Township 31 South, Range 15 East,
Pinellas County. The minimum annual fee of $100 has been
tendered. No dredging is required for this project.

The Department of Natural Resources, the Game and Fresh Water
Fish Commission and the Department of Air and Water Pollution
Control have no objections to the proposed mooring facility.

Staff recommends approval of the marina license.

ACTION OF THE TRUSTEES:

Motion was made by Mr. Christian, seconded by Mr. Conner and
adopted without objection, that the marina license be issued
to the applicant.

358

-19-

BROWARD COUNTY - Maintenance Dredge Permit,
          File No. 253.123-775

    Bradford Marine, Inc.
    c/o Jenkins and Charland, Inc.
    2120 Northeast 21 Street, Ft. Lauderdale, Florida 33705,

requests a permit to dredge a navigation channel entrance into
an existing boat basin and to remove two shoal areas in the South
Fork North New River canal in Sections 16 and 20, Township
50 South, Range 42 East to fill uplands owned by the applicant.

This project is a modification of an existing installation and
conforms with recommendations of the Department of Natural
Resources.

The shoal areas are not biologically productive and the proposed
work should not have significant adverse effects on marine
biological resources.

The Department of Air and Water Pollution Control and the Game
and Fresh Water Fish Commission, have no objections to the project.

A total of 4,282 cubic yards will be excavated, and payment of
$4,282 has been remitted for the material.

Staff requests authority to issue dredge permit.

ACTION OF THE TRUSTEES:

On motion by Mr. Conner, seconded by Mr. Christian and adopted
without objection, the Board authorized issuance of the dredge
permit.

-20-

MANATEE COUNTY - Channel Dredge Permit 253.123-809
          Outfall Pipe Installation 253.03

    Florida Power and Light Company
    Post Office Box 3100, Miami, Florida 33101

applies for a permit to dredge a cooling water inlet channel in
Tampa Bay, adjacent to Section 12, Township 33 South, Range 17
East. Approximately 50,500 cubic yards will be excavated
creating a channel 223 feet wide, top cut, by 500 feet long
on sovereignty land. The remaining segment of the proposed
channel will be 5,500 feet on the applicant's uplands. The
outfall will be constructed of 10-foot diameter concrete pipe
buried by dredging to a maximum depth of 19.5 feet below existing
ground level of Tampa Bay. This pipe will extend approximately
8,000 feet into Tampa Bay. Approximately 60,000 cubic yards of
material, to be removed for the installation of the pipeline,
will be stockpiled to be used to backfill the dredged area.

The applicant proposes to dedicate in perpetuity approximately
260 acres of marginal lands as a permanent wildlife sanctuary.
An appropriate corporate resolution will be recorded in the
public records of Manatee County. The applicant will further
resolve to refrain from utilizing the balance of the tract,
except for that part to be used as the plant site and related
appurtenances, to the detriment of the dedicated parcel. Representatives of the applicant have indicated that the 60-acre parcel
abutting the port facility has been excluded from the company's
option with the Hendry Corporation.

The biological report of July 8, 1971, from the Department of
Natural Resources states that, "Construction of the intake
channel and outfall will have adverse effects on marine biological
resources." This report also considers the effects of the heated
effluent on marine biological resources and recommends that the
heated effluent be cooled prior to being returned to the Bay.

8-17-71

The Department of Air and Water Pollution Control has advised that its Board would review all applications submitted by the power industry and rescinds comments of July 8, 1971, whereby it advised that there were no objections to the project.

As of this date no response has been received from the Game and Fresh Water Fish Commission regarding this project.

The matter has been placed on the agenda at the request of the applicant. Trustees staff does not have sufficient data to properly evaluate the project in the absence of recommendations from two of the three environmental agencies which the Trustees require to comment.

Staff requests this matter be deferred pending receipt and evaluation of the required agency comments.

ACTION OF THE TRUSTEES:

Consideration of this application was deferred until August 31, 1971.

On motion duly adopted, the meeting was adjourned.

_____
SECRETARY OF STATE, ACTING CHAIRMAN

ATTEST: _____
EXECUTIVE DIRECTOR

*   *   *

Tallahassee, Florida
August 31, 1971

The State of Florida Board of Trustees of the Internal Improvement Trust Fund met on this date in the auditorium of the Department of Transportation, with the following members present:

Reubin O'D. Askew	Governor
Robert L. Shevin	Attorney General
Fred O. Dickinson, Jr.	Comptroller
Thomas D. O'Malley	Treasurer
Floyd T. Christian	Commissioner of Education
Doyle Conner	Commissioner of Agriculture

Joel Kuperberg	Executive Director

The minutes of the meeting held on August 3, 1971, were approved as submitted.

-1-

AQUATIC PRESERVES

1. St. Lucie County, North Fork, St. Lucie River extension
2. Franklin-Wakulla Counties, Ochlockonee Bay
3. Jefferson, Taylor, and Wakulla Counties, St. Marks Wildlife Refuge.

The Interagency Advisory Committee on Aquatic Preserves has taken the following action and recommends;

(1) That the North Fork St. Lucie River Aquatic Preserve be extended to include the area between White City Road (S.R. 712) and Selvitz Road (S.R. 611B). It is recommended that the following clause be included in the resolution establishing the North Fork St. Lucie River Aquatic Preserve:

8-31-71

"Nothing contained herein, nor in the basic implementing
resolution adopted by the Board of Trustees on the 21st
day of October, 1969, shall be construed to preclude the Board
of Trustees from considering and acting upon applications
for permits from city, county or other public bodies for
contruction and maintenance of drainage and flood control
facilities, including but not necessarily limited to the
maintenance of the river bottom to assure free passage of
water."

(2) The committee requests that action on the proposed Ochlockonee
Bay Aquatic Preserve be deferred for another 90 days at which
time a recommendation shall be submitted.

(3) It was brought to the Committee's attention that its recommendation to include sovereignty lands within the St. Marks
Wildlife Refuge in an aquatic preserve has never been presented
to the Trustees for their consideration due to an inadvertent
omission in preparation of the Trustees' agenda.

The Committee recommends that the St. Marks Wildlife Aquatic
Preserve be established with the seaward boundary coinciding with
the offshore boundary of the federal wildlife refuge, and limited
to the mean high water line at other points in the Refuge.

(4) Under its present organizational status the life of the
Committee would expire on August 31, 1971. Because of unfinished
business related to the Ochlockonee Bay matter and other proposals
recently submitted, it is recommended that the life of the Committee
be extended for another 6 months.

ACTION OF THE TRUSTEES:

At the request of Mr. Conner, action was deferred for two weeks
on (1) the extension of the North Fork St. Lucie River Aquatic
Preserve.

Consideration of the proposed Ochlockonee Bay Aquatic Preserve was
deferred for another 90 days as requested by the committee.

With reference to (3), Dr. Andre Clewell of Florida State University
biology department, representing Conservation 70's, urged the inclusion of the sovereignty lands between the St. Marks and the Aucilla
Rivers in an aquatic preserve. It would be a part of the St. Marks
Wildlife Refuge that the Bureau of Sports Fisheries and Wildlife
has proposed for inclusion in the National Wilderness System. The
Cabinet was asked to endorse the wilderness concept, already
supported by a number of local groups.

Mr. Christian said that many of the elected officials of the local
governing bodies in this area were very much opposed to the preserve, and he thought they should be heard on the issue. Mr.
Kuperberg said he was not aware of any opposition, that no additional
areas would be taken as the state would be ratifying an existing
federal wildlife refuge. The Director was asked to contact those
objectors, and at Mr. Christian's request the Trustees deferred
action for two weeks.

On motion by Mr. Dickinson, seconded by Mr. O'Malley and adopted
without objection, the Trustees extended the Interagency Advisory
Committee on Aquatic Preserves for six months because of the
unfinished work related to the Ochlockonee Bay preserve and the
other proposals recently submitted.

-2-

BREVARD COUNTY - Murphy Act Land Sale

The City Council of Cocoa by resolution adopted June 8, 1971,
requests conveyance of Lot 13, Block A, Hughlett's Washington
Heights Subdivision, Plat Book O, Page 18, Brevard County.

The lot is 42.6 feet by 160 feet, two blocks northwest of the intersection of State Road 520 and U. S. Highway No. 1, and within Lot 10 of a 16-lot industrial park subdivision developed by the city with streets, curbs, drainage, sewer, water and electricity in place.

Under Section 197.350(b), Florida Statutes, the Trustees may sell Murphy Act lands to municipalities without notice and public sale.

The staff appraiser made inspection and valued the lot at $1,500.

Recommend conveyance of Lot 13 to the City of Cocoa for the appraised value of $1,500 without notice or public sale.

ACTION OF THE TRUSTEES:

On motion by Mr. Dickinson, seconded by Mr. Christian and adopted without objection, the Trustees approved the application of the City of Cocoa for conveyance of Lot 13 for $1,500 under the provisions of Section 197.350(b) Florida Statutes.

-3-

MANATEE COUNTY - City of Bradenton,
              Dedication No. 24748 (2051-41)

On February 27, 1968, the Trustees dedicated without monetary consideration 54.25 acres of sovereignty lands for public municipal purposes only in the Manatee River abutting uplands owned by the City of Bradenton. The city was charged with the supervision and management of the land.

The restrictive covenant in the dedicatory instrument states:

> "...it being agreed and understood that the public
> municipal purposes for which this land is hereby
> dedicated shall include, but not necessarily be
> limited to the following: a municipal complex,
> parking area, facilities for sports programs, including
> aquatic sports, buildings and docks, including sanitary
> facilities necessary or desirable to construct and
> operate and lease a marina, along with a food service
> facility. Also, grantee named herein is authorized
> to grant concessions and leases for facilities built
> or to be built on said land for a period of time not
> in excess of thirty (30) years, subject to the formal
> approval of the Trustees,..."

The parcel has been seawalled and filled; however, to date no facilities or structures have been constructed.

A plan has been prepared and submitted by the city which calls for development of "DeSoto Center", a combination of private commercial development and public facilities. This plan calls for construction of retail merchandising and commercial entertainment facilities, hotel/motel complex, commercial office space and multiple rental dwellings. The public sector of the plan contemplates construction of a convention/exhibit hall, theater/auditorium, galleries, lobbies, concourses, educational, cultural, recreational, and parking areas.

The city desires to be advised if the proposed development concept complies with the restrictive covenants in Trustees' Dedication 24748(2051-41) and requests approval of the plan as submitted.

Objections to the proposed project have been filed by the Manatee Chapter of the Izaak Walton League and Mrs. Mary U. Blackburn, President, League of Women Voters of Manatee County. Mr. Allen S. Hitch of the Manatee County Audubon Society desired that public hearings be held so that the society could present their views.

The project has been endorsed by the Kiwanis Club of Bradenton and the Downtown Bradenton Association.

The staff recommends that the Trustees approve the project in principle on the following conditions: (1) that the ratio of the area to be utilized by private interests be no greater than 25% of the 54-acre parcel, (2) that the area reserved for public use be adjacent to the open waters of the Manatee River, (3) that a "blue ribbon" ad hoc committee be created by the city with membership subject to Trustees' approval, that would act in an advisory capacity to the development program, (4) that a time table for public development be submitted within 180 days subsequent to this action, and (5) that quarterly reports be furnished to the Trustees' staff on the progress of development and activities of the "blue ribbon" committee.

ACTION OF THE TRUSTEES:

Mr. Kuperberg advised the Governor that there had been no request for deferral of this application.

On motion by Mr. Christian, seconded by Mr. Dickinson and Mr. O'Malley, adopted without objection, the staff recommendations were accepted as the action of the Trustees.

-4-

VOLUSIA COUNTY - Disclaimer, File No. 2412-64-253.129

> Charles H. Strasser, et ux,
> Ormond Beach, Florida,

represented by Bernard H. Strasser, attorney of Daytona Beach, submits an application for a disclaimer for a parcel of filled sovereignty land embracing .77 acre in the Halifax River, abutting Government Lot 2, Section 3, Township 14 South, Range 32 East, Volusia County.

All required exhibits have been furnished including two affidavits indicating that the parcel was filled by a predecessor in title, and prior to May 29, 1951.

Recommend that disclaimer be issued for the usual processing fee of $100.

ACTION OF THE TRUSTEES:

On motion by Mr. Christian, seconded by Mr. Conner and adopted without objection, the Trustees authorized issuance of the disclaimer for $100 processing fee.

-5-

HILLSBOROUGH COUNTY - Bulkhead Lines, Section 253.122
Florida Statutes

In accordance with request of the Trustees on July 6, 1971, the Tampa Port Authority, by Resolution No. R-71-15 dated August 10, 1971, relocated bulkhead lines to the mean high water line in the McKay Bay area north of 22nd Street Causeway.

Staff recommends approval of bulkhead lines.

ACTION OF THE TRUSTEES:

On motion by Mr. Dickinson, seconded by Mr. Christian and adopted without objection, the Trustees approved the bulkhead lines as relocated by Tampa Port Authority by Resolution No. R-71-15 dated August 10, 1971.

MONROE COUNTY - Bulkhead Line, Dredge and Fill Permits,
Sections 253.122, 253.123 and 253.124,
Florida Statutes

Florida Keys Aqueduct Authority
Post Office Box 1239, Key West, Florida

The Board of County Commissioners of Monroe County by Resolution
No. 60-1970, adopted July 21, 1970, established a bulkhead
line pursuant to Section 253.122, Florida Statutes, 1,960 feet
long offshore from Stock Island adjacent to Section 35, Township
67 South, Range 25 East, and Section 2, Township 68 South,
Range 25 East, Monroe County.

The County Commissioners also granted a permit to dredge 96,000
cubic yards of material from a proposed channel 150 feet wide,
420 feet long and 35 feet deep, mean low water, and a permit to
fill 7.47 acres of submerged land conveyed by Trustees' Deed
No. 24409.

The biological report applicable to the original project is
adverse and the Department of Air and Water Pollution Control
has indicated filling would adversely affect water quality.

On January 26, 1971, the staff recommended approval of the
original plan. Action on the matter was deferred for the
purpose of ascertaining if any alternate site was available for
the plant.

It has been determined that no other economically feasible site
is available.

This project for the expansion of the existing desalination plant
has been modified by reducing the fill area to 2.3 acres and
requiring only 40,000 cubic yards of fill material.

Staff recommends approval with waiver of all fees conditioned
upon (1) the Authority relocating the Bulkhead line landward
to coincide with limits of fill and (2) reconveyance by the
Authority of the 3.17 acres of submerged land parcel not
comtemplated to be filled.

ACTION OF THE TRUSTEES:

Mr. Kuperberg said the applicant had made an additional request,
that in exchange for the reconveyance of 3.17 acres in the recommendation, the Trustees look with favor on an application for
a different parcel containing 1 1/2 acres lying immediately south
of the Aqueduct Authority's upland parcel to fulfill the need
for a public water supply.

On motion by Mr. Dickinson, seconded by Mr. O'Malley and Mr. Christian,
the recommendation of the staff was accepted without objection as the
action of the Board.

7

CITRUS COUNTY - Dredge Permit, 253.123-799

Gulf Coast Aggregates, Inc.
Post Office Box 5797, Tampa, Florida,

requests a permit for excavation of a barge mooring slip 1,000
feet by 150 feet (bottom cut) by -10 feet mean low water,
removing 300,000 cubic yards of material. The slips will connect
with the land cut section of the Cross Florida Barge Canal in
Section 10, Township 17 South, Range 16 East, Citrus County.

This project is located entirely upon uplands in private ownership
approximately three miles landward of the Gulf of Mexico.

8-31-71

The biological report is not adverse but recommends that the upland portion of the barge slip be completed before connecting it to the barge canal. The Department of Air and Water Pollution Control has no objections. The Game and Fresh Water Fish Commission has no objections providing that the Department of Natural Resources recommendation is followed.

Staff request authority to issue a dredge permit.

ACTION OF THE TRUSTEES:

On motion by Mr. O'Malley, seconded by Mr. Christian and adopted without objection, the Trustees approved issuance of the dredge permit to Gulf Coast Aggregates, Inc.

-8-

COLLIER COUNTY - Marco Island Development Corporation
    (A) File No. 253.123-51
    (B) File Nos. 253.123-678, 253.124-149

On July 20, 1971, staff recommended the extension of the Roberts Bay permit (File 253.123-51) to December 1972, and the Marco River permit (File 253.123-678, 253.124-149) to December 1971, to correspond with the existing Corps of Engineers permits, the time of extension to be conditioned upon the execution of the final agreement within 45 days.

Staff has made significant progress but has not yet a final agreement to present.   .

Staff recommends an additional 45 days extension on the subject permits, subject to conditions in the memorandum of August 31 from the Executive Director to the Trustees as follows:

> Preliminary procedural policy leading to
> acceptance of a memorandum of understanding
> between Marco Island Development Corporation
> and the State of Florida

Staff recommends:

1. Dredging operations shall not proceed until such time as adequate turbidity control "diapers" shall have been installed and approved by the Trustees' staff.

2. Bond shall be posted in the amount of $50,000 to be paid to the State as liquidated damages in the event turbidity produced by dredging operations exceeds 50 Jackson Units as related to standard candle turbidimeter above background.

3. Trustees' staff shall establish a full-time inspection program to oversee all Marco Island Development Corporation activities requiring State permits, with all expenses for such program to be reimbursed to the Trustees by Marco Island Development Corporation.

4. Marco Island Development Corporation shall immediately place in escrow the title to Kice Island, with said title to be conveyed to the State by warranty deed, a fee simple absolute title showing a good and marketable title, on January 3, 1972, subject to the entering of a memo of understanding between Marco Island Development Corporation and the state.

ACTION OF THE TRUSTEES:

Motion was made by Mr. Christian, seconded by Mr. O'Malley, for approval of the extension subject to the staff recommendations in the memorandum.

Mr. O'Malley asked about the expense involved and the Director advised that the applicant had approved the proposed full-time inspection program and would reimburse the Trustees' office.

8-31-71

The work would be done by an inspector employed by the Trustees' office for this work, or by a private inspecting laboratory.

Without objection, the motion was adopted.

-9-

DADE COUNTY - Fill Permit, 253.124(8)-212

> Muriel Williams
> c/o Max Henry Larson
> Dock and Marine Construction Corporation
> 750 Northeast 78th Terrace, Miami, Florida,

requests approval of a construction permit issued by the City of Miami (permit number 33) March 8, 1971, for the applicant to reconstruct approximately 30 to 40 feet of an existing rubble wall built in 1937 that has fallen into the Little River Canal.

Our Field Operations report states that no sovereignty land will be filled by the project. The application is in accordance with Section 253.124(8) pertaining to reconstruction of existing coastal structures.

Staff recommends approval of the construction permit issued by the City of Miami.

ACTION OF THE TRUSTEES:

On motion by Mr. Christian, seconded by Mr. Conner and adopted without objection, the Trustees approved the construction permit.

-10-

LEE COUNTY - Fill Permit, 253.124(8)-193

> R. M. Harby
> 156 Ibis Street
> Ft. Myers Beach, Florida,

requests approval of a fill permit, in accordance with Section 253.124(8) pertaining to the reclamation of land lost by avulsion and/or artificially-induced erosion, issued by the Board of County Commissioners of Lee County on June 16, 1971. Applicant proposes to construct a seawall and fill approximately 0.2 acre of submerged land that was formerly upland lost by action of Hurricane Donna in Estero Bay, Section 34, Township 46 South, Range 24 East, Lee County.

The Field Operations report substantiates the applicant's claim. The applicant has submitted two affidavits signed by James M. Sweeney, Jr., Commissioner District 3, Lee County, and E. G. Nordstrom, former owner of the property, stating that the area the applicant proposes to fill was eroded by the storm.

Staff recommends approval of the fill permit issued by Lee County Board of County Commissioners.

ACTION OF THE TRUSTEES:

On motion by Mr. Dickinson, seconded by Mr. Conner and adopted without objection, the Trustees approved the fill permit issued by Lee County.

Mr. Shevin said he had no objection but for the record noted that this was not an exception to the normal conservation review becasue this affected the building of the new seawall as opposed to the reconstruction of an old one, and affected only a very small parcel. The Governor added that the damage had been caused by avulsion.

8-31-71

MANATEE COUNTY - Settlement of Unauthorized Construction

> Gwynne D. Pearsall, President,
> Trader Jack of Lauderdale by the Sea, Inc.
> 700 Gulf Drive North, Bradenton Beach, Florida

To prevent damage to an existing commercial structure adjacent to the Gulf of Mexico, the applicant engaged in unauthorized construction consisting of placing riprap and pouring concrete in the area subject to erosion 20 to 30 feet seaward of the property line on sovereignty lands abutting Government Lot 1, Section 4, Township 35 South, Range 17 East, Manatee County.

The applicant has acknowledged the encroachment, and to settle the matter has prepared a deed quitclaiming all right, title and interest to the land in question.

The Department of Natural Resources indicates that there has not been significant damage to the biological resources because of this construction.

The Florida Game and Fresh Water Fish Commission endorses the settlement.

The Department of Air and Water Pollution Control indicates that certification would have been required in accordance with Section 21(b), Public Law 91-224, and that the work was performed in violation of this law.

The Bureau of Beaches and Shores indicated it would recommend favorably on a variance to Section 161.052, Florida Statutes, that requires a 50-foot set back from the mean high water line.

The staff recommends acceptance of the quitclaim. No other remedial action is waived thereby.

ACTION OF THE TRUSTEES:

The Department of Natural Resources on this date had granted a variance for the seawall that was built to protect a restaurant that had been in existence a long time but was in danger of being undermined. There had been a complete staff investigation in cooperation with the Division of Beaches and Shores.

On motion by Mr. O'Malley, seconded by Mr. Dickinson and Mr. Christian, adopted without objection, the Trustees approved the staff recommendation.

-12-

OKALOOSA COUNTY - Dredge Permit, Marina License,
File No. 253.123-813

The application of Marlborough, Inc., of Destin, Florida was withdrawn from the agenda by the staff.

-13-

PATENTS, COPYRIGHTS AND TRADEMARKS.

On the request of the Commissioner of Agriculture, the Trustees deferred action on the request of the Department of Citrus for two weeks for some further negotiations on the matter of patents.

-14-

TRUSTEES' FUNDS

On motion by Mr. O'Malley, seconded by Mr. Dickinson and Mr. Christian, adopted without objection, the Trustees granted authority to pay Fred Vidzes for 40 hours of unused, accumulated annual leave earned while he served as division director and interim executive director during the period from November 1, 1969, through August 31, 1971.

-15-

MANATEE COUNTY - Channel Dredge Permit 253.123-809
                 Outfall Pipe Installation 253.03

        Florida Power and Light Company
        Post Office Box 3100, Miami, Florida 33101

applies for a permit to dredge cooling water inlet and outlet channels in Tampa Bay, adjacent to Section 12, Township 33 South, Range 17 East. Approximately 50,500 cubic yards will be excavated creating an inlet channel 223 feet wide, top cut, by 500 feet long on sovereignty land. The proposed inlet channel will continue, extending 5,500 feet on the applicant's upland. All fill will be deposited on applicant's upland. The outfall will consist of a 10-foot diameter concrete pipe buried by dredging to a maximum depth of 19.5 feet below the existing bottom of Tampa Bay. This pipe will extend approximately 8,000 feet into Tampa Bay. Approximately 60,000 cubic yards of material, to be removed from the installation of the pipeline, will be stockpiled and used to backfill the pipe/ditch. The applicant proposes to dedicate in perpetuity approximately 260 acres of marginal lands as a permanent wildlife sanctuary. An appropriate corporate resolution will be recorded in the public records of Manatee County. The applicant will further resolve to refrain from utilizing the balance of the tract, except for that part to be used as the plant site and related appurtenances, to the detriment of the dedicated parcel. Representatives of the applicant have indicated that a 60-acre parcel abutting Port Manatee has been excluded from the purchase option with the Hendry Corporation.

The biological report of July 8, 1971, from the Department of Natural Resources states that, "Construction of the intake channel and outfall will have adverse effects on marine biological resources." This report also considers the effects of heated effluent on marine biological resources and recommends that the heated effluent be cooled prior to being returned to the Bay.

The Game and Fresh Water Fish Commission states, "...numerous adverse conditions will result from construction and operation of this facility." The report recommends: (1) relocation of the inlet channel, (2) extension of the outfall pipe to the deep water Tampa Bay navigation channel to increase dilution of the heated effluent or (3) redesign of the proposed cooling system so that outfall water releases can be closer to natural water temperatures in Tampa Bay.

Trustees staff is of the opinion that relocation of the inlet canal to preserve less than one acre of sovereign bottom dredging would complicate further the ultimate resolution of the Hendry Dredging Company case. Extension of the proposed outfall pipe would increase retention time of the heated effluent and might result in a greater kill of entrained marine organisms. Introduction of a greater volume of cooling water in order to reduce the temperature of effluent might also increase the number of organisms entrained and killed.

The Department of Air and Water Pollution Control by letter of August 27, 1971, has advised that their Board will hear an application for a construction permit covering all air and water quality aspects of the subject steam electric generating plant, September 7, 1971. Their comments re the subject dredge permit will be reserved, pending completion of the hearing procedures.

Trustees staff has sought additional factual guidance from the marine science departments of three Florida universities and a federal agency. The lack of adequate information by which to evaluate the impact of the proposed plant was laid bare. It was impossible,

despite diligent efforts, to properly evaluate the cost to the public
in lost marine resources of the construction and operation of a
seventh steam electric generating plant on the shores of Tampa Bay.

Staff recommends that, in view of the alleged overriding public need
for electric power, the Trustees issue the required channel dredging
permit, subject to execution of the proposed dedications of land
by Florida Power and Light and further subject to the design and
authorization of a continuing study, paid for by Florida Power and
Light and approved by Trustees staff, to determine the before and
after operation status and the possible cumulative effects upon
the planktonic and other marine resources of Tampa Bay of this proposed Port Manatee generating plant.

ACTION OF THE TRUSTEES:

Mr. Kuperberg said it was a difficult decision, a value judgment
as to whether the demand for electricity represents sufficient demonstration of public interest to justify the, at this time, unassessable
damage to the Tampa Bay marine environment; and the impact of this
plant would help the staff evaluate such generating systems in the
future. There had been much research and it was difficult to
determine the true cost to the public of the use of public waters
to cool a privately owned power plant.

After further discussion, the motion by Mr. Dickinson, seconded by
Mr. Christian, to approve the staff recommendations was adopted
without objection.

-16-

CHARLOTTE COUNTY - Dredge Permit, File No. 253.123-802

At the applicant's request, the Trustees deferred until September 21
consideration of a dredge permit applied for by Punta Gorda Isles,
Inc., to connect an upland canal with the south branch of Alligator
Creek in Charlotte County.

-17-

HILLSBOROUGH COUNTY - Mr. Robert Thomas and others from Hillsborough
County Port Authority were present in connection with an application
at Port Sutton. He did not object to some delay but would like full
investigation and a place on the agenda, as he was not aware of any
objections on the basis of turbidity.

Mr. Kuperberg explained that the problem was one of water quality
and the staff, according to the Trustees' policy, endeavored to
obtain approval of all three environmental agencies before placing
an application on the agenda. Also, there had been a moratorium
in Tampa Bay, now resolved with the relocation of bulkhead lines
back to mean high water.

Governor Askew asked that the matter be worked out and placed on
the agenda soon.

DUVAL COUNTY - Attorney General Shevin brought up the spoil areas
for the Jacksonville Harbor deepening project, asking for consideration of alternate spoil areas suggested by conservationists.

Mr. Kuperberg advised that the alternate areas were either marsh
areas equal in value in the opinion of the Department of Natural
Resources, or one upland area at Mayport Naval Air Station that was
restricted by the Navy for maintenance dredging of their port.

The marsh areas had been patented 80 to 100 years ago to the
railroad companies by the State of Florida, hundreds of thousands
of acres of marsh were in private ownership with state-owned
tidal creeks running throughout, virtually impossible to develop
because of the intermingling of state and private ownerships.

Mr. Kuperberg explained something of the negotiations with the
North Shore Corporation, trying to restore to state ownership
some marshes now in private ownership on Fanning Island in return
for the value of the fill dredged from a public channel and placed
on private property, and to obtain reconveyance to the Trustees of
tidal creeks.

On motion duly adopted, the meeting was adjourned.

GOVERNOR   -   CHAIRMAN

ATTEST:

EXECUTIVE DIRECTOR

* * *

Tallahassee, Florida
September 7, 1971

The State of Florida Board of Trustees of the Internal Improvement
Trust Fund met on this date in the auditorium of the Department
of Transportation, with the following members present:

Reubin O'D. Askew	Governor
Richard (Dick) Stone	Secretary of State
Robert L. Shevin	Attorney General
Fred O. Dickinson, Jr.	Comptroller
Thomas D. O'Malley	Treasurer
Floyd T. Christian	Commissioner of Education
Doyle Conner	Commissioner of Agriculture

Joel Kuperberg	Executive Director

The minutes of the meeting of August 17, 1971, were approved as
submitted.

Senator William Dean Barrow of Crestview, Florida, was present
in connection with the application of Marlborough, Inc., for a
dredge permit and marina license in Okaloosa County that had
been withdrawn from the agenda on August 31. He requested that
the matter be deferred rather than withdrawn.

On motion by Mr. Stone, seconded by Mr. O'Malley and adopted
without objection, the Marlborough application was scheduled
for consideration on October 12, 1971.

-1-

PASCO COUNTY - Application to Purchase,
          File No. 2142-51-253.12

     Staff Description: A parcel of sovereignty land in the
     Gulf of Mexico embracing 301 acres abutting Section 32 and 33,
     Township 34 South, Range 16 East, and Section 5 in Township
     25 South, Range 16 East in the Town of Hudson, Pasco County.

     Applicant: Leisure Lands, Inc.
                Post Office Box 1081
                New Port Richey, Florida 33552

     Acreage: 301 acres
     Rate Per acre: $150

9-7-71

```
Total Offer:      $45,150
Appraisal:        Has not been requested

Purpose:          Development for homesites and apartments
```

The biological report dated June 3, 1969 is adverse, stating that "Filling of the 301 acres sought for purchase and dredging a 2,000 foot by 5,380 foot area seaward of the 301 acre parcel would have massive adverse effects on marine biological resources." The biological report dated May 26, 1971, concludes: "To best conserve wildlife and marine biological resources, development should be restricted to the uplands."

The Interagency Advisory Committee on Submerged Land Management on August 6, 1968, recommended that the Pasco County bulkhead line be established at the line of mean high water.

Staff recommends that the application be denied, the $75 application fee be refunded and the file be deactivated, as the sale of the parcel would not be in the public interest.

ACTION OF THE TRUSTEES:

On motion by Mr. Stone, seconded by Mr. Christian and adopted without objection, the staff recommendations were accepted as the action of the Board.

-2-

DADE COUNTY - Biscayne Bay, Campsite Lease No. 2213

Francis X. Knuck, Esther T. Knuck
60 Olive Drive, Hialeah, Florida 33101

made application for renewal of Campsite Lease No. 2213. Applicant has tendered his check for $300 as yearly rental on this lease.

Staff recommends that the Board renew the existing lease at annual rental of $300.

ACTION OF THE TRUSTEES:

On motion by Mr. O'Malley, seconded by Mr. Dickinson and adopted without objection, the Board authorized renewal at $300 annual rental.

-3-

LEE COUNTY - Lease for Wildlife Refuge, 79.2 acres

Florida Audubon Society makes application for lease for wildlife refuge purposes of a sovereignty area 1,500 feet East and West by 2,300 feet North and South in the East 1/2 of Section 3, Township 44 South, Range 21 East, which includes 3 mangrove keys or islands known as "Broken Keys" in Pine Island Sound, Lee County. The parcel is not riparian to any upland and is more than one mile from the route of the Intracoastal Waterway. The mangrove islands and adjacent area are reported to be strategic for protection of wading birds, and presentation of this request has been deferred about 2 years pending location of the waterway route. The applicant has furnished acceptable legal description using coordinates to fix the location accurately.

Recommend 10-year lease at $1 per year for wildlife refuge purposes only, with requirement of annual report on use of the area and its effectiveness, subject to cancellation by the Trustees on 6 months' written notice.

ACTION OF THE TRUSTEES:

On motion by Mr. O'Malley, seconded by Mr. Dickinson and
adopted without objection, the Board granted the request of
the Florida Audubon Society for 10-year lease for wildlife refuge
purposes only at one dollar per year, subject to the conditions
recommended by the staff.

-4-

BROWARD COUNTY - Marina License, Section 253.03, F. S.

>George Harrison, President
>Capital Growth Corporation
>2942 N. E. 32nd Avenue, Ft. Lauderdale, Florida,

requests a marina license covering 753 square feet in the
Intracoastal Waterway abutting Section 30, Township 49 South,
Range 43 East, Broward County. No dredging is required. The
minimum annual fee of $100 has been tendered.

The Department of Natural Resources, the Game and Fresh Water
Fish Commission, the Department of Air and Water Pollution
Control, the Florida Inland Navigation District, the Board of
County Commissioners of Broward County and the City of Ft. Lauder-
dale have no objections to the proposed project.

Staff recommends approval of marina license.

ACTION OF THE TRUSTEES:

On motion by Mr. Dickinson, seconded by Mr. Conner and Mr. O'Malley,
adopted without objection, the Trustees approved issuance of the
marina license.

-5-

BROWARD COUNTY - Marina License, Section 253.03, F. S.

>Lauderdale Yacht Basin, Inc.
>2000 S. W. 20th Street
>Ft. Lauderdale, Florida 33315,

applies for a marina license covering 14,820 square feet in the
South Fork of New River abutting upland in Section 16, Township
15 South, Range 42 East, Broward County. Dolphin piles are to
be placed 20 feet channelward of the proposed wharf, and
no dredging is required. The minimum annual fee of $296.40 has
been tendered.

The Department of Natural Resources, the Game and Fresh Water
Fish Commission and the Department of Air and Water Pollution
Control have no objections to the proposed project.

Staff recommends approval of marina license.

ACTION OF THE TRUSTEES:

On motion by Mr. Dickinson, seconded by Mr. Conner and Mr. O'Malley,
adopted without objection, the Trustees approved issuance of the
marina license.

-6-

MONROE COUNTY - Construction Permit, Mooring Dolphins,
             Section 253.03, F. S.

>Utility Board of the City of Key West
>Post Office Box 1060, Key West, Florida 33040

9-7-71

requests approval of the installation of dolphins at the existing fuel unloading dock facility in Key West Harbor abutting Section 31, Township 67 South, Range 25 East, Monroe County. Applicant requests waiver of any fees.

The Department of Natural Resources, the Game and Fresh Water Fish Commission, and the Department of Air and Water Pollution Control have no objections to the proposed project.

Staff recommends issuance of construction permit and waiver of fees.

ACTION OF THE TRUSTEES:

On motion by Mr. O'Malley, seconded by Mr. Dickinson and adopted without objection, the Trustees authorized issuance of the construction permit without charge.

-7-

VOLUNTARY DISMISSAL OF CONDEMNATION SUIT

On September 22, 1970, upon staff recommendation, the Trustees disapproved the relocation of a bulkhead line from its mean high water line location to an offshore location as adopted by the City of Port Orange due to adverse biological reports. Disapproval prohibited C. K. Walley from commercially developing 4.5 acres of submerged lands on the south side of the Port Orange Causeway in the Halifax River. The submerged lands had been conveyed previously by the Trustees in 1952 for $150 per acre.

Upon further staff recommendation, the Trustees voted to condemn Mr. Walley's 4.5 acres under the newly enacted Florida Statute, 253.02(4)(1970). Previous attempts to purchase the property were unsuccessful. Mr. Jack Pierce of the Department of Natural Resources was asked to handle the matter. The state values the property at around $35,000; Mr. Walley, at more than two and a half times that amount.

Pretrial hearing and several depositions are scheduled for September 9, 1971; trial is set for October 4, 1971. Although dismissal of the suit would require payment of attorneys' fees and other costs incurred to date, these costs will increase as trial approaches. The current staff believes that condemnation of the 4.5 acres is not justified.

Staff requests permission to voluntarily dismiss the condemnation suit, Case No. 18,987, now pending in the Circuit Court of the Seventh Judicial Circuit, Division D, Volusia County, Florida.

ACTION OF THE TRUSTEES:

On motion by Mr. Dickinson, seconded by Mr. O'Malley and adopted without objection, the Trustees authorized the staff to voluntarily dismiss the condemnation suit.

In response to Mr. Shevin's question, the Executive Director said the Chief Counsel was reviewing about 55 cases now pending.

-8-

PINELLAS COUNTY - Utility Installation with Dredging
          File No. 253.123(2)(b)-903

     Pinellas County Board of County Commissioners
     315 Haven Street, Clearwater, Florida 33516

requests approval of Dredge Only Permit No. 197 issued by the Pinellas County Water and Navigation Control Authority on July 6, 1971, to install a 20" sewage force main across Boca Ciega Bay at Madeira Beach. Applicant requests waiver of the $100 processing fee for utility installation.

The biological report is not adverse. The Game and Fresh Water Fish Commission and the Department of Air and Water Pollution Control have no objections.

Staff requests approval of Permit No. 197 issued by the Pinellas County Water and Navigation Control Authority and that the fee be waived because of the public works nature of the project.

ACTION OF THE TRUSTEES:

On motion by Mr. O'Malley, seconded by Mr. Dickinson and adopted without objection, the Trustees approved the permit issued by Pinellas County Water and Navigation Control Authority and waived the fee as recommended by the staff.

-9-

OKEECHOBEE COUNTY - Marina Licenses, Bait and Tackle Shops, Section 253.03, F. S.

    (1) Ray's Fish Camps, c/o Ray Watson
        601 West North Street, Okeechobee, Florida

    (2) Earl's Fish Camp, c/o Earl W. Bertram
        1310 Avenue B, Okeechobee, Florida

Pursuant to investigations by Field Operations Division, applications have been filed by the above parties for after the fact marina licenses for the existing bait and tackle sales barges along the northwest shore of Lake Okeechobee.

The Game and Fresh Water Fish Commission has filed an amended comment, objecting on the basis of water quality, blockage of public boat ramp. The Board of County Commissioners of Okeechobee County and the Central and Southern Florida Flood Control District have objected to the existing facilities.

This item appeared on the August 3, 1971, agenda and was deferred.

Staff recommends denial and requests authorization to have the facilities removed from the premises.

ACTION OF THE TRUSTEES:

On motion by Mr. O'Malley, seconded and adopted without objection, the Board approved the recommendation for denial and authorized the staff to have the facilities removed from the premises.

-10-

DADE COUNTY - Dredge Permit, 253.123-849

    Herbert W. Hoover, Jr.
    70 Park Drive, Bal Harbour, Florida 33154,

requests a permit to excavate an access channel 100 ft. long x 15 feet wide (bottom cut) x -7 feet deep mean high water and a docking area 70 feet x 50 feet x -7 feet (mean high water) in Biscayne Bay, Dade County.

Applicant proposes to remove 2,200 cubic yards of material to be placed on his upland. A check for $2,200 has been tendered. The biological report is not adverse. The Game and Fresh Water Fish Commission and the Department of Air and Water Pollution Control have no objections.

Staff recommends approval of dredge permit.

ACTION OF THE TRUSTEES:

On motion by Mr. Dickinson, seconded by Mr. Conner and adopted without objection, the Board authorized issuance of the dredge permit.

-11-

TRUSTEES' FUNDS - Request authority to enter into a contract with the Environmental Information Center of the Florida Conservation Foundation, Inc. to study the effects of waterfront development and associated labyrinthine canal systems on Florida's natural resources. The contract would not exceed $5,000 and funds are available within the existing budget.

ACTION OF THE TRUSTEES:

Motion was made by Mr. Dickinson, seconded by Mr. Conner and Mr. O'Malley, and adopted without objection, that the contract in an amount not to exceed $5,000 be approved.

-12-

HILLSBOROUGH COUNTY - Dredge Permit, 253.123

    Seaboard Coast Line Railroad
    Jacksonville, Florida,

requests approval of Dredge Permit No. 71-17 issued by the Tampa Port Authority on July 19, 1971. The applicant proposes to excavate by dragline landward of the existing sheet steel piling and subsequently to remove the piling to improve the existing docking facility.

All material removed will be placed on applicant's upland.

The biological report indicates the limited construction should not have significant adverse effects on marine life.

The Game and Fresh Water Fish Commission and the Department of Pollution Control have no objections.

Staff recommends approval of Dredge Permit No. 71-17 issued by Tampa Port Authority.

ACTION OF THE TRUSTEES:

On motion by Mr. Stone, seconded by Mr. Dickinson and adopted without objection, the Trustees approved the dredge permit issued by Tampa Port Authority to Seaboard Coast Line Railroad.

-13-

HILLSBOROUGH COUNTY - Dredge Permit, File No. 253.123-908

    Florida Portland Cement
    Post Office Box 1002, Tampa, Florida 33601

requests approval of Dredge Permit No. 71-19 issued by Tampa Port Authority on August 10, 1971. Applicant proposes to excavate approximately 18,000 cubic yards of material from an existing docking facility in Sparkman Channel.

Spoil will be placed on privately-owned upland.

The biological report is not adverse.

The Game and Fresh Water Fish Commission and the Department of Pollution Control have no objections.

Staff recommends approval of the dredge permit issued by Tampa Port Authority.

ACTION OF THE TRUSTEES:

On motion by Mr. Dickinson, seconded by Mr. Conner and adopted without objection, the Trustees approved the dredge permit issued by Tampa Port Authority to Florida Portland Cement.

-14-

PINELLAS COUNTY - Core Borings

Department of Coastal & Oceanographic Engineering
University of Florida, Gainesville, Florida,

requests a permit to conduct fourteen core borings in
Anclote Anchorage and St. Joseph Sound along the route of an
existing navigation channel to augment cores taken by Corps of
Engineers. The cores each will be approximately 6 feet long
with a diameter of less than 4 inches.

The Department of Natural Resources, the Game and Fresh Water
Fish Commission and the Department of Air and Water Pollution
Control have no objections.

Applicant requests that all fees be waived.

Staff recommends approval of a permit for the core borings and
that all fees be waived.

ACTION OF THE TRUSTEES:

On motion by Mr. Conner, seconded by Mr. Dickinson and adopted
without objection, the Trustees approved issuance of permit
for the core borings without charge as recommended by the staff.

-15-

BROWARD COUNTY - Hallandale Beach Restoration Project

The Board of Trustees in meeting on March 19, 1969, agreed to a
beach nourishment project for the City of Hallandale Beach,
Florida

Upon approval of this nourishment project by the Department of
Natural Resources, the Board of Trustees was to issue ex parte
disclaimers to any land lying landward of the restoration line
in exchange for quitclaim deeds from the riparian upland owners
to any land oceanward of this restoration line.

Staff received quitclaim deeds from the following applicants:
Morris Gates and Anna Gates, husband and wife; Co-executors of
the Estate of Samuel Rizzo, deceased; Windrift Enterprises, Inc.
and B. B. Weisberg and Thelma Weisberg his wife; Dakar Investment
Corp; Acmar Engineering Corp; John Rosen, Sol Berger and Security
Management Corp.

Request authority to issue ex parte disclaimers to these applicants.

ACTION OF THE TRUSTEES:

On motion by Mr. Stone, seconded by Mr. Dickinson and adopted
without objection, the Trustees authorized issuance of ex parte
disclaimers to the applicants listed above.

-16-

WAKULLA COUNTY - Dredge Permit, 253.123-688

Wakulla Outdoor Enterprises, Inc.
833 West Tharpe Street, Tallahassee, Florida 32303

requests a permit to excavate an access channel approximately 180
feet long x 20 feet wide (bottom cut) x (-4) feet deep mean low
water and a second access channel approximately 100 feet long x
20 feet wide (bottom cut) x (-4) feet deep mean low water. Both
channels will connect to the Wakulla River in Lot 3 Hartsfield
Survey in Township 3 South, Range 1 West, Wakulla County.

Applicant proposes to remove 2,600 cubic yards of material from
sovereignty land to be placed upon privately-owned upland.
A check for $1,300 representing the payment at the established
rate of 50¢ per cubic yard has been tendered.

9-7-71

The Department of Natural Resources forwarded the biological survey conducted by the Game and Fresh Water Fish Commission that was initially adverse but does not object to the revised project providing all dredging will be done by dragline or end-loader, all spoil placed on the applicant's upland above the mean high water line, and all upland dredging completed before removing the earthern plugs at the mouth of the canals.

The Department of Pollution Control recommended two channels for flushing within the interior network of canals and boat basin. The applicant has revised the project to meet this recommendation.

Staff recommends approval of the permit providing that all work be done as recommended by the Game and Fresh Water Fish Commission.

ACTION OF THE TRUSTEES:

On motion by Mr. O'Malley, seconded by Mr. Stone and adopted without objection, the Trustees approved issuance of the dredge permit to Wakulla Outdoor Enterprises, Inc., subject to all work being done as recommended by the Game and Fresh Water Fish Commission.

-17-

DUVAL COUNTY - Jacksonville Harbor Channel Deepening Project

The Board of Trustees and the North Shore Corporation granted perpetual spoil disposal easements over certain lands on the north side of Fanning Island for the disposal of spoil and dredged material from the construction and maintenance of the Jacksonville Harbor deepening project. These certain lands are comprised of marsh and sovereignty lands.

To avoid depositing of spoil and dredged material in the dedicated spoil disposal areas and the subsequent destruction of these valuable marsh and sovereignty lands, the Jacksonville Port Authority sought upland spoil disposal areas from the North Shore Corporation which has agreed to grant an easement to previously spoiled areas on Fanning Island provided, however, that they will not be charged for the spoil material.

The staff appraiser has indicated the placement of the fill material in this upland area will not materially enhance the property, since fill from previous channel dredgings exists on the site in sufficient quantities to raise the spoil area to a usable grade. Therefore the additional fill will be surplus to the needs of the designated spoil areas as of this date and represents a material inventory having some removal and sale potential as of this date.

Recommend that there be no charge levied for this material provided that the spoil areas be adequately diked and provided that the North Shore Corporation will not take any action to cause any spoil or dredged material placed on its upland property on Fanning Island to be spread in or otherwise invade or damage the adjacent marsh or sovereignty lands lying within the existing perpetual spoil area.

ACTION OF THE TRUSTEES:

Mr. Kuperberg said the staff carefully reviewed the matter discussed briefly last week and found no satisfactory alternate spoil sites, the public spoil areas being productive biological marsh on which none of this spoil would be placed. He thanked the North Shore Corporation for working with the staff to reach the best possible solution to this particular project, under way when he found out about it. He felt that there was a further question to be investigated regarding equities when sovereign lands are dug and placed on private properties.

Governor Askew pointed out that as a condition to having the spoil placed there without charge, unsolicited by the corporation,

North Shore Corporation would take ⅿ action to spread any of
the material into the marsh lands. The delay had worked for
the better by finding the site that would cause the least
possible damage.

Mr. Herman Ulmer of Ulmer, Murchison, Ashby and Ball, attorney
for the corporation, assured the Trustees that the conditions
in the recommendation were satisfactory, that the firm would
not spread any material on the adjacent marsh but would provide
an alternate area for the Port Authority and the Corps of Engineers
to do the work in order to save the marshes that were originally
requested of the corporation by the Corps. His client would
not be in control of the work but would contribute money towards
erection of the dikes to be built under contract with Jacksonville Port Authority as designed by the Corps of Engineers. The
corporation had nⅽt solicited the spoil in 1967 - the Corps of
Engineers had requested a spoil area that the Corporation had
agreed to provide.

Attorney General Shevin said he understood and thought that was
all the corporation could be responsible for.

Motion was made by Mr. Christian, seconded by Mr. Dickinson and
adopted without objection, that the staff recommendation be
approved as the action of the Board.

On motion duly adopted without objection, the meeting was adjourned.

GOVERNOR   CHAIRMAN

ATTEST:

EXECUTIVE DIRECTOR

        *   *   *   *

Tallahassee, Florida
September 14, 1971

The State of Florida Board of Trustees of the Internal Improvement
Trust Fund met on this date in the auditorium of the Department
of Transportation with the following members present:

Reubin O'D. Askew	Governor
Richard (Dick) Stone	Secretary of State
Robert L. Shevin	Attorney General
Fred O. Dickinson, Jr.	Comptroller
Thomas D. O'Malley	Treasurer
Floyd T. Christian	Commissioner of Education
Doyle Conner	Commissioner of Agriculture

Joel Kuperberg	Executive Director

Attorney General Shevin expressed concern regarding recent
action of the cabinet approving an application as an emergency
addendum from Florida Power and Light Company, and then four
days later the Department of Pollution Control had denied
that company's application. He felt that the staffs of the
two agencies should work more closely together so that the
Trustees would know whether the other agency was going to
approve or deny an application to be considered by the Trustees.

Mr. Kuperberg explained that he had been requested to agenda
that dredging application because of the overriding public
interest. The staff of the Department of Pollution Control had

approved issuance of the channel dredge permit and then, after
that board determined that it would consider all applications
involving power plants, revoked that approval. Mr. Kuperberg
said the staff would like to be involved in site selection
for power plants.

Governor Askew said the Trustees' approval was in the area of
their responsibility, the channel dredging, not approval of
operation of the power plant; and every effort should be made
to have complete cooperation between staffs of the two agencies.

-1-

DADE COUNTY - Purchase Application Denial
             File No'. 679-13-253.12, Swan Key,
             City of Islandia

Applicant: Richard B. Swanson
             Spring Mill, Harpers Ferry, West Virginia 25425

     By: T. H. Teasley
             Padgett, Teasley, Niles and Davison
             2505 Ponce de Leon Boulevard, Coral Gables,
             Florida 33134

The application was submitted to the Trustees on October 9, 1956.
It was submitted on June 1, 1960, advertised for objections, and
scheduled for final action on December 19, 1961. Action was
deferred, along with numerous other applications in the City of
Islandia. The application was again considered by the Trustees on
February 20, 1962, and the Board on August 28, 1962, agreed to
complete the sale subject to the purchaser coming to an agreement with the City of Islandia and Dade County.

On October 4, 1963, the applicant was notified that the matter
was being placed in the inactive file; and reactivation of the
application would be subject to future changes in policy, rules and
regulations. The application, on the agenda December 2, 1969, with
recommendation for denial, was deferred at the request of the
applicant.

Although Swan Key was not included in the Biscayne National
Monument, the sovereignty lands abutting it are in Aquatic Pre-
serve A-12 (Biscayne Bay - Cape Florida to South Dade County
Line) established by the Trustees on October 21, 1969.

Staff recommends that the Trustees rescind the action of August
28, 1962, as it relates to this purchase application, and that the
request for purchase of 66.2 acres of submerged bay bottoms be
denied and the file be deactivated, and that the $50 application
fee be refunded.

ACTION OF THE TRUSTEES:

Motion was made by Mr. Stone, seconded by Mr. O'Malley and
adopted without objection, that the staff recommendation be
approved.

The applicant had requested that the denial be without
prejudice, as he might submit a modified application. The
Executive Director said in the staff's judgment a simple
denial would be without prejudice. Governor Askew said it
was understood that the denial would be without prejudice.
The Attorney General questioned return of the filing fee. The
Director advised that in the case of the Swanson application
the administrative rule required payment of $50 for advertising
costs, and since the application did not reach that stage the
staff recommended refund of the unexpended fee. Under present
administrative rules an applicant must submit $75, of which
$50 is for advertising the proposed purchase and $25 is the
processing fee which may be refunded. He had directed the Land
Management Division that in the future the processing fee will
not be refunded, as often there is more work involved in gathering
data to justify a denial.

9-14-71

Mr. Shevin accepted the explanation in this case, but at his suggestion the Director would consult the chief counsel regarding possible change of the rules.

-2-

PALM BEACH COUNTY - Land Sale, File No. 2414-50-253.36

Staff description: A parcel of reclaimed lake bottom land 100 ft. wide in Lake Okeechobee in unsurveyed Sections 18 and 19, Township 43 South, Range 35 East, Palm Beach County, 3.78 acres

Applicant: Clewiston Syrup Mill, Clewiston, Florida
By: Howard S. Rhoads,
Post Office Box 1480, Fort Myers, Florida 33902
Acreage: 3.78 acres (100 ft. wide by 1600 ft. long)
Offer: Appraised value
Appraisal:. $3,000 for the parcel
Date: July 6, 1971
Appraiser: John H. Kline, S.R.A., Reviewed by Staff Appraiser
Purpose: To acquire land which separates present ownership on which to create a privately-operated public recreational camping park
Biological
Report: Not applicable

On August 3, 1971, the Trustees authorized advertisement of this parcel, which is surplus canal right-of-way.

The Board of County Commissioners of Palm Beach County and of Hendry County, the City Commission and Board of Directors of the Chamber of Commerce of Clewiston, all state that the creation of the proposed recreational camping park would be in the public interest. The Department of Natural Resources, the Game and Fresh Water Fish Commission and the Department of Pollution Control have no objections.

Staff remarks: The applicant has offered to purchase this land or to trade a ten-acre parcel of land 10 miles south of Arcadia for it. The ten-acre parcel does not have vehicular access. Staff recommends sale of the 3.78 acres of land for $1,000 per acre.

ACTION OF THE TRUSTEES:

On motion by Mr. Conner, seconded by Mr. Stone and adopted without objection, the Trustees approved sale of the 3.78 acres for $1,000 per acre, it being the decision of the Board that the sale was in the public interest.

-3-

SANTA ROSA COUNTY - Consideration of Oil and Gas Lease Bids

On August 3 the Trustees authorized advertisement for sealed bids for a five-year oil and gas drilling lease covering the one-half undivided interest held by the State in Lots 1 and 2, Section 28, Township 6 North, Range 29 West, containing 80 surface acres in Santa Rosa County.

The lease requires an annual rental of $1 per net mineral acre, $50,000 surety bond, 1/6 royalty and at least one test well every 2 1/2 years to a depth of 6,000 feet or to a depth sufficient to test the Norphlet Sands, whichever is deeper. No drilling will be permitted in the waters of streams, rivers or lakes within the leased area.

Invitation to bid was advertised pursuant to law in the Tallahassee Democrat and the Milton Press-Gazette with bids to be opened at 10:00 a.m. (DST) on September 14, 1971, for consideration by the Trustees.

ACTION OF THE TRUSTEES:

Mr. James T. Williams of the Trustees' Land Records Division
reported that one bid had been received from Louisiana Land
and Exploration Company in the total amount of $7,040.00, the bid
was in order, and he recommended awarding the lease.

On motion by Mr. Christian, seconded by Mr. Stone and adopted
without objection, the Trustees accepted the bid and authorized the
oil and gas drilling lease issued to Louisiana Land and Exploration
Company.

-4-

SANTA ROSA COUNTY - Consideration of Oil and Gas Lease Bids

On August 3 the Trustees authorized advertisement for sealed bids
for a five-year oil and gas lease covering the one-half undivided
interest held by the State in privately-owned N 1/2 of NW 1/4 of
SE 1/4 of SE 1/4 of Section 22, Township 5 North, Range 29 West,
containing 5 surface acres in Santa Rosa County.

The lease requires an annual rental of $1 per net mineral acre,
$50,000 surety bond, 1/6 royalty and at least one test well every
2 1/2 years to a depth of 6,000 feet or to a depth sufficient to
test the Norphlet Sands, whichever is deeper. No drilling will
be permitted in the waters of streams, rivers and lakes within
the leased area.

Invitation to bid was advertised pursuant to law in the Tallahassee
Democrat and the Milton Press-Gazette, with bids to be opened at
10:00 a.m. (DST) on September 14, 1971, for consideration by
the Trustees.

ACTION OF THE TRUSTEES:

Mr. James T. Williams reported the following six bids received:

1. $13,187.50 from Harris R. Fender, Harris R. Fender, Jr.,
    David M. Fender and Phillip B. Berry
2. $7,732.50 from Sun Oil Company
3. $10,780.00 from Dalco Oil Company
4. $6,264.00 from Humble Oil Company
5. $3,802.00 from Chevron Oil Company
6. $4,002.50 from Frederick Gillmore III

All were in order with the exception that cashier's or certified
check was required and Mr. Fender had submitted a bank money
order. Attorney General Shevin said there was no problem in
that regard.

On motion by Mr. Conner, seconded by Mr. O'Malley and adopted
without objection, the Trustees accepted the high bid of
$13,187.50 and authorized oil and gas drilling lease issued
to the high bidder.

-5-

DADE COUNTY - Campsite Lease No. 2210

    Nicola and Associates
    922 Alfred I. DuPont Building, Miami, Florida,

made application for renewal of Campsite Lease No. 2210. Applicant tendered check for $300 as yearly rental on lease of 1/4 acre
in the south shoal area in Biscayne Bay.

Staff recommends renewal of lease at annual rental of $300 for
1/4 acre.

9-14-71

ACTION OF THE TRUSTEES:

Motion was made by Mr. O'Malley, seconded by Mr. Stone that renewal of the lease be approved.

Mr. Kuperberg said it had been suggested that although there were no federal requirements concerning sanitary sewerage facilities, the Trustees might want to include in the renewal a requirement in that regard.

The motion was amended by Mr. O'Malley, seconded by Mr. Stone and adopted without objection, that the lease renewal be approved contingent upon provision being made by the lessee to prevent discharge of any raw sewage from this site.

Mr. Christian noted that other similar leases had been approved without such a provision. Mr. Kuperberg stated that the staff would include a recommendation for that provision in any future renewal applications.

-6-

LEON COUNTY - Sewer Line Easement

The City of Tallahassee requests an easement 10 feet by 968 feet for an underground sanitary sewer line across the western portion of the Sunland Hospital property in Section 29, Township 1 North, Range 1 East, Leon County.

The Department of Health and Rehabilitative Services has reviewed and approved the request for easement.

Recommend issuance of the easement.

ACTION OF THE TRUSTEES:

On motion by Mr. Dickinson. seconded by Mr. Conner and adopted without objection, the Trustees authorized issuance of the easement requested by the City of Tallahassee.

-7-

POLK COUNTY - Road Right of Way

The City of Haines City requests an easement 12 feet wide on the south side of the Haines City National Guard Armory property for street widening purposes. The strip is described as the South 12 feet of Lots 10 and 11, Block 43, of Haines City per plat book 3A, Page 12B, public records of Polk County, Florida.

The Armory Board has reviewed and approves the proposed road easement.

Recommend issuance of the easement for public road purposes only.

ACTION OF THE TRUSTEES:

On motion by Mr. Dickinson, seconded by Mr. Conner and adopted without objection, the Trustees authorized issuance of the easement requested by the City of Haines City.

-8-

ST. LUCIE COUNTY - Road Right of Way

The Board of County Commissioners of St. Lucie County by resolution adopted January 19, 1971, requests an easement for public road purposes across the north 40 feet of NE 1/4 of NE 1/4 of Section 33, Township 35 South, Range 40 East, St. Lucie County. The right of way requested is that portion of an existing county

9-14-71

road known as Bell Avenue across the North 40 feet of N 1/2 of NE 1/4 of NE 1/4 of Section 33 owned by the Trustees, in use by the Department of Transportation and known as the old Ft. Pierce Convict Camp. That department has reviewed and approved the easement.

Recommend issuance of the easement for public road purposes only.

ACTION OF THE TRUSTEES:

On motion by Mr. Dickinson, seconded by Mr. Conner and adopted without objection, the Trustees authorized issuance of the easement requested by the Board of County Commissioners of St. Lucie County for public road purposes.

-9-

BROWARD COUNTY - Utility Installation with Dredging
              File No. 253.123-431A

   Florida Power and Light Company, by W. B. Flewellen, Jr.,
      Division Engineer
   Post Office Box 8248, Ft. Lauderdale, Florida 33310,

applies for a permit to dredge for installation of 2 additional submarine cables in Section 26, Township 51 South, Range 42 East, Intracoastal Waterway, Broward County. The cables will be placed in the same location authorized by Permit No. 431.

The biological report is not adverse. The Game and Fresh Water Fish Commission and the Department of Pollution Control have no objections.

Staff recommends approval.

ACTION OF THE TRUSTEES:

On motion by Mr. Stone, seconded by Mr. Dickinson and adopted without objection, the Trustees authorized issuance of the permit requested by Florida Power and Light Company for installation of the submarine cables.

-10-

MARTIN COUNTY - State Construction Permit, Section 253.03, F. S.

   Royal American Industries, Inc.
   1001 Park Avenue, Lake Park, Florida 33403

requests a state permit for the construction of a bridge across the northwest prong of the Loxahatchee River in Section 22, Township 40 South, Range 42 East, Martin County. $100 processing fee has been tendered.

The bridge will be placed on privately-owned submerged land conveyed by Trustees' Deed No. 21253-B.

The Department of Natural Resources, the Game and Fresh Water Fish Commission, the Department of Pollution Control, the Board of County Commissioners of Martin County, the Central and Southern Florida Flood Control District, and the U. S. Coast Guard have no objections to the proposed structure.

Staff recommends approval.

ACTION OF THE TRUSTEES:

On motion by Mr. Dickinson, seconded by Mr. Conner and adopted without objection, the Trustees approved issuance of state construction permit for the bridge. Mr. Kuperberg said the problems had been resolved and the local authority approved the application.

SANTA ROSA COUNTY - Dredge permit 253.123-504, Refund

> Robert A. Duncan
> 614 Fairpoint Drive, Gulf Breeze, Florida,

on April 28, 1970, was issued a permit to excavate 173 cubic yards
of material from Pensacola Bay. Mr. Duncan advises that due to
his inability to get a dredge to do the work that was authorized,
he obtained the needed material from upland sources. He would
like a refund of the $50 he paid for the material.

Field Operations made an on-site inspection and confirms that no
dredging has been done.

Recommend authorization be granted for refund of the $50 paid
for the material and cancellation of the permit.

ACTION OF THE TRUSTEES:

Mr. Kuperberg said $50 was paid for material that was to have been
excavated, but the permittee had the material trucked to the site
instead of dredging.

On motion by Mr. O'Malley, seconded by Mr. Stone and adopted
without objection, the Trustees approved cancellation of the
permit and refund of the $50.

-12-

MONROE COUNTY - Bulkhead Line, Dredge and Fill
                Section 253.122, F. S.

The Board of County Commissioners of Monroe County by Resolution
No. 62-1970 adopted on July 21, 1971, established a bulkhead line
2,876.97 feet long adjacent to upland on Stock Island in Section
35, Township 67 South, Range 25 East, and Section 2, Township
68 South, Range 25 East, Monroe County.

The biological survey report is adverse. The Game and Fresh Water
Fish Commission has objected to the proposed project.

Dedication No. 24168A was rescinded by action of the Trustees
on December 16, 1969.

Staff recommends modification of the bulkhead line, dredge and fill
permit applications in accordance with the bulkhead line recommended
to the Florida Keys Aqueduct Authority at the August 31 meeting
of the Board of Trustees.

ACTION OF THE TRUSTEES:

On motion by Mr. Shevin, seconded by Mr. Christian and Mr. O'Malley
adopted without objection, the Trustees denied the application
with a recommendation to the Board of County Commissioners that
modifications be made in accordance with the bulkhead line
recommended to the Florida Keys Aqueduct Authority at the August
31 meeting of the Trustees.

-13-

TRUSTEES' FUNDS - Water Resources Investigations

Request authority to enter into an agreement with the United
States Department of the Interior, Geological Survey, for the
purpose of continuing water resources investigations during the
1971-72 year.

As in the past, various counties and conservation districts contribute approximately $12,000 which is to be matched by funds of the
Trustees. The total of these amounts is matched by the USGS for the

total effort.

The total 1971-72 cost for the Trustees will not exceed $12,000 and funds are available within the current operating budget.

ACTION OF THE TRUSTEES:

Mr. Kuperberg said that water resources investigation was one of the best uses of Trustees' funds.

On motion by Mr. Stone, seconded by Mr. Conner and adopted without objection, the Trustees authorized the Executive Director to enter into the agreement with the United States Department of the Interior, Geological Survey, that would commit funds of the Trustees to match the local contributions for the purpose of continuing water resources investigations.

-14-

MARTIN COUNTY - Beach Protective Devices

The staff has received a report that drivers of dune buggies are damaging federal and state park property on the north end of Jupiter Island by holding dune buggy rallies in this area.

Request authority to install the necessary protective devices subject to approval by affected state and federal agencies and post no trespassing signs to protect this area from further damage.

ACTION OF THE TRUSTEES:

Mr. Kuperberg said that Mr. Bill Lund had called to the staff's attention the great damage being done by dune buggies to lands in state park or federal ownership. He recommended installation of devices to prevent free access to the beach by the vehicles.

On motion by Mr. O'Malley, seconded by Mr. Dickinson and adopted without objection, the Trustees granted the authority requested.

On motion duly adopted, the meeting was adjourned.

GOVERNOR - CHAIRMAN

ATTEST: EXECUTIVE DIRECTOR

* * *

Tallahassee, Florida
September 21, 1971

The State of Florida Board of Trustees of the Internal Improvement Trust Fund met on this date in the auditorium of the Department of Transportation, with the following members present:

Reubin O'D. Askew   Governor
Richard (Dick) Stone   Secretary of State
Robert L. Shevin   Attorney General
Thomas D. O'Malley   Treasurer
Floyd T. Christian   Commissioner of Education

Joel Kuperberg   Executive Director

9-21-71

The minutes of the meetings of August 31 and September 7 were approved as submitted.

-1-

BROWARD COUNTY - Seminole Indian Lease

The Board of Trustees by Chapter 71-286, Laws of Florida was designated Trustee of the State Indian reservation lands superseding the Department of General Services. These reservation lands consist of 104,800 acres lying in Broward and Palm Beach Counties.

The Seminole Agency requests the Board, acting in its capacity as Trustee of the State Indian reservation lands, to approve an agricultural improvement lease, negotiated between the Seminole Tribe of Florida and Mr. and Mrs. Bill Osceola, members of the Seminole Tribe.

The lease is for a term of 25 years with option to renew for an additional 25 years. The lease has been approved by the office of the Attorney General. The proposed lease area is all of Section 33 and that part of Section 32 lying East of State Road 833 in Township 48 South, Range 35 East, containing 960 acres. The land lies outside of Conservation Area No. 3.

Recommend approval of the lease.

ACTION OF THE TRUSTEES:

Mr. Shevin noted that his office had approved the lease as to form and legality, and the content was being approved by the Board.

On motion by Mr. Stone, seconded by Mr. Christian and adopted without objection, the Trustees approved the lease.

-2-

OKALOOSA COUNTY - Advertise Oil and Gas Lease

Southern Natural Gas Company, Houston, Texas,

requests the Board to advertise for sealed bids for a five-year oil and gas drilling lease covering the reserved one-half interest of the state in the petroleum and petroleum products in nine scattered parcels of privately-owned land containing 363 surface acres in Section 34, Township 4 North, Range 24 West and Sections 2, 3, 4, 9, 10 and 15, Township 3 North, Range 24 West, Okaloosa County.

This request has been reviewed by the State Geologist who concurs in the following recommendation.

Recommend advertising for sealed bids for lease with an annual rental of $1 per net mineral acre, 1/6 royalty, five-year primary term, $50,000 surety bond, and at least one test well to 6,000 feet or to a depth sufficient to test the Norphlet Sands, whichever is deeper.

ACTION OF THE TRUSTEES:

On motion by Mr. Stone, seconded by Mr. Christian and adopted without objection, the Trustees authorized the land advertised for lease.

9-21-71

-3-

SANTA ROSA COUNTY - Advertise for Oil and Gas Leases

Phillips Petroleum Company, Shreveport, Louisiana,

requests the Board to advertise the following tracts for five-year oil and gas drilling leases covering the reserved undivided interest in the petroleum and petroleum products held by the state as shown:

Blackwater River State Forest

Tract 2 - S 1/2 and NE 1/4, Section 32, Township 3 North, Range 26 West, 1/4 interest, 480 surface acres

Tract 3 - All of Section 9, Township 2 North, Range 26 West, 1/4 interest, 636.48 surface acres

Private Ownership, Chapter 18296 (Murphy Act)

Tract 4 - E 1/2 of NW 1/4 of SW 1/4, Section 22, Township 2 North, Range 26 West; NE 1/4, Section 28, Township 2 North, Range 26 West; N 1/2 of NW 1/4, Section 34, Township 2 North, Range 26 West, 1/2 interest, 260 surface acres

Tract 5 - NW 1/4, NW 1/4 of NE 1/4 and N 1/2 of SW 1/4, Section 26, Township 2 North, Range 26 West, 1/2 interest, 280 surface acres

Tract 6 - S 1/2 of SW 1/4 and NE 1/4 of SW 1/4, Section 24, Township 2 North, Range 26 West; E 3/4 of SW 1/4 of SE 1/4, Section 25, Township 2 North, Range 26 West, 1/2 interest, 150 surface acres.

Each lease would prohibit drilling operations in the waters of streams, rivers and lakes within the leased area. The lessees would be required to notify the Division of Forestry and the Game and Fresh Water Fish Commission prior to entering the lands wthin the forest to conduct exploration operations.

The Game Commission and Division of Forestry have reviewed and approved offering the forest lands under the conditions listed above.

The State Geologist has reviewed this request and concurs in the following recommendation.

Recommend advertising each tract for a separate five-year primary term lease with a 1/6 royalty, $50,000 surety bond and at least one test well to 6,000 feet or to a depth sufficient to test the Norphlet Sands, whichever is deeper.

ACTION OF THE TRUSTEES:

On motion by Mr. Stone, seconded by Mr. Christian and adopted without objection, the Trustees authorized the land advertised for lease.

-4-

SANTA ROSA COUNTY - Oil and Gas Lease, Public Hearing

On April 27, 1971, the Trustees awarded a five-year oil and gas drilling lease covering 13.62 acres of State Road No. 89 right of way to Chevron Oil Company for its high bid of $42,917, subject to receiving the consent of the Town of Jay as required by Section 253.61(a), Florida Statutes. The consent of the town is necessary, as a portion of the leased area is within its corporate limits.

The Town of Jay by resolution adopted on August 24, 1971, has consented to the Trustees issuing this lease. Before lease can be issued a public hearing is required pursuant to Section 253.52, Florida Statutes, to give all interested persons an opportunity to be heard with respect to the issuance of the lease, because a portion of the road right of way lies within a radius of three miles of an incorporated town.

Recommend that James T. Williams of the Trustees' staff be designated to conduct the required public hearing pursuant to law and report to the Trustees the results of the hearing.

ACTION OF THE TRUSTEES:

On motion by Mr. Stone, seconded by Mr. Christian and adopted without objection, the Trustees approved the recommendation that Mr. Williams conduct the public hearing and report the results to the Board.

-5-

DADE COUNTY - Spoil Island Lease

    Mr. George R. Headley, Executive Director, Interama, Post Office Box 456, North Miami, Florida,

requests that the Trustees lease to Interama Sandspur Island in Biscayne Bay, a designated spoil island (MSA 1282) located in projected Sections 22 and 27, Township 52 South, Range 42 East, lying opposite Bakers Haulover Inlet in Dade County.

On December 15, 1970, the Trustees authorized the staff to proceed to have the island released from the easement and dedicate it as a preserve in conformity with the desire of Interama.

The Corps of Engineers requirements are such that securing the release is economically unfeasible as it is necessary that Florida Inland Navigation District procure an alternate spoil area.

The purpose of the lease is to preserve the spoil island in its natural state to provide a windbreak and wave barrier for a proposed marina installation. As part of the consideration, Interama will be responsible for policing and maintaining the area free of debris, trash and refuse and will allow public use.

Staff recommends annual lease period, with rental at $100 per annum, subject to a 90-day cancellation clause and subordinate to any interests of the Corps of Engineers.

ACTION OF THE TRUSTEES:

Motion was made by Mr. O'Malley, seconded by Mr. Stone and adopted without objection, that the Trustees approve lease of the spoil island to Interama at $100 per annum, subject to a 90-day cancellation clause and subordinate to any interest of the U. S. Corps of Engineers.

-6-

DADE COUNTY - Water and Sewerage Line Easement

    The Board of County Commissioners of Dade County

by resolution No. R 1129-71 adopted August 31, 1971, requests an easement covering the east 55 feet of the SE 1/4 of SE 1/4 of Section 28, Township 53 South, Range 40 East, Dade County, for installation and maintenance of underground water and sanitary sewage transmission lines.

The Trustees hold title to the S 1/2 of SE 1/4 which is under lease to the Federal Aviation Administration as a radio communications site. The FAA has reviewed and approved the proposed easement.

Recommend issuance of the easement.

9-21-71

ACTION OF THE TRUSTEES:

On motion by Mr. Stone, seconded by Mr. O'Malley and adopted without objection, the Trustees authorized issuance of the easement requested by the Board of County Commissioners of Dade County.

-7-

PALM BEACH COUNTY - Telephone Easement

Southern Bell Telephone and Telegraph Company,
Boca Raton, Florida,

requests an easement over and under that portion of the South 75 feet of Section 13, Township 47 South, Range 42 East and Section 18, Township 47 South, Range 43 East, Palm Beach County, lying in the Florida Atlantic University property. The easement is required for the relocation of a telephone cable from Glades Road right of way to a buried location on the existing overhead electric transmission line right of way along the south boundary of the campus. Relocation is necessary due to construction of Interstate 95.

The request was reviewed and approved by the Board of Regents on May 3, 1971.

Recommend issuance of the easement.

ACTION OF THE TRUSTEES:

On motion by Mr. Stone, seconded by Mr. O'Malley and adopted without objection, the Trustees authorized issuance of the easement to Southern Bell Telephone and Telegraph Company.

-8-

ESCAMBIA COUNTY - Marina License, Section 253.03, F. S.

Chemical Terminal and Storage Company
Post Office Box 1200, Tallahassee, Florida, 32302,

requests a marina license covering 3,875 square feet in Bayou Chico abutting Section 38, Township 2 South, Range 30 West, Escambia County. The minimum annual fee of $100 has been tendered. No dredging or filling is required for the proposed dock construction.

The Department of Natural Resources, the Game and Fresh Water Fish Commission and the Department of Pollution Control have offered no objections to the proposed construction.

Staff recommends approval.

ACTION OF THE TRUSTEES:

Motion was made by Mr. O'Malley, seconded by Mr. Christian and adopted without objection, that the application for a marina license be approved.

-9-

CHARLOTTE COUNTY - Dredge Permit, File No. 253.123-802

At the request of the applicant, Punta Gorda Isles, Inc., consideration of a dredge permit was deferred. It was scheduled for the agenda on October 5, 1971.

-10-

HILLSBOROUGH COUNTY - Fill Permit, File No. 253.124(8)-205

At the request of the staff, the Trustees deferred consideration of an application from University Downtowner Motel, Howard Sharps, President, Associated Franchises, Inc.

Mr. Kuperberg said the staff had thought the matter resolved and placed it on the agenda, but there was an alternate proposal from the applicant to be studied.

-11-

PALM BEACH COUNTY - Fill Permit 253.124-181

Mayfran, Inc.
c/o Brockway, Owen and Anderson
Post Office Box 3331, West Palm Beach, Florida 33402

requests approval of a fill permit issued by the Town of Palm Beach on June 8, 1971, to fill an area of submerged land embracing 0.698 acre in Section 11, Township 44 South, Range 43 East, Palm Beach County. This parcel was purchased from the Trustees as a sovereignty land sale on February 25, 1971, by Trustees Deed No. 25188.

Applicant proposes to truck in the fill material. The Department of Pollution Control has no objections.

The biological report states that the proposed fill area was productive prior to the removal in June, 1970, of the red mangroves; the parcel is now much less productive and filling it should not have significant adverse effects on marine biological resources.

The applicant paid $1200 for the unauthorized removal of the mangroves as a condition to the Trustees' conveyance of the sovereignty land.

The Game and Fresh Water Fish Commission recommends that the applicant develop a sloped intertidal zone waterward of the bulkhead. This may be accomplished by spreading enough fill to bring the bottom elevation up to the intertidal elevation. The area should then be planted with red mangroves to replace the trees prematurely destroyed by the applicant.

The Area Planning Board of Palm Beach County has no objections to the seawall and the fill permit.

Staff recommends approval of the fill permit issued by the Town of Palm Beach providing the applicant complies with the recommendation of the Game and Fresh Water Fish Commission.

ACTION OF THE TRUSTEES:

Mr. Kuperberg stated that this did not violate the moratorium imposed by Palm Beach County.

On motion by Mr. O'Malley, seconded by Mr. Stone and adopted without objection, the Board approved issuance of the fill permit on the basis recommended by the staff.

-12-

MONROE COUNTY - Request for Refund

Mrs. Josephine Giovannielli, a widow,
by Mr. Fred A. Bee, Marathon, Florida,

requests refund of the $800 purchase price for a .43 acre portion of an unsurveyed island conveyed by Trustees' Deed No. 19690, October 17, 1950, to Joseph Giovannielli and wife, Josephine Giovannielli. These lands were conveyed as sovereignty lands.

9-21-71

Subsequently, the United States Department of the Interior, Bureau of Land Management, surveyed the island and described the island as Government Lot 6, Section 20, Township 65 South, Range 34 East. This land was classified as public land of the United States. The plat of the survey was accepted by the Bureau of Land Management on November 23, 1954.

The Bureau of Land Management by Patent No. 1208091, May 2, 1960, conveyed the island to an individual.

Request authority to refund to Josephine Giovannielli the $800 purchase price for Deed No. 19690, under Chapter 253.29, Florida Statutes, as title to this land has failed.

ACTION OF THE TRUSTEES:

On motion by Mr. Stone, seconded by Mr. O'Malley and adopted without objection, the Trustees authorized refund of the purchase price for the land to which title had failed.

-13-

MINUTES OF THE TRUSTEES - Printing

Pursuant to authorization on August 17, invitation for bids for printing Volume 37 of the minutes of the Trustees for the period from July 1968 through June 1970 was duly advertised and the following two bids were received:

> Rose Printing Co., Tallahassee $6.95 per page
>   Estimated total $6,032.60
>
> St. Petersburg Printing Company $7.85 per page
>   Estimated total $6,813.80

Recommend that the bid be awarded to the low bidder.

ACTION OF THE TRUSTEES:

On motion by Mr. O'Malley, seconded by Mr. Shevin and adopted without objection, the Trustees awarded the bid to the low bidder, Rose Printing Company of Tallahassee.

Mr. O'Malley stated that volumes of the minutes were being sold at $10 each to members of the public, or agencies, which did not appear realistic in view of the cost of printing. He requested Mr. Kuperberg to review the basic cost and make a recommendation to the Board on increasing that price.

-14-

PATENTS, COPYRIGHTS AND TRADEMARKS

Mr. Kuperberg said the matter was placed on the agenda as requested, but that Mr. Monterey Campbell of the Department of Citrus was present and did not wish to have the matter considered on this date.

Governor Askew asked for a week's deferment and an opinion from the Attorney General, as there was a difference of opinion between the Trustees' legal counsel and the Department of Citrus counsel.

-15-

VOLUSIA COUNTY - Dredge Permit No. 253.123-944

Mr. J. Kermit Coble and Mr. William J. Roberts, attorneys for Daytona Beach Marina and Boat Works, were present to request an emergency permit for maintenance dredging to remove silt from channels and turning basin.

The staff had determined that the proposed work involved submerged bottoms in state ownership and ordered the necessary biological studies by the Department of Natural Resources, the Game and Fresh Water Fish Commission, and requested applicant to apply to the Department of Pollution Control for certification. Under the law the biological studies must be made within 90 days, but the applicant had been advised that the staff would process the application as quickly as possible and the environmental agencies indicated that they would expedite the studies.

Governor Askew stated that the Board always tried to hear those present, but they were being asked to make a decision on a technical matter without a staff recommendation. The Director had not determined that it was an emergency with no alternative.

On motion by Mr. O'Malley, seconded by Mr. Stone and adopted, the Trustees waived the rules to hear the extent of the emergency.

Mr. Coble explained that the boating season was at hand, a dredge nearby, and although an application should have been made prior to this time any delay of maintenance dredging would put many people out of work. He said the Board on five affirmative votes could waive biological studies and urged approval now of dredging necessary to get boats into the marina.

Mr. O'Malley requested deferment a week in order for the Director to furnish information for a decision to be made on waiving the regular procedure and asked for an aerial photograph of the area. Mr. Stone agreed, suggesting that the dredging might be permitted only in the slips until biological and environmental reports are received.

It was so ordered.

On motion duly adopted, the meeting was adjourned.

GOVERNOR   -   CHAIRMAN

ATTEST: EXECUTIVE DIRECTOR

*   *   *

Tallahassee, Florida
September 28, 1971

The State of Florida Board of Trustees of the Internal Improvement Trust Fund met on this date in the auditorium of the Department of Transportation, with the following members present:

Reubin O'D. Askew	Governor
Richard (Dick) Stone	Secretary of State
Robert L. Shevin	Attorney General
Fred O. Dickinson, Jr.	Comptroller
Thomas D. O'Malley	Treasurer
Floyd T. Christian	Commissioner of Education

Joel Kuperberg	Executive Director

9-28-71

-1-

TRUSTEES' FUNDS - Coastal Coordinating Council

The 1971 Legislature appropriated $207,016 from the operating trust fund of the Board of Trustees of the Internal Improvement Trust Fund to finance the operations of the Coastal Coordinating Council for the 1971-72 fiscal year.

Staff requests authority to transfer up to $207,016 to the Coastal Coordinating Council as the need arises.

ACTION OF THE TRUSTEES:

Mr. Kuperberg explained that the Council under the Department of Natural Resources was funded by the Legislature from the Internal Improvement Trust Fund. The budgeted amount is requested.

On motion by Mr. Stone, seconded by Mr. Shevin and adopted without objection, the Trustees authorized transfer up to $207,016 to the Coastal Coordinating Council as the funds are needed.

-2-

BREVARD COUNTY - Lease for Public Park

The Division of Recreation and Parks, Department of Natural Resources, requests the Trustees to lease to the City of Cocoa Beach for a term of 99 years a parcel in Sections 2 and 3, Township 25 South, Range 37 East, Brevard County, containing 6.95 acres, for public park development.

This parcel known as Fischer Park is located on the Atlantic Ocean with 300 feet of beach frontage. The city has deeded the land to the Trustees to be eligible for a $50,000 grant of park development money from the Department of Natural Resources. The department approved the park development project on May 26, 1971, committing the funds to the City of Cocoa Beach.

Recommend issuance of the lease to the City of Cocoa Beach for park and recreational purposes only.

ACTION OF THE TRUSTEES:

On motion by Mr. Dickinson, seconded by Mr. Stone and adopted without objection, the Trustees approved leasing the parcel to the City of Cocoa Beach for park and recreational purposes only as recommended by the staff.

-3-

SANTA ROSA COUNTY - Oil and Gas Lease, Public Hearing

On September 14 the Trustees awarded a five-year oil and gas lease covering a reserved 1/2 interest in 5 surface acres in the N 1/2 of NW 1/4 of SE 1/4 of SE 1/4 of Section 22, Township 5 North, Range 29 West, Santa Rosa County, to the highest bidder, Harris R. Fender, Harris R. Fender, Jr, David M. Fender and Philip B. Berry, from Tyler, Texas.

Before lease can be issued a public hearing is required pursuant to Section 253.52, Florida Statutes, to give all interested persons an opportunity to be heard with respect to issuance of the lease, because the leased area is within a radius of three miles of the incorporated Town of Jay.

Recommend that James T. Williams of the Trustees staff be designated to conduct the public hearing pursuant to law and report to the Trustees the results of the hearing.

ACTION OF THE TRUSTEES:

On motion by Mr. Dickinson, seconded by Mr. Stone, and adopted
without objection, the Board approved the recommendation.

Mr. Kuperberg said the staff planned to combine this public
hearing with one previously requested.

-4-

ESCAMBIA COUNTY - Consideration of Oil and Gas Lease Bids

On August 3 the Trustees authorized advertisement for sealed
bids for a five-year oil and gas drilling lease covering the
one-half undivided interest held by the State in a privately-
owned tract in the NW 1/4 of NW 1/4 of Section 11, Township 5
North, Range 33 West, Escambia County, containing 3.1 surface
acres.

The lease requires an annual rental of $1 per net mineral acre,
$50,000 surety bond, 1/6 royalty and at least one test well
every 2 1/2 years to a depth of 6,000 feet or to a depth sufficient
to test the Norphlet Sands, whichever is deeper.

Invitation to bid was advertised pursuant to law in the Tallahassee
Democrat and the Pensacola Journal, with bids to be opened at
10:00 a.m.(DST) on September 28, 1971, for consideration by the
Trustees.

ACTION OF THE TRUSTEES:

Mr. James T. Williams, Land Records Director of the Trustees
office, reported one bid received for the lease. Southeastern
Exploration Limited submitted a bid of $17.05 for lease of the
one-half interest in 1.55 net mineral acres held by the State
of Florida under a Murphy Act deed reservation.

Answering Governor Askew's question, Mr. Williams said that the
bid was good even though only one was received.

On motion by Mr. Christian, seconded by Mr. Stone and adopted
without objection, the Trustees accepted the bid and authorized
issuance of the oil and gas drilling lease.

-5-

ESCAMBIA COUNTY - Consideration of Oil and Gas Lease Bids

On August 17 the Trustees authorized advertisement for sealed
bids for a five-year oil and gas drilling lease covering the
one-half undivided interest held by the State in a privately-
owned tract in NE 1/4 of NE 1/4 of Section 10, Township 5 North,
Range 33 West, Escambia County, containing 6.9 surface acres.

The lease requires an annual rental of $1 per net mineral acre,
$50,000 surety bond, 1/6 royalty and at least one test well
every 2 1/2 years to a depth of 6,000 feet or to a depth
sufficient to test the Norphlet Sands, whichever is deeper.

Invitation to bid was advertised pursuant to law in the Tallahassee
Democrat and the Pensacola Journal, with bids to be opened at
10:00 a.m. (DST) on September 28, 1971, for consideration by the
Trustees.

ACTION OF THE TRUSTEES:

Mr. James T. Williams, Land Records Director, reported one bid
received from Southeastern Exploration Limited in the amount
of $37.95 for lease of one-half interest on the privately-
owned parcel in the same vicinity as land in the preceding item.

The land was approximately 20 miles west of the Jay area and considered a wildcat area. All costs of advertising such leases are paid by the successful bidder.

On motion by Mr. Stone, seconded by Mr. Christian and adopted without objection, the Trustees accepted the bid and authorized issuance of the oil and gas drilling lease.

-6-

PALM BEACH COUNTY - File No. 2370-50-253.12
                    1. Bulkhead Line Establishment
                    2. Application to Purchase

    Multicon Properties, Inc., applicant

On June 29, the Board authorized advertisement for objections to a proposed sale of 3.67 acres of sovereignty land along the north bank of the Hillsboro Canal in Section 31, Township 47 South, Range 43 east, City of Boca Raton, Palm Beach County. The notice showed August 17 as the date for consideration of the proposed sale.

The matter was deferred on August 17, as it was reported by Royal Palm Audubon Society that the applicant had already filled some sovereignty land.

The applicant furnished a topographic survey which indicated that fill material had been placed on land lying below the mean high water line elevation of 1.6 feet above mean sea level. This amounted to an encroachment on .583 acre of the 3.67 acres under consideration. Based on past Board action, the land encroached upon, if sold, should be priced at three times the appraised value.

The staff appraiser indicated the value of the 3.67 acres to be $70,000. The filled .583 acre parcel is valued at $12,500. Three time this amount is $37,500. The value of the unfilled 3.087 acres is $57,500. The total value of the land would be $95,000.

The staff has received several letters of endorsement and two letters of objection to this sale.

The Department of Natural Resources biological report indicates the proposed bulkhead line is a close approximation of the mean high water line, and that approval and subsequent development would not have significant adverse effects on marine biological resources.

The Game and Fresh Water Fish Commission has no objections to this project.

The Department of Pollution Control has indicated certification will be issued upon receipt of a copy of the Board of Trustees' permit.

Applicant has furnished extensive data representing this sale to be in the public interest.

Staff recommends the sale with use of the funds to reaoquire productive marine bottoms in an area and of a shape to be capable of protection from manmade erosion, overuse and the accompanying hazards of the high density urban environment.

ACTION OF THE TRUSTEES:

Mr. Kuperberg said the staff worked very hard on this application with the objectors and property owners, made several on-site inspections, and arrived at a solution satisfactory to all. Some 3.67 acres along the Hillsboro Canal apparently was not shown in the original survey as being submerged land. As a result of a staff investigation it was determined that the mean high water line did not follow smoothly along the line of the canal but did invade the Multicon property. Because it appeared that the 3.67 acres, if retained, ultimately would be lost to problems of high density and high boat uses of the canal, the staff felt it was in the public interest to sell the land and use the money to reacquire productive marine bottoms in an area and of a shape to be capable of protection from man-made erosion and the accompanying hazards of high density urban environment.

Governor Askew made it clear that the basis of the public interest determination was not that the money from the sale could be used for something else in the public interest, but that an integral part of the determination of public interest involved the present status and condition of the land and the proper uses for this particular land. The sale would not be a precedent, but the staff judgment was that this sale was in the public interest.

Motion was made by Mr. Dickinson, seconded by Mr. Stone and adopted without objection, that the Trustees approve the bulkhead line established by the City of Boca Raton on April 6, 1971, along the Northwesterly shore of the Hillsboro Canal in Section 31, Township 47 South, Range 43 East, Palm Beach County; and that sale of the advertised parcel of sovereignty land to Multicon Properties, Inc., be confirmed at the total price of $95,000 with the understanding that the money will be committed for use as recommended by the staff.

Treasurer O'Malley noted that the filled land was sold for three times its appraised value and that the Royal Palm Audubon Society should be commended for its investigation and calling attention to the matter. Mr. Kuperberg said officers of the Society were informed and agreed to the settlement although they would have preferred an acquisition of a suitable parcel of land in Palm Beach County that could be traded.

-7-

MONROE COUNTY - Dredge Permit, File 253.03-294

   Marine Harvesters Association, Inc., c/o Mr. Bela Zeky, President, Post Office Box 2081, Key West, Florida 33040

requests a permit to blow out a channel 560 feet by 25 feet (top cut) by -3 feet to -4 feet deep m.h.w. by use of a tug boat at Loggerhead Key in Hawk Channel in Sections 15 and 16, Township 67 South, Range 28 East, Monroe County. The spoil material will be blown over an area 1 foot deep within 50 feet on both sides of the proposed channel. The channel would gain access to the island for research on future aquaculture projects.

The Department of Natural Resources biological report states that the proposed 20 to 30 feet wide by -2 feet deep channel which will cut through the grass flat should have only limited adverse effects on marine biological resources.

The Game and Fresh Water Fish Commission states that the proposed operation will have very temporary adverse effects on the area and that full recovery can be expected.

The Department of Pollution Control has no objections.

Staff recommends approval of the dredge permit provided applicant notifies Trustees staff so that an on-site inspection can be made during channel clean-out operations and the work shall be stopped if it is determined that this operation has significant adverse effects on the marine resources in the area.

ACTION OF THE TRUSTEES:

Mr. Kuperberg said this kind of work in another county recently was unsatisfactory because of the nature of the bottom material, but the staff did not want to preclude cleaning out of a channel through the use of a large propeller provided the work could be properly supervised.

On motion by Mr. O'Malley, seconded by Mr. Stone and adopted without objection, the Trustees approved the dredge permit subject to the provision recommended.

-8-

BROWARD COUNTY - Construction Permit, 253.03 F. S., Bridge

> Island Club of Pompano, Inc.
> c/o G. W. Martin Seawall, Inc.
> 201 North Federal Highway,
> Deerfield Beach, Florida 33441

requests approval for the placement of a bridge structure across a land cut portion of the Pompano Canal in Section 6, Township 49 South, Range 43 East, Broward County. The applicant has tendered $100 processing fee.

The Department of Natural Resources, the Game and Fresh Water Fish Commission, the Department of Pollution Control and the Florida Inland Navigation District have no objections to the proposed project.

Staff recommends approval.

ACTION OF THE TRUSTEES:

On motion by Mr. Stone, seconded by Mr. Christian and Mr. O'Malley, and adopted without objection, the Trustees authorized issuance of the construction permit.

-9-

DUVAL COUNTY - Marina License, Section 253.03, F. S.

> Harrell's Marine, Inc.
> 2315 Beach Boulevard
> Jacksonville Beach, Florida 32250

applies for a marina license covering 5,500 square feet of sovereignty land in the Intracoastal Waterway abutting Section 32, Township 2 South, Range 29 East, Duval County. The minimum annual fee of $110 has been tendered. The proposed dredging has been authorized under State Permit No. 253.123-658.

The Department of Natural Resources, the Department of Pollution Control and the Game and Fresh Water Fish Commission have no objections to the proposed marina facility.

Staff recommends approval of the marina license.

ACTION OF THE TRUSTEES:

Mr. Kuperberg said that a problem regarding placement of the fill had been resolved. There were two Harrell's Marinas on opposite sides of the same road, there had been a misunderstanding, but everything is in order.

On motion by Mr. O'Malley, seconded by Mr. Stone and adopted without objection, the Trustees approved issuance of the marina license.

-10-

PINELLAS COUNTY - Marina License, Section 253.03, F. S.

    Department of Natural Resources
    Division of Recreation and Parks
    Room 613 Larson Building, Tallahassee, Florida,

requests a marina license 59,448 square feet in St. Joseph Sound
at Caladesi Island State Park in Section 20, Township 28 South,
Range 15 East, Pinellas County. Applicant has requested waiver of
all fees. No dredging or filling is required for the proposed
marina facility.

The Department of Natural Resources, the Game and Fresh Water Fish
Commission and the Department of Pollution Control have no objections
to the proposed project.

Staff recommends approval of license and waiver of fees.

ACTION OF THE TRUSTEES:

On motion by Mr. O'Malley, seconded by Mr. Stone and adopted
without objection, the license was approved without fees.

-11-

VOLUSIA COUNTY - Maintenance Dredging, File No. 253.123-944

    Daytona Marina and Boat Works,
    c/o Kermit Coble, Daytona Beach, Florida,

requests emergency consideration of a permit to perform
maintenance dredging in the existing channel and boat basin.
15,750 cubic yards of material will be removed and placed on
a previously filled area. Applicant has submitted a check for
$7,875 as payment for the material to be removed.

The biological report from the Department of Natural Resources
is not adverse.

The Game and Fresh Water Fish Commission has no objections.

The Department of Pollution Control has not been able to review
the project, however, staff believes that all turbidity problems
can be met by installing a silt screen across the mouth of the
channel.

Recommend approval provided that spoil areas are adequately
diked and a silt screen placed across the boat channel to protect
adjacent marine bottoms from siltation, subject to certification
by the Department of Pollution Control.

ACTION OF THE TRUSTEES:

The applicant agreed to protect adjacent marine bottoms as
recommended and staff counsel advised that the dredging operation
could be authorized subject to a final conclusion on an ownership
problem involving land built out into the Halifax River, the
original filling having been done in 1938.

On motion by Mr. O'Malley, seconded by Mr. Dickinson and adopted
without objection, the Trustees approved the permit for maintenance
dredging subject to the staff recommendations.

Mr. Kermit Coble, attorney for the applicant, requested waiver
of the $7,875 charge for material removed from the boat basin,
which he said was worthless silt. He indicated that an engineer's
certificate would be submitted.

Mr. O'Malley said the Board had previously waived payment in
the event an engineering determination showed the removed

9-28-71

material was silt and not useful for fill material. Mr. Stone
suggested that an applicant requesting waiver of the charge
for material could employ and pay an engineer of the Director's
choice to establish the value of the material. Mr. O'Malley
said the Director might designate his choice of three engineers,
the Trustees could consider the engineering report, 'and the
applicant had indicated he would pay the cost. Also professional
biologists paid by the applicant might make the analysis the
Director needed as to marine damage, Mr. Stone added.

Mr. Kuperberg discussed the difficulty of determining the value
of material in some cases, and the necessity to consider the
damage to the bottoms for which the state should be compensated.
While there might be some inequities, he was endeavoring to
protect the state's marine environment with a limited field
staff and a new policy for dredged material.

Governor Askew said he saw the problem, not only from the standpoint of whether the material was usable but also that the state did
not have to allow disruption of bottoms for the benefit of the
user. It would be helpful for the Director to develop some
policy fair to all concerned, including the state.

The Governor said this application was approved with the $7,875
charge for material, and if a refund could be justified the Board
would consider it at a later date.

Mr. Douglas Crane, representing Harrell's Marine, Inc., was
present in connection with Dredge Permit No. 253.123-787
approved by the Trustees on July 20, 1971, with payment for
the material removed from maintenance dredging of the existing
channels to be waived conditioned upon the Director receiving
adequate evidence that it was worthless silt. Mr. Crane said
the applicant immediately complied with the Cabinet's request
for core borings and an analysis by a registered laboratory
to establish that the material was not suitable for fill material,
but had not received refund of the $3,700 submitted in June.

He mentioned the other application from the same firm and that
nothing was said on the agenda today about refund or charge for
the silt at $1 per yard.

Governor Askew asked Mr. Crane to discuss it with the Director
who would do what was necessary to dispose of the matter.

Mr. Kuperberg explained that Mr. Crane's application was the
first issue of this kind, Mr. Coble's the second, the Trustees had
recently adopted a new fill policy designed to protect the
environment, and it would be very difficult to develop a policy
that would apply to all cases or to decide at what point the
charge should be refunded. The equities concerned him but he
intended to protect the state's marine environment.

Governor Askew stated that he supported the Director's position.

-12-

Joint Resolution with the State Board of Education

On motion by Mr. Shevin, seconded by Mr. Christian and Mr.
O'Malley, and adopted without objection, the rules were waived
and the Trustees of the Internal Improvement Trust Fund in
concurrence with the State Board of Education of Florida adopted
a resolution with respect to certain real property in Section 1,
Township 10 South, Range 19 East, Alachua County (a golf course)
of the University Athletic Association, Inc., a Florida Corporation not for profit. By the resolution both boards in concert
declined to accept the delivery of the deed described in the
resolution, now being held by the Atlantic National Bank of
Jacksonville as escrow depositary, and that bank was authorized
and directed to return and re-deliver the said deed to the
Association for such disposition as it deems necessary or proper
effective immediately upon passage of the resolution.

Last week Attorney General Shevin was requested to prepare an
opinion with regard to the powers of the Trustees and/or the
Citrus Commission regarding patents. He furnished an opinion
concluding that the assignment of a patent to a state agency
in the sense that all right, title and interest of the Trustees
becomes vested in such agency is not within the intent and
purpose of the statute and would violate the trust responsibilities
that have been imposed upon the Trustees.

The matter would be placed on the agenda next week.

On motion duly adopted, the meeting was adjourned.

GOVERNOR - CHAIRMAN

ATTEST:

EXECUTIVE DIRECTOR

Tallahassee, Florida
October 5, 1971

The State of Florida Board of Trustees of the Internal
Improvement Trust Fund met on this date in the auditorium
of the Department of Transportation, with the following members
present:

Reubin O'D. Askew	Governor
Richard (Dick) Stone	Secretary of State
Robert L. Shevin	Attorney General
Fred O. Dickinson, Jr.	Comptroller
Thomas D. O'Malley	Treasurer
Floyd T. Christian	Commissioner of Education
Doyle Conner	Commissioner of Agriculture

Joel Kuperberg	Executive Director

The minutes of the meetings of September 14 and 21 were approved
as submitted.

-1-

TRUSTEES' BUDGET. The staff requested acceptance and trans-
mittal of the 1972-73 legislative budget request to the Governor
and Secretary of Administration.

ACTION OF THE TRUSTEES:

Attorney General Shevin said that with the exception of the
Board of Education the law did not clearly set out responsibilities with respect to budgets, but he had determined that
the members had the authority to do more than accept and transmit
unless they delegated budgetary responsibilities to the secretary
or executive director. Mr. Stone commented on the insufficient
time for staff work on this year's budget.

It was the consensus that in the future the members could
exercise their responsibility by analyzing the budgets con-
structively, but this budget would not be delayed. Motion was
made by Mr. O'Malley to accept and transmit the budget to
the Department of Administration.

10-5-71

General Shevin felt strongly that operating expenses should not come from trust funds that should be used only for acquiring lands. He did not wish to delay this budget but to make known to the Governor and the Department of Administration that position.

Mr. Shevin offered an amendment to the motion, seconded by Mr. O'Malley, that the Board request the Governor and the Legislature to consider funding all operations of the Trustees' office and staff in the General Revenue Act for 1972-73 and to consider restoring the integrity of the public lands trust fund by restricting its use solely for the acquisition, protection and enhancement of the value of lands, waters and other irreplaceable natural resources which are essential to maintaining the quality of the natural environment.

Mr. Dickinson was not against the philosophy but suggested delay for further research and review, noting that the Legislature had considered this matter for some time.

Mr. Conner said that a policy proposition regarding trust funds could have resounding effects and he would like to give it more consideration.

Mr. Christian was assured that the provision of one-fourth of land sales proceeds for the public school fund would not be affected.

Governor Askew said the point was whether or not they would continue using trust funds for operations. He would be happy to receive any recommendations, but would abstain from voting as it would be referred to him for consideration of the budget.

Mr. O'Malley agreed that it had been considered in the past, and felt that the cabinet should express itself on the concept and request consideration.

On the amendment, Messrs. Shevin, Christian, Conner, Stone and O'Malley voted "Aye", Mr. Dickinson voted "No".

Governor Askew then called for a vote on the original motion to accept and transmit the budget, as amended by Mr. Shevin, which was adopted.

Secretary of State Stone said it was an appropriate time for him to change his vote to approval of Mr. Kuperberg as Executive Director, as he was well pleased by the staff work, orientation and approach since Mr. Kuperberg was nominated by the Governor and appointed.

-2-

ST. LUCIE COUNTY - Aquatic Preserve Extension, North Fork, St. Lucie River

The Board on August 31 deferred action on a proposed northerly extension of the North Fork of the St. Lucie River Aquatic Preserve that would include the area between White City Road (S. R. 712) and Selvitz Road (S. R. 611B).

The Interagency Advisory Committee on Aquatic Preserves recommended that the following clause be included in the resolutions establishing this extension of the preserve along the North Fork of the St. Lucie River:

"Nothing contained herein, nor in the basic implementing resolution adopted by the Board of Trustees on the 21st day of October, 1969, shall be construed to preclude the Board of Trustees from considering and acting upon applications for permits from city, county or other public bodies for construction and maintenance of drainage and flood control facilities, including but not limited to the maintenance of the river bottom to assure free passage of water."

The Board of County Commissioners of St. Lucie County and the Board of Supervisors of the North St. Lucie River Drainage District, the St. Lucie Cattlemen's Association and others are opposed to this extension.

Recommend approval of the Interagency Advisory Committee's recommendations for extension of the North Fork of the St. Lucie River Aquatic Preserve to include the area between White City Road and Selvitz Road.

ACTION OF THE TRUSTEES:

Mr. Kuperberg discussed the proposed extension as a buffer zone to protect the downstream section but not to preclude existing uses of the river for drainage or to prevent dredging with proper permits. He thought the clause was acceptable at one time but the staff was not able to reconcile the objections. He was not aware of the title questions raised today, but the wording of all aquatic preserve resolutions took care of questions of private and public ownership present in every area. He said many in favor of the extension had attended the public hearing but were not present at this meeting.

About twenty were present opposing the extension, including Mr. Weldon Lewis, County Administrator of St. Lucie County, Mr. Frank Fee, Sr., attorney of North St. Lucie River Drainage District, members of St. Lucie County Commission, St. Lucie Farm Bureau, City of Fort Pierce, Chamber of Commerce and property owners. Mr. Lewis said the river continually shoaled and required management to provide water control and drainage for that agricultural area. Placing the waterway in an aquatic preserve would make present uses difficult.

Mr. Frank Fee explained that the language of the clause was not acceptable to all concerned and made no reference to maintenance of that stream. He discussed opposition based on the opinion that it would harm the economy of St. Lucie County and would incorporate into a state preserve a stream largely not sovereignty land but privately-owned channels constructed by land owners. He spoke of the peculiar geographic aspect of the county, the present difficulties in obtaining permits from the various regulatory bodies, and the additional red tape that would result from inclusion in an aquatic preserve.

The Governor also had questions regarding the private ownership involved but noted that other aquatic preserves involved title questions, also. Mr. Conner said the burden of determining private ownership and precluding the private lands from the preserve should be shifted from private individuals to the state.

Mr. Conner made a motion, seconded by Mr. Dickinson, that the recommendation be denied.

Unless there was something unique in the northerly extension, Mr. Stone felt that the two purposes of the extension were already served (1) as to control of state land, and (2) dredging, which the Board had the right to prevent anyway.

Mr. Randolph Hodges, Chairman of the Interagency Advisory Committee, explained that the recommendation sought to accommodate drainage uses of the area because they would have to go to the Department of Pollution Control or the Trustees for permits, anyway.

Mr. Christian thought the hearings should determine those areas where an economic hardship would not be created, and this extension appeared to disturb local governments in carrying out their responsibilities.

Mr. Dwight Goforth, a biologist with the Game and Fresh Water
Fish Commission, explained why this area was unique as the
headwaters of the river, a buffer to protect downstream water
quality and the entire ecosystem.

It was suggested that legal questions regarding land titles
should be resolved, but the Attorney General did not see
anything that would prevent voting. Governor Askew said it
appeared that those present wanted a decision made. The Director
did not favor further delay. He pointed out that it should be
considered a state and not just a county problem, as the river
runs through more than one county.

On Mr. Conner's motion, seconded by Mr. Dickinson and adopted
four to three against the northerly extension of the North Fork
St. Lucie River Aquatic Preserve, the vote was as follows:

> For the motion: Messrs. Conner, Dickinson, Christian
> and Stone
> Against the motion: Governor Askew, Mr. Shevin and
> Mr. O'Malley.

-3-

MANATEE COUNTY - Paid-up Purchase Contract

On November 22, 1966, the Trustees issued Purchase Contract
No. 24446(1902-41) to Jerome V. Ansel, New York, New York
for the purchase of 6.4 acres of submerged land in Sarasota
Bay in Section 25, Township 35 South, Range 16 East, Manatee
County.   .

On-site inspections revealed that no filling of the purchase area
had taken place.

All contract payments have been paid and under the terms of
the contract the purchaser is entitled to a deed.

Recommend issuance of deed.

ACTION OF THE TRUSTEES:

On motion by Mr. Christian, seconded by Mr. Conner and adopted
without objection, the Trustees authorized issuance of the
deed to the land purchased under contract.

-4-

MARION COUNTY - Murphy Act Land Sale

On September 14 the Clerk of the Circuit Court of Marion County,
acting as agent for the Board, offered for public sale a parcel
105 feet by 210 feet, located in Section 14, Township 13 South,
Range 23 East. The parcel had reverted to the State under
Chapter 18296, Laws of Florida, Acts of 1937 (Murphy Act.) Notice of
sale was published in the Ocala Star-Banner pursuant to provisions
of Section 197.350, Florida Statutes. The value of $262.50 was
approved by staff appraiser.

John Collins and Annie Collins, his wife, bid $262.50 for the
parcel of land.

Recommend approval of the sale and issuance of deed to John Collins
and Annie Collins, his wife.

ACTION OF THE TRUSTEES:

On motion by Mr. Conner, seconded by Mr. Christian and adopted
without objection, the Board approved the land sale and
authorized issuance of the deed.

-5-

ORANGE COUNTY - Temporary Road Right of Way Easement

The Department of Transportation requests a temporary easement over and across a portion of a Highway Patrol Station located on State Road 50 in Orlando in Section 28, Township 22 South, Range 30 East, Orange County. State Road 50 will be widened and the Department is seeking authority to make the necessary driveway changes caused by the construction of the road.

The Department of Highway Safety and Motor Vehicles has reviewed and approved granting of the easement.

Recommend issuance of the temporary easement.

ACTION OF THE TRUSTEES:

On motion by Mr. Christian, seconded by Mr. Conner and adopted without objection, the temporary easement to the Department of Transportation was approved.

-6-

OKALOOSA COUNTY - Oil Lease Assignment

On March 24, 1969, an oil and gas lease was issued by the Florida Board of Forestry to Arthur E. Meinhart covering the 1/4 interest in the petroleum held by the State in 14,648.04 acres in Blackwater River State Forest in Okaloosa County.

Continental Oil Company, as holder of this lease by assignment, desires to assign its full interest to Continental Oil Limited, a limited partnership, Houston, Texas.

Executed assignment has been reviewed and approved by staff legal counsel as to form and legality. The Division of Forestry approves the assignment.

Recommend approval of assignment.

ACTION OF THE TRUSTEES:

Motion was made by Mr. O'Malley, seconded by Mr. Dickinson and adopted without objection, that assignment of the oil lease as recommended by the Division of Forestry be approved by the Trustees.

-7-

HILLSBOROUGH COUNTY - Dredge Permit, File No. 253.123-820

Tampa Electric Company
Post Office Box 111, Tampa, Florida 33601,

requests approval of Tampa Port Electric Authority Permit No. 71-10 to perform dredging for the maintenance of an existing breakwater at Big Bend, Hillsborough Bay, near Tampa in Township 31 South, Range 19 East, Hillsborough County. The applicant proposes to dredge alongside an existing breakwater which is 150 feet to 300 feet wide and about 2,600 feet in length. The applicant proposes to deposit the spoil material in the fill area to rebuild the breakwater to an elevation of +9.0 feet. The existing breakwater was intended to protect docking facilities and reduces re-circulation of warm water.

The Department of Natural Resources, the Game and Fresh Water Fish Commission, and the Department of Pollution Control have no adverse comments.

Staff recommends approval of the permit issued by the Tampa Port Authority.

10-5-71

ACTION OF THE TRUSTEES:

On motion by Mr. O'Malley, seconded by Mr. Dickinson and adopted
without objection, the Trustees approved the permit issued by
Tampa Port Authority for the maintenance dredging.

-8-

LEE COUNTY - Dredge Permit, File No. 253.123-900

    J. Hilbert Sapp
    Post Office Box 7757, Orlando, Florida, 32804,

requests a permit to connect applicant's upland boat basin to
Whiskey Creek in Section 15, Township 45 South, Range 24 East,
Lee County. 62 cubic yards of material will be removed from
sovereignty land and placed on privately-owned uplands. The
applicant has tendered a check for $62 in payment.

The Lee County Board of County Commissioners approved the
application on August 11, 1971.

The biological report is not adverse. The Game and Fresh Water
Fish Commission and the Department of Pollution Control have
no objections.

Staff requests authority to issue the dredge permit.

ACTION OF THE TRUSTEES:

Motion was made by Mr. Christian, seconded by Mr. Dickinson
and adopted without objection, authorizing issuance of the
dredge permit to Mr. Sapp.

-9-

MONROE COUNTY - Dredge Permit 253.03-234

    Long Duck Key Corporation
    by W. J. Roberts, Tallahassee, Florida,

requests a permit to connect an upland marina with the Bay of
Florida and to construct a navigation channel 350 feet long,
50 feet wide (top cut) and 7 feet deep at mean low water, in
Section 25, Township 66 South, Range 30 East, Monroe County,
4,355 cubic yards of material will be removed from this channel.

This application has been amended to conform with the recommendations of the Department of Natural Resources biological report
dated January 29, 1971. This channel will not have adverse
effects on the marine resources in the area.

The Game and Fresh Water Fish Commission recommends limiting the
channel to a top cut of 50 feet.

The Department of Pollution Control would have no objections to
the proposed project providing the problems with the boat basins
are resolved.

Applicant has offered to convey to the State of Florida a 1.4 acre
parcel of land on Ohio Key for a parking and turn-around area,
and a small island offshore from Ohio Key. The Department of
Natural Resources, Division of Recreation and Parks, along with
the Long Duck Key Corporation, proposes to establish a Rachel
Carson Memorial on these lands.

Staff recommends issuance of a dredge permit provided the
applicant restores any of the red mangrove fringe which may have
been destroyed along the perimeter of Ohio Key. Applicant should
post a $1,000 bond to insure that mangroves are restored to the
satisfaction of the Department of Natural Resources biologist.
Staff recommendation is further conditioned on applicant conveying by warranty deed to the State of Florida the 1.4 acre
parcel of upland adjacent to U. S. No. 1 and the unnamed offshore
key.

ACTION OF THE TRUSTEES:

Mr. Kuperberg advised the members that the red mangrove fringe was intact, mangroves had not been removed, and recommended approval of the application.

On motion by Mr. O'Malley, seconded by Mr. Christian and adopted without objection, the Trustees approved issuance of the dredge permit with the provisions recommended by the staff.

-10-

PINELLAS COUNTY - Utility Installation,
File No. 253.123(2)(b)-902

Pinellas County Sewer System
315 Haven Street, Clearwater, Florida 33516,

requests approval of Dredge Only Permit No. 196 issued by the Pinellas County Water and Navigation Control Authority on July 6, 1971, to install a 24" sewage force main across Long Bayou and Cross Bayou in Pinellas County.

The biological report recommends that construction be done in a manner to carefully conserve oyster bars and adjoining stands of intertidal red mangroves. Also, the sanitary sewer force main should be inserted deep enough to allow for the future construction of a small boat channel (50 feet wide by -5 feet deep mean low water) close to the West shore of Long Bayou.

The Department of Pollution Control and the Game and Fresh Water Fish Commission have no objections.

Applicant requests waiver of the $100 processing fee for utility installation.

Staff requests approval of Permit No. 196 by the Pinellas County Water and Navigation Control Authority subject to recommendation of the Department of Natural Resources and that the fee be waived because of the public works nature of the project.

ACTION OF THE TRUSTEES:

On motion by Mr. O'Malley, seconded by Mr. Dickinson and adopted without objection, the Trustees authorized waiver of the processing fee and approved the permit issued by the Authority subject to the recommendations of the Department of Natural Resources.

-11-

PATENTS, COPYRIGHTS AND TRADEMARKS
Consideration of the request of the Department of Citrus for assignment of right, title and interest in and to patents and patent applications was deferred for one additional week with the understanding that action will be taken then.

-12-

HILLSBOROUGH COUNTY - Fill Permit, File 253.124(8)-205

University Downtowner Motel
c/o Howard Scharps, President
Associated Franchises, Inc.

requests approval of fill permit No. 71-16 issued by Tampa Port Authority on March 11, 1971, to fill an area of submerged land in accordance with Section 253.124(8) pertaining to the reclamation of land lost by artificially induced erosion.

185 cubic yards of sand fill will be hauled to the site.

Applicant has amended his application in accordance with recommendations of the Department of Natural Resources to re-establish the intertidal zone and plant red mangroves in this area.

Guy N. Verger, Port Director of Tampa Port Authority, states that the Authority feels that this bulkheading would straighten up the shorelines and provide sound bulkheads and would have beneficial value.

The applicant states that placing the seawall at the line of mean high water will cause irreparable damage to the construction plans, as that is the area for the pool.

The Game and Fresh Water Fish Commission and the Department of Pollution Control have no adverse comments.

Staff recommends approval of Fill Permit No. 71-16 issued by the Tampa Port Authority subject to the stipulations of the Department of Natural Resources.

ACTION OF THE TRUSTEES:

On motion by Mr. O'Malley, seconded by Mr. Stone and adopted without objection, the Trustees approved the fill permit issued by Tampa Port Authority subject to the stipulations of the Department of Natural Resources.

On motion duly adopted, the meeting was adjourned.

GOVERNOR - CHAIRMAN

ATTEST:

EXECUTIVE DIRECTOR

Tallahassee, Florida
October 12, 1971

The State of Florida Board of Trustees of the Internal Improvement Trust Fund met on this date in the auditorium of the Department of Transportation, with the following members present:

Reubin O'D. Askew   Governor
Richard (Dick) Stone   Secretary of State
Robert L. Shevin   Attorney General
Thomas D. O'Malley   Treasurer
Floyd T. Christian   Commissioner of Education
Doyle Conner   Commissioner of Agriculture

Joel Kuperberg   Executive Director

-1-

The minutes of the meeting of September 28 were approved.

COLLIER COUNTY - File No. 253.123-51
          File Nos. 253.123-678, 253.124-149

   Marco Island Development Corporation

Staff will present proposed final agreement in this matter,
pursuant to the action taken on August 31 to allow an additional
45 days' extension on the permits subject to the staff memorandum
of August 31.

ACTION OF THE TRUSTEES:

The Executive Director briefly summarized his position, stating
that with the help of the Trustees and the particular help of
the Governor, the agreements submitted today have been accepted by
the staff and Marco Island Development Corporation. It was not entirely
satisfactory to Mr. Kuperberg as a biologist and a conservationist,
but it was the best he could do since the Board's attorneys advised
that an attempt to halt all construction would be a long, legal
battle over lands sold by the state in 1926.

Mr. Christian made a motion, seconded by Mr. Stone, that the
agreements be accepted.

Governor Askew said the Board recognized the difficulties involved
in reaching agreement on developments caught up in changing times
and new environmental protection laws. The Trustees had driven
a hard bargain but he thought it was a fair agreement and the
Board would go forward and extend some permits in the existing
development areas on Marco Island, and would work with the
developers in other areas consistent with the rules and the law,
which had been made clear to Marco Island Development Corporation
(Deltona). The Trustees had secured Kice Island which could be
the key to protection of one of the most valuable estuarine areas
in the state, and further acquisitions were anticipated in that
southwesterly part of Florida through the help of the federal
government and others.

Mr. Stone expressed approval of the agreements which as an ultimate
approach would help the environment, while it might have some
adverse points. He realized they could not always say "no"
in such cases.

Mr. O'Malley also commended the Director and the staff for the
settlement. In his opinion the objections and a demand for a
public hearing were inappropriate as all the transactions had been
open to the public and he was convinced the agreements were in the
best interest of the state, which would get approximately 4,000 acres.

The Governor pointed out that the agreement in no way obligated
the Governor or the Board to insure permits for any other areas,
and while they would not turn back or make technical objections,
Deltona was aware that it was a matter of good faith between
the firm and the agencies of the state, and the Department of
Pollution Control had full authority in the area of its
responsibility.

On the motion by Mr. Christian adopted without objection, the
Trustees approved the agreements as set out hereafter and made a
part of these minutes.

The Agreement to Convey was signed by the Trustees, and the
Articles of Agreement would be signed after the Trustees exercise
their discretion under Chapter 253 in reviewing the biological
reports submitted by the Department of Natural Resources on
the applications that include (1) Barfield Bay, (2) Blue Hill Bay,
and (3) the Big Key Bay-John Stevens Creek area.

AGREEMENT TO CONVEY

   THIS AGREEMENT made and entered into this 12th day of
October, 1971, by and between MARCO ISLAND DEVELOPMENT CORPORA-

10-12-71

TION (and the Deltona Corp., both hereinafter called MIDC), and
REUBIN O'D. ASKEW, RICHARD B. (DICK) STONE, ROBERT L. SHEVIN,
FRED O. DICKINSON, JR., THOMAS D. O'MALLEY, FLOYD T. CHRISTIAN,
and DOYLE E. CONNER, as being the Board of Trustees of the Internal
Improvement Trust Fund, a statutory agency of the State of Florida
(hereinafter called Trustees).

W I T N E S S E T H:

WHEREAS, the parties hereto have negotiated a detailed
settlement covering the numerous items of agreement relating
to MIDC'S holdings; and

WHEREAS, said agreement contemplates the exercise of the
discretion vested by Chapter 253, Florida Statutes, in the
Trustees who must comply with statutory prerequisites including
consideration of various studies prior to exercise of their
discretion; and

WHEREAS, the Trustees desire that an immediate conveyance
be made of the lands owned by MIDC known generally as Kice Island
and the submerged lands appurtenant thereto now owned by MIDC
which the Trustees previously conveyed under Trustees' Deed
No. 17,738, together referred to as Kice Island; and

WHEREAS, the attached Articles of Agreement provide that
MIDC will convey other lands to the Trustees as MIDC receives
the governmental permits (not including renewals) required to
develop its land in Collier County now platted as Units 1
through 24, excluding those units for which the Trustees agree
to issue permits herein; and

WHEREAS, the subsequent discretionary execution of said
Articles of Agreement by the Trustees will form part of the
consideration for this agreement; and

WHEREAS, all exhibits (numbers 1-16) attached hereto are
helpful to clearly express the intention of the parties hereto,
and all such exhibits are to be construed as part of this agreement and part of the attached Articles of Agreement, except
insofar as they may be inconsistent with the provisions of either;

NOW THEREFORE, in consideration of the mutual covenants
and promises herein contained, the parties do agree as follows:

1. MIDC will execute, to the Trustees or the State of
Florida, a fee simple conveyance of the lands of Kice Island,
said conveyance being subject to all outstanding mortgages or
other liens, which liens or mortgages MIDC will covenant to pay
and satisfy according to the terms of said mortgages or liens;
said executed conveyance to be delivered to the Trustees to be
held by said Trustees under the terms and conditions of this
Agreement.

2. The conveyance described in Paragraph 1 above shall
not become effective and no rights shall vest thereunder unless
and until all the following actions and all approvals required thereunder are taken and completed:

(a) Trustees issue to MIDC a renewal permit for
MIDC'S development area known as Marco River (Trustees'
permits #253.123-678 and #253.124-149), said renewal permit
to expire December 31, 1971.
MIDC agrees that it will revise its application
for renewal of the Marco River permit by restricting its
dredge area (exclusive of the Factory Bay portion of said
permit) to a total of 1,500,000 cubic yards encompassing
an area of 100 acres (formerly 3,000,000 and 240 respectively). Exhibit 9 delineates the revised dredge area.

(b) Trustees shall issue to MIDC a renewal permit
for MIDC'S development area known as Robert's Bay (Trustees'
Permit #253.123-51), said renewal permit to expire December
31, 1972.

(c) Trustees issue to MIDC its dredge and fill permit
for MIDC'S Collier Bay permit area (Trustees file #253.123-
679). (Said permit was previously approved by the Trustees
subject to certain restrictions, which have, under the terms
of the Articles of Agreement, been resolved.)

10-12-71

MIDC agrees to revise its application for the Collier Bay permit by restricting its dredge area to 42 acres (formerly 65). Exhibit 10 delineates the revised dredge area.

Although no governmental (state or federal) approval is required to fulfill this condition, the Trustees do agree that the three year term of the Collier Bay permit shall be stated to begin on the date the last required governmental permit (state or federal) is issued with respect to the Collier Bay permit area as long as MIDC pursues applications for such permits with due diligence.

(d) Trustees enter into a boundary line agreement with MIDC to immediately relinquish and convey to MIDC any and all interests the Trustees or the State of Florida may have in and to any of the lands included within the platted areas of MIDC known as Units 1 through 23. In return, MIDC shall agree to immediately relinquish and convey to the Trustees all of its interests outside the established bulkhead lines which MIDC obtained under and by virtue of Trustees' Deed #17,748 and all of its interests in those submerged areas adjacent to the recorded plats of Marco Beach Subdivision in Units 1 through 23. In further consideration of the relinquishment and conveyance of submerged lands by MIDC to the Trustees, the Trustees agree that MIDC will be allowed to remove sufficient fill material without charge from outside the platted lot line in Units 1 through 23 (as close to the construction sites as biologically feasible) in order to raise the platted properties to the elevation required under Exhibit 13, if MIDC has necessary permits, renewals or extensions approving or sanctioning such dredging and filling.

(e) Trustees execute the Articles of Agreement referred to above. It is understood that execution of the Articles of Agreement can only occur after the Trustees have given proper consideration to all matters required under the terms of Chapter 253, Florida Statutes, and only if after such due consideration the Trustees in the proper exercise of their discretion, approve each of the items stated therein.

3. Trustees shall, as soon as practicable, issue the permits described in paragraph 2(a), 2(b), and 2(c) and execute the boundary line agreement described in 2(d).

4. MIDC will, on or before December 1, 1971, file with Trustees, all necessary applications for dredge and fill permits to be granted under the terms of the attached Articles of Agreement.

5. In the event that each of the conditions described in paragraph 2 above do not occur within a reasonable period of time, (which shall in no event exceed one (1) year from date hereof), the Trustees shall return to MIDC the conveyance described in paragraph 1 above, the Trustees shall have no further right, claim or interest in or to the lands described therein; provided that the failure of such conditions to occur is not the result of a breach of this agreement by MIDC or otherwise attributable to the malfeasance or misfeasance of MIDC.

6. Upon the receipt of all the items set forth in paragraph 2 above, the conveyance described in paragraph 1 shall be considered delivered and fee simple title shall vest in the Trustees (or State of Florida) subject only to the aforementioned liens or mortgages, and the restriction against private use described in paragraph 12 of the attached Articles of Agreement. The parties hereto specifically acknowledge that the conveyance described in paragraph 1 is not conditioned upon any governmental action or approval other than as required of the Trustees by the terms of paragraph 2 above.

IN WITNESS WHEREOF, the parties hereto have executed this agreement the day and year first above written.

10-12-71

MARCO ISLAND DEVELOPMENT CORPORATION
(and the Deltona Corp.)
By FRANK E. MACKLE, JR.
President

STATE OF FLORIDA BOARD OF TRUSTEES
OF THE INTERNAL IMPROVEMENT TRUST
FUND

REUBIN O'D. ASKEW
GOVERNOR

RICHARD (DICK) STONE
SECRETARY OF STATE

ROBERT L. SHEVIN
ATTORNEY GENERAL

FRED O. DICKINSON, JR.
COMPTROLLER

THOMAS D. O'MALLEY
TREASURER

FLOYD T. CHRISTIAN
COMMISSIONER OF EDUCATION

DOYLE E. CONNER
COMMISSIONER OF AGRICULTURE

AS AND CONSTITUTING THE STATE OF
FLORIDA BOARD OF TRUSTEES OF THE
INTERNAL IMPROVEMENT TRUST FUND

ARTICLES OF AGREEMENT

THIS AGREEMENT made and entered into this _____
day of _____, _____, by and between MARCO ISLAND
DEVELOPMENT CORPORATION (and the Deltona Corp., both hereinafter
called MIDC), and REUBIN O'D. ASKEW, RICHARD (DICK) STONE, ROBERT
L. SHEVIN, FRED O. DICKINSON, JR., THOMAS D. O'MALLEY, FLOYD T.
CHRISTIAN, and DOYLE E. CONNER, as and being the Board of Trustees
of the Internal Improvement Trust Fund, a statutory agency of the
State of Florida (hereinafter called Trustees).

W I T N E S S E T H :

WHEREAS, the parties hereto, after protracted negotiations, executed an Agreement to Convey on October 12, 1971, in
which the execution of these Articles of Agreement was contemplated;
and

WHEREAS, the Trustees after consideration of the
required biological and ecological reports and other statutory
prerequisites, have determined that the execution of this
Agreement is in the public interest;

NOW THEREFORE, in consideration of the mutual covenants
and promises herein contained, the parties do agree as follows:

1. MIDC will convey to the Trustees, subject to the
conditions set forth herein, the lands described in Exhibit 6
and 7. These lands do not include the title to Kice Island and its
appurtenant submerged lands which will have absolutely vested in
the Trustees under the Agreement to Convey upon the signing of these
Articles of Agreement.

2. MIDC agrees that it will not sell or offer for
sale, prior to the issuance of all necessary dredge and fill
permits, state and federal, any lands except those now embraced
within the recorded plats of Marco Beach Subdivision, Units 1
through 24.

3. MIDC agrees to establish experimental mangrove islands
and a natural preserve area in Barfield Bay as indicated on Exhibit

10-12-71

.11; provided, however, that the design and ultimate issuance of the required dredge permits in Barfield Bay may necessitate a modification and/or deletion of one or more of the experimental mangrove islands shown on Exhibit 11.

4. MIDC agrees to continue its support and funding of a current study by the University of Miami which study will provide baseline ecological information, MIDC'S support and funding of said study being pursuant to the terms and conditions of agreement entered into by and between MIDC and the University of Miami.

5. MIDC agrees to continue through its environmental department its program of environmental studies and enhancement.

6. MIDC agrees that, pending the conveyances of lands described in paragraph 1 above, it will undertake no development or otherwise disturb the natural condition of the lands that lie south of Caxambas Pass (the parties acknowledge that the lands described in paragraph 1 include portions of Barfield Bay, Roberts Bay and Blue Hill Bay, all north of Caxambas Pass, in which there will be some dredge activity).

7. Trustees agree to issue for the term provided in paragraph 14 herein the permits necessary to enable MIDC to con-struct and develop the presently platted Units 1 through 23 as shown on the recorded plats according to the specifications and representations under which said lots were designed, advertised, offered for sale and sold as generally indicated on Exhibit 13; provided, however, that the Trustees agree hereunder to issue only those permits necessary for the development of Units 1 through 23 that were not issued or renewed as conditions of the conveyance of Kice Island under the Agreement to Convey; and further provided that the Trustees make no commitment to renew or further extend any permits to develop Units 1 through 23 under the Agreement to Convey or under these Articles of Agreement.

8. The Trustees have previously issued a dredge and fill permit for MIDC'S Unit 24. The parties specifically acknowledge that MIDC'S dredge and fill permit with respect to Unit 24 is now the subject of a pending proceeding before the Department of Air and Water Pollution Control and that modifi-cation to such permit may be required by said Department of Air and Water Pollution Control under the provisions of the Federal Water Quality Act of 1970, and further acknowledge that this Agreement does not and should not be construed as advocating the approval by any other governmental agency of MIDC'S Unit 24 as presently designed.

9. The Trustees make no commitment to issue a permit for the development of Horr's Island. However, in the spirit of working toward comprehensive land planning, the Trustees do agree to grant to MIDC reasonable navigational access through the preserve area, provided that MIDC applies to these Trustees during the term of their current administration. In return, MIDC agrees that when it does apply to the Trustees for the development of Horr's Island, it will restrict its application for development to only those areas shown on Exhibit 12 so that at minimum the remainder of the island is assured to continue in its natural state. The navigation access areas shown on Exhibit 12 do not necessarily represent the parties' understanding of "reasonable navigational access" since the number and location of specific access points shown thereby are subject to modi-fications as may be required when biological studies of the area are completed and application is made for the appropriate permits.

10. The improvement of MIDC'S lands in Collier County other than the now platted Units 1 through 24 will proceed according to the ecological and development principles which MIDC and the Trustees may agree upon at the time application is presented to the Trustees for development of those lands [i.e., those lands not covered by the Agreement to Convey or these Articles of

Agreement, which include the 7,500 acres more or less located north and east of Marco River as well as Horr's Island (except as specified in paragraph 9)].

11. Exhibit 7 identifies two separate parcels of land (upland and submerged) from which the Trustees may select the acreage to be conveyed by MIDC as agreed in paragraph 1 herein, provided, however, that all acreage within land area number one (1) must be used before any selection may be made in land area number two (2). Conveyances of the lands described in Exhibits 6 and 7 shall be made as and when MIDC receives all governmental permits, state and federal, necessary to permit MIDC three years of construction time with respect to each area to be permitted herein by the Trustees (with the exception relating to Unit 24 as set forth in paragraphs 8 and 14). Such conveyances shall be made in the amounts shown on Exhibits 6 and 7. Any modification or restriction of a Trustees' permit which is accepted by MIDC shall be deemed a permit issuance by that governmental agency. If MIDC does receive federal and state permits, but is not allowed to complete the full construction period authorized by the Trustees for any reason other than violation by MIDC of the terms of any state or federal permit, then the lands conveyed with respect to that area shall revert to MIDC and the Trustees shall forthwith issue to MIDC a quitclaim deed with respect to that acreage.

12. The conveyance of lands to the Trustees agreed upon in paragraph 1 herein shall be restricted against any private use. Exhibit 15 contains a copy of the restrictive convenants which shall be included in each conveyance from MIDC to the Trustees, except that such access facilities as are acceptable under federal laws pertaining tq Wilderness Areas shall be allowed without the consent of MIDC or its successors.

13. Trustees and MIDC agree that, as between the parties hereto, the section lines and designation contained in the survey entitled "Boundary and partial topographic survey, in Township 52 South, Range 25 East - Marco Island and vicinity, Collier County, Florida", prepared by Carl E. Johnson, Registered Land Surveyor, and recorded in the Public Records of Collier County, Florida, in Plat Book 187, Pages 1 through 74, shall be controlling in any legal descriptions required for conveyances or permitting purposes.

14. Construction permits (dredge and/or fill) to be issued under the terms of this Agreement (excluding the permit already issued for Unit 24, shall authorize three (3) years of actual construction time from the date MIDC secures the last governmental authorization (state or federal) necessary or required to commence construction provided MIDC diligently pursues all applications for such permits. Failure by MIDC to diligently pursue its applications for other governmental permits shall be equivalent to their issuance.

IN WITNESS WHEREOF, the parties hereto have executed these Articles of Agreement the day and year first above written.

MARCO ISLAND DEVELOPMENT CORPORATION
(and the Deltona Corp.)

(Not executed on this date)

STATE OF FLORIDA BOARD OF TRUSTEES
OF THE INTERNAL IMPROVEMENT
TRUST FUND

EXHIBIT 7

Lands to be conveyed to the Trsutees related to the development of Units 1-24.

The total acres to be conveyed to the "Trustees" as listed in Exhibit 6 is approximately 4032.3 acres. This total area is to be conveyed as three separate areas.

1. The land known as Kice Island is to be conveyed to the Trustees as the initial transfer, this area consists of approximately 1277.7 acres and is recited in Exhibit 6 as legal descriptions 62 through 86 inclusive.

2. The area North of Caxambas Channel and South of the Recorded Plats of Marco Beach Subdivision. This area consists of approximately 1697.4 acres and is recited in Exhibit 6 as legal description numbers 1 through 36 inclusive.

3. The area South of Caxambas Pass and East of Snook Hole Channel, this area consists of approximately 1057.2 acres and is recited in Exhibit 6 as legal descriptions 37 through 61 inclusive.

The areas scheduled for development in Units 1 through 24 Marco Beach Subdivision as recited in Exhibit 4 are grouped into permit areas and related to relative size to provide a means of prorating the transfer of the property to be conveyed to the Trustees as recited in Exhibit 6. The following is a list of Permit Areas that will, upon issuance and completion, provide for the development of Units 1 through 24 Marco Beach Subdivision.

The area of Kice Island as described in Area 1 above, is to be transferred initially to the Trustees in return for Marco River permit extension, Roberts Bay permit extension and the State Dredge and Fill permit for Collier Bay, also included in the agreement of initial transfer is the exchange of Quitclaim Deeds or Land Line Agreement mentioned elsewhere in this document. The remainder of the permits to develop Marco Beach Subdivision Units 1 through 24 will each be related to a relative size and upon issuance of all necessary permits for completion of this work, the remainder of the land described in Exhibit 6 will be conveyed. The amount of land conveyed for each of the related permits will be as follows:

Permit Area	Relative Size	Acres Lands to be Conveyed to Trustees
Unit 24	36%	990.6 acres
Bayside Waterway	5%	138 acres
Clam Pass	5%	138 acres
Clam Bay	9%	248 acres
Barfield Bay	18%	496 acres
Big Key	27%	744 acres
TOTAL	100%	2754.6 acres

Land shall be conveyed to the Trustees in the amount shown on the above schedule at the time of receipt of the final Government Permit Authorization for commencement of the work. Lands to be conveyed shall be selected by the Trustees from the legal description shown as Exhibit 6 in the amounts shown in the above schedule of permits subject to the following provision.

Lands first conveyed shall be those described in Paragraph 1 (Kice Island); Lands next conveyed shall be from those lands described in Area 2 above (between Caxambas Pass on the South and Marco Island); After and only after complete conveyance of Areas 1 and 2 may lands be conveyed from Area 3.

10-12-71

OKALOOSA COUNTY - Bulkhead Line, Section 253.122, F. S.

Consideration of a bulkhead line established by the City of
Niceville in Okaloosa County was postponed until November 9
at the request of Senator William Dean Barrow.

-4-

MANATEE COUNTY - Dedication No. 24748(2051-41)

City of Bradenton

On August 31, 1971, the Board of Trustees approved the staff
recommendations: (1) that the ratio of the area to be utilized
by private interests be no greater than 25% of the 54-acre
parcel, (2) that the area reserved for public use be adjacent
to the open waters of the Manatee River, (3) that a "blue
ribbon" ad hoc committee be created by the city with membership
subject to Trustees' approval, that would act in an advisory
capacity to the development program, (4) that a time table for
public development be submitted within 180 days subsequent to
this action, and (5) that quarterly reports be furnished to the
Trustees' staff on the progress of development and activities
of the "blue ribbon" committee.

The City of Bradenton has created a committee comprised of seven
persons selected by the Mayor subject to approval of the Board
of Trustees.

Committee appointments are:

Mr. Ken Barnaby, Mr. Wheeler Leath,
Mrs. Steven Sparkman, Dr. Robert Johnson,
Mr. A. Sterling Hall, Mr. Irving H. Stewart,
Mrs. Mary Blackburn.

Recommend approval of these appointments.

ACTION OF THE TRUSTEES:

On motion by Mr. Stone, seconded by Mr. O'Malley and adopted
without objection, the Trustees approved the committee appointments.

Mr. Stone stated that there would be news of this fine
development in a few days.

-5-

HIGHLANDS COUNTY - Grazing Lease Renewal,

Lykes Brothers, Inc.
Tampa, Florida,

holder of Grazing Lease No. 2122-S which expired July 28,
requests renewal or extension for an additional three years.

Lease area is all of Section 16, Township 36 South, Range 32
East, Highlands County, containing 640 acres. This section is
located approximately 16 miles southeast of Sebring and six miles
east of Lake Istokpoga. The land is typical of the pine, palmetto
and wire grass land in this region and is completely surrounded
by Lykes Brothers ownership.

The lease was for grazing purposes only with annual rental of
$1 per acre and contained a clause allowing cancellation by
the Trustees after 90-day written notice. Appraisal has recently
been made by the staff appraiser who recommends future fair rental
should be $1.61 per acre with lessee to pay any and all taxes law-
fully assessed against the land.

Recommend renewal of lease under same terms and conditions

axes.

ACTION OF THE TRUSTEES:

Mr. Kuperberg said that all grazing leases contained a 90-day cancellation clause.

On motion by Mr. O'Malley and Mr. Conner, seconded by Mr. Stone and adopted without objection, the Trustees approved renewal of the lease with increased rental and terms and conditions as recommended.

-6-

LEON COUNTY - Land Exchange

The Board of Regents requests approval of the Board of Trustees to exchange a parcel of Florida State University land on Copeland Street described as the North 50 feet of the West 120 feet of Lot 39 in the Northwest Addition to the City of Tallahassee with a lot on West Call Street 49 feet by 115.5 feet in Lot 57 of the Northwest Addition which is owned by the Westcott Trust for the benefit of the University.

Although appraisals of the two Leon County parcels indicate the Westcott Trust property to be less valuable, the exchange appears justified.

Clear title to the Westcott Trust parcel is needed in order to include the parcel with adjoining University land for the construction of a telephone exchange building. The Westcott Trust property is under the control of the University; however, restrictions prohibit the construction of a non-revenue producing facility such as that contemplated.

The Board of Education approved the proposed exchange on October 20, 1970.

Recommend exchange of land as requested.

ACTION OF THE TRUSTEES:

On motion by Mr. Stone, seconded by Mr. Conner and Mr. Christian, the Trustees approved the land exchange requested by the Board of Regents.

-7-

Mineral Interest - Estate of Dolores Ruthenberg, Florida
National Bank of Jacksonville, Executor

On November 24, 1970, the Board authorized sale to Bailey M. Theus, Jr. of all of the interest of the Board in certain subdivision lots in DeSoto County which were bequeathed to the Council for the Blind and State Board of Health under the will of Dolores Ruthenberg.

In addition to the real property, a 2/3 interest of an undivided 1/160th interest in and to all of the oil, gas and other minerals in a forty-acre parcel in Marion County, Illinois, valued at $63.62, was bequeathed to the Council for the Blind and State Board of Health.

Staff legal counsel has reviewed this matter and concluded that the interest in the oil, gas and minerals passed through the Department of Health and Rehabilitative Services to the Board of Trustees by virtue of Section 253.03(6), Florida Statutes, as an interest in real property under Florida and Illinois law.

The Department has requested quitclaim of the 2/3 interest in the oil, gas and minerals held by the Board to Bailey M. Theus, Jr., the other residuary beneficiary of the Estate which will allow

10-12-71

approximately $20,000 to be distributed to the Division of Health under the will of Dolores Ruthenberg.

Recommend quitclaim of the interest of the Board in the oil, gas and mineral interest to Bailey M. Theus, Jr.

ACTION OF THE TRUSTEES:

On motion by Mr. Conner, seconded by Mr. Christian and adopted without objection, the Trustees approved the recommendation to quitclaim the oil, gas and mineral interest of the Board to Bailey M. Theus, Jr.

-8-

BREVARD AND INDIAN RIVER COUNTIES - Beach Nourishment Project
File No. 253.123-910

    Sebastian Inlet District
    Melbourne, Florida

requests a permit to remove 300,000 cubic yards of sand from a sand trap in the Indian River to artificially nourish approximately 2,400 feet of public beach in Sections 20 and 21, Township 30 South, Range 39 East, Brevard and Indian River Counties.

This beach nourishment project is being financed by state and local funds and is on the Department of Natural Resources' agenda.

The biological report from the Department of Natural Resources indicates the proposed project would not have significant adverse effects on marine resources.

The Game and Fresh Water Fish Commission has no objections to this project.

The Department of Pollution Control has no objections provided that stringent controls are used to prevent siltation of shellfish areas north and south of the inlet.

Recommend issuance of permit subject to stipulations by Department of Pollution Control and waiver of fees for this public interest project.

ACTION OF THE TRUSTEES:

On motion by Mr. Stone, seconded by Mr. Christian and adopted without objection, the Board authorized issuance of the permit without fee subject to the stipulations by the Department of Pollution Control.

-9-

BROWARD COUNTY - Seawall and Fill, File No. 253.124(8)

    Howard Rau
    Arthur V. Strock & Associates, Inc.
    829 Southeast Ninth Street
    Deerfield Beach, Florida 33441

requests a permit to install a seawall and backfill landward and along the east right-of-way line of the Intracoastal Waterway in Section 30, Township 48 South, Range 43 East, Broward County. The material placed behind the seawall will be hauled in from upland sources.

Field inspection confirms that the seawalls which have been constructed on either side of this parcel of land have contributed to artificially induced erosion caused by boat traffic.

The biological report from the Department of Natural Resources indicates this project will have only limited adverse effects on marine biological resources.

The Game and Fresh Water Fish Commission has no objection to
the project.

The Department of Pollution Control issued certification on
March 23, 1971.

Recommend issuance of requested permit.

ACTION OF THE TRUSTEES:

Mr. Kuperberg said this was an application under the avulsion
restoration section of the statute. The staff had obtained
a biological report in accordance with the Attorney General's
request.

On motion by Mr. Christian, seconded by Mr. O'Malley and adopted
without objection, the Board authorized issuance of the permit.

-10-

PALM BEACH COUNTY - Fill Permit No. 253.124(8)

> C. H. Carrington
> P. O. Box 311, Jupiter, Florida 33458,

requests approval of a fill permit issued by the Building Inspector
of Jupiter, Florida, on May 13, 1971, to fill approximately .12
acre of submerged land in Section 6, Township 41 South, Range 43
East in accordance with the provisions of Section 253.124(8).

Our Field Operations Division reports that the applicant proposes
to truck in approximately 150 cubic yards of fill to place behind
a proposed seawall; at no point will the seawall exceed 12-20 feet
waterward of the existing shoreline. The proposed seawall is
aligned precisely with an extension of an existing seawall to
the south.

It is the opinion of a staff field investigator that the seawall
to the south together with boat wakes, winds and tides has caused
shoreline avulsion.

The Department of Natural Resources biological report indicates
that this project should not have significant adverse effects on
marine biological resources.

Staff requests approval of the fill permit issued by the Building
Inspector of Jupiter, Florida.

ACTION OF THE TRUSTEES:

Mr. Kuperberg advised the Board that the area was above water
and there was no objection.

On motion by Mr. O'Malley, seconded by Mr. Stone and adopted
without objection, the Trustees approved the fill permit issued
by the City of Jupiter.

-11-

VOLUSIA COUNTY - Artificial Reef, File No. 253.03-284

> Board of County Commissioners of Volusia County

requests permit to construct an artificial reef offshore from
Daytona Beach, Florida, located at latitude 29° 08' 54" North
and longitude 80° 49' 26" West in 70 feet of water, with a
minimum vehicle clearance of 45 feet.

The proposed reef will be constructed of 3,000 automobile tires,
bonded and weighted with concrete in bundles of 6 to 10 tires,

10-12-71

418

500 old cars and miscellaneous rubble such as old sewer pipes.

The Department of Natural Resources advises that local fisherman have reviewed the proposal and have no objections. The Department of Natural Resources has no objection.

The Game and Fresh Water Fish Commission has no objection. The Department of Pollution Control has no objection provided that old automobile bodies are not used.

Staff recommends approval of the proposed project subject to stipulation by the Department of Pollution Control.

ACTION OF THE TRUSTEES:

Treasurer O'Malley commented on objections from the United States Navy to the use of automobiles for artificial reef construction in Dade County. The Director said that clearance was required from the Coast Guard and Army Corps of Engineers, and the staff recommended omitting automobile bodies as requested by the Department of Pollution Control.

The Secretary of State said that after thorough review, the Coast Guard, Navy, Corps of Engineers and Bureau of Sport Fisheries had given approval for the reefs being built in the Dade County area.

On motion by Mr. Stone, seconded by Mr. Conner and adopted without objection, the Trustees approved the artificial reef permit subject to the provision that automobile bodies not be used.

-12-

COLLIER COUNTY - Dredge Permit, File No. 253.123(2)(b)-816 and 817

City of Naples
735 Eighth Street South, Naples, Florida 33940

requests permit to install 20 inch subaqueous sewage force main across Rock Creek and Gordon River in Collier County, Florida.

The Department of Natural Resources, the Game and Fresh Water Fish Commission, and the Department of Pollution Control have no objections to this project.

The City of Naples requests that $100.00 processing fee be waived.

Staff requests authority to issue permit without fee because of the public works nature of the project.

ACTION OF THE TRUSTEES:

Mr. Kuperberg pointed out that the application involved a minor amount of dredging.

Motion was made by Mr. Christian, seconded by Mr. Stone and adopted without objection, that the permit be issued without fee as a public project.

-13-

TRUSTEES' OFFICE

Due to a backlog of work in the Trustees' legal section, which has been compounded by changes in the legal staff, authority is requested to employ an attorney on a temporary basis from budgeted OPS funds to assist the Trustees' general counsel. It is recommended that Chris H. Bentley be employed at the rate of $1,062 a month.

419

ACTION OF THE TRUSTEES:

The Director said the Trustees' office was operating with only
one attorney, the chief counsel, and having a problem finding
qualified men for the legal division.

On motion by Mr. Stone, seconded by Mr. O'Malley and adopted
without objection, the Trustees approved the temporary
employment of Mr. Bentley as recommended.

-14-

PATENTS, COPYRIGHTS AND TRADEMARKS

The Department of Citrus has requested that the Trustees transfer
by assignment all of their right, title and interest in and to
the following eight patents and patent applications to the
Department of Citrus:

1. U. S. Patent Application No. 109,922
   Item: Improved Essence for Enhancing the Flavor of Citrus
         Juices

2. U. S. Patent Application No. 079,422
   Item: Full-flavored Citrus Juice Energy Supplement

3. U. S. Patent Application No. 24,820
   Item: Full-flavored Citrus Juice Energy Supplement

4. No U. S. Patent Application number has been assigned at
   this time.
   Item: Full-flavored Citrus Juice Energy Supplement

5. U. S. Patent Application No. 844,984
   Item: Citrus Seed Clouding Agent for Beverage Bases and
         food products

6. U. S. Patent Application No. 867,886
   Item: Natural Orange Base

7. U. S. Patent Application No. 14,672
   Item: High Protein Citrus Food Products

8. U. S. Patent Application No. 61,385
   Item: Enhancement of Color in Reconstituted Juice by
         Natural Means

Under Section 286.021, Florida Statutes, the Trustees are vested
with title to all patents, trademarks and copyrights held by
the State or any of its boards, commissions or agencies. Section
286.031, Florida Statutes, charges the Trustees with the use,
management and control of patents, copyrights, etc. Staff legal
counsel is of the opinion that the Trustees can permit the Department of Citrus to use the patent. The Attorney General in 1969
by letter to the Department of Citrus and Opinion 069.81 indicated
a license arrangement would be the proper means of granting use
of patents to other boards, commissions or agencies of the State.
However, title to the patent and the right to approve how the patent
is used by private industry must remain in the Trustees.

It is recommended that the Trustees grant to the Department of
Citrus a license to develop and use the eight patents and
applications and to receive royalties therefrom upon transfer
of the right to use to third parties - provided such transfer is
approved by the Trustees.

On September 21 the Trustees requested an opinion from the
Attorney General on the question of transfer of title to patents
held by the State of Florida. Based on the Attorney General's
Opinion No. 071-298 dated September 28, 1971, the recommendation of the staff is reaffirmed.

10-12-71

ACTION OF THE TRUSTEES:

Mr. Kuperberg reviewed the position of the staff as supported by the opinion of the Attorney General.

Mr. Monterey Campbell, attorney of the Department of Citrus, said it was not the position they would like, but the Department was willing to accept the decision. Mr. Kuperberg assured him that the staff would work in complete cooperation with the Department of Citrus in this matter.

On motion by Mr. O'Malley, seconded by Mr. Stone and adopted without objection, the Trustees accepted the recommendation of the staff.

On motion duly adopted, the meeting was adjourned.

GOVERNOR - CHAIRMAN

ATTEST:

EXECUTIVE DIRECTOR

* * * *

Tallahassee, Florida
October 19, 1971

The State of Florida Board of Trustees of the Internal Improvement Trust Fund met on this date in the auditorium of the Department of Transportation, with the following members present:

Reubin O'D. Askew	Governor
Richard (Dick) Stone	Secretary of State
Robert L. Shevin	Attorney General
Fred O. Dickinson, Jr.	Comptroller
Thomas D. O'Malley	Treasurer
Doyle Conner	Commissioner of Agriculture
Joel Kuperberg	Executive Director

-1-

On motion adopted without objection, the Trustees approved the minutes of the meeting of October 5, 1971, and authorized correction of the minutes of September 28 to change $7,800 in item 11 to $7,875, the correct amount shown on the agenda as payment for the material to be removed by Daytona Marina and Boat Works.

-2-

MARTIN COUNTY - Advertise Grazing Lease

Several parties have expressed an interest in leasing a 147.58 acre parcel of vacant school land for grazing purposes.

The tract, described as all of Section 16, Township 39 South, Range 41 East, lying south and west of the Sunshine State Parkway, is uncommitted school land with title vested in the Trustees. It is located 7.5 miles southwest of Stuart and is accessible only over land under other ownership. The soil is sandy, overgrown in native grass, pine and palmetto, with good drainage. The staff appraiser indicates highest and

10-19-71

best use at this time would be interim grazing at annual rental of $2 per acre.

Recommend advertising for sealed bids for a three-year grazing lease with a base or starting bid of $2 per acre per year, with lease to contain a 90-day cancellation provision.

ACTION OF THE TRUSTEES:

On motion by Mr. Conner, seconded by Mr. Dickinson and adopted without objection, the recommendation was approved as the action of the Board.

-3-

DADE COUNTY - Campsite Lease No. 2210A

> Richard Nichols, William Hicks, William Colson,
> Doing business as Nicohick Associates,
> 601 Concord Building, Miami, Florida

On September 14, 1971, the Trustees approved renewal of Campsite Lease No. 2210A of a shoal area in South Biscayne Bay to Perry Nichols, William C. Lantaff and Richard Nichols.

On September 29, 1971, Richard Nichols requested permission to assign the interest of William Lantaff, who passed away subsequent to September 14, 1971, to William Colson, and the interest of Perry Nichols to William Hicks.

Since Lease No. 2210A was improperly executed, staff recommends that the Board grant a reassignment of Lease No. 2210A to Richard Nichols, William Hicks and William Colson, with annual rental of $300 per 1/4 acre and the lease renewal be approved with the provision that no raw sewage will be discharged from this site.

ACTION OF THE TRUSTEES:

On motion by Mr. Shevin, seconded by Mr. Stone and adopted without objection, the Trustees authorized issuance of a reassignment instrument of Lease No. 2210A as recommended.

-4-

MONROE COUNTY - Aquaculture Lease

> Marine Harvesters Associates, Inc., c/o Mr. Bela Zeky,
> Post Office Box 2081, Key West, Florida 33040,

has filed an aquaculture lease application embracing approximately 75 acres in Section 22 and 23, Township 66 South, Range 28 East, Monroe County, Florida for the purpose of experimental planting of varieties of seaweed. The erection of 1 1/2" mesh nylon netting suspended on metal poles spaced 20 feet apart is proposed, to contain the prospective crop from drifting out on storm tides.

Upland riparian owners have no objection.

The Department of Natural Resources has no objection. The biological survey report is not adverse.

The Department of Pollution Control has no objection.

The Game and Fresh Water Fish Commission has no adverse comments.

Request authority to advertise for objections in accordance with the provisions of Section 253.70, Florida Statutes.

10-19-71

ACTION OF THE TRUSTEES:

Mr. Kuperberg said that while the Department of Natural
Resources offered no objection in the biological survey,
because of the problem of introducing exotic marine seaweed
the staff wished to add a stipulation in the lease.

Mr. O'Malley called attention to the aquaculture lease guidelines adopted in 1969 that included, among other things, requirements pertaining to accounting records and statements of financial
position and net income of the lessee. The Director said the
staff would require conformance to the guidelines.

On motion by Mr. Dickinson, seconded by Mr. Stone and adopted
without objection, the Trustees authorized advertisement of the
proposed aquaculture lease for objections in accordance with the
provisions of Section 253.70, Florida Statutes, subject to the
stipulation that seaweed culture be coordinated with and have
the approval of the Department of Natural Resources in accordance
with the statutes, and subject to the aquaculture lease guidelines
of 1969.

-5-

OKALOOSA COUNTY - Dredge Permit, File No. 253.123-813,
                Marina License, Section 253.03,
                Florida Statutes

    Marlborough, Inc.
    Post Office Box 37, Destin, Florida,

applies for a marina license covering 31,574 square feet in East
Pass Lagoon abutting upland in Township 2 South, Range 23 West,
Okaloosa County. The minimum annual fee of $631.48 was tendered.
980 cubic yards of material will be removed to allow adequate depth
for navigation.

This was withdrawn from the August 31, 1971, agenda at the request
of the staff.

The biological survey report submitted with respect to the original
plan was adverse, but the applicant has revised the project in
accordance with the recommendations of the Department of Natural
Resources.

The Game and Fresh Water Fish Commission has no objection to
the proposed project.

The Department of Pollution Control has objected to the proposed
project.

Objections to the proposed project received from adjacent owners
cite devaluation of property and interference with view, but staff
does not consider the objections valid. The county has indicated
that applicant's property has no county zoning.

Staff recommends denial of the project based on objections from
The Department of Pollution Control.

ACTION OF THE TRUSTEES:

Mr. Shevin made a motion, seconded by Mr. Stone, to deny the
application as recommended.

Mr. Ben Holley, attorney for the applicant, exhibited photographs
of the Destin area showing many other docks and marinas. He said
the Board of County Commissioners unanimously approved the project,
after considering the local objections. The applicant changed the
original plan as recommended by the Department of Natural Resources,
and recent objection from the Department of Pollution Control of
restriction of water flow did not seem fair to his client.

Secretary of State Stone said the time had come to try to improve water quality and he could vote for the project only if the applicant made the changes necessary to satisfy the objections of the Department of Pollution Control, from which the applicant would have to obtain a permit, also.

Treasurer O'Malley was concerned at the contradictory agenda recommendations and the reversal of position by the Department of Pollution Control. Objections based on flushing action did not appear justified to him in view of the photographs showing this project at the widest part of the bay, and might reflect other motives. He asked for two week's deferral and additional information from the Trustees' office.

Mr. Kuperberg thought there was concern that at some point there must be a cut-off based on a determination that only the Department of Pollution Control could make on long-term damage that might occur to the water quality.

Governor Askew said the inquiry as to the changed recommendation was a valid one, but he thought the answer would lie with environmental considerations.

Mr. Ross Marler, resident of Destin and former president of the area Chamber of Commerce, said a negative vote would affect the economy that depended on boating and fishing. In his opinion additional docking facilities were needed and the placing of pilings would not create any problem in the flushing capabilities, as the harbor was shut off at one end with no water flow except that created by the tides and surface winds.

Mr. Joe Jacobs, attorney for a local objector, said he would present what he believed to be the contrary position when the Board considered the matter in two weeks.

Without objection, action was deferred for two weeks on the request of the State Treasurer.

-6-

ST. LUCIE COUNTY - Marina License,
          Section 253.03, F. S.

    General Development Corporation
    111 South Bayshore Drive, Miami, Florida 33131

applies for a marina license covering 234,666 square feet of sovereignty land in the North Fork, St. Lucie River, abutting Section 23, Township 37 South, Range 40 East, St. Lucie County. The minimum annual fee of $4,693.32 has been tendered. No dredging is required.

The Department of Natural Resources has no objection to the license.

The Game and Fresh Water Fish Commission has no objection.

The Department of Pollution Control has no objection to the proposed facility.

Staff recommends approval of the marina license, with commencement of construction subject to certification by the Department of Pollution Control.

ACTION OF THE TRUSTEES:

On motion by Mr. Stone, seconded by Mr. Shevin and adopted without objection, the Trustees approved issuance of the marina license.

-7-

SEMINOLE COUNTY - Marina License and Dredge Permit
          File No. 253.123-951

Sanford Boat Works and Marina, Inc.
c/o G. Andrew Speer, Attorney At Law
Post Office Box 698
Sanford, Florida 32771

applies for a marina license covering 12,567 square feet of submerged land in Indian Mound Slough westerly of the St. Johns
River in unsurveyed Section 27, Township 19 South, Range 31
East, Seminole County. The minimum annual fee of $251.34 has
been tendered.

Application has also been filed for a permit to complete a
dredging operation, whereby approximately 3,000 cubic yards
of material will be removed and placed on applicant's upland.
The applicant has indicated that approximately 1,000 cubic
yards had been removed prior to September 1970, and no
dredging has taken place since that date.

The Department of Natural Resources has no objection to the
project.

The Department of Pollution Control has no objection.

The Field Operation Division of the Trustees' staff has no
objection to the proposed facility.

The Game and Fresh Water Fish Commission has no objection
provided (1) all spoil material must be placed above the
mean high water line within diked spoil areas, and (2) if at
any time the operation is considered detrimental to the
aquatic habitat, it should cease.

Staff recommends approval and issuance of the marina license
and dredge permit subject to the following stipulations:

1. Applicant shall submit payment for the 1,000 cubic yards
    previously removed at three times the rate at the time
    of removal (0.10¢ per cubic yard), $300.

2. Applicant shall submit payment for the remaining material
    (2,000 cubic yards), $1,000.

3. Applicant shall post bond in the amount of $754.02 as
    required for the marina license, and submit $50 for the
    required dredge permit processing fee.

4. All operations shall meet the stipulations cited by the
    Game and Fresh Water Fish Commission.

5. Certification by Department of Pollution Control to occur
    as tentatively indicated.

ACTION OF THE TRUSTEES:

On motion by Mr. Stone, seconded by Mr. Conner and adopted
without objection, the Trustees approved issuance of the marina
license with the stipulations recommended.

-8-

DADE COUNTY - Dredge Permit, File No. 253.123(2)(b)-855

City of Miami
Department of Public Works
3332 Pan American Drive, Miami, Florida 33133

Applicant requests approval of City of Miami Permit No. 42357
to install a 10-inch sanitary sewer force main across the
Intracoastal Waterway at Venetian Causeway in Section 35,
Township 53 South, Range 41 East, in Dade County, Florida.

The Department of Natural Resources has no objections to the project as proposed.

The Game and Fresh Water Fish Commission has no objection.

The Department of Pollution Control has no objection.

Staff recommends approval of the application and waiver of the fee, as this is a public works project.

ACTION OF THE TRUSTEES:

Mr. Stone said he was very much in favor of using waterways to pipe sewage because right of way did not have to be bought, it was easily spotted and repaired, and it was better to put effluent in a pipe in a waterway than in the waterway.

On motion by Mr. Stone, seconded by Mr. Shevin and adopted without objection, the Trustees approved the dredge permit without charge for the public project.

-9-

LEON COUNTY - Blanket Dredge Permit, 253.123-936

Leon County Board of County Commissioners
Room 214 Courthouse, Post Office Box 726,
Tallahassee, Florida

requests a blanket maintenance dredging permit to cover twenty county boat ramp projects located on Lake Jackson, Lake Talquin, and Lake Iamonia. The applicant proposes to confine limits of dredging to 5 feet lakeward of the mean low water line. All material will be placed on county-owned upland.

The Game and Fresh Water Fish Commission has no objection to issuance of the permit.

The Department of Pollution Control has no objection.

Staff recommends approval of the permit and waiver of processing fee since the proposal is in the public interest.

ACTION OF THE TRUSTEES:

Mr. Kuperberg explained that the staff processed this application for a blanket dredge permit within fifty days, as rapidly as possible - even without receiving a formal application and on the promise of the $100 fee for the Department of Natural Resources biological survey.

On motion by Mr. Conner, seconded by Mr. Stone and adopted without objection, the Trustees approved the permit and waived the processing fee as the application was in the public interest.

-10-

PASCO COUNTY - Dredge Permit, File No. 253.123-882

Coastal Bonded Title Company, as Trustee
706 West Main Street, New Port Richey, Florida 33552

Applicant requests approval of permit issued by the City Council of the City of New Port Richey to dredge 500 cubic yards of material from the Pithlachascotee River in the City of New Port Richey adjacent to South Boulevard Bridge. Spoil is to be deposited on private uplands. Applicant has remitted $500 payment for the spoil to be removed.

The Department of Natural Resources recommended that the proposed 100 foot wide channel cut be reduced to 80 feet.

10-19-71

Applicant revised the proposed plan to conform to that request.

The Game and Fresh Water Fish Commission has no objection.

The Department of Pollution Control has no objection.

<u>Staff recommends approval of the permit issued by the City of New Port Richey.</u>

ACTION OF THE TRUSTEES:

On motion by Mr. Stone, seconded by Mr. Conner and adopted without objection, the Board approved the permit issued by the City of New Port Richey.

-11-

PINELLAS COUNTY - Dredge and Fill Permit
          File Nos. 253.123-810 and 253.124-185

     Arthur, Ashley, Williams Foundation
     129-A Concord Street, Framingham, Massachusetts 01701,

     Represented by George F. Young, Inc.
     819 Arlington Avenue North, St. Petersburg, Florida,

requests approval of Pinellas County Water and Navigation Control Authority Permit No. DF-271 to conduct maintenance dredge and fill operations in Section 30, Township 29 South, Range 15 East, Pinellas County, Clearwater Harbor, Belleair Beach, for the purpose of cleaning out runoff and creating a final seawall. The work is to be accomplished by drag line.

The original application was revised to conform with the Game and Fresh Water Fish Commission recommendations.

The Department of Natural Resources reports that the project should have limited adverse effects on marine life and wildlife.

The Game and Fresh Water Fish Commission recommends that the seawalls be in place prior to any work on the proposed project, to control siltation and turbidities in the project area, and has no objection provided this suggestion is followed. The applicant has agreed to follow the recommendation.

The Department of Pollution Control has no objection.

<u>Staff recommends approval of Permit DF-271 provided the seawalls are in place prior to back-filling.</u>

ACTION OF THE TRUSTEES:

A new owner desired to install seawalls and redredge in a development started many years ago.

On motion by Mr. Stone, seconded and adopted without objection, the Trustees approved permit DF-271 subject to the stipulations recommended by the Game and Fresh Water Fish Commission.

On motion duly adopted, the meeting was adjourned.

GOVERNOR   CHAIRMAN

ATTEST:

EXECUTIVE DIRECTOR

*   *   *   *   *

10-19-71

Tallahassee, Florida
October 26, 1971

The State of Florida Board of Trustees of the Internal Improvement Trust Fund met on this date in the auditorium of the Department of Transportation, with the following members present:

Reubin O'D. Askew	Governor
Richard (Dick) Stone	Secretary of State
Robert L. Shevin	Attorney General
Thomas D. O'Malley	Treasurer
Floyd T. Christian	Commissioner of Education
Doyle Conner	Commissioner of Agriculture
Joel Kuperberg	Executive Director

-1-

The Director withdrew the request for approval of the minutes of October 12.

-2-

LEE COUNTY - Bulkhead Line, Section 253.122, Florida Statutes

At the request of the applicant, consideration of a bulkhead line along the southerly shoreline of the Caloosahatchee River at Shell Point in Lee County was withdrawn from the agenda.

-3-

BREVARD COUNTY - Application for Quitclaim
File No. 2381-05-253,12(6)   0.24 acre

Staff Description: A parcel of filled sovereignty land adjacent to Section 24, Township 28 South, Range 37 East, Brevard County.

A. CITY AND COUNTY: Brevard County

B. APPLICANT: Trailer Town Development Corporation
315 Indian River Drive, Palm Bay, Florida

C. ACREAGE: 0.24 acre
RATE PER ACRE: $3,332; $800 for the parcel

D. APPRAISAL: By staff appraiser on February 16, 1971

E. PURPOSE: To construct dock and boat launching facilities for trailer park.

F. BIOLOGICAL
REPORT: Not applicable

G. STAFF REMARKS: The applicant applied for a quitclaim deed pursuant to Section 253.12(6), Florida Statutes, which provided that "Where any person, state agency, county, city or other political subdivision prior to June 11, 1957, extended or added to existing lands or islands bordering on or being in the navigable waters as defined in this section by filling in or causing to be filled in such lands, the Board shall upon application therefor convey said land so filled to the riparian owner or owners of the upland so extended or added to. The consideration for such conveyance shall be the appraised value of said lands as they existed prior to such filling."

10-26-71

Two affidavits have been submitted stating that the lands in question had been filled prior to June 11, 1957.

The applicant holds a conditional quitclaim deed from an adjoining owner, the Florida East Coast Railway Company, dated June 12, 1970, for any interest the company may have in the parcel.

The applicant has paid a $100 processing fee and the $350 fee for a staff appraisal.

The applicant has also submitted $800 in payment for the parcel of land.

Request authority to issue a quitclaim deed for consideration of $800.

ACTION OF THE TRUSTEES:

On motion by Mr. Stone, seconded by Mr. Christian and adopted without objection, the Trustees authorized issuance of the quitclaim for $800 consideration.

-4-

VOLUSIA COUNTY - Application for a Quitclaim
File No. 2425-64-253.12(6)   0.70 acre

Staff description: A parcel of filled sovereignty land adjacent to Government Lot 1, Section 27, Township 15 South, Range 33 East

A. CITY AND COUNTY: Volusia County

B. APPLICANT: Charlotte Holland Ennis

C. APPLICANT'S
    REPRESENTATIVE: Thomas C. Simpson, P. A.
                     Post Office Box 1390, Daytona Beach, Florida

D. ACREAGE: 0.70 acre
    RATE PER ACRE: $300; $210 for the parcel

E. APPRAISAL: By staff appraiser on September 7, 1971

                     The staff appraiser indicates that the value
                     of this 0.70 parcel of land prior to filling
                     was $300 per acre. The value of this parcel
                     of land is $210.

F. PURPOSE: Residential development

G. BIOLOGICAL
    REPORT: Not applicable

H. STAFF REMARKS: The applicant applied for a quitclaim deed
    pursuant to Section 253.12(6) Florida Statutes, which provided
    that "Where any person, state agency, county, city or other
    political subdivision prior to June 11, 1957, extended or
    added to existing lands or islands bordering on or being in the
    navigable waters as defined in this section by filling in or
    causing to be filled in such lands, the Board shall upon applica-
    tion therefor convey said land so filled to the riparian owner
    or owners of the upland so extended or added to. The considera-
    tion for such conveyance shall be the appraised value of said
    lands as they existed prior to such filling."

Two affidavits have been submitted stating that the lands in question had been filled sometime between 1951 and 1954.

Applicant has submitted the $100 application fee and $210 for the parcel of land.

Request authority to issue a quitclaim for consideration of $210.

ACTION OF THE TRUSTEES:

On motion by Mr. Stone, seconded by Mr. Christian and adopted
without objection, the Trustees authorized issuance of the quitclaim for $210 consideration.

-5-

LEON COUNTY - Sanitary Sewer Line Easement

    The City of Tallahassee

requests an easement 30 feet wide under and across a portion
of the Florida State University Golf Course in Sections 4 and 9,
Township 1 South, Range 1 West, Leon County, for construction
of an underground sanitary sewer line.

The Board of Regents has reviewed this matter and at its meeting
on September 17 approved the request.

Recommend issuance of the easement requested for underground
sanitary sewer line purposes only.

ACTION OF THE TRUSTEES:

On motion by Mr. Stone, seconded by Mr. Conner and adopted without
objection, the Trustees approved the application from the City of
Tallahassee and authorized issuance of the easement for underground sanitary sewer line purposes only.

-6-

SANTA ROSA COUNTY - Advertise Oil and Gas Lease

    W. A. Moncrief, Fort Worth, Texas,

requests the Board to offer for competitive sealed bids an oil
and gas drilling lease covering the 10.4-acre parcel in Section
41, Township 5 North, Range 29 West, Santa Rosa County, known
as the Jay State Livestock Market, now under the control and
management of the Department of Agriculture and Consumer Services.

That Department has reviewed this request and recommends offering
the parcel for lease with the understanding that lease will be
awarded only if the Board considers that the best interest of the
State will be served under a lease arrangement. All proceeds
from a lease will go to the Department of Agriculture and Consumer Services.

This parcel is located within the corporate limits of the Town
of Jay. The State Geologist has reviewed this request and
concurs in the following recommendation.

Recommend advertising the parcel of land for sealed bids pursuant
to law, with an annual rental of $1 per net mineral acre, 1/6
royalty, five-year primary term, $100,000 surety bond and at
least one test well required to be drilled to a depth of 6,000 feet
or to a depth sufficient to test the Norphlet Sands, whichever is
deeper. The right to reject any or all bids will be reserved.

ACTION OF THE TRUSTEES:

On motion by Mr. Christian, seconded by Mr. Conner and adopted
without objection, the advertisement was approved as recommended.

10-26-71

SANTA ROSA COUNTY - Oil Lease Public Hearing

On October 18 a public hearing was held in the Town of Jay as
required by Section 253.52, Florida Statutes, to give all
interested persons an opportunity to be heard with respect to
issuance of two proposed oil and gas drilling leases.

One proposed lease covers the reserved one-half interest of
the State in a five-acre parcel in the N 1/2 of NW 1/4 of SE 1/4
of SE 1/4 of Section 25, Township 5 North, Range 29 West, Santa
Rosa County. Harris R. Fender, et al, made the high bid of
$13,187.50 for this lease on September 14, 1971. All proceeds
from this lease of Murphy Act land will go to General Revenue
Unallocated.

The other proposed lease covers that portion of State Road No. 89
lying within Section 40, Township 5 North, Range 29 West, containing 13.62 acres in Santa Rosa County. Chevron Oil Company
made the high bid of $42,917 on April 27, 1971, for this lease.
All proceeds from this lease will go to the Department of
Transportation.

Notice of the public hearing was published the required one
time in the Milton Press-Gazette. No one appeared at the
hearing in opposition to issuance of the leases.

It is recommended that the two leases be issued to the high
bidders.

ACTION OF THE TRUSTEES:

On motion by Mr. Christian, seconded by Mr. Stone and adopted
without objection, the Board authorized issuance of the two
leases to the high bidders, Harris R. Fender, et al, and Chevron
Oil Company, respectively.

-8-

PALM BEACH COUNTY - Fill Permit, File 253.124(8)-

    DiVosta Construction Company,
    251 River Drive, Tequesta-Jupiter, Florida 33458

requests approval of a permit to construct a seawall and backfill,
issued by the Village of Tequesta to reclaim a triangular strip
of land 4 feet at the base by 60 feet in length (120 sq. feet)
landward of the east right of way line of the Intracoastal
Waterway in the Gomez Grant in Township 38 South, Range 42 East,
Palm Beach County.

The fill material will come from upland sources.

An on-site inspection indicates this land has been lost by
artificially induced erosion caused by boat traffic traversing
the Intracoastal Waterway and by construction of a new bridge
south of this parcel of land.

Recommend approval of the permit as requested.

ACTION OF THE TRUSTEES:

On motion by Mr. Christian, seconded by Mr. Conner and adopted
without objection, the Trustees approved the permit to DiVosta
Construction Company.

-9-

WALTON COUNTY - Utility Permit
        File 253.03(7)-290

        Mechanical Equipment Co., Inc., c/o Poole Engineering Co.
        225 Eglin Parkway Southeast, Fort Walton Beach, Florida,

requests permit to install four 2-inch P. V. C. pipelines a
short distance into the Gulf of Mexico in Section 33, Township
2 South, Range 21 West, Walton County. These pipelines will be
used as seawater supply lines for a desalting plant.

The Department of Natural Resources biological report indicates
the installation should not have significant adverse effects on
marine biological resources.

The Game and Fresh Water Fish Commission does not object to
issuance of the permit.

The Department of Pollution Control has no objection, and has
already issued a construction permit for the project.

The applicant must obtain a variance from the Bureau of Beaches
and Shores, Department of Natural Resources, under the provisions
of Section 161.052, Florida Statutes.

Recommend issuance of the requested permit subject to the necessary variance from the Department of Natural Resources.

ACTION OF THE TRUSTEES:

On motion by Mr. Conner, seconded by Mr. Stone and adopted
without objection, the Trustees approved the permit subject to
the necessary variance from the Department of Natural Resources.

-10-

PINELLAS COUNTY - Marina License,
        Section 253.03, F. S.

        Charles Armitage
        699 Bay Esplanade, Clearwater Beach, Florida

applies for a marina license covering 702 square feet in Clearwater Bay abutting uplands in Section 5, Township 29 South,
Range 15 East, Pinellas County. The proposed structure will
replace an existing structure and shall be used by apartment
tenants without charge.

The minimum annual fee of $100 has been tendered. No dredging
will be done.

The Department of Natural Resources indicates this project will
not have significant adverse effects on marine resources.

The Game and Fresh Water Fish Commission has no objection to the
permit.

The Department of Pollution Control has no objection to the
project as proposed.

Staff recommends approval of the marina license.

ACTION OF THE TRUSTEES:

On motion by Mr. Conner, seconded by Mr. Stone and adopted
without objection, the Trustees authorized issuance of the marina
license.

-11-

PINELLAS COUNTY - Marina License,
                 Section 253.02, Florida Statutes

    Points West Apartments (Greenfeathers, Inc.)
    c/o Mr. James R. Moody
    12000 Capri Circle, Treasure Island, Florida 33706

applies for a marina license covering 540 square feet in Boca
Ciega Bay, abutting uplands in Section 23, Township 31 South,
Range 15 East, Pinellas County. The facility is to be for
the private use of apartment owners as a sun deck, and no
fees will be charged.

The minimum annual fee of $100 has been tendered. No dredging
is required.

The Department of Natural Resources has no objection to the
permit.

The Game and Fresh Water Fish Commission has no objection to
the project.

The Department of Pollution Control has no objection to the
project.

Staff recommends approval of the marina license.

ACTION OF THE TRUSTEES:

On motion by Mr. Stone, seconded by Mr. Christian and adopted
without objection, the Trustees authorized issuance of the
marina license.

-12-

MARINA LICENSES - Renewals

The required annual fees for the following marina licenses have
been submitted:

Marina License No.	Licensee	Annual Fee
ML-1	Port Tarpon Marina, Inc., Anclote River, Sec.2,T27-R15E, Pinellas County	$ 749.00
ML-5	Sailfish Club of Florida, Lake Worth, Sec.3,T43S-R43E, Palm Beach County	1896.30
ML-10	City of South Daytona, Halifax River, Sec.33,T15S-R43E, Volusia County	(waived)

Staff recommends renewal of the marina licenses for one year at
the fees indicated.

ACTION OF THE TRUSTEES:

On motion by Mr. Stone, seconded by Mr. Christian and adopted without
objection, the Board authorized renewal of the three marina licenses
for one year as recommended.

On motion duly adopted, the meeting was adjourned.

ATTEST:

EXECUTIVE DIRECTOR

GOVERNOR - CHAIRMAN

10-26-71

Tallahassee, Florida
November 9, 1971

The State of Florida Board of Trustees of the Internal Improvement Trust Fund met on this date in the auditorium of the Department of Transportation, with the following members present:

Reubin O'D. Askew	Governor
Richard (Dick) Stone	Secretary of State
Robert L. Shevin	Attorney General
Fred O. Dickinson, Jr.	Comptroller
Thomas D. O'Malley	Treasurer
Floyd T. Christian	Commissioner of Education
Doyle Conner	Commissioner of Agriculture

Joel Kuperberg	Executive Director

-1-

The minutes of the meetings on October 12, 19 and 26, 1971, were approved as submitted.

-2-

OKALOOSA COUNTY - Consideration of Oil and Gas Lease Bids

On September 21, 1971, the Trustees authorized advertisement for sealed bids of a five-year oil and gas drilling lease covering the reserved one-half interest of the State in nine scattered parcels of privately-owned land containing 363 surface acres in Section 34, Township 4 North, Range 24 West, and Sections 2, 3, 4, 9, 10, and 15, Township 3 North, Range 24 West, Okaloosa County.

The lease will require an annual rental of $1 per net mineral acre, $50,000 surety bond, 1/6 royalty, five-year primary term, and at least one test well every 2 1/2 years to 6,000 feet or to a depth sufficient to test the Norphlet Sands, whichever is deeper.

All proceeds from this lease will go to General Revenue Unallocated.

Invitation to bid was advertised pursuant to law in the Tallahassee Democrat and Okaloosa News-Journal, with bids to be opened at 10:00 A.M. (EST) on November 2, 1971, for consideration by the Trustees.

Recommend that prior to issuance of lease, James T. Williams of the Trustees' staff be designated to conduct the public hearing required by Section 253.52, Florida Statutes, as several of the parcels lie within three miles of the incorporated Town of Crestview.

ACTION OF THE TRUSTEES:

As there was no meeting of the Board of Trustees on November 2, bids were received and held for opening on this date.

Mr. James T. Williams of the Land Records Division opened and read the following two bids for the oil and gas drilling lease: $7,713.75 from J. Milton Newton, Inc., of Jackson, Mississippi, and $7,459.65 from Southern Natural Gas Company of Houston, Texas. Mr. Williams recommended award of the bid to the high bidder subject to the public hearing that he would conduct and report on before issuance of the lease.

On motion by Mr. Christian, seconded by Mr. Conner and passed without objection, the Trustees accepted the high bid of $7,713.75 subject to the required public hearing being conducted by Mr. Williams and report made to the board prior to issuance of the lease.

-3-

SANTA ROSA COUNTY - Consideration of Oil and Gas Lease Bids

On September 21 the Trustees authorized advertisement for sealed bids for five oil and gas drilling leases covering the reserved interest in the following five tracts in Santa Rosa County:

A. Blackwater River State Forest

   Tract 2 - S 1/2 and NE 1/4, Section 32, Township 3 North, Range 26 West, 1/4 interest, 480 surface acres

   Tract 3 - All of Section 9, Township 2 North, Range 26, West, 1/4 interest, 636.48 surface acres

   All proceeds from these leases will go to the Department of Agriculture and Consumer Services.

B. Private Ownership, Chapter 18296 (Murphy Act)

   Tract 4 - E 1/2 of NW 1/4 of SW 1/4, Section 22, Township 2 North, Range 26 West; NE 1/4, Section 28, Township 2 North, Range 26 West; N 1/2 of NW 1/4, Section 34, Township 2 North, Range 26 West, 1/2 interest, 260 surface acres

   Tract 5 - NW 1/4, NW 1/4 of NE 1/4 and N 1/2 of SW 1/4, Section 26, Township 2 North, Range 26 West, 1/2 interest, 280 surface acres

   Tract 6 - S 1/2 of SW 1/4 and NE 1/4 of SW 1/4, Section 24, Township 2 North, Range 26 West; E 3/4 of SW 1/4 of SE 1/4, Section 25, Township 2 North, Range 26 West, 1/2 interest, 150 surface acres

   All proceeds from these leases will go to General Revenue Unallocated.

Each lease requires an annual rental of $1 per net mineral acre, $50,000 surety bond, five-year primary term, 1/6 royalty and at least one test well every 2 1/2 years to a depth of 6,000 feet or to a depth sufficient to test the Norphlet Sands, whichever is deeper.

Invitations to bid were advertised pursuant to law in the Tallahassee Democrat and the Milton Press-Gazette with bids to be opened at 10:00 A.M.(EST) on November 2, 1971, for consideration by the Trustees.

ACTION OF THE TRUSTEES:

Two tracts were within and a part of the Blackwater River State Forest. The United States held a reserved three-fourths interest in minerals and over the years had issued leases, approximately 96% of the Forest now being under leases issued by the United States. Three tracts outside the Blackwater River State Forest were on privately-owned land in which the state had reserved one-half interest in oil.

There was discussion regarding oil exploration in state forests. Mr. Kuperberg said this area was probably less subject to pro-blems than the Big Cypress, that actual drilling operations could probably be accomplished with little damage to the environment. There is the problem that additional roads to drilling sites could further segment a state forest that now has a number of private in-holdings and roads.

Governor Askew suggested receiving the bids that had been held for opening in this date as there had been no meeting on November 2, but the Board should defer acceptance of bids for some policy recommendations on permitting oil exploration on state-owned land and particularly state forests. The Governor said the policy might well be to continue what was now being done, and he did not see any real problem in this area.

The Governor named the following committee to re-evaluate oil exploration policies with a view toward minimizing hazards and aiding the Board to reach future decisions on oil exploration in state-owned land and particularly in state forests:

> Chairman, Mr. Joel Kuperberg, Executive Director of
>   the Trustees of the Internal Improvement Trust Fund
> Mr. Randolph Hodges, Executive Director of the Department
>   of Natural Resources
> Mr. John M. Bethea, Director of the Division of Forestry,
>   Department of Agriculture and Consumer Services
> Mr. Vincent D. Patton, Executive Director of the Department
>   of Pollution Control
> Dr. O. E. Frye, Jr., Director of the Florida Game and
>   Fresh Water Fish Commission.

Mr. Conner agreed that the staff should investigate and make recommendations. He said the situation here was unique and the entire economy of that part of the state might be changed, that an oil well here would be a small installation but any hazard that might exist should be thoroughly explored.

Mr. Stone made a motion, seconded by Mr. Christian and Mr. O'Malley, and adopted, that the bids be opened and read into the record, and that the committee re-evaluate oil exploration policies with respect to all state forests and state-owned lands.

Mr. James T. Williams read the bids received from Phillips Petroleum Company, the only bidder, as follows:

A. For reserved interest in land in Blackwater River State
   Forest, $3,321.20 for Tract 2, $6,788.06 for Tract 3;

B. For reserved interest in land in private ownership
   (Murphy Act Land), $8,275.80 for Tract 4, $3,872.40
   for Tract 5, and $499.50 for Tract 6.

On motion by Mr. Christian, seconded by Mr. Conner and adopted without objection, the Trustees accepted the bids for lease of the reserved interest in the land under private ownership and authorized issuance of the oil and gas lease to Phillips Petroleum Company as to those lands only.

The staff was directed to hold the bids for the reserved interest in land under "A" pending receipt of recommendations from the committee appointed by the Governor.

-4-

OFFSHORE GULF AREA - Geophysical Survey

> Tidelands Geophysical Co., Inc.
> Houston, Texas,

requests permission to conduct a gravity and magnetic survey in the Gulf of Mexico. The area extends from the coastline outward to the 100-fathom line from Key West to Apalachicola.

The survey will be conducted without explosives. The Department of Natural Resources approved this request on October 26 and issued Permit No. 102 covering this operation.

Recommend approval of the survey insofar as the interest of the Trustees extends.

ACTION OF THE TRUSTEES:

On motion by Mr. O'Malley, seconded by Mr. Dickinson and adopted without objection, permission was granted insofar as the interest of the Trustees extends.

11-9-71

CHARLOTTE COUNTY - Electric Transmission Easement

Florida Power and Light Company requests an easement 170 feet
wide across an unnamed island in Section 11, Township 40 South,
Range 23 East in the Peace River in Charlotte County, for the
erection of three power line structures in the 1,765 foot long
easement area containing 7.0 acres, more or less.

Florida Power and Light Company has offered the appraised value,
$1,400, for the easement. The appraisal has been reviewed by the
staff appraiser who approved the sum offered as reasonable for
the easement.

The Interagency Advisory Committee for State Wilderness Systems
reviewed the first application received from Florida Power and
Light Company consisting of a 2,215-foot long easement crossing
the island with five structures. The Committee recommended that
Florida Power and Light Company submit an alternate route.
Such an alternate route was submitted, crossing the island in
a location where fewer structures would be required and where a
smaller portion of the island would be affected. The Committee
has reviewed and recommended the alternate route.

The Division of Recreation and Parks has reviewed the proposed
easement and states that the line would not be detrimental even
if the island should be used as a wildlife preserve or if the
river is included in the State's Wild and Scenic River System.

The Game and Fresh Water Fish Commission in its review of the
proposed easement states that if clearing of vegetation, either
upland or marsh type, be kept to an absolute minimum there are
no objections to the granting of the easement. Florida Power
and Light Company has agreed to these conditions.

Recommend issuance of easement for the consideration of $1,400.

ACTION OF THE TRUSTEES:

On motion by Mr. O'Malley, seconded by Mr. Stone and adopted
without objection, the application was approved as recommended.

-6-

ORANGE COUNTY - Power Line Easement

Florida Power Corporation
St. Petersburg, Florida

requests a ten-foot wide easement across a portion of Trustees'
land for the purpose of furnishing electric power to the Driver
Testing building being constructed by the Department of Highway
Safety and Motor Vehicles. The power line will be placed underground.

The Department has reviewed and approved issuance of the easement.

Recommend issuance of the easement requested.

ACTION OF THE TRUSTEES:

On motion by Mr. O'Malley, seconded by Mr. Dickinson and adopted
without objection, the easement was approved.

-7-

FRANKLIN COUNTY - Dredge Permit, 253.123-593

Applicant: Dr. A. C. Tuck

On July 21, December 1 and 15, 1970 the Board considered an application from Dr. A. C. Tuck for a permit to dredge a navigation channel in Alligator Harbor adjacent to Section 6, Township 7 South, Range 1 West, Franklin County.

The application has been amended to conform with the recommendations of the Department of Natural Resources and the Game and Fresh Water Fish Commission. All material removed from the channel and upland boat basin will be deposited behind dikes on the applicant's upland.

The Department of Natural Resources biological report indicates the revised application will involve much less destruction of the biologically productive intertidal marsh than would the original application.

The Game and Fresh Water Fish Commission has reviewed the October 14, 1971 revision and offers no objection to this project.

The Department of Pollution Control has previously certified this project.

Dr. Tuck has offered to convey to the State of Florida 1 3/4 acres of marsh in exchange for the permit.

Recommend issuance of the permit upon receipt of deed to the 1 3/4 acre parcel of marsh.

ACTION OF THE TRUSTEES:

Mr. Kuperberg said the problems had been resolved to the satisfaction of all the environmental agencies, and staff recommended that the marina and all deposited material be placed above the high water mark. The channel would be 30 feet wide at the top of the cut.

On motion by Mr. Dickinson, seconded by Mr. Christian and adopted without objection, the recommendations of the staff were approved.

———

-8-

PINELLAS COUNTY - Marina License,
Section 253.03, Florida Statutes

X. F. Albores
11755 Third Street East, Treasure Island, Florida 33706,

applies for a marina license covering 702 square feet in Boca Ciega Bay abutting uplands in Section 14, Township 31 South, Range 15 East, Pinellas County. The proposed structure will be used by apartment tenants at no charge. The $100 minimum annual fee has been tendered and no dredging will be done.

The Department of Natural Resources has no objection to the proposed facility.

The Department of Pollution Control has no objection to the proposed facility; however, certification will be required.

The Game and Fresh Water Fish Commission has no objection to the proposed facility.

Staff recommends approval of the marina license.

11-9-71

ACTION OF THE TRUSTEES:

On motion by Mr. Christian, seconded by Mr. Dickinson and adopted
without objection, the marina license was approved.

-9-

PINELLAS COUNTY - Shell Lease Application

The application by Bay Dredging and Construction Company was
withdrawn from the agenda as requested by the present lease holder.

-10-

OKALOOSA COUNTY - Bulkhead Line, Section 253.122 F. S.

At the request of the applicant, the Trustees deferred for one
week consideration of a bulkhead line established by the City
of Niceville.

-11-

OKALOOSA COUNTY - Dredge Permit, File No. 253.123-813,
                  Marina License, Section 253.03,
                  Florida Statutes

    Marlborough, Inc.
    Post Office Box 37, Destin, Florida,

applies for a marina license covering 28,617 square feet in
East Pass Lagoon abutting upland in Township 2 South, Range
23 West, Okaloosa County. The minimum annual fee of $572.34
was tendered. 980 cubic yards of material will be removed to
allow adequate depth for navigation.

The application was withdrawn from the August 31, 1971, agenda
at the request of the staff.

The biological survey report submitted with respect to the original
plan was adverse, but the applicant has revised the project in
accordance with the recommendations of the Department of Natural
Resources.

The Game and Fresh Water Fish Commission has no objection to
the proposed project.

The Department of Pollution Control objected to the application
as it was previously submitted, but by letter of October 29
indicated approval of a revised plan.

Objections to the proposed project which were received from adjacent
owners have been resolved. The county has indicated that applicant's
property has no county zoning.

Staff recommends issuance of dredge permit and marina license for
the revised project as approved by the Department of Pollution
Control.

ACTION OF THE TRUSTEES:

Mr. Kuperberg advised that both the applicant and the objectors
were represented, that staff understood the differences had
been resolved and the project revised as approved by the Department of Pollution Control.

On motion by Mr. Dickinson, seconded by Mr. Christian and
adopted without objection, the staff recommendation was approved
as the action of the Board.

-12-

PINELLAS COUNTY - Dredge Permit
File No. 253.123-838

Pinellas County Water and Navigation Control Authority issued
Dredge Only Permit No. DO-195 to

Field Hotel Corporation
Clearwater Beach, Florida,

to perform maintenance dredging in its marina area in Clearwater
Harbor in Section 17, Township 29 South, Range 15 East, Pinellas
County. Dredge will be restricted to the sandy unvegetated
area in accordance with the recommendations in the biological
reports.

2,108 cubic yards of material will be removed from the dredge
area and placed behind dikes on the applicant's upland
property. Applicant tendered check for $2,108 as payment for
the material.

The Department of Natural Resources biological report indicates
that if the dredging is confined to the unvegetated bottoms,
there would be no significant adverse effects on marine biological
resources.

The Game and Fresh Water Fish Commission does not object to the
dredging provided it is confined to the non-vegetated areas.

The Department of Pollution Control has no objection to this
project as proposed.

Recommend approval and issuance of the permit.

ACTION OF THE TRUSTEES:

The project was modified in accordance with the Game and Fresh
Water Fish Commission recommendation.

On motion by Mr. O'Malley, seconded by Mr. Christian and adopted
without objection, the Trustees authorized issuance of the permit
for the project as modified.

-13-

CITRUS COUNTY - Dredge Permit
File No. 253.123-907

Lt. Col. R. D. Briercheck
General Delivery, Crystal River, Florida,

requests a permit to dredge a boat slip in the Crystal River in
Section 28, Township 18 South, Range 18 East, Citrus County,
and deposit approximately 59 cubic yards of material on his
uplands. Applicant has submitted a check for $50 representing
minimum payment for material removed from sovereignty lands at
50¢ per cubic yard.

The Department of Natural Resources has no objections.

The Game and Fresh Water Fish Commission has no objections.

The Department of Pollution Control has no objections.

Staff recommends that the application be approved.

ACTION OF THE TRUSTEES:

On motion by Mr. O'Malley, seconded by Mr. Christian and adopted
without objection, the Trustees approved the application.

11-9-71

-14-

TRUSTEES' FUNDS - Topographic Mapping

Request authority to transfer $250,000 to the U. S. Geological
Survey for the 1971-72 contribution for the accelerated topographic
mapping program. These funds were appropriated by the Legislature
and are currently available within the budget.

ACTION OF THE TRUSTEES:

On motion by Mr. Stone, seconded by Mr. O'Malley and adopted
without objection, the Trustees authorized the transfer of
funds requested for the topographic mapping program.

-15-

TRUSTEES' FUNDS - Shoreline Mapping

Request authority to transfer $125,000 to the U. S. Coast and
Geodetic Survey for the 1971-72 contribution for the shoreline
mapping program. These funds were appropriated by the Legislature
and are currently available within the budget.

ACTION OF THE TRUSTEES:

On motion by Mr. Stone, seconded by Mr. O'Malley and adopted
without objection, the Trustees authorized transfer of $125,000
as requested for the shoreline mapping program.

-16-

TRUSTEES' FUNDS - Repayment of Funds Used for Repairs to the
                  Capitol

On January 26, and later reaffirmed on February 2, 1971, the Board
of Trustees authorized use of up to $100,000 of Trustees' funds
for repairs of the Capitol Building. To date $85,885.86 of these
funds have been expended for the project. During the discussion at
the Board meetings, it was indicated that this transaction would
be a loan and the Legislature would be asked to repay the Trust Fund.
Your staff drafted legislation for repayment but failed to get
the proposal introduced in the 1971 Legislature.

Request authority for the staff to again request repayment from the
1972 Legislature.

ACTION OF THE TRUSTEES:

Governor Askew said that he would recommend .to the Special Session
of the Legislature the repayment of those funds, and also that the
operating budget of the Trustees' staff be funded by General Revenue
for the latter half of this fiscal year in order to preserve the
trust fund, and hopefully to work out legislation during the regular
session to preserve this fund for environmental purposes.

On motion by Mr. Shevin, seconded by Mr. Stone and adopted
unanimously, the Trustees approved the recommendations of the
Governor that the Legislature be asked to repay the amount
expended for the capitol project and to fund the operations of
the Trustees' office from General .Revenue.

-17-

CASCADES PARK

On motion by Mr. Stone, seconded by Mr. Dickinson and adopted
without objection, the Trustees concurred in action taken by the
Department of General Services on this date approving the revised

11-9-71

Cascades Park proposal for which the Board of Trustees of the Internal Improvement Trust Fund will execute the required documents to implement the purposes of the resolution.

On motion duly adopted, the meeting was adjourned.

GOVERNOR – CHAIRMAN

ATTEST:

EXECUTIVE DIRECTOR

*   *   *   *

Tallahassee, Florida
November 16, 1971

The State of Florida Board of Trustees of the Internal Improvement Trust Fund met on this date in the auditorium of the Department of Transportation, with the following members present:

Reubin O'D. Askew	Governor
Richard (Dick) Stone	Secretary of State
Robert L. Shevin	Attorney General
Fred O. Dickinson, Jr.	Comptroller
Doyle Conner	Commissioner of Agriculture
Joel Kuperberg	Executive Director

-1-

OKALOOSA COUNTY - Road Right of Way and Drainage Easement

The Department of Transportation

(1)   requests an easement across 11.12 acres in the Blackwater River State Forest in Sections 20 and 21, Township 5 North, Range 24 West, Okaloosa County, for construction and/or improvement of State Road No. S-2-B; and

(2)   requests a drainage easement over portions of the Blackwater River State Forest in Sections 20 and 21, Township 5 North Range 24 West, Okaloosa County, for construction of five (5) outfalls, drainage ditches and drains in connection with the construction of State Road No. S-2-B.

The Division of Forestry, Department of Agriculture and Consumer Services, has reviewed and approved this request.

Recommend issuance of the easement for public highway purposes only, and issuance of the drainage easement as requested.

ACTION OF THE TRUSTEES:

On motion by Mr. Dickinson, seconded by Mr. Stone and adopted without objection, the Trustees granted the request of the Department of Transportation for road right of way and drainage easements.

-2-

VOLUSIA COUNTY - Application for Disclaimer
                File No. 2426-64-253.129   0.60 acre

Staff Description: A parcel of filled sovereignty land in the
Halifax River abutting Government Lot 1, Section 27, Township
15 South, Range 33 East, Volusia County

A. CITY AND COUNTY: Volusia County
B. APPLICANT: Everette F. Wendler, et ux
                       2712 South Peninsula Drive
                       Daytona Beach, Florida 32018
C. APPLICANT'S
    REPRESENTATIVE: Kinsey, Vincent and Pyle
                       Post Office Box 3096, Daytona Beach, Florida
D. ACREAGE: 0.60
    RATE PER ACRE: Not applicable
                       $100 minimum handling charge
E. APPRAISAL: Not applicable
F. PURPOSE: Residential and private boat basin
G. BIOLOGICAL
    REPORT: Not applicable
H. STAFF REMARKS: The applicant applied for a disclaimer pursuant
    to Section 253.129, Florida Statutes, which provides that "The
    title to all lands heretofore filled or developed is herewith
    confirmed in the upland owners and the Trustees shall on
    request issue a disclaimer to each such owner."

    Two affidavits have been submitted stating that the lands in
    question had been filled prior to May 29, 1951.

    Staff legal counsel reviewed the application and recommended
    a disclaimer for the parcel.

    The applicant has also submitted $100 for the processing fee.

Request authority to issue the disclaimer.

ACTION OF THE TRUSTEES:

On motion by Mr. Dickinson, seconded by Mr. Stone and adopted
without objection, the Trustees authorized issuance of the
disclaimer requested by Mr. Wendler.

-3-

MONROE COUNTY - Application for Quitclaim
               File No. 2391-44-253.12(6)   33.58 acres

Staff Description: Two parcels of filled sovereignty lands
containing, respectively, 31.62 and 1.96 acres, more or less,
adjacent to Government Lot 1, Section 20, and Government
Lot 3, Section 21, Township 64 South, Range 36 East, Monroe
County

A. CITY AND COUNTY: Monroe County
B. APPLICANT: The Branigar Organization, Inc.
                       Irving Park and Medinah Roads
                       Medinah, Illinois 60157
C. APPLICANT'S
    REPRESENTATIVE: William J. Roberts, P. A.
                       Post Office Box 1386, Tallahassee, Florida
D. ACREAGE: 33.58 acres
    TOTAL OFFER: $10,000
E. APPRAISAL: By staff appraiser on April 7, 1971 (as of
                       January 1, 1957)
F. PURPOSE: Not applicable
G. BIOLOGICAL
    REPORT: Not applicable
H. STAFF REMARKS: The applicant applied for a quitclaim deed
    pursuant to Section 253.12(6) Florida Statutes, which pro-
    vided that "Where any person, state agency, county, city or

other political subdivision prior to June 11, 1957, extended
or added to existing lands or islands bordering on or being
in the navigable waters as defined in this section by filling
in or causing to be filled in such lands, the Board shall
upon application therefor convey said land so filled to the
riparian owner or owners of the upland so extended or added
to. The consideration for such conveyance shall be the
appraised value of said lands as they existed prior to such
filling."

Seven affidavits have been submitted stating that prior
to 1957 the tract was completely covered with mangrove,
except for a small land-locked pond and there was no
break in the shoreline along Florida Bay; prior to and
in the spring of 1957 a predecessor in title dredged a canal
into the mangrove lands filling the submerged land and a
substantial portion of the mangrove land; and after the
initial dredging prior to June, 1957, additional fill has
been placed on the original fill, raising the ground to
the existing elevation.

The larger of the two parcels was a meandered bayou as
shown on the original township survey and is verified by
reference to old coast charts. A Coast and Geodetic topographic
map compiled from 1935 and 1938 information shows a pond
having no connection with the ocean.

A sovereignty land conveyance by Trustees' Deed No. 20770,
dated October 1, 1954, vested title in the applicant's
predecessor to a 100 foot wide strip abutting the northwesterly side of the 31.62 acre parcel. The applicant now
owns all lands surrounding the former bayou except those lots
which have been sold under sales contracts.

The application of the Branigar Organization, Inc. was
withdrawn from the agenda August 3, 1971, because only four
members of the Board were present. Since that date, additional supporting information has been received. Applicant has
submitted the $100 application fee.

Request authority to issue a quitclaim deed for consideration of
$10,000 plus $475 for appraisal services, provided applicant withdraws his request for a permit to fill submerged lands.

ACTION OF THE TRUSTEES:

On motion by Mr. Shevin, seconded by Mr. Conner and adopted
without objection, the Trustees authorized issuance of the
quitclaim deed for $10,000 consideration plus payment of
$475 for the appraisal, subject to the applicant withdrawing his
request for a fill permit.

-4-

DUVAL COUNTY - Bulkhead Line, Section 253.122, Florida Statutes

The Board of County Commissioners of Duval County

by resolution dated July 8, 1968, established a bulkhead line
2195.03 feet long in the St. Johns River adjacent to uplands in
Section 51, Township 1 South, Range 27 East, Duval County.

The Department of Pollution Control has no objection to the proposed bulkhead line; however, it reserves the right to review any
proposed future development.

The Game and Fresh Water Fish Commission objects to the proposed
bulkhead line and recommends insuring the continued maintenance
of this important marsh area by locating the bulkhead line at
the mean high water line.

The Department of Natural Resources objects to the proposed bulkhead line and recommends "that the bulkhead line be set along the

11-16-71

mean high water line and that upland development be done without harm to the marsh grasses."

Staff recommends denial of the proposed bulkhead and return of the application to the county with the suggestion that the county consider establishing a bulkhead line at the mean high water line.

ACTION OF THE TRUSTEES:

On motion by Mr. Conner, seconded by Mr. Stone and adopted without objection, the staff recommendations for denial and return were accepted as the action of the Board.

Mr. Shevin said the Trustees might take action with respect to Duval County bulkhead lines similar to the case of Hillsborough County several months ago when the Board made it known that they would not consider any applications for dredge and fill in that area until the bulkhead lines were set according to recommendations. He noted that number "6" on this agenda was an application for a dredge permit and marina license in Duval County, and the Director said that the permit would not issue if there was any problem in this case.

Governor Askew asked the Director to check on the status of any bulkhead line problems and applications that might be pending in Hillsborough County.

-5-

DADE COUNTY - Permit No. 253.03(7)-297

> U. S. Department of Commerce
> Atlantic Oceanographic and Meteorological Laboratories
> 901 South Miami Avenue, Miami, Florida,

requests approval of permit for laying approximately 6 nautical miles of cable in coordination with Southeast Florida Coastal Circulation Study.

The Department of Natural Resources offers no adverse comments.

Game and Fresh Water Fish Commission offers no adverse comments.

Department of Pollution Control offers no adverse comments.

Request waiver of fees due to public interest in project.

Staff recommends issuance of permit and waiver of fees, as this is a federal project.

ACTION OF THE TRUSTEES:

On motion by Mr. Conner, seconded by Mr. Dickinson and carried without objection, the application was approved and fees waived for the federal project.

-6-

DUVAL COUNTY - Dredge Permit 253.123-898
                and Marina License, ML-56

> Colonial Point Apartments, Inc.
> 5201 Atlantic Boulevard
> Jacksonville, Florida 32207

applies for a marina license covering 3,000 square feet in Little Pottsburg Creek abutting Section 42, Township 2 South, Range 27 East, Duval County. The proposed structure will be used by tenants of the apartment complex. The minimum annual fee of $100 has been tendered.

The applicant also wishes to excavate 2,500 cubic yards of material from an area under and adjacent to the proposed pier site and dispose of the material on upland. Payment of $2,500 has been submitted for the material to be removed.

The Game and Fresh Water Fish Commission has no objection to the proposed project.

The Department of Pollution Control has no objection to the proposed project and will issue certification upon receipt of Trustees' permit.

The Department of Natural Resources has indicated that dredging should not have significant adverse effects on marine biological resources unless water turbidity and siltation limits are exceeded. Precautions should be taken to keep spoil sediments off intertidal bottoms during the preparation and use of the proposed disposal area.

The staff recommends approval of the dredge permit and marina license, subject to stipulations by the Department of Natural Resources.

ACTION OF THE TRUSTEES:

On motion by Mr. Shevin, seconded and adopted without objection, the Trustees approved the dredge permit and marina license as recommended by the staff, subject to review of the bulkhead line in the area as suggested by Mr. Kuperberg.

-7-

MANATEE COUNTY - Dredge Permit 253.123-100A

    Mr. Robert C. Hutches, Chairman
    Manatee County Port Authority

makes application for permit to complete the work authorized under Dredge Permit 253.123-100. The South side of the basin was not dredged to project depth due to lack of funds. The new cut will complete the project as originally authorized. Applicant requests that the state permit expiration date coincide with the Corps permit, which expires on December 31, 1973. All material removed will be placed on diked upland owned by the Port Authority.

The Department of Natural Resources biological report indicates dredging in the existing boat basin should not have significant adverse effects on marine biological resources provided dredging is carefully done to minimize siltation.

The Game and Fresh Water Fish Commission has no objection to issuance of the permit.

The Department of Pollution Control has no objection to the issuance of the permit.

Recommend issuance of the permit as requested.

ACTION OF THE TRUSTEES:

Mr. Kuperberg explained that consideration of the application was delayed awaiting a court decision on a case that the Army Corps of Engineers had against the Port Authority and against Hendry Dredging Corporation.

On motion by Mr. Stone, seconded by Mr. Conner and adopted without objection, the Board approved issuance of the permit.

11-16-71

8

PINELLAS COUNTY - Dredge Permit 253.123-800

> Florida Power Corp., c/o John A. Hancock, Manager
> Generation Environmental and Regulatory Affairs
> St. Petersburg, Florida

requests approval of Dredge Only Permit No. 193 issued by
Pinellas County Water and Navigation Control Authority on
May 18, 1971, to perform maintenance dredging in Tampa Bay
at Weedon Island at Bartow Plant, in Sections 21 and 22,
Township 30 South, Range 17 East, Pinellas County.

Approximately 414,372.51 cubic yards of material will be removed
to restore the existing channel to the -34 feet Mean Low Water
depth, and placed on privately-owned upland. Of this quantity,
31,840.89 cubic yards of material will be removed from submerged
lands owned by the State of Florida. Applicant has tendered a
check for $31,840.89 as payment for this material.

The Department of Natural Resources biological survey states
that the proposed maintenance dredging should be carefully
monitored and reviewed by Pollution Control Agencies to assure
the protection of natural habitat and the maintenance of water
quality.

The Game and Fresh Water Fish Commission requests the right to
shut down the operation if siltation problems develop.

The Department of Pollution Control has no objection.

Staff recommends approval of dredge permit 253.123-800 subject
to monitoring and review by Pollution Control Agencies.

ACTION OF THE TRUSTEES:

On motion by Mr. Stone, seconded by Mr. Dickinson and adopted
without objection, the dredge permit was approved subject to
monitoring and review by Pollution Control Agencies.

9

MARINA LICENSES - Renewals

The required annual fees for the following marina licenses have
been submitted:

Marina License No.	Licensee	Annual Fee
ML-4	William Bachstet (Bill's Sailfish Marina), Lake Worth, Sec. 26, T42S-R43E, Palm Beach County	$255.00
ML-8	Arvida Corp, Lake Boca Raton, Sec. 29, T47S-R43E, Palm Beach Co.	231.83
ML-9	Miracle Strip Yacht Basin, St. Andrews Bay, Sec. 34, T3S-15W, Bay County	570.00
ML-12	John A. Herbert, Hobe Sound, Sec.19,T40S-R43E, Martin County	380.40
ML-15	L. E. Files, Steinhatchee River, Sec.25,T9S-R9E, Taylor County	100.00
ML-42	Frederick F. Lutz, Phillippi Creek, Sec.7,T37S,R18E, Sarasota County	100.00

Staff recommends renewal of the marina licenses for one year at
the fees indicated.

ACTION OF THE TRUSTEES:

On motion by Mr. Dickinson, seconded by Mr. Stone and adopted
without objection, the Trustees approved renewal of the six
marina licenses as recommended.

-10-

OKALOOSA COUNTY - Bulkhead Line, Section 253.122, F. S.

Senator William Dean Barrow, the applicant's attorney, had asked
for the application to be placed on the agenda but was not able
to be present because of a conflict. He had requested another
postponement.

Governor Askew noted that the matter had been deferred several
times, that the request would be granted but he hoped action
could be taken next week as it was hard for the staff to have
applications unduly pending. Mr. Kuperberg said the staff
recommendation would not change as long as the application was
for a bulkhead line in the water.

On motion by Mr. Conner, duly adopted, the Trustees deferred
consideration of the bulkhead line for one week.

-11-

MANATEE COUNTY - Dredge Permit No. 253.123-916

APPLICANT: Manatee County Highway Department

PROJECT: To improve boat ramp and dredge channel on
                  Anna Maria Key, Sarasota Pass, in Section 28,
                  Township 34 South, Range 16 East, Manatee
                  County.

MATERIAL: Spoil will be placed on county public beach
                  lands.

PAYMENT: Public works project

ENVIRONMENTAL
     ASPECTS: Department of Natural Resources biological survey
                  has no objection.

                  Game and Fresh Water Fish Commission has no
                  objection.

                  Department of Pollution Control has no objection.

Staff recommends issuance of permit and waiver of fees.

ACTION OF THE TRUSTEES:

On motion by Mr. Dickinson, seconded by Mr. Stone and adopted
without objection, the recommendation was approved as the action
of the Board.

-12-

DIXIE COUNTY - Federal Surplus Land

     The Department of Health and Rehabilitative Services

requests the Trustees to adopt a resolution to be submitted to the
United States Department of Health, Education and Welfare in support of the application by the state department to acquire
approximately 10.30 acres of land and 35 buildings consisting of
the Cross City Air Force Radar Station in Sections 1 and 2,
Township 10 South, Range 12 East, Dixie County.

11-16-71

This property is surplus to the federal government and available to the state for educational purposes. The Department of Health and Rehabilitative Services has determined that the facility could readily and economically be converted into a medium or minimum custody institution by the Division of Corrections.

Application by the Department must be submitted to the United States by November 19 and accompanied by a resolution executed by the Trustees, as the appropriate agency of the State of Florida to hold title to the land, designating Mr. Emmett S. Roberts, Secretary of the Department of Health and Rehabilitative Services, to act on behalf of the Trustees in doing all acts and things necessary to secure the transfer of this property to the state.

Funds of the Trustees will not be involved in this transaction.

Recommend execution of the resolution.

ACTION OF THE TRUSTEES:

On motion by Mr. Dickinson, seconded by Mr. Conner and adopted without objection, the Trustees approved the request and executed the resolution.

-13-

BREVARD COUNTY - Quitclaim Deed, File 1869-05-253.12

C. P. C. Properties of Florida, Inc.,

requests issuance of a corrective deed to its predecessor in title of certain formerly submerged lands in the Indian River. The lands in question, prior to development, were riparian to Lots 1 and 2 and part of Lot 3 of Block 1 of a subdivision lying east of U. S. Highway 1 near Titusville.

The subdivision upland adjoining the submerged land came to Roy and Ruby Stackhouse in 1965 and was re-deeded by them to Washington Plaza, Inc., their wholly owned subsidiary, later that year. Roy and Ruby Stackhouse also owned adjoining waterfront property to the north.

On September 13, 1966, the Trustees approved deeding the submerged land riparian to their upland to Washington Plaza, Inc. and Roy and Ruby Stackhouse. A contract for purchase was executed on October 6, 1966.

The following day, October 7, 1966, Washington Plaza, Inc., deeded its interest to the upland to Washington Plaza Land, Inc. The purchase contract was fulfilled and the Trustees' deed to the land was executed on May 14, 1968. The deed was executed in accordance with the purchase contract in favor of Roy and Ruby Stackhouse and Washington Plaza, Inc. (Trustees Deed No. 24402).

F. S. Section 253.12(4) provides that submerged lands "shall be sold only to the upland riparian owner and to no other person, firm or corporation." This section was also in effect at the time of the Trustees' deed. The land in question has been filled and condominiums placed upon it. A title company has questioned the validity of the Trustees' deed to other than a riparian owner. At the time of the Trustees' deed in 1968, Washington Plaza, Inc., the party to the contract, was no longer the upland owner.

Washington Plaza, Inc., was dissolved in May of 1969, but its surviving trustees, pursuant to F. S. Section 608.30, have executed a deed of the submerged lands to C. P. C. Properties of Florida, Inc., as well as a resolution consenting to the Trustees' execution of a deed to that corporation. C. P. C. Properties of Florida, Inc., is the present record holder of title to the upland and submerged lands.

In light of all the transactions, it appears that the deed of October 7, 1966, from Washington Plaza, Inc., to Washington Plaza Land, Inc., carried with it an assignment of the right to receive submerged lands from the Trustees. The Trustees were not informed of the intended assignment and consequently deeded to the incorrect party. No prejudice has resulted since Washington Plaza, Inc., has not deeded the submerged lands out except to rectify title of C. P. C. Properties of Florida, Inc. Further, Roy and Ruby Stackhouse, the major principals of both corporations, obviously believed that Washington Plaza, Inc., did not participate in the quitclaiming of the entire land area on January 28, 1969, to Stackhouse Corporation, the immediate predecessor in title of C. P. C. Properties of Florida, Inc.

Since Washington Plaza Land, Inc., is also dissolved, staff legal counsel has determined that a quitclaim deed to C. P. C. Properties of Florida, Inc., should be issued to clear title. The deed should contain the following language:

> "This instrument is issued to cure Trustees Deed No. 24402(1869-05) issued to Roy D. Stackhouse and Ruby J. Stackhouse, his wife, and Washington Plaza, Inc., a Florida corporation, which deed did not convey submerged lands to all of the upland riparian owners."

Recommend issuance of the quitclaim deed subject to the language above, for the usual $100 processing fee.

ACTION OF THE TRUSTEES:

On motion by Mr. Dickinson, seconded by Mr. Conner and carried without objection, the Board of Trustees authorized issuance of the quitclaim deed subject to the above language, for the usual $100 processing fee.

On motion duly adopted, the meeting was adjourned.

GOVERNOR — CHAIRMAN

ATTEST: EXECUTIVE DIRECTOR

Tallahassee, Florida
November 23, 1971

The State of Florida Board of Trustees of the Internal Improvement Trust Fund met on this date in the auditorium of the Department of Transportation, with the following members present:

Reubin O'D. Askew	Governor
Richard (Dick) Stone	Secretary of State
Robert L. Shevin	Attorney General
Fred O. Dickinson, Jr.	Comptroller
Thomas D. O'Malley	Treasurer
Floyd T. Christian	Commissioner of Education
Doyle Conner	Commissioner of Agriculture

Joel Kuperberg	Executive Director

Attorney General Shevin introduced a resolution regarding a public hearing to be held on November 30 at Miami-Dade Jr. College South, on legislation introduced by U. S. Senator Lawton Chiles of Florida proposing federal acquisition of key watershed areas

11-23-71

in the Big Cypress Swamp and referring to a letter dated July 20 from the Governor to the Secretary of the Interior urging the acquisition.

The Trustees unanimously adopted the resolution approving Governor Askew's letter of July 20 as the official policy of the State of Florida and transmitting a copy of this resolution and of the Governor's letter to Chairman Jackson and the U. S. Senate Committee on Interior and Insular Affairs with the specific request that it be entered into the record of the public hearing. Copy of the resolution is attached as a part of these minutes.

-1-

On motion by Mr. Stone, seconded by Mr. Conner and adopted, the Trustees approved the minutes of November 9 subject to showing the correct size, 28,617 square feet, for the reduced marina area for which the Board approved issuance of a marina license in item 11.

-2-

MARTIN COUNTY - Consideration of Grazing Lease Bids

On October 19 the Trustees authorized advertisement for sealed bids for a three-year grazing lease of 147.58 acres in Section 16, Township 39 South, Range 41 East, Martin County, at a base or starting bid of $2 per acre per year. The lease will contain a 90-day cancellation provision.

The land is 7.5 miles southwest of Stuart and accessible only over land under other ownership. The soil is sandy, overgrown in native grass, pine and palmetto, with good drainage.

Invitation to bid was published for four consecutive weeks in the Belle Glade Herald and Stuart News with bids to be opened at 10:00 a.m. (EST) on November 23, 1971, for consideration by the Trustees.

ACTION OF THE TRUSTEES:

Mr. James T. Williams, staff member, said that only one bid had been received and that Martin County had requested the use of 60 acres of the land for a sanitary land fill. He suggested holding the bid for at least two weeks for the staff to review the county's request and make a recommendation to the Board.

Wayne R. Page of Stuart, Florida, bid $4.40 per acre per year rental for the grazing lease. Staff appraiser had indicated that a starting bid of $2 per acre would be a fair rental.

Mr. Christian was opposed to the use of 60 acres for the purpose requested by the county.

On motion by Mr. Dickinson, seconded by Mr. Stone and adopted without objection, the Board received the bid and directed it be held for at least two weeks pending a staff review of the request of the county.

-3-

MARINA LICENSES - Renewals

The required annual fees for the following marina licenses have been submitted:

Marina License No.	Licensee	Annual Fee
ML-6	Sunbeam Television Corporation Section 9, Township 53 South, Range 42 East, Biscayne Bay, Dade County	$100.00

ML-11   Keystone Harbor Condominium $157.50
        Section 28, Township 52 South;
        Range 42 East, New Arch Creek,
        Dade County

Staff recommends renewal of the marina licenses for one year at the fees indicated.

ACTION OF THE TRUSTEES:

On motion by Mr. Christian, seconded by Mr. Dickinson and adopted without objection, the renewals were approved at the fees indicated.

Mr. Kuperberg advised the Attorney General that the staff was undertaking a review of the rental fees charged per square foot.

-4-

CHARLOTTE COUNTY - Dredge Permit 253.123-720

APPLICANT: West Coast Inland Navigation District
     Post Office Box 786, Bradenton, Florida 33505

PROJECT: To dredge approximately 20,000 cubic yards of material from Cut C-2 of the West Coast Intracoastal Waterway located in Charlotte County, Township 42 South, Range 20 East, in connection with channel realignment work required in rebuilding the center span of the SCL Railroad bridge leading from Placida to Gasparilla Island.

MATERIAL: Dredge material will be placed on existing spoil islands in the immediate vicinity, which will be adequately diked to provide settling basins.

ECOLOGICAL
 REPORTS: Department of Natural Resources has no objection to the project; requests material be contained behind dikes to maintain water quality.

     Game and Fresh Water Fish Commission has no objection to the project; requests all spoil be placed on present spoil islands in vicinity.

     Department of Pollution Control has no objection to project; requests precautions during dredging to insure water quality.

Staff recommends issuance of permit with stipulation that spoil be placed on existing spoil areas and that areas be diked to protect water quality, and waiver of fees since the project is in the public interest.

ACTION OF THE TRUSTEES:

On motion by Mr. Christian, seconded by Mr. Conner and adopted without objection, the dredge permit was approved as recommended.

-5-

MARTIN COUNTY - Dredge Permit, 253.123-887

APPLICANT: Roger M. Skillman
     Post Office Box 2287
     Delray Beach, Florida 33444

PROJECT: To remove 1,655 cubic yards of material from sovereignty lands in St. Lucie Inlet, Intracoastal Waterway, in Section 20, Township 38 South, Range 42 East, for a boat channel to Rocky Point Estates.

11-23-71

MATERIAL: Spoil material will be placed landward of the mean high water line. A check for $827.50 was sent to pay for 1,655 cubic yards of material to be removed from sovereignty lands.

ECOLOGICAL
COMMENTS: Department of Natural Resources biological report has no objections to the project.

Game and Fresh Water Fish Commission has no objection to the project.

Department of Pollution Control has no objection to the project.

Staff recommends issuance of permit.

ACTION OF THE TRUSTEES:

On motion by Mr. Stone, seconded by Mr. Dickinson and adopted without objection, the dredge permit was approved.

-6-

MONROE COUNTY - Dredge Permit 253.03-169
                Modification and Refund

APPLICANT: The Branigar Organization, Inc.
Post Office Box 349, Islamorada, Florida

PROJECT: On September 22, 1970, the Board of Trustees authorized issuance of a permit to remove 15,000 cubic yards of material from a navigation channel in Florida Bay adjacent to Sections 20 and 21, Township 64 South, Range 36 East, Monroe County. The material was to be placed on upland and submerged land previously purchased from the Board of Trustees.

The applicant wishes to amend his permit to eliminate the offshore dredging and to permit channel maintenance dredging of an existing channel across privately-owned lands.

MATERIAL: Applicant requests refund of $1,500 previously paid for material to be removed from sovereignty land. There will not be any charge for the material to be removed from the existing channel, since the channel is located on privately-owned lands. All material to be removed will be placed on diked uplands.

ECOLOGICAL
COMMENTS: The Department of Natural Resources reports the elimination of the offshore dredging area will significantly lessen adverse effects on marine biological resources.

The Game and Fresh Water Fish Commission has no objection to the channel maintenance dredging provided appropriate measures are taken to prevent suspended marl from spreading to productive adjacent areas and all fill is placed above the mean high water line.

Department of Pollution Control has no objections to the modified project.

Staff recommends issuance of modified dredge permit, subject to appropriate measures being taken to prevent siltation of productive adjacent areas, and refund of $1,500 to the applicant.

ACTION OF THE TRUSTEES:

Mr. Kuperberg said that this long-standing problem had been resolved to the satisfaction of all environmental agencies concerned.

On motion by Mr. Stone, seconded by Mr. Dickinson and adopted without objection, the dredge permit and refund were approved as recommended.

-7-

OSCEOLA COUNTY - Dredge Permit 253.123-893

APPLICANT: City of Kissimmee
                Lake Tohopekaliga, Osceola County

PROJECT: Request approval of dredging two navigation channels 5 feet deep, 30 feet wide and 500 feet in length in Sections 27 and 28, Township 25 East, Range 29 South, Osceola County. These channels are necessary because of the drawdown of Lake Tohopekaliga.

MATERIAL: The material will be removed to a public upland location.

ECOLOGICAL
  COMMENTS: Department of Natural Resources requested the Game and Fresh Water Fish Commission to do the biological reports and comments.

                Game and Fresh Water Fish Commission offers no adverse comments.

                Department of Pollution Control offers no adverse comments.

Staff recommends issuance of dredge permit with waiver of fees since the project is in the public interest.

ACTION OF THE TRUSTEES:

On motion by Mr. Stone, seconded by Mr. Conner and adopted without objection, the dredge permit was approved as recommended.

-8-

OKALOOSA COUNTY - Bulkhead Line, Section 253.122 Florida Statutes

A bulkhead line established by the City Council of Niceville in Boggy Bayou, Okaloosa County, deferred previously several times, was listed again with an adverse recommendation by the staff.

Mr. Kuperberg had received a request from the City of Niceville for withdrawal of the matter, as the city in special council meeting on November 22 had voted unanimously to rescind approval of their resolution fixing the bulkhead line so that the council might consider any alternate plan that might be submitted which would be in the best interest of the public.

On motion by Mr. Stone, seconded by Mr. Shevin and adopted without objection, consideration of the bulkhead line was withdrawn at the request of the applicant.

-9-

OKALOOSA COUNTY - Dredge Permit 253.123-866

APPLICANT: Department of Transportation

PROJECT: Perform maintenance dredging in an existing boat basin in Township 2 South, Range 22 West, at East Pass Marina, Destin, Florida, to remove silt deposited

11-23-71

by runoff during the four-laning of State Road 30.

MATERIAL: 1,351 cubic yards will be removed by dragline and trucked to public uplands.

PAYMENT: Waived, since the material will be deposited on public property

ECOLOGICAL
REPORTS: Department of Natural Resources has no objection to the project.

Game and Fresh Water Fish Commission has no objection to the project.

Department of Pollution Control has issued Certificate No. DF46-248.

Staff recommends issuance of Permit 253.123-866 and that the fee be waived.

ACTION OF THE TRUSTEES:

On motion by Mr. Dickinson, seconded by Mr. Stone and adopted without objection, the Trustees approved the application and waived the fee for the Department of Transportation project.

-10-

PINELLAS COUNTY - Dredge Permit 253.123-662

APPLICANT: City of St. Petersburg

PROJECT: A variance of Trustees' Permit 253.123-662 (Pinellas County Permit DO-184) to allow use of a hydraulic dredge to pump approximately 6,000 cubic yards of material from channels "J" and "K" to be placed under that portion of the municipal pier which is over land. Approximately 400 feet of the St. Petersburg Municipal Pier has experienced extensive deterioration of concrete and failure of reinforcing steel in this overland portion.

MATERIAL: 6,000 cubic yards of material from channels "J" and "K".

PAYMENT: Waived, since this is a public works project.

ECOLOGICAL
REPORTS: Department of Natural Resources has no objection to the project.

Game and Fresh Water Fish Commission has no objection to the project.

Department of Pollution Control has no objection to the project.

Staff recommends issuance of the variance to Permit 253.123-622 and that the fee be waived.

ACTION OF THE TRUSTEES:

On motion by Mr. O'Malley, seconded by Mr. Christian and adopted without objection, the Trustees approved issuance of the variance to Permit 253.123-622 without fee.

11-23-71

-11-

ST. JOHNS COUNTY - Dredge Permit, 253.123-904

APPLICANT: Harry E. Xynides Boatyard
                   258 Riberia, St. Augustine, Florida 32084

PROJECT: Maintenance dredging at applicant's boatyard
                   adjacent to the San Sebastian River in Section
                   19, Township 7 South, Range 30 East, St. Johns
                   County.

MATERIAL: Spoil will be deposited on an upland area.

PAYMENT: Payment of $50 was tendered for 100 cubic yards
                   of material to be removed.

ECOLOGICAL
  REPORTS: Department of Natural Resources has no objection
                   to the project.

                   Game and Fresh Water Fish Commission has no objec-
                   tion to the project provided the spoil is placed
                   on uplands and retained.

                   Department of Pollution Control has no objection
                   to the project.

Staff recommends issuance of Permit 253.123-904 provided the
environmental departments' stipulations are met.

ACTION OF THE TRUSTEES:

On motion by Mr. Dickinson, seconded by Mr. Christian and adopted
without objection, the permit was approved subject to compliance
with the stipulations of the Game and Fresh Water Fish Commission
with reference to the spoil material.

————————————

-12-

POLK COUNTY - Marina License, Modification
              Section 253.03, Florida Statutes

APPLICANT: Lake Development Company, c/o Nelson Steiner
                   8800 Sheldon Road, Tampa, Florida, 33615

PROJECT: Modification of State Marina License No. ML-21 to
                   allow for lengthening the proposed structure to
                   a maximum length of 66 feet and construction of
                   a floating facility in lieu of a 54-foot open-
                   trestle design. The revised area would cover
                   2,244 square feet, which falls within the minimum
                   fee of $100 per year (previously tendered).

ECOLOGICAL
  RESPONSES: The Department of Natural Resources offers no objec-
                   tion to the proposed modification.

                   The Game and Fresh Water Fish Commission has no
                   objections to the proposed modification.

                   The Department of Pollution Control has no objection
                   to the proposed modification.

Staff recommends approval of the proposed structural modifications
and dimensions.

ACTION OF THE TRUSTEES:

On motion by Mr. Conner, seconded by Mr. Dickinson and adopted
without objection, the recommended marina license modification
was approved.

————————————

11-23-71

-13-

POLK COUNTY - Avon Park Correctional Institution

On April 20, 1971, the Trustees approved acquisition by the
Department of Health and Rehabilitative Services of the
455.32-acre surplus portion of the Avon Park Air Force Bombing
Range from General Services Administration for $425,000.

Prior to completion of this purchase the Air Force found need
for the retention of 44.86 acres of the 455.32 acres due to a
recent change in Air Force mission requirements at the
Avon Park Bombing Range. This matter has been reviewed by the
Division of Corrections and the Department of Health and
Rehabilitative Services who offer no objection to the Air Force
retaining the 44.86 acres. General Services advises that the
purchase price has been revised to $391,350 as opposed to the
original price of $425,000.

Recommend approval of the reduced acreage and price.

ACTION OF THE TRUSTEES:

On motion by Mr. Conner, seconded by Mr. Dickinson and adopted
without objection, the Trustees approved the reduced acreage and
price for land to be acquired by the Department of Health and
Rehabilitative Services.

-14-

MONROE COUNTY - Dredge and Fill Permit 253.03-288

APPLICANT: Bryn Mawr Group, Inc., Key Largo
                c/o William J. Roberts, Tallahassee, Florida

PROJECT: Navigation Channel - 220 feet long by 50 feet
                wide by 5 feet deep across sovereignty lands and
                to excavate a channel 280 feet long by 50 feet
                wide by 5 feet deep; also a boat basin 300 feet
                long by 130 feet wide by 5 feet deep and a swimming
                pool 260 feet long by 120 feet wide by 10 feet deep.
                A 10 foot wide breakwater is to be constructed along
                the outside perimeter of the boat basin and swimming
                pool.

MATERIAL: 750 cubic yards of this material is to come from
                sovereignty land.

APPRAISAL: Staff appraiser indicates value of submerged
                land would not exceed $400 per acre.

ENVIRONMENTAL
ASPECTS: Department of Natural Resources: This revised project
                will have significantly less adverse effect on marine
                biological resources than would the original proposal.
                The dredging and filling should be carefully controlled
                to limit siltation, especially during filling of the
                15 foot deep area.

                Bureau of Beaches and Shores advises that a hydrographic
                survey will not be required.

                Game and Fresh Water Fish Commission has no objection.

                Department of Pollution Control has no objection.

PAYMENT: Applicant offers to convey back to Trustees all of the
                submerged land not used for the swimming area, boat
                basin, dock and navigation channel.

Recommends issuance of permit upon receipt of the deed conveying
the submerged lands and subject to the stipulations by the Department of Natural Resources.

ACTION OF THE TRUSTEES:

On motion by Mr. Conner, seconded by Mr. Stone and adopted without objection, the Trustees approved issuance of 'the permit with the provision and stipulations recommended by the staff.

PALM BEACH COUNTY - Lake Osborne Litigation

On March 1971, the Trustees considered reports of dredging in Lake Osborne in Palm Beach County and authorized the Attorney General to intervene as counsel for the Trustees of the Internal Improvement Trust Fund in a case brought by the Federated Conservation Council, Inc., to obtain a permanent injunction against the Palm Beach County Commission and R. R. Barnes and Company to stop dredging operations in the lake by the latter under a sand lease from the county. Some thirty years ago the property was deeded to the county by the Trustees (Deed 18516) to be used only for park purposes.

Mr. Shevin said the Circuit Court of Palm Beach County entered a permanent injunction from further dredging in Lake Osborne on August 5, 1971, until defendants complied with the permit requirements, there was a further petition for rehearing that was denied, and the appeal period has now run. The suit was successful.

LEE COUNTY - General Acceptance Corporation, Cape Coral

Mr. Kuperberg announced that after extended negotiations that preceded his appointment as Executive Director, the staff had worked out an arrangement for settlement of the Cape Coral matter which the staff considered a good settlement that could be recommended to the Trustees. Briefly, it was a package settlement and purchase wherein GAC Corporation would retain certain land ownership, develop certain land under today's ecological standards, preserve the water system from the top end of the Fakahatchee Strand to Alligator Alley, and pay the settlement the Trustees had proposed in December 1970, that was approximately $200,000 more than what the company offered at that time.

Mr. Kuperberg said details were contained in a letter dated November 22, 1971, from GAC Corporation and a formal presentation would be made to the Board at a later date.

On motion duly adopted, the meeting was adjourned.

GOVERNOR CHAIRMAN

ATTEST: EXECUTIVE DIRECTOR

RESOLUTION

WHEREAS, a public hearing will be held by the U. S. Senate Committee on Interior and Insular Affairs, Senator Henry Jackson presiding, beginning at 2:30 p.m. on November 30, 1971, at Miami-Dade Jr. College South, on legislation introduced by U. S. Senator Lawton Chiles of Florida proposing federal acquisition of key watershed areas in the Big Cypress Swamp; and

WHEREAS, protection of this watershed area is essential to the safeguarding of vital water supplies, irreplaceable wildlife and the rich estuarine resources of the Big Cypress-Ten Thousand Islands ecosystem; and

WHEREAS, the Honorable Reubin O'D. Askew, Governor of Florida, in a letter dated July 20, 1971, to the Honorable Rogers Morton, Secretary of the Interior of the United States, declared that "acquisition is the only sure method to protect the heart of this natural ecosystem and at the same time treat the landowners fairly. Therefore, of the alternatives outlined in the report my recommendation is the acquisition of the portion of subdrainage area 'C' described in alternative I (of the Department's Big Cypress study)".

In addition, the Governor's letter stated that he also joined with the recommendation of the Bureau of Sports Fisheries and Wildlife in urging the acquisition of the Ten Thousand Islands; and

WHEREAS, Governor Askew properly stated that since this major ecosystem has such an important role in the water resources of southernmost Florida, it is his feeling that "state government should play a major role in its management" -- and he suggested consultations between federal and state agencies with respect to the most effective preservation of this vital area;

NOW, THEREFORE BE IT RESOLVED that the Governor and Cabinet of the State of Florida, sitting as the Board of Trustees of the Internal Improvement Trust Fund which holds title to all state lands, hereby approve and adopt Governor Askew's letter of July 20, 1971, as the official policy of the State of Florida; and

BE IT FURTHER RESOLVED that a copy of this resolution and of the Governor's letter be transmitted forthwith to Chairman Jackson and the Senate Committee on Interior and Insular Affairs with the specific request that it be entered into the record of the public hearing.

IN TESTIMONY WHEREOF, the Trustees for and on behalf of the State of Florida Board of Trustees of the Internal Improvement Trust Fund have hereunto subscribed their names and have caused the official seal of said State of Florida Board of Trustees of the Internal Improvement Trust Fund to be hereunto affixed, in the City of Tallahassee, Florida, on this the 23rd day of November, A. D. 1971.

REUBIN O'D. ASKEW
GOVERNOR

RICHARD (DICK) STONE
SECRETARY OF STATE

ROBERT L. SHEVIN
ATTORNEY GENERAL

FRED O. DICKINSON, JR.
COMPTROLLER

THOMAS D. O'MALLEY
TREASURER

FLOYD T. CHRISTIAN
COMMISSIONER OF EDUCATION

DOYLE CONNER
COMMISSIONER OF AGRICULTURE

Tallahassee, Florida
November 30, 1971

The State of Florida Board of Trustees of the Internal Improvement Trust Fund met on this date in the auditorium of the
Department of Transportation, with the following members present:

Reubin O'D. Askew	Governor
Richard (Dick) Stone	Secretary of State
Robert L. Shevin	Attorney General
Fred O. Dickinson	Comptroller
Floyd T. Christian	Commissioner of Education
Doyle Conner	Commissioner of Agriculture

James T. Williams	Staff Member

-1-

The Trustees approved the minutes of November 16 as submitted.

-2-

PINELLAS COUNTY - Settlement

APPLICANT: Charles H. Zutes
757 Clinton Avenue
Rochester, New York 14605

Represented by H. H. Baskin, Jr.
Attorney at Law, Clearwater, Florida

PROJECT: Placed fill on .98 acres of sovereignty land in the
Anclote River adjacent to Government Lot 4, Section
11, Township 27 South, Range 15 East, Pinellas
County.

SETTLEMENT
PROPOSAL: Applicant agrees to remove fill but requests that
some fill be allowed to remain for access to land.

ECOLOGICAL
REPORTS: Florida Game and Fresh Water Fish Commission
recommends that Mr. Zutes remove illegal fill
immediately.

Florida Department of Pollution Control indicates
there was no certification for the work.

Florida Department of Natural Resources states
that the fill has adverse effects on marine
biological resources.

RECOMMEND: Removal of fill from sovereignty land to the
original high water line, use of diapers around
dredge to limit siltation, and reimbursement by
Mr. Zutes for expenses of land survey and biological
survey, which amount to $700.00 and $100.00 respectively.

Any filling for access to land should be applied for
under normal permit procedures.

ACTION OF THE TRUSTEES:

Attorney General Shevin commended the staff for taking the proper
kind of action, and made a motion, seconded by Mr. Christian and
adopted without objection, that the staff recommendations be
approved as the action of the Board.

11-30-71

460

-3-

CITRUS COUNTY - Dredge Permit 253.123-883

APPLICANT: Raymond Donnersberger
                407 South Dearborn Street, Chicago, Illinois 60605

PROJECT: Dredging to improve navigation adjacent to a proposed
           boat basin by removing 35 cubic yards of material from
           an area 20 feet by 20 feet to a depth of 4.2 feet in
           front of Lot 16, Block "A", Magnolia Shores, Citrus
           County, Florida.

MATERIAL: Spoil to be placed on upland.

PAYMENT: Minimum charge of $50 has been paid.

REPORTS: Department of Natural Resources biological report
           has no objection to the project.

           Game and Fresh Water Fish Commission has no objec-
           tion to the project.

           Department of Pollution Control has no objection
           to the project.

Staff recommends issuance of Dredge Permit 253.123-883.

ACTION OF THE TRUSTEES:

On motion by Mr. Christian, seconded by Mr. Conner and adopted
without objection, the staff recommendation was approved.

-4-

MONROE COUNTY - Dredge Permit 253.03-216

APPLICANT: William V. Payne
           Payne & Company
           303 South Ninth Street, Lafayette, Indiana 47901

PROJECT: Dredge a navigation channel 30 feet wide, approxi-
           mately 90 feet in length connecting two existing
           channels, in Section 14, Township 66 South, Range
           29 East, in Bogie Channel, Big Pine Key, Monroe
           County.

MATERIAL: Spoil will be placed on applicant's upland.

PAYMENT: A check for $615.00 has been submitted to cover 410
           cubic yards of material to be removed.

ECOLOGICAL
REPORTS: Department of Natural Resources has no objection to
           the project.

           Game and Fresh Water Fish Commission has no objec-
           tion to the project.

           Department of Pollution Control has issued Certifica-
           tion No. DF-44-102.

Staff recommends issuance of Dredge Permit 253.03-216, Monroe
County.

ACTION OF THE TRUSTEES:

On motion by Mr. Christian, seconded by Mr. Conner and
adopted without objection, the Trustees approved issuance of
the dredge permit.

11-30-71

-5-

SARASOTA COUNTY - Dredge Permit 253.123-828

APPLICANT: Board of County Commissioners of Sarasota County
               Post Office Box "B", Sarasota, Florida

PROJECT: Perform maintenance dredging in Phillipi Creek,
               Section 8, Township 37 South, Range 18 East,
               in Sarasota County.

MATERIAL: 11,000 cubic yards of material to be removed and
               transported by truck to Gregg Beach where it is
               to be deposited on county owned uplands.

ECOLOGICAL
  REPORTS: Department of Natural Resources has no objection.

               Game and Fresh Water Fish Commission has no objec-
               tion.

               Department of Pollution Control has no objection.

PAYMENT: Public works project.

Staff recommends issuance of permit with waiver of fees.

ACTION OF THE TRUSTEES:

On motion by Mr. Stone, seconded by Mr. Shevin and adopted
without objection, the Trustees approved issuance of the
dredge permit without requiring the fee.

-6-

MINUTES, VOLUME 37

The cost of printing 140 paper-bound copies of Volume 37 of
the minutes of the Board of Trustees of the Internal Improvement Trust Fund was $5,509 or $39.35 each.

Staff recommends establishment of a sales price of $40 per
paper-bound copy.

ACTION OF THE TRUSTEES:

On motion by Mr. Christian, seconded by Mr. Stone and adopted
without objection, the Trustees fixed a price of $40 for sale
of each paper-bound copy of Volume 37 of the Minutes of the
Trustees.

-7-

DADE, BROWARD AND PALM BEACH COUNTIES - Power Line Easements

     Florida Power and Light Company
     Miami, Florida,

proposes to construct a cross-state transmission line from
Turkey Point in Dade County to Fort Myers crossing certain
state-owned lands, for which the following five easements
have been requested.

ACTION OF THE TRUSTEES:

The five power line easements were approved by the Board as
shown below following each recommendation listed for A, B,
C, D and E.

A. DADE COUNTY

Florida Power and Light Company applies for a 330-foot wide easement over and across thirteen parcels of land in Dade County owned by the Trustees for construction, operation and maintenance of one or more overhead electric transmission and distribution lines in Sections 3, 15, 20 and 22 in Township 53 South, Range 39 East; Sections 24, 25, 35 and 36 in Township 53 South, Range 38 East; and Hiatus Lots 2 and 3 in Township 53/54 South, Range 38 East, Dade County.

The easement would cross a portion of Conservation Area 3 and three parcels of Trustees' land subject to flowage easement held by Central and Southern Florida Flood Control District. The District has approved the alignment of the proposed cross-state transmission line and has entered into a written agreement with Florida Power and Light Company specifying that all matters pertaining to construction on the easement must be approved by the District in order to insure that no violence is done to the flowage easement obtained from the Trustees.

Approval also has been obtained from the Game and Fresh Water Fish Commission that leased Conservation Area 3 for game and fish management purposes.

The Division of Forestry has reviewed this request and commented that the proposed route is far better than an earlier one bisecting Conservation Area 3-A. Further, the Division of Forestry recommended that in clearing right of way all resources which will be removed or destroyed, such as timber, should be salvaged for the benefit of the state. A provision will be incorporated in the easement to provide for this.

The thirteen parcels of Trustees' land have been appraised and Florida Power and Light Company offers $69,314.40 for easement. Staff appraiser reviewed the appraisals and considers the offer reasonable.

One parcel of land in the proposed easement is subject to Rock Mining Lease No. 2429 dated April 14, 1970, held by Seminole Rock Products, Inc. Lessee has consented to the easement by an instrument of consent dated September 9, 1971.

In the proposed easement the Trustees reserve the right to utilize the right of way for agricultural and all other purposes except the right to construct buildings or structures other than fences.

Correcte
in minute
8/29/72

Recommend granting the easement for electric transmission and distribution line purposes only for the consideration offered, $69,314.40.

On motion by Mr. Conner, seconded by Mr. Christian and adopted without objection, the Board of Trustees approved the easement for electric transmission and distribution line purposes only for $69,314.40 consideration as recommended.

B. BROWARD COUNTY

Florida Power and Light Company applies for an easement over and across 87.5 acres in Section 16, Township 49 South, Range 39 East, Broward County, that has been appraised by Florida Power and Light Company. Staff appraiser reviewed the appraisal and considers the offer of $4,200 to be equitable. Consideration offered for the easement across this parcel will be deposited in the School Fund.

The easement would be within Conservation Area 3-A. Central and Southern Florida Flood Control District, holder of a flowage easement over the land, has approved issuance of the easement and entered into a written agreement with Florida Power and Light Company in which is specified that all matters pertaining to construction on the easement area must be approved by the District in order to insure that no violence is done to the flowage easement obtained from the Board of Education. Approval also has been obtained from the Game and Fresh Water Fish Commission that leased Conservation Area 3 for game and fish management purposes.

The Division of Forestry has reviewed this request and commented that the proposed route is far better than an earlier one bisecting Conservation Area 3-A. Further, the Division of Forestry recommended that in clearing right of way all resources which will be removed or destroyed, such as timber, should be salvaged for the benefit of the state. A provision will be incorporated in the easement to provide for this.

In the proposed easement the Trustees reserve the right to utilize the right of way for agricultural and other purposes except the right to construct buildings or structures other than fences.

Recommend granting the easement for electric transmission and distribution line purposes only for the $4,200 consideration offered.

On motion by Mr. Conner, seconded by Mr. Christian and adopted without objection, the Board of Trustees approved the easement for electric transmission and distribution line purposes only for $4,200 consideration as recommended.

    C.   BROWARD COUNTY

       Florida Power and Light Company applies for a 660-foot wide easement over and across a parcel of land in Section 3, Township 50 South, Range 39 East, owned by Broward County in which the Trustees hold a reversionary interest by virture of Deed No. 21007 dated September 1, 1955, from the Trustees to the county.

Broward County by official action on February 9, 1971, approved issuance of an easement to Florida Power and Light Company for transmission line purposes.

The interest of the Trustees was appraised by Florida Power and Light Company. Staff appraiser reviewed the appraisal and considers the offer of $1,516 reasonable.

Recommend granting the easement for electric transmission and distribution line purposes only for the consideration of $1,516.

On motion by Mr. Conner, seconded by Mr. Christian and adopted without objection, the Board of Trustees approved the easement for electric transmission and distribution line purposes only for $1,516 consideration as recommended.

    D.   BROWARD AND PALM BEACH COUNTIES

       Florida Power and Light Company applies for an easement for construction, operation and maintenance of one or more overhead electric transmission and distribution lines over and across 16 parcels of land in Broward and Palm Beach Counties owned by the Trustees in the following sections:

Broward County:

Sections	Township South	Range East
7 through 12	47	36
25 through 30	47	37
27,28,29,30,34 and 35	47	38
1, 2, 11, 12 and 13	48	38
18, 20 and 32	48	39
4 and 33	49	39
4 and 34	50	39

Palm Beach County:

| 1 through 6 | 48 | 36 |
| 19, 20 and 21 | 47 | 37 |

The easement would cross a portion of Conservation Area 3 and three parcels of Trustees' land subject to a flowage easement held by Central and Southern Florida Flood Control District. The District approved the alignment of the proposed cross-state transmission line and has entered into a written agreement with Florida Power and Light Company in which is specified that all matters pertaining to construction on the easement must be approved by the District in order to insure that no violence is done to the flowage easement obtained from the Trustees by the District.

Approval also has been obtained from the Game and Fresh Water Fish Commission that leased Conservation Area 3 for game and fish management purposes.

The Division of Forestry has reviewed this request and commented that the proposed route is far better than an earlier one bisecting Conservation Area 3-A. Further, the Division of Forestry recommended that in clearing the right of way all resources which will be removed or destroyed, such as timber, should be salvaged for the benefit of the state. A provision will be incorporated in the easement to provide for this.

The 16 parcels of land were appraised and Florida Power and Light Company offers $161,591.74 for the easement. Staff appraiser reviewed the appraisals and considers the offer reasonable.

The Trustees reserve the right to utilize the easement right of way for agricultural and all other purposes except growing sugar cane or construction of buildings or structures other than fences.

Recommend granting the easement for electric transmission and distribution line purposes only for the consideration of $161,591.74.

On motion by Mr. Conner, seconded by Mr. Christian and adopted without objection, the Board of Trustees approved the easement for electric transmission and distribution line purposes only for $161,591.74 consideration as recommended.

E. PALM BEACH COUNTY - Seminole Indian Land

Florida Power and Light Company has entered into a right of way agreement with the Seminole Tribe of Florida to cross a portion of the tribe's land.

In 1965 the Seminole Tribe granted an easement for a power line across the State Reservation covering 594 acres, but due to objections to the location of the right of way the line was not built. A new route was established using only 242 acres of the Reservation in Palm Beach County. The Seminole Tribe on July 7, 1971, in regular meeting authorized issuance of the 242-acre easement. The $17,482.50 paid to the tribe for the earlier route will be retained as consideration for the new route.

Trustees' staff counsel has reviewed and approved the right of way agreement as to form and legality.

Recommend that the Board of Trustees, acting in its capacity as Trustee for the Seminole Tribe of Florida, consent to issuance of the right of way easement.

On motion by Mr. Conner, seconded by Mr. Christian and adopted without objection, the Board of Trustees, acting as Trustee for the Seminole Tribe of Florida, consented to issuance of the right of way easement as recommended.

11-30-71

-8-

BAY COUNTY - Marina License, 253.03 F. S.
                Dredge Permit No. 253.123-986

APPLICANT: Grand Lagoon Marina, c/o Guy-Rogers Marine, Inc.
                5323 North Lagoon Drive, Panama City, Florida 32401

PROJECT: Modify and enlarge existing marina facility in
                Grand Lagoon adjacent to Section 9, 10, 15, and
                16, Township 4 South, Range 15 West, Bay County.

                Applicant proposed to enlarge existing facility
                covering 14,300 square feet of sovereignty land and
                16,000 square feet of privately-owned submerged land
                (total area of 31,300 square feet). The modification
                will add 28,600 square feet of sovereignty land to
                the existing facility. The total sovereignty land
                to be encompassed within the proposed facility will
                be 43,900 square feet.

                Applicant also proposes to remove 1,500 cubic yards
                of material from the artificial cut portion of the
                existing facility.

ECOLOGICAL
    REPORTS: Department of Natural Resources has no objection.

                Game and Fresh Water Fish Commission has no object-
                tion.

                Department of Pollution Control has no objection.

Staff recommends approval of marina license for annual fee of
$878.00, and dredge permit.

ACTION OF THE TRUSTEES:

On motion by Mr. Dickinson, seconded by Mr. Christian and
Mr. Stone, adopted without objection, the Board authorized
issuance of the dredge permit and a marina license for the
annual fee of $878.00.

-9-

PALM BEACH COUNTY - Dredge and Fill Permits 253.123-890 and
                253.124-206

APPLICANT: City of Boca Raton

PROJECT: To construct a seawall and fill by performing
                necessary dredging to reclaim eroded material at
                the city's Spanish River Park

LOCATION: The lagoon at Spanish River Park in Section 16,
                Township 47 South, Range 43 East, Palm Beach County

PAYMENT: Request fees be waived since this is a public works
                project.

ECOLOGICAL
    REPORTS: Department of Natural Resources biological report
                indicates limited adverse effects as to the dredging
                portion of the project. Filling the near shore area
                will have adverse effects on marine biological
                resources, and siltation from the dredging would
                probably have adverse effects, also, on the shallow
                vegetated bottoms adjacent to the fill area.

Game and Fresh Water Fish Commission has no objection
to the project provided the seawall is constructed
before filling is done and adequate steps are taken
to prevent turbidity and siltation in the surrounding
areas.

Department of Pollution Control has no objection to
this project.

OTHER
REPORTS: The Board of County Commissioners of Palm Beach
County is of the opinion that this project is in
the public interest.

The Area Planning Board of Palm Beach County considers
this project to be truly in the public interest.

Recommend issuance of the permit provided the stipulations in the
Game and Fresh Water Fish Commission report are met, and that
fees be waived since this is a public works project.

ACTION OF THE TRUSTEES:

On motion by Mr. Dickinson, seconded by Mr. Christian and
adopted without objection, the application was approved without
fee subject to the recommended stipulations.

On motion duly adopted, the meeting was adjourned.

GOVERNOR   CHAIRMAN

ATTEST:
STAFF MEMBER

*   *   *   *   *

Tallahassee, Florida
December 14, 1971

The State of Florida Board of Trustees of the Internal Improvement Trust Fund met on this date in the Capitol with the following members present:

Reubin O'D. Askew	Governor
Richard (Dick) Stone	Secretary of State
Fred O. Dickinson, Jr.	Comptroller
Thomas D. O'Malley	Treasurer
Floyd T. Christian	Commissioner of Education
Doyle Conner	Commissioner of Agriculture
Joel Kuperberg	Executive Director

-1-

The Trustees approved the minutes of November 23 and 30 as
submitted.

12-14-71

2

ESCAMBIA COUNTY - Surplus State Fire Tower Site

A change in the forest fire protection system has caused the
Walnut Hill Towersite to be surplus to the needs of the
Division of Forestry. All fixed improvements have been removed
or sold. The 10-acre parcel site in Section 4, Township 4
North, Range 33 West, Escambia County, was donated to the
Board of Forestry on December 14, 1937, by J. H. and Mary
A. Sherrill. Although the deed does not contain a reverter
clause, the Department of Agriculture and Consumer Services
recommends returning the land at no cost to the heirs of
J. H. and Mary A. Sherrill who own all the adjacent land.

This matter was before the Board on August 11, 1970, when the
Attorney General asked that the matter be deferred so that he
might review the legal situation. The Department of Agriculture
and Consumer Services has furnished four affidavits indicating
the State's intent to hold title to this property for towersite
purposes only. The Attorney General has reviewed these affidavits and the history of this transaction and can find no legal
objection to reconveying the surplus parcel to the J. H. Sherrill
heirs.

Recommend reconveyance of the 10-acre parcel without cost to
Frontis W. Sherrill, John H. Sherrill, Jr., Alan P. Sherrill,
Margaret S. Bach and Mary S. Baranco, heirs of J. H. and Mary A.
Sherrill.

ACTION OF THE TRUSTEES:

On motion by Mr. Stone, seconded by Mr. O'Malley, adopted without objection, the reconveyance was approved as recommended.

3

PALM BEACH COUNTY - Road Right of Way

The Board of County Commissioners of Palm Beach County requests
an easement for road right of way over and across a parcel
containing forty square feet located in the NE 1/4 of Section
6, Township 43 South, Range 43 East, and the Southwest corner of
the University of Florida's Genesys facility. The land will
be utilized as a turnout to improve access to the Genesys
facility.

The Board of Regents on August 20, 1971, reviewed and approved
this request.

Recommend issuance of the easement for road right of way purposes only.

ACTION OF THE TRUSTEES:

On motion by Mr. O'Malley, seconded by Mr. Christian and adopted
without objection, the Trustees granted the 40 sq.ft. easement
to Palm Beach County for road right of way purposes only.

SANTA ROSA COUNTY - Consideration of Oil and Gas Lease Bids

On October 26, 1971, the Trustees authorized advertisement for
sealed bids for a five-year oil and gas drilling lease covering
the 10.4-acre Jay State Livestock Market located within the
corporate limits of the Town of Jay in Santa Rosa County.

The lease will require royalty payments of 1/6 in kind or value
for all oil and gas produced, annual rental of $1 per net

mineral acre, $100,000 surety bond and at least one test well
be drilled to a depth of 6,000 feet or to a depth sufficient
to test the Norphlet Sands, whichever is deeper.

Invitation to bid was advertised in the Tallahassee Democrat
and the Press-Gazette of Milton. Prior to issuance of this
lease, a resolution will be necessary from the Town of Jay
consenting to the lease as required by Section 253.61(a),
Florida Statutes.

All proceeds from this lease will go to the Department of
Agriculture and Consumer Services which department requests
that bids be received, opened and reviewed to determine if
the best interest of the State will be served under a lease
arrangement. Right to reject any or all bids has been reserved.

ACTION OF THE TRUSTEES:

The Director called on Mr. James T. Williams, staff member, to
report on the bids received pursuant to advertised bid invitation.
The eleven bids were read, each total amount comprising the first
year's rental plus a bonus bid on the 10.4 acres of land in
Section 41, Township 5 North, Range 29 West, Santa Rosa County,
as follows:

$ 83,886.40	Sun Oil Company
55,374.00	Spencer Brothers
132,704.00	Dalco Oil Company
104,108.40	M. B. Rudman
105,415.00	Chevron Oil Company
80,205.94	Arden A. Anderson
95,790.00	Humble Oil and Refining Company
105,248.00	Victor P. Smith
83,375.00	Harris R. Fender, David M. Fender, Harris R. Fender, Jr., and Philip B. Berry
161,777.72	W. A. Moncrief
80,790.15	William D. Mounger

There was considerable interest in leasing the 10.4 acre parcel
of land, as evidenced by the bids. The high bid amounted to
$15,554 per acre which appeared to be the all-time high for a
state lease.

The Town of Jay had submitted a resolution to the Trustees
consenting to issuance of the lease.

The motion by Mr. Christian, seconded by Mr. Conner, to accept
the high bid and award the oil and gas drilling lease to W.
A. Moncrief was adopted on a vote of five to one. Mr. Stone
voted "no" because while there was an evacuation plan for the
Town of Jay, there were people in the area where the oil well
would be drilled.

-5-

MONROE COUNTY - Aquaculture Lease

    Wometco Enterprises, Inc.
    c/o Charles Francis, Director
    Subsidiary Services
    Rickenbacker Causeway, Miami, Florida

The applicant, who is the riparian upland owner, has filed an
aquaculture lease application embracing approximately 1.87
acres in part of Government Lot 2, Section 19, Township 65
South, Range 34 East, on Grassy Key, Monroe County, Florida,
for the purpose of experimental breeding of bottle-nose dolphins.

The construction of 1" mesh metal fencing spaced 4 to 5 feet
apart is proposed to contain these dolphins.

The Department of Natural Resources has no objection.

The Department of Pollution Control has no objection.

The Florida Game and Fresh Water Fish Commission has no objection.

Request authority to advertise for competitive bids and objections in accordance with the provisions of Section 253.70, Florida Statutes.

ACTION OF THE TRUSTEES:

On motion by Mr. Stone, seconded by Mr. Dickinson and adopted without objection, the Trustees authorized advertisement for competitive bids and objections.

———————

-6-

COLLIER COUNTY - Fill Permit 253.124(8)-195

APPLICANT:	Key Island, Inc. c/o Tri-County Engineering, Inc. Post Office Box 578, Naples, Florida
PROJECT:	To fill land behind a groin (rubble revetment) that eroded due to recent dredging by Corps of Engineers, boat traffic, wind and current damage.
MATERIAL:	Approximately 1,200 cubic yards of material will be used as backfill.
PAYMENT:	Waived. Material will come from dredge area authorized under Permit 253.123-660.
ECOLOGICAL REPORTS:	Department of Natural Resources comments that "The dredging and filling proposed should have only insignificant effects on marine biological resources, particularly if all or most of the fill is placed above the line of mean high water."
	Game and Fresh Water Fish Commission has no objection to the project.
	Department of Pollution Control has no objection to the project.

Staff recommends issuance of Fill Permit No. 253.124(8)-195 to Key Island, Inc.

ACTION OF THE TRUSTEES:

On motion by Mr. Stone, seconded by Mr. Christian and adopted without objection, the Board authorized issuance of the fill permit to Key Island, Inc.

———————

-7-

MARTIN COUNTY - Dredge Permit 253.123-935

APPLICANT:	James Burgess Lot 18 Bay Shore Village, Salerno, Florida
PROJECT:	To dredge a navigation channel 70 feet by 40 feet by -4.0 feet, and to dredge an upland boat basin and construct a seawall around the perimeter of the boat basin.
MATERIAL:	Approximately 200 cubic yards of material to be removed from sovereignty land will be placed on owner's upland.
PAYMENT:	$100 check has been tendered as payment for the material at standard 50¢ per cubic yard rate for Martin County.

12-14-71

ECOLOGICAL
REPORTS: Department of Natural Resources has no objection to
the project.

Game and Fresh Water Fish Commission has no objec-
to the project.

Department of Pollution Control has no objection to
the project.

Staff recommends issuance of dredge permit 253.123-935.

ACTION OF THE TRUSTEES:

On motion by Mr. Dickinson, seconded by Mr. Christian and
adopted without objection, the Board authorized issuance of
the dredge permit.

-8-

PASCO COUNTY - Extension of Dredge Permit
                253.123-146

James V. Hodnett, Jr.
Sea Pines, Inc.
Post Office Box 1023, Hudson, Florida,

requests extension of State Permit 253.123-146 to coincide with
the December 31, 1972 expiration date of the U. S. Corps of
Engineers permit for the sole purpose of removing the balance
of spoil placed alongside channel during construction work
authorized under this permit but not yet complete.

Recommend extension of Permit No. 253.123-146 to December 31,
1972.

ACTION OF THE TRUSTEES:

On motion by Mr. Dickinson, seconded by Mr. Christian and
adopted without objection, the Board authorized extension of
the dredge permit as recommended.

-9-

BREVARD COUNTY - Refund, 253.123-154

Dr. L. R. Wells
2210 South Atlantic Avenue, Cocoa Beach, Florida

requests refund of $508.40 which represents payment for fill
material for which a permit issued to secure 10,210 cubic
yards on February 4, 1964. The permittee did not exercise
his privilege and the permit expired.

A request was submitted to renew the permit. However, the
proposed dredge area lies in the Banana River Aquatic Preserve.
Plans for disposal of fill material on submerged land require
that a bulkhead line be established offshore from the mean high
water line.

The Game and Fresh Water Fish Commission and various administrative branches of Brevard County are opposed to this project.

On February 3, 1970, at the request of the Governor, action was
deferred on the staff request for authority to make a refund.

Staff recommends authority to refund $508.40 to Dr. L. R. Wells.

ACTION OF THE TRUSTEES:

Mr. Kuperberg stated that on a biological basis the extension of
this permit was not recommended.

12-14-71

On motion by Mr. Dickinson, seconded by Mr. Christian and adopted without objection, the Board authorized refund of $508.40 to Dr. Wells.

-10-

BREVARD AND ORANGE COUNTIES - Right of Way Easement
                    File 2430-05-48-253.03

APPLICANT: Department of Transportation

PROJECT: Bridge Construction for State Road 524 (Bee Line
             Expressway) No dredging or filling required.

LOCATION: A parcel of submerged land, estimated 2.50 acres,
             in the St. Johns River in Section 26, Township 23
             South, Range 34 East, Brevard and Orange Counties

ECOLOGICAL
RESPONSES: The Department of Natural Resources has no objection.
             The Game and Fresh Water Fish Commission has no
             objection.
             The Department of Pollution Control has no objection.
             The Central and Southern Florida Flood Control District
             has no objection.
             The Corps of Engineers has no objection to the pro-
             ject.

Staff requests authority to issue right of way easement.

ACTION OF THE TRUSTEES:

On motion by Mr. Stone, seconded by Mr. Dickinson and adopted
without objection, the Board approved the right of way easement.

-11-

The minutes of November 23 were approved as shown in #1 above.

-12-

DUVAL COUNTY - Land Sale
         File No. 2422-16-253.12

Staff Description: 0.11 acre parcel of filled sovereignty land
in St. Johns River abutting Section 37, Township 3 South, Range
26 East.

A. CITY AND COUNTY: Duval County

B. APPLICANT: Alvin M. Coplan, 4040 San Remo Drive,
                      Jacksonville, Florida

C. APPLICANT'S
    REPRESENTATIVE: Not applicable

D. ACREAGE: 0.11
    RATE PER ACRE: $650 for the parcel

E. APPRAISAL: Boyce Taylor, S.R.A., A.S.A., adjusted by
                      staff appraiser on August 6, 1970

F. PURPOSE: Residential

G. BIOLOGICAL REPORT:Not applicable

H. STAFF REMARKS: The parcel is landward of the established
    bulkhead line. The predecessor in title, Bart Peaden, on
    October 6, 1970, stated that during September 1964 Hurricane
    Dora washed out an old retaining wall and eroded several feet
    under the bluff-line, almost caving in a line of very old
    trees. He applied to the Small Business Administration for

12-14-71

472

an emergency loan. After a survey, the loan was approved and with the approval of adjoining property owner, Mr. Peaden contracted for construction of the seawall in line with the seawalls on each side of his property. 0.11 acre of sovereignty land was inadvertently filled.

A July 7, 1971, field investigation report indicated that the entire shore line in the area has been bulkheaded. It is the opinion of the staff investigator that the sale would be in the public interest.

The applicant gives the following reasons why the sale is in the public interest:

> "First, if I have to tear down by bulkhead it would create a bad health hazard because my bulkhead would not be even with the other ones. Scum would build up in the corners and create a serious health problem to children playing around the area. Second, if I tear down the bulkhead the property next to me on both sides would erode and cause construction damage to their property. Last, the shore line would lose it beauty because of the unevenness."

Staff legal counsel is of the opinion that nothing of the public would be sacrificed since there is no public access, and the environment would not be damaged. The public interest would be furthered because title clearing would be facilitated.

Staff requests authority to advertise for objections only.

ACTION OF THE TRUSTEES:

Mr. Kuperberg explained that application could not be filed under Section 253.124(8) because the damage occurred prior to passage of that statute. He believed it was in the public interest in the case of this 0.11 acre parcel of land.

Mr. Dickinson referred to past instances where advertisements had been authorized although it appeared that ecological and conservation reports would be adverse and sale denied. The Director said the biological reports had been received and the staff knew of no reason for denial assuming the advertisement did not result in the filing of valid objections.

On motion by Mr. Stone, seconded by Mr. Christian and adopted without objection, the Trustees authorized advertisement for objections only.

-13-

MANATEE COUNTY - Application for Quitclaim
    File No. 2423-41-253.12(6)

Staff description: A parcel of filled sovereignty land in Sportsman's Harbor abutting Government Lot 1, Section 28, Township 34 South, Range 16 East, Manatee County

A. CITY AND COUNTY: Holmes Beach, Manatee County

B. APPLICANT: Edith G. Ward

C. APPLICANT'S
   REPRESENTATIVE: Clyde C. Goebel, P.A.
                  Post Office Box 155, Bradenton, Florida 33506

D. ACREAGE: 0.024
   RATE PER ACRE: $275 for the parcel

E. APPRAISAL: By staff appraiser on November 19, 1971

12-14-71

F. PURPOSE: Home site

G. BIOLOGICAL
    REPORT: Not applicable

H. STAFF REMARKS: The applicant applied for a quitclaim deed
    pursuant to Section 253.12(6) Florida Statutes, which provided
    that "Where any person, state agency, county, city or other
    political subdivision prior to June 11, 1957, extended or
    added to existing lands or islands bordering on or being in
    the navigable waters as defined in this section by filling
    in or causing to be filled in such lands, the Board shall
    upon application therefor convey said land so filled to the
    riparian owner or owners of the upland so extended or added
    to. The consideration for such conveyance shall be the
    appraised value of said lands as they existed prior to such
    filling."

    Two affidavits have been submitted stating that the lands in
    question had been filled prior to June 11, 1957, by a prede-
    cessor in title.

    The applicant has submitted payment of $100 for the processing
    fee, $275 for the parcel, and $250 for the appraisal fee.

    Staff requests authority to issue a quitclaim deed for considera-
    tion of $275 plus $250 for the appraisal services.

ACTION OF THE TRUSTEES:

Motion was made by Mr. Stone, seconded by Mr. Dickinson and
adopted without objection, that the quitclaim deed be issued
for $275 consideration plus $250 for the appraisal service.

-14-

COLLIER COUNTY - Artificial Reef, 253.03-270A

APPLICANT: Marco Island Development Corp.
            Post Office Box 280, Miami, Florida 33129

PROJECT: Permit 253.03-270 approved May 26, 1971, authorized
            the placing of 15,000 used tires annually on the reef
            site for a period of five years. Revised application
            is requested to allow the placing of 90,000 used tires
            annually.

MATERIAL: 90,000 used tires, plastics and several shapes and sizes
            of wooden material placed as follows:

            A. The northern third of the reef will be divided into
            9-acre squares. The central acre will be a research
            site in which the tires are grouped in various forma-
            tions and in various numbers ranging from 1,000 to
            15,000 per acre. Concrete anchors will be placed on
            the corner of each acre plot and all tires will be
            fastened to these anchors by nylon or polyethylene
            rope. This area will be open to fishing.

            B. The middle third will be similar except that we
            will attempt to discourage fishing to determine if
            this practice facilitates the building up of a fish
            population.

            C. The bottom third will be divided into 120 1-acre
            plots and every other plot will be used as a site for
            research on the efficiency of several types of wood and
            plastics in various shapes and colors as fish attractors.

            Each test structure will be anchored by a suitable con-
            crete block. None of these structures will be more than

12-14-71

ten feet from the bottom allowing a clear depth of at least ten feet from the surface at mean low water.

PAYMENT: $50 processing fee was tendered.

ECOLOGICAL
 REPORTS: Department of Natural Resources has no objection to the project.

Game and Fresh Water Fish Commission has no objection to the project.

Department of Pollution Control has no objection to the project.

Staff recommends issuance of Artificial Reef Permit No. 253.03-270A.

ACTION OF THE TRUSTEES:

On motion by Mr. Stone, seconded by Mr. Dickinson and adopted without objection, the Trustees approved the artificial reef permit.

-15-

PINELLAS COUNTY - Dredge Permit 253.123-913

APPLICANT: Maximo Harbor, Inc.
3800--46th Avenue South, St. Petersburg, Florida

PROJECT: **To dredge a channel 50 feet wide by 5 feet deep in** Boca Ciega Bay, Section 3, Township 32 South, Range 16 East, Pinellas County

MATERIAL: Approximately 10,000 cubic yards of material will be dredged by dragline and placed on uplands.

PAYMENT: Waived. Applicant owns the submerged lands to be dredged.

BIOLOGICAL
 REPORTS: Department of Natural Resources has no objection to the project.

Game and Fresh Water Fish Commission has no objection to the project.

Department of Pollution Control has no objection to the project.

Staff recommends issuance of dredge permit 253.123-913 to Maximo Harbor, Inc.

ACTION OF THE TRUSTEES:

On motion by Mr. Stone, seconded by Mr. Dickinson and adopted without objection, the Trustees approved issuance of the dredge permit.

-16-

MARINA LICENSE - Renewals

The required annual fees for the following marina licenses have been submitted:

Marina License	Licensee	Annual Fee
ML-7	Ronald G. Sinn, Lake Worth, Section 28, Township 42 South Range 43 East, Palm Beach County	$128.69
ML-13	Motel Miramar Apartments,	100.00

Santa Rosa Sound, Section 23
Township 2 South, Range 24 West,
Okaloosa County

ML-18   Alligator Point Marina, Inc.   2,099.59
             Alligator Harbor, Sections 2
             and 3, Township 7 South,
             Range 2 West, Franklin County

Staff recommends renewal of the marina licenses for one year at
the fees indicated.

ACTION OF THE TRUSTEES:

On motion by Mr. Stone, seconded by Mr. Dickinson and adopted
without objection, the Trustees approved renewal of the three
marina licenses as recommended.

-17-

BAY COUNTY - State Construction Permit

APPLICANT: Federal Aviation Administration

PROJECT: Concrete boat ramp

LOCATION: Little Goose Bayou, adjacent to Panama City-Bay
              County Airport in Section 19, Township 3 South,
              Range 14 West, Bay County.

ECOLOGICAL
  REPORTS: Department of Natural Resources has no objection.

              Game and Fresh Water Fish Commission has no objection.

              Department of Pollution Control has no objection, but
              certification is required.

Recommend approval of state construction permit for placement of
boat ramp and request waiver of fee for the facility for the use and
benefit of the United States.

ACTION OF THE TRUSTEES:

On motion by Mr. Stone, seconded by Mr. Dickinson and adopted
without objection, the Trustees approved issuance of state
construction permit without fee as recommended by the staff.

-18-

MANATEE COUNTY - Application for ex parte disclaimer,
                 File No. 2429-41-253.03

The application of Longbeach, Inc., for a disclaimer was
withdrawn from the agenda.

-19-

BROWARD COUNTY - Fill Permit, 253.124(8)-225

APPLICANT: Cam-Dur Development Corporation, c/o McLaughlin
              Engineering Co., 400 Northeast Third Avenue,
              Ft. Lauderdale, Florida

PROJECT: Requests approval of a permit issued by the City
              of Ft. Lauderdale for construction of a seawall
              along the west bank of the Middle River in Section
              36, Township 49 South, Range 42 East, Broward County.
              The proposed seawall will connect and be in line with
              existing seawalls on the north and south ends of
              applicant's property.

12-14-71

MATERIAL: The seawall will average about 10 feet riverward of the mean high water line. The shoreline has suffered erosion due to boat traffic in the area. Material needed to backfill will come from upland sources.

ECOLOGICAL
RESPONSES: The Department of Natural Resources biological report indicates the proposed seawall and filling should have only limited adverse effects on marine biological resources.

The Game and Fresh Water Fish Commission has no objection to issuance of the permit.

The Department of Pollution Control has no objection to the proposed project.

Staff recommends issuance of Fill Permit 253.124(8)-225.

ACTION OF THE TRUSTEES:

On motion by Mr. Stone, seconded by Mr. Dickinson and adopted without objection, the Trustees approved issuance of the fill permit.

LITIGATION - Peace River

Executive Director Kuperberg recommended that the Trustees, as holders of the fee title to public lands and waters of the State of Florida, join with the Department of Pollution Control in the lawsuit against Cities Service Oil Company with regard to the pollution and degradation of the Peace River lands and waters by the breaking of a dike and phosphate slime spillage.

On motion by Mr. Stone, seconded by Mr. Christian and adopted without objection, the rules were waived to allow consideration of the matter, and the Trustees voted to enter into the suit as title holder of the lands and waters in public trust.

Governor Askew, commenting that the Trustees were involved in terms of being the proper party for some elements of damage, called on Mr. James R. Brindell of the Environmental Law Section of the Department of Pollution Control, who briefly discussed the compensatory and punitive damage aspects and the grounds upon which the lawsuit was instituted, temporary and permanent injunctive relief sought under the pollution statute, protection of the public interest and welfare, conservation and protection of the state's natural resources and scenic beauty, liability aspects and abatement of a public nuisance.

Mr. Brindell explained that under Department of Pollution Control rules there are specific standards for dams that are used by the phosphate industry, and one basis for negligence claim was that these standards had not been met.

On motion duly adopted the meeting was adjourned.

GOVERNOR - CHAIRMAN

ATTEST:
EXECUTIVE DIRECTOR

12-14-71

Tallahassee, Florida
December 21, 1971

The State of Florida Board of Trustees of the Internal Improvement Trust Fund met on this date in the auditorium of the Department of Transportation, with the following members present:

Reubin O'D. Askew	Governor
Richard (Dick) Stone	Secretary of State
Robert L. Shevin	Attorney General
Fred O. Dickinson, Jr.	Comptroller
Floyd T. Christian	Commissioner of Education
Doyle Conner	Commissioner of Agriculture

Joel Kuperberg   Executive Director

-1-

LEE COUNTY - Bulkhead Line, Section 253.122, Florida Statutes

At the applicant's request, the staff asked for consideration of the bulkhead line to be withdrawn from the agenda. Mr. Kuperberg said the staff position for denial of the bulkhead line would not change.

Without objection, the Board withdrew the bulkhead line from the agenda.

-2-

BREVARD COUNTY - Application to Advertise
File No. 2428-05-253.12, 0.264 acre

STAFF DESCRIPTION: A parcel of filled sovereignty land in the Indian River abutting Government Lot 1, Section 9, Township 27 South, Range 37 East, Brevard County

A. CITY AND COUNTY: Eau Gallie, Brevard County

B. APPLICANT: Donald R. Bang, et ux
Post Office Box 1376
Eau Gallie, Florida 32935

C. APPLICANT'S
REPRESENTATIVE: G. W. Hedman
1103 Hibiscus Boulevard,
Melbourne, Florida 32901

D. ACREAGE: 0.264
RATE PER
ACRE: $2800 for the parcel

E. APPRAISAL: By staff appraiser on June 14, 1971

F. PURPOSE: Home site

G. BIOLOGICAL
REPORTS: Department of Natural Resources dated July 27, 1971, not adverse.

Game and Fresh Water Fish Commission dated August 2, 1971, adverse.

Department of Pollution Control dated July 16, 1971, not adverse.

12-21-71

H.   STAFF REMARKS: The parcel was bulkheaded and filled without
     authorization in 1963-5, by a predecessor in title. It is
     landward of the bulkhead line approved by the Trustees on
     August 8, 1967.

     Staff legal counsel is of the opinion that nothing of the
     public would be sacrificed since there is no public access,
     and the environment would not be damaged. The public interest
     would be furthered because title clearing would be facilitated.

Staff requests authority to advertise for objections only.

ACTION OF THE TRUSTEES:

Mr. Stone noted that the staff recommended advertising while
preserving the Board's right to negotiate with the applicant.

On that basis, motion was made by Mr. Stone, seconded by
Mr. Christian, and adopted without objection, that the land
be advertised for objections only.

Attorney General Shevin remarked that when the application is
considered again, the applicant should demonstrate that sale
would be in the public interest more than just the clearing of
title.

-3-

ALACHUA COUNTY - Murphy Act Land Sale

     Henry L. Gray, Jr., Attorney
     Gainesville, Florida,

on behalf of Ronnie Coleman Davis and Norita Vanzant Davis,
his wife, Leonard Onile Nadeau and Pauline Mary Nadeau, his
wife, and Richard S. Bloodworth and Beth Bloodworth, his wife,
applies to purchase the interest of the state in the NW 1/4 of
SW 1/4 of Section 17, Township 10 South, Range 22 East, 40 acres,
more or less, in Alachua County, under Section 197.355, Florida
Statutes ("Hardship Act", Chapter 28317, Acts of 1953).

This land was acquired by the state under the Murphy Act,
Chapter 18296, Laws of Florida, Acts of 1937. Tax sale
certificates were redeemed by W. F. Townsend in 1934, except
Certificate No. 1112, sale of July 3, 1899, for $2.32, that
apparently was overlooked. W. F. Townsend was the record owner
of this parcel of land on June 9, 1939, and according to Section
197.355, F. S., the Board may convey to this owner or his heirs
or assigns for such consideration as the Board shall deem
equitable and proper without advertisement and public sale.

All taxes and assessments have been regularly assessed and paid
to current date subsequent to the redemption in 1934.

The applicant, representing Ronnie Coleman Davis, et al, the
record owners of this land with their title based upon a chain
derived from W. F. Townsend, deceased, offers $400 for the
state's interest which conforms to policy to accept not less
than $10 per acre when the interest of the state is conveyed
under Section 197.355 F. S.

The application appears to qualify under the so-called "Hardship
Act."

Recommend conveying the interest of the state in this parcel
of land to Ronnie Coleman Davis, et al, for the consideration
of $400.

ACTION OF THE TRUSTEES:

On motion by Mr. Conner, seconded by Mr. Stone and adopted
without objection, the Trustees approved conveyance of the
interest of the state to Ronnie Coleman Davis for $400 under
provisions of Section 197.355, Florida Statutes.

-4-

ALACHUA COUNTY - Murphy Act Land Sale

> A. Curtis Powers, Clerk
> Alachua County Circuit Court
> Gainesville, Florida,

on behalf of Nathaniel Brockington, applies to purchase the
interest of the state in the NE 1/4 of NE 1/4 in Section 5,
Township 8 South, Range 19 East, 25.5 acres in Alachua County,
under Section 197.355, Florida Statutes ("Hardship Act", Chapter
28317, Acts of 1953).

This parcel of land was acquired by the state under the Murphy
Act, Chapter 18296, Laws of Florida, Acts of 1937, by Tax Sale
Certificate No. 524 of the year 1929 in the amount of $18.05.
Mr. H. A. H. Brockington, father of Nathaniel Brockington, present
record owner, has maintained his home on this property for over
fifty years and holds a life estate in the property. All taxes
have been paid for more than 20 years after June 9, 1939, the date
title vested in the state under the Murphy Act.

The applicant has offered $100 for the 25.5 acres. Policy has
been to accept not less than $10 per acre when the interest of
the state is conveyed under Section 197.355, Florida Statutes.

This application appears to qualify under the so-called "Hardship
Act."

Recommend conveying the interest of the state in this parcel
of land to Nathaniel Brockington for the consideration of $255.

ACTION OF THE TRUSTEES:

On motion by Mr. Conner, seconded by Mr. Stone and adopted
without objection, the Trustees approved conveyance of the
interest of the state to Nathaniel Brockington for $255
under provisions of Section 197.355 Florida Statutes.

-5-

DADE COUNTY - Modification of Power Line Easement

> Florida Power and Light Company
> Miami, Florida

requests modification of Easement Agreement No. 25027 dated
November 21, 1969, between the Trustees and Florida Power and
Light Company by the addition of 5.75 acres in Sections 22 and
23, Township 53 South, Range 39 East, Dade County, adjacent to
the existing power line easement. The additional right of way
is needed to accommodate suitable structures to tie in these
facilities with extra-high voltage lines of the cross-state
transmission line.

The ownership of the Trustees in Sections 22 and 23 is under
lease to Seminole Rock Products, Inc., for lime rock excavation
subject to the power line easement granted in 1969. Seminole
Rock Products, Inc., has reviewed and consented to the proposed
addition requested by Florida Power and Light Company. $6,550
has been offered for the additional 5.75 acres based on appraisal
furnished by the company and approved by staff appraiser.

12-21-71

Recommend issuance of the modification easement as requested for the consideration of $6,550.

ACTION OF THE TRUSTEES:

On motion by Mr. Stone, seconded by Mr. Christian and adopted without objection, the Trustees approved modification of the easement for $6,550 consideration.

-6-

DUVAL COUNTY - Road Right of Way Easement

The Department of Transportation

requests an easement for public highway purposes across state land adjacent to the new St. Johns Bluff Road in Section 5, Township 3 South, Range 28 East, containing 0.18 acre in Duval County. This additional right of way is required to install a right turn lane outside of the normal roadway for the benefit of the University of North Florida.

The Board of Regents has reviewed and approved issuance of the easement.

Recommend granting the right of way easement.

ACTION OF THE TRUSTEES:

On motion by Mr. Dickinson, seconded by Mr. Christian and adopted without objection, the Trustees granted the right of way easement to the Department of Transportation.

-7-

BAY COUNTY - Dredge Permit 253.123-851

APPLICANT: International Paper Company
             Post Office Box 2487, Panama City, Florida

PROJECT: Maintenance dredging adjacent to existing dock
             in Sections 14 and 15, Township 4 South, Range
             14 West, St. Andrews Bay, to excavate 9,200 cubic
             yards of material to restore docking area to
             original depth of 32 feet. The spoil material to
             be removed will be placed on diked upland owned
             by applicant. The sketches have been revised to
             meet environmental stipulations.

PAYMENT: Applicant tendered his check for $9,200 as payment
             at the standard yardage rate for the material to
             be removed.

ECOLOGICAL
  REPORTS: Department of Natural Resources has no objection
             provided weir is constructed so that overflow
             returns south into St. Andrews Bay.

             Game and Fresh Water Fish Commission has no objection
             provided the upland spoil area is diked to prevent
             siltation from running into the estuary.

             Department of Pollution Control has no objection
             to the project.

Staff recommends issuance of permit 253.123-851.

ACTION OF THE TRUSTEES:

Motion was made by Mr. Stone, seconded by Mr. Dickinson and adopted without objection, that the permit for maintenance dredging be approved.

12-21-71

-8-

DUVAL COUNTY - Dredge Permit 253.123-853 and Fill Permit
        253.124(8)-197

APPLICANT: Jacksonville Shipyards, Inc.
              Post Office Box 2347, Jacksonville, Florida

PROJECT: To remove a deteriorated seawall in St. Johns River
              in Sections 13 and 38, Township 2 South, Range 26
              East, and to replace with sheet steel piling.

MATERIAL: 2,800 cubic yards of material will be removed
              landward of the existing seawall. This material
              will be stockpiled for later use as backfill
              behind the new seawall.

PAYMENT: $50 check tendered for processing fee. Fee for
              material waived under Florida Statutes 253.124(8).

ECOLOGICAL
  REPORTS: Department of Natural Resources has no objection
              to the project.

              The Game and Fresh Water Fish Commission has no
              objection to the project.

              The Department of Pollution Control has no objection
              to the project.

Staff recommends issuance of permits 253.123-853 and 253.124(8)-
197 to Jacksonville Shipyards, Inc.

ACTION OF THE TRUSTEES:

Motion was made by Mr. Dickinson, seconded by Mr. Stone and
adopted without objection, that the dredge and fill permits be
approved as recommended.

-9-

MONROE COUNTY - Dredge Permit 253.03-213

APPLICANT: Rosemary Hoyle
              Florida Bay at Plantation Key

PROJECT: To excavate a boat basin and construct a boulder
              breakwater in front of Lot 24, Section 18, Township
              63 South, Range 38 East, Monroe County. Mrs. Hoyle
              owns the submerged land. TIITF Deed Nos. 24157 and
              24379.

MATERIAL: Approximately 2,000 cubic yards of spoil will be
              removed and used for construction of the breakwater.

PAYMENT: Waived because material comes from private ownership.
              $50 check tendered for processing fee.

ECOLOGICAL
  REPORTS: Department of Natural Resources has no objection.

              Game and Fresh Water Fish Commission has no objection.

              Department of Pollution Control has no objection.

Staff recommends issuance of Dredge Permit 253.03-213 to Mrs.
Rosemary Hoyle.

12-21-71

ACTION OF THE TRUSTEES:

Governor Askew asked what progress was being made by Duval
County on bulkhead lines. Mr. Kuperberg said the staff would
submit a report on an overall review being made of all counties
where bulkhead lines had not been established as recommended.

On motion by Mr. Dickinson, seconded by Mr. Stone and Mr.
Christian, the Trustees approved issuance of the dredge permit.

-10-

MONROE COUNTY - Permit 253.03-260

APPLICANT: Donald Stone
              c/o James T. Glass, P. E., Post Office Box 349,
              Islamorada, Florida

PROJECT: To extend an existing jetty 35 feet into Florida Bay
              to protect applicant's upland property on Upper
              Matecumbe Key in Section 28, Township 63 South,
              Range 27 East, Monroe County and to provide a
              protected area for docking of boats and swimming
              activities.

MATERIAL: To be constructed of boulders with a concrete cap.

PAYMENT: $50 check tendered for processing fee.

ECOLOGICAL
  REPORTS: Department of Natural Resources has no objection.

              Game and Fresh Water Fish Commission has no objection.

              Department of Pollution Control has no objection.

Staff recommends issuance of Permit 253.03-260 to Donald Stone.

ACTION OF THE TRUSTEES:

On motion by Mr. Christian, seconded by Mr. Stone and adopted
without objection, the permit was approved as recommended.

-11-

POLK COUNTY - Permit 253.03(7)-312

APPLICANT: Southwest Florida Water Management District
              Post Office Box 457, Brooksville, Florida 33512

PROJECT: To remove major fallen trees from the Peace River
              from the Route 60 Bridge East of Bartow to the
              Route 98 Bridge in Fort Meade.

PAYMENT: Fees waived, since the project is in the public
              interest.

ECOLOGICAL
  REPORTS: Department of Natural Resources has no objection to
              the project.

              Game and Fresh Water Fish Commisssion has no
              objection to the project.

              Department of Pollution Control has no objection to
              the project.

Staff recommends issuance of Permit 253.03(7)-312 to the Southwest
Florida Water Management District.

ACTION OF THE TRUSTEES:

It was noted that there was another similar application on the agenda, No. 18.

On motion by Mr. Stone, seconded by Mr. Christian and adopted without objection, the Trustees authorized issuance of a permit to Southwest Florida Water Management District for removal of the fallen trees from the Peace River as recommended.

-12-

VOLUSIA COUNTY - Permit 253.123(2)(b)-842

APPLICANT: County Council of Volusia County
c/o Public Works Department
Post Office Box 125, Deland, Florida

PROJECT: Extending Northeasterly and Southeasterly a 48"
R.C.P. from an existing 48" R.C.P. for the purpose
of relieving stagnant impounded water in Section 15,
Township 14 South, Range 32 East, Ormond Beach,
Volusia County.

MATERIAL: No dredging or filling will be required.

PAYMENT: Request fees be waived because of public interest.

ECOLOGICAL
  REPORTS: Department of Natural Resources has no objection.

  Game and Fresh Water Fish Commission has no objection.

  Department of Pollution Control has no objection.

Recommend issuance of Utility Permit 253.123(2)(b)-842 and waiver of fees, since the project is in the public interest.

ACTION OF THE TRUSTEES:

On motion by Mr. Stone, seconded by Mr. Conner and adopted without objection, the Trustees authorized issuance of permit without fee for installation of the utility culvert.

-13-

LEVY COUNTY - Submerged Land Donation

    Mr. P. C. Crapps, Jr.
    Live Oak, Florida

offers to donate to the Trustees a 3.65 acre, more or less, parcel of submerged land adjacent to State Road No. 24 in the Town of Cedar Key in Section 29, Township 15 South, Range 13 East, Levy County.

The parcel is a shallow area consisting of oyster bars on a mud-sand bottom partially exposed at low tide with salt water grasses near the shoreline. Mr. Crapps purchased this parcel on November 23, 1960, from J. F. Hembree for $10,000.

Recommend acceptance of the donation and expression of appreciation.

ACTION OF THE TRUSTEES:

The Director said a problem was resolved by the owner of the land agreeing to donate to the state his title to this sub-merged land. Director Randolph Hodges of the Department of Natural Resources had been helpful in the matter.

12-21-71

On motion by Mr. Stone, seconded by Mr. Dickinson and adopted, the Trustees accepted the land donation with an expression of gratitude to Mr. Crapps, and also thanked Senator Hodges for his assistance.

-14-

MARTIN COUNTY - Grazing Lease Award

On November 23 bids were opened for a three-year grazing lease covering all of Section 16, Township 39 South, Range 41 East, Martin County, west of Sunshine State Parkway containing 147.58 acres. One bid was received from Wayne R. Page in the amount of $4.40 per acre per year rental.

Award of lease was deferred until a request from Martin County to use sixty acres of the parcel for a sanitary land fill could be reviewed and considered. Martin County has subsequently withdrawn its request due to a problem of access to the site.

Recommend award of the three-year grazing lease to the high bidder, Wayne R. Page.

ACTION OF THE TRUSTEES:

On motion by Mr. Conner, seconded by Mr. Christian and adopted without objection, the Trustees awarded the grazing lease to Mr. Page at $4.40 per acre per year rental.

-15-

MONROE COUNTY - Dredge Permit 253.03-248

APPLICANT: J. H. T. Inc.
c/o E. V. Timmons
6825 Northwest 17th Avenue, Miami, Florida

PROJECT: To excavate a navigational channel 25 feet wide x 700 feet long x 5 feet deep from the mean high water line of applicant's property to an existing channel in Section 21, Township 60 South, Range 40 East, Monroe County.

MATERIAL: 2,600 cubic yards of material will be excavated from sovereignty land and placed on privately owned uplands.

PAYMENT: Check for $3,900 tendered as payment for 2,600 cubic yards of material to be removed.

ECOLOGICAL
  REPORTS: Department of Natural Resources - No objection to the project.

Game and Fresh Water Fish Commission - No objection to the project.

Department of Pollution Control - No objection to the project.

Staff recommends issuance of Dredge Permit 253.03-248.

ACTION OF THE TRUSTEES:

On motion by Mr. Christian, seconded by Mr. Stone and adopted without objection, the Trustees approved issuance of the dredge permit as recommended .

12-21-71

MARINA LICENSES - Renewals

The required annual fees for the following marina licenses
have been submitted:

Marina License	Licensee	Annual Fee
ML-16	Lakeside Hills Estates, Inc., Lake Gibson, Section 25, Township 27 South, Range 23 East, Polk County	$346.50
ML-17	City of Daytona Beach, Halifax River, Section 39, Township 15 South, Range 33 East, Volusia County	waived

Staff recommends renewal of the marina licenses for one year
at the fees indicated.

ACTION OF THE TRUSTEES:

On motion by Mr. Stone, seconded by Mr. Christian and adopted
without objection, the Trustees authorized renewal of the two
marina licenses for one year as recommended.

-17-

DUVAL COUNTY - Dredge Permit 253.123-821

APPLICANT: Bellinger Shipyards, Inc.
13911 Atlantic Boulevard, Jacksonville, Florida

PROJECT: To perform maintenance dredging in ship basin
constructed on applicant's upland landward of
Pablo Creek in Section 24, Township 2 South, Range
28 East, Duval County

MATERIAL: To be removed, will be deposited on adequately diked
uplands previously used as a spoil disposal area.

PAYMENT: None. All material to be removed comes from
applicant's land.

ECOLOGICAL
RESPONSES: Department of Natural Resources - no objection
provided old spoil area is used.

Game and Fresh Water Fish Commission - no objection
provided old spoil area is used.

Department of Pollution Control - no objection
provided that:

1. The westernmost area be used as a spoil area.
2. The existing dikes be removed in the eastern
spoil area.
3. Culverts emptying into marsh areas are removed.
4. Proper overflow structures be constructed to
contain runoff from the spoil area during
disposition of the dredged material.

Recommend issuance of Permit No. 253.123-821 subject to the
recommendations of the Department of Pollution Control.

12-21-71

ACTION OF THE TRUSTEES:

Mr. Kuperberg said the applicant revised plans to comply
with the above provisions.

On motion by Mr. Dickinson, seconded by Mr. Stone and adopted
without objection, the Board authorized issuance of the permit
subject to the recommendations of the Department of Pollution
Control.

-18-

PASCO COUNTY - Permit 253.03(7)-313

APPLICANT: Southwest Florida Water Management District
             Post Office Box 457, Brooksville, Florida 33512

PROJECT: To remove major fallen trees from the Anclote River,
             from the Anclote Acres Bridge to the mouth of the
             Anclote River.

PAYMENT: Fees waived, since this project is in the public
             interest.

ECOLOGICAL
RESPONSES: Department of Natural Resources - no objection to
             the project.

             Game and Fresh Water Fish Commission - no objection
             to the project.

             Department of Pollution Control - no objection to
             the project.

Staff recommends issuance of Permit 253.03(7)-313 to the Southwest Florida Water Management District.

ACTION OF THE TRUSTEES:

On motion by Mr. Christian, seconded by Mr. Stone and adopted
without objection, the Trustees authorized issuance of permit
to Southwest Florida Water Management District for removal of
the fallen trees from the Anclote River as recommended by the
staff.

BROWARD COUNTY - Seawall Application.

The rules were waived on motion by Mr. Stone, seconded by Mr.
Shevin, and adopted, to hear a request by William J. Roberts
on behalf of Resources Development and Mortgage Company for
permission to construct a seawall and backfill on the
Hillsboro Canal in Deerfield Beach. Because of an adverse
biological report, Mr. Kuperberg said the staff would oppose
the permit and try to negotiate with the owner to move the
seawall inland that in some places was as much as 50 feet offshore.

Mr. Roberts explained that it was necessary to fill in portions
of the property about 40 feet back into the upland lost by
erosion that was continuing because of heavy boat traffic in
this portion of the Hillsboro Canal which he described as
artificially created submerged land. He did not think the
riprap seawall recommended in the biological report was
practical to connect two sheet piling seawalls in this
developed area. A permit obtained by the former owner in
1963 from the Corps of Engineers (no state seawall permit then
required) expired in 1966 with no construction having taken
place, and the property was now under purchase option with
lender's funds withheld until the seawall problem was resolved.

Mr. Kuperberg said the staff did not have comments from the
Department of Pollution Control or Game and Fish Commission or

12-21-71

enough information to determine whether the area was artificially created land or part of the old Hillsboro River
shoreline and therefore state-owned submerged land. Another
applicant had paid a large sum for some parcels of land on the
Hillsboro River determined to be state-owned.

On motion by Mr. Christian, seconded by Mr. Dickinson and
adopted without objection, the Trustees declined to approve
issuance of an emergency permit and referred the request to
the staff for proper procedures and recommendations.

On motion duly adopted, the meeting was adjourned.

GOVERNOR — CHAIRMAN

ATTEST:

EXECUTIVE DIRECTOR

*

Tallahassee, Florida
January 4, 1972

The State of Florida Board of Trustees of the Internal Improvement Trust Fund met on this date with the following members
present:

Reubin O'D. Askew	Governor
Richard (Dick) Stone	Secretary of State
Robert L. Shevin	Attorney General
Fred O. Dickinson, Jr.	Comptroller
Thomas D. O'Malley	Treasurer
Doyle Conner	Commissioner of Agriculture

Joel Kuperberg	Executive Director

-1-

The minutes of December 14, 1971, were approved as submitted.

-2-

OKALOOSA COUNTY - Oil Lease Public Hearing

On December 16 a public hearing was held in Crestview as required
by Section 253.52, Florida Statutes, to give all interested
persons an opportunity to be heard with respect to the issuance
of a proposed oil and gas drilling lease involving several
parcels lying within three miles of the corporate limits of
the Town of Crestview.

Notice of the public hearing was published one time as required,
in the Okaloosa News-Journal. No one appeared at the hearing
in opposition to issuance of the lease.

The proposed lease covers the reserved one-half interest of
the state (Murphy Act) in nine scattered parcels of privately-
owned land containing a total of 363 surface acres in Townships
3 and 4 North, Range 24 West, Okaloosa County.

J. Milton Newton, Inc., Jackson, Mississippi, made the high bid
of $7,713.75 for this lease on November 9, 1971. All proceeds
from this lease will go to General Revenue Unallocated.

Recommend that the lease be issued to the high bidder,
J. Milton Newton, Inc.

ACTION OF THE TRUSTEES:

On motion by Mr. Stone, seconded by Mr. O'Malley and adopted
without objection, the Board authorized issuance of oil and
gas drilling lease to the high bidder.

-3-

MONROE COUNTY - Application for Quitclaim

File No. 2427-44-253.12(6), 0.124 acre

Staff Description: A parcel of filled sovereignty land in
the Atlantic Ocean abutting Government Lot 6, Section 5,
Township 63 South, Range 38 East, Plantation Key.

A. City and County: Monroe County

B. Applicant: Mrs. S. A. Howard

C. Applicant's
   Representative: W. L. Todd
                       Bailey, Glass & Post
                       Post Office Box 349, Islamorada, Florida

D. Acreage: 0.124 acre
   Rate Per acre: Not applicable

E. Appraisal: By staff appraiser on December 8, 1971,
                       Minimum nominal value of $100 as of June 10,
                       1957, for the parcel.

F. Purpose: Solid-fill dock and abutment for owners' use.

G. Biological
   Report: Not applicable

H. Staff Remarks: The applicant applied for a quitclaim deed
   pursuant to Section 253.12(6) Florida Statutes, which provided
   that "Where any person, state agency, county, city or other
   political subdivision prior to June 11, 1957, extended or
   added to existing lands or islands bordering on or being in
   the navigable waters as defined in this section by filling
   in or causing to be filled in such lands, the board shall
   upon application therefor convey said land so filled to the
   riparian owner or owners of the upland so extended or added
   to. The consideration for such conveyance shall be the
   appraised value of said lands as they existed prior to such
   filling."

   Two affidavits have been submitted stating that the project
   was constructed prior to May, 1957.

   The applicant has submitted payment of $100 for the processing
   fee.

Request authority to issue a quitclaim deed for consideration of
$100 plus $100 for appraisal services.

ACTION OF THE TRUSTEES:

On motion by Mr. O'Malley, seconded by Mr. Stone and adopted
without objection, the Board authorized issuance of the quitclaim
for $100 consideration plus $100 for the appraisal.

-4-

LEE COUNTY - Dredge Permit 253.123-949

APPLICANT: Benson Associates
Post Office Box 1043, Bradenton, Florida 33505

PROJECT: To dredge several upland canals varying in width
from 60 feet to 120 feet and having a maximum depth
of 10 feet. These canals will connect with existing
canals in Sections 34 and 35, Township 45 South,
Range 22 East, Lee County.

There will be no dead-end canals since culverts will
be installed under the road to provide water circulation.

MATERIAL: To be deposited on applicant's upland.

PAYMENT: None, since all work is to be done on applicant's
upland.

ECOLOGICAL
RESPONSES: Department of Natural Resources - no objection to
project provided that small canals parallel the
access parkway across the preserve and a culvert
is installed for a small tidal creek.

Game and Fresh Water Fish Commission - no objection to
project provided no alterations are permitted seaward of the upper limit of red mangroves.

Department of Pollution Control - no objection to
project.

Staff recommends issuance of Permit 253.123-949 provided that the
stipulations from the Department of Natural Resources and the
Game and Fresh Water Fish Commission are met.

ACTION OF THE TRUSTEES:

Mr. Kuperberg said the request to do dredging work represented
a new concept in tide operated valves, an effort to improve
flushing in canal systems, and the staff recommended issuance
of the permit.

On motion by Mr. Stone, seconded by Mr. Conner and adopted without
objection, the application was approved as recommended.

-5-

HILLSBOROUGH COUNTY - Bulkhead Line, Section 253.122, F. S.

APPLICANT: Department of Transportation
Tallahassee, Florida

PROJECT: Bulkhead line 201.41 feet long adjacent to the
Westerly shoreline of Sweetwater Creek in Sections
1 and 12, Township 29 South, Range 17 East, approved
and established by the Tampa Port Authority on
September 14, 1971, by Resolution No. 71-18.

ECOLOGICAL
RESPONSES: Department of Natural Resources - No objection.

Game and Fresh Water Fish Commission - No objection.

Department of Pollution Control - No objection.

Staff recommends approval of bulkhead line.

ACTION OF THE TRUSTEES:

Motion was made by Mr. Stone, seconded by Mr. O'Malley and adopted without objection, that the bulkhead line be approved.

-6-

HILLSBOROUGH COUNTY - Dredge Permit 253.123-964
                      Fill Permit 253.124-241

APPLICANT: Department of Transportation
             Tallahassee, Florida

PROJECT: Relocate Sweetwater Creek at State Road No. S-576
           in Sections 1 and 12, Township 29 South, Range 17
           East. Dredged material removed from easterly bank
           will be used to fill 0.14 acre along the westerly
           bank landward of the bulkhead line.

MATERIAL: Dredge 4,800 cubic yards.

PAYMENT: None, as the submerged land is owned by Tampa Port
           Authority.

ECOLOGICAL
RESPONSES: Department of Natural Resources - Only limited adverse
             effects.

  Game and Fresh Water Fish Commission - Only short
  term effects provided dredging is done in such a
  manner as to prevent turbidity problems.

  Department of Pollution Control - No objection.

Staff recommends issuance of dredge and fill permits, subject
to stipulations by the Department of Natural Resources and the
Game and Fresh Water Fish Commission.

ACTION OF THE TRUSTEES:

On motion by Mr. Stone, seconded by Mr. O'Malley and adopted
without objection, the Trustees approved issuance of the dredge
and fill permits as recommended by the staff.

-7-

MONROE COUNTY - Dredge Permit 253.03-181

APPLICANT: Mr. Craig Estes, Route 1, Box 108,
             La Orilla Resort, Islamorada, Florida

PROJECT: To excavate a channel 800' long x 30' wide x 5'
           deep from Mr. Estes' property to an existing channel
           located in Section 5, Township 64 South, Range 37
           East, Monroe County.

MATERIAL: Approximately 2,600 cubic yards of material will
            be removed from sovereignty land and placed on
            privately owned upland.

PAYMENT: A check for $3,900 has been tendered for payment of
           2,600 cubic yards of material.

ECOLOGICAL
RESPONSES: Department of Natural Resources - no objection to
             the project.

  Game and Fresh Water Fish Commission - no objection
  to the project.

  Department of Pollution Control - no objection to the
  project.

1-4-72

Staff recommends issuance of Dredge Permit 253.03-181 to Mr. Craig Estes, Islamorada, Florida.

ACTION OF THE TRUSTEES:

On motion by Mr. O'Malley, seconded by Mr. Stone and adopted without objection, the Trustees approved issuance of the dredge permit.

-8-

MONROE COUNTY - Dredge Permit 253.03-241

APPLICANT: Dr. Frank Woods
              Lot 35, Block 10, Plantation Beach
              c/o James T. Glass, P. O. Box 349, Islamorada, Florida

PROJECT: To excavate a basin and to construct a breakwater on
              a parcel of land he owns (TIITF Deed No. 22,606)
              in Section 18, Township 63 South, Range 38 East,
              Plantation Key, Monroe County. The breakwater would
              protect the basin and upland property from adverse
              wave action.

MATERIAL: Approximately 300 cubic yards of material will be
              removed from the basin and placed in a breakwater.

PAYMENT: $50.00 check has been tendered for processing fee.
              Payment for material will be waived, because the
              required material is coming from private ownership.

ECOLOGICAL
RESPONSES: Department of Natural Resources - no objection to
              the project.

              Game and Fresh Water Fish Commission - no objection
              to the project.

              Department of Pollution Control - no objection to
              the project.

Staff recommends issuance of Dredge Permit 253.03-241 to Dr. Frank Woods.

ACTION OF THE TRUSTEES:

On motion by Mr. O'Malley, seconded by Mr. Stone and adopted without objection, the Trustees approved the request to excavate a boat basin and construct a breakwater on privately-owned submerged land.

-9-

PALM BEACH COUNTY - Dredge Permit 253.123-937

APPLICANT: South Lake Worth Inlet District
              P. O. Box 3465, Lantana, Florida 33460

PROJECT: To dredge the sand shoal east of the Intracoastal
              Waterway, south of South Lake Worth Inlet, in
              Section 15, Township 45 South, Range 43 East, Palm
              Beach County.

MATERIAL: Approximately 45,000 cubic yards of material will
              be removed and placed south of the inlet for beach
              nourishment.

PAYMENT: Fee waived because project is in the public interest.

ECOLOGICAL
RESPONSES: Department of Natural Resources - no objections to
              project. Suggest that only those areas in parcels A

and D, where sand from beach continually is deposited, should be dredged for beach nourishment purposes and that spoil be concentrated along the intertidal zone.

Game and Fresh Water Fish Commission - No objection to project. Request they be notified when project begins.

Department of Pollution Control - No objections to project.

Staff recommends issuance of Dredge Permit 253.123-937 provided the stipulations of the Department of Natural Resources and the Game and Fresh Water Fish Commission are met, and further recommends that the fees be waived as the project is deemed to be in the public interest.

ACTION OF THE TRUSTEES:

On motion by Mr. Stone, seconded by Mr. O'Malley and adopted without objection, the Trustees approved the application for channel dredging and beach nourishment without charge, subject to the requirements recommended by the environmental agencies.

-10-

PINELLAS COUNTY - Fill Permit, FO-277- Denial

APPLICANT: G. J. Apple
            3 Palms Point, Unit 9, 79th Street South,
            St. Petersburg, Florida 33707

PROJECT: To dredge and fill approximately 1.5 acres of land
            that had eroded from the tip of a finger fill located
            at three Palms Point Unit 9, St. Petersburg Beach,
            in Section 31, Township 31 South, Range 16 East,
            Pinellas County.

MATERIAL: 900 cubic yards of material is to be used.

ECOLOGICAL
RESPONSES: Department of Natural Resources - Adverse comments

            Game and Fresh Water Fish Commission - None requested

            Department of Pollution Control - None requested

Staff recommends confirmation of action taken by the Pinellas County Water and Navigation Control Authority on November 16, 1971, denying Permit FO-277.

ACTION OF THE TRUSTEES:

On motion by Mr. Stone, seconded by Mr. O'Malley and adopted without objection, the Trustees accepted the staff recommendation, thus confirming Pinellas County's denial of a fill permit.

-11-

VOLUSIA COUNTY - Marina License ML-87
                Dredge Permit 253.123-878

APPLICANT: Smyrna Yacht Club
            Post Office Box 83, New Smyrna Beach, Florida

PROJECT: Enlargement of an existing docking facility
            and dredge to improve navigation in the Indian River
            abutting Section 20, Township 17 South, Range 34
            East, Volusia County. The marina license will
            include 17,563 square feet of submerged land.

MATERIAL: 6,850 cubic yards of material is to be placed in an upland spoil area.

PAYMENT: $351.26 annual fee for marina license and $3,425 payment for dredged material at standard yardage rate of 50¢ per cubic yard.

ECOLOGICAL
RESPONSES: Department of Natural Resources - limited adverse effects provided silt is contained during dredging operations.

Game and Fresh Water Fish Commission - temporary damage if siltation is minimized and turbidity restricted to dredge area.

Department of Pollution Control - no objection.

Staff recommends issuance of dredge permit and marina license subject to stipulations recommended by the Department of Natural Resources and Game and Fresh Water Fish Commission.

ACTION OF THE TRUSTEES:

On motion by Mr. Stone, seconded by Mr. O'Malley and adopted without objection, the Trustees approved issuance of the dredge permit and marina license subject to the recommendations of the environmental agencies.

––––––––––

-12-

Consideration of the request from Radcliff Materials, Inc., to renew a shell lease on sovereignty lands in several counties on the Gulf of Mexico was deferred for two weeks at the request of Comptroller Dickinson.

––––––––––

-13-

Consideration of a request from Fort Myers Shell & Dredging Co., Inc., to renew a shell lease on sovereignty land in Lee County was deferred for two weeks at the request of Comptroller Dickinson.

On motion duly adopted, the meeting was adjourned.

GOVERNOR   CHAIRMAN

ATTEST:
EXECUTIVE DIRECTOR

* *   * *

1-4-72

Tallahassee, Florida
January 11, 1972

The Trustees of the Internal Improvement Trust Fund met on this
date in the auditorium of the Department of Transportation, with
the following members present:

-1-

Approval of the minutes of December 21, 1971, was deferred for
one week.

-2-

ALACHUA COUNTY - Murphy Act Land Sale

Donald MacLean and Mildred H. MacLean, his wife,
Represented by A. Curtis Powers, Clerk,
Alachua County Circuit Court, Gainesville, Florida,

apply to purchase the interest of the State in a 69.35-acre
parcel of land located in the S 1/2 of Section 18, Township 9
South, Range 21 East, in Alachua County, under Section 197.355,
Florida Statutes ("Hardship Act", Chapter 28317, Acts of 1953).

This land was acquired by the State under the Murphy Act, Chapter
18296, Laws of Florida, Acts of 1937. Tax Sale Certificate
No. 346 for the year of 1902 was redeemed in 1903 by Nancy Wood,
and her heirs redeemed Tax Sale Certificate No. 1324 for the year
of 1935. Tax Sale Certificate No. 796 for the year 1900 in the
amount of $3.50 was apparently overlooked. The applicants, who
are the present record owners, claim title through the heirs
of Nancy Wood, deceased, the record owner as of June 9, 1939.
According to Section 197.355, Florida Statutes, the Board may
convey the interest of the State to the owner in 1939 or his
heirs or assigns for such consideration as the Board shall deem
equitable and proper without advertisement and public sale.

An amount has been deposited with the Clerk of the Circuit Court
equal to the unpaid state and county taxes and assessments on
this property from 1899 to June 9, 1939, plus interest and
costs. All taxes which have accrued since June 9, 1939, have
been paid.

The applicant offers $693.50 for the State's interest, which
conforms to policy to accept not less than $10 per acre when
the interest of the State is conveyed under Section 197.355,
Florida Statutes.

This application appears to qualify under the so-called
"Hardship Act."

Recommend conveying the interest of the State of Florida in this
parcel of land to Donald and Mildred H. MacLean for the consideration of $693.50.

ACTION OF THE TRUSTEES:

On motion made by Mr. Stone, and adopted without objection,
the Board authorized conveyance of the state's interest in the
parcel of Murphy Act land to the applicants for $693.50.

DADE COUNTY - Telephone Cable Easement

Southern Bell Telephone and Telegraph Company
Miami, Florida

requests a ten-foot wide easement under and across the west ten
feet of the east fifty-five feet of the S 1/2 of the SE 1/4 of
Section 28, Township 53 South, Range 40 East, Dade County,
for installation of underground telephone lines and cables.

The area of the requested easement lies within an easement
granted to Dade County for sanitary sewer line purposes and
across a portion of the state land under lease to the Federal
Aviation Administration. Dade County and FAA have reviewed
and approved issuance of the telephone cable easement.

Recommend granting the easement.

ACTION OF THE TRUSTEES:

On motion by Mr. Conner, seconded by Mr. Dickinson and Mr.
Christian, adopted without objection, the Board granted the
easement to Southern Bell Telephone and Telegraph Company for
underground lines and cables.

-4-

HENDRY COUNTY - Advertise Oil and Gas Lease

Tribal Oil Company, Lafayette, Louisiana

requests the Board to offer for competitive sealed bids
a five-year oil and gas drilling lease covering the reserved
one-half interest of the Board of Education in the petroleum
and petroleum products in privately-owned Section 16, Township
44 South, Range 28 East, 640 acres more or less in Hendry County.
This section is approximately eight miles southwest of La Belle
and 16 miles north of the northern boundary of the Big Cypress
Watershed area. All proceeds from this lease will go to the
School Fund.

This request has been reviewed by the State Geologist who
concurs in the following recommendation.

Recommend advertising for sealed bids for lease with annual
rental of $1 per net mineral acre, 1/8 royalty, five-year
primary term, $50,000 surety bond and at least one test well
to 6,000 feet or to the Roberts zone of the Sunniland Formation,
whichever is deeper.

ACTION OF THE TRUSTEES:

On motion by Mr. Stone, seconded by Mr. Dickinson and Mr.
Christian, and adopted without objection, the Board authorized
the advertisement for bids as recommended.

-5-

SANTA ROSA COUNTY - Advertise Oil and Gas Lease

Humble Oil and Refining Company
New Orleans, Louisiana,

requests the Board to offer for competitive sealed bids a
five-year oil and gas drilling lease covering the reserved
one-half interest of the State in the petroleum and petroleum
products in privately-owned W 1/2 of NW 1/4 of NW 1/4 of Section
13, Township 4 North, Range 29 West, containing 20 surface

1-11-72

acres in Santa Rosa County approximately six miles southeast of the Town of Jay. All proceeds from this lease will go to General Revenue Unallocated (Murphy Act Lands).

The request has been reviewed by the State Geologist who concurs in the following recommendation.

Recommend advertising for sealed bids for lease with annual rental of $1 per net mineral acre, 1/6 royalty, five-year primary term, $50,000 surety bond and at least one test well to 6,000 feet or to a depth sufficient to test the Norphlet Sands, whichever is deeper.

ACTION OF THE TRUSTEES:

On motion by Mr. Stone, seconded by Mr. Dickinson and Mr. Christian, and adopted without objection, the Board authorized the advertisement for bids as recommended.

-6-

BROWARD COUNTY - Fill Permit 253.124(8)-221

APPLICANT: John Charles Petrie
1401 Northwest Seventh Avenue, Boca Raton, Florida

PROJECT: To reclaim a strip of land approximately 85 feet long with a maximum offshore distance of 10 feet by constructing a seawall and backfilling with trucked-in material. This strip of land was lost due to artificially induced erosion caused by boat traffic.

MATERIAL: To come from upland sources

PAYMENT: None

ECOLOGICAL
RESPONSES: Department of Natural Resources reported that the project should not have significant adverse effects on marine biological resources in the canal. To prevent creation of debris-collecting inside corners, the seawall could be constructed even with seawall on Lot 12 and connect to boulder rip-rap on Lot 14, thus creating a uniform shoreline.

Game and Fresh Water Fish Commission has no objection if applicant will agree to place the seawall at or behind the historic mean high water line.

Department of Pollution Control has no objection to proposed realignment of the seawall.

Recommend issuance of permit as amended to conform with recommendations of the environmental agencies.

ACTION OF THE TRUSTEES:

Motion was made by Mr. Dickinson, seconded by Mr. Stone and adopted without objection, that the permit be approved subject to amendment to conform with the recommendations of the environmental agencies.

-7-

DADE COUNTY - Permit 253.124(8)-226

APPLICANT: Metropolitan-Dade County, Public Works Department
1351 NW 12th Street, Miami, Florida

PROJECT: To repair recently eroded shorelines to prevent
erosion

LOCATION: Haulover Beach Park, Biscayne Bay, Dade County

MATERIAL: To be trucked in

PAYMENT: None

ECOLOGICAL
RESPONSES: Department of Natural Resources does not object
provided there is no dredging of submerged land or
filling beyond recently eroded shorelines.

Department of Pollution Control does not object.

Game and Fresh Water Fish Commission does not object
provided mangroves are not disturbed.

Recommend issuance of permit 253.124(8)-226 to Metropolitan-Dade
County Public Works Department subject to the stipulations in the
environmental reports.

ACTION OF THE TRUSTEES:

Motion was made by Mr. Dickinson, seconded by Mr. Stone and
adopted without objection, that the permit be approved subject
to the stipulations in the environmental reports.

-8-

MANATEE COUNTY - Dredge Permit 253.123-844

APPLICANT: Honorable Harry W. Cole, Mayor,
City of Anna Maria

PROJECT: Dredge approximately 5,000 cubic yards of material
for maintenance of existing channel in Tampa Bay,
Anna Maria Key, Section 28, Township 34 South,
Range 16 East, Manatee County.

MATERIAL: Material will be placed on city-owned upland for
beach nourishment

PAYMENT: Fees waived since project is in the public interest.

ECOLOGICAL
RESPONSES: Department of Natural Resources has no objection to
project.

Game and Fresh Water Fish Commission has no objection to the project.

Department of Pollution Control has no objection to
the project.

Staff recommends issuance of Dredge Permit 253.123-844 to the
City of Anna Maria and that the fee be waived since the project
is in the public interest.

ACTION OF THE TRUSTEES:

On motion by Mr. Dickinson, seconded by Mr. Stone and adopted
without objection, the Trustees authorized issuance of the
dredge permit to the City of Anna Maria without charge.

-9-

PINELLAS COUNTY - Marina License No. ML-67

APPLICANT: Victor A. Milloy
            7201 Bay Street, St. Petersburg, Florida 33738

PROJECT: Removal of existing dock and mooring piles and
            construction of fishing pier covering 1,950 square
            feet of sovereignty land in Boca Ciega Bay abutting
            Section 34, Township 31 South, Range 15 East,
            Pinellas County.

ECOLOGICAL
  REPORTS: Department of Natural Resources has no objection.

            Game and Fresh Water Fish Commission has no objec-
            tion.

            Department of Pollution Control has no objection.

Staff recommends approval of marina license for annual fee of
$100.

ACTION OF THE TRUSTEES:

On motion by Mr. Stone, seconded by Mr. Dickinson and adopted
without objection, the Trustees authorized issuance of the
marina license for $100 annual fee.

-10-

PINELLAS COUNTY - State Construction Permit

APPLICANT: Parks Department,
            Board of County Commission of Pinellas County

PROJECT: Reconstruct existing public fishing pier.

LOCATION: Tampa Bay adjacent to Fort DeSoto Park on Mullet
            Key in Section 18, Township 33 South, Range 16
            East, Pinellas County

ECOLOGICAL
RESPONSES: Department of Natural Resources has no objection.

            Game and Fresh Water Fish Commission has no objection.

            Department of Pollution Control has no objection.

Staff recommends approval of state construction permit for
reconstruction of existing pier and waiver of fee for the facility
for the use and benefit of the general public.

ACTION OF THE TRUSTEES:

On motion by Mr. Dickinson, seconded by Mr. Stone and adopted
without objection, the Trustees approved state construction
permit without fee as recommended.

-11-

DUVAL COUNTY - Fill Permit 253.124-191

APPLICANT: Mode, Inc.
            St. Johns River, Duval County

PROJECT: To fill approximately 6.0 acres located in Sections
            34 and 38, Township 2 South, Range 27 East on the
            St. Johns River in Duval County.

MATERIAL: All material will come from owner's upland.

1-11-72

PAYMENT: None

ECOLOGICAL
RESPONSES: Department of Natural Resources has no objection
             to the project provided that marsh grass is planted
             in an area provided for its growth.

             Game and Fresh Water Fish Commission has no objection
             as long as no fill is required on stream bottom.

             Department of Pollution Control objects to project
             as proposed and suggests that plan be revised to
             eliminate proposed fill.

Staff recommends denial of permit application as submitted.

ACTION OF THE TRUSTEES:

Mr. Kuperberg discussed supplemental reports from environmental
agencies including a hydrographic report indicating that while
there may be no adverse effects from the coastal engineering
point of view from this individual project, the long-range effects
of several such projects may well be adverse and therefore
consideration should be given to the total effects on a much
larger portion of the river. Supplemental reports from the
Game and Fresh Water Fish Commission were adverse. Dr. E. O.
Frye, Jr., Director of that agency, and Mr. Barney Barnes from
the Department of Pollution Control were present to answer any
questions the members might have.

Mr. Kuperberg said the staff recommended alternate techniques
that might be used to prevent filling the water column, such as
a floating marina or one on pilings.

Mr. Quinton Rumph, representing the applicant, reviewed the
background starting in 1966 with conveyance by the Trustees of
submerged land to predecessor in title by deeds containing oil
and mineral reservations but no other restrictions. He said the
state had conveyed only three parcels of submerged land in that
area, his client had agreed to several modifications recommended
by the staff including reducing the area from 13 to 6 acres, but
one agency objected to any fill being placed in the river. He
referred to recent findings of the court in the Gables-by-the-Sea
suit that denial of that owner's right to fill his submerged land
was not justified.

At Mr. Conner's questioning, Mr. Rumph stated that his client
would agree to deed back the 50 feet not included in the amended
marina plan.

Mr. O'Malley thought the land should never have been sold, but
since it had been, he was impressed with the concept and type
of this development. He was concerned that the particular project should not damage the ecology and noted that the evaluations from the environmental agencies were based on what might
happen as a longe-range effect of many such projects. He suggested
deferment for the applicant to secure his own evaluations and
work out something with the staff.

Mr. Shevin said he would want the record to show denial based
upon an adequate showing of damage to this specific area.

At Mr. O'Malley's request, further consideration was deferred
for one week.

1-11-72

500

-12-

MONROE COUNTY - Modified Dredge Permit 253.03-248

At the request of the applicant, J. H. T., Inc., consideration
of a modified dredge permit was deferred one week for further
revision of the project and reduction of the dredge area.

-13-

MONROE COUNTY - Aquaculture Lease
On October 19, 1971, the Board of Trustees authorized
advertisement for objections to the proposed aquaculture lease
of approximately 75 acres of submerged land in Sections 22
and 23, Township 66 South, Range 28 East, Monroe County.

Three letters objecting to the proposed lease have been received.

According to the provisions of Section 253.70, Florida Statutes,
the Board of Trustees or its designee shall, if written objections
are received, hear and consider the same at a public hearing
which shall be held in the county from which the application
was received.

Recommend that a designee of the Board be appointed to hold
a public hearing in Key West, Florida on February 4, 1972.

ACTION OF THE TRUSTEES:

On motion by Mr. Stone, seconded by Mr. Dickinson and Mr.
O'Malley and adopted without objection, the staff recommendation was approved.

-14-

DADE COUNTY - Permit 253.124(8)-249

APPLICANT: Florida East Coast Properties, Inc.
             1605 Biscayne Boulevard, Miami, Florida 33132

PROJECT: To construct a seawall and fill to approximate
             elevation +5.0 between the existing shoreline and
             Harbor line on the south bank of the Miami River
             in Section 38, Township 54 South, Range 41 East,
             and directly west of Brickell Avenue (U. S. No.1).
             The seawall will form part of the building face on
             the north elevation.

MATERIAL: All material will be trucked in from upland sources.

PAYMENT: Waived, since no sovereignty material or land is
             used.

ECOLOGICAL
RESPONSES: Department of Natural Resources suggests that the
             proposed seawall be built at either the Mean high
             water line along the existing seawall or at the
             mean high water line along the eroded shore.

             Department of Pollution Control has no objection to
             the project.

             Bureau of Beaches and Shores - should not be con-
             structed channelward of existing bulkhead.

Staff recommends issuance of Permit 253.124(8)-249 subject to
the relocation of the seawall as recommended by the Department
of Natural Resources.

ACTION OF THE TRUSTEES:

On motion by Mr. Dickinson, seconded by Mr. Stone and adopted
without objection, issuance of the permit was approved subject
to the relocation of the seawall as recommended.

-15-

MARTIN COUNTY - Fill Permit 253.124(8)248

APPLICATION: Board of Trustees of the Internal Improvement
Trust Fund
Tallahassee, Florida

PROJECT: Construct a seawall 200 feet in length along the
north side of the SR S707A causeway across the
Indian River in Section 15, Township 37 South,
Range 41 East. This seawall shall be a westerly
prolongation of the seawall constructed under the
authority of Board of Trustees Permit No. 253.124(8)-
170. Material to fill the eroded area lying between
the present mean high water line and the proposed
seawall shall come from upland sources.

MATERIAL: None

PAYMENT: None

ECOLOGICAL
RESPONSES: Department of Natural Resources - The eroded shoreline could be restored by fill.

Staff recommends issuance of Fill Permit 253.124(8)248 and assignment to Board of County Commissioners of Martin County who shall
bear the cost of and shall be responsible for the construction
authorized.

ACTION OF THE TRUSTEES:

On motion by Mr. O'Malley, seconded by Mr. Dickinson and adopted
without objection, the rules were waived for consideration of an
emergency permit application received after preparation of the
agenda, pertaining to erosion damage along the side of a picnic
area along the Jensen Beach Causeway in Martin County that needed
to be seawalled and protected. The land is owned by the Trustees.

Motion was made by Mr. O'Malley, seconded by Mr. Dickinson and
adopted without objection, that the application be approved.

There was discussion of the application for a dredging permit
for Harrell's Marine, Inc., File 253.123-787, approved by the
Trustees on July 20, 1971, and a subsequent request by the applicant that payment for the material be waived as it was worthless
silt. The check had not been deposited and was now stale-dated.
The work had not been done as the applicant had not secured a
permit from the U. S. Corps of Engineers.

Mr. Kuperberg obtained permission to distribute to the Board
a newspaper article on damage to the John Pennekamp Coral Reef
Park and other portions of the coral reef that, in the opinion
of many scientists, was dying because of pollution from dredging,
sewage and other man-made causes.

The Director had met with representatives of the federal government in discussions of the evidence that was factual of the
danger of loss of this valued coral reef asset, verifying the

1-11-72

newspaper article. He would have recommendations soon to submit to the Trustees.

On motion duly adopted, the meeting was adjourned.

GOVERNOR - CHAIRMAN

ATTEST:

EXECUTIVE DIRECTOR

* * * * *

Tallahassee, Florida
January 18, 1972

The State of Florida Board of Trustees of the Internal Improve-ment Trust Fund met on this date in the auditorium of the Burns Building with the following members present:

Reubin O'D. Askew	Governor
Richard (Dick) Stone	Secretary of State
Robert L. Shevin	Attorney General
Thomas D. O'Malley	Treasurer
Floyd T. Christian	Commissioner of Education
Doyle Conner	Commissioner of Agriculture

Joel Kuperberg   Executive Director

-1-

The minutes of the meetings on December 21, 1971, and January 4, 1972, were approved as submitted.

-2-

DADE COUNTY - Dredge Permit 253.123-982

APPLICANT: Metropolitan Dade County
Public Works Department
Water Control Division
1351 Northwest 12th Street, Miami, Florida 33125

PROJECT: Maintenance repairs to bulkhead, construction of a concrete dock, and the dredging of approximately 300 cubic yards of material to improve navigation at Crandon Park Marina in Section 21, Township 54 South, Range 42 East, Dade County. The property is owned by the Parks and Recreation Department of Dade County.

MATERIAL: Approximately 300 cubic yards to be removed and placed on county-owned upland south of the work site.

PAYMENT: Request fees be waived since this project is in the public interest.

ECOLOGICAL
RESPONSES: Department of Natural Resources - no objection to project.

Game and Fresh Water Fish Commission - no objection to the project.

1-18-72

Department of Pollution Control - no objection to the project.

Staff recommends issuance of Dredge Permit 253.123-982 to Metropolitan Dade County with waiver of fees, as project is in the public interest.

ACTION OF THE TRUSTEES:

On motion by Mr. Stone, seconded by Mr. O'Malley and adopted without objection, the Trustees approved this public works project without requiring payment of the fee.

-3-

HERNANDO COUNTY - Right of Way Easement
                  File 2433-27-253.03

APPLICANT: Department of Transportation

PROJECT: Bridge construction for State Road 50. No dredging or filling required.

LOCATION: 1.39 acre parcel of sovereignty land in the Withlacoochee River in the NE 1/4 of Section 4, Township 23 South, Range 21 East, Hernando County.

ECOLOGICAL
RESPONSES: Department of Natural Resources has no objection.

            Department of Pollution Control has no objection.

            Game and Fresh Water Fish Commission comments that minimum damage to water quality and wildlife habitat will be incurred if certain precautions are utilized during construction.

Staff requests authority to issue right of way easement.

ACTION OF THE TRUSTEES:

On motion by Mr. Christian, seconded by Mr. O'Malley and adopted without objection, the request of the Department of Transportation was approved.

-4-

HILLSBOROUGH COUNTY - Dredge Permit 253.123-924

APPLICANT: Detsco Terminals, Inc.
            Post Office Box 5067 Y, Tampa, Florida 33605

PROJECT: To excavate approximately 4,500 cubic yards of material from Northerly end of Ybor Channel in Tampa, Section 18, Township 29 South, Range 19 East, Hillsborough County.

MATERIAL: Spoil will be placed on uplands and properly diked to prevent siltation.

PAYMENT: Fees waived since work will be on privately-owned land.

ECOLOGICAL
RESPONSES: Department of Natural Resources - no objection provided spoil is placed on upland.

            Game and Fresh Water Fish Commission - no objection provided spoil is placed on upland that has been properly diked.

            Department of Pollution Control - no objection to

1-18-72

the project.

Staff recommends issuance of Dredge Permit 253.123-924 to Detsco Terminals, Inc.

ACTION OF THE TRUSTEES:

Motion was made by Mr. Christian, seconded by Mr. O'Malley and adopted without objection, that the dredge permit be issued.

-5-

ALACHUA COUNTY - Land Conveyance

At the request of the Department of Health and Rehabilitative Services, the Trustees deferred consideration of a request from the Board of County Commissioners of Alachua County for conveyance of 102.09 acres of state land on which to locate an agricultural center and county fairgrounds. The land was a portion of an area northeast of Gainesville leased to the Department of Health and Rehabilitative Services and used by the Division of Corrections.

-6-

WASHINGTON COUNTY - Land Conveyance

The Town of Ebro by resolution adopted December 8, 1971, requests the Trustees to convey to the town 18.59 acres of land located in the Pine Log State Forest to be used for municipal purposes and installation of civic improvements.

The Town of Ebro has submitted a site location plan indicating the parcel of land will be utilized for the location of a fire station, community building and outdoor recreation facilities. The land is in the extreme north portion of the forest and within the incorporated area of the town on State Road No. 79. The Department of Agriculture and Consumer Services has reviewed this request and recommends that the parcel be granted to the city for municipal purposes provided that the location of the buildings and recreation areas be placed in a manner to retain as much of the vegetation and trees as possible.

Recommend that the 18.59 acre parcel of land located in the NW 1/4 of NW 1/4 of Section 5, Township 1 South, Range 16 West, Washington County, be dedicated to the Town of Ebro for public recreation and fire control purposes as set forth on the site location plan, with a reverter clause in event of use for other than public recreation and fire control purposes and for non-use for a period of three years, subject to the restrictions recommended by the Department of Agriculture and Consumer Services.

ACTION OF THE TRUSTEES:

On motion by Mr. Stone, seconded by Mr. Christian and adopted without objection, the Trustees granted the request of the Town of Ebro for dedication of the 18.59 acre parcel of land for public recreation and fire control purposes, with a reverter clause and restrictions as recommended.

-7-

At the request of the Commissioner of Agriculture Doyle Conner, action was deferred for two weeks on the request from Radcliff Material, Inc., for renewal of Shell Lease No. 1718.

-8-

At the request of Commissioner of Agriculture Doyle Conner, action was deferred for two weeks on the request from Fort Myers Shell and Dredging Company, Inc., for renewal of Shell Lease No. 2235.

-9-

Request authority to engage Dr. O. Edward Cunningham, Ph.D., to undertake basic research on the history of Florida Bay for use by the Department of Legal Affairs in connection with the U. S. Supreme Court case U. S. v. Florida 52 Original. This action involves settlement of the outer boundary line of Florida and many thousands of acres of submerged land. Total costs shall not exceed $6,400 and funds are available within the approved budget of the Board of Trustees.

ACTION OF THE TRUSTEES:

Upon motion by Mr. Stone, seconded by Mr. Christian and Mr. O'Malley, adopted without objection, the rules were waived to consider this and the following addendum items and the Board approved the request to engage Dr. O. Edward Cunningham for the work stated, the total cost not to exceed $6,400 to be paid from available funds.

-10-

LEVY COUNTY - Dredge Permit 253.123-1051

APPLICANT: Department of Natural Resources, Division of Recreation and Parks, Larson Building Tallahassee, Florida

PROJECT: To dredge 200 cubic yards of material from within the existing basin located at Cedar Key in Levy County; also minor construction of a boat ramp and dock.

MATERIAL: All material will be trucked away to the county dump. This material is muck and considered of no value.

PAYMENT: Request fees be waived as the project is in the public interest.

ECOLOGICAL
RESPONSES: Department of Natural Resources - No objections to project.

Game and Fresh Water Fish Commission - No objection to project.

Department of Pollution Control - No objection to project.

Staff recommends issuance of dredge permit 253.123-1051 to the Department of Natural Resources.

ACTION OF THE TRUSTEES:

On motion made by Mr. Stone, seconded by Mr. Christian and adopted without objection, the Board approved the request for issuance of a dredge permit to the Department of Natural Resources, Division of Recreation and Parks.

-11-

MONROE COUNTY - Modified Dredge Permit 253.03-248

APPLICANT: J. H. T. Inc., c/o E. V. Timmons
6825 Northwest 17th Avenue, Miami, Florida

PROJECT: Applicant requests modification of original permit
by reducing navigation channel to 25' x 700' x -3'
instead of 25' x 700' x 5' from the mean high water
line of applicant's property to an existing channel
in Section 21, Township 60 South, Range 40 East
Monroe County.

MATERIAL: 1,100 cubic yards (instead of 2,600) will be excavated
from sovereignty land and placed on privately-owned
uplands.

PAYMENT: Check for $3,900 tendered as payment for 2,600 cubic
yards of material to be removed.

ECOLOGICAL
RESPONSES: Department of Natural Resources has no objection
to the project.

Game and Fresh Water Fish Commission has no objection
to the project.

Department of Pollution Control has no objection
to the project.

Staff recommends issuance of modified Dredge Permit 253.03-248
and refund of $2,250, since the charge for sovereignty material
will be $1,650 instead of $3,900 as approved by the Board on
December 21, 1971, for Permit 253.03-248, Monroe County.

ACTION OF THE TRUSTEES:

Mr. Kuperberg discussed modification of the permit issued in
December 1971, at which time he was not aware that it was in
that portion of John Pennekamp Coral Reef Park boundaries
included by the Trustees in the park in 1967 subject to
riparian rights and private navigation access rights held by
owners of the upland abutting the land included in the park.

The owner applied for reduction of the channel depth and a
refund because less material would be removed. The staff
recommended approval of the revised permit because it was for
a minimum navigation channel connecting to an existing navigation channel into deeper water, but the Director expressed
some concern because of the problems now affecting the coral
reef.

Mr. Kuperberg advised that at some time in the past the Division
of Recreation and Parks and Trustees' staff had worked to develop
a master plan for navigation channels to which all private owners
could have access, which plan apparently was not completed.
In view of the conditions, the federal government was taking
a close look at all dredging in the keys.

Governor Askew said of course there was still some private
ownership within the park, and the Director should recommend
a general policy in that area.

On motion by Mr. Stone, seconded by Mr. O'Malley and adopted
without objection, the staff recommendation was approved.

-12-

LEE COUNTY - Cape Coral Encroachment and G.A.C. Corporation
          Settlement

December 15, 1970, the Board proposed settlement in the amount of
$983,800 consisting of $33,800 cash for engineering costs and
$950,000 credit on the acquisition of G.A.C. land in or near the
Fahkahatchee Strand based on the 1962 value thereof.

S. H. Wills, Chairman of the Board, on behalf of G.A.C. Corporation
by letter to the Board dated January 3, 1972, agréed to the proposed
settlement. Prior negotiations arrived at a quantum of land
approximating 9,523 acres in or near the Fahkahatchee Strand,
Collier County, in satisfaction of the $950,000 portion of the
Cape Coral settlement. In exchange the state must deliver to
G.A.C. a release, deeds, and any other assurances deemed necessary to establish good and marketable title to the land in
controversy along the northerly banks of the Caloosahatchee River
in Sections 32 and 33, Township 44 South, Range 24 East, Sections
5, 8, 17, 18 and 19, Township 45 South, Range 24 East, and in
Sections 23 and 24, Township 45 South, Range 23 East, Lee County,
and the state is to approve the bulkhead line previously submitted
to the state by the County of Lee as outlined in the resolution
passed by the Board of County Commissioners on August 28, 1968.
This land had been filled in the development of the Cape Coral
Subdivision.

The Fahkahatchee Strand land is set forth as 9,523 acres, more
or less, in Collier County, Florida, and being all those following
described lands LESS those portions thereof which are described
as being specifically excepted therefrom.

A. In Township 53 South, Range 28 East:
      All of Section one (1), thereof, and

B. In Township 52 South, Range 29 East:
      All of Sections thirty-one (31) and thirty-two (32), thereof
    and

C. In Township 52 South, Range 28 East:
    (1) All of Sections fifteen (15), twenty-two (22), twenty-three
        (23), twenty-four (24), twenty-five (25), twenty-six (26),
        twenty-seven (27), thirty-five (35) and thirty-six (36);
        and

    (2) The East halves (E 1/2) of Sections twenty-one (21),
        twenty-eight (28) and thirty-four (34); and

    (3) All of those portions of Sections ten (10), eleven (11)
        and fourteen (14) which lie Southerly of the Right of Way
        (R/W) of U. S. Highway 41, RESERVING UNTO THE GRANTOR
        THEREFROM a 350 foot wide navigational canal easement and
        237 foot wide spoil easement for construction and maintenance
        of said canal (which reservation shall not be construed to
        vest in the grantor, or its successors or assigns, any
        special equities respecting the issuance of a dredge
        permit or the granting of any waiver of the necessity
        for such permit)comprising a strip of land running
        adjacent and contiguous to the south side of the Right
        of Way of U. S. Highway 41, and more particularly
        described as follows:

            Commencing with a Point of Beginning at Intersection
            of the South Line of the Right of Way of U. S. Highway
            41 and the West line of said Section ten (10), Township
            52 South, Range 28 East, then South along the West line
            of Section ten (10), for 1,034.13 feet, then East at
            right angles to said section line for 350 feet to a
            corner; thence North and parallel to said West line of
            Section ten (10) to a point 587 feet South of South
            line of said Right of Way, then Easterly and South-

1-18-72

easterly along a line 587 feet Southerly and parallel to
the South Right of Way line of said U. S. Highway 41,
to a point where said line intersects with the West
section line of Section eleven (11), then Northeasterly
along a line which is at right angles to the Right of
Way of said U. S. Highway 41 for 587 feet to the South
line of said Right of Way, then Northwesterly and
Westerly along the South line of said Right of Way to
a point where said line intersects with the West line
of Section ten (10) said point of intersection being
also the Point of Beginning.

The lands to be conveyed as settlement of a problem not of G.A.C.
Corporation's making, constitute an important addition to the
state's reservoir of natural resources.

Staff recommends acceptance of the lands to be conveyed as part of
the settlement and the granting of releases, deeds, and other
assurances deemed necessary to vest good and marketable title in
G.A.C. Corporation to the land in controversy.

ACTION OF THE TRUSTEES:

On motion by Mr. Conner, seconded by Mr. Christian, the rules
were waived for consideration of the addition to the agenda of
the Trustees and also the related addendum of the Department of
Conservation concerning a five-year option on some 17,500 acres
of GAC land also in the Fahkahatchee Strand area. When deferment
was suggested by Mr. Christian, the Director advised that there
was no urgency on the part of the staff but representatives of
GAC were present and desired to make settlement. The cabinet
aides had been informed from time to time during the two and one-
half years of negotiations.

Mr. Kuperberg said it was an excellent settlement arrived at
after extended negotiations which, as reviewed briefly, included
everything south of the Tamiami Trail between Everglades
National Park and The Nature Conservancy's holdings in The
Ten Thousand Islands. The acquisition was described as part of
an overall plan that ultimately, hopefully, would bring the
Ten Thousand Islands under public ownership. He described
today's recommendation as the second step, the first being the
settlement with Marco Island and acquisition of all the islands
in MIDC ownership south of Marco Island.

In return the Board would give clear title to those GAC lands
along the Caloosahatchee River, title to which had been in
controversy for several years. It was actually the same
settlement originally proposed by the previous Director of
the Trustees, with the exception of some shifting to block
up Fahkahatchee land ownership into an ecologically manageable
portion.

Senator Randolph Hodges, Director of the Department of Natural
Resources, explained the related proposal on his agenda and
recommended approval. He said it did not obligate the state
but gave the state five years to explore the possibility of
acquiring parcels in the Fahkahatchee Strand that would be
desirable to acquire in his opinion.

The Governor pointed out that the settlement did not commit
the Board in any way toward furnishing salt water access to
a canal in the southwestern corner of the area.

In response to questions, Mr. Gerard Turner, general counsel
for GAC Corporation, said the company desired to settle the
long-pending controversy and he had no authority to extend
the time stated in the company's letter. He referred to the
previous resolution that tied together the exchange of lands
in the Fahkahatchee Strand for the Cape Coral settlement.

Mr. O'Malley spoke of the many staff meetings to review the history and final negotiation stages. He was satisfied that it was a reasonable settlement and was prepared to vote.

Mr. Christian said he had not had an opportunity to hear the presentations referred to, but he would not request delay if the members were ready to proceed.

Motion was made by Mr. O'Malley, seconded by Mr. Stone, and adopted without objection, that the Board of Trustees approve the recommendation of the staff for acceptance of the lands to be conveyed as part of the settlement and the granting of releases, deeds, and other assurances deemed necessary to vest good and marketable title in GAC Corporation to the land in controversy.

The cabinet in its capacity as the Board of the Department of Natural Resources took action to approve the recommendation on that agenda.

Governor Askew thanked Senator Hodges and Ney Landrum who had worked for a long time in this regard, and thanked Mr. Kuperberg for his efforts toward what represented a fair settlement and one that would assist in clearing up a difficult problem related to all the boundary disputes along the river, Cape Coral, and also try to reconcile problems within the Fahkahatchee Strand.

On motion duly adopted, the meeting was adjourned.

GOVERNOR — CHAIRMAN

ATTEST:

EXECUTIVE DIRECTOR

Tallahassee, Florida
January 25, 1972

The State of Florida Board of Trustees of the Internal Improvement Trust Fund met on this date in the auditorium of the Burns Building, with the following members present:

Reubin O'D. Askew	Governor
Richard (Dick) Stone	Secretary of State
Robert L. Shevin	Attorney General
Fred O. Dickinson, Jr.	Comptroller
Thomas D. O'Malley	Treasurer
Floyd T. Christian	Commissioner of Education
Doyle Conner	Commissioner of Agriculture

Joel Kuperberg	Executive Director

-1-

The minutes of the January 11, 1972, meeting were approved as submitted.

1-25-72

2

PALM BEACH COUNTY - Grazing Lease Assignment

APPLICANT: Terry Cattle Company
             P. O. Box 192, Orlando, Florida

REQUEST: Assignment of Grazing Lease No. 2004 to United
             States Sugar Corporation

LOCATION: 640 acres in Section 5, Township 43 South, Range
             39 East, Palm Beach County

LEASE TERM: 10 years from May 13, 1964

Executed instrument of assignment has been filed and approved
by the Trustees' legal staff as to form and legality.

The Division of Corrections has consented to this assignment.

Recommend consent to assignment.

ACTION OF THE TRUSTEES:

On motion by Mr. Stone, seconded by Mr. Conner and adopted
without objection, the Board consented to the lease assignment.

3

MARTIN COUNTY - Dredge Permit 253.123-969

APPLICANT: Archipelago Community Association, Inc.
             c/o George M. Booth
             Route 1, Box 508, Jensen Beach, Florida 33457

PROJECT: To dredge an existing channel to a depth of minus
             7 feet with a bottom width of 50 feet. This
             channel is the entrance to Sewall's Point from the
             Intracoastal Waterway.

MATERIAL: All dredge material will be placed on Lots 21 and
             22 of Archipelago Subdivision. Approximately 1,000
             cubic yards of material will be removed.

PAYMENT: A check for $500 has been tendered to cover the
             cost of material removed from sovereignty land at
             the standard yardage rate of 50¢ per cubic yard.

ECOLOGICAL
RESPONSES: Department of Natural Resources - No objection
             provided the spoil area is diked

             Game and Fresh Water Fish Commission - No objection

             Department of Pollution Control - No objection

Staff recommends issuance of Dredge Permit 253.123-969.

ACTION OF THE TRUSTEES:

Motion was made by Mr. Dickinson, seconded by Mr. Stone and
unanimously carried, authorizing issuance of the dredge permit.

4

MONROE COUNTY - Marina License No. ML-83

APPLICANT: Sun'n Surf Motel, c/o Anita Kram
             508 South Street, Key West, Florida 33040

PROJECT: Construction of concrete pier covering 2,250
             square feet of sovereignty land in the Atlantic

Ocean abutting Section 31, Township 67 South,
Range 25 East, Monroe County.

ECOLOGICAL
RESPONSES: Department of Natural Resources - No objection.

Game and Fresh Water Fish Commission - No objection.

Department of Pollution Control - No objection.

Staff recommends approval of marina license for annual fee of
$100.

ACTION OF THE TRUSTEES:

Motion was made by Mr. Stone, seconded by Mr. Conner and
unanimously carried, that the marina license be issued as
recommended, for $100 annual fee.

-5-

WAKULLA COUNTY - Marina License ML-106

APPLICANT: Panacea Bridgehouse, Inc.,
              c/o William J. Roberts, Attorney at Law
              135 West Jefferson Street, Tallahassee, Florida

PROJECT: Construction of a pier facility and restaurant
              covering 26,810 square feet of submerged land in
              Ochlocknee Bay abutting Section 12, Township 6
              South, Range 2 West, Wakulla County. No dredging
              is required.

PAYMENT: $336.20 minimum annual fee for marina license.

ECOLOGICAL
RESPONSES: Department of Natural Resources - No objection.

Game and Fresh Water Fish Commission - No objection.

Department of Pollution Control - No objection.

Staff recommends issuance of marina license for annual fee of
$336.20.

ACTION OF THE TRUSTEES:

Motion was made by Mr. Stone, seconded by Mr. Conner and adopted,
that the staff recommendation be accepted.

Attorney General Shevin was not opposed to the recommendation,
commenting that it would be difficult to raise prices with regard
to the water column in this area, but he called attention to
his earlier request that consideration be given to increasing the
rental the state charges for use of the water column.

Mr. Kuperberg advised that the staff was researching the question
of rates in an attempt to be equitable, to determine whether
rates should be different or a flat rate state-wide with an
increase in the square foot rental. Since marina licenses are
reviewed annually, this one would be subject to review in a year
for any change in rates that might be accepted.

-6-

OKALOOSA COUNTY - Fill Permit 253.124(8)-228

APPLICANT: American Marine Repair Facility
              c/o A. G. Rowley
              330 Race Track Road, Ft. Walton Beach, Florida

PROJECT: To construct a seawall to prevent further erosion
           in Joes Bayou in Township 2 South, Range 23 West,
           Okaloosa County. The area to be filled will extend
           less than 25 feet offshore from the MHW mark.

MATERIAL: All material will be trucked in.

PAYMENT: None

ECOLOGICAL
RESPONSES: Department of Natural Resources - no objection to
            project as revised.

            Game and Fresh Water Fish Commission - no objection
            provided dikes are built to control siltation

            Department of Pollution Control - no objection to
            project.

Staff recommends issuance of Fill Permit 253.124(8)-228 to
American Marina Repair Facility subject to siltation control
requested by the environmental agencies.

ACTION OF THE TRUSTEES:

The Director asked that the minutes reflect that the recommendation was amended to include "subject to siltation control
requested by the environmental agencies."

Motion was made by Mr. Stone, seconded by Mr. Christian and
adopted without objection, that the staff recommendation as
amended be accepted as the action of the Board.

-7-

MANATEE COUNTY — File No. 253.123-926

APPLICANT: City of Bradenton
            Post Office Drawer 730
            Bradenton, Florida 33505

PROJECT &
LOCATION: To dredge approximately 5,000 cubic yards of
            material from an existing municipal yacht basin
            to a depth of 6 feet below mean low water in the
            Manatee River in Section 26, Township 34 South,
            Range 17 East in Manatee County, Florida.

MATERIAL: 5,000 cubic yards of material will be hauled away
            and deposited on diked city-owned uplands.

PAYMENT: Applicant is requesting waiver of the $50 processing
            fee and waiver of the fee for materials at $1 per
            cubic yard, since it is a municipality and the
            material is of no value to the City.

ECOLOGICAL
RESPONSES: The Department of Natural Resources has no objection
            to the proposed project.

            The Game and Fresh Water Fish Commission concurs with
            the report of the Department of Natural Resources
            and, therefore, has no objection.

            The Department of Pollution Control has no objection
            to the proposed project.

Staff recommends approval of Permit No. 253.123-926 and waiver
of fees.

ACTION OF THE TRUSTEES:

Motion was made by Mr. Dickinson, seconded by Mr. Stone and carried unanimously, that the permit be authorized without fee as recommended by the staff.

-8A-

BAY COUNTY - Bulkhead Line, Section 253.122, F. S.

APPLICANT: Department of Transportation
              Tallahassee, Florida

PROJECT: Bulkhead line 886.00 feet long in Martin Bayou
              abutting Section 1, Township 4 South, Range 14·West,
              Bay County, Florida approved and established by the
              Board of County Commissioners of Bay County by
              resolution adopted April 20, 1971.

ECOLOGICAL
RESPONSES: Department of Natural Resources - no objection

              Game and Fresh Water Fish Commission - no objection

              Department of Pollution Control - no objection

Staff recommends approval of bulkhead line.

ACTION OF THE TRUSTEES:

On moton by Mr. Stone, seconded by Mr. Dickinson and adopted unanimously, the bulkhead line was approved as established by the Board of County Commissioners of Bay County.

-8B-

BAY COUNTY - Right of Way Easement, File 2437-03-253.03

APPLICANT: Department of Transportation

PROJECT: Highway and bridge construction for State Road S-22.
              Dredging and filling is required.

LOCATION: 0.84 acre parcel of sovereignty land in Martin Bayou,
              Section 1, Township 4 South, Range 14 West, Bay County.

ECOLOGICAL
RESPONSES: Department of Natural Resources - no objection

              Game and Fresh Water Fish Commission - no objection

              Department of Pollution Control - no objection

Staff requests authority to issue right of way easement.

ACTION OF THE TRUSTEES:

Motion was made by Mr. Stone, seconded by Mr. Dickinson and carried unanimously, that the right of way easement be granted to the Department of Transportation.

-8C-

BAY COUNTY - Fill Permit 253.124-252

APPLICANT: Department of Transportation

PROJECT: To remove approximately 6,176 cubic yards of muck and
              replace with 10,670 cubic yards of fill to stabilize the
              foundation for the proposed bridge in Section 1, Town-
              ship 4 South, Range 14 West, State Road S-22, Bay County,

1-25-72

Martin Bayou.

MATERIAL: Will be trucked in from upland sources.

PAYMENT: Fees waived since project is in the public interest.

ECOLOGICAL
RESPONSES: Department of Natural Resources - no objection to
project

Game and Fresh Water Fish Commission - no objection
provided the proper procedures are taken to prevent
siltation.

Department of Pollution Control - no objection provided
the proper procedures are taken to prevent siltation.

Staff recommends issuance of Fill Permit 253.124-252 to the Department of Transportation and waiver of fees, since the project is in
the interest of the public.

ACTION OF THE TRUSTEES:

Motion was made by Mr. Stone, seconded by Mr. Dickinson and
carried unanimously, that the Trustees authorize issuance of
the fill permit to the Department of Transportation without
fee, because the project is in the public interest.

-9-

BROWARD COUNTY - Permit 253.124(8)-246

APPLICANT: Hillsboro River View Corporation
3100 East Oakland Park Boulevard
Ft. Lauderdale, Florida 33308

PROJECT: Reclamation of a strip of land lost by artificially
induced erosion caused by boat traffic. A seawall
will be constructed to connect with existing seawalls.
Riprap will be placed along the seawall and mangroves
will be planted along the riprap in areas suitable
for their growth. All work lies in Section 5,
Township 48 South, Range 43 East, Broward County.

MATERIAL: All material needed to backfill will be hauled in
from upland sources.

PAYMENT: None

ECOLOGICAL
RESPONSES: Department of Natural Resources has no objection to
to the project amended to include riprap and planting
of mangroves.

Game and Fresh Water Fish Commission objects to the
project since it is doubtful that the establishment
of such a productive area is possible because the
area is subjected to extreme wave action caused by
large boats utilizing the waterway.

Department of Pollution Control has no objection.

Staff recommends issuance of Permit 253.124(8)-246 as amended
to include riprap and planting of mangroves.

ACTION OF THE TRUSTEES:

Mr. Kuperberg asked that the minutes reflect a change in the
agenda requested by the applicant, so that the permit will
be issued to the Hillsboro River View Corporation, the firm
taking title to the land, rather than the Resources Development
and Mortgage Company, the firm that held title when the application was filed.

The work would be outside the boundaries of the river, that had been widened into an artificial waterway with seawalls on each side in an urbanized area. The work would go no further waterward than the line of the seawalls and represented restoration of eroded land.

On motion by Mr. Dickinson, seconded by Mr. Conner and Mr. Dickinson, adopted unanimously, the Board approved issuance of the permit as amended to include riprap and planting of mangroves.

Announcement was made that the next meeting would be on Monday, January 31, at 2 p.m., instead of on February 1; and the next meeting following that was scheduled for February 15, 1972.

On motion duly adopted, the meeting was adjourned.

GOVERNOR - CHAIRMAN

ATTEST:

EXECUTIVE DIRECTOR

* .   * * *

Tallahassee, Florida
January 31, 1972

The State of Florida Board of Trustees of the Internal Improvement Trust Fund met in the auditorium of the Burns Building on this date at 2:00 p.m. with the following members present:

Reubin O'D. Askew	Governor
Richard (Dick) Stone	Secretary of State
Robert L. Shevin	Attorney General
Fred O. Dickinson, Jr.	Comptroller
Thomas D. O'Malley	Treasurer
Floyd T. Christian	Commissioner of Education
Doyle Conner	Commissioner of Agriculture

Joel Kuperberg   Executive Director

-1-

The minutes of the January 18, 1972, meeting were approved as submitted.

-2-

ALACHUA COUNTY - Murphy Act Land Sale

LAND
DESCRIPTION: Lots 1 through 4, Block A
                 Lots 10 through 12, Block G
                 Lots 7 through 11, & N 1/2 of Lot 12, Block H
                 Lots 2, 3, 4 and 7, Block I
                 Lots 1, 2 and 3, Block J
                 Lots 7 through 12, Block K
                 Lots 6 through 9, Block L
                 Lots 1 through 8, Block M
                 Lots 1 through 12, Block N
                 Lots 1 through 6, Block S
                 Lots 1 through 4, Block T
                 Futch Clayton Addition subdivision, Plat Book A,

1-31-72

Page 126, Public Records of Alachua County in
Section 4, Township 8 South, Range 17 East.

LOCATION: A 1920 subdivision of small (50' x 150' average)
lots within High Springs city limits, zoned A-1
(agricultural) with scattered modest frame homes
fronting dirt trail roads. 60% of the lots are
cleared and planted in pasture grass. The lots
comprise a total area of 9.86 acres in an area
where residential lots are not in demand.

APPRAISAL: By staff appraiser, $335 per acre or $3,300.

AUTHORITY
FOR SALE: Section 197.350, Florida Statutes

DATE OF
SALE: December 8, 1971, by Clerk of Circuit Court of
Alachua County

HIGH BIDDER: R. N. Peacock
Post Office Box 6243, High Springs, Florida

HIGH BID: $3,300

Recommend confirmation of sale of the lots to R. N. Peacock
for $3,300 plus costs of advertising and clerk's fee.

ACTION OF THE TRUSTEES:

Motion was made by Mr. Dickinson, seconded by Mr. Christian
and unanimously carried, that sale of the lots be confirmed
as recommended.

-3-

FLAGLER COUNTY - Quitclaim Deed

On May 26, 1958, the Florida Board of Forestry conveyed to
Rayonier, Incorporated, a parcel of land in a land exchange.
On November 14, 1967, pursuant to Section 253.03, Florida
Statutes, as amended by Chapter 67-2236, Laws of Florida, the
Board of Forestry conveyed to the Trustees all of the land
owned by the Board of Forestry. The parcel conveyed in 1958
to Rayonier, Incorporated, was inadvertently included in the
deed to the Trustees in 1967, thereby creating a cloud on the
title.

To remove this cloud, ITT Rayonier, Incorporated, successor
to Rayonier, Incorporated, requests a quitclaim from the
Trustees covering the parcel previously conveyed by the Board
of Forestry.

Staff legal counsel has reviewed this matter and recommends the
quitclaim as requested.

Recommend that the Board quitclaim to Rayonier, Incorporated,
its interest in the parcel conveyed by the Board of Forestry
on May 26, 1958.

ACTION OF THE TRUSTEES:

Motion was made by Mr. Dickinson, seconded by Mr. Christian and
unanimously carried, that the interest of the Trustees in the
parcel conveyed by the Board of Forestry be quitclaimed as requested.

1-31-72

-4-

SANTA ROSA COUNTY - Oil Lease Assignment

APPLICANT: Philip B. Berry
             Post Office Box 642, Tyler, Texas

REQUEST: Assignment to Harris R. Fender, Post Office Box
             449, Tyler, Texas, of Philip B. Berry's one-fourth
             undivided interest in Oil and Gas Drilling Lease
             No. 2559-MA.

LOCATION: One-half interest of the State of Florida (Murphy
             Act) in N 1/2 of NW 1/4 of SE 1/4 of SE 1/4 of
             Section 22, Township 5 North, Range 29 West,
             containing 5 surface acres in Santa Rosa County.

LEASE TERM: Five years from September 14, 1971.

Executed instrument of assignment has been filed and approved as
to form by the Trustees' legal staff.

Recommend approval and consent to assignment.

ACTION OF THE TRUSTEES:

On motion by Mr. Dickinson, seconded by Mr. Stone and carried
unanimously, the Trustees approved and consented to the assignment as requested.

-5-

CHARLOTTE COUNTY - Campsite Lease Renewals

(1) Lease No. 2257, Ralph J. Brandon and Stephen R. Roddy
request renewal of Campsite Lease No. 2257 for one year
with option to renew for an additional four years at $300
annual rental.

(2) Lease No. 2261, James A. Kelly requests renewal of Campsite
Lease No. 2261 for one year with option to renew for an additional
four years at $300 annual rental.

These requests conform to policy of April 7, 1970, that allows
lease as long as the structure remains on the site and the
policy of October 6, 1970, that established an annual rental of
$300 for a quarter-acre site.

Recommend renewal of Campsite Leases No. 2257 and No. 2261,
provided that sanitary facilities are installed by the lessee
to prevent discharge of any raw sewage from the site.

ACTION OF THE TRUSTEES:

Motion was made by Mr. Christian, seconded by Mr. Stone and
carried unanimously, that the two campsite leases be renewed
as requested, provided that sanitary facilities be installed
by the lessees to prevent discharge of any raw sewage, as
recommended by the staff.

-6-

DADE COUNTY - Assignment and Renewal of Campsite Lease No.
             2156A

Gilbert L. O'Neal, holder of Campsite Lease No. 2156A which
expires February 1, 1976, requests assignment of the lease to
Stilts, Inc., a Florida corporation, c/o Raphael Steinhardt,
1896 79 Street Causeway, Miami Beach, Florida 33141.

1-31-72

Instruments of assignment, and acceptance of terms and conditions executed by both parties, have been approved by staff legal counsel.

Applicants have tendered $25 assignment fee in accordance with the Trustees' policy of December 1, 1970.

Stilts, Inc., requests renewal of Campsite Lease No. 2156A for one year with option to renew on a year to year basis for four additional years at an annual rental of $300.

Recommend assignment and renewal of Campsite Lease No. 2156A provided that sanitary facilities are installed by the lessee to prevent discharge of any raw sewage from the site.

ACTION OF THE TRUSTEES:

Motion was made by Mr. Christian, seconded by Mr. Stone and carried unanimously, authorizing the assignment and renewal of Campsite Lease 2156A subject to the installation by the lessee of sanitary facilities to prevent raw sewage discharge.

———————

-7-

DADE COUNTY - Fill Permit 253.124-216

APPLICANT: H. P. Forrest, Trustee
Suite 1220 DuPont Building, Miami, Florida

PROJECT: To fill 4.4 acres and construct a seawall in Biscayne Bay west of Lots 1, 2, 3, 4, 5, 6, 7, 8 and 9, Block 15, Island View Subdivision, Plat Book 6, Page 115, Miami Beach, in Section 33, Township 53 South, Range 42 East, Dade County

MATERIAL: Will be trucked in from other sources

PAYMENT: Fees waived, since no sovereignty land will be used

ECOLOGICAL
RESPONSES: Department of Natural Resources made adverse comments; recommends denial.

Game and Fresh Water Fish Commission made adverse comments; recommends denial.

Department of Pollution Control reported adversely; recommends denial.

Staff recommends denial of project based on the recommendations from the environmental agencies.

ACTION OF THE TRUSTEES:

Mr. Kuperberg explained that the staff, faced with adverse responses from three environmental agencies, could only support the adverse recommendation and bring the public interest aspects to the Board for a decision.

Secretary of State Stone asked for postponement until after the Pollution Control Board had made its decision. If approved by the Trustees, the application still had to have pollution Control approval and Mr. Stone did not wish to make a decision before that Board. He noted that in the event the Trustees act negatively they would not have had an opportunity to see if public interest considerations and modifications could correct the situation.

Answering questions raised by the Attorney General regarding the validity of the public interest aspect and efforts to weigh the public interest as against biological damage, the Director said the Trustees in 1970 had decided the sale was in the public interest, that in other cases one adverse environmental report

1-31-72

had been overruled in consideration of other aspects, but there were three adverse environmental reports on this applica- tion. A possible alternative might be for the staff to meet with the Pollution Control staff to try to resolve the problem as suggested by Comptroller Dickinson.

Mr. William J. Roberts, present with Mr. H. P. Forrest and Dr. Conger representing Island View Special Services Hospital, Inc., reviewed the various applications including the bulkhead line approved by the Trustees and confirmed by the Interagency Advisory Committee, sale by the Trustees in 1970 of the strip of land needed for added width for the building site, the tax- exempt, non-sectarian, non-profit status of the hospital, the exception in favor of the hospital in the City of Miami Beach no-fill ordinance, various determinations that the hospital was in the public interest and need for it particularly in the winter months, earlier biological reports of little to preserve in that area, additional reports and the applicant's willingness to construct riprap seawall and take steps necessary to eliminate debris entrapment. He explained that the Department of Pollution Control required permit from the Trustees before action except on an informal basis.

Governor Askew said the Trustees could not vote affirmatively today, and while the applicants had expended time and money relying on using the land, it could not be said that any decision made by the Trustees in the past could bind the present board. He suggested that the application would have a better chance if the staff could confer further with the Pollution Control staff. Without that Department's permit the applicant could not proceed, in any case.

Mr. O'Malley said that in view of past actions and the sale in 1970 in anticipation of hospital construction, they might consider as a last alternative giving the applicant an oppor- tunity to return the land to state ownership if a solution could not be found.

Mr. Kuperberg commented briefly on the one reversal by the Board of Pollution Control since he became Director because of a change in policy for power plants, the policy that requests would not go to the Pollution Control Board in event of staff denial, and the work of the three-man committee that established the guidelines for alignments of bulkhead lines all around the state that did not, however, relieve the Trustees of the responsi- bility of reviewing, individually, biological reports on each application site.

Motion was made by Mr. Dickinson, seconded by Mr. Stone and carried without objection, that action be deferred for two weeks pending further study by the staffs of the Trustees and the Pollution Control Department in an effort to resolve the adverse aspects and legal technicalities.

-8-

BROWARD COUNTY - Dredge Permit 253.123-1005

APPLICANT: Lauderdale Yacht Basin, Inc.
c/o Williams, Hatfield and Stoner, Inc.
2312 Wilton Drive, Ft. Lauderdale, Florida 33305

PROJECT: To remove approximately 8,000 cubic yards of material that was previously placed in the river to form a breakwater. This is now being replaced by concrete and steel, all work to be done along South Fork New River in Section 16, Township 50 South, Range 42 East, Broward County.

MATERIAL: 8,000 cubic yards will be removed and placed on owner's upland.

PAYMENT: $50 check was tendered to pay the processing fee. No charge for material since it will come from private property.

ECOLOGICAL
RESPONSES: Department of Natural Resources - No objection

    Game and Fresh Water Fish Commission - No objection provided adequate barriers are placed to prevent siltation.

    Department of Pollution Control - No objection; issued Certificate DF-06-254.

Staff recommends issuance of Dredge Permit 253.123-1005.

ACTION OF THE TRUSTEES:

On motion by Mr. Christian, seconded by Mr. Conner and carried unanimously, the application for a dredge permit was approved.

-9-

DUVAL COUNTY - Dredge, Fill and Seawall Permit
    File 253.123-829 and 253.124-191

APPLICANT: Mode, Inc.
    3614 St. Augustine Road, Jacksonville, Florida

PROJECT: To construct a seawall, place riprap along the shore outside of boat basin, to dredge a boat basin 625 feet by 225 feet, to a depth of minus 6 ft., and to fill 1.5 acres of privately-owned submerged land in Section 34 and 38, Township 2 S, R27E on the St. Johns River, Duval County.

MATERIAL: 36,000 cubic yards of material will be removed from the boat basin and placed behind seawall and riprapping.

PAYMENT   None. All dredging will be accomplished on privately-owned submerged land.

BIOLOGICAL
RESPONSES: Department of Natural Resources has no objection to the project provided that marsh grass is planted in areas flanking the boat basin.

    Game and Fresh Water Fish Commission feels that the applicant has made considerable concessions in order to mitigate damages to the aquatic environment; and even though there will be some environmental damage, they feel that the final proposal represents an acceptable compromise between development and environmental protection.

    Department of Pollution Control has no objection to the project as revised, provided the bulkheading for the boat basin is constructed and the opening temporarily closed off prior to dredging the basin itself.

Staff recommends issuance of the requested seawall, dredge and fill permits 253.123-829 and 253.124-191 provided the requirements of the environmental agencies are met.

ACTION OF THE TRUSTEES:

Motion was made by Mr. Christian, seconded by Mr. Stone, and carried on a vote of six to one with Mr. Shevin voting "No", that the application to construct a seawall, dredge and fill be approved provided the requirements of the environmental agencies are met as recommended by the staff.

521

BAY COUNTY - Dredge Permit No. 253.123-1004

APPLICANT: Anderson's Pier, Inc,
550 North Lagoon Drive, Panama City, Florida 32401

PROJECT: To dredge approximately 1700 cubic yards of material
in front of a dock located in Section 9, Township
4 South, Range 15 West, Block 8, Plat of Port Lagoon,
Bay County, and construct 160 feet of seawall to
connect with an existing seawall.

MATERIAL: 1700 cubic yards will be used for beach nourishment.

PAYMENT: $1700 has been tendered as payment at standard yardage
rate. If it is proved that the material is suitable
for beach nourishment, the fee for the material will
be refunded.

ECOLOGICAL
RESPONSES: Department of Natural Resources - No objection to
project.

Game and Fresh Water Fish Commission - No objection
to project.

Department of Pollution Control - No objection to
project.

Department of Beaches and Shores - No objection,
provided that any unsuitable material will be removed
by applicant immediately after pumping.

Staff recommends issuance of Permit No. 253.123-1004 to Anderson's
Pier, Inc.

ACTION OF THE TRUSTEES:

Motion was made by Mr. Christian, seconded by Mr. Dickinson and
Mr. Conner, carried unanimously, that the dredge permit be
approved and the $1,700 tendered as payment for the material be
refunded if the material is suitable to be used for beach
nourishment.

SHELL DREDGING LEASES

Fort Myers Shell and Dredging Co., Inc., Lease No. 2235
in Lee County

Radcliff Materials, Inc., Lease No. 1718 in Wakulla,
Franklin, Gulf, Bay, Walton, Okaloosa and Santa Rosa
Counties

The Director asked for instructions regarding the outstanding
shell leases about to expire, which were on the agenda on
January 4 and 18, 1971, with recommendation to advertise for
competitive bids pursuant to Section 253.45, Florida Statutes,
with the requirement that prior to dredging, permits will be
obtained in accordance with the provisions of Section 253.123,
Florida Statutes, to bring shell dredging under the same
requirements as other dredging. On those dates the Trustees
had deferred action at the request of members of the Board.
Based on the Attorney General's opinion that the leases might
be extended, the Director recommended temporary extension
pending completion of a report he would work on in coordination with Senator Randolph Hodges, Director of the Department
of Natural Resources.

On motion by Mr. O'Malley, seconded by Mr. Conner and carried
unanimously, the rules were waived for consideration of the
shell leases.

1-31-72

Mr. O'Malley made a motion that the Fort Myers Shell and Dredging Company, Inc., lease expiring January 31, 1972, and the Radcliff Materials, Inc., lease expiring February 5, 1972, be extended six months subject to the permit requirement recommended by Mr. Kuperberg. There was no second.

Mr. Conner was concerned about dredging in such wholesale fashion while some individual requests for dredging small projects had been denied.

Mr. Hodges said the marine research program was funded by proceeds from shell leases. While Radcliff had not operated since 1970 the firm paid the $40,000 minimum stipulated in the lease in advance each year to hold the lease; but if permits were required for each dredging operation, Mr. Hodges thought the firm would not make that advance payment without which he would have a fund shortage as the Legislature had not funded the program.

Mr. O'Malley made a motion, seconded by Mr. Dickinson, that the Trustees extend those two leases through June 30, 1972, and that Mr. Hodges meet with Mr. Ireland and Mr. Kuperberg to resolve the question of the future of such leases. He felt that shell leases originating in the past probably should never have been approved. No vote was taken on the motion.

Governor Askew pointed out that Mr. Kuperberg recommended dredge permits, a provision he did not think the Board could waive. He asked the staff of the Trustees and Department of Natural Resources to recommend a policy with respect to any leasing of state-owned bottoms and any lease extensions beyond December 31, 1972.

Attorney General Shevin said the statutes require permits for removal of sand, rock and earth from the navigable waters and submerged bottoms which, in his opinion, certainly would be involved in removal of shell. With reference to certain other leases he felt that the Board also could require permits regardless of who owned the bottom lands.

Mr. Kenneth Ireland entered into the discussion of possible replacement funds that would be needed immediately to administer the research program in the event the leases were not extended and the $40,000 was not available to the Department of Natural Resources.

Mr. Kuperberg recommended extension of the Radcliff lease to the end of the calendar year subject to requirement of permits for dredging, and that the Fort Myers shell lease be extended for thirty days and by that time a recommendation would be prepared by Senator Hodges and Mr. Kuperberg for consideration of the Board.

Motion was made by Mr. Christian, seconded by Mr. Shevin and adopted unanimously, that the Director's recommendation be accepted as the action of the Board.

FLORIDA KEYS REPORT

The Director asked Mr. Glenn Ulrich, Trustees' field inspector in the Keys and a marine biologist, to hand each member a report consisting of reviews on the environmental impact of urbanization with particular reference to dredge and fill on the Florida Keys and John Pennekamp State Park. The report was prepared individually by four separate agencies, one federal and three state agencies, and would be supplemented by a report by the Department of Pollution Control. Mr. Kuperberg commented on the thoroughness and unanimity of opinion, and seriousness of the problem.

In answer to Mr. Shevin's question regarding illegal dredge and fill operations in the Keys, Mr. Kuperberg reported receipt of the results of another aerial survey showing some flagrant violations, some dredge and fill operations stopped last year but started up again.

Mr. Dickinson expressed the concern of the Board to protect and preserve the great natural reefs and habitat. He commended the Director for the speed with which he moved to obtain and report the information.

On motion duly adopted, the meeting was adjourned.

GOVERNOR - CHAIRMAN

ATTEST:

EXECUTIVE DIRECTOR

* * * * *

Tallahassee, Florida
February 15, 1972

The State of Florida Board of Trustees of the Internal Improvement Trust Fund met in the auditorium of the Burns Building on this date with the following members present:

Reubin O'D. Askew	Governor
Richard (Dick) Stone	Secretary of State
Robert L. Shevin	Attorney General
Fred O. Dickinson, Jr.	Comptroller
Thomas D. O'Malley	Treasurer
Doyle Conner	Commissioner of Agriculture

Joel Kuperberg	Executive Director

-1-

The minutes of the meetings on January 25 and 31 were approved as submitted.

-2-

LEVY COUNTY - School Land Transfer

The School Board of Levy County by resolution adopted January 4, 1972, requested transfer of a ten-acre parcel described as W 1/2 of W 1/2 of SE 1/4 of NW 1/4 of Section 8, Township 12 South, Range 17 East, Levy County, to the Board for location of its proposed administration offices, transportation unit and maintenance unit.

This parcel was donated to the State Board of Education on March 22, 1966, by Irene Camille O'Neill for "educational purposes to honor Haydon Burns, Governor of Florida." The parcel has been under lease to the Board of Regents for the use and benefit of the University of Florida. The Board of Regents on December 7, 1971, considered and approved the transfer of the property to the Levy County Public School system.

The State Board of Education at its meeting on January 18 approved the transfer by the Trustees to the School Board of Levy County.

Recommend dedication to the School Board of Levy County for

2-15-72

school administration offices, transportation and maintenance
units, with a reverter provision in event of other use and
non-use for a period of five consecutive years.

ACTION OF THE TRUSTEES:

On motion by Mr. O'Malley, seconded by Mr. Conner and Mr. Stone,
adopted without objection, the Trustees approved the dedication
as recommended.

-3-

SANTA ROSA COUNTY - Oil and Gas Lease Bids,Blackwater River
                    State Forest

On November 9, 1971, bids were received for oil and gas drilling
leases covering the one-quarter interest of the State in two
parcels of land located within the Blackwater River State
Forest. These parcels are identified as Tract 2 - S 1/2 and
NE 1/4 of Section 32, Township 3 North, Range 26 West, 480
surface acres, and Tract 3 - all of Section 9, Township 2 North,
Range 26 West, Santa Rosa County, 636.48 surface acres. Phillips
Petroleum Company, the only bidder, submitted bids on Tract 2
for $3,331.20 and Tract 3 for $6,788.06.

These tracts are in the Southwestern portion of the forest and
watershed, and if drilling should take place it would have
minimal impact upon the environment.

Due to the concern expressed by the Governor and Board regarding
oil exploration in State forests, the bids received were opened
and read into the record and held pending a review by a
committee composed of the following members:

    Chairman, Mr. Joel Kuperberg, Executive Director of
      the Trustees of the Internal Improvement Trust Fund

    Mr. Randolph Hodges, Executive Director of the Department
      of Natural Resources

    Mr. John M. Bethea, Director of the Divison of Forestry,
      Department of Agriculture and Consumer Services

    Mr. Vincent D. Patton, Executive Director of the Department
      of Pollution Control

    Dr. O. E. Frye, Jr., Director of the Florida Game and Fresh
      Water Fish Commission.

The committee was instructed to re-evaluate oil exploration
policies with respect to all state forests and state-owned lands.

The committee met and discussed the need for the adoption of
rules and regulations to protect the environment, preserve
the water quality of the streams, lakes and rivers and limit the
construction of new roads in the forest.

The committee will bring its report to the Board in the near
future. The staff will not recommend further leasing of the
one-quarter interest held by the state in the forest until the
committee recommendations have been considered.

The committee further recommends that the Board accept the
bids received for Tracts 2 and 3, and award the leases to
Phillips Petroleum Company.

525

ACTION OF THE TRUSTEES:

The Director said the committee re-evaluating oil exploration policies had agreed that these particular leases would have minimal impact on the forest resources because of the location at the southern edge of the forest.

Motion was made by Mr. Conner, seconded by Mr. O'Malley and adopted without objection, that the bid be accepted and the leases awarded to Phillips Petroleum Company.

The special committee would have additional time to bring its report with respect to all state forests and state-owned lands.

-4-

COLLIER COUNTY - Oil and Gas Lease Assignment

APPLICANT: Mobil Oil Corporation
1001 Howard Avenue
New Orleans, Louisiana 70113

REQUEST: Assignment of Oil and Gas Drilling Lease No. 2350-S, to Exchange Oil and Gas Corporation

LOCATION: Reserved one-half interest in 640 surface acres in Section 16, Township 47 South, Range 28 East, Collier County

LEASE
TERM: Five years from October 15, 1968.

Executed instrument of assignment has been filed and approved by the Trustees' legal counsel as to form.

Recommend approval and consent to assignment.

ACTION OF THE TRUSTEES:

On motion by Mr. O'Malley, seconded by Mr. Conner and adopted without objection, the Trustees approved and consented to the assignment of Lease No. 2350-S to Exchange Oil and Gas Corporation.

-5-

DADE COUNTY - Lease Assignment and Renewal

Robert W. Sudbrink, holder of Lease No. 1627 covering 7.16 acres of sovereignty land in Dade County for use for radio transmitter towers, requests assignment of this lease to Sudbrink Broadcasting, Inc. Executed copy of assignment and acceptance of the terms of the lease by assignee are on file in the Land Office.

Sudbrink Broadcasting, Inc., requests five-year renewal of Lease No. 1627 which expired September 21, 1971, covering 7.16 acres of sovereignty submerged shoal area in Township 55 South, Range 42 East, Dade County, for radio antenna and towers. The lease requires compliance with all applicable regulations and requirements of the U. S. Army Corps of Engineers, Federal Communications Commission and the Federal Aviation Administration, as well as the state and local regulations. Annual rental will be $1,200, or $167.60 per acre, an increase of $842 over the previous annual rental. Rent of $1,200 has been paid for the year September 21, 1971 through September 21, 1972.

Recommend approval of the assignment and lease renewal at the increased annual rental of $1,200.

2-15-72

ACTION OF THE TRUSTEES:

On motion made by Mr. O'Malley, seconded by Mr. Dickinson and
adopted without objection, the Trustees approved the assignment
and renewal of the lease at the increased annual rental of $1,200.

-6-

CHARLOTTE COUNTY - Application for Disclaimer
                   File 2418-08-253.129

Staff description: A parcel of filled sovereignty land in the
Peace River abutting Section 6, Township 41 South, Range 23 East,
7.6 acres

A. CITY AND
    COUNTY: Punta Gorda, Charlotte County

B. APPLICANT: City of Punta Gorda

C. APPLICANT'S
    REPRESENTATIVE: John R. Gargis, Tri-County Engineering, Inc.,
                     121 East Charlotte Avenue, Punta Gorda, Florida

D. ACREAGE: 7.6 acres
    RATE PER ACRE: Not applicable

E. APPRAISAL: Not applicable

F. PURPOSE: City Park

G. BIOLOGICAL
    REPORT: Not applicable

H. STAFF REMARKS: The applicant applied for a disclaimer pursuant
    to Section 253.129, Florida Statutes, which provided that
    "The title to all lands heretofore filled or developed is
    herewith confirmed in the upland owners and the Trustees
    shall on request issue a disclaimer to each such owner."

    Two affidavits have been submitted stating that the fill
    material has been in place since the year 1943 or prior
    thereto.

    Staff legal counsel is of the opinion that the application
    qualifies under the provision of Section 253.129, Florida
    Statutes.

    The applicant has submitted payment of $100 for the
    processing fee.

Request authority to issue a disclaimer.

ACTION OF THE TRUSTEES:

Modion was made by Mr. Dickinson, seconded by Mr. Stone and adopted
without objection, that the disclaimer be issued.

-7-

The staff withdrew from consideration at this time an illegal
dredging operation in Monroe County.

2-15-72

527

-8-

COLLIER COUNTY - Bulkhead Line, Section 253.122, F. S.

APPLICANT: Mayflower Realty, Inc.
             c/o Thompson, Wadsworth and Messer
             Post Office Box 1876, Tallahassee, Florida

PROJECT: Bulkhead Line 1,496.38 feet long in Section 29,
             Township 48 South, Range 25 East, Collier County,
             approved and established by the Board of County
             Commissioners of Collier County by resolution adopted
             May 4, 1971.

ECOLOGICAL
RESPONSES: Department of Natural Resources - no objection

             Game and Fresh Water Fish Commission - no objection

             Department of Pollution Control - no objection

Staff recommends approval of bulkhead line.

ACTION OF THE TRUSTEES:

Motion was made by Mr. Stone, seconded by Mr. O'Malley and
carried without objection, that the Trustees approve the
bulkhead line established by the Board of County Commissioners
of Collier County on May 4, 1971.

-9-

COLLIER COUNTY - Dredge Permit 253.123-1066
                 Fill Permit 253.124-257

APPLICANT: Mayflower Realty, Inc.
             c/o Thompson, Wadsworth & Messer
             P. O. Box 1876, Tallahassee, Florida

PROJECT: To excavate approximately 110,000 cubic yards of
             material from an existing artificially created
             waterway and to excavate a boat basin to a depth
             of 20 feet below mean sea level in Section 29,
             Township 48 South, Range 25 East, Collier County,
             Florida. Dredged material removed will be used to
             fill along the westerly bank landward of the bulkhead
             line.

PAYMENT: None, as material is being removed from an artificially
             created waterway.

ECOLOGICAL
RESPONSES: Department of Natural Resources - no significant
             adverse effects on marine resources.

             Game and Fresh Water Fish Commission - no objection
             but recommend waterway be excavated only to 8 feet below
             mean sea level.

             Department of Pollution Control - no objection.

Staff recommends approval of Dredge permit No. 253.123-1066 and
Fill Permit No. 253.124-257 subject to recommendation of Game
and Fresh Water Fish Commission.

2-15-72

ACTION OF THE TRUSTEES:

Motion was made by Mr. Stone, seconded by Mr. O'Malley and
adopted without objection, that the dredge and fill permit
be approved subject to the recommendation by the Game and
Fresh Water Fish Commission.

-10-

DADE COUNTY - Fill Permit No. 253.124-230

Consideration of an application from the City of Miami to fill
an area under proposed Southeast 8th Street Bridge was withdrawn for three weeks at the request of the applicant.

-11-

DADE COUNTY - Fill Permit No. 253.124-179
The application from Charles E. Gottlieb to construct a seawall
and fill in Biscayne Bay was withdrawn from the agenda for
three weeks at the request of the applicant.

-12-

DADE COUNTY - Fill Permit No. 253.124-232
At the request of the staff, an application from Ransom School
to fill land in Biscayne Bay was withdrawn. The Director said
it involved an unauthorized fill that had not been resolved.

-13-

DADE COUNTY - Dredge Permit 253.123-1071

APPLICANT: Metropolitan Dade County
             c/o Public Works Department
             Miami, Florida 33125

PROJECT: To dredge approximately 1,100 cubic yards of
             material from an existing marina at Haulover Beach
             Park in Section 23, Township 52 South, Range 42
             East, Dade County. Dredged material will be removed
             to a depth of 6 feet below mean low water and all
             material will be placed on uplands.

PAYMENT: Applicant is requesting waiver of the $50 processing
             fee and waiver of the fee for materials at $1 per
             cubic yard, because the project is a public recreation
             facility.

ECOLOGICAL
RESPONSES: Department of Natural Resources - No objection.

             Game and Fresh Water Fish Commission - No objection.

             Department of Pollution Control - No objection

Staff recommends approval of Dredge Permit No. 253.123-1071 and
waiver of charge.

ACTION OF THE TRUSTEES:

On motion by Mr. Stone, seconded by Mr. O'Malley and adopted
without objection, the Board approved issuance of the dredge
permit without charge.

529

-14-

DADE COUNTY - Marina License ML-107

APPLICANT: Metropolitan Dade County
c/o Public Works Department
Miami, Florida 33125

PROJECT: Construction of additional mooring facilities at
Haulover Beach Park in Biscayne Bay adjacent to
Section 23, Township 52 South, Range 42 East,
Dade County.

PAYMENT: Request waiver of fees as the facility is for the
benefit of the public.

ECOLOGICAL
RESPONSES: Department of Natural Resources - No objection

Game and Fresh Water Fish Commission - No objection

Department of Pollution Control - No objection.

Staff recommends issuance of marina license and waiver of
license fee.

ACTION OF THE TRUSTEES:

On motion by Mr. Stone, seconded by Mr. O'Malley and adopted
without objection, the Board authorized issuance of the marina
license without fee.

-15-

PALM BEACH COUNTY - Dredge Permit No. 253.123-970
At the request of the staff, action was deferred for one week
on the application for a dredge permit from Jupiter Inlet
Commission.

-16-

PINELLAS COUNTY - Marina License ML-91

APPLICANT: Continental Towers
c/o A.A.A. Marine Construction
10029 Gulf Boulevard, Treasure Island, Florida

PROJECT: Construction of a pier facility covering 795 square
feet of submerged land in the Gulf of Mexico abutting
Section 17, Township 29 South, Range 15 East, Pinellas
County. No dredging or filling is required.

PAYMENT: $100 minimum annual fee for marina license.

ECOLOGICAL
RESPONSES: Department of Natural Resources - No objection

Game and Fresh Water Fish Commission - No objection

Department of Pollution Control - No objection

Staff recommends issuance of marina license for annual fee of $100.

ACTION OF THE TRUSTEES:

On motion by Mr. Dickinson, seconded by Mr. Stone, adopted
without objection, the Trustees approved issuance of the
marina license.

-17-

PINELLAS COUNTY - Marina License ML-69

APPLICANT: L. P. Construction Company, Inc.
             Post Office Box 6675
             St. Petersburg, Florida 33705

PROJECT: Construction of a docking facility in Boca Ciega
             Bay abutting Section 31, Township 31 South, Range
             16 East, Pinellas County. The facility will cover
             3,600 square feet of sovereignty land. No dredging
             or filling is required.

PAYMENT: $100 minimum annual fee for marina license.

ECOLOGICAL
RESPONSES: Department of Natural Resources - No objection

             Game and Fresh Water Fish Commission - No objection

             Department of Pollution Control - No objection

Staff recommends issuance of marina license for annual fee of $100.

ACTION OF THE TRUSTEES:

On motion by Mr. Dickinson, seconded by Mr. Stone and adopted
without objection, the Trustees approved issuance of the
marina license.

-18-

POLK COUNTY - Marina License ML-71

APPLICANT: Spring Lake Towers, Inc.
             212 South Summerlin Street
             Orlando, Florida 32801

PROJECT: Construction of a pier facility covering 480 square
             feet of submerged land in Lake Spring abutting
             Section 20, Township 28 South, Range 26 East,
             Polk County, Florida. No dredging or filling is
             required.

PAYMENT: $100 minimum annual fee for marina license.

ECOLOGICAL
RESPONSES: Department of Natural Resources - No objection

             Game and Fresh Water Fish Commission - No objection

             Department of Pollution Control - No objection

Staff recommends issuance of marina license for annual fee of $100.

ACTION OF THE TRUSTEES:

Motion was made by Mr. Stone, seconded by Mr. Dickinson and
carried, that the marina license be approved.

-19-

FLORIDA KEYS - Monroe County Survey

The Director presented a progress report from Field Operations
on the study made by state and federal inspection personnel
of dredge and fill activities in the Florida Keys with particular
attention to the main area of concern, the John Pennekamp Coral

Reef along the Atlantic side of Key Largo. He reported on
several large projects, a land survey to determine areas of
encroachment, extension or new starts on a number of dredging
projects, unauthorized work and overdredging, an arrest for
improper dragline work, and a suit filed for work on state-
owned submerged land.

A conference was held between the state attorney and the
Trustees' attorney to establish procedures for handling
established violations. The information needed to institute
a trespass suit is as follows:

    A. Aerial photography, old and new made to scale
    B. A survey showing existing mean high water line and
        U. S. Government meander line.
    C. A biological report showing the extent of the
        ecological damage
    D. Witness statements
    E. General information concerning ownership

Mr. Kuperberg said the staff was anxious to resolve the
problems, some of which were caused by the exemption of
Monroe County from applicable state laws, without trespassing on
private property rights. Up-to-date vertical aerial photography
was needed because oblique aerials were not proper to use for
survey and court purposes. Mr. Kuperberg said it would take at
least six months to make a complete study by field surveying and
office research to resolve the problem of trespass upon the public
lands alone. Approximately half the Keys were covered in this
study which was continuing in order to develop the necessary
details.

If all activity were stopped, it might be difficult to determine
the impact of dredging and filling on the reefs. Mr. Kuperberg
was exploring the possibility of federal-state funding of
a research project to determine exactly what was killing the
coral reefs.

Attorney General Shevin clarified the request of the staff as
withholding issuance of new permits but not curtailing existing
permits. Commenting on the size of the task force working in
the Keys, he recommended that state agencies and his office be
called on for additional assistance to try to concentrate man-
power in that area to ferret out the violations and move toward
legal action.

On motion by Mr. Shevin, seconded by Mr. Stone and carried
without objection, the rules were waived and expenditure of
$1,500 from budgeted funds was authorized for up-to-date vertical
aerial photography.

-20-

PASCO COUNTY - Campsite Lease

Crawford A. Deems, Post Office Box 423, Leesburg, Florida, applies
for a private campsite lease in the Gulf of Mexico, off New Port
Richey, Florida. This structure was severely damaged by Hurricane
Gladys in October of 1968 and affidavits were furnished to
establish this fact. The area for lease will not exceed 1/4 acre,
at annual rental of $300 for one-year lease with option to renew
for four additional years.

Recommend issuance of lease in accordance with policy adopted
on April 7, 1970, which states, in part: "Require all structures
in existence to be under lease for so long as the structure remains
in existence", provided that sanitary facilities are installed
by the lessee to prevent discharge of any raw sewage from the site.

2-15-72

ACTION OF THE TRUSTEES:

Motion was made by Mr. Dickinson, seconded by Mr. O'Malley
and carried without objection, that the staff recommendation
be accepted as the action of the Board.

-21-

MONROE COUNTY - Aquaculture Lease

Wometco Enterprises, Inc., Charles Francis, Director
Rickenbacker Causeway, Miami, Florida

The applicant, who is the riparian upland owner, has filed an
application for an aquaculture lease embracing approximately
1.87 acres in part of Government Lot 2, Section 19, Township 65
South, Range 34 East, on Grassy Key, Monroe County, Florida,
for the purpose of experimental breeding of bottle-nose dolphins.

To contain the dolphins, the applicant proposes to construct 1"
mesh metal fencing spaced 4 to 5 feet apart.

The Department of Natural Resources has no objection.

The Department of Pollution Control has no objection.

The Florida Game and Fresh Water Fish Commission has no objection.

On December 14, 1971, the Trustees authorized advertisement for
competitive bids and objections. As of this date, no objections
or other bids have been received. The advertised notice called for
bids on February 8, 1972. The bids received will be opened today.

ACTION OF THE TRUSTEES:

The only sealed bid received was from the applicant. It was
opened and read into the record as annual rental of $435.60
per acre for the first through the fifth year, annual rental for
the sixth through the tenth year of $871.20 per acre, royalty of
7 1/2% on gross income, such income limited to the sale of
porpoises commencing after 1 1/2 years of operation.

Mr. Kuperberg recommended that the bid be received and held for
two weeks, as there was a problem regarding use of the land
prior to 1970.

Motion was made by Mr. Conner, seconded by Mr. Dickinson and
Mr. O'Malley, and carried, that the bid be received and held
pending review by the staff.

-22-

ESCAMBIA COUNTY - Marina License ML-106

APPLICANT: Gulf Power Company
             Post Office Box 1151, Pensacola, Florida

PROJECT: Construction of unloading facility covering 12,500
             square feet of submerged land in Governor's Bayou
             abutting Section 25, Township 1 North, Range 30 West,
             Escambia County. No dredging is required.

PAYMENT: $250 minimum annual fee for marina license.

ECOLOGICAL
RESPONSES: Department of Natural Resources - No objection

             Game and Fresh Water Fish Commission - No objection

2-15-72

Department of Pollution Control - No objection, subject
to: (1) Water inside of the cells should be evacuated
prior to filling them with soil. Turbid water should
not be overflowed from the cells. (2) Precautions
must be taken to ensure that soil is not
accidentally spilled outside of the cells during the
filling operation. (4) Coal handling and storage
facilities must be well drained to a ponded area to
allow adequate settling or treatment of storm water
discharge prior to discharge.

Staff recommends issuance of marina license for annual fee of
$250 subject to stipulations made by the Department of Pollution
Control.

ACTION OF THE TRUSTEES:

Motion was made by Mr. Dickinson, seconded by Mr. Conner and
carried without objection, that the Trustees approve issuance
of the marina license subject to the stipulations of the
Department of Pollution Control.

-23A-

MONROE COUNTY - Dredge Permit 253.03-235

APPLICANT: Key Motels, Inc., Ralph E. Cunningham, Attorney
              P. O. Box 938, Marathon, Florida

PROJECT: To dredge a channel 220 ft. long x 50 ft. wide x 5 ft.
              deep to connect two existing perimeter channels, and
              to dredge a channel 200 ft. long x 50 ft. wide x 5 ft.
              deep to connect an existing perimeter channel to Bone-
              fish Bay in Section 5, Township 66 South, Range 33
              East, Monroe County

MATERIAL: Approximately 2,400 cubic yards will be removed from
              sovereignty land and placed on privately-owned
              uplands.

PAYMENT: $50 for processing fee, and $3,600 for dredged material
              at standard yardage rate of $1.50 per cubic yard.

ECOLOGICAL
RESPONSES: Department of Natural Resources - Completion of the
              dredging should have only limited adverse effects on
              the marine biological resources. The proposed alternate
              route for the access channel shown on the sketch would
              reduce damage to marine life from dredging and filling.

              Game and Fresh Water Fish Commission - No objection

              Department of Pollution Control - No objection

Staff recommends issuance of Dredge Permit 253.03-235 subject to
(1) relocation of a 35 ft. segment of the existing seawall to a
point landward of the mean high water line, and (2) relocation of
access channel as recommended by Department of Natural Resources.

ACTION OF THE TRUSTEES:

On motion by Mr. Conner, seconded and carried without objection,
the Trustees accepted the staff recommendation for issuance
of the permit subject to certain requirements for relocation
of a portion of the seawall and the access channel.

534

-23B-

MONROE COUNTY - Marina License ML-62

APPLICANT: Key Motels, Inc.
             c/o Ralph E. Cunningham, Attorney
             P. O. Box 938, Marathon, Florida

PROJECT: Construction of a marina facility covering 10,500
             square feet of submerged land in Bonefish Bay abutting
             Section 5, Township 66 South, Range 33 East, Monroe
             County, Florida.

PAYMENT: $210 minimum annual fee for marina license.

ECOLOGICAL
RESPONSES: Department of Natural Resources - No objection

             Game and Fresh Water Fish Commission - No objection

             Department of Pollution Control - No objection

Staff recommends issuance of marina license for annual fee of $210.

ACTION OF THE TRUSTEES:

On motion by Mr. Conner, seconded and carried without objection,
the Trustees authorized issuance of the marina license.

-24-

PINELLAS COUNTY - Dredge Permit 253.123-912
                  Construction Permit

APPLICANT: W. W. Ericson
             Post Office Box 4426, Ozona, Florida

PROJECT: To dredge in an existing man-made lagoon to a depth of
             minus 5 feet and to enlarge existing mooring facilities.
             The lagoon connects to the Anclote River and abuts
             Section 12, Township 27 South, Range 15 East, Pinellas
             County.

MATERIAL: Approximately 7,820 cubic yards of material will be
             removed and all material will be placed on privately-
             owned upland.

PAYMENT: $50 standard dredge permit processing fee and $100
             construction permit fee. No sovereignty material will
             be removed.

ECOLOGICAL
RESPONSES: Department of Natural Resources - No objections
             provided dredging is performed by dragline.

             Game and Fresh Water Fish Commission - No objection.

             Department of Pollution Control - No objection.

Staff recommends issuance of Dredge Permit No. 253.123-912 and
construction permit subject to stipulations of Department of
Natural Resources.

ACTION OF THE TRUSTEES:

Motion was made by Mr. Conner, seconded by Mr. O'Malley and
carried without objection that Pinellas County Permit DO-198 be
approved and the application for dredge and construction permits
be approved subject to the stipulations of the Department of
Natural Resources.

2-15-72

-25-

MARTIN COUNTY - Artificial Reef Permit 253.03-310

APPLICANT: Stuart Sailfish Club
             Post Office Box 2005, Stuart, Florida

PROJECT: Construction of an artificial fishing reef in the
             Atlantic Ocean approximately 3,000 feet long by 300
             feet wide.

LOCATION: In 60 feet of water at 27.93 degrees North Latitude,
             and 80.33 degrees West Longitude, which is about
             4.8 miles from the nearest land near St. Lucie Inlet.

MATERIAL: Automobile tires weighted with cement in the bottom
             third of the casings plus concrete rubble and slabs.

ECOLOGICAL
RESPONSES: Department of Natural Resources - No objection

             Game and Fresh Water Fish Commission - No objection

             Department of Pollution Control - No objection

Staff recommends issuance of Artificial Reef Permit 253.03-310.

ACTION OF THE TRUSTEES:

On motion by Mr. Conner, seconded by Mr. Shevin and adopted
without objection, the Trustees authorized issuance of the
artificial reef permit to Stuart Sailfish Club.

─────────────

-26-

TRUST FUNDS - Purchase Lands Pursuant to Chapter 71-981.

Your Executive Director has been advised that the legislative
interpretation of Chapter 71-981 relating the the use of the
Internal Improvement Trust Fund, by the Senate Ways and Means
Committee, requires the following submission to the Committee:

    1. Description of the land to be acquired
    2. Purpose of acquisition
    3. Estimate of cost of such land
    4. Recommended order of priorities

The Committee has indicated an early submission of the information
if it is anticipated that lands are to be acquired by purchase
during the fiscal year 1972-73.

Pursuant to the foregoing requirements, your Director recommends
that the Trustees establish an order of priorities from among
the following recommended purchases.

Palm Beach County land	$ 95,000
10,000 Islands (60,000 acres)	6,000,000
Cape Romano (455 acres)	450,000
St. Joe Bay (985 acres)	2,500,000
Beach frontage (25,000 feet)	
Port Charlotte Beach frontage	1,150,000
(98 acres; 7,700 feet)	
Gilchrist County - Suwannee and Santa Fe	1,085,000
River frontage (1,446 acres)	
Glades County - Conservation Area (640 acres)	192,000
Sarasota County - Adjacent to Myakka State	2,973,500
Park (6,260 acres)	
Tomoka Marshes (2,500 to 3,000 acres)	(price information not complete)
North Indian River Lagoon	(price information
(4,000 acres, 1,500 private)	not complete)

2-15-72

ACTION OF THE TRUSTEES:

Mr. Kuperberg asked that the Board place at the top of the list $95,000 obtained through a settlement with Multicon Properties for Palm Beach County land. The Trustees on September 28, 1971, had agreed to use the money for reacquiring productive marine bottom lands.

Mr. O'Malley said the Board made the commitment to the Royal Palm Audubon Society and its committee on site selection had suggested three parcels that the Director should review.

On motion by Mr. O'Malley, seconded by Mr. Shevin and adopted without objection, the Trustees placed the $95,000 at the top of the priority list to honor the commitment made to the Palm Beach County group, and deferred action for one week for the Director to contact the Outdoor Recreation Advisory Committee with respect to the tracts listed and the information requested by the Senate Ways and Means Committee.

-27-

DADE COUNTY - Fill Permit 253.124-216
        Applicant: H. P. Forrest, Trustee
                   Island View Special Services Hospital, Inc.
At the request of the staff the Board deferred for one week consideration of this application previously considered on January 31, 1972. The staff had not received reports that were necessary to formulate recommendations to the Trustees.

On motion duly adopted, the meeting was adjourned.

_____
GOVERNOR   CHAIRMAN

ATTEST: _____
        EXECUTIVE DIRECTOR

Tallahassee, Florida
February 22, 1972

The State of Florida Board of Trustees of the Internal Improvement Trust Fund met in the auditorium of the Burns Building on this date, with the following members present:

-1-

BROWARD COUNTY - Miccosukee Tribe Lease

The Miccosukee Tribe of Indians of Florida requests the Board
in its capacity as Trustee of all Seminole Indian lands, to
approve a 15-year farming lease between the tribe and C&G Farms,
Inc., and Goodno Farms, Inc.

The lease authorized by the tribal council by Resolution No.
MB-3-71 dated April 15, 1971, covers 24 sections of land in
Townships 49 and 50 South, Range 35 East, Broward County,
outside of Conservation Area No. 3.

The annual rental will be 50¢ per acre for unimproved land
and $1 per acre for improved land after the first six years of
the lease. Rental was reviewed by staff appraiser who considers
the rent not unreasonable.

The form of the lease has been reviewed and approved by staff
legal counsel.

Recommend approval of the lease as amended.

ACTION OF THE TRUSTEES:

The land was near Conservation Area No. 3, and action was
deferred for the staff to request review of the lease proposal by the Central and Southern Florida Flood Control
District.

Also, the Director was asked to provide population information
on the Miccosukee Tribe.

-2-

HENDRY COUNTY - Consideration of Oil and Gas Lease Bids

On January 11, 1972, at the request of Tribal Oil Company, the
Trustees authorized advertisement for sealed bids for a five-
year oil and gas drilling lease covering the reserved one-
half interest of the Board of Education in privately-owned
Section 16, Township 44 South, Range 28 East, 640 surface acres,
more or less, in Hendry County approximately eight miles southwest of LaBelle and 16 miles north of the Big Cypress Watershed
area.

All proceeds will go to the School Fund.

The lease requires an annual rental of $1 per net mineral acre,
$50,000 surety bond, 1/8 royalty and at least one test well
every 2 1/2 years of the lease to a depth of 6,000 feet or to the
Roberts Zone of the Sunniland Formation.

Invitation to bid was advertised pursuant to law in the Tallahassee
Democrat and Hendry County News with bids to be opened at 10:00
a.m. (EST) on February 22, 1972, for consideration by the Trustees.
The right to reject any or all bids is reserved.
ACTION OF THE TRUSTEES:

The oil and gas drilling lease had been advertised and one
sealed bid was received from Tribal Oil Company offering a
total of cash consideration of $3,600.00 which was a bonus
bid per acre of $10.25. Proceeds from this lease would go
to the State School Fund.

Motion was made by Mr. Christian, seconded by Mr. Conner and
adopted without objection, that the bid be accepted and lease
awarded to Tribal Oil Company as recommended by Mr. James T.
Williams.

2-22-72

538

-3-

SANTA ROSA COUNTY - Consideration of Oil and Gas Lease Bids

On January 11, 1972, at the request of Humble Oil and Refining
Company, the Trustees authorized advertisement for sealed bids
for a five-year oil and gas drilling lease covering the reserved
one-half interest of the State (Murphy Act) in privately-owned
W 1/2 of NW 1/4 of NW 1/4 of Section 13, Township 4 North, Range
29 West, containing 20 surface acres in Santa Rosa County
approximately six miles southeast of the Town of Jay.

All proceeds will go to General Revenue Unallocated (Murphy Act).
The lease requires an annual rental of $1 per net mineral acre,
1/6 royalty and at least one test well every 2 1/2 years of the
lease term to a depth of 6,000 feet or to a depth sufficient to
test the Norphlet Sands, whichever is deeper.

Invitation to bid was advertised pursuant to law in the
Tallahassee Democrat and the Milton Press-Gazette with bids
to be opened at 10:00 a.m. (EST) on February 22 for consideration
by the Trustees. The right to reject any or all bids is reserved.

ACTION OF THE TRUSTEES:

The oil and gas drilling lease had been advertised and six
sealed bids were received and opened. Bids were on the
reserved one-half interest covering 20 surface acres, or a
net 10 acres held by the state under the Murphy Act. All
proceeds from leasing would go to the General Revenue.

Mr. James T. Williams read the following total consideration
offers:

Arden A. Anderson	$ 44,444.44
Humble Oil and Refining Company	51,110.00
Spencer Brothers	58,000.00
Headwaters Oil Company	77,510.00
W. A. Moncrief	101,111.11
Amoco Production Company	125,079.82

In analyzing the bids, the high bid was a bonus per acre of
$12,506.98. Mr. Williams recommended acceptance and awarding
lease to that bidder.

In the discussion that followed Mr. Christian said this was a
very high bid for the right to explore for the possibility of
oil in land owned by others on which the state held the reserved
mineral rights. Mr. Stone noted that the environmental impact
studies had been favorable. Mr. Conner added that this was the
most active discovery in the United States for at least the past
five years, a good grade of oil was being recovered, and the
severance tax of about five million dollars a year would accrue
to the benefit of the state.

Motion was made by Mr. Conner, seconded by Mr. Christian and
adopted without objection, that the Trustees accept the high
bid from Amoco Production Company and award oil and gas drilling
lease to that firm.

-4-

INDIAN RIVER COUNTY - Trustees File 253.123-389 - Refund

APPLICANT: Lost Tree Village Corporation
c/o Lloyd and Associates
1835 20th Street, Vero Beach, Florida 32960

PROJECT &
MATERIAL: Trustees Permit 253.123-389 issued on October 7,
1969, authorized the excavating of 60,000 cubic yards

of material from sovereignty land. The project was completed and cross-section furnished indicates that only 29,955 cubic yards of sovereignty material were excavated.

LOCATION: Section 12 and 13, Township 32 South, Range 39 East, Indian River at John's Island, Indian River County.

PAYMENT: Applicant paid for 60,000 cubic yards of material. Since only 29,955 cubic yards were excavated, applicant has requested refund.

Staff recommends refund in the amount of $3,004.50 since the quantity of material paid for was not used.

ACTION OF THE TRUSTEES:

On motion by Mr. Christian, seconded by Mr. Conner and adopted without objection, the refund was authorized by the Board.

-5-

BROWARD COUNTY - Marina License ML-92
            Dredge Permit 253.123-1035

APPLICANT: Hatteras of Lauderdale, Inc.
           c/o McLaughlin Engineering Co.
           Ft. Lauderdale, Florida

PROJECT: Excavate a boat slip and construct piers covering 1,102 square feet of submerged land in New River abutting Section 10, Township 50 South, Range 42 East, Broward County. All excavation is on applicant's upland and all material will be removed prior to removal of the seawall plug.

PAYMENT: $100 minimum annual fee for marina license. No fee for permit or charge for material. All excavation work is on applicant's upland.

ECOLOGICAL
RESPONSES: Department of Natural Resources - No objection provided all upland excavation is completed prior to seawall plug removal.

Game and Fresh Water Fish Commission - No objection.

Department of Pollution Control - No objection.

Staff recommends issuance of marina license for annual fee of $100, and Dredge Permit 253.123-1035 subject to the stipulation of the Department of Natural Resources.

ACTION OF THE TRUSTEES:

On motion by Mr. Christian, seconded by Mr. Conner and adopted without objection, the Board approved the application subject to the stipulation of the Department of Natural Resources.

-6-

DUVAL COUNTY - Marina License ML-93
           Dredge Permit 253.123-1043

APPLICANT: U. S. Naval Air Station, Jacksonville, Florida 32212

PROJECT: Construct additional mooring facilities at the existing marina in the St. Johns River abutting Section 23, Township 3 South, Range 26 East, Duval County. The enlarged facility will cover approximately 76,250 square feet of submerged land.

The original proposal included dredging the area to a depth of 8 feet below mean low water and removal of 9,000 cubic yards of material. Applicant has revised proposal in accordance with the recommendations of the Department of Natural Resources. All material will be placed on applicant's upland.

PAYMENT: Request waiver of all fees as the project is for a federal agency.

ECOLOGICAL
RESPONSES: Department of Natural Resources - No objections since the shallow productive bottoms within 60 feet of shoreline have been excluded from dredge area.

Game and Fresh Water Fish Commission - No objections.

Department of Pollution Control - No objection.

Staff recommends issuance of marina license and Dredge Permit 253.123-1043 for the project as revised, and waiver of all fees.

ACTION OF THE TRUSTEES:

Motion was made by Mr. Dickinson, seconded by Mr. Conner and adopted without objection, that the application be approved and fees waived.

-7-

ST. LUCIE COUNTY - Dredge Permit 253.123-980

APPLICANT: City of Fort Pierce
C. W. Temby, Director of Engineering
Post Office Box 3191, Fort Pierce, Florida 33450

PROJECT: To dredge an upland area and install a boat ramp and riprap bulkhead as a part of a wayside park to be located in the north side of the proposed New South Bridge adjacent to the Indian River.

LOCATION: Section 3, Township 35 South, Range 40 East, St. Lucie County

MATERIAL: All material removed will be placed on upland.

PAYMENT: None, since the material removed comes from the uplands.

ECOLOGICAL
RESPONSES: Department of Natural Resources - No objection

Game and Fresh Water Fish Commission - No objection

Department of Pollution Control - No objection

Staff recommends issuance of Dredge Permit 253.123-980.

ACTION OF THE TRUSTEES:

On motion made by Mr. Christian, seconded by Mr. Conner and adopted without objection, the application was approved.

-8-

VOLUSIA COUNTY - Marina License ML-109

APPLICANT: Daniel Amster & Ralph Antonelli
137 Sunrise Boulevard, Daytona Beach, Florida

PROJECT: Construction of docking facility covering 5,000 square feet of submerged land in the Halifax River

2-22-72

abutting Section 37, Township 15 South, Range 33
East, Volusia County. No dredging is required.

PAYMENT: $100 minimum annual fee for marina license.

ECOLOGICAL
RESPONSES: Department of Natural Resources - No objection

Game and Fresh Water Fish Commission - No objection

Department of Pollution Control - No objection

Staff recommends issuance of marina license for annual fee of
$100.

ACTION OF THE TRUSTEES:

On motion by Mr. Conner, seconded by Mr. Christian and adopted
without objection, the Trustees authorized issuance of marina
license for $100 annual fee.

-9-

DADE COUNTY - Fill Permit 253.124-216, Island View Hospital

At the request of the staff and concurrence of the applicant,
action was deferred. The Attorney General requested the
inclusion of a covenant that would run with the land which
would permit the land to be used only for hospital purposes
and applicant should furnish proof of financing prior to
actual filling.

Mr. Kuperberg said the City of Miami Beach made that clear in
its zoning action; but the state also should include protective
conditions and since the sale was determined to be in the
public interest, the use of that land should be for a public
interest function. Language to be incorporated in the fill
permit was being developed by staff legal counsel for consideration by the Trustees.

-10-

DADE COUNTY - Dredge and Fill Permit 253.124 and 253.123-212

APPLICANT: Robert Gould
             c/o Lee Crouch, Attorney
             1820 East Beach Boulevard, Hallandale, Florida 33009

The Board of Trustees authorized issuance of Dredge and Fill
Permit 253.124 and 253.123-212 on January 28, 1969. The permit
was accepted by the applicant on March 4, 1969.

This permit, which has not been exercised, will expire before the
U. S. Army Corps of Engineers' permit issues.

The applicant has tried with all due effort and diligence over the
past 3 years to obtain a Corps of Engineers' permit.

This application has been resubmitted to Washington and the
permit will be issued upon renewal of Trustees' permit.

The applicant indicated all work authorized can be completed within
six months after the U. S. Army Corps of Engineers permit is issued
and requests that the Board of Trustees permit be extended to
expire six months after issuance of the U. S. Corps of Engineers'
permit.

Staff recommends dredge and fill permits 253.124 and 253.123-212
be extended for one year or six months after issuance of the U. S.
Army Corps of Engineers' permit, whichever comes first.

2-22-72

ACTION OF THE TRUSTEES:

Mr. Dickinson made a motion that the applicant be granted a
year's time after issuance of the Corps of Engineers permit. He
pointed out that the applicant had complied with all state
requirements and waited three years for action at the Washington
level and the Corps of Engineers, that in 1969 Board members had
viewed the area and felt that the proposed improvement was
needed.

Mr. Conner seconded the motion that was adopted on a vote of
four to one, with Mr. Shevin voting in the negative.

-11-

DADE COUNTY - Dredge and Fill Permits 253.124 and 253.123-204

APPLICANT: Atlas Terminals of Florida, Inc.,
            c/o R. B. Gautier, Jr.
            200 Southeast First Street, Miami, Florida 33131

The Board of Trustees authorized the issuance of Dredge and Fill
Permits 253.124 and 253.123-204 on February 18, 1969. The
permit was accepted by the applicant on February 26, 1969.

This permit which has not been exercised will expire before the
U. S. Army Corps of Engineers permit issues.

The applicant has with all due effort and diligence over the
past three years attempted to obtain a Corps of Engineers
permit. This application has been resubmitted to Washington
and the permit will be issued upon renewal of the Trustees
permit.

The applicant indicated all work authorized can be completed
within six months after the U. S. Army Corps of Engineers permit
is issued and requests that the Board of Trustees permit be
extended to expire six months after issuance of the U. S. Army
Corps of Engineers permit.

Staff recommends dredge and fill permits 253.124 and 253.123-204
be extended for one year or six months after issuance of the
U. S. Army Corps of Engineers permit, whichever comes first.

ACTION OF THE TRUSTEES:

On this application Mr. Dickinson made a motion that the applicant be granted a year's time after issuance of the Corps of
Engineers permit. He pointed out that the applicant had complied with all state requirements and waited three years for
action at the Washington level and the Corps of Engineers, that in
1969 the Board members had viewed the area and felt that the
proposed improvement was needed.

Mr. Conner seconded the motion that was adopted on a vote of four
to one, with Mr. Shevin voting "No."

-12-

MARTIN COUNTY - Dredge Permit No. 253.123-1065

APPLICANT: Multicon Properties, Inc.,
            Suite 101, 3081 East Commercial Boulevard
            Ft. Lauderdale, Florida 33308

PROJECT: To dredge waterways in upland and the St. Lucie River
            to provide for navigation to upland housing develop-
            ment. Two channels in St. Lucie River will each be
            50 feet wide by 400 feet long and cut 5 feet below
            the mean low water.

LOCATION: Section 8, Township 38 South, Range 41 East, South Fork of the St. Lucie River, Martin County

MATERIAL: Estimated 3,250 cubic yards of sovereignty material will be removed and placed on owner's upland.

PAYMENT: $1,625 is offered for 3,250 cubic yards of material at 50¢ per cubic yard.

ECOLOGICAL
RESPONSES: Department of Natural Resources - No objection.

Game and Fresh Water Fish Commission - Applicant has agreed to stipulations contained in Commission's letter of February 14, 1972.

Department of Pollution Control - No objection.

OTHERS: Martin County Board of County Commissioners has no objection.

Staff recommends issuance of dredge permit 253.123-1065 to Multicon Properties, Inc., subject to stipulations contained in the Game and Fresh Water Fish Commission letter of February 14, 1972.

ACTION OF THE TRUSTEES:

On motion by Mr. Christian, seconded by Mr. Dickinson and adopted without objection, the recommendation was approved as the action of the Board.

-13-

PALM BEACH COUNTY - Dredge Permit 253.123-970

APPLICANT: Jupiter Inlet Commission
c/o Brockway, Owen & Anderson Engineers, Inc.
Post Office Box 3331, West Palm Beach, Florida

PROJECT: To perform biennial maintenance dredging of Jupiter Inlet Channel in Section 32, Township 40 South, Range 43 East, Palm Beach County.

The Area Planning Board of Palm Beach County has no objection.

The Board of County Commissioners has no objection.

MATERIAL: Spoil removed will be used for beach nourishment.

PAYMENT: Fees waived because the spoil material will be used for beach nourishment.

ECOLOGICAL
RESPONSES: Department of Natural Resources - No objection

Game and Fresh Water Fish Commission advises that this is a very important sea turtle nesting area and any spoiling should be done at a time when it would not destroy valuable sea turtle nests. (Mr. Frank Lund, Jupiter, Florida, advised that this area is a prime nesting ground for sea turtles. The nesting occurs from May through October.)

Department of Pollution Control - No objection

Staff recommends issuance of dredge permit 253.123-970 and waiver of fees as the project is in the public interest, provided all dredging and spoiling is to be done so as to minimize the impact on sea turtle nesting cycles.

2-22-72

ACTION OF THE TRUSTEES:

Mr. Kuperberg said the staff was satisfied that proper
precautions would be taken to protect the sea turtles.

Motion was made by Mr. Dickinson, seconded by Mr. Christian
and adopted without objection, that the application be approved
without fee with the provision recommended by the staff that
all dredging and spoiling shall be done so as to minimize the
impact on sea turtle nesting cycles.

-14-

PALM BEACH COUNTY - Dredge Permit 253.123-999

APPLICANT: Fine Builders, Inc., c/o Adair & Brady
            Post Office Box 967, Lake Worth, Florida 33460

PROJECT: To dredge an access channel approximately 1120
            feet long, 50 feet top cut, -5 feet deep, from
            the applicant's upland to the intracoastal waterway
            channel, located on Government Lot 5, Section 34,
            Township 44 South, Range 43 East, Palm Beach County.

            The Area Planning Board of Palm Beach County has no
            objection.

            The Board of County Commissioners of Palm Beach County
            has determined the project to be in the public interest
            and therefore has no objection.

MATERIAL: Approximately 6,500 cubic yards of material will be
            dredged and placed on upland.

PAYMENT: A check for $6,500 has been tendered for payment of
            sovereignty material.

ECOLOGICAL
RESPONSES: The Department of Natural Resources has no objection
            provided no fill material will be placed below the
            mean high water line.

            The Game and Fresh Water Fish Commission has no
            objection, provided all spoil is placed on upland.

            The Department of Pollution Control has no objection
            to the project as amended.

Staff recommends issuance of Permit No. 253.123-999 provided all
material is placed on diked uplands.

ACTION OF THE TRUSTEES:

On motion made by Mr. Christian, seconded by Mr. Conner and
adopted without objection, the permit was approved with the
provision recommended by the staff.

-15-

TRUST FUNDS - Purchase Lands Pursuant to Chapter 71-981.

Your Executive Director has been advised that the legislative
interpretation of Chapter 71-981 relating to the use of the
Internal Improvement Trust Fund, by the Senate Ways and Means
Committee, requires the following submission to the Committee:

    1. Description of the land to be acquired
    2. Purpose of acquisition
    3. Estimate of cost of such land
    4. Recommended order of priorities

The Committee has indicated an early submission of the information

2-22-72

if it is anticipated that lands are to be acquired by purchase during the fiscal year 1972-73.

Pursuant to the foregoing requirements, your Director recommends that the Trustees establish an order of priorities from among the following recommended purchases.

Palm Beach County natural resource lands	$ 95,000
10,000 Islands (60,000 acres)	6,000,000
Cape Romano (455 acres)	450,000
St. Joe Bay (985 acres) Beach frontage (25,000 feet)	2,500,000
Port Charlotte Beach frontage (98 acres; 7,700 feet)	1,150,000
Gilchrist County - Suwannee and Santa Fe River frontage (1,446 acres)	1,085,000
Glades County - Conservation Area (640 acres)	192,000
Sarasota County - Adjacent to Myakka State Park (6,260 acres)	2,973,500
Tomoka Marshes (2,500 to 3,000 acres)	(price information not complete)
North Indian River Lagoon (4,000 acres, 1,500 private)	(price information not complete)

Reacquisition of submerged lands as need and opportunity favors, statewide

ACTION OF THE TRUSTEES:

The Director had reviewed the priority list with Mr. Ney Landrum of the Division of Recreation and Parks, had the concurrence of Mr. Randolph Hodges, the matter had been on the agenda of a meeting of the Outdoor Recreation Advisory Committee, and the Trustees' staff recommended approval of the priorities and acquisition of the land to fulfill legislative directive but thought it unwise to disclose cost estimates and that the appropriation should be a lump sum from the trust fund.

Mr. Conner agreed that it would not be a good thing for the state to publish values as it would place the staff in an untenable position in negotiating purchases. Mr. Christian said the price estimates would hurt future bargaining positions and should not bind the Board. Mr. Dickinson added that the priority list should not prevent the Board from considering other desirable property that might become available.

The members discussed the directive from the Senate Ways and Means Committee that required listing of estimated costs, order of priorities, and other information. Mr. Wallace Henderson said the Committee proposed to include this item in a separate appropriations bill with details on the land to be acquired, but he had urged them not to put dollar amounts in the bill to give the Trustees the latitude to negotiate for the very best prices.

Motion was made by Mr. Dickinson, seconded by Mr. Conner, and carried, that the rules be waived and the list adopted but not to bind the Board as an exclusive list, as the Trustees felt they had the right to consider additional desirable parcels of land that might become available.

Mr. Dickinson suggested that the Chairman and members of the Senate Ways and Means Committee be furnished a list of the lands acquired under this program from the acquisition of Cape Florida in Dade County to the beach property recently purchased in Gulf County, as he thought the Cabinet had done a fine job in the proper use of public funds to acquire lands for all the citizens of Florida and future generations.

———————

Mr. Kuperberg distributed to the members the most recent staff progress report on the Florida Keys.

———————

2-22-72

At the beginning of the cabinet meeting on this date, Environment Tallahassee, represented by Miss Nancy Catlin, had asked the Florida Cabinet to show state-wide leadership action in several areas of concern to that organization including a request for immediate help to remove a fence from the Wakulla River below Wakulla Springs.

Mr. Tom Morrill was granted permission to appear on the Trustees' agenda with remarks concerning Wakulla Springs and Wakulla River. He said copies of his remarks would be furnished to the Cabinet. He posed several questions regarding the Trustees' jurisdiction over the springs and the river north of U. S. 319, whether Mr. Edward Ball was preserving nature at Wakulla Springs, the position of conservationists on the issue of the fence across the river, and why the Trustees had not taken to court a suit to have the fence removed and protect the spring and river from destruction of natural resources.

It was pointed out to Mr. Morrill by Mr. Christian and Mr. Dickinson that the matter had never been brought to Board for for action, that some of his statements were out of order, misleading and indicated lack of knowledge.

Mr. Kuperberg said the staff had been working diligently to resolve the problem in other ways than by going to court, that they were making significant progress and the staff would make a proper report and recommendations to the Board prior to the date set by the Court for action.

On motion duly adopted, the meeting was adjourned.

GOVERNOR — CHAIRMAN

ATTEST: _____
EXECUTIVE DIRECTOR

* * * * * *

Tallahassee, Florida
February 28, 1972

The State of Florida Board of Trustees of the Internal Improvement Trust Fund met this date in the auditorium of the Burns Building with the following members present:

Reubin O'D. Askew	Governor
Richard (Dick) Stone	Secretary of State
Robert L. Shevin	Attorney General
Fred O. Dickinson, Jr.	Comptroller
Thomas D. O'Malley	Treasurer
Floyd T. Christian	Commissioner of Education
Doyle Conner	Commissioner of Agriculture

| Joel Kuperberg | Executive Director |

-1-

The minutes of the February 15, 1972, meeting were approved.

2-28-72

RESOLUTION - On motion by Mr. Dickinson, seconded by Mr. Christian and adopted without objection, the rules were waived and the following resolution presented by Commissioner of Agriculture Doyle Conner was adopted:

> WHEREAS, it is the responsibility of the Governor and the Cabinet to carry out the clear legislative mandate for the protection of the environment of the State of Florida, and
>
> WHEREAS, it has come to the attention of the Governor and members of the Cabinet through legislative hearings and testimony that there exist undue delay and unnecessary costs in the processing of applications for dredge and fill permits, marinas, bulkheads, docks and coastal construction permits in the State of Florida, and
>
> WHEREAS, it is the intent of the Governor and Cabinet that all applications submitted by citizens of Florida receive due process consistent with the protection of the environment of our great state,
>
> NOW, THEREFORE, BE IT RESOLVED that the Governor and Cabinet, in a regular meeting assembled in Tallahassee, Florida, do direct the Florida Department of Natural Resources, the Trustees of the Internal Improvement Trust Fund, the Game and Fresh Water Fish Commission, and the Department of Pollution Control to submit a report to this body at its regular meeting on Tuesday, March 14, 1972, which report shall include a listing of all applications pending for six months or more, together with an explanation for such delay.

-2-

BREVARD COUNTY - Land Sale Deferment
             File No. 2428-05-253.12

For the reason that a proposed land sale to Donald R. Bang was advertised to be considered on February 29, the Trustees deferred action until the next meeting after that date, March 7.

-3-

DUVAL COUNTY - Land Sale Deferment
             File No. 2422-16-253.12

For the reason that the proposed land sale to Alvin M. Coplan was advertised to be considered on February 29, the Trustees deferred action until the next meeting after that date, March 7.

-4-

MARION COUNTY - Murphy Act Land Sale

APPLICANT: Business Sales, Inc., a Florida corporation,
            Represented by John F. Nicholson, Clerk of
            Marion County Circuit Court, Ocala, Florida,

makes application under Section 197.355, Florida Statutes "Hardship Act", Chapter 28317, Acts of 1953), to purchase the undivided 1/2 interest of the state in the SE 1/4 of NE 1/4 of Section 9, Township 15 South, Range 21 East, containing 40 acres in Marion County.

The 1/2 interest in this parcel was acquired by the state under the Murphy Act, Chapter 18296, Acts of 1937, by Tax Sale Certificate No. 1049 of June 5, 1922. The certificate in the amount of $2.98 apparently was overlooked when other certificates were redeemed in 1936 by H. A. Fausett.

The applicant who is the present record owner claims title
through the heirs of H. A. Fausett, deceased, the record owner
on June 9, 1939. According to Section 197.355, F. S., the Board
may convey the interest of the state to the owner in 1939 or
those claiming by, through or under that owner, for such consideration as the Board shall deem equitable and proper without
advertisement and public sale.

The amount has been deposited with the Clerk of the Circuit Court
equal to the unpaid state and county taxes, plus interest on
the tax certificate.

The applicant offers $200 for the state's undivided 1/2 interest,
which conforms to the policy to accept not less than $10 per
acre when the interest of the state is conveyed under Section
197.355, Florida Statutes.

This application appears to qualify under the so-called
"Hardship Act."

Recommend conveying the interest of the State of Florida in
this parcel of land to Business Sales, Inc., for $200.

ACTION OF THE TRUSTEES:

Motion was made by Mr. Stone, seconded by Mr. Dickinson and
carried unanimously, that the application be approved and the
deed issued to Business Sales, Inc., for $200.

-5A-

SANTA ROSA AND ESCAMBIA COUNTIES - Oil and Gas Royalty Division
Orders, Jay Field

On September 1, 1970, the Trustees issued Oil and Gas Drilling
Lease No. 2464 covering a 205-acre portion of the Escambia
River to Marshall R. Young Co. The lease provides for a royalty
of 1/8 and prohibits drilling of wells on any submerged land.
On July 6, 1971, the lease was divided into three parcels and
31.80 acres assigned to Humble Oil and Refining Co., and 15.00
acres to Marshall R. Young, et. al.

L L & E has drilled and completed two producing oil and gas
wells identified as Unit 30-1 and Unit 31-1. Each drilling
unit contains 176 acres located in Section 31, Township 6 North,
Range 29 West (Unit 30-1) and Section 30, Township 6 North, Range
29 West (Unit 30-1). A portion of the Escambia River under Lease
No. 2464 is within each drilling unit. The two wells were not
drilled in the river, but that portion of the river in each of
these two drilling units will earn royalty from each well, ful-
filling the drilling requirements contained in the lease.

L L & E has submitted two oil, gas and sulphur division orders
which set forth the division of interest of the Trustees under
Lease No. 2464 in each producing well, as follows:

Unit 30-1 well - $\frac{18.06 \text{ acres}}{176.00 \text{ acres}}$ of 1/8 or .0128267 Royalty Interest

Unit 31-1 well - $\frac{23.15 \text{ acres}}{176.00 \text{ acres}}$ of 1.8 or .0164417 Royalty Interest

The two orders have been reviewed and approved by staff legal
counsel and correctly set forth the number of acres contained in
the river under lease within each drilling unit.

It is recommended that the executive director be authorized to
execute each division order on behalf of the Trustees and further
be granted the authority to execute future division orders when
received, after they are reviewed by the staff and found to be in
order.

ACTION OF THE TRUSTEES:

Motion was made by Mr. Shevin, seconded by Mr. Conner and carried
unanimously, that the Executive Director be authorized to
execute the two division orders and others in the future on
behalf of the Trustees.

-5B-

Representatives of Louisiana Land and Exploration Company, New
Orleans, expect to attend to present to the Board of Trustees
the first royalty check from two producing oil and gas wells
under a state oil and gas drilling lease in the Jay Field.

SANTA ROSA AND ESCAMBIA COUNTIES - Lease No. 2464 Royalty

Mr. Kuperberg said that royalty to the state from the Jay field
was an historic first and Mr. Lawrence Davis and others representing
Louisiana Land and Exploration Company had expected to attend
the meeting to present to the Trustees the first royalty check
from two producing oil and gas wells under State Oil and Gas
Drilling Lease No. 2464.

Travel difficulties having prevented Mr. Davis' attendance, Mr.
James T. Williams had been asked to present the check for
$5,405.13 representing the Board's share of royalties for oil
and gas recovered during the period from the last of November
1971 through January 1972, from two wells identified as Unit
30-1 and Unit 31-1 under Lease No. 2464. Mr. Williams said
that Louisiana Land and Exploration Company anticipated six
producing wells by the end of this year, in which the Trustees
had an interest and would receive royalties.

The Trustees received the royalty check.

In response to an inquiry, Mr. Kuperberg advised the Board that
the staff was bonded to handle funds to a limit of liability of
$25,000 per person, with all employees covered.

-6-

COLLIER COUNTY - Construction Permit, Marina License ML-114

APPLICANT: Marco Towers, Inc.
            c/o Bruce Green & Associates, Inc.
            365 Fifth Avenue South, Naples, Florida

PROJECT: Construct pier facilities covering 5,000 square feet
            of submerged land in Big Marco Pass abutting Section
            6, Township 52 South, Range 26 East, Collier County.
            No dredging is required.

PAYMENT: $100 minimum annual fee for marina license.

ECOLOGICAL
RESPONSES: Department of Natural Resources - No objection.

            Game and Fresh Water Fish Commission - No objection.

            Department of Pollution Control - No objection.

Staff recommends issuance of construction permit and marina
license for annual fee of $100.

ACTION OF THE TRUSTEES:

Motion was made by Mr. Stone, seconded by Mr. Christian and
Mr. Dickinson, carried unanimously, that the application for
construction permit and marina license be approved.

2-28-72

-7-

FRANKLIN COUNTY - Dredge Permit 253.123-195

APPLICANT: N. R. Robinson, Town Motel and Marina
Box 585, Carrabelle, Florida

PROJECT: One-year extension of Permit 253.123-195 to complete
construction. Delay resulted from the Corps of Engineers
and State Highway Department decision to realign the
channel. Mr. Robinson is asking for this extension
so the work can be accomplished in conjunction with
the state highway channel realignment.

MATERIAL: At the time the permit was issued in February 1969,
there was no requirement for payment of material
removed from navigation projects nor was there a
calculation of the quantity of material to be
removed.

PAYMENT: Fees tendered for permit 253.123-195

ECOLOGICAL
RESPONSES: Department of Natural Resources - No adverse comments.

Game and Fresh Water Fish Commission - No objection.

Department of Pollution Control - No objection.

Staff recommends one-year extension of Permit 253.123-195.

ACTION OF THE TRUSTEES:

On motion by Mr. Stone, seconded by Mr. Dickinson and adopted
without objection, the one-year extension of Permit 253.123-195
was approved.

-8-

FRANKLIN COUNTY - Permit for Planting Marsh Grasses.

APPLICANT: Florida Agricultural and Mechanical University
c/o Dr. Charles L. Coultas, School of Agriculture
Tallahassee, Florida

PROJECT: Experimental plantings of three marsh plant species,
Spartina Alterniflora, Juncus Roemerianus and
Distichlis Spicata, on three of a group of four recently
created spoil islands.

LOCATION: Four spoil islands in Ochlockonee Bay easterly of the
channel marked by markers 33, 35 and 37 and westerly
of U. S. Highway 98 Bridge, in Section 1, Township 6
South, Range 2 West, Franklin County.

ECOLOGICAL
RESPONSES: Department of Natural Resources - No objection.

Game and Fresh Water Fish Commission - No objection.

Department of Pollution Control - No objection.

Staff requests authority to issue a permit for a five-year term
for planting marsh grasses.

ACTION OF THE TRUSTEES:

Mr. Kuperberg informed the Board that no payment was involved,
and requested that the record so indicate. The staff
strongly urged approval of the project as being very important
research.

Governor Askew said it was a commendable experiment.

Motion was made by Mr. Stone, seconded by Mr. Dickinson, and carried unanimously, that the application be approved as amended to show no payment was involved in the marsh grass planting permit.

-9-

LEE COUNTY - Marina License ML-88 and Construction Permit

APPLICANT: Department of the Interior
Bureau of Sport Fisheries and Wildlife
Atlanta, Georgia

PROJECT: Construction of a fishing pier covering 2,640 square
feet of submerged land in San Carlos Bay at Point
Ybel, Lee County. No dredging is required.

PAYMENT: Requests waiver of annual fee for marina license.

ECOLOGICAL
RESPONSES: Department of Natural Resources - No objection.

Game and Fresh Water Fish Commission - No objection.

Department of Pollution Control - No objection.

Staff recommends issuance of construction permit and marina license and waiver of annual fee.

ACTION OF THE TRUSTEES:

Motion was made by Mr. Stone, seconded by Mr. Dickinson and carried unanimously, that the construction permit and marina license be approved and annual fee waived for building the fishing pier at "Ding" Darling Wildlife Refuge headquarters on Sanibel Island.

-10-

NASSAU COUNTY - Dredge Permit 253.123-888

APPLICANT: E. L. Dell, Dell Industries
1000 Garlington Avenue, Waycross, Georgia

PROJECT: To deepen an existing access channel to -8 feet
mean low water with a bottom width of 50 feet,
and to enlarge and seawall an existing upland
boat basin.

LOCATION: Section 46, Township 2 North, Range 28 East, Nassau
County.

MATERIAL: Approximately 36,000 cubic yards of material to be
removed from upland channel and boat basin and placed
on diked upland spoil sites.

PAYMENT: None. All material to be removed from private property.

ECOLOGICAL
RESPONSES: Department of Natural Resources - No objection provided
spoil is placed on diked upland.

Game and Fresh Water Fish Commission - No objection
provided spoil area is adequately diked and diapers
are used to control turbidity.

Department of Pollution Control - No objection to project.

Staff recommends issuance of Dredge Permit 253.123-888 subject to stipulations of the environmental agencies.

2-28-72

ACTION OF THE TRUSTEES:

Mr. Kuperberg having advised the members that an application had been filed and everything was now in order, the application was approved as recommended on the motion of Mr. Stone, seconded by Mr. O'Malley and carried without objection, subject to the stipulations of the environmental agencies.

-11-

BROWARD COUNTY - Corrective Deed
            File No. 2441-06-253.42

APPLICANT: City of Ft. Lauderdale, by City Engineer
            Post Office Drawer 1181
            Ft. Lauderdale, Florida 33302

LOCATION: Sovereignty land in New River Sound in the East half
            of Section 12, Township 50 South, Range 42 East, City
            of Ft. Lauderdale, Broward County.

PROPOSAL: The City of Ft. Lauderdale would like a corrective
            deed to the parcel of land which is presently occupied
            by its Bahia Mar marina.

PAYMENT: None.

STAFF REMARKS: The Trustees, by virtue of authority of Chapter
12427, Laws of Florida 1927, conveyed two parcels of sovereignty water bottoms in New River Sound embracing a total
of 44.6 acres to the City of Ft. Lauderdale by Deed No. 18397
dated March 31, 1937.

The city in 1948, prior to enactment of the bulkhead act, received
a Department of the Army permit to construct a marina complex in
the area now known as Bahia Mar. The Trustees' staff had protested the original request, the application was revised and the
staff withdrew its objections.

In 1962, the Trustees' staff filed with the Department of Army
Corps of Engineers a waiver of objection to an application
by the city for a proposed fill and bulkhead at Bahia Mar. The
information furnished to the staff identified the work area as
being in city ownership.

A recent title search for the City of Ft. Lauderdale revealed
state ownership of a strip of land between the land conveyed by
the Trustees' deed in 1937 and the uplands owned by the city.

Due to the vague boundaries in the Trustees' deed and through
oversight, the city has occupied 18.1 acres of sovereignty
land in connection with a city-owned marina complex.

Staff requests authority to issue corrective deed.

ACTION OF THE TRUSTEES:

There had been an error in the description in the 1937 conveyance
that would be corrected by the instrument.

On motion by Mr. Dickinson, seconded by Mr. Stone and Mr. O'Malley
and adopted unanimously, the Trustees authorized issuance of the
corrective deed.

At the request of the Attorney General, there is submitted for
the Trustees' consideration a resolution

> That the Trustees of the Internal Improvement Trust
> Fund will not consider any applications relating to
> dredging or filling within the Consolidated City of
> Jacksonville and Duval County, except those involving
> emergency maintenance, until such time as the City of
> Jacksonville and Duval County has reviewed all bulkhead
> lines and established them at the mean high water line
> except where the locations of lines farther offshore can
> be fully justified as being in the public interest, in
> accordance with recommendations of the Interagency
> Committee on Submerged Land Management which recommen-
> dations and request were transmitted to all counties
> and municipalities in 1968.

Staff recommends adoption of the resolution requested by the
Attorney General.

ACTION OF THE TRUSTEES:

The Consolidated City of Jacksonville and Duval County, and the
Jacksonville Port Authority were represented at the meeting.
Mr. Lynwood Roberts, President of the Council of the Consolidated
City and County said they understood and concurred with the
objective of the Attorney General to obtain correction of
deficiencies in bulkhead lines noted in the 1968 report of the
Interagency Advisory Committee on Submerged Land Management;
and the council had enacted a resolution to hold public hearing,
review and consider, as rapidly as possible, the relocation of
the relatively small area of deficiences noted in the report
being about four miles of bulkhead lines whereas there were
more than 5,000 miles of waterfront on navigable waterways in
Duval County. He urged the Trustees not to impose a moratorium
on applications but permit them to continue to operate on a
voluntary basis as they proceed with public hearings, engineering
reports and whatever details are necessary.

Attorney General Shevin noted that the council's resolution was
a start but after three and a half years he hoped for a stronger
resolution than to merely consider the relocation of bulkhead
lines and to review the ramifications of establishing such lines
at the mean high water line. He was concerned and thought it
incumbent upon the Board to set a hard and firm policy, but he did
not object to the Governor's suggestion that the Board delay
consideration of the moratorium for a period of 90 days to allow
time for the local government to accomplish what would otherwise
be required in the moratorium.

Mr. Shevin made a motion that consideration of the moratorium
be withdrawn from the agenda for a temporary period of 90 days
during which time it was assumed and hoped that the council
would establish the bulkhead lines pursuant to the Interagency
report of some three and one-half years ago.

Mr. Dickinson and Mr. Christian seconded the motion that carried
unanimously.

Governor Askew said it should be pointed out that in the
absence of action to relocate the bulkhead lines they might
anticipate imposition of such a moratorium, but since the
local government now had 90 days he did not see any problem
in accomplishing it without the restriction that such a
moratorium would impose.

2-28-72

554

-13-

DADE COUNTY - Permit No. 253.124(8)-267

APPLICANT: Jose Milton
1400 Southwest 27 Avenue, Miami, Florida

PROJECT: The City of Miami issued a permit to construct a
seawall 229.94 feet long and to reclaim a triangular
strip of land 25 feet by 180 feet lost by artificially
induced erosion. This land was originally filled under
Permit No. 1216.

LOCATION: Biscayne Bay, Section 19, Township 53 South, Range
42 East, Dade County.

MATERIAL: Needed for backfill will be hauled in.

PAYMENT: None. Sovereignty land not involved.

ECOLOGICAL
RESPONSES: The Department of Natural Resources reports that
completion of the project should not have significant
effects on marine biological resources.

The Department of Pollution Control has certified the
project.

The Staff recommends issuance of Permit No. 253.124(8)-267 to
construct a seawall and backfill.

ACTION OF THE TRUSTEES:.

Motion was made by Mr. Christian, seconded by Mr. Conner and
adopted without objection, that the permit application be
approved.

-14-

MONROE COUNTY - Aquaculture Lease

Wometco Enterprises, Inc.
c/o Charles Francis, Director of Subsidiary Services
Rickenbacker Causeway, Miami, Florida

Submitted the following bid for an aquaculture lease over 1.87
acres of sovereignty land in Section 19, Township 65 South, Range
34 East, Monroe County:

Annual rental 1 through 5 years $435.60 per acre
Annual rental 6 through 10 years   871.20 per acre

Plus a royalty of 7 1/2% on gross income, such income
limited to the sale of porpoises (Tursiops truncatus)
commencing after the first 1 1/2 years of operation,

and has offered $1,475.57 as payment for use of the land by
its predecessors in title.

Staff recommends issuance of aquaculture lease to Wometco
Enterprises, Inc., and acceptance of $1,475.57 as payment for
prior use of land.

ACTION OF THE TRUSTEES:

Motion was made by Mr. Dickinson, seconded by Mr. Stone and
carried without objection, that the staff recommendation be
accepted as the action of the Board.

On motion duly adopted, the meeting was adjourned.

ATTEST: _____
EXECUTIVE DIRECTOR

GOVERNOR   CHAIRMAN

*   *   *   *   *

Tallahassee, Florida
March 7, 1972

The State of Florida Board of Trustees of the Internal Improvement Trust Fund met on this date in the auditorium of the Burns Building with the following members present:

Reubin O'D. Askew	Governor
Richard (Dick) Stone	Secretary of State
Robert L. Shevin	Attorney General
Fred O. Dickinson, Jr.	Comptroller
Thomas D. O'Malley	Treasurer
Floyd T. Christian	Commissioner of Education
Doyle Conner	Commissioner of Agriculture
Joel Kuperberg	Executive Director

Announcement was made that there would be no cabinet meeting on March 14, Election Day, and the next meeting would be on March 21, 1972.

-1-

The minutes of the meeting on February 22, 1972, were approved as submitted.

-2-

HENDRY COUNTY - Advertise Oil and Gas Lease

APPLICANT: Sun Oil Company
                Post Office Box 2880, Dallas, Texas

REQUEST: Advertise for oil and gas drilling lease

LOCATION: All of Sections 15, 16, 17, 19, 21, N 1/2 of 27 and N 1/2 of 29, Township 46 South, Range 32 East, 3,840 surface acres (1,920 net mineral acres) in Hendry County.

INTEREST
OF STATE: Board of Education holds an undivided one-half interest in Section 16 and Trustees hold an undivided one-half interest in the remainder of the land.

These privately-owned lands lie on the northerly boundary of the Big Cypress Watershed Area. The Advisory Committee on Oil Exploration in the Big Cypress reviewed this request, inspected the lands on January 25, 1972, and advised that the lands are crossed by State Roads 833 and 846 and are sandy, dry uplands planted in grass and used for grazing. The Committee found no environmental reason why the lands should not be leased.

Proceeds from this lease will go to the Internal Improvement Trust Fund except for Section 16, which will go to the School Fund.

3-7-72

This request has been reviewed by the Director of Interior Resources, Department of Natural Resources, who concurred in the following recommendation.

Recommend advertising for sealed bids for lease with annual rental of $1 per net mineral acre, 1/8 royalty, five-year primary term, $50,000 surety bond and at least one test well every 2 1/2 years drilled to 6,000 feet or to the Roberts Zone of the Sunniland Formation or other anticipated oil horizons, whichever is deeper.

ACTION OF THE TRUSTEES:

On motion by Mr. Christian, seconded by Mr. Conner and adopted unanimously, the Board authorized the lease advertised for sealed bids as recommended by the staff.

-3-

OKALOOSA AND SANTA ROSA COUNTIES - Oil Lease Assignments

APPLICANT: Penzoil United, Inc.
             Post Office Box 1407, Shreveport, Louisiana

REQUEST: Approval to assign an undivided 50% interest in
             five concurring State oil and gas leases issued
             by Florida Board of Forestry, each dated March 24,
             1969, to Champlin Petroleum Company, Post Office
             Box 9365, Fort Worth, Texas.

LOCATION: Township 6 North, Range 24 West: Section 30

             Township 6 North, Range 25 West: Sections 25, 26,
             27, 29, 30, 32, 33, 34, and 35

             Township 5 North, Range 24 West: Sections 5, 6, 7,
             8, 17, 18 and 32

             Township 5 North, Range 25 West: Section 2, 3, 4,
             5, 6, 7, 10, 11, 12, 13, 14, 15, 16, 17, 18, 19, 20,
             21, 22, 23, 24, 25, 26, 27, 28 and 29

Lease Term: Five years from March 24, 1969.

The Division of Forestry, Department of Agriculture and Consumer Services, reviewed and approved the assignment.

Executed instruments of assignment have been filed and approved as to form by the Trustees' legal staff.

Recommend approval and consent to assign.

ACTION OF THE TRUSTEES:

On motion by Mr. O'Malley, seconded by Mr. Conner and adopted unanimously, the Board approved and consented to the assignment.

-4-

SARASOTA COUNTY - Lease Amendment
                File No. 23588(1344-58)

APPLICANT: William C. Strode, City Attorney
             City of Sarasota
             Post Office Box 1058, Sarasota, Florida 33578

Requests approval of an amendment to a lease agreement between the City of Sarasota and Jack Graham, Inc., a Florida Corporation.

The amendment would extend the term of the original lease agreement from thirty years to forty-four years and grant the necessary rights and privileges unto tenant in that area designated as "marina operations area" on schedule "B", plus an additional

200 feet northwesterly along the bulkhead toward Ringling Boulevard so as to allow said tenant to fully implement uses for which this lease is made.

Staff recommends approval of the amendment to the lease with respect to the time extension. Staff further recommends that lessee make application for a marina license for the additional area sought.

ACTION OF THE TRUSTEES:

On motion by Mr. Dickinson, seconded by Mr. Christian and adopted unanimously, the staff recommendation was approved as the action of the Board.

-5-

MANATEE COUNTY - File No. 2051-41-253.12

APPLICANT: City of Bradenton
            Post Office Drawer 730, Bradenton, Florida

The Board of Trustees in meeting on October 12, 1971, approved the "blue ribbon" ad hoc committee, appointed to act in an advisory capacity to the city for the development of the 54-acre parcel of land dedicated to the city. A time table for the development was to be submitted within 180 days.

In December there was a general election and some of the officials involved in this project were not reelected. The "blue ribbon" ad hoc committee resigned en masse effective January 4, 1972, the date the newly elected officials took office.

The "blue ribbon" ad hoc committee recommended that the current mayor and city council request a sixty-day extension of time to produce and submit a plan of development.

Staff recommends that the sixty-day extension of time be granted.

ACTION OF THE TRUSTEES:

Motion was made by Mr. O'Malley, seconded by Mr. Shevin and Mr. Conner, and adopted unanimously, that the request for sixty-day time extension be granted.

-6-

PALM BEACH COUNTY - Sewage Lift Station Easement

The City of West Palm Beach by Resolution No. 164-71 dated November 29, 1971, requested an easement for construction and installation of a sanitary sewage lift station on property of the University of Florida College of Engineering in the NE 1/4 of Section 6, Township 43 South, Range 43 East, Palm Beach County.

The lift station will service this University facility and will occupy an area of 400 square feet in the southwest corner of the property. The Facilities Committee of the Board of Regents has reviewed and approved the granting of the easement.

Recommend issuance of the easement for the construction, operation and maintenance of a lift station only.

ACTION OF THE TRUSTEES:

Motion was made by Mr. Christian, seconded by Mr. Conner and adopted unanimously, authorizing issuance of the easement for construction, operation and maintenance of a lift station only.

3-7-72

-7-

OKALOOSA COUNTY - Marina License ML-118
                    and Construction Permit, 253.03, F. S.

APPLICANT: American Marine Repair Facility
             c/o A. G. Rowley
             330 Race Track Road, Fort Walton Beach, Florida
                                                    4,580   Correc
PROJECT: Construct a docking facility covering ~~2,320~~ square   April 4,
             feet of submerged land in Joe's Bayou abutting
             Township 2 South, Range 23 West, Okaloosa County.
             No dredging is required.

PAYMENT: $100 minimum annual fee for marina license.

ECOLOGICAL
RESPONSES: Department of Natural Resources - No objection.

             Game and Fresh Water Fish Commission - No objection.

             Department of Pollution Control - No objection.

Staff recommends issuance of construction permit and marina
license for annual fee of $100.

ACTION OF THE TRUSTEES:

Motion was made by Mr. O'Malley, seconded by Mr. Stone and
carried unanimously, to approve the construction permit and
marina license as recommended.

———————————

-8-

JACKSON COUNTY - Road Easement

The Department of Transportation requests an easement containing
11.75 acres across a parcel of land in Section 17, Township 4
North, Range 10 West for road right of way purposes for the
construction and maintenance of State Road 8 (I-10), and a
0.40-acre parcel in Section 7, Township 4 North, Range 10 West,
for road right of way purposes in connection with State Road
276 in Jackson County.

The two parcels are portions of the land in use by the Department
of Health and Rehabilitative Services and a part of the Arthur
G. Dozier School for Boys.

This request has been reviewed and approved by the Department
of Health and Rehabilitative Services and the Division of Youth
Services and the Division of Corrections.

Recommend issuance of the easement requested for public highway
purposes only.

ACTION OF THE TRUSTEES:

Motion was made by Mr. Conner, seconded by Mr. O'Malley and
carried unanimously, to approve the easement for public highway
purposes only.

———————————

-9-

PALM BEACH COUNTY - The Board of County Commissioners of
Palm Beach County by Resolution No. R-71-453, dated November 16,
1971, requested a long-term lease covering 56.2 acres of reclaimed
Lake Okeechobee bottom land outside the Herbert Hoover Dike in
Section 35, Township 43 South, Range 35 East and Section 2,
Township 44 South, Range 35 East, Palm Beach County for develop-
ment and maintenance as a public recreational center named
John H. Stretch Park.

This land is being deeded to the State by Palm Beach County in

return for a 99-year lease back to the county in order to be
eligible for assistance from the 15% portion of the Land
Acquisition Trust Fund in the amount of $50,000. This money
will be utilized by the county in constructing outdoor recreational facilities on the parcel.

The Department of Natural Resources on October 26, 1971, authorized $50,000 grant to Palm Beach County following conveyance
of title back to the Trustees and lease back to the county.
Immediate and long range development plans have been filed and
approved by the Division of Recreation and Parks which division,
under the terms of the proposed lease, will inspect the land
and development to insure that terms of the lease are carried out.

Recommend leasing the 56.2-acre parcel to Palm Beach County for
public outdoor recreation, park, conservation and related purposes for a period of 99 years.

ACTION OF THE TRUSTEES:

On motion by Mr. Christian, seconded by Mr. Conner and adopted
without objection, the Trustees granted the request of Palm
Beach County to lease the parcel for public outdoor recreation,
park, conservation and related purposes for 99 years.

-10-

BAY COUNTY - Permit 253.123-833

APPLICANT: Panama City Port Authority
            Post Office Box 388, Panama City, Florida

PROJECT: Dredging to provide sufficient depth to allow ocean
            vessels to take on bulk cargo adjacent to new bulk-
            head wall. New bulkhead wall proposed 3 feet land-
            ward of existing bulkhead line.

LOCATION: Section 34, Township 3 South, Range 15 West, St.
            Andrews Bay at Panama City.

MATERIAL: Propose to dredge 30,000 cubic yards of material and
            deposit material on adequately diked upland.

PAYMENT: Request waiver of payment for material to be removed.
            Applicant has agreed to convey to the Board of
            Trustees by quitclaim deed the offshore area
            previously dedicated as a spoil disposal site.

ECOLOGICAL
RESPONSES: Department of Natural Resources - No objection
            provided spoil area "A" is carefully diked to
            limit siltation.

            Game and Fresh Water Fish Commission - No objection.

            Department of Pollution Control - No objection.

Staff recommends issuance of Dredge Permit 253.123-1005 and
waiver of payment for material because the project is in the
public interest.

ACTION OF THE TRUSTEES:

Motion was made by Mr. O'Malley, seconded by Mr. Conner and
adopted unanimously, that the dredge permit be issued without
payment for the material for the public interest project.

3-7-72

-11-

BREVARD COUNTY - State Construction Permit and
                 Marina License ML-121

APPLICANT: Division of Marine Resources
             Department of Natural Resources
             Tallahassee, Florida

PROJECT: Constructon of pier covering 800 square feet of
             sovereignty land in the Indian River abutting
             Section 28, Township 29 South, Range 38 East,
             Brevard County. No dredging is required.

PAYMENT: Waiver of minimum annual fee for marina license,
             as the facility is for a public agency.

ECOLOGICAL
RESPONSES: Department of Natural Resources - No objection.

             Game and Fresh Water Fish Commission - No objection.

             Department of Pollution Control - No objection.

Staff recommends issuance of marina license and waiver of annual
fee.

ACTION OF THE TRUSTEES:

Motion was made by Mr. Christian, seconded by Mr. O'Malley and
adopted unanimously, that the application be approved and the
annual fee waived in the public interest.

-12-

DADE COUNTY - Fill Permit 253.124-247

APPLICANT: Adler-Donner Associates
             4001 South Ocean Drive, Hollywood, Florida

PROJECT: Dade County issued a permit to construct a 600-foot
             long seawall along the East right-of-way line of the
             existing land-cut segment of the Intracoastal
             Waterway, to connect with seawalls to the north and
             south. This upland has eroded due to boat traffic
             using the Intracoastal Waterway. The material to
             backfill would be hauled in from upland sources.

LOCATION: Land-cut segment of the Intracoastal Waterway in
             Section 2, Township 52 South, Range 42 East, Dade
             County.

MATERIAL: From upland sources.

PAYMENT: None. Sovereignty lands not involved.

ECOLOGICAL
RESPONSES: The Department of Natural Resources reported that the
             bottoms consist of sand and coral rock. Although
             not vegetated, the shallow shoreline area is
             important to marine productivity. The proposed
             project would have only limited adverse effects on
             marine productivity if plans were revised to more
             closely follow the shoreline to conserve some of
             the shallow bottoms.

             The Game and Fresh Water Fish Commission reports
             that this is one of the last remaining sections of
             natural shoreline in North Dumfoundling Bay and as
             such provides a productive exception to neighboring
             areas. To minimize biological damage it recommends
             that the seawall be constructed along the existing
             high water line.

The Department of Pollution Control has no objection
to the project; recommends riprap be placed on the
water side of the seawall.

Staff recommends issuance of Permit No. 253.124-247 provided riprap
is placed on the water side of the seawall.

ACTION OF THE TRUSTEES:

Motion was made by Mr. Christian, seconded by Mr. O'Malley and
Mr. Conner, carried unanimously, that the permit be approved
with the stipulations recommended by the environmental agencies
and staff.

-13-

PUTNAM COUNTY - Permit No. 253.123-795

APPLICANT: Nancy Pearce Johnson
             Post Office Box 416, East Palatka, Florida

PROJECT: To connect an upland boat canal with the St. Johns
            River by draglining a channel 30 feet long, 35 feet
            wide (top cut), by 5 feet deep. Also to reconstruct a
            deteriorated retaining wall landward of the mean
            high water line.

LOCATION: Section 6, Township 10 South, Range 27 East, Putnam
            County.

MATERIAL: 125 cubic yards of material to be removed from
            sovereignty land.

PAYMENT: $62.50 has been tendered as payment at standard yardage
            rate of 50¢ per cubic yard.

ECOLOGICAL
RESPONSES: Department of Natural Resources - The Game and Fresh
            Water Fish Commission made the biological report.

            The Game and Fresh Water Fish Commission - No objec-
            tion provided spoil is placed on upland.

            The Department of Pollution Control - No objection.

OTHERS: Approved by the Board of County Commissioners on
            February 23, 1971.

Staff recommends issuance of Dredge Permit No. 253.123-795
provided all material is placed behind dikes on the upland.

ACTION OF THE TRUSTEES:

Motion was made by Mr. O'Malley, seconded by Mr. Stone and
carried unanimously, that the dredge permit be issued subject
to the provision that all material be placed behind dikes on
the upland.

-14-

DADE, BROWARD AND PALM BEACH COUNTIES

APPLICANT: Florida Power and Light Company
           Post Office Box 1900, Miami, Florida

On November 30, 1971, the Trustees authorized issuance of 5
easements to Florida Power and Light Company for rights of way
in connection with its cross-state transmission line from
Turkey Point to Ft. Myers. The consideration offered and accepted
by the Trustees for these easements totals $238,817.72, of which
$4,200 will go the School Fund.

Florida Power and Light has offered to deed to the Trustees, as part of the consideration for the easements, 150 acres of unimproved land in Section 9, Township 53 South, Range 39 East, Dade County. The tract, located 10 miles west of Miami in the vicinity of several tracts of state-owned land, has a current appraised value of $120,000.

Recommend acceptance of the land offered as part of the consideration for the five easements.

ACTION OF THE TRUSTEES:

On motion by Mr. O'Malley, seconded by Mr. Stone and carried unanimously, the Trustees agreed to accept the land offered as part of the consideration for the five easements.

On motion by Mr. Christian, seconded by Mr. O'Malley and adopted without objection, the rules were waived to allow consideration of all the following items that were addenda to the original printed agenda.

-15-

COLLIER COUNTY - Construction Permit No. 253.03(7)320

APPLICANT: Key Island, Inc.
             c/o Tri-County Engineering, Inc.
             Post Office Box 578, Naples, Florida 33940

PROJECT: To rebuild an existing groin on the south side of
             Gordon Pass.

LOCATION: Section 28, Township 50 South, Range 25 East,
             Collier County.

MATERIAL: None. All material will be hauled in.

PAYMENT: None. No sovereignty lands involved.

ECOLOGICAL
RESPONSES: Department of Natural Resources - No objection.

             Game and Fresh Water Fish Commission - No objection.

             Department of Pollution Control - No objection.

OTHERS: Bureau of Beaches and Shores, Department of Natural
             Resources, cannot issue permit, since all work will
             be done on land in private ownership.

Staff recommends issuance of construction permit 253.03(7)320.

ACTION OF THE TRUSTEES:

Mr. Kuperberg explained that the application involved installing additional rock on top of an existing groin to bring it above the high water level.

On motion by Mr. O'Malley, seconded by Mr. Stone and adopted without objection, the application was approved.

-16-

DUVAL COUNTY - Construction and Marina License, ML-111

APPLICANT: Jacksonville Shipyards, Inc.
             Post Office Box 2347, Jacksonville, Florida

PROJECT: To enlarge existing facility by constructing
             a new pier, and to extend two existing piers. Two
             dry docks will be moored in this area. The piers

and dry dock will preempt 226,773 square feet of
water surface. Applicant has applied for a marina
license.

LOCATION: St. Johns River in Sections 13 and 38, Township 2
South, Range 26 East, Duval County.

MATERIAL: No dredging involved.

PAYMENT: The annual fee for the marina license will be
$4,535.46.

ECOLOGICAL
RESPONSES: Department of Natural Resources - No objection.

Department of Pollution Control - No objection.

Staff recommends issuance of construction permit and marina license.

ACTION OF THE TRUSTEES:

Motion was made by Mr. Stone, seconded by Mr. Christian and
carried without objection, that the Board approve issuance
of the construction permit and marina license.

-17-

INDIAN RIVER COUNTY - Dredge Permit No. 253.123-1092
and State Construction Permit

APPLICANT: Division of Recreation and Parks
Florida Department of Natural Resources,
Tallahassee, Florida

PROJECT: Dredge to remove an existing sand point and to install
two boat ramps at the Sebastian Inlet State Park along
the Indian River.

LOCATION: Section 29, Township 30 South, Range 31 East,
Indian River County.

MATERIAL: Approximately 100 cubic yards of material will be
removed from an existing sand point and placed on
state park upland.

PAYMENT: Request waiver of all fees as the project is for a
state park.

ECOLOGICAL
RESPONSES: Department of Natural Resources - No objection,
provided spoil is placed on uplands.

Game and Fresh Water Fish Commission - No objection.

Department of Pollution Control - No objection.

Staff recommends issuance of Dredge Permit No. 253.123-1092 and
Construction permit, with waiver of all fees.

ACTION OF THE TRUSTEES:

On motion by Mr. O'Malley, seconded by Mr. Stone and carried
unanimously, the Board approved issuance of dredge permit and
construction permit, waiving all fees for this application from
the Division of Recreation and Parks.

-18-

DADE COUNTY - Permit 253.124(8)-124

APPLICANT: Mahi Shrine, c/o Joseph G. Moretti
Post Office Box 35-868, Miami, Florida

PROJECT: To construct a seawall 5 feet offshore from the existing bank of the Miami River.

LOCATION: Section 35, Township 53 South, Range 41 East, Dade County.

MATERIAL: To be hauled in from upland sources.

PAYMENT: None. Sovereignty land not involved.

OTHER
STATEMENTS: The City of Miami recommends a vertical seawall to beautify the river, eliminate erosion and permit proper mooring of boats.

ECOLOGICAL
RESPONSES: Department of Natural Resources reports that to better conserve marine biological resources the existing rubble wall and intertidal area should not be replaced by a vertical seawall. The westerly end of the wall should connect with the southeasterly corner of an existing seawall.

Game and Fresh Water Fish Commission recommends that a vertical seawall not be constructed on this site. Additional riprap should be used if more erosion protection is needed.

Department of Pollution Control - No objection to project as proposed.

Staff recommends issuance of Permit 253.124(8)-242 provided riprap seawall is constructed in accordance with ecological agencies' recommendations.

ACTION OF THE TRUSTEES:

Mr. Kuperberg said the staff recommended the work provided a riprap rather than vertical seawall was used. Because of the many problems in the Miami River, whatever biological productivity that remains should not be damaged.

Mr. Conner made a motion, seconded by Mr. Christian, to approve that recommendation.

Mr. O'Malley pointed out that the applicant had written each member to explain the desire to construct a vertical seawall, which he thought was reasonable if the adjoining properties on each side had vertical walls. He asked for deferral and descriptions and photographs of this and the adjoining properties.

Mr. Conner had no objection, and the matter was deferred for two weeks for further information.

-19-

DUVAL COUNTY - Land Sale
File No. 2422-16-253.12

Staff Description: 0.11 acre parcel of filled sovereignty land in St. Johns River abutting Section 37, Township 3 South, Range 26 East.

A. CITY AND COUNTY: Duval County

B. APPLICANT: Alvin M. Coplan, 4040 San Remo Drive,
                              Jacksonville, Florida

C. APPLICANT'S
    REPRESENTATIVE: Not applicable

D. ACREAGE: 0.11
    RATE PER ACRE: $650 for the parcel

E. APPRAISAL: Boyce Taylor, S.R.A., A.S.A., adjusted by
                              staff appraiser on August 6, 1970

F. PURPOSE: Residential

G. BIOLOGICAL REPORT:Not applicable

H. STAFF REMARKS: The parcel is landward of the established
bulkhead line. The predecessor in title, Bart Peaden, on
October 6, 1970, stated that during September 1964 Hurricane
Dora washed out an old retaining wall and eroded several feet
under the bluff-line, almost caving in a line of very old
trees. He applied to the Small Business Administration for
an emergency loan. After a survey which depicted the 0.11
acre involved, the loan was approved and with the approval
of adjoining property owner, Mr. Peaden contracted for
construction of the seawall in line with the seawalls on
each side of his property.

A July 7, 1971, field investigation report indicated that the
entire shore line in the area has been bulkheaded. The
seawall was constructed in line with seawalls already
constructed. The public interest was not harmed at the
time the work was done, and in fact was furthered since
erosion has been prevented and a debris pocket between two
neighboring seawalls has been eliminated.

The applicant gives the following reasons why the sale is
in the public interest:

> "First, if I have to tear down my bulkhead, it would
> create a bad health hazard because my bulkhead would
> not be even with the other ones. Scum would build
> up in the corners and create a serious health pro-
> blem to children playing around the area. Second,
> if I tear down the bulkhead the property next to me
> on both sides would erode and cause construction
> damage to their property. Last, the shore line
> would lose its beauty because of the unevenness."

Advertisement (notice of proposed sale) was authorized December
14, 1971, and no objections have been received.

The item appeared on the agenda February 28, 1972, and was
deferred for one week, since the Trustees' meeting was one
day ahead of the advertised date for consideration of the
sale.

Staff recommends sale of the parcel for consideration of $650
and requests authority to issue deed.

ACTION OF THE TRUSTEES:

On motion by Mr. Stone, seconded by Mr. Christian and adopted
unanimously, the Board approved sale of the small parcel of
filled sovereignty land to Mr. Copland for $650.

3-7-72

-20-

DADE COUNTY - Seawall and Fill Permit No. 253.124-230

APPLICANT: City of Miami,
                c/o Rader and Associates
                First National Bank Building
                Miami, Florida 33131

PROJECT: To fill an area 70 feet wide to the Dade County
                Bulkhead Line 61 feet away. The area is under the
                proposed Southeast 8th Street Bridge and will serve
                as a bridge approach.

LOCATION: Biscayne Bay, Section 38, Township 54 South, Range
                42 East, Dade County.

MATERIAL: Will be hauled in.

PAYMENT: Fees waived because the project is in the public
                interest.

ECOLOGICAL
RESPONSES: Department of Natural Resources - States that the
                area should not be filled, but that subject property
                has been adversely affected by past dredging.

                Game and Fresh Water Fish Commission - States that
                the additional placement of fill would only add to
                the destruction that has already taken place and
                recommends that permit be denied.

                Department of Pollution Control - No objection.

OTHERS: 1. City of Miami by letter of February 22, 1972,
                indicates that it has no equipment to maintain pockets
                under bridge.

                2. University of Miami report of February 1972 states
                there is little justification for preservation of
                this area either as an example of an unspoiled com-
                munity or as an important energy source within the
                Biscayne Bay ecosystem.

<u>Staff recommends issuance of Permit 253.124-230 provided seawall
is constructed prior to filling with upland materials.</u>

ACTION OF THE TRUSTEES:

Mr. Kuperberg said the staff decisions on the several projects
on this agenda that infringed on Biscayne Bay had been difficult
but as this particular application involved an area owned by
the city that would be covered by the bridge, filling of the
small parcel was considered to be in the public interest. The
City of Miami had insisted on filling and supplemented its position with a report from the University of Miami.

Motion for approval made by Mr. Conner and seconded by Mr.
Christian was withdrawn when Mr. Shevin expressed opposition
to any filling in Biscayne Bay without any exceptions.

Mr. O'Malley in making a motion for approval that was seconded
by Mr. Christian, commented that the area would serve as a
bridge approach and without being filled would become a pocket
with no tidal action where debris would accumulate.

On Mr. O'Malley's motion to approve the application, those
in favor were Mr. Christian, Mr. Stone, Mr. Dickinson and
Governor Askew. Those opposed were Mr. Shevin and Mr. Conner.
The motion carried.

———————

3-7-72

-21-

BREVARD COUNTY - Land Sale
           File No. 2428-05-253.12, 0.264 acre

STAFF DESCRIPTION: A parcel of filled sovereignty land in the
                     Indian River abutting Government Lot 1,
                     Section 9, Township 27 South, Range 37 East,
                     Brevard County

A. CITY AND COUNTY: Eau Gallie, Brevard County

B. APPLICANT: Donald R. Bang, et ux
               Post Office Box 1376
               Eau Gallie, Florida 32935

C. APPLICANT'S
   REPRESENTATIVE: G. W. Hedman
                     1103 Hibiscus Boulevard,
                     Melbourne, Florida 32901

D. ACREAGE: 0.264
   RATE PER
    ACRE: $2800 for the parcel

E. APPRAISAL: By staff appraiser on June 14, 1971

F. PURPOSE: Home site

G. BIOLOGICAL
     REPORTS: Department of Natural Resources dated July 27,
               1971, not adverse.

               Game and Fresh Water Fish Commission dated
               August 2, 1971, adverse.

               Department of Pollution Control dated July 16,
               1971, not adverse.

H. STAFF REMARKS: The parcel was bulkheaded and filled without
   authorization in 1963-5, by a predecessor in title. It is
   landward of the bulkhead line approved by the Trustees on
   August 8, 1967.

   The constitutional amendment adopted on November 3, 1970,
   specified that sale of lands under navigable waters may be
   authorized only when in the public interest. However, the
   staff believes that the sale of submerged lands that were
   filled prior to the constitutional amendment should be
   processed under the law effective at the time of the filling.

   Nevertheless, a review of this file indicates that filling
   was done by applicant's predecessor in title sometime
   between 1963 and 1965. More than four years later, on
   February 11, 1969, the applicant innocently purchased the
   upland and filled parcel by warranty deed with guaranteed
   title. The filled parcel is roughly 300 feet by 40 feet
   comprising 0.264 acre, and its existence is not detrimental
   to navigation or to use of surrounding riparian lands.

   The Department of Natural Resources reports that allowing
   the fill to remain would-have less damaging effect on
   marine resources than removing it.

   The Department of Pollution Control reports that removing
   the fill would have adverse effects on the water quality
   in this area of the Indian River.

   The applicant did not discover the unauthorized filling
   until he offered the parcel for sale. Effecting sale without
   title to the filled parcel will be extremely difficult.

3-7-72

Since the public cannot make beneficial use of the parcel, the staff believes the applicant should not be penalized for another's violation of which he could not reasonably have knowledge.

Advertising (notice of proposed sale) was authorized December 21, 1971, and no objections have been received.

The item appeared on the agenda February 28, 1972, and was deferred for one week since the Trustees' meeting was held one day ahead of the advertised date.

The applicant's legal counsel submits the following reasons as to why the sale would be in the public interest: the land is located in an area where there is a very narrow strip of land between the road right of way and the river, the biological services report that from an ecology point of view, it would be better for the property to remain as it is than for it to be restored; this property is remote from other government holdings, and there is no access to it.

Staff recommends sale of the parcel for consideration of $2,800 and requests authority to issue deed.

ACTION OF THE TRUSTEES:

Motion was made by Mr. Christian, seconded by Mr. O'Malley and carried unanimously, that sale of the parcel of filled sovereignty land to Mr. Bang for $2,800 be approved.

-22-

DADE COUNTY - Fill Permit 253.124-179

At the request of the attorney for the applicant, Charles E. Gottlieb, the application to construct a seawall and fill in Biscayne Bay was withdrawn from the agenda for two weeks.

-23-

DADE COUNTY - Fill Permit 253.124-216

APPLICANT: H. P. Forrest, Trustee
            Suite 1220 DuPont Building, Miami, Florida

PROJECT: Has been amended to fill 3 acres, more or less, and con-
            struct a riprap seawall set back 15 feet from the approved
            bulkhead line in Biscayne Bay west of Lots 1, 2, 3,
            4, 5, 6, 7, 8 and 9, Block 15, Island View Subdivision,
            Plat Book 6, Page 115, Miami Beach, in Section 33,
            Township 53 South, Range 42 East, Dade County.

MATERIAL: Will be trucked in from other sources.

PAYMENT: Fees waived, since no sovereignty land will be used.

ECOLOGICAL
RESPONSES: Department of Natural Resources - The application has
            been amended to substitute riprap seawall for the
            previously proposed vertical seawall. While a riprap
            seawall is preferable to a vertical seawall since it
            provides more surface area for attachment of marine
            organisms, this project will still involve filling of
            over three acres of submerged land. The project will
            have adverse effects on marine biological resources.

            Game and Fresh Water Fish Commission still objects
            to the project as amended.

            Department of Pollution Control - The revised project
            will be considerably less damaging from a water quality

3-7-72

standpoint. The previously reported pocket at the south end of the project would be eliminated. The previous objections are withdrawn.

OTHER
COMMENTS: Applicant has agreed to a deed covenant stating that:

1. The land described therein, when filled, shall be used solely for the construction and operation of a non-profit hospital as defined by Section 501(c)(3) of the Internal Revenue Code, and appurtenant facilities for the care and treatment of human ailments and the furnishing of hospital services and allied activities, excluding patient services which are primarily residential in nature.

2. In the event that the grantee fails to commence bulkheading and filling for construction of a non-profit hospital on the subject property on or before December 31, 1978, the grantee shall have the option to require the grantor to repurchase the subject property free and clear of all liens, at the lesser of $95,000 or fair market value.

Staff recommends approval of fill permit 253.124-216 as amended, provided that the permit shall not be issued until the deed covenant has been recorded in the public records of Dade County and evidence of such recording has been furnished.

ACTION OF THE TRUSTEES:

Mr. Kuperberg explained that the staff was trying to honor a commitment of former Trustees who had determined that sale of the submerged parcel for a hospital was in the public interest. A question was raised as to whether or not construction of the hospital was in the public interest and whether, in fact, a hospital was to be built on the site. At the request of the staff the applicant agreed to return the original deed with no reverter, whereupon the staff would recommend the reissuance of a deed with a reversion provision that the land may be used only for a general hospital.

There was discussion of the nonprofit status of the hospital. Statements on behalf of the application were made by William J. Roberts, attorney for the Island View Hospital Group, Mr. H. O. Forrest, Dr. Stephen Cogen and Dr. Paul Unger.

Considerable local opposition had been expressed. Mr. Shepard Broad appeared as an official of Mt. Sinai Hospital, and other Miami Beach officials were present opposing the application. Mr. Broad requested postponement to allow local differences to be resolved.

Mr. O'Malley said the matter apparently was the subject of political ramifications in the local community that were irrelevant to the fill permit, that the Board should consider the ecological criteria, and apparently submerged land had been sold and filled for St. Francis and Mt. Sinai Hospital projects, over-riding similar adverse biological aspects.

Motion was made by Mr. O'Malley that the staff recommendation be followed and provisions 1 and 2 be included in the deed to be reissued to contain the reverter clause. The motion died for lack of a second.

Mr. Shevin opposed the permit based on his belief that there should not be any filling in Biscayne Bay unless there was an overriding public interest, which had not been demonstrated to him. As two environmental agencies reported adversely, he would vote to deny the permit and thought there was an obligation for the Board to repurchase the submerged land.

3-7-72

Mr. Christian asked if there was moral obligation to continue with the project since the land had been sold for a nonprofit hospital and considerable costs incurred, but Mr. Shevin expressed the opinion that there was no legal obligation and the statutes gave the Board the prerogative and discretion to grant or deny fill permits on primarily ecological considerations.

Mr. O'Malley renewed his motion which was seconded by Mr. Christian.

Mr. Stone explained why he would vote against the extension of filled land into the Bay. He read from a statement made before the Miami Beach City Commission that indicated that the hospital officials had an alternate plan if they were not able to go out into the Bay.

The motion was defeated on the following vote: Ayes, Mr. O'Malley and Mr. Christian; Nays, Mr. Shevin, Mr. Conner, Mr. Dickinson, and Mr. Stone. The Governor was recorded as voting in the negative.

Attorney General Shevin then made a motion that the Trustees go on record to repurchase the submerged land for either the $95,000 figure that they originally sold it to the applicant for, or the fair market value based upon a current appraisal to be obtained by the Trustees' staff, whichever is higher. The motion was seconded by Mr. Christian and carried on a vote of six to one with Mr. O'Malley voting in the negative.

-24-

DADE COUNTY -

    Florida Power and Light Company
    c/o A. M. Davis, Vice President
    Post Office Box 3100, Miami, Florida 33101

Sections 28, 32, 33 and 34, Township 57 South, Range 40 East; Sections 1, 3, 4, 5, 7, 8, 9, 10, 14, 15, 17, 18, 19, 20, 21, 22, 27, 28, 29, 31, 32, 33 Township 58 South, Range 40 East; and Sections 5 and 6, Township 59 South, Range 40 East were patented to the State of Florida as swamp and overflowed lands and subsequently conveyed into private ownership.

Section 16, Township 58 South, Range 40 East was patented to the School Board under the School Act of Congress, March 3, 1945 and subsequently conveyed into private ownership.

PROJECT: The Florida Power and Light Company wishes to construct a series of north-south canals for the Turkey Point generating plant across Sections 4, 5, 7, 8, 9, 16, 17, 18, 19, 20, 21, 28, 29, 30, 31, 32 and 33, Township 58 South, Range 40 East, and fractional section 6, Township 59 South, Range 40 East. This work is necessary to comply with a court order requiring the phased development of a closed cycle cooling system with a completion date of November 30, 1974. These canals will be constructed on both sides of an existing canal connecting the Turkey Point facilities with Card Sound.

Florida Power and Light Company is claiming ownership to the U. S. G. L. O. meander line as located in these sections. The Board of Trustees claims jurisdiction to those lands lying bayward of the mean high water line. The mean high water line in this area is difficult to establish.

To resolve this dispute, the Florida Power and Light Company has offered a boundary line agreement wherein the State would convey all right, title and interest to the six thousand acres, more or less, upon which the canal system will be constructed and the Florida Power and Light Company will convey all its right, title and interest in a 12-mile strip of land lying along Lower Biscayne Bay and Card Sound comprising 2,505 acres.

The proposed agreement specifically is made applicable to the lands involved and specifically excludes the use for determination of MHW with respect to any other lands.

Staff recommends approval of the proposal because of the critical need for power in the South Florida area, and the necessity for the protection of the environment against the consequences of the location of the plant at its existing site makes this transaction one of overriding public interest, and the granting of an easement over, through and across all lands lying between the open waters of Card Sound and the mean high water line of fractional Section 27 lying south of the easterly extension of Government Lot 1, Section 28, Fractional Section 28 and the North one-half of Government Lot 1, Section 33, Township 58 South, Range 40 East, for carrying out the needful works for the Turkey Point generating plant.

ACTION OF THE TRUSTEES:

Motion was made by Mr. Christian, seconded and adopted without objection, that the proposal be approved as recommended by the staff.

On motion duly adopted, the meeting was adjourned.

GOVERNOR   CHAIRMAN

ATTEST:

EXECUTIVE DIRECTOR

*   *   *   *   *

Tallahassee, Florida
March 21, 1972

The State of Florida Board of Trustees of the Internal Improvement Trust Fund met on this date in the auditorium of the Burns Building with the following members present:

Reubin O'D. Askew	Governor
Richard (Dick) Stone	Secretary of State
Robert L. Shevin	Attorney General
Fred O. Dickinson, Jr.	Comptroller
Thomas D. O'Malley	Treasurer
Floyd T. Christian	Commissioner of Education
Doyle Conner	Commissioner of Agriculture
Joel Kuperberg	Executive Director

-1-

The minutes of the February 28 meeting were approved without objection.

3-21-72

572

BROWARD COUNTY - Permit 253.123-973

APPLICANT: Powell Brothers, Inc.,
c/o Striker Aluminum Yachts, Inc.
Post Office Box 281, Ft. Lauderdale, Florida

PROJECT: To dredge, fill and construct a seawall for a boat
yard facility, all dredging and other work to be
performed in an artificially constructed upland
boat basin.

LOCATION: Section 20, Township 50 South, Range 42 East, South
Fork New River at Fort Lauderdale in Broward County.

MATERIAL: None. All work to be done within an upland boat basin.

PAYMENT: Not applicable since material is on privately-owned
property.

ECOLOGICAL
RESPONSES: Department of Natural Resources - No objection.

Game and Fresh Water Fish Commission - Since applicant
proceeded with the operation prior to their investigation, they will not approve the action.

Department of Pollution Control - No objection.

Staff recommends issuance of permit since project is entirely
on applicant's private property.

ACTION OF THE TRUSTEES:

Motion was made by Mr. Christian, seconded by Mr. Conner and
unanimously carried, to approve issuance of the permit.

-3-

DADE COUNTY - Dredge Permit No. 253.123-1003

APPLICANT: Little River Marine Construction Company, Inc.
6301 Northwest 74 Avenue, Miami, Florida 33166

PROJECT: To construct a steel sheet pile retaining wall and
dredge 500 cubic yards of material from sovereignty
land to permit the loading and unloading of ships at
the wall.

LOCATION: Miami River, Section 37, Township 54 South, Range
41 East, Dade County.

MATERIAL: Will be placed behind proposed retaining wall for fill.

PAYMENT: Check for $500 tendered for payment of sovereignty
material.

ECOLOGICAL
RESPONSES: Department of Natural Resources - No objection to
project.

Game and Fresh Water Fish Commission - No objection
to permit provided the bulkhead is constructed
behind the mean high water line.

Department of Pollution Control - No objection to
project.

OTHERS: Construction permit issued by City of Miami.

Staff recommends issuance of Dredge Permit No. 253.123-1003 to
Little River Marine Construction Company, Inc., with stipulation
that the retaining wall for fill be placed at the mean high water
line.

3-21-72

ACTION OF THE TRUSTEES:

Motion was made by Mr. Christian, seconded by Mr. Conner and unanimously carried, to approve issuance of the permit with the stipulation recommended.

-4-

PALM BEACH COUNTY - Utility Permit No. 253.123(2)(b)-946

APPLICANT: City of Riviera Beach
c/o Brockway, Owen & Anderson Engineers, Inc.
Post Office Box 3331, West Palm Beach, Florida

PROJECT: Installation of a 16-inch water main north of the Blue Heron Boulevard Bridge and a 16-inch sewage force main south of the bridge across Lake Worth.

LOCATION: Intracoastal Waterway, Lake Worth, Section 27, Township 42 South, Range 43 East, Palm Beach County.

MATERIAL: No material to be used.

PAYMENT: Waiver of processing fee has been requested since the project is in the public interest.

ECOLOGICAL
RESPONSES: Department of Natural Resources - No objection.

Game and Fresh Water Fish Commission - No objection.

Department of Pollution Control - No objection.

OTHERS: 1. Area Planning Board - No objection as long as standard environmental protective measures are taken.

2. Board of County Commissioners approved the project as being in the public interest.

Staff recommends issuance of Permit No. 253.123(2)(b)-946 and waiver of fees as the project is in the public interest.

ACTION OF THE TRUSTEES:

On motion by Mr. Conner, seconded by Mr. Christian and adopted unanimously, the Board approved issuance of the permit without charge as recommended.

-5-

PALM BEACH COUNTY - Dredge Permit No. 253.123-983

APPLICANT: Royal American Industries, Inc.
1001 Park Avenue, Lake Park, Florida

PROJECT: To dredge in the Intracoastal Waterway between the south line of Section 5 and the P.G.A. Boulevard Bridge to a depth of 16 feet at mean low water.

MATERIAL: Approximately 56,000 cubic yards of material will be removed and deposited on privately-owned upland.

LOCATION: Section 5, Township 42 South, Range 43 East, Palm Beach County.

ECOLOGICAL
RESPONSES: Department of Natural Resources - No objection, but to best preserve natural marine biological resources silt should be kept out of the creek along the south side of Garden Lane.

3-21-72

Game and Fresh Water Fish Commission - No objection.

Department of POllution Control - No objection, but does not recommend dredging of finger canal.

OTHERS: Area Planning Board - No objection.

Board of County Commissioners - Not in the public interest.

Staff recommends denial of Permit Application No. 253.123-983 as it is in conflict with Palm Beach County moratorium on dredging projects.

ACTION OF THE TRUSTEES:

On motion made by Mr. Shevin, seconded by Mr. Stone and carried by a six to one vote, with Mr. Dickinson voting "No", the Board denied approval of the permit.

-6-

DADE COUNTY - Power Line and Substation Easement

APPLICANT: Florida Power and Light Company
Post Office Box 3100, Miami, Florida

REQUEST: Easement for location of an electric substation and rights of way for underground electric distribution lines on the campus of Florida International University.·

DESCRIPTION: Electric substation - 2.5 acres in the SW corner of campus in Section 7, Township 54 South, Range 40 East, Dade County. Distribution lines as needed on campus.

The Board of Regents recommended the easement at its meeting on November 19, 1971.

Trustees' staff confirmed with Regents' Chairman Kibler that the Board of Regents, its facilities committee and university officials, concur in the shared use of this state land.

Recommend issuance of easement.

ACTION OF THE TRUSTEES:

Motion was made by Mr. Christian, seconded by Mr. Conner and unanimously carried, to approve issuance of the easement.

-7-

MONROE COUNTY - Dredge Permit No. 253.03-287

APPLICANT: Valhalla Yacht Service, Inc.
c/o E. R. Brownell
3152 Coral Way, Miami, Florida

PROJECT: To dredge material for beach nourishment from an existing channel. Depth of dredge area would be 8 feet. For some of this project, permit has already been issued to B. M. Manno, State Permit No. 253.03-209.

LOCATION: Hawk Channel, Section 35, Township 65 South, Range 33 East, near Marathon, in Monroe County.

MATERIAL: Approximately 8,000 cubic yards of sand to be removed and deposited on upland beaches and low spots

PAYMENT: Requests waiver of fees since project is in the public interest. $50 check tendered for processing fee.

ECOLOGICAL
RESPONSES: Department of Natural Resources - Would have definite
adverse effects.

Game and Fresh Water Fish Commission - Recommend that
permit application be denied because approval has been
previously given for the necessary part of this work.

Department of Pollution Control - Cannot comment
favorably on a project that is an obvious duplication
of a previously approved project.

Staff recommends denial of Permit No. 253.03-287, since the project is more extensive than one that has already been approved
under State Permit No. 253.03-209 and ecological responses are
unfavorable.

ACTION OF THE TRUSTEES:

Motion was made by Mr. Stone, seconded by Mr. Shevin and
carried unanimously, that the staff recommendation to deny
the permit be accepted as the action of the Board.

-8-

PALM BEACH COUNTY - State Construction Permit and Marina
License ML-63

APPLICANT: Tideway Construction Co.
c/o William G. Wallace, Inc.
105-106 Lakeview Building
North Palm Beach, Florida

PROJECT: Construct marina facility covering 5576 square feet
of submerged land in Lake Worth abutting Section 28,
Township 42 South, Range 43 East, Palm Beach County.
No dredging is required.

PAYMENT: $111.52 minimum annual fee for marina license.

ECOLOGICAL
RESPONSES: Department of Natural Resources - No objection.

Game and Fresh Water Fish Commission - No objection.

Department of Pollution Control - No objection.

OTHERS: Area Planning Board of Palm Beach County - No comments.

Staff recommends issuance of marina license for annual fee of
$111.52.

ACTION OF THE TRUSTEES:

On motion by Mr. Christian, seconded by Mr. Conner and carried
unanimously, the Trustees approved issuance of the marina license.

-9-

SANTA ROSA COUNTY - Oil and Gas Drilling Lease Bond

On January 11, 1972, the Trustees authorized advertising for
sealed bids for a five-year oil and gas drilling lease of the
reserved one-half interest of the state in the W 1/2 of the
NW 1/4 of the NW 1/4 of Section 13, Township 4 North, Range
29 East, containing 20 surface acres in Santa Rosa County, with
a surety bond in the amount of $50,000.

On February 22, 1972, sealed bids were received and opened and
the Trustees awarded the lease to Amoco Production Company, which
submitted $125,079.82, the highest of six bids for the lease.

3-21-72

Subsequent to the award of the lease it was discovered that due to an administrative error the legal notice calling for bids stated that a $40,000 surety bond was required.

Pursuant to Section 253.571, Florida Statutes, the bond is required by the lessee prior to the time the lessee mines, drills, or extracts in any manner petroleum products, gas sulphur or any other minerals from the leased land.

Section 253.52, Florida Statutes, requires the form of lease to be available to the general public during the period of time when the legal notice of lease sale is being published. As the amount of the bond in the lease form and legal notices was listed as $40,000 and all bidders submitted their bids on that basis, a change in the amount of bond to $50,000 following award of lease would subject the validity of the lease to question.

It is recommended that the Board amend its action of January 11, 1972, by reducing the amount of the bond required for this lease to $40,000 in order to validate the lease awarded on February 22 to Amoco Production.

ACTION OF THE TRUSTEES:

Motion was made by Mr. O'Malley, seconded by Mr. Stone and carried unanimously, that the staff recommendation be accepted as the action of the Board.

-10A-

DUVAL COUNTY - Temporary Easement Extension

    Jacksonville Port Authority
    Post Office Box 3005, Jacksonville, Florida 32206

requests one-year extension of Temporary Spoil Easement No. 2414 dated April 28, 1970. Current dredging in connection with the Jacksonville Harbor Deepening Project will extend beyond the April 28, 1972, expiration date of the easement. The spoil area located on a portion of the Huguenot Memorial State Park contains approximately 95 acres in Duval County.

The Department of Natural Resources has reviewed the request and approves the extension, provided every effort will be made to avoid dumping spoil on any of the remaining salt marshes within the area.

Recommend the extension for one year with a special provision prohibiting placing spoil on any salt marsh area.

ACTION OF THE TRUSTEES:

The Director said the spoil area was in the state park and not spoil area CS-2. Motion was made by Mr. Stone, seconded by Mr. Dickinson and Mr. Christian, and adopted without objection, to extend for one year the temporary easement with the special provision as recommended by the staff.

-10B-

DUVAL COUNTY - Temporary Pipeline Easement

    Jacksonville Port Authority

requests a temporary pipeline easement for one year over and across a parcel of land adjacent to the water's edge in Section 19, Township 1 South, Range 29 East, Duval County, to provide upland access to the spoil area described in item "10A" above.

The easement area will be sixty feet wide and 1550 feet long in a part of the Huguenot Memorial State Park.

The Department of Natural Resources has reviewed and approved
the route of the pipeline easement provided the easement is
relocated farther from the edge of the water to minimize
siltation of adjacent waters in event of accidental spillage.

Recommend issuance of the temporary pipeline easement for one
year at a location twenty feet from the water's edge.

ACTION OF THE TRUSTEES:

Motion was made by Mr. Stone, seconded by Mr. Dickinson and
Mr. Christian, and adopted without objection, to authorize
issuance of the temporary pipeline easement for one year at
a location twenty feet from the water's edge.

-11-

The minutes of the March 7 meeting were approved as submitted.

-12-

DADE COUNTY - Fill Permit 253.124-179

APPLICANT: Charles E. Gottlieb
DuPont Plaza Center, Miami, Florida 33131

PROJECT: To construct a seawall and fill in Biscayne Bay at
Southeast 15 Road and South Bayshore Drive in Section
39, Township 54 South, Range 41 East, Dade County.

MATERIAL: All material will come from upland sources.

PAYMENT: No fees charged since no sovereignty land will be used.

ECOLOGICAL
RESPONSES: Department of Natural Resources - Will have adverse
effects on marine biological resources.

Game and Fresh Water Fish Commission - will have adverse
effects; recommends that permit be denied.

Department of Pollution Control - No objection to project.

(See Exhibit No. 11 on February 15 agenda)

OTHERS: Dade County - issued permit. No objection to project.

Staff recommends that application be denied and applicant's purchase
price plus 6% interest since time of sale be refunded.

ACTION OF THE TRUSTEES:

Motion was made by Mr. Stone, seconded by Mr. Dickinson, to
approve the application for a fill permit. Mr. O'Malley and
Mr. Christian voted in favor. Mr. Shevin, expressing again
his opposition to any more filling in Biscayne Bay, voted
against the motion as did Mr. Conner and Governor Askew. The
motion carried four to three.

After consideration of the next application on the agenda, motion
was made by Mr. Stone, seconded by Messrs. Christian and Conner,
carried without objection, to reconsider the Gottlieb permit.

Mr. Stone made a motion, seconded by Mr. Conner, to follow the
staff recommendation to deny approval. Mr. Christian voted "No",
stating that the area was landward of the approved bulkhead line
and he thought the Board's past action had led the owner to
believe he would be allowed to use the parcel he had bought.
Mr. Dickinson was of the same opinion, and voted against denial
of the permit.

3-21-72

Mr. Gottlieb argued that filling the small parcel purchased in 1969 with no adverse reports at that time and with the understanding that it would be filled and used, could pose no threat to the ecology of Biscayne Bay, that the Board in 1970 allowed filling of five acres just south of his property, there was other filling taking place in the bay now, and there was something unfair when a different administration would deny his application to fill within the bulkhead line approved by the Interagency Advisory Committee in 1968.

Dr. O. E. Frye, Jr., Director of Florida Game and Fresh Water Fish Commission, stated that at the time of the Delphi matter the commission felt obligated by the 1968 Interagency Advisory Report it had participated in, but since then the Commission had been assured that it was not obligated. Consequently an adverse biological report was issued on the Gottlieb application.

Mr. Shevin pointed out that the Delphi permit was issued not by this Cabinet with its present members, he did not feel bound by the action in 1970 of a prior board, and he would not accept the concept that everything out to the bulkhead line should be allowed to be filled.

Mr. Stone said the bulkhead line was drawn to allow filling landward of it, with filling outside it only in the public interest. He added that if the bulkhead line was wrong a new line should be established and denial now was unfair treatment of this property owner.

Mr. O'Malley also felt it might be unfair. He disagreed with a blanket no-fill vote but would vote against this permit and asked for reconsideration of the approval two weeks ago of the City of Miami permit to fill a small parcel under a bridge.

Mr. Christian recalled that the Board had authorized advertisement with the understanding that the land would be sold for use, and the director at that time felt it was justified. In his opinion denial now was unfair to this applicant.

Mr. Dickinson felt very strongly that the government had an obligation to all of the people and this upland owner had bought the submerged land under the assumption that he would be granted a fill permit. He understood that some members thought the ecology outweighed the equity of the human being, but this land was behind the bulkhead line and in his judgment the equities were with the applicant and these matters should be determined on their individual merits. He would not vote for the staff recommendation to deny.

A substitute motion to approve the application was offered by Mr. Christian and seconded by Mr. Dickinson.

Mr. Kuperberg, asked to comment on the problem, said at some point in time filling had to stop to preserve marine resources; he was sympathetic but the applicant was not being deprived of use of his land as he could build a smaller high-rise.

The substitute motion to approve the fill application failed to pass on the following vote: Ayes, Messrs, Christian and Dickinson; Nays, Messrs, Shevin, Conner, Stone, O'Malley and the Governor.

Mr. Shevin proposed an amendment that the Trustees offer to repurchase the submerged land at, rather than the 6% figure recommended by staff, what the Board had sold it for or the fair market value based on a current appraisal to be obtained by the Trustees. The amendment was seconded by Mr. O'Malley and carried without objection.

The motion, recurring on the staff recommendation as amended to deny the permit and offer to repurchase the land for what was paid for it or the fair market value today, whichever is higher, carried on the following vote: Ayes, Messrs. Shevin, Conner, Stone, O'Malley and the Governor; Nays, Messrs. Christian and Dickinson.

3-21-72

DADE COUNTY - Application for Dedication
            File No. 2364-13-253.03   (0.092 acres)

Staff Description: A parcel of sovereignty land, in Biscayne
                    Bay southeasterly of Southeast 15 Road
                    abutting Section 39, Township 54 South,
                    Range 41 East.

A. CITY AND
    COUNTY: City of Miami, Dade County

B. APPLICANT: City of Miami

C. APPLICANT'S
    REPRESENTATIVE:Director of Public Works

D. ACREAGE: 0.092
    RATE PER ACRE: Not applicable

E: APPRAISAL: Not applicable

F. PURPOSE: For street purposes

G. BIOLOGICAL
    RESPONSES: Department of Natural Resources - March 29,
                    1971, adverse.

                    Game and Fresh Water Fish Commission - adverse

                    Department of Pollution Control - No objection
                    to the proposed dedication.

H. The parcel is landward of the approved bulkhead line as con-
    firmed by the Interagency Advisory Committee.

Staff recommends application for dedication be denied.

ACTION OF THE TRUSTEES:

Mr. Kuperberg explained that in order to be consistent the
staff recommended against the dedication because the next
request would be to fill the submerged parcel of land.

Motion was made by Mr. O'Malley, seconded by Mr. Christian,
that the application of the city be approved, but the motion
failed to pass. Mr. Stone voted "No", asked for reconsideration
of Item 12, and much of the discussion shown for the previous
item in these minutes followed.

On Item 13, motion was made by Mr. Shevin, seconded by Mr.
Conner that the staff recommendation for denial be followed.
The motion carried with Messrs. Shevin, Christian, Conner,
Dickinson, Stone and O'Malley voting for denial.

Governor Askew announced that the Board's action on 12 and
13 was to uphold the recommendations of the staff to deny both
applications.

Treasurer O'Malley made a motion that the Executive Director
request the Interagency Advisory Committee, Dade County, and
the City of Miami to inquire into the advisability of changing
the existing bulkhead line to pull it back to the mean high
water line, if there is a mean high water line at that point in
Biscayne Bay, before other property owners burden themselves
with financial arrangements to carry out plans involving filling.
Mr. Stone seconded the motion.

Mr. Shevin also seconded the motion and had no objection to
urging the county to re-examine the bulkhead line, but he felt
that the establishment of a bulkhead line did not obligate the
Board to allow filling to the line. Mr. O'Malley thought the
Cabinet did need some recommendations from the county and a

580

general policy with respect to that controversial part of
Biscayne Bay. The Governor commented that there were
differences of opinion and members wished the Executive
Director to review again that sensitive area.

Motion was made by Mr. O'Malley, seconded by Mr. Shevin and
adopted, with the Governor voting in the negative, that the
Board reconsider the permit approved two weeks ago for filling
in the City of Miami under a portion of the structure of the
bridge that would go to Claughton Island.

Mr. O'Malley made a motion that the application be denied,
seconded by Mr. Shevin.

Mr. Stone's request that the matter be scheduled next week,
so that the City of Miami would have an opportunity to be
heard, was granted and action was deferred one week.

-14-

DADE COUNTY - Dredge Permit 253.123.691

APPLICANT: Florida Power and Light Company
              c/o A. M. Davis, Vice-President
              Post Office Box 3100, Miami, Florida

PROJECT: To construct berms along each side of the discharge
              channel leading into Card Sound in accordance with
              Final Judgment (Civil Action No. 70-328-CA) Part
              IV, Paragraph 6A, "No discharge will be allowed to
              flow over the shallow substrate which is exposed
              at low tide."

              Applicant wishes to amend the permit to allow
              the material temporarily deposited on each side
              of the discharge channel to remain in place. This
              material if left in place would comply with the
              requirements of the Final Judgment.

MATERIAL: To be left in place on sovereignty land.

PAYMENT: None Required.

ECOLOGICAL
RESPONSES: Department of Natural Resources - No objection.

              Division of Beaches & Shores - No objection.

              Game and Fresh Water Fish Commission - No objection.

              Department of Pollution Control - No objection.

Staff recommends issuance of a modified permit as requested.

ACTION OF THE TRUSTEES:

On motion by Mr. Conner, seconded by Mr. O'Malley and adopted
without objection, the Board authorized issuance of the modified
permit as recommended to allow the berms to remain in place.

-15-

LEE COUNTY - Dredge Permit No. 253.123-1052

APPLICANT: Andy Reiber
              c/o Duane Hall and Associates, Inc.
              Villa Plaza, Suite 3, Fort Myers, Florida

PROJECT: To construct a navigation channel 140 feet in length
              to connect with an existing channel in front of the
              property, and to remove a small sand bar in the mouth

3-21-72

of the existing channel.

LOCATION: Section 36, Township 45 South, Range 23 East,
Caloosahatchee River, Lee County.

MATERIAL: Approximately 657 cubic yards to be removed from
sovereignty lands and deposited on upland spoil areas.

PAYMENT: Check for $657 tendered as payment for material at
a standard yardage rate of $1 per cubic yard.

ECOLOGICAL
RESPONSES: Department of Natural Resources - Project has been
revised to meet suggestions of the Department of
Natural Resources.

Game and Fresh Water Fish Commission - No objection.

Department of Pollution Control - No objection.

OTHERS: Approved by Lee County Commissioners.

Staff recommends issuance of Dredge Permit No. 253.123-1052 to
Andy Reiber with the stipulation that spoil areas be properly
diked.

ACTION OF THE TRUSTEES:

On motion by Mr. Stone, seconded by Mr. Christian and Mr. Conner,
adopted without objection, the Board authorized issuance of the
permit with the recommended stipulation.

-16-

MONROE COUNTY - Dredge Permit No. 253.03-326

APPLICANT: Ronald Lockenbach
c/o Bailey and Associates
Post Office Box 349, Islamorada, Florida

PROJECT: To perform maintenance dredging in an existing channel
to improve navigation between two existing canals.
Depth will be 5.0' below mean low water.

LOCATION: Vaca Key, Hawk Channel, Section 11, Township 66
South, Range 32 East, Monroe County

MATERIAL: No sovereignty material involved. Spoil will be placed
on upland.

PAYMENT: Not applicable.

ECOLOGICAL
RESPONSES: Department of Natural Resources - No objection.

Game and Fresh Water Fish Commission - No objection.

Department of Pollution Control - No objection to
project provided two submerged tanks be removed
from the channel and riprap be placed on Lot 14 to
hold the spoil.

Staff recommends issuance of Dredge Permit No. 253.03-326 to Ronald
Lockenbach, with the provision that the two existing submerged
tanks be removed from the channel and riprap be placed on Lot 14
to hold the spoil.

ACTION OF THE TRUSTEES:

On motion by Mr. Christian, seconded by Mr. Stone and adopted
unanimously, the Board approved issuance of the permit subject to
the recommended conditions to which the applicant had agreed.

3-21-72

-17-

BREVARD AND INDIAN RIVER COUNTIES - Beach Nourishment Project
253.123-910

APPLICANT: Sebastian Inlet District
c/o Biendorf and Associates, Inc.
Post Office Box 849, Vero Beach, Florida

PROJECT: To amend permit authorizing removal of 300,000
cubic yards of sand, to authorize the removal of
500,000 cubic yards of sand from the sand trap in
the Indian River to artificially nourish approximately 2,400 feet of public beach along the Atlantic
Ocean in Sections 20 and 21, Township 30 South, Range
39 East, Brevard and Indian River Counties.

MATERIAL: The beach nourishment is covered by the Department of
Natural Resources, Bureau of Beaches and Shores
Permit BBS 71-35.

PAYMENT: This beach nourishment project is being financed by
state and local funds.

ECOLOGICAL
RESPONSES: Department of Natural Resources - No objection.

Game and Fresh Water Fish Commission - No objection.

Department of Pollution Control - No objection to
the project provided that stringent controls are
used to prevent siltation of shell fish areas North
and South of the Inlet.

Staff recommends modification of Permit 253.123-910 subject to
stipulations of the Department of Pollution Control.

ACTION OF THE TRUSTEES:

The scope of the project would be enlarged because a favorable price
had been obtained for the fill material in the beach nourishment
project.

Motion was made by Mr. Conner, seconded by Mr. Stone and
Mr. Christian, carried unanimously, that the permit be modified
subject to the stipulations of the Department of Pollution Control.

-18-

HILLSBOROUGH COUNTY - Fill Permit No. 253.123-161(TPA Permit 71-5)

APPLICANT: Port Sutton, Inc. and Tampa Port Authority
Post Office Box "E", Tampa, Florida

PROJECT: The Tampa Port Authority issued TPA Permit 71-5 to
fill a two hundred foot strip of land south of the
south finger of Port Sutton. The project was modified
to reduce the original width from 300 feet to 200 feet,
and fill will not be placed in the westerly 1000 feet
of the original spoil disposal area.

This item first appeared on the Trustees' agenda of
February 23, 1971, and was deferred at the request of
the Secretary of State.

It again appeared on March 3, 1971, and was again
deferred at the request of the Secretary of State.

On March 9, 1971, the item was postponed upon staff
recommendation until the bulkhead lines had been
re-established by the Tampa Port Authority.

3-21-72

This item was not placed on the agenda following the relocation of the bulkhead lines as there were two adverse biological reports and the Department of Pollution Control indicated it would not certify the project. In a letter of February 24, 1972, the Department of Pollution Control withdrew the previously submitted objections to this project.

LOCATION: Section 3, Township 30 South, Range 19 East, Hillsborough Bay.

MATERIAL: Removed from pierside maintenance dredging of a strip of land 6,170 feet long by 34 feet deep by 100 feet wide.

PAYMENT: None. State-owned sovereignty land not involved.

ECOLOGICAL
RESPONSES: Department of Natural Resources - The proposed fill area to the South of Pendola Point has been reduced from an area of 30 acres to an area of 18 acres of submerged land. To conserve a developing cordgrass marsh on silted bay bottoms, no additional filling of submerged land should be permitted. It is evident that some damage to marine biological resources would result from filling of submerged land.

Game and Fresh Water Fish Commission - The area is at present a most valuable and productive portion of the marine ecosystem. If the permit application is approved, spoil will cover a portion of the shallow productive area and another important portion of the ecosystem will be lost. The commission recommends that the permit application as presented be denied.

Department of Pollution Control - Original objections to this project were based in part on the following: "That any fill on the south side of Pendola Point would have definite adverse effects on water quality in the area. The normal flow of water in the area of the tidal creek that existed on the natural shoreline to the east would be disrupted by filling the south side of Pendola Point."

The tidal areas to the east have been filled. Based on the above, this Department withdraws the previously submitted objections to the 200 foot fill on the south side of Pendola Point. Drawings and information will be required from the applicant to define the bulkheading, method of fill, and controls to be utilized during the filling operation.

Staff recommends approval of Tampa Port Authority Permit 71-5 (Fill Permit 253.123-161) as modified to permit completion of this project.

ACTION OF THE TRUSTEES:

Mr. Christian made a motion, seconded by Mr. Conner, to approve the staff recommendation. Mr. Stone voted against it, stating that the Board should take a strict position in Tampa Bay. Mr. Shevin and Mr. O'Malley voted "No", whereupon Mr. Conner said he would vote "No" to follow the action of the legal counsel of the Board, the Attorney General.

Mr. O'Malley questioned the staff position that the property owner had greater rights to the use of the bay bottoms in Tampa Bay because it was commercial and industrial than the private property owner in a zoned business classification area in Biscayne Bay. Mr. Kuperberg said the staff, trying to make a judgment of the public interest, thought a port area had more public values than an apartment house area. Also, the

Trustees' jurisdiction was reduced by the fact that Tampa Port
Authority owned the bottom lands by Legislative Act, and the Trustees
only reviewed the permits that were issued by the Tampa Port
Authority. Mr. O'Malley asked the Attorney General to
provide an opinion on the differences between the rights of the
two property owners.

Noting that the Board tried to maintain a consistent position,
Mr. Conner asked for deferral for two weeks. It was agreed.

Mr. Shevin asked the Director for information on conditions
imposed when the Trustees in July 1971 approved a fill permit
in Biscayne Bay for Florida East Coast Railway Company.

-19-

ST. LUCIE COUNTY - Utility Permit No. 253.123(2)(b)-1101

APPLICANT: Florida Power and Light Company
              Post Office Box 3100, Miami, Florida

PROJECT: To excavate and backfill two trenches 2,450 ft.
              apart in the Atlantic Ocean. The two subaqueous
              intake pipes installed in the south trench will
              end 1,200 feet offshore. These pipes will be
              buried 20 feet below grade at the shoreline and
              13 feet below the bottom at the offshore end. The
              subaqueous discharge pipe and Y-type diffuser
              installed in the north trench will also end 1,200
              feet offshore. This pipe will be buried 26 feet
              below grade at the shoreline and will be exposed at
              the offshore end. The ocean bottom in the immediate
              vicinity of the discharge will be protected against
              scour by use of riprap or other appropriate material.

LOCATION: Hutchinson Island, Township 36 South, Range 41 East,
              St. Lucie County.

MATERIAL: No sovereignty material involved.

ECOLOGICAL
RESPONSES: Department of Natural Resources -
              1. Beaches and Shores requires variance of
                  setback provisions of Chapter 161.052, F. S.
                  This will be scheduled on D. N. R. agenda
                  on the same date as Trustees' agenda.
              2. If dikes constructed in conjunction with
                  dredging of canals upland of pipe ends do
                  not further impede the flow of water to and
                  from the area between them, there will be
                  limited adverse effects on marine biological
                  resources.

              Game and Fresh Water Fish Commission - The only
              areas that will be adversely affected by the proposed
              project will be those either dredged or filled to
              construct the canals.

              Department of Pollution Control - No objection.

Staff recommends issuance of Permit 253.123(2)(b)-1101 with the
applicant responsible for satisfying federal requirements as
to hazard-to-navigation markings.

ACTION OF THE TRUSTEES:

The Director expressed staff approval of the project as
planned, for which the Department of Natural Resources on this
date had granted a permit, also.

On motion by Mr. Christian, seconded by Mr. Conner and carried
unanimously, the utility permit was approved.

3-21-72

-20-

SARASOTA COUNTY - Dredge Permit No. 253.123-987

APPLICANT: Dee S. Harpham
c/o Archie B. Brown Surveys
Post Office Box 752, Venice, Florida

PROJECT: The Sarasota County Water and Navigation Control
Authority issued its permit for construction of
a 30' wide x 4' deep access channel and a boat
basin located above the mean high water line.
The width was reduced to comply with the recommendations of the Department of Natural Resources.

LOCATION: Section 31, Township 40 South, Range 20 East,
Gottfried Creek, Sarasota County.

MATERIAL: 329.38 cubic yards of sovereignty material to be
dredged and placed on upland.

PAYMENT: Check for $329.38 tendered for payment of sovereignty
material.

ECOLOGICAL
RESPONSES: Department of Natural Resources - No objection
to project, provided construction is accomplished
with a dragline.

Game and Fresh Water Fish Commission - No objection.

Department of Pollution Control - No objection.

Staff recommends issuance of Dredge Permit No. 253.123-897 to
Dee S. Harpham with the stipulation that dredging be accomplished
by dragline.

ACTION OF THE TRUSTEES:

Motion was made by Mr. Christian, seconded by Mr. Stone and
carried unanimously, to approve the dredge permit with the
recommended stipulation.

_____

-21-

SANTA ROSA COUNTY - Advertise Oil and Gas Lease

APPLICANT: P. R. Rutherford, Houston, Texas
and
Texas Gas Exploration Company

REQUEST: Advertise for oil and gas drilling lease.

LOCATION: That portion of Big Coldwater Creek lying in
Sections 31 and 32, Township 3 North, Range 27
West and Sections 5, 6, 8, 17, and 20, Township
2 North, Range 27 West, containing 71.8 acres,
more or less, in Santa Rosa County.

INTEREST
OF STATE: Full interest held by Trustees.

Well drilling in the waterbottoms will be specifically
prohibited by this lease. Pooling will allow compliance with requirement to drill.

Proceeds from this lease will go to the Internal
Improvement Trust Fund. This request has been
reviewed by the Director of Interior Resources,
Department of Natural Resources, who concurs with
the following recommendation.

Recommend advertising for sealed bids for a five-year lease with
annual rental of $1 per net mineral acre, 1/6 royalty, $50,000
surety bond and at least one test well every 2 1/2 years drilled
to 6,000 feet or to a depth sufficient to test the Norphlet Sands,
whichever is deeper.

ACTION OF THE TRUSTEES:

On motion by Mr. Stone, seconded by Mr. Conner and Mr. O'Malley,
the rules were waived for consideration of all the addendum
items, and advertisement of the oil and gas lease was approved
without objection.

-22-

DADE COUNTY - Permit 253.124(8)-124

APPLICANT: Mahi Shrine, c/o Joseph G. Moretti
Post Office Box 35-868, Miami, Florida

PROJECT: To construct a seawall 5 feet offshore from the
existing bank of the Miami River.

LOCATION: Section 35, Township 53 South, Range 41 East, Dade
County.

MATERIAL: To be hauled in from upland sources.

PAYMENT: None. Sovereignty land not involved.

OTHER
STATEMENTS: The City of Miami recommends a vertical seawall to
beautify the river, eliminate erosion and permit
proper mooring of boats.

ECOLOGICAL
RESPONSES: Department of Natural Resources reports that to better
conserve marine biological resources the existing
rubble wall and intertidal area should not be replaced
by a vertical seawall. The westerly end of the wall
should connect with the southeasterly corner of an
existing seawall.

Game and Fresh Water Fish Commission recommends that
a vertical seawall not be constructed on this site.
Additional riprap should be used if more erosion
protection is needed.

Department of Pollution Control - No objection to
project as proposed.

OTHERS: 1. City of Miami indicates that it has long been
the wish and intention to have the banks of the Miami
River seawalled. It is felt that a proper bulkhead
would beautify the river, eliminate erosion and
avulsion problems, and would permit proper mooring
of boats. A similar view has been expressed by both
the Coast Guard and the Corps of Engineers. Private
development of the river has proceeded according to
this plan.

2. A March 15, 1972, letter and photographs furnished
by Nick Leischen, Administrative Aide, Secretary of
State, indicates entire south shore of Miami River in
this area has vertical seawalls. This river as
determined by its activity is a commercial industrial
river and not a scenic passive one. Any type of construction such as riprap, sand bagging or berms, will
be causative of problems.

Staff recommends issuance of Permit 253.124(8)-242 provided a riprap
seawall is installed in accordance with ecological agencies'
recommendations.

3-21-72

ACTION OF THE TRUSTEES:

Secretary of State Stone made a motion, seconded by Mr. O'Malley, that the application for a vertical seawall be approved as it seemed to be logical and right in that area of the river for property located between two other seawalled properties.

Mr. O'Malley said that no dredging and filling was involved, and Senator Randolph Hodges had commented that although the biological report showed some marine life in the area he believed the construction of a vertical seawall to connect with existing seawalls would be desirable.

In response to a question by the Governor, Mr. Kuperberg advised that, as in the Town of Naples, docks for tieing up boats could be built out over riprap, and the riprap would absorb wave action and contribute to preservation of biological values. The applicant had been advised of the staff recommendation but did not desire to change the plans.

Without objection, action was deferred.

-23A-

LEE COUNTY - Bulkhead Line, Section 253.122, F. S.

APPLICANT: City of Fort Myers
Post Office Box 2217, Fort Myers, Florida

PROJECT: Revised bulkhead line 465.00 feet long in the Caloosahatchee River abutting Section 13, Township 44 South, Range 24 East, Lee County, Florida, approved and established by the City Council of the City of Fort Myers, Florida, by Ordinance No. 794, adopted January 3, 1972, and reconfirmed on March 20, 1972.

ECOLOGICAL
RESPONSES: Department of Natural Resources - No objection.

Game and Fresh Water Fish Commission - Not received.

Department of Pollution Control - No objection.

Staff recommends approval of bulkhead line.

ACTION OF THE TRUSTEES:

On motion by Mr. Christian, seconded by Mr. Dickinson and carried without objection, the bulkhead line was approved.

-23B-

LEE COUNTY - Dredge Permit No. 253.123-1082

APPLICANT: City of Fort Myers

PROJECT: To perform maintenance dredging in an existing marina and to construct a channel 300 feet by 150 feet wide connecting the existing marina to the Okeechobee Waterway Channel in the Caloosahatchee River.

LOCATION: Section 13, Township 44 South, Range 24 East, Lee County.

MATERIAL: Approximately 17,000 cubic yards of material to be dredged from the proposed access channel and the existing marina is to be placed in U. S. Corps of Engineers spoil areas.

PAYMENT: None. Sovereignty land not involved.

3-21-72

ECOLOGICAL
RESPONSES: Department of Natural Resources - Should have only
limited adverse effects on the marine biological
resources.

Game and Fresh Water Fish Commission - Reports that
we encourage the marina concept since it allows
numerous boats to use the same navigation channels,
thus eliminating massive environmental damage. However, the filling of one acre of submerged river
bottom will cause degradation of the river ecosystem.

Department of Pollution Control - Awaiting concurrence
from regional office for this project.

Staff recommends issuance of Dredge Permit 253.123-1082.

ACTION OF THE TRUSTEES:

On motion by Mr. Christian, seconded by Mr. Dickinson and
carried without objection, the Trustees approved issuance of
the dredge permit.

-23C-

LEE COUNTY - Fill Permit No. 253.124-273

APPLICANT: City of Fort Myers

PROJECT: To fill approximately 1.0 acre of submerged land
in the existing marina for additional vehicle
parking. The submerged land was conveyed to the
City of Fort Myers by Chapter 6962, Laws of Florida,
1915.

LOCATION: Caloosahatchee River in Section 13, Township 44 South,
Range 24 East, Lee County.

MATERIAL: Approximately 17,000 cubic yards of fill material will
come from Corps of Engineers channel dredging project.

PAYMENT: None. Sovereignty land not involved.

ECOLOGICAL
RESPONSES: Department of Natural Resources - Only limited adverse
effects if spoil is adequately contained.

Game and Fresh Water Fish Commission - Reports that
we encourage the marina concept since it allows
numerous boats to use the same navigation channels thus
eliminating massive environmental damage. However,
the filling of one acre of submerged river bottom will
cause degradation of the river ecosystem.

Department of Pollution Control - Awaiting concurrence
from regional office for this project.

Staff recommends issuance of Fill Permit No. 253.124 provided dikes
and turbidity screens are installed prior to filling submerged land.

ACTION OF THE TRUSTEES:

On motion by Mr. Christian, seconded by Mr. Dickinson and
carried without objection, the Trustees authorized issuance of
the fill permit with the provisions recommended by the staff.

589

-23D-

LEE COUNTY - Construction Permit, Section 253.03

APPLICANT: City of Fort Myers

PROJECT: Construction of breakwater and a public marina
facility, covering approximately 288,500 square
feet in the Caloosahatchee River abutting Section
13, Township 44 South, Range 24 East, Lee County.

PAYMENT: None.

ECOLOGICAL
RESPONSES: Department of Natural Resources - No objection.

Game and Fresh Water Fish Commission - No response.

Department of Pollution Control - No objection
provided adequare openings allowed in breakwater to
allow circulation of basin water.

Staff recommends approval of construction permit subject to
recommendation of the Department of Pollution Control.

ACTION OF THE TRUSTEES:

Motion was made by Mr. Christian, seconded by Mr. Dickinson and
carried unanimously that the construction permit be approved
subject to the recommendation of the Department of Pollution
Control.

On motion duly adopted, the meeting was adjourned.

GOVERNOR - CHAIRMAN

ATTEST:
EXECUTIVE DIRECTOR

* * *   * * *

Tallahassee, Florida
March 28, 1972

The Board of Trustees of the Internal Improvement Trust Fund
met on this date in the auditorium of the Burns Building
with the following members present:

Reubin O'D. Askew	Governor
Richard (Dick) Stone	Secretary of State
Robert L. Shevin	Attorney General
Thomas D. O'Malley	Treasurer
Floyd T. Christian	Commissioner of Education
Doyle Conner	Commissioner of Agriculture
Joel Kuperberg	Executive Director

There was brief discussion of the report submitted by the staff
in response to the resolution presented by Commissioner of
Agriculture Conner and adopted by the Cabinet on February 28.
There had been no meeting on March 14, the agenda of the next
meeting was lengthy, and Mr. Conner had requested consideration
as the first matter on the agenda on this date.

3-28-72

Each member had been furnished the most recent up-dated list of applications pending six months or more. The Executive Director explained that, while many applications had been shown as pending because applicants had been requested by the Trustees' office to obtain comments from the Department of Pollution Control, in most instances the applicants had failed to make application to that department.

-1-

LEON COUNTY - Road Easement

The Department of Transportation

requests an easement containing 0.5 acre across a parcel of land in Section 12, Township 1 South, Range 1 West, Leon County, for road right of way purposes for widening Orange Avenue (State Road 373) west of South Adams Street.

The parcel is a portion of the Florida A & M University campus. The request has been reviewed and approved by the Board of Regents.

Recommend issuance of the easement for public highway purposes.

ACTION OF THE TRUSTEES:

Motion was made by Mr. O'Malley, seconded by Mr. Stone and carried unanimously, to grant the easement for public highway purposes.

-2-

DADE COUNTY - Construction Permit and Marina License ML-120

APPLICANT: Jose Milton
              1400 Southwest 27 Avenue
              Miami, Florida

PROJECT: Construction of a mooring facility covering 8,820
              square feet of submerged land in Biscayne Bay
              adjacent to Section 19, Township 53 South, Range 42
              East, Dade County. No dredging is required. Seawall
              and backfill are to be placed under Trustees' Permit
              No. 253.124(8) issued February 29, 1972.

PAYMENT: $176.40 minimum annual fee for marina license.

ECOLOGICAL
RESPONSES: Department of Natural Resources - No objection.

              Game and Fresh Water Fish Commission - No objection.

              Department of Pollution Control - No objection.

Staff recommends issuance of construction permit and marina license for annual fee of $176.40.

ACTION OF THE TRUSTEES:

Motion was made by Mr. Stone, seconded by Mr. Christian and carried unanimously, to authorize issuance of construction permit and marina license for an annual fee of $176.40.

-3-

At the request of the Department of Transportation, Dredge Permit No. 253.123-869 for that department to perform work in Deep Bottom Branch in Duval County was withdrawn from the agenda.

-4-

FRANKLIN COUNTY - Construction Permit

APPLICANT: Department of Natural Resources
Larson Building
Tallahassee, Florida

PROJECT: 15 feet by 32 feet covered boat shed on the Carrabelle River adjacent to the Marine Patrol Office in Section 20, Township 7 South, Range 4 West, Franklin County.

No dredging is required.

PAYMENT: Request waiver of fee.

ECOLOGICAL
RESPONSES: Department of Natural Resources - No objection.

Game and Fresh Water Fish Commission - No objection.

Department of Pollution Control - No objection.

Staff recommends issuance of construction permit and waiver of fee.

ACTION OF THE TRUSTEES:

Motion was made by Mr. Christian, seconded by Mr. Stone and adopted unanimously, to approve the construction permit for the Department of Natural Resources without fee.

-5-

HILLSBOROUGH COUNTY - Dredge Permit No. 253.123-792(TPA 71-9)

APPLICANT: Tampa Electric Company
J. D. Hicks, Vice President, Operations
Post Office Box 111, Tampa, Florida

PROJECT: Tampa Port Authority issued Permit 71-9 authorizing maintenance dredging in the cooling water discharge slip on Black Point.

LOCATION: Section 4, Township 30 South, Range 19 East, Hillsborough County.

MATERIAL: 2,145 cubic yards of material will be removed and placed on adequately diked spoil area and in accordance with U. S. Corps of Engineers Permit No. 57-463.

PAYMENT: None. State-owned sovereignty land not involved.

ECOLOGICAL
RESPONSES: Department of Natural Resources - No objection.

Game and Fresh Water Fish Commission - No objection.

Department of Pollution Control - No objection.

Staff recommends issuance of Permit 253.123-792(TPA 71-9).

3-28-72

ACTION OF THE TRUSTEES:

Motion was made by Mr. Christian, seconded by Mr. Stone and
adopted unanimously, to approve issuance of the dredge permit
for Tampa Electric Company to perform maintenance dredging in a
cooling water discharge channel.

-6-

LAKE COUNTY - Dredge Permit No. 253.123-959

APPLICANT: Mid-Florida Lakes, Inc.
            Route 2, Box 289
            Leesburg, Florida

PROJECT: To connect an upland canal and an upland boat basin
            and canal to a tributary of Haines Creek

LOCATION: Haines Creek, Section 1, Township 19 South, Range
            25 East, Lake County.

MATERIAL: No sovereignty material involved.

PAYMENT: None involved.

ECOLOGICAL
RESPONSES: Department of Natural Resources - See Game and Fresh
            Water Fish Commission report for this fresh water
            project.

            Game and Fresh Water Fish Commission - Long deadend
            canals do not provide high quality habitat for fish
            and wildlife and they usually have a detrimental
            effect on the connecting body of water. For these
            reasons, recommend that the permit be denied.

            Department of Pollution Control - The connection of the
            canals to the waters of a tributary to Haines Creek
            will have a detrimental effect on the water quality
            of Haines Creek. The project is not recommended for
            approval.

Staff recommends denial of Permit No. 253.123-959.

ACTION OF THE TRUSTEES:

On motion by Mr. Stone, seconded by Mr. Shevin and adopted
without objection, the Trustees accepted the staff recommendation
for denial of the dredge permit.

-7-

MONROE COUNTY - Dredge Permit No. 253.03-289

APPLICANT: Key Largo KOA, Key Largo, Florida

PROJECT: To excavate a channel 50 feet wide by 1850 feet long
            by 5 feet deep. 350 feet will be through mangrove
            (Pennekamp Park Property) into an existing canal
            of South Sound Creek. Excavating will be done by
            shooting the rock with dynamite and digging with
            dragline.

LOCATION: Section 22, Township 61 South, Range 39 East,
            Newport Bay, Key Largo, Monroe County.

MATERIAL: Approximately 10,000 cubic yards of material will be
            excavated and placed on privately-owned upland.

3-28-72

ECOLOGICAL
RESPONSES: Department of Natural Resources - Since the proposed
              navigation channel would cut through a very scenic
              and important mangrove area of the park and add
              additional boat traffic to the already congested
              condition in South Sound Creek, we have no choice
              but to object.

              Game and Fresh Water Fish Commission - The proposed
              channel and spoil site as presently designed will
              destroy a portion of intertidal mangroves as well as
              turtlegrass flats. The mangrove creek which would
              connect to the proposed channel is a scenic portion
              of John Pennekamp State Park and should not be
              altered. Piecemeal destruction of lands set aside
              for scenic and biological purposes will render the
              objectives of such sites meaningless. We recommend
              that a permit not be granted for the above referenced
              channel construction.

              Department of Pollution Control - Dredging, along
              with the destruction of mangrove shoreline, will
              have an effect on water quality. The waters are
              suitable for recreation and the propagation of fish
              and wildlife. The construction and operation of
              the channel will eliminate to some extent the ability
              of the waters to support fish propagation. It is
              recommended that the permit application be rejected
              and the applicant consider an alternate route.

Staff recommends denial of Dredge Permit No. 253.03-289 to Key
Largo KOA based on adverse ecological reports.

ACTION OF THE TRUSTEES:

The Director pointed out that since there were objections from
all three environmental agencies to the proposed channel
dredging in grass flats and mangroves within the boundaries of
the John Pennekamp State Park, the staff could take no other
position than to recommend denial.

Motion was made by Mr. O'Malley, seconded by Mr. Stone, to
deny the application.

Mr. David B. Cable, owner and operator of Key Largo KOA Kamp-
ground and Marina, explained the need for deep water access and
urged approval of a navigation channel for use by the many
boaters using his recreation and camping facilities. He said
the channel presently in use was longer, too shallow with
several hairpin curves, hazardous to boats, and the proposed
new channel would have the advantage of also being available
for use by an adjacent development. In response to Mr. Christian's
suggestion that the channel he was using might be improved,
Mr. Cable explained that it would be a greater distance and
also in mangroves.

A substitute motion was made by Mr. O'Malley, seconded by
Mr. Stone and carried without objection, to defer action for
thirty days for the staff of the Trustees and the environmental
agencies to explore the possibility of an alternate route that
the applicant could accept.

-8-

MONROE COUNTY - Fill Permit No. 253.03-318

APPLICANT: Utility Board of the City of Key West
              Post Office Drawer 1060, Key West, Florida

PROJECT: To enlarge the present site of the existing electric
              power substation by filling a parcel of submerged

3-28-72

land 35 feet wide by 125 feet long. This submerged
land was previously conveyed by Trustees Deed No.
23855. Boulder riprap will be placed around the
perimeter area to protect the area from erosion.

LOCATION: North of U. S. 1 between Stock Island and Racoon
Key in Section 26, Township 67 South, Range 25 East,
Monroe County.

MATERIAL: Will be hauled in.

PAYMENT: None. Sovereignty land not involved. Request waiver
of processing fee.

ECOLOGICAL
RESPONSES: Department of Natural Resources - The proposed filling
of the productive grassy area, 43 feet by 125 feet,
is not recommended. The 8-foot wide fill area on
the North and East side of the existing fill area should
be filled with boulders.

Game and Fresh Water Fish Commission - Recommend that
permission to conduct this operation be denied.

Department of Pollution Control - No objection.

Staff recommends issuance of Permit 253.03-318 with the stipulation
that a silt screen be used to prevent siltation of the surrounding
area, and recommend waiver of the fee since the project is in the
public interest.

ACTION OF THE TRUSTEES:

Mr. Kuperberg said the staff had worked extensively with the
applicant, a reduced fill area and riprap had been agreed on
and there appeared to be no alternate to the substation site
according to the representation of the Key West Utility Board.
Nonetheless there was an objection from the Game and Fresh Water
Fish Commission.

Motion was made by Mr. Christian, seconded by Mr. Stone and
carried, to approve the application. Immediately after the
meeting Mr. Shevin said he had intended to vote against the
permit and requested that his vote be recorded as "No."

-9A-

OKALOOSA COUNTY - Construction Permit and Marina License ML-108

APPLICANT: City of Ft. Walton Beach
Post Office Box 1449, Ft. Walton Beach, Florida

PROJECT: Construction of three piers and two concrete boat
ramps in Santa Rosa Sound at the proposed Liza M.
Jackson Park (Santa Rosa Sound Park) in Section
15, Township 2 South, Range 24 West, Okaloosa County.

The Bureau of Beaches and Shores, Department of
Natural Resources, has issued Permit No. BBS-72-5
for the proposed groined piers.

PAYMENT: Request waiver of annual fee for marina license.

ECOLOGICAL
RESPONSES: Department of Natural Resources - No objection.

Game and Fresh Water Fish Commission - No objection.

Department of Pollution Control - No objection.

Staff recommends issuance of construction permit and marina license
and waiver of annual fee.

3-28-72

ACTION OF THE TRUSTEES:

On motion by Mr. Stone, seconded by Mr. O'Malley and carried
without objection, the Trustees authorized issuance of
construction permit and marina license, and waived the
annual fee for the City of Fort Walton Beach.

-9B-

OKALOOSA COUNTY - Dredge Permit No. 253.123-1047

APPLICANT: City of Ft. Walton Beach

PROJECT: To provide access for boat traffic at proposed loading
             ramps and docks. Depth to be -4 feet Mean Low Water.

LOCATION: Section 15, Township 2 South, Range 24 West, Santa
             Rosa Sound at Liza M. Jackson Park.

MATERIAL: 345 cubic yards of material to be dredged and deposited
             on upland.

PAYMENT: Request waiver of all fees.

ECOLOGICAL
RESPONSES: Department of Natural Resources - No objection.

             Game and Fresh Water Fish Commission - No objection.

             Department of Pollution Control - No objection subject
             to applicant's using a hydraulic dredge and diked
             upland spoil area.

Staff recommends issuance of Dredge Permit No. 253.123-1047, and
waiver of fees since project is in the public interest.

ACTION OF THE TRUSTEES:

On motion by Mr. Stone, seconded by Mr. Christian and Mr.
O'Malley, and carried unanimously, the Trustees agreed to
waive the fee and approve issuance of the dredge permit for
the public interest project.

-10-

POLK COUNTY - Dredge Permit No. 253.123-827

At the request of the applicant, the staff withdrew from the
agenda the dredge permit application of G. A. C. Properties,
Inc., to connect a series of deadend upland canals with the
Kissimmee River, a long-pending matter that the staff had
attempted to resolve by placing it on the agenda.

In response to Mr. Shevin's question whether an applicant
could get anything withdrawn from an agenda upon request, the
Director explained that as a matter of policy it had been
done that way, that if an applicant submits an application
and wants to negotiate further, it had been the staff
practice to withdraw the matter; but if this placed the
staff in a position of delay, perhaps such a request should
constitute a deactivation of the file and a new beginning
would then have to be made.

Mr. Shevin requested the staff to review that policy.

3-28-72

-11-

ST. LUCIE COUNTY - Construction Permit

APPLICANT: City of Fort Pierce
Post Office Box 1480, Fort Pierce, Florida

PROJECT: Construct a fender piling cluster adjacent to the
city pier in the Indian River of Seaway Drive
(S.R.A-1-A) in Section 3, Township 35 South, Range
40 East, St. Lucie County.

PAYMENT: $100 processing fee.

ECOLOGICAL
RESPONSES: Department of Natural Resources - No objection.

Game and Fresh Water Fish Commission - No objection.

Department of Pollution Control - No objection.

Staff recommends issuance of construction permit.

ACTION OF THE TRUSTEES:

Motion made by Mr. O'Malley, seconded by Mr. Christian, to
approve the permit was carried unanimously.

As this city paid the $100 fee, Mr. Christian asked why fees
were waived for 9A and 9B, and he thought all should pay.
Governor Askew expressed the opinion that obviously the city
was unaware that the fee could be waived, but there should
be a standard policy for governmental units. The Director
responded that as a policy decision of a previous Board of
Trustees, a waiver was recommended by the staff when a request
was submitted by a municipality. The staff on several occasions had been asked to increase the income commensurate
with operating costs, and there was nothing in the statutes
requiring waiver of the fee.

A motion was made by Mr. Christian, seconded by Mr. O'Malley,
and adopted without objection, that the processing fee be waived
for this municipality, also.

Governor Askew asked the Director to give some consideration to
this question and prepare a recommendation as to whether any
fees should be waived since the money will go into the General
Revenue Fund.

_____

-12A-

SARASOTA COUNTY - Bulkhead Line, Section 253.122, F. S.

APPLICANT: Carl E. Weller
c/o R. F. Sutton and Associates, Inc.
Post Office Box 852, Venice, Florida

PROJECT: Bulkhead line 1538.41 feet long in Section 17,
Township 39 South, Range 19 East, Sarasota County,
approved and established by the Board of County
Commissioners of Sarasota County, sitting as the
Sarasota County Water and Navigation Control Authority,
by Resolution adopted January 18, 1972.

ECOLOGICAL
RESPONSES: Department of Natural Resources - No objection.

Game and Fresh Water Fish Commission - No objection.

Department of Pollution Control - No objection.

Staff recommends approval of bulkhead line.

3-28-72

ACTION OF THE TRUSTEES:

Mr. Kuperberg informed the members that the Sarasota County
Water and Navigation Control Authority asked the Trustees to
ratify all their actions, even though this was in an upland area.

Motion was made by Mr. O'Malley, seconded by Mr. Christian and
adopted without objection, that the bulkhead line be approved.

-12B-

SARASOTA COUNTY - Dredge Permit No. 253.123-1076

APPLICANT: Carl E. Weller
c/o R. F. Sutton and Associates, Inc.
Post Office Box 852, Venice, Florida

PROJECT: To dredge an upland boat basin and connect it
with the landcut segment of the Intracoastal
Waterway.

LOCATION: Intracoastal Waterway at U. S. Highway 41 in Section
17, Township 39 South, Range 19 East, Sarasota County.

MATERIAL: Approximately 112,000 cubic yards of material to be
dredged and removed from property. No sovereignty
material involved.

PAYMENT: None. Sovereignty land not involved.

ECOLOGICAL
RESPONSES: Department of Natural Resources - No objection.

Game and Fresh Water Fish Commission - No objection.

Department of Pollution Control - Requested maximum
depth be held to -7 feet MLW. Drawings have been
revised to show -7 feet MLW depth.

OTHERS: Approved by Sarasota County Water and Navigation
Control Authority.

Staff recommends issuance of Dredge Permit 253.123-1076.

ACTION OF THE TRUSTEES:

Motion was made by Mr. O'Malley, seconded by Mr. Christian and
adopted without objection, that the dredge permit be approved.

-13-

WALTON COUNTY - Artificial Reef Permit No. 2399-Extension

APPLICANT: Walton County Chamber of Commerce
Post Office Box 29, DeFuniak Springs, Florida

PROJECT: Request for time extension of Artificial Reef Permit
No. 2399 covering 4 sites each 1 acre in size.

LOCATION: (1) 30° 24' 38" North Latitude
86° 08' 48" West Longitude
(2) 30° 25' 56" North Latitude
86° 14' 18" West Longitude
(3) 30° 27' 58" North Latitude
86° 14' 34" West Longitude
(4) 30° 24' 36" North Latitude
86° 17' 35" West Longitude

MATERIAL: Old tires and concrete held in place with stainless
steel cables.

3-28-72

PAYMENT: $50 processing fee tendered.

ECOLOGICAL
RESPONSES: Department of Natural Resources - No objection.

             Game and Fresh Water Fish Commission - No objection.

             Department of Pollution Control - No objection.

Staff recommends authorization to extend expiration time for
Artificial Reef Permit No. 2399.

ACTION OF THE TRUSTEES:

Motion was made by Mr. Stone, seconded by Mr. O'Malley and carried
without objection, to authorize extension of the expiration
time for the artificial reef permit.

-14-

MARINA LICENSES - Renewal

The required annual fee for the following marina license has
been submitted:

Marina License	Licensee	Annual Fee
ML-1	Port Tarpon Marina, Inc., Anclote River, Section 2, Township 27 South, Range 15 East, Pinellas County.	$749.00

Staff recommends renewal of the marina license for one year at
the fee indicated.

ACTION OF THE TRUSTEES:

Motion was made by Mr. O'Malley, seconded by Mr. Stone and
Mr. Conner, and adopted without objection, to authorize
renewal of the marina license for one year at the fee indicated.

-15-

The discussion of the report on pending applications was
recorded at the beginning of these minutes.

-16-

MANATEE COUNTY - File No. 2429-41-253.03

The Trustees deferred for one week consideration of an application from Frank J. Conrad and wife for an ex parte disclaimer.

-17-

DADE COUNTY - Seawall and Fill Permit No. 253.124-230

The City of Miami's application was placed on the agenda for
reconsideration on this date, and was deferred for one
additional week.

-18-

FRANKLIN COUNTY - Dredge Permit No. 253.123-952

APPLICANT: General Engineering Services, Inc.
              c/o W. B. Miller
              Star Route, Lanark Beach, Florida

PROJECT: To dredge a channel 950 feet long varying in width
              from 100 feet to 150 feet by 12.5 feet deep
              paralleling the shore line; to construct a seawall
              and an upland boat slip.

LOCATION: Carrabelle River in Section 20, Township 7 South,
              Range 4 West, Franklin County.

MATERIAL: 33,000 cubic yards of material will be removed and
              stockpiled on applicant's upland for use by the
              Franklin County School Board (17,000 cubic yards)
              and the City of Carabelle (16,000 cubic yards).

PAYMENT: Request waiver of payment for the material to be
              removed since it will be given to the County and
              City.

ECOLOGICAL
RESPONSES: Department of Natural Resources - No objection,
              provided the spoil area is adequately diked.

              Game and Fresh Water Fish Commission - No objection,
              provided the area is diked and waste water facilities
              used to prevent turbid water from escaping.

              Department of Pollution Control - No objection to
              project.

Staff recommends issuance of Permit 253.123-952 and waiver of
the payment for the material, as the material will be used for
public interest projects.

ACTION OF THE TRUSTEES:

Mr. Kuperberg explained that there had been a problem in
determining whether the fill would be used for public purposes
or would be paid for. Substantiating letters had been received
from both the city and county verifying public use of the fill
material.

Motion was made by Mr. Christian, seconded by Mr. Conner and
carried without objection, to approve the staff recommendation
as the action of the Board.

-19-

DADE COUNTY - Permit 253.124(8)-124

APPLICANT: Mahi Shrine, c/o Joseph G. Moretti
              Post Office Box 35-868, Miami, Florida

PROJECT: To construct a seawall 5 feet offshore from the existing
              bank of the Miami River.

LOCATION: Section 35, Township 53 South, Range 41 East, Dade
              County.

MATERIAL: To be hauled in from upland sources.

PAYMENT: None. Sovereignty land not involved.

3-28-72

OTHER
STATEMENTS: The City of Miami recommends a vertical seawall
to beautify the river, eliminate erosion and
permit proper mooring of boats.

ECOLOGICAL
RESPONSES: Department of Natural Resources reports that to better
conserve marine biological resources the existing
rubble wall and intertidal area should not be replaced
by a vertical seawall. The westerly end of the wall
should connect with the southeasterly corner of an
existing seawall.

Game and Fresh Water Fish Commission recommends that
a vertical seawall not be constructed on this site.
Additional riprap should be used if more erosion
protection is needed.

Department of Pollution Control - No objection to
project as proposed.

OTHERS: 1. City of Miami indicates that it has long been
the wish and intention to have the banks of the Miami
River seawalled. It is felt that a proper bulkhead
would beautify the river, eliminate erosion and
avulsion problems, and would permit proper mooring
of boats. A similar view has been expressed by both
the Coast Guard and the Corps of Engineers. Private
development of the river has proceeded according to
this plan.

2. A March 15, 1972, letter and photographs furnished
by Nick Leischen, Administrative Aide, Secretary of State,
indicates entire south shore of Miami River in this
area has vertical seawalls. This river as determined
by its activity is a commercial industrial river and
not a scenic passive one. Any type of construction
such as riprap, sand bagging or berms, will be
causative of problems.

Staff recommends issuance of Permit 253.124(8)-242 provided a riprap
seawall is installed in accordance with ecological agencies'
recommendations.

ACTION OF THE TRUSTEES:

On motion by Mr. Stone, seconded by Mr. O'Malley and carried
without objection, the rules were waived for consideration of
the matter.

Motion was made by Mr. O'Malley and Mr. Stone, seconded by Mr.
Conner and carried, to approve the application for construction of the
vertical seawall.

On motion duly adopted, the meeting was adjourned.

GOVERNOR - CHAIRMAN

ATTEST:
EXECUTIVE DIRECTOR

3-28-72

Tallahassee, Florida
April 4, 1972

The State of Florida Board of Trustees of the Internal
Improvement Trust Fund met on this date in the auditorium
of the Burns Building, with the following members present:

Reubin O'D. Askew	Governor
Richard (Dick) Stone	Secretary of State
Robert L. Shevin	Attorney General
Fred O. Dickinson, Jr.	Comptroller
Floyd T. Christian	Commissioner of Education
Doyle Conner	Commissioner of Agriculture

Joel Kuperberg	Executive Director

On behalf of the State Treasurer, Thomas O'Malley, absent
because of illness, the Secretary of State offered the
following resolution and made a motion for its adoption.
The motion was seconded by Mr. Dickinson and carried without
objection.

RESOLUTION

WHEREAS, it is the responsibility of the Governor
and the Cabinet to carry out the clear legislative mandate
for the protection of the environment of the State of
Florida, and,

WHEREAS, it has come to the attention of the Governor
and members of the Cabinet through legislative hearings
and testimony that there exists undue delay and unnecessary
costs in the processing of applications for dredge and fill,
marinas, bulkheads, docks and coastal construction permits
in the State of Florida, and

WHEREAS, it is the intent of the Governor and Cabinet
that all applications submitted by citizens of Florida
receive due process consistent with the protection of the
environment of our great State,

NOW THEREFORE BE IT RESOLVED that the Governor and
Cabinet, in a regular meeting assembled in Tallahassee,
Florida, do formally designate the Board of Trustees of
the Internal Improvement Trust Fund as the agency for
coordinating permit applications for agencies jointly under
the Governor and Cabinet, and further direct the Department
of Natural Resources, and request the Game and Fresh Water
Fish Commission and the Department of Pollution Control
to join in this endeavor by processing applications with
the Board of Trustees of the Internal Improvement Trust
Fund as expeditiously as possible, but in no case shall
the processing and subsequent action by the Board
extend beyond 120 days from the date of receipt of a complete
and correct application unless the time requirement is
waived by the Board or extended in writing by the applicant.

Adopted this 4th day of April, 1972.

REUBIN O'D. ASKEW
GOVERNOR

RICHARD (DICK) STONE
SECRETARY OF STATE

4-4-72

602

-14-

The minutes of March 21, 1972, were approved as submitted.

-15-

On motion by Mr. Stone, seconded by Mr. Christian and adopted
without objection, the Trustees authorized correction of a
scrivener's error in the agenda and minutes of March 7, and
the issuance of a marina license covering an area of 4,580
square feet to American Marine Repair Facility that was
approved on that date but incorrectly shown to encompass
2,320 square feet. The minimum annual fee of $100 would
still apply.

-2-

BREVARD COUNTY - Bulkhead Line Relocation
Section 253.122, Florida Statutes

APPLICANT: City of Melbourne

PROJECT: Relocation of bulkhead line along the westerly shore
of the Indian River and Crane Creek within the city
limits of the City of Melbourne, Florida, approved
and established by the City Council of the City of
Melbourne, by Ordinance No. 71-22 adopted July 20,
1971.

ECOLOGICAL
RESPONSES: Department of Natural Resources - No objection to
portion where line approximates mean high water
line. Filling landward of the 3,100 foot offshore
portion would have definite adverse effects on
marine biological resources; recommend the line be
relocated to the mean high water line.

Game and Fresh Water Fish Commission - No objection to
areas where line approximates mean high water line.
Recommend relocating 3,100 foot offshore area to the
mean high water line to insure continued maintenance
of an area as a productive estuarine resource.

Department of Pollution Control - No objection.

Staff recommends approval of bulkhead line excepting that 3,100
foot (more or less) portion lying between Lot 11, Block B of
Riverside Drive (at Cherry Street) and Lot 1 of the Caroline
Tract.

ACTION OF THE TRUSTEES:

Motion was made by Mr. Stone, seconded by Mr. Christian, to approve the staff recommendation.

Mr. Elting L. Storms, City Attorney, Mr. Michael Donoghue, City Engineer, and others were present in opposition to the staff recommendation to deny that portion of the line lying seaward of the mean high water line. Mr. Storms reviewed the establishment of the bulkhead line in 1959, the recommendation in 1969 that the line be relocated, four letters from the Trustees office in 1970 requesting relocation except in those areas where bottom lands had been sold, the public hearing held by the City of Melbourne and relocation of the bulkhead line on July 20, 1971. Mr. Storms urged approval, since the city had relocated the line as recommended by the Trustees staff (former staff).

Mr. Kuperberg pointed out that the agenda recommendation was in accordance with present-day thinking that the bulkhead line should be at the mean high water line, the staff did not think ownership of submerged bottoms automatically carried with it the right to fill, and that under their regulatory function the Trustees retained a reserved trust in public waters, and the authority to affirm or deny the right to fill.

Governor Askew said changing times necessitated changing policies in all departments, a decision must be made as to whether there was in fact any commitment of prior Trustees to allow filling of all lands sold, and establishment of the bulkhead line might make it more difficult to deny filling.

Mr. Christian expressed the opinion that the sales were made with the understanding that the buyers could use the land, and now that the city had relocated the bulkhead line as recommended by the Board through its staff, a subsequent change of policy should not be retroactive. He felt there was an obligation to uphold decisions of previous Boards.

A substitute motion was offered by Mr. Christian, seconded by Mr. Dickinson, and carried without objection, that the staff be directed to review the matter further and enter into discussions with the officials of the City of Melbourne.

-3-

BREVARD COUNTY - File No. 23775(790-05) Application to Fill

The application from Edward Shablowski to fill a parcel of submerged land in the North 1/2 of Section 34, Township 27 South, Range 37 East, Brevard County, landward of the bulk-head line proposed by the City of Melbourne, was deferred on motion by Mr. Christian, seconded by Mr. Dickinson, and carried without objection.

-4-

ST. JOHNS COUNTY - Bulkhead Line, Section 253.122, Florida Statutes

APPLICANT: City of St. Augustine
            Post Office Box 1453, St. Augustine, Florida

PROJECT: Bulkhead Line 9,812.37 feet long in the San Sebastian
            River and Matanzas River abutting Sections 19, 20, 29
            and 30, Township 7 South, Range 30 East, St. Johns
            County, approved and established by the City Commission
            of the City of St. Augustine by Resolution No. 2230
            adopted September 27, 1971.

            No plans for development have been submitted.

ECOLOGICAL
RESPONSES: Department of Natural Resources - A report dated

    4-4-72

June 5, 1970, indicates that the proposed bulkhead, "if approved and followed by filling would have significant adverse effects on marine biological resources. The bulkhead line should be located at the mean high tide line and exclude the cord grass marsh."

Game and Fresh Water Fish Commission - Comments not requested.

Department of Pollution Control - Comments not requested.

Interagency Advisory Committee Report No. 3 dated December 31, 1968, recommended setting the bulkhead line at the line of mean high water.

<u>Staff recommends denial of the bulkhead line</u>.

ACTION OF THE TRUSTEES:

The Director explained that there were no development plans, the Department of Natural Resources had objections, and the staff recommended denial of a bulkhead line considerably off-shore in that very productive marine resource area where the Interagency Advisory Committee had recommended setting the bulkhead line at the mean high water.

Mr. Hamilton Upchurch, member of the City Commission of St. Augustine, present with officials of the city and the county, explained that a 1925 Special Act of the Legislature vested title in the city to all river bottoms within city limits in fee simple, there was city and county property within the bulkhead line and no objections to the proposed line at the public hearing, the area though small and marshy was greatly needed for future planning for public uses but there was no specific plan at present.

Mr. Shevin, pointing out that the Interagency Advisory Committee report recommended the bulkhead line at the mean high water line and the Trustees should insist on it or change the policy, made a motion, seconded by Mr. Conner, to deny the bulkhead line that intruded into the river.

Mr. Kuperberg commented on the biological productivity of the land, the notice given three and a half years ago by the Interagency report that the land should be retained in its present condition, the trust function of the Board in all navigable waters regardless of ownership, and the probability that the federal government would not allow development in the water.

Mr. Conner felt that he might view differently some minor deviation from the mean high water line in order to improve the mud flat shore. He withdrew his second in order to suggest remanding the line to the staff for further work.

Mr. Stone then seconded Mr. Shevin's motion to deny the bulkhead line.

Mr. Conner offered a substitute motion to remand the bulkhead line back to the staff for review with the local officials. Mr. Dickinson seconded the motion in order to afford the staff and the city an opportunity to try to resolve differences in a reasonable way, as he was impressed with the long-range planning and felt that no city on a navigable stream would desire excessive filling.

Governor Askew thought the staff needed some direction from the members as to how to proceed. Mr. Stone expressed the opinion that members were not ready to approve an extension 600 feet into the river but desired to assist the city and county use the land they own. He suggested conferences and local hearing with state and federal representatives on the site to work out an alternate.

Representative A. H. Craig commented that a very small portion

605

of the marsh grass area of the St. Johns River was involved, the bulkhead line was in the public interest, and they should be able to resolve the problems.

Without objection, the substitute motion carried to refer the matter back to the staff to work with the applicants in coordination with other agencies and the Corps of Engineers to try to find an alternate that, if possible, would be satisfactory to the city.

-1-

HILLSBOROUGH COUNTY - Fill Permit No. 253.123-161(TPA Permit 71-5)

APPLICANT: Port Sutton, Inc. and Tampa Port Authority
Post Office Box "E", Tampa, Florida

PROJECT: The Tampa Port Authority issued TPA Permit 71-5 to fill a two hundred foot strip of land south of the south finger of Port Sutton. The project was modified to reduce the original width from 300 feet to 200 feet, and fill will not be placed in the westerly 1000 feet of the original spoil disposal area.

This item first appeared on the Trustees' agenda of February 23, 1971, and was deferred at the request of the Secretary of State.

It again appeared on March 3, 1971, and was again deferred at the request of the Secretary of State.

On March 9, 1971, the item was postponed upon staff recommendation until the bulkhead lines had been re-established by the Tampa Port Authority.

This item was not placed on the agenda following the relocation of the bulkhead lines as there were two adverse biological reports and the Department of Pollution Control indicated it would not certify the project. In a letter of February 24, 1972, the Department of Pollution Control withdrew the previously submitted objections to this project.

LOCATION: Section 3, Township 30 South, Range 19 East, Hillsborough Bay.

MATERIAL: Removed from pierside maintenance dredging of a strip of land 6,170 feet long by 34 feet deep by 100 feet wide.

PAYMENT: None. State-owned sovereignty land not involved.

ECOLOGICAL
RESPONSES: Department of Natural Resources - The proposed fill area to the South of Pendola Point has been reduced from an area of 30 acres to an area of 18 acres of submerged land. To conserve a developing cordgrass marsh on silted bay bottoms, no additional filling of submerged land should be permitted. It is evident that some damage to marine biological resources would result from filling of submerged land.

Game and Fresh Water Fish Commission - The area is at present a most valuable and productive portion of the marine ecosystem. If the permit application is approved, spoil will cover a portion of the shallow productive area and another important portion of the ecosystem will be lost. The commission recommends that the permit application as presented be denied.

4-4-72

Department of Pollution Control - Original objections to this project were based in part on the following: "That any fill on the south side of Pendola Point would have definite adverse effects on water quality in the area. The normal flow of water in the area of the tidal creek that existed on the natural shoreline to the east would be disrupted by filling the south side of Pendola Point."

The tidal areas to the east have been filled. Based on the above, this Department withdraws the previously submitted objections to the 200 foot fill on the south side of Pendola Point. Drawings and information will be required from the applicant to define the bulkheading, method of fill, and controls to be utilized during the filling operation.

Staff recommends approval of Tampa Port Authority Permit 71-5 (Fill Permit 253.123-161) as modified to permit completion of this project.

ACTION OF THE TRUSTEES:

Mr. Kuperberg reviewed the background of this fill proposal that had been reduced from an original 70 acres to 30 and then to 18 at the recommendation of the Department of Natural Resources. Negotiation on the bulkhead line had been concluded by Tampa Port Authority agreeing to restore it to the mean high water in Tampa Bay except in those areas where previous contractual commitments had been made, one being the Port Sutton fill. Objections of the Department of Pollution Control had been withdrawn, and the staff felt that all requirements and obligations were fulfilled.

Mr. Robert Thomas and Mr. Clint Brown, Chairman of Tampa Port Authority, were present.

On motion by Mr. Christian, seconded by Mr. Conner and adopted, with Mr. Shevin voting in the negative, the fill permit was approved as recommended by the staff. Governor Askew voted in support of the staff recommendation.

-5-

ST. LUCIE COUNTY - Bulkhead Line, Section 253.122, F. S.

APPLICANT: Board of County Commissioners
of St. Lucie County

PROJECT: Bulkhead line 1,664.71 feet long in Fort Pierce Cut abutting Section 26, Township 34 South, Range 40 East, St. Lucie County, approved and established by the Board of County Commissioners of St. Lucie County by Resolution No. 70-85 adopted November 10, 1970.

ECOLOGICAL
RESPONSES: Department of Natural Resources - No objection.

Game and Fresh Water Fish Commission - Recommends mean high water line and existing seawalls.

Department of Pollution Control - No objection.

Staff recommends approval of 1,208.52-foot portion of bulkhead line lying north of Tract "B".

ACTION OF THE TRUSTEES:

Motion was made by Mr. Christian, seconded by Mr. Stone and adopted without objection, that the staff recommendation be approved as the action of the Board.

-6-

ST. LUCIE COUNTY - State Construction Permit and
                   Marina License ML-102

APPLICANT: City of Fort Pierce, Engineering Department
             Post Office Box 3191, Fort Pierce, Florida

PROJECT: Enlargement of existing city marina facility in
             the Indian River at Moores Creek abutting Section
             10, Township 35 South, Range 40 East, St. Lucie
             County. Approximately 6,693.75 square feet of
             sovereignty land will be used.

             No dredging is required.

PAYMENT: Request waiver of minimum annual fee for marina
             license.

ECOLOGICAL
RESPONSES: Department of Natural Resources - No objection.

             Game and Fresh Water Fish Commission - No objection.

             Department of Pollution Control - No objection.

Staff recommends issuance of construction permit and marina license
and waiver of all fees.

ACTION OF THE TRUSTEES:

On motion by Mr. Christian, seconded by Mr. Dickinson and
adopted without objection, the Trustees approved the
construction permit and marina license without charge.

-17-

MANATEE COUNTY - Application for ex parte disclaimer
                 File No. 2429-41-253.03'

On December 14, 1971, application for disclaimer was withdrawn
from the agenda. On March 28 consideration of the application
was deferred one week.

Staff description: A parcel of land abutting Block 39,
Longbeach Subdivision, Government Lots 3 and 5, Section 15,
Township 35 South, Range 16 East, Manatee County.

A.   CITY AND
     COUNTY: Town of Longboat Key, Manatee County

B.   APPLICANT: Frank J. Conrad and Marjorie Conrad, his wife.

C.   APPLICANT's
     REPRESENTATIVE: Robert J. Carr

D.   ACREAGE:
     RATE PER ACRE: Not applicable

E.   APPRAISAL: Not applicable

F.   PURPOSE: Not applicable

G.   BIOLOGICAL
     REPORTS: Not applicable

H.   STAFF REMARKS: Applicant has submitted supporting documents
     and a series of aerial photographs and coastal charts of the
     north end of Longboat Key which indicate that the subject
     land is a natural accretion onto existing upland owned by
     the applicant. The staff has found no documentary evidence
     to contradict that evidence presented by the applicant.

     It appears that there is a great deal of public interest
     in Manatee County in retaining the subject land in its

4-4-72

natural state as a public recreation area. The Town of Longboat Key and the Manatee County Board of County Commissioners argue that the subject property is not accretion. Town and County officials have requested that the Board of Trustees convey the subject land by a quitclaim deed to Manatee County so that the county can pursue whatever interest the people may have.

Although no evidence has been found to support a claim by the state to the subject land, the Staff feels that because of the substantial local interest in retaining the subject land as a public recreational area and because of the stated willingness of the county to undertake the pursuit of any interest the public may have, the matter would be more appropriately settled at the local level.

Staff recommends denial of the application for disclaimer and granting of request by Manatee County for a quitclaim deed to the property.

ACTION OF THE TRUSTEES:

The Director discussed the staff work and original recommendation in favor of disclaimer to the owner of the upland, the objections of private citizens, the Town of Longboat Key and Manatee County, subsequent conferences with town and county officials, and the request from the town and county for a quitclaim to the county. The staff in no way wanted to abandon any possible public interest, because of adverse possession or other public claims.

Representative John Harlee spoke of the keen local interest in the matter and asked for support of the staff recommendation.

Mr. Robert J. Carr, attorney for the applicants, with maps and explanations of the formation of the land known as Beer Can Island, sought to clarify his clients' position as owners of the accretion.

Mr. Dewey Dye, attorney retained in March by applicants, had filed suit to quiet title, including an injunction against deeding the land to anyone other than the applicants. His clients' position was that because of evidence of fact, under common law the title to the accretion was in the upland owner as one of his riparian rights. Mr. Dye said this was not a matter of policy but of statutory procedures and the Board of Trustees of the Internal Improvement Trust Fund, a special statutory agency, should follow the procedure outlined in the law.

Motion was made by Mr. Stone, seconded by Mr. Shevin and adopted without objection, that the staff recommendation be approved as the action of the Board.

-7-

DUVAL COUNTY - Right of Way Easement, File 2447-16-253.03

APPLICANT: Jacksonville Port Authority

PROJECT: Highway and bridge construction for State Road 9-A. No dredging or filling is required.

LOCATION: 2.80 acre parcel of sovereignty land in the St. Johns River in Section 18 and 19, Township 1 South, Range 28 East, Duval County.

ECOLOGICAL
RESPONSES: Department of Natural Resources - "If precautions are taken to protect the cordgrass marsh adjacent to the proposed bridge, the project should have only very limited adverse effects on marine biological resources."

Game and Fresh Water Fish Commission - No objection.

Department of Pollution Control - No objection.

Staff remarks: This is a joint project by the Jacksonville Port Authority and the Department of Transportation to construct a two-lane concrete bridge to serve the Blount Island terminal area.

Staff requests authority to issue right of way easement.

ACTION OF THE TRUSTEES:

On motion by Mr. Christian, seconded by Mr. Dickinson and adopted without objection, the easement was approved.

-8A-

GULF COUNTY - Right of Way Easement, File No. 2445-23-253.03

APPLICANT: Department of Transportation
Haydon Burns Building, Tallahassee, Florida

PROJECT: Highway and boat ramp construction for State Road S-30-B. Dredging is required.

LOCATION: 0.13 acre parcel of sovereignty land in the Gulf of Mexico abutting Government Lot 1, Section 22, Township 9 South, Range 10 West, Gulf County.

ECOLOGICAL
RESPONSES: Department of Natural Resources - No objection.

Game and Fresh Water Fish Commission - No objection.

Department of Pollution Control - No objection.

Staff requests authority to issue right of way easement.

ACTION OF THE TRUSTEES:

Motion was made by Mr. Christian, seconded by Mr. Dickinson and carried without objection, to approve the easement to the Department of Transportation.

-8B-

GULF COUNTY - Dredge Permit No. 253.123-1103

APPLICANT: Department of Transportation
Haydon Burns Building
Tallahassee, Florida

PROJECT: To construct a concrete boat ramp for public use at the end of State Road No. S-30-B.

LOCATION: Indian Pass in Section 22, Township 9 South, Range 10 West, Gulf County.

MATERIAL: 20 cubic yards of material will be removed and used in the construction of the boat ramp.

PAYMENT: Request waiver of the fees since the project is in the public interest.

ECOLOGICAL
RESPONSES: Department of Natural Resources - No objection.

Game and Fresh Water Fish Commission - No objection.

Department of Pollution Control - No objection.

OTHERS: Dredge permit issued by Gulf County.

Staff recommends issuance of Permit 253.123-1103 and waiver of

4-4-72

all fees as the project is in the public interest.

ACTION OF THE TRUSTEES:

Motion was made by Mr. Christian, seconded by Mr. Dickinson
and carried without objection, to approve the dredge permit
without fee for the public interest project.

-9A-

CITRUS COUNTY - Dredge Permit No. 253.123-938

APPLICANT: Pete's Pier, Inc.
Post Office Box 633, Crystal River, Florida

PROJECT: Dredge to restore navigability by removing remains
of previous docks and sunken barges, and to dredge
to -5 feet mean low water.

LOCATION: Crystal River, Section 21, Township 18 South, Range
17 East, Citrus County.

MATERIAL: Dredge 2,472 cubic yards of material which will
be placed in a diked spoil site on privately-owned
upland.

PAYMENT: $50 processing fee and $1,236 for dredge material
at the standard rate of 50¢ per cubic yard.

ECOLOGICAL
RESPONSES: Department of Natural Resources - Proposed dredging
should not have significant adverse effects.

Game and Fresh Water Fish Commission - No objection,
provided there is no dredging within 45 feet of
existing shoreline. Walkways across the preserved
beach, for access, would not be objectionable.

Department of Pollution Control - No objection.

OTHERS: Field Operations Division - No objection.

Applicant has agreed to the suggested modifications.

Staff recommends issuance of Dredge Permit No. 253.123-938 amended
to conform with the recommendations of the Department of Natural
Resources and the Game and Fresh Water Fish Commission.

ACTION OF THE TRUSTEES:

Motion was made by Mr. Stone, seconded by Mr. Conner and Mr.
Dickinson, and carried without objection, to approve the
dredge permit amended to conform to the recommendations
of the environmental agencies.

-9B-

CITRUS COUNTY - State Construction Permit and Marina License
No. 53

APPLICANT: Pete's Pier, Inc.
Post Office Box 633, Crystal River, Florida

PROJECT: Construction of marina facility and wet storage
covering 59,400 square feet of sovereignty land in
Crystal River abutting Section 21, Township 18 South,
Range 17 East, Citrus County.

PAYMENT: $1,188 minimum annual fee for marina license.

ECOLOGICAL
RESPONSES: Department of Natural Resources - No objection.

Game and Fresh Water Fish Commission - No objection, provided no structures except access walkways are placed within 45 feet of existing shoreline.

Department of Pollution Control - No objection.

<u>Staff recommends issuance of construction permit and marina license amended to conform with the recommendations of the Game and Fresh Water Fish Commission.</u>

ACTION OF THE TRUSTEES:

On motion by Mr. Stone, seconded by Mr. Conner and Mr. Dickinson, carried without objection, the Trustees approved construction permit and marina license amended to conform to the recommendations of the Game and Fresh Water Fish Commission.

-10-

ESCAMBIA COUNTY - Artificial Reef Permit No. 253.03-330

APPLICANT: Santa Rosa Island Authority
Post Office Box 9008, Pensacola Beach, Florida

PROJECT: To construct an artificial fishing reef in the Gulf of Mexico along the 60-foot contour 2,200 yards offshore from Santa Rosa Island. This reef will have a minimum clearance of -50 feet mean low water.

LOCATION: The ends of the reef will be located at the following coordinates: East end, 30° 18' 46" North latitude and 87° 07' 00" West Longitude; West end, 30° 18' 46" North Latitude and 87° 08' 00" West Longitude.

MATERIAL: 1,500 cubic yards of concrete rubble obtained from the demolished Casino Building at Pensacola Beach.

PAYMENT: $50 processing fee.

ECOLOGICAL
RESPONSES: Department of Natural Resources - No objection. Florida Marine Patrol reports that construction of reef should not interfere with commercial fishing activities.

Game and Fresh Water Fish Commission - No objection.

Department of Pollution Control - No objection, providing (1) site survey determines that the bottom is suitable, no existing reef and (2) inert materials used for construction of the reef.

<u>Staff recommends issuance of Permit 253.03-330 for the artificial reef.</u>

ACTION OF THE TRUSTEES:

Motion was made by Mr. Dickinson, seconded by Mr. Stone and carried without objection, to approve the artificial reef permit.

-11-

GADSDEN COUNTY - Construction Permit 253.03, F. S.

APPLICANT: Department of Transportation
Burns Building, Tallahassee, Florida

PROJECT: Construct a concrete boat ramp 50 feet long by 30 feet in the Ochlockonee River south of State Road No. 10 (U. S. 90) in Section 23, Township 1 North, Range 2 West, Gadsden County.

612

No dredging is required.

PAYMENT: Request waiver of fee.

ECOLOGICAL
RESPONSES: Department of Natural Resources - No objection.

Game and Fresn Water Fish Commission - No objection.

Department of Pollution Control - No objection.

Staff recommends issuance of construction permit and waiver of fee.

ACTION OF THE TRUSTEES:

On motion by Mr. Christian, seconded by Mr. Stone and adopted without objection, the Trustees approved the construction permit and authorized addition of the words "No objection" following the words "Department of Natural Resources" that was an inadvertent omission on the agenda.

-12-

HENDRY COUNTY - Dredge Permit No. 253.123-968

APPLICANT: R. E. Hawker
            Star Route 2, Box 201
            LaBelle, Florida

PROJECT: To construct an upland boat slip 40 feet by 70 feet by 7 feet deep in a land cut segment of the Caloosahatchee River Canal.

LOCATION: The North bank of the Caloosahatchee River in the vicinity of Fort Denaud, Florida, five miles west of LaBelle in Section 10, Township 43 South, Range 28 East, Hendry County.

MATERIAL: Material taken from dredge area will be placed on upland.

PAYMENT: None. Sovereignty land not involved.

ECOLOGICAL
RESPONSES: Department of Natural Resources - Requested Game And Fresh Water Fish Commission to perform biological survey.

Game and Fresh Water Fish Commission - No objection.

Department of Pollution Control - No objection.

Staff recommends issuance of Dredge Permit 253.123-968 to R. E. Hawker.

ACTION OF THE TRUSTEES:

Motion made by Mr. Christian, seconded by Mr. Stone, to approve the dredge permit carried without objection.

-13-

MARTIN COUNTY - Fill Permit No. 253.124(8)-253

APPLICANT: Sea Gate Harbor Home Owners Association
            Mr. Frederick G. Sundheim
            Post Office Box 768, Palm City, Florida

PROJECT: To construct a seawall 107 feet along the entrance to a canal and 114 feet along the north fork of

4-4-72

the St. Lucie River to reduce erosion and improve navigation.

LOCATION: Section 6, Township 38 South, Range 41 East, Martin County.

MATERIAL: All material will be trucked in from upland sources.

PAYMENT: No sovereignty material involved.

ECOLOGICAL
RESPONSES: Department of Natural Resources, Survey and Management - Should have no significant adverse effects on marine biological resources.

Beaches and Shores - Bulkhead line should more nearly coincide with the line of mean high water and should be designed to dissipate wave energy.

Game and Fresh Water Fish Commission - No objection to the proposed project provided that stone riprap material rather than the proposed vertical seawall be used.

Department of Pollution Control - No objection to the proposed bulkheading, but it should be at the approximate line of mean high water and should be of riprap construction.

OTHERS: Board of County Commissioners has no objection.

Trustees' Field Operations Division recommends issuance of permit.

Staff recommends issuance of Fill Permit No. 253.124(8)-253 subject to the stipulation that stone riprap material be used for construction and that the seawall generally coincide with the line of mean high water along the river.
ACTION OF THE TRUSTEES:

Mr. Kuperberg pointed out that riprap material was recommended for the construction and the staff recommended issuance on that basis.

Motion was made by Mr. Christian, seconded by Mr. Stone and adopted without objection, to approve issuance of the fill permit subject to the stipulations recommended by the staff.

-16-

GADSDEN COUNTY - School Land Exchange

The University of Florida proposes to exchange with the Gadsden County School Board a 37.06-acre tract of state land for a 84.5-acre tract.

The 37.06-acre parcel in Section 18, Township 2 North, Range 3 West and Section 13, Township 2 North, Range 4 West is the original state agricultural experiment tract in Gadsden County acquired in 1921. Today this tract is in the City of Quincy surrounded by county school facilities and residences. In 1929 a 617-acre tract of land was acquired by the state 3 1/2 miles south of Quincy on the Lake Talquin Road (State Road 267).

The land offered to the State is contiguous to the 617-acre experiment station. The proposed exchange offers many advantages to the State, the greatest advantage being consolidation of facilities and obtaining additional acreage of excellent, highly fertile soils. Other advantages would be the elimination of moving farm machinery along a busy highway between the present two separate experiment stations and eliminating trespass and safety hazards at the 37.06-acre tract, both of which have become major problems.

Three appraisals have been made of each tract. The lowest appraisal of the 37.06-acre state tract is $77,000. The lowest appraisal of the 84.5-acre county tract is $84,982. The County School Board is willing to trade on an even basis with the University of Florida paying one-half of the cost of the appraisals.

The Board of Regents reviewed and approved the exchange at its March 6 meeting. The Board of Education approved the exchange at its meeting on March 21.

Recommend the exchange of land as proposed.

ACTION OF THE TRUSTEES:

Motion was made by Mr. Christian, seconded by Mr. Stone and adopted without objection, to approve the proposed land exchange.

-18-

DADE COUNTY - Seawall and Fill Permit No. 253.124-230

This application was considered and approved on March 7. Placed on the agenda on March 28 for reconsideration, it was deferred one week.

APPLICANT: City of Miami,
c/o Rader and Associates
First National Bank Building
Miami, Florida 33131

PROJECT: To fill an area 70 feet wide to the Dade County Bulkhead Line 61 feet away. The area is under the proposed Southeast 8th Street Bridge and will serve as a bridge approach.

LOCATION: Biscayne Bay, Section 38, Township 54 South, Range 42 East, Dade County.

MATERIAL: Will be hauled in.

PAYMENT: Fees waived because the project is in the public interest.

ECOLOGICAL
RESPONSES: Department of Natural Resources - States that the area should not be filled, but that subject property has been adversely affected by past dredging.

Game and Fresh Water Fish Commission - States that the additional placement of fill would only add to the destruction that has already taken place and recommends that permit be denied.

Department of Pollution Control - No objection.

OTHERS: 1. City of Miami by letter of February 22, 1972, indicates that it has no equipment to maintain pockets under bridge.

2. University of Miami report of February 1972 states there is little justification for preservation of this area either as an example of an unspoiled community or as an important energy source within the Biscayne Bay ecosystem.

Staff recommends issuance of Permit 253.124-230 provided seawall is constructed prior to filling with upland materials.

615

ACTION OF THE TRUSTEES:

Governor Askew said the matter was back for reconsideration as if no action had been taken, involving a very small fill under the bridgehead of the new bridge to Claughton Island.

Motion by Mr. Christian to approve the permit passed with the Attorney General and Commissioner of Agriculture voting in the negative.

Mr. Christian brought up the permit application from Charles E. Gottlieb on the agenda of March 21 as item 12 for filling and construction of a seawall in Biscayne Bay at Southeast 15 Road and South Bayshore Drive in Section 39, Township 54 South, Range 41 East, Dade County. After much discussion the permit was denied on March 21. (Fill Permit 253.124-179)

Mr. Christian asked for reconsideration, as in his opinion the private filling in this case was justified as much as the public filling (by the City of Miami).

There was some discussion as to whether the matter had been previously reconsidered, in which case it might technically require a waiver of the rules for another reconsideration. Mr. Christian offered to make a motion to waive the rules but the Governor said that in the absence of anyone pointing out that action should be to the contrary, he would entertain a motion on reconsideration.

Motion by Mr. Christian to reconsider, seconded by Mr. Dickinson, carried on the following vote:

    Ayes: Messrs. Christian, Dickinson, Conner and Stone
    Nays: Mr. Shevin and Governor Askew

Mr. Christian recalled that the Treasurer had suggested that if the public fill was approved the private fill permit should also be approved. Therefore, he made a motion that the Trustees approve Mr. Gottlieb's fill permit, noting that it would not require any dredging.

Mr. Dickinson seconded the motion that passed with the following vote:

    Ayes: Messrs. Christian, Conner, Dickinson and Stone
    Nays: Mr. Shevin and Governor Askew

After discussion of the next item there was added to the approval the condition that the end of the seawall be modified as recommended by the staff to avoid creation of a pocket at the adjoining property line.

Governor Askew brought up the denial on March 21 of the dedication request of the City of Miami for a sliver of sovereignty land in Biscayne Bay immediately adjacent to the Gottlieb parcel. (File No. 2364-13-253.02)

Mr. Christian made a motion to reconsider that, also. Mr. Dickinson seconded the motion that passed with Mr. Shevin voting "No."

Motion by Mr. Christian, seconded by Mr. Dickinson, to approve the dedication failed to pass on a vote of three to three, as follows:

    Ayes: Messrs. Christian, Dickinson and Stone
    Nays: Messrs. Shevin, Conner and Governor Askew

The Governor noted that the staff recommended against both the Gottlieb fill and the dedication, but approved the fill under the bridgehead. Mr. Kuperberg explained that it had not been made clear what the city intended to do with the

4-4-72

616

dedication area, but in effect a dedication was a precursor
to filling the land. In his opinion it would not be necessary
to fill the parcel to avoid a pocket, provided Mr. Gottlieb
modified his seawall at that end so it would not create a
right angle corner.

After that explanation Mr. Christian withdrew his motion to
reconsider the dedication and no further action was taken.

In response to the Attorney General's question on a report
with respect to the Marco Island matter, Mr. Kuperberg said
he had not seen the Burgess Report, learned of it only last
night from a newsman, the two charges that the Executive
Director knowingly concealed information from the
Trustees and that permits were violated were completely untrue -
as had been other charges for which the staff had repeatedly
tried to discover the basis and Mr. Burgess had never presented
any supporting facts. The Director and staff had no knowledge
of violations "that should have been brought to the Board's
attention" and had never refused to respond to any report of
any alleged unauthorized action.

Mr. Kuperberg, speaking of the two reported "massive violations",
explained that the Smokehouse Bay area was covered by the state
permit but as sometimes happens the federal permit did not cover
exactly the same area as the state permit and the work appeared
to be unpermitted by the United States Corps of Engineers permit.
Mr. Kuperberg called the Corps and had been told that when the
Corps contacted Marco Island Development Corporation the corp-
ration voluntarily stopped all work in the questioned area
as Trustees' staff field reports verified. The other alleged
violation was an upland cut, a channel cut into the upland where
the Trustees had no jurisdiction, the Corps was advised
subsequently and informed the Trustees' staff that the channel
was used as a runoff from the dredge area to prevent siltation
from the dredging, an approved pollution control technique.

In response to a question by Mr. Christian, the Director
indicated he did not know whether the report was a part of the
intention in a suit filed against the Trustees by Mr. George
Matthews.

On motion duly adopted, the meeting was adjourned.

GOVERNOR

CHAIRMAN

TEST:

EXECUTIVE DIRECTOR

4-4-72

The Board of Trustees of the Internal Improvement Trust Fund
met on this date in the auditorium of the Burns Building with
the following members present:

Reubin O'D. Askew   Governor
Richard (Dick) Stone   Secretary of State
Fred O. Dickinson, Jr.   Comptroller
Floyd T. Christian   Commissioner of Education
Doyle Conner   Commissioner of Agriculture

Joel Kuperberg   Executive Director

-1-

The minutes of the March 28 meeting were approved as submitted.

-2-

CITRUS AND HERNANDO COUNTIES

APPLICANT: United States Department of the Interior
Fish and Wildlife Service
Bureau of Sport Fisheries and Wildlife
Peachtree-Seventh Building, Atlanta, Georgia 30323

PROJECT: Applicant wishes to acquire private lands within
the Chassahowitzka National Wildlife Refuge as
Federal Duck Stamp funds become available in accordance with the Migratory Bird Act and the so-called
Wetlands Act which requires state approval. The
purpose of this acquisition is to more adequately
protect and develop this refuge for use by wildlife
and people.

LOCATION: Homosassa Bay in Township 20 South, Ranges 16 and 17
East, and Chassahowitzka Bay in Township 21 South,
Range 17 East, Citrus and Hernando Counties.

PAYMENT: Not required.

STAFF
COMMENTS: Section 372.771, Florida Statutes, gives consent to
the United States for acquisition of lands for the
purpose of managing, protecting and propagating fish
and wildlife subject to approval by the Board of
Trustees.

Staff recommends granting approval for acquisition of the private
lands as authorized under Section 372.771, Florida Statutes.

ACTION OF THE TRUSTEES:

Mr. Kuperberg advised that there would be no expense to the
state, required by law to indicate approval or disapproval.

Motion was made by Mr. Stone, seconded by Mr. Conner and
Mr. Christian, adopted without objection, that the land
acquisition be approved.

-3-

GADSDEN COUNTY - Road Right of Way

City of Chattahoochee,

on behalf of the Gadsden County School Board, requests a 100-
foot wide easement for public road purposes across a portion
of the Florida State Hospital land in Section 33, Township
4 North, Range 6 West, Gadsden County, for construction of
a new street approximately 1,150 feet in length for access to
a new public school under construction.

The Department of Health and Rehabilitative Services has
reviewed and approved the request.

The impact the proposed street will have on the environment
has been reviewed by the State Planning and Development
Clearinghouse and other environmental agencies. The Department
of Health and Rehabilitative Services, Department of Community
Affairs and Game and Fresh Water Fish Commission offer no
adverse comments. The Division of Forestry, Department of
Agriculture had no objection but suggested that precautions
be taken during construction to assure that erosion does not
occur. The City, advised of this, agreed to take all precautions during construction as suggested by the Division of
Forestry and, further, to provide adequate drainage to prevent
any erosion following completion of the street. All merchantable
timber will be removed by the Division of Corrections for the
benefit of the State.

Recommend granting the easement for public road purposes only.

ACTION OF THE TRUSTEES: .

Motion was made by Mr. Christian, seconded by Mr. Stone and
carried without objection, to grant the easement for public
road purposes only.

-4-

LEE COUNTY - Bulkhead Line, Section 253.122, Florida Statutes

The staff recommended denial of a bulkhead line 1,726.65 feet
long at the north end of Hickory Island at Big Hickory Pass
in Section 24, Township 47 South, Range 24 East, Lee County.
The attorney for the applicant had requested a deferral, but the
Director pointed out that denial would be without prejudice,
the bulkhead line was not recommended by the Interagency Advisory
Committee report or the Department of Natural Resources, and
regardless of modifications the staff felt that this particular
line should be denied which would not preclude the county's
submitting a modified bulkhead line.

Motion was made by Mr. Stone and seconded by Mr. Christian to
accept the staff recommendation for denial of the bulkhead line.

After brief discussion and in deference to the right of
the county to be heard, Mr. Stone withdrew his motion and the
substitute motion by Mr. Dickinson, seconded by Mr. Conner and
Mr. Stone, to defer action until next week, carried without
objection.

-5-

PALM BEACH COUNTY - Bulkhead Line, Section 253.122, Florida
                    Statutes

At the request of Treasurer O'Malley, the Trustees deferred
for one week consideration of a bulkhead line established by
the City of Riviera Beach 7,755.28 feet long in Lake Worth
west of Sections 10, 15, and 22, Township 42 South, Range 43
East, Palm Beach County.

4-11-72

6

DUVAL COUNTY - Dredge Permit No. 253.123-721

APPLICANT: Fred L. Ahern
c/o Harbor Engineering Co.
1039 Flagler Avenue, Jacksonville, Florida

PROJECT: To perform maintenance dredging in a series of
canals near the Intracoastal Waterway. This
property is located between the Intracoastal
Waterway and San Pablo Road in Sections 38 and
39, Township 2 South, Range 29 East, Duval County.

MATERIAL: Plans have been revised so that no dredging of
state land will take place.

PAYMENT: Not applicable.

ECOLOGICAL
RESPONSES: Department of Natural Resources - No objection to
project.

Game and Fresh Water Fish Commission - No objection
provided measures are taken to minimize turbidity,
and place spoil on areas designated by the
Department of Pollution Control.

Department of Pollution Control - No objection
provided spoil is placed on existing spoil areas.

Staff recommends issuance of Dredge Permit No. 253.123-721 to
Fred L. Ahern with the stipulation that spoil shall be placed
on existing spoil areas.

ACTION OF THE TRUSTEES:

On motion by Mr. Christian, seconded by Mr. Stone and Mr. Conner,
passed without objection, the dredge permit was approved with
the stipulation recommended as to placement of spoil.

7

MONROE COUNTY - Dredge Permit No. 253.03-273

APPLICANT: Maradocks, Inc.
955-122 Street, Marathon, Florida

PROJECT: To dredge a navigation channel 50 feet wide by 650
feet long by 5 feet deep and perform maintenance
dredging in an existing channel between Hog Key
and Vaca Key. The mangrove areas will not be
disturbed.

LOCATION: Sections 8 and 17, Township 66 South, Range 32 East,
Monroe County.

MATERIAL: Will be placed on privately-owned diked uplands.
Spoil will not be placed on the mangrove area.

PAYMENT: None. All work will be done on submerged lands
owned by the applicant.

ECOLOGICAL
RESPONSES: No objection as long as the 50 foot wide tidal
red mangrove strip is not filled.

Game and Fresh Water Fish Commission - No objection.

Department of Pollution Control - No objection.

OTHERS: 1. Field Operations Division reports that the red
mangrove area to the east of the channel will be

4-11-72

left undisturbed.

Staff recommends issuance of Permit 253.03-273.

ACTION OF THE TRUSTEES:

On motion by Mr. Dickinson, seconded by Mr. Christian and passed without objection, the dredge permit was approved.

-8A-

OKALOOSA COUNTY - Construction Permit and Marina License ML-113

APPLICANT: Hudson Marina, Inc.
9 Marina Drive, Ft. Walton Beach, Florida

PROJECT: Construction of additional docking structures covering 11,520 square feet at an existing marina in Garnier Bayou abutting Section 1, Township 2 South, Range 24 West, Okaloosa County. No dredging is required.

PAYMENT: $230.40 minimum annual fee for marina license.

ECOLOGICAL
RESPONSES: Department of Natural Resources - No objection.

Game and Fresh Water Fish Commission - No objection.

Department of Pollution Control - No objection.

Staff recommends issuance of marina license for annual fee of $230.40.

ACTION OF THE TRUSTEES: ·

Motion was made by Mr. Dickinson, seconded by Mr. Christian and carried without objection, that the marina license be approved.

-8B-

OKALOOSA COUNTY - Fill Permit No. 253.124(8)-275

APPLICANT: Hudson Marina, Inc.
9 Marina Drive, Ft. Walton Beach, Florida

PROJECT: To reclaim an 8 foot strip of land 147 feet long lost by avulsion and artificially induced erosion by constructing a seawall in line with an existing seawall.

No dredging is required.

LOCATION: Section 1, Township 2 South, Range 24 West, Okaloosa County.

MATERIAL: Fill material to be trucked in from upland source.

PAYMENT: None - Sovereignty land not involved.

ECOLOGICAL
RESPONSES: Department of Natural Resources - No objection.

Game and Fresh Water Fish Commission - No objection.

Department of Pollution Control - No objection.

OTHERS: Field Operations Division has no objection to the proposed project.

Staff recommends issuance of Fill Permit No. 253.124(8)-275.

ACTION OF THE TRUSTEES:

Motion was made by Mr. Dickinson, seconded by Mr. Christian and carried without objection, that the fill permit be approved.

-9-

ESCAMBIA COUNTY

By Act of Congress dated January 8, 1971 (Public Law 91-660), establishment of the Gulf Islands National Seashore was authorized.

On January 11, 1972, the Department of Natural Resources considered and approved the donation and transfer of Fort Pickens State Park to the National Park Service subject to the United States taking steps as soon as possible to stabilize the deteriorating condition of the fort and to continue to seek funds for actual restoration as circumstances might permit.

Staff recommends transfer of Fort Pickens State Park to the United States by appropriate instrument subject to the above conditions recommended by the Department of Natural Resources.

ACTION OF THE TRUSTEES:

On motion by Mr. Stone, seconded by Mr. Dickinson and adopted without objection, the rules were waived for consideration of the two items on the addendum.

Motion was made by Mr. Stone, seconded by Mr. Dickinson and carried without objection, that the Trustees approve the transfer of Fort Pickens State Park to the United States subject to the conditions recommended.

-10-

PALM BEACH COUNTY - Fill Permit No. 253.123-5

APPLICANT: Boat Square Holding Corporation
c/o Brockway, Owen and Anderson Engineers, Inc.
Post Office Box 3331, West Palm Beach, Florida

PROJECT: To complete the filling project authorized by the Board of Trustees on November 7, 1967, by placing fill in an unfilled 50' x 150' riprap diked area.

LOCATION: Lake Worth in Section 10, Township 45 South, Range 43 East, Palm Beach County.

MATERIAL: Will be hauled in from upland sources.

PAYMENT: $50 processing fee.

ECOLOGICAL
RESPONSES: Department of Natural Resources - No objection.

Game and Fresh Water Fish Commission - No objection.

Department of Pollution Control - No objection.

OTHERS: Area Planning Board of Palm Beach County - No objection.

City of Hypoluxo - No objection.

Staff recommends issuance of Permit No. 253.123-5.

ACTION OF THE TRUSTEES:

Motion was made by Mr. Dickinson, seconded by Mr. Christian and carried without objection, to approve the fill permit for Boat Square Holding Corporation.

4-11-72

Mr. Tom Morrill of Tallahassee had asked to be heard on the subject of Wakulla Springs and the fence across the Wakulla River above the bridge on U. S. 319. He opined that the Attorney General's opinion dated August 10, 1971, was arrived at in conjunction with the Trustees' legal staff, that it held that if title to the submerged sovereignty land of the Wakulla River had passed into private ownership, that fact would not give riparian owners the right to dredge, fill or otherwise encroach upon the public waters or navigation rights without permission of the state through the Trustees of the Internal Improvement Trust Fund.

Mr. Morrill urged the Board to take legal action now, as he claimed there had been months of excuses regarding the case for illegality of Mr. Ed Ball's development. Mr. Morrill alleged that a plan conforming closely to what the Director had been suggesting was passed by the Natural Resources Committee of the House of Representatives but did not pass both Chambers of the Legislature. He further alleged that the plan was untenable as it would include retention of the river and the artificial structures and allow continued commercialization in the spring itself by the private developers. He charged that it would compromise public owner-ship of other springs and rivers and of coastal submerged lands of the Forbes purchase, and would be underwriting continued exploitation.

Governor Askew thanked Mr. Morrill and referred the matter to the staff for preparing some type of definitive recommendation as to the best way to proceed in regard to his suggestion.

Mrs. Clifton Lewis of Environment Tallahassee called attention to the need to halt Florida's chaotic growth and need for concurrent state and federal action for a moratorium on the cutting of trees. She said architects and defenders of the environment were calling for a halt to I-10, I-90 and 75 realizing that what was happening was similar to the great loss of natural resources in other states.

Mrs. Lewis then specifically urged the Cabinet to look into the possible purchase and an immediate binder of $20,000 on the Gwynn property across from the Governor's mansion to save great trees threatened by building plans of the owner. She indicated that federal matching funds were available for saving trees and that Environment Tallahassee might lead a fund drive for the Cabinet.

Governor Askew expressed the Board's appreciation for Mrs. Lewis' willingness to come forward with a challenge to preserve the area, and while it was not a decision that could be made immediately without knowing the legal basis and the extent of available federal funds, the Board would refer the matter to the Department of General Services for a recommendation.

On motion duly adopted, the meeting was adjourned.

ATTEST:

GOVERNOR   CHAIRMAN

EXECUTIVE DIRECTOR

* * *   * * *   * * *

4-11-72

623

Tallahassee, Florida
April 18, 1972

The Board of Trustees of the Internal Improvement Trust Fund
met on this date in the auditorium of the Burns Building with
the following members present:

Reubin O'D. Askew	Governor
Richard (Dick) Stone	Secretary of State
Robert L. Shevin	Attorney General
Fred O. Dickinson, Jr.	Comptroller
Floyd T. Christian	Commissioner of Education
Doyle Conner	Commissioner of Agriculture

Joel Kuperberg	Executive Director

-1-

The minutes of the April 4, 1972, meeting were approved as
submitted.

-2-

HENDRY COUNTY - Consideration of Oil and Gas Lease Bids

On March 7, 1972, at the request of Sun Oil Company, the
Trustees authorized advertisement for sealed bids for a five-
year oil and gas drilling lease covering the reserved one-
half interest of the Board of Education in Section 16, Township
46 South, Range 32 East and the reserved one-half interest of
the Trustees in all of Sections 15, 17, 19, 21, N 1/2 of Section
27, and N 1/2 of Section 29, Township 46 South, Range 32 East,
containing 3,840 surface acres (1,920 net mineral acres) in
Hendry County.

All proceeds from this lease will go to the Internal Improvement Trust Fund except for Section 16, which will go to the
School Fund.

The lease requires an annual rental of $1 per net mineral acre,
1/8 royalty, $50,000 surety bond and at least one test well
every 2 1/2 years drilled to 6,000 feet or to the Robert Zone
of the Sunniland Formation or other anticipated oil horizons,
whichever is deeper.

Invitation to bid was advertised pursuant to law in the
Tallahassee Democrat and the Hendry County News with bids
to be opened at 10:00 a.m. (EST) on April 18 for consideration
by the Trustees. The right to reject any or all bids is reserved.

ACTION OF THE TRUSTEES:

Mr. James T. Williams of the Land Records Division of the
Trustees' office opened the one bid received in response to
the advertisement and recommended acceptance of the bid.

Sun Oil Company offered as total consideration for the lease
$26,131.20, representing a bonus bid of $12.61 per acre.

Motion was made by Mr. Christian, seconded by Mr. Conner and
carried without objection, that the bid be accepted and the
oil and gas drilling lease awarded to Sun Oil Company.

-3-

SANTA ROSA COUNTY - Oil and Gas Lease Assignment

APPLICANT: Humble Oil and Refining Company
              Post Office Box 61812, New Orleans, Louisiana

REQUEST: Assignment of State Oil and Gas Lease No. 2521-MA

4-18-72

dated February 16, 1971, between the Trustees and Humble Oil and Refining Company from Humble's undivided leasehold interests to the following parties:

W. A. Moncrief - 46.875% of a 1/3 interest

W. A. Moncrief, Jr. - 46.875% of an undivided 1/3 interest

Mary Wiley Black - 3.125% of an undivided 1/3 interest

Mary Wiley Black, independent executrix of the Estate of Richard Barto Moncrief, Sr. - 3.125% of an undivided 1/3 interest

George M. Young - 30% of an undivided 1/6 interest

William K. Young - 30% of an undivided 1/6 interest

Frank G. Young - 25% of an undivided 1/6 interest

Marshall R. Young, Jr. - 15% of an undivided 1/6 interest

LOCATION: 1/2 interest of the State (Murphy Act) in 70 surface acres in Section 20, Township 5 North, Range 29 West, 2 miles west of the Town of Jay, Santa Rosa County.

Executed instrument of Assignment has been filed and approved by the Trustees' legal counsel.

Recommend approval and consent to assignment.

ACTION OF THE TRUSTEES:

On motion by Mr. Conner, seconded by Mr. Christian and Mr. Dickinson, carried without objection, the Trustees approved and consented to the lease assignment as requested.

-4-

OKALOOSA AND SANTA ROSA COUNTIES - Oil and Gas Lease
Assignment

APPLICANT: Maui Oil Corporation
2000 Classen Center, Oklahoma City, Oklahoma 73106

REQUEST: Assignment to Beard Oil Company of the interest of Maui Oil Corporation in State Oil and Gas Lease dated March 24, 1969, between Florida Board of Forestry as lessor and Arthur E. Meinhart and Irwin Rubenstein as lessees.

LOCATION: 14,648.04 acres of the Blackwater River State Forest in Township 3 North, Range 25 West; Township 3 North, Range 27 West; Township 2 North, Range 26 West and Township 3 North, Range 26 West, Okaloosa and Santa Rosa Counties.

LEASE TERM: Ten years.

Executed instrument of assignment has been filed and approved by the Trustees' legal counsel as to form and legality. The Division of Forestry has no objections to the assignment.

Recommend approval and consent to assignment.

ACTION OF THE TRUSTEES:

On motion by Mr. Conner, seconded by Mr. Christian and Mr.
Dickinson, carried without objection, the Trustees approved
and consented to the lease assignment as requested.

-5-

DIXIE COUNTY - Fire Tower Land Exchange

In 1936 Mr. P. C. Crapps, Sr., and Mr. P. C. Crapps, Jr.,
deeded to the Board of Forestry at no cost 10.5 acres of land
in Section 32, Township 8 South, Range 11 East, Dixie County,
for use as a towersite.

The Division of Forestry in recent years realigned its
detection or tower system and eliminated or relocated a
number of towers. In the process this 10.5-acre Hines
Towersite and another towersite southwest of the Hines
Tower can be eliminated by locating a new tower midway
between the two.

It has been found that Mr. P. C. Crapps, Jr. has a 2-acre
parcel in SW 1/4 of Section 11, Township 9 South, Range 10
East, on U. S. Highway 19 that is ideally situated for the
new tower location. Mr. Crapps is willing to convey to the
State the 2-acre site in exchange for return of the 10.5-acre
Hines Towersite, provided the deed for the 2-acre new site
contains a reverter clause stating "the land shall revert to
the grantor if not used for state forestry purposes for a
period of five years."

Staff appraiser has appraised both parcels. The market
value of the 10.5-acre Hines site is $3,875 and the market
value of the new 2-acre site is $3,885.

The Department of Agriculture has reviewed and recommends
the proposed exchange since it will be advantageous to the
Division of Forestry and will require no expenditure of funds.
The State has had the use of the 10.5-acre Hines towersite
at no cost since 1936 and the Department feels it would be
fair to return the parcel to the donors, the Crapps family.

Staff recommends approval of the land exchange.

ACTION OF THE TRUSTEES:

On motion by Mr. Conner, seconded by Mr. Stone and carried
without objection, the Trustees approved the land exchange
as recommended.

-6-

HIGHLANDS COUNTY - Quitclaim Former Armory Site

The Department of Military Affairs advises that a new National
Guard Armory for Avon Park was completed and occupied on
April 1, 1972, on a ten-acre tract leased by the City of
Avon Park to the Department for 99 years, replacing the former
armory.

The former armory is located on a parcel of land described as
Lots 5 and 8, Block 48, Section 22, Township 33 South, Range
28 East, a site deeded by the City of Avon Park to the Armory
Board on February 24, 1937. The deed contained a clause stating
that should the Armory Board cease to use the property for
military purposes, title would revert to the City.

Due to the relocation of the Armory, the Department of Military
Affairs recommends the return of the former site and improvements to the City of Avon Park by quitclaim deed.

The staff recommends issuance of a quitclaim deed to the City

4-18-72

of Avon Park of Lots 5 and 8, Block 48, Section 22, Township
33 South, Range 28 East, Highlands County by the Trustees as
successor in title to the Department of Military Affairs
pursuant to Chapter 67-2236, Laws of Florida.

ACTION OF THE TRUSTEES:

Motion was made by Mr. Stone, seconded by Mr. Dickinson and
carried without objection, that the quitclaim deed be issued
to the City of Avon Park as recommended by the staff.

-7-

JACKSON COUNTY - State Road Easement

   The Department of Transportation

requests an easement containing 0.10 of an acre in Section 30,
Township 4 North, Range 7 West, Jackson County, for road right
of way purposes across the west 17 feet of the Grand Ridge
Forest Towersite.

The request has been reviewed and approved by the Division of
Forestry, Department of Agriculture and Consumer Services.

Recommend issuance of easement for public highway purposes.

ACTION OF THE TRUSTEES:

Motion was made by Mr. Christian, seconded by Mr. Stone and
carried without objection, granting the request of the Department of Transportation for an easement for public highway
purposes.

-8-

ORANGE COUNTY - Application for Sale, File No. 2421-48-253.36

Staff Description: A parcel of reclaimed Lake Conway bottom
                     land, Lots 17 and 18, Block C, Venetian
                     Gardens, in Section 18, Township 23 South,
                     Range 30 East, 0.172 acre.

A. City and County: City of Belle Isle, Orange County.
B. Applicant: Mrs. Mary Ann Curtis
C. Applicant's
   Representative: W. Scott Gabrielson, P. A.
                     Post Office Box 3146, Orlando, Florida
D. Acreage: 0.172 acre
   Rate: $2,000 for the parcel
E. Appraisal: Memorandum of Appraisal by Staff Appraiser
                     February 3, 1972
F. Purpose: Private residence
G. Biological
   Remarks: Not applicable

H. Staff Remarks: On May 28, 1952, the Board established a
   policy for perfecting title to lands which were artificially
   created in Lake Conway. In cooperation with the United States
   Geological Survey and the County Surveyor of Orange County,
   the Board established the elevation of the ordinary high
   water mark at 86.4 feet mean sea level as a result of the
   permanent lowering of Lake Conway.

   The parcel is above the 86.4 ft. contour and does not
   border on the present lake shore.

   Application was made to the Lake Conway Water and Navigation
   Control Authority. Advertisement was made and a public
   hearing held on October 26, 1971. There was no opposition
   to the proposed purchase. The Authority had no objection
   to the purchase.

4-18-72

The applicant submits the following statement: "I feel it is definitely in the public interest for this sale to be approved. My late husband and I had invested our entire life savings in this home as have many of my neighbors. Many of us have been depending on the proceeds we could raise from the sale of our homes to support us in our later years. However, I have discovered that my property, and much of the surrounding property, is unmarketable unless a deed can be obtained out of the Trustees Internal Improvement Fund. I urge you to take affirmative action on my request to purchase the above described property, both for my sake and that of others who are in the same situation as I and will need to sell their land in the future."

The staff recommends approval of the application and requests authority to issue a deed for the consideration of $2,000.

ACTION OF THE TRUSTEES:

Mr. Kuperberg recommended the sale in accordance with the previously established policy.

On motion by Mr. Christian, seconded by Mr. Conner and Mr. Dickinson, carried without objection, the Trustees approved the recommendation and authorized sale of the parcel of reclaimed Lake Conway bottom land for $2,000.

-9-

PALM BEACH COUNTY - Dredge Permit No. 253.123-1048

APPLICANT: Enoch K. Sprague, Old Slip Marina
              108 Old Slip Road, Riviera Beach, Florida

PROJECT: To perform periodic maintenance dredging in an
              existing marina basin to maintain -7 feet at mean
              low water.

LOCATION: Intracoastal Waterway, Lake Worth at Riviera Beach,
              Sections 33 and 34, Township 42 South, Range 43
              East, Palm Beach County.

MATERIAL: To be deposited on upland and used by the City of
              Riviera Beach.

PAYMENT: Waiver of fees for material is requested.

ECOLOGICAL
RESPONSES: Department of Natural Resources - No objection.

              Game and Fresh Water Fish Commission - No objection.

              Department of Pollution Control - No objection.

OTHERS: 1. Area Planning Board of Palm Beach County - No
              objection.

              2. Palm Beach County Board of County Commissioners -
              project is in the public interest.

              3. Field Operations - No objection.

Staff recommends issuance of Permit No. 253.123-1048 and waiver of fee for material.

ACTION OF THE TRUSTEES:

On motion by Mr. Stone, seconded by Mr. Christian and carried without objection, the Trustees approved issuance of the permit without fee.

4-18-72

-10-

PINELLAS COUNTY - Dredge Permit No. 253.123-811

APPLICANT: W. W. Caruth, Jr.
4900 Gulf Boulevard, St. Petersburg, Florida

PROJECT: To dredge approximately 2900 cubic yards of material from Boca Ciega Bay in Section 6, Township 32 South, Range 16 East, St. Petersburg Beach, Florida, to deepen and widen a channel to existing boat docks. There will be no dredging within 10 to 15 feet of an existing seawall.

MATERIAL: 2900 cubic yards of dredged sovereignty material will be placed on the upland portion of Upham Park, City of St. Petersburg Beach.

PAYMENT: Request waiver of fee since the material will be used by the City of St. Petersburg Beach.

ECOLOGICAL
RESPONSES: The Department of Natural Resources - Has no objection provided a strip of land 10 feet to 15 feet wide extending from the seawall is protected.

The Game and Fresh Water Fish Commission - Has no objection provided the stipulation from the Department of Natural Resources is met.

The Department of Pollution Control has no objection.

OTHER: Pinellas County Water and Navigation Control Authority issued dredge permit.

Staff recommends issuance of Dredge Permit 253.123-811 as revised to conform with ecological recommendations and waiver of fee since spoil material will be used for public park purposes.

ACTION OF THE TRUSTEES:

Motion was made by Mr. Christian, seconded by Mr. Dickinson and carried without objection, authorizing issuance of the dredge permit as revised to conform with ecological recommendations, without charge for the public purpose project.

-11-

POLK COUNTY - Refund

APPLICANT: David A. Despard, Despard Constructors, Post Office Box 2237, Winter Haven, Florida

PROJECT: To dredge and fill. Dredging was not done.

LOCATION: Section 4, Township 29 South, Range 26 East, Lake Lulu in Polk County.

MATERIAL: An estimated 2,800 cubic yards of sovereignty material was to be dredged from lake.

PAYMENT: $140 was paid for fill material. Since the material was not dredged, applicant requests refund.

Staff recommends refund of $140 to applicant.

ACTION OF THE TRUSTEES:

On motion by Mr. Stone, seconded by Mr. Conner and adopted without objection, the Trustees authorized refund of $140 to the applicant.

-12-

SANTA ROSA COUNTY - State Construction Permit

APPLICANT: Orgulf Transport Co.
             Post Office Box 6098, New Orleans, Louisiana

PROJECT: Placement of buoys in Escambia Bay for the temporary
             mooring of commercial barges.

             No dredging is required.

PAYMENT: $100.

ECOLOGICAL
RESPONSES: Department of Natural Resources - No objection.

             Game and Fresh Water Fish Commission - No objection.

             Department of Pollution Control - No objection.

Staff recommends issuance of construction permit for $100 fee.

ACTION OF THE TRUSTEES:

Motion was made by Mr. Stone, seconded by Mr. Christian and
adopted without objection, approving issuance of the construction permit for $100 fee.

-13-

LEE COUNTY - Bulkhead Line, Section 253.122, F. S.

APPLICANT: Board of County Commissioners
             Of Lee County

PROJECT: Bulkhead line 1,726.65 feet long at the north
             end of Hickory Island at Big Hickory Pass in
             Section 24, Township 47 South, Range 24 East,
             Lee County, approved and established by the Board
             of County Commissioners of Lee County by resolution
             adopted July 15, 1970.

             No development plans or dredge and fill applications
             have been submitted.

ECOLOGICAL
RESPONSES: Department of Natural Resources - The biological
             survey report is not adverse; however indication
             was made that ..."The subject area appears subject
             to tidal scouring." The Bureau of Beaches and
             Shores is opposed to the establishment of a bulkhead
             line along sandy beaches.

             Game and Fresh Water Fish Commission - No comments
             requested.

             Department of Pollution Control - No comments
             requested.

Staff recommends denial of bulkhead line.

ACTION OF THE TRUSTEES:

Motion was made by Mr. Stone, seconded by Mr. Conner and
carried without objection, that the rules be waived for
consideration of the three addendum items that had been added
to the original printed agenda.

The Director advised that the applicant's attorney had
requested permanent withdrawal of the application from the
agenda and from further consideration. A new application will
be filed when a modified bulkhead line has been set.

4-18-72

Governor Askew said no action was necessary as the item had been permanently withdrawn.

-14-

PALM BEACH COUNTY - Bulkhead Line, Section 253.122, F. S.

APPLICANT: City of Riviera Beach
2214 Avenue E, Riviera Beach, Florida

PROJECT: Bulkhead line 7,755.28 feet long in Lake Worth west of Sections 10, 15 and 22, Township 42 South, Range 43 East, Palm Beach County, approved and established by the City Council of the City of Riviera Beach by Ordinance No. 805 adopted May 7, 1969.

ECOLOGICAL
RESPONSES: Department of Natural Resources - To prevent massive and irreversible adverse effects on marine biological and wildlife resources, the bulkhead line should be set at the mean high water line as recommended in Report No. 1 of the Interagency Advisory Committee on Submerged Land Management.

Game and Fresh Water Fish Commission - Recommend that the bulkhead line be established at the mean high water line.

Department of Pollution Control - No objection to the establishment of a bulkhead line at the mean high water line.

OTHER: 1. Palm Beach County Area Planning Board recommends mean high water line.

2. Interagency Advisory Committee Report No. 1 dated May 27, 1968, recommends mean high water line.

Staff recommends denial of bulkhead line.

ACTION OF THE TRUSTEES:

Mr. Stone made a motion, seconded by Mr. Conner and carried without objection, that the staff recommendation for denial of the bulkhead line adopted by the City of Riviera Beach in Ordinance No. 805 be accepted.

Mr. Eugene W. Potter said Lake Worth had already been damaged and he would support any moratorium that would eliminate further filling in that lake and uphold the line that the Cabinet in 1957 set in Lake Worth.

-15-

ORANGE COUNTY - Permit Application Not Filed

APPLICANT: MGIC-Janis Properties, Inc.
c/o Mr. Robert Ervin
Tallahassee, Florida

PROJECT: To dredge 500,000 cubic yards of material from Lake Wekiva; to make minor alteration to the shoreline; and proposes to give this lake to the State of Florida

LOCATION: Sections 4, 5 and 8, Township 22 South, Range 29 East, Orange County.

MATERIAL: Will be used to fill uplands and to alter the shore of Lake Wekiva.

4-18-72

PAYMENT: Ownership of this land has not been determined, as the sections in which this lake lies were patented to the State of Florida as swamp and overflow lands and subsequently conveyed by the Trustees. The staff believes that regardless of ownership, a permit would be required prior to beginning dredging operation. The processing fee would be $50.

ECOLOGICAL
RESPONSES: Department of Natural Resources -

Game and Fresh Water Fish Commission - Requested April 7, 1972

Department of Pollution Control - Has determined that a permit under Public Law 91-224 will be required; also need to consider the effect dredging will have on the aquifer, the dead-end finger canals, the provisions for storm drainage treatment prior to entering the lake, and the controls which will be used.

Staff recommends that an application for permit be filed.

ACTION OF THE TRUSTEES:

Mr. Kuperberg advised that the staff had met with Mr. Ervin, the owners, and a number of staff members and others interested in the project that came to the staff's attention early this month. He respected the request for speed and agendaed the application at the request of a member of the Board, but the staff could not make a recommendation without a proper application. The staff considered the lake navigable in fact and therefore that Trustees had jurisdiction to regulate construction and modification of the shoreline. Mr. Kuperberg said the Trustees' office would expedite processing of an application in every way possible to protect the quality of water and the biological system. The staff wanted an opportunity to cooperate with the developer in a design that might improve the body of water, however he felt that the state should not be in the position of receiving a lake which may be irreparably damaged by dredge and fill work over which we had no control. Attorney General Shevin made a motion that the Board act on the staff recommendation. He said it was a sound position and his office would help to expedite the matter; but it was necessary to have a staff investigation through normal channels as it is a non-meandered but navigable fresh water lake and a permit from the Trustees is required for dredging.

Mr. Robert Ervin, attorney for MGIC-Janis Properties, Inc., maintained that his client owned the lake bottom which the staff apparently considered publicly-owned; it had been in private ownership for some 90 years and never been considered as public property; his client had obtained three independent title reports and he did not consider it covered by the law requiring a permit. Complete studies obtained from responsible environmental engineers disclosed that the lake was a deteriorating natural resource, according to Mr. Ervin. He said the offer was advantageous to the state but if the Trustees were not disposed to accept the gift subject to the conditions under which it was proffered, his client could not keep the offer open because of the expense keeping the dredging equipment on the site. The land might be given to a citizen's committee or the City of Orlando, he indicated.

The Governor noted that the staff position was that regardless of ownership, a permit would be required. He added that if the Board did not accept the offer, and could not require the applicant to file an application, the result could only be litigation if work proceeds without a permit.

Comptroller Dickinson made a motion to accept the offer which, upon receiving no second, failed.

Secretary of State Stone said he might agree but only after the

Board had full information as a prerequisite to accepting title
to the lake. He read from a letter from Dr. O. E. Frye, Jr.,
Director of Florida Game and Fresh Water Fish Commission, that
indicated no objection to the project as the marshes were not
extensive and the fishery in Lake Wekiva of little value because
of the severely degraded water quality, but recommended formula-
tion of draw-down plans and coordination with Orange County
before issuance of a permit by the Trustees. Mr. Stone thought
the project could probably be worked out in coordination with
Orange County.

Governor Askew pointed out Dr. Frye's presumption that there
would be an application for a permit, and ruled that no action
on the part of the Board was required in the absence of
acceptance of the applicant's offer.

On motion duly adopted, the meeting was adjourned.

GOVERNOR   CHAIRMAN

ATTEST: _____

EXECUTIVE DIRECTOR

^ ^ ^   * * *

Tallahassee, Florida
April 25, 1972

The Board of Trustees of the Internal Improvement Trust Fund
met on this date in the auditorium of the Burns Building with
the following members present:

Reubin O'D. Askew	Governor
Richard (Dick) Stone	Secretary of State
Robert L. Shevin	Attorney General
Floyd T. Christian	Commissioner of Education
Doyle Conner	Commissioner of Agriculture

Joel Kuperberg	Executive Director

-1-

The minutes of the April 11 meeting were approved as submitted.

-2-

Since only five members were present and any conveyance of land
requires five affirmative votes, action on land conveyances was
approved by all five members listed above unless otherwise
stated in the minutes.

ALACHUA COUNTY - Conveyance of Land to County

On January 18, 1972, this item was deferred at the request of
the Department of Health and Rehabilitative Services.

The Board of County Commissioners of Alachua County,

by resolution adopted October 26, 1971, requested the Trustees
to convey to the county a 102.09-acre tract of state land on which
to locate an agricultural center and county fairgrounds, to
promote Alachua County and its agriculture products.

This tract is a portion of 3,337 acres northeast of Gainesville
leased to the Department of Health and Rehabilitative Services

and used by the Division of Corrections, Sunland Training Center and the University of Forida. The 102.09-acre tract is in Section 26, Township 9 South, Range 20 East, Alachua County, on the north side of Northeast 39th Avenue (State Road S-232) and east side of Waldo Road (State Road 24). The county has furnished a plan of the proposed location of livestock pavilion, exhibit building, concession stand, office building, wayside park and picnic area.

The Department of Health and Rehabilitative Services has reviewed and approved transferring the 102.09 acres to the county for an agriculture center and county fairground purposes only, subject to inclusion in the instrument of conveyance of a covenant providing for reversion if the land is used for commercial purposes or other uses inconsistent with the purposes of the conveyance, and also subject to a reservation in the Department of Health and Rehabilitative Services of the right to harvest any timber that is required to be removed prior to construction.

The Department of Agriculture and Consumer Services recommends the location as being excellent for the desired purposes and of sufficient size to be useful.

Recommend conveyance of the tract to Alachua County for use as a county agriculture center and county fairgrounds with provision for reversion should the land be used for commercial or purposes other than enumerated above or for non-use for a period of three years and reserving the right to harvest timber.

ACTION OF THE TRUSTEES:

Motion was made by Mr. Stone, seconded by Mr. Conner and carried unanimously, that the tract of land be conveyed to Alachua County for a county agriculture center and county fairgrounds with the reversion provision recommended by the staff.

The Chairman of the Board of County Commissioners, Mr. Ralph W. Cellon, Jr., other county officials, members of the Jaycees and other interested parties were recognized by the Governor.

-3-

GADSDEN COUNTY - Conveyance of Land

The Department of Transportation

requests fee title to a one-acre parcel of land owned by the State of Florida under Chapter 18296, Acts of 1937 (Murphy Act), and located in Section 8, Township 1 North, Range 2 West, Gadsden County. All except 0.01 acre is within the proposed right of way for State Road 8 (I-10) and is 9 1/2 miles south-east of Quincy, without paved road access, and surrounded by private ownership.

The Department's offer of $200 for the land has been reviewed and approved by the staff appraiser as being fair market value.

Staff recommends sale of the entire parcel of land to the Department of Transportation for $200, the appraised value, without notice or public sale pursuant to Section 197.350, Florida Statutes.

ACTION OF THE TRUSTEES:

Motion was made by Mr. Christian, seconded by Mr. Stone and carried unanimously, approving sale of the small parcel of land to the Department of Transportation pursuant to Section 197.350, Florida Statutes, for the appraised value of $200.

-4-

SANTA ROSA COUNTY - Seismic Survey

Amoco Production Company
Post Office Box 50879, New Orleans, Louisiana,

requests permission to conduct seismic survey in a portion of
the Blackwater River from its mouth up to Section 20, Township
2 North, Range 27 West, a distance of approximately six miles
in Santa Rosa County. The survey will be conducted by the air
gun method with no explosives being used.

The Department of Natural Resources has issued Permit 109 to
Amoco for seismic survey by air gun in East Bay and tidal
area of the river. The time of the survey in the river should
not exceed five days.

The Game and Fresh Water Fish Commission reviewed the request
and has no objection.

Staff recommends granting Amoco Production Company permission
to conduct the seismic survey as requested.

ACTION OF THE TRUSTEES:

Mr. Kuperberg pointed out that the work would be done in
fresh water.

Motion was made by Mr. Stone, seconded by Mr. Christian and
carried unanimously, granting permission to conduct the
seismic survey.

-5-

INDIAN RIVER COUNTY - Application for Quitclaim
File No. 2386-31-253.12(6)
(November 21, 1971)

Staff Description: A parcel of filled sovereignty land in the
Indian River abutting Section 8, Township
31 South, Range 31 East, 0.717 acre.

A. CITY AND COUNTY: Indian River County

B. APPLICANT: F. M. Points (successor in title
to W. G. Bosworth estate)

C. APPLICANT'S
REPRESENTATIVE: Walter T. Rose, Jr. P. A.
Post Office Box 1255, Cocoa Beach, Florida

D. ACREAGE: 0.717 acre
RATE PER ACRE: $165 for the parcel, in its unfilled state
in 1955

E. APPRAISAL: By staff appraiser, last revised February
24, 1972

F. PURPOSE: Home site and boat basin

G. BIOLOGICAL REPORT: Not applicable

H. STAFF REMARKS: The applicant applied for a quitclaim deed
pursuant to Section 253.12(6) Florida Statutes, which
provided that "Where any person, state agency, county, city
or other political subdivision prior to June 11, 1957,
extended or added to existing lands or islands bordering
on or being in the navigable waters as defined in this
section by filling in or causing to be filled in such
lands, the Board shall upon application therefor convey
said land so filled to the riparian owner or owners of
the upland so extended or added to. The consideration
for such conveyance shall be the appraised value of said lands

4-25-72

as they existed prior to such filling."

Three affidavits have been submitted stating that the land in question had been filled and improved prior to June 11, 1957.

Staff recommends issuance of a quitclaim deed for the considera-tion of $165, and that applicant be required to pay $850 for appraisal fees.

ACTION OF THE TRUSTEES:

On motion by Mr. Christian, seconded by Mr. Stone, carried without objection, the Trustees authorized issuance of the quitclaim deed for $165 consideration subject to payment of the $850 appraisal fees.

-6-

POLK COUNTY - Application to Advertise
             File No. 2435-53-253.36, 0.27 acre, more or less
             (September 8, 1971)

Staff Description: A parcel of filled reclaimed lake bottom
                     land abutting Government Lot, Section 4,
                     Township 29 South, Range 26 East, Lake Lulu.

A. CITY AND COUNTY: Polk County

B. APPLICANT: Despard Constructors, Inc.
                      Post Office Box 2237, Winter Haven, Florida

C. APPLICANT'S
    REPRESENTATIVE: William J. Roberts
                       Post Office Box 1386, Tallahassee, Florida

D. ACREAGE: 0.27 acre, more or less
    RATE PER ACRE: Appraised value

E. APPRAISAL: To be requested.

F. PURPOSE: Residential townhouses.
G. BIOLOGICAL REPORT: Not applicable

H. STAFF REMARKS: The Board of Trustees on April 22, 1968, authorized the issuance of a dredge and fill permit to the applicant for the purpose of improving his upland with material from Lake Lulu. The Game and Fresh Water Fish Commission had no objection to the project. All material removed from Lake Lulu was to be placed landward of the ordinary high water line.

An application was made for a dock permit. The survey furnished with this application was prepared on March 19, 1968, and was in conflict with the one furnished with the dredge and fill application.

By letter on May 20, 1968, the Trustees staff notified the applicant's surveyor of the discrepancies between the two surveys, that fill could not be placed in the additional area shown in the later survey, and suggested that his client make application to purchase the additional area as reclaimed lake bottom land.

On July 24, 1968, Mr. Despard requested a refund of monies paid for material since he decided not to take material from Lake Lulu.

On August 8, 1968, in response to Mr. Despard's request for refund, the staff wrote to Mr. Despard telling him of a possible encroachment based on the comparison between the 1952 and 1968 surveys, and that in order for him to protect his interest and to remove any doubt about an encroachment on reclaimed lake bottom land, we should be furnished an up-to-date survey showing thereon the original G. L. O. meander line and the normal ordinary high water line of Lake Lulu. There was no response to

4-25-72

this letter until June 18, 1971, when a letter was received
from a surveyor requesting we quitclaim this land to Mr.
Despard.

Lake Lulu has been lowered and the controlled elevation is
131.2 feet above mean sea level. The land lying between the
controlled elevation and the original ordinary high water line
would be classified as reclaimed lake bottom land. In lieu of
other evidence it has been the practice of the staff to accept
the G. L. O. meander corners as an indication of the elevation
of the ordinary high water line.

The applicant has built several apartments on his upland and
what may be reclaimed lake bottom land. The survey furnished
the bank for permanent financing indicated parts of the
building were constructed lakeward of the G. L. O. meander
line. Permanent financing is being held up pending title
clearance.

The section corner used by local surveyors to locate the
G. L. O. meander line has not been proven to be the true and
correct corner. Local surveyors indicate that they think
this corner may be as much as two hundred feet east of the
true corner. If this is true then the apparent encroachment
may be non-existent.

The original lender is about to foreclose its interest in
the apartments. This would relieve Mr. Despard of his
problem but would not resolve anything since the apparent
encroachment would still exist.

Mr. Despard would like to purchase that part of the reclaimed
lake bottom land upon which the apartments are built and
obtain an easement or lease over the balance of the land. The
amount to be purchased is approximately 0.27 of an acre, and
the lease area 0.112 of an acre.

Staff requests authority to advertise for objections only.

ACTION OF THE TRUSTEES:

Motion was made by Mr. Stone, seconded by Mr. Conner, carried
without objection, that the parcel of filled reclaimed lake
bottom land be advertised for objections only.

-7-

BAY COUNTY - Dredge Permit No. 253.123-1002
              November 16, 1971

APPLICANT: Marifarms, Inc.
             Post Office Box 2239, Panama City, Florida

PROJECT: To dredge a channel 40 feet wide, -5 feet deep at
             mean low water which will extend 200 feet along
             the shore and thence 1,200 feet into the bay.

LOCATION: West Bay, Section 9, Township 30 South, Range 16
             West, Bay County.

MATERIAL: 6,700 cubic yards of sovereignty material to be
             removed and placed on uplands leased by the company
             from St. Joe Paper Company.

PAYMENT: $6,700 has been paid for sovereignty material.

ECOLOGICAL
RESPONSES: Department of Natural Resources - Dredging should
             have only limited adverse effects on marine
             biological resources.

             Game and Fresh Water Fish Commission - No objection
             provided precautions are taken to prevent excess
             turbidity.

637

Department of Pollution Control - No objection.

OTHERS: 1. State of Florida Division of Health - No objection.

2. Field Operations - No objection.

Staff recommends issuance of Permit No. 253.123-1002 provided precautions are taken to prevent excess turbidity.

ACTION OF THE TRUSTEES:

Mr. Kuperberg recommended approval of the permit in connection with the state's first shrimp farming operation.

Attorney General Shevin had pointed out to the staff that this was the second anniversary of the lease that provided that the rate and total amount to date of royalties based upon production could begin on February 19. He questioned whether additional permits should be given if there had not been any royalty agreement or audit of the company books. Responding, the Director explained that the applicant had suffered more delays than anticipated and the staff felt it appropriate to delay royalties that might be too low at this point since the work had not reached full operating scale, and in the judgment of the staff a delay in setting the royalty payment might result in additional income to the state. Mr. Kuperberg said no options were lost or injuries incurred by the state, the applicant had proceeded in good faith and had requested postponement of the decision on royalty payments, but the staff should have made a timely report to the Trustees.

Answering a question by the Governor as to a possible encroach- on sovereignty tidal lands, the Director advised that the staff was conducting a survey of some diking on the other side of the bay where the applicant had leased privately-owned land, to determine whether there was any encroachment on sovereignty land.

Motion was made by Mr. Christian, seconded by Mr. Stone and carried without objection, to approve the dredge permit provided precautions are taken to prevent excess turbidity.

-8-

MONROE COUNTY - Aquaculture Lease

The office of the Commissioner of Agriculture had asked for withdrawal for one week of the application from Marine Harvesters, Inc., represented by Mr. Bela Zeky, for lease of sovereignty land for experimental planting of seaweed.

Consideration of the application was deferred one week.

-9-

SARASOTA COUNTY - Fill Permit No. 253.124(8)-211
                  November 11, 1971

APPLICANT: Graydon A. Ellis
            1630 Ravine Terrace, Highland Park, Illinois 60035

PROJECT: To reclaim land which has been lost by artificially induced erosion by constructing a seawall between the existing seawalls and to backfill with material from upland sources.

LOCATION: Little Sarasota Bay, Section 18, Township 36 South, Range 18 East, Sarasota County.

4-25-72

MATERIAL: Will be hauled in from upland sources.

PAYMENT: None. Sovereignty land not involved.

ECOLOGICAL
RESPONSES: Department of Natural Resources - No objection.

Game and Fresh Water Fish Commission - No objection.

Department of Pollution Control - Exempt from
certification.

OTHERS: 1. Water and Navigation Control Authority, Sarasota
County - Approved.

2. Field Operations - Land was lost and the loss was
caused by artificially induced erosion.

Staff recommends issuance of Permit No. 253.124(8)-211.

ACTION OF THE TRUSTEES:

Motion was made by Mr. Christian, seconded by Mr. Conner and carried
without objection, approving issuance of the fill permit.

-10A-

HILLSBOROUGH COUNTY - Bulkhead Line, Section 253.122, F. S.
                     (Tampa Port Authority Permit 72-1)
                     February 10, 1972

APPLICANT: Department of Transportation

PROJECT: Bulkhead line 13,932.55 feet long in Old Tampa Bay
adjacent to the Courtney Campbell Causeway, State
Road No. 60, Hillsborough County, approved and
established by the Tampa Port Authority by
Resolution No. R-75-2 adopted March 14, 1972.

ECOLOGICAL
RESPONSES: Department of Natural Resources - No objection.

Game and Fresh Water Fish Commission - No objection.

Department of Pollution Control - No objection.

OTHERS: Field Operations Division - No objection.

Staff recommends approval of the bulkhead line.

ACTION OF THE TRUSTEES:

On motion by Mr. Stone, seconded by Mr. Conner and adopted
without objection, the Trustees approved the bulkhead line
as established by the Tampa Port Authority on March 14, 1972.

-10B-

HILLSBOROUGH COUNTY - Fill Permit 253.124-264
                     February 10, 1972

APPLICANT: Department of Transportation

PROJECT: To fill approximately 2.2 acres and construct
seawalls adjacent to the Courtney Campbell Causeway,
State Road No. 60, in Old Tampa Bay, Hillsborough
County.

MATERIAL: Approximately 10,500 cubic yards of material will
be trucked in from upland sources.

PAYMENT: Fees waived since project is in the public interest.

ECOLOGICAL
RESPONSES: Department of Natural Resources - No objection.

            Game and Fresh Water Fish Commission - No objection
            provided riprap habitat installed.

            Department of Polluton Control - No objection.

OTHERS: Field Operations Division - No objection.

Staff recommends issuance of Fill Permit 253.124-264 to the
Department of Transportation and waiver of fees, since the
project is in the public interest.

ACTION OF THE TRUSTEES:

On motion by Mr. Stone, seconded by Mr. Conner and carried
without objection, the Trustees authorized issuance of the
fill permit to the Department of Transportation without fee
for the public interest project.

-11A-

PINELLAS COUNTY - Bulkhead Line, Section 253.122, F. S.
                (April 10, 1972)

APPLICANT: Department of Transportation
            Tallahassee, Florida

PROJECT: Bulkhead line 866.00 feet long in Old Tampa Bay
            adjacent to the Courtney Campbell Causeway, State
            Road No. 60, Pinellas County, approved and
            established by the Board of County Commissioners
            of Pinellas County by Resolution No. B-346, adopted
            March 30, 1972.

ECOLOGICAL
RESPONSES: Department of Natural Resources - No objection.

            Game and Fresh Water Fish Commission - No objection.

            Department of Pollution Control - No objection.

OTHERS: Field Operations Divison - No objection.

Staff recommends approval of the bulkhead line.

ACTION OF THE TRUSTEES:

Motion was made by Mr. Stone, seconded by Mr. Conner, carried
without objection, that the bulkhead line be approved as
established by the Board of County Commissioners of Pinellas
County on March 30, 1972.

-11B-

PINELLAS COUNTY - Fill Permit 253.124-265
                (April 10, 1972)

APPLICANT: Department of Transportation

PROJECT: To fill approximately 0.10 acre and construct
            seawalls adjacent to the Courtney Campbell Causeway,
            State Road No. 60, in Old Tampa Bay, Pinellas County.

MATERIAL: Approximately 200 cubic yards of material will be
            trucked in from upland sources.

PAYMENT: Fees waived since project is in the public interest.

ECOLOGICAL
RESPONSES: Department of Natural Resources - No objection.

Game and Fresh Water Fish Commission - No objection
provided riprap habitat installed.

Department of Pollution Control - No objection.

OTHERS: Field Operations Division - No objection.

Staff recommends approval of Fill Permit 253.124-265 to the
Department of Transportation and waiver of fees, since the
project is in the public interest.

ACTION OF THE TRUSTEES:

Motion was made by Mr. Stone, seconded by Mr. Conner and
carried without objection, that the fill permit be approved
without fee for the public interest project.

The City of Lake Worth had submitted request for extension
of an existing permit (No. 253.124-250). The Director advised
that responses had not been obtained from Palm Beach County
Planning Board or the County Commissioners, and the staff
policy was to review all applications for work in Palm Beach
County. He asked that the record reflect that the permit did
not expire until May 27, 1972. The matter would be placed on
the agenda when the local authorities' comments were received.

Mr. Conner made a motion, seconded by Mr. Christian, to
waive the rules and approve the Director's report.

Mr. Kuperberg submitted a progress report on the resolution
of April 4 to the environmental agencies. Commenting that
the staff had excellent cooperation from the other three
agencies, he distributed a plan to streamline permitting
procedures as tentatively agreed upon by the agencies involved.

Attorney General Shevin said it had become apparent, in view
of the many new policies and changes in the statutory language,
that the administrative rules of the Trustees needed revision.
He made a motion that the Board instruct Mr. Kuperberg to
begin a systematic and comprehensive review of all the rules
in a joint effort with the staffs of each of the members of
the Board. Mr. Kuperberg advised that the work was already
under way.

It was so ordered.

On motion duly adopted, the meeting was adjourned.

GOVERNOR   -   CHAIRMAN

ATTEST:
EXECUTIVE DIRECTOR

*

4-25-72

Tallahassee, Florida
May 2, 1972

The State of Florida Board of Trustees of the Internal Improvement Trust Fund met on this date in the auditorium of the Burns Building with the following members present:

Reubin O'D. Askew	Governor
Richard (Dick) Stone	Secretary of State
Robert L. Shevin	Attorney General
Fred O. Dickinson, Jr.	Comptroller
Thomas D. O'Malley	Treasurer
Floyd T. Christian	Commissioner of Education

Joel Kuperberg	Executive Director

-1-

The minutes of the April 18, 1972, meeting were approved as submitted.

-2-

DADE COUNTY - Sewer Line Easement
           (March 17, 1972)

    Metropolitan Dade County

requests an easement 30 feet wide across and under a portion of the Florida International University in NW 1/4 of Section 7, Township 54 South, Range 40 East, Dade County, for the installation of a pressure sanitary sewer transmission and underground water line to serve the University.

The request has been reviewed and approved by the Facilities Committee of the Board of Regents.

Recommend issuance of the easement to Metropolitan Dade County for sanitary sewer transmission and underground water line purposes.

ACTION OF THE TRUSTEES:

Motion was made by Mr. Christian, seconded by Mr. Dickinson and passed without objection, granting the application from Metropolitan Dade County for easements for sanitary sewer and underground water line purposes.

-3-

PALM BEACH COUNTY - Easement for Electric Distribution Lines
               (March 16, 1972)

    Florida Power and Light Company
    Miami, Florida,

requests an easement twelve feet wide across a portion of the Florida Atlantic University campus to provide electrical service to the experimental fish farm in Palm Beach County.

The Facilities Committee of the Board of Regents has reviewed and approved this request.

Recommend issuance of the easement for electric distribution line purposes.

ACTION OF THE TRUSTEES:

Motion was made by Mr. Stone, seconded by Mr. O'Malley and passed
without objection, authorizing issuance of the easement for
electric distribution line requested by Florida Power and Light
Company.

-4-

HILLSBOROUGH COUNTY - Mortgage on Shell Lease No. 1788
                     (April 6, 1972)

APPLICANT: Benton and Company, Inc., and R. C. Huffman and
             R. C. Huffman, Jr., individually, St. Petersburg

PROJECT: Dredge to remove dead shell from the Tampa Bay
             area for a period of 10 years.

PAYMENT: $30,000 minimum annual payment for the 10 year
             period. A $300,000 mortgage dated February 1,
             1962, was given to secure a forfeiture bond of
             $300,000.

STAFF REMARKS: Department of Natural Resources reports that the
final payment has been made in accordance with the terms of the
lease and mortgage.

Staff recommends issuance of a satisfaction of mortgage to Benton
and Company, Inc., and R. C. Huffman and R. C. Huffman, Jr.,
individually.

ACTION OF THE TRUSTEES:

Motion was made by Mr. Dickinson, seconded by Mr. Stone and
passed without objection, approving issuance of satisfaction
of mortgage as recommended by the staff.

-5-

PINELLAS COUNTY - Lease or Dedicate Filled Land
                  (January 28, 1972)

APPLICANT: City of Madeira Beach
             c/o W. Furman Betts, Jr., City Attorney
             Post Office Box 8635, Madeira Beach, Florida

PROJECT: Long term lease over 1.266 acre parcel of filled
             sovereignty land. This land was filled
             in accordance with an agreement between the city
             and the Trustees on March 29, 1961, for a beach
             nourishment project. 'This land will·be used
             for public recreation.

             A major portion of the riparian upland
             is in private ownership.

LOCATION: At Johns Pass in Section 15, Township 31 South,
             Range 15 East, Pinellas County

MATERIAL: None.

PAYMENT: None.

ECOLOGICAL
RESPONSES: Not applicable

OTHERS: The City of Madeira Beach has $75,000 tentatively
             allocated for public beach and recreational
             facilities for the Johns Pass area.

Staff recommends that the Board of Trustees agree to lease or dedicate this filled land to the City of Madeira Beach exclusively for public beach and public recreational facilities if and when the city has acquired those uplands contiguous to the filled area.

ACTION OF THE TRUSTEES:

Mr. Kuperberg said action was to show the intent on the part of the Board of Trustees to lease or dedicate to the city land filled in the beach nourishment program if the city obtains the upland interest.

On motion by Mr. O'Malley, seconded by Mr. Stone and carried without objection, the staff recommendation was approved as the action of the Trustees.

-6-

SANTA ROSA COUNTY - Consideration of Oil and Gas Lease Bids

On March 21, 1972, at the request of P. R. Rutherford, Houston, Texas, and Texas Gas Exploration Company, the Trustees authorized advertisement for sealed bids for a five-year oil and gas drilling lease covering a portion of Big Coldwater Creek in Sections 31 and 32, Township 3 North, Range 27 West and Sections 5, 6, 8, 17 and 20, Township 2 North, Range 27 West, containing 71.8 acres, more or less, in Santa Rosa County.

All proceeds from this lease will go to the Internal Improvement Trust Fund.

The lease requires an annual rental of $1 per net mineral acre, 1/6 royalty, $50,000 surety bond and at least one test well every 2-1/2 years. Drilling in the waterbottoms of the creek is specifically prohibited. Pooling will allow compliance with requirement to drill.

Invitation to bid was advertised pursuant to law in the Tallahassee Democrat and the Press-Gazette, Milton, Florida, with bids to be opened at 10:00 A. M. (EDST) on May 2 for consideration by the Trustees. The right to reject any or all bids is reserved.

ACTION OF THE TRUSTEES:

Mr. James T. Williams, Land Records Division, reported the following four bids received in response to the advertised call for sealed bids:

Floyd T. Domingue, Lafayette, Louisiana	$53,993.80
P. R. Rutherford, Houston, Texas	15,221.60
Ernest B. Ross, Houston, Texas	4,810.60
Humble Oil & Refining Co., New Orleans, La.	1,500.00

and advised that the high bid represented a bonus bid of $751.00 per acre.

On motion by Mr. O'Malley, seconded by Mr. Christian and carried without objection, the Trustees accepted the high bid and awarded the oil and gas drilling lease to Floyd J. Domingue.

-7-

MARION COUNTY - Murphy Act Land Sale (February 29, 1972)

William J. Day
Represented by Seymour H. Rowland, Jr., attorney,
Ocala, Florida,

makes application under Section 197.355, Florida Statutes, "Hardship Act" (Chapter 28317, Acts of 1953), to purchase the SW 1/4 of SE 1/4 of SE 1/4 of Section 11, Township 13 South, Range 21 East, 10 acres in Marion County.

5-2-72

The interest of the State in this parcel was acquired under the Murphy Act, Chapter 18296, Acts of 1937, by Tax Certificate No. 556 of August 1, 1932. This certificate in the amount of $8.61 apparently was overlooked by the Clerk when the owner, James Day, attempted to redeem other outstanding certificates. This certificate did not qualify for cancellation under the Futch Act.

The applicant is the present record owner and heir of James Day, the record owner on June 9, 1939. Section 197.355, Florida Statutes, provides that the Board may convey the interest of the State to the owner in 1939 or those claiming by, through or under that owner, for such consideration as the Board shall deem equitable and proper without advertisement and public sale.

There has been deposited with the Clerk of Marion County an amount equal to the sum of all state, county taxes and assessments due to the date of the application.

The applicant offers $100 for the ten acres of land which conforms to the policy to accept not less than $10 per acre when the interest of the state is conveyed under Section 197.355, Florida Statutes.

This application appears to qualify under the so-called "Hardship Act".

Recommend conveying the interest of the State of Florida in this parcel of land to William J. Day for $100.

ACTION OF THE TRUSTEES:

On motion by Mr. Stone, seconded by Mr. O'Malley and Mr. Christian, carried without objection, the Trustees approved conveyance of the interest of the State of Florida in the parcel of land to the applicant for $100.

-8-

INDIAN RIVER COUNTY - Dredge Permit No. 253.123-1004

At the request of the applicant, General Development Corporation, action was deferred for six weeks on the application for a dredge permit.

-9-

ST. JOHNS COUNTY - Dredge Permit NO. 253.123-1014
                   (July 26, 1971)

APPLICANT: Rudolph K. Hall
              8030 Almar Place, Jacksonville, Florida

PROJECT: To perform maintenance dredging in existing upland
              canals which connect with the St. Johns River and
              to excavate 3,500 cubic yards by dragline method.

LOCATION: Approximately three miles south of State Road 16 bridge
              at Colee Cove in St. Johns County.

MATERIAL: All material will be placed along-side the canals
              on uplands.

PAYMENT: Not applicable.

ECOLOGICAL
RESPONSES: Department of Natural Resources - No objection as
              long as silt and turbid waters are contained
              within the canal systems.

              Game and Fresh Water Fish Commission - No objection.

5-2-72

645

Department of Pollution Control - No objection.

OTHERS: Field Operations Division - No objection.

Staff recommends issuance of Dredge Permit No. 253.123-1014.

ACTION OF THE TRUSTEES:

In response to the Treasurer's questions, Mr. Kuperberg said
the work would consist of maintenance dredging in upland
canals connecting with the St. Johns River, and placement of
spoil material on upland areas with no filling of submerged
land.

Motion was made by Mr. Stone, seconded by Mr. Dickinson and
Mr. Christian, and carried without objection, that the Trustees
approve issuance of the dredge permit.

-10-

LAKE COUNTY - Road Easements
              (April 21, 1972)

APPLICANT: First National Bank of Leesburg, as Trustee
            by P. B. Howell, Jr., attorney
            Leesburg, Florida

REQUEST: Non-exclusive perpetual road easements over two
            30-foot wide strips of land owned by the Trustees and
            in use by the University of Florida Agriculture
            Research Center (formerly Watermelon and Grape
            Experimental Laboratory). Consideration for the
            easements is fee title to a parcel of land 15 feet
            wide, 180 feet long, lying adjacent to and west of
            the University Research Center.

LOCATION: Requested 50-foot by 30-foot easements are in the
            NE 1/4 of Section 23, Township 20 South, Range 24
            East, Lake County. The 15-foot wide parcel of land
            to be received by Trustees in exchange for the
            easements is in the NE 1/4 of Section 25, Township 20
            South, Range 24 East, Lake County.

The Board of Regents' Facilities Committee on April 4, 1972,
approved giving the two easements in exchange for title to the
15-foot wide strip contiguous to the present laboratory office
site.

Recommend approval of the easements and acceptance of the 15-foot
wide strip.

ACTION OF THE TRUSTEES:

On motion by Mr. O'Malley, seconded by Mr. Stone and carried
without objection, the Trustees approved the easements in
return for the acquisition of the 15-foot wide strip of land
adjacent to and west of the University of Florida Agriculture
Research Center.

-11-

DADE COUNTY - Application for Disclaimer
              File 2453-13-253.129, 0.405 acre
              (April 7, 1972)

Staff Description: A parcel of filled sovereignty land abutting
                    Section 9, Township 52 South, Range 42 East.

A. CITY AND COUNTY: Dade County

B. APPLICANT: Richard I. Thayer, et ux

5-2-72

C. APPLICANT'S
   REPRESENTATIVE: John P. McNutt, P. A.
                   First National Bank Building, Miami, Florida

D. ACREAGE: 0.405

E. APPRAISAL: Not applicable
F. PURPOSE: Not applicable
G. BIOLOGICAL
   REMARKS: Not applicable

H. STAFF REMARKS: The applicant has made application pursuant
   to Section 253.129 which provides that "The title to all
   lands heretofore filled or developed is herewith confirmed
   in the upland owners and the trustees shall on request issue
   a disclaimer to each such owner."

   Two affidavits have been submitted that show the parcel
   to have been filled prior to May 9, 1951.

   $100 processing fee has been submitted.

Staff requests authority to issue the disclaimer.

ACTION OF THE TRUSTEES:

On motion by Mr. O'Malley, seconded by Mr. Stone and carried
without objection, the Trustees authorized issuance of the
disclaimer requested by Mr. Thayer.

-12-

BROWARD COUNTY - Dredge Permit No. 253.123-965
               (July 26, 1972)

APPLICANT: Town of Hillsboro Beach
           Hillsboro Beach, Florida

PROJECT: To artificially nourish approximately 5000 feet of
         Atlantic Ocean shoreline with approximately 1,550,000
         cubic yards of material to be dredged from two offshore
         borrow areas.

LOCATION: Atlantic Ocean at Hillsboro Beach, Section 8, Township
          48 South, Range 43 East, Broward County.

PAYMENT: Waiver of fee for material requested as a project
         in the public interest.

ECOLOGICAL
RESPONSES: Department of Natural Resources - Bureau of Beaches
           and Shores - item will be placed on agenda for same
           date as Trustees agenda.

           Bureau of Planning and Grants, Division of Recreation
           and Parks - approves.

           Division of Survey and Management - No objection to the
           proposed offshore dredging (May 24, 1971). Recommends
           reducing the 600 foot wide spoil area to a maximum
           of 200 feet to reduce possible damage to productive
           offshore reefs (February 8, 1972).

           The Executive Director, Department of Natural Re-
           sources, has reviewed this project and finds it to be
           in the public interest.

           Game and Fresh Water Fish Commission - No objection
           to the proposed project.

           Department of Pollution Control - No objection, but
           special emphasis should be placed on controlling
           turbidity.

OTHERS: 1. Department of Health and Rehabilitative Services - approved.
2. U. S. Department of Commerce - No objection.
3. U. S. Department of Interior, Fish and Wildlife Service - No objection.

Staff recommends issuance of Dredge Permit No. 253.123-965.

ACTION OF THE TRUSTEES:

On motion by Mr. O'Malley, seconded by Mr. Stone and carried without objection, the Board authorized issuance of the dredge permit for the artificial nourishment program.

-13-

MONROE COUNTY - Aquaculture Lease

The application of Marine Harvesters, Inc., was withdrawn from the agenda pending review and processing of permit by the Department of Pollution Control.

-14-

TRUSTEES' FUNDS

In furtherance of Trustees' Resolution of April 4, 1972, a survey has been conducted, at staff's request, by Mr. Nelson Hanover of Financial Controls, Inc., who has agreed to perform the following services:

1. Evaluate the adequacy of all classes of current permitting applications with respect to the providing of complete environmental and technical descriptions to allow proper and speedy processing.

2. Make detailed recommendations concerning engineering and scientific study requirements of the permitting activity.

3. Assist in the technical exchange necessary for coordinating new approaches to the permitting activity between state agencies.

All of the activities described above are to be completed by June 30, 1972, and the fee for these services is not to exceed $3,400, plus reasonable travel expenses in compliance with Section 112.061, Florida Statutes.

Staff requests Trustees' authorization to order the study and to expend the funds necessary for this work.

ACTION OF THE TRUSTEES:

On motion by Mr. O'Malley, seconded by Mr. Stone and carried without objection, the Trustees authorized the study and expenditure of funds necessary for the work as recommended by the staff.

-15-

VOLUSIA COUNTY - Seawall, Ponce Inlet Club South

In response to complaints received from citizens in Volusia County, and in accordance with Section 253.05, Florida Statutes, Governor Askew requested the Honorable Stephen L. Boyles, State Attorney for the Seventh Judicial Circuit, to determine if legal proceedings were necessary to protect and preserve the public interest in Atlantic Ocean beach front property in the area involved.

The State Attorney has completed his investigation and recommends that the Trustees authorize appropriate legal action.

5-2-72

Recommend that the State Attorney, in cooperation with the Attorney General and Counsel for the Board of Trustees, be authorized to institute appropriate legal proceedings on behalf of the Board.

ACTION OF THE TRUSTEES:

The situation was explained by Mr. Kuperberg as the public interest involvement in land long used as a public beach in the Daytona Beach area. Adding details, Mr. Stephen L. Boyles, State Attorney in the Seventh Judicial Circuit, said that PIA, Inc., was constructing a condominium about eight miles south of Daytona Beach with a seawall extending about 50 feet seaward of the line of natural sand dunes and natural vegetation, that three theories involved in the case of the sky tower were involved here - whether it was on sovereignty land, whether it was a public highway, and whether the public acquired a prescriptive right. Mr. Boyles recommended, in order to preserve the beach, that the Trustees authorize him to proceed with litigation to have the seawall and any encroachments beyond the line of natural vegetation or seaward of the dune line removed and stopped.

Mr. O'Malley asked for a week's deferment for study of aerial maps, but upon examining exhibits submitted by Mr. Boyles he withdrew his request, remarking that had there been better zoning in Dade County 40 years ago, there might be beaches there now instead of concrete.

Mr. Fletcher Rush of Orlando, attorney for Mr. Robert Langford and Mr. William Slemons, discussed Mr. Langford's known conservation record, the securing of permits for building the seawall and for the five-story condominium on property about a mile north of Ponce de Leon Inlet from the South Peninsula Zoning Commission that under legislative act of 1949 had jurisdiction and had adopted a seawall line in 1965 by resolution recorded in the public records of Volusia County, and his clients' compliance with all known legal requirements. Mr. Rush advised that the building was up five stories with the south 400 feet of seawall in front of the condominium completed and capped, and properties a short distance to the north and south followed the same seawall line. He and his clients had met with the State Attorney and Mr. W. T. Carlton and proposed as a settlement keeping the completed and capped portion of the seawall but moving back the remaining 900 feet of the planned seawall.

Mr. Langford and Mr. Slemons felt that they had complied with all known legal requirements as good citizens, that with hindsite there might have been different design possibilities but the building and seawall plan including swimming pool and patio had been used as the basis for the sale of one-fourth of the apartments. Mr. Langford asked if the Board referred to removal of the seawall only, or the building. Mr. Rush raised a question regarding jurisdiction of the Trustees, stating that the seawall line was at least 60 feet upland from the mean high water line established by the Trustees at 2.35 feet above mean sea level at Daytona Beach.

There was discussion by Treasurer O'Malley and other members of the need for county-wide zoning to protect the beaches and planning that might have located the condominium further from the beach. The Governor pointed out that the equities would be determined by the court if the Board decided against a settlement. The Attorney General said there was ample precedent for proceeding to litigation if the object was to protect the public beach, regardless of how far along the project was under construction.

Mr. Shevin made a motion, seconded by Mr. O'Malley and adopted without objection, to support the staff recommendation and to authorize and direct the State Attorney to institute appropriate legal proceedings on behalf of the Board of Trustees, in cooperation with the Attorney General and the counsel for the Board.

Mr. Dickinson voted aye with an explanation that if he could be the swing vote it would be for Mr. Langford whose equities were

heavy, and there was a continuing obligation on the part of the
Board to live up to commitments, if not contrary to the public
good. He thought there would be litigation anyway, as well
as the public sentiment element, and the vote would point
up the kind of corrective actions being initiated by the present
Board.

Mr. O'Malley tended to concur in terms of the equity and felt
that Volusia County, through South Peninsula Zoning Board, had
made mistakes but, nevertheless, zoning action had to be taken
locally. Mr. Stone added that every County Commission should
caution its building department regarding shorelines and the
fact that the Board of Trustees was in the process of reworking
all the bulkhead lines.

The Director said he would work with Senator Randolph Hodges to,
jointly, work out something appropriate to advise affected
communities.

On motion duly adopted, the meeting was adjourned.

GOVERNOR   CHAIRMAN

ATTEST:
EXECUTIVE DIRECTOR

Tallahassee, Florida
May 9, 1972

The Board of Trustees of the Internal Improvement Trust Fund
met on this date in the auditorium of the Burns Building with
the following members present:

Reubin O'D. Askew   Governor
Richard (Dick) Stone   Secretary of State
Robert L. Shevin   Attorney General
Fred O. Dickinson, Jr.   Comptroller
Thomas D. O'Malley   Treasurer
Floyd T. Christian   Commissioner of Education

Joel Kuperberg   Executive Director

-1-

The minutes of the April 25 meeting were approved as submitted.

-2-

SANTA ROSA COUNTY - Oil and Gas Lease Assignment
                (March 15, 1972)

APPLICANT: W. A. Moncrief, Fort Worth, Texas

REQUEST: Assignment of State Oil and Gas Lease No. 2568-ACS
           dated December 14, 1971, between the Trustees and
           W. A. Moncrief, from W. A. Moncrief to the following:

5-9-72

R. W. Moncrief - 40% of an undivided 2/3 interest

W. A. Moncrief and W. A. Moncrief, Jr., Trustees of
Tom O. Moncrief Trust, dated November 7, 1967 -
30% of an undivided 2/3 interest

W. A. Moncrief and W. A. Moncrief, Jr., Trustees of
Charles B. Moncrief Trust, dated November 7, 1967 -
30% of an undivided 2/3 interest

George M. Young - 30% of an undivided 1/3 interest

William K. Young - 30% of an undivided 1/3 interest

Frank G. Young - 25% of an undivided 1/3 interest

Marshall R. Young, Jr.- 15% of an undivided 1/3 interest

LOCATION: Jay State Livestock Market in Section 41, Township 5
North, Range 29 West, Santa Rosa County

Executed instrument of assignment has been filed and approved
by the Trustees' legal counsel as to form and legality. The
Department of Agriculture and Consumer Services has no objections
to the assignment.

Recommend approval and consent to assignment.

ACTION OF THE TRUSTEES:

Motion was made by Mr. Stone, seconded by Mr. Dickinson and
adopted without objection, to approve and consent to the
assignment as requested.

-3-

DADE COUNTY - Road Right of Way
(April 13, 1972)

APPLICANT: Metropolitan Dade County

REQUEST: Easement for the widening and improving of
Southwest 107th Avenue.

LOCATION: A strip of land containing 1.368 acres being
29.02 feet wide at its widest point and extending
along the east boundary of the Florida International
University in Section 7, Township 54 South; Range
40 East, Dade County.

The Board of Regents' Facilities Committee on April 4, 1972,
approved granting the easement, as the widening of Southwest
107th Avenue is for the benefit of the University.

Recommend issuance of the easement to Dade County for road
purposes only.

ACTION OF THE TRUSTEES:

Motion was made by Mr. Dickinson, seconded by Mr. Christian
and adopted without objection, authorizing issuance of the
easement to Dade County for road purposes only.

-4A-

HILLSBOROUGH COUNTY - Bulkhead Line, Section 253.122, F. S.
(March 16, 1972)

APPLICANT: Department of Transportation
Tallahassee, Florida

PROJECT: Bulkhead line 4,304.22 feet long in Tampa Bay in
                Hillsborough County adjacent to the Sunshine
                Skyway (State Road No. 55), approved by the Board of
                County Commissioners of Hillsborough County by
                resolution adopted September 10, 1970.

ECOLOGICAL
RESPONSES: Department of Natural Resources - No objection.

                Game and Fresh Water Fish Commission - No objection.

                Department of Pollution Control - No objection.

OTHERS: Field Operations Division - No objection as long
                as dredging and filling is held to a minimum.

Staff recommends approval of bulkhead line.

ACTION OF THE TRUSTEES:

Mr. Kuperberg pointed out that agenda items numbered 4A through
4F represented bulkhead line, dredge and fill applications for
the Sunshine Skyway passing through three counties, and the
total area of fill was 2.947 acres to protect the right of way
for the four-laning.

On motion by Mr. Christian, seconded and adopted without objections, the Trustees approved the bulkhead line 4,304.22 feet
long in Tampa Bay in Hillsborough County as established by
the county on September 10, 1970.

                            -4B-

HILLSBOROUGH COUNTY - Dredge Permit No. 253.123-1110 and
                      Fill Permit No. 253.124-281 (TPA 71-12)
                      (March 16, 1972)

APPLICANT: Department of Transportation
                Tallahassee, Florida

PROJECT: To fill approximately 1.276 acres of submerged
                land adjacent to the Sunshine Skyway (S. R. 55 -
                U. S. 19). The area to be filled lies within
                existing right of way of the Department of
                Transportation. Construction also includes minor
                dredging for installation of a concrete boat ramp.

LOCATION: Tampa Bay, Hillsborough County.

MATERIAL: Approximately 10,000 cubic yards of fill material
                will come from upland sources.

PAYMENT: Waive fees for public project.

ECOLOGICAL
RESPONSES: Department of Natural Resources - No objection.

                Game and Fresh Water Fish Commission - No objection.

                Department of Pollution Control - No objection.

OTHERS: Field Operations Division - No objection as long
                as dredging and filling is held to a minimum.

Staff recommends issuance of Dredge Permit No. 253.123-1110,
Fill Permit No. 253.124-281, and waiver of fees.

ACTION OF THE TRUSTEES:

On motion by Mr. Christian, seconded and adopted without objection, the Trustees authorized issuance of Dredge Permit No.
253.123-1110 and Fill Permit No. 253.124-281 to the Department
of Transportation without fee.

-4C-

MANATEE COUNTY - Bulkhead Line, Section 253.122, F. S.
                 (March 16, 1972)

APPLICANT: Department of Transportation
              Tallahassee, Florida

PROJECT: Bulkhead Line 20,918.96 feet long in Tampa Bay in
              Manatee County adjacent to the Sunshine Skyway
              (State Road No. 55), approved by the Board of
              County Commissioners of Manatee County by
              Resolution No. R-71-4 adopted April 13, 1971.

ECOLOGICAL
RESPONSES: Department of Natural Resources - No objection.

              Game and Fresh Water Fish Commission - No objection.

              Department of Pollution Control - No objection.

OTHERS: Field Operations Division - No objection as long
              as dredging and filling is held to a minimum.

Staff recommends approval of the bulkhead line.

ACTION OF THE TRUSTEES:

On motion by Mr. Christian, seconded and adopted without objection, the Trustees approved the bulkhead line 20,918.96 feet
long in Tampa Bay in Manatee County as established by the county
on April 13, 1971.

-4D-

MANATEE COUNTY - Fill Permit No. 253.124-279
                 (March 16, 1972)

APPLICANT: Department of Transportation
              Tallahassee, Florida

PROJECT: To fill approximately 0.017 acre of submerged land
              adjacent to the Sunshine Skyway (S. R. 55 - U. S. 19).
              The area to be filled lies within existing right of
              way of the Department of Transportation.

LOCATION: Tampa Bay, Manatee County.

MATERIAL: Approximately 150 cubic yards of fill material will
              come from upland sources.

PAYMENT: Waive fees for public project.

ECOLOGICAL
RESPONSES: Department of Natural Resources - No objection.

              Game and Fresh Water Fish Commission - No objection.

              Department of Pollution Control - No objection.

OTHERS: Field Operations Division - No objection as long
              as dredging and filling is held to a minimum.

Staff recommends issuance of Fill Permit No. 253.124-279, and
waiver of fees.

ACTION OF THE TRUSTEES:

On motion by Mr. Christian, seconded and adopted without
objection, the Trustees authorized issuance of Fill Permit No.
253.124-279 to the Department of Transportation without fee.

-4E-

PINELLAS COUNTY - Bulkhead Line, Section 253.122, F. S.
(March 16, 1972)

APPLICANT: Department of Transportation
Tallahassee, Florida

PROJECT: Bulkhead line 32,957.01 feet long in Tampa Bay in
Pinellas County adjacent to the Sunshine Skyway
(State Road No. 55), approved by the Board of County
Commissioners sitting as the Pinellas County Water
and Navigation Control Authority on June 16, 1970.

ECOLOGICAL
RESPONSES: Department of Natural Resources - No objection.

Game and Fresh Water Fish Commission - No objection.

Department of Pollution Control - No objection.

OTHERS: Field Operations Division - No objection as long
as dredging and filling is held to a minimum.

Staff recommends approval of bulkhead line.

ACTION OF THE TRUSTEES:

On motion by Mr. Christian, seconded and adopted without
objection, the Trustees approved the bulkhead line 32,957.01 feet
long in Tampa Bay in Pinellas County as established by the county
on June 16, 1970.

-4F-

PINELLAS COUNTY - Fill Permit No. 253.124-280
(March 16, 1972)

APPLICANT: Department of Transportation
Tallahassee, Florida

PROJECT: To fill areas totaling approximately 1.654 acres
of submerged land in Pinellas County adjacent to
the Sunshine Skyway (S. R. 55 - U. S. 19). The
area to be filled lies within existing right of
way of the Department of Transportation.

LOCATION: Tampa Bay, Pinellas County.

MATERIAL: Approximately 7,000 cubic yards of fill material
will come from upland sources.

PAYMENT: Waive fees for public project.

ECOLOGICAL
RESPONSES: Department of Natural Resources - No objection.

Game and Fresh Water Fish Commission - No objection.

Department of Pollution Control - No objection.

OTHERS: Field Operations Division - No objection as long
as dredging and filling is held to a minimum.

Staff recommends issuance of Fill Permit No. 253.124-280 and
waiver of fees.

ACTION OF THE TRUSTEES:

On motion by Mr. Christian, seconded and adopted without
objection, the Trustees authorized issuance of Fill Permit
No. 253.124-280 to the Department of Transportation without
fee.

5-9-72

-5A-

VOLUSIA COUNTY - Bulkhead Line, Section
253.122, Florida Statutes
(March 24, 1972)

APPLICANT: City of New Smyrna Beach
Post Office Box 490
New Smyrna Beach, Florida

PROJECT: Bulkhead line 1594.65 feet long in the Indian River
abutting Section 20, Township 17 South, Range 34
East, Volusia County, approved and established by
the City Council of New Smyrna Beach by Ordinance
No. 838 adopted December 14, 1971.

ECOLOGICAL
RESPONSES: Department of Natural Resources - No objection.

Game and Fresh Water Fish Commission - No objection.

Department of Pollution Control - No objection.

OTHERS: Field Operations Division - No objection.

Staff recommends approval of bulkhead line.

ACTION OF THE TRUSTEES:

The Director stated agenda items 5A, 5B and 5C represented a
"package", and the applicant agreed to comply with the
recommendations.

On motion by Mr. Dickinson, seconded by Mr. Stone and adopted
without objection, the Trustees approved the bulkhead line in
the Indian River in Volusia County as established by the City
Council of New Smyrna Beach on December 14, 1971.

-5B-

VOLUSIA COUNTY - State Construction Permit and
Marina License ML-110
(March 24, 1972)

APPLICANT: Yacht Club Island Corporation
c/o Mr. John C. Gross, President
Post Office Box 596, New Smyrna Beach, Florida

PROJECT: Construct marina facility covering 34,376 square
feet of submerged land in the Indian River abutting
Section 20, Township 17 South, Range 34 East,
Volusia County.

PAYMENT: $687.52 minimum annual fee for marina license.

ECOLOGICAL
RESPONSES: Department of Natural Resources - No objection.

Game and Fresh Water Fish Commission - No objection.

Department of Pollution Control - No objection.

OTHERS: Field Operations Division - No objection.

Staff recommends issuance of construction permit and marina
license for annual fee of $687.52.

ACTION OF THE TRUSTEES:

On motion by Mr. Dickinson, seconded by Mr. Stone and adopted
without objection, the Trustees approved issuance of construction
permit and marina license for $687.52 annual fee.

VOLUSIA COUNTY - Dredge Permit No. 253.123-1049
(March 24, 1972)

APPLICANT: Yacht Club Island Corporation
c/o John C. Gross, President
Post Office Box 596, New Smyrna Beach, Florida

PROJECT: Redredge an existing navigation channel 900 feet
long, 75 feet wide, -5 feet deep and a turning
basin 100 by 100 feet by 5 feet deep.

LOCATION: Section 20, Township 17 South, Range 34 East,
in the Indian River, Volusia County.

MATERIAL: Approximately 12,870 cubic yards of material will
be removed from sovereignty land and placed on
upland spoil area.

PAYMENT: $6,435 as payment for material at the standard
yardage rate of 50¢ per cubic yard.

ECOLOGICAL
RESPONSES: Department of Natural Resources - No objection
provided applicant replants mangroves and uses
energy-absorbing seawall construction.

Game and Fresh Water Fish Commission - No objection
provided dredge area is diapered to prevent excessive
turbidity and all water run-off is discharged to the
east side of the spoil area.

Department of Pollution Control - Concurs with
stipulations by the Game and Fresh Water Fish Commission.

OTHERS: Field Operations Division - No objection.

Staff recommends approval of Dredge Permit No. 253.123-1049
subject to stipulations by the Game and Fresh Water Fish
Commission and the Department of Natural Resources.

ACTION OF THE TRUSTEES:

On motion by Mr. Dickinson, seconded by Mr. Stone and adopted
without objection, the staff recommendation was approved as the
action of the Board. It was noted that the applicant had agreed
to the stipulations.

VOLUSIA COUNTY - Bulkhead Line, Section 253.122, F. S.
(April 17, 1972)

APPLICANT: Board of County Commissioners
of Volusia County

PROJECT: Bulkhead line 2,716.67 feet long along the east shore
of the Halifax River in Section 27, Township 15 South,
Range 33 East, Volusia County, approved and established
by the Board of County Commissioners of Volusia County
by Resolution No. 71-85 adopted February 17, 1972.

ECOLOGICAL
RESPONSES: Department of Natural Resources - No objection.

Game and Fresh Water Fish Commission - No objection.

Department of Pollution Control - No objection.

Staff recommends approval of bulkhead line.

ACTION OF THE TRUSTEES:

On motion by Mr. Stone, seconded by Mr. Christian and Mr. O'Malley, adopted without objection, the Trustees approved the bulkhead line along the east shore of the Halifax River as established by the Board of County Commissioners of Volusia County on February 17, 1972.

-7-

COLLIER COUNTY - Dredge Permit No. 253.123-942
                 (January 21, 1972)

APPLICANT: James B. Morgan
                218 Banyan Boulevard, Naples, Florida

PROJECT: To dredge a turning basin 80 feet long by 30 feet wide by 4 feet deep, dredge an upland boat slip, and install a seawall.

LOCATION: Champney Bay in Section 21, Township 50 South, Range 25 East, Collier County, Government Lot 1.

PAYMENT: A check for $270 has been tendered as payment for the sovereignty material to be removed.

ECOLOGICAL
RESPONSES: Department of Natural Resources - Project has been revised as recommended by Department of Natural Resources.

                Game and Fresh Water Fish Commission - No objection.

                Department of Pollution Control - No objection.

OTHERS: Field Operations Division - No objection.

Staff recommends issuance of Dredge Permit No. 253.123-942 as revised to conform to suggestions of the Department of Natural Resources.

ACTION OF THE TRUSTEES:

On motion by Mr. Stone, seconded by Mr. Dickinson and adopted without objection, the Trustees approved issuance of the dredge permit revised as stipulated by the environmental agency.

-8-

PALM BEACH COUNTY - State Construction Permit
                    253.03, Florida Statutes
                    (March 22, 1972)

APPLICANT: Kassuba Inns, Inc.
                350 Royal Palm Way, Palm Beach, Florida

PROJECT: Construct bridge and install force main and water main crossing an artificial canal in Section 5, Township 41 South, Range 43 East, Palm Beach County. No dredging or filling is required.

PAYMENT: $100 fee submitted.

ECOLOGICAL
RESPONSES: Department of Natural Resources - No objection.

                Game and Fresh Water Fish Commission - No objection.

                Department of Pollution Control - No objection.

OTHERS: Field Operations Division - No objection.

Staff recommends issuance of state construction permit.

5-9-72

ACTION OF THE TRUSTEES:

On motion by Mr. Dickinson, seconded by Mr. Christian and
adopted without objection, the Trustees approved issuance of
the state construction permit.

-9-

PINELLAS COUNTY - File No. 2450-52-253.03

At the meeting of the Board of Natural Resources on this date,
action was deferred for one week on a matter related to the
application for easements to the United States for the Treasure
Island beach nourishment project. Treasurer O'Malley was concerned
about the source of the fill material.

Without objection, the Trustees deferred action one week.

-10-

PINELLAS COUNTY - State Construction Permit, 253.03, F. S.
               (January 17, 1972)

APPLICANT: City of St. Petersburg
            Municipal Building, St. Petersburg, Florida

PROJECT: Floating dock facility at Crisp Park in Placido
            Bayou in Section 8, Township 31 South, Range 17
            East, Pinellas County. The proposed construction
            lies within an artificial cut portion of Placido
            Bayou. No dredging or filling is required.

PAYMENT: City requests waiver of $25 processing fee.

ECOLOGICAL
RESPONSES: Department of Natural Resources - No objection.

            Game and Fresh Water Fish Commission - No objection.

            Department of Pollution Control - No objection.

OTHERS: Field Operations Division - No objection.

Staff recommends waiver of fee and issuance of construction
permit.

ACTION OF THE TRUSTEES:

On motion by Mr. Stone, seconded by Mr. Christian and adopted
without objection, the Trustees authorized issuance of the
construction permit to the city without charge.

-11-

PINELLAS COUNTY - Dredge Permit No. 253.123-1039

The staff recommended approval of the modified application of
Gale J. Apple and issuance of a dredge permit upon receipt of
$2,500 for material to be dredged from a small boat channel and
placed on applicant's previously filled upland.

Attorney General Shevin questioned placing an application on the
agenda when payment had not been tendered on request, and dredging
in Boca Ciega Bay. The Director advised that the staff is endeavoring to comply with the Board's directive to agenda applications promptly and with the auditor's directions not to hold
checks. Assurance was given the Attorney General that the staff would
not issue the permit until was payment was received. The Director
further stated that his personal feeling was that there should be
no dredging unless it could be shown to be in the public interest,
but as Executive Director it was his responsibility to weigh the

5-9-72

equities. This project area had been reduced to one-quarter
of the original size and consists of maintenance dredging in
an existing silted-in channel to restore a navigable depth of
minus 5 feet. It was pointed out that the Board regularly
grants maintenance dredging permits in existing waterways.

Mr. Christian knew the area well and considered it a reasonable
request to allow the owners boat access.

Mr. O'Malley made a motion for a week's deferral since payment
had not been received, and at Mr. Kuperberg's request for two weeks,
so the check would be in hand when the application was considered,
he amended his motion.

Mr. Stone seconded the amended motion to defer for two weeks,
which passed without objection.

-12-

TRUSTEES' FUNDS

Staff requests authorization to expend up to $10,000 from
budgeted funds for expert witness fees and related court
costs in connection with litigation (growing out of the Port
Manatee project) against Hendry Corporation now pending in
Hillsborough County Circuit Court.

Staff expects the majority of these expenses to be incurred
in the next fiscal year with eventual reimbursement from the
defendant if we are successful in this litigation.

ACTION OF THE TRUSTEES:

On motion by Mr. O'Malley, seconded by Mr. Christian and
Mr. Stone, carried without objection, the Board authorized
expenditure of up to the $10,000 requested for expert witness
fees and related court costs.

On motion by Mr. Stone, seconded by Mr. O'Malley and carried
without objection, the rules were waived to consider the
addendum items.

-13-

TRUSTEES' FUNDS - Shoreline Mapping

Request authority to transfer $25,000 to the Department of
Natural Resources, Division of Interior Resources, for the
continuation of various shoreline survey projects. These funds
were appropriated by the Legislature and are available for
transfer within the approved operating budget.

ACTION OF THE TRUSTEES:

Mr. Kuperberg said the sum would be a routine transfer of funds
that had been budgeted to pay for the shoreline survey.

On motion by Mr. O'Malley, seconded by Mr. Dickinson and adopted
unanimously, the Board authorized transfer of $25,000 to the
Department of Natural Resources, Division of Interior Resources.

-14-

WAKULLA COUNTY - Marina License, ML-106

On January 25, 1972, upon recommendation of the staff, the Board
approved issuance of a marina license to Panacea Bridgehouse,
Inc., for the construction of a pier facility and restaurant
covering 26,810 square feet of submerged land in Ochlockonee
Bay. The recommendation cited that no dredging was required.

Pursuant to approval of the Board, a license was prepared and
sent to the applicant for signature on February 16, 1972. Shortly
thereafter, Mr. Elliott Messer advised the executive director of
objection to the issuance of this license and that neighboring
property owners, including his client, had not received notice
of the proposed issuance in time to make a presentation to the
Trustees. A staff legal opinion was requested on the applica-
bility of statutory advertising requirements to this project.
On March 14, 1972, staff counsel rendered the following opinion:

"In this instance, I believe the public notice provisions of F.S. 253.12(3) are applicable. That statute
requires public notice and notice to nearby riparian
owners when the Board sells or conveys submerged lands.
I believe this license to use sovereign bottoms with
its privilege of indefinite automatic renewal is a
conveyance of the type for which the statute contemplates public notice."

On March 24, 1972, Mr. Elliott Messer confirmed previous oral
objections by letter stating, in part:

"Your file will reflect that the applicant filed a list
setting forth the names and addresses of five persons
or families owning those lots in White Beaches Subdivision which are located closest to the project.
Yet, no notice or opportunity to be heard was given
to Mr. Toney or to any of the other persons described
in the list.

Approval of the subject application was accomplished by
the granting of a 'marina license', notwithstanding the
fact that the contemplated project is not in fact a
marina facility. It is our understanding, gained from
a review of correspondence between counsel for the
applicant and the United States Corps of Engineers,
that Panacea Bridgehouse, Inc., owns or controls sufficient upland upon which it could locate the restaurant
facility. We can only assume that the applicant's
desire to construct the commercial facility on state
owned land in the navigable waters of the Ochlocknee
River is prompted by the fact that the laws of Wakulla
County do not permit the sale of alcoholic beverages
within that county.

Finally, while the foregoing deficiencies are important, the gist of Mr. Toney's complaint rests in the
fact that: (1) a 'marina license' was used to
authorize private use of public lands and waters for
a purpose unconnected with public recreational use
of our natural resources; (2) the location of the
facility will be detrimental to the peace and enjoyment of adjoining private property owners; and (3)
no notice or opportunity to be heard was afforded
those persons that will be vitally affected."

Pursuant to the Board's administrative rules, an immediate informal conference was called in an attempt to evaluate the objection
which was treated as a request for reconsideration of the Board's
decision. During discussions, it became apparent that the applicant would probably apply for a dredge permit in the immediate
future to dig a channel to accommodate the licensed pier. The
executive director's original recommendation, of course, had
not considered that dredging would be required. The conference
concluded with the attorneys for each side agreeing to negotiate
to resolve the objection. By subsequent letter, however, Mr.
Messer advised that no settlement had been reached, that his
client continued to maintain strong objection to licensing of the
project, and that the Bureau of Sport Fisheries and Wildlife
has strong objection to the issuance of a Corps permit. Mr.
Messer has requested to make a presentation to the Trustees to
ask reconsideration of issuance of the license. While the staff

is obliged to take the necessary steps to implement action of the Board, it is also duty-bound to point out facts and problems that are discovered after such action.

Staff recommends that the Board entertain Mr. Messer's petition for the Board to reconsider its decision of January 25, 1972, to withdraw its approval of the license application, and to advertise for objections and conduct appropriate public hearing.

ACTION OF THE TRUSTEES:

Mr. Kuperberg stated that objections were received after the Board approved a license for a restaurant over the water with attached dock.

Mr. O'Malley made a motion, seconded by Mr. Shevin, to approve the staff recommendation.

Mr. William J. Roberts, attorney for Mr. Finley McMillan, principal stockholder of Panacea Bridgehouse, Inc., furnished maps of the unzoned area. He stated that prior to approval by the Trustees, the Department of Pollution Control advertised for objections and none were received, no environmental agency had any objections, and a number of similar licenses had been approved recently with the same type of notice. The applicant had furnished names and addresses of adjacent property owners when the application was filed. Subsequent to approval the applicant had requested issuance of the permit, and a question was raised as to whether adequate notice was given because of the objections that had been received. Mr. Roberts said his client had no objection to all the facts being aired by the objectors, and asked for an early hearing before a hearing examiner.

Mr. Elliott Messer represented Mr. Gunter Toney and wife, whose residence was adjacent to the application area. The Toneys and others objected to the restaurant facility to be constructed 295 feet into the river because of the expected noise and their concern that the use of a marina license was somewhat misleading as the project did not appear to be for marine activities. It was suggested that the restaurant might be constructed on the applicant's upland property. Mr. Messer asked for a hearing and, if it should be determined that the requested use of the public water bottoms was in the public interest, that there might be some modification to lessen the noise.

The Governor commented that in the absence of zoning, this was a difference between private owners, that a public hearing would give all an opportunity to be heard. Mr. O'Malley added that all facts had not been known when the application was considered in January.

The Director commented that he felt the marina rule needed overhauling. He suggested that approval of the staff recommendation would be a way to resolve this particular application.

Without objection, the motion was passed to reconsider the decision of January 25, 1972, to withdraw approval of the license application, and to advertise for objections and conduct an appropriate public hearing.

-15-

MARTIN COUNTY - Dredge Permit 253.123-265
(issued May 6, 1969)

APPLICANT: William R. Dean, Trustee, c/o James F. Littman
P. O. Box 1154, Stuart, Florida

PROJECT: To construct a navigation channel 75 feet wide, 5 feet deep and 500 feet long.

LOCATION: Indian River in Section 25, Township 37 South, Range 41 East, Martin County

MATERIAL: 590 cubic yards to be removed from the oversize cut.

PAYMENT: $59 paid for material at the rate of 10¢ per cubic yard.

STAFF
REMARKS: Permit expires May 10, 1972. Applicant requests 90-day extension of this permit since, until now, he has not been able to get a contractor to do the work as authorized. This work lies within an aquatic preserve which the Board now has under advisement.

ECOLOGICAL
RESPONSES: Department of Natural Resources - In report dated April 23, 1969, indicated that the reduction of channel width and depth from 100' x 6' x 600' to 75' x 5' x 500' would reduce resultant damage to marine resources.

OTHERS: Martin County issued its permit to construct the navigation channel.

Applicant is here today and requests to be heard.

ACTION OF THE TRUSTEES:

The Director said Mr. Skelton, representing the deceased applicant, had requested renewal of a permit that would expire on May 14, three years from the effective date of the dredge permit. The staff felt it had not been pursued with diligence and a new application should be made under today's guidelines.

Mr. O'Malley made a motion that carried, to allow Mr. Skelton time for a brief presentation.

On behalf of Mr. Arthur Quinn, successor trustee appointed by the court, Mr. Ronald L. Skelton said there had been a company reorganization, responsibility for the permit was assigned to him and although he tried diligently since January 1, it had been very difficult to get the small dredging job done. He now had assurance that one dredge company could do the work in June and had requested extension of the Corps of Engineers permit for 90 days. He explained that the canal had been dug but the channel to the intracoastal waterway was not dredged, that the project was part of properties extending from ocean to river, that the ocean side was developed but not the land on the river side.

Mr. O'Malley indicated he might have approved the extension if there were homes for which the channel would provide access and if there was a firm contract commitment to do the dredging, but under the circumstances he made a motion, seconded by Mr. Stone, that the permit be allowed to expire and the applicant might then refile under the existing rules.

Mr. Christian suggested extension along with the Corps permit time, and Mr. Kuperberg advised that the law did allow extension for good cause and showing of diligence but the staff felt that work delayed for three years should come under present regulations. There were problems as it was in an aquatic preserve area, had not been approved by the Department of Pollution Control, and was connected to a 700 ft. long dead-end canal.

In response to Mr. Dickinson's question, Mr. Skelton explained something of the legal delay and trusteeship.

Mr. O'Malley expressed the opinion that the members appreciated the problems but there was nothing to prevent the filing of a new application which the staff would try to accommodate within the time limitations allowed by the Corps permit.

On motion by Mr. O'Malley, seconded by Mr. Stone and carried, with Mr. Dickinson voting in the negative, the Board accepted the Director's recommendation to allow the permit to expire.

Mr. Kuperberg reported that the staff was making progress in expediting permit processing procedures and preparing new procedures and new administrative rules for consideration by the Trustees in the near future.

On motion duly adopted, the meeting was adjourned.

GOVERNOR   CHAIRMAN

ATTEST:
EXECUTIVE DIRECTOR

*   *   *   *

Tallahassee, Florida
May 16, 1972

The State of Florida Board of Trustees of the Internal Improvement Trust Fund met on this date in the auditorium of the Burns Building with the following members present:

Reubin O'D. Askew	Governor
Richard (Dick) Stone	Secretary of State
Robert L. Shevin	Attorney General
Fred O. Dickinson, Jr.	Comptroller
Floyd T. Christian	Commissioner of Education
Doyle Conner	Commissioner of Agriculture

John DuBose   Staff Member

-1-

The minutes of the May 2, 1972, meeting were approved as submitted.

-2-

PUTNAM AND FLAGLER COUNTIES - Advertise Oil and Gas Lease

APPLICANT: Thayer-Davis and Associates,
Tampa, Florida

REQUEST: Advertise oil and gas drilling lease.

LOCATION
AND
INTEREST
OF STATE:
Reserved 1/2 interest in Government Lot 1, Section 27, Township 11 South, Range 27 East, and full interest in the north portion of Lake Crescent described as follows: those parts of Sections 22, 23, 24, 27 and 34 and all of Sections 25 and 26, Township 11 South, Range 27 East, Putnam County, and that part of Section 30, Township 11 South, Range 28 East, Flagler County, in Lake Crescent, containing a total of 2,792.09 net mineral acres, more or less.

Proceeds from lease will go to Internal Improvement Trust Fund.

Drilling operations will be prohibited in the portion of the lease covering the lake bottom.

The request has been reviewed by the Director of Interior Resources, Department of Natural Resources, who concurs in the following recommendation.

Recommend advertising for sealed bids for lease with annual rental of $1 per net mineral acre, 1/8 royalty, five-year primary term, $50,000 surety bond and at least one test well every 2 1/2 years drilled to 6,000 feet or to the top of the Paleozoics, igneous implacements or metamorphic rocks, whichever is deeper.

ACTION OF THE TRUSTEES:

On motion by Mr. Christian, seconded by Mr. Stone and carried unanimously, the staff recommendation was approved as the action of the Board.

-3-

BROWARD COUNTY - State Construction Permit
               Marina License ML-99
               (April 17, 1972)

APPLICANT: Bayshore Towers of Fort Lauderdale, Inc.
             c/o McLaughlin Engineering Co.
             400 Northeast Third Avenue, Ft. Lauderdale, Florida

PROJECT: Construction of additional docking structures covering 9,125 square feet of sovereignty land in the Intracoastal Waterway abutting Section 1, Township 50 South, Range 43 East, Broward County. No dredging is required.

PAYMENT: $182.50 minimum annual fee for marina license.

ECOLOGICAL
RESPONSES: Department of Natural Resources - No objection.

             Game and Fresh Water Fish Commission - No objection.

             Department of Pollution Control - No objection.

OTHERS: 1. Florida Inland Navigation District - No objection.

             2. Field Operations Division - No objection.

Staff recommends issuance of construction permit and marina license for annual fee of $182.50.

ACTION OF THE TRUSTEES:

Attorney General Shevin considered the annual fee of $182.50 insufficient for use of a very valuable water column in the Intracoastal Waterway, which pointed up the need for revision. Mr. DuBose assured him the staff was working on fee schedules and administrative rules revision.

Motion was made by Mr. Christian, seconded by Mr. Stone and carried without objection, authorizing issuance of the construction permit and marina license as recommended by the staff.

-4-

PALM BEACH COUNTY - Marina License No. ML-7
                    Revision - 253.03, F. S.
                    (February 23, 1972)

APPLICANT: Ronald Sinn
              2308 Avenue A, Riviera Beach, Florida

PROJECT: Revision of existing marina facility by the addition
              of a marine railway lift, all construction to be
              within the area previously authorized. No dredging
              is required.

PAYMENT: None required.

ECOLOGICAL
RESPONSES: Department of Natural Resources - No objection.

              Game and Fresh Water Fish Commission - No objection.

              Department of Pollution Control - No objection.

OTHERS: Field Operations Division - No objection.

Staff recommends approval of proposed revision.

ACTION OF THE TRUSTEES:

Motion was made by Mr. Stone, seconded by Mr. Christian and
carried without objection, to approve the proposed revision
of the marina.   _____.
                          -5-
LEE COUNTY - Application for Land Exchange, File 2413-36-253.12,
              9.39 acres to applicant, 59.04 acres to Trustees.

The application of Lover's Key, Inc., for a proposed land
exchange had been requested to be deferred for two weeks by
the State Treasurer.

Parties present on behalf of this application included
Stanley W. Hole, president of the consultant firm, and Howard
S. Rhoads, attorney. Mr. Rhoads expressed no objection to
deferral and was advised that the advertising could not be
started during the deferral period.

Mr. Dickinson said it should be understood that when approval
is granted for an advertisement, it did not carry any assurance that the final decision on a project would be favorable.

Based on the Treasurer's request for deferral, the Board
postponed action until the meeting on June 6.

                    _____

                        -6-

PINELLAS COUNTY - File No. 2450-52-253.03
                  (March 9, 1972)

ON May 9 at request of the State Treasurer, the Board deferred
consideration of this application for one week.

APPLICANT: United States of America, by the
              Board of County Commissioners of Pinellas County

PROJECT: Perpetual borrow easement 17.40 acres,
              perpetual pipeline easement 9.90 acres, and
              perpetual construction easement 8.14 acres,
              for Pinellas County Beach Erosion Control
              Project, Treasure Island (south end) Nourishment.

              The Department of Natural Resources, Bureau of Beaches
              and Shores, File No. 72-20, will present a request for
              approval of the project on its agenda on this date.

LOCATION: Three parcels of sovereignty land in Gulf of Mexico in Section 36, Township 31 South, Range 15 East, Pinellas County.

MATERIAL: 120,000 cubic yards from the offshore borrow easement.

PAYMENT: None.

ECOLOGICAL
RESPONSES: Department of Natural Resources on January 5, 1972, commented that the project would have limited adverse effects and suggested alternate dredge areas. On January 6, 1972, Executive Director Randolph Hodges commented that the project would have limited adverse effects but expressed the opinion that public benefit would outweigh adverse effects.

Game and Fresh Water Fish Commission concurs with Department of Natural Resources Survey and Management comments of January 5, 1972.

Department of Pollution Control - No objection.

OTHERS: February 1, 1972, the U. S. Army Corps of Engineers advised that one suggested alternate spoil area did not have suitable material and the other would require excessive transport cost.

Staff remarks: This is the second beach nourishment project with adverse biological responses.

Staff recommends that authority be granted to issue the easements.

ACTION OF THE TRUSTEES:

On motion by Mr. Stone, seconded by Mr. Christian and Mr. Conner, adopted without objection, the rules were waived to consider the addendum.

The Board of Natural Resources approved a related matter on its agenda on this date.

Motion was made by Mr. Christian, seconded by Mr. Stone and carried unanimously, to grant the easements as recommended by the staff.

On motion duly adopted, the meeting was adjourned.

_____
GOVERNOR - CHAIRMAN

ATTEST:_____
STAFF MEMBER

*

5-16-72

The Board of Trustees of the Internal Improvement Trust Fund
met on this date in the auditorium of the Burns Building with
the following members present:

-1-

The minutes of the meeting of May 9, 1972, were approved with
corrections in agenda item 5C to show Dredge Permit No. 253.123-
1049, channel 900 feet long, $6,435 as payment for material,
and $0.50 per cubic yard.

-2A-

BAY COUNTY - Bulkhead Line, Section 253.122, F. S.
             (January 27, 1972)

APPLICANT: Department of Transportation

PROJECT: Bulkhead line 514.00 feet long in Martin Bayou
            abutting Section 12, Township 4 South, Range 14
            West, Bay County, established by the Board of County
            Commissioners of Bay County by Resolution No. 567
            adopted October 26, 1971.

ECOLOGICAL
RESPONSES: Department of Natural Resources - No objection.

            Game and Fresh Water Fish Commission - No objection.

            Department of Pollution Control - No objection.

            Department of Transportation indicates cost
            of proposed box culvert extension would be $70,000
            and cost of replacing the existing facility with 200
            foot bridge would cost $250,000.

Staff recommends approval of bulkhead line.

ACTION OF THE TRUSTEES:

Motion was made by Mr. O'Malley, seconded by Mr. Stone and
adopted unanimously, to approve the bulkhead line established
by Bay County on October 26, 1972.

-2B-

BAY COUNTY - Right of Way Easement, File 2440-03-253.03
             (March 9, 1972)
APPLICANT: Department of Transportation

PROJECT: Highway and box culvert construction for State Road
            22. Dredging and filling are required.

LOCATION: 0.06 acre parcel of sovereignty land in Martin
            Bayou in Section 12, Township 4 South, Range 14 West,
            Bay County.

ECOLOGICAL
RESPONSES: Department of Natural Resources - No objection.

Game and Fresh Water Fish Commission - No objection.

Department of Pollution Control - No objection.

Staff requests authority to issue right of way easement.

ACTION OF THE TRUSTEES:

Motion was made by Mr. O'Malley, seconded by Mr. Stone and
adopted unanimously, to grant to the Department of Transportation the right of way easement for State Road 22.

-2C-

BAY COUNTY - Permits 253.123-1069 and 253.124-260
             (March 9, 1972)

APPLICANT: Department of Transportation

PROJECT: Dredging and filling for highway and box culvert con-
            struction for State Road 22.

LOCATION: Section 12, Township 4 South, Range 14 West, Martin
            Bayou, Bay County.

MATERIAL: Approximately 200 cubic yards of material to be
            dredged and 0.06 acre to be filled.

PAYMENT: Fees waived, since project is in the public interest.

ECOLOGICAL
RESPONSES: Department of Natural Resources - No objection to
            project, but if the causeways were replaced by
            bridge structures, the increased circulation should
            significantly improve the quality of the bayou
            waters and enhance its biological productivity.

            Game and Fresh Water Fish Commission - No objection
            to project provided a diaper is employed on both
            sides of the roadway during dredging and filling
            operations, the bulkhead is completed before any
            fill is deposited, and driving rather than jetting
            down of concrete sheet piling is recommended for
            bulkhead construction.

            Department of Pollution Control - No objection to
            project.

Staff recommends issuance of Fill Permit 253.124-260 and Dredge
Permit 253.123-1069 to the Department of Transportation and
waiver of fees, since the project is in the public interest.

ACTION OF THE TRUSTEES:

Mr. Kuperberg asked that the staff recommendation be amended to
include the words, "subject to the requirements of the Game
and Fresh Water Fish Commission."

On motion by Mr. O'Malley, seconded by Mr. Stone and adopted
unanimously, the Trustees approved issuance of the fill and
dredge permits without fee subject to the stipulations of the
Game and Fresh Water Fish Commission.

-3A-

COLLIER COUNTY - Bulkhead Line, Section 253.122, Florida Statutes
            (April 13, 1972)

APPLICANT: Department of Transportation

PROJECT: Bulkhead line 496.90 feet long in Goodland Bay and
            Marco River abutting State Road No. 92 in Section
            18, Township 52 South, Range 27 East, Collier County,
            approved and established by the Board of County
            Commissioners of Collier County, by resolution
            adopted May 4, 1971.

ECOLOGICAL
RESPONSES: Department of Natural Resources - No objection.

            Game and Fresh Water Fish Commission - No objection.

            Department of Pollution Control - No objection.

OTHERS: Field Operations Division - No objection.

Staff recommends approval of bulkhead line.

ACTION OF THE TRUSTEES:

On motion by Mr. O'Malley, seconded by Mr. Dickinson and
adopted without objection, the bulkhead line was approved
as established by the Board of County Commissioners of Collier
County on May 4, 1971.

-3B-

COLLIER COUNTY - Right of Way Easement, File No. 2455-11-253.03
            (April 13, 1972)

APPLICANT: Department of Transportation

PROJECT: Highway and bridge construction for State Road
            No. 92. Some filling of submerged land is
            proposed but no dredging is required.

LOCATION: Two parcels of sovereignty land abutting Section 13,
            Township 52 South, Range 26 East, and Section 18,
            Township 52 South, Range 27 East, Collier County.

PAYMENT: None.

ECOLOGICAL
RESPONSES: Department of Natural Resources - No objection.

            Game and Fresh Water Fish Commission - No objection.

            Department of Pollution Control - No objection.

OTHERS: Field Operations Division - No objection.

Staff requests authority to issue right of way easement upon being
furnished proof that all abutting upland ownership has been secured.

ACTION OF THE TRUSTEES:

On motion by Mr. O'Malley, seconded by Mr. Dickinson and adopted
without objection, the Board authorized issuance of right of way
easement subject to proof being furnished that all abutting
upland ownership had been secured as recommended by the staff.

5-23-72

-3C-

COLLIER COUNTY - Fill Permit No. 253.124-291 and
                Utility Permit No. 253.123(2)(b)-1146
                (April 13, 1972)

APPLICANT: Department of Transportation

PROJECT: To fill 0.379 acres needed for relocation of the
             right of way and bridge construction of SR-92
             and to install storm sewer outfalls.

LOCATION: Section 18, Township 52 South, Range 27 East,
             Collier County.

MATERIAL: No sovereignty material involved.

PAYMENT: Request waiver of permit fees.

STAFF
REMARKS: Field Operations has no objection.

ECOLOGICAL
RESPONSES: Department of Natural Resources - No objection.

             Game and Fresh Water Fish Commission - No objection.

             Department of Pollution Control - No objection.

OTHERS: Board of County Commissioners approved permit.

Staff recommends issuance of Fill and Utility Permits provided
turbidity curtains are installed and maintained in place
during construction.

ACTION OF THE TRUSTEES:

On motion by Mr. O'Malley, seconded by Mr. Dickinson and adopted
unanimously, the Trustees approved issuance of the fill and
utility permits subject to the provisions recommended by the
staff.

-4A-

DUVAL COUNTY - Bulkhead Line Relocation
               (May 5, 1972)

APPLICANT: City of Jacksonville
             City Hall, Jacksonville, Florida

PROJECT: Relocation of the bulkhead line to the line of
             mean high water on the easterly side of the St. Johns
             River at the Mathews Bridge in accordance with the
             recommendations of the Interagency Advisory Committee
             recommendations.

Staff recommends approval of the bulkhead line.

ACTION OF THE TRUSTEES:

The Director reported an irregularity in the agendaed matter
as the staff had been informed that the local governmental unit
had taken the necessary action to relocate the bulkhead line;
but when details were furnished, it was learned that the
action that had been taken was the adoption of a resolution of
intent as to what they planned to do. Therefore, there was no
relocated bulkhead line before the Trustees at this time and
Mr. Shevin's 90-day deferral period, which the Board had granted
on February 28, 1972, would expire at the end of May.

Attorney General Shevin had expressed his concern to Mr. Lynwood
Roberts, President of the Council of the Consolidated City and
County, who had outlined the local action. The Attorney General
said there would be no problem on one line and the city could
complete the advertising and other necessary procedures.

On motion by Mr. O'Malley, seconded by Mr. Shevin and adopted without objection, the Trustees indicated their approval of the bulkhead line that the city intends to establish on the easterly side of the river as recommended in 4A, and extended for 90 days the time during which the City of Jacksonville might accomplish this relocation. The bulkhead line in 4A would be brought back to the Board for approval after it had been properly established by the local governing body.

———————

-4B-

DUVAL COUNTY - Bulkhead Line Relocation
            (May 4, 1972)

APPLICANT: City of Jacksonville
             City Hall, Jacksonville, Florida

PROJECT: Relocation of the bulkhead line on the southerly
             side of the St. Johns River from a point on the
             mean high water line at the southeasterly corner
             of the lands conveyed by Trustees Deed No. 24640-
             (1923-16), thence easterly along the mean high
             water line to the easterly extremity of the existing
             bulkhead, except for those portions of bulkhead
             line where submerged lands were sold to upland
             owners prior to the adoption of this resolution.

Staff recommends that approval of the bulkhead line be denied
and that the City of Jacksonville be requested to relocate this
bulkhead line to the mean high water line extending from a point
on the existing bulkhead line, which point bears S89° 08' West
from Reddie Point, thence easterly to the mean high water line
at Reddie Point and thence easterly along the mean high water
line to an intersection with the existing seawall at the Fort
Caroline Club Estates Unit 9, thence northerly, easterly and
southerly along the face of this seawall to its termination at
the mean high water line.

ACTION OF THE TRUSTEES:

Attorney General Shevin spoke of the problem in regard to the
bulkhead line jutting out about one thousand feet in the Reddie
Point area. He recommended that the Board today indicate its
rejection of the lines that are not at the mean high water line
as recommended, involving privately-owned submerged bottom
lands. The staff recommended relocation both as to the Wurn
property and the Charter property.

Mr. Lynwood Roberts pointed out on a map those bulkhead lines
established in 1961, submerged lands sold to upland owners in
the 1950's, and said the Council was concerned about arbitrary
pull-back of bulkhead lines after people had purchased land in
good faith and paid taxes yearly. He explained that the Council
did pass a resolution of intent, was in the process of advertising,
and on June 25 would hold the final public hearing, but the
Council had addressed itself to the two locations in the 1968
Interagency·Advisory Committee report. To include the 1,000-
foot area would require starting the advertisement again.

Mr. Shevin and Mr. O'Malley pointed out that all the bulkhead
lines should be relocated at the mean high water line, that the
Board would then be in a position to consider compensation to
the landowner as the Trustees have funds for the purchase of
lands for the state, and the 90-day period of time could be
extended to allow for completion of the necessary procedures.

Motion was made by Mr. Shevin, seconded by Mr. Christian, that
the Board approve the staff recommendation for denial of the
bulkhead line relocation as the city had indicated in its intention,
and that the city be requested to relocate the lines to the mean
high water line as recommended by the staff.

Mr. Shevin proposed an amendment, seconded by Mr. Christian, that the time be extended for an additional 90 days during which period the city might accomplish relocation of the bulkhead lines in this area.

The motion as amended passed unanimously.

-5-

PALM BEACH COUNTY - File No. 2434-50-253.36

At the request of the Comptroller, action was deferred for two weeks on the request from M. L. Lairsey for advertisement of a parcel of reclaimed Lake Okeechobee bottom land in Section 33, Township 41 South, Range 37 East, 0.077 acre at Canal Point in Palm Beach County.

-6-

SEMINOLE COUNTY - Electric Distribution Line Easement
(March 30, 1972)

APPLICANT: Florida Power Corporation
             Winter Park, Florida

PROJECT: Construction of a power line to provide electric
             service to the State Fish Hatchery near Oviedo.

LOCATION: North 8 feet of the south 454 feet of the west
             420 feet of Lots 373 and 376 and the West 1/2 of
             Lots 374 and 375, O. P. Swopes Addition to
             Black Hammock, Plat Book 2, Page 110, Public
             Records of Seminole County, Florida. The proposed
             easement will be in Section 25, Township 20 South,
             Range 31 East, Seminole County.

PAYMENT: Not applicable as the state will benefit from this
             service.

The Game and Fresh Water Fish Commission has reviewed this easement request and on April 25 approved granting the easement.

Staff recommends granting the easement requested for electric distribution line purposes only.

ACTION OF THE TRUSTEES:

Motion was made by Mr. Christian, seconded by Mr. Conner and adopted unanimously, granting the requested easement to Florida Power Corporation for electric distribution line purposes only.

-7-

See #7 at the end of these minutes.

-8-

DADE COUNTY - State Construction Permit
(March 16, 1972)

APPLICANT: Metropolitan Dade County
             Public Works Department

PROJECT: Install mooring piles and loading ramp in Biscayne
             Bay at Vizcaya in Section 40, Township 54 South,
             Range 41 East, Dade County.

             No dredging is required.

PAYMENT: City requests waiver of fees.

ECOLOGICAL
RESPONSES: Department of Natural Resources - No objection.

Game and Fresh Water Fish Commission - No objection.

Department of Pollution Control - No objection.

OTHERS: Field Operations Division - No objection.

Staff recommends issuance of construction permit and waiver of
fees.

ACTION OF THE TRUSTEES:

Motion was made by Mr. Dickinson, seconded by Mr. Christian and
carried unanimously, to approve the construction permit without
fee.

-9-

DADE COUNTY - Dredge Permit No. 253.123-1100
              (March 14, 1972)

APPLICANT: Palm Bay Towers, Inc.
            c/o G. W. Martin Seawall, Inc.
            201 North Federal Highway, Deerfield Beach, Florida

PROJECT: To dredge approximately 8,700 cubic yards of material
            for deposit on upland. Approximately 500 cubic yards
            will be excavated bayward of the mean high water line.

LOCATION: Section 18, Township 53 South, Range 42 East, Biscayne
            Bay, City of Miami.

MATERIAL: Will be removed from privately-owned uplands and from
            privately-owned submerged lands.

PAYMENT: None, since no sovereignty material is involved.

STAFF
REMARKS: Field Operations has no objection.

ECOLOGICAL
RESPONSES: Department of Natural Resources - No objection.

            Game and Fresh Water Fish Commission - No objection.

            Department of Pollution Control - No objection.

Staff recommends issuance of Dredge Permit No. 253.123-1100,
provided that upland excavation is done prior to excavation of
the 15 foot strip of land in the bay.

ACTION OF THE TRUSTEES:

Motion was made by Mr. Dickinson, seconded by Mr. Conner and
carried unanimously, to approve the dredge permit subject to
the provision recommended by the staff that the upland excavation be done prior to excavation of the 15-foot strip of land
in the bay, to reduce turbidity.

-10-

HILLSBOROUGH COUNTY - Dredge Permit No. 253.123-1106
                      (March 3, 1972)

APPLICANT: Westinghouse Electric Corporation
            Post Office Box 19218, Tampa, Florida

PROJECT: To perform maintenance dredging in an existing access
            channel.

LOCATION: Old Tampa Bay, Section 8, Township 30 South, Range
            18 East, Hillsborough County.

MATERIAL: Approximately 70,000 cubic yards of material to be removed and placed on applicant's upland.

PAYMENT: Not applicable. State-owned sovereignty land not involved.

STAFF
REMARKS: Field Operations reports the spoil will be placed on diked uplands with a series of sediment basins to retain silt.

ECOLOGICAL
RESPONSES: Department of Natural Resources - No objection provided spoil is carefully contained on uplands.

     Game and Fresh Water Fish Commission - No objection.

     Department of Pollution Control - No objection.

OTHERS: Tampa Port Authority has issued Permit TPA 71-22.

Staff recommends issuance of Permit 253.123-1106 provided that turbidity curtains are used to prevent siltation and turbidity increase.

ACTION OF THE TRUSTEES:

Motion was made by Mr. Christian, seconded by Mr. Conner and Mr. Stone and carried unanimously, to approve the dredge permit subject to the provision for use of turbidity curtains to prevent siltation and turbidity increase.

-11-

PALM BEACH COUNTY - Dredge and Fill Permit No. 253.124-250

On April 25, 1972, the Board was advised that the subject permit would not expire until May 27, 1972, and that the application of the City of Lake Worth to extend the permit would be placed on the agenda when comments were received from the local authorities.

Mr. Raphael Steinhardt by telegram received May 22 had requested extension until August 1. The staff recommended a two-weeks' deferment and extension of the permit.

On motion by Mr. Dickinson, seconded by Mr. Stone and adopted without objection, the Board deferred consideration of the application and extended the existing permit for two weeks.

-12-

PASCO COUNTY - Dredge Permit No. 253.123-1091
     (May 1, 1972)

APPLICANT: Florida Power Corporation
     Post Office Box 14042, St. Petersburg, Florida

PROJECT: To dredge intake and discharge canals to provide water cooling for the Anclote site power plant.

LOCATION: Gulf of Mexico and Anclote River, Sections 27 and 34, Township 26 South, Range 15 East, Pasco County.

MATERIAL: 142,053.54 cubic yards of sovereignty material to be removed and placed on upland.

PAYMENT: $142,053.54 has been paid for sovereignty material.

STAFF
REMARKS: Field Operations has no objections except to spoiling below the mean high water line.

ECOLOGICAL
RESPONSES: Department of Natural Resources - Revised dredging
              plan is a significant improvement over the original
              plan and will better conserve marine biological
              resources, but to best conserve marine biological
              resources power plant effluent should be cooled
              before being discharged into Florida's coastal
              waters.

              Game and Fresh Water Fish Commission - Because of
              the loss of approximately 22.5 productive acres
              and the heating of discharge water plus various
              indirect effects, there will be an adverse impact
              on the estuarine ecosystem which cannot be ignored;
              however, it is recognized that applicant is attempting
              to minimize this intrusion and making efforts to gain
              knowledge which may be applied to future pow r plant
              construction.

              Department of Pollution Control - No objection.

OTHERS: Board of County Commissioners, Pasco County -
              Approved.

Staff recommends issuance of Dredge Permit No. 253.123-1091
provided no material is placed seaward of the mean high water
line.

ACTION OF THE TRUSTEES:

Motion was made by Mr. Christian, seconded by Mr. Conner, that
the staff recommendation be approved.

Mr. Hayward Matthews, a' biologist representing S.A.V.E. (Suncoast
Active Volunteers for Ecology), objected that the project was
hastily planned, would damage grass flats and the bay north of
the Anclote River, that draglines and cooling ponds should be
used. While he did not suggest that the project be disapproved,
he suggested that the Board require the five scientists at the
University of South Florida who made the studies to bring to the
cabinet statements that the plan will not damage the grass flats
and that cooling ponds would not protect the environment.

Commissioner of Education Christian was sure that scientific,
biological studies were available on the project, and requested
postponement for two weeks.

Without objection, further consideration of the application was
deferred for two weeks.

-13-

PINELLAS COUNTY - State Construction Permit, Marina License
                  ML-126
                  (April 13, 1972)

APPLICANT: Arlene M. Lawrence, c/o Bailey Weldon
              500 - 139th Avenue, Madeira Beach, Florida

PROJECT: Construct a. docking facility containing 768 square
              feet in Boca Ciega Bay at Madeira Harbor adjacent
              to Section 15, Township 31 South, Range 15 East,
              Pinellas County.

              No dredging is required.

PAYMENT: $100 minimum annual fee for marina license.

ECOLOGICAL
RESPONSES: Department of Natural Resources - No objection.

              Game and Fresh Water Fish Commission - No objection.

5-23-72

Department of Pollution Control - No objection.

OTHERS: Field Operations Division - No objection.

Staff recommends issuance of construction permit and marina
license for annual fee of $100.

ACTION OF THE TRUSTEES:

Motion was made by Mr. Conner, seconded by Mr. Christian and
carried unanimously, authorizing issuance of the construction
permit and marina license for $100 annual fee.

-14-

ST. LUCIE COUNTY - State Construction Permit
                  Marina License ML-143
                  (March 8, 1972)

APPLICANT: The Colonnades, Real Estate Capital Corporation
             1166 Bayshore Drive, Fort Pierce, Florida

PROJECT: Construct a docking facility covering 4,140 square
             feet in Faber Cove adjacent to the Indian River in
             Section 1, Township 35 South, Range 40 East, St.
             Lucie County.

             No dredging or filling is required.

PAYMENT: $100 minimum annual fee for marina license.

ECOLOGICAL
RESPONSES: Department of Natural Resources - No objection.

             Game and Fresh Water Fish Commission - No objection.

             Department of Pollution Control - No objection.

OTHERS: Field Operations Division - No objection.

Staff recommends issuance of construction permit and marina
license for annual fee of $100.

ACTION OF THE TRUSTEES:

Motion was made by Mr. Stone, seconded by Mr. Christian and
Mr. Dickinson, carried unanimously, authorizing issuance of
the construction permit and marina license for $100 annual
fee.

On motion by Mr. Stone, seconded by Mr. Christian and Mr.
O'Malley, and carried unanimously, the rules were waived for
consideration of the three applications on the addendum agenda.

-15-

PINELLAS COUNTY - Dredge Permit No. 253.123-1039
                  (May 15, 1972)

On May 9 action was deferred pending receipt of payment for the
sovereignty material.

APPLICANT: Gale J. Apple
             1187 - 79 Street South
             St. Petersburg, Florida 33707

PROJECT: To dredge for construction of a small boat channel
             50 feet wide by 5 feet deep, 15 feet offshore of the
             southwest side of the north fill area at Palm Point
             for a distance of approximately 683 feet.

LOCATION: Boca Ciega Bay, St. Petersburg Beach, 64 Avenue at

Palm Point.

MATERIAL: Approximately 2,500 cubic yards of sovereignty
material to be removed and placed on applicant's
previously filled upland.

PAYMENT: $2,500 paid for sovereignty material.

ECOLOGICAL
RESPONSES: Department of Natural Resources - Project was
modified to meet recommendations of Department of
Natural Resources.

Game and Fresh Water Fish Commission - Recommends
that these shallow productive areas remain undisturbed.

Department of Pollution Control - No objections.

OTHERS: 1. Pinellas County Water and Navigation Control
Authority - issued modified permit in keeping
with the Department of Natural Resources'
recommendations.

2. Field Operations Division - Dredging will affect
water quality in the area and will set back
revegetation and natural construction of lands
that have been disturbed too many times in the
past.

Staff recommends issuance of Permit No. 253.123-1039 as modified.

ACTION OF THE TRUSTEES:

Mr. Kuperberg advised that the applicant had submitted a
certified check in payment for the material.

Attorney General Shevin commented that there was an adverse
biological report on this work in Boca Ciega Bay, and the
Director assured him that it was for maintenance dredging of a
canal to improve navigability.

On motion by Mr. Christian, seconded by Mr. Dickinson and adopted
without objection, the Trustees authorized issuance of the permit
as modified.

-16-

ORANGE COUNTY - Conveyance of Land for School Purposes

APPLICANT: Orange County School Board
Orlando, Florida

REQUEST: Acquisition of a 30.01-acre parcel of land for
development of a proposed Special Education Center

LOCATION: 30.01 acres described as the south 1326 feet of the
west 986 feet of SE 1/4 of SW 1/4 of Section 14,
Township 22 South, Range 28 East, being a portion of
the 160-acre tract on which is located the Sunland
Hospital in Orlando

This site has been requested by the Orange County School Board
for the purpose of constructing facilities for trainable mentally
retarded, physically handicapped and emotionally disturbed
children under the State Exceptional Child Facilities Projects
Program. Funds to finance the project have been pledged by the
state in the amount of $670,891.

The Department of Health and Rehabilitative Services has reviewed
and approved the use of the site for this project.

This matter was requested by Mr. Christian to be brought before
the Board on this date.

Recommend conveyance of the parcel to the Orange County School
Board for use as a Special Education Center with provision for
reversion of all or any portion of the parcel should the land be
used for other purposes or for non-use for a period of three years.

ACTION OF THE TRUSTEES:

Motion was made by Mr. Dickinson, seconded by Mr. Christian and
carried unanimously, to accept the staff recommendation as the
action of the Board on the land conveyance for school purposes.

-17-

TRUSTEES' FUNDS - Litigation Costs

On motion by Mr. Stone, seconded by Mr. Shevin and carried
unanimously, the Trustees authorized expenditure of up to
$10,000 for expert witness fees and related costs in the
United States Supreme Court case U. S. vs. Florida 52 Original
concerning settlement of Florida's outer boundaries. The funds
will be used to engage the services of Dr. Proctor of the
University of Florida and Dr. Tebeau of the University of Miami
and for related expenses.

-7-

DUVAL COUNTY - Dredge and Fill Permits 253.123-1153 & 253.124
            (April 21, 1972)

APPLICANT: Jacksonville Port Authority
             Post Office Box 3005, Jacksonville, Florida

PROJECT: To dredge for fill by widening and deepening
             the existing channel in St. Johns River along the
             the northeasterly, easterly and southerly sides of
             Blount Island and to fill to the existing bulkhead
             line as established along the northeasterly, easterly
             and southerly sides of Blount Island. All material
             unsuitable for fill material will be placed behind
             dikes at remote spoil areas.

LOCATION: St. Johns River in Sections 19, 20, 29 and 30,
             Township 1 South, Range 28 East, Duval County.

MATERIAL: 8.02 million cubic yards of material are to be
             removed; 6.76 million cubic yards of material are to
             be placed on Blount Island. 1.26 million cubic yards
             of silt are to be placed on diked upland spoil areas.

PAYMENT: Jacksonville Port Authority requests "waiver of payment
             for the material to be removed since the authority is
             a public agency and the development is being undertaken
             in the public interest." The Trustees yardage rate for
             fill material in this area is $1 per cubic yard.

ECOLOGICAL
RESPONSES: Department of Natural Resources - "This proposed
             project will result in the irreversible and irretrie-
             vable commitment of a large area of productive marine
             habitat and will have massive adverse effects on the
             marine biological resources of northeast Florida. An
             alternate site should be found for this industrial plant
             and Back River should be conserved so that it can
             continue to function as an important part of the
             St. John's estuary."

             Game and Fresh Water Fish Commission - "... in concert
             with representatives of the Department of Natural
             Resources and the United States Bureau of Sport
             Fisheries has made a full investigation and biological
             assessment of the area for dredge and fill operations

5-23-72

678

by Jacksonville Port Authority. In concurring with this
report, we offer our additional observation. We believe
that the construction of offshore power plants has the
likelihood of posing less damage to the environment
than power plants situated on fresh or brackish water
sites. If the ultimate decision is to sacrifice the
environmental values associated with Blount Island
because of such potential compensating factor then
some definite commitment should be made that the site
would be irrevocably used for production of
offshore power plants before any dredge and fill
permit is granted."

Department of Pollution Control - Comments will be
forwarded after the Department of Pollution Control
Board acts on this application at its meeting on
May 22, 1972.

OTHERS: 1. A hydrographic survey prepared for Jacksonville
Port Authority by Dr. B. A. Christenson of the
University of Florida indicates that, "Back River
will cease to exist and function physically as a
river due to siltation ten to fifteen years from
today."

2. Trustees legal staff: Believes that there may be some
title problems if the Jacksonville Port Authority conveys
to Westinghouse-Tenneco any portion of the 128 acres of
land previously conveyed by the Board of Trustees in
1967. Aside from the title problems, difficulty
might arise if this project is abandoned during
construction or in later years.

In accordance with the Board's policy of having all comments in hand,
staff is unable to present its recommendation until all environmental statements have been received and evaluated.

The Executive Director had received the unofficial record of
the action of the Pollution Control Board approving water
quality effects of the proposed factory site on Blount Island,
and by memorandum to the Board dated May 23, 1972, he pointed
out three basic issues in need of resolution:

(1) Clearing title to the submerged land areas adjacent
to Blount Island and to a 600-foot strip of land
within the easement of the Fulton-Dame Point right
of way.

(2) Establishing the value of the state's interest in
the lands and fill material required by the project and
securing payment for same. This should include a
consideration of lost productivity of Back River.

(3) Securing a guarantee to the state that its interest
in the 1,000 acres, more or less, which is declared
surplus by the Jacksonville Port Authority, will not
be converted to another use, subverting the intent of
the proposal presently before the Trustees (ala Aerojet
General's intended conversion of land to uses other than
a rocket engine factory site).

In the memorandum the staff recommended that one of the following
options be selected:

(1) The item be deferred for thirty days to permit the
further investigation of the above questions.

(2) Any action prior to such time be conditioned upon
the satisfactory resolution, by the State, Jacksonville
Port Authority and Westinghouse-Tenneco, of the above
three matters;

(3) The Trustees, Jacksonville Port Authority and Westinghouse-
Tenneco jointly appoint a blue-ribbon commission to

review the bio-socio-economic impact of this project
and make a recommendation to the Trustees.

ACTION OF THE TRUSTEES:

Attorney General Shevin proposed a resolution as an amendment
to the staff recommendations, many of which he said were
included in his resolution. Certain revisions were made shortly
before the meeting. After discussion of some of the language,
the resolution was referred to members of the staffs of the
Governor, the Attorney General and other Trustees, along
with representatives of the Port Authority and the city to try
to work out further revisions that would furnish the desired
guarantees and assurances.

A large delegation of officials, representatives of groups,
and citizens in favor of the application made statements,
including the following:

    Mr. Ed Austin, General Counsel of the City of Jacksonville,
    Mr. William B. Mills, Chairman, and Mr. Bob Pease,
      Managing Director, of Jacksonville Port Authority
    Mr. William Staten of Westinghouse-Tenneco
    Mr. Pat Conroy, General Counsel of Title and Trust
      Company of Florida
    Mr. John Buchanan, President, and Mr. Wallace Parker,
      Research Director, of Jacksonville Area Chamber of
      Commerce
    Mr. Cecil Hardesty, Superintendent of Duval County Schools
    Mr. Wesley Paxon, Chairman of Jacksonville Transportation
      Authority
    Mr. Clarence L. Brown, Jacksonville Urban League
    Mr. Arnett Girardeau, President of Black Committee Coalition
    Mr. Jim Deaton, President of AFL-CIO Council of Jacksonville
    Mr. John W. Bowden, President of Northeast Florida Building
      Construction Trade Council
    Mr. DeWitt Dawkins, Chairman of the Committee of 100 of
      Jacksonville Area Chamber of Commerce
    Mr. Earl Johnson
    Mr. Harvey Vickers and Mr. Allen Harrell, Organized Fishermen
      of Florida, St. Johns River Chapter
    Mr. Harold A. Martin, retired vice president for development
      of the Barnett Banks of Florida
    Mr. Landon Williams, President of Longshoremen's Union
      of Port of Jacksonville
    Mr. Alton W. Yates, Executive Director of Greater Jacksonville
      Economic Opportunity, Inc.
    Mr. Lynwood Roberts, President of City Council
    Mr. A. C. Thomas, President of Jacksonville Jaycees
    Mayor Hans Tanzler of Jacksonville

During the discussion, Mr. Staten on behalf of Westinghouse-
Tenneco agreed to the reverter provision, and Mr. Conway affirmed
that the title was insured and in his opinion was not questionable.

Mr. Austin concluded the applicant's presentation by submitting
a certificate from the Jacksonville Port Authority certifying
that all fill material used for filling submerged land pursuant
to the construction permit would be placed on public land; and
if any submerged land owned by the Port Authority, upon which
fill material acquired from sovereignty lands was placed
pursuant to said permit, is disposed of to private interests,
that the private interests shall take said land subject to a
lien in favor of the Board of Trustees in an amount equal to
one dollar per cubic yard for each cubic yard of fill material
so deposited. Mr. Austin requested waiver as to the productivity
value of the Back River area.

Governor Askew commented that the intent of the offer was that
the application be conditioned upon reimbursement of a dollar
per cubic yard to the state for any fill taken from any areas
to which the state holds title, which could be a substantial
amount to the trust fund.

Mr. Charles Lee opposed the application on behalf of the Florida
Audubon Society, expressing special concern regarding
any dredging to deepen the channel that leads to the
Jacksonville Harbor, and the larger environmental problem of
thermal pollution. He suggested that there should be public
policy regarding energy generation and recommended a delay
of thirty days for solving the biological and legal questions,
noting that the power companies in Florida did not appear to
consider the proposed plants entirely feasible.

Dr. Robert B. Ragland of Jacksonville charged that there had
been a massive propaganda push of the project and insufficient
concern for the effects of so much growth.

Mr. Jack Rudloe, president of Gulf Specimen Company, spoke of
the worth of the biological resources in the tidal marshes in
Back River, exhibited living aquatic specimens collected in
Back River and asked the Board to consider the highest and best
possible use of this land as its natural state.

Members of the Board asked a number of questions during the
lengthy presentations of the proponents and the opponents.

Mr. Kuperberg reported on the 22 letters filed from various
organizations and persons, 17 for and 4 against the project.

Governor said a strong case for the project had been presented,
pointing out that any money paid for fill material would be placed
in the trust fund for purchase of environmental lands.

Mr. Shevin expressed the apparent consensus of the Board that
the decision was a hard one to make, that the ecological loss
was not being disregarded and the Board has asked for assurances
that the economic benefits would come to the city and county.

Attorney General Shevin offered as a motion the resolution that
had been revised during the meeting, containing guarantees and
assurances that the Board required without impairing the
ability of Westinghouse-Tenneco to move forward. He explained
that in his opinion it obviated the necessity of the options
recommended by the staff and he did not think the Board should
get into the title questions as a condition of granting the permit.

Mr. O'Malley seconded the motion to grant the permit contingent
upon conditions in the resolution, with the statement that he
had some disagreement with some language in the whereas clauses
but that was not pertinent to the actual motion to grant the
permit subject to certain conditions. The Governor added that
the motion did not encompass the whereas clauses that were
expressions of intent and did not represent necessarily findings
of the Trustees.

Mr. O'Malley offered an amendment, accepted without objection,
that the commitment to pay for fill material be included in
the motion.

On the amended motion, carried unanimously, the Trustees adopted
the following resolution, the resolving clauses constituting the
actual motion approving issuance of the dredge and fill permits
to the Jacksonville Port Authority:

RESOLUTION

TRUSTEES OF THE INTERNAL IMPROVEMENT TRUST FUND

BE IT RESOLVED BY THE TRUSTEES OF THE INTERNAL IMPROVEMENT
TRUST FUND:

That its decision to grant the fill permit necessary for
the Westinghouse-Tenneco joint venture requested by the
Jacksonville Port Authority is contingent upon:

(1) A written agreement by the Westinghouse-Tenneco

joint venture to accept Jacksonville's offer of the Blount
Island site and to stipulate in writing that said site shall
be used for construction of a manufacturing plant to produce
the contemplated offshore power plants.

(2)   Written assurances by the Jacksonville Port Authority
that any lands conveyed by the Port Authority to Westinghouse-
Tenneco shall be upon the conditions that said lands revert
back to the Jacksonville Port Authority if the lands are not
in fact used by Westinghouse-Tenneco to construct a manufacturing
plant to produce platform mounted nuclear power plants.

(3)   That should it be determined by the Trustees of the
Internal Improvement Trust Fund that the State has any right,
title or interest in any of the lands subject to the dredge
and fill permit, the State shall receive reasonable compensation
for the legal interest it holds and any conveyance of said
interest by the State shall be upon the condition that any
and all lands revert back to the State if the land is not in
fact used by Westinghouse-Tenneco to construct platform
mounted nuclear power plants.

(4)   In consideration of the approval by the Board of
Trustees of the Internal Improvement Trust Fund of the State
of Florida of the application by the Jacksonville Port Authority,
a body politic and corporate created by Chapter 63-1447, Laws
of Florida, as amended, for a construction permit to dredge
and fill in the vicinity of and on Blount Island, located in
the St. Johns River in Duval County, Florida, which permit
was authorized by Resolution 72-395-105 of the Council of the
City of Jacksonville on May 4, 1972, subject to approval by
the Board of Trustees of the Internal Improvement Trust Fund,
the Jacksonville Port Authority hereby certifies that all fill
material which will be used for the purpose of filling submerged land pursuant to the construction permit will be placed
on public land. The Jacksonville Port Authority hereby gives
notice that if any submerged land, owned by the Jacksonville
Port Authority upon which fill material acquired from
sovereignty lands has been placed pursuant to the foregoing
construction permit, is disposed of to private interests,
that said private interest shall take said land subject to a
lien in favor of the Board of Trustees of the Internal
Improvement Trust Fund of the State of Florida in an amount
equal to One Dollar ($1.00) per cubic yard for each cubic
yard of fill material so deposited.

(5)   That the Director of the Trustees of the Internal
Improvement Trust Fund is hereby directed to allow no dredging
of filling of the area subject to the Port Authority's
application pursuant to the permit prior to the above conditions having been fulfilled and appearing in the records of
his office.

On motion duly adopted, the meeting was adjourned.

GOVERNOR   CHAIRMAN

ATTEST:
            EXECUTIVE DIRECTOR

5-23-72

Tallahassee, Florida
June 6, 1972

The Board of Trustees of the Internal Improvement Trust Fund
met on this date in the auditorium of the Burns Building with
the following members present:

-1-

The minutes of the meeting of May 16, 1972, were approved as
submitted.
-2-

DADE COUNTY - Road Right of Way Easement
              (December 28, 1971)

APPLICANT: Department of Transportation
            by J. E. Greiner Company, Inc., Tampa, Florida

REQUEST: Easements for construction of the Homestead
            Extension of Florida Turnpike, State Road 821.

LOCATION: East 415 feet, more or less, of Tracts 1, 2, 4,
            6, 8, 49, 50 and 51, Florida Fruit Lands Subdivision,
            Plat Book 2, Page 17, in Section 1, Township 53
            South, Range 39 East, Dade County Public Records,
            and a part of Tract 55 of Florida Fruit Lands
            Company's Subdivision No. 1 of Section 5,
            Township 52 South, Range 40 East, Plat Book 2,
            Page 17, Dade County Public Records, containing
            a total of 35.225 acres, more or less, in Dade County.

PAYMENT: $133,400 offered. Reviewed and approved by staff
            appraiser.

These parcels requested for road right of way purposes are part
of ten-acre scattered tracts owned by the Trustees as state
public land which is uncommitted for use at this time. The
tracts are located approximately thirteen miles northwest of downtown Miami in an unincorporated area where ground elevation
is marginal. The land is subject to flooding and principally
used for limerock mining. Use of the remainder of each of the
five parcels will be unimpaired.

Recommend issuance of easement to Department of Transportation
for road purposes only.

ACTION OF THE TRUSTEES:

On motion by Mr. Christian, seconded by Mr. Stone and adopted
without objection, the Trustees granted the request of the
Department of Transportation for an easement for road purposes
only.

3

ALACHUA COUNTY - Public Sale of Murphy Act Land
            (May 10, 1972)

Description: Lots 6, 7 and 10, South of State Road 20
                Extension, Original Hawthorne, in Section 26,
                Township 10 South, Range 22 East, Plat Book A,
                Page 78, Public Records of Alachua County

LOCATION: The land, within the incorporated limits of the
                Town of Hawthorne, is triangular in shape with
                130 feet of frontage on Virginia Street, 134
                front feet on State Road 20 exit, and is
                approximately 450 feet west of the Seaboard
                Coast Line Railroad and U. S. 301.

APPRAISAL: By staff appraiser, $900.

AUTHORITY
FOR SALE: Section 197.350, Florida Statutes.

DATE OF
SALE: May 8, 1972, by Clerk of Circuit Court of Alachua
                County.

HIGH
BIDDER: T. M. Powell and wife, Neva W. Powell
                Hawthorne, Florida

HIGH BID: $900

Recommend confirmation of sale of the lots to T. M. Powell and
wife, Neva W. Powell, for $900 plus costs of advertising and
clerk's fee.

ACTION OF THE TRUSTEES:

Motion was made by Mr. Stone, seconded by Mr. Christian and
carried without objection, to confirm the sale as recommended
by the staff, under the provisions of the Murphy Act.

4

COLUMBIA COUNTY - Murphy Act Land Sale (Hardship Act)
                (May 9, 1972)

    Clarence E. Brown
    Executor of the Estate of Perdita H. Graham, Deceased
    Lake City, Florida

makes application under Section 197.355, Florida Statutes
Chapter 28317, Acts of 1953 (Hardship Act) to purchase E 1/2
of Lot 6, Ways Subdivision, Block 304, Southern Division of
Lake City, Florida, in Columbia County.

The interest of the state in this parcel was acquired under the
Murphy Act, Chapter 18296, Acts of 1937, by tax sale certificate
No. 752 of August 5, 1929. This certificate in the amount of
$3.22 apparently was overlooked by the Clerk when the former
owner, George R. Graham attempted to redeem other outstanding
tax sale certificates. This certificate did not qualify for
cancellation under the Futch Act.

Section 197.355, Florida Statutes, provides that the Board may
convey the interest of the State to the owner in 1939 or those
claiming by, through or under that owner, for such consideration
as the Board shall deem equitable and proper without advertisement
and public sale.

There has been deposited with the Clerk of the Circuit Court of
Columbia County an amount equal to the sum of all state, county
taxes and assessments due to the date of the application.

684

The applicant offers $470, the appraised value, for this parcel of land.

Recommend conveying the interest of the State of Florida in this parcel of land to Clarence E. Brown, Executor of the Estate of Perdita H. Graham, Deceased, for $470.

ACTION OF THE TRUSTEES:

Motion was made by Mr. Stone, seconded by Mr. Christian and carried without objection, to approve the sale as recommended by the staff.

-5-

INDIAN RIVER COUNTY - Murphy Act Conveyance
(April 27, 1972)

APPLICANT: Indian River Farms Drainage District,
             represented by Charles E. Smith, Attorney
                for the District
             Vero Beach, Florida

REQUEST: Purchase of 0.74 acre under
             Section 197.350(1)(c), Florida Statutes

DESCRIPTION: East 0.74 acre of the West 30.74 acres of
             Tract 1, Indian River Farms Company Subdivision,
             Plat Book 2, Page 25, St. Lucie County
             Public Records, lying in Section 22, Township
             33 South, Range 39 East, Indian River County.

OFFER: $444 for the parcel - Staff appraised value

Tract 1 contains 40.74 acres of which the west 30.74 acres was certified to the State under the Murphy Act in Certificate No. 2214 dated August 5, 1929, and Certificate No. 6944 dated September 4, 1933, but was described in the certificates as the west 30 acres. The east 10 acres of the west 30 acres were deeded to the Indian River Farms Drainage District by Deed No. 746, and the west 20 acres of the west 30 acres were deeded to the Indian River Farms Drainage District by Deed No. 886. There remained vested in the State 0.74 acre which went unnoticed until recently. The 0.74 acre is a strip of 24.42 feet wide and 1,320 feet long, contiguous to several private ownerships.

The District has requested the parcel be deeded to it for conveyance to the various owners of property adjoining the 0.74 acre strip, thereby clearing title at the least expense and preventing third parties who are not adjoining owners from acquiring the strip of land and holding it as a nuisance.

Recommend issuance of deed to the Indian River Farms Drainage District under Section 197.350 without advertisement and public sale for the appraised price of $444.

ACTION OF THE TRUSTEES:

Motion was made by Mr. Stone, seconded by Mr. Christian and carried without objection, to approve issuance of the deed as recommended by the staff.

-6-

SUMTER COUNTY - Public Sale of Murphy Act Land
(May 8, 1972)

Description: Lot 5, Block 5, Bushnell Park Plat 22, in
             Section 17, Township 21 South, Range 22 East,
             Sumter County.

LOCATION: The unzoned land is a 50' x 125' platted lot
             fronting a paved street outside of any municipality.

6-6-72

APPRAISAL: By staff appraiser, $250.

AUTHORITY
FOR SALE: Section 197.350, Florida Statutes.

DATE OF
SALE: May 4, 1972, by Clerk of Circuit Court of Sumter
County.

HIGH BIDDER: Joe D. Merritt of Bushnell, Florida

HIGH BID: $250

Recommend confirmation of sale of the lot to Joe D. Merritt
for $250 plus costs of advertising and clerk's fee.

ACTION OF THE TRUSTEES:

Motion was made by Mr. Stone, seconded by Mr. Christian and
carried without objection, to confirm sale of the land as
recommended by the staff, under provisions of the Murphy Act.

-7-

BROWARD COUNTY - Miccosukee Tribe Farm Lease

The Miccosukee Tribe of Indians of Florida requests the Board
in its capacity as Trustee of all Seminole Indian lands to
approve a 15-year farming lease between the tribe and C&G
Farms, Inc., and Goodno Farms, Inc., authorized by the tribal
council by Resolution No. MB-3-71 dated April 15, 1971, covering
24 sections of land in Townships 49 and 50 south, Range 35 East,
Broward County, outside of Conservation Area No. 3.

The annual rental will be 50¢ per acre for unimproved land and
$1 per acre for improved land after the first six years of the
lease. Rental was reviewed by staff appraiser who considers the
rent not unreasonable.

On February 22, 1972, when this matter was considered by the
Board, the staff was requested to review the lease proposal
with the Central and Southern Florida Flood Control District.
The District has advised that the lease is acceptable providing
Provision Six is expanded to include reference to the fact that
the lease is subject to any easement in favor of the District.
The lease has been modified as requested by the District and
approved by the Miccosukee Tribe.

Recommend approval of the lease as amended and modified.

ACTION OF THE TRUSTEES:

Motion was made by Mr. Christian, seconded by Mr. Stone and
carried unanimously, to approve the lease as amended and
modified.

-8-

PALM BEACH COUNTY - Application for Disclaimer
                     File No. 2459-50-253.129
                     (May 5, 1972)

Staff description: A parcel of filled sovereignty land in
Lake Worth abutting Government Lot 2, Section 35, Township 44
South, Range 43 East, 3.22 acres.

A.   CITY AND COUNTY: South Palm Beach, Palm Beach County

B.   APPLICANT: Mark M. Kane

C.   APPLICANT'S
     REPRESENTATIVE: J. A. Plisco
                        Post Office Box 947, West Palm Beach

D. ACREAGE: 3.22 acres

E. APPRAISAL: Not applicable

F. BIOLOGICAL REMARKS: Not applicable

G. STAFF REMARKS: The applicant has made application pursuant
    to Section 253.129, Florida Statutes, which provides that
    "The title to all land heretofore filled or developed is
    herewith confirmed in the upland owners and the Trustees shall
    on request issue a disclaimer to each such owner."

    Three affidavits have been submitted that show the parcel to
    have been filled prior to June 1, 1957.

    $100 processing fee has been submitted.

Staff requests authority to issue the disclaimer.

ACTION OF THE TRUSTEES:

Motion was made by Mr. Dickinson, seconded by Mr. Stone and
carried unanimously, authorizing issuance of the disclaimer
pursuant to the provisions of Section 253.129, Florida Statutes.

-9-

MARTIN COUNTY - Request for Refund, File No. 207.7-43-253.12
                (May 15, 1972)

APPLICANTS: Warren S. Tucker, Sr., and Warren S. Tucker, Jr.

APPLICANTS'
REPRESENTATIVE: James F. Littman
                 Post Office Box 1154, Stuart, Florida 33494

DESCRIPTION: Two parcels of sovereignty land in the Indian
                 River embracing 1.85 acres abutting Section 5,
                 Township 38 South, Range 42 East, Martin County.

STAFF REMARKS: On May 14, 1968, the Trustees confirmed the sale
of the two parcels for the sum of $559.59. On May 21, 1968, and
June 14, 1968, the Board directed that the deed not be issued and
referred the matter to the Interagency Advisory Committee. This
committee in Report No. 4 recommended that the bulkhead line in
this area be set at the mean high water line.

Applicants' representative requests that the money paid for this
land be refunded.

Staff recommends that the action of the Trustees on May 14, 1968,
be rescinded and requests authority to refund to J. F. Littman the
purchase price of $559.59.

ACTION OF THE TRUSTEES:

On motion by Mr. Christian, seconded by Mr. Conner and adopted
unanimously, the Trustees rescinded the action on May 14, 1968,
and authorized the refund as recommended by the staff.

-10-

BAY COUNTY - Bulkhead Line, Section 253.122, Florida Statutes
             (March 27, 1972)

APPLICANT: Board of County Commissioners of Bay County

PROJECT: Bulkhead lines totaling 4,416.35 feet in Grand Lagoon
            along the mean high water line in Sections 9, 15 and
            16, in Township 4 South, Range 15 West, Bay County,

approved and adopted by the Board of County Commissioners of Bay County by Resolution No. 592 adopted March 7, 1972.

STAFF
REMARKS: No objection.

ECOLOGICAL
RESPONSES: Department of Natural Resources indicates that the revised proposed bulkhead lines should not have any significant adverse effects.

Game and Fresh Water Fish Commission has no objection.

Department of Pollution Control has no objection.

Staff recommends approval of the proposed bulkhead lines.

ACTION OF THE TRUSTEES:

Motion was made by Mr. Stone, seconded by Mr. O'Malley and carried unanimously, approving the bulkhead lines as located by the Board of County Commissioners of Bay County by Resolution No. 592 adopted on March 7, 1972.

-11-

DADE COUNTY - Dredge Permit No. 253.123-1007
           (December 13, 1971)

APPLICANT: Henry Burks, Maule Industries, Inc.
             100 Biscayne Boulevard, North Miami, Florida

PROJECT: To construct a quarry overflow ditch which leads
             into the Miami Canal.

LOCATION: South of Miami Canal and U. S. 27, three miles west
             of Ralmetto Expressway in Dade County.

MATERIAL: Will be placed on upland.

PAYMENT: None required - No sovereignty material used.

STAFF
REMARKS: No objection.

ECOLOGICAL
RESPONSES: Department of Natural Resources - No objection.

             Game and Fresh Water Fish Commission - No objection.

             Department of Pollution Control - No objection.

OTHERS: Central and Southern Florida Flood Control District -
             No objection.

Staff recommends issuance of Dredge Permit No. 253.123-1007.

ACTION OF THE TRUSTEES:

Motion was made by Mr. Dickinson, seconded by Mr. Christian and carried unanimously, approving issuance of the dredge permit.

688

-12-

DUVAL COUNTY - Dredge Permit No. 253.123-869
    (April 26, 1972)

APPLICANT: Department of Transportation

PROJECT: To restore navigability to Deep Bottom Branch by
           removing 12,000 cubic yards of material deposited
           in the channel by runoff during construction of
           Interstate 295. The restored channel will extend
           from Lynwood Terrace to the St. Johns River and will
           have a bottom cut varying from 18 to 26 feet and
           depth varying from 5 to 6 feet.

LOCATION: Section 38, Township 4 South, Range 27 East, and
           Section 11, Township 4 South, Range 26 East, Duval
           County.

MATERIAL: Will be deposited and retained on uplands designated by
           applicant.

PAYMENT: Request payment be waived since restoration of naviga-
           bility of Deep Bottom Creek is in the public interest.

STAFF
REMARKS: Field Operations has no objection provided the project
           is limited to maintenance dredging only and spoil
           is placed above the mean high water line.

BIOLOGICAL
RESPONSES: Department of Natural Resources - No objection.

           Game and Fresh Water Fish Commission - No objection
           provided channel depth is limited to -5 feet mean
           low water, and width is limited to 40 feet. All
           material must be placed on upland and diked, to
           prevent return to the creek.

           Department of Pollution Control - No objection.

Staff recommends issuance of Permit No. 253.123-869.

ACTION OF THE TRUSTEES:

Mr. Kuperberg advised that questions had been raised at the
meeting of the Trustees' aides regarding placement of the fill
material and waiver of payment.

Mr. John Harris from the Department of Transportation explained
that the material hampered navigation and should be removed, that
when government land was available that would benefit from spoil
material it was pumped there but in this instance none was
available and to move the material by truck was not feasible.
He said the material would go on private land, that maps had
been supplied to the Trustees, but he could not identify the
ownership of the private land and suggested deferral.

The Governor said the only question was whether the fill material
was silt or usable material that would accrue to the benefit of
the receiver, that the Board needed to know if there was a choice
of sites for deposit of the spoil, if a person wanted the material
for fill to benefit his land, or if it was just a matter of
getting rid of the spoil.

Mr. O'Malley asked the Director to find out just what substance
the material was, but indicated no objection to the project.

Motion was made by Mr. O'Malley, seconded by Mr. Christian and
carried without objection, that the dredge permit be approved
but that a decision on waiver of charge for the spoil material
be deferred for further information.

-13-

MARTIN COUNTY - Dredge Permit No. 253.123-840
                (September 7, 1971)

APPLICANT: Mr. Herman Reitz, President
             Stuart Marina Center, Inc.
             500 West Monterey Road
             Stuart, Florida

PROJECT: To remove approximately 200 cubic yards of material
             from sovereignty land parallel to the upland boat
             basin to provide a connection with the south fork
             of the St. Lucie River.

LOCATION: South Fork of St. Lucie River, North 600 feet of
             Government Lot 1, being in Section 17, Township 36
             South, Range 41 East, Martin County.

MATERIAL: To be trucked to upland spoil areas.

PAYMENT: Check for $100 has been tendered to cover the
             removal of 200 cubic yards of sovereignty material.

ECOLOGICAL
RESPONSES: Department of Natural Resources - Has no objection
             to the proposed project.

             Game and Fresh Water Fish Commission - The applicant
             proceeded with the operation prior to our investi-
             gation and therefore we were unable to make a
             biological assessment of the resources involved, or
             offer any modification to preserve or enhance these
             resources.

             Department of Pollution Control - Has no objection
             to the proposed project.

OTHERS: Board of County Commissioners - No objection.

             Field Operations Division reports that applicant
             excavated an upland boat basin leaving a strip of
             land 7 feet in width between the basin and the open
             water. A washout occurred due to bad weather.

Staff recommends issuance of Dredge Permit 253.123-840 to Stuart
Marina Center, Inc.

ACTION OF THE TRUSTEES:

Motion was made by Mr. O'Malley, seconded by Mr. Christian and
carried unanimously, approving issuance of the dredge permit.

-14-

PUTNAM COUNTY - Dredge Permit No. 253.123-1117
                (April 28, 1972)

APPLICANT: Hudson Pulp and Paper Corporation
             Post Office Box 919
             Palatka, Florida 32077

PROJECT: To perform maintenance dredging in an existing canal
             and turning basin to improve navigation.

LOCATION: Rice Creek - Etonia Creek, Section 27, Township 9
             South, Range 26 East, Putnam County.

MATERIAL: No sovereignty material involved.

PAYMENT: Not applicable.

STAFF
REMARKS: No objection.

ECOLOGICAL
RESPONSES: Department of Natural Resources - No objection.

Game and Fresh Water Fish Commission - No objection.

Department of Pollution Control - No objection.

OTHERS: Board of County Commissioners - approved as a project
in the public interest.

Staff recommends issuance of Permit 253.123-1117.

ACTION OF THE TRUSTEES:

Motion was made by Mr. Christian, seconded by Mr. Conner and
carried unanimously, approving issuance of the dredge permit.

On motion by Mr. O'Malley, seconded by Mr. Christian and
carried unanimously, the rules were waived for consideration of
the following applications on the addendum agenda.

-15-

LEE COUNTY - Application for Land Exchange, File 2413-36-253.12,
9.39 acres to applicant, 59.04 acres to Trustees
(February 29, 1972)

On May 16 consideration was deferred at the request
of the State Treasurer.

Staff Description: Sovereignty land in Sections 10 and 11,
Township 47 South, Range 24 East.

A.   CITY AND COUNTY: Lee County.

B.   APPLICANT: Lover's Key, Inc.
Naples, Florida

C.   APPLICANT'S
REPRESENTATIVE: Suboceanic Consultants, Inc.,
Post Office Box 1516, Naples, Florida

ESCROW HOLDER: Allen, Knudsen, Swartz, DeBoest,
Rhoads and Edwards
Post Office Box 1480, Ft. Myers, Florida

D.   ACREAGE: 9.39 acres Trustees' submerged land
59.04 acres privately-owned submerged land

E.   APPRAISAL: The appraisal submitted has been reviewed
and reports the value of the parcels as
follows:

59.04 acre parcel owned by
Lover's Key, Inc. $1,250,000

9.39 acre parcel owned by
the state   500,000

Credit to Lover's Key, Inc. $ 750,000

Note: Applicant wishes to apply $430,000 as credit
towards purchase of sovereignty material at $1 per
yard. The balance of the credit would inure to the
state.

F.   PURPOSE: Development according to plan.

G.   STAFF REMARKS: In 1963 the State Road Department, in order
to obtain the necessary right of way for the Bonita Beach
Causeway, entered into agreements with the land owners whereby
certain submerged lands would be conveyed to them in exchange
for right of way and cash.

Applicant wants to exchange 59.04 acres of submerged land
previously acquired from the Board of Trustees for 9.39 acres
of submerged land lying between the mean high water line and
the proposed relocated bulkhead line. The proposed comprehensive
development plan for the property consists of:

    a.   Development of a public beach area 50 feet wide by
         2,400 feet long. Easements no less than 90 feet for
         public access to the beach shall be provided at least
         every one-half mile along the beach from the southern
         boundary line of the property extending to the main
         access road leading into the property from Black Island.
         The location of the easements will be subject to the
         approval of the Bureau of Beaches and Shores.

    b.   Construction of navigation and circulation channels
         to and from the property to Big Carlos Pass.

    c.   Construction of an interior boat basin at the northerly end
         of applicant's submerged land and to excavate an area at
         the southerly end of applicant's submerged land to improve
         water circulation through the area.

    d.   If there is dredge material available that is not suitable
         for beach stabilization, applicant wished to purchase
         up to 1,000,000 cubic yards of material at the standard
         yardage rate of $1 per cubic yard. Applicant will apply
         only $430,000 of the difference in land value as payment
         for the material not suitable for beach stabilization.

    e.   Three easements for bridge access

    f.   Relocation of the bulkhead line to encompass the land
         to be filled. The bulkhead line will also serve as the
         boundary line between private and public lands.

H.   ECOLOGICAL
     RESPONCES: Department of Natural Resources - No objection.

                 Bureau of Beaches and Shores will agenda request
                 for coastal construction permit upon execution
                 of proposed exchange agreement.

                 Game and Fresh Water Fish Commission recommends
                 against this project as presented because of the
                 resulting destruction of biological resources.

                 Department of Pollution Control - No objection.

                 Field Operations Division offers no objection to
                 this item being placed before the Board of Trustees
                 for consideration.

     OTHERS: 1. Lee County has issued a dredge and fill permit
                 for this project subject to the exchange of land
                 being accomplished.

                 2. Trustees' Executive Director wished the record
                 to indicate that he served as a private conserva-
                 tion consultant on this project prior to being
                 employed by the State of Florida.

Staff recommends advertising the proposed exchange of lands for
objections only.

ACTION OF THE TRUSTEES:

Because of his prior work with the project planning, the Director disqualified himself and asked Mr. John DuBose, member of the Trustees' staff, to explain the application. Mr. DuBose reviewed the June 6 report from the Department of Natural Resources biologist, Mr. Bob Routa, that emphasized rapidly changing conditions favoring marine growth in the area.

The Attorney General made a motion to advertise for objections only, making it clear that it did not indicate any approval of the application itself.

Mr. Conner raised a question regarding approval of fill permit applications for the private property. Mr. O'Malley suggested that if objections were received to the advertised proposal, there might be a local public hearing.

Mr. Shevin withdrew his motion and seconded a motion by Mr. O'Malley that the land exchange application be advertised and in the event objections are received that the staff be instructed to hold a public hearing in the area. The motion carried unanimously, the Governor commenting that this was no commitment for approval of the application.

-16-

PALM BEACH COUNTY - Application to Advertise
            File No. 2434-50-253.36
            (March 3, 1972)

On May 23, consideration of this application was deferred at the request of the State Comptroller.

Staff description: A parcel of reclaimed Lake Okeechobee bottom land in Section 33, Township 41 South, Range 37 East, 0.077 acre.

A. CITY AND COUNTY: Canal Point, Palm Beach County.

B. APPLICANT: M. L. Lairsey, et ux.

C. APPLICANT'S
   REPRESENTATIVE: Ralph O. Johnson, P. A.
                    147 Bacom Point Road, Pahokee, Florida

D. ACREAGE: 0.077 acre.

E. APPRAISAL: To be requested.

F. PURPOSE: Private residence.

G. BIOLOGICAL
   REMARKS: Not applicable.

H. STAFF
   REMARKS: The parcel is landward of Lake Okeechobee
                    Hoover Levee and the Florida East Coast
                    Railroad.

I. OTHER: The applicant believes that such sale would be in
   the public interest as required by Article X, Section 11
   of the Constitution of the State of Florida for the following
   reasons:

   (1) The lands have been filled lands for many years.

   (2) Public access to the lands is blocked because of
       private ownership on all sides of the parcel sought
       to be purchased, except to the westerly side, which is
       bordered by the Florida East Coast Railroad right of
       way.

(3) None of the lands in fact front upon any presently existing navigable waters.

(4) The property has no practical or suitable use for recreational or public purposes because of its size and location.

Accordingly, applicant would appreciate your giving this matter special consideration because of the hardship to the land owner in making any improvements, or plans for further use of his property, and in view of the fact that such would not seem to be prejudicial to the public interest.

The building has existed for many years and until a recent survey, the owners did not know of the encroachment. The original owners are now deceased and the applicants are purchasers from the estate of the decedents. They desire to repair and improve the property.

J.   <u>Staff requests authority to advertise for objections only.</u>

-17-

PASCO COUNTY - Dredge Permit No. 253.123-1091

On May 23 the Trustees, after hearing objections from Mr. Hayward Matthews, a biologist, deferred action on the application of Florida Power Corporation to dredge intake and discharge canals for the Anclote site power plant in the Gulf of Mexico and the Anclote River in Sections 27 and 34, Township 26 South, Range 15 East, Pasco County.

Mr. Kuperberg said that objectors were present, about 42 letters of objection had been received, and while there are serious problems with power generating plants in shallow estuaries, this project had been thoroughly studied and the staff recommendation was based on the preeminent power shortage existing in Florida and the acceptance by the corporation of many of the recommendations of a study team of biologists and conservationists.

Mr. Christian and Mr. O'Malley expressed the opinion that there had been much study and investigation and the staff recommendation appeared proper.

Governor Askew said those present would be heard but suggested that the speakers recognize the time limitations.

Mr. Bill Crown, President of S.A.V.E., and Mr. Hayward Matthews objected because of concern for water quality and suggested alternatives of cooling ponds and reversal of intake and discharge canals.

Mr. Ray Sirman, representing Florida Power Corporation, introduced speakers who discussed the project and the effort the corporation had made to protect the environment, including Mr. Joel Rodgers; Dr. Bernard Ross, professor of engineering at the University of South Florida, Dr. Kendall Carder, University of South Florida. Others were present to answer any questions the board might have.

There was discussion and in response to Mr. Shevin's question regarding the suggested alternatives, the Director said that with reference to cooling ponds there were problems with salt water intrusion and the staff had made no study of the flow reversal, basing its position on the work of the study teams and modifications of plans by the applicant. Mr. Kuperberg discussed the state's need for a team to deal with the complexities of power plant construction and suggested a delay of thirty days to secure information on questions brought up today.

Mr. O'Malley commented that after much investigation of the project there had been a local hearing, and many experts were present in support of the plan that the study group indicated would cause no significant water quality difference. He felt that delay was unjustified and was prepared to support the staff recommendation for approval.

Mr. Christian made a motion for approval, amending it to include requirement that the Department of Pollution Control monitor the project, and Mr. Conner seconded the amended motion.

Mr. O'Malley suggested an amendment that the staff bring to the Trustees recommendations for guidelines and reasonable standards for such a monitoring program, whereupon Mr. Rodgers advised that the Pollution Control permit required monitoring and the original design of the plant had been modified with respect to the water temperature. Mr. Stone then added that the Department of Pollution Control was vigorous in its review and therefore he was ready to vote.

Governor Askew said it appeared that the study team had made an assessment covering the question of water quality.

The Attorney General requested two weeks' deferment which was ordered. The Director was asked to be prepared to respond with staff recommendations at that time.

Mr. O'Malley commended the Director for pointing up needs with respect to power plant applications and suggested assigning adequate personnel to handle filing of such applications in all respects through this agency and others to avoid overlapping and delays.

-18-

VOLUSIA COUNTY - Fill Permit No. 253.123-(2)(c)1172
        (May 26, 1972)

APPLICANT: Department of Natural Resources
             Bureau of Beaches and Shores
             Larson Building, Tallahassee

PROJECT: To restore an eroded beach area 500 feet wide by
             2,800 feet long immediately north of the North Jetty
             being constructed at Ponce de Leon Inlet. This
             beach area was lost by avulsive action due to
             unseasonal weather conditions and by the inlet
             improvement project.

LOCATION: Ponce de Leon Inlet, Township 16 South, Range 34
             East, in Volusia County.

MATERIAL: Approximately 600,000 cubic yards is to be removed
             from inside the inlet adjacent to the North Jetty.

PAYMENT: None. This project would come under the Board of
             Trustees policy which states, "The economic value of
             Florida's beaches is such that upon recommendation
             of the Department of Natural Resources, the state
             should not charge for the material used to nourish
             beaches."

ECOLOGICAL
RESPONSES: Department of Natural Resources - No objection.

             Division of Beaches and Shores - Advises that
             an emergency condition exists along the shoreline in
             Volusia County immediately north of and adjacent to
             the Ponce de Leon Inlet, and recommends this project
             as being in the public interest to restore and
             maintain the dunes in this area for the protection
             of the beach and to prevent a possible "breakthrough"
             to the Intracoastal Waterway north of the inlet.

Staff recommends issuance of Permit No. 253.123(2)(c).

ACTION OF THE TRUSTEES:

Motion was made by Mr. Christian, seconded by Mr. Conner and
carried unanimously, to approve the application of the Department
of Natural Resources, Bureau of Beaches and Shores, for a fill
permit to restore an eroded beach area.

-19-

PALM BEACH COUNTY - Dredge and Fill Permit 253.123-250
(February 10, 1972)

On April 25, 1972, the Board was advised that this permit would
not expire until May 27, 1972, and that this matter would be
placed on the agenda when the local authority's comments
were received. On May 23, action was deferred and permit
extended two weeks.

APPLICANT: City of Lake Worth, c/o Malcolm Anderson, City
            Attorney, 414 Lake Avenue, Lake Worth, Florida

PROJECT: To extend the existing dredge and fill permit
            issued on April 30, 1969, for an additional three-
            year period of time. The original permit authorized
            the filling of an area of submerged land 490 feet,
            more or less, by 1,200 feet, more or less. This
            project was held up by litigation until a court order
            was signed January 12, 1972, dismissing the complaint.

LOCATION: Sections 26 and 27, in Township 44 South, Range 43
            East, Lake Worth, Palm Beach County.

MATERIAL: 88,000 cubic yards of material to be removed from
            sovereignty land.

PAYMENT: Previously paid.

OTHERS: 1. Palm Beach County: The Board of County Commis-
                sioners made the determination that this application
                was not in the public interest.

            2. Area Planning Board of Palm Beach County objects
                to the approval of this application.

            3. Several individuals representing various groups
                are here and wish to be heard.

Staff recommends denial of the application for the extension of
time of Dredge and Fill Permit 253.123-250.

ACTION OF THE TRUSTEES:

Mr. Kuperberg advised that six different groups, represented by
Mr. Herbert P. Benn, opposed the permit, that Mr. Raphael
Steinhardt who holds a contract from the applicant (City of
Lake Worth) felt he did not have a proper hearing before the
local authorities and wished an extension of the permit until
August 2. The project was originally attacked by local
interests, had been in the courts, and was not approved by
Palm Beach County or the Area Planning Board as being in the
public interest.

Motion was made by Mr. O'Malley, seconded by Mr. Shevin, to
deny the application.

Comptroller Dickinson offered a substitute motion for one month's
delay which died without a second, whereupon the Governor said
the merits of the application should be considered.

Mr. Steinhardt felt that the project had been fully considered
in 1969, discussed the history of efforts to develop the marina
complex under lease from the city but hampered by legal actions,
delays in correspondence and inability to secure from state

agencies certain information or to be placed on the agenda. He
desired time to prepare the necessary ecological studies for a
hearing before the local authorities, considered it unfair for
the state to allow filling to build a bridge but to deny his
client's filling of adjacent property, and said that delays
and filing a new application would prejudice his client's case
after efforts for six years to proceed under the original permit.

Mr. O'Malley recognized the problems and suggested filing a new
application that would be considered on its merits without delay.
Mr. Stone also recommended that a new application be filed that
would be given a quick hearing, and Mr. Dickinson was concerned
that any citizen felt he had been subjected to unnecessary delays.

Representing Save Lake Worth, Inc., Environmental Defense Fund,
Inc., Audubon Society of Everglades, Federated Conservation
Council, Citizens to Save the County, Inc., Lake Worth Boating
and Fishing Club, and other objectors, Mr. Herb Benn said there
had been four local hearings and urged against delay on a project
that he charged was in the interest of only the developer. He
discussed reasons for considering this application against the
public interest, referring to various lawsuits and charging
inconsistencies in statements of the proponent.

Mr. Ben Oehlert, Councilman, and Mr. G. R. Frost, Town Manager,
both of the Town of Palm Beach, opposed the permit. Mr. Frost
said other municipalities in the area complied with the 1969
request to pull back bulkhead lines as recommended by the
Interagency Advisory Committee but the City of Lake Worth did
not, and that approval of this application would hamper efforts
to relocate bulkhead lines at the mean high water line.

The staff might not have handled the matter as expeditiously as
possible, the Director acknowledged, but most of the letters were
notices that extension might be needed and not until February 23
was extension applied for. The staff then tried to assist and
did respond to the City of Lake Worth.

Mr. O'Malley pointed out two options open to the applicant - court
action or refiling under existing standards; and while he was not
sure he would favor the project he thought mistakes had been made.

Mr. Dickinson felt that the Board should not be voting on the
merits today in view of the testimony, but should have a
chance for properly hearing all the facts in the application.
He would vote "No" today - not against the marina itself but
because he thought this applicant had not received fair treatment.

On Mr. O'Malley's motion, seconded by Mr. Shevin, the Trustees
approved the staff recommendation for denial of the application
for extension of the time of dredge and fill permit on a vote
of six to one, with the Comptroller voting "No" for the reasons
explained.

-20-

DADE COUNTY - Fill Permit No. 253.124-237

The application of the Town of Bay Harbor Islands to extend
the existing seawall on each side of the Broad Causeway in
Biscayne Bay, Township 52 South, Range 42 East, Dade County,
was deferred at the request of the State Treasurer.

Comptroller Dickinson said the Trustees might be fairly near
a settlement that would be to the public's advantage by gaining
use of the island and beach, in the Munyon Island lawsuit
(Bankers Life and Casualty Company vs Village of North Palm
Beach, et al). He made a motion that the Board direct the
chief counsel to request opposing counsel, with permission of
the court, to postpone oral argument.

Attorney General Shevin recommended that, if the court grants the postponement, some reasonable time such as sixty or ninety days be requested.

Governor Askew suggested that the Board have an evaluation by independent counsel of any type of compromise or offer of settlement.

The motion by the Comptroller, with amendment of a time limitation of ninety days, was seconded by Treasurer O'Malley and carried without objection.

On motion duly adopted, the meeting was adjourned.

_____
GOVERNOR   -   CHAIRMAN

ATTEST:

_____
EXECUTIVE DIRECTOR

*   *   *

Tallahassee, Florida
June 20, 1972

The Board of Trustees of the Internal Improvement Trust Fund met on this date in the auditorium of the Burns Building with the following members present:

Reubin O'D. Askew	Governor
Richard (Dick) Stone	Secretary of State
Robert L. Shevin	Attorney General
Fred O. Dickinson, Jr.	Comptroller
Floyd T. Christian	Commissioner of Education
Doyle Conner	Commissioner of Agriculture

Joel Kuperberg	Executive Director

-1-

Request for approval of minutes of May 23 and June 6 was withdrawn.

-2-

JACKSON COUNTY - Surplus Compass Lake Fire Tower Site

On September 29, 1951, Otis A. Rosborough, Jr., conveyed without cost to the Board of Forestry a one-acre parcel of land in the SE 1/4 of Section 36, Township 3 North, Range 12 West, in Jackson County, for a fire tower site. The deed contains a restriction that the property could be used only for forestry purposes and title would revert if not used for forestry purposes continuously for a period of five years.

The Division of Forestry advises that this site has been abandoned, will no longer be utilized in its forestry program, and recommends that the property be deeded to Nortek Properties, Inc., successor to the reversionary interest retained by Otis A. Rosborough, Jr.

6-20-72

Recommend that the Board of Trustees quitclaim its interest in
this one-acre parcel of land to Nortek Properties, Inc.

ACTION OF THE TRUSTEES:

Motion was made by Mr. Stone, seconded by Mr. Conner and
adopted without objection, approving the staff recommendation
to quitclaim interest in the parcel of land that was no longer
needed in the forestry program.

-3-

HILLSBOROUGH COUNTY - Water Meter Easement
                     (May 18, 1972)

APPLICANT: City of Tampa, a municipal corporation

REQUEST: Easement for location of a water meter to serve
            the University of South Florida Medical Center

LOCATION: An area 10 feet by 35 feet in Section 8, Township
            28 South, Range 19 East, Hillsborough County.

The Board of Regents reviewed this request, and at its meeting
on May 3, 1971, approved the easement.

Recommend issuance of the easement to the City of Tampa for
meter installation purposes only.

ACTION OF THE TRUSTEES:

Motion was made by Mr. Stone, seconded by Mr. Conner and
adopted without objection, to authorize issuance of the
easement requested by the City of Tampa for meter installation purposes only.

-4-

POLK COUNTY - Drainage Easement
              (May 23, 1972)

APPLICANT: Board of County Commissioners of Polk County

REQUEST: Easement for drainage purposes across land in
            use by the Florida Experiment Station near
            Lake Alfred to connect with an existing
            storm sewer on privately-owned land. The
            easement will be used for installation of an
            underground pipeline.

LOCATION: An area 10 feet wide and 706 feet long in the
            NW 1/4 of SE 1/4 of Section 28, Township 27 South,
            Range 26 East, Polk County.

The Facilities Committee of the Board of Regents has reviewed
this request and on May 8 approved the request, stating that
the easement will be to the mutual advantage of the state and
county by helping to develop low cost housing which will be
available for employees of the Citrus Experiment Station.

Recommend granting the easement for drainage purposes only.

ACTION OF THE TRUSTEES:

Motion was made by Mr. Stone, seconded by Mr. Conner and
adopted unanimously, to grant the request of Polk County
Commission for an easement for drainage purposes only.

-5-

BROWARD COUNTY - Utility Permit No. 253.123(2)(b)-1112

At the request of the Secretary of State, action was deferred for two weeks on the application from the Board of County Commissioners of Broward County for a permit for construction of a waste water outfall into the Atlantic Ocean.

-6-

COLLIER COUNTY - Construction Permit No. CP-2171
              (April 5, 1972)

APPLICANT: Deltona Corporation
           3250 Southwest Third Avenue, Miami, Florida

PROJECT: To construct bridge across Copeland Waterway at Marco Island.

LOCATION: Section 28, Township 52 South, Range 26 East, Collier County.

MATERIAL: No dredging required.

PAYMENT: $25 fee received April 5, 1972.

STAFF
REMARKS: Field Operations - No objection.

ECOLOGICAL
RESPONSES: Department of Natural Resources - No objection.

Game and Fresh Water Fish Commission - No objection.

Department of Pollution Control - No objection.

Staff recommends issuance of construction permit.

ACTION OF THE TRUSTEES:

On motion by Mr. Christian, seconded by Mr. Stone and carried without objection, the construction permit was approved.

-7-

DUVAL COUNTY - Dredge Permit No. 253.123-1085
             (March 27, 1972)

APPLICANT: Atlantic Marine, Inc.
           Post Office Box 138
           Fort George Island, Florida 32226

PROJECT: To perform maintenance dredging in an existing boat basin.

LOCATION: Sisters Creek, Section 26, Township 1 South, Range 28 East, Duval County.

MATERIAL: 500 cubic yards of material is to be removed and placed in an upland disposal area 100 feet landward of the mean high water line.

PAYMENT: $500 has been paid for sovereignty material.

STAFF
REMARKS: No objection.

ECOLOGICAL
RESPONSES: Department of Natural Resources - No objection provided precautions are taken to contain the dredged material at the upland site.

Game and Fresh Water Fish Commission - No objection.

Department of Pollution Control - No objection.

Staff recommends issuance of Dredge Permit 253.123-1085
subject to containment of the spoil at the upland disposal site.

ACTION OF THE TRUSTEES:

On motion by Mr. Stone, seconded by Mr. Christian and carried
without objection, the dredge permit was approved subject to
containment of the spoil at the upland disposal site.

-8-

MARTIN COUNTY - Marina License ML-116 and Construction Permit
(March 10, 1972)

APPLICANT: Monterey Yacht & Country Club
1900 Palm City Road, Stuart, Florida 33494

PROJECT: Construct docking facility and boat ramp in the
AND South Fork of the St. Lucie River abutting Section
LOCATION: 8, Township 38 South, Range 41 East, Martin County.

MATERIAL: No dredging is required.

PAYMENT: $128.52 minimum annual fee for marina license.

STAFF
REMARKS: Field Operations - No objection.

ECOLOGICAL
RESPONSES: Department of Natural Resources - No objection.

Game and Fresh Water Fish Commission - No objection.

Department of Pollution Control - No objection.

OTHERS: Martin County Board of County Commissioners -
No objection.

Staff recommends issuance of construction permit and marina
license No. 116.

ACTION OF THE TRUSTEES:

Mr. Kuperberg pointed out that the application was for a marina
license and a construction permit.

On motion by Mr. Christian, seconded by Mr. Stone and carried
without objection, the application was approved as clarified
by the Executive Director.

-9-

PALM BEACH COUNTY - Contruction Permit No. CP-2172
January 10, 1972)

APPLICANT: City of Boynton Beach
120 Northeast Second Avenue, Boynton Beach, Florida

PROJECT: To repair and extend existing pier at the city boat
ramp and recreational area on the west shore of
Lake Worth.

LOCATION: Section 15, Township 45 South, Range 43 East, Palm
Beach County.

MATERIAL: No dredging required. Submerged land has been dedicated
to City of Boynton Beach for public municipal purposes.

PAYMENT: Fee waiver requested by City of Boynton Beach as project is a public facility and is maintained by the city at no charge to the public.

STAFF
REMARKS: Field Operations - No objection.

ECOLOGICAL
RESPONSES: Department of Natural Resources - No objection.

Game and Fresh Water Fish Commission - No objection.

Department of Pollution Control - No objection.

OTHERS: 1. Area Planning Board - No objection.

2. Board of County Commissioners of Palm Beach County - No objection.

Staff recommends issuance of construction permit and waiver of fees.

ACTION OF THE TRUSTEES:

Motion was made by Mr. Christian, seconded by Mr. Stone and carried unanimously, authorizing issuance of construction permit without charge.

-10-

MANATEE COUNTY - File No. 2051-41-253.12
(May 8, 1972)

APPLICANT: City of Bradenton
Post Office Drawer 730, Bradenton, Florida

The Board of Trustees in meeting on October 12, 1971, approved the "blue ribbon" ad hoc committee appointed to act in an advisory capacity to the city for the development of the 54-acre parcel of land conveyed to the City of Bradenton.

In December there was a general election and some of the officials involved in the project were not reelected. The "blue ribbon" ad hoc committee resigned en masse effective January 4, 1972, the date the newly elected officials took office.

The City of Bradenton has created a new "blue ribbon" ad hoc committee comprised of seven persons selected by the Mayor subject to approval of the Board of Trustees.

Committee appointments are :

Mr. Douglas E. Croll, A.I.A., Mrs. Doris M. Stalker, Mrs. June Arnold, Mrs. Mary Upshaw Blackburn, Mr. R. J. Rutledge, Mr. A. Sterling Hall and Mr. A. Q. Winn.

Staff recommends approval of these appointments.

ACTION OF THE TRUSTEES:

Motion was made by Mr. Stone, seconded by Mr. Christian and carried unanimously, approving the appointments.

-11-

HENDRY COUNTY - Advertise for Oil and Gas Lease
(March 9, 1972)

APPLICANT: Robert Mosbacher by William M. Register, Jr.
Post Office Box 3239, Tampa, Florida

REQUEST: Advertise for bids for an oil and gas drilling lease.

LOCATION: W 1/2 of Section 19; N 1/2 and SW 1/4 of Section 21;
            N 1/2 of Section 29 and all of Section 31, Township
            46 South, Range 31 East, containing 1,760 surface
            acres (880 net mineral acres) in Hendry County,
            approximately 6 miles east of Immokalee.

INTEREST
OF STATE: Trustees hold an undivided one-half interest in the
            petroleum and petroleum products.

These privately-owned lands lie immediately south of the
northerly boundary of the Big Cypress Watershed Area. The
Advisory Committee on Oil Exploration in the Big Cypress reviewed
this request and advises that 75% of these lands consists of
cleared grazing land or land that had been grazed and is well
drained sandy land. The Committee was unanimous in recommending
the area be leased for oil exploration.

Proceeds from this lease will go to the Internal Improvement
Trust Fund.

The request has been reviewed by the Director of Interior
Resources, Department of Natural Resources, who concurs in
the following recommendation.

Recommend advertising for sealed bids for a five-year primary
term lease with annual rental of $1 per net mineral acre, 1/8
royalty, $50,000 surety bond and at least one test well every
2 1/2 years drilled to 6,000 feet or to the Roberts Zone of
the Sunniland Formation or other anticipated oil horizons,
whichever is deeper.

ACTION OF THE TRUSTEES:

Motion was made by Mr. Conner, seconded by Mr. Christian and
carried unanimously, authorizing advertising for sealed bids
as recommended by the staff.

-12-

PUTNAM AND FLAGLER COUNTIES - Consideration of Oil and Gas
                    Lease Bids

On May 16, 1972, at the request of Gilbert E. Thayer and Sam F.
Davis, Tampa, Florida, the Trustees authorized advertisement
for sealed bids for a five-year oil and gas drilling lease
covering 2,792.09 net mineral acres in Government Lot 1, Section
27 and the north portion of Lake Crescent, all in Township 11
South, Ranges 27 and 28 East, Putnam and Flagler Counties.

Drilling operations will be prohibited in the portion of the
lease covering the lake bottom.

Proceeds from the lease will go to the Internal Improvement Trust
Fund.

The lease requires an annual rental of $1 per net mineral acre,
$50,000 surety bond, 1/8 royalty and at least one test well
every 2 1/2 years.

Invitation to bid was advertised pursuant to law in the
Tallahassee Democrat and the Palatka Daily News with bids
to be opened at 10:00 a.m. (EDST) on June 20 for consideration
by the Trustees. The right to reject any or all bids is
reserved.

ACTION OF THE TRUSTEES:

At the Director's request, Mr. James T. Williams opened one
bid received for the advertised lease and reported that Thayer-
Davis and Associates of Tampa offered the amount of $3,025 as
cash consideration for an oil and gas lease of the 2,792.09 net
mineral acres in Putnam and Flagler Counties. Mr. Williams
said the price was in keeping with what might be received in
that area.

Motion was made by Mr. Stone, seconded by Mr. Conner and
carried unanimously, that the Board accept the bid and award
the oil and gas drilling lease to Thayer-Davis and Associates.

-13-

BREVARD COUNTY - Application for Disclaimer
              (May 17, 1972)

APPLICANT: Kenneth D. Rosen, Trustee

REPRESENTATIVE: Joseph B. Reisman
                 Suite 1002, Ainsley Building
                 Miami, Florida

REQUEST: Disclaimer to a parcel in Section 31, Township 24
          South, Range 37 East, containing 0.61 acre in
          Brevard County.

STAFF
REMARKS: Disclaimer is requested to remove a cloud from the
          title to the 0.61-acre parcel owned by Kenneth D. Rosen,
          Trustee, by reason of two road easements (Easements Nos.
          24589 and 24590) issued by the Trustees to the State
          Road Department covering rights of way across sovereignty
          land in Banana River and New Found Harbor for the
          construction of State Road 520. Survey furnished by
          applicant clearly shows the 0.61-acre parcel to be
          upland. Further evidence submitted shows title to
          the 0.61-acre parcel was in private ownership in 1940
          when the Trustees issued the two easements.

          Staff legal counsel has reviewed this request and
          recommends issuance of a disclaimer.

Recommend issuance of an exparte disclaimer for a processing fee
of $25 disclaiming interest in the 0.61-acre parcel as a result
of the two road rights of way easements numbered 24589 and 24590,
dated April 23, 1940, and June 25, 1940.

ACTION OF THE TRUSTEES:

Mr. Kuperberg explained that an erroneous description had
been furnished that covered upland as well as submerged lands.
The purpose of the disclaimer was to eliminate from the easement
those upland areas not in Trustees' ownership.

On motion by Mr. Stone, seconded by Mr. Christian and carried
unanimously, the Board authorized issuance of ex parte disclaimer
for $25 processing fee.

-14-

BAY COUNTY - Dredge Permit No. 253.123-1021
           (May 2, 1972)

APPLICANT: Woodlawn Community Club
            c/o Benton Associates, Inc.,
            512 East 15th Street, Panama City, Florida

PROJECT: To perform maintenance dredging in an existing canal
          to improve navigation.

6-20-72

LOCATION: St. Andrews Bay, Section 28, Township 3 South, Range
             15 West, Bay County.

MATERIAL: Approximately 1,390 cubic yards to be dredged and
             placed on dedicated county roads.

PAYMENT: Waiver of fees is requested.

STAFF
REMARKS: Field Operations - No objection.

ECOLOGICAL
RESPONSES: Department of Natural Resources - No objection.

             Game and Fresh Water Fish Commission - No objection.

             Department of Pollution Control - No objection.

OTHERS: Board of County Commissioners - Approved.

Staff recommends issuance of Permit 253.123-1021 and waiver of
fee for material.

ACTION OF THE TRUSTEES:

Motion was made by Mr. Stone, seconded by Mr. Christian and
carried unanimously, to authorize issuance of the permit
without charge for the material to be placed on dedicated
county roads.

-15-

FRANKLIN COUNTY - Dredge Permit No. 253.123-952-Rescind
               (June 2, 1972)

APPLICANT: General Engineering Services, Inc.
             c/o W. B. Miller
             Star Route, Carrabelle, Florida

PROJECT: To dredge a channel 950 feet long ranging in width
             from 100 feet to 150 feet by 12.5 feet deep paralleling
             the shoreline; to construct a seawall and an upland
             boat slip.

LOCATION: Carrabelle River in Section 20, Township 7 South,
             Range 4 West, Franklin County.

MATERIAL: 33,000 cubic yards of material will be removed and
             stockpiled on applicant's upland for use by the
             Franklin County School Board (17,000 cubic yards)
             and the City of Carrabelle (16,000 cubic yards).

PAYMENT: Request waiver of payment for the material to be
             removed since it will be given to the county and city.

STAFF
REMARKS: Permit was issued but was not accepted by the permittee
             in accordance with stipulations on face of permit.
             This permit should be cancelled since General
             Engineering Services, Inc., no longer has any
             interest in the adjacent upland. This action has
             been approved by new owner who will apply for a
             new permit to construct a marina at this site.

ECOLOGICAL
RESPONSES: Department of Natural Resources - No objection,
             provided the spoil area is adequately diked.

             Game and Fresh Water Fish Commission - No objection,
             provided the area is diked and waste water facilities
             used to prevent turbid waters from escaping.

Department of Pollution Control - No objection.

OTHERS: Mr. Nick Fallier, by letter dated May 29, 1972, advised that the Crooked River Marina interests had acquired the land and interests of the General Engineering Services, Inc. and propose to construct a marina in the area, which will require a new application.

Staff recommends the Board of Trustees rescind the March 28, 1972, action authorizing issuance of Permit 253.123-952 as the applicant has abandoned this project.

ACTION OF THE TRUSTEES:

Mr. Kuperberg advised that the staff had information that the applicant had sold the land and did not propose to do the work. The new owner had asked for a massive revision of the plans which the staff considered should come under a new application.

Motion was made by Mr. Stone, seconded by Mr. Christian and carried unanimously, to approve the staff recommendation and rescind the existing Permit No. 253.123-952.

-16-

MONROE COUNTY - Dredge Permit No. 253.03-224
          (July 30, 1971)

APPLICANT: Henry Staples
1120 West 37 Street, Hialeah, Florida

PROJECT: To dredge a channel 50 feet wide and 5 feet deep to connect to an existing upland canal.

LOCATION: Florida Bay, Section 27, Township 62 South, Range 38 East, Monroe County.

MATERIAL: All material will be used to fill privately-owned submerged land (TIITF Deed No. 21935) approximately 5,000 cubic yards.

PAYMENT: None. Sovereignty land not involved.

STAFF
REMARKS: Approve dredging of proposed navigation canal but retain shoreline in its present condition.

ECOLOGICAL
RESPONSES: Department of Natural Resources - No objection.

Game and Fresh Water Fish Commission - No objection.

Department of Pollution Control - No objection.

Staff recommends issuance of Dredge Permit 253.03-224.

ACTION OF THE TRUSTEES:

On motion by Mr. Conner, seconded by Mr. Christian and carried unanimously, the dredge permit was approved.

-17-

OKALOOSA COUNTY - Dredge Permit No. 253.123-1046
          (January 4, 1972)

APPLICANT: Ruckel Properties, Inc.
Post Office Box 187, Valparaiso, Florida

PROJECT: To construct a 50 feet wide by 120 feet long by 5 feet deep channel in Rocky Bayou. This channel will connect to a proposed interior dead end canal 50 feet wide by 700 feet long by 5 feet deep.

6-20-72

LOCATION: Section 10, Township 1 South, Range 22 West, Okaloosa County.

MATERIAL: 382 cubic yards of material to be removed and placed on upland.

PAYMENT: $191.00 check has been tendered as payment for sovereignty material at the standard rate of 50¢ per cubic yard.

STAFF
REMARKS: Field Operations - No objection.

ECOLOGICAL
RESPONSES: Department of Natural Resources - No objection.

     Game and Fresh Water Fish Commission - No objection.

     Department of Pollution Control - Requests application be denied because there is not reasonable assurance that the water quality standards of Rocky Bayou will not be affected.

OTHERS: County Commissioners - approved the application.

Staff recommends denial of Dredge Permit 253.123-1046.

ACTION OF THE TRUSTEES:

Motion was made by Mr. Stone, seconded by Mr. Christian, and carried without objection, that the permit be denied as recommended by the staff, based on the adverse report from the Department of Pollution Control.

-18-

SANTA ROSA COUNTY - Dredge Permit No. 253.123-176
            (May 8, 1972)

APPLICANT: Air Products & Chemicals, Inc. (formerly Escambia Chemical Corp.), Post Office Box 467 Pensacola, Florida 32502

PROJECT: To return funds paid for sovereignty material which was not used.

LOCATION: Santa Rosa County, Township 1 North, Range 29 West.

MATERIAL: None used.

PAYMENT: $12,600 was paid for material.

STAFF
REMARKS: Field Operations has verified that material was not used.

ECOLOGICAL
RESPONSES: Department of Natural Resources - Not applicable.

     Game and Fresh Water Fish Commission - Not applicable.

     Department of Pollution Control - Not applicable.

Staff recommends refund of $12,600 to applicant.

ACTION OF THE TRUSTEES:

It was ascertained that Mr. Joe McClure, who expected to be present in regard to this matter, was not on hand.

On motion by Mr. Stone, seconded by Mr. Dickinson and carried without objection, the Board authorized refund of $12,600 to the applicant for the reason that the sovereignty material was not used.

-19-

VOLUSIA COUNTY - Dredge Permit No. 253.123-1083
           (May 3, 1972)

APPLICANT: Florida Power and Light Company
              Post Office Box 3100, Miami, Florida 33101

PROJECT: To dredge to improve navigation for fuel oil unloading
              in applicant's plant cooling water intake canal.

LOCATION: St. Johns River at Sanford, Florida, Section 16,
              Township 19 South, Range 30 East, Volusia County.

MATERIAL: Approximately 1,500 cubic yards of sovereignty
              material is to be removed and placed on applicant's
              upland.

PAYMENT: $1,500 has been paid for material. At the rate of
              50¢ per cubic yard in Volusia County, this represents
              an overpayment by the applicant of $750.

STAFF
REMARKS: Field Operations - No objection, provided turbidity
              curtains are used and the Trustees are notified at least
              5 days in advance of start of dredging.

              Land Management - Project was revised to reduce damage
              to the St. Johns River in the event of accidental oil
              spillage.

ECOLOGICAL
RESPONSES: Department of Natural Resources - Requested that
              Game and Fresh Water Fish Commission prepare the
              biological report for this fresh water project.

              Game and Fresh Water Fish Commission - Recommends
              permit be granted provided a diaper be used at the
              mouth of the canal during dredging, applicant initiate
              corrective measures on the discharge canal if turbid
              water goes into the river and all spoil be placed
              landward of the cypress trees and suitably diked.

              Department of Pollution Control - No objection.

OTHERS: Volusia County Public Works Director - Commends company
              for taking action to provide better control over
              accidental oil spillages.

<u>Staff recommends issuance of Dredge Permit 253.123-1083 with stipulations as recommended by Game and Fresh Water Fish Commission and Field Operations, plus refund of $750 overpayment for material</u>.

ACTION OF THE TRUSTEES:

On motion by Mr. Conner, seconded by Mr. Christian and carried without objection, the Board authorized issuance of dredge permit with the recommended stipulations, and approved refund of $750 overpayment.

-20-

DADE COUNTY - Fill Permit No. 253.124-237

Attorney General Shevin requested deferral of the application to the Town of Bay Harbor Islands to extend the existing seawall on each side of Broad Causeway in Biscayne Bay. He commented that Dade County Commissioner Joyce Goldberg had asked for deferral two weeks ago which was granted by the Board at

Mr. O'Malley's request. Mrs. Goldberg, unable to be present on this date, had contacted Mr. Shevin who agreed to request deferral. He expected that she would be present at the next meeting to explain her objections.

-21-

PASCO COUNTY - Dredge Permit No. 253.123-1091
      (May 1, 1972)

APPLICANT: Florida Power Corporation
               Post Office Box 14042, St. Petersburg, Florida

PROJECT: To dredge intake and discharge canals to provide water cooling for the Anclote site power plant.

LOCATION: Gulf of Mexico and Anclote River, Sections 27 and 34, Township 26 South, Range 15 East, Pasco County.

MATERIAL: 142,053.54 cubic yards of sovereignty material to be removed and placed on upland.

PAYMENT: $142,053.54 has been paid for sovereignty material.

STAFF
REMARKS: Field Operations has no objections except to spoiling below the mean high water line.

ECOLOGICAL
RESPONSES: Department of Natural Resources - Revised dredging plan is a significant improvement over the original plan and will better conserve marine biological resources, but to best conserve marine biological resources power plant effluent should be cooled before being discharged into Florida's coastal waters.

            Game and Fresh Water Fish Commission - Because of the loss of approximately 22.5 productive acres and the heating of discharge water plus various indirect effects, there will be an adverse impact on the estuarine ecoystem which cannot be ignored; however, it is recognized that applicant is attempting to minimize this intrusion and making efforts to gain knowledge which may be applied to future power plant construction.

            Department of Pollution Control - No objection.

OTHERS: Board of County Commissioners, Pasco County - Approved.

Staff recommends issuance of Dredge Permit No. 253.123-1091 provided no material is placed seaward of the mean high water line.

ACTION OF THE TRUSTEES:

Mr. Kuperberg reported that the Florida Power Corporation had prepared additional data and had representatives present; and by letter received this morning the conservation group, S.A.V.E., had withdrawn its objections. Mr. Shevin added the group was satisfied that the alternatives had been properly investigated.

Motion was made by Mr. Stone, seconded by Mr. Christian and carried unanimously, to approve issuance of the dredge permit subject to the provision recommended by the staff.

On motion made by Mr. Christian, seconded by Mr. Dickinson and adopted without objection, the rules were waived to allow consideration of the following applications on the addendum.

-22-

PALM BEACH COUNTY - Land Exchange

APPLICANT: Gulf and Western Food Products Company

REPRESENTATIVE: William C. Herrell
Tallahassee Bank Building
Tallahassee, Florida

REQUEST: Exchange of 1,558 acres of land owned by
Gulf and Western in Palm Beach County for
1,501.02 acres owned by the Trustees in
Palm Beach County.

PURPOSE OF
EXCHANGE: To place Gulf and Western lands in a location
contiguous to other Gulf and Western land and
also consolidate state lands in this area,
thereby allowing each owner to better utilize
its lands.

Gulf and Western offers to exchange all of Sections 2 and 31
and all of Section 10 lying east of Miami Canal in Township 46
South, Range 35 East, containing 1,558 acres with an appraised
value of $428,450, for the following ownership of the Trustees -
all of Section 3 West of Miami Canal, all of Section 18, 608.50
acres in Section 20 and 70 acres in Section 30, Township 46 South,
Range 35 East, containing 1,501.02 acres with an appraised value
of $425,965.50. Section 3 is Public School Land.

In this proposal the state would gain 56.98 acres with a value
of $2,484.50.

These lands are located in the southwestern portion of Palm Beach
County and are all undeveloped at the present time having the
same general soil conditions.

Gulf and Western has furnished an appraisal report prepared by
Jerome R. Wedekind, M.A.I., of Palm Beach, Florida.

Review of this appraisal report has been made by staff appraiser
who states that the exchange is equitable.

Exchange of Trustees' land for privately-owned land is provided
for in Section 253.42, Florida Statutes and conveyance of Trustees'
land without reserving the statutory reservation of oil and minerals
is permissible provided the land received in the exchange is
without such reservation.

This exchange will be beneficial to the State due to the
consolidation of lands in an area where large acreage tracts
are more desirable than scattered parcels.

Recommend exchange of lands as proposed subject to Gulf and
Western being able to convey marketable title without reservation
as evidenced by title.insurance or complete abstract of title.

ACTION OF THE TRUSTEES:

Mr. Kuperberg advised that a procedural question was raised at the
cabinet aides' meeting, but investigation revealed that the Trustees'
resolution of January 26, 1971, pertained only to exchanges of
sovereignty lands whereas this was an upland exchange.

Motion was made by Mr. Dickinson, seconded by Mr. Christian and
adopted unanimously, to approve the land exchange subject to
the condition in the staff recommendation.

-23A-

ST. LUCIE COUNTY - Bulkhead Line
(May 19, 1972)

APPLICANT: Department of Transportation
Tallahassee, Florida

6-20-72

PROJECT: Bulkhead line enclosing a parcel of sovereignty
lands 200 feet x 258 feet (51,600 square feet) on
the West shore of the Indian River within the
Department of Transportation right of way at
Fort Pierce, Florida

LOCATION: Section 3, Township 35 South, Route 40 East,
St. Lucie County.

MATERIAL: None required.

PAYMENT: None required.

ECOLOGICAL
RESPONSES: Department of Natural Resources - No objection.
Hydrographic adverse.

            Game and Fresh Water Fish Commission - No objection.

            Department of Pollution Control - No objection.

Staff recommends approval of Bulkhead Line as proposed. Recommend
issuance of Construction Permit for bridge construction on piling.

ACTION OF THE TRUSTEES:

Responding to the Attorney General's question, Mr. Kuperberg
said the bulkhead line was not entirely at the mean high water
mark but was a compromise. The Game and Fresh Water Fish Commission objected because it would reduce the size of the park.
It was a city park, the city had approved the project, and for
that reason and because it was for a public road project, the staff
recommended approval.

The Governor added that he understood the bridge was in a bad
condition and the work was needed.

On motion by Mr. Dickinson, seconded by Mr. Stone and carried
without objection, the staff recommendation was approved.

-23B-

ST. LUCIE COUNTY - Right of Way Easement, File No. 2469-56-253.03
                 (May 19, 1972)

APPLICANT: Department of Transportation
Tallahassee, Florida

PROJECT: Highway and bridge construction for state Road A-I-A.
Some filling of submerged land is proposed but no
dredging is required.

LOCATION: An 11.34-acre parcel of submerged land in the
Indian River abutting Sections 2 and 3, Township
35 South, Range 40 East, St. Lucie County.

MATERIAL: To be secured from upland source.

PAYMENT: None.

ECOLOGICAL
RESPONSES: Department of Natural Resources - No objection.

            Game and Fresh Water Fish Commission - No objection.

            Department of Pollution Control - No objection.

Staff requests authority to issue easement.

ACTION OF THE TRUSTEES:

On motion by Mr. Dickinson, seconded by Mr. Stone and carried without objection, the staff recommendation was approved as amended, with correction of "permit" to "easement."

-23C-

ST. LUCIE COUNTY - Fill and Utility Permit No. 253.03-(7)-371
                   and 253.124-303
                   (May 19, 1972)

APPLICANT: Department of Transportation
              Tallahassee, Florida

PROJECT: Installation of storm sewer outfalls and fill in conjunction with construction of a new bridge as an improvement to State Road A-I-A across the Indian River.

LOCATION: Indian River at the City of Fort Pierce in St. Lucie County.

MATERIAL: No sovereignty material involved.

PAYMENT: Not applicable

STAFF
REMARKS: (Comments have been requested from Field Operations)

ECOLOGICAL
RESPONSES: Department of Natural Resources - Survey and Management - The proposed fill should not have significant adverse effects on the marine life in the area. Referred to Beaches and Shores for hydrographic comments.

              Beaches and Shores indicates the installation of culverts in the fill area would negate the possibility of poor water circulation and the collection of floating debris.

              Game and Fresh Water Fish Commission - No objection to the fill and bulkheading, but objects to the road alignment which would reduce the size of Indian River Memorial Park. Recommends the old bridge be retained as a fishing pier.

              Department of Pollution Control - No objection.

OTHERS: City Commission of the City of Fort Pierce - Approved.

Staff recommends issuance of Permits 253.03(7)0371 and 253.124-303 subject to the installation of culverts of a size and at the location designated by the Department of Natural Resources, Bureau of Beaches and Shores.

ACTION OF THE TRUSTEES:

On motion by Mr. Dickinson, seconded by Mr. Stone and carried without objection, the Board approved issuance of the permits subject to installation of culverts as recommended by the Department of Natural Resources, Bureau of Beaches and Shores.

-24-

At the request of the staff, consideration of marina license regulations was deferred.

-25-

HERNANDO COUNTY - Dredge Permit No. 253.123-1141
              (March 29, 1972)

APPLICANT: Hernando County Board of County Commissioners
             Post Office Box 185, Brooksville, Florida

PROJECT: To dredge a channel 40 feet wide and about 5,000
             feet long to -3 feet at mean low water to improve
             navigation for public recreational purposes.

LOCATION: Bayport Park, Section 25, Township 22 South, Range 16
             East, Hernando County.

MATERIAL: 6,000 cubic yards of material will be removed and
             placed on upland in a properly diked spoil area.

PAYMENT: Waiver of charge for material is requested since
             project is in the public interest. However, the
             spoil area is owned by Leon Whitehurst & Association
             Realtors.

STAFF
REMARKS: Field Operations has no objection.

ECOLOGICAL
RESPONSES: Department of Natural Resources - No objection,
             provided the material is placed on upland spoil
             disposal area.

             Game and Fresh Water Fish Commission - No objection.

             Department of Pollution Control - No objection.

OTHERS: This item is placed on the agenda at the request of
             Treasurer O'Malley.

Staff recommends issuance of Dredge Permit 253.123-1141 upon
receipt of check for $3,000 as payment for the material or upon
receipt of certification from the Board of County Commissioners
that the material will be deposited on public lands.

ACTION OF THE TRUSTEES:

Mr. Kuperberg said a check for $3,000 was reported to be in the
mail, that the staff would not issue the permit unless one of
the two conditions in the recommendation was met, either payment
for the material or certification that the material is deposited
on public lands.

Motion was made by Mr. Christian, seconded by Mr. Stone and
carried without objection, to approve the staff recommendation.

-26-

Under Chapter 253.03 (7) Florida Statute, the Board of
Trustees of the Internal Improvement Trust Fund is charged
with the responsibility of maintaining a current inventory
of all state-owned lands. Over the past several months, the
Trustees' staff has engaged in discussions with Dr. Edward
Fernald, Director of the Florida Resources Analysis Center,
Florida State University, towards the accomplishment of this
goal. The Florida Environmental Land and Water Management
Act of 1972, Chapter 72-317 Laws of Florida, requires that
before any "area of critical state concern" may be designated
by the Governor and Cabinet, there must be filed with the new
Division of State Planning, an inventory of state-owned lands.

In addition, the 1972-73 General Appropriations Act directs all
agencies, boards, commissions and departments to complete the
required transfer of title to state lands as required in
Section 253.03, Florida Statute no later than December 31, 1972.
The Department of Administration is directed to withhold further

releases of appropriated funds after that date to any commission, board, agency or department which has not complied with this statute.

This directive should permit the staff working with Dr. Fernald to comply with the existing requirements that a current inventory be developed and maintained.

Staff requests authority to enter into an agreement with the Florida Resources Analysis Center, Florida State University, to produce a current inventory of all state-owned lands by no later than December 1, 1972, at a total cost not to exceed $30,000.

ACTION OF THE TRUSTEES:

On motion by Mr. Stone, seconded by Mr. Dickinson and Mr. Christian, carried without objection, the Trustees approved the staff recommendation.

-27-

DADE COUNTY - Dredge and Fill Permit 253.123-1185-253.124-306

The Circuit Court of the Second Judicial Circuit in and for Leon County, Florida in Civil Action No. 69-984 styled Gables By the Sea, Inc., a Florida Corporation, Plaintiff vs Claude R. Kirk, Jr. Governor of the State of Florida, et al, as the Board of Trustees of the Internal Improvement Trust Fund of the State of Florida, ordered the Board of Trustees to issue a dredge and fill and to allow use of such material to fill its privately-owned submerged land indicated on such application for a period of time consisting of 223 days beginning on the date this judgement becomes final by the expiration of the time of appeal, or the filing of the mandate of an Appellate Court affirming this judgement, whichever is the later date.

This decision went upon appeal.

The District Court of Appeal First District, State of Florida, July Term, A.D. 1971, in Case No. 0-167 styled Claude R. Kirk, Jr., Governor of the State of Florida, et al, Appellants vs. Gables By the Sea, Inc., a Florida Corporation, Appellee, ordered that the judgement in the lower court be amended so that the same shall read, as amended, that the Appellee shall have the lawful right to dredge material from the areas indicated on the application for a dredge and fill permit and to use such material to fill its privately-owned submerged land indicated on such application for a period of time consisting of 223 days, beginning either as the day after the Army Corps of Engineers issues its final permit permitting the appellee to dredge and fill as aforesaid, or beginning on the first day after there are no legal impediments to the appellee commencing its filling operation. In all other respects the final judgement is affirmed.

The Department of Pollution Control pursuant to the order of the. Circuit Court of the Second Judicial Circuit, In and For Leon County, Florida, in Case No. 69-904 styled Gables By the Sea, Inc., a Florida Corporation vs. Reubin O'Donovan Askew, Governor, etc., et al, Defendants, issued its certification of the dredge and fill project proposed by Gables By the Sea, Inc.

Staff requests authority to issue Dredge and Fill Permits 253.123-1185 and 253.124-306 pursuant to the order of the District Court of Appeal First District, State of Florida.

ACTION OF THE TRUSTEES:

Mr. Stone made a motion, seconded by Mr. Dickinson, authorizing issuance of the dredge and fill permits pursuant to the order of the District Court of Appeal First District, State of Florida.

Aerojet-General Corporation Litigation

Attorney General Shevin reported on litigation involving 25,313 acres of land in southwest Dade County (in Lease-Option No. 1640-1640-S dated in 1961 which the Board in 1969 had declared in default and on March 16, 1971, had rejected a settlement offer).

Dade County has appealed to the Florida Supreme Court under a statute that gives the county first option when land is sold to private interests.

Mr. Shevin related that Judge D. L. Middlebrooks in emergency hearing this morning denied a petition for stay, that the Board intended to implead Aerojet before the Florida Supreme Court and was under a court order in the federal court pursuant to a mandate of the Fifth Circuit in an order entered by Judge Middlebrooks to convey the property to Aerojet by June 21, 1972. Also, there was pending in the United States Supreme Court a petition for certiorari that had not been acted upon, and the Supreme Court had denied a petition for a stay order sought earlier in regard to Judge Middlebrooks' order.

Summarizing, Mr. Shevin said the clerk of the court had authority under the federal ruling to convey for the cabinet which the judge said would be acceptable, that the cabinet's Supreme Court case was still pending in Washington, the Florida Supreme Court case was pending, that if Dade County receives the relief it is seeking then Aerojet would be required to convey to Dade County. But in the interim the land had to be conveyed to Aerojet. Mr. Shevin said a lis pendens would be filed as notice of the fact that there are pending lawsuits involving the property.

The Trustees accepted without objection the report of the Attorney General.

On motion duly adopted, the meeting was adjourned.

GOVERNOR   -   CHAIRMAN

ATTEST:

EXECUTIVE DIRECTOR

-E-

-F-

-K-

Permits (continued)
  Dredge and Fill

Trustees
  Policies (continued)
    Rules repealed, 18-031, 18-1.032   136
    Stilt houses, Marquesas Keys   175,182,230
    Spoil islands in natural state   42-3
    Staff employment review   334
    Submarine cable permits, no charge   17
    Surveying state-owned land   160
    Wilderness systems - Interagency committee   309
    Utility crossings, staff authority   . 18
  Resolutions
    Cascades Park in capitol center   440
    Collier County violations   39,56
    Governor as Chairman   171
    Hendry Corp. fill   121
    Land exchange   189-190
    Old Tampa Bay permit moratorium   141-2
    Palm Beach County dredging moratorium   294
    Pending permits, 120-day processing   547,601
    Public interest   26
    Univ. Athletic Assoc. golf course   398
  Miscellaneous
    Agenda with payment in hand   658
    All properties centralized   335
    Capitol center surplus buildings   321
    Committee review oil exploration, state forests   524
    Indians
      Miccosukee Tribe lease, Broward Co.   537
      Reservation lands, Ch. 71-286   385
      Seminole Tribe of Florida   464
    Office building, Madison St.   204
    Patents, copyrights, trademarks   335,419
    Peace River pollution suit   476
    Quarterly operations reports   153,183,269
    Records disposal   233
Tuck, A. C. - Permit, deed, Franklin Co.   24,146,156-7,222,437
Tucker, J. C. - Lease, Dade Co.   228
Tucker, W. S. - Refund, Martin Co.   686
Turner, Gerard:
  General Acceptance Corp. settlement, Lee Co.   508
Turner, J. G.:
  G.A.C. Cape Coral fill, Lee County   40,70,97-9
Turner, Steve, Trustees counsel   334
Tyndall Air Force Base permit, Bay County   181
Tyre, R. C. - Protest Lake Swan fill   44-47

-U-

Ulmer, Herman - North Shore spoil area   376
Ulrich, Glenn - Florida Keys report   522
Unger, Paul - Island View Hospital   569
United States of America
  Army Corps of Engineers
    Caloosahatchee, Okeechobee Waterway, spoil areas   183
    Coastal Petroleum Company litigation   9
    Escambia County easement   149
    Gould, R. - Permit, Dade County   541
    Hillsborough Co. permits   7,25
    Jacksonville Harbor deepening project   376
    Lee County easement, right of way   165
    Marco Island Development Corp.   616
    Okeechobee County easement   147,148
    Palm Beach County easement   15
    Payment to state for maintenance dredging material   200
    Release spoil area policy   288
    Santa Rosa County easement   149
    Spoil island to Interama   387
    Telegram, dredging   159
    Treasure Is. Erosion Control easements   664

-z-